RICHARD GROSS

PSYCHOLOGY

THE SCIENCE OF MIND AND BEHAVIOUR

FIFTH EDITION

Hodder Arnold

A MEMBER OF THE HODDER HEADLINE GROUP

DEDICATION

To my 'three girls', the common thread running through all five editions of this labour of love.

Orders: please contact Bookpoint Ltd, 130 Milton Park, Abingdon, Oxon OX14 4SB. Telephone: +44 (0)1235 827720. Fax: +44 (0)1235 400454. Lines are open from 9.00–5.00, Monday to Saturday, with a 24-hour message-answering service. You can also order through our website www.hoddereducation.co.uk

British Library Cataloguing in Publication Data
A catalogue record for this title is available from the British Library

ISBN-10: 0 340 90098 9
ISBN-13: 978 0 340 90098 7

First published 2005

Impression number 10 9 8 7 6 5 4 3
Year 2009 2008 2007 2006

Typeset by GreenGate Publishing Services, Tonbridge, Kent.

Printed and bound in Dubai for Hodder Arnold, an imprint of Hodder Education, a member of the Hodder Headline Group, 338 Euston Road, London NW1 3BH.

CONTENTS

PREFACE TO THE FIFTH EDITION

The first edition of this book was published in 1987. Eighteen years and four editions later, the same issues seem to recur. How to decide what goes in, what stays in, and what comes out if the book isn't to run into more than one volume.

So, what were my guiding principles?

- The overriding aim was to provide a general introduction to psychology, which means that all the major topic areas are covered.
- Within each topic area, some of the material from the fourth edition has been retained, some removed or pruned, and some given greater emphasis and extended. The extent to which this has been done varies considerably between chapters and sections. For example, Chapter 4 on the Nervous System and Chapter 15 on Perception: Processes and Theories have changed very little, while Interpersonal Relationships (Chapter 28) and Psychopathology (Chapter 44) have been extensively expanded and updated. Overall, most changes have been made to the Social Psychology and Individual Differences sections.
- At the end of each section there is an applied chapter. The aim of these chapters is to demonstrate how the theory and research discussed in the preceding chapters has been used in attempts to understand current real-life issues and problems and to implement practical interventions (such as trying to help people lead safer and healthier lives, interviewing eyewitnesses, enhancing the performance of sports teams, and preventing crime and re-offending).

What's stayed the same?

- The basic structure of the fourth edition is retained – 50 chapters grouped into seven major sections. There are five applied chapters, coming at the ends of Parts 2–6.
- Chapter contents are clearly shown in the panel at the beginning of each chapter, and there's a comprehensive summary at the end of each chapter.
- Throughout each chapter there are '*Ask Yourself…*' breaks. These are designed to encourage you to think about the text that follows, to have questions in your mind (if not always answers) to help you understand and digest the studies and theories that you read about. So, instead of just reading in a fairly passive way, you'll adopt a more critical approach, equipped with some idea of what to expect and what to look out for.

Sometimes, the questions are quite specific, and the answers are given, directly, in the text that immediately follows. At other times, the questions are more general and abstract, and the answers unfold throughout the next few paragraphs. Another kind of question will require you to think about your own experiences and views on a particular issue – in these cases, of course, there's no 'correct' answer.

In all cases, the aim is to engage you, to make the process of reading the text more active and interactive, and, consequently, more interesting. Sometimes, the questions can easily be used as the basis for a seminar or class debate.

What's new?

- Every chapter (except Chapter 1) ends with a section called 'Links with other topics/chapters'. This is intended to supplement the cross-referencing that occurs within every chapter, and sometimes cross-references are repeated in this end-of-chapter section. There's always a degree of artificiality about how course syllabuses, and textbooks, are organised into distinct topics, sections and chapters. In reality, there's considerable overlap and interrelatedness between these different 'chunks' of psychological knowledge, and part of the ability to evaluate a particular theory or piece of research is to see its connections with others. This new section is designed to help you develop this ability.
- This fifth edition is in full-colour, with different sections being 'colour-coded' to make it easier to find your way around the book – and generally to make it more attractive.
- The major new feature is an accompanying CD-Rom. This provides extra resources that couldn't be included in the text – either for practical or technological reasons. For every chapter in the text, there are:
  - *drag-and-drop* exercises to help you check your understanding of some of the major terms and concepts;

- *self-assessment questions*: these are essay-style questions, which require you to display both basic understanding and evaluation of a range of topics;
- *sample essay answers*: these are 650–1000-word sample answers, drawing on material in the chapter, showing the various skills required in essay-writing. I must stress that these are 'samples'/'examples' only – there's no one correct way to answer any essay-style question (although they are meant to show what a 'good' standard of essay might look like);
- *downloadable schemas*: these are schematic summaries of the entire chapter, condensed into a single 'screen' (and printable on to a single page). Some are much more detailed than others (largely reflecting the density of chapter content and the nature of the topic). They are designed as revision aids and could suggest how you might prepare your own schemas;
- *websites and further reading*: the websites are hyperlinked, so that you can go straight to them (by clicking on the website address). Some contain online questionnaires or experiments, and many have links with other useful sites. These, and the recommendations for further reading, appeared in the fourth edition text.

Hopefully, all that was good about the previous edition is still here, mixed in with much that's different. The appeal of the fourth edition was that it catered for the needs of students on a wide variety of courses, without being written specifically or exclusively for any one group. I hope – and trust – that the same can be said of this fifth edition. As before, please let me know what you think of my efforts (via the publisher) – it's not just students who need feedback!

Good luck – and enjoy!

ACKNOWLEDGEMENTS

I'd like to thank Lynn Brown for her meticulous editing and everyone at Greengate for their typesetting of the text. Thanks also to 'the team' at Hodder Arnold, especially Jo Lincoln for all her hard work and support during a project that seems to have been going on forever, and, of course, Emma Woolf, whose good humour and general 'being there' has made this long journey far less arduous than it might otherwise have been.

The author and publishers would like to thank the following for permission to reproduce material in this book:

Pages 3, 777 (left), Images.com/CORBIS; page 4, reproduced by permission of Icon Books Ltd; page 6, Zephyr/Science Photo Library; pages 8 (left), 10 (right), Paul Doyle/Photofusion; pages 8 (top right), 274, 314, 330, 547, 554, 608, 632, 638, 645, 662 (top), 909, Bubbles; page 8 (bottom right), Ulrike Preuss/Photofusion; pages 10 (left), 11 (left), 591 (top and bottom), Sally & Richard Greenhill; page 11 (right), Jacky Chapman/Photofusion; page 12 (left), Brian Lee/Corbis; pages 12 (right), 146 (bottom), 180, 588, 859 (right), BDI Images Ltd; pages 13, 168, reproduced with permission of www.CartoonStock.com; page 14, Bridgeman Art Library; pages 16, 25, 648, Roger Ressmeyer/CORBIS; pages 17, 411, 641, Associated Press; page 19, George Disario/CORBIS; pages 20, 21 (top left, top right and bottom right), 24, 37 (right), 38 (top), 38 (bottom), 94, 113, 198, 347, 349 (left), 429, 446, 454, 483 (right), 685 (left), 713, 732, 758, 764, 867, 901, Bettmann/CORBIS; pages 21 (bottom left), 764, National Library of Medicine/Science Photo Library; pages 22, 44, 45, 71 (left and right), 77, 358 (right), 402, 415, 630, 707, 879 (right), 882 (right), Getty Images; pages 26, 141, 217, 375, 425, 642, 643 (right), 657, 662 (bottom), 670, 768 (right), CORBIS; page 27, Debbie Joffe/Albert Ellis; page 29 (left), World Religions Photo Library/Claire Stout; page 29 (right), Sophie Bassouls/CORBIS SYGMA; page 30, The Independent; pages 32 (left), 327, Rick Friedman/CORBIS; pages 32 (right), 156, 170, 186, 306, 310, 468, 566, 581, 666, 705, 747 (right), 775, 874, 887, AKG Images; page 36, Cambridge University Press; pages 37 (left), 42, Archivo Iconografico, S.A./CORBIS; page 39, Underwood & Underwood/CORBIS; pages 40, 172 (bottom left and bottom right), 396, 596, The Archives of the History of American Psychology, The University of Akron; pages 46 (top), 167, 309, 861, 881, Ian West; page 46 (bottom), William Vandivert, Dennis, MA, USA/Scientific American; page 47, 'Construction Workers', 1951, Fernand Leger © ADAGP, Paris and DACS, London 2005/Pushkin Museum, Moscow/AKG Images; page 53, Eye of Science/Science Photo Library; page 60, from Penfield, W. & Boldrey, E. (1937) Brain, 60, 389–442, Oxford University Press; page 61 (bottom right), Sovereign, ISM/Science Photo Library; page 61 (left), Guardian Newspaper, 1996; page 61 (middle right), CNRI/Science Photo Library; page 61 (top right), Scott Camazine/Science Photo Library; page 82, Steve Percival/Science Photo Library; page 84 (top), Colin Taylor Productions; pages 84 (bottom), 151 (right), 496 (left), 512, 571, 590, 661, 862 (left), 886, Still Pictures; pages 92, 125 (left), 126, 147 (top), 346, 426 (left), 456, 483 (left), 511, 568, 578, 684 (right), 735 (top right), 801, 804 (top), 837, 844, 847, 848, 849, Rex Features Ltd; pages 93, 125 (right), 189 (right), 389, 401, 451, 471, 474, 476, 482 (left), 494, 601, 603, 654, 671 (left), 761, 777 (right), 791, 793, 821, 846, 908, British Film Institute; page 95, 'Visions from a dying brain', reproduced by permission of Liz Pyle; page 97, Jeremy Walker/Science Photo Library; page 104, 'The Sleep', 1974 © Salvador Dali, Gala-Salvador Dali Foundation, DACS, London 2005/AKG Images; page 108, Jack Hollingsworth/CORBIS; page 112 (top), Baumgartner Olivia/CORBIS SYGMA; page 112 (bottom), Michael Pole/CORBIS; page 116, Ed Young/Science Photo Library; page 120, Dorothea Tanning 'Eine kleine Nachtmusik', 1944, T07346, Tate, London 2005 © ADAGP, Paris and DACS, London, 2005; page 123, Stuart Saunders/Photofusion; page 132, Lawrence Manning/CORBIS; page 133, Frank Trapper/CORBIS; page 134, Douglas Kirkland/CORBIS; page 136, Erich Lessing/AKG Images; pages 139, 367 (top), 522, 560, 627, 783, 832, 893, Reuters/CORBIS; page 142, Sheila Terry/Science Photo Library; page 146 (top), Mark Thomas/PictureArts/CORBIS; page 147 (bottom), from Psychology: Science, Behaviour & Life 2nd edition by Robert Crooks, permission of Holt, Rinehart & Winston; pages 148, 194, 400, The Advertising Archive; page 151 (left), University of Wisconsin Primate Laboratory; pages 159, 349 (right), 545, Science Photo Library; page 165, Robert Estall Photo Library; pages 172 (top left), 175, 698, 748, Wellcome Photo Library, London; page 176, Oxford Scientific Films Ltd; page 177, Stephanie Diani/CORBIS; pages 189 (left), 864 (left), Henning Christoph/Still Pictures; page 195, Randy M. Ury/CORBIS; pages 199, 658, Anthea Sieveking/ Wellcome Photo Library; page 201, Sam Tanner/ Photofusion; page 204, Mark M. Lawrence/CORBIS; page 206, Life File Photo Library/Andrew Ward; page 215, Kelly Harriger/CORBIS; page 216, Carl & Ann Purcell/CORBIS; page 227, courtesy BSM; page 236, reproduced with permission from Dr Helmut Leder, University of Vienna; page 238, 'Gazzaker', reproduced with permission from Dr Derek Carson, University of Abertay, Dundee; page 243, M.C. Escher's *Sky and Water* © 2005 The M.C. Escher Company-Holland. All rights reserved. www.mcescher.com; page 248, Julius/CORBIS; page 251, M.C. Escher's *Relativity* © 2005 The M.C. Escher Company-Holland. All rights reserved. www.mcescher.com; page 259, Phil Schermeister/ CORBIS; page 264, Laura Dwight/CORBIS; page 265, D. Roberts/Science Photo Library; page 273, Professor Mark Johnson, Centre for Brain and Cognitive Development; page 281, Philip James Corwin/CORBIS; page 286, Lanz Von Horsten; Gallo Images/CORBIS; page 288, Hilary Shedel/ArenaPAL; page 291, Rev. Ronald Royer/Science Photo Library; page 293, Farina Christopher/CORBIS SYGMA; pages 308, 712 (right), Rob Howard/CORBIS; page 319, Anna Clopet/CORBIS; page 320, Graham Rawle; page 321, Thomas Philip Morgan/Mary Evans Picture Library; page 335, Georgia State University; page 338, Haruyoshi Yamaguchi/CORBIS; page 344, Jerry Cooke/CORBIS; page 352, Peter Menzel/Science Photo Library; pages 355, 394, 417 (left), 455, 503 (left and right), 604, 611, 636, 730, 749, 815, 835, 888, The Ronald Grant Archive; pages 365, 380, 430 (left), 533, 614, 735 (bottom right), 735 (top right), Empics; page 367 (bottom), Associated Press, US Army; pages 378, 737, 762, 767, 858, 889, Mary Evans Picture Library; pages 379, 405, 517, 631, 660, 839, 842, PA News Photo Library; pages 386, 684 (left), Reuters NewMedia Inc./CORBIS; page 397, John Frost Newspapers (Telegraph); page 413, Imperial War Museum; page 414, British Heart Foundation anti-smoking advertising campaign 2004; page 417 (right), Steve Jennings/CORBIS; page 423, Nathan Benn/CORBIS; page 426 (right), reproduced by permission of The Commission for Racial Equality; page 427, Hulton Archive/Contributor Getty Images; page 430 (right), Flip Schulke/CORBIS; page 431, KTLA/Associated Press; pages 435, 621, Brian Rasic/Rex Features Ltd; page 436, David Roger/Getty Images; page 439, Concord Video & Film Council; pages 441, 497, 508, 528, 535, 607, ActionPlus; page 444, Scientific American; page 452, Marvin Koner/CORBIS; pages 457, 820 (left), Arthur W. Melton Library, Washington DC; page 459, copyright 1965 by Stanley Milgram from the film Obedience, distributed by Pennsylvania State University, Audio Visual Services; page 460, Hulton Archive/Getty Images; page 461, Barry Lewis/CORBIS; page 464, from Psychology & Life by P.G. Zimbardo, permission of Philip Zimbardo, Inc.; page 470, Nik Wheeler/CORBIS; pages 472, 677, 780, Russell Underwood/CORBIS; page 482 (right), Dr Judith H. Langlois, University of Texas at Austin; page 486, Gabe Palmer/CORBIS; page 487, Granada Media; page 496 (right), APTN/Associated Press; page 501, Daniel Aubry NYC/CORBIS; page 507 (left), reprinted by permission of Philip G. Zimbardo, Inc.; page 507 (right), Andy Clark/Reuters/CORBIS; page 515, Brenda Prince/ Photofusion; page 519, Peter Turnley/CORBIS; page 526, Allsport Concepts/Getty Images; pages 529, 541, 712 (left), 791, 877, Hulton-Deutsch Collection/CORBIS; page 531, Getty Images Sport; page 534, Randy Faris/CORBIS; page 543, Rob Goldman/CORBIS; page 544, Harlow Primate Laboratory, University of Wisconsin; page 550, Charles & Josette Lenars/CORBIS; page 552, Concord Films Council/Joyce Robertson; page 569, Steve Azzara/CORBIS; page 573, Brian Mitchell/Photofusion; page 575, Bonaventura Apicella/Photofusion; page 582, Farrell Grehan/CORBIS; page 592, by permission of Harvard University Press; page 593, Julie Houck/CORBIS; page 606, Craig Hammell/CORBIS; page 609, David King Collection; page 616, Albert Bandura, Stanford University; page 620, John Raffo/ Science Photo Library; page 623 (left and right), from Man & Woman, Boy & Girl, Money, J. & Ehrhardt, A. (1972), Johns Hopkins University Press; page 624, Jennie Woodcock; Reflections Photolibrary/CORBIS; page 629 (top), Jose Luis Pelaez, Inc./CORBIS; page 629 (bottom), David Turnley/CORBIS; page 635, © Munch Museum/Munch-Ellingsen Group, BONO, Oslo/DACS, London 2005; page 640 (left), David Robinson/Bubbles; page 640 (right), David H. Wells/CORBIS; page 643 (left), Per-Anders Pettersson/Getty Images; page 651, Sipa Press/Rex Features Ltd; page 652, Darama/CORBIS; page 667, Parrot Pascal/CORBIS; page 671 (right), Alfred Pasieka/Science Photo Library; page 673, Peter Poby/CORBIS; page 674 (top), Topham Picturepoint; page 674 (bottom), Ariel Skelley/CORBIS; page 676, BBC; page 679, Nati Harnik/Associated Press TLV104; page 682, Stephen Wiltshire 2004; pages 685 (right), 687 (top), Ethan Hill; page 687 (bottom), courtesy The Magstim Company Ltd; page 688, Private Collection/The Bridgeman Art Library; page 691 (left), reproduced by permission of the National Autistic Society; page 691 (top right), Bernard Bisson/CORBIS SYGMA; page 691 (bottom right), Paula Solloway/Photofusion; page 720, Barbara Herbert; page 722 (left), courtesy Richard Plomin; page 722 (right), Neil Bromhall/Science Photo Library; page 723, James Leynse/CORBIS; page 725, Ray Roberts/Photofusion; page 726, TDY/Rex Features Ltd; page 734, Dieter E.Hoppe (www.berlin-fotographie.de); page 735 (bottom right), Brooks Kraft/CORBIS; page 747 (left), Colin Garratt; Milepost 92½/CORBIS; page 748, OSU Photo Archives; page 753 (left), Wolfgang Kaehler/CORBIS; page 753 (right), Christie's Images/CORBIS; page 757, 'Cat in a Rainbow', Louis Wain (1860–1939)/Bonhams, London, UK/Bridgeman Art Library; page 768 (left), David Lees/CORBIS; page 769, Garcon Mathieu/CORBIS; pages 771, 820 (right), 870, Lucy Tizard/Bubbles; page 776, Jim Zuckerman/CORBIS; pages 778, 878, Aaron Horowitz/ CORBIS; page 779, Bob Watkins/Photofusion; page 790, Greg Baker/Associated Press; page 792, Bethlem Royal Hospital Archives and Museum; page 799, Allen Ginsberg/CORBIS; page 800, from Let me be by A.H. Crisp, Harcout Publishers Ltd; page 802, Anthony Redpath/CORBIS; page 804 (bottom), Mitchell Gerber/CORBIS; page 807, British Library; page 809, Richard T. Nowitz/CORBIS; page 811, John Greim/Science Photo Library; page 813, Najlah Feanny/Corbis; page 818, Peter Aprahamian/CORBIS; page 825, Paula Glassman/Photofusion; page 827, Aaron Beck; page 836, Adam Butler/Associated Press; page 851, Richard T. Nowitz/Science Photo Library; page 855, St Bartholomew's Hospital/Science Photo Library; page 857, Celia Kitzinger; page 859 (left), Priscilla Coleman; page 860 (right), Wellesley College; page 862 (right), Lisa Woollett/Photofusion; page 864 (right), Gideon Mendel/CORBIS; page 871, Philip G. Zimbardo, Ph.D., Professor Emeritus of Psychology, Stanford University; page 873, Paul Baldesare/Photofusion; page 879 (left), courtesy Medical Research Council; page 882 (left), Mo Wilson/Photofusion; page 890, Mike Walker/Rex Features Ltd; page 896, Charles O'Rear/CORBIS; page 900, Tom & Dee Ann McCarthy/CORBIS; page 903 (left), courtesy www.dumbletons.co.uk; page 903 (right), James King-Holmes/Science Photo Library.

Every effort has been made to obtain necessary permission with reference to copyright material. The publishers apologise if inadvertently any sources remain unacknowledged and will be glad to make the necessary arrangements at the earliest opportunity.

ONE
THE NATURE AND SCOPE OF PSYCHOLOGY

1

WHAT IS THIS THING CALLED PSYCHOLOGY?

INTRODUCTION AND OVERVIEW

When a psychologist meets someone for the first time at, say, a party and replies truthfully to the standard opening line, 'What do you do for a living?', the reaction of the newly made acquaintance is likely to fall into one of the following categories:

- 'Oh, I'd better be careful what I say from now on' (partly defensive, partly amused)
- 'I bet you meet some right weirdos in your work' (partly intrigued, partly sympathetic)
- 'What exactly is psychology?' (partly inquisitive, partly puzzled).

ASK YOURSELF...

- If you're completely new to psychology, how might you react?
- If you've studied it before, how would you define it and what's the range of topics/subjects it covers?
- How does it differ from other disciplines, such as physiology, sociology, and anthropology?

What these reactions betray – especially the first two – is an inaccurate and incomplete understanding of the subject. The first seems to imply that psychologists are mind readers and have access to other people's thoughts (they *don't*), while the second seems to imply that psychologists work only or largely with people who are 'mentally ill' or 'mad' (again, they *don't*, although many do). The third reaction perhaps implies that the boundaries between psychology and other subject disciplines aren't clearly drawn (they *aren't*), and what this chapter aims to do is make them sufficiently clear to enable you, the reader, who may be 'visiting' psychology for the first time, to find your way around this book – and the subject – relatively easily.

The opening chapter in any textbook is intended to 'set the scene' for what follows, and this normally involves defining the subject or discipline. In most disciplines, this is usually a fairly simple task. With psychology, however, it's far from straightforward. Definitions of psychology have changed frequently during its relatively short history as a separate field of study. This reflects different, and sometimes conflicting, theoretical views regarding the nature of human beings and the most appropriate methods for investigating them.

A BRIEF HISTORY

The word 'psychology' is derived from the Greek *psyche* (mind, soul or spirit) and *logos* (knowledge, discourse or study). Literally, then, psychology is the 'study of the mind'.

In Greek mythology, Psyche was represented by a butterfly. She became the wife of Eros, the god of love (renamed Cupid by the Romans).
And logos means "knowledge", "study": like all "ologies"!

The emergence of psychology as a separate discipline is generally dated at 1879, when Wilhelm Wundt opened the first psychological laboratory at the University of Leipzig in Germany. Wundt and his co-workers were attempting to investigate 'the mind' through *introspection* (observing and analysing the structure of their own conscious mental processes). Introspection's aim was to analyse conscious thought into its basic elements and perception into its constituent sensations, much as chemists analyse compounds into elements. This attempt to identify the structure of conscious thought is called *structuralism*.

Wundt and his co-workers recorded and measured the results of their introspections under *controlled conditions*, using the same physical surroundings, the same 'stimulus' (such as a clicking metronome), the same verbal instructions to each participant, and so on. This emphasis on measurement and control marked the separation of the 'new psychology' from its parent discipline of philosophy.

Philosophers had discussed 'the mind' for thousands of years. For the first time, *scientists* (Wundt was a physiologist by training) applied some of scientific investigation's basic methods to the study of mental processes. This was reflected in James's (1890) definition of psychology as:

> ... the Science of Mental Life, both of its phenomena and of their conditions ... The Phenomena are such things as we call feelings, desires, cognition, reasoning, decisions and the like.

However, by the early twentieth century, the validity and usefulness of introspection were being seriously questioned, particularly by an American psychologist, John B. Watson. Watson believed that the results of introspection could never be proved or disproved, since if one person's introspection produced different results from another's, how could we ever decide which was correct? *Objectively*, of course, we cannot, since it's impossible to 'get behind' an introspective report to check its accuracy. Introspection is *subjective*, and only the individual can observe his/her own mental processes.

Consequently, Watson (1913) proposed that psychologists should confine themselves to studying *behaviour*, since only this is measurable and observable by more than one person. Watson's form of psychology was known as *behaviourism*. It largely replaced introspectionism and advocated that people should be regarded as complex animals and studied using the same scientific methods as those used in chemistry and physics. For Watson, the only way psychology could make any claim to being scientific was to emulate the natural sciences and adopt its own objective methods. He defined psychology as:

> ... that division of Natural Science which takes human behaviour – the doings and sayings, both learned and unlearned – as its subject matter. (Watson, 1919)

The study of inaccessible, private, mental processes was to have no place in a truly scientific psychology.

Especially in America, behaviourism (in one form or another) remained the dominant force in psychology for the next 40 years or so. The emphasis on the role of *learning* (in the form of *conditioning*) was to make that topic one of the central areas of psychological research as a whole (see Chapter 2, pages 17–19 and Chapter 11).

Box 1.1 Psychoanalytic theory and Gestalt psychology

- In 1900, Sigmund Freud, a neurologist living in Vienna, first published his *psychoanalytic theory* of personality in which the *unconscious* mind played a crucial role. In parallel with this theory, he developed a form of psychotherapy called *psychoanalysis*. Freud's theory (which forms the basis of the *psychodynamic* approach) represented a challenge and a major alternative to behaviourism (see Chapter 2, pages 19–23).
- A reaction against both structuralism and behaviourism came from the *Gestalt* school of psychology, which emerged in the 1920s in Austria and Germany. Gestalt psychologists were mainly interested in perception, and believed that perceptions couldn't be broken down in the way that Wundt proposed (see Chapter 3) and behaviourists advocated for behaviour (see Chapters 3 and 11). Gestalt psychologists identified several 'laws' or *principles of perceptual organisation* (such as 'the whole is greater than the sum of its parts'), which have made a lasting contribution to our understanding of the perceptual process (see Chapter 15 for a detailed discussion).

In the late 1950s, many British and American psychologists began looking to the work of computer scientists to try to understand more complex behaviours which, they felt, had been either neglected altogether or greatly oversimplified by learning theory (conditioning). These complex behaviours were what Wundt, James and other early scientific psychologists had called '*mind*' or mental processes. They were now called *cognition* or *cognitive processes*, and refer to all the ways in which we come to know the world around us, how we attain, retain and regain information, through the processes of perception, attention, memory, problem-solving, decision-making, language and thinking in general.

Cognitive psychologists see people as *information-processors*, and cognitive psychology has been heavily influenced by computer science, with human cognitive processes being compared to the operation of computer programs (the *computer analogy*). Cognitive psychology now forms part of *cognitive science*, which emerged in the late 1970s (see Figure 1.1). The events which together constitute the 'cognitive revolution' are described in Box 3.3 (page 40).

Although mental or cognitive processes can only be *inferred* from what a person does (they cannot be observed literally or directly), mental processes are now accepted as being valid subject matter for psychology, provided they can be made 'public' (as in memory tests or problem-solving tasks). Consequently, what people say and do are perfectly acceptable sources of information *about* their cognitive processes, although the processes

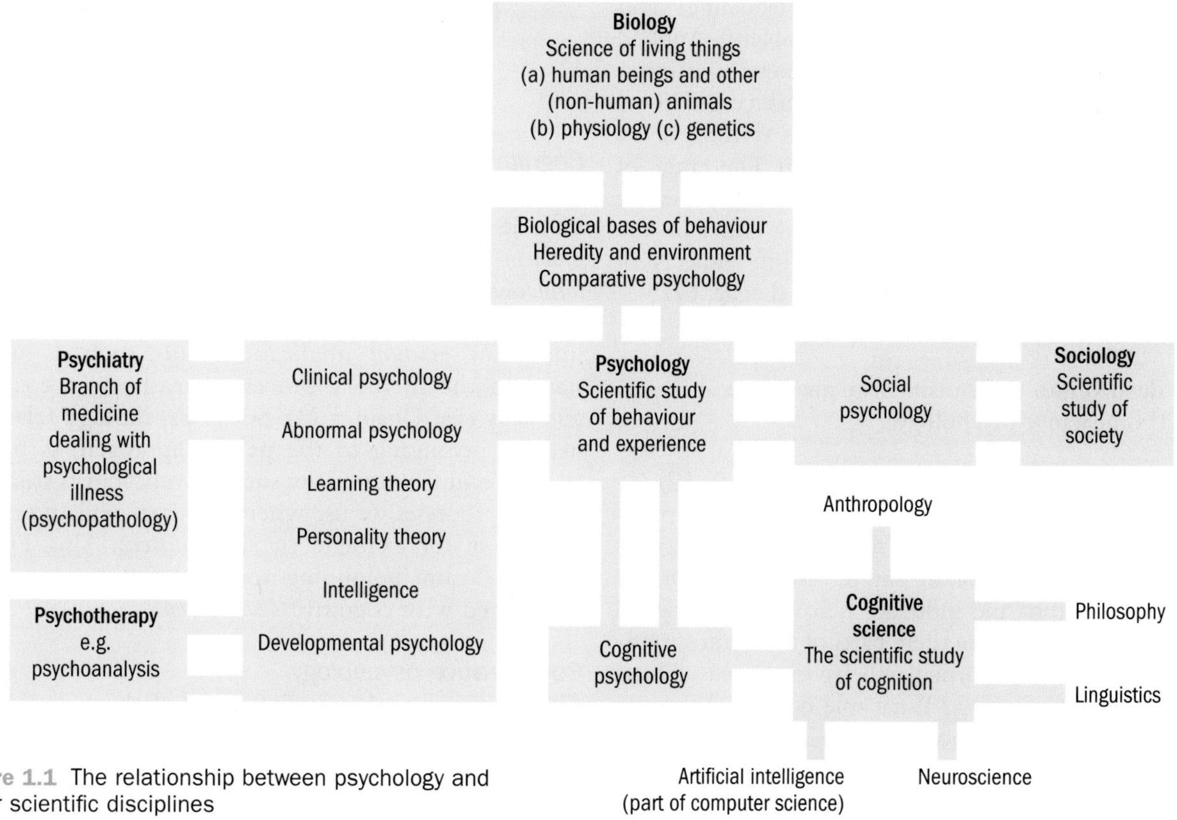

Figure 1.1 The relationship between psychology and other scientific disciplines

themselves remain inaccessible to the observer, who can study them only *indirectly*.

The influence of both behaviourism and cognitive psychology is reflected in Clark and Miller's (1970) definition of psychology as:

> ... the scientific study of behaviour. Its subject matter includes behavioural processes that are observable, such as gestures, speech and physiological changes, and processes that can only be inferred, such as thoughts and dreams.

Similarly, Zimbardo (1992) states that:

> Psychology is formally defined as the scientific study of the behaviour of individuals and their mental processes.

CLASSIFYING THE WORK OF PSYCHOLOGISTS

Despite behaviourist and cognitive psychology's influence on psychology's general direction in the last 90 years or so, much more goes on within psychology than has been outlined so far. There are other theoretical approaches or orientations, other aspects of human (and non-human) activity that constitute the special focus of study, and different kinds of work that different psychologists do.

A useful, but not hard and fast, distinction can be made between the *academic* and *applied* branches of psychology (see Figure 1.2). Academic psychologists carry out research and are attached to a university or research establishment, where they'll also teach undergraduates and supervise the research of postgraduates. Research is both *pure* (done for its own sake and intended, primarily, to increase our knowledge and understanding) and *applied* (aimed at solving a particular problem). Applied research is usually funded by a government institution like the Home Office, National Health Service (NHS) or the Department for Education and Skills (DfES), or by some commercial or industrial institution. The range of topics that may be investigated is as wide as psychology itself, but they can be classified as focusing either on the processes or *mechanisms* underlying various aspects of behaviour, or more directly on the *person* (Legge, 1975).

The process approach

This is divided into three main areas: physiological, cognitive and comparative psychology.

Physiological (or bio-)psychology (Chapters 4–12)

Physiological (or *bio-*)*psychologists* are interested in the physical basis of behaviour, how the functions of the nervous system (in particular the brain) and the *endocrine* (*hormonal*) system are related to and influence behaviour and mental processes. For example, are there parts of the brain specifically concerned with particular behaviours and abilities (*localisation of brain function*)? What role do hormones play in the experience of emotion and how are these linked to brain processes? What is the relationship between brain activity and different *states of consciousness* (including sleep)?

A fundamentally important biological process with important implications for psychology is *genetic transmission*. The *heredity and environment* (or *nature–nurture*) issue draws on what geneticists have discovered about the characteristics that can be passed from parents to offspring, how this takes place, and how genetic factors interact with environmental ones (see Chapters 41, 44 and 50). Other topics within physiological psychology include motivation and stress (an important topic within *health psychology*: see Chapter 12), and sensory processes, which are closely connected with perception (see Chapter 15).

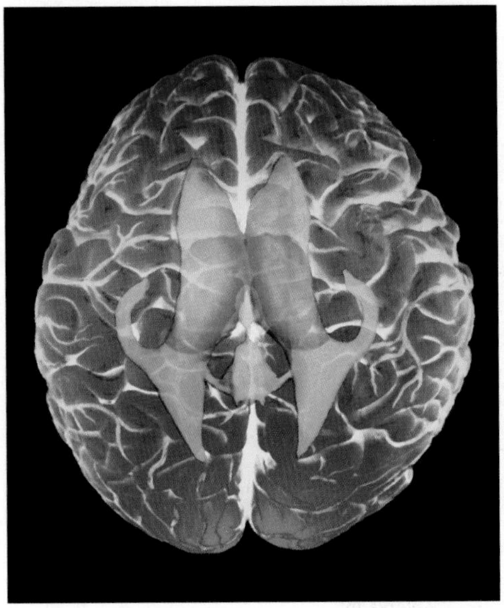

Cognitive psychology (Chapters 13–21)

As we saw earlier, cognitive (or mental) processes include *attention*, *memory*, *perception*, *language*, *thinking*, *problem-solving*, *decision-making*, *reasoning* and *concept-formation* ('higher-order' mental activities). Although these are often studied for their own sake, they may have important *practical* implications too, such as understanding the memory processes involved in *eyewitness testimony* (see Chapter 21). Social psychology (classified here as belonging to the person approach) is heavily cognitive in flavour: many social psychologists study the mental processes we use when trying to explain people's behaviour, for example (*social cognition*). Also, Piaget's theory (again, belonging to the person approach) is concerned with cognitive *development*.

Comparative psychology

Comparative psychology is the study of the behaviour of non-human animals, aimed at identifying similarities and differences between species. It also involves studying non-human animal behaviour to gain a better understanding of human behaviour. The basis of comparative psychology is *evolutionary theory*. Research areas include classical and operant conditioning (see Chapter 11), animal communication, language and memory (see Gross *et al.*, 2000), and evolutionary explanations of human behaviour (see Chapter 2, pages 30–33, and Clamp, 2001). Teaching language to non-humans is discussed in relation to language development (Chapter 19).

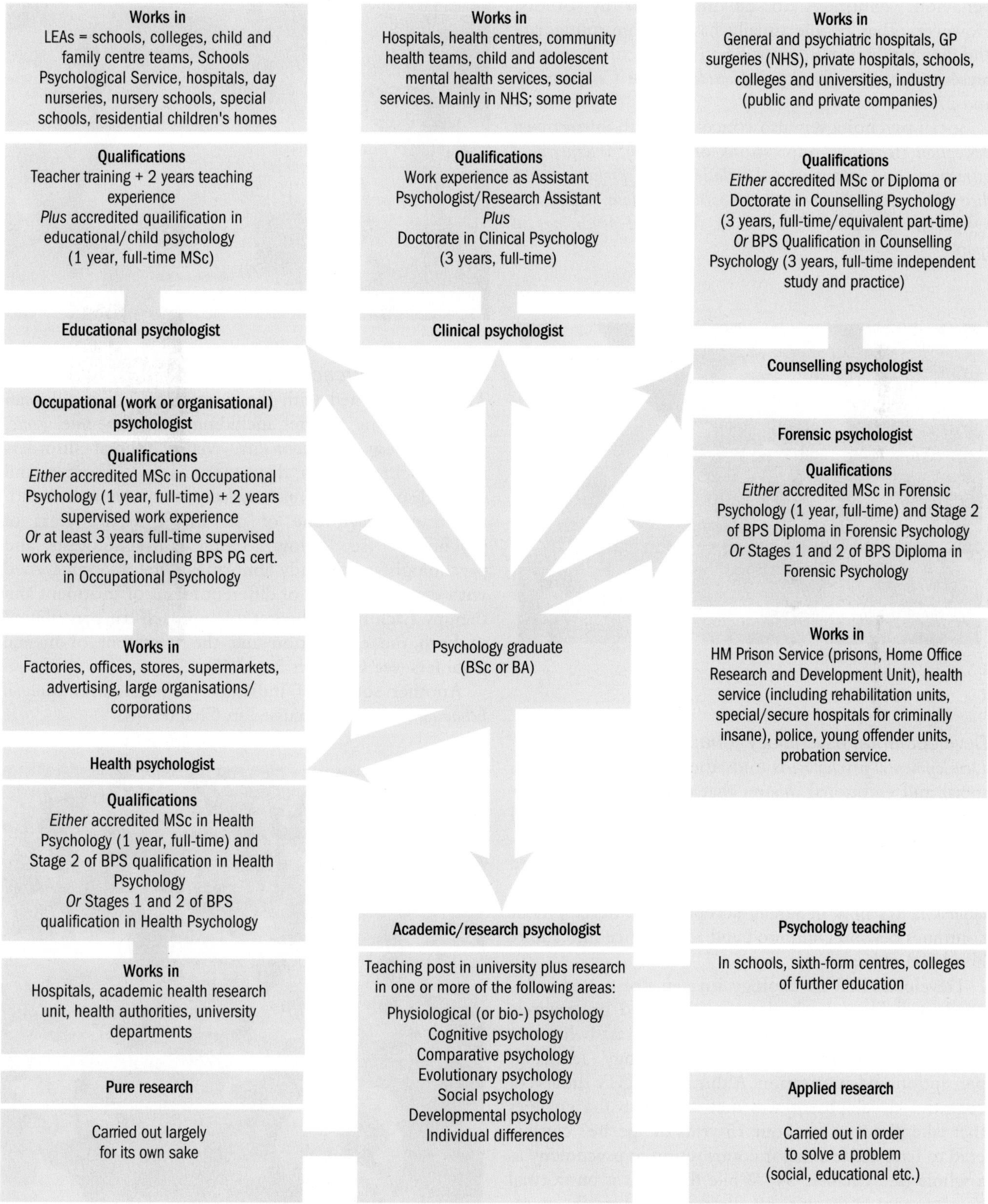

Works in
LEAs = schools, colleges, child and family centre teams, Schools Psychological Service, hospitals, day nurseries, nursery schools, special schools, residential children's homes
Qualifications
Teacher training + 2 years teaching experience
Plus accredited quailification in educational/child psychology (1 year, full-time MSc)
Educational psychologist
Works in
Hospitals, health centres, community health teams, child and adolescent mental health services, social services. Mainly in NHS; some private
Qualifications
Work experience as Assistant Psychologist/Research Assistant
Plus
Doctorate in Clinical Psychology (3 years, full-time)
Clinical psychologist
Works in
General and psychiatric hospitals, GP surgeries (NHS), private hospitals, schools, colleges and universities, industry (public and private companies)
Qualifications
Either accredited MSc or Diploma or Doctorate in Counselling Psychology (3 years, full-time/equivalent part-time)
Or BPS Qualification in Counselling Psychology (3 years, full-time independent study and practice)
Counselling psychologist
Occupational (work or organisational) psychologist
Qualifications
Either accredited MSc in Occupational Psychology (1 year, full-time) + 2 years supervised work experience
Or at least 3 years full-time supervised work experience, including BPS PG cert. in Occupational Psychology
Works in
Factories, offices, stores, supermarkets, advertising, large organisations/corporations
Psychology graduate
(BSc or BA)
Forensic psychologist
Qualifications
Either accredited MSc in Forensic Psychology (1 year, full-time) and Stage 2 of BPS Diploma in Forensic Psychology
Or Stages 1 and 2 of BPS Diploma in Forensic Psychology
Works in
HM Prison Service (prisons, Home Office Research and Development Unit), health service (including rehabilitation units, special/secure hospitals for criminally insane), police, young offender units, probation service.
Health psychologist
Qualifications
Either accredited MSc in Health Psychology (1 year, full-time) and Stage 2 of BPS qualification in Health Psychology
Or Stages 1 and 2 of BPS qualification in Health Psychology
Works in
Hospitals, academic health research unit, health authorities, university departments
Academic/research psychologist
Teaching post in university plus research in one or more of the following areas:
Physiological (or bio-) psychology
Cognitive psychology
Comparative psychology
Evolutionary psychology
Social psychology
Developmental psychology
Individual differences
Psychology teaching
In schools, sixth-form centres, colleges of further education
Pure research
Carried out largely for its own sake
Applied research
Carried out in order to solve a problem (social, educational etc.)

Figure 1.2 The main areas of academic and applied psychology open to psychology graduates

Social psychology (Chapters 22–31)

Some psychologists would claim that 'all psychology is social psychology', because all behaviour takes place within a social context and, even when we're alone, our behaviour continues to be influenced by others. However, other people usually have a more immediate and direct influence upon us when we're actually in their presence (as in *conformity and obedience*: see Chapters 26 and 27).

Social psychology is also concerned with *interpersonal perception* (forming impressions of others), *interpersonal attraction*, and *interpersonal relationships*, *prejudice* and *discrimination*, and *pro-* and *anti-social behaviour* (especially *aggression*). Chapter 31 looks at the *social psychology of sport*.

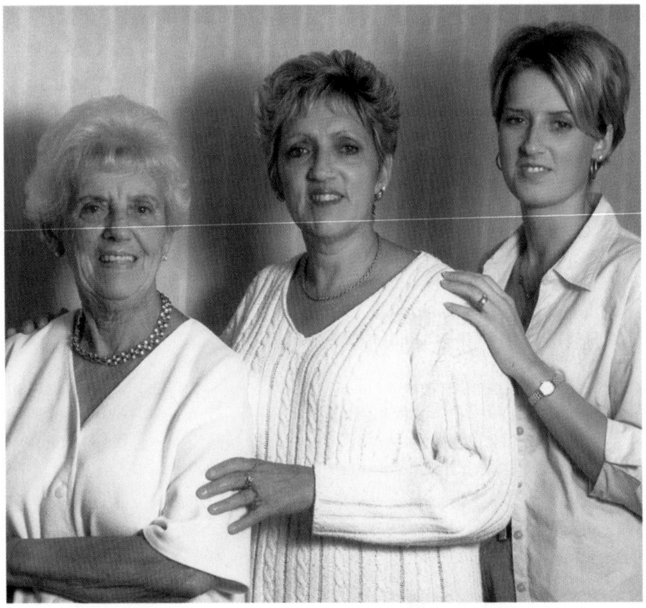

Developmental psychology (Chapters 32–40)

Developmental psychologists study the biological, cognitive, social and emotional *changes* that occur in people over time. One significant change within developmental psychology during the past 30 years or so is the recognition that development isn't confined to childhood and adolescence, but is a lifelong process (the *lifespan approach*). It's now generally accepted that development continues beyond childhood and adolescence into adulthood and old age.

Developmental psychology isn't an isolated or independent field, and advances in it depend on progress within psychology as a whole, such as behaviour genetics, (neuro)physiological psychology, learning, perception and motivation. Although Piaget's theory of cognitive development was meant to map the changes that take place up to about 15 years of age, he's considered to have made a major contribution to psychology as a whole (see Chapter 34). While the focus is on normal development, Chapter 40 is concerned with *exceptional/atypical development*.

Individual differences (Chapters 41–46)

This is concerned with the ways in which people can differ from one another, including *personality*, *intelligence*, and *psychological abnormality*. Major mental disorders include schizophrenia, depression, anxiety disorders and eating disorders. *Abnormal psychology* is closely linked with *clinical psychology*, one of the major *applied* areas of psychology (see below). Clinical psychologists and psychologists who study abnormality are also concerned with the effectiveness of different forms of treatment and therapy. Each major theoretical approach has contributed to both the explanation and the treatment of mental disorders (see Chapters 2 and 45).

Another source of individual differences is *criminal behaviour*, which is discussed in Chapter 46.

Comparing the process and person approaches

In practice, it's very difficult to separate the two approaches, even if it can be done theoretically. However, there are important relative differences between them.

Box 1.2 Some important differences between the process and person approaches

- **The process approach** is typically confined to the laboratory (where experiments are the method of choice). It makes far greater experimental use of non-human animals and assumes that psychological processes (particularly learning) are essentially the same in all species, and that any differences between species are only *quantitative* (differences of degree).
- **The person approach** makes much greater use of field studies (such as observing behaviour in its natural environment) and of non-experimental methods (e.g. correlational studies: see Coolican, 1999). Typically, human participants are studied, and it's assumed that there are *qualitative* differences (differences in kind) between humans and non-humans.

Areas of applied psychology

Discussion of the person/process approaches has been largely concerned with the *academic* branch of psychology. Since the various areas of applied psychology are all concerned with people, they can be thought of as the *applied* aspects of the person approach.

According to Hartley and Branthwaite (1997), most applied psychologists work in four main areas: *clinical*, *educational* and *occupational psychology*, and *government service* (such as *forensic psychologists*). In addition, Coolican *et al.* (1996) identify *forensic* (or *criminological*), *sport*, *health* and *environmental psychologists*. Hartley and Branthwaite argue that the work psychologists do in these different areas has much in common: it's the *subject matter* of their jobs that differs, rather than the skills they employ. Consequently, they consider an applied psychologist to be a person who can deploy specialised skills appropriately in different situations.

Box 1.3 Seven major skills (or roles) used by applied psychologists

- **The psychologist as counsellor**: helping people to talk openly, express their feelings, explore problems more deeply, and see these problems from different perspectives. Problems may include school phobia, marriage crises and traumatic experiences (such as being the victim of a hijacking), and the counsellor can adopt a more or less directive approach (see Chapter 2, pages 24–25, and Chapter 45).
- **The psychologist as colleague**: working as a member of a team and bringing a particular perspective to a task, namely drawing attention to the human issues, such as the point of view of the individual end-user (be it a product or a service of some kind).
- **The psychologist as expert**: drawing upon psychologists' specialised knowledge, ideas, theories and practical knowledge to advise on issues ranging from incentive schemes in industry to appearing as an 'expert witness' in a court case.
- **The psychologist as toolmaker**: using and developing appropriate measures and techniques to help in the analysis and assessment of problems. These include questionnaire and interview schedules, computer-based ability and aptitude tests, and other *psychometric tests* (see Chapters 41 and 42).
- **The psychologist as detached investigator**: many applied psychologists carry out evaluation studies to assess the evidence for and against a particular point of view. This reflects the view of psychology as an objective science, which should use controlled experimentation whenever possible. The validity of this view is a recurrent theme throughout psychology (see, in particular, Chapter 3).
- **The psychologist as theoretician**: theories try to explain observed phenomena, suggesting possible underlying mechanisms or processes. They can suggest where to look for causes and how to design specific studies that will produce evidence for or against a particular point of view. Results from applied psychology can influence theoretical psychology, and vice versa.
- **The psychologist as agent for change**: applied psychologists are involved in helping people, institutions, and organisations, based on the belief that their work will change people and society for the better. However, some changes are much more controversial than others, such as the use of psychometric tests to determine educational and occupational opportunities, and the use of behaviour therapy and modification techniques to change abnormal behaviour (see Chapters 41, 45, 47 and 48).

(Based on Hartley and Branthwaite, 2000)

Clinical psychology

Clinical psychologists are the largest single group of psychologists, both in the UK (Coolican *et al.*, 1996) and the USA (Atkinson *et al.*, 1990). A related group is counselling psychologists, who tend to work with younger clients in colleges and universities rather than in hospitals.

Box 1.4 The major functions of the clinical psychologist

A clinical psychologist has had work experience as an assistant psychologist/research assistant, plus three years' postgraduate training (Doctorate in Clinical Psychology) (BPS, 2004). The clinical psychologist's functions include:

- assessing people with learning difficulties, administering psychological tests to brain-damaged patients, devising rehabilitation programmes for long-term psychiatric patients and assessing the elderly for their fitness to live independently
- planning and carrying out programmes of therapy, usually *behaviour therapy/modification* (both derived from learning theory principles), or *psychotherapy* (group or individual) in preference to, or in addition to, behavioural techniques (see Chapter 45)
- carrying out research into abnormal psychology, including the effectiveness of different treatment methods ('outcome' studies); patients are usually adults, many of whom will be elderly, in psychiatric hospitals, psychiatric wards in general hospitals, and psychiatric clinics
- involvement in community care, as psychiatric care in general moves out of the large psychiatric hospitals
- teaching other groups of professionals, such as nurses, psychiatrists and social workers.

Clinical psychologists work largely in health and social care settings, including hospitals, health centres, community mental health teams, child and adolescent mental health services and social services. They usually work as part of a team with, for example, social workers, medical practitioners and other health professionals. In the UK, most work in the National Health Service (NHS), but some work in private practice.

Psychotherapy is usually carried out by psychiatrists (medically qualified doctors specialising in psychological medicine) or psychotherapists (who've undergone special training, including their own psychotherapy). In all its various forms, psychotherapy is derived from Freud's psychoanalysis (see Chapters 2 and 45), and is distinguished from both behavioural treatments and physical (somatic) treatments (those based on the medical model: see Chapters 43 and 45).

Counselling psychology

Counselling psychologists have either (a) an accredited MSc or Diploma or Doctorate in Counselling Psychology (three years' full-time or equivalent part-time), or (b) the British Psychological Society's (BPS's) Qualification in Counselling Psychology (three years' full-time independent study and practice).

They work within the NHS (in general and psychiatric hospitals and GP surgeries), in private hospitals and in private practice, within education in schools, colleges and universities, in industry and in public and private corporate institutions. They may work directly with individuals, couples, families and groups, or act as consultants (see Chapter 45).

Forensic psychology

This is a branch of psychology that attempts to apply psychological principles to the criminal justice system. It is rooted in empirical research and draws on cognitive, developmental, social and clinical psychology. One main focus is the study of criminal behaviour and its management, but in recent years research interests have expanded to include other areas, most notably those with a high media profile (such as stalking: see Chapter 46).

Forensic psychologists have either (a) an accredited MSc (one year full-time) in Forensic Psychology plus Stage 2 of the BPS's Diploma in Forensic Psychology, or (b) Stages 1 and 2 of the BPS's Diploma in Forensic Psychology (BPS, 2004). Like clinical psychologists, a crucial part of their work involves research and evaluation of what constitutes successful treatment.

The largest single employer of forensic psychologists in the UK is HM Prison Service (which includes the Home Office Research and Development Unit as well as prisons). Forensic psychologists also work in the health service (including rehabilitation units and special/secure hospitals for the criminally insane, such as Broadmoor and Rampton), the police service, young offender units and the probation service. Some work in university departments or in private consultancy.

Box 1.5 Some recent areas of research interest among forensic psychologists

- Jury selection
- The presentation of evidence
- Eyewitness testimony (see Chapter 21)
- Improving the recall of child witnesses
- False memory syndrome and recovered memory (see Chapter 21)
- Offender profiling (see Chapter 46)
- Crime prevention (see Chapter 46)
- Devising treatment programmes (like anger management)
- Assessing the risk of releasing prisoners (see Chapter 46)

(From Coolican *et al.*, 1996)

Educational psychology

Traditionally, educational psychologists in England, Scotland and Northern Ireland have needed teacher training plus at least two years' teaching experience, and have gained an accredited postgraduate qualification in educational or child psychology (one year, full-time MSc). It's proposed that the teacher status and experience requirement will be dropped from 2005 (Dunsmuir and Turner, 2004). In Scotland, teaching qualifications or experience aren't required, but a two-year, full-time MSc course plus one year supervised practice as an educational psychologist are necessary (BPS, 2004).

Educational psychologists are mostly employed by local education authorities (LEAs), working in schools, colleges, child and family centre teams (previously called 'child guidance'), the Schools Psychological Service, hospitals, day nurseries, nursery schools, special schools (day and residential), and residential children's homes. Clients are aged up to 18 years, but most fall into the 5–16 age group. They regularly liaise with other professionals from the departments of education, health and social services. A growing number work as independent or private consultants (BPS, 2004).

Box 1.6 Some of the responsibilities of the educational psychologist

- Administering psychometric tests, particularly intelligence (or IQ) tests, as part of the assessment of learning difficulties (LDs) (see Chapters 40 and 41)
- Planning and supervising remedial teaching; research into teaching methods, the curriculum (subjects taught), interviewing and counselling methods and techniques
- Planning educational programmes for those with mental and physical impairments (including the visually impaired and autistic), and other groups of children and adolescents who aren't attending ordinary schools (special educational needs: see Chapter 40)
- Advising parents and teachers how to deal with children and adolescents with physical impairments, behaviour problems or LDs
- Teacher training

Occupational (work or organisational) psychology

Occupational psychologists are involved in the selection and training of individuals for jobs and vocational guidance, including administration of aptitude tests and tests of interest. (This overlaps with the work of those trained in *personnel management*.)

Occupational psychologists have either (a) an accredited MSc in Occupational Psychology (one year, full-time) plus two years' supervised work experience, or (b) at least three years' full-time supervised work experience, including the BPS's Postgraduate Certificate in Occupational Psychology.

Box 1.7 Other responsibilities of the occupational psychologist

- Helping people who, for reasons of illness, accident or redundancy, need to choose and retrain for a new career (*industrial rehabilitation*)

- Designing training schemes, as part of *'fitting the person to the job'*; teaching machines and simulators (such as an aeroplane cockpit) often feature prominently in these schemes
- 'Fitting the job to the person' (*human engineering/engineering psychology* or *ergonomics*) – findings from experimental psychology are applied to the design of equipment and machinery in order to make the best use of human resources and to minimise accidents and fatigue; examples include telephone dialling codes (memory and attention) and the design of decimal coinage (tactile and visual discrimination)
- Advising on working conditions in order to maximise productivity (another facet of ergonomics – the study of people's efficiency in their working environments); occupational groups involved include computer/VDU operators, production line workers and air traffic controllers
- Helping the flow of communication between departments in government institutions, or 'industrial relations' in commerce and industry (*organisational psychology*); the emphasis is on the social, rather than the physical or practical, aspects of the working environment
- Helping to sell products and services through *advertising* and *promotions*; many psychologists are employed in the advertising industry, where they draw on what experimental psychologists have discovered about human motivation, attitudes and cognition (see Chapter 24)

Health psychology

This is one of the newer fields of applied psychology. Health psychologists have either (a) an accredited MSc in Health Psychology (one year, full-time) plus Stage 2 of BPS's qualification in Health Psychology, or (b) Stages 1 and 2 of the BPS's Health Psychology qualification.

Box 1.8 The breadth of health psychology

This involves the use of psychological principles to promote changes in people's attitudes, behaviour and thinking about health and illness (see Chapter 12). This may involve:

- the use of psychological theories and interventions to prevent damaging behaviours (such as smoking, drug abuse, poor diet), and to change health-related behaviour in community and workplace settings
- promoting and protecting health by encouraging behaviours such as exercise, healthy diet, teeth brushing, health checks/self-examination
- health-related cognitions – investigating the processes that can explain, predict and change health and illness behaviours
- processes influencing health care delivery – the nature and effects of communication between health care practitioners and patients, including interventions to improve communication, facilitate adherence (such as taking medication), prepare for stressful medical procedures, and so on
- psychological aspects of illness – looking at the psychological impact of acute and chronic illness on individuals, families and carers.

(Based on BPS, 2004)

Health psychologists work in a variety of settings, such as hospitals, academic health research units, health authorities, and university departments. They may deal with problems identified by health care agencies, including NHS Trusts and health authorities, health professionals (such as GPs, nurses, and rehabilitation therapists), and employers outside the health care system.

Chartered psychologists

Since 1987, the British Psychological Society (BPS), the only professional body for British psychologists incorporated by Royal Charter, has been authorised under its

Charter to keep a Register of Chartered Psychologists. Entry to the Register is restricted to members of the Society who've applied for registration and who have the necessary qualifications or experience to have reached a standard sufficient for professional practice in psychology without supervision (Gale, 1990).

All the applied areas described above (clinical, counselling, forensic, educational, occupational and health) lead to chartered status. This is also true of *Teaching and Research*, which requires either (a) a PhD in Psychology or (b), for teachers, at least three years' full-time experience as a teacher of psychology including the BPS's Diploma in the Applied Psychology of Teaching. As yet, sport psychology and psychotherapy don't grant chartered status (BPS, 2004).

> *ASK YOURSELF...*
> • What, if anything, has come as a surprise to you regarding what goes on in the name of 'psychology'?

The language of psychology

- As in all sciences, there's a special set of technical terms (jargon) to get used to, and this is generally accepted as an unavoidable feature of studying the subject. But over and above this jargon, psychologists use words that are familiar to us from everyday speech in a *technical way*, and it's in these instances that 'doing psychology' can become a little confusing.
- Some examples of this are 'behaviour' and 'personality'. For a parent to tell a child to 'behave yourself' is meaningless to a psychologist's ears: behaving is something we're all doing all the time (even when we're asleep). Similarly, to say that someone 'has no personality' is meaningless because, as personality refers to what makes a person unique and different from others, you cannot help but have one!
- Other terms that denote large portions of the research of experimental psychology, such as memory, learning and intelligence, are *hypothetical constructs* – that is, they don't refer to anything that can be directly observed but only *inferred* from observable behaviour (see above, page 5). They're necessary for explaining the behaviour being observed, but there's a danger of thinking of them as 'things' or 'entities' (*reification*), rather than as a way of trying to make sense of behaviour.
- Another way in which psychologists try to make sense of something is by comparing it with something else using an *analogy*. Often something complex is compared with something more simple. Since the 1950s and the development of computer science, the *computer analogy* has become very popular as a way of trying to understand how the mind works. As we saw earlier, the language of computer science has permeated the cognitive view of human beings as information processors (see Chapter 2, pages 25–27).
- A *model* is a kind of *metaphor*, involving a single, fundamental idea or image; this makes it less complex than a *theory* (although sometimes the terms are used interchangeably). A theory is a complex set of inter-related statements that attempt to explain certain observed phenomena. But in practice, when we refer to a particular theory (for example, Freud's or Piaget's), we often include *description* as well. Thomas (1985) defines a theory as 'an explanation of how the facts fit together', and he likens a theory to a lens through which to view the subject matter, filtering out certain facts and giving a particular pattern to those it lets in. A *hypothesis* is a testable statement about the relationship between two or more variables, usually derived from a model or theory (see Chapter 3).

Psychology and common sense

> *ASK YOURSELF...*
> • What do you understand by the term 'common sense'?
> • In what ways are we all psychologists?
> • How might a 'common sense' understanding of human behaviour and experience differ from that of professional psychologists?

A common reaction among psychology students, when discussing the findings of some piece of research, is to say, 'But we knew that already' (implying that it's mere 'common sense'). Alternatively, they might say, 'But that's not what we normally understand by such-and-such', implying that the research is in some way wrong. So psychology often seems to be in a no-win situation: either it merely confirms common sense or it contradicts it, in which case psychology seems to be the less credible of the two.

We all consider we know something about people and why they behave as they do, and so there's a sense in which we're all psychologists (see Chapters 22 and 23).

"Ok, let's try reverse psychology.
Andrew ... don't eat all your dinner up!"

The Last Evening, by Tissot

This is a theme explored at length by Joynson in *Psychology and Common Sense* (1974). He begins by stating that human beings aren't like the objects of natural science – we understand ourselves and can already predict and control our behaviour to a remarkable extent. This creates for the psychologist a paradoxical task: what kind of understanding can you seek of a creature that already understands itself?

For Joynson, the fundamental question is, 'If the psychologist did not exist, would it be necessary to invent him?' Conversely, for Skinner (1971), 'it is science or nothing' and Broadbent (1961) also rejects the validity of our everyday understanding of ourselves and others (Joynson calls this 'the behaviourists' prejudice'). Yet we cannot help but try to make sense of our own and other people's behaviour (by virtue of our cognitive abilities and the nature of social interaction), and to this extent we're all psychologists. Heather (1976) points to ordinary language as embodying our 'natural' understanding of human behaviour: as long as human beings have lived they've been psychologists, and language gives us an 'elaborate and highly refined conceptual tool, developed over thousands of years of talking to each other'.

Formal vs informal psychology

Legge (1975) and others resolve this dilemma by distinguishing between *formal* and *informal psychology* (or professional versus amateur, scientific versus non-scientific).

Our common sense, intuitive or 'natural' understanding is unsystematic and doesn't constitute a body of knowledge. This makes it very difficult to 'check' an individual's 'theory' about human nature, as does the fact that each individual has to learn from his/her own experience. So part of the aim of formal psychology is to provide such a systematic body of knowledge, which represents the unobservable basis of our 'gut reactions'.

Yet it could be argued that informal psychology *does* provide a 'body of knowledge' in the form of proverbs or sayings or folk wisdom, handed down from generation to generation (for example, 'Birds of a feather flock together', 'Too many cooks spoil the broth' and 'Don't cross your bridges before you come to them'). While these may contain at least a grain of truth, for each one there's another proverb that states the opposite ('Opposites attract', 'Many hands make light work' and 'Time and tide wait for no man' or 'Nothing ventured, nothing gained').

However, formal psychology may help us reconcile these contradictory statements. For example, there's evidence to support both proverbs in the first pair (see Chapter 28). Formal psychology tries to identify the conditions under which each statement applies, and they *appear* contradictory if we assume that only one or the other can be true! In this way, scientific psychology throws light on our everyday, informal understanding, rather than negating or invalidating it.

Legge (1975) believes that most psychological research should indeed be aimed at demonstrations of 'what we know already', but that it should also aim to go one step further. Only the methods of science, he believes, can provide us with the public, communicable body of knowledge that we're seeking. According to Allport (1947), the aim of science is 'Understanding, prediction and control above the levels achieved by unaided common sense', and this is meant to apply to psychology as much as to the natural sciences (see Chapters 3 and 42).

CONCLUSIONS

Psychology is a diverse discipline. Psychologists investigate a huge range of behaviours and mental or cognitive processes. There's a growing number of applied areas, in which theory and research findings are brought to bear in trying to improve people's lives in a variety of ways. During the course of its life as a separate discipline, definitions of psychology have changed quite fundamentally, reflecting the influence of different theoretical approaches. Rather than having to choose between our common-sense understanding of people and the 'scientific' version, psychology as a scientific discipline can be seen as complementing and illuminating our 'everyday' psychological knowledge.

CHAPTER SUMMARY

- Early psychologists, such as Wundt, attempted to study the mind through **introspection** under controlled conditions, aiming to analyse conscious thought into its basic elements (**structuralism**).
- Watson rejected introspectionism's **subjectivity** and replaced it with **behaviourism**. Only by regarding people as complex animals, using the methods of natural science and studying observable behaviour, could psychology become a true science.

- **Gestalt psychologists** criticised both structuralism and behaviourism, advocating that 'the whole is greater than the sum of its parts'. Freud's **psychoanalytic theory** was another major alternative to behaviourism.
- Following the **cognitive revolution**, people came to be seen as **information-processors**, based on the **computer analogy**. Cognitive processes, such as perception and memory, became an acceptable part of psychology's subject matter.
- **Academic** psychologists are mainly concerned with conducting **research** (**pure or applied**), which may focus on underlying **processes/mechanisms** or on the **person**.
- The **process approach** consists of **physiological psychology**, **cognitive processes** and **comparative psychology**, while the **person approach** covers **developmental** and **social psychology** and **individual differences**.
- While the process approach is largely confined to **laboratory experiments** using **non-humans**, the person approach makes greater use of field studies and **non-experimental** methods involving **humans**. The two approaches see species differences as **quantitative** or **qualitative** respectively.
- Most **applied psychologists** work in **clinical**, **counselling**, **forensic**, **educational** or **occupational psychology**. Newer fields include **health** and **sport** psychology.
- There's a sense in which we're all psychologists, creating a dilemma for psychologists: are they necessary? One solution is to distinguish between **informal/common-sense** and **formal/scientific psychology**. The latter aims to go beyond common-sense understanding and to provide a public, communicable body of knowledge.

2

THEORETICAL APPROACHES TO PSYCHOLOGY

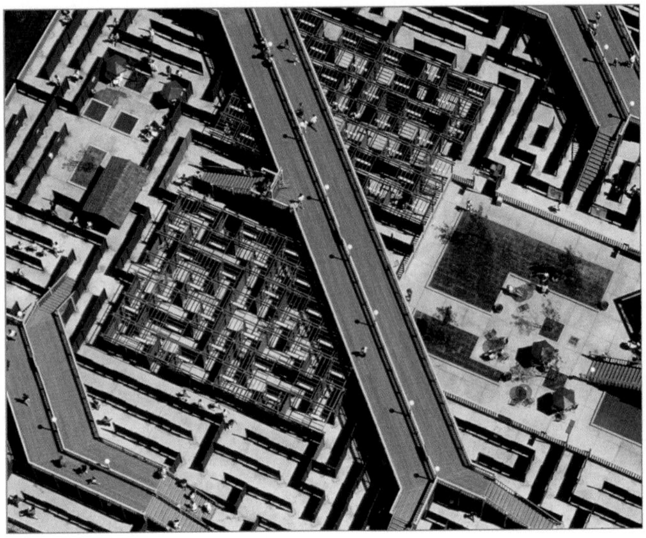

INTRODUCTION AND OVERVIEW

Different psychologists make different assumptions about what particular aspects of a person are worthy of study, and this helps to determine an underlying model or image of what people are like. In turn, this model or image determines a view of psychological normality, the nature of development, preferred methods of study, the major cause(s) of abnormality, and the preferred methods and goals of treatment.

An approach is a perspective that isn't as clearly outlined as a theory and that:

... provides a general orientation to a view of humankind. It says, in effect, we see people as operating according to these basic principles and we therefore see explanations of human behaviour as needing to be set within these limits and with these or those principles understood. (Coolican *et al.*, 1996)

As we shall see, all the major approaches include two or more distinguishable theories, but within an approach they share certain basic principles and assumptions that give them a distinct 'flavour' or identity. The focus here is on the *behaviourist, psychodynamic, humanistic, cognitive, social constructionist* and *evolutionary* approaches.

THE BEHAVIOURIST APPROACH

Basic principles and assumptions

As we saw in Chapter 1, Watson (1913) revolutionised psychology by rejecting the introspectionist approach and advocating the study of observable behaviour. Only by modelling itself on the natural sciences could psychology legitimately call itself a science. Watson was seeking to transform the very subject matter of psychology (from 'mind' to 'behaviour') and this is often called *methodological behaviourism*. According to Skinner (1987):

'Methodological' behaviourists often accept the existence of feelings and states of mind, but do not deal with them because they are not public and hence statements about them are not subject to confirmation by more than one person.

In this sense, what was revolutionary when Watson (1913) first delivered his 'behaviourist manifesto' (see Box 3.2, page 39) has become almost taken for granted, 'orthodox' psychology. It could be argued that all psychologists are methodological behaviourists (Blackman, 1980). Belief in the importance of empirical methods, especially the experiment, as a way of collecting data about humans (and non-humans), which can be quantified and statistically analysed, is a major feature of *mainstream psychology* (see Chapter 3). By contrast, as Skinner (1987) asserts:

'Radical' behaviourists ... recognise the role of private events (accessible in varying degrees to self-observation and physiological research), but contend that so-called mental activities are metaphors or explanatory fictions and that behaviour attributed to them can be more effectively explained in other ways.

For Skinner, these more effective explanations of behaviour come in the form of the principles of reinforcement derived from his experimental work with rats and pigeons. What's 'radical' about Skinner's *radical behaviourism* is the claim that feelings, sensations and other private events cannot be used to explain behaviour but are to *be explained* in an analysis of behaviour. Methodological behaviourism proposes to *ignore* such inner states (they're *inaccessible*). But Skinner *rejects* them as variables that can explain behaviour (they're *irrelevant*) and argues that they can be translated into the language of reinforcement theory (Garrett, 1996).

According to Nye (2000), Skinner's ideas are also radical because he applied the same type of analysis to covert behaviour (thoughts and feelings) occurring 'within the skin' as he did to overt, publicly observable, behaviours. He stressed the importance of identifying *functional relations* (cause-and-effect connections) between environmental conditions and behaviours. As Nye (2000) points out:

Radical behaviourists are able to describe with considerable detail various observable factors that affect learning, thereby buttressing the arguments that human behaviour is controlled in many ways by circumstances that can be objectively specified and manipulated.

Given this important distinction between methodological and radical behaviourism, we need to consider some principles and assumptions that apply to behaviourism in general.

Box 2.1 Basic principles and assumptions made by the behaviourist approach

- Behaviourists emphasise the role of environmental factors in influencing behaviour, to the near exclusion of innate or inherited factors (see Chapter 50). This amounts essentially to a focus on learning. The key form of learning is conditioning, either classical (Pavlovian or respondent), which formed the basis of Watson's behaviourism, or operant (instrumental), which is at the centre of Skinner's radical behaviourism. Classical and operant conditioning are often referred to (collectively) as learning theory, as opposed to 'theories of learning', which usually imply theories other than conditioning theories – that is, non-behaviourist theories (see Chapter 11).

B.F. Skinner (1904–90)

- Behaviourism is often referred to as 'S–R' psychology ('S' standing for 'stimulus' and 'R' for 'response'). Both classical and operant conditioning explain observable behaviour (responses) in terms of environmental events (stimuli), but they define the stimulus and response relationship in fundamentally different ways. Only in classical conditioning is the stimulus seen as triggering a response in a predictable, automatic way, and this is what's conveyed by 'S–R' psychology. It is, therefore, a mistake to describe operant conditioning as an 'S–R' approach (see Chapter 11).

- Both types of conditioning are forms of *associative learning*, whereby associations or connections are formed between stimuli and responses that didn't exist before learning took place.
- Part of Watson's rejection of introspectionism was his belief that it invoked too many vague concepts that are difficult, if not impossible, to define and measure. According to the *law of parsimony* (or 'Occam's razor'), the fewer assumptions a theory makes, the better (more 'economical' explanations are superior).
- The mechanisms proposed by a theory should be as simple as possible. Behaviourists stress the use of *operational definitions* (defining concepts in terms of observable, measurable, events).
- The aim of a science of behaviour is to *predict* and *control* behaviour.

Theoretical contributions

Behaviourism made a massive contribution to psychology, at least up to the 1950s, and explanations of behaviour in conditioning terms recur throughout this book. For example, apart from a whole chapter on learning and conditioning (Chapter 11), imagery as a form of organisation in memory and as a memory aid is based on the principle of association, and the interference theory of forgetting is largely couched in stimulus–response terms (Chapter 17). Language, moral and gender development (Chapters 19, 35 and 36) have all been explained in terms of conditioning, and some influential theories of the formation and maintenance of relationships focus on the concept of reinforcement (Chapter 28). The behaviourist approach also offers one of the major models of abnormal behaviour (Chapter 45). Finally, Skinner's notorious views on free will are discussed in detail in Chapter 49.

Theorists and researchers critical of the original, 'orthodox' theories have modified and built on them, making a huge contribution in the process. Noteworthy examples are Tolman's (1948) *cognitive behaviourism* (see Chapter 11) and *social learning theory* (see Chapters 29, 35 and 36).

ASK YOURSELF...

- Dip into some of these chapters, just to familiarise yourself with the range of topic areas to which the behaviourist approach has been applied (and to help you find your way round the book).

Practical contributions

Methodological behaviourism, with its emphasis on experimentation, operational definitions, and the measurement of observable events (see Box 2.1), has been a major influence on the practice of scientific psychology in general (what Skinner, 1974, called the 'science of behaviour'). This is quite unrelated to any views about the nature and role of mental events. Other, more 'tangible' contributions include:

- *behaviour therapy* and *behaviour modification* (based on classical and operant conditioning respectively) as major approaches to the treatment of abnormal behaviour (see Chapter 45) and one of the main tools in the clinical psychologist's 'kit bag' (see Box 1.4, pages 8–9)
- *behavioural neuroscience* is an interdisciplinary field of study, using behavioural techniques to understand brain function and neuroscientific techniques to throw light on behavioural processes; while many believe that behaviour can be explained by (*reduced* to) brain processes (see Chapter 49), the evidence shows that each is dependent on the other (Leslie, 2002)
- *behavioural pharmacology* involves the use of *schedules of reinforcement* (see Chapter 11) to assess the behavioural effects of new drugs that modify brain activity; most importantly, the research has illustrated how many behavioural effects of drugs are determined as much by the current behaviour and reinforcement contingencies as by the effects of the drug on the brain (Leslie, 2002: see Chapter 8)
- *biofeedback* as a non-medical treatment for stress-related symptoms, derived from attempts to change rats' autonomic physiological functions through the use of operant techniques (see Chapter 12)
- *teaching machines* and *programmed learning*, which now commonly take the form of *computer-assisted learning* (CAL).

An evaluation of behaviourism

In addition to the criticisms – both general and specific – that occur in the particular chapters where behaviourist explanations are presented, two evaluative points will be made here:

1. the 'Skinner box' is an 'auto-environmental chamber', in which rats' and pigeons' environments can be totally controlled by the experimenter (see Chapter 11). This is central to Skinner's analysis of behaviour. A rat pressing a lever was intended to be equivalent to a cat operating an escape latch in Thorndike's puzzle box (1898), so counting the number of lever presses (the *response rate*) became the standard measure of operant learning. Despite Skinner's claim that he doesn't have a *theory*, 'the response' in operant conditioning has largely considered only the *frequency* of

behaviour, ignoring intensity, duration and quality. As Glassman (1995) observes:

> While the focus on frequency was a practical consideration, it eventually became part of the overall conceptual framework as well – a case of research methods directing theory.

But in everyday life, frequency isn't always the most meaningful aspect of behaviour. For example, should we judge an author's worth by how many books s/he publishes, rather than their content?

> *ASK YOURSELF...*
> - Do you agree with Skinner's claim that thoughts and other 'covert behaviours' don't *explain* our behaviour (because they cannot *determine* what we do)?

2. Skinner's claim that human behaviour can be predicted and controlled in the same way as the behaviour of non-humans is usually accepted only by other behaviour analysts. Possessing language allows us to communicate with each other and to think about 'things' that have never been observed (and may not even exist), including rules, laws and principles (Garrett, 1996). While these can only be expressed in or thought about in words, much of our behaviour is governed by them. According to Garrett, when this happens:

> ... behaviour is now shaped by what goes on inside their [people's] heads ... and not simply by what goes on in the external environment.

So, what people *think* is among the important variables determining what they do and say, the very *opposite* of what Skinner's radical behaviourism claims.

Behaviourists find it very difficult to explain creativity or novel behaviour of any kind

However, behaviour analysts recognise the limitations of their approach. For example, Leslie (2002) admits that:

> ... operant conditioning cannot provide a complete account of psychology from a behavioural perspective, even in principle.

Similarly, O'Donohue and Ferguson (2001) acknowledge that the science of behaviour cannot account for creativity, as in music, literature and science.

THE PSYCHODYNAMIC APPROACH

The term 'psychodynamic' denotes the active forces within the personality that motivate behaviour, and the inner causes of behaviour (in particular the *unconscious conflict* between the different structures that compose the whole personality). While Freud's was the original psychodynamic theory, the approach includes all those theories based on his ideas, such as those of Jung (1964), Adler (1927) and Erikson (1950). Freud's *psychoanalytic theory* is psychodynamic, but the psychodynamic theories of Adler, Jung and Erikson aren't psychoanalytic. So the two terms *aren't* synonymous. However, because of their enormous influence, Freud's ideas will be emphasised in the rest of this section.

Basic principles and assumptions

Freud's concepts are closely interwoven, making it difficult to know where a description of them should begin (Jacobs, 1992). Fortunately, Freud himself stressed the acceptance of certain key theories as essential to the practice of *psychoanalysis*, the form of psychotherapy he pioneered and from which most others are derived (see page 22).

> **Box 2.2 The major principles and assumptions of psychoanalytic theory**
>
> - Much of our behaviour is determined by *unconscious* thoughts, wishes, memories, and so on. What we're consciously aware of at any one time represents the tip of an iceberg: most of our thoughts and ideas are either not accessible at that moment (*pre-conscious*) or are totally inaccessible (*unconscious*). These unconscious thoughts and ideas can become conscious through the use of special techniques, such as *free association*, *dream interpretation* and *transference*, the cornerstones of psychoanalysis (see Chapter 45).
> - Much of what's unconscious has been made so through *repression*, whereby threatening or unpleasant experiences are 'forgotten' (see Chapter 21, pages 366–370). They become inaccessible, locked away from our conscious awareness. This is a major form of *ego defence* (see Chapter 42). Freud singled out repression as a special cornerstone 'on which the whole structure of psychoanalysis rests. It is the most essential part of it' (Freud,

1914). Repression is closely related to *resistance*, interpretation of which is another key technique used in psychoanalysis (see Chapter 45).

- According to the theory of *infantile sexuality*, the sexual instinct or drive is active from birth and develops through a series of five *psychosexual stages*. The most important of these is the *phallic stage* (spanning the ages 3–5/6), during which all children experience the Oedipus complex (see Chapter 35). In fact, Freud used the German word *'Trieb'*, which translates as 'drive', rather than *'Instinkt'*, which was meant to imply that experience played a crucial role in determining the 'fate' of sexual (and aggressive) energy (see Box 50.2, page 902).
- Related to infantile sexuality is the general *impact of early experience* on later personality (see Chapter 32). According to Freud (1949):

> *It seems that the neuroses are only acquired during early childhood (up to the age of six), even though their symptoms may not make their appearance until much later ... the child is psychologically father of the man and ... the events of its first years are of paramount importance for its whole subsequent life.*

Sigmund Freud (1856–1939)

Theoretical contributions

As with behaviourist accounts of conditioning, many of Freud's ideas and concepts have become part of mainstream psychology's vocabulary. You don't have to be a 'Freudian' to use concepts such as 'repression', 'unconscious', and so on, and many of the vast number of studies of different aspects of the theory have been conducted by critics hoping to discredit it (such as Eysenck, 1985; Eysenck and Wilson, 1973).

Like behaviourist theories, Freud's can also be found throughout psychology as a whole. His contribution is extremely rich and diverse, offering theories of motivation (see Chapter 9), dreams and the relationship between sleep and dreams (Chapter 7), forgetting (Chapter 21), attachment and the effects of early experience (Chapter 32), moral and gender development (Chapters 35 and 36), aggression (Chapter 29), and abnormality (Chapter 45). Psychoanalytic theory has also influenced Gould's (1978, 1980) theory of the evolution of adult consciousness (Chapter 38) and Adorno *et al.*'s (1950) theory of the authoritarian personality (a major account of prejudice: see Chapter 25).

Finally, and as noted earlier, Freud's theories have stimulated the development of alternative theories, often resulting from the rejection of some of his fundamental principles and assumptions, but reflecting his influence enough for them to be described as psychodynamic.

ASK YOURSELF...

- Repeat the exercise suggested for the behaviourist approach (see page 18).

Some major alternative psychodynamic theories

- *Ego psychology*, promoted by Freud's daughter, Anna, focused on the mechanisms used by the *ego* to deal with the world, especially the ego defence mechanisms. Freud, by contrast, stressed the influence of the *id*'s innate drives (especially sexuality and aggression) and is often described as an instinct theorist (but see the third point in Box 2.2). The ego, as well as the id, originates in basic human inheritance and has its own developmental course. It uses neutralised (non-sexual) energy, which makes possible an interest in objects and activities that aren't necessarily related to underlying sexual and aggressive drives.

According to Nye (2000), the increased attention given to an independent ego has probably resulted partly from a change in the types of patients psychoanalysts are treating. In recent years, patients are more likely to be troubled by the problems of an increasingly complex society (vague anxieties, insecurities and dissatisfaction), and are seeking ways to find meaning and value in work, family and social roles:

> Since the ego is the part of the personality that must deal with the external world in some rational, decision-making way, it seems natural that more emphasis should be given to it. Perhaps for the contemporary patient it is important to focus more attention on conscious thought processes and coping mechanisms; he or she is less likely to be plagued by unconscious guilt and repressed sexuality than by the uncertainties and rootlessness of modern society that requires the ego to grapple with existential problems. (Nye, 2000)

- Erik Erikson, trained by Anna Freud as a child psychoanalyst, also stressed the importance of the ego, as well as the influence of social and cultural factors on individual development. He pioneered the *lifespan approach* to development, proposing eight *psychosocial stages*, in contrast with Freud's five psychosexual stages that end with physical maturity (see Chapters 37 and 38).

- Two of Freud's original 'disciples', Carl Jung and Alfred Adler, broke ranks with Freud and formed their own 'schools' (*analytical psychology* and *individual psychology*, respectively). Jung attached relatively little importance to childhood experiences (and the associated personal unconscious) but considerable importance to the *collective* (or *racial*) *unconscious*, which stems from the evolutionary history of human beings as a whole (see Chapter 42).
- Like Jung, Adler rejected Freud's emphasis on sexuality, stressing instead the *will to power* or *striving for superiority*, which he saw as an attempt to overcome feelings of inferiority faced by all children as they grow up. He also shared Jung's view of the person as an *indivisible unity* or whole, and Erikson's emphasis on the *social* nature of human beings.
- Melanie Klein (1932) is often seen as a key transitional figure between Freud's instinct theory and the *object relations school* (see Box 2.3). Like Anna Freud, she adapted Freud's techniques (such as pioneering play therapy) in order to tap a young child's unconscious, and maintained that the superego and Oedipus complex appear as early as the first and second years of life (see Chapter 35).

Anna Freud (1895–1982)

Erik Erikson (1902–1994)

Carl Gustav Jung (1875–1961)

Alfred Adler (1870–1937)

Box 2.3 Object relations theory

- The *object relations school* (the 'British school') was greatly influenced by Klein's emphasis on the infant's earliest (pre-Oedipal) relationships with its mother. It places far less emphasis on the role of instincts and more on the *relationship with particular love objects* (especially the mother), seeing early relationships as crucial for later patterns of relationships with others.
- Fairbairn (1952), for example, saw the aim of the libido as *object-seeking* (as opposed to pleasure-seeking), and this was extended by Bowlby (1969) in his *attachment theory* (see Chapter 32).
- According to Nye (2000):

> Although both object relations theory and Freudian theory are concerned with childhood experiences and the inner world of the person, the former puts more emphasis on discrepancies between inner-world and real-world persons and situations. The latter puts more emphasis on the role of factors such as instinctual drives and unresolved Oedipus conflicts ...

- Object relations theory isn't a single, widely accepted theory. Rather, it refers to a number of separate ideas proposed by different theorists. However, they all stress that internal images ('representations') of one's self and of 'objects' (a technical term usually denoting another person toward whom we direct emotion and action – *significant others*) can have powerful effects on our relationships with others.
- Mahler (1975) and Winnicott (1965) stress the movement from the newborn's absolute dependence to the independence and autonomy of adults as the primary and lifelong developmental task. Development proceeds from *symbiotic fusion* with the mother, through various stages of partial differentiation of the self and other, to a state of *increased individuation* and independence (see Chapter 38). The internalised images of others (objects) in the infant (and the psychotic adult: see Chapter 44) are primitive, engulfing, devouring and otherwise menacing. Only when separation from the mother has been successfully achieved are we capable of empathising with others and seeing them as they really are (rather than projections of our primitive fantasies).

(Based on Holmes, 1993; Nye, 2000; Zeldow, 1995)

Practical contributions

The current psychotherapy scene is highly diverse, with only a minority using Freudian techniques (see Chapter 45), but, as Fancher (1996) points out:

Most modern therapists use techniques that were developed either by Freud and his followers or by dissidents in explicit reaction against his theories. Freud remains a dominating figure, for or against whom virtually all therapists feel compelled to take a stand.

Both Rogers, the major humanistic therapist (see below) and Wolpe, who developed *systematic desensitisation* (a major form of behaviour therapy: see Chapter 45), were originally trained in Freudian techniques. Perls, the founder of *Gestalt therapy*, Ellis, the founder of *rational emotive therapy* (RET) (see Chapter 45) and Berne, who devised *transactional analysis* (TA) were also trained psychoanalysts.

Even Freud's fiercest critics concede his influence, not just within world psychiatry but in philosophy, literary criticism, history, theology, sociology, and art and literature generally. Freudian terminology is commonly used in conversations between therapists well beyond Freudian circles, and his influence is brought daily to therapy sessions as part of the cultural background and experience of nearly every client (Jacobs, 1992).

Many mental health practitioners (including psychotherapists, counsellors and social workers), although not formally trained as psychoanalysts, have incorporated elements of Freudian thought and technique into their approaches to helping their patients (Nye, 2000).

An evaluation of the psychodynamic approach

- A criticism repeatedly made of Freudian (and other psychodynamic) theories is that they're unscientific because they're *unfalsifiable* (incapable of being disproved). For example, if the Freudian prediction that 'dependent' men will prefer big-breasted women is confirmed, then the theory is supported. However, if such men actually prefer small-breasted women (Scodel, 1957), Freudians can use the concept of *reaction formation* (an ego defence mechanism: see Table 42.6, page 749) to argue that an unconscious fixation with big breasts may manifest itself as a conscious preference for the opposite, a clear case of 'heads I win, tails you lose' (Eysenck, 1985; Popper, 1959).

Hans J. Eysenck (1916–1997)

- However, it's probably a mistake to see reaction formation as typical of Freudian theory as a whole. According to Kline (1984, 1989), for example, the theory comprises a collection of hypotheses, some of which are more easily tested than others, some of which are more central to the theory than others, and some of which have more supporting evidence than others. Also, different parts of the theory have been tested using different methods (see Chapter 42, pages 750–752).
- According to Zeldow (1995), the history of science reveals that those theories that are the richest in explanatory power have proved the most difficult to test empirically. For example, Newton's Second Law couldn't be demonstrated in a reliable, quantitative way for 100 years, and Einstein's general theory of relativity is still untestable. Eysenck, Popper and others have criticised psychoanalytic theory for being untestable. But even if this were true:

> ... the same thing could (and should) be said about any psychological hypotheses involving complex phenomena and worthy of being tested...psychoanalytic theories have inspired more empirical research in the social and behavioural sciences than any other group of theories ... (Zeldow, 1995)

RESEARCH UPDATE: 2.1 Evidence supporting Freudian theory

- Fisher and Greenberg (1996) conducted an extensive reappraisal of studies of psychoanalytic theory carried out up to the early 1990s. Along with Kline (1989), they argue that Freud's theory should be evaluated in terms of a series of specific hypotheses (or mini-theories), rather than as a whole. They also believe that what should be considered are overall trends across studies.
- Fisher and Greenberg concluded that there's evidence to support Freud's notion of oral and anal personality tendencies (see Chapter 42), and some aspects of his ideas on the origins of depression and paranoia (see Chapters 44 and 45). But they found only weak and indirect support for the notion of the Oedipal conflict, and no support for their impact on later development, or for his views on women's sexuality and how their development differs from men's (see Chapters 35 and 47).
- While their review is extremely broad, it's not comprehensive (for example, it doesn't cover repression and other defence mechanisms, or transference). The strength of the evidence presented is variable and sometimes indirect, and where it's supportive it rests on Fisher and Greenberg's interpretation of the results (Andrews & Brewin, 2000). However, for Zeldow (1995) the mere existence of such reviews:

> *... gives the lie to the notion that all psychoanalytic ideas are too vague or abstruse to be tested scientifically.*

- According to Andersen & Miranda (2000), *transference* is a normal, non-pathological process that's part of our normal mechanisms of social interaction. They claim that their research represents the first experimental demonstration of transference. Within the framework of social cognition, they've shown that mental representations of significant others, developed in one's family and elsewhere, are linked to representations of self in memory. These representations are 'heavily laden with affect and motivation', and are often activated and used in responding to new people that resemble a significant other. Their experimental procedure in effect assesses transference in terms of how much participants 'go beyond the information given' (Bruner, 1957) about the new person (see Chapters 15, 22 and 23).
- According to Reason (2000), Freud was probably not right in asserting that (nearly) all slips (of the tongue) are in some way intended. But he was certainly correct in claiming that 'Freudian slips' represent minor eruptions of unconscious processing (see Chapter 42). Instead of taking a strictly psychoanalytic interpretation of 'unconscious', Reason prefers one that relates to processes that aren't directly accessible to consciousness, i.e. automatic processing or habitual performance (see Chapter 13).
- Similarly, much of modern cognitive psychology and neuropsychology (see Chapter 4) is consistent with the Freudian view that behaviour isn't dependent on conscious experience (Power, 2000). For example, modern theories of the display of facial affect explicitly recognise a role for the conscious and unconscious control of behaviour (Ekman, 1986: see Chapter 10). Another example is blindsight (Weiskrantz, 1986: see Case Study 5.1, page 85). According to Power (2000):

... Whereas cognitive psychology has emphasised the co-operation between conscious and automatic processes (essential, for example, whilst driving), psychoanalysis has always emphasised conflict instead. The most recent models in psychology have come to consider both co-operation and conflict between conscious and unconscious processes.

- Freud's theory provides methods and concepts that enable us to interpret and 'unpack' underlying *meanings* (it has great *hermeneutic strength*). Popper's and Eysenck's criticism above helps to underline the fact that these meanings (both conscious and unconscious) cannot be measured in any precise way. Freud offers a way of understanding that's different from theories that are easily testable, and it may actually be *more* appropriate for capturing the nature of human experience and action (Stevens, 1995: see Chapter 3). According to Fancher (1996):

> Although always controversial, Freud struck a responsive chord with his basic image of human beings as creatures in conflict, beset by irreconcilable and often unconscious demands from within as well as without. His ideas about repression, the importance of early experience and sexuality, and the inaccessibility of much of human nature to ordinary conscious introspection have become part of the standard Western intellectual currency.

- Reason (2000) believes it's time to re-acknowledge Freud's greatness as a psychologist. Like James, he had a rare gift for describing and analysing the phenomenology of mental life. Perhaps Freud's greatest contribution was in recognising that apparent trivia we now commonly call 'Freudian slips' are 'windows on the mind'. According to Kline (1998):

> ... after 100 years, Freudian theory cannot be uncritically accepted just as it cannot be totally rejected. However ... Freudian theory contains some profound observations and understanding of human behaviour. These must be incorporated into any adequate human psychology, not only its theory but also its methods ...

THE HUMANISTIC APPROACH

Basic principles and assumptions

As we noted earlier, Rogers, a leading humanistic psychologist (and therapist), was trained as a psychoanalyst. Although the term 'humanistic psychology' was coined by Cohen (1958), a British psychologist, this approach emerged mainly in the USA during the 1950s. Maslow (1968), in particular, gave wide currency to the term 'humanistic' in America, calling it a 'third force' (the other two being behaviourism and Freudianism). However, Maslow didn't reject these approaches but hoped to unify them, thus integrating both subjective and objective, the private and public aspects of the person, and providing a complete, holistic psychology.

Box 2.4 Some basic principles and assumptions of the humanistic approach

- Both the psychoanalytic and behaviourist approaches are *deterministic*. People are driven by forces beyond their control, either unconscious forces from within (Freud) or reinforcements from outside (Skinner). Humanistic psychologists believe in free will and people's ability to choose how they act (see Chapter 49).
- A truly scientific psychology must treat its subject matter as fully human, which means acknowledging individuals as interpreters of themselves and their world. Behaviour, therefore, must be understood in terms of the individual's *subjective experience*, from the perspective of the actor (a *phenomenological approach*, which explains why this is sometimes called the 'humanistic-phenomenological' approach). This contrasts with the positivist approach of the natural sciences, which tries to study

people from the position of a detached observer. Only the individual can explain the meaning of a particular behaviour and is the 'expert' – not the investigator or therapist.

- Maslow argued that Freud supplied the 'sick half' of psychology, through his belief in the inevitability of conflict, neurosis, innate self-destructiveness, and so on, while he (and Rogers) stressed the 'healthy half'. Maslow saw *self-actualisation* at the peak of a hierarchy of needs (see below and Chapter 9), while Rogers talked about the *actualising tendency*, an intrinsic property of life, reflecting the desire to grow, develop and enhance our capacities. A fully functioning person is the ideal of growth. Personality development naturally moves towards healthy growth (unless it's blocked by external factors), and should be considered the norm (see Chapter 42).
- Maslow's contacts with Wertheimer and other Gestalt psychologists (see Chapter 15) led him to stress the importance of understanding the *whole person*, rather than separate 'bits' of behaviour.

(Based on Glassman, 1995)

Theoretical contributions

Maslow's *hierarchy of needs* (see Chapter 9, pages 140–142) distinguishes between motives shared by both humans and non-humans and those that are uniquely human, and can be seen as an extension of the psychodynamic approach. Freud's id would represent physiological needs (at the hierarchy's base), Horney (a major critic of the male bias in Freud's theory: see Chapter 35) focused on the need for safety and love (corresponding to the next two levels), and Adler (see above) stressed esteem needs (at the fourth level). Maslow added self-actualisation to the peak of the hierarchy (Glassman, 1995).

According to Rogers (1951), while awareness of being alive is the most basic of human experiences, we each fundamentally live in a world of our own creation and have a unique perception of the world (the *phenomenal field*). It's our *perception* of external reality that shapes our lives (*not* external reality itself). Within our phenomenal field, the most significant element is our sense of *self*, 'an organised consistent gestalt, constantly in the process of forming and reforming' (Rogers, 1959: see Chapter 42). This view contrasts with those of many other self theorists, who see it as a central, unchanging core of personality (see Chapter 33).

Abraham H. Maslow (1908–1970)

ASK YOURSELF...

- Repeat the exercise as for the behaviourist and psychodynamic approaches.

Practical contributions

By far the most significant practical influence of any humanistic psychologist is Rogers' *client-* (or *person-*) *centred therapy* (see Chapter 45). Originally (in the 1950s) it was called 'client-centred' (CCT), but since the mid-1970s it has been known as 'person-centred' therapy (PCT):

> ... psychotherapy is the releasing of an already existing capacity in a potentially competent individual. (Rogers, 1959)

The change in name was meant to reflect more strongly that the person, in his/her full complexity, is the centre of focus. Also, Rogers wanted to convey that his assumptions were meant to apply broadly to almost all aspects of human behaviour – not just to therapeutic settings. For example, he saw many parallels between therapists and teachers: they're both 'facilitators' of an atmosphere of freedom and support for individual pursuits (Nye, 2000). For Nye:

> At the level at which Rogers' ideas were developed originally, in therapy and counselling situations, his impact certainly has been significant and far-reaching. A wide range of individuals – psychotherapists, counsellors, social workers, clergy and others – have been influenced by Rogers' assumptions that, if one can be a careful and accurate listener, while showing acceptance and honesty, one can be of help to troubled persons.

Less well known is the prolific research that Rogers undertook during the 1940s, 1950s and 1960s into this form of therapy. According to Thorne (1992):

> This body of research constituted the most intensive investigation of psychotherapy attempted anywhere in the world up to that time ... The major achievement of these studies was to establish beyond all question that psychotherapy could and should be subjected to the rigours of scientific enquiry.

Rogers helped develop research designs (such as Q-sorts) which enable objective measurement of the self-concept, ideal self and their relationship over the course of therapy, as well as methodologies (such as rating scales and the use of external 'consultants') for exploring the importance of therapist qualities. These innovations continue to influence therapeutic practice, and many therapists are now concerned that their work should be subjected to research scrutiny. Research findings are now more likely than ever before to affect training procedures and clinical practice across many different therapeutic orientations (Thorne, 1992: see Chapter 45).

By emphasising the therapist's personal qualities, Rogers opened up psychotherapy to psychologists and contributed to the development of therapy provided by non-medically qualified therapists (*lay therapy*). This is especially significant in the USA, where (until recently) psychoanalysts had to be psychiatrists (medically qualified). Rogers originally used the term 'counselling' as a strategy for silencing psychiatrists who objected to psychologists practising 'psychotherapy'. In the UK, the outcome of Rogers' campaign has been the evolution of a counselling profession whose practitioners are drawn from a wide variety of disciplines, with neither psychiatrists nor psychologists dominating. Counselling skills are used in a variety of settings throughout education, the health professions, social work, industry and commerce, the armed services, and international organisations (Thorne, 1992).

Carl Rogers (1902–1987)

An evaluation of the humanistic approach

- According to Wilson *et al.* (1996), the humanistic approach isn't an elaborate or comprehensive theory of personality, but should be seen as a set of uniquely personal theories of living created by humane people optimistic about human potential. It has wide appeal to those who seek an alternative to the more mechanistic, deterministic theories.
- However, like Freud's theory, many of its concepts are difficult to test empirically (such as self-actualisation), and it cannot account for the origins of personality. Since it describes but doesn't explain personality, it's subject to the *nominal fallacy* (Carlson & Buskist, 1997).
- Nevertheless, for all its shortcomings, the humanistic approach represents a counterbalance to the psychodynamic (especially Freud) and the behaviourist approaches, and has helped to bring the 'person' back into psychology. Crucially, it recognises that people help determine their own behaviour and aren't simply slaves to environmental contingencies or to their past. The self, personal responsibility and agency, choice, and free will are now legitimate issues for psychological investigation.

THE COGNITIVE APPROACH

Basic principles and assumptions

Despite its undoubted influence within psychology as a whole (see below and Chapter 3), it's more difficult to define the boundaries of cognitive psychology compared with the other major approaches. Its identity isn't as clearly established, and it cannot be considered to be a specific, integrated set of assumptions and concepts. It has several contemporary forms, with many theories, research programmes and forms of psychotherapy having a 'cognitive tilt' (Nye, 2000).

Also, there's no specific figure who can be identified as being central to its development in the same way as Watson, Freud and Rogers can with their respective approaches. As Wade & Tavris (1990) say:

> Cognitive psychology does not yet have a unifying theory, and unlike other 'brands' of psychology ... it lacks an acknowledged spokesperson.

Box 2.5 Some basic principles and assumptions of the cognitive approach

- According to Parkin (2000), psychologists in general, and cognitive psychologists in particular, face a problem not faced by other scientists:

  The human brain is not like other organs of the body in that looking at its structure does not reveal anything about how it functions. We can see that the wall of the small intestine acts as an absorptive surface, the heart as a pump, and the kidney as a filter. The brain, however, is a large mass of cells and fibres which, no matter how clearly we look at it, gives no indication of how we think, speak and remember ...

For these reasons, cognitive psychologists are forced to seek *analogies* and *metaphors* when trying to describe a construct within the brain – that is, how the brain works is compared with the operation of something we already understand.

- Many different analogies have been used in cognitive psychology. By far the most dominant is that internal mental abilities are *information processing systems* (drawing on ideas from telecommunications and computer science: the *computer analogy*). Included within this overall analogy are several central ideas or concepts, such as *coding*, *channel capacity*, and *serial/parallel processing* (see Chapter 20).

- Every telecommunication system uses some form of *coding*. For example, a telephone receives and translates our voice into an electromagnetic code, which is then decoded back into our voice at the other end. Cognitive psychologists realised that the concept of coding was central to understanding the representations used by the brain. When we see a picture, for example, we extract information from it that forms a code, which is, therefore, a symbol of the original stimulus (see Chapters 5 and 15).
- *Channel capacity* is the idea that any transmission system has a finite limit to the amount of information it can hold. Nowadays, with the advent of optic fibres, channel capacity can be huge – but it's still limited. This is also true of human beings: most of our mental activities are capacity-constrained, such as our attentional processes (see Chapter 13). But compared with physical communication devices, human coding is more flexible, and can take account of the form of the input in order to reduce the amount and nature of information that's actually formed into a code (as demonstrated in *span of apprehension experiments* and *chunking* (see Chapter 17). Unlike humans, physical systems reduce all information to fundamental units ('bits'), which in turn allows the absolute capacity of the system to be defined (which is impossible for human information processing).

(Based on Parkin, 2000)

The mind as an information-processing device

Theoretical contributions

We noted earlier (see page 18) that two major modifications to 'orthodox' learning theory are Tolman's *cognitive behaviourism* and *social learning theory* (associated primarily with Bandura). Both these theories stress the central role of cognitive processes in the learning process. The influence of the information-processing approach is obvious in relation to attention, pattern recognition and memory (see Box 2.6), but it has permeated many other areas of psychology. As we noted in Chapter 1, *social cognition* is now a commonly used term to refer to many aspects of the perception of people (see Chapter 22), attribution (see Chapter 23), attitudes and attitude change (including prejudice: see Chapters 24 and 25), and other areas of social psychology.

The information-processing approach also represents an increasingly influential view of cognitive development (see Chapter 34) and of the nature of intelligence (see Chapter 41). Cognitive behaviour therapy also represents a major approach to the treatment of mental disorders (see Chapter 45 and the section entitled 'Practical contributions', below).

ASK YOURSELF...
- Repeat the exercise as for the behaviourist, psychodynamic and humanistic approaches.

Practical contributions

In relation to counselling and psychotherapy, Ellis's *rational emotive behaviour therapy* (REBT: previously just called rational emotive therapy or RET) deserves special attention (Nye, 2000). According to Rorer (1998), 'the cognitive revolution in psychotherapy began with the publication of [Ellis's 1962 book] *Reason and Emotion in Psychotherapy*'. REBT is the predecessor of the current cognitive and cognitive-behaviour therapies (see Chapter 45), and continues to evolve and gain in popularity. His emphasis on the primacy of cognition in psychopathology is at the forefront of practice and research in clinical psychology (Nye, 2000).

REBT attempts directly and actively to get clients to dispute their irrational and unscientific beliefs, and replace them with rational beliefs, which are less likely to be associated with extremely negative emotional states or maladaptive behaviours. The key concept underlying REBT (and other cognitive approaches) is that people are disturbed not by events themselves but by their *perception* of them. (This is similar to Rogers' *phenomenal field*: see above.)

Although Ellis (1987) believes that people have a biological tendency to think irrationally, REBT is an optimistic approach. It emphasises that:

> ... people have enormous power to think about their thinking, to use rationality and the scientific method, and to radically control and change their emotional destiny – providing they really work at doing so. (Ellis, 1987)

Albert Ellis (born 1913)

An evaluation of the cognitive approach

- The parallels between human beings and computers are compelling (Parkin, 2000). According to Lachman *et al.* (1979):

> Computers take a symbolic input, recode it, make decisions about the recoded input, make new expressions from it, store some or all of the input, and give back a symbolic input. By analogy that is what most cognitive psychology is about. It is about how people take in information ... recode and remember it, how they make decisions, how they transform their internal knowledge states, and how they translate these states into behavioural outputs.

Box 2.6 Some other similarities between computers and humans as information processors

- Computers operate in terms of *information streams*, which flow between different components of the system. This is conceptually similar to how we assume symbolic information flows through human information channels (for example, see Atkinson and Shiffrin's multi-store model (MSM) of memory, Chapter 17, page 287).
- All computers have a *central processing unit*, which carries out the manipulation of information. At the simplest level, a central processor might take a sequence of numbers and combine them according to a particular rule in order to compute an average. This was seen by many as analogous to the mechanism that would be responsible for the same type of mental operation.
- Computers have *databases* and *information stores*, which are permanent representations of knowledge the computer has acquired. In many ways this is comparable to our permanent (long-term) memory.
- Information sometimes needs to be held for a period of time while some other operation is performed. This is the job of the *information buffer*, which is a feature of computers and information-processing models of human attention (see Chapter 13) and memory (again, see the section on the MSM in Chapter 17).

(Based on Parkin, 2000)

ASK YOURSELF...

- Can you think of some limitations of the computer analogy? (See Box 2.9 and Chapter 20, pages 351–353.)

- Information-processing accounts invariably address some specific aspect of mental processing, rather than being all-embracing accounts of cognition. A good example (in addition to those given in Box 2.6) is Bruce and Young's (1986) model of *face recognition* (see Chapter 14, pages 240–241). A *model* is more than a mere analogy (see Chapter 1): the proposed information-processing system is specified in sufficient detail to enable clear predictions to be made about how humans would behave in certain situations.
- Cognitive psychologists implicitly adopted, at least initially, a strong *nomothetic* view of human mental processes – that is, they assumed that any information-processing model would apply equally to everyone (see Chapter 42). But the influence of *individual differences* soon became apparent. The general rule is that the more complex the cognitive process, the more likely there are to be individual differences (Parkin, 2000).
- Until the mid-1980s, mainstream cognitive psychologists took little interest in the study of how brain damage affects subsequent cognitive and behavioural functioning. *Cognitive neuropsychologists* now study people with acquired cognitive deficits in order to learn about the nature and organisation of cognitive functioning in normal people (the *cognitive architecture* of mental processes: see Chapter 4).

THE SOCIAL CONSTRUCTIONIST APPROACH

Basic principles and assumptions

Social constructionism (SC) has played a central role in the various challenges that have been made to mainstream, academic psychology (see Chapter 3) during the last 30 years or so. The emergence of SC is usually dated from Gergen's (1973) paper 'Social psychology as history'. In this, he argued that all knowledge, including psychological knowledge, is historically and culturally specific, and that we therefore must extend our enquiries beyond the individual into social, political and economic realms for a proper understanding of the evolution of present-day psychology and social life. Since the only constant feature of social life is that it's continually *changing*, psychology in general – and social psychology in particular – becomes a form of *historical undertaking*: all we can ever do is try to understand and account for how the world appears to be *at the present time*.

Gergen's paper was written at the time of 'the crisis in social psychology'. Starting in the late 1960s and early 1970s, some social psychologists were becoming increasingly concerned that the 'voice' of ordinary people was being omitted from social psychological research. By concentrating on *decontextualised* laboratory behaviour, it was ignoring the real-world contexts that give human action its meaning. Several books were published, each proposing an alternative to positivist science and focusing on the accounts of ordinary people (e.g. Harré and Secord, 1972). These concerns are clearly seen today in SC.

> *ASK YOURSELF...*
> - Try to formulate some arguments for and against the view that people are basically the same, regardless of culture and historical period (the *universalist assumption*).

While there's no single definition of SC that would be accepted by all those who might be included under its umbrella, we could categorise as social constructionist any approach that is based on one or more of the following key attitudes (as proposed by Gergen, 1985). Burr (2003) suggests we might think of these as 'things you would absolutely have to believe in order to be a social constructionist'.

- *A critical stance towards taken-for-granted knowledge:* our observations of the world don't reveal in any simple way the true nature of the world, and conventional knowledge isn't based on objective, unbiased 'sampling' of the world (see Table 3.1, page 42). The categories with which we understand the world don't necessarily correspond to natural or 'real' categories/distinctions. Belief in such natural categories is called *essentialism*, so social constructionists are *anti-essentialism*.
- *Historical and cultural specificity:* how we commonly understand the world, and the categories and concepts we use, are historically and culturally *relative*. Not only are they specific to particular cultures and historical periods, they're seen as products of that culture and history, and this must include the knowledge generated by the social sciences. The theories and explanations of psychology thus become time- and culture-bound, and cannot be taken as once-and-for-all descriptions of human nature:

> The disciplines of psychology and social psychology can therefore no longer be aimed at discovering the 'true' nature of people and social life ... (Burr, 2003)

- *Knowledge is sustained by social processes:* our current accepted way of understanding the world ('truth') doesn't reflect the world as it really is (*objective reality*), but is constructed by people through their everyday interactions. Social interaction of all kinds, and particularly language, is of central importance for social constructionists: it's other people, both past and present, who are the sources of knowledge.

> We are born into a world where the conceptual frameworks and categories used by the people of our culture already exist ... Concepts and categories are acquired by each person as they develop the use of language and are thus reproduced every day by everyone who shares a culture and language. This means that the way a person thinks, the very categories and concepts that provide a framework of meaning for them, are provided by the language that they use. Language therefore is a necessary pre-condition for thought as we know it ... (Burr, 2003)

CRITICAL DISCUSSION 2.1: Transcultural and cross-cultural psychology, and the universalist assumption

- If knowledge is culturally created, then we shouldn't assume that our ways of understanding are necessarily any better (closer to 'the truth') than other ways. Yet this is precisely what mainstream (social) psychology has done. According to Much (1995), a new *(trans)cultural psychology* has emerged in North America (e.g. Bruner, 1990; Cole, 1990; Shweder, 1990) as an attempt to overcome the bias of *ethnocentrism* that has too often limited the scope of understanding in the social sciences (see Chapter 47).
- Shweder (1990) makes the crucial distinction between *cultural psychology* and *cross-cultural psychology* (C-CP), which is a branch of experimental social, cognitive and personality psychology.

(a) Most of what's been known as 'cross-cultural' psychology has presupposed the categories and models that have been based on (mostly experimental) research with (limited samples of) Euro-American populations. It has mostly either 'tested the hypothesis' or 'validated the instrument' in other cultures or 'measured' the social and psychological characteristics of members of other cultures with the methods and standards of western populations, usually assumed as a valid universal norm.

(b) The new 'cultural psychology' rejects this *universalist* model (Much, 1995). It's become almost a 'standing joke' that experimental (social) psychology is really the psychology of the American undergraduate/psychology major (see Chapter 47). Apart from their accessibility, the argument commonly assumed to justify the practice of studying mostly student behaviour is based upon a sweeping and gratuitous universalist assumption: since we're all human, we're all fundamentally alike in significant psychological functions, and cultural/social contexts of diversity don't affect the important 'deep' or 'hard-wired' structures of the mind. The corollary of this assumption is that the categories and standards developed on western European/North American populations are suitable for 'measuring', understanding and evaluating the characteristics of other populations.

- By contrast, a genuinely transcultural psychology – 'the interplay between the individual and society and [symbolic] culture' (Kakar, 1982, quoted in Much, 1995) – would base its categories, discriminations and generalisations upon empirical knowledge of the fullest possible range of existing human forms of life, without privileging one form as the norm or standard for evaluation.

Penitents in Mauritius, participating in a Hindi religious ceremony. The lower lip is pierced through for the insertion of a copper or brass ring, often with a view to maintain strict silence

By giving a central role to *social interactions* and seeing these as actively producing taken-for-granted knowledge of the world, it follows that language itself is more than simply a way of expressing our thoughts and feelings (as typically assumed by mainstream psychology). When people talk to each other, they (help to) *construct* the world, such that language use is a form of action (it has a '*performative*' role (see Chapter 18).

- *Knowledge and social action go together:* these 'negotiated' understandings could take a wide variety of forms, so that there are many possible 'social constructions' of the world. But each different construction also brings with it, or invites, a different kind of action: how we account for a particular behaviour (what caused it) will dictate how we react to and treat the person whose behaviour it is (see Chapter 23).

Mainstream psychology looks for explanations of social phenomena *inside* the person – for example, by hypothesising the existence of attitudes, motives, cognitions, and so on (*individualism*: see Box 47.1, page 856). This can also be seen as *reductionist* (see Chapter 49). Social constructionists reject this view: explanations are to be found neither inside the individual psyche, nor in social structures or institutions (as advocated by sociologists), but in the *interactive processes* that take place routinely between people. For Burr (2003):

> Knowledge is therefore seen not as something that a person has or doesn't have, but as something that people do together ...

Theoretical contributions and an evaluation of social constructionism

Social constructionism and social representation theory

- According to *social representation theory* (SRT), people come to understand their social world by way of images and social representations (SRs) shared by members of a social group. These representations act like a map which makes a baffling or novel terrain familiar and passable, thereby providing evaluations of good and bad areas. Attitudes are secondary phenomena, underpinned by SRs. SRT tries to provide a historical account of people's understanding of the world (Potter, 1996).
- During the 1950s, the French psychologist, Moscovici, conducted one of the classic pieces of research on SRs. He was interested in how the ideas/concepts of psychoanalytic theory could be absorbed within a culture (post-Second World War France), based on women's magazines, church publications and interviews. He concluded that psychoanalytic theory had trickled down from the analytic couch and learned journals into both 'high' culture and popular common sense: people 'think' with psychoanalytic concepts, without it seeming as if they are doing anything theoretical at all. But rather than the general population of Paris being conversant with/conversing with psychoanalytic theory in all its complexities, they were working with a simplified image of it, with some concepts having a wide currency (such as repression) and others not (such as libido) (Potter, 1996).

Serge Moscovici (born 1925)

- SRT is a *constructionist* theory: instead of portraying people as simply perceiving (or misperceiving) their social worlds, it regards these worlds as constructed, and an SR is a device for doing this construction. It allows someone to make sense of something potentially unfamiliar and to evaluate it. For Moscovici, all thought and understanding are based on the working of SRs, each of which consists of a mixture of concepts, ideas and images; these are both in people's minds and circulating in society.

Box 2.7 What's social about social representations (SRs)?

According to Potter (1996), SRs are truly social for the following reasons:

- they're *generated in communication*. When people interact through gossip, argue with one another or discuss political scandals, they're building up shared pictures of the world: 'social representations are the outcome of an increasing babble and a permanent dialogue between individuals' (Moscovici, 1985). The media play a major role in sustaining, producing and circulating SRs, which cannot be reduced to images inside people's heads;
- they *provide a code for communication*. As a consequence of people sharing SRs, they can clearly understand each other and have free-flowing conversations, since they share a stable version of the world. Communication between people with different SRs is likely to produce conflict;
- they *provide a way of distinguishing social groups*. According to Moscovici, one way of defining a group is in terms of a shared set of SRs, which provide a crucial *homogenising* force for groups.

Newspaper of the Year
THE INDEPENDENT
Arts&BooksReview
£20m in 24 hours
Shocked by the devastation caused by the tsunami, Britons responded yesterday with unprecedented generosity to the appeal for donations

The power of the media to circulate social representations by capturing the 'national mood'

- SRT wasn't published in English until the early 1980s. Since then research has snowballed, especially in Europe, Australia and South America (though it's been largely ignored by mainstream North American social psychologists in the experimental cognitive tradition). Potter (1996) suggests that one reason for this may be that the latter's pursuit of general laws and processes is directly challenged by SRT's emphasis on the specific content of a culture's or group's SR as the main object of analysis.

Social constructionism and feminist psychology

- For Stainton Rogers *et al.* (1995),

> ... there is no conceptual vacuum we can occupy where we can be 'outside' the pressing 'social facts' that constitute our understanding of the world. All we can ever do is ... begin to recognise the illusions which constitute our 'social realities' as illusions and not as really real realities.

- Feminist scholars are concerned with trying to identify and challenge those illusory aspects of our social realities that specifically relate to women. According to Nicolson (1995), they've been consistently developing critiques of *positivist science* (see Chapter 3) for the past 100 years, with momentum and influence gathering especially since the early 1970s.
- Part of this feminist critique involves demonstrating how positivist science, far from being value-free, displays a clear bias towards the 'pathologisation' of women (see Chapters 36, 43, 44 and 47). Nicolson (1995) argues that the scientific method is gender-biased (see Chapters 3 and 47), claiming that the priority western society attaches to science is more problematic today than ever before, because of the relationship of science to the media, which influences human socialisation (cf. the role of the media in circulating SRs: see above). She argues that:

> Psychology relies for its data on the practices of socialised and culture-bound individuals, so that to explore 'natural' or 'culture-free' behaviour (namely that behaviour unfettered by cultural, social structures and power relations) is by definition impossible, which is a state of affairs that normally goes unacknowledged ...

'Normally' denotes *mainstream psychology*. SC, in its various forms, is concerned with acknowledging this 'state of affairs'. The view that 'science as knowledge is fabricated rather than discovered' (Fox, 1993) is gaining popularity among feminist psychologists.

- Although within feminism itself there are many different 'voices', feminism is essentially a reaction to and a product of *patriarchal* culture (or *patriarchy*), and one of its significant roles has been to account for women's subordination. Patriarchy commonly refers to the context and processes through which men and male-dominated institutions (including universities and other organisations that foster scientific endeavour) promote male supremacy. Feminist psychologists seek to *contextualise* women's lives and to explain the constraints, attributed by some to biology, within a social framework: women's lack of social power is made to seem 'natural' by the practice of academic psychology. They also offer a critical challenge to psychological knowledge on gender issues by drawing on other disciplines (such as sociology and anthropology). This rarely occurs in psychology, because, traditionally, it is 'jealous' of its boundaries (Nicolson, 1995).

THE EVOLUTIONARY APPROACH

Basic principles and assumptions

Sociobiology (Wilson, 1975) grew out of the work of evolutionary biologists in the 1960s. Wilson set out to explain all non-human and human social behaviour in terms of evolution and other biological principles. It concentrated on the evolutionary origins of behaviour and tended to imply rigid genetic control (Archer, 1996). Since then, many of these principles have been used to study topics covered by the social sciences – including psychology.

Evolutionary psychology (Buss, 1995) is a development of sociobiology (and is often referred to as '*neo-* or *modern Darwinism*'). According to evolutionary psychology (EP), evolutionary principles are used to link the original *function* of behaviour to current psychological mechanisms, and *flexibility of responding* is central to those mechanisms. Starting with the principle of natural selection, evolutionary psychologists construct a theory of human nature – that is, an overall view of how we should expect humans to behave. From this, they derive and test more specific theories and hypotheses (Archer, 1996).

According to Rose (2000):

> The declared aim of evolutionary psychology is to provide explanations for the patterns of human activity and the forms of organisation of human society which take into account the fact that humans are animals, and like all other currently living organisms, are the present-day products of some four billion years of evolution ...

Box 2.8 Some basic principles and assumptions of evolutionary psychology (EP)

- EP rejects the Standard Social Science Model (SSSM), which makes two broad assumptions about human beings: (a) there's no such thing as human nature, or if there is, it has so little effect on people's social lives that it can be ignored; (b) explanations of social behaviour can be derived from considering only social roles, socialisation and culture.
- Human social behaviour, like that of non-humans, can be understood in terms of its past contribution to survival and reproduction. For example, instead of regarding young males' proneness to violence in terms of social learning (modelling) or frustration (Berkowitz, 1993), EP views it as the result of its past contributions to obtaining resources, status and access to women (Daly and Wilson, 1988a, 1988b: see Chapter 29).
- While acknowledging their debt to sociobiology, evolutionary psychologists contend that sociobiologists often ignored the role of *mind* in mediating links between genes and behaviour. According to Barkow, Cosmides and Tooby (1992), the mind consists of a collection of specialised, independent mechanisms or *modules*, designed by natural selection to solve problems that faced our hunter-gatherer ancestors, such as acquiring a mate, raising children and dealing with rivals. The solutions often involve such emotions as lust, fear, affection, jealousy and anger. Together, these modules and the related emotions constitute *human nature*.
- EP is, in general, about *universal* features of the mind. In so far as individual differences exist, the default assumption is that they're expressions of the same universal human nature as it encounters different environments. *Gender* is the crucial exception to this rule. Natural selection has constructed the mental modules of men and women in very different ways as a result of their divergent reproductive roles (*sexual dimorphism*).
- EP *isn't* a form of *genetic determinism* (or *nativism*). Like most modern biologists and social scientists, evolutionary psychologists argue that 'nature or nurture' is a false dichotomy, and they distinguish themselves from behaviour geneticists (see Chapter 50).

(Based on Horgan, 1995; Rose, 2000)

Theoretical contributions

As indicated in Box 2.8, EP (and sociobiological) explanations can be found throughout psychology. For example, fear is commonly regarded as an adaptive response to threatening stimuli and events, while anxiety is an 'aberration' (see Chapter 44). Similarly, the harmful effects of stress have been explained in evolutionary terms. While the body's stress response evolved to help us cope with life-threatening situations (emergencies), most 'modern-day' stressors aren't like this. Consequently, our bodies react in an inappropriate, and potentially life-threatening, way to 'chronic' stress (see Chapter 12).

Rather more controversially, Buss (1994) claims that men, because they can in principle father a virtually infinite number of children, are much more inclined towards promiscuity than women are. Women, because they can average only one child per year, are choosier in selecting a mate. Men in all cultures place greater emphasis on youth and physical attractiveness, while women look to men's 'resources' (see Chapter 28). Similarly, because men can never be sure that a child is theirs, their jealousy tends to be triggered by fears of a mate's sexual infidelity. Women, on the other hand, become more upset at the thought of losing a mate's emotional commitment – and thus his resources. In turn, women make greater 'parental investment' in their children than men do (see Chapter 32).

Perhaps the best-known, and also one of the most controversial, claims of sociobiology is Dawkins' (1976) 'selfish-gene' theory (see Chapter 30).

Is language an instinct?

According to Pinker (1994), a linguist 'converted' to EP, language is far too complex to be learned: it must stem from an innate 'program' hardwired into our brains. Language almost certainly arose, he claims, because it was adaptive – that is, it conferred benefits on our hunter-gatherer ancestors. It would have allowed early hominids to share learned tool-making, hunting and other skills, and those especially adept at language could manipulate others and form alliances that would increase their chances of producing offspring.

Steven Pinker (born 1954)

Ironically, these claims are *denied* by Chomsky, a fellow linguist and colleague of Pinker's. Chomsky first argued in the 1950s that language represents a distinct mental module (or 'language organ') unique to human beings and independent of general cognitive ability, and that we all possess an innate Language Acquisition Device (LAD: see Chapter 19). In this way, he laid the foundation for EP, and evolutionary psychologists are, in a sense, his heirs (Horgan, 1995; Kohn, 1998).

However, Chomsky disputes the assumption that language is a 'selected trait': just because language is adaptive now, doesn't mean that it *arose* in response to selection pressures. Given the enormous gap between human language and the relatively simple communication systems of other species, and given our fragmentary knowledge of our evolutionary past, science can tell us little about how language evolved. It may have been an incidental/accidental by-product of a spurt in intelligence or of the human brain's large size (Horgan, 1995; Kohn, 1998). The same may be true of other properties of the human mind.

ASK YOURSELF...

- Repeat the exercise as for the other approaches.
- Look at the arguments you formulated for and against the universalist assumption (in relation to social constructionism). Are any of these relevant in evaluating EP?

An evaluation of EP

Our hunter-gatherer past

- EP is based on the belief that the human mind is adapted to cope with life as a Pleistocene hunter-gatherer (which we were for about two million years before the ancient Chinese, Indian, Egyptian and Sumerian civilisations: Abdulla, 1996). Forms of behaviour and social organisation that evolved adaptively over many generations in human hunter-gatherer society may or may not be adaptive in modern industrialised society; but they have become, to a degree, fixed by humanity's evolutionary experience in the Palaeolithic *Environment of Evolutionary Adaptation* (EEA), thought to be the African savannah (Rose, 2000).
- However, just as Chomsky's argument with Pinker concerned *how* language evolved (rather than whether or not it evolved), so the story of our human hunter-gatherer ancestors is, inevitably, partly a work of fiction (Turney, 1999). According to Rose (2000), the descriptions offered by EP of what hunter-gatherer societies were like read little better than 'Just so' accounts:

> There is a circularity about reading this version of the present into the past, and then claiming that this imagined past explains the present.

In other words, based on what human beings are capable of *now*, evolutionary psychologists imagine how these abilities may have evolved, then propose this *constructed past* as the cause of these current abilities.

Can we use 'images' like these of our hunter-gatherer ancestors to explain how our current human abilities evolved?

- Evolutionary psychologists also claim that the timescale of human history has been too short for evolutionary selection pressures to have produced significant change; but we know very little about just how quickly such change can occur (Rose, 2000). Evolutionarily, modern humans appeared 100,000 years ago. Allowing 15–20 years for each generation, there have been 5000–6600 generations between human origins and modern times. We really have no idea whether these generations are 'time enough' for substantial evolutionary change:

> However, granted the very rapid changes in human environment, social organisation, technology, and mode of production that have clearly occurred over that period, one must assume significant selection pressures operating ... the automatic assumption that the Palaeolithic was an EEA in which fundamental human traits were fixed, and that there has not been time since to alter them, does not bear serious inspection. (Rose, 2000)

Box 2.9 EP, computers and emotion

- Drawing heavily on the jargon and conceptual framework of computer science and artificial intelligence (see Chapter 20), evolutionary psychologists see the mind as a *cognitive machine*, an information-processing device that is 'run' by the brain. It's *not* a general-purpose computer, but is composed of several specific modules (see Box 2.8). For Rose (2000), however:

> *... it is not adequate to reduce the mind/brain to nothing more than a cognitive 'architectural' information-processing machine. Brains/minds do not just deal with information. They are concerned with living meaning ... the key feature which distinguishes brains/minds from computers is their/our capacity to experience emotion. Indeed, emotion is primary – which may be why Darwin devoted an entire book to it rather than to cognition.* (Rose, 2000)

- Several neuroscientists have devoted considerable attention to the mechanisms and survival advantages of emotion (e.g. LeDoux, 1998: see Chapter 44). This makes it all the more surprising that evolutionary psychologists give so much emphasis to cognitive functions. For Rose:

> *... affect and cognition are inextricably engaged in all brain and mind processes, creating meaning out of information – just one more reason why brains aren't computers.*

- Most remarkable of all is the phrase used by Cosmides, Tooby and others, namely the 'architecture of the mind', implying a static, stable structure, built to a blueprint. Nothing could be less appropriate for capturing the fluid, dynamic process whereby our minds/brains develop, creating 'order out of the blooming buzzing confusion of the world which confronts us moment by moment'. (Rose, 2000)

Phylogeny and ontogeny

- According to Karmiloff-Smith (2000), developmental psychologists see *plasticity* during brain growth as the rule rather than the exception or a response to brain injury (see Chapter 4). Cosmides & Tooby (1994) compare the newborn brain to a Swiss army knife, crammed with independent functional tools, each designed for a specific problem that faced our hunter-gatherer ancestors (see Box 2.8).
- But even if we set aside the problem of knowing just what the problems faced by our ancestors were (and, therefore, what tools they needed), Karmiloff-Smith believes that it's just as plausible that, unlike the gross macro-structure of the brain, cortical micro-circuitry *isn't* innately specified by evolution but is progressively constructed by the postnatal experience of different kinds of input. She argues that:

> Evolution has helped to guarantee human survival by raising the upper limits on complexity and avoiding too much prespecification of higher cognitive functions ...

Development requires both evolution (*phylogeny*) and *ontogeny* (individual development):

> A multitude of different learning mechanisms which may have emerged from evolution might, during ontogeny, each discover inputs from the environment that are more or less suited to their form of processing. Gradually, with development and with trying to process different kinds of input, each mechanism would become progressively more domain-specific.

Hence:

> Evolutionary psychology's Swiss army knife view of the brain is inappropriate for understanding higher cognitive functions, particularly for children ... (Karmiloff-Smith, 2000)

Violent stepfathers and the problem of unfalsifiability

- According to Daly & Wilson (1988a, 1988b), children under the age of two were at least 60 times more likely to be killed by a step-parent – and almost always a stepfather – than by a natural parent. This is exactly what evolutionary theory would predict, since step-parents and step-children are genetically unrelated, while a child inherits half its genes from each biological parent.
- However, most stepfathers *don't* kill or abuse, and a minority of biological fathers do; these findings are difficult to square with any explanation based on shared/non-shared genes.
- More seriously, in discussing women who kill their newborn babies, Pinker (1997b) claimed that when such an act takes place in conditions of poverty, it could be regarded as an *adaptationist* response. The psychological module that normally induces protectiveness in mothers of newborns is switched off by the challenge of an impoverished environment. This means that both killing and protecting are explained by evolutionary selection. As Hilary Rose (2000) says, this explains everything and, therefore, nothing.

CONCLUSIONS

The focus of this discussion of various theoretical approaches within psychology has been on how each conceptualises human beings. Freud's 'tension-reducing person', Skinner's 'environmentally controlled person' and Rogers' 'growth-motivated person' really are quite different from each other (Nye, 2000). The person-as-information-processor and the person-as-shaped-by-our-evolutionary-past are different again – both from each other and from the first three approaches. SC's image of the person is rather less concrete and more elusive: what people are like and what they do is *relative* to their culture, historical period, and so on.

However, we've also noted some important similarities between different approaches, such as the deterministic nature of Freud's and Skinner's theories, and the in-fluence of the information-processing approach on we shall see throughout this book, each approach has something of value to contribute to our understanding of ourselves – even if it is only to reject the particular explanation it offers. The diversity of approaches reflects the complexity of the subject matter, so, usually, there's room for a diversity of explanations.

CHAPTER SUMMARY

- Different theoretical **approaches/perspectives** are based on different models/images of the nature of human beings.
- **Methodological behaviourism** focuses on what can be quantified and observed by different researchers. Skinner's **radical behaviourism** regards mental processes as both **inaccessible** and **irrelevant** for explaining behaviour.
- The **behaviourist approach** stresses the role of environmental influences (**learning**), especially **classical** and **operant conditioning**. Psychology's aim is to **predict** and **control** behaviour.
- Tolman's **cognitive behaviourism** and **social learning theory** represent modifications of 'orthodox' learning (conditioning) theory.
- Methodological behaviourism has influenced the practice of scientific psychology in general. Other practical contributions include **behaviour therapy** and **modification**, **behavioural neuroscience** and **pharmacology**, and **biofeedback**.
- The **psychodynamic approach** is based on Freud's **psychoanalytic theory**. Central aspects are the **unconscious** (especially **repression**), **infantile sexuality**, and the impact of **early experience**.
- Freud's ideas have become part of **mainstream psychology**, contributing to our understanding of motivation, sleep and dreams, forgetting, attachment, aggression and abnormality.
- Major modifications/alternatives to Freudian theory include **ego psychology**, Erikson's **psychosocial theory**, and the **object relations school**.
- All forms of **psychotherapy** stem directly or indirectly from **psychoanalysis**. Many trained psychoanalysts have been responsible for developing radically different therapeutic approaches, including Rogers, Perls and Wolpe.
- Maslow called the **humanistic approach** the 'third force' in psychology. It believes in free will, adopts a **phenomenological perspective**, and stresses the **positive** aspects of human personality.
- Rogers was a prolific researcher into the effectiveness of his **client/person-centred therapy**, opened up psychotherapy to psychologists and other non-medically qualified practitioners, and created a counselling profession that operates within a wide diversity of settings.
- The **cognitive approach** lacks both a central figure and a unifying theory. It uses **analogies** and **metaphors** when trying to describe what's going on inside the brain, in particular the **computer analogy** and the view of people as **information processors**.
- Other important features of the cognitive approach include the concepts of **coding**, **channel capacity** and **serial/parallel processing**.
- A major application of the cognitive approach has been **cognitive behaviour therapy**, as in Ellis's **rational emotive behaviour therapy** (REBT).
- While the computer analogy is a useful way of understanding cognitive processes, there are also some important **differences** between how computers and people process information.
- One of the goals of **social constructionism** (SC) is to correct the tendency of mainstream psychology to **decontextualise** behaviour. Related to this is the **universalist assumption**, which is challenged by **(trans)cultural** (as distinct from **cross-cultural**) **psychology**.
- **Social representation theory** (SRT) is a social constructionist theory, and many **feminist psychologists** adopt a social constructionist approach in challenging mainstream psychology.
- **Evolutionary psychology** (EP) grew out of **sociobiology**. Unlike the latter, EP puts the **mind** in centre stage, identifying several independent mental mechanisms or **modules**. These form the core of **human nature**.
- A major assumption of EP is that these mental modules have become fixed by our hunter-gatherer ancestors' experience in the Palaeolithic **Environment of Evolutionary Evolution** (EEA). But knowledge of the EEA is largely speculative, and there's good reason to believe that human traits have changed since that time.
- The notion of the 'architecture of the mind' is contradicted by the dynamic nature of brain activity and development, which requires both evolution (**phylogeny**) and individual development (**ontogeny**).

Links with other topics/chapters

- The description of classical and operant conditioning as forms of associative learning reflects the philosophical roots of behaviourism, namely the *empiricist* philosophy of John Locke. This was a major influence on the development of science in general, as well as on behaviourism in particular (Chapter 3).
- Defining the aims of a science of behaviour as prediction and control raises both *conceptual* questions (about the *nature of science*, in particular the role of theory: Chapter 3) and *ethical* questions (for example, about

power and the role of *psychologists as agents of change*: Chapter 48).

- The *ethics* of some forms of *behaviour modification* (such as the token economy) and certain aspects of *applied behaviour analysis* (especially the use of punishment with vulnerable individuals) have been seriously questioned (Chapters 45 and 48).
- Many psychologists would agree that there are degrees or levels of *consciousness*, but most wouldn't share Freud's distinction between the conscious, preconscious and unconscious mind (Chapter 7).
- The distinction between cultural psychology and cross-cultural psychology corresponds to the *emic–etic distinction* (Chapter 47).
- Social constructionism is consistent with Whorf's *linguistic relativity hypothesis* and the more general theory of *linguistic determinism* (language determines thought) (Chapter 18).
- Discursive psychology (a social constructionist approach) finds nothing odd about the common finding that *attitudes are often poor predictors of behaviour* (see Critical Discussion 24.1, page 411).
- Social representations are an important part of *social cognition* and *social perception* (Chapter 22, pages 379–381).

3

PSYCHOLOGY AS A SCIENCE

INTRODUCTION AND OVERVIEW

As we saw in Chapter 1, psychology is commonly defined as the scientific study of behaviour and cognitive processes (or mind or experience). In effect, this book as a whole looks at how different psychologists have put this definition into practice, through their use of various investigative methods to study a wide variety of behaviours and cognitive processes.

This chapter turns the spotlight once more on the definition of psychology given above. It does this by examining the nature of science (including the major features of scientific method), and by tracing some of the major developments in psychology's history as a scientific discipline. This enables us to address the question of how appropriate it is to use scientific method to study human behaviour and cognitive processes, and to assess the validity of this widely accepted definition.

SOME PHILOSOPHICAL ROOTS OF SCIENCE AND PSYCHOLOGY

The seventeenth-century French philosopher Descartes was the first person to distinguish formally between mind and matter (*philosophical dualism*: see Chapter 49), which had an enormous impact on the development of both psychology as a science and science in general. Dualism allowed scientists to treat matter as inert and completely distinct from human beings, which meant that the world could be described *objectively*, without reference to the human observer. *Objectivity* became the ideal of science, and was extended to the study of human behaviour and social institutions in the mid-1800s by Comte, who called it *positivism*.

Descartes also promoted *mechanism*, the view that the material world comprises objects which are assembled like a huge machine and operated by mechanical laws. He extended this view to living organisms, including, eventually, humans. Because the mind (unlike the physical world) is non-material, Descartes believed that it can be investigated only through *introspection* (observing one's own thoughts and feelings: see Chapter 1, page 4). He was also one of the first advocates of *reductionism* (see Chapter 49).

René Descartes (1596–1650)

Empiricism refers to the ideas of the seventeenth- and eighteenth-century British philosophers, Locke, Hume and Berkeley. They believed that the only source of true knowledge about the world is sensory experience (what comes to us through our senses or can be inferred about the relationship between such sensory facts). Empiricism is usually contrasted with *nativism* (or *rationalism*), according to which knowledge of the world is largely innate or inborn.

The word '*empirical*' ('through the senses') is often used to mean 'scientific', implying that what scientists do, and what distinguishes them from non-scientists, is carry out experiments and observations as ways of collecting data or 'facts' about the world (hence, 'empirical methods' for 'scientific methods'). Empiricism proved to be one of the central influences on the development of physics and chemistry.

Empiricism and psychology

Prior to the 1870s, there were no laboratories devoted specifically to psychological research, and the early scientific psychologists had trained mainly as physiologists, doctors, philosophers, or some combination of these. The two professors who set up the first two psychological laboratories deserve much of the credit for the development of academic psychology. They were Wundt (1832–1920) in Germany, and James (1842–1910) in the USA (Fancher, 1979).

Wundt's contribution

A physiologist by training, Wundt is generally regarded as the 'founder' of the new science of experimental psychology, or what he called 'a new domain of science' (1874). Having worked as Helmholtz's assistant (see Chapter 15), Wundt eventually became professor of 'scientific philosophy' at Leipzig University in 1875, illustrating the lack of distinct boundaries between the various disciplines that combined to bring about psychology's development (Fancher, 1979).

Wilhelm Wundt (1832–1920)

In 1879, Wundt converted his 'laboratory' at Leipzig into a 'private institute' of experimental psychology. For the first time, a place had been set aside for the explicit purpose of conducting psychological research, and hence 1879 is widely accepted as the 'birth date' of psychology as a discipline in its own right. From its modest beginnings, the institute began to attract people from all over the world, who returned to their own countries to establish laboratories modelled on Wundt's.

Box 3.1 Wundt's study of the conscious mind: introspective psychology and structuralism

- Wundt believed that conscious mental states could be scientifically studied through the systematic manipulation of *antecedent variables* (those that occur before some other event), and analysed by carefully controlled techniques of *introspection*.
- Introspection was a rigorous and highly disciplined technique for analysing conscious experience into its most basic elements (*sensations* and *feelings*). Participants were always advanced psychology students, who'd been carefully trained to introspect properly.
- Sensations are the raw sensory content of consciousness, devoid of all 'meaning' or interpretation, and all conscious thoughts, ideas and perceptions were assumed to be combinations of sensations. Based on his experiment in which he listened to a metronome beating at varying rates, Wundt concluded that feelings could be analysed in terms of *pleasantness–unpleasantness*, *tension–relaxation* and *activity–passivity*.
- Wundt believed that introspection made it possible to cut through the learned categories and concepts that define our everyday experience of the world, and so expose the 'building blocks' of experience.
- Because of introspection's central role, Wundt's early brand of psychology was called *introspective psychology* (or *introspectionism*), and his attempt to analyse consciousness into its elementary sensations and feelings is known as *structuralism*.

(Based on Fancher, 1979)

ASK YOURSELF...

- Consider the difficulties that might be involved in relying on introspection to formulate an account of the nature of conscious experience (i.e. an account that applies to *people in general*).
- In what ways is structuralism *reductionist*? (See Chapter 49.)
- Which major theory of perception rejects this structuralist approach, and what are its principal features? (See Chapter 15.)

James's contribution

James taught anatomy and physiology at Harvard University in 1872, and by 1875 was calling his course 'The Relations Between Physiology and Psychology'. In the same year, he established a small laboratory, used mainly for teaching purposes. In 1878, he dropped anatomy and physiology, and for several years taught 'pure psychology'.

His view of psychology is summarised in *The Principles of Psychology* (1890), which includes discussion of instinct, brain function, habit, the stream of consciousness, the self (see Chapter 33), attention (Chapter 13), memory (Chapter 17), perception (Chapters 15 and 16), free will (Chapter 49), and emotion (Chapter 10).

William James (1842–1910)

The Principles of Psychology provided the famous definition of psychology as 'the science of mental life' (see Chapter 1). But ironically, James was very critical both of his book and of what psychology could offer as a science. He became increasingly interested in philosophy and lost interest in psychology, although in 1894 he became the first American to call favourable attention to the recent work of the then little known Viennese neurologist, Sigmund Freud (Fancher, 1979).

James proposed a point of view (rather than a theory) that directly inspired *functionalism*, which emphasises the purpose and utility of behaviour (Fancher, 1979). Functionalism, in turn, helped to stimulate interest in *individual differences*, since they determine how well or poorly individuals adapt to their environments. These attitudes made Americans especially receptive to Darwin's (1859) ideas about individual variation, evolution by natural selection, and the 'survival of the fittest' (see Chapter 2).

Charles Darwin (1809–1882)

Watson's behaviourist revolution

Watson took over the psychology department at Johns Hopkins University in 1909, and immediately began cutting psychology's ties with philosophy and strengthening those with biology. At that time, Wundt's and James's studies of consciousness were still the 'real' psychology, but Watson was doing research on non-human animals and became increasingly critical of the use of introspection.

John Broadus Watson (1878–1958)

In particular, Watson argued that introspective reports were unreliable and difficult to verify. It's impossible to check the accuracy of such reports, because they're based on purely *private experience*, to which the investigator has no possible means of access. As a result, Watson redefined psychology in his famous 'behaviourist manifesto' of 1913.

Box 3.2 Watson's (1913) 'behaviourist manifesto'

- Watson's article 'Psychology as the behaviourist views it' is often referred to as the 'behaviourist manifesto', a charter for a truly scientific psychology. It was behaviourism that was to represent a rigorous empiricist approach within psychology for the first time. According to Watson:

psychology as the behaviourist views it is a purely objective natural science. Its theoretical goal is the prediction and control of behaviour. Introspection forms no essential part of its methods, nor is the scientific value of its data dependent upon the readiness with which they lend themselves to interpretation in terms of consciousness. The behaviourist ... recognises no dividing line between man and brute. The behaviour of a man ... forms only a part of the behaviourist's total scheme of investigation.

- Three features of this 'manifesto' deserve special mention:

1. Psychology must be purely *objective*, excluding all subjective data or interpretations in terms of conscious experience. This redefines psychology as the '*science of behaviour*' (rather than the 'science of mental life').
2. The goals of psychology should be to *predict* and *control* behaviour (as opposed to describing and explaining conscious mental states), a goal later endorsed by Skinner's *radical behaviourism* (see Chapter 2).
3. There's no fundamental (*qualitative*) distinction between human and non-human behaviour. If, as Darwin had shown, humans evolved from more simple species, then it follows that human behaviour is simply a more complex form of the behaviour of other species (the difference is merely *quantitative* – one of degree). Consequently, rats, cats, dogs and pigeons became the major source of psychological data. Since 'psychological' now meant 'behaviour' rather than 'consciousness', non-humans that were convenient to study, and whose environments could be easily controlled, could replace people as experimental subjects.

(Based on Fancher, 1979; Watson, 1913)

ASK YOURSELF...

- Try to formulate arguments for and against Watson's claim that there's only a quantitative difference between the behaviour of humans and non-humans.

In his 1915 presidential address to the American Psychological Association, Watson talked about his recent 'discovery' of Pavlov's work on conditioned reflexes in dogs. He proposed that the conditioned reflex could become the foundation for a full-scale human psychology.

The extreme environmentalism of Locke's empiricism (see above) lent itself well to the behaviourist emphasis on learning (through the process of Pavlovian or classical conditioning). While Locke had described the mind at birth as a *tabula rasa* ('blank slate') on which experience writes, Watson, in rejecting the mind as suitable for a scientific psychology, simply swapped mind for *behaviour*: it's now behaviour that's shaped by the environment.

According to Miller (1962), empiricism provided psychology with both (a) a *methodology* (stressing the role of observation and measurement) and (b) a *theory*, including *analysis into elements* (such as stimulus–response units) and *associationism* (which explains how simple elements can be combined to form more complex ones).

Behaviourism also embodied positivism, in particular the emphasis on the need for scientific rigour and objectivity. Humans were now conceptualised and studied as 'natural phenomena', with subjective experience, consciousness, and other characteristics (traditionally regarded as distinctive human qualities) no longer having a place in the behaviourist world.

The cognitive revolution

Academic psychology in the USA and the UK was dominated by behaviourism for the next 40 years. However, criticism and dissatisfaction with it culminated in a number of 'events', all taking place in 1956, which, collectively, are referred to as the 'cognitive revolution'.

Box 3.3 The 1956 'cognitive revolution'

- At a meeting at the Massachusetts Institute of Technology (MIT), Chomsky introduced his theory of language (see Chapter 19), Miller presented a paper on the 'magical number seven' in short-term memory (see Chapter 17), and Newell and Simon presented a paper on the logical theory machine (or logic theorist), with a further paper by Newell *et al.* (1958), which Newell and Simon (1972) extended into the general problem-solver (GPS: see Chapter 20).
- The first systematic attempt to investigate concept formation (in adults) from a cognitive psychological perspective was reported (Bruner *et al.*, 1956).
- At Dartmouth College, New Hampshire (the 'Dartmouth Conference'), ten academics met to discuss the possibility of producing computer programs that could 'behave' or 'think' intelligently. These academics included McCarthy (generally attributed with having coined the term 'artificial intelligence'), Minsky, Simon, Newell, Chomsky and Miller (see Chapter 20).

(Based on Eysenck and Keane, 1995)

George A. Miller (born 1920)

This new way of thinking about and investigating people was called the *information-processing approach*. At its centre is the *computer analogy*, the view that human cognition can be understood by comparing it with the functioning of a digital computer. It was now acceptable to study the mind again, although its conceptualisation was very different from that of Wundt, James and the other pioneers of the 'new psychology' prior to Watson's 'behaviourist revolution'.

Science, scientism and mainstream psychology

Despite this major change in psychology after 1956, certain central assumptions and practices within the discipline have remained essentially the same, and these are referred to as *mainstream psychology*. Harré (1989) refers to the mainstream as the 'old paradigm', which he believes continues to be haunted by certain 'unexamined presuppositions'. One of these is *scientism*, defined by Van Langenhove (1995) as:

> ... the borrowing of methods and a characteristic vocabulary from the natural sciences in order to discover causal mechanisms that explain psychological phenomena.

Scientism maintains that all aspects of human behaviour can and should be studied using the methods of natural science, which claims to be the sole means of establishing 'objective truth'. This can be achieved by studying phenomena removed from any particular context ('*context-stripping*' exposes them in their 'pure' form), and in a *value-free* way (there's no bias on the investigator's part). The most reliable way of doing this is through the laboratory experiment, the method providing the greatest degree of control over relevant variables (see Box 3.7, page 47). As noted earlier, these beliefs and assumptions add up to the traditional view of science known as positivism.

ASK YOURSELF...

- Try to find examples of experimental studies of human behaviour that fit the definition of 'context-stripping' given above. Probably the 'best' examples will come from social psychology, which in itself should suggest criticisms of this approach to studying behaviour. (See also Chapter 47.)

Although much research has moved beyond the confines of the laboratory experiment, the same positivist logic is still central to how psychological enquiry is conceived and conducted. Method and measurement still have a privileged status:

> Whether concerned with mind or behaviour (and whether conducted inside or outside the laboratory), research tends to be constructed in terms of the separation (or reduction) of entities into independent and dependent variables and the measurement of hypothesised relationships between them. (Smith *et al.*, 1995)

Despite the fact that since the mid-1970s the natural sciences model has become the subject of vigorous attacks, psychology is still to a large extent dominated by it. The most prominent effect of this is the dominance of experiments (Van Langenhove, 1995). This has far-reaching effects on the way psychology *pictures* people as more or less passive and mechanical information-processing devices, whose behaviour can be split up into variables. It also affects the way psychology *deals* with people. In experiments, people aren't treated as single individuals, but as interchangeable 'subjects'. There's no room for individualised observations.

WHAT DO WE MEAN BY 'SCIENCE'?

The major features of science

Most psychologists and philosophers of science would probably agree that for a discipline to be called a science, it must possess certain characteristics. These are summarised in Box 3.4 and Figure 3.1.

Box 3.4 The major features of science

- **A definable subject matter.** This changed from conscious human thought to human and non-human behaviour, then to cognitive processes, within psychology's first 80 years as a separate discipline.
- **Theory construction.** This represents an attempt to *explain* observed phenomena, such as Watson's attempt to account for (almost all) human and non-human behaviour in terms of classical conditioning, and Skinner's subsequent attempt to do the same with operant conditioning (see Chapters 2 and 11).
- **Hypothesis testing.** This involves making specific *predictions* about behaviour under certain conditions (for example, predicting that by combining the sight of a rat with the sound of a hammer crashing down on a steel bar just behind his head, a small child will learn to fear the rat, as in the case of Little Albert: see Key Study 11.1, page 174).
- **Empirical methods.** These are used to collect *data* (*evidence*) relevant to the hypothesis being tested.

What is 'scientific method'?

The account given in Box 3.4 and Figure 3.1 of what constitutes a science is non-controversial. However, it fails to tell us how the *scientific process* takes place, the sequence of 'events' involved (such as where the theory comes from in the first place, and how it's related to observation of the subject matter), or the exact relationship between theory construction, hypothesis testing, and data collection.

Collectively, these 'events' and relationships are referred to as (the) *scientific method*. Table 3.1 summarises some common beliefs about both science and scientific method, together with some alternative views.

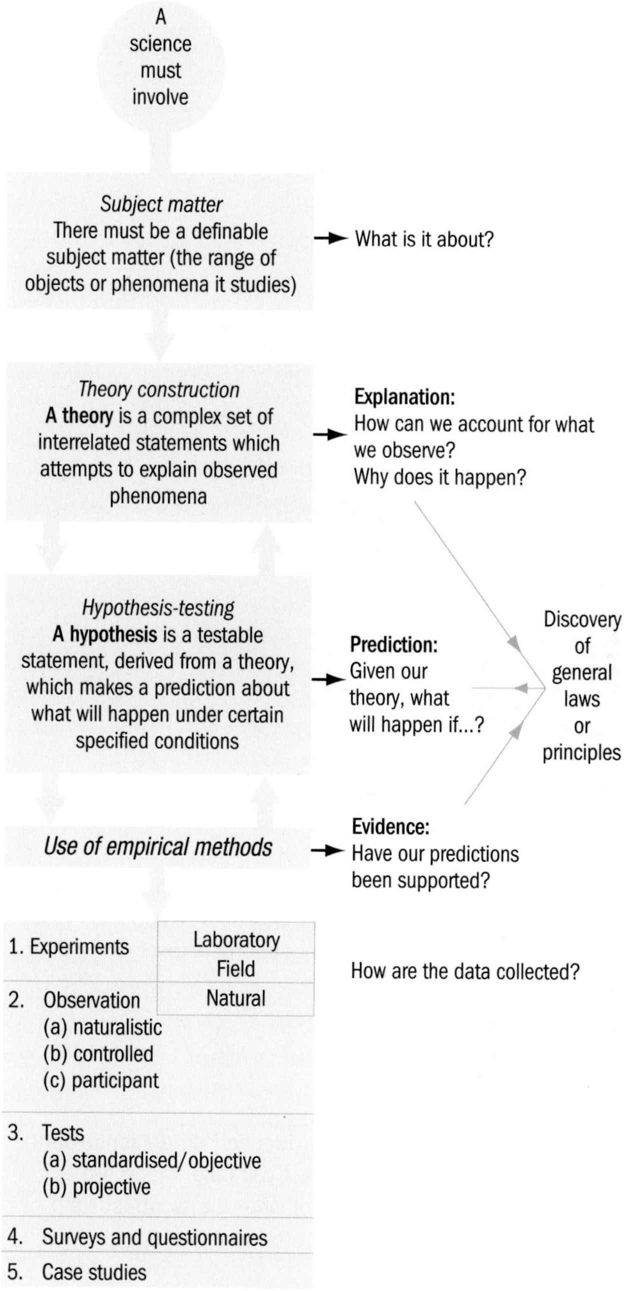

Figure 3.1 A summary of the major features of a science

Box 3.5 The inner world of scientists

- According to Richards and Wolpert (1997), scientists, outside their own habitat, are a poorly understood species. If they feature in popular awareness at all, it's through a limited set of media stereotypes. With a few exceptions, if scientists aren't mad or bad, they're perceived as personality-free, their measured tones and formal reports implying ways of thinking and working far removed from the intellectual and emotional 'messiness' of other human activities.

- Richards and Wolpert engaged in a series of conversations with several eminent scientists (including chemists, immunologists, biologists, biochemists, neuro- and evolutionary biologists) in an attempt to redress the balance, and give a rare glimpse of the human reality of scientific life.
- Scientists think and feel about their work using the same psychological apparatus as the rest of us. The human qualities of science come over very strongly: its energy and imaginative richness, the frustration, love and despair that enslave its practitioners.
- For example, Mitchison (an immunologist) says that experiments start with 'the act of creation':

Not all experiments you think of are good experiments, but thinking of one is just wonderful, eureka! It's fantastic.

- According to Edelman (an immunologist and neurobiologist), stumbling upon the solution to a problem when you least expect to find it is a 'remarkable pleasure'. Some scientists are like voyeurs, with 'almost a lustful feeling of excitement when a secret of nature is revealed'.

(Adapted from Richards and Wolpert, 1997)

The original 'Eureka' ('I have found it') moment – Archimedes (287–212 BC) discovering the principle of buoyancy

Table 3.1 Some common beliefs and alternative views about 'science' and 'scientific method'

Common beliefs	Alternative views
● Scientific discovery begins with simple, unbiased, unprejudiced observation: the scientist simply 'samples' the world without any preconceptions, expectations or predetermined theories.	● There's no such thing as 'unbiased' or 'unprejudiced' observation. Observation is always selective, interpretative, prestructured, and directed: we must have at least some idea of what we're looking for, otherwise we cannot know when we've found it. Goldberg (2000) cites a philosophy professor who asserted that what we call 'data' (that which is given) should more accurately be called 'capta' (that which is taken).
■ From the resulting sensory evidence ('data'/sense-data), generalised statements of fact will take shape: we gradually build up a picture of what the world is like based on a number of separate 'samples'.	■ 'Data' don't constitute 'facts': evidence usually implies measurements, numbers, and recordings, which need to be interpreted in the light of a theory. Facts don't exist objectively and cannot be discovered through 'pure observation'. 'Fact' = Data + Theory (Deese, 1972).
▲ The essential feature of scientific activity is the use of empirical methods, through which the sensory evidence is gathered: what distinguishes science from non-science is performing experiments etc.	▲ Despite the central role of data collection, data alone don't make a science. Theory is just as crucial, because without it data have no meaning (see point above).
▼ The truth about the world (the objective nature of things, what the world is 'really like') can be established through properly controlled experiments and other ways of collecting 'facts': science can tell us about reality as it is *independently* of the scientist or the activity of observing it.	▼ Scientific theory and research reflect the biases, prejudices, values and assumptions of the individual scientist, as well as of the scientific community s/he belongs to. Science *isn't* value-free (see Chapter 47).
◆ Science involves the steady accumulation of knowledge: each generation of scientists adds to the discoveries of previous generations.	◆ Science involves an endless succession of long, peaceful periods ('normal science') and 'scientific revolutions' (Kuhn, 1962: see Table 3.3, page 43).
	✻ Science has a warm, human, exciting, argumentative, creative 'face' (Collins, 1994: see Box 3.5).

(Based on Medawar, 1963; Popper, 1972)

Table 3.2 Comparison between the classical, inductive view of science and Popper's revised version

Inductive method	**Popper's version**
Observation and method	Problem (usually a refutation of an existing theory or prediction)
Inductive generalisation	Proposed solution or new theory
Hypothesis	Deduction of testable statements (hypotheses) from the new theory. This relates to the *hypothetico-deductive method*, which is usually contrasted with/opposed to the inductive method. In practice, both approaches are involved in the scientific process and are complementary
Attempted verification of hypothesis	Tests or attempts to refute by methods including observation and experiment
Proof or disproof	Establishing a preference between competing theories
Knowledge	

(Based on Popper, 1972)

As a result of the first two beliefs identified in Table 3.1, Popper (1972) has revised the stages of the scientific process as proposed by the classical view (the *inductive method*). This, together with Popper's revised version, is shown in Table 3.2.

Can psychology be a science if psychologists cannot agree what psychology is?

As we noted earlier, definitions of psychology have changed during its lifetime, largely reflecting the influence and contributions of its major theoretical approaches or orientations. In this chapter (and Chapter 2) we've seen that each approach rests upon a different image of what people are like. This, in turn, determines what's considered worthy of investigation, as well as the methods of study that can and should be used to investigate it. Consequently, different approaches can be seen as self-contained disciplines, as well as different facets of the same discipline (Kline, 1988; Kuhn, 1962).

ASK YOURSELF...

- What is the underlying image of the person associated with each of the major theoretical approaches within psychology?
- Which of these do you consider captures your own experience, and your experience of others, most accurately, and why? (You might find it helpful to refer to both Chapters 2 and 45.)

Kuhn argues that a field of study can only legitimately be considered a science if a majority of its workers subscribe to a common, global perspective or *paradigm*. According to Kuhn, this means that psychology is *preparadigmatic*: it lacks a paradigm, without which it's still in a state (or stage) of *prescience*. Whether psychology has, or has ever had, a paradigm, is hotly debated.

Is a theoretical approach the same as a paradigm?

As Table 3.3 shows, Kuhn (a philosopher of science), along with some psychologists, maintains that psychology is still a prescience. Others believe that psychology has already undergone at least two revolutions, and is in a stage of normal science, with cognitive psychology the current paradigm. A third view, which represents a blend of the first two, is that psychology currently, and simultaneously, has a number of paradigms.

For example, Smith *et al.* (1998) identify psychoanalysis, behaviourism, sociobiology, and the information-processing, and cognitive–developmental approaches as paradigms, with the last being the most important as far as child development is concerned (see Chapters 34 and 35).

Table 3.3 Stages in the development of a science (▲) and their application to psychology (■)

▲ *Prescience:* No paradigm has evolved, and there are several schools of thought or theoretical orientations.

■ Like Kuhn, Joynson (1980) and Boden (1980) argue that psychology is preparadigmatic. Kline (1988) sees its various approaches as involving different paradigms.

▲ *Normal science:* A paradigm has emerged, dictating the kind of research that's carried out and providing a framework for interpreting results. The details of the theory are filled in, and workers explore its limits. Disagreements can usually be resolved within the limits allowed by the paradigm.

■ According to Valentine (1982), *behaviourism* comes as close as anything could to a paradigm. It provides: (a) a clear definition of the subject matter (behaviour as opposed to 'the mind'); (b) fundamental assumptions, in the form of the central role of learning (especially conditioning), and the analysis of behaviour into stimulus–response units, which allow prediction and control; (c) a methodology, with the controlled experiment at its core.

▲ *Revolution:* A point is reached in most established sciences where the conflicting evidence becomes so overwhelming that the old paradigm has to be abandoned and is replaced by a new one (*paradigm shift*). For example, Newtonian physics was replaced by Einstein's theory of relativity. When this paradigm shift occurs, there's a return to *normal science*.

■ Palermo (1971) and LeFrancois (1983) argue that psychology has already undergone several paradigm shifts. The first paradigm was *structuralism*, represented by Wundt's introspectionism. This was replaced by Watson's *behaviourism*. Finally, *cognitive psychology* largely replaced behaviourism, based on the computer analogy and the concept of information processing. Glassman (1995) disagrees, claiming that there's never been a complete reorganisation of the discipline, as has happened in physics.

Thomas Kuhn (1922–1996)

For Davison *et al.* (2004) the current paradigms in psychopathology and therapy are the biological, psychoanalytic, humanistic and existential, learning (behaviourist) and cognitive (see Chapter 45).

Lambie (1991) believes it's a mistake to equate 'paradigm' with 'approach'. As noted in Table 3.2, while theory is an essential part of a paradigm, there's much more involved than this. For example, different theories can coexist within the same overall approach, such as classical and operant conditioning within 'learning theory' (the behaviourist approach), and Freud's and Erikson's theories within the psychodynamic approach.

One of the 'ingredients' that makes a paradigm different from an approach is its *social psychological* dimension. Paradigms refer to assumptions and beliefs held in common by most, if not all, the members of a given scientific community. This issue is discussed further in the following section.

THE SCIENTIFIC STUDY OF HUMAN BEHAVIOUR

The social nature of science: the problem of objectivity

'Doing science' is part of human behaviour. When psychologists study what people do, they're engaging in some of the very same behaviours they're trying to understand (such as thinking, perceiving, problem-solving and explaining). This is what's meant by the statement that psychologists are part of their own subject matter, which makes it even more difficult for them to be objective than other scientists.

According to Richards (1996b):

> Whereas in orthodox sciences there is always some external object of enquiry – rocks, electrons, DNA, chemicals – existing essentially unchanging in the non-human world (even if never finally knowable 'as it really is' beyond human conceptions), this is not so for psychology. 'Doing psychology' is the human activity of studying human activity; it is human psychology examining itself – and what it produces by way of new theories, ideas and beliefs about itself is also part of our psychology!

Knowable 'as it really is' refers to objectivity, and Richards is claiming that it may be impossible for any scientist to achieve complete objectivity. One reason for this relates to the social nature of scientific activity. As Rose (1997) says:

> How biologists – or any scientists – perceive the world is not the result of simply holding a true reflecting mirror up to nature: it is shaped by the history of our subject, by dominant social expectations and by the patterns of research funding.

Does this mean that 'the truth' only exists 'by agreement'? Does science not tell us about what things are 'really' like, but only what scientists happen to believe is the truth at any particular time?

> *ASK YOURSELF...*
> - Given what was said earlier about the sometimes very intense feelings aroused in individual scientists during the course of their work (see Box 3.5), in what ways do you think science can be described as a social activity? (It might be useful to think about why you do practical work/labs – other than because you have to!)

According to Richardson (1991), whatever the *logical* aspects of scientific method may be (deriving hypotheses from theories, the importance of refutability, and so on), science is a very *social* business. Research must be qualified and quantified to enable others to replicate it, and in this way the procedures, instruments and measures become standardised, so that scientists anywhere in the world can check the truth of reported observations and findings. This implies the need for universally agreed conventions for reporting these observations and findings (Richardson, 1991).

Collins (1994) takes a more extreme view, arguing that the results of experiments are more ambiguous than is usually assumed, while theory is more flexible than most people imagine:

> This means that science can progress only within communities that can reach consensus about what counts as plausible. Plausibility is a matter of social context so science is a 'social construct'. (Collins, 1994)

Kuhn's concept of a paradigm also stresses the role of agreement or consensus among scientists working within a particular discipline. Accordingly, 'truth' has more to do with the popularity and widespread acceptance of a particular framework within the scientific community than with its 'truth value'. The fact that revolutions do occur (paradigm shifts: see Table 3.3) demonstrates that 'the truth' can and does change.

Science is essentially a social process

For example, the change from Newtonian to Einsteinian physics reflected the changing popularity of these two accounts. For Planck (in Kuhn, 1970), who helped to shape the 'Einsteinian revolution':

> A new scientific theory does not triumph by convincing its opponents and making them see the light, but rather because its opponents eventually die, and a new generation grows up that is familiar with it.

The popularity or acceptability of a theory, however, must be at least partly determined by how well it explains and predicts the phenomena in question. In other words, *both* social and 'purely' scientific or rational criteria are relevant.

However, even if there are widely accepted ways of 'doing science', 'good science' doesn't necessarily mean 'good psychology'. Is it valid to study human behaviour and experience as part of the natural world, or is a different kind of approach needed altogether? After all, it isn't just psychologists who observe, experiment and theorise (Heather, 1976).

The psychology experiment as a social situation

To regard empirical research in general, and the experiment in particular, as objective involves two related assumptions:

1. researchers only influence the participants' behaviour (the outcome of the experiment) to the extent that they decide what hypothesis to test, how the variables are to be operationalised, what design to use, and so on;
2. the only factors influencing the participants' performance are the objectively defined variables manipulated by the experimenter.

ASK YOURSELF...

- Try to formulate some arguments against these two assumptions.
- What do the experimenter and participant bring with them to the experimental situation that isn't directly related to the experiment, and how may this (and other factors) influence what goes on in the experimental situation? (See Chapter 47.)

Experimenters are people too: the problem of experimenter bias

According to Rosenthal (1966), what the experimenter is *like* is correlated with what s/he *does*, as well as influencing the participant's perception of, and response to, the experimenter. This is related to *experimenter bias*.

Box 3.6 Some examples of experimenter bias

- According to Valentine (1992), experimenter bias has been demonstrated in a variety of experiments, including reaction time, psychophysics, animal learning, verbal conditioning, personality assessment, person perception, learning and ability, as well as in everyday life situations.
- What these experiments consistently show is that if one group of experimenters has one hypothesis about what it expects to find and another group has the opposite hypothesis, *both* groups will obtain results that support their respective hypotheses. The results *aren't* due to the mishandling of data by biased experimenters, but the experimenter's bias somehow creates a changed environment, in which participants actually behave differently.
- When experimenters were informed that rats learning mazes had been specially bred for this ability ('maze-bright'), they obtained better learning from their rats than did experimenters who believed their rats were 'maze-dull' (Rosenthal & Fode, 1963; Rosenthal & Lawson, 1964). In fact, both groups of rats were drawn from the same population and were *randomly* allocated to the 'bright' or 'dull' condition. The crucial point is that the 'bright' rats did actually learn faster. The experimenters' expectations in some way concretely changed the situation, although how this happened is far less clear.
- In a natural classroom situation, children whose teachers were told they'd show academic 'promise' during the next academic year showed significantly greater IQ gains than children for whom such predictions weren't made (although this latter group also made substantial improvements). In fact, the children were *randomly* allocated to the two conditions. But the teachers' expectations actually produced the predicted improvements in the 'academic promise' group – that is, there was a *self-fulfilling prophecy* (Rosenthal & Jacobson, 1968).

(Based on Valentine, 1992; Weisstein, 1993)

ASK YOURSELF...

- How could you explain the findings from the studies described in Box 3.6?
- How could experimenter expectations actually bring about the different performances of the two groups of rats and children?

Participants are psychologists too: demand characteristics

Instead of seeing the person being studied as a passive responder to whom things are done ('subject'), Orne (1962) stresses what the person *does*, implying a far more *active* role. Participants' performance in an experiment could be thought of as a form of *problem-solving behaviour*. At some level, they see the task as working out the true purpose of the experiment and responding in a way which will support (or not support, in the case of the unhelpful participant) the hypothesis being tested.

In this context, the cues that convey the experimental hypothesis to participants represent important influences on their behaviour, and the sum total of those cues are called the *demand characteristics* of the experimental situation. These cues include:

> ... the rumours or campus scuttlebutt [gossip] about the research, the information conveyed during the original situation, the person of the experimenter, and the setting of the laboratory, as well as all explicit and implicit communications during the experiment proper. (Orne, 1962)

This tendency to identify the demand characteristics is related to the tendency to play the role of a 'good' (or 'bad') experimental participant.

KEY STUDY 3.1 The lengths that some people will go to to please the experimenter (Orne, 1962)

- Orne points out that if people are asked to do five push-ups as a favour, they'll ask 'Why?', but if the request comes from an experimenter, they'll ask 'Where?'
- Similarly, he reports an experiment in which people were asked to add sheets of random numbers, then tear them up into at least 32 pieces. Five and a half hours later, they were still doing it, and the experimenter had to tell them to stop!
- This demonstrates very clearly the strong tendency of people to want to please the experimenter, and not to 'upset the experiment'. It's mainly in this sense that Orne sees the experiment as a social situation, in which the people involved play different but complementary roles. In order for this interaction to proceed fairly smoothly, each must have some idea of what the other expects of him or her.

The expectations referred to in Key Study 3.1 are part of the culturally shared understandings of what science in general, and psychology in particular, involves and

What we only do for the sake of science

without which the experiment couldn't 'happen' (Moghaddam *et al.*, 1993). So, not only is the experiment a social situation, but science itself is a *culture-related phenomenon*. This represents another respect in which science cannot claim complete objectivity.

The problem of representativeness

Traditional, mainstream experimental psychology adopts a *nomothetic* ('law-like') approach. This involves generalisation from limited samples of participants to 'people in general', as part of the attempt to establish general 'laws' or principles of behaviour (see Figure 3.1 and Chapter 42).

ASK YOURSELF...

- The photograph below captures a fairly typical scene as far as participant characteristics in mainstream psychological research are concerned.
- In this photograph of one of Asch's famous conformity experiments (see Chapter 26, page 444), what are the most apparent characteristics of the experimental participants, and how are they similar to/different from those of Asch (who's pictured furthest right)?

Despite the fact that Asch's experiments were carried out in the early 1950s, very little has changed as far as participant samples are concerned. In American psychology, at least, the typical participant is a psychology undergraduate, who's obliged to take part in a certain number of studies as a course requirement, and who receives 'course credits' for so doing (Krupat and Garonzik, 1994).

Mainstream British and American psychology has implicitly equated 'human being' with 'member of western culture'. Despite the fact that the vast majority of research participants are members of western societies, the resulting findings and theories have been applied to 'human beings', as if culture made no difference (they are 'culture-bound and culture-blind': Sinha, 1997). This *Anglocentric* or *Eurocentric bias* (a form of *ethnocentrism*) is matched by the *androcentric* or *masculinist bias* (a form of *sexism*), according to which the behaviours and experiences of men are taken as the standard against which women are judged (see Chapter 47).

In both cases, while the bias remains implicit and goes unrecognised (and is reinforced by psychology's claim to be objective and value-free), research findings are taken as providing us with an objective, scientifically valid, account of what 'women/people in general are like'. Once we realise that scientists, like all human beings, have prejudices, biases and values, their research and theories begin to look less objective, reliable and valid than they did before.

The problem of artificiality

Criticisms of traditional empirical methods (especially the laboratory experiment) have focused on their *artificiality*, including the often unusual and bizarre tasks that people are asked to perform in the name of science (see Key Study 3.1). Yet we cannot be sure that the way people behave in the laboratory is an accurate indication of how they're likely to behave outside it (Heather, 1976).

What makes the laboratory experiment such an unnatural and artificial situation is the fact that it's almost totally structured by one 'participant' – the experimenter. This relates to *power differences* between experimenters and their 'subjects', which is as much an *ethical* as a practical issue (see Chapter 48).

Traditionally, participants have been referred to as 'subjects', implying something less than a person, a dehumanised and depersonalised 'object'. According to Heather (1976), it's a small step from reducing the person to a mere thing or object (or experimental 'subject'), to seeing people as machines or machine-like ('mechanism' = 'machine-ism' = mechanistic view of people). This way of thinking about people is reflected in the popular definition of psychology as the study of 'what makes people tick' (see Chapter 1).

The term 'subject' reduces a person to something less than human: 'man as machine'

The problem of internal versus external validity

If the experimental setting (and task) is seen as similar or relevant enough to everyday situations to allow us to generalise the results, we say that the study has high *external* or *ecological validity*. But what about *internal validity*? Modelling itself on natural science, psychology attempts to overcome the problem of the complexity of human behaviour by using experimental control. This involves isolating an independent variable (IV) and ensuring that extraneous variables (variables other than the IV likely to affect the dependent variable) don't affect the outcome (see Coolican, 1999). But this begs the crucial question 'How do we know when all the relevant extraneous variables have been controlled?'

Box 3.7 Some difficulties with the notion of experimental control

- While it's relatively easy to control the more obvious *situational variables*, this is more difficult with *participant variables* (such as age, gender and culture), either for practical reasons (such as the availability of these groups), or because it isn't always obvious exactly what the relevant variables are. Ultimately, it's down to the experimenter's judgement and intuition: what s/he believes is important (and possible) to control (Deese, 1972).
- If judgement and intuition are involved, then control and objectivity are matters of degree, whether in psychology or physics (see Table 3.1).
- It's the *variability/heterogeneity* of human beings that makes them so much more difficult to study than, say, chemicals. Chemists don't usually have to worry about how two samples of a particular chemical might be different from each other, but psychologists need to allow for *individual differences* between participants.

- We cannot just assume that the IV (or 'stimulus' or 'input') is identical for every participant, definable in some objective way, independent of the participant, and exerting a standard effect on everyone. The attempt to define IVs (and DVs) in this way can be regarded as a form of *reductionism* (see Chapter 49).
- Complete control would mean that the IV alone was responsible for the DV, so that experimenter bias and the effect of demand characteristics were irrelevant. But even if complete control were possible (in other words, if we could guarantee the *internal validity* of the experiment), a fundamental dilemma would remain. The greater the degree of control over the experimental situation, the more different it becomes from real-life situations (the more artificial it gets and the lower its *external validity*).

As Box 3.7 indicates, in order to discover the relationships between variables (necessary for understanding human behaviour in natural, real-life situations), psychologists must 'bring' the behaviour into a specially created environment (the laboratory), where the relevant variables can be controlled in a way that's impossible in naturally occurring settings. However, in doing so, psychologists have constructed an artificial environment and the resulting behaviour is similarly artificial. It's no longer the behaviour they were trying to understand!

CONCLUSIONS

Psychology as a separate field of study grew out of several other disciplines, both scientific (such as physiology), and non-scientific (in particular philosophy). For much of its life as an independent discipline, and through what some call revolutions and paradigm shifts, it has taken the natural sciences as its model (scientism). This chapter has highlighted some of the major implications of adopting methods of investigating the natural world and applying them to the study of human behaviour and experience. In doing this, the chapter has also examined what are fast becoming outdated and inaccurate views about the nature of science. Ultimately, whatever a particular science may claim to have discovered about the phenomena it studies, scientific activity remains just one more aspect of human behaviour.

CHAPTER SUMMARY

- **Philosophical dualism** enabled scientists to describe the world **objectively**, which became the ideal of science. Its extension by Comte to the study of human behaviour and social institutions is called **positivism**.
- Descartes extended **mechanism** to the human body, but the mind remained accessible only through **introspection**.
- **Empiricism** emphasises the importance of sensory experience, as opposed to **nativism's** claim that knowledge is innate. 'Empirical' implies that the essence of science is collecting data/facts through experiments and observations.
- Wundt is generally regarded as the founder of the new science of experimental psychology. He used **introspection** to study conscious experience, analysing it into its basic elements (**structuralism**).
- James is the other pioneer of scientific psychology. As well as helping to make Freud's ideas popular in America, he influenced **functionalism** which, in turn, stimulated interest in **individual differences**.
- Watson argued that for psychology to be objective, it must study **behaviour** rather than mental life, its goals should be **prediction** and **control**, and there are only **quantitative differences** between human and animal behaviour.
- Dissatisfaction with behaviourism culminated in the 1956 '**cognitive revolution**'. At the centre of this new **information-processing approach** lay the **computer analogy**.
- **Scientism** maintains that all aspects of human behaviour can and should be studied using the methods of natural science. It involves '**context-stripping**' and the **value-free**, objective use of **laboratory experiments** in particular.
- A science must possess a **definable subject matter**, involve **theory construction** and **hypothesis testing**, and use **empirical methods** for **data collection**. However, these characteristics fail to describe the **scientific process** or **scientific method**.
- While the **classical view** of science is built around the **inductive method**, Popper's revised view stresses the **hypothetico-deductive method**. The two methods are complementary.
- Different **theoretical approaches** can be seen as self-contained disciplines, making psychology **pre-paradigmatic** and so still in a stage of **prescience**.
- Only when a discipline possesses a **paradigm** has it reached the stage of **normal science**, after which **paradigm shifts** result in **revolution** (and a return to normal science).
- Science is a very **social** activity. Consensus among the scientific community is paramount, as shown by the fact that revolutions involve redefining 'the truth'.
- Environmental changes are somehow produced by experimenters' expectations (**experimenter bias**), and **demand characteristics** influence participants' behaviours by helping to convey the experimental hypothesis. The experiment is a social situation and science itself is **culture-related**.
- The **artificiality** of laboratory experiments is largely due to their being totally structured by experimenters. Also, the higher an experiment's **internal validity**, the lower its **external validity** becomes.

Links with other topics/chapters

- Empiricism and nativism lie at the heart of the *nature–nurture debate* (or the *heredity and environment issue*). Sometimes, this concerns the causes of universal abilities or behaviours, such as *perception* (Chapter 16), *language* (Chapter 19), *aggression* (Chapter 29), *attachment* (Chapter 32) and *development of gender* (Chapter 36). Most controversially, the debate focuses on *individual differences*, in particular *intelligence* (Chapter 41) and *mental disorders*, such as schizophrenia and depression (Chapter 44). Chapter 50 is devoted to the debate as a whole.
- *Feminist psychologists* are highly critical of the scientific method in general and context-stripping (and the related *individualism*) in particular. They also argue that *sexism* and *androcentrism* (together with *ethnocentrism*) demonstrate how psychology is far from being objective and value-free (Chapter 47).
- The treatment of people as 'subjects' in psychology experiments has both methodological and *ethical* implications (Chapter 48). Treating subjects as interchangeable (group data are all-important) represents a *nomothetic approach* to studying people (Chapter 42).
- Rose (1997) calls experimental control *reductionism as methodology* (Chapter 49).

TWO

THE BIOLOGICAL BASIS OF BEHAVIOUR AND EXPERIENCE

4

THE NERVOUS SYSTEM

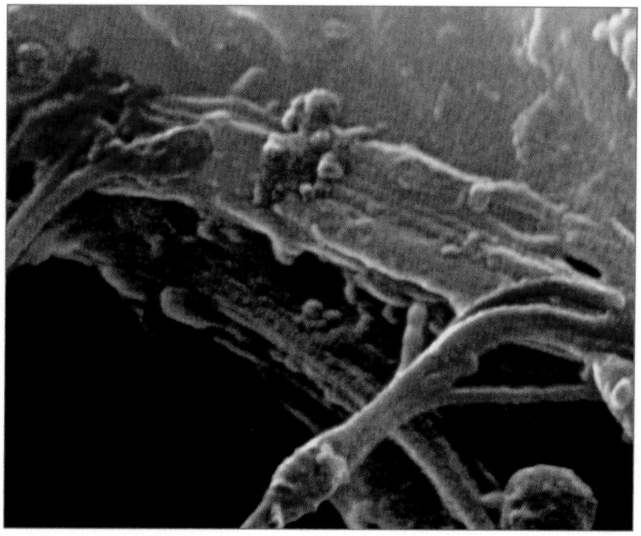

INTRODUCTION AND OVERVIEW

Biopsychology is the study of the biological bases, or the physiological correlates, of behaviour and is a branch of neuroscience (or the 'brain sciences'), the study of the nervous system. Biopsychology is also sometimes referred to as 'psychobiology', 'behavioural neuroscience' and 'physiological psychology'. But Pinel (1993) prefers the term 'biopsychology', because it denotes a biological approach to the study of psychology, where psychology 'commands centre stage'. According to Pinel:

> biopsychology's unique contribution to neuroscientific research is a knowledge of behaviour and of the methods of behavioural research ... the ultimate purpose of the nervous system is to produce and control behaviour.

In other words, biopsychologists aren't interested in biology for its own sake, but for what it can tell them about behaviour and mental processes. In general terms:

- the kind of behaviour an animal is capable of depends very much on the kind of body it possesses; for example, humans can flap their arms as much as they like but they'll never fly (unaided) – arms are simply not designed for flying, while wings are; however, we're very skilled at manipulating objects (especially small ones), because that's how our hands and fingers have developed during the course of evolution
- the possession of a specialised body is of very little use unless the nervous system is able to control it; of course, evolution of the one usually mirrors evolution of the other
- the kind of nervous system also determines the extent and nature of the learning a species is capable of. As you move along the phylogenetic (evolutionary) scale, from simple, one-celled amoebae, through insects, birds and mammals, to primates (including Homo sapiens), the nervous system gradually becomes more complex. At the same time, behaviour becomes increasingly the product of learning and environmental influence, rather than instinct and other innate, genetically determined factors.

BIOPSYCHOLOGY AND OTHER DISCIPLINES

According to Pinel (1993), biopsychology draws together knowledge from the other neuroscientific disciplines, in particular:

- *neuroanatomy* – the study of the structure of the nervous system (NS)
- *developmental neurobiology* – the study of how the NS changes as the organism matures and ages
- *neurochemistry* – the study of the chemical bases of neural activity, especially those underlying the transmission of signals through and between neurons (nerve cells)
- *neuroendocrinology* – the study of the interactions between the NS and the endocrine (hormonal) system (see pages 73–75);
- *neuropathology* – the study of NS disorders; related to this is *neuropsychology*, the study of the behavioural deficits produced in people by brain damage
- *neuropharmacology* – the study of the effects of drugs on the NS, especially those influencing neural transmission; related to this is *psychopharmacology*, which is concerned with the effects of drugs on behaviour (see pages 57–59 and Chapter 8)
- *neurophysiology* – the study of the responses of the NS, particularly those involved in transmission of electrical signals through and between neurons; this is related to (a) *physiological psychology*, which involves manipulation of the NS through surgical, electrical and chemical means under strictly controlled experimental conditions (*invasive methods*, using mainly non-human animal subjects), and (b) *psychophysiology*, which uses *non-invasive methods*, mainly with human participants, to study the physiology of psychological processes such as attention, emotion, information processing and, increasingly, major mental disorders (especially schizophrenia: see Chapter 44).

AN OVERVIEW OF THE HUMAN NERVOUS SYSTEM (NS): STRUCTURE AND FUNCTION

As Figure 4.1 (page 55) shows, the NS involves a number of sub-divisions. Before looking at these in detail, we need to look at some of the general characteristics of the NS.

Neurons

The NS as a whole comprises approximately 100 billion (100,000,000,000) nerve cells or *neurons*, the basic structural units, or building blocks, of the NS. About 80 per cent of all neurons are found in the brain, particularly in the *cerebral cortex*, the topmost outer layer. Information is passed from neuron to neuron in the form of *electrochemical impulses*, which constitute the 'language' of the NS. There are three main kinds of neuron:

- *sensory* (or *afferent*), which carry information from the sense organs to the central nervous system (CNS)
- *motor* (or *efferent*), which carry information from the CNS to the muscles and glands
- *interneurons* (or *connector neurons*), which connect neurons to other neurons and integrate the activities of sensory and motor neurons; interneurons are the most numerous and constitute about 97 per cent of the total number of neurons in the CNS.

Although no two neurons are identical, most share the same basic structure, and they work in essentially the same way. Figure 4.2 (page 56) shows a typical motor neuron.

The cell body (or *soma*) houses the *nucleus* (which contains the genetic code), the *cytoplasm* (which feeds the nucleus) and the other structures common to all living cells. The *dendrites* branch out from the cell body, and it's through the dendrites that the neuron makes electrochemical contact with other neurons, by receiving incoming signals from neighbouring neurons. The *axon* is a thin cylinder of protoplasm, which projects away from the cell body and carries the signals received by the dendrites to other neurons. The *myelin sheath* is a white, fatty substance, which insulates the axon and speeds up the rate of conduction of signals down the axon and towards the *terminal buttons* (or *boutons* or *synaptic knobs*). The myelin sheath isn't continuous but is interrupted by the *nodes of Ranvier*.

In the spinal cord, a neuron may have an axon two to three feet long, running from the tip of the spine down to

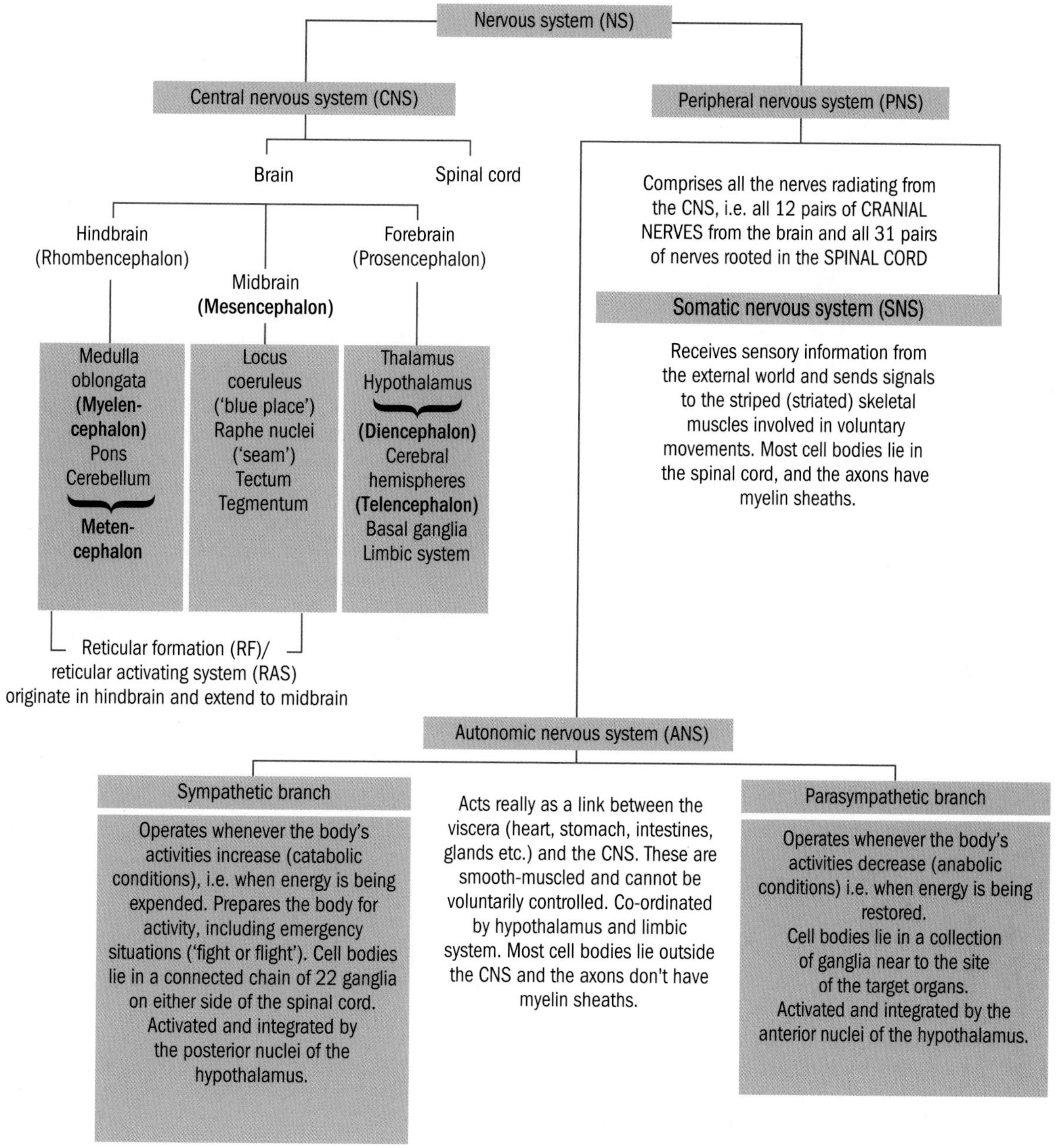

Figure 4.1 Major subdivisions of the human nervous system (including the main subdivisions of the brain)

the big toe. In the brain, neurons are only a few one-thousandths of an inch long. Axons of motor neurons that terminate in muscles end in a series of branches, tipped by *motor endplates*, each of which is attached to a single muscle fibre. Impulses at the motor endplate cause the muscle to contract (as in raising the arm).

A *nerve* is a bundle of elongated axons belonging to hundreds or thousands of neurons. Nerves spread out to every part of the body and connect with sense receptors, skin, muscles and internal organs. Twelve pairs of *cranial nerves* leave the brain through holes in the skull, and 31 pairs of *spinal nerves* leave the spinal cord through the vertebrae. Together, they constitute the nerves of the *peripheral nervous system* (PNS: see Fig. 4.1). Nerves are usually large enough to be seen with the naked eye, while neurons can only be seen with the help of a powerful microscope.

Communication between neurons

As Figure 4.3 (page 56) shows, the terminal buttons house a number of tiny sacs, or *synaptic vesicles*, which contain between 10 and 100,000 molecules of a chemical messenger called a *neurotransmitter*. When an *electrochemical impulse* has passed down the axon, it arrives at a terminal button and stimulates the vesicles to discharge their contents into the minute gap between the end of the terminal button (the *presynaptic membrane*) and the dendrite of the receiving neuron (the *postsynaptic membrane*) called the *synaptic cleft* (or *gap*).

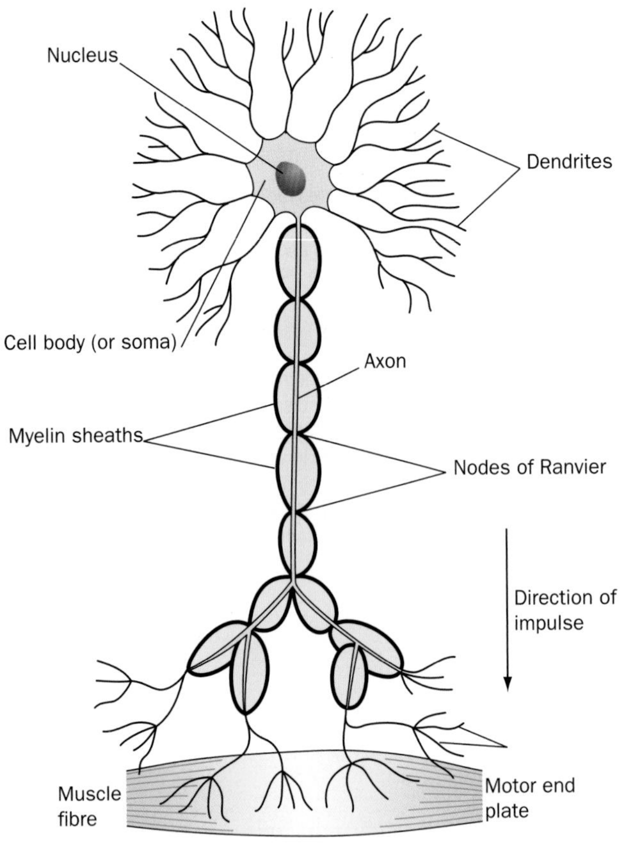

Figure 4.2 A typical motor neuron

The neurotransmitter molecules cross the synaptic gap and combine with special receptor sites in the postsynaptic membrane of the dendrite of the receiving neuron. So, the term 'synapse' refers to the junction between neurons (although there's no actual physical contact between them), at which signals are passed from a sending to a receiving neuron through the release of neurotransmitters. Although this *synaptic transmission* is the most common form of communication between neurons (Iversen, 1979), 20 per cent of the brain is completely devoid of neurons. Instead of forming a solid mass, the neurons are interspersed with a convoluted network of fluid-filled spaces or cavities. According to Mitchell (1999), there's a growing body of opinion that neurons can communicate with large regions of the brain by releasing chemicals into these watery spaces. This is called *volume transmission*, which is seen as *complementary* to synaptic transmission.

RESEARCH UPDATE 4.1: What evidence is there for 'volume transmission?

- Researchers tracked a neurotransmitter (neuropeptide Y) in rats' brains and found receptors that were sometimes several millimetres (a million times the width of a synaptic gap) away from the source of the neurotransmitter. Synaptic transmission couldn't work on this sort of scale – but volume transmission could.
- Receptors for *serotonin* and *dopamine* (two major transmitters: see Table 4.1, page 58) have also been identified away from their most likely locations. For example, serotonin receptors have been found on *axons*: only if serotonin could travel via volume transmission would you expect to find receptors there.
- Although not everyone accepts the idea of volume transmission, there are certain global patterns of activity that it's very difficult to explain in any other way. For example, Parkinson's disease sufferers seem to lose neurons in the substantia nigra, a brain region that normally supplies the neighbouring striatum with dopamine (which initiates and controls signalling to the muscles). However, sufferers don't develop symptoms until a massive 80 per cent of the dopamine-producing neurons have been lost. So, signalling must have continued during this period of neuron loss. Volume transmission would account for this far better than synaptic transmission.
- Sleep is another good example of why the brain needs volume transmission (see Chapter 7). A molecule called *prostaglandins D2* sends us off to sleep, whereas *prostaglandins E2* helps to wake us up. The enzyme that produces *D2* comes mainly from non-neuronal cells in the brain; it may reach its target by diffusing through the cerebrospinal fluid (CSF), which surrounds and bathes the neurons.

(Source: based on Mitchell, 1999)

Electrochemical impulses

The electrochemical signal that passes down the axon is called an *action potential*. Before the action potential occurs, an inactive neuron contains positively charged potassium (K^+) ions (electrically charged potassium atoms) and large, negatively charged protein molecules. Outside the neuron, in the surrounding fluid, there are

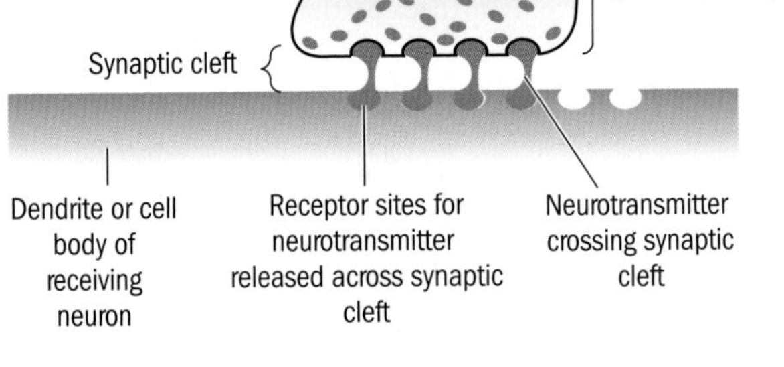

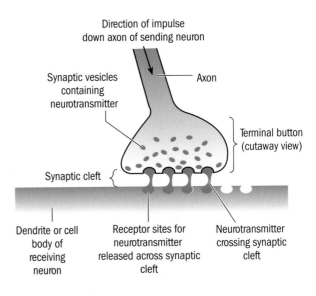

Figure 4.3 The synapse

concentrations of positively charged sodium ions (Na^+) and negatively charged chloride ions (Cl^-). The large, negatively charged, protein ions are trapped inside the neuron, while the positively charged sodium ions are kept out by the action of the *sodium-potassium pumps* in the cell membrane, which allow potassium (and chloride) ions to move in and out fairly freely.

The overall effect of this uneven distribution of ions is that the inside of the cell is electrically negative relative to the outside (by about 70 millivolts). The neuron is said to be *impermeable* to the positively charged sodium ions (its resting state or *resting potential*). When an action potential occurs, the inside of the neuron momentarily changes from negative to positive (+40 millivolts), the sodium channels are opened (for one millisecond) and sodium ions flood into the neuron (it's now permeable to sodium ions). This sets off a chain reaction, whereby the sodium channels open at adjacent membrane sites all the way down the axon. But almost as soon as the sodium channels are opened, they close again: potassium channels are opened instead, allowing potassium ions out through the membrane and restoring the negative resting potential.

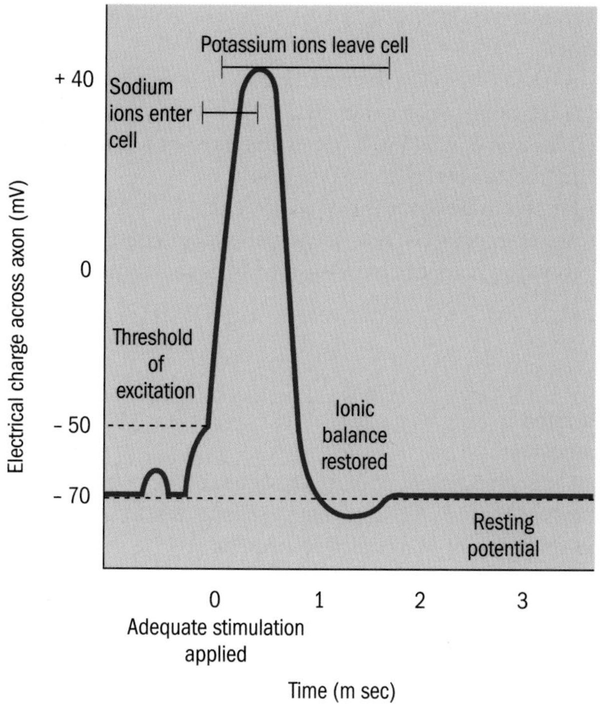

Figure 4.4 The sequence of events when a neuron 'fires'. The small 'bump' on the left represents an incoming message that was not strong enough to cause the neuron to fire

Because the myelin sheath isn't continuous, but is segmented (the axon is actually exposed at the nodes of Ranvier: see Figure 4.2), the action potential jumps from one node to another down the axon. This is called *saltatory conduction*, which is actually faster than if the sheaths were continuous.

Response threshold

The stimulus to the neuron must be intense enough to produce an action potential (it must exceed the *threshold of response*). But once this has occurred, it travels at the same speed to the end of the axon. So, an impulse is either present or absent (the *all-or-none rule*). Action potentials are all of the same strength (*amplitude*), so the intensity of the stimulus is measured by:

- the *frequency of firing* – the stronger the stimulus, the more often the neuron will fire (a very strong stimulus producing a volley of impulses)
- the *number of neurons stimulated* – the stronger the stimulus, the greater the number of neurons stimulated.

However strong the stimulus, there's always a very short interval after each firing (1–2 milliseconds), during which no further impulse can pass (the *absolute refractory period*). This is followed by a *relative refractory period*: the stronger the stimulus, the shorter the interval between the absolute refractory period and the next impulse.

Different types of synapses

Some synapses are *excitatory* (they 'instruct' the receiving neuron to 'fire' – that is, to conduct an action potential), while others are *inhibitory* (they 'instruct' the receiving neuron not to 'fire'). Because each neuron may have between 1000 and 10,000 synapses, some of which will be excitatory and some inhibitory, the 'decision' to fire or not will depend on the combined effect of all its receiving synapses. If enough excitatory synapses are active, their combined effect may add up to exceed the threshold for firing of the receiving neuron (this is called *summation*).

Inhibitory synapses are important because they help control the spread of excitation through the highly interconnected NS, keeping activity channelled in appropriate networks or 'circuits'. Epileptic seizures (fits), for example, may be caused by excitation of many different brain circuits at the same time and, if it weren't for inhibition, we might all be having seizures much of the time.

Different types of neurotransmitter

What makes a synapse either excitatory or inhibitory is the particular neurotransmitter(s) contained within the vesicles of the synaptic button. A region on the surface of the receptor site is precisely tailored to match the shape of the transmitter molecule (in a lock-and-key fashion). The effect of the transmitter is brought to an end either by *deactivation* (where it's destroyed by special enzymes) or by *reuptake* (where it's pumped back into the presynaptic axon, either for destruction or recycling).

According to Iversen (1979), there are at least 30 different neurotransmitters in the brain, each with its specific excitatory or inhibitory effect on certain neurons. Neurotransmitters aren't randomly distributed throughout the brain, but are localised in specific groups of neurons and pathways. Some of the major transmitters and their effects are shown in Table 4.1.

As a general rule, a single neuron will store and release the same neurotransmitter in all its axon terminals. So, *cholinergic*, *noradrenergic*, *dopaminergic* and *serotonergic* neurons use ACh, noradrenaline, dopamine and serotonin respectively. However, there's some evidence that more than one kind of transmitter may be released from the same synaptic button, depending on the pattern of action potentials reaching it (Lloyd *et al.*, 1984).

Neurotransmitters have a fairly direct influence on receiving neurons. But *neuromodulators* 'tune' or 'prime' neurons, enabling them to respond in a particular way to later stimulation by a neurotransmitter. Neuromodulators include certain *neuropeptides* (see Table 4.1), notably the *enkephalins* ('in the head') and the *endorphins* ('morphine within').

Box 4.1 Opioids: the brain's natural painkillers?

- The enkephalins and endorphins are also known as opioids, because functionally they resemble the opium drugs morphine, heroin and opium itself (see Chapter 8). Morphine is commonly used for the relief of severe, intractable pain, and the discovery of 'opiate receptors' in the neurons strongly suggested that the brain creates its own powerful painkiller.
- Enkephalins and endorphins seemed to fit the bill, and they may work by interfering with the release of transmitters from the presynaptic membrane of neurons that transmit information about pain.
- It's thought that they're released during acupuncture and hypnosis, producing a reduction in perceived pain, although pain information probably still reaches the brain (as it's not the pain receptors that are directly influenced: see Chapter 12).
- It's also believed that placebos ('dummy drugs') work by influencing the release of endorphins in response to the belief that an active drug was given (Hamilton & Timmons, 1995: see Chapters 12 and 45).

Other neuropeptides are found as hormones, including:

- *vasopressin*, which is thought to play a role in memory (see Chapter 17)
- *corticosteroids* ('stress hormones') and *adrenocorticotrophic hormone* (ACTH), which are involved in stress reactions (see Chapter 12) and emotional arousal (see Chapter 10)
- *androgens* (male sex hormones), which regulate sex drive in both sexes (see Table 4.3, page 74 and Box 36.1, pages 621–622).

RESEARCH UPDATE 4.2: Glial cells: the other half of the brain

- Glial cells (or glia) are mostly smaller than neurons and 9–10 times more numerous.
- They come in different forms, the most important being astrocytes and oligodendrocytes.
- It used to be thought that they merely 'fill in the space' between neurons, and serve just a maintenance role (bringing nutrients from the blood vessels to neurons,

Table 4.1 Major transmitters and their effects

Neurotransmitter	Effect on receiving neuron	Related behaviour
Acetylcholine (ACh)	Generally *excitatory*, but can be *inhibitory*,depending on the type of receptor molecule involved	Voluntary movement of muscles, behavioural inhibition, drinking, memory. In Alzheimer's disease, there's a degeneration of ACh-producing neurons
Noradrenaline (norepinephrine)*	*Inhibitory* (in CNS); *excitatory* (in ANS)	Wakefulness and arousal (behavioural and emotional), eating, depression and mania (see Chapters 44 and 45)
Dopamine*	*Inhibitory* and *excitatory*	Voluntary movement, emotional arousal. Parkinson's disease involves degeneration of dopamine-releasing neurons. Schizophrenia is associated with excess of dopamine (see Chapter 44)
Serotonin*	*Inhibitory* and *excitatory*.	Sleep (see Chapter 7), temperature regulation
GABA (gamma aminobutyric acid)	*Inhibitory* (the most common inhibitor in CNS)	Motor behaviour. Huntington's disease may result from degeneration of GABA cells in the corpus striatum
Glycine	*Inhibitory* (found in spinal cord)	Spinal reflexes and other motor behaviour
Neuromodulators (neuropeptides; e.g. enkephalins and endorphins)	*Inhibitory* and *excitatory*	Sensory transmission, especially pain (see Chapter 12)

* Monoamine (MAO) transmitters

maintaining a healthy balance of ions in the brain, and warding off pathogens that evaded the immune system: see Figure 12.7, page 207).

- Imaging studies have shown, however, that neurons and glial cells engage in a two-way dialogue, beginning in the embryo and continuing through to old age. Glial cells help to determine which neural connections get stronger or weaker over time. These changes are essential to learning and storing long-term memories.
- Glial cells also communicate between themselves, in a separate but parallel network to the neural network, influencing the brain's overall level of performance.
- They influence the formation of synapses, and oligodendrocytes provide the insulating myelin sheath around the axon of the neuron (see page 56).
- Astrocytes regulate signalling across the synapse. They may (a) strengthen it by secreting the same neurotransmitter, or (b) weaken it by absorbing the neurotransmitter or secreting proteins that bind to it, thereby preventing it from reaching its target. Modifying the connections between neurons is one way the brain revises its responses to stimuli as it accumulates experience (in other words, how it learns).
- The proportion of glial cells to neurons increases considerably as animals move up the evolutionary ladder. Extensive connectivity among astrocytes might contribute to greater learning capacity. It could be that what distinguishes geniuses (such as Einstein) from 'mere mortals' is a higher concentration of glial cells, or a more potent type of glia.
- According to Fields (2004), neuroscientists 'are excited by the prospect that more than half the brain has gone largely unexplored and may contain a trove of information about how the mind works'.

(Source: based on Fields, 2004).

THE CENTRAL NERVOUS SYSTEM (CNS)

Methods of studying the brain

Box 4.2 A classification of methods used to study the brain

- *Clinical/anatomical methods:* studying the effects on behaviour of accidental injury to the brain or brain disease in human beings, or patients who've undergone brain surgery for the treatment of disorders such as epilepsy (in particular, 'split-brain' patients: see pages 70–72).
- *Invasive methods:* surgically removing areas of brain tissue (*ablation*) or causing damage or injury (*lesions*) to particular brain sites or stimulation of the brain, either electrically or chemically. Also included is the recording of the electrical activity of very small areas of the brain, or even single neurons, through the insertion of very fine electrodes (*microelectrode recording*). These methods involve animal subjects and are extremely controversial from an ethical point of view (see Chapter 48).
- *Non-invasive methods:* either the brain's electrical activity is recorded by attaching electrodes to the scalp, or *computerised scanning/imaging techniques* are used to study the living human brain. In either case, the brain isn't interfered with in any way and there's no risk of damage or injury.

Clinical/anatomical methods

One of the earliest methods used to study the CNS was the study of patients who'd suffered brain damage following an accident, or a stroke or tumour. A famous and early example is Paul Broca's discovery of a specialised area of the brain for speech. In 1869, Broca, a French physician, reviewed evidence from a number of cases of brain damage. He concluded that injury to a certain part of the left cerebral hemisphere (the left half of the brain) caused the patient's speech to become slow and laboured, but that the ability to understand speech was almost completely unaffected. What's now called *Broca's area* seems to control the ability to produce speech, and damage to it causes *motor* (or *expressive*) *aphasia*. In 1874, Carl Wernicke reported that injury to a different part of the left hemisphere caused *receptive aphasia*, the inability to understand speech (one's own or someone else's).

These clinical studies of the brain have normally been conducted in parallel with anatomical studies, usually during the course of postmortem examinations. Studying structure and function in a complementary way is essential for an adequate understanding of such a complex organ as the brain. *Split-brain patients* have undergone surgery for epilepsy when all other treatments have failed. The surgery (*commissurotomy*) involves cutting the tissue which connects the two halves of the brain (the corpus callosum). Roger Sperry and his colleagues in the 1960s and 1970s made full use of the unique opportunity to study these 'split brains'. Their work is discussed in detail later in the chapter (see pages 70–72).

Invasive methods

As noted in Box 4.2, parts of the brain may be surgically removed (*ablation*) or an area of the brain may be damaged (rather than removed: the *lesion method*). An early user of the first method was Karl Lashley, working with rats in the 1920s, and it has been used extensively to study the role of the brain in eating (see Chapter 9).

Psychologists are usually interested in destroying areas or structures located deep within the brain. To do this, a *stereotaxic apparatus* is used, which allows the researcher to operate on brain structures that are hidden from view (see Figure 4.5). While the subjects are exclusively non-human animals, stereotaxic surgery is also used with humans, including psychiatric patients (see Chapter 45).

ASK YOURSELF...

- Is it ethically acceptable to use invasive methods with non-human animals?
- How could you justify their use?

(See Chapter 48, pages 878–881.)

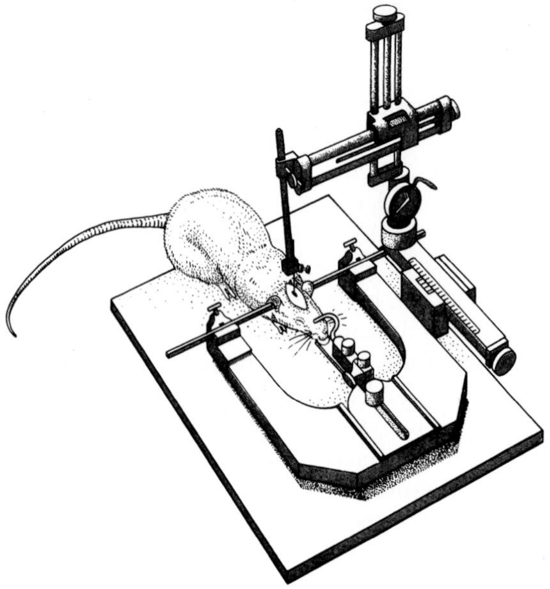

Figure 4.5 A stereotaxic apparatus, used to insert an electrode into a specific portion of an animal's brain (from N. Carlson, 1992, *Foundations of Physiological Psychology*, 2nd edition, Boston, Allyn & Bacon)

Instead of surgically removing or damaging the brain, it can be stimulated. This can be done either (a) *chemically* (using micropipettes to drop drugs known to either increase or decrease the activity of particular neurotransmitters on to specific areas of the brain) or, more commonly, (b) *electrically*, using microelectrodes, whereby precise locations can be stimulated. Again, it's usually non-human animals that are involved (see Figure 4.6 and Chapter 9), but sometimes patients already undergoing surgery for a brain tumour or some other abnormality (such as epilepsy) are studied. Here, the neurosurgeon takes advantage of the fact that the patient is conscious, alert and able to report memories, sensations, and so on, produced by the stimulation. Wilder Penfield pioneered this kind of research in the 1950s (and through it discovered the 'Penfield homunculus': see Figure 4.9, page 64).

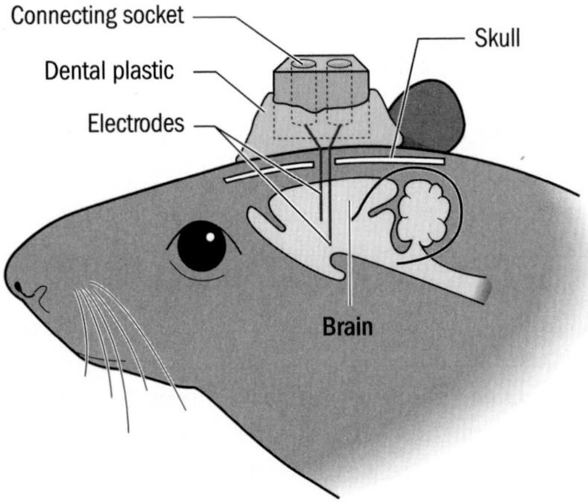

Figure 4.6 Electrical stimulation of the brain

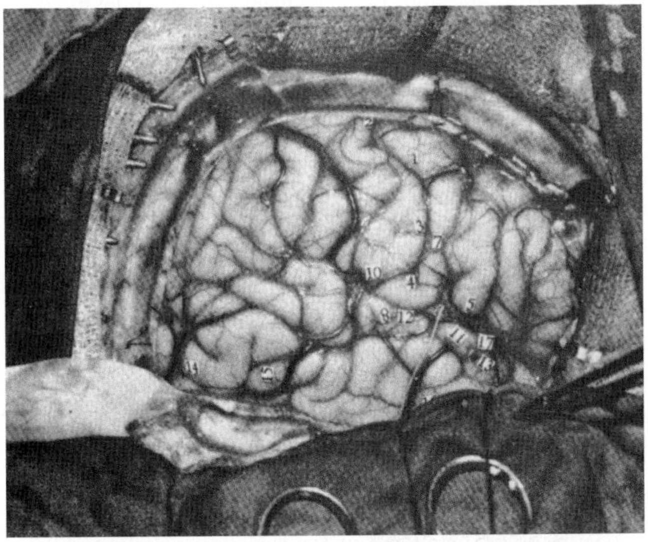

Photograph taken during surgery carried out by Penfield. The numbers refer to the parts of the cortex stimulated (Oxford University Press)

Microelectrodes are also used to record the electrical activity in individual neurons when the subject (usually a cat or monkey) is presented with various kinds of stimuli. This method was used by Hubel and Wiesel in the 1960s to study visual feature detectors (see Chapters 5 and 14).

Non-invasive methods

The electroencephalogram (EEG)

The electrical activity of the brain can also be recorded from the outside, by fitting electrodes (passive sensors) to the scalp. The activity can be traced on paper, and typical brainwave patterns associated with various states of arousal have been found. The EEG records action potentials for large groups of neurons and has been used extensively in the study of states of consciousness, including sleep. Related to this is the *electromyogram* (EMG), which records the electrical activity of muscles, and the *electrooculogram* (EOG), which records eye movements, both of which are, like the EEG, used in sleep research (see Chapter 7).

Average evoked potentials (AEPs)

A brief change in the EEG may be produced by the presentation of a single stimulus, but the effect may well be lost (or obscured) in the overall pattern of waves. However, if the stimulus is presented repeatedly and the results averaged by a computer, other waves cancel out and the evoked response can be detected. This technique has shown that an identical visual stimulus yields different AEPs according to the meaning the participant attaches to it.

EEG imaging and the geodesic net

While the EEG involves a small number of electrodes, EEG *imaging* records the brain's electrical activity using 32 electrodes. This is fed to a computer, which translates it into coloured moving images on a TV monitor. While originally developed for investigating convulsive seizures, it has been adapted for studying brain development in babies in the form of a *geodesic net*. This consists of 64 or 132 electrodes, whose combined output produces a map of the active regions across the baby's head. The computer then calculates the likely brain areas that generated the voltages observed on the scalp. The geodesic net is unlikely to rival the spatial accuracy of adult scanning methods (see below), but its resolution over time is far superior, allowing the study of brain events 'at the speed of thought' (Johnson, 2000). One area of research that has made use of the geodesic net is infants' perception of faces (see Chapter 16).

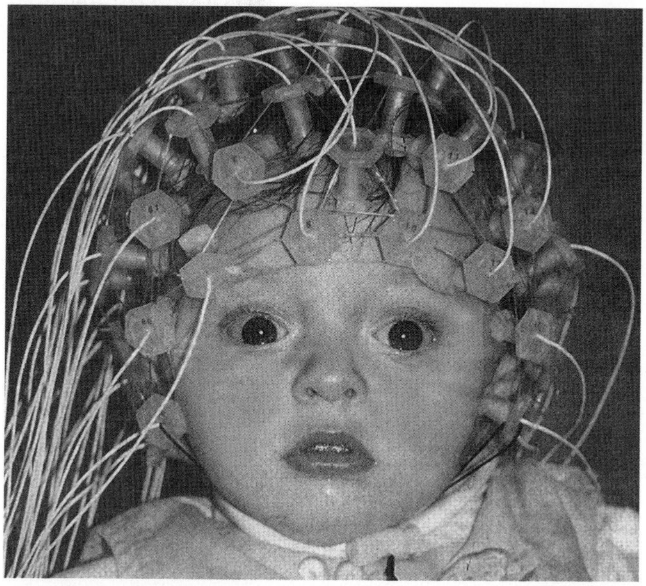

A geodesic sensor net being used to study brain activity in an infant

Radioactive labelling

This is a relatively recent method of studying the CNS, which takes advantage of the brain's flexible use of blood-borne oxygen. A radioactive isotope is added to the blood, causing low levels of radioactivity, which increase as greater blood flow occurs in more active areas of the brain. A scanner next to the head feeds radiation readings to a computer, which produces a coloured map of the most and least active brain regions: different regions change colour as the person attempts a variety of tasks or is presented with a variety of stimuli.

Computerised axial tomography (CAT)

A moving X-ray beam takes pictures from different positions around the head, and these are converted by the computer into 'brain slices' (apparent cross-sections of the brain). CAT scanning is used primarily for the detection and diagnosis of brain injury and disease.

Positron emission tomography (PET)

This uses the same computer-calculation approach as CAT, but uses radiation for the information from which the brain slices are computed. A radioactive tracer is added to a substance used by the body (such as oxygen or glucose). As the marked substance is metabolised, PET shows the pattern of how it's being used. For example, more or less use of glucose could indicate a tumour, and changes are revealed when the eyes are opened or closed. PET diagnoses brain abnormalities more efficiently than CAT.

Magnetic resonance imaging (MRI)

This is like a CAT scan, but instead of using radiation, it passes an extremely strong magnetic field through the

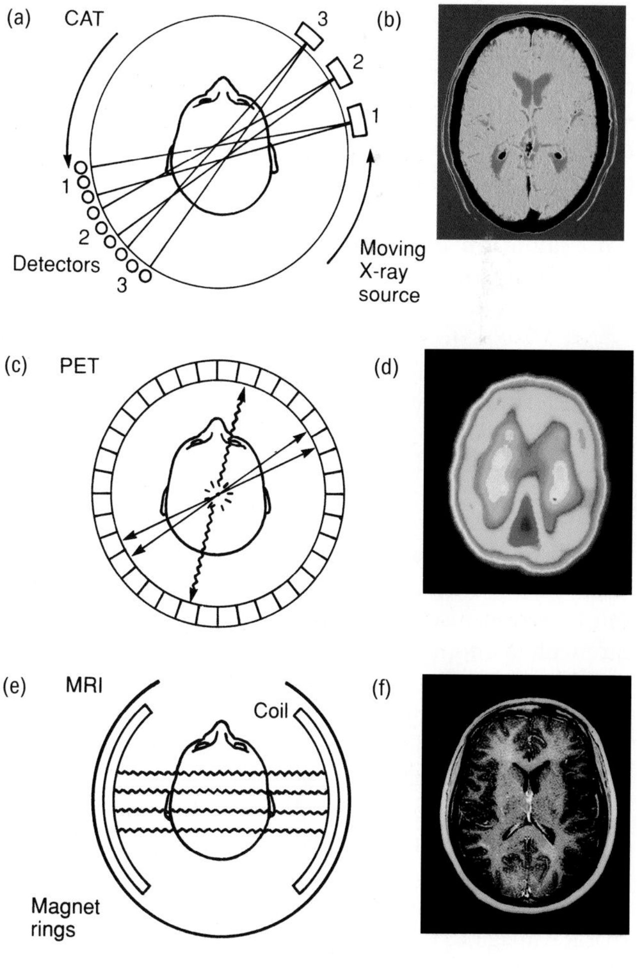

Figure 4.7 Non-invasive techniques (a), (c) and (e) used to study detailed sections of the living human brain (b), (d) and (f)

head and measures its effects on the rotation of atomic nuclei of some element in the body. Again, a computerised cross-sectional image is produced. So far only hydrogen nuclei have been used. Because hydrogen molecules are present in substantially different concentrations in different brain structures, the MRI can use the information to prepare pictures of brain slices which are much clearer (higher resolution) than CAT pictures.

Functional MRI (fMRI)

The MRI can identify the smallest tumour, or the slightest reduction in blood flow in a vein or artery. But it shares with CAT the limitation of only providing *still* images of brain slices. This tells us very little about brain *function*. To remedy this, fMRI monitors blood flow in the brain over time as people perform different kinds of task, so it's used as much to study the normal as the damaged/diseased brain.

SPECT and SQUID

The most recent imaging techniques are *single-photon/positron emission computerised tomography* (SPECT) (which, like PET, tracks blood flow through the brain), and *superconducting quantum imaging/interference device* (SQUID) (which detects tiny changes in magnetic fields). Their main advantage is that they can focus on tiny areas of the brain. SPECT has revealed that there is significant loss of functioning in the front part of the brain in patients with *Korsakoff's syndrome*, caused by prolonged and heavy use of alcohol (see Chapter 8).

An evaluation of scanning/imaging techniques: what they can and cannot tell us

ASK YOURSELF...

- What would you say are the main advantages of using scanning/imaging techniques compared with other methods?

Neuroscientists no longer have to rely on laboratory animals or brain-damaged patients requiring surgery to view what's taking place inside the brain as it happens. We can now peer into a healthy living brain and observe the moment-to-moment changes that occur in relation to mental activity. But this *doesn't* mean that we can literally look inside someone's *mind* (see Chapter 49 for a discussion of the long-standing philosophical debate about the relationship between mind and brain).

As we noted in the *Introduction and overview* section, psychologists aren't interested in the brain for its own sake, but for what it can tell us about the control of psychological functions and abilities. It's tempting to infer that if damage to (or loss of) a particular brain area is associated with the loss of (or reduction in) a particular ability, then that part of the brain normally controls that ability. Unfortunately, there are other possibilities. For example, the damaged area might itself be controlled by a different (undamaged) area, or the damage may have disrupted the normal functioning of nearby, or related, intact areas. (See the discussion of split-brain patients below, pages 70–72.)

How does the brain develop?

One of the most remarkable things about the human brain is the staggering complexity of the *interconnections* between the neurons. Given the 8–10 billion neurons in the brain, each of which may have 1000–10,000 synaptic connections with other neurons, it's been estimated that there are more possible ways in which the neurons of a single human brain can be interconnected than there are atoms in the known universe!

At birth, the baby has almost its full complement of neurons, and the brain is closer to its adult size than any other organ. It represents 10 per cent of the baby's total body weight compared with 2 per cent of the adult's. At six months, the brain is already half its eventual adult weight; at 12 months, 60 per cent; at five years, 90 per cent; and at 10 years 95 per cent. The brain reaches its maximum weight by about 20 years.

Box 4.3 Major aspects of infant brain development

While the major development *before* birth is the growth of neurons, brain growth *after* birth is the result of four major changes.

1. The growth of *synaptic connections* between neighbouring neurons accounts for much of the increase in brain volume. However, there are also *regressive/subtractive events*: the density of synapses increases until it's even greater than in adults (usually about 150 per cent of adult levels), followed by the death of many synapses. This reduces the overall number to those normally observed in adults. It seems that the less useful connections are 'pruned', leaving only those that have proved useful. A similar pattern is found for complexity of dendrites and for measures of energy used by the brain (Johnson, 2000).
2. Neurons *increase in size* (but not in number), as do synapses.
3. *Glial cells* develop (see Research Update 4.2, page 58).
4. The oligodendrocytes produce the *myelin sheaths*, which grow around the axons to insulate the neuron and speed up the conduction of action potentials (again, see Research Update 4.2).

If the absolute size of the brain determined level of intelligence, then humans would certainly be surpassed by many species. Even if we take the brain size/body size ratio, house mice, porpoises, tree shrews and squirrel monkeys would still come higher in the intelligence league than humans. Clearly, it's the *kind* of brain that matters. What seems to be unique about the human brain is the proportion of it that isn't devoted to particular physical and psychological functions, and that is 'free' to facilitate our intelligence, our general ability to think, reason, use language and learn.

THE MAJOR STRUCTURES AND FUNCTIONS OF THE BRAIN

As Figure 4.8 shows, during the first five weeks of foetal life, the neural tube changes its shape to produce five bulbous enlargements. These are generally accepted as the basic divisions of the brain, namely the *myelencephalon* (the medulla oblongata), the *metencephalon* (the pons and cerebellum), the *mesencephalon* (the tectum and tegmentum), the *diencephalon* (thalamus and hypothalamus) and the *telencephalon* (the cerebral hemispheres or cerebrum, basal ganglia and limbic system). 'Encephalon' means 'within the head'.

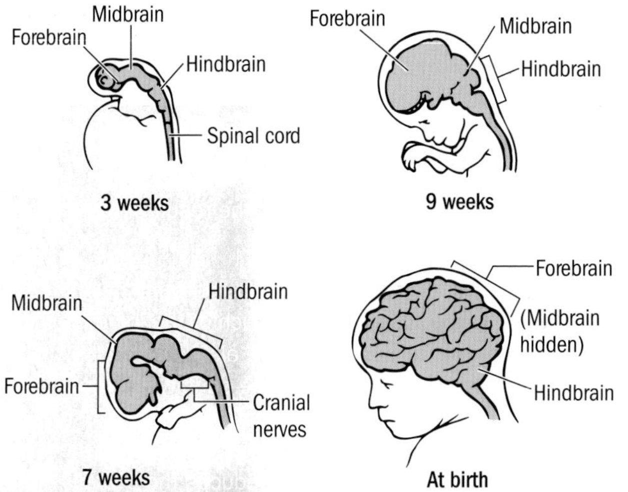

Figure 4.8 The human brain at four stages of development

As shown in Figure 4.1, the myelencephalon and metencephalon together make up the *hindbrain*, the mesencephalon constitutes the *midbrain*, and the diencephalon and telencephalon make up the *forebrain*.

The forebrain

The cerebral hemispheres (or cerebrum)

The cerebral hemispheres are the two largest structures at the top of the brain, which enfold (and, therefore, conceal from view) most other brain structures. If you removed an intact brain, its appearance would be dominated by the massive hemispheres, with just the cerebellum showing at the back (see Figure 4.9).

The top layer of the cerebrum (about 1 cm at its deepest) is the *cerebral cortex* (usually just called 'cortex', which means 'bark'). It is highly convoluted (wrinkled), which is necessary in order to pack its 2.5-square-foot surface area into the relatively small space inside the skull. The cortex is pinkish-grey in colour (hence 'grey matter'), but below it the cerebrum consists of much thicker white matter, composed of myelinated axons (the cortex consists of cell bodies).

There's a large crevice running along the cerebrum from front to back (the *longitudinal fissure/sulcus*), which divides the two hemispheres. But they're connected further down by a dense mass of commissurial ('joining') fibres called the *corpus callosum* (or 'hard body').

There are two other natural dividing lines in each hemisphere: the *lateral fissure* (or *fissure of Sylvius*) and the *central fissure* (or *fissure of Rolando*). The lateral fissure separates the *temporal lobe* from the *frontal lobe* (anteriorly: towards the front) and from the *parietal lobe* (posteriorly: from the back), while the central fissure separates the frontal and parietal lobes. The *occipital lobe* is situated behind the parietal lobe and is at the back of the head. This division of the cortex into four lobes – named after the bones beneath which they lie – is a feature of *both* hemispheres, which are mirror images of each other.

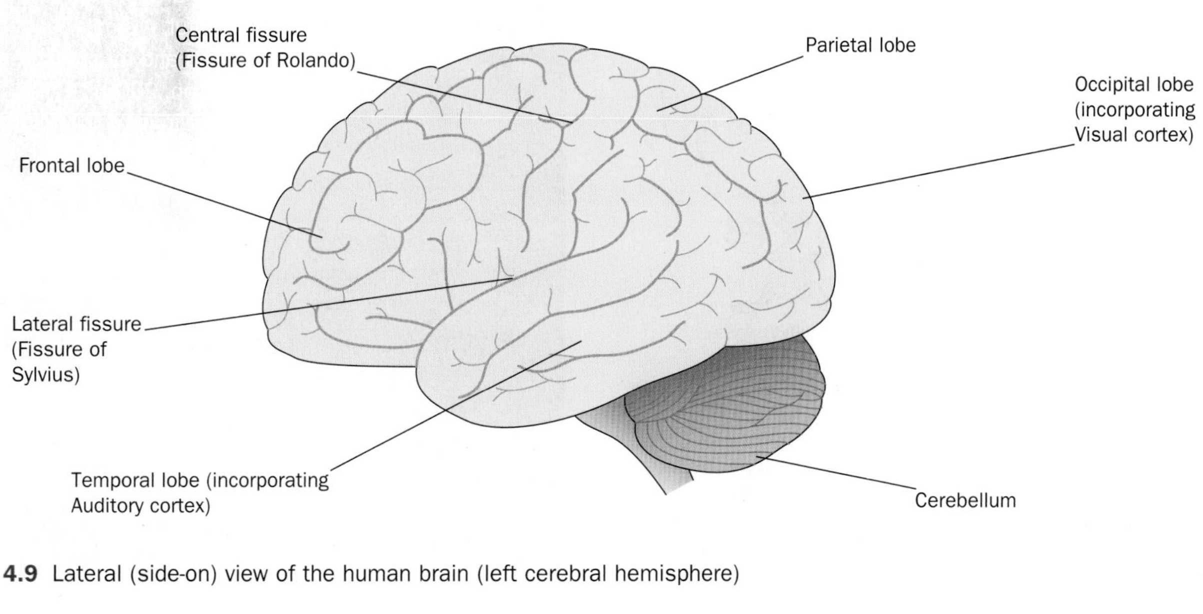

Figure 4.9 Lateral (side-on) view of the human brain (left cerebral hemisphere)

The *primary visual cortex* is found in the occipital lobe, the *primary auditory cortex* in the temporal lobe, the *primary somatosensory* (or *body-sense*) cortex in the parietal lobe, and the *primary motor cortex* in the frontal lobe (see Chapter 5). The somatosensory cortex and motor cortex are perhaps the most well-defined areas, both showing *contralateral control*: areas in the right hemisphere receive information from, and are concerned with the activities of, the left side of the body, and vice versa. The crossing over (*corticospinal decussation*) takes place in the medulla (part of the brainstem). These areas represent the body in an upside-down fashion, so information from the feet, for example, is received by neurons at the top of the area.

Furthermore, the amount of cortex devoted to different parts of the body is related to the *sensitivity* and *importance* of that part of the body – *not* to its size. For example, fingers have much more cortex devoted to them than the trunk in the motor cortex, and the lips have a very large representation in the somatosensory cortex (see Figure 4.10). Broca's area is found in the frontal lobe and Wernicke's area borders the temporal and parietal lobes, but only in the left hemisphere. (We shall say more about this under localisation of brain function: see pages 68–70)

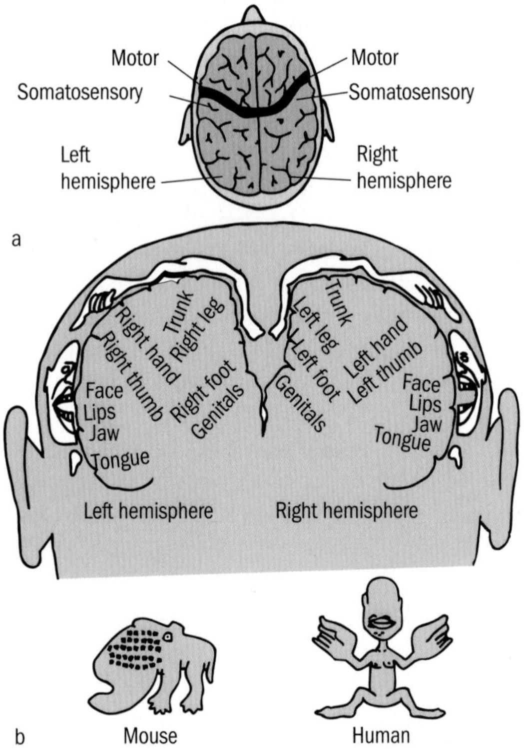

Figure 4.10 Animunculi and homunculi showing how much cortical tissue is devoted to each body area. The mouse explores with its nose and each whisker has its own cortical area. We can use our hands for sensing, although we normally rely more on vision. The large face of the homunculus reflects the large cortical areas necessary for the control of speech. This is sometimes called the Penfield homunculus, after Wilder Penfield who discovered it

The cortex and body image

> *ASK YOURSELF...*
> - What do you understand by the term 'body image'?
> - Do you have a sense of being 'in' your body, or is your body just a part or extension of 'you'?

The *homunculus* ('little man') in Figure 4.10 depicts how the body is represented by the brain. We each have a 'body image', which forms a fundamental part of our overall sense of ourselves as a stable, embodied 'self' (see Chapter 33). Usually, we just 'know' what our arms and legs are doing without having to look: they do what we 'ask' them to. The 'body map' represented by the homunculus may appear to be 'hard-wired' into our brain. But our body image can become distorted, and when it does, the disability it causes can be every bit as devastating as injuring the equivalent part of the body. If a stroke or accident damages the brain region housing the body map, patients may lose the use of a perfectly healthy limb – even though the brain areas that directly control movement remain intact (Phillips, 2000). Conversely, amputees can continue to experience their missing arm or leg as if it were still attached: this is the *phantom limb* phenomenon.

As Ramachandran & Blakeslee (1998) point out, the Penfield 'map' doesn't represent precisely the body's basic organisation. For example, the face isn't near the neck, where it 'should be', but is below the hand. The genitals, instead of being between the thighs, are located *below the foot* (they cite the case of a female leg amputee, who had strange sensations in her phantom foot after sex!). This lack of a perfect match can help explain at least some cases of phantom limbs.

Box 4.4 The case of the phantom hand

Tom Sorenson lost a hand in a car accident, after which his arm was amputated just above the elbow. When his *face* was touched in various places, he experienced sensations in his phantom thumb, index finger, little finger and so on. The whole surface of his hand was mapped out beautifully on his cheek. As Figure 4.11 shows, Tom also had a second 'map' of the missing hand, tucked into his left upper arm a few inches above the amputation line. Stroking the skin surface on this second map also produced precisely localised sensations on individual fingers.

How can we explain this apparently bizarre phenomenon? Ramachandran & Blakeslee (1998) believe the secret lies in the peculiar mapping of body parts in the brain. On the Penfield map, the hand area in the brain is flanked below by the face area and above by the upper arm/shoulder area. Sensory fibres originating from Tom's face (which normally activate *only* the face area in the cortex) invaded space left vacant by the amputated hand. The same happened with fibres originating in the upper arm/shoulder. The brain generated the feeling of the hand from the signals coming from another part of the body.

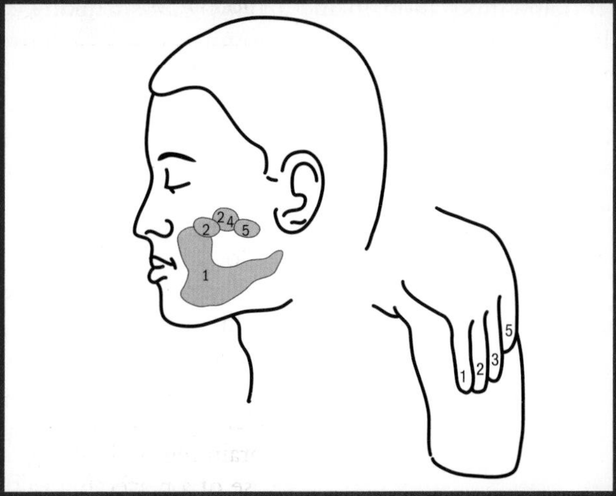

Figure 4.11 Points on the body surface that produced referred sensations in the phantom hand (from Ramachandran & Blakeslee, 1998, reproduced with permission from HarperCollins Publishers Ltd)

ASK YOURSELF...

- What conclusions can you draw from the case of Tom's phantom hand regarding the potential for change in brain circuitry in adulthood?

These findings imply that very precise and highly organised new connections can be formed in the adult brain extremely quickly – at least in some patients. According to Ramachandran and Blakeslee, cases such as Tom's contradict the widely held belief that once neurological circuitry is laid down in the foetus or early infancy, little modification is possible in adulthood. They argue that the phantom doesn't reside in the stump, but in the cortex, where the re-mapping has occurred. As they say:

> ... every time Tom smiles or moves his face and lips, the impulses activate the 'hand' area of his cortex, creating the illusion that his hand is still there. Stimulated by all these spurious signals, Tom's brain literally hallucinates his arm and perhaps this is the essence of the phantom limb ...

Box 4.5 Demonstrating the flexibility of your brain's body image

- Sit at a table and recruit a helper. Hide one hand under the table, resting palm down on your knee. Then ask your helper to tap, touch and stroke with his/her fingertips the back of your hidden hand and the table top directly above the hand with an identical pattern of movements, for a minute or two.
- It's important to concentrate on the table, where your helper is touching, and to make sure you cannot see your hand or your helper's hand under the table. The more irregular the pattern, and the more synchronised the touches you can see and feel, the more likely you are to feel something very strange. The table starts to feel like part of your body – as though the hand is transferred into the table!
- According to Ramachandran and Blakeslee, just as an amputee might experience a phantom limb, so our entire body image is a phantom – something the brain constructs for convenience.

(Source: based on Phillips, 2000)

Can the brain repair itself?

If Ramachandran and Blakeslee's explanation of phantom limbs is correct, then the adult brain seems capable of compensating for damage or loss quite well, by making new connections between *existing* neurons. But this is very different from the claim that the brain can *repair* itself (produce new neurons to replace damaged ones). Until very recently, most neurobiologists firmly believed that the brain lacks the remarkable *stem cells* that account for much of the repair involved in skin, bone and other body cells. However, Kempermann & Gage (1999) cite research showing that the mature human brain *does* produce new neurons at least in one site – the hippocampus (see below, page 67). According to Kempermann and Gage:

> ... Current data suggest that stem cells probably make new neurons in another part of the human brain and also reside, albeit dormantly, in additional locations. Hence, the adult brain, which repairs itself so poorly, might actually harbour great potential for neuronal regeneration ...

If we can learn how to induce existing stem cells to produce useful numbers of functioning neurons in selected brain regions, the practical benefits for people suffering from Alzheimer's and Parkinson's disease, and disabilities caused by strokes and trauma, would be enormous (Kempermann & Gage, 1999).

Association areas in the cortex

The primary motor and sensory areas account for only about 25 per cent of the cortex's surface area, leaving about 75 per cent without an obvious sensory or motor function. This *association cortex* is where the 'higher mental functions' (cognitive processes, such as thinking, reasoning, planning and deciding) probably 'occur'. However, much less is known about where these functions are localised, compared with certain aspects of memory, perception and language.

What is clear is that cortex isn't necessary for biological survival (which is controlled by various *subcortical* structures). Some species (birds, for example) don't have one to begin with, and in those that do, surgical removal doesn't prevent the animal from displaying a wide range of behaviour (although it becomes much more automatic and stereotyped). The human brain has a greater proportion of association cortex than any other species.

The thalamus ('deep chamber')

There are actually two thalami, situated deep in the forebrain (between the brainstem and the cerebral hemispheres). Each is an egg-shaped mass of grey matter and represents a crucial link between the cerebrum and the sense organs. All sensory signals pass through the thalamus, which serves as a relay station or major integrator of information flowing in from the sense organs to the cortex. Each contains nuclei that are specialised to handle particular types of signal:

- the *ventrobasal complex* takes information fed in from the body via the spinal cord
- the *lateral geniculate* ('bent') *body* (LGB) processes visual information (see Chapter 5)
- the *medial geniculate body* (MGB) processes auditory information.

The thalamus also receives information from the cortex, mainly dealing with complex limb movements, which are directed to the cerebellum. Another part of the thalamus plays a part in sleep and waking (see Chapter 7).

> ***ASK YOURSELF...***
> - What role does the thalamus play in theories of emotion? (See Chapter 10, pages 159–168.)

The hypothalamus ('under the thalamus')

For its size (about equal to the tip of your index finger), the hypothalamus is a remarkable and extremely important part of the brain. It plays a major part in homoeostasis (control of the body's internal environment) and motivation, including eating and drinking (see Chapter 9), sexual behaviour, emotional arousal and stress (see Chapter 12). Seven areas can be identified, each with its own special function: *posterior* (sex drive); *anterior* (water balance); *supraoptic* (also water balance); *presupraoptic* (heat control); *ventromedial* (hunger); *dorsomedial* (aggression); and *dorsal* (pleasure).

The hypothalamus works basically in two ways:

1. by sending electrochemical signals to the entire ANS (see Figure 4.1), so that it represents a major link between the CNS and the ANS
2. by influencing the *pituitary gland*, to which it's connected by a network of blood vessels and neurons.

The pituitary gland is situated in the brain, just below and to one side of the hypothalamus. However, it's actually part of the endocrine (hormonal) system (see pages 73–75).

Basal ganglia ('nerve knots')

These are embedded in the mass of white matter of each cerebral hemisphere. They are themselves small areas of grey matter, comprising a number of smaller structures:

- the *corpus striatum* ('striped body'), composed of the *lentiform nucleus* and *caudate nucleus*
- the *amygdala* ('almond')
- the *substantia nigra* (which is also part of the tegmentum, usually classified as part of the midbrain).

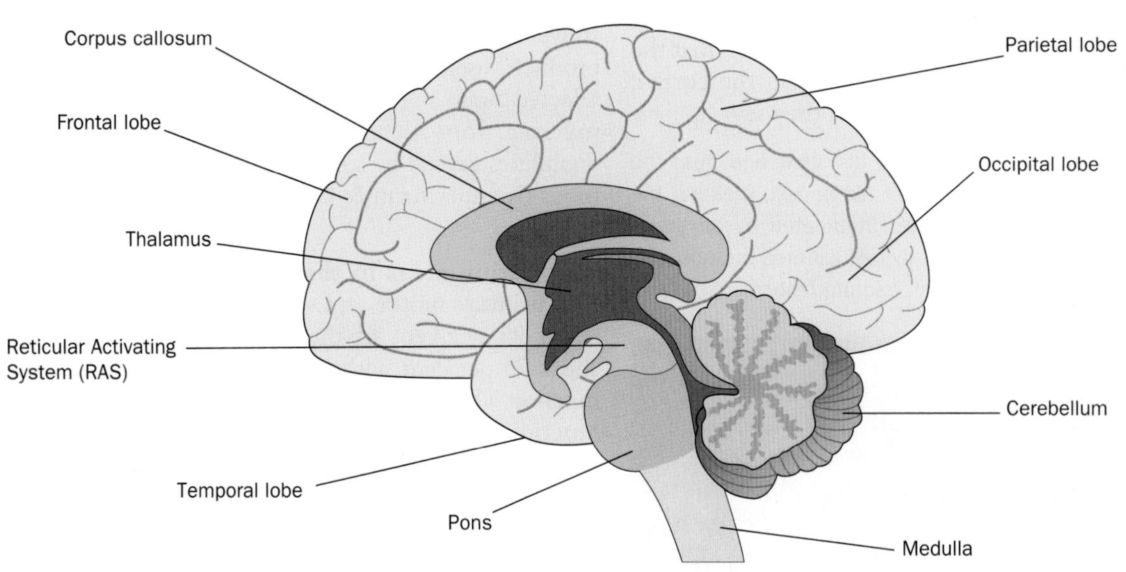

Figure 4.12 Front-to-back cross-section of the right cerebral hemisphere

These structures are closely linked to the thalamus, and they seem to play a part in muscle tone and posture by integrating and coordinating the main voluntary muscle movements, which are the concern of the great descending motor pathway (the *pyramidal system*). Information from the cortex is relayed to the brainstem and cerebellum.

The limbic system ('bordering')

This isn't a separate structure, but comprises a number of highly inter-related structures which, when seen from the side, seem to nest inside each other, encircling the brainstem in a 'wishbone' (see Figure 4.13). The major structures are: (i) the thalami bodies; (ii) hypothalamus; (iii) mamillary bodies; (iv) septum pellucidum; (v) cingulate gyrus; (vi) hippocampus; (vii) amygdala; (viii) fornix; and (ix) olfactory bulbs.

The human limbic system is very similar to that of primitive mammals, and so is often called 'the old mammalian brain'. It's also sometimes called the 'nose brain', because much of its development seems to have been related to the olfactory sense (and, of course, the olfactory bulb, which is concerned with the sense of smell, is one of its components). It's closely involved with behaviours that satisfy certain motivational and emotional needs, including feeding, fighting, escape and mating.

The limbic system as a whole serves as a meeting place between the cortex (or 'neocortex', in evolutionary terms the most recent part of the brain to have developed) and older parts of the brain, such as the hypothalamus. From the cortex it receives interpreted information about the world, and from the hypothalamus information about the body's internal state. These are integrated and the 'conclusions' are fed back to the cortex and to the older, subcortical areas.

The midbrain

This is really an extension of the brainstem connecting the forebrain to the spinal cord. The main structure is the *reticular activating system* (RAS) or *reticular formation* (RF). This ascends from the spinal cord to the forebrain carrying mainly sensory information (the ARAS), and descends from the forebrain to the spinal cord carrying mainly motor information. Since it begins in the spinal cord and passes through the brainstem, it's often classified as part of the hindbrain in addition to the midbrain.

Box 4.6 Major functions of the ARAS

- The ARAS is vitally important in maintaining our general level of arousal or alertness (it's often called the '*consciousness switch*') and plays an important part (but by no means the only one) in the sleep–wake cycle (see Chapter 7).
- It also plays a part in selective attention. Although it responds unselectively to all kinds of stimulation, it helps to screen extraneous sensory information by, for example, controlling *habituation* to constant sources of stimulation, and making us alert and responsive mainly to *changes* in stimulation (see Chapter 7).
- Sleeping parents who keep 'one ear open' for the baby who might start to cry are relying on their ARAS to let only very important sensory signals through. So, it acts as a kind of sentry for the cortex. Damage can induce a coma-like state of sleep.

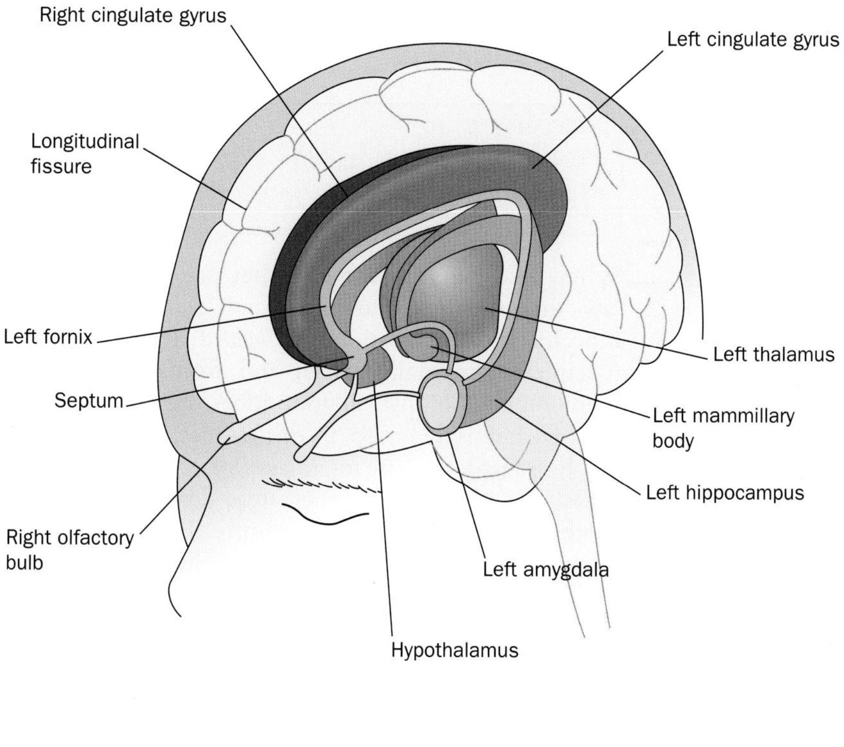

Figure 4.13 The major structures of the limbic system: the thalami bodies, the hypothalamus, the mammillary bodies, the hippocampus, the amygdala, the septum, the fornix and the cingulate gyrus. Also illustrated are the olfactory bulbs, which are connected to several limbic structures (from J. Pinel, 1993, *Biopsychology*, Boston, Allyn & Bacon)

The midbrain also contains important centres for visual and auditory reflexes, including the *orienting reflex*, a general response to a novel stimulus. Other structures include the *locus coeruleus* (see Chapter 7), the *raphne nuclei*, the *tectum* and the *tegmentum*.

The hindbrain

Cerebellum ('little brain')

Like the cerebrum, the cerebellum consists of two halves or hemispheres, and is even more convoluted than the cortex. It plays a vital role in the coordination of voluntary (skeletal) muscle activity, balance and fine movements (such as reaching for things). Motor commands that originate in higher brain centres are processed here before transmission to the muscles. Damage to the cerebellum can cause hand tremors, drunken movements and loss of balance. The inability to reach for objects normally (*ataxia*) and hand tremors are quite common among the elderly.

The cerebellum also controls the intricate movements involved in the swimming of a fish, the flying of a bird, playing a musical instrument and driving a car. Once learned, complex movements like those involved in picking up a glass, walking and talking seem to be 'programmed' into the cerebellum. This allows us do them 'automatically' without having to think consciously about what we're doing (it acts as an 'automatic pilot' inside the brain).

The cerebellum accounts for about 11 per cent of the brain's entire weight; only the cerebrum is larger. Its grey matter in fact consists of three layers of cells, the middle layer of which – the *Purkinje cells* – can link each synapse with up to 100,000 other neurons, more than any other kind of brain cell.

The pons ('bridge')

This is a bulge of white matter that connects the two halves of the cerebellum. It's an important connection between the midbrain and the medulla, and is vital in integrating the movements of the two sides of the body. Four of the 12 cranial nerves (which originate in the brain) have their nuclei ('relay stations') here, including the large *trigeminal* nerve. It's the middle portion of the brainstem.

The medulla oblongata ('rather long marrow')

This is a fibrous section of the lower brainstem (about 2 cm long), and is really a thick extension of the spinal cord. In evolutionary terms, it's the oldest part of the brain and is the site of the crossing over of the major nerve tracts coming up from the spinal cord and coming down from the brain. It contains vital reflex centres, which control breathing, cardiac function, swallowing, vomiting, coughing, chewing, salivation and facial movements. The midbrain, pons and medulla together make up the *brainstem*.

THE SPINAL CORD

The spinal cord is about the thickness of a little finger. It passes from the brainstem down the whole length of the back and is encased in the vertebrae of the spine. The spinal cord is the main communication 'cable' between the brain (CNS) and the peripheral nervous system (PNS), providing the pathway between body and brain.

Messages enter and leave the spinal cord by means of 31 pairs of spinal nerves. Each pair innervates a different and fairly specific part of the body and are 'mixed nerves': they contain both *motor neurons* (carrying information from the NS to the muscles) and *sensory neurons* (carrying information from the sensory receptors to the NS) for most of their length. But at the junction with the cord itself, the nerves divide into two roots – the *dorsal root* (towards the back of the body), which contains sensory neurons, and the *ventral root* (towards the front of the body), which contains motor neurons.

The basic functional unit of the NS is the *spinal reflex arc*, such as the knee-jerk reflex. This involves just two kinds of neuron: a sensory neuron conveys information about stimulation of the patella tendon (knee cap) to the spinal cord, and this information crosses a single synapse within the grey 'butterfly' (which runs inside the centre of the cord: see Figure 4.14, page 69). This causes a motor neuron to stimulate the appropriate muscle groups in the leg, which causes the leg to shoot up in the air.

However, most spinal reflexes are more complex than this. For example, withdrawing your hand from a hot plate will involve an interneuron (as well as a sensory and motor neuron) and two synapses. Commonly, the experience of pain follows one to two seconds after you have withdrawn your hand – this is how long it takes for sensory information to reach the cortex.

THE LOCALISATION AND LATERALISATION OF BRAIN FUNCTION

ASK YOURSELF...
- What do you understand by these two terms?
- How are they different?

When describing the cortex earlier (see pages 63–65), we saw that different functions, such as vision, hearing, movement and sensation, are *located* in different lobes (occipital, temporal, parietal and frontal, respectively). Remember also that all four lobes are found in both cerebral hemispheres, so, in this respect, the hemispheres can be regarded as mirror images of each other. We also noted that there are distinct areas dealing with speech production and comprehension (Broca's area and Wernicke's area, respectively), again illustrating *functional localisation*. However, these are found *only* in the left hemisphere, illustrating *functional lateralisation* (or *hemispheric asymmetry*).

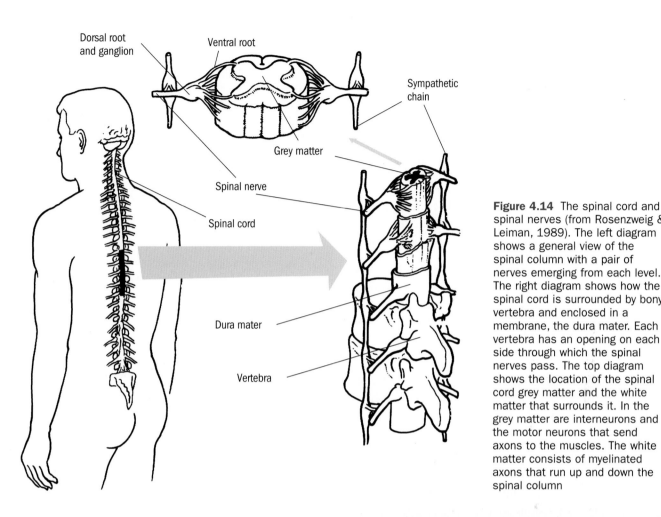

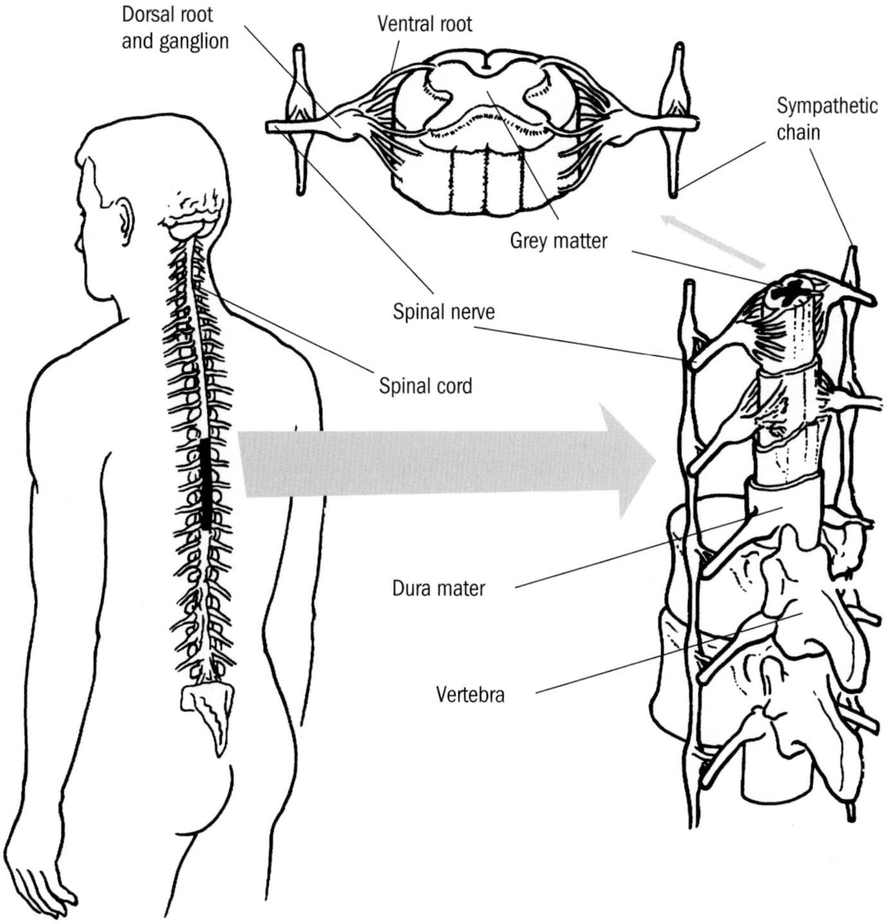

Figure 4.14 The spinal cord and spinal nerves (from Rosenzweig & Leiman, 1989). The left diagram shows a general view of the spinal column with a pair of nerves emerging from each level. The right diagram shows how the spinal cord is surrounded by bony vertebra and enclosed in a membrane, the dura mater. Each vertebra has an opening on each side through which the spinal nerves pass. The top diagram shows the location of the spinal cord grey matter and the white matter that surrounds it. In the grey matter are interneurons and the motor neurons that send axons to the muscles. The white matter consists of myelinated axons that run up and down the spinal column

Lateralisation, language and handedness

Much of the discussion of lateralisaton has focused on language. From studies of stroke victims in particular, it's generally agreed that for the majority of right-handed people, their left hemisphere is dominant for speech (and language ability in general). People paralysed down their *right* side must have suffered damage to the *left* hemisphere and, if they've also suffered aphasia (see page 59), then we can infer that language is normally controlled by the *left* hemisphere.

One of the difficulties associated with generalisations in psychology (even with something as 'biological' as cerebral function) is the existence of *individual differences*. Some people seem to have much more lateralised brains than others, while some have language more or less equally represented on both sides (*bilateral representation*: Beaumont, 1988). The left hemisphere seems to be dominant for language for 95 per cent of right-handed patients, while only 5 per cent had their right hemisphere dominant. But with left-handers, things are much less clear-cut: 75 per cent had their left hemisphere dominant, none had the right dominant, but 25 per cent showed bilateral representation (based on a review by Satz (1979) of all studies between 1935 and 1975; cited in Beaumont, 1988).

Box 4.7 Are women really superior when it comes to language?

- Over and above this left/right-handed difference, women show *less lateralisation* than men for both linguistic and other abilities. This means that left-hemisphere damage would produce greater deficits in language ability for men (at least, most right-handed men) than it would in (most right-handed) women.
- This difference is thought to underlie females' advantage over males on a variety of linguistic tasks, from detection of dichotic syllables (where different auditory signals are presented to the two ears) to the generation of synonyms.
- However, neuroimaging studies using fMRI (see page 62) have shown that men and women can perform identical language processes with the same degree of functional capacity – but, apparently, using very differently organised brain systems.
- One attempt to replicate these findings (Frost *et al.*, 1999) found that both sexes showed very similar, strongly left-lateralised activation patterns. Although sex differences may exist at a microscopic neural level, these aren't detectable using currently available fMRI methods.

(Source: based on Esgate, 1999)

The effects of brain damage: is it 'where' or 'how much' that matters?

In the majority of right-handed people, is the dominance of the left hemisphere a built-in characteristic or is it modifiable? According to Zaidel (1978), the two hemispheres are fairly equal up until about age five. In general, a child's brain is much more *plastic* (flexible) than an adult's (Rose, 1976). For example, in children up to three years, brain trauma produces similar effects regardless of which site is damaged. Provided the lesion isn't too severe, or that it occurs on one side only, considerable recovery is possible: the corresponding area on the other side takes over the function of the damaged area, and this seems to be especially true of language (see Chapter 19).

This seems to support the conclusions of Lashley, who (in the 1920s) studied the effects of brain destruction on rats' learning ability. His (1929) *law of mass action* states that the learning of difficult problems depends upon the *amount of damage* to the cortex, and not on the position or site of the damage. In other words, the greater the cortical damage, the greater the learning difficulty. However, Lashley couldn't find specific neural circuits related to the learning of, or memory for, particular types of problem. The *law of equipotentiality* states that corresponding parts of the brain are capable of taking over the function normally performed by the damaged area.

Similarly, the *principle of multiple control* maintains that any particular part of the brain is likely to be involved in the performance of many different types of behaviour. For example, rats with lesions in their lateral hypothalamus show deficits in certain learning situations, as well as impaired feeding (see Chapter 9). Conversely, the same behaviour (such as aggression or emotion) normally involves a number of brain sites. The logical conclusion of this seems to be that the brain functions as a complete unit, an integrated whole. We shall return to this issue below.

Split-brain patients

Remember that split-brain patients have undergone surgery (normally in the treatment of epilepsy) to cut their corpus callosum, which joins the two hemispheres and allows them to exchange information. While the surgery may relieve the epilepsy, it has a major side-effect: the two hemispheres become functionally separate (they act as two separate, independent brains). Sperry (based on a number of studies in the 1960s and 1970s, for which he was awarded the Nobel Prize for Medicine in 1981) and Ornstein (1975) believe that split-brain studies reveal the 'true' nature of the two hemispheres, and that each embodies a different kind of consciousness (see Chapter 7). A typical split-brain experiment is described in Key Study 4.1.

> ***ASK YOURSELF...***
> - What do the following examples suggest regarding the right hemisphere's linguistic abilities?

KEY STUDY 4.1 When the left brain literally doesn't know what the left hand is doing (Sperry, 1968)

- Participants sit in front of a screen, their hands free to handle objects that are behind the screen but which are obscured from sight. While fixating on a spot in the middle of the screen, a word (for example, 'key') is flashed on to the left side of the screen for a tenth of a second (this ensures that the word is only 'seen' by the right hemisphere).
- If asked to select the key from a pile of objects with the left hand (still controlled by the right hemisphere), this can be done quite easily. However, the participant is unable to say what word appeared on the screen (because the left hemisphere doesn't receive the information from the right as it normally would), and literally doesn't know why s/he chose the key.
- This time, a word (for example, 'heart') is flashed on the screen, with 'he' to the left and 'art' to the right of the fixation point. If asked to name the word, participants will say 'art', because this is the portion of the word projected to the left hemisphere. However, when asked to point with the left hand to one of two cards on which 'he' and 'art' are written, the left hand will point to 'he', because this is the portion projected to the right hemisphere.

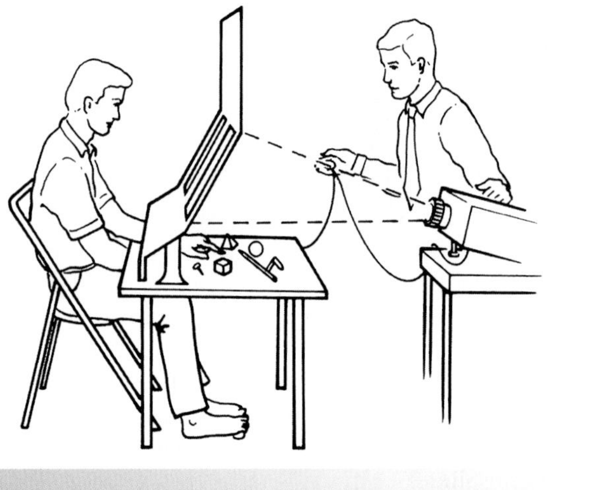

Figure 4.15 Apparatus for studying lateralisation of visual, tactile, lingual and associated functions in the surgically separated hemispheres (from Sperry, 1968)

These examples show that the right hemisphere doesn't completely lack language ability – otherwise participants couldn't successfully point or select. However, it clearly lacks the left hemisphere's ability to name and articulate what has been experienced. In the second example, both hemispheres are handicapped if information isn't conveyed from one to the other – the whole word ('heart') isn't perceived by either!

A similar, but perhaps more dramatic, example involved sets of photographs of different faces. Each photo was cut down the middle and halves of two different faces were pasted together. They were then presented in such a way that the left side of the photo would only be visible to the right hemisphere, and vice-versa.

> *ASK YOURSELF...*
> - If a picture of an old man were presented to the left hemisphere and a young boy to the right, and participants were asked to *describe what they'd seen* (the *left hemisphere* responding), what would they have said?
> - If asked to *point with their left hand* to the complete photo of the person they'd seen (the *right hemisphere* responding), which picture would they have pointed to?

In the first case, they said 'an old man', and in the second case, they pointed to the young boy. It seems that two completely separate visual worlds can exist within the same head!

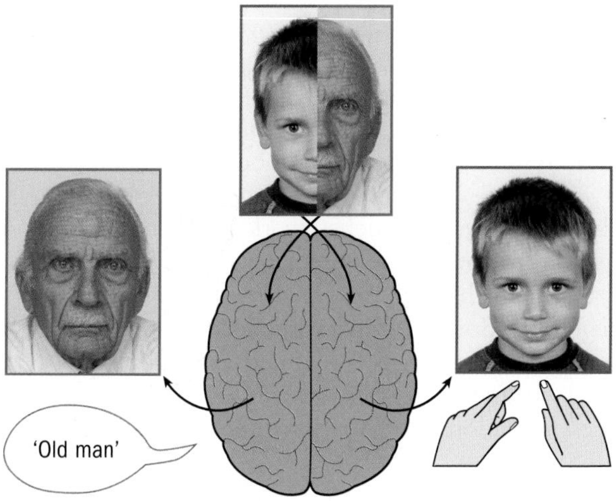

Figure 4.16 Responses given by the left and right hemispheres to a chimeric

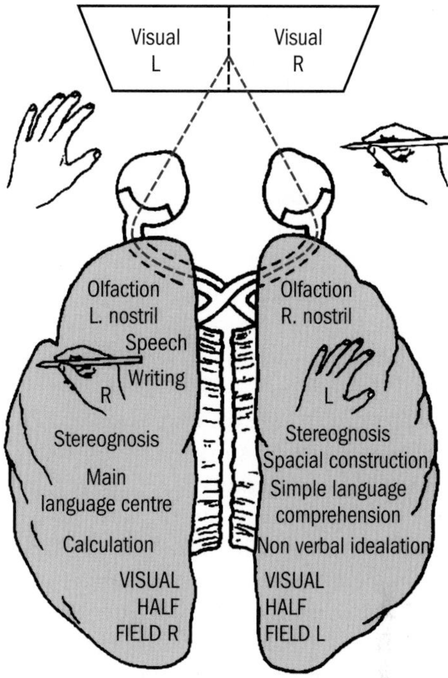

Figure 4.17 Schematic outline of the functional lateralisation evident in behavioural tests of patients with forebrain commissurotomy (from Sperry, 1968)

One brain or two? One mind or two?

These and many more equally dramatic experiments led Sperry, Ornstein and others to conclude that each of the separated hemispheres has its own private sensations, perceptions, thoughts, feelings and memories. In short, they constitute two separate minds, two separate spheres of consciousness (Sperry, 1964; see Figure 4.17). Levy-Agresti & Sperry (1968) concluded that the:

> ... mute, minor hemisphere is specialized for Gestalt perception, being primarily a synthesist in dealing with information input. The speaking, major hemisphere, in contrast, seems to operate in a more logical, analytic, computer-like fashion ...

Cohen (1975) argues that long-standing presurgical pathology might have caused an abnormal reorganisation of the brains of these split-brain patients, so that generalising to normal people might not be valid. Several attempts have been made to move beyond the simplistic left hemisphere/right hemisphere, verbal/non-verbal distinction, both in normal participants and in split-brain patients. In a review of research, Annett (1991) says that 'it is evident that each hemisphere has some role in the functions assigned to the other'. For example, the right hemisphere has a considerable understanding of language and it's been suggested that it might be responsible for semantic errors made by deep dyslexics (see Chapter 40). Similarly, the left hemisphere is almost certainly responsible for the production of imagery, 'which is likely to be required in much spatial thinking'.

Box 4.8 The major differences between the left and right hemispheres

Ornstein (1986) summarises the differences as follows:

- the *left* is specialised for *analytic and logical thinking* (breaking things down into their component parts), especially in verbal and mathematical functions, processes information *sequentially* (one item at a time), and its mode of operation is primarily *linear* (straight line);
- the *right* is specialised for *synthetic thinking* (bringing different things together to form a whole), particularly in the area of spatial tasks, artistic activities, crafts, body image and face recognition, processes information more *diffusely* (several items at once), and its mode of operation is much *less linear* (more *holistic*).

ASK YOURSELF...

- Should we generalise about hemispheric differences from studies of split-brain patients?

According to Gazzaniga (1985), the brain is organised in a *modular fashion* – that is, organised into relatively independent functioning units, which work in parallel. Many of the modules operate at a non-conscious level, in parallel to our conscious thought, with the left hemisphere interpreting the processing of these modules. So, brains are organised such that many mental systems co-exist in a 'confederation'.

Sternberg (1990) believes that Gazzaniga's view isn't widely accepted by neuropsychologists; but many would also reject the degree of separation between the hemispheres suggested by Sperry and his co-workers. An alternative view is one of *integration*: the two hemispheres should be seen as playing different parts in an integrated performance (Broadbent, 1985, cited in Sternberg, 1990). Cohen (1975) agrees that, when normal participants are studied, the two sides of the brain don't function in isolation but form a highly integrated system. Most everyday tasks involve a mixture of 'left' and 'right' skills. For example, in listening to speech, we analyse both the words and the intonation pattern, and when reading we analyse visual shapes and draw on our linguistic knowledge. Far from doing their own thing, the two hemispheres work very much together (Cohen, 1975).

McCrone (1999) concludes that researchers have come to see the distinction between the two hemispheres as a subtle one of *processing style*, with every mental faculty shared across the brain, and each side contributing in a *complementary*, not exclusive, fashion. Evidence from imaging studies suggests that the left hemisphere 'prefers' (or pays more attention to) detail (such as grammar and specific word production), while the right prefers the overall meaning of what's being said (as conveyed by intonation and emphasis). This is consistent with the finding that people with right-hemisphere stroke damage become much more *literal* in their interpretation of language. However, a 'smart' brain is one that responds in *both* ways. As McCrone (1999) says:

> ... whatever the story about lateralization, simple dichotomies are out. It is how the two sides of the brain complement and combine that counts.

THE AUTONOMIC NERVOUS SYSTEM (ANS)

As shown in Figure 4.1, the ANS is the part of the PNS that controls the internal organs and glands of the body over which we have little (or no) voluntary control. It comprises two branches:

1. the *sympathetic*, which takes over whenever the body needs to use its energy (as in emergencies: the 'fight or flight' syndrome), and
2. the *parasympathetic*, which is dominant when the body is at 'rest' and energy is being built up.

Although the two branches work in essentially opposite ways, they're both equally necessary for the maintenance of the delicately balanced internal state of *homoeostasis* (see Chapter 9). Sometimes, a sequence of sympathetic and parasympathetic activity is required. For example, in sexual arousal in men, erection is primarily parasympathetic, while ejaculation is primarily sympathetic.

Table 4.2 Major sympathetic and parasympathetic reactions

	Organ or function affected	Sympathetic reaction	Parasympathetic reaction
1	Heart rate	Increase	Decrease
2	Blood pressure	Increase	Decrease
3	Secretion of saliva	Suppressed (mouth feels dry)	Stimulated
4	Pupils	Dilate (to aid vision)	Contract
5	Limbs (and trunk)	Dilation of blood vessels of the voluntary muscles (to help us run faster, for example)	Contraction of these blood vessels
6	Peristalsis (contraction of stomach and intestines)	Slows down (you don't feel hungry in an emergency)	Speeds up
7	Galvanic skin response (GSR) (measure of the electrical resistance of the skin)	Decreases (due to increased sweating associated with increased anxiety)	Increases
8	Bladder muscles	Relaxed (there may be temporary loss of bladder control)	Contracted
9	Adrenal glands	Stimulated to secrete more adrenaline and noradrenaline	Reduced secretion
10	Breathing rate	Increased (through dilation of bronchi)	Decreased
11	Liver	Glucose (stored as glycogen) is released into the blood to increase energy	Sugar is stored
12	Emotion	Experience of strong emotion	Less extreme emotions

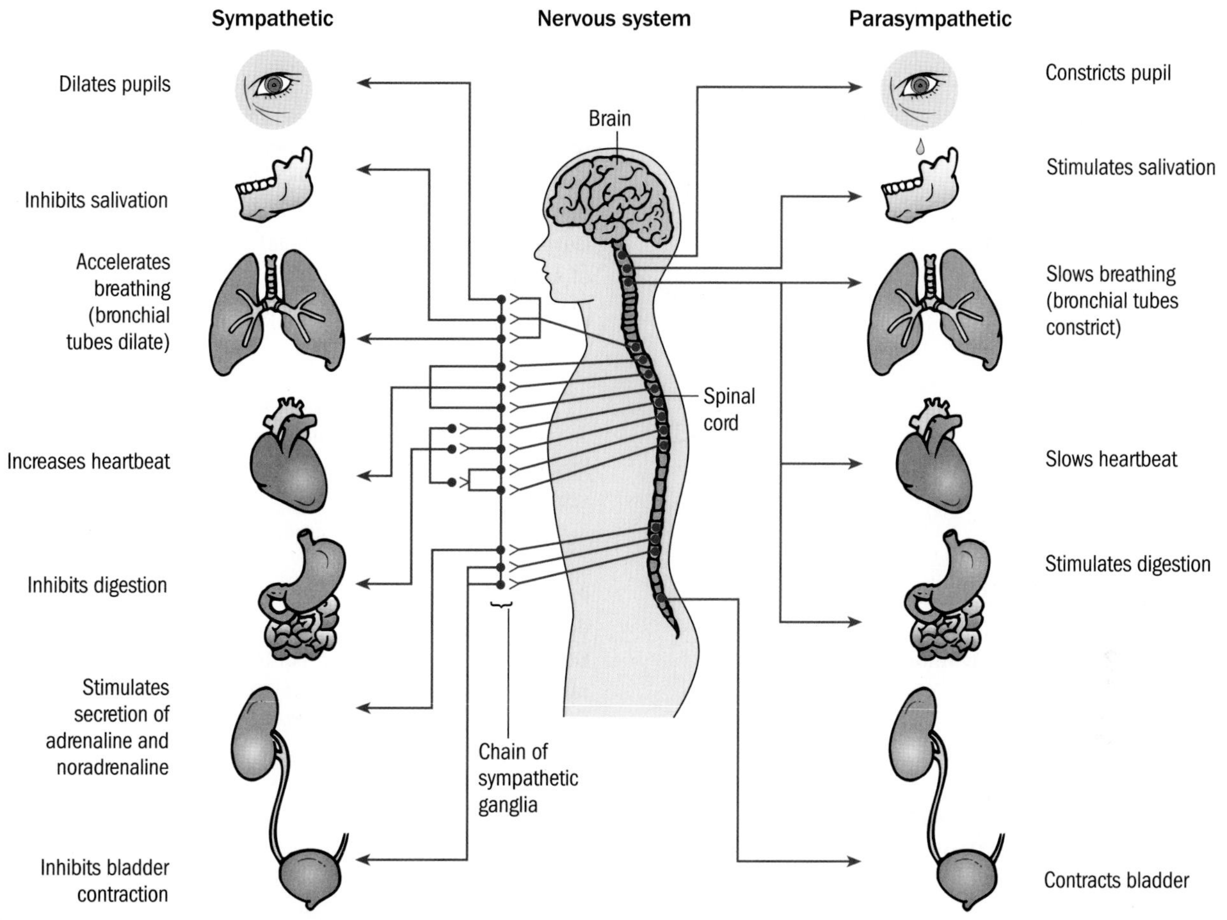

Figure 4.18 Some of the organs affected by the two branches of the ANS (from Hassett & White, 1989)

The ANS produces its effects in two ways:

1. by direct neural stimulation of body organs
2. by stimulating the release of hormones from the endocrine glands (see below).

In both cases, the *hypothalamus* is the orchestrator. The ANS is discussed further in Chapter 10, in relation to emotion, and in Chapter 12, in relation to stress.

THE ENDOCRINE SYSTEM

Endocrine glands secrete *hormones* (chemical messengers) which, unlike neurotransmitters, are released directly into the bloodstream and are carried throughout the body. While an electrochemical impulse can convey a message in a matter of milliseconds, it may take several seconds for a hormone to be stimulated, released and reach its destination. Consequently, where an immediate behavioural reaction is required (for example, a reflex action), the NS plays a major role. Hormones are better suited to communicating steady, relatively unchanging messages over prolonged periods of time (for example, the body changes associated with puberty: see Chapter 37).

Box 4.9 The pituitary gland

- The major endocrine gland is the *pituitary gland*, which is physically (but not functionally) part of the brain (situated just below the hypothalamus).
- It is often called the 'master gland', because it produces the largest number of different hormones, and also because it controls the secretion of several other endocrine glands.
- The pituitary comprises two independently functioning parts: the *posterior* and the *anterior*. The former transmits hormones that are thought to be manufactured in the hypothalamus, while the latter is stimulated by the hypothalamus to produce its own hormones.
- The major hormones of the posterior and anterior lobes of the pituitary are shown, along with their effects, in Table 4.3, page 74.

Other important endocrine glands are the *adrenals* (situated just above the kidneys), each of which comprises the *adrenal medulla* (inner core) and the *adrenal cortex* (outer layer). As Table 4.3 shows, the medulla secretes *adrenaline* and *noradrenaline*, which are the transmitter substances for the sympathetic branch of the ANS.

Table 4.3 Major pituitary hormones and their effects

	Hormone	Endocrine gland or organ stimulated	Effects
Anterior pituitary	**Growth hormone (somatotrophin)**	Body tissues	Increases growth of bones and muscles, particularly in childhood and adolescence Too little produces pituitary dwarfism and too much gigantism
Anterior pituitary	**Gonadotrophic hormones** **1 Luteinising hormone (LH)**	Gonads (Testes–male, Ovaries–female)	Development of sex (germ) cells: Ova (female); Sperm (male) Production of sex hormones: Oestrogen and progesterone (female); Testosterone (male)
Anterior pituitary	**2 Follicle-stimulating hormone (FSH)**	Ovaries	Production of follicles in ovary during ovulation
Anterior pituitary	**Thyrotrophic hormone (TTH)**	Thyroid gland	Secretion of thyroxin which controls metabolic rate – too little causes lethargy and depression, too much causes hyperactivity and anxiety
Anterior pituitary	**Lactogenic hormone (Prolactin)**	Breasts	Milk production during pregnancy
Anterior pituitary	**Adrenocorticotrophic hormone (ACTH)**	Adrenal glands 1 Adrenal medulla 2 Adrenal cortex	 Secretion of adrenaline and noradrenaline Secretion of adrenocorticoid hormones (or corticosteroids), e.g. cortisol and hydrocortisone (important in coping with stress) (see Chapter 12)
Posterior pituitary	**Oxytocin**	Uterus (womb)	Causes contractions during labour and milk release during breast feeding
Posterior pituitary	**Vasopressin (also a neurotransmitter)**	Blood vessels	Causes contraction of the muscle in the walls of the blood vessels and so raises blood pressure
Posterior pituitary	**Antidiuretic hormone (ADH)**	Kidneys	Regulates the amount of water passed in the urine

Other endocrine glands include:

(a) Thymus – situated in the chest; functions unknown, but thought to involve production of antibodies (see Chapter 12)

(b) Pancreas – secretes insulin (anti-diabetic hormone), given in the treatment of diabetes. Controls the body's ability to absorb glucose and fats

(c) Pineal body/gland – situated near corpus callosum, functions unknown but may play a role in sleep–waking cycle (see Chapter 7)

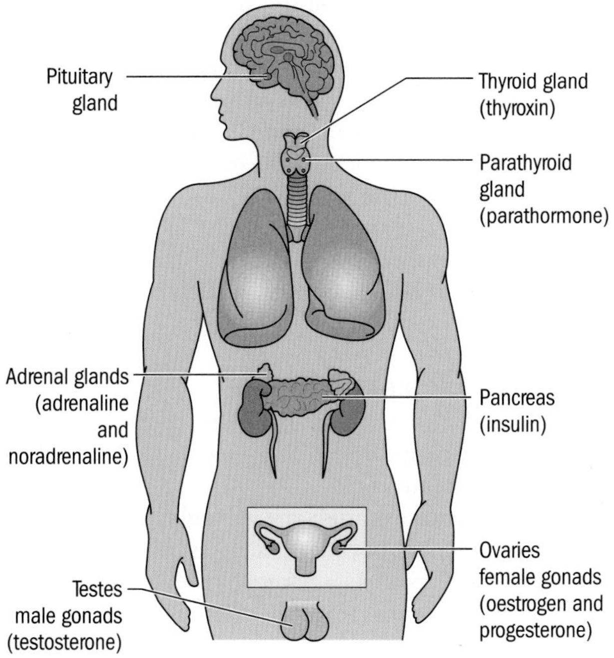

Figure 4.19 Some major glands of the endocrine system and the hormones they produce

CHAPTER SUMMARY

- **Biopsychology** is the branch of neuroscience that studies the biological bases of behaviour. Biopsychologists are only interested in biology for what it can tell them about behaviour and mental processes.
- The **nervous system (NS)** comprises 10–12 billion **neurons**, 80 per cent of which are found in the brain, mainly in the cerebral cortex. There are nine to ten times as many **glial cells**.
- Neurons are either **sensory/afferent**, **motor/efferent** or **interneurons/connector**. They vary enormously in length, but share a basic structure.
- A **nerve** is a bundle of **elongated axons**. Twelve pairs of **cranial nerves** leave the brain through holes in the skull, while 31 pairs of **spinal nerves** leave the spinal cord through the vertebrae. Together, they constitute the nerves of the **peripheral nervous system (PNS)**.
- When an **electrochemical signal/action potential** occurs, the inside of the neuron momentarily changes from negative to positive. The **resting potential** is almost immediately restored. Once the **threshold of response** has been exceeded, action potentials travel according to the **all-or-none rule**.
- **Synapses** are either **excitatory** or **inhibitory**, depending on the particular **neurotransmitter** contained within the **synaptic button**. Whether or not a particular neuron will fire depends on the combined effect of all its receiving synapses (**summation**). Once the transmitter molecules have crossed into the **post-synaptic membrane**, their effect is ended either by **deactivation** or **reuptake**.
- **Neuromodulators** 'prime' receiving neurons for later stimulation by a neurotransmitter. Neuromodulators include **neuropeptides**, in particular the **enkephalins** and **endorphins/opioids**.
- **Clinical/anatomical methods** of studying the brain involve patients who've suffered accidental brain damage or disease, or **split-brain** patients.
- **Invasive methods** involve **ablation**, **stimulating** the brain (either electrically or chemically), and **micro-electrode recording**.
- **Non-invasive methods** include the **electroen-cephalogram** (EEG), **electromyogram** (EMG), **electrooculogram** (EOG) and **average evoked potentials** (AEPs).
- Computers are also used in a number of **scanning/imaging devices**. These include **comput-erised axial tomography** (CAT), **positron emission tomography** (PET), **magnetic resonance imaging** (MRI), **single-photon emission comput-erised tomography** (SPECT), and **superconducting quantum imaging/interference device** (SQUID). These techniques provide access to processes associated with mental activity, inside the healthy living brain as they happen.
- The **cerebral hemispheres/cerebrum** enfold and conceal most other brain structures. The top layer is the highly convoluted **cortex**. Each hemisphere is naturally divided into the **occipital lobe** (which houses

the **visual cortex**), the **temporal lobe** (**auditory cortex**), the **parietal lobe** (**somatosensory/body-sense cortex**), and the **frontal lobe (motor cortex**).

- Highly sensitive parts of the body and those over which we have precise motor control have much more cortex devoted to them than other parts. The whole body is represented on the surface of the cortex as a 'body map' (**homunculus**).
- The **association cortex** is where higher mental processes 'occur', but as yet most have not been localised. The cortex isn't necessary for biological survival, which is controlled by various **subcortical** structures.
- The cerebral hemispheres are part of the **forebrain**, together with the **thalamus**, **hypothalamus**, **basal ganglia** and the **limbic system**.
- The **midbrain** is an extension of the brainstem and connects the forebrain to the spinal cord. The **reticular activating system** (RAS) begins in the spinal cord and passes through the brainstem.
- The **hindbrain** consists of the **medulla oblongata**, the **pons** and the **cerebellum**.
- The **spinal cord** is encased in the vertebrae and is the main communication cable between the CNS and the PNS. Messages enter and leave via 31 pairs of **spinal nerves**. At the junction with the cord itself, the nerve divides into the **dorsal root** (**sensory neurons**) and the **ventral root** (**motor neurons**).
- There's considerable evidence for both **functional localisation** and **functional lateralisation**. The left hemisphere is dominant for language in most right-handed people, but some people seem to have much more lateralised brains than others, while others display **bilateral representation**.
- Children's brains show considerable **plasticity**, which supports Lashley's **laws of mass action** and **equipotentiality**.
- The **phantom limb** phenomenon suggests that the adult brain is also very malleable, and there's some evidence of neurons being capable of regeneration.
- The findings from **split-brain studies** have led to the view that each hemisphere constitutes a separate mind or sphere of consciousness. An alternative interpretation is that the brain is organised in the form of **modules**, which work in parallel and often non-consciously. A third view is that the two hemispheres differ in their **processing styles**, yet represent a highly **integrated** system.
- The **autonomic nervous system** (ANS) comprises the **sympathetic** and **parasympathetic branches**. It works either by direct neural stimulation of body organs, or by stimulating the release of **hormones** from the **endocrine system**.
- The **pituitary gland** produces the largest number of different hormones and controls the secretion of several other endocrine glands, such as the **adrenal glands**.

Links with other topics/chapters

- Both neuropharmacology and psychopharmacology are relevant to understanding *substance dependence and abuse* (see Chapter 8).
- Several neurotransmitters are thought to be involved in major mental disorders, such as *schizophrenia* and *depression* (Chapter 44). Some of the most important evidence for their role in causing these disorders comes from what's known about how *drugs used to treat them* affect these neurotransmitters (Chapter 45).
- Some neuropeptides occur as hormones, including those that are involved *in emotional arousal* (Chapter 10), *stress reactions* (Chapter 12), and *sex drive* (Chapter 36).
- One of the ways the ANS produces its effects is by stimulating the release of hormones from the endocrine glands. The ANS is relevant to understanding *emotion* (Chapter 10) and *stress* (Chapter 12).
- Much of the *ethical controversy* surrounding the *use of non-human animals in experiments* focuses on the invasive methods used to study the brain (Chapter 48). These methods have been used in relation to *sensory processes* (Chapter 5), *eating* (Chapter 9), *stress* (Chapter 12), *pattern recognition* (Chapter 14) and *perceptual development* (Chapter 16).
- Non-invasive methods (in particular, the EEG, EMG and EOG) have been used extensively in relation to *sleep* (Chapter 7).
- Body image is one important component of the *self-concept* (Chapter 33).
- The study of split-brain patients raises fundamental issues regarding the *relationship between the brain and mind/consciousness* (Chapter 49).

5

SENSORY PROCESSES

INTRODUCTION AND OVERVIEW

When we move our eyes or our heads, the objects we see around us remain stable. Similarly, when we follow a moving object, we attribute the movement to the object and not to ourselves. When we walk towards someone in the street, we don't experience them as gradually growing 'before our eyes', and we recognise objects seen from various angles.

These examples of how we experience the world may seem mundane and obvious, until we realise what's actually taking place physically. If we compare what we experience (a world of objects that remain stable and constant) with what our sense organs receive in the form of physical stimulation (a world in an almost continuous state of flux), it's almost as if there were two entirely different worlds involved. The one we are aware of is a world of objects and people (*perception*), and the one we're not aware of is a world of sense data (*sensation*).

While perception cannot occur without sensation (the physical stimulation of the sense organs), the sense data constitute only the 'raw material' from which our awareness of objects is constructed. Although we feel we're in direct and immediate contact with the world as it really is, in fact our awareness of things is the end-product of a long and complex process. This begins with physical energy stimulating the sense organs (light in the case of vision, sound waves in the case of hearing), and ends with the brain interpreting the information received from the sense organs.

This chapter concentrates on sensation, the physical processes necessary for the psychological process of perception (see Chapters 15 and 16). However, when we talk about *vision*, for example, we're referring not just to the eyes, but to the whole *visual system*. The system also includes pathways between the eyes and the brain, as well as the brain itself.

THE SENSES: PROVIDING THE RAW MATERIAL OF PERCEPTION

According to Ornstein (1975), we don't perceive objective reality but, rather, our *construction* of reality. Our sense organs gather information, which the brain modifies and sorts, and this 'heavily filtered input' is compared with memories, expectancies, and so on, until, finally, our consciousness is constructed as a 'best guess' about reality.

In a similar vein, James (1902) maintained that 'the mind, in short, works on the data it receives much as the sculptor works on his block of stone'. However, different artists use different materials, and, similarly, different sensory systems provide different kinds of sense data for the perceiver-sculptor to 'model'. Each of our various sensory systems is designed to respond only to a particular kind of stimulation. But a related and equally important point (often overlooked) is that our sensory systems also function as *data reduction systems* (Ornstein, 1975).

If something cannot be sensed (because our senses aren't responsive or sensitive to it), *it doesn't exist for us*. While we normally regard our senses as the 'windows' to the world, a major job they perform is to discard 'irrelevant' information and to register only what's likely to be of practical value (clearly, something that has occurred as a result of evolutionary forces). We'd be overwhelmed if we responded to the world as it is: different forms of energy are so diverse they're still being discovered. Each species has developed particular sensitivity to certain of these different forms of energy, which have aided their survival. According to Bruce & Green (1990):

> Sensitivity to diffusing chemicals and to mechanical energy gives an animal considerable perceptual abilities but leaves it unable to obtain information rapidly about either its inanimate world or about silent animals at a distance from itself ... The form of energy that can provide these kinds of information is light, and consequently most animals have some ability to perceive their surroundings through vision ...

Box 5.1 The nature of light

- *Light* is one form of *electromagnetic radiation*, which includes radio waves, microwaves, infrared and ultraviolet light, as well as the visible spectrum.
- Although the entire spectrum ranges from less than 1 billionth of a metre to more than 100 metres, the human eye, by design, responds only to the tiny portion between 380 and 780 billionths of a metre (nanometres) which we call light. (Although pressure on the eyeball produces sensations of light, it's external sources of light that normally produce the sensation: see Figure 5.1.)

(Source: based on Bruce & Green, 1990)

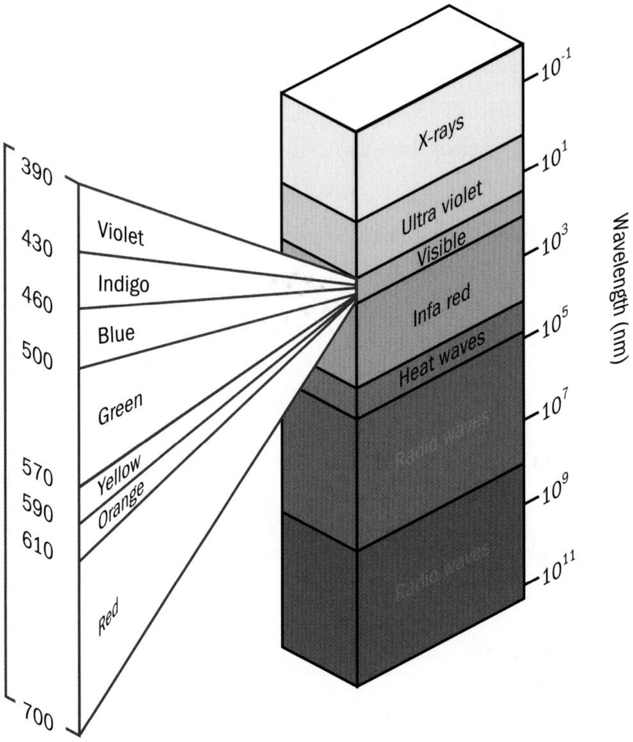

Figure 5.1 The spectrum of electromagnetic radiation. Wavelengths are given in nanometres (1 nm = 10^{-9} m). The visible part of the spectrum is shown on the left, with the colours of different wavelengths of light (redrawn from Bruce & Green, 1990)

CLASSIFYING SENSORY SYSTEMS

The senses have been classified in several ways. For example, Sherrington (1906) identified three kinds of receptor:

1. *exteroceptors*, which tell us about the external environment
2. *interoceptors*, which tell us about the internal environment
3. *proprioceptors*, which deal with the position of our body in space and its movement through space.

Exteroception includes the five 'traditional' senses of sight (*vision*), hearing (*audition*), smell (*olfaction*), taste (*gustation*) and touch (*cutaneous* or *skin senses*). Interoception includes the internal receptors for oxygen, carbon dioxide, blood glucose, and so on. Proprioception is usually sub-divided into: (i) the *kinaesthetic sense*, which monitors movements of the limbs, joints and muscles; and (ii) the *vestibular sense*, which responds to gravity and the movements of the head.

Gibson (1966) rejected proprioception as a distinct sensory system (and saw taste and smell as representing the same system), and Legge (1975) includes proprioception under the general heading of interoception.

CHARACTERISTICS OF SENSORY SYSTEMS

However we classify them, all sensory systems (or modalities) share certain characteristics.

- They each respond to particular forms of energy or information.
- They each have a *sense organ* (or *accessory structure*), which is the first 'point of entry' for the information that will be processed by the system (the sense organ 'catches' the information).
- They each have *sense receptors* (or *transducers*), specialised cells that are sensitive to particular kinds of energy, and which then convert it into electrical nerve impulses, the only form in which this physical energy can be dealt with by the brain (see Chapter 4).
- They each involve a *specialised part of the brain* that interprets the messages received from the sense receptors and (usually) results in perception of an object, a person, a word, a taste etc.
- A certain *minimum stimulation* of the sense receptors is necessary before any sensory experience will occur (the *absolute threshold*). In practice, instead of finding a single intensity value below which people never detect the stimulus and above which they always detect it, a range of values is found and the absolute threshold is taken to be the value at which the stimulus is detected 50 per cent of the time.

These characteristics for the six major sense modalities are described in Table 5.1.

Sensory thresholds

Not only does the absolute threshold vary from individual to individual, but it varies for the same individual at different times, depending on physical state, motivation, physical conditions of presentation, and so on.

The *difference threshold* is the minimum amount of stimulation necessary to discriminate between two stimuli, and is also known as the *just noticeable difference*

Table 5.1 Sense organs, sense receptors and brain areas for the six major sense modalities

Sense modality	Sense organ (accessory structure)	Sense receptor (transducer)	Brain area
Vision (sight)	Eye (in particular, the lens)	Rods and cones (in the retina)	Occipital lobe (striate cortex, extrastriate/prestriate cortex) (via optic nerve)
Audition (hearing)	Outer ear (pinna), middle ear (eardrum and ossicles), inner ear (cochlea)	Specialised hair cells in organ of Corti (in cochlea)	Temporal lobe (via auditory nerve)
Gustation (taste)	Tongue (in particular the taste buds and papillae, the ridges around the side of the tongue)	Specialised receptors in taste buds, which connect with sensory neurons	Temporal lobe (via gustatory nerve)
Olfaction (smell)	Nose (in particular the olfactory mucosa of nasal cavity)	Transducers in the olfactory mucosa	Temporal lobe and limbic system (via olfactory bulb and olfactory tracts)
Skin/cutaneous senses (touch)	Skin	There are about 5 million sensors, of at least 7 types, including: • Meissner's corpuscles (touch); • Krause end bulbs (cold)	Parietal lobe (somatosensory cortex) and cerebellum
Proprioception (kinaesthetic and vestibular senses)	Inner ear (semicircular canals, vestibular sacs)	Vestibular sensors (otoliths or 'earstones'), tiny crystals attached to hair cells in vestibular sacs which are sensitive to gravity	Cerebellum (via vestibular nerve)

(jnd). Weber's law states that the jnd is a constant value, but this, of course, will differ from one sense modality to another. For example, 1/133 is the value needed to tell apart the pitch of two different tones, and 1/5 for discriminating between saline solutions.

Box 5.2 Psychophysics and the Weber–Fechner law

- Fechner (1860) reformulated Weber's law and the Weber–Fechner law (as it's come to be known) states that large increases in the intensity of a stimulus produce smaller, proportional increases in the perceived intensity.
- Fechner's was one of the first attempts to express a psychological phenomenon mathematically, and was an important contribution to *psychophysics*. This studies the relationship between physical stimuli and how they're subjectively experienced.
- Psychophysics is of enormous historical importance in the development of psychology as a science (see Chapter 3).

The Weber–Fechner law holds only approximately through the middle ranges of stimulus intensities. An alternative approach is *signal detection theory*, which rejects the notion of thresholds altogether. Each sensory channel always carries *noise* (any activity that interferes with the detection of a signal): the stronger the stimulus, the higher the *signal-to-noise ratio* and the easier it is to detect the stimulus. The detection of a stimulus, therefore, then becomes a statistical matter (a question of *probabilities*).

THE VISUAL SYSTEM

The fundamental job of a single-chambered eye (such as the human eye) is to map the spatial pattern in the *optic array* onto the retina by forming an *image*. The optic array is the pattern of light reaching a point in space from all directions (Gibson, 1966: see Chapter 15). All light rays striking the eye from one point in space are brought to a focus at one point on the retina (Bruce & Green, 1990). *Visual acuity* is a way of describing the efficiency with which the eye does this. Pinel (1993) defines acuity as 'the ability to see the details of objects'. Acuity is limited by several processes, in particular:

- the efficiency with which the optical apparatus of the eye maps the spatial pattern of the optic array on to the retina
- the efficiency with which the receptor cells convert that pattern into a pattern of electrical activity
- the extent to which information available in the pattern of receptor cells activity is detected by the neural apparatus of the retina and the brain.

We'll now look at each of these aspects of acuity in turn.

The sense organ: the eye

ASK YOURSELF...
- Why do you think vision is considered to be the most important of the human sense modalities?

Ornstein (1975) describes the eye as 'the most important avenue of personal consciousness', and it's estimated that 80 per cent of the information we receive about the external world reaches us through vision (Dodwell, 1995). Research interest has focused largely on vision, both as a sensory system and a perceptual system. The sense organ of vision is the eye and its major structures are shown in Figure 5.2 (page 81).

The *conjunctiva* is a transparent, delicate membrane, covering the inside of the eyelids and the front of the eye. It contains nerves and many tiny blood vessels, which dilate (expand) if the eye is irritated or injured (the eye becomes bloodshot). The *cornea* is a transparent membrane, which protects the lens and through which light enters the eye.

Box 5.3 The pupil and the ANS

- The *pupil* (the hole in the iris) regulates the amount of light entering the eye via the iris (the coloured part of the eye), which has tiny sets of muscles that dilate and contract the pupil. (Pupil size is also regulated by the ciliary muscles.)
- In bright light, the pupil contracts to shut out some of the light rays; when light is dim or we're looking at distant objects, the pupils dilate to let more light in. *Sensitivity* rather than acuity is what's crucial.
- Ultimately, pupil size is controlled by the *autonomic nervous system* (ANS), and so is outside conscious control. The *parasympathetic branch* of the ANS controls change in pupil size as a function of change in illumination. The *sympathetic branch* dilates the pupils under conditions of strong emotional arousal, as in an 'emergency' situation when we need to see 'better' (see Chapters 9, 10 and 12).

The *lens*, situated just behind the iris, is enclosed in a capsule held firmly in place by the *suspensory ligaments*. It focuses light on the retina as an *inverted* (upside-down) image, and its shape is regulated by the ciliary muscles. As with certain reptiles, birds and other mammals, the lens of the human eye thickens and increases its curvature (and the ciliary muscles contract) when focusing on nearby objects. When viewing more distant objects, it becomes flatter (and the ciliary muscles are fully relaxed). This process is called *accommodation* (see Figure 5.3).

Between the cornea and the lens is the anterior chamber filled with *aqueous humour*, a clear, watery fluid, and behind the lens is the larger posterior chamber filled

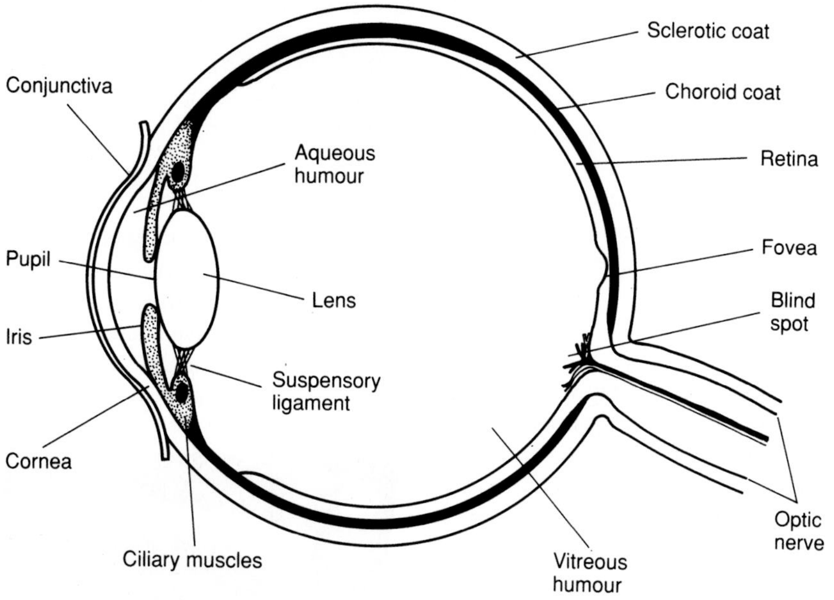

Figure 5.2 The major structures of the human eye

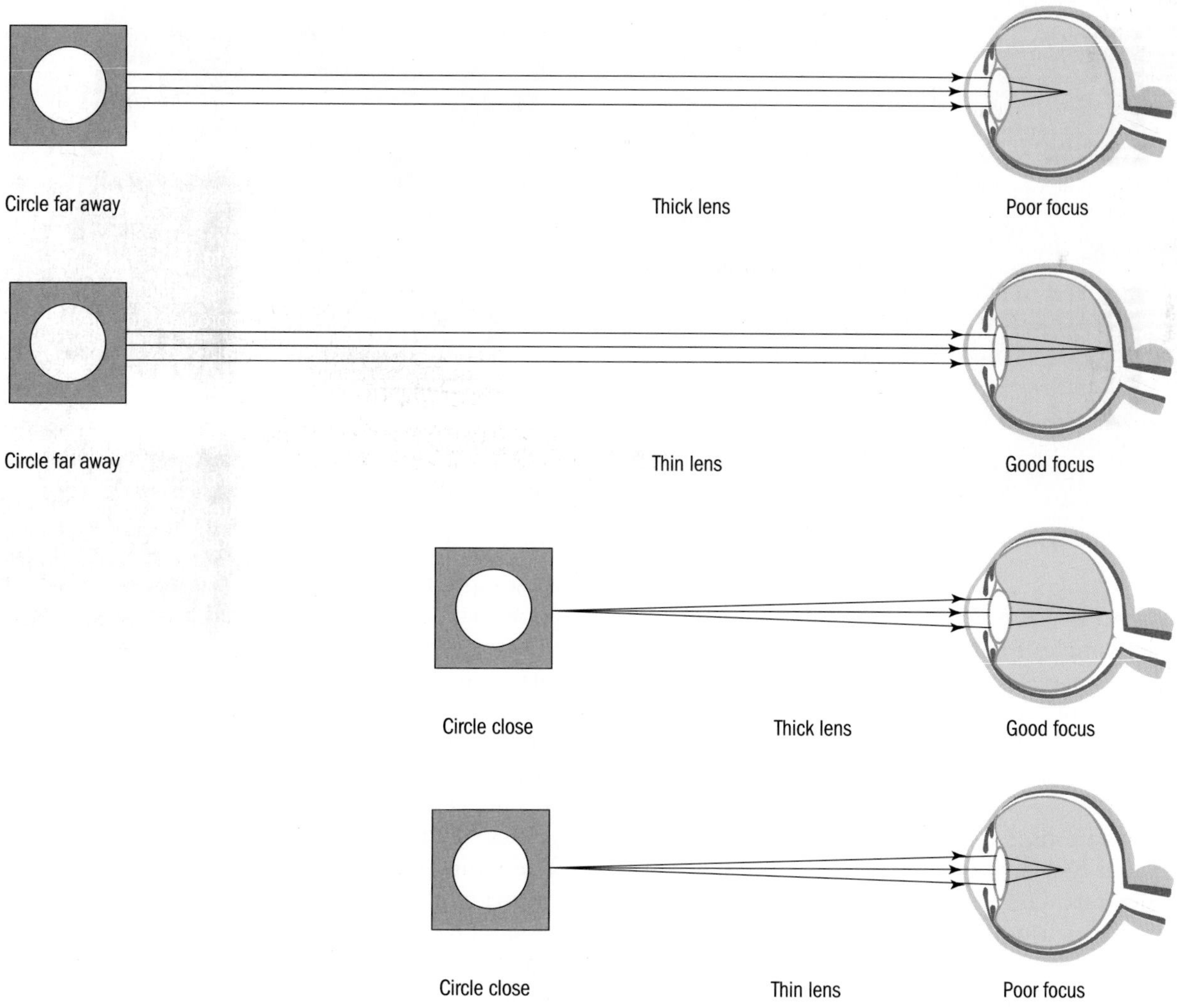

Figure 5.3 An illustration of accommodation
(from Matlin & Foley, *Sensation & Perception* 4th edition, Copyright © 1992 by Allyn & Bacon, Boston, MA. Copyright © 1992 by Pearson Education. Adapted by permission of the publisher.)

with *vitreous humour*, a jelly-like substance. Both fluids give the eyeball its shape and help to keep it firm.

The *sclerotic coat* is the thickest layer of the eyeball and forms the outer, white part of the eye. It consists of a strong, fibrous membrane, except in the front where it bulges to form the *cornea*. The *choroid coat* is a dark layer containing black-coloured matter, which darkens the chamber of the eye and prevents reflection of light inside the eye. In front, it becomes the iris, which is seen through the transparent cornea.

Eye movements

Primates' eyes make the largest, most rapid and most precisely controlled eye movements of all animals except the chameleon. The human eye is held in position by a dynamic balance between three pairs of antagonistic muscles, and instability in this balance produces a continuous, small-amplitude tremor, which means that the retinal image is in constant motion.

Box 5.4 Different types of eye movement

Sampling the optic array is achieved by three kinds of movement.

1. Sudden, intermittent jumps of eye position (*saccades*) occur while trying to fixate an object when looking directly at it (*foveal vision*). Even when we think we're looking steadily at something, or when we read or look at a picture, our eyes make several saccades each second to scan it.
2. Once an object has been fixated, smooth and continuous pursuit movements keep it in foveal vision as the object or the observer moves.
3. If the distance of the object from the observer changes, smooth and continuous *convergence movements* keep it fixated by the foveas of both eyes.

(Source: based on Bruce & Green, 1990)

According to Bruce & Green (1990), the human eye at any instant samples a relatively large portion of the optic array (the *peripheral visual field*) with low acuity, and a much smaller portion (the *central* or *foveal visual field*) with high acuity. Beaumont (1988) believes that constant alteration of the retinal image serves three useful purposes:

1. it gives more time to the pigments to replace themselves after bleaching (see below)
2. any nervous tissue becomes less responsive with repeated stimulation, and so also needs a chance to recover
3. it helps reduce the probability that parts of the retina will become obscured by blood vessels, by giving an opportunity for slightly different parts of the stimulus to be viewed by different sets of receptors.

Is the eye a camera?

ASK YOURSELF...
- In what ways can the eye be thought of as a camera?
- What are some of the major similarities and differences?

In a camera, light striking each light-sensitive grain in the film comes from a narrow segment of the optic array, and this is also true of the retinal image (Bruce & Green, 1990). Both also have a lens that projects the image on to the film or the retina. So the camera is a useful analogy for understanding the optics of the eye.

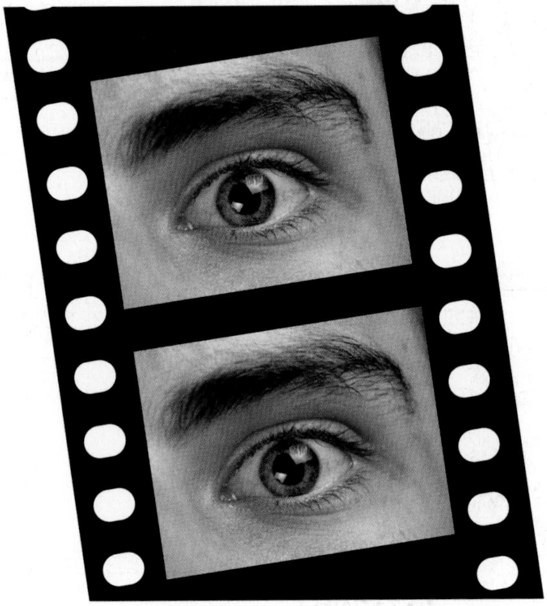

The eye as a camera?

However, Bruce and Green point out a number of important differences.

- If judged by the same standards as a camera, even the most sophisticated eye forms an image of an extremely poor quality. Optical aberrations produce blur, aberrations of the lens and cornea cause distortions in the image, and the curvature of the retina means that images of straight lines are curved and metrical relations in the image don't correspond to those in the world.
- A camera that moved as much as the eye would produce blurred pictures.
- The retinal image has a yellowish cast, particularly in the macular region, and contains shadows of the blood vessels that lie in front of the receptor cells in the retina.
- While the purpose of a camera is to produce a static picture for people to look at, the purpose of the eye and brain is to extract the information from the changing optic array needed to guide a person's

actions or to specify important objects or events. The optic nerve doesn't transmit a stream of pictures to the brain (as a TV camera does to a TV set), but instead transmits information about the pattern of light reaching the eyes. The brain then has to interpret that information.

The *retina* is the innermost layer of the eyeball, formed by the expansion of the optic nerve, which enters at the back and a little to the nasal side of the eye.

Box 5.5 The three layers of the retina

1. *Rods* and *cones*, photosensitive cells that convert light energy into electrical nerve impulses (and form the rear layer of the retina)
2. *Bipolar cells*, connected to the rods, cones and ganglion cells
3. *Ganglion cells*, whose fibres (axons) form the beginning of the optic nerve leading to the brain

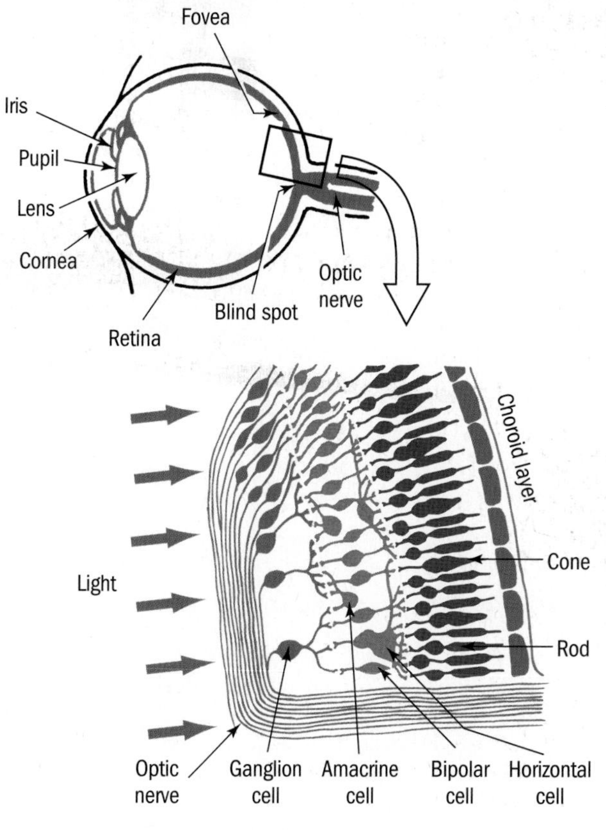

Figure 5.4 A diagrammatic section through the eye and a section through the retina at the edge of the blind spot (from Atkinson *et al*., 1983)

The receptors: rods and cones

Gregory (1966) has estimated that only about 10 per cent of the light entering the eye actually reaches the transducers (rods and cones), the rest being absorbed by the accessory structures (the rest of the eye).

Box 5.6 The distribution of rods and cones

- The rods are 1000 times more sensitive than the cones – that is, they are far more likely to respond to *low levels* of illumination.
- They're also far more numerous: in each retina there are 120 million rods and 7 million cones.
- Their distribution around the retina also differs. Cones are much more numerous towards the *centre* of the retina. The *fovea*, a pit-like depression, is part of a cone-rich area (the *macula lutea*), where there's a concentration of about 50,000 cones. By contrast, the rods are distributed fairly evenly around the *periphery* (but aren't found in the fovea).

What do rods and cones do?

The *rods* are specialised for vision in dim light (including night-time vision) and contain a photosensitive chemical (*rhodopsin*), which changes structure in response to low levels of illumination. They help us see black, white and intermediate greys (*achromatic colour*), and this is referred to as *scotopic vision*. The *cones* are specialised for bright-light vision (including daylight) and contain *iodopsin*. They help us see *chromatic colour* (red, green, blue, and so on) and provide *photopic vision* (from 'photon', the smallest particle of light that travels in a straight line).

This chemical difference between the rods and cones explains the phenomenon of *dark adaptation*. If you go into a dark cinema from bright sunlight, you'll experience near blindness for a few seconds. This is because the rods need a little time to take over from the cones, which were responding outside. The rhodopsin in the rods is being regenerated (resynthesised), having been 'bleached' by the bright sunlight. It takes 30 minutes for the rods to reach their maximum level of responding.

Rods, cones and adaptation

Human vision, like that of most species, must be adapted to operate in a range of light intensities, and this is reflected in the structure of the retina. Rods have a deeper stack of pigment-filled layers of folded membrane in the outer segment than cones; this means that a photon passing through a rod is less likely to come out the other end, making rods far more sensitive than cones (see Box 5.6).

According to Bruce & Green (1990), this difference explains the correlation between the rod:cone ratio in an animal's retina and its ecology. *Diurnal animals* (which are active by day and sleep at night) have a higher *proportion of cones* than *nocturnals* (which are active by night and sleep by day: see Chapter 7). Pure-cone retinas are rare (mostly confined to lizards and snakes), as are pure-rod retinas (confined to bats and deep-sea fish, which never leave their dark habitats).

Box 5.7 What's the best way of looking at an object?

- When focusing on objects in bright light, the most sharply defined image is obtained by looking directly at them, thereby projecting the light on to the fovea (which, remember, is packed with cones).
- In night light, however, the sharpest image is actually produced by looking slightly to one side of the object (for example, a star in the sky), thereby stimulating the rods (which are found in the periphery of the retina).
- The dense packing of cones helps explain *acuity*: the more densely packed the receptors, the finer the details of a pattern of light intensity that can be transformed into differences in electrical activity. The difference between a human's acuity and, say, a falcon's is the result of a difference in receptor packing, with receptors being three times more densely packed in the falcon (Bruce & Green, 1990).

Dogs are diurnal and have relatively more cones than nocturnal animals, such as bats

Rods, cones and ganglion cells

The 127 million rods and cones are 'reduced' to 1 million ganglion cells, which make up the optic nerve. This means that information reaching the brain has already been 'refined' to some extent compared with the relatively 'raw' information received from other sensory nerves. However, the degree of reduction (or summation) differs considerably for different areas of the retina. In the *periphery*, up to 1200 rods may combine to form a single ganglion cell, and so connect to a single axon in the optic nerve. This provides only *very general visual information*. At the *fovea*, only 10–12 cones may be summed for each ganglion cell, providing *much more detailed information*.

Two other kinds of cell, *horizontal* and *amacrine*, interconnect with groups of the other cells and connect them together. This further increases the degree of information processing that takes place in the retina itself. Horizontal cells connect receptors and bipolar cells, while amacrine cells connect bipolar and ganglion cells.

Ganglion cells and receptive fields

Each ganglion cell has a *receptive field*, a (usually) roughly circular region of the retina, in which stimulation affects the ganglion cell's *firing rate*. There are (at least) three kinds of ganglion cell, each with a different kind of receptive field:

1. *on-centre cells* are more neurally active when light falls in the centre of the receptive field, but less active when it falls on the edge
2. *off-centre cells* work in the opposite way
3. *transient cells* have larger receptive fields and seem to respond to movements, especially sudden ones.

The combined activity of on-centre and off-centre cells provides a clear definition of *contours* ('edges'), where there is a sudden change in brightness. These contours are essential in defining the shape of objects to be perceived (Beaumont, 1988). Further analysis of contours takes place in the striate cortex by simple, complex and hypercomplex cells (see below).

Box 5.8 Is the retina back-to-front?

- As Beaumont (1988) points out, the retina appears to be built back-to-front: the receptors don't point to the source of the light but towards the supporting cells at the back of the eye. Before it arrives at the receptors, light must pass through the layers of retinal cells and blood vessels inside the eye (see Figure 5.4). In view of this, it's surprising that such high-quality vision can still be achieved.
- If you've ever looked directly at a flash of lightning, you may well have experienced a tree-like after-image, which is the shadows of the blood vessels thrown upon the retina. Or when you look up at the sky, especially a cloudless blue sky, you see small transparent bubbles floating in front of you: these are red blood cells.

Visual pathways: from eye to brain

As Figure 5.5 shows, the pathways from the half of each retina closest to the nose cross at the *optic chiasma* (or *chasm*) and travel to the *opposite hemisphere* (crossed pathways). The pathways from the half of each retina furthest from the nose (uncrossed pathways) travel to the hemisphere on the *same* side as the eye. So, when you fixate on a point straight ahead (such that the eyes converge), the image of an object to the *right* of fixation falls on the *left*

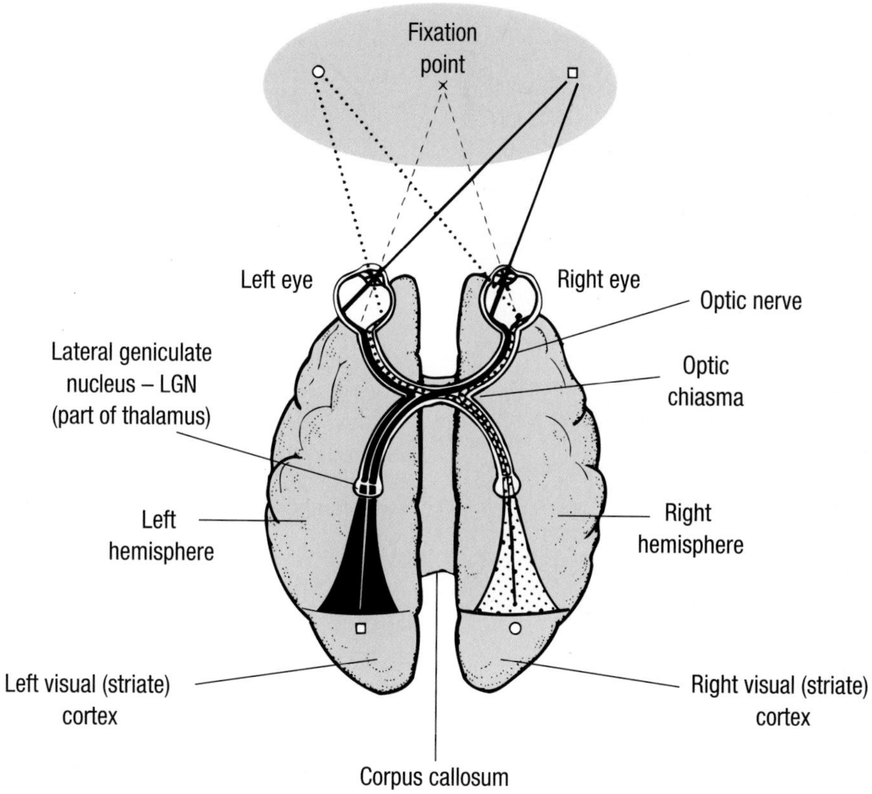

Figure 5.5 The visual system

half of each retina, and information about it passes along the *crossed pathway* from the right eye to the left hemisphere and along the *uncrossed pathway* from the left eye to the left hemisphere. No information is passed directly to the right hemisphere.

All these relationships are reversed for an object to the *left* of the fixation point, so that information is passed directly only to the *right* hemisphere. It follows that any damage to the visual area of just one hemisphere will produce blind areas in both eyes; however, the crossed pathway ensures that complete blindness in either eye won't occur.

Before reaching the cortex, the optic nerve travels through the *lateral geniculate nucleus* (LGN), which is part of the thalamus (see Chapter 4). Optic nerve fibres terminate at synapses with LGN cells arranged in layers (*laminae*), each lamina containing a *retino-optic map* of half the visual field.

LGN cells have concentric receptive fields similar to those of retinal ganglion cells, and the axons of LGN cells project to the *occipital lobe*. In monkeys, all LGN cells project to area 17, which is the *visual* or *striate cortex* (called the *geniculostriate path*).

CASE STUDY 5.1 D.B. and blindsight

- In humans, the *geniculostriate path* must be intact for conscious experience of vision to be possible. People with damage to their visual cortex will report complete blindness in part or all of the visual field. Even so, they'll show some ability to locate or even identify objects that they cannot consciously see; Weiskrantz (1986) called this *blindsight*.
- The most thoroughly investigated patient is D.B., who had an operation meant to reduce the number of severe migraines he suffered. Despite being left with an area of subjective blindness, he could detect whether or not a visual stimulus had been presented to the blind area and also identify its location. However, he seemed to possess only a rudimentary ability to discriminate shapes.
- This suggests that, while most visual functions rely on the 'primary' geniculostriate path, the 'secondary' *retino-tectal path* (some ganglion cells are projected to the paired superior colliculi structures in the midbrain) carries enough information to guide some actions in an unconscious way. In the intact brain, these two paths function interdependently: the *corticotectal path* provides the superior colliculi with input from the cortex.

Hubel and Wiesel's studies of cortical cells

The first recordings from single cells in the striate cortex of cats and monkeys were made by Hubel & Wiesel (1959, 1962, 1968). They identified three kinds of cortical cell.

Box 5.9 Simple, complex and hypercomplex cells

- *Simple cells* respond only to particular features of a stimulus (such as straight lines, edges and slits) in particular orientations and in particular locations in the animal's visual field. For example, a bar presented vertically may cause a cell to 'fire', but if the bar is moved to one side or out of vertical, the cell will not respond.
- *Complex cells* also respond to lines of particular orientation, but location is no longer important. For example, a vertical line detector will respond wherever it is in the visual field. It seems that complex cells receive inputs from larger numbers of simple cells sharing the same orientation sensitivity.
- *Hypercomplex cells* are 'fed' by large numbers of complex cells and are similar to complex cells, except that they take length into account too (that is, they are most responsive to a bar or edge not extending beyond their receptive field).

Some researchers have questioned the existence of hypercomplex cells as a distinct class of cell (Bruce & Green, 1990). However, Hubel and Wiesel's research demonstrates that the visual cortex isn't a homogeneous mass of tissue, with randomly scattered cells of different kinds. Rather, it shows an astonishingly precise and regular arrangement of different cell types, which Hubel & Wiesel (1962) called the *functional architecture* of the visual cortex.

The six main layers of the striate cortex can be recognised under the microscope. The cortical area devoted to the central part of the visual field is proportionately larger than that devoted to the periphery. Hubel & Wiesel (1977) suggest that the cortex is divided into roughly square blocks of tissue (about 1 mm square), extending from the surface down to the white matter (*hypercolumns*).

The extrastriate (prestriate) cortex

Single-cell recordings have revealed many regions of the *extrastriate* (or *prestriate*) cortex, to the front of the striate, which can be considered 'visual areas'. However, it's proved more difficult to map these, compared with the striate cortex.

Maunsell & Newsome (1987) reviewed studies involving macaque monkeys. They concluded that there are 19 visual areas, covering large areas of the occipital, temporal and parietal lobes (see Figure 5.6). The deep folding of the cortex means that some areas, lying within folds (*sulci*), aren't visible from the exterior. This is why two important areas aren't shown in Figure 5.6, namely V3 (lying between V2 and V4) and the middle temporal area (MT: in front of V4).

Each area sends output to several others and most, if not all, connections are matched by reciprocal connections running in the opposite direction. Van Essen (1985) lists 92 pathways linking the visual areas. Most can be classified as either *ascending* (leading away from V1) or *descending* (leading towards V1). When the pathways are classified in this way, a consistently hierarchical pattern emerges, with areas placed at different levels (as shown in Figure 5.7).

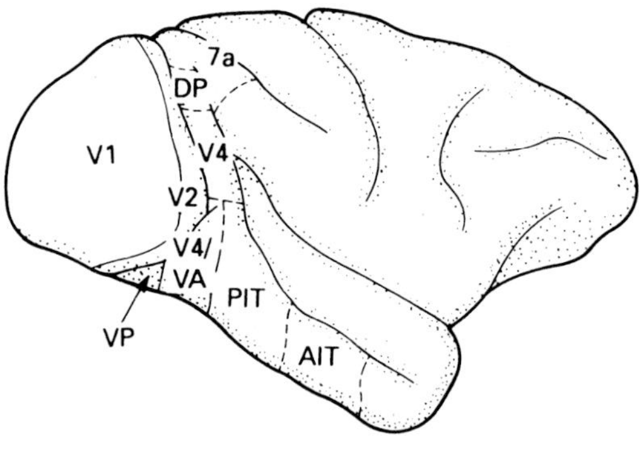

Figure 5.6 Side view of the right cerebral hemisphere of a macaque monkey. Area VI is the striate cortex (from Maunsell & Newsome, 1987)
Reprinted, with permission, from the *Annual Review of Neuroscience*, Volume 10 © 1987 by Annual Reviews www.annualreviews.org

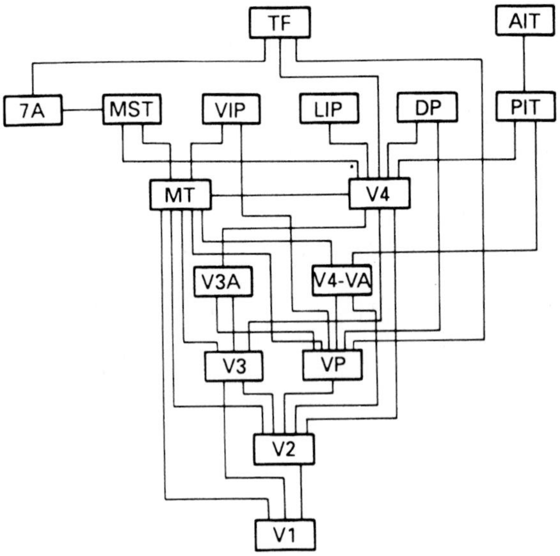

Figure 5.7 The hierarchical organisation of extrastriate visual areas in the macaque monkey as proposed by Maunsell and Newsome (from Maunsell & Newsome, 1987)
Reprinted, with permission, from the *Annual Review of Neuroscience*, Volume 10 © 1987 by Annual Reviews www.annualreviews.org

The hierarchical processing of colour and number

According to Ramachandran & Hubbard (2003), neural signals from the retina initially travel to area 17 in the occipital lobe. The image is processed further within local clusters or blobs into such simple attributes as colour, motion, form and depth. The information about these separate features is then sent forward and distributed to several far-flung regions in the temporal and parietal lobes.

In the case of colour, information is sent to V4 in the fusiform gyrus of the temporal lobe. It's then passed to areas lying further up in the hierarchy of colour centres, including a region near a patch of cortex called TPO (standing for the junction of the temporal, parietal and occipital lobes). These areas may be concerned with more sophisticated aspects of colour processing, such as *colour constancy* (see below, pages 89–90).

Numerical computation also occurs in stages. An early step also occurs in the fusiform gyrus, where the actual shapes of numbers are represented. A later stage occurs in the angular gyrus, a part of the TPO concerned with numerical concepts such as ordinality (sequence) and cardinality (quantity).

The way in which colour and number are processed could help explain the fascinating phenomenon of *synaesthesia* (see below).

Does each area have its own specified function?

Zeki (1978) proposed a 'parcelling model', whereby the simple representation of the visual field in V1 and V2 is parcelled out to be analysed by a number of areas working in parallel. For example, V3 analyses form, V4 colour and V5 motion. However, Maunsell & Newsome (1987) and Van Essen (1985) believe that there might be two main pathways operating in parallel, one concerned with the analysis of motion and spatial layout, the other with colour, form and object recognition. Some of the evidence regarding processing of colour is discussed in the next section. Zeki himself later came to cast doubt on the parcelling model.

CASE STUDY 5.2 G.Y. and motion detection in the blind

- Zeki (1992, 1993) studied G.Y., a man blinded in an accident when he was seven.
- He could detect fast-moving objects, such as cars, and the direction they were travelling in.
- Scans confirmed that G.Y.'s V5 was active when he was 'seeing' fast motion, but his V1 wasn't.
- This suggests that fast movements are first processed by V5, while signals from *slow* movements arrive initially in V1. In Zeki's view, signals must go through V1 to see clearly, but even the blind can sometimes see through other areas in a rudimentary way.

The case of G.Y. still supports the view that different aspects of visual processing occur in different parts of the brain. This view is further supported by other examples of very specific visual impairments caused by brain damage. For example, V5 damage produces *akinetopsia*, in which moving objects appear invisible, even though the same objects can be seen quite clearly when stationary. Patients with *chromatopsia* (caused by widespread damage due to carbon monoxide poisoning) have intact colour vision, but almost all other visual abilities are impaired. Similarly, P.B. awoke from a four-month coma to find he was blind, *except* for the ability to make out colours (Zeki, cited in Highfield, 1999). The converse of this is *achromatopia*. Following a stroke, E.H. reported that everything looked grey, although all other visual abilities were normal. An MRI scan revealed damage to V4 (Shuren *et al.*, 1996).

Synaesthesia

ASK YOURSELF...

- Does it make sense to say that we can taste shapes, see sounds, or hear colours?
- Have you ever associated particular numbers with particular colours?
- Could the way that different kinds of visual information (colour, motion, form and depth) are processed help explain these phenomena (see above)

A small number of otherwise 'normal' people experience the ordinary world in extraordinary ways, and

> ... seem to inhabit a mysterious no-man's land between fantasy and reality. For them, the senses – touch, hearing, vision and smell – get mixed up instead of remaining separate. (Ramachandran & Hubbard, 2003)

Examples include associating letters of the alphabet, or musical notes played on the piano, with colours, and numbers and shapes with tastes. *Synaesthesia* is commonly defined as a joining of the senses, where sensations in one modality (e.g. hearing) produce sensations in another (e.g. colour vision). But this is an oversimplification, because synaesthetic experiences are often driven by symbolic rather than sensory representations (as the examples above involving letters and numbers demonstrate) (Ward, 2003).

How does synaesthesia happen?

According to Ramachandran & Hubbard (2003), recent research has begun to uncover brain processes that could account for this phenomenon. One possibility is *cross-wiring*. As we noted earlier, both colours and numbers are initially processed in the fusiform gyrus, and subsequently near the angular gyrus. Number–colour synaesthesia might be caused by (a) cross-wiring between V4 and the number-appearance area (both located within the fusiform gyrus), or (b) between higher-colour areas and the number-concept area (both located within the TPO). The hearing centre in the temporal lobes is also close to the higher brain area that receives colour signals from V4. This could explain sound–colour synaesthesia.

ASK YOURSELF...

- Look at the figures on the next page.
- Which of these is a 'bouba' and which a 'kiki'?

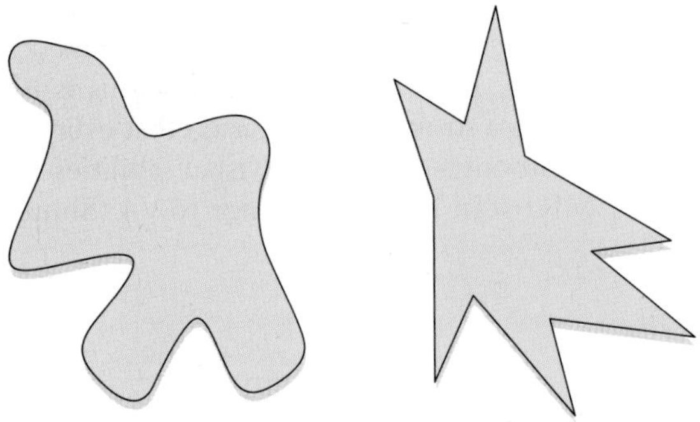

Are we all 'closet synaesthetes'?
According to Ramachandran and Hubbard, 98 per cent of people pick the inkblot as 'bouba'. Why? Perhaps the gentle curves of the amoeba-like figure *metaphorically* mimic the gentle undulations of the sound 'bouba' as represented in the brain's hearing centres, as well as the gradual inflections of the lips as they produce the curved 'bouba' sound. The sharp inflection of the tongue on the palate when saying 'kiki' mimics the sudden changes in the jagged visual shape. People with damage to their angular gyrus fail to make the bouba/kiki distinction. Ramachandran and Hubbard suggest that the angular gyrus (which is disproportionately large in humans compared with apes and monkeys) evolved originally for cross-modal associations – but then was taken over for other, more abstract functions, such as metaphor. Significantly, synaesthetes are seven times more common among creative people, many of whom share the skill of using metaphor (in some form or another). It's as if their brains are set to make links between seemingly unrelated conceptual domains.

ASK YOURSELF...
- How does your perception of the world differ from mine?
- How could we possibly find out?

Box 5.10 Is 'my' red the same as 'your' red?

- According to Ward (2003), synaesthesia challenges the implicit assumption that other people's perceptual experiences of the world are the same as our own. This an age-old philosophical question, which many would say is insoluble.
- But according to Breslin (in Hollingham, 2004), a neuroscientist, 'No two people live in the same sensory world'. Recent genetic research has identified a huge number of genes involved in taste, smell, touch and vision.
- Not only are sensory genes vastly abundant, they are also highly variable. This means that individuals rarely have the same set of sensory genes – for smell, light sensitivity, pain perception – and colour perception (see the section on colour blindness, below).

COLOUR VISION AND COLOUR BLINDNESS

Light can be described physically by its *energy spectrum* (intensities at different wavelengths) or phenomenologically by three dimensions:

1. *brightness* (perceived intensity)
2. *hue* (perceived colour)
3. *saturation* (the purity of hue: how much colour or how much white).

Although both hue and saturation are aspects of 'colour', hue is what theories of colour vision and discussion of colour vision defects are concerned with.

As we've seen, cones are the photoreceptors responsible for chromatic vision, and rods and cones contain photosensitive pigments (which change their chemical constitution on exposure to light, namely rhodopsin and iodopsin, respectively).

Rushton & Campbell (1954, cited by Rushton, 1987) were the first to measure the visual pigments in the living human eye, applying the familiar observation that a cat's eye will reflect back light shone in its eye. Instead of the cat's shining *tapetum lucidium*, we have a very black surface behind the retina – the choroid coat – which reflects very faint light. Rushton and Campbell identified rhodopsin, plus red and green pigments. However, insufficient blue light is reflected to measure the blue cone pigment (Rushton, 1987).

Later, Marks *et al.* (1964, cited by Rushton, 1987) used fresh retinas from monkeys and human eyes removed during surgery to measure visual pigments in single cones. They found the blue-green and red-sensitive cones, thus supporting the Young–Helmholtz trichromatic theory (see below). Rushton and Campbell's findings were also confirmed using living colour-blind participants, who possessed only one of the two pigments they measured.

Theories of colour vision

The Young–Helmholtz trichromatic theory

The trichromatic theory (Young, 1801) claims that colour is mediated by three different kinds of cone, each responding to light from a different part of the visible spectrum. *Blue-sensitive*, *green-sensitive* and *red-sensitive* cones are maximally responsive to short, medium and long wavelengths, respectively. While the sum of the three wavelengths (B + G + R) determines brightness, their *ratio* or pattern (B:G:R) determines colour. This is essentially what is believed today (Rushton, 1987).

This explains the painter's experience that mixing a few paints will produce a whole range of colours. It also implies that every colour (including white) should excite B, G and R cones in a characteristic set of ratios, so that a mixture of red and green and blue lights, adjusted to produce this same set of ratios, should appear white or whatever the initial colour was. This was systematically tested by Maxwell (1854), who found that every colour can be matched by a suitable mixture of blue, green and red 'primaries' (the *trichromacy of colour*). This was later confirmed by Helmholtz (Rushton, 1987). Hence, this is often called the *Young–Helmholtz trichromatic theory*.

The opponent process theory

While the Young–Helmholtz theory can explain the effects of mixing colours of different wavelengths, it has difficulty explaining *colour blindness* (see Box 5.11) and the phenomenon of *negative after-images*. Both of these can be explained more easily by the major alternative to the trichromatic theory, namely the opponent process (*tetrachromatic*) theory (Hering, 1878). This claims that colour analysis depends on the action of two types of detector, each having two modes of response. One signals red *or* green, the other signals yellow *or* blue. A third type of detector, black–white, contributes to the perception of brightness and saturation.

Evidence for the opponent process theory

- If you stare at a coloured surface (for example, red) and then look at a plain surface, you'll perceive an after-image that is coloured in the 'opposite direction' (i.e. green). This is called a *complementary* (or *negative*) after-image.
- The retina encodes in terms of three constituent components (a blue-green-red 'component' system: *stage one* of colour vision). But output through the bipolar and ganglion cells and on to the LGN (*stage two*) becomes re-coded in terms of opponent processes (DeValois & Jacobs, 1984). There seem to be *four* kinds of LGN cell: those that increase activity to red light but decrease with green (R+ G-); those that increase activity to green light but decrease with red (G+ R-); and similarly for blue and yellow (B+ Y-) and yellow and blue (Y+ B-). Still other LGN cells simply respond to black and white (Beaumont, 1988).

Box 5.11 Colour blindness

- People with defective colour vision (usually called '*colour-blind*') usually fail to distinguish between *red and green*. This is the most common form of defect, caused by a recessive sex-linked gene that affects more males (about 8 per cent) than females (about 0.4 per cent).
- Sufferers have *dichromatic* vision (normal vision is *trichromatic*): they possess only red- *or* green-sensitive cone pigments, but they can match every colour of the rainbow exactly with a suitable mix of only two coloured lights (for example, red and blue). Most people need the green primary as well if every colour is to be matched.
- Next most common is true colour-blindness, which involves an absence of any cones at all (*monochromatic vision*).
- Least common of all is *yellow-blue* blindness. These findings are clearly consistent with the opponent colour theory.
- Men's greater susceptibility to colour-blindness (of any kind) is due to their possessing only one X chromosome. Women possess two X chromosomes, so they carry the normal genes, plus (sometimes) one or more variant genes. This makes them potentially *tetrachromatic* ('super-sighted'), able to distinguish, for example, between two apparently identical shades of green (Hollingham, 2004).

Must we choose between the two theories?

The generally held view is that a complete theory of colour vision must draw on elements from *both* theories. Indeed, Helmholtz himself showed that the two theories aren't incompatible, as a simple transformation could change the three receptor outputs to two different signals, plus one additive signal (Troscianko, 1987). According to Harris (1998), both theories are compatible, and neurophysiological evidence exists for both.

Colour constancy

Any chromatic light hitting the retina is composed of different amounts of the three primary colours (for example, turquoise might be 70 per cent blue, 30 per cent green). So, blue-sensitive cones would 'fire' quite quickly, and green-sensitive ones quite slowly (and red-sensitive wouldn't fire at all). However, perceived colour isn't solely determined by the wavelength composition of the light reflected from the object (the *spectral reflectance* of the object).

Box 5.12 Factors influencing the perception of colour

- The relative proportions of different wavelengths in the light falling on the object (the *spectral composition* of the illumination)
- Prior stimulation of the retina (as shown by complementary or negative after-images)
- The nature of the surroundings, such as the simultaneous contrast created by adjacent areas of different colour or brightness; for example, a grey square will look brighter set against a black background than against a white background)

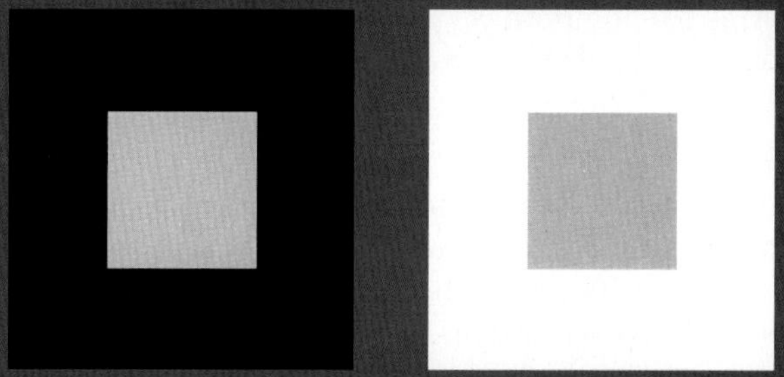

- Our familiarity with, and knowledge of, an object's colour, which is part of the psychological phenomenon of *colour constancy*.

According to McCann (1987), our visual system is built to tell us about the permanent colours of objects, as opposed to the spectral composition of the light falling on a local area of the retina. Land (1977), the inventor of the Polaroid camera, provided a powerful demonstration of colour constancy.

KEY STUDY 5.1 Land's (1977) 'Mondrian' experiment

- Land used a *colour Mondrian*, a patchwork of different-coloured matt papers, randomly arranged so that each colour was surrounded by several others. The display was illuminated by mixed light from projectors with red, green and blue filters. Each projector also had an independent brightness control.
- Observers then selected one of the papers (for example, white) and Land measured the amounts of red, green and blue light coming from the white paper. They then selected a second paper (for example, red), and again the amounts of red, green and blue light were measured.
- Land then changed the illumination so that the red light from the red paper was exactly equal to the red light from the white paper (this required only a small change, since roughly equal amounts of red light are reflected from a red and a white paper). However, a substantial change was required to adjust the other projectors to produce exactly the same amounts of green and blue (much less green and blue are reflected from a red than a white paper).
- When all three projectors were switched on together, each observer reported 'red', despite the fact that the physical properties of the light from the red paper *were the same* as the light from the white paper.
- Using this method with other pairs of coloured papers, Land showed that almost the full range of colour sensations could be produced from a single mixture of red, green and blue light (thus supporting the trichromatic theory).

Retinex theory

ASK YOURSELF...

- If perceived colour were determined solely by the spectral composition of the reflected light, how would the first and second colours have been seen?
- Explain your answer.

If the spectral composition of the reflected light was all that determined perceived colour, they'd have been seen *as the same*. The fact that they *weren't*, means that the observers were displaying *colour constancy*. To explain this, Land proposed the *retinex theory of colour constancy* ('retinex' is a combination of 'retina' and 'cortex'). According to the theory, there are three separate visual systems or retinexes, responsive primarily to long-, medium- and short-wavelength light. Each produces a separate lightness image, and a comparison of these images is made. The comparison determines the colour that's perceived.

The three lightnesses provide the coordinates of a three-dimensional space. A colour space based on the *absolute* absorptions in the three classes of receptor predicts only whether two stimuli will *match*. But a space based on the three lightnesses predicts how colours actually *look*. This is because, between them, they give the reflectance of the object in different parts of the spectrum (that is, a measure of their *relative absorptions*). Land's theory implies that the formation of lightnesses could occur in the retina or cortex, and that the *retina-cortical structure* acts as a whole.

Cells with suitable properties for retinex theory exist in the LGN, and Zeki (1980) found that the response of individual cells in V4 of macaque monkeys mirrored his own perception of surface colour as opposed to the physical composition of the light. These V4 cells seem to be genuinely colour- (rather than wavelength-) selective (Harris, 1998).

CHAPTER SUMMARY

- **Sensation** is necessary for **perception**, since sense data represent the 'raw material' from which conscious awareness of the world is constructed.
- Each **sensory system** or **modality** is sensitive to a particular form of physical energy, but each also acts as a **data reduction system**. Being able to detect information rapidly about the inanimate world or other animals is very important for survival, which is why most species have evolved visual abilities.
- **Light** is one form of **electromagnetic radiation**. The human eye responds to only a tiny fraction of the visible electromagnetic spectrum.
- **Exteroceptors** include the five traditional senses of sight, hearing, smell, taste and touch; **interoceptors** include receptors for the internal environment; **proprioceptors** are usually sub-divided into the **kinaesthetic** and **vestibular senses**.
- Every sense modality comprises a **sense organ/accessory structure**, sense **receptors/transducers**, a **specialised brain area** that processes the sensory messages, and an **absolute threshold**.
- The **Weber–Fechner law** is an attempt to predict **difference threshold/jnd** and is an important part of **psychophysics**, which studies the relationship between physical stimuli and subjective experience.
- **Signal detection theory** rejects the notion of thresholds, and instead uses the concept of **signal-to-noise ratio**.
- The fundamental job of the human eye is to focus an image of the **optic array** on to the retina with maximum **acuity**. About 80 per cent of our information about the world comes through vision.

- The **pupil** regulates the amount of light entering the eye by contracting or dilating. Pupil size is controlled by the ciliary muscles and by the ANS.
- The **lens** focuses light on the retina as an inverted image, and its shape is regulated through **accommodation**. The retinal image is continuously moving, and other kinds of movement include **saccades**, **pursuit movements** and **convergence**.
- Although the camera is a useful analogy for understanding the optics of the eye, a particularly important **difference** is that what is sent to the brain is not a picture, but information about the pattern of light reaching the eyes. This information must then be interpreted.
- The **retina** contains 120 million **rods** and 7 million **cones**, the **photosensitive cells** that convert light energy into electrical nerve impulses. It also comprises **bipolar** and **ganglion cells**.
- The rods help us see **achromatic colour** (**scotopic vision**), and the cones help us see **chromatic colour** (**photopic vision**). When focusing on objects in bright light, the sharpest image is obtained by projecting the image on to the **fovea**, which is densely packed with cones.
- The rods and cones are 'reduced' to 1 million ganglion cells (**summation**) but this varies according to which part of the retina is involved. There are (at least) three kinds of ganglion cell, each with a different kind of **receptive field**.
- The pathways from the half of each retina closest to the nose cross at the **optic chiasma/chasm**, through the LGN, then on to the **visual/striate cortex** in the occipital lobe. This is called the **geniculostriate path**. Cases of **blindsight** suggest that the **retinotectal path** carries enough information to allow some 'unconscious' vision. Normally, these two paths work together.
- **Simple**, **complex** and **hypercomplex** cells in the striate cortex of cats and monkeys respond to particular stimulus features. These cells are arranged in **hypercolumns**.
- Research with monkeys has shown that large areas of the occipital, temporal and parietal lobes are involved in vision.
- **Synaesthesia** may result from the **cross-wiring** between parts of the brain that normally process different types of information separately.
- The **Young–Helmholtz trichromatic theory of colour vision** stresses the ratio or pattern of the three wavelengths of light, while the **opponent process/tetrachromatic theory** is based on the two modes of response of two types of detector.
- Some of the evidence supporting the opponent process theory comes from the study of **colour-blind** people. Both theories are seen as valid and complementary.
- According to **retinex theory**, perceived colour isn't solely determined by the wavelength of the light reflected from the object, but also by a number of other factors, including **colour constancy**.

Links with other topics/chapters

- Sensation provides the 'raw material' for *perception* (Chapters 15 and 16).
- Sensory information is fed to the CNS via the SNS (part of the PNS). We've seen how sensory information is processed in various parts of the *brain*, and that 'vision' denotes the sense organ, sense receptor and specialised area of the brain working as a system (Chapter 4).
- Psychophysics was a significant development in psychology's emergence as a discipline in its own right (Chapters 1 and 3).

6

PARAPSYCHOLOGY

INTRODUCTION AND OVERVIEW

For at least most psychologists, the sensory systems or modalities described in Chapter 5 are the only means by which we can acquire information about our environment (both physical objects and other people). However, there are some phenomena that seem to involve meaningful exchanges of information between organisms and their environment, and yet at the same time appear somehow to exceed the capacities of the sensory and motor systems as they are currently understood (Rao and Palmer, 1987). For these reasons, such phenomena are considered to be *anomalous*, and are commonly referred to as *paranormal* (or 'psi', short for 'psychic ability').

Such phenomena include 'extra-sensory perception' (ESP). The term unambiguously implies that there *are* ways of acquiring information about the world that *don't* depend on vision, hearing and so on. Similarly, psychokinesis (PK) refers to the influence of physical events by purely mental means. So, 'paranormal' is used for phenomena apparently lying outside the range of normal scientific explanations and investigations. However, most parapsychologists consider themselves to be scientists applying the usual rules of scientific enquiry to admittedly unusual phenomena. Indeed, the term 'parapsychology' was first introduced in the 1930s to refer to the scientific investigation of paranormal phenomena (Evans, 1987a).

PARAPSYCHOLOGY AND SCIENCE

> *ASK YOURSELF...*
> - How is it possible to believe in paranormal phenomena and be a scientist at the same time?

Agents Mulder and Scully in a scene from *The X Files*. While Scully believes there is a 'scientific' explanation for everything, Mulder believes in the existence of other life-forms

Perhaps the crucial phrase in the previous paragraph is 'apparently lying outside'. Parapsychologists who apply 'normal' scientific methods are following a long tradition of scientists who investigated phenomena that *at the time* seemed mysterious (Utts & Josephson, 1996) or were given what we'd now consider bizarre, 'unscientific', explanations. Gregory (1987a) gives the example of thunder and lightning:

> ... once considered to be the wrath of the Gods, but now understood as the same electricity that we generate and use for wonders of our technology.

In other words, 'paranormal' is a convenient label for certain aspects of human behaviour and experience that can be investigated scientifically and are subject to 'scientific' explanation. Once they've been accounted for scientifically, they'll no longer be called 'paranormal':

> ... Yet the phenomena of psi are so extraordinary and so similar to what are widely regarded as superstitions that some scientists declare psi to be an impossibility and reject the legitimacy of parapsychological inquiry ... (Atkinson *et al.*, 1990)

Sometimes, 'extraordinary' can be construed as 'not real', and the history of parapsychology is littered with accusations of fraud on the part of 'believers' by those who, for whatever reason, reject their claims. However, if psi 'really exists', what does this imply for many of our fundamental scientific beliefs about the world? While strong opposition to parapsychology is understandable, pre-judgements about the impossibility of psi are inappropriate in science. Many psychologists who are not yet convinced that psi has been demonstrated are nevertheless open to the *possibility* that new evidence may emerge that would be more compelling. Many parapsychologists believe that the case for psi has already been 'proven', or that experimental procedures exist that have the potential for doing so (Atkinson *et al.*, 1990).

We shall return to these issues later in the chapter (see pages 97–101).

THE HISTORICAL ROOTS OF PARAPSYCHOLOGY (PP)

According to Evans (1987a), the history of PP can be conveniently divided into three overlapping phases or periods: *spiritualistic research/spiritualism*, *psychical research*, and *modern PP*.

Spiritualistic research/spiritualism

Most Victorian scientists brought up as orthodox Christians were expected to believe in the reality of an immortal, non-physical soul. So a substantial number of them became involved in the minority religion of *spiritualism*: if souls or spirits survived the death of the physical body, they must exist *somewhere* in the universe and should, in principle, be contactable (for example, through mediums). Some of the outstanding brains of the time, including physicists, biologists and anthropologists, solemnly tried to induce spirit forms to materialise in their laboratories. The Society for Psychical Research was founded in London in 1882 and, soon after, the *Journal of the Society for Psychical Research*.

Other, more critical or sceptical colleagues conducted their own experiments. Medium after medium was exposed as fraudulent, and the pioneers were shown to be gullible, incompetent, or both. By 1900, scientific interest was moving away from seances and towards 'more plausible' aspects of the paranormal.

In the heyday of spiritualism, mediums were tied up inside a 'cabinet' in front of an audience. In a deep trance, they claimed to exude ectoplasm from various bodily orifices, and so create fully-formed spirits that could move around the room, touching the astounded sitters (Blackmore, 2003)

Psychical research

This was the era of the 'ghost hunter'. Scientists and affluent amateurs turned to phenomena such as manifestations in haunted houses, poltergeist activity, demonic possession, apparitions and premonitions. There was also a growing number of casual studies of telepathy and precognitive dreams.

Modern PP

According to Blackmore (1995), a British parapsychologist, credit for the founding of PP (in the 1930s) was almost entirely due to J.B. Rhine and Louisa Rhine (although Louisa is often not mentioned, as in Evans', 1987a, account). They were biologists who wanted to find evidence against a purely materialist view of human nature. Despite sharing the same objectives, they wanted to dissociate themselves from spiritualism and bring their new science firmly into the laboratory. They renamed their research 'parapsychology', established a department of PP at Duke University in the USA, began to develop new experimental methods, and defined their terms operationally.

VARIETIES AND DEFINITIONS OF PARAPSYCHOLOGICAL PHENOMENA

ASK YOURSELF...

- What do you understand parapsychological/paranormal phenomena to be?
- Do you believe they exist as real phenomena (regardless of how you might explain them)?

J.B. Rhine introduced the term 'extrasensory perception' (ESP) in 1934. This was a general term used to cover three types of communication that supposedly occur without the use of the senses, namely *telepathy*, *clairvoyance* and *precognition*. These, and other commonly researched phenomena in PP, are defined in Box 6.1.

Box 6.1 The four types of psi

- **Telepathy:** '... the transmission of information from one mind to another, without the use of language, body movements, or any of the known senses ...' (Evans, 1987b). It was previously called 'thought transference'.
- **Clairvoyance:** '... the acquisition by a mind or brain of information which is not available to it by the known senses, and, most important, which is *not known at the time to any other mind or brain* ...' (Evans, 1987b).
- **Precognition:** '... the apparent ability to access information about future events before they happen ...' (Morris, 1989).

These are all forms of extrasensory perception (ESP). In all cases, the direction of influence is from environment to person.

- **Psychokinesis (PK):** '... the supposed power of the mind to manipulate matter at a distance without any known physical means ...' (Evans, 1987b), or the apparent ability to '... influence events simply by a direct volitional act of some sort, by wanting the event to happen in a certain way ...' (Morris, 1989).

For PK, the direction of influence is from person to environment (the reverse of ESP).

One consequence of definitions such as those in Box 6.1 is that the field of PP is ever-shrinking. For example, hypnosis, hallucinations, and lucid dreams used to be considered part of PP, until psychologists made progress in understanding them. As Boring (1966) said, a scientific success is a failure for psychical research; in other words, PP is concerned with those phenomena that 'mainstream' or 'regular' psychology cannot explain with its currently available models and theories (see above).

Other paranormal experiences which are increasingly becoming part of mainstream psychology are *near-death* and *out-of-body experiences*. The title of an article by Blackmore (1988) illustrates this 'shrinkage' of PP very well : '*Visions from the dying brain – Near-death experiences may tell us more about consciousness and the brain than about what lies beyond the grave*'. In it, Blackmore discusses near-death experiences and considers alternative explanations in terms of known or hypothesised *physiological processes*, in particular those relating to brain mechanisms. While seeing such experiences as deserving of serious study (they are real, powerful experiences), she rejects the claim that they are evidence of life-after-death (the occult/supernatural explanation). Instead, she argues that they should be understood in terms of brain function (neuropsychological explanations). Not only can we apply what we already know (about the brain) to these experiences, but they can also teach us much about the brain.

A representation of near-death experience (NDE) (© Liz Pyle, 1988)

METHODS USED TO STUDY PSI

According to Alcock (1981), definitions of ESP and PK are all negative, in the sense that they depend on ruling out 'normal' communication before the paranormal can be assumed. Progression in PP's experimental methods has necessarily been designed to exclude the 'normal' with even greater confidence. However, this inevitably leaves it open for critics to argue for even more devious ways in which sensory communication or outright fraud might occur (Blackmore, 1995).

ESP and Zener cards

The Rhines were convinced that the supposedly paranormal powers of the mind were essentially psychological phenomena, and so should be investigated with the tools of traditional psychological research. Throughout the 1930s, they conducted a lengthy series of *telepathy* experiments, in which a *receiver* had to guess the identity of a target being looked at by an *agent*. To make the task as easy as possible, a set of simple symbols was developed and made into *Zener cards* (named after their designer) or 'ESP cards'. They come as a pack of 25 cards, consisting of five circles, five squares, five crosses, five stars and five wavy lines.

The rationale for these studies was that they allowed the experimenter to compare the results achieved with what would be expected by chance. So, in a pack of 25 cards comprising five of each of five distinct symbols, we'd expect, on average, five to be *guessed* correctly (i.e. by chance alone). If receivers repeatedly scored above chance over long series of trials, this would suggest that they were 'receiving' some information about the cards. This would, in turn, imply that, if the experiments had been sufficiently tightly controlled as to exclude all normal or known sensory cues, then the information must be coming via ESP (Evans, 1987a). In *clairvoyance* experiments, the cards were randomised out of sight of anyone, and in *precognition* experiments, the card order was decided only *after* the receiver had made his/her guesses.

The order was determined initially by shuffling, and later by the use of random number tables. It's extremely important for targets in ESP experiments to be properly randomised, so that results cannot be affected by any kind of systematic biases: shuffling *isn't* adequate (Blackmore, 1995).

What were the Rhines' findings?

The technique seemed to be successful, and the Rhines reported results that were way beyond what could be expected by chance (Blackmore, 1995). They claimed that they'd established the existence of ESP. However, these claims produced considerable opposition from the psychological establishment.

For example, were the Rhines' receivers physically completely isolated from the experimenter, so that information couldn't be passed unwittingly (for example, by unconsciously whispering or other non-deliberate cues)? Were checks on the data records precise enough to ensure minor errors weren't made (unconsciously or deliberately) to bias the results in a pro-ESP direction?

The Rhines tightened up their procedures on both counts by (a) separating receiver and experimenter in different buildings, and (b) arranging independent verification and analysis of the results. As a consequence, the above-chance results became more rare, although they remained sufficiently common to constitute apparently indisputable evidence for ESP. However, then came another, more fundamental criticism. When psychologists not committed to a belief in ESP tried to replicate the Rhines' findings in their own laboratories, they simply failed to produce any positive results.

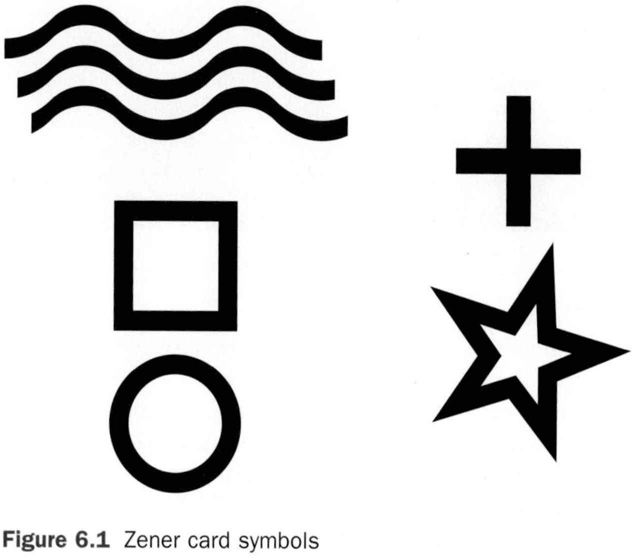

Figure 6.1 Zener card symbols

In response to this potentially fatal blow, the parapsychologists argued that a significant factor in ESP might be the *experimenter's attitude* to the phenomenon under investigation: sceptical or dismissive experimenters ('goats') might have a 'negative effect' on the results (the Rhines, and other believers, being 'sheep'). This argument seems to imply that only believers are fit to investigate ESP, which is contrary to the spirit of scientific research (Evans, 1987a: see Chapter 3). The director of research at the Duke University Laboratory (the Rhines themselves had retired) was later caught flagrantly modifying some experimental data in a pro-ESP direction. Fortunately, or unfortunately (depending on whether you're a goat or a sheep), this wasn't an isolated example. (We'll return to this issue later in the chapter: see Research Update 6.1, page 100.)

ASK YOURSELF...
- Are you a sheep or a goat?

Box 6.2 The problem of fraud

- According to Colman (1987), the history of PP is '... disfigured by numerous cases of fraud involving some of the most "highly respected scientists", their colleagues and participants ...'
- For example, Soal (Soal & Bateman, 1954), a mathematician at Queen Mary College, London, tried to replicate some of the Rhines' telepathy experiments using Zener cards. Despite his rigid controls and the involvement of other scientists as observers throughout, accusations of fraud resulted in a series of re-analyses of the data.
- Marwick, a member of the Society for Psychical Research in London, finally proved (in 1978) that Soal *had* cheated (Blackmore, 1995).
- Against this, it's misleading to suggest that experimenter fraud is rife in PP, or even that it's more common here than in other disciplines. According to Roe (personal communication), books such as *Betrayers of the Truth* (Broad & Wade, 1982) show that fraud is more likely when the rewards are high and the chances of being caught (publicly exposed) are low. This characterises mainstream science (especially medicine), and is certainly *not* characteristic of PP.

Free-response ESP

One drawback of the early Rhine research was that guessing long series of cards is extremely boring. By contrast, reports of psychic dreams, premonitions and other cases of spontaneous psi abounded. The challenge was to capture these under laboratory conditions (Blackmore, 1995). Free-response ESP represents the most important attempts to meet this challenge.

Remote viewing

Free-response methods include *remote viewing (RV) studies* (Targ & Puthoff, 1974, 1977). RV is a form of *clairvoyance*, in which an individual is able to 'see' a specific location some distance away, without receiving any information about it through the usual sensory channels. Targ and Puthoff reported a series of field studies involving Pat Price, a former California police commissioner, which sparked a debate between researchers as to whether Price's successes constituted genuine clairvoyance. Despite the controversy, the research was sufficiently convincing for the US military to fund a substantial research programme. The CIA declassified this information and released details of more than 20 years of RV research (Blackmore, 1996). RV has been put to practical use in 'psychic archaeology' (finding lost sites), criminal investigations (see Chapter 46) and, most controversially, predicting price fluctuations of silver futures on the stock market!

The Ganzfeld

The most successful free-response method has been the *Ganzfeld* ('ganz' = 'whole'; 'feld' = 'field'), first used for psi research by Honorton in 1974. He argued that why ESP occurs in dreams, meditation and reverie is that they're all states of reduced sensory input and increased internal attention. He tried to find a way of producing such a 'psi-conducive' state without the expense of a dream laboratory (see Chapter 7).

Box 6.3 The Ganzfeld

- Halved ping-pong balls are taped over the *receiver's* eyes, and red light is shone into them, so all that can be seen is a pinkish glow. Soothing sea sounds or hissing 'white noise' (like a radio that's not properly tuned in) are played through headphones while the participant lies on a comfortable couch or reclining chair. While this doesn't constitute total sensory deprivation (see Chapter 9), the Ganzfeld deprives receivers of patterned input and encourages internal imagery. They typically report a pleasant sensation of being immersed in a 'sea of light'.
- The *sender* (an experimenter acting as an agent) is situated in a separate, acoustically isolated room. A visual stimulus (a picture, slide or brief video sequence) is randomly selected from a large pool of similar stimuli to serve as the *target*. While the sender concentrates on the target (for about 15 minutes), the receiver tries to describe it by providing a continuous verbal report of his/her ongoing imagery and free associations.
- The sender stays in the room for another 10 minutes. From a separate room, the experimenter can both hear (via a microphone) and see (via a one-way mirror) the receiver, and is blind to the target (doesn't know what the target is).

- At the end of the experimental session, the receiver is presented with four stimuli (one of which is the target), and is asked to rate the degree to which each one matches the imagery and associations experienced during the session. A 'direct hit' is recorded if the receiver assigns the highest rating to the target.
- The sender is then called in and reveals the target. A typical experiment involves about 30 sessions.

A receiver in the Ganzfeld

The 'Ganzfeld debate'

Honorton (1985) analysed 28 studies using the Ganzfeld procedure (totalling 835 sessions, conducted in ten different laboratories). He reported a 38 per cent correct selection of the target, which compares with a 25 per cent success rate by chance alone (i.e. by guessing). Statistically, this is highly significant: the chances of obtaining a 38 per cent success rate by chance alone is less than one in a billion (Honorton, 1985).

However, a critical review by Hyman (in the *Journal of Parapsychology*, 1985) pointed out discrepancies in the scoring systems used, and procedural flaws (such as the failure to use proper randomisation for selecting the targets). Hyman also claimed to have found correlations between the quality ratings for studies and outcome, with the sloppier studies giving the 'better' results. However, in the same journal, Honorton claimed to have found *no* evidence of such a correlation. Rosenthal provided a commentary on the debate, generally regarded as favouring Honorton's interpretation (Blackmore, 1995).

Hyman & Honorton issued a joint 'communiqué' (Hyman and Honorton, 1986), in which they agreed that the studies as a whole fell short of ideal, but that something beyond selective reporting, or inflated significance levels, seemed to be producing the non-chance outcomes. They also agreed that the significant outcomes had been produced by several different researchers. Further replication would decide which of their interpretations was correct.

This debate, which Morris (1989) describes as 'an outstanding example of productive interaction between critic and researcher', brought parapsychologists and sceptics together to try to agree what would constitute an acceptable experiment. As a consequence, Honorton designed a *fully automated* Ganzfeld experiment, leaving little scope for human error or deliberate fraud. Several experiments produced significant results, which were published in the *Psychological Bulletin* in 1994. This is one of the world's most prestigious psychology journals, and meant that 'The Ganzfeld had achieved respectability' (Blackmore, 1997). However, despite many parapsychologists believing that the Ganzfeld is a genuinely repeatable experiment, most other scientists seem to reject the evidence:

> ... 'Unfair' say the parapsychologists. But we still do not know who is right. (Blackmore, 1997)

Clairvoyance vs telepathy

Some Ganzfeld experiments didn't use a sender, so that the target images could be acquired through *clairvoyance* (telepathy would require the involvement of another mind – the sender's). Honorton (1985) reported that where a sender was involved (*telepathy condition*), the results were generally more positive – but only when the experimenters were already experienced in using both sender and no-sender methods. Where experimenters consistently used one or other method, the *no-sender/clairvoyance condition* produced slightly more positive results.

SOME RECURRING ISSUES IN ESP RESEARCH

In our discussion of ESP research so far, we've seen just how divided opinion is between those who believe in the reality of ESP ('sheep') and those who don't ('goats'). We've also seen that accusations of fraud – the deliberate invention or modification of procedures or results – have been a feature of the history of PP research. Arguably, this makes the study of psi unique as an area of psychological enquiry. At least as far as goats are concerned, parapsychologists are guilty unless proven innocent. In other words, if psi doesn't exist (as goats maintain), then any claims by sheep that it does must be based on fraudulent (or, at best, unreliable and/or invalid) data. So, rather than simply trying to produce evidence that supports the existence of psi, parapsychologists are constantly having to show that they are *not cheating*! But how can you prove a negative?

The history of PP also seems to highlight a number of methodological issues that, while they recur throughout all areas of psychological research, assume a more exaggerated or extreme form in relation to psi. These include:

- the question of *the 'conclusive' experiment*
- the *replication problem*
- *publication bias* (or the *file-drawer problem*)
- the *inadequacy of controls*
- *experimenter effects*.

The question of the 'conclusive' experiment

According to Abelson (1978), then editor of *Science*, 'extraordinary claims require extraordinary evidence' (quoted in Rao & Palmer, 1987). This implies that the strength of evidence needed to establish a new phenomenon is directly proportional to how incompatible the phenomenon is with our current beliefs about the world. If we reject the possibility of this new phenomenon (its *subjective probability* is zero), then no amount of empirical evidence will be sufficient to establish the claim. However, as Rao and Palmer point out:

> ... In serious scientific discourse ... few would be expected to take a zero-probability stance because such a stance could be seen to be sheer dogmatism, and the very antithesis of the basic assumption of science's open-endedness.

Abelson's 'extraordinary evidence' sometimes means, in practice, demands for a 'foolproof' experiment that would control for all conceivable kinds of error, including experimenter fraud. This assumes that at any given time, one can identify all possible sources of error and how to control for them (see Chapter 3).

> ***ASK YOURSELF...***
> - Is this assumption valid? (See Box 3.7, page 47.)

According to Rao & Palmer (1987):

> ... The concept of a 'conclusive' experiment, totally free of any possible error or fraud and immune to all skeptical doubt, is a practical impossibility for empirical phenomena. In reality, evidence in science is a matter of degree ... a 'conclusive' experiment [should] be defined more modestly as one in which it is highly *improbable* that the result is artifactual ...

In other words, there are *no absolutes* in science (no certainty, no once-and-for-all 'proof'), only *probabilities* (see Chapter 3). In *this* sense, Rao and Palmer believe that a case can be made for 'conclusive' experiments in PP.

> **Box 6.4 Schmidt's (1969) random event generator (REG)**
>
> - Schmidt, a physicist at the Boeing Scientific Research Laboratories in the USA, designed a test for the possibility of ESP.
> - A specially built machine seemed to rule out all artefacts arising from recording errors, sensory cues or receiver cheating. The machine randomly selected targets with equal probability, and recorded both target selections and receivers' responses. The receiver's task was to guess which of four lamps would light and press the corresponding button if aiming for high scores (or avoid pressing if aiming for low scores).
> - Random lighting of the lamps was achieved by a sophisticated electronic *random event generator* (REG), which was tested extensively in control trials and found not to deviate significantly from chance.

The REG experiments:

- represent one of the major experimental paradigms in contemporary PP
- are regarded by most parapsychologists as providing good evidence for psi
- have been subjected to detailed scrutiny by critics.

Despite this, and almost inevitably, they have been criticised. For example, Hansel (1980) claimed that Schmidt's highly significant results haven't been replicated by other researchers (see below), and these criticisms are routinely taken as valid by most sceptics (such as Alcock, 1981). Although Hyman (1981, cited in Rao & Palmer, 1987) is one of the few psi goats who has questioned Hansel's basic reasoning, he still agrees with Hansel's claim that the REG experiments don't provide an adequate case for the existence of psi. However:

> There is no such thing as an experiment immune from trickery ... Even if one assembles all the world's magicians and scientists and puts them to the task of designing a fraud-proof experiment, it cannot be done. (Rao & Palmer, 1987)

The replication problem

Rao & Palmer (1987) argue that science is concerned with establishing general laws, not unique events (this relates to the *idiographic–nomothetic debate*: see Chapter 42). The ability to repeat an experiment would seem to be a reasonable thing to demand of a field aiming to achieve scientific respectability (*New Scientist*, 2004: see Chapter 3).

However, many sceptics argue that only 'replication on demand' can produce conclusive proof of psi. According to Rao and Palmer, an experiment isn't either replicable or not replicable, but rather it's on a continuum:

> ... In this sense of statistical replication, an experiment or an effect may be considered replicated if a series of replication attempts provides statistically significant evidence for the original effect when analysed as a series. (Rao & Palmer, 1987)

In other words, does the evidence *overall* support the existence of the effect being investigated? On *balance*, does the accumulated evidence, based on a large number of replication attempts, point towards the existence of psi, or not? But while this is fine in principle, in practice it's proved impossible to reach any kind of consensus.

Between 1995 and 1999, 30 Ganzfeld experiments were conducted. Four different *meta-analytic* studies of these experiments were also performed. (A meta-analysis (MA) is a 'study of studies' using a statistical technique that allows diverse studies to be compared on a single measure, called an *averaged effect size*: see Box 45.10, page 830). Two of these MAs concluded that the findings were significant, while the other two concluded that they weren't! The biggest discrepancy between them was the inclusion (or not) of a hugely successful study by Dalton (1997) carried out at Edinburgh University. It was omitted from two of the MAs on the grounds that it was an 'outlier': because its results were so much better than any others, it should be discounted (an accepted practice in MA). But another accepted practice is that MAs must use *all* available data. So, the other two included Dalton's study (*New Scientist*, 2004). So much for scientific objectivity!

Rao & Palmer (1987) argue that, once we give up the idea of *absolute* replication ('replication on demand'), parapsychological phenomena have been replicated in a statistically significant sense. Also, many parapsychologists argue that any failure to replicate should be taken as a *positive* result: it confirms what they knew all along, namely that paranormal phenomena are inherently elusive. You cannot expect to pin them down in the laboratory (*New Scientist*, 2004).

Publication bias (or the 'file-drawer' problem)

The so-called *file-drawer problem* refers to the claim that non-significant results may systematically go unreported: if a study fails to find evidence of psi, it's 'consigned to the filing-cabinet drawer', so that no one except the researchers who conducted the study know of its existence. This would mean that those that are published (the database of known studies) may not accurately reflect the true state of affairs: there will be a strong bias in favour of psi.

According to Rao & Palmer (1987), close scrutiny of the field suggests that the file-drawer problem cannot explain away the significant number of replications in PP. But isn't it impossible ever to establish how many studies may have been 'binned'?

Box 6.5 Solving the file-drawer problem

- Parapsychologists are more sensitive to the possible impact of unreported negative results than most other scientists. In the USA, the Parapsychological Association (PA) has advocated publishing all methodologically sound experiments, regardless of the outcome. Since 1976, this policy has been reflected in publications of all affiliated journals (such as the *Journal of Parapsychology*) and in papers accepted for presentation at annual PA conventions.
- There are relatively few parapsychologists, and most are aware of ongoing work in the various laboratories around the world. When conducting an MA, parapsychologists actively seek out unpublished negative studies at conventions and through personal networks.
- A technique developed by Rosenthal (1979, cited in Rao & Palmer, 1987) makes it possible to estimate the number of unpublished, non-significant experiments that would be necessary to reduce an entire database to non-significance. For example, Honorton (1985) estimated that 423 non-significant Ganzfeld studies would be needed to reduce the direct-hit studies to a non-significant level (the equivalent of 12,000 sessions: see Box 6.3).

  ... Given the complex and time-consuming nature of the ganzfeld procedure, it is unreasonable to suppose that so many experiments exist in the 'file drawer'... (Rao & Palmer, 1987)

- There are also some areas where we can be reasonably certain we have access to *all* the experiments conducted – for example, research into the relationship between ESP performance and ratings obtained on the Defence Mechanism Test (DMT: Kragh & Smith, 1970, cited in Rao & Palmer, 1987). Because the administration and scoring of the test requires specialised training available to only a few individuals, Johnson (at the University of Utrecht and a leading authority on DMT) has been able to keep track of the relevant experiments, conducted by qualified people. In all ten experiments identified by Johnson & Haraldsson (1984, cited in Rao & Palmer, 1987), the less defensive participants scored higher on ESP tests, seven studies proving significant at the 0.05 level.

(Source: based on Atkinson *et al.*, 1990; Rao & Palmer, 1987)

The inadequacy of controls

According to Alcock (1981), replication of an experimental result by other experimenters:

> ... does not assure that experimental artifacts were not responsible for the results in the replication as well as in the original experiment.

This is perhaps like saying that 'two wrongs don't make a right'. While it's true that replicating an effect implies nothing directly about its cause, it's also a basic premise of experimental science that replication reduces the probability of *some* causal explanations, particularly those related to the honesty or competence of individual experimenters (Rao & Palmer, 1987). As Alcock (1981) himself says in another context:

> It is not enough for a researcher to report his observations with respect to a phenomenon; he could be mistaken, or even dishonest. But if other people, using his methodology, can independently produce the same results, it is much more likely that error and dishonesty are not responsible for them.

Some more specific criticisms of ESP research relating to inadequacy of controls were discussed in the sections on 'Methods used to study psi', above (see pages 95–97).

Experimenter effects

Alcock (1981) and others have argued that replications must be conducted by investigators *unsympathetic to psi* (goats). This would exclude most – but not all – parapsychologists (Blackmore being a good example of one who would 'qualify'). Researchers' personal beliefs are rarely reported and may often be difficult to determine reliably. Rao & Palmer (1987) believe that if such a criterion were to be applied retrospectively to published research in psychology as a whole, there wouldn't be much left. Why should parapsychologists be singled out in this way, and why have critics not suggested that negative results from 'disbelievers' in psi also be rejected? It's impossible to know how many 'disbelievers' have obtained positive results, nor can we assume that such results would necessarily be acknowledged as such.

However, one of the most consistent findings in parapsychological research is that some experimenters, using well-controlled methods, repeatedly produce significant results, while others, using exactly the same methods, consistently produce non-significant results. As we saw in Chapter 3 (Box 3.6, page 45), experimenters can affect the outcome of experiments unwittingly, through tone of voice and other forms of bodily communication, which can subtly (and unconsciously) convey expectations to the participants. These *experimenter effects* have long been explicitly recognised and discussed in PP.

Box 6.6 Psi-permissive, psi-inhibitory and psi-conducive experimenters

- Some experimenters seem capable of creating a climate in which participants' psi abilities are allowed to express themselves (*psi-permissive* experimenters), while others have the opposite effect and produce consistently negative results (*psi-inhibitory* results). These differences seem to be related to:
  - (i) the pleasantness/unpleasantness of the experimental setting for the participant – a relaxed participant is more likely to display psi abilities (Crandall, 1985)
  - (ii) the experimenter's expectations – participants are more likely to display psi abilities if the experimenter expects positive results (Taddonio, 1976).
- According to Schmiedler (1997), some experimenters have produced particularly high levels of positive results with participants who fail to repeat their performance later. This could be explained in terms of a highly motivated experimenter, who has strong psi abilities him/herself. S/he may somehow *transfer* these abilities to participants during the course of the experiments (but not beyond). These are referred to as *psi-conducive* experimenters. This transfer can distort the experimental findings.

How should we interpret these findings?

The experimenter effect (EE) is one of parapsychology's longest-standing controversies. This is largely due to the 'heads I win, tails you lose' interpretation that many parapsychologists (sheep) place on the findings described in Box 6.6. In other words, the fact that positive results are obtained by researchers with psi abilities – but not by those without – 'proves' that psi exists. Rather than being a confounding variable as sceptics would claim (see Chapter 3), believers argue that experimenter effects in the context of parapsychological research actually demonstrate the phenomena under investigation.

According to Palmer, of the Rhine Research Centre (in McCrone, 2004), 'the strongest predictor of ESP results generally is the identity of the experimenter'. The EE itself is now the object of intense research. New explanations for it are also emerging. For example, some parapsychologists claim that it arises not through experimenters' influence over mind or matter, but because they use their extra-sensory powers to pick the right moments to sample a fluctuating process and catch any 'fluky', but natural, departures from randomness (McCrone, 2004).

RESEARCH UPDATE 6.1: Investigating the experimenter effect

- Ongoing research into the experimenter effect is being conducted jointly by Wiseman (University of Hertfordshire, UK) and Schlitz (Institute of Noetic Sciences, California, USA). This is a classic sceptic (Wiseman) versus believer (Schlitz) experiment.
- The experiment is an example of *Direct Mental Interaction with Living Systems* (DMILS) – that is, attempts to use mental connection to influence distant biological systems. This can take the form of remote staring (as in the Wiseman–Schlitz research), and affecting the growth rates of seedlings and yeast cultures.
- Participants sit in an isolated room, hooked up to electrodes that measure arousal levels through slight changes in sweating of the hands (galvanic skin response/GSR: see Chapter 4).
- In another room, the experimenter can see the participant on CCTV.
- The experimenter has either to stare at the participant or look away, according to a random 16-minute schedule divided into 30-second blocks.
- The hypothesis being tested is that if participants know they're being stared at, they should show detectable shifts in arousal while they're under surveillance.
- Schlitz and others have been claiming small but statistically significant results for more than a decade. In the mid-1990s, Wiseman (a professional magician before he trained as a psychologist) tried the same experiment and found no effect. The collaboration between them began in 1996. They've swapped laboratories and shared

participant pools. According to Wiseman, Schlitz's results are on 'the very knife-edge of significance'.

- But does the experimenter effect come from somewhere other than the experimenter's psychic powers?
- In the latest study, the 'meet and greet' part of the experiment is being split from the experimental phase. On some trials, the experimenter will do both; on others, these jobs will be shared with another experimenter. Interactions between experimenters and participants are videotaped and independently rated for factors such as warmth.

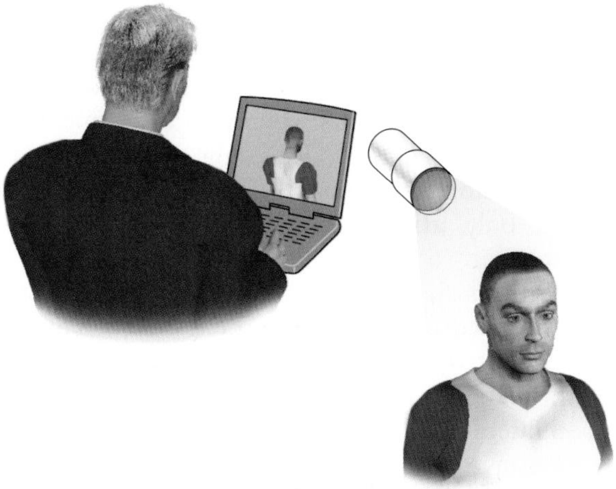

The Wiseman-Schlitz experiment tests whether participants can tell if they're being watched via a CCTV link

(Source: based on McCrone, 2004)

Paranormal phenomena and the mind–brain relationship

ASK YOURSELF...

- What implications do paranormal phenomena have for belief in the existence of mind as separate from the brain?
- Do you believe that the mind exists separately from the brain?

As we noted earlier, PP grew out of spiritualism and psychical research. What seems to underlie accounts of psi is the notion of mind affecting other minds (as in ESP) or matter (as in PK), but this is exactly what most of us believe happens whenever we do anything at all, such as waggling a finger. 'Common sense' seems to assume *dualism*, the philosophical theory according to which mind and body (or mind and brain) are distinct. This contrasts with *identity theories* of the mind–body/brain relationship, which maintain that there's only 'matter' (see Chapter 49). According to Gregory (1987a):

> ... Clear-cut paranormal phenomena demonstrating disembodied mind might conceivably show identity theories to be untenable. So paranormal accounts do have empirical consequences, even though ... we may seriously doubt whether there are any such phenomena.

Similarly, if it could be shown that psi exists:

> ... Not only would strictly mechanistic models of psychology – such as Skinnerian behaviourism ... have to be scrapped, but many of the assumptions and theories of physical science would need at least to be thoroughly overhauled ... (Evans, 1987b)

According to Beloff (1987), not all parapsychologists are necessarily dualists, just as they aren't necessarily 'believers'. Blackmore is a good example of a parapsychologist who regards psi as a function of the brain (see above, page 94).

Box 6.7 Psi and consciousness

- According to Blackmore (1996), the popular view is that if ESP exists, it proves that mental phenomena are *non-local* (independent of space and time). If PK exists, it proves that mind can reach out beyond brain to affect things at a distance.
- If you equate mind with consciousness, then, hey presto, ESP and PK prove the power of consciousness. Blackmore argues that it's a desire for this 'power of consciousness' that fuels much of the enthusiasm for the paranormal.
- However, the more we look into the workings of the brain, the less it looks like a machine run by a conscious self. There's no place inside the brain where consciousness 'resides', where mental images are 'viewed' or where instructions are 'issued'. There's just massive parallel throughput and no centre (see Chapter 4).
- Indeed, Blackmore argues that there are even a few crucial experiments suggesting that conscious experience takes some time to build up and is much too slow to be responsible for making things happen (see Chapter 7):

> *... the brain seems to be a machine that runs itself very well and produces an illusion that there is someone in charge ...*

- PP is trying to prove that consciousness really does have power, that our minds really can reach out and 'do' things, not only within our own bodies but beyond them.

CONCLUSIONS: THE CONTROVERSY GOES ON

According to Scott (1987):

> Perhaps the only non-controversial statement that can be made about the present position is that the controversy continues ...

Eysenck & Sargent (1993), two psychologists known for being hard-nosed scientists, who demand rigorous, objective standards of experimentation, conclude that:

Human beings do seem to use sensory abilities beyond their 'conventional' senses. They do seem to influence distant events and objects through will alone.

Some parapsychologists and physicists are working actively on possible meeting points between PP and the 'new physics' (*quantum theory/mechanics*). For example, there's evidence that the conscious act of making an experimental observation can directly influence the random events in the apparatus (Simpson, 2000). The new physics represents a major revolution in science since the beginning of the twentieth century. According to Morgan (2000), it

> ... has challenged the very basis of classical materialism and caused a fundamental re-examination of the traditional division between mind and matter ...

Perhaps the real significance of psi and of PP as areas of research is that they force us to question some of our basic beliefs and assumptions about the world and ourselves. Both scientists and non-scientists are capable of prejudice and closed-mindedness, and PP can be seen as a case study in 'doing science', which isn't the unbiased, objective activity many scientists take it to be (see Chapters 3 and 47).

Matthews (2004) believes that parapsychological studies are often better designed, and their results more impressive, than clinical drug trials:

> ... by all the normal rules for assessing scientific evidence, the case for ESP has been made. And yet most scientists still refuse to believe the findings, maintaining that ESP simply does not exist ...

Matthews concludes that science alone cannot give us what we seek – an objective view of reality. As he says:

> More than any other scientific discipline, parapsychology pushes the scientific process to its limits and reveals where its faults lie. In particular, it has highlighted that, contrary to the insistence of many scientists, data alone can never settle this or any other issue. (Matthews, 2004)

CHAPTER SUMMARY

- **Parapsychology (PP)** is the scientific study of paranormal phenomena (or 'psi'), which appear to exceed the sensory means by which we normally acquire information about the environment. Because they are so extraordinary, many psychologists have denied the possibility of their existence, and the history of PP is littered with accusations of fraud.
- Modern PP was founded in the 1930s by the Rhines, and grew out of **spiritualistic research/spiritualism** and **psychical research** dating back to the 1880s.
- **Extra-sensory perception (ESP)** consists of **telepathy**, **clairvoyance** and **precognition**. The direction of influence is from environment to person. The other major type of psi is **psychokinesis (PK)**, in which the influence is from person to environment.
- PP is concerned with phenomena that mainstream psychology cannot explain. As psychological understanding increases, so the field of PP shrinks. **Near-death** and **out-of-body experiences** are increasingly being explained in terms of widely accepted **neuropsychological processes** (as opposed to occult or supernatural explanations).
- Early ESP research used **Zener cards**, which allowed the experimenter to compare the results with what would be expected by chance (i.e. guessing). In **telepathy** experiments, a **receiver** had to guess the identity of a **target** symbol being looked at by an **agent/sender**. In **clairvoyance** experiments, the cards were randomised out of sight of everyone, and in **precognition** experiments, card order was determined only **after** the receiver had made his/her guesses.
- The Rhines claimed to have established the existence of ESP, based on their use of Zener cards. This claim was disputed by critics who pointed out several methodological flaws (or potential flaws), resulting in the tightening up of the Rhines' procedures. However, revelations of fraud, together with the monotonous nature of the task, led to the search for alternative methods.
- **Free-response methods** include **remote-viewing** and the **Ganzfeld**. The so-called **Ganzfeld debate** between Honorton and Hyman, resulting in their joint statement identifying areas of agreement between them, brought parapsychologists and sceptics together in an effort to define an acceptable experiment. This resulted in a **fully automated Ganzfeld**, but the dispute between 'sheep' and 'goats' continues.
- Parapsychologists continually have to prove that they are *not* cheating, and there are also several methodological issues that, while not unique to PP, assume a more extreme form in relation to psi. These include the **'conclusive' experiment**, the **replication problem**, **publication bias** (or the **file-drawer problem**), the **inadequacy of controls** and **experimenter/participant effects**.
- Schmidt's **random event generator (REG)** is regarded by many parapsychologists as constituting a 'conclusive' experiment, but critics disagree. The safest conclusion is that there is no such thing as a fraud-proof experiment.
- Parapsychologists are more sensitive to the file-drawer problem than most other scientists, and they have taken a number of steps to get round it. These include calculating the number of studies with negative results needed to cancel out a series of positive results.
- One of the most consistent findings in parapsychological research concerns the consistency with which

different experimenters produce positive or negative results. These experimenter differences have been classified as **psi-permissive**, **psi-inhibitory** and **psi-conducive**. Important individual differences between participants relevant to psi abilities have also been identified.

- Belief in psi supports a **dualist** theory of the **mind–body/brain relationship**, as opposed to **identity theories**. However, not all parapsychologists are necessarily dualists, and mind or consciousness can be explained in terms of brain processes alone.
- **Quantum theory/mechanics** in physics, which challenges the traditional division between mind and matter, may offer a revolutionary way of thinking about the world that could accommodate paranormal phenomena.

Links with other topics/chapters

- Parapsychology raises fundamental questions regarding the *nature of science* – in particular, its objectivity (Chapter 3). This is related to the *biases and prejudices* of scientists themselves (Chapter 47). These issues are relevant to all aspects of psychological (and other scientific) research, but are highlighted in PP.
- The reality of psi has fundamental implications for theories of the *mind–brain relationship*, especially those *reductionist* theories which claim that any psychological account of 'the mind' can be replaced by a neurophysiological one (Chapters 4 and 49). It also has implications for the *free will versus determinism* debate (Chapter 49 again).
- There's evidence that people with particular personality characteristics (such as extroverts: Honorton *et al.*, 1990) may be more likely to display psi abilities (Chapter 42).

7

STATES OF CONSCIOUSNESS AND BODILY RHYTHMS

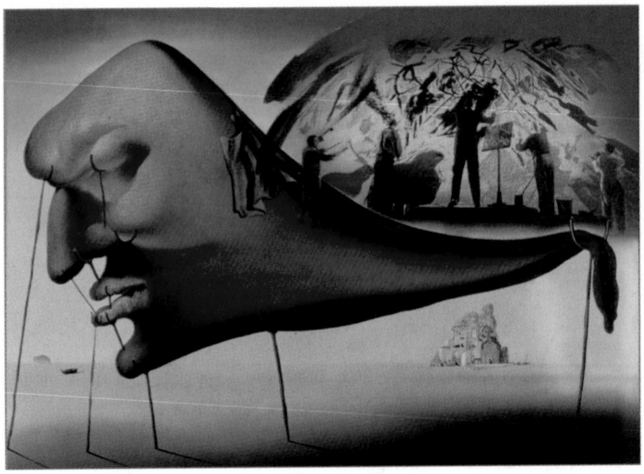

INTRODUCTION AND OVERVIEW

For the first 30 or so years of its life as a separate discipline, pioneered by figures such as William James and Wilhelm Wundt, psychology took conscious human experience as its subject matter. As we saw in Chapter 1, *introspection* – the observation of one's own mind – was the primary method used to study it. This interest in consciousness shouldn't come as a surprise, given how fundamental it is to everything we do (Rubin & McNeill, 1983).

Yet it is the very *subjectivity* of our experience that led Watson to reject introspectionism in favour of a truly scientific (i.e. *objective*) approach to the study of psychology, namely behaviourism. Writing from the perspective of a modern neuroscientist, Greenfield (1998) states that:

> Any scientific explanation of consciousness must be objective and embrace physical properties of the brain: but at the same time it must, nonetheless, somehow take account of the subjective. This is why consciousness has been such an anathema to scientists, because the whole essence of science is objectivity. And yet we are going to deal with a phenomenon that is subjective ...

However, as part of the 'cognitive revolution' in the 1950s (which removed behaviourism from its dominant position within psychology), 'the mind' once more became an acceptable, respectable focus of psychological research. Reflecting the current interest in consciousness among neuroscientists, philosophers and psychologists, one of the questions we'll be asking is: How might the brain generate consciousness?

There's been a considerable amount of research, since the 1950s, into *sleep* as a state of consciousness, much of which involves trying to find correlations between objective measures of physiological activity and subjective experience, in particular *dreaming*. Sleep is increasingly being discussed in relation to *bodily rhythms*; disruption of these through our modern lifestyle is increasingly being seen as a risk to health. According to Hobson (1995), the rhythm of rest and activity, 'the primordial of sleeping and waking', represents one of the most universal and basic features of life. So, the study of sleep is of interest to biologists as well as to psychologists.

WHAT IS 'CONSCIOUSNESS'?

Are only human beings 'conscious'?

ASK YOURSELF...
- In what sense could non-human animals be described as conscious?

If being conscious means having sensations of pain, cold, hunger, fear, and so on, then most species can be said to be conscious (although *sentient* might be a better term than 'conscious': see Chapter 48).

If by conscious we mean having *self-consciousness*, then humans may be unique (with the possible exception of some higher primates: see Chapters 19 and 33). According to Singer (1998), *self-awareness* (normally used synonymously with 'self-consciousness') is the experience of one's own individuality, the ability to experience oneself as an autonomous individual with subjective feelings. It's considered to be 'the result of social interactions, and hence of cultural evolution'. This suggests that it's a rather human thing to have.

Singer also claims that when we say we're conscious, we usually mean that we perceive and remember in a way that makes it possible to report about the perceived and remembered content, or to make it the object of intentional deliberations. Given the crucial role of language in these processes, and given that language is regarded by many as unique to humans (but see Chapter 19), the rest of this chapter will focus on consciousness as a characteristic of human beings.

ASK YOURSELF...
- Can you think of some other ways in which we use the term '(un)conscious/consciousness' in everyday conversation?

Some other definitions

- When we're awake we are *conscious*, but when we're asleep, in a coma or have been 'knocked out' by a punch to the head, we're *unconscious*. The term 'unconscious' is often reserved for the last two examples but, as we shall see, when we fall asleep, we do 'lose consciousness'.
- When we do something *consciously*, we do it deliberately or knowingly, but to do something *unconsciously* means doing it automatically or without having to think about it (for example, an experienced driver or typist: see Chapter 13)
- Public health campaigns (such as those promoting safe sex) are aimed at increasing *public consciousness* or awareness of the dangers of certain types of behaviour (see Chapters 12 and 24).

Freud's theory of consciousness

Freud saw consciousness as a whole comprising three levels:

1. the *conscious* – what we're fully aware of at any one time;
2. the *preconscious* – what we could become aware of quite easily if we switched our attention to it
3. the *unconscious* – what we've pushed out of our conscious minds, through repression, making it extremely inaccessible, although it continues to exert an influence on our thoughts, feelings and behaviour (see Chapters 2 and 42).

Most psychologists would agree that thoughts, feelings, memories, and so on, differ in their degree of accessibility. But most wouldn't accept Freud's formulation of the unconscious (based on repression). Indeed, other psychodynamic theorists, in particular Jung, disagreed fundamentally with Freud's view of the unconscious (see Chapter 42).

Rubin & McNeil (1983) define consciousness as 'our subjective awareness of our actions and of the world around us'. So, consciousness points *inwards*, towards our thoughts, feelings, actions, and so on, and *outwards*, towards external, environmental events (including other people). This mirrors the 'mental' orientation of Wundt and James, and cognitive psychologists since the mid-1950s, and Watson's (and Skinner's) behaviourist orientation, respectively.

CONSCIOUSNESS, AROUSAL AND ALERTNESS

Objective physiological measures, such as the electroencephalogram (EEG), electromyogram (EMG), electrooculogram (EOG) (see below), breathing and heart rates, and other correlates of consciousness, are often described as measures of level of *arousal* or *alertness*. Both subjectively and in terms of overt behaviour, there's an obvious difference between being sleepy and being wide awake in terms of degree of arousal or alertness. Less obvious are the smaller changes that occur during normal wakefulness and that are of two kinds – *tonic* and *phasic* These are mediated by different brain systems (Lloyd *et al.*, 1984).

Tonic alertness

Changes in tonic alertness reflect intrinsic (and usually quite slow) changes of the basic level of arousal throughout a 24-hour period (or even across a lifetime). They are closely related to various *biological rhythms*, in particular the *circadian rhythm* (see below). It was originally thought that the reticular formation (RF)/reticular activating system (RAS) was solely responsible for arousing and maintaining consciousness (in Chapter 4, the RAS was described as a 'consciousness switch'). For instance, if the brainstem is severed *below* the RAS, the animal will be paralysed but will remain fully alert when awake and will show normal sleep–wake EEG patterns. However, if it's sectioned *above* the RAS, it will fall into a state of continuous slow-wave sleep (see below).

KEY STUDY 7.1 Moruzzi & Magoun's (1949) study of cats' RAS

- Moruzzi and Magoun found that electrical stimulation of the RAS of sleeping cats woke them up. In anaesthetised cats it produced long-lasting signs of arousal in their EEGs. In cats that weren't anaesthetised, RAS stimulation produced behavioural signs of arousal, alertness and attention.
- According to Moruzzi and Magoun, sleep occurs when the activity of the RAS falls below a certain critical level.
- In sleep, sensory input to the RAS is reduced, and the electrical activity sweeping from the RAS up through the cortex drops below the level required to keep us awake (Diagram Group, 1982).

It's now known that other brain structures (both in the thalamus and hypothalamus) are involved in the sleep–wake cycle, and the coordination of all these systems is necessary for the initiation and maintenance of conscious awareness. Both during wakefulness and sleep, there are periodic, fairly predictable changes in the degree of alertness: the daytime changes are governed by a *diurnal rhythm* and the sleep (night-time) changes by an *ultradian rhythm*.

Phasic alertness

Changes in *phasic alertness* involve short-term, temporary variations in arousal, over a period of seconds, initiated by novel and important environmental events. An important component of these changes is the *orienting response* to arousing stimuli. It involves a decrease in heart rate and breathing rate, pupil dilation, tensing of the muscles and characteristic changes in the EEG, which becomes desynchronised.

If the stimuli are continuously presented, the orienting response is replaced by *habituation*: the person or animal stops responding to them. Habituation is, in fact, a form of *adaptation*. It's more important from a survival point of view to respond to novel stimuli rather than constant ones, and since most stimuli are relatively constant, we need to be able to attend selectively to those that are different and/or unexpected. It's the *changing* aspects of the environment that demand, and usually receive, our attention, and the nervous systems of animals and humans have evolved so as to make them especially responsive to change.

CONSCIOUSNESS AND ATTENTION

Although consciousness is difficult to describe because it's fundamental to everything we do (Rubin & McNeil, 1983), one way of trying to 'pin it down' is to study what we're paying attention to – what is in the forefront of our consciousness. According to Allport (1980a), 'attention is the experimental psychologist's code name for consciousness'.

Focal attention

Focal attention/awareness is what we're currently paying deliberate attention to and what's in the centre of our awareness (this corresponds to Freud's conscious). All those other aspects of our environment (as well as our own thoughts and feelings), which are on the fringes of our awareness, but which could easily become the object of our focal attention, are within our *peripheral attention/awareness* (corresponding to Freud's preconscious).

We seem to be capable of doing many things quite unconsciously or automatically (without having to think about what we're doing). A good illustration of this is perception. It's difficult to imagine what it would be like if we were aware of how we perceive.

Box 7.1 Perception as an automatic process: doing what comes naturally

ASK YOURSELF...
- If you haven't seen the picture below before, what do you see?
- If you have seen it before, try to explain how you saw what you saw when you first saw it.

Figure 7.1

- To select *consciously* one version of the ambiguous duck/rabbit figure, we must *either* know that there's a duck and a rabbit 'in' the picture, *or* we must have already perceived both versions. (In which case, how did the original perception come about?)
- You may have had difficulty yourself perceiving the duck if your immediate perception was of the rabbit, even though you consciously 'searched' for, and tried to see, the alternative version.
- This illustrates the very important difference between *conception* and *perception*: most of the time, perception is something that we 'just do' (see Chapter 15).

Conversely, something we normally do quite automatically, such as walking down stairs, might well be disrupted if we try to bring it into focal awareness (for example, thinking about each step as we take it – don't try this at home!). In general, being able to do things automatically makes sense in terms of freeing us to attend to those environmental events that are unfamiliar or threatening in some way. If we had to think about our bodily movements when walking, this would add to the already long list of sources of stimulation competing for our attention (see Chapter 13).

Even with skills that definitely do require focal attention when first acquired (such as driving or playing the piano), once they've been mastered, they become automatic. As Lloyd *et al.* (1984) put it, unconscious processes seem to be 'precipitates' of earlier conscious processes.

Nisbett & Wilson (1977) go so far as to claim that all psychological activities (including social behaviour) are governed by processes *of which we are unaware*. If people are asked about what they think governed their behaviour after participating in a social psychology experiment, the answers they give don't usually correspond very well with the explanations psychologists offer for the same behaviour (and which they believe are the *real reasons*).

Nisbett and Wilson argue that our belief that we can account for our own behaviour ('common sense' or *intuitive explanations*) is illusory, because what *really* guides our behaviour isn't available to consciousness. We don't have direct or 'privileged' access to our cognitive processes themselves, only to the *products/outputs* of those processes. Joynson (1974), Heather (1976) and other psychologists present an opposing view, arguing that people are psychologists, and that common-sense explanations may be as valid as theoretical, scientific ones (see Chapter 1).

ASK YOURSELF...
- Do you lean towards Nisbett and Wilson on this issue, or Joynson and Heather?
- How might you try to choose between them?
- Is there a convergence between Nisbett and Wilson's ideas, and Freud's, regarding the reasons 'ordinary' people give for their own behaviour and the explanations provided by psychologists? (See Chapter 42).

CONSCIOUSNESS AND BRAIN ACTIVITY

Passingham (at Oxford University) and his colleagues from the Institute of Neurology in London (1998, in McCrone, 1999) conducted a finger-tapping experiment, which may have revolutionary implications for our understanding of what it means consciously to experience something.

Box 7.2 Could finger-tapping be the key to conscious experience?

- Participants positioned their head into the heart of a brain scanner and rested one hand on a keypad. Then, by trial-and-error, they started to work out an unknown sequence of eight finger taps.
- A tick would flash up on a screen whenever they pressed the correct key. Once they knew the sequence, their instruction was to keep drumming out the pattern until it became an unthinking rhythm. After an hour, their fingers were skipping through the complex routine almost of their own accord, and they were barely conscious of what they were doing.
- In the learning phase, having to remember what they'd just discovered while groping for the next step, regions all over the brain were clearly very active. These included a range of high-level cognitive areas in the forebrain (such as those involved with planning and memory), as well as other, lower-brain areas that regulate movements (such as the basal ganglia and the cerebellum: see Chapter 4).
- Yet, within minutes of 'getting' the sequence, this 'wash' of activity began to fade. The job of moving the fingers became confined to just a small set of motor areas:

> *... It seems, having used the whole brain consciously to establish the individual finger movements, just the bare bones of the routine are left. The brain now has a template or habit that can produce the same behaviour 'as if' it were still going through all the hoops of being consciously aware. (McCrone, 1999)*

McCrone believes that Passingham *et al.*'s results aren't especially surprising. After all, we'd expect the brain to be capable of 'automating' motor tasks, such as typing or riding a bike. However, he refers to other imaging studies, which have shown that a similar process occurs when we learn more cognitive skills, such as matching verbs to nouns (e.g. 'hammer' and 'hit'), learning to play a computer game, and learning a path through a drawn maze. What studies using these various tasks show is that:

> ... paying focal, effortful attention to something calls large regions of the brain into action. The brain does not behave like a collection of isolated pathways, each doing their own thing, but as a coherent system. (McCrone, 1999)

It's not just in the learning of psychomotor skills that the whole (conscious) brain gives way to more specific (automatic) 'bare-bones' processing

There seem to be general-purpose planning centres that come into play whenever the brain is dealing with any kind of novel or difficult mental situation. These guide the more specialist language and motor centres to an appropriate output. Once the brain has found an optimal way to respond to a certain situation, the 'wider scaffolding' quickly falls away. It's not a case of practice making more efficient use of the pathways that were active during conscious learning, but rather that the response can be reduced to its bare essentials. When Passingham *et al.* asked their participants to pay close attention to their finger-tapping rhythm (after this had become automatic), their pre-frontal cortex immediately became active again. Just as significantly, their actual performance became more ragged, as if their brains were being put back into exploratory mode.

How might the brain generate consciousness?

Greenfield (1998) suggests that consciousness may have three properties.

1. Where might a 'consciousness centre' in the brain be? She claims that a recurring problem in neuroscience in general is the difficulty of 'location of function' (see Chapter 4). Vision, memory, movement and other brain/mind functions seem almost certainly *not* to be related in a modular way to single respective brain regions. Many different regions play parallel roles, analysing the outside world in various ways and reintegrating it into a connected whole. This is likely to be true of consciousness: it could be spatially multiple, but also temporally unitary (that is, we're usually only conscious of any one state at a time). This view is consistent with Passingham *et al.*'s research discussed above.
2. Rather than being all-or-nothing (either you're conscious or you're not), a more plausible scenario is that consciousness is more like the light on a dimmer switch that grows as the brain does. The more complex the brain, the greater the consciousness, with a continuum running from minimal to profound. This view can accommodate non-human animal consciousness and children's consciousness, as well as differences between the same individuals on different occasions (for example, changes in consciousness induced by drugs (see Chapters 8 and 45), religious experience, or listening to music).
3. We're always conscious of *something*: there's always some kind of focus, epicentre or trigger.

Box 7.3 Epicentres and neuronal connectivity

- The circuitry of the brain changes with learning and development. As we noted in Chapter 4, it's connections between neurons, rather than neurons themselves, that are established as a result of postnatal experience.
- This *plasticity* is especially marked in humans, and the brain remains adaptable and sensitive to life experiences even in adults (see Ramachandran's explanation of phantom limbs, pages 64–65). Experience changes the connectivity of neurons according to whatever circuits are most stimulated, and hence the most active.
- The *epicentre* is like a stone thrown into a pond, causing ripples to spread out over the surface of the water. The extent of these neuronal 'ripples' would affect the degree of consciousness at any one time. The epicentre that's going to trigger consciousness at any one moment is mediated by a group of neurons with relatively long-lasting connections between them. The activated hub of neurons generates the ripples in the brain that constitute consciousness.

(Source: Greenfield, 1998)

How might this happen? Greenfield cites an experiment by Libet, in which he pricked participants' skin and recorded the activity of large parts of the brain surface using the EEG (see Chapter 4). There was a huge amount of activity in the somatosensory cortex, but participants reported *no* conscious experience of tingling or any other sensations. They felt nothing, although their brain was registering signals of the touch to the skin, via the spinal cord. In Greenfield's model, it's this early component in the response that is equivalent to the 'epicentre'. But then, after about 500 m/sec, the activity evoked by the skin prick spread away from the somatosensory cortex to a much larger area of the brain. Only at this stage did participants report feeling a tingle.

Because we never have the same conscious experience on two separate occasions, the same number of neurons will never be stimulated to exactly the same extent or in exactly the same way more than once. Greenfield's model, therefore, needs a neuronal mechanism that can bias a large number of neurons to become activated simultaneously, and she believes that *neuromodulators* fit the bill. We saw in Chapter 4 that these chemicals 'prime' (*bias* or *modulate*) neurons for stimulation by neurotransmitters.

THE FUNCTIONS OF CONSCIOUSNESS: WHAT IS IT FOR?

Like perception, many cases of problem-solving seem to involve processes that are 'out of consciousness'. For example, solutions often seem to 'pop into our head' and we don't know how we reached them. If what's important is the solution (as opposed to the process involved in reaching it), then consciousness may be seen as incidental to information processing (consistent with Nisbett and Wilson's view). But while perception and other basic cognitive and behavioural processes may not *require* consciousness, they're at least usually *accompanied by* consciousness. Assuming that most other species lack our kind of consciousness, then we can infer that it evolved in human beings for some purpose.

ASK YOURSELF...
- From an evolutionary perspective, what advantages do you think (self-)consciousness might have conferred on human beings?
- What does it allow you to do in relation to other people?

The complexity of our nervous system, which makes our consciousness possible, provided our ancestors with the flexibility of behaviour that helped them survive. However, it's less obvious whether consciousness was itself adaptive or simply a side-effect or by-product of a complex nervous system. Some psychologists and biologists believe that consciousness is a powerful agent for controlling behaviour, which has evolved *in its own right*. Accordingly, non-conscious problem-solving systems are seen as the *servants of consciousness* (Ruch, 1984).

Box 7.4 Evolution of the 'inner eye'

- Humphrey (1986, 1993) argues that if consciousness (what he calls the 'inner eye') is the answer to anything at all, it must be to a biological challenge that human beings have had to meet, namely the human need to understand, respond to and manipulate the behaviour of other human beings:

> *... The first use of human consciousness was – and is – to enable each human being to understand what it feels like to be human and so to make sense of himself and other people from the inside. (Humphrey, 1993)*

- This inner eye allowed our ancestors to raise social life to a new level, so that consciousness is essential for human social activity. We are natural psychologists in a way that species lacking consciousness cannot be (see Gross, 2003b).

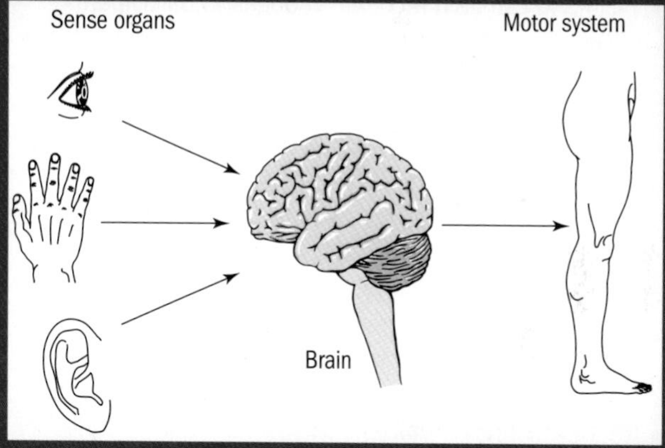

Figure 7.2a How an animal without insight works (from Humphrey, 1986)

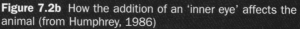

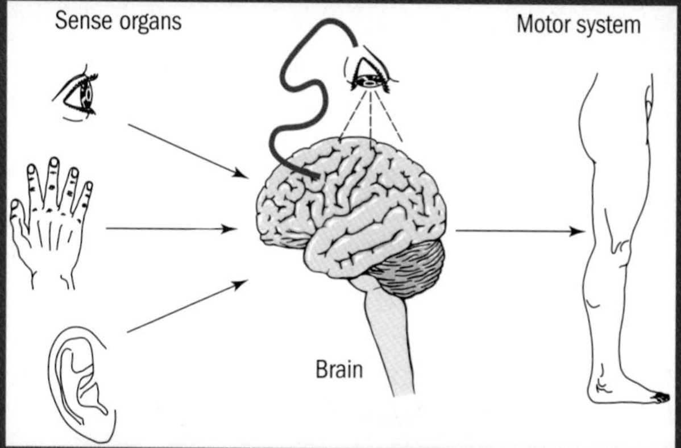

Figure 7.2b How the addition of an 'inner eye' affects the animal (from Humphrey, 1986)

According to Hilgard's (1974) *'neo-dissociation' theory of hypnosis* (see Gross, 2003a), the consciousness which solves a problem may be different from that which reports the solution: neither is 'higher' or 'lower' than the other – they're simply different. This is consistent with work on *split-brain patients*. As we saw in Chapter 3, some psychologists believe that the two cerebral hemispheres are specialised (although they share the potential for many functions and both participate in most psychological activities), so that each is dominant with respect to particular functions.

Ornstein (1986) believes that these two modes of operation represent two distinct modes of consciousness. In daily life, we normally just alternate between them and, although they might complement each other, they don't readily substitute for one another (as when you try to describe a spiral staircase or how you tie a shoelace). Is there any evidence to support these claims?

KEY STUDY 7.2 Alpha rhythms and hemispheric lateralisation (Galin & Ornstein, 1972, cited in Ornstein, 1986)

- Galin and Ornstein recorded changes in participants' EEGs when presented with either verbal or spatial tasks.
- On verbal tasks, *alpha rhythms* (associated with a waking adult with the eyes closed) in the *right* hemisphere *increased* relative to the left, while on spatial tasks, the reverse was true.
- The appearance of alpha rhythms indicates a 'turning off' of information processing in the area of the brain involved. So, on verbal tasks, information processing is being turned off in the right hemisphere. This is the side of the brain not being used (as if to reduce the interference between the two conflicting modes of operation of the two hemispheres).
- Similarly, people with damage to the left hemisphere have greater problems with consciously executed writing, while those with right hemisphere damage have greater problems with more automatic writing, such as signing their name.
- This suggests that the left hemisphere may be more involved in highly conscious processes that require intentional behaviour and the focusing of attention. The right may be more involved with automatic or unconscious actions, and more sensitive to material outside the conscious focus of attention.

CONSCIOUSNESS AND THE ELECTROENCEPHALOGRAM (EEG)

As we saw in Chapter 4, a major method (since the 1930s) of studying the working of the brain is to monitor its electrical activity. Exactly the same information can be used to throw light on consciousness, because particular patterns of electrical activity are correlated with other measures of arousal and alertness.

Electroencephalography (literally, 'electric-in-head writing') detects the output of minute electrical 'ripples', caused by changes in the electrical charges in different parts of the brain (usually the synchronised activity of large groups of neurons). Although there are characteristic patterns common to all individuals of a particular age or developmental stage, individuals' brain activity is as unique and distinctive as their fingerprints.

The electroencephalogram (EEG) has wires, an amplifier, electromagnetic pens and paper revolving on a drum. One end of each wire is attached to the scalp (with the help of special jelly) and the other to the amplifier, which can register impulses of 100 microvolts (1/10,000 of a volt) or less and magnifies them a million times. The impulses are traced on paper by pens and appear as rows of oscillating waves.

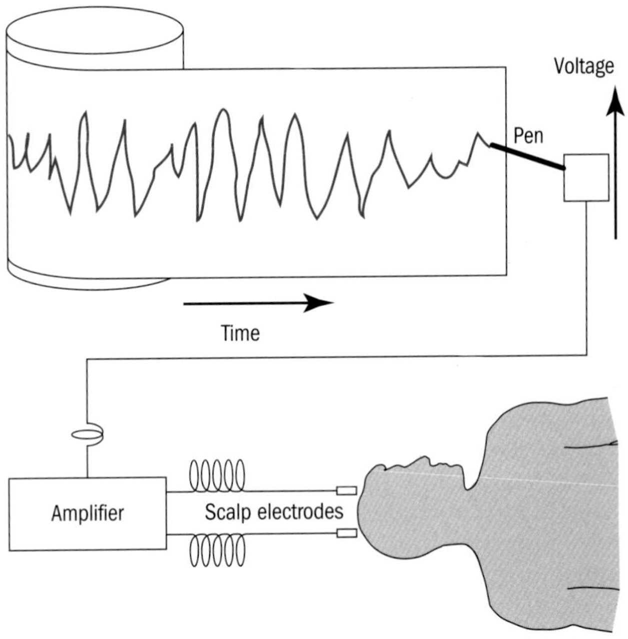

Figure 7.3 Schematic diagram of EEG recording (from Figure 3.20, page 87, from *Psychology*, third edition, by Henry Gleitman. Copyright © 1991, 1986, 1981 by W.W. Norton & Company, Inc. Used by permission of W.W. Norton & Company, Inc.)

The waves vary in frequency and amplitude.

- *Frequency* is measured as the number of oscillations per second – the more oscillations, the higher the frequency. One complete oscillation is a cycle, and the frequency is expressed as cycles per second (cps) or hertz (Hz).
- *Amplitude* is measured as half the height from the peak to the trough of a single oscillation. Frequency is the more important of the two measures.

Box 7.5 The four major types of brain wave (measured in frequency)

- **Delta (1–2 Hz):** found mainly in infants, sleeping adults or adults with brain tumours
- **Theta (3–7 Hz):** found mainly in children aged two to five years, and in psychopaths (see Chapter 46); may be induced by frustration
- **Alpha (8–12 Hz):** found mainly in adults who are awake, relaxed and whose eyes are closed; most reliably recorded from the back of the scalp
- **Beta (13 Hz and over):** found mainly in adults who are awake and alert, whose eyes are open, and who may be concentrating on some task or other; most reliably recorded from the middle of the scalp, and related to activity in the somatosensory and motor cortex

(See Table 7.1, page 115.)

Computerised electroencephalography has recently been used to detect evoked potentials, minute voltage changes induced in the brain by fairly specific visual and auditory stimuli. Often the average of a number of responses to similar kinds of stimuli is used – the *average evoked potential* (AEP) – in order to amplify the signal-to-noise ratio. AEPs are used to study newborns, some children with learning problems, patients in a coma, stroke victims, tumour patients and patients with multiple sclerosis. However, for certain brain conditions, brain scanning has largely replaced the EEG (Diagram Group (1982): see Chapter 4).

SLEEP

Sleep and the circadian rhythm

ASK YOURSELF...

- Blakemore (1988) asks what would happen if we removed all the external cues to the nature of time (*Zeitgebers*), both natural (day and night) and manufactured (clocks, mealtimes).
- Would our bodies still have their own rhythmic existence?

CASE STUDY 7.1: Siffre and the 25-hour day

- In 1972, Michel Siffre, a young French cave explorer, spent seven months underground with no cues as to the time of day.
- He had adequate food, water, books and exercise equipment, and his only contact with the outside world was via a telephone that was permanently staffed. He was linked up to a computer and video camera, by which scientists on the surface could monitor his physiological functions and state of mind.
- He organised his life into a fairly normal pattern of alternating periods of activity and sleep, and his 'day' was broken up by a normal meal pattern.
- The remarkable finding was that he chose to live a 25-hour day (not 24). For every real day that passed, he rose an hour later – the clock in his brain was running a little slow.

(Source: Blakemore, 1988)

According to Blakemore (1988):

> For all the advances of modern society, we cannot afford to ignore the rhythms of the animal brain within us, any more than we can neglect our need to breathe or eat. Without the biological clocks in our brains, our lives would be chaotic, our actions disorganized. The brain has internalized the rhythms of Nature, but can tick on for months without sight of the sun ...

Most animals display a *circadian rhythm* (from the Latin *circa dies* = 'about one day'). This is a periodicity or rhythmical alternation of various physiological and behavioural functions, synchronised to the 24-hour cycle of light and dark. So, during a 24-hour period, there's a cycle of several physiological functions (heart rate, metabolic rate, breathing rate, body temperature, hormonal secretion, urine excretion, immune function, alertness, and so on), which all tend to reach maximum values during the late afternoon and early evening, and minimum values in the early hours of the morning. (The disruption of circadian rhythms is discussed in Chapter 12 as a source of stress.)

The internal or biological clock

Rats, like humans, have an inherent rhythm of about 25 hours, which dictates their cycle of sleep and waking if they're put in the dark. This internal clock is as reliable and regular as most manufactured ones – the rhythm deviates by no more than a few minutes over several months. So how is the internal (biological) clock reset each day to the cycle of the real world, and where is the 'clock' to be found?

It's thought to be a tiny cluster of neurons, the *suprachiasmatic nucleus* (SCN), situated in the medial hypothalamus. For example, damage to the SCN in rats produces complete disappearance of the circadian rhythm: the sleep–wake cycle, eating and drinking, hormone secretion, and so on, become completely random during the course of the 24-hour period. Most of what's known about the SCN is based on experiments with non-human animals using ablation (see Chapter 4), and we cannot make direct electrophysiological recordings from the human brain. But anatomical studies show that humans have an SCN (Empson, 1993). The function of the SCN is to synchronise all the bodily functions that are governed by the circadian rhythm.

The SCN is situated directly above the optic chiasma (the junction of the two optic nerves en route to the brain: see Chapter 5). A tuft of thin nerve fibres branches off from the main nerve and penetrates the hypothalamus above, forming synaptic connections with cells in the SCN. This anatomically insignificant pathway is the link between the outside world and the brain's own clock (Blakemore, 1988). So the retina projects directly onto the SCN, which ensures that the sleep–wake cycle is tuned to the rhythm of night and day. If this connection with the retina is severed, the cycle goes 'haywire'.

The effects of disrupting the biological clock

So, in human adults at least, it appears that the circadian rhythm doesn't depend primarily on external cues, although it's surprisingly easy to outsmart our body clock by external means such as alarm clocks.

> **ASK YOURSELF…**
> • What is an average night's sleep for you?
> • Is that as much as you really need?
> • If not, what ill effects are you experiencing?

According to Melton (2000), scientists are warning that we ignore our natural bodily rhythms at our peril:

… Fighting our natural sleep tendencies … may be grinding away at our health, triggering a string of maladies … Giving up the late nights and weekend lie-ins in favour of a strict daily routine and a regular bedtime might be as important to our health as quitting smoking or cutting back on saturated fat.

So, how much sleep do we need?

We're biologically ill prepared to function on minimal sleep: our prehistoric genetic blueprint for sleep hasn't evolved fast enough to keep up with the pace of twenty-first-century life. Humans are more likely to need an average of ten hours of sleep a night than the four that Margaret Thatcher famously claimed to get by on. In the sleep laboratory, people who average eight hours a night, and maintain they're fully alert during the day, and who then get an extra hour's sleep at night, find their productivity levels increase by 25 per cent.

It's been suggested that each of us maintains a personal sleep bank account. We need enough sleep in the account to be able to function properly during the day. This means at least eight hours for most people, in order to cancel out the sleep debt incurred by 16 hours of continuous alertness. Similarly, Dement (2000), one of the pioneers of sleep research and the founder of the world's first sleep disorders centre (see below), proposes a rough rule of thumb: most people require about an hour's sleep for every two waking hours.

Whatever happened to lunch-breaks? Our work-hungry society demands that we eat at our work-stations

CRITICAL DISCUSSION 7.1: Are children getting enough sleep?

· Four-year-olds are thought to need about 12 hours' sleep per night, seven-year-olds ten hours, and ten-year-olds eight hours.
· Many children regularly sleep one or two hours' less than recommended.
· Part of the blame is the extended use of computer games, PCs and television in children's bedrooms – enjoyed by 67 per cent of four- to ten-year-olds in the UK.
· One American study has linked disturbed sleep among 11–13-year-olds to increased rates of depression and low self-esteem, and reduced academic performance.
· An Italian study reported that reduced sleep in children aged 14 and under was associated with an 86 per cent increase in the risk of accidents and injury.

Late-night viewing can be a health risk for children

We're living in a *sleep-deprived society* (Griffey, 2004; Williams, 1998). For example, in the past 20 years, we've added about 158 hours to our annual working and commuting time – equal to a full month of working hours. (The British work longer hours than any other nation in Europe.) Young mothers with children have added an astonishing 241 hours since the 1960s (see Chapter 38). According to the National Sleep Survey (2004), we have just 6.5 hours' sleep per night (rather than eight), although the almost 2000 respondents were mainly younger than in other surveys. This is more than two hours less than our grandparents slept every night. In our 24-hour society, the pace of life is becoming faster and harder, and the stresses and pressures of work are leading to longer working hours and disrupted sleep. But, as Griffey (2004) says:

> ... sleep isn't a social inconvenience, it's a physical necessity and more and more studies are showing that sleep deprivation is a growing problem ...

How does sleep deprivation produce negative effects on health?

Dement (2000) believes that most of us carry a heavy 'sleep debt', a deficit of sleep built up over days, weeks and months. Sleep debt is dangerous, and potentially lethal. Examples are drivers who fall asleep at the wheel, pilots who are too sleepy to land planes safely, and surgeons who botch surgical procedures because they're exhausted. Both the *Exxon Valdez* and the *Challenger* space shuttle disasters were attributed to human error caused by extreme sleep deprivation. Dement also links high blood pressure, heart attacks and strokes to *sleep apnoea*, a chronic failure to sleep well because of problems breathing during sleep.

According to Melton (2000), reduced sleep can interfere with the regulation of the *immune system* (see Chapter 12). Griffey (2004) reports on the findings of several studies showing why sleep deprivation is so harmful. The metabolic and endocrine changes resulting from a significant sleep debt mimic many of the hallmarks of ageing. Chronic sleep loss could not only speed up the onset, but could also increase the severity of age-related diseases such as diabetes, hypertension, obesity and memory loss. This might happen through chronic increases in the level of cortisol. This is a stress-related hormone, which in large quantities acts as neurotoxin, killing billions of brain cells. It's also associated with increased risk of heart disease (again see Chapter 12). Shift workers are especially at risk.

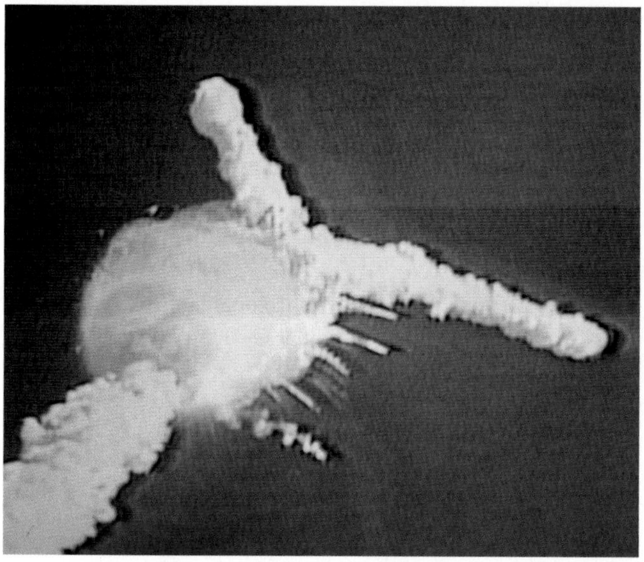

The 1986 *Challenger* space shuttle exploding on live TV, killing all seven astronauts on board

Box 7.6 Are you a lark or an owl?

- Larks (*morning types/early birds*) wake early, ready to face the day, while owls (*night-adepts/night-birds*) wake later, struggle to wake up, and stay up later at night.
- There's some evidence that owls' circadian rhythms are longer than 24 hours, while larks' cycles are much closer to the 'classic' 24 hours (but see Case Study 7.1). Only 5–10 per cent of the population falls at either end of this spectrum, with most of us falling somewhere in between.
- Nevertheless, morning types endure the punishing schedule of late shifts better, and suffer fewer physical problems than evening types. Why? The crucial factor is how easily a person's body clock can be reset. Because morning people's clocks are stable and need no tuning – they're almost exactly 24 hours – even on shifts the clock remains constant.
- These findings suggest that night workers should try to orient their whole life towards being a daytime person, who just occasionally stays up all night to work. Shifts should be broken into units of just a few days to minimise circadian disruption. For example, working two successive nights is preferable to working four or five in a row. By contrast, most *chronobiologists* (those who study biological rhythms) recommend that the way to maintain alertness and reduce the risk of accidents is to try adapting the body clock to suit fully the new work pattern, making shift changes less frequent, not more (see Chapter 12). According to Folkard (in Melton, 2000):

> *People have to accept that they are designed to be members of a daytime species ... Asking people to work at night is a bit like throwing them in the sea and asking them to be aquatic for a week. It is possible, but we are not designed to do it, so there are risks.*

(Source: based on Melton, 2000)

ASK YOURSELF...

- Are you a lark or an owl?
- Has this changed as you've got older?
- What are the advantages and disadvantages of being what you are?

The physiology of sleep

When darkness falls, the eyes indirectly inform the *pineal gland* (the 'third eye'). This is a tiny structure at the top of the brainstem, which keeps track of the body's natural cycles and registers external factors such as light and darkness. The pineal gland secretes *melatonin* in response to darkness, making us drowsy. Downing (1988) calls melatonin 'nature's sleeping draught'. Melatonin is a hormone that affects brain cells, which produce serotonin, concentrated in the *raphe nuclei* (situated near the pons), and these secrete a substance that acts on the RAS to induce light sleep. Jouvet (1967) found that lesions of the raphe nuclei in cats produced severe insomnia, and naturally occurring lesions in humans seem to have a very similar effect.

Another important sleep centre is the *locus coeruleus* (LC), a tiny structure on each side of the brainstem, whose cells are rich in noradrenaline, thought to be involved in inducing active (or rapid eye movement/REM) sleep (see below). The LC may well serve many of the functions previously attributed to the RAS. Studies with rats suggest that the LC regulates the animal's level of *vigilance* to environmental stimuli (Empson, 1993).

There's also evidence that a substance called *factor S* accumulates gradually in the brains of animals while they're awake. If this is removed from the fluid surrounding the brain and transferred into another animal, sleep will be induced. It's likely that factor S contributes to our feelings of sleepiness (Diagram Group, 1982).

Varieties of sleep and the ultradian rhythm

In the typical sleep laboratory, a volunteer settles down for the night with not only EEG wires attached, but also wires from an electro-oculogram (EOG) ('oculo' meaning eye) and an electromyogram (EMG) ('myo' meaning muscle).

A typical night's sleep comprises a number of *ultradian cycles* (lasting approximately 90 minutes), and each cycle consists of a number of stages.

The cycle then goes into reverse, so we re-enter stage 3 and then stage 2, but instead of re-entering stage 1, a different kind of sleep (*active sleep*) appears. Pulse and respiration rates increase, as does blood pressure, and all three processes become less regular. EEGs begin to resemble those of the waking state, showing that the brain is active, supported by increases in oxygen consumption, blood flow and neural firing in many brain structures. But it's even *more* difficult to wake us from this kind of sleep than the deep stage 4 sleep, which is why it's called *paradoxical sleep* (Aserinsky & Kleitman, 1953).

Another characteristic of active sleep is the rapid eye movements (the eyeballs moving back and forth, up and down, together) under the closed lids (hence *rapid eye movement* (REM) *sleep*). Finally, while the brain may be very active, the body isn't. REM sleep is characterised by muscular paralysis (especially the muscles of the arms and legs), so that all the tossing and turning and other typical movements associated with sleep in fact only occur during stages 1–4 (non-rapid eye movement/NREM sleep). The distinction between REM and NREM sleep was originally made by Dement & Kleitman (1957).

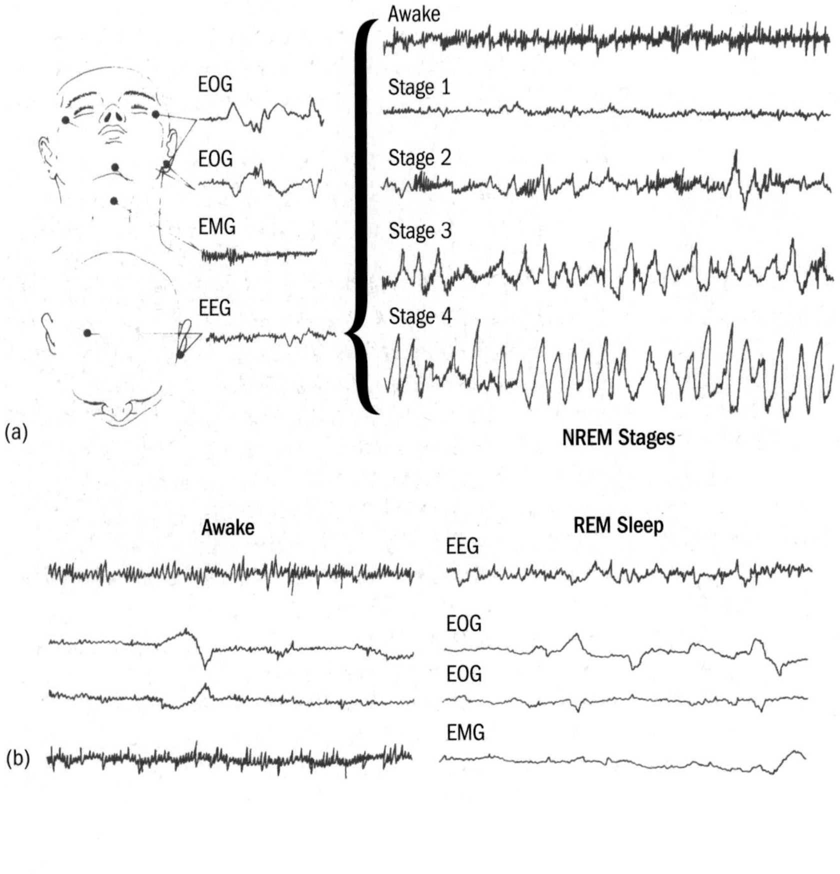

Figure 7.4 Comparison of physiological measures for different types of sleep. (a) The non-rapid eye movement (NREM) stages are represented in typical order of appearance; in reality each one gradually blends into the next. (b) Rapid eye movement (REM) sleep is in some ways similar to waking but in others quite different; the EEG is more similar to waking than to that of any NREM stage and REMs are present, but the body muscles are deeply inhibited

Table 7.1 A typical night's sleep: The four stages of non-rapid eye movement (NREM) sleep

After we shut our eyes and prepare to sleep, alpha waves begin to punctuate the high frequency beta waves of active wakefulness. The transition from being awake to entering stage 1 sleep is called the *hypnagogic period*, and is sometimes included in stage 1.
Stage 1: When we first fall asleep, the EEG is irregular and lacks the pattern of alpha waves which characterises the relaxed waking state. At first there's a reduction in frequency of alpha waves, which are then replaced by low voltage, slow theta waves, accompanied by slow rolling eye movements. Heart rate begins to slow down, the muscles relax, but we can still be woken up easily.
Stage 2: This is a deeper state of sleep, but we can still be woken fairly easily. The EEG shows bursts of activity called sleep spindles (one– to two–second waxing and waning bursts of 12–14 Hz waves). There are also occasional sharp rises and falls in amplitude of the whole EEG (*K complexes*), which last up to two seconds.
Stage 3: Sleep becomes deeper, the spindles disappear and are replaced by long, slow delta waves for up to 50 per cent of the EEG record. We're now quite unresponsive to external stimuli, and so it's difficult to wake us up. Heart rate, blood pressure and body temperature all continue to drop.
Stage 4: We now enter delta sleep (deep or 'quiet sleep': 50 per cent and more of the record consists of delta waves) and will spend up to 30 minutes in stage 4. About an hour has elapsed since stage 1 began. As in stage 3, it's difficult to wake us, unless something happens that's of great personal significance (such as our baby crying).
Stages 2–4 collectively are called *slow-wave sleep (SWS)*. As we pass from stages 1 to 4, the frequency of the waves decreases, and the amplitude/voltage increases. Also, muscle tone steadily declines.

Another feature of REM sleep is the appearance of *pontine-geniculo-occipital* (PGO) *spikes/waves*, which are generated in the pons and travel through the lateral geniculate nucleus (LGN: see Chapter 5). These were discovered by Jouvet working with cats in the 1960s. PGO spikes typically occur in bursts, often preceding individual eve movements. According to the activation-synthesis model of dreaming (see below), PGO activity is the prime source of dreaming experience (Empson, 1993).

> *ASK YOURSELF...*
> • Construct a summary table of differences between REM and NREM sleep.

After 15 minutes or so in REM sleep, we re-enter NREM sleep (stages 2–4), and so another ultradian cycle begins. However, with each 90-minute cycle (of which there are four to five on average per night), the duration of the REM sleep *increases* and that of NREM sleep *decreases*. The first cycle normally provides the deepest sleep and the shortest REM period. As the night goes on, we spend relatively more time in REM and less in NREM sleep. In later cycles, it's quite common to go from REM to stage 2, and then straight back into REM sleep (bypassing stages 3 and 4). Natural waking usually occurs during a period of REM sleep.

According to Empson (1993):

> While most all-night recording experiments are over brief periods (of up to a week), some very extended studies have been done and there is no evidence that the patterns of sleep we observe over short periods (after the first night) are in any way peculiar to the unfamiliarity of the laboratory environment.

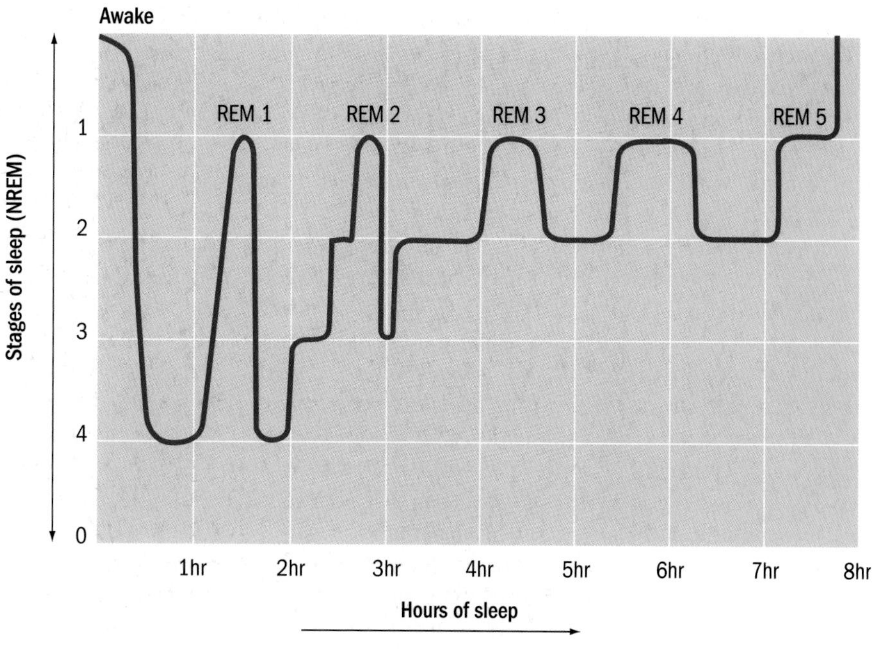

Figure 7.5 A typical night's sleep (note the disappearance of stages 3 and 4 and the relative increase in the length of REM periods)

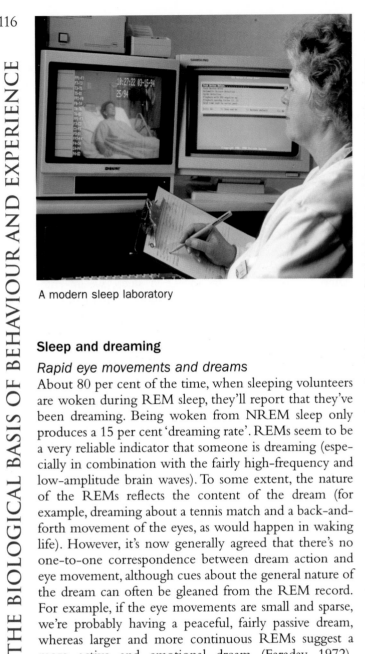

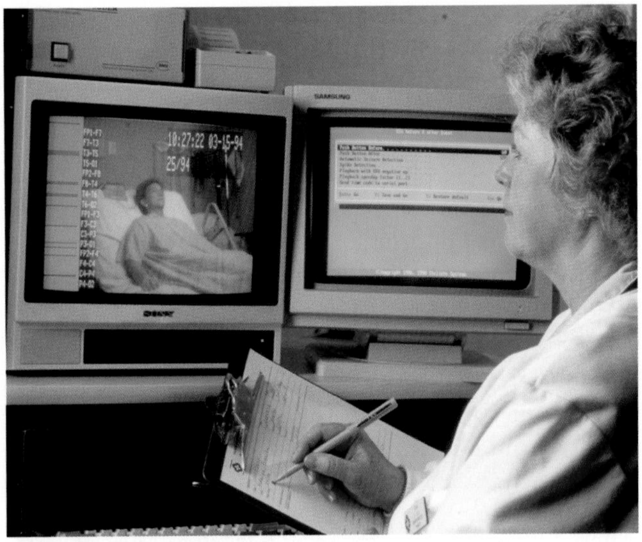

A modern sleep laboratory

Sleep and dreaming

Rapid eye movements and dreams

About 80 per cent of the time, when sleeping volunteers are woken during REM sleep, they'll report that they've been dreaming. Being woken from NREM sleep only produces a 15 per cent 'dreaming rate'. REMs seem to be a very reliable indicator that someone is dreaming (especially in combination with the fairly high-frequency and low-amplitude brain waves). To some extent, the nature of the REMs reflects the content of the dream (for example, dreaming about a tennis match and a back-and-forth movement of the eyes, as would happen in waking life). However, it's now generally agreed that there's no one-to-one correspondence between dream action and eye movement, although cues about the general nature of the dream can often be gleaned from the REM record. For example, if the eye movements are small and sparse, we're probably having a peaceful, fairly passive dream, whereas larger and more continuous REMs suggest a more active and emotional dream (Faraday, 1972). According to Faraday, research has shown that movements of the inner ear also occur during sleep and may be correlated with the auditory content of dreams.

Not only is there a difference in the number of times that dreams are reported when participants are woken from REM and NREM ('orthodox') sleep, the kind of mental activity associated with each is very different. Participants woken from NREM sleep tend to report dreams that are shorter, less vivid and less visual than REM dreams; in fact, they often describe themselves as having been 'thinking' rather than dreaming. NREM sleep is also associated with sleepwalking (somnambulism), sleeptalking and some types of nightmare.

REM sleep has been called 'dream sleep' or the 'D-state' and some have gone as far as to call it the 'third state of existence', because in many ways it's as different from NREM sleep (the 'S-state') as it is from waking. This leads us to ask why we need to dream.

Box 7.7 Are REM dreams simply more easily recalled?

- Is it possible that the difference between dreams in REM and NREM sleep is actually an artefact of the ability to recall dreams following the 'rude awakening'?
- Beaumont (1988) argues that being woken from NREM sleep may lead to the dream being forgotten before the participant is sufficiently awake to report it (since this is a deeper kind of sleep in which the brain is much less active).
- By contrast, being woken from REM sleep may allow the ongoing dream to be remembered and then reported (here the brain is much more active).
- Clearly, if this is so, then we've stumbled upon a major confounding variable that challenges the very basis of much of the sleep/dream research. An appreciable amount of mental activity occurs during NREM sleep, and there are no completely consistent differences between dream reports obtained when participants are woken from either kind of sleep.
- However, evidence from studies of *sleep deprivation* seems to support the view of REM sleep as a dream-state sleep quite independently of the sleeper's report of having dreamed (or not).

The effects of sleep deprivation

As far as rats are concerned, long-term sleep deprivation is definitely not good for their health: it causes impaired thermoregulation, metabolic dysfunction and eventually death (Hobson, 1995). For example, Rechtschaffen *et al.* (1989a, 1989b) selectively deprived rats of either REM or both REM and NREM sleep. After a week of total deprivation, they showed progressive weight loss despite increased food intake. This became more pronounced after two weeks, and after four weeks they died. During this time, body weight plummeted, while food consumption soared and body temperature became progressively more unstable.

In the case of human beings, studies have been remarkably consistent in failing to show any marked changes in heart and breathing rates, blood pressure, skin conduction, body temperature, EMG or EEG, even when deprivation continues for up to 200 hours (Pinel, 1993). But as we saw above (page 113), this is very different from the *chronic* sleep deprivation that is symptomatic of our modern (western) lifestyle.

Webb & Bonnet (1979) limited participants to two hours' sleep on one particular night; they suffered no ill effects the following day, but that night they fell asleep more quickly and slept longer than usual. Longer periods of sleep deprivation may result in some unpleasant psychological effects, but people are remarkably able to do without sleep. Webb and Bonnet gradually reduced the length of sleep in a group of volunteers from eight to four hours per night over a two-month period, with no detectable effect.

Box 7.8 The REM rebound

- When sleep is *abruptly* reduced (as, for example, in the case of hospital doctors, who may be on duty for 50 hours at a stretch), the effects are rather more serious. These effects include irritability, intellectual inefficiency, and an intense fatigue and need for sleep.
- These effects mirror those produced by depriving participants of approximately two hours of REM sleep (but otherwise allowing them to sleep normally). The following night, there's an increase in REM sleep (to compensate for the previous night's loss). This is called the *REM rebound*.
- When volunteers are able to get by on greatly (but gradually) reduced amounts of sleep, it's apparently because they pack their two hours of REM tightly into their sleeping time (thus reducing the amount of NREM sleep in between their dreams). When sleep is abruptly reduced, there's no time to adopt this alternative dreaming-sleep pattern.

What evidence is there for the REM rebound?

- Dement (1960) woke participants from their REM sleep on five successive nights (while those in a control group were only woken during NREM sleep periods). When they were allowed to sleep uninterruptedly, they did 60 per cent more dreaming until they'd made up their lost REM time. For as many as five nights following their REM deprivation, they spent more time in REM sleep than usual, and on some nights they doubled their REM time.

Theories of sleep

According to Blakemore (1988):

> Our planet is a dangerous place; there is ruthless competition for limited resources and only the fittest survive. And yet all the most advanced animals, normally alert, shrewd, watchful, drop their defences to sleep. Even human beings, the most spectacularly successful species, spend one-third of their lives more or less paralysed and senseless. If sleep is so risky, it must bestow a huge benefit on animals that indulge in it, or it would have been eliminated by the powerful forces of natural selection. Animals that did not need sleep would surely have evolved and prevailed over their sleepy competitors ... sleep must surely be valuable ... (Blakemore, 1988)

Empson (1993) maintains that even though physiologists have made great strides in understanding sleep mechanisms, this hasn't greatly helped in understanding what sleep is for. While sleep has the features of a primary drive (such as hunger and sex), what makes it unique as a primary biological drive is that the need for sleep is reflected in *decreased levels of arousal*, and its satisfaction is associated with further decreases. Sleep, therefore, represents a serious exception to the view that organisms seek a single optimal level of (non-specific) arousal (Lloyd *et al.*, 1984: see Chapter 9).

The restoration theory

Oswald (1966) maintains that both REM and NREM sleep serve a restorative, replenishing function. NREM restores bodily processes that have deteriorated during the day, while REM sleep is a time for replenishing and renewing brain processes, through the stimulation of protein synthesis.

Box 7.9 REM sleep and the developing brain

- Restoration theory helps explain the large proportion of babies' sleeping time spent in REM sleep.
- During much of their first year, babies are sleeping for about 18 hours per 24, and by about 12 months they have two periods of sleep every 24 hours (one during the day and one at night). Not until about five years has an 'adult' pattern become established, probably as a result of both environmental and maturational factors.
- Within these changing patterns, the relative proportions of REM and NREM sleep change quite dramatically. Whereas newborns spend half their 18 hours in REM sleep, adults usually spend only one-quarter of their eight hours in REM sleep.
- The developing brain needs a great deal of protein synthesis for cell manufacture and growth, and REM sleep helps to achieve this.

An evaluation of restoration theory

- Patients who survive drug overdoses and withdrawal, and other brain 'insults', such as intensive electroconvulsive therapy (see Chapter 45), experience prolonged increases in REM sleep. These increases are consistent with the estimated time for the half-life of proteins in the brain – that is, in a six-week period, about half the brain's total protein is replaced, and this is the approximate length of the increased REM period.
- Nocturnal secretion of growth hormone (which produces bodily protein synthesis) depends on uninterrupted stage 4 sleep. In adults, a chronic lack of normal stage 4 is found in fibrositis sufferers, whose EEG during sleep is characterised by 'alpha-delta' patterns, a mixture of sleeping and waking EEG (typically experienced as fitful, 'unrestorative sleep'). The disturbance of stage 4 in healthy volunteers produces the symptoms of fibrositis.
- According to Empson (1993), all this evidence is consistent with a general *anabolic function* for sleep: REM sleep underlies brain growth, repair and

memory functions, and slow-wave (stage 4) sleep promotes bodily growth and repair. However, cell repair goes on 24 hours a day (even though it reaches a peak at night).

- A more serious objection is that REM sleep is an active state (at least as far as the brain is concerned), and probably burns up a substantial amount of energy. Indeed, blood flow to the brain *increases* during REM sleep, and this would actually *prevent* high levels of protein synthesis. In view of this kind of evidence, Oswald (1974) maintains that *both* types of sleep are involved in the process of restoring *bodily tissue*.
- However, Oswald may have been a little premature. According to Siegel (2003), although most brain cells are at least as active during REM sleep as in waking, there's a specific group of cells that goes against this trend. These are the cells that produce the monoamine neurotransmitters (noradrenaline, serotonin and histamine). These key neurotransmitters inhibit body movement and reduce awareness of the environment, and the cells that produce them stop discharging completely during REM sleep. This cessation of neurotransmitter release is vital for the functioning of these neurons and their receptors on recipient neurons. This interruption may allow the receptor systems to 'rest' and regain full sensitivity, which may be crucial during waking for mood regulation. The monoamines also play a part in rewiring the brain to respond to new experiences. So, turning them off during REM may help prevent changes in brain connections that might otherwise be 'accidentally' created as a consequence of the activation of other neurons during REM sleep. The REM rebound might result from the need to rest monoamine systems and other 'off' systems (Siegel, 2003).

Evolutionary theory

Different species characteristically sleep for different periods. Those at risk from predators, which cannot find a safe place to sleep, or which spend large parts of each day searching for and consuming food and water (such as herd animals), sleep very little (for example, zebras sleep for only two to three hours per day). Predators that sleep in safe places, and can satisfy their food and water needs fairly quickly, sleep for much of the day. Lions, for example, often sleep more or less continuously for two to three days after gorging themselves on a kill.

According to Meddis (1975), sleep is an advantage, because it keeps the animal immobilised for long periods, making it less conspicuous to would-be predators and, therefore, safer. The safer the animal from predators, the longer it's likely to sleep. Meddis also argues that the long sleep periods of babies have evolved to prevent exhaustion in their mothers and, in this sense, sleep is still functional – at least for mothers of babies and small children! As to the need for immobilisation, this no longer seems viable as an explanation of sleep in humans, and so may be regarded as a remnant of our evolutionary past.

An evaluation of evolutionary theory

- According to the theory, a preyed-upon species may sleep for *shorter* periods (because of the constant need to stay on guard against predators) as well as *longer* periods (because this makes it safer from predators). In other words, whatever sleep pattern a species has, it can be explained in 'evolutionary' terms – an example of *non-falsifiability* (see Chapter 3). This represents a serious limitation of evolutionary theory.
- Empson (1993) characterises Meddis's theory as a 'waste of time' theory. He believes that the fact that all animals sleep contradicts the theory, as does the finding that sleep deprivation can be fatal (Kleitman, 1927; Rechtschaffen *et al.*, 1989a, 1989b).
- A weaker version of the 'waste of time' theory was proposed by Horne (1988), who distinguishes between *core sleep* (which is necessary) and *optional sleep* (which isn't). Evidence from sleep deprivation experiments (both partial and total) shows that accumulated sleep 'debts' are made up to some extent on recovery nights, but never entirely. For example, REM rebound accounts for approximately 50 per cent of the REM sleep lost during selective awakenings. This suggests that only the first three hours of sleep are truly necessary (core sleep), and the rest is optional (having no physiological function).
- But most of us eat more than we absolutely need to in order to keep body and soul together, yet no biologist would say that because a proportion of feeding was optional that feeding was only partly functional (Empson, 1993). He concludes by saying:

> ... sleep appears to be ubiquitous and necessary; it is a complex function of the brain involving far-reaching changes in body physiology as well as brain physiology. It is difficult to believe that it does not have an important function and the restorative theories provide a coherent account of what this might be.

Hobson's levels

Although not a discrete theory, Hobson (1995) proposes that the function of sleep can be analysed at different levels.

- At the *behavioural level*, sleep suppresses activity at a time (night-time/darkness) when the chances of finding food or a mate are relatively low. Also, such activities have a high energy cost in warm-blooded animals when the temperature is low. This makes sleep behaviourally very efficient. In addition, the enforced nature of sleep and its relation to resting activity serves to unite animals in a family or pair-bonded situation, which may encourage sexual behaviour and promote the care and development of the young. Hobson finds it incredible that ethologists have failed to recognise and systematically study sleep as a form of behaviour (see Chapter 2).

- At the *developmental level*, a function of REM sleep for developing organisms could be the guaranteed activation of neural circuits underlying crucial, survival behaviours (see Box 7.9). From an evolutionary point of view, there would be great advantages gained from ensuring the organised activation of the complex systems of the brain before the organism has developed the ability to test them in the real world. In both the developing and the adult animal, REM sleep could constitute a form of *behavioural rehearsal*.
- At the *metabolic level*, the recurring cycles of NREM/REM sleep are accompanied by major changes in all the body's physiological systems. NREM sleep involves decreased blood pressure, heart and breathing rates, as well as the release of growth and sex hormones from the pituitary (consistent with the restoration theory), while REM sleep involves increased blood pressure, heart and breathing rates, as well as penile erection and clitoral engorgement.

DREAMING

> *ASK YOURSELF...*
> - From what we've described above about NREM and REM sleep, is it valid to say that dreaming and REM sleep are the same thing?
> - If subjective descriptions of a dream are correlated with various physiological, neurochemical and behavioural variables, can we then reduce or equate dreams with those variables?

Box 7.10 Why dreams and REM sleep aren't the same thing

- The correlation between dreams and REM sleep is real enough – but it isn't perfect. Earlier, we noted that (vivid) dreaming is reported from 80 per cent of REM awakenings, but only 15 per cent of NREM awakenings. Blackmore (2003) gives figures of 70–95 per cent and 5–10 per cent respectively. Mentation (mental activity) of some sort is reported in about 50 per cent of NREM awakenings. The figures vary according to the criteria used (Empson, 2001). So, being in REM sleep doesn't guarantee dreaming, and, conversely, dreaming can and does occur in NREM sleep.
- Human foetuses spend about 15 hours per day in REM sleep – but they couldn't be 'dreaming' (since experience of the world is the 'raw material' of dreams: see below).
- From what we know about REM sleep in other species, and from what we believe about their dreams and state of consciousness, we must conclude that dreaming and REM sleep aren't the same thing (Blackmore, 2003).

> *ASK YOURSELF...*
> - How do dreams differ from waking consciousness?

Although dreaming and REM sleep aren't the same thing, dreaming is associated with REM sleep, and psychologists have developed reliable techniques for establishing when someone is likely to be dreaming. But there's been no equivalent progress in understanding the *nature* of dreams. According to Empson (1993), a starting point must be to establish clearly how dreaming differs from waking consciousness. Empson identifies four such differences:

1. Dreams *happen to us* as opposed to being a product of our conscious control:

   > ... When dreaming we are the spectators of an unfolding drama, and only rarely does one have the impression of being in control ...

   Lucid dreaming, in which the dreamer 'knows' s/he is dreaming and decides how the dream plot should develop, is very rare.
2. The *logic* of waking consciousness is suspended (see Freud's theory, Chapter 42).
3. Dreams reported in the laboratory tend to be mundane and lack the *bizarre quality* of 'normal' dreams, probably because only the strangest experiences are remembered when we wake normally after a night's sleep.
4. Dreams have a *singlemindedness*: the imagery of the dream totally dominates the dreamer's consciousness. But when we're awake, we normally reflect on the stream of consciousness as it goes on, and can be aware of one thing but simultaneously imagine something else. (Recall that Greenfield, 1998, claims that waking consciousness is single-minded: see above, page 108).

Hobson (1995) describes dreams as typically including:

- *hallucinations* (predominantly visual, although auditory, tactile and movement sensations are also prominent, with taste and smell under-represented and pain extremely rare)
- *delusions* (believing that the events are real)
- *cognitive abnormalities* (such as the occurrence of events that would be physically impossible in the real world)
- *emotional intensification* and *amnesia* (we forget over 95 per cent of our dreams).

These characteristics have led to a comparison between dreams and abnormal states of mind, as in schizophrenia and organic mental disorders, in particular delirium (see Chapter 44).

Dorothea Tanning's *Eine Kleine Nacht Musik* (1944). The impossible nature of the imagery depicted in the painting is what gives dreams their distinctive flavour

Theories of dreaming

> *ASK YOURSELF...*
> - What's dreaming for?
> - Do dreams have a function of their own, or are they just an accompaniment to certain sleep states?
> - Why do we dream?

Reorganisation of mental structures

According to Ornstein (1986), REM sleep and dreaming may be involved in the reorganisation of our *schemas* (mental structures), so as to accommodate new information. People placed in a 'disturbing and perplexing' atmosphere for four hours just prior to sleep (asked to perform difficult tasks with no explanation) spend longer in REM sleep than normal. REM time also increases after people have had to learn complex tasks.

This may explain why REM sleep decreases with age. As we have seen, newborns spend 50 per cent of their (approximately) 18 hours of sleep in REM sleep compared with 25 per cent spent by adults in their (approximately) eight hours. Oswald suggested that babies' brains need to process and assimilate the flood of new stimuli pouring in from the outside world, and that this is (partly) achieved through REM sleep (see Box 7.9, page 117).

Activation-synthesis model (Hobson & McCarley, 1977; McCarley, 1983)

The cortex is highly active during REM sleep (*activation*), although it receives little external stimulation. While the motor cortex is highly active (generating activity that would normally produce bodily movement), these commands don't reach the muscles of the limbs but are 'switched off' at a 'relay station' at the top of the spinal column: we're effectively paralysed (*output blockade*).

Not only is the cortex isolated (unable to control muscles), but there's also inhibition of incoming signals produced by the sensory systems. Consequently, perceptions of the 'real' world are selectively attenuated (*input blockade*). Hindbrain and midbrain structures, normally associated with relaying sensory information to the cortex, spontaneously generate signals (*PGO waves*; see page 115) responsible for cortical activation. These are indistinguishable from signals that would normally have been relayed from the eyes/ears. This activity is under the control of a periodic triggering mechanism in the *pontine brainstem* (top of the spinal column, at the base of the brain).

Dreams are a conscious interpretation (*synthesis*) of all this activity. The cognitive system, which organises sensory information into the simplest meaningful interpretation when we're awake, processes all the internally generated signals as if they came from the outside world. In combination with oculomotor activity, PGO waves are sent to the visual and association cortex and the thalamus.

What we call a dream is the simplest way of interpreting these internally produced signals, by combining them into some meaningful whole. It's the unusual intensity and rapidity of brain stimulation (often involving simultaneous activation of areas not usually activated together during waking), which account for the highly changeable and sometimes bizarre content of dreams. According to Hobson (1995):

> ... the now autoactivated and autostimulated brain processes these signals and interprets them in terms of information stored in memory ...

Many dream experiences do seem to reflect the brain's and body's state, and so can be thought of as interpretations of these physical states. For example, being chased, locked up or frozen with fear may well reflect the blocked motor commands to the muscles. Floating, flying and falling experiences may reflect vestibular activation, and the sexual content of dreams may reflect clitoral engorgement and penile erection (Ornstein, 1986).

Evaluation of the activation-synthesis model

- In a sense, we dream instead of acting (perhaps suggesting the need for rest/restoration for the body). Cats with brainstem injury act out their dreams by, for example, chasing the mouse of their dreams while ignoring the real mouse in their cage: they aren't paralysed in the normal way during REM sleep.
- Crick & Mitchison (1983) proposed a modified version of the model, which they called *reverse learning*. The basic idea is that we dream in order to forget. The cortex (unlike other parts of the brain) is composed of richly interconnected neuronal networks. The problem with such a network system is that it malfunctions when there's overload of incoming information. To deal with such overload, the brain needs a mechanism to 'debug' or 'clean up' the network, and REM sleep is that mechanism. In this way, we awake with a cleaned-up network, and the

brain is ready for new input. According to Crick and Mitchison, trying to remember our dreams may not be a good idea: they are the very patterns of thought the system is trying to tune out.

- For others, especially psychoanalysts and other psychodynamic psychologists, it's *essential* that we do remember our dreams, so that we can try to understand their meaning. For example, Freud saw dreams are *wish fulfilments*. Both he and Jung saw *symbolism* as being of central importance in dreams, which put the dreamer in touch with parts of the self usually inaccessible during waking life (see Chapter 42). Hall (1966) saw dreams as 'a personal document, a letter to oneself' and, like Jung, advocated the study of *dream series*, rather than single, isolated dreams.

CONCLUSIONS: INTEGRATING NEUROBIOLOGICAL, EVOLUTIONARY AND PSYCHOLOGICAL ACCOUNTS OF DREAMING

Winson (1997), a neuroscientist, argues that neural and psychological theories of dreams are *not* mutually exclusive. While Crick and Mitchison argue that we need to forget our dreams, Winson claims that

> ... dreams may reflect a memory-processing mechanism inherited from lower species, in which information important for survival is reprocessed during REM sleep. This information may constitute the core of the unconscious.

To maintain sleep, locomotion had to be suppressed by inhibiting motor neurons. But suppressing *eye movements* wasn't necessary, because these don't disturb sleep. With the evolution of REM sleep, each species could process the information most needed for its survival (such as the location of food, and means of predation or escape). In REM sleep, this information may be re-accessed and integrated with past experience to provide an ongoing strategy for behaviour. Similarly, *threat simulation theory* (Revonso, 2000) claims that dreaming evolved to simulate the very real threats to individuals' physical survival (and hence to reproductive success) during human evolution. Ways of dealing with these threats could be 'practised' in dreams.

According to Humphrey (1986, 1993), dreams are also about practising all sorts of physical, intellectual and social skills ('dreaming as play'):

> Dreaming represents the most audacious and ingenious of nature's tricks for educating her psychologists ... (Humphrey, 1986)

It may be true that dreams are just an evolutionary 'epiphenomenon', without any adaptive function (Flanagan, 2000), and it may also be true that many people function perfectly well without remembering their dreams (Hobson, 2002). Nevertheless, we can still use dreaming in our waking lives:

> ... studying our own dreams can be valuable in all sorts of ways. They can reveal our inner motivations and hopes, help us face our fears, encourage growing awareness, and even be a source of creativity and insight ... (Blackmore, 2003)

CHAPTER SUMMARY

- Since the cognitive revolution dislodged behaviourism from its dominant position in psychology, cognitive processes and consciousness have once more become important areas of psychological research.
- Freud distinguished three levels of consciousness: **conscious**, **preconscious** and **unconscious**. Most psychologists do not accept Freud's view of the unconscious as based on repression, but they would accept that there is a **continuum of consciousness**.
- **Arousal/alertness** can be defined objectively in terms of various physiological measures, such as EEGs, EOGs, EMGs, breathing and heart rates. These are **correlates** of consciousness.
- Changes in **tonic alertness** are closely linked to various biological rhythms, especially the circadian rhythm. The RF/RAS plays an important role in arousing/maintaining consciousness. Alertness changes in fairly predictable ways both during wakefulness (controlled by a **diurnal rhythm**) and sleep (**ultradian rhythm**).
- Changes in **phasic alertness** involve changes in the **orienting response** to arousing stimuli. This is complemented by **habituation**, a form of adaptation. Human and non-human nervous systems have evolved such that they are especially responsive to **change**.
- Consciousness can be experimentally pinned down by studying **attention** (**focal** or **peripheral**). Perception seems to take place largely unconsciously, and many behaviours are carried out quite automatically, allowing us to attend consciously to the unfamiliar or threatening aspects of our environment.
- Nisbett and Wilson claim that all psychological activities are governed by processes that are not available to consciousness. However, Humphrey maintains that the 'inner eye' of consciousness evolved to allow our ancestors to relate to others based on understanding others' experience of being human.
- Most animals display a **circadian rhythm** synchronised to the 24-hour cycle of light and dark, involving a rhythmical alternation of various physiological and behavioural functions.
- The internal/**biological clock** is thought to be the **suprachiasmatic nucleus (SCN)**, part of the hypothalamus. The retina projects directly onto the SCN, ensuring that the sleep–wake cycle is tuned to the rhythm of night and day.
- When darkness falls, the **pineal gland** begins to secrete **melatonin**, making us drowsy. It affects brain cells that produce **serotonin** concentrated in the

raphe nuclei; these secrete a substance that acts on the RAS to induce light sleep. The **locus coeruleus (LC)** is rich in noradrenaline, which induces REM sleep.

- Modern living increases the likelihood that the circadian rhythm will be disrupted, and people are sleeping less than human beings are designed for by evolution. This is having harmful effects on people's mental and physical health.
- Sleep is measured in the laboratory using an **electrocephalogram (EEG)**, **electrooculogram (EOG)** and **electromyogram (EMG)**. A typical night's sleep comprises four to five **ultradian cycles**, each consisting of several stages. Stages 2–4 are collectively called **slow-wave sleep (SWS)** or 'deep' sleep; stages 1–4 are collectively called **non-rapid eye movement (NREM)** sleep.
- **Rapid eye movement (REM)** or **active** sleep replaces stage 1 at the beginning of the next cycle. Physiological processes increase and EEGs begin to resemble those of the waking state, yet it is more difficult to wake someone than from stage 4 sleep (making it **paradoxical**). With each ultradian cycle, the duration of REM sleep increases.
- Depriving people of REM sleep produces the **REM rebound**, suggesting that dreaming associated with REM sleep is perhaps the most important function of sleep. But psychologists are still very unclear about the functions of sleep. It is unique as a primary biological drive in that the need for sleep is reflected in **decreased** levels of arousal.
- According to Oswald's **restoration theory**, REM and NREM sleep help replenish bodily and brain processes respectively. However, the fact that cell repair goes on 24 hours a day, and that the brain is highly active during REM sleep, led Oswald to claim that *both* REM and NREM sleep are involved in restoration of bodily tissue.
- Meddis's **evolutionary theory** claims that sleep keeps the animal immobilised and so safer from predators, so longer sleep is associated with greater safety. But danger from predators is also associated with shorter sleep, because of the need to stay alert, and longer sleep is also characteristic of certain predators such as lions. This makes the theory **unfalsifiable**. **Hibernation theory** is a variant of evolutionary theory.
- According to the **activation-synthesis model**, dreams are the simplest way of interpreting all the internal, brain-produced signals that occur during REM sleep. This **activation** of the brain is consciously interpreted (**synthesis**) in the form of a dream. Psychological theories of dreams, such as those of Freud, Jung and Hall, focus on the synthesis component, stressing their significance for the dreamer.
- According to Crick and Mitchison's **reverse learning theory**, dreams are a way of 'cleaning up' the cortex's neural networks and preparing them for new input. So, we need to forget our dreams. Psychological theories, however, stress the need to remember them.
- Different theories of dreaming are *not* mutually exclusive. REM sleep may have evolved to help animals' biological survival, but they continue to serve a vital function for individuals, helping them to survive psychologically.

Links with other topics/chapters

- The distinction between conscious(ness) and self-conscious(ness)/self-awareness is crucial for understanding the *difference between humans and non-humans* (Chapters 1, 3 and 48). Self-awareness is a key feature of the *self-concept* and there's debate as to whether humans are the only primates who possess it (Chapter 33). This debate is also relevant when assessing attempts to teach language to chimpanzees and other non-human primates (Chapter 19).
- Definitions of consciousness are relevant to *attention and performance* (Chapter 13), and Freud's *psychoanalytic theory* (Chapters 2 and 42).
- Ways of measuring consciousness (in terms of arousal and alertness, sleep and dreams) involve methods used to study the *nervous system* in general (Chapter 4).
- Explanations of the functions of consciousness (including theories of sleep and dreams) often take an *evolutionary* perspective (Chapter 2).

8

SUBSTANCE DEPENDENCE AND ABUSE

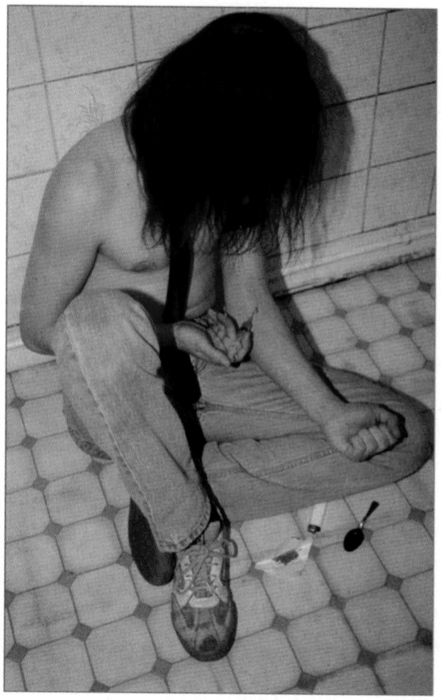

INTRODUCTION AND OVERVIEW

For thousands of years, people have taken substances to alter their perception of reality, and societies have restricted the substances their members are allowed to take. These substances, which we usually call drugs, are *psychoactive*, denoting a chemical substance that alters conscious awareness through its effect on the brain. Most drugs fit this definition. Some – for example, aspirin – are *indirectly* psychoactive: their primary purpose is to remove pain, but being headache-free lifts our mood. Others, however, are designed to change mood and behaviour. These are collectively referred to as *psychotherapeutic* drugs, such as those used in the treatment of anxiety, depression and schizophrenia (see Chapter 45).

This chapter is concerned with psychoactive drugs used to produce a temporarily altered state of consciousness for the purpose of *pleasure*. These include *recreational drugs*, which have no legal restrictions (such as alcohol, nicotine and caffeine), and *drugs of abuse*, which are illegal. However, just as recreational drugs can be abused (such as alcohol), so illegal drugs are taken recreationally (such as ecstasy). 'Substance abuse', therefore, doesn't imply particular types of drug, but refers to the extent to which the drug is used, and the effects – emotional, behavioural and medical – on the abuser.

What counts as a recreational drug or a drug of abuse changes over time within a society, as well as between societies. For example, cocaine had been freely available over the counter in a huge variety of tonics and pick-me-ups before the 1930s, and was an ingredient of the original blend of Coca-Cola in the 1890s. At that time, it was seen as a harmless stimulant (Plant, 1999); now it's a Class A drug. Conversely, in the UK cannabis was reclassified in 2004 from a Class B to a Class C drug (still illegal but seen as less dangerous and carrying a more lenient, if any, punishment). Its therapeutic (medical) use is likely to become legalised within three years (Bennetto, 2000). According to Veitia & McGahee (1995):

> Cigarette smoking and alcohol abuse permeate our culture and are widespread enough to be considered ordinary addictions ... The degree to which these drugs permeate our culture and the extent to which they are accepted by our society distinguish them from other addictive but illegal substances such as heroin and cocaine.

DEFINING ABUSE

The concept of addiction

> *ASK YOURSELF...*
> - What do you understand by the term 'addiction'?

Until recently, the study and treatment of drug problems were organised around the concept of *addiction*: people with drug problems have problems because they're addicted to the drug (Hammersley, 1999). Addicts are compelled by a physiological need to continue taking the drug, experience horrible physical and psychological symptoms when trying to stop, and will continue taking it despite these symptoms because of their addictive need. Their addiction will also change them psychologically for the worse, they will commit crimes to pay for the drug, neglect their social roles and responsibilities, and even harm the people around them. In addition, some drugs are considered inherently much more addictive than others (see below), and substance users can be divided into addicts and non-addicts.

Criticisms of the concept

- It's an oversimplification. Most professionals who deal with people with any kind of problem – medical, criminal, educational, social – will have seen many clients who aren't exactly addicts, but whose drug use seems to have contributed to, or worsened, their other problems (Hammersley, 1999).
- It's based on the *addiction-as-disease* model. While medical models such as this are generally persuasive, because they offer a diagnosis, definition and a pathology, they also appear to relieve the 'addict' of responsibility for his/her behaviour (Baker, 2000: see Chapter 43).

CRITICAL DISCUSSION 8.1: Limitations of the addiction-as-disease model

Sussman & Ames (2001) identify four major problems with this model.

1. *There's no independent means of verifying the existence of the disease*. In several conditions, the factors that produce certain symptoms can be assessed (for example, a viral infection can be measured through a throat culture, antibody production or high temperature). Also, the factors can be assessed independently of the resulting symptoms (for example, it can be established that high temperature is caused either by a poison, virus or bacterium).

   But with behavioural disorders it's often difficult to separate factors from symptoms (Davison & Neale, 1990). If the problem were merely one of *behaviour*, then no longer taking the drug would stop the problem. But relapse rates never fall to zero and are 65 per cent in the first year following treatment, halving each year after that. This is true regardless of the substance involved. High relapse rates imply underlying factors, but there are no independent measures of assessing the underlying factors.

   However, recent research evidence has thrown light on the 'addicted brain', and this might provide the independent assessment of underlying factors required by the disease model (see Research Update 8.1, page 126)
2. *Variation in disordered behavioural symptoms*. Behavioural symptoms may be defined as more or less disordered depending on the social context. For example, someone who gets drunk and obnoxious once a month may be seen as an alcoholic in a church-going community – but not in a college dorm. Also, drug abuse can be seen as falling somewhere on a continuum, rather than a binary (yes/no) state, which is often used to define a disease ('you're either an addict or you're not') (see Chapter 43). However, heart disease, for example, also falls along a continuum, which is why it can be 'missed' or misdiagnosed (even though there are objective tests that can detect it).

3. *Variation in behavioural symptoms may not reflect the same underlying processes*. For example, it's unclear whether or not a person who drinks alcohol very occasionally, or one who drinks heavily periodically, or one whose drinking is always out of control, are subject to the same underlying influences. In other words, there are many patterns of drug abuse, but it's unclear whether they all reflect the same cause.
4. *The aetiological factors for drug abuse as a behavioural disorder aren't known*. We don't know what makes people abuse drugs. If there's a common underlying cause, it's plausible that this has nothing to do with drug abuse behaviour. Indeed, drug abuse is associated with various problem behaviours, including crime, violence, sensation-seeking and poor diet, which may precede the abuse as a disease.

George Best, gifted footballer and famous alcoholic

According to Hammersley (1999), the more modern view is to see drug problems as two-fold: *substance abuse* and *substance dependence* (hence the title of this chapter). This view is adopted in the American Psychiatric Association's (2000) *Diagnostic and Statistical Manual of Mental Disorders* (DSM-IV-TR: see Boxes 8.1 and 8.2). 'Addiction' now usually refers to a field of study, covering substance use, abuse and dependence, rather than to a theory of why people become dependent.

Is there more to addiction than drugs?

ASK YOURSELF...
- What do terms such as 'workaholic', 'shopaholic' and 'chocaholic' tell you about the nature of addictive behaviour?
- Can you define addiction in a way that can cover such non-drug behaviours?
- What might they all have in common?

Rather than rejecting the concept of addiction, some researchers argue that the concept should be *broadened*, in order to cover certain recent forms of 'addictive' behaviour that don't involve chemical substances at all. According to Shaffer *et al.* (1989):

> Addictive behaviours typically serve the addict in the short run at the price of longer-term destructiveness. Physical dependence is not a requisite for addiction ... addictive behaviours organise the addict's life. All of life's other activities fit in the gaps that the addictive behaviour permits.

The addiction can be to a substance or an experience: shopping, gambling or eating (or abstaining from eating: see Chapter 44) could equally fit this definition. Drawing on current definitions of substance dependence, pathological gambling, and eating disorders, Walters (1999) suggests that addiction may be defined as 'the persistent and repetitious enactment of a behaviour pattern', which includes:

- *progression* (increase in severity)
- *preoccupation* with the activity
- *perceived loss of control*
- *persistence* despite negative long-term consequences.

Similarly, Griffiths (1999b) maintains that addiction isn't confined to drugs. Several other behaviours, including gambling, watching TV, playing amusement machines, overeating, sex, exercise, playing computer games, and using the Internet, are potentially addictive. Social pathologies are beginning to surface in cyberspace in the form of *technological addictions*, which are:

> ... non-chemical (behavioural) addictions that involve human–machine interaction. They can be either passive (e.g. television) or active (e.g. computer games). The interaction usually contains inducing and reinforcing features (e.g. sound effects, colour effects ...) that may promote addictive tendencies. (Griffiths, 1995)

Michael Douglas, Hollywood star and self-confessed sex addict

Griffiths (1996) argues that these behaviours display the same *core components* of addiction (complementing Walters' 'four Ps' above), namely:

- *salience* – the activity becomes the most important one in the person's life; it dominates thinking (preoccupations), feelings (cravings) and behaviour (socialised behaviour deteriorates)
- *mood modification* – for example, the activity produces an arousing 'buzz' or 'high'
- *tolerance* – increasing amounts of the activity are needed to achieve the same effects
- *withdrawal symptoms* – discontinuation or sudden reduction of the activity produces unpleasant feelings and physical effects
- *conflict* – this may be between the addict and those around him/her, with other activities (such as work, social life, and other interests) or within the individual him/herself
- *relapse* – reverting to earlier patterns of the activity soon after a period of abstinence or self-control.

RESEARCH UPDATE 8.1: The 'addicted brain'

- Neurobiologists have long known that drugs have their effect because they ultimately boost the activity of the brain's reward system: a complex circuit of neurons which evolved to make us feel 'flush' after eating or sex. At least initially, stimulating this system makes us feel good, which encourages us to repeat whatever induced the pleasure.
- But new research indicates that chronic drug use can induce changes in the structure and function of the system's neurons that last for weeks, months or years after the fix.
- A key part of the circuit is the pathway extending from dopamine-producing neurons of the ventral tegmental area (VTA) to dopamine-sensitive neurons in the nucleus accumbens (NA), situated deep beneath the frontal cortex. These changes contribute significantly to the tolerance, dependence and craving (see below) that fuel repeated use and that lead to relapses even after long periods of abstinence.
- There are also pathways linking the NA and VTA with other brain regions that can help make addicts highly sensitive to reminders of past highs (such as drug paraphernalia and places where they've scored), vulnerable to relapse when stressed and unable to control the urge to seek drugs.
- The VTA–NA pathway acts as a 'rheostat of reward': it 'tells' other brain centres how rewarding an activity is. The more rewarding, the more likely the organism is to remember it well and repeat it.
- fMRI and PET scans (see Chapter 4) show that the NA in cocaine addicts' brains 'lights up' when offered a snort, shown a video of someone using cocaine or even a photograph of white lines on a mirror.

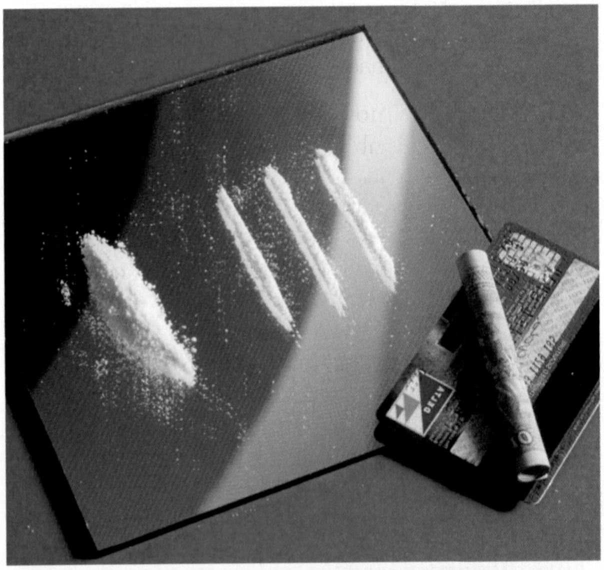

This image is enough to excite a cocaine addict's brain

The amygdala and some areas of the cortex also respond. While being scanned, they rate their feelings of rush and craving on a scale of 0–3. Such studies show that (a) the VTA and sublenticular extended amygdala are important to the cocaine-induced rush, and (b) the amygdala and NA influence both the rush *and* the craving for more of the drug, which becomes stronger as the euphoria wears off (as shown in Figure 8.1).

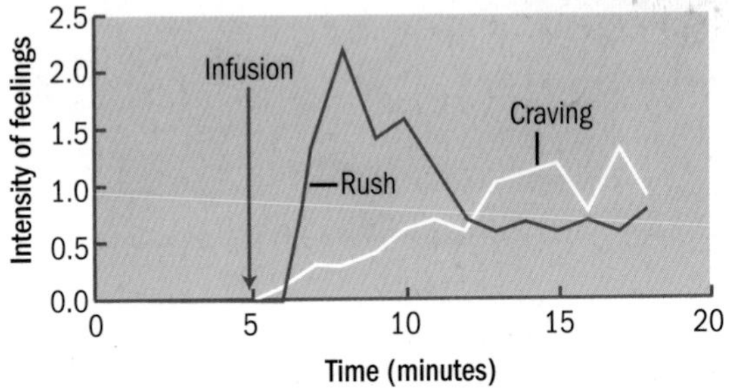

Figure 8.1 from Nestler & Malenka (2004) (reprinted with permission from Hans C. Breiter, Massachusetts General Hospital)

The same regions react in compulsive gamblers shown images of slot machines.

Substance use and abuse

According to Hammersley (1999), abuse is the use of a substance in a harmful or risky manner, without medical sanction. The concept is something of a compromise, because it's debatable whether *any* use of a substance can be entirely risk-free. It also suggests that some risks are negligible, while others are substantial. Hammersley claims that:

... The health risks of tobacco smoking now seem so substantial that all smoking is probably abuse – there is no negligible-risk use of tobacco ...

But he believes that most other drugs *can* be used in ways that make risks negligible.

Box 8.1 The DSM-IV-TR criteria for substance abuse

- A maladaptive pattern of substance use leading to clinically significant impairment or distress, as manifested by one (or more) of the following, occurring within a 12-month period:

  1. recurrent substance use resulting in a failure to fulfil major role obligations at work, school or home (e.g. repeated absences or poor work performance related to substance use, substance-related absences, suspensions, or expulsions from school; neglect of children or household);
  2. recurrent substance use in situations where it is physically hazardous (e.g. driving an automobile or operating a machine when impaired by substance use);
  3. recurrent substance-related legal problems (e.g. arrests for substance-related disorderly conduct);
  4. continued substance use despite having persistent or recurrent social or interpersonal problems caused or exacerbated by the effects of the substance (e.g. arguments with spouse about consequences of intoxication, physical fights).

- The symptoms have never met the criteria for Substance Dependence for this class of substance.

Dependence

How does dependence differ from abuse?

Box 8.2 DSM-IV-TR criteria for substance dependence

- A maladaptive pattern of substance use leading to clinically significant impairment or distress, as manifested by three (or more) of the following, occurring at any time in the same 12-month period:

  1. Tolerance, as defined by either of the following:
     (a) a need for markedly increased amounts of the substance to achieve intoxication or desired effect;
     (b) markedly diminished effect with continued use of the same amount of the substance.
  2. Withdrawal, as manifested by either of the following:
     (a) the characteristic withdrawal syndrome for the substance (varies from substance to substance);
     (b) the same (or a closely related) substance is taken to relieve or avoid withdrawal symptoms.
  3. The substance is often taken in larger amounts and over a longer period than was intended.
  4. There is a persistent desire or unsuccessful efforts to cut down or control substance use.
  5. A great deal of time is spent in activities necessary to obtain the substance (e.g. visiting multiple doctors or driving long distances), use the substance (e.g. chain-smoking), or recover from its effects.
  6. Important social, occupational, or recreational activities are given up or reduced because of substance use.
  7. The substance use is continued despite knowledge of having a persistent physical or psychological problem that is likely to have been caused or exacerbated by the substance (e.g. current cocaine use despite recognition of cocaine-induced depression, or continued drinking despite recognition that an ulcer was made worse by alcohol consumption).

Specify if:

- *With physiological dependence* – evidence of tolerance or withdrawal (i.e. either item 1 or 2 is present).
- *With psychological dependence* – no evidence of tolerance or withdrawal (i.e. neither item 1 or 2 is present).

The concept of dependence is based around a constellation of symptoms and problems, not just on the idea of physiological need for a drug. Only items 1 and 2 in Box 8.2 refer to physiological dependence. Anyone who fits three or more of these criteria would be diagnosed as substance dependent. Dependence, therefore, is quite varied, and few people fit all seven criteria (Hammersley, 1999).

Most substance-dependent people have tried to give up several times, always returning to use after weeks, months or even years. They often report strong craving or desire for the substance, and are at particular risk of resuming use when stressed, anxious, depressed, angry or happy. They also often feel they have difficulty controlling the amount they take once they start. When they relapse, they often return very quickly to their old, often destructive, habits.

Physiological vs psychological dependence

It's also important to highlight the difference between physiological and psychological dependence. As Box 8.2 shows, *physiological dependence* is related to *withdrawal* and/or *tolerance* (which relates to the traditional concept of *addiction*), while *psychological dependence* isn't. However, being deprived of a substance that's highly pleasurable can induce anxiety. Since the symptoms of anxiety (rapid pulse, profuse sweating, shaking, and so on) overlap with withdrawal symptoms, people may mistakenly believe that they're physiologically dependent. Psychological dependence is, though, part of the overall *dependence syndrome* (see Figure 8.2).

A good example of the difference between the two types of dependence is imipramine, used to treat depression (see Chapter 45). When it's stopped after prolonged use, there may be nausea, muscle pain, anxiety and difficulty in sleeping, but there's *never* a compulsion to resume

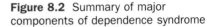

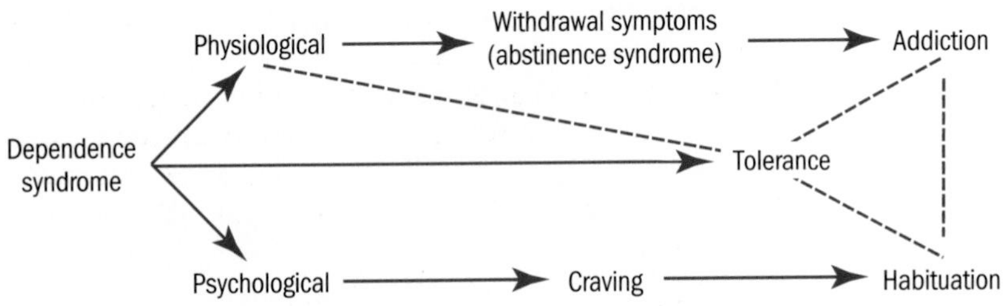

Figure 8.2 Summary of major components of dependence syndrome

taking it (Lowe, 1995). However, Lowe claims that 'psychological' dependence has little scientific meaning beyond the notion that drug-taking becomes part of one's habitual behaviour. Giving it up is very difficult, because the person has become *habituated* to it:

> Habituation is the repeated use of a drug because the user finds that use increases pleasurable feelings or reduces feelings of anxiety, fear, or stress. Habituation becomes problematic when the person becomes so consumed by the need for the drug-altered state of consciousness that all his or her energies are directed to compulsive drug-seeking behaviour ... (Lowe, 1995)

Physiologically addictive drugs, such as heroin and alcohol, typically cause habituation *as well*. Most widely used recreational drugs, including cannabis, cocaine, LSD, PCP (see Table 8.1), and *methylenedioxymethamphetamine* (*MDMA*: otherwise known as '*ecstasy*'), *don't* cause physiological dependence – but people *do* become habituated.

Some dependent people can stay dependent for long periods *without* suffering any other problems. This applies particularly to people who otherwise fit well into society, and who haven't experienced financial, legal or health problems as a result of their substance use – such as many smokers. Some very heavy drinkers 'only' damage their livers, and even some heroin or cocaine users fit this pattern. Nevertheless:

> ... one of the most striking things about the counselling of substance dependent people is that they will continue to use the substance even when they have suffered very severe problems as a result ... (Hammersley, 1999)

Some of these severe problems are discussed in the section on the effects of drugs, below.

Classifying drugs

Psychoactive drugs have been classified in several different ways. For example, Hamilton & Timmons (1995) identify three broad groups:

1. *stimulants* temporarily excite neural activity, arouse bodily functions, enhance positive feelings and heighten alertness; in high doses, they cause overt seizures
2. *depressants* (or *sedatives*) depress neural activity, slow down bodily functions, induce calmness and produce sleep; in high doses, they cause unconsciousness
3. *hallucinogens* produce distortion of normal perception and thought processes; in high doses, they can cause episodes of psychotic behaviour (see Chapters 43 and 44).

Table 8.1 Some examples of the major categories of psychoactive drugs

Major category	Examples	Slang name(s)
Depressants (sedatives)	alcohol	
	barbiturates:	'downers', 'barbs', various other names derived from names or colour of pill/capsule (e.g.'blueys').
	tranquillisers:	'tranx'.
	solvents	
Stimulants	caffeine	
	nicotine	
	amphetamines:	'uppers', 'speed', 'sulphate','sulph','whizz'.
	MDMA:	'ecstasy', 'E', and many names derived from shape/colour of drugs.
	cocaine:	'coke', 'snow', 'crack', 'freebase', 'base','wash', 'rock'.
Opiates	morphine:	
	heroin	'junk', 'skag','H', 'smack'.
	codeine	
	methadone:	'amps' (injectable), 'linctus' (oral).
Hallucinogens	lysergic acid diethylamide (LSD):	'acid'.
	mescaline:	
	psilocybin:	'magic mushrooms', 'mushies'.
	phencyclidine (PCP):	'angel dust'.
Cannabis	cannabis sativa:	'pot', 'dope', 'blow', 'draw','smoke'.
	herbal cannabis:	'grass', 'marijuana', 'ganja'.
	cannabis resin:	'weed', 'the herb', 'skunk'.
	cannabis oil:	'hash', 'hashish'.

(Based on Cooper, 1995)

A fourth category is *opiates*. These also depress activity in the CNS, but have an *analgesic* property – that is, they reduce sensitivity to pain without loss of consciousness. The Royal College of Psychiatrists (1987) identified *minor tranquillisers* as a separate category, but in Table 8.1 (page 128) they've been included under the general category of depressants. *Cannabis* doesn't fall easily into any of these other categories.

THE EFFECTS OF DRUGS

According to Greenfield (in Ahuja, 2000):

> As a person, you are the configuration of your brain cells ... Drugs are specifically designed to alter that configuration. So when you blow your mind on drugs, you really are blowing your mind. They may not kill you, but they may dramatically alter the person you are ...

Children and teenagers, whose relatively malleable brains are still being moulded, are particularly vulnerable (see Chapter 4). Teenagers, for various social and cultural reasons, are especially likely to take drugs, including those that pose the greatest threat to physical and mental health (see Chapter 37).

Depressants

Alcohol

Despite the difficulties in assessing the relationship between level of intake and harmful effects, certain '*safe levels*' are widely accepted (Gelder *et al.*, 1999). These are expressed in terms of *units* of alcohol, which is equal to eight grammes of ethanol (the equivalent of half a pint of beer, a small glass of wine, a glass of sherry or a standard (pub) measure of spirits).

For *men*, up to *21 units* per week, and for *women*, up to *14 units* is considered safe, provided the whole amount isn't taken all at once and that there are occasional drink-free days. Anything over 50 and 35 units, respectively, is considered '*dangerous*'. The British legal driving blood alcohol limit is 80 mg per 100 ml (equivalent to two or three drinks).

How does alcohol affect us?

> *ASK YOURSELF...*
> - Either from your own experience, or from observing others, how would you describe the effects of alcohol?

According to Motluk (1999), it's possible to identify a number of stages, based on the amount of alcohol consumed.

- With our first drink, and with blood alcohol levels remaining fairly low, *stimulation* is the first effect. At these low levels, alcohol sensitises one of the brain's major excitatory message pathways, the *N*-methyl-*D*-aspartate (NMDA) system (not to be confused with ecstasy). This makes certain NMDA receptors more readily activated by the brain's main neurotransmitter, glutamate. Some of the most sensitised brain regions are the cortex (thinking), hippocampus (remembering) and nucleus accumbens (NA) (pleasure-seeking), and our inhibitions begin to decrease.
- After two or three drinks, alpha rhythms (see Chapter 7) increase, extra blood flows to the prefrontal cortex and to the right temporal cortex. Mood is heightened and we may even feel euphoric.
- After three or four drinks, a turning point is reached, reflecting the complex 'biphasic' relationship with alcohol. With our blood now awash with alcohol, the very NMDA receptors that helped to perk us up after just one drink are refusing to respond. Also, the brain's *gamma-aminobutyric acid* (GABA) *system* becomes activated. GABA is an *inhibitory* neurotransmitter (see Table 4.1, page 58), which dulls activity (it's the system activated by benzodiazepines, such as Valium: see Chapter 45). From this point, alcohol begins to act more like a *depressant/sedative*. The hippocampus and thalamus are both slowed down.
- Any more drinks, and our speech and other motor functions begin to fail us. The cerebellum seems to be most affected by this stage. A common experience is that the room is spinning. This is called *positional alcohol nystagmus*, a booze-induced version of an eye reflex normally triggered by the inner ear's balance organs when they detect head rotation (Motluk, 1999: see Chapter 5).
- A blood alcohol concentration of 500 mg per 100 ml is considered lethal. At this concentration, the brain centres that keep us breathing shut down.

Box 8.3 Some physiological effects of alcohol

- Ethanol is a *diuretic*, so you end up *expelling* more water than you drink. It acts on the pituitary gland, blocking production of the hormone *vasopressin*, which directs the kidneys to re-absorb water that would otherwise end up in the bladder. So, the body borrows water from other places, including the brain, which shrinks temporarily. Though the brain itself cannot experience pain, it's thought that dehydration shrivels the *dura* (a membrane covering the brain). As this happens, it tugs at pain-sensitive filaments connecting it to the skull. Water loss may also account for pains elsewhere in the body.
- Frequent trips to the toilet also result in loss of essential sodium and potassium ions, which are central to how nerves and muscles work (see Chapter 4). Subtle chemical imbalances caused by ion depletion could account for a cluster of symptoms, including headaches, nausea and fatigue.

- Alcohol also depletes our reserves of sugar, leading to hypoglycaemia. The body's store of energy-rich glycogen in the liver is broken down into glucose; this quickly becomes another constituent of urine. This can account for feelings of weakness and unsteadiness the morning after.

(Source: based on *New Scientist*, 1999)

Heavy drinkers suffer malnutrition. Since alcohol is high in calories, appetite is suppressed. It also causes vitamin deficiency, by interfering with absorption of vitamin B from the intestines. Long term, this causes brain damage. Other physical effects include liver damage, heart disease, increased risk of a stroke and susceptibility to infections due to a suppressed immune system (see Chapter 12). Women who drink while pregnant can produce babies with *foetal alcohol syndrome* (see Chapter 40).

Alcohol and memory

Alcohol interferes with normal sleep patterns. Although it causes sedation, alcohol also suppresses REM sleep by as much as 20 per cent (see Chapter 7). There also appears to be a link between alcohol-induced sleepiness and memory loss. People who get drunk and then forget what happened have memory impairments similar to those suffered by people with sleep disorders, such as daytime sleepiness (Motluk, 1999).

In both cases, the person cannot recall how they got home, or what happened while at work or at the pub. It's the *transfer* of information into long-term memory that seems to be disrupted. The GABA signals that induce the sleepiness can interfere with both the early and late stages of memory formation (*stimulus registration* and *consolidation*, respectively). Chemicals that mimic GABA can do this, and there are many GABA receptors in the hippocampus. Another memory disorder associated with chronic alcohol consumption is *Korsakoff's syndrome* (see Chapter 17).

Alcohol and sex

Alcohol lowers levels of testosterone, the male sex hormone, in the blood. One of testosterone's functions is to maintain and regulate sex drive, so excessive drinking can explain loss of sexual appetite and/or the inability to 'perform' (that is, get an erection – otherwise known as 'brewer's droop'). While sexual function returns after blood alcohol levels have fallen again, habitual overindulgence over a five- to ten-year period can permanently damage a man's virility (erectile dysfunction and impotence). Even more worrying, alcohol can actually reduce the size of a man's genitalia (Burke, 1999)!

In women, the reverse seems to happen: even a couple of drinks can very quickly *increase* testosterone levels in the blood, thus increasing their libido (making them *more* randy). This is especially marked in women on the pill and non-pill users who are ovulating. However, as with men, chronic heavy women drinkers can suffer loss of libido and performance, as well as infertility (Burke, 1999).

Who drinks, and why?

The heaviest drinkers are young men in their late teens/early twenties, but there have been recent increases among 15–16-year-olds. Fewer women drink dangerous amounts, but rates among women are rising faster than in men, especially those in professional and managerial jobs (Gelder *et al.*, 1999).

A recent Mori poll (in Waterhouse *et al.*, 2000) showed that 17 per cent of those under 25 say they drink in order to get 'trolleyed'. A European School Survey Project on Alcohol and Other Drugs indicates that more than half of 15–16-year-old British teenagers admitted 'binge drinking' in the previous month. Under-16s are drinking twice as much as they were ten years ago (Ahmed, 2004). A UK survey by the Alcohol and Health Research Centre in Edinburgh of more than 2600 school students (2001) revealed that 57 per cent of boys and 54.8 per cent of girls had drunk five or more drinks in a row in the previous 30 days. Among 16–24-year-olds, 38 per cent of men and 21 per cent of women regularly drink twice the recommended daily limit (Waterhouse *et al.*, 2000: see above).

Box 8.4 The influence of socio-economic changes on alcohol consumption

- Alcohol is much more affordable than it used to be. Although the cost of alcohol has increased 22 per cent more than house prices generally since 1976, households' disposable income has risen by 81 per cent in real terms. As Figure 8.3 shows, in the 1960s, the British drank the equivalent of about 4.5 litres of pure alcohol per head per year (compared with 7.5 litres in 1998).
- The alcohol industry is at least partly to blame for the increase in drinking among young people. Responding to a decline in traditional beer drinking, it has created a 'postmodern market', tempting young people to drink strong, designer drinks in glitzy theme bars. From 1978–98, the number of pubs and bars in England and Wales rose by 16 per cent to 78,000, and nightclubs by 25 per cent to 4000 (Waterhouse *et al.*, 2000). New-style 'drinking warehouses' and superpubs are encouraging a growing culture of drinking to excess (Ahmed, 2004).
- Another reason for the increase is the trend towards 'extended youth'. Puberty starts earlier (see Chapter 37), and men and women are postponing both marriage and having children, creating a state of 'perpetual adolescence' (see Chapter 38).

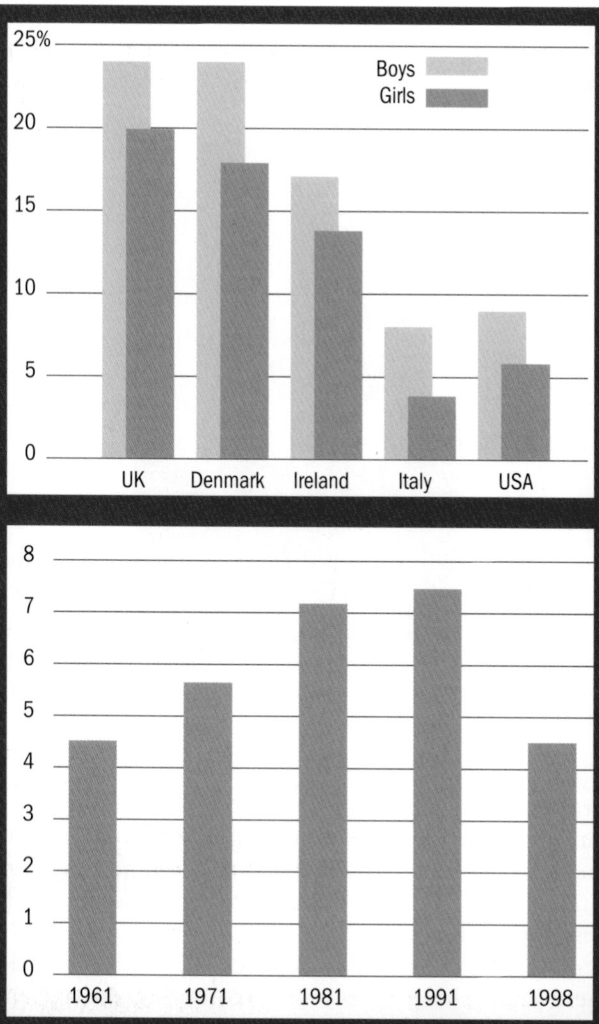

Figure 8.3 (above) Percentages of boys and girls drunk three times in the last 30 days; (below) Litres of pure alcohol drunk per head per year (UK) (from 'Young people are drinking to "get trolleyed" like never before', by Rosie Waterhouse, Mark Macaskill and Senay Boztas, © Times Newspapers Ltd, 23 July 2000, reproduced by permission)

Stimulants

Amphetamines

These were first synthesised in the 1920s. Their general effect is to increase energy and enhance self-confidence. For this reason, they were used extensively by the military in the Second World War to reduce fatigue and give soldiers going into battle more confidence. Amphetamines also suppress appetite and are hence the main ingredient of 'slimming pills' such as Methedrine, Dexedrine and Benzedrine.

Amphetamines are swallowed in pill form, inhaled through the nose in powder form or injected in liquid form. Small amounts cause increased wakefulness, alertness and arousal. Users experience a sense of energy and confidence, and feel that any problem can be solved and any task accomplished. Once the drug wears off, users experience a 'crash' or 'hangover', characterised by extreme fatigue and depression, irritability, disorientation and agitated motor activity. They counteract this by taking the drug again. Large amounts can cause restlessness, hallucinations and *paranoid delusions* (or *amphetamine psychosis*), which is virtually indistinguishable from *paranoid schizophrenia* (see Chapter 44). Long-term use has also been linked with severe depression, suicidal tendencies, disrupted thinking and brain damage.

Tolerance and *psychological dependence* develop quickly. The amphetamine 'hangover' is indicative of *withdrawal*, suggesting that there's also *physiological dependence*.

Cocaine

Cocaine hydrochloride is a powerful CNS stimulant extracted from the leaves of the coca shrub, native to the Andes mountains in South America. The Peruvian Indians originally discovered that chewing the leaves could increase stamina and relieve fatigue and hunger. While they still chew the leaves, elsewhere in the world cocaine is inhaled in powder form, injected into the veins in liquid form or smoked. When smoked, the drug reaches the brain in five to ten seconds, much faster than the other methods. It can also be swallowed, rubbed on the gums or blown into the throat.

In general the effects of cocaine are similar to those of amphetamines, but they tend to last only 15–30 minutes (compared with several hours). Typically, the user experiences a state of euphoria, deadening of pain, increased self-confidence, energy and attention. There's also a 'crash' when the drug wears off.

Even in small amounts, the stimulating effects can cause cardiac arrest and death. Recent research suggests that young people who use cocaine (and amphetamines) may be increasing their risk of having a stroke (brain haemorrhage) (Laurance, 2000). The growing pandemic of cocaine use in western society is overshadowing the traditional risk factors for stroke, such as high blood pressure. This is much more common in older people, as are strokes, but it's becoming increasingly common for people under 30 to suffer strokes after taking drugs.

Cocaine (and amphetamines) produces a surge in blood pressure. People with abnormal blood vessels in their brain, such as a cerebral aneurysm, are at greatest risk. But, it's also possible that the drug-taking caused the deformed blood vessels (Laurance, 2000). Repeated inhalation constricts the blood vessels in the nose. The nasal septum may become perforated, necessitating cosmetic surgery.

Formication refers to the sensation that 'insects' ('coke bugs') are crawling beneath the skin. Although this is merely random neural activity, users sometimes try to remove the imaginary insects by cutting deep into their skin. Cocaine definitely produces *psychological dependence*, but there's much more doubt regarding *physiological dependence*, *tolerance* and *withdrawal*.

Both amphetamines and cocaine increase ANS activity. Increased brain activation is probably due to secretion of increased levels of noradrenaline and dopamine, whose re-uptake is then inhibited (see Chapter 4). This results in an excess of these neurotransmitters, which increases neuronal activity, producing a persistent state of arousal. Dopamine probably accounts for the euphoric effect, while noradrenaline explains the increased energy. Cocaine stimulates neural circuits that are normally triggered by reinforcing events such as eating or sex. The 'crash' is caused by the fairly sudden depletion of dopamine and noradrenaline.

Box 8.5 Crack

- *Crack* is a form of cocaine, which first appeared in the 1980s.
- It's made using cocaine hydrochloride, ammonia or baking soda and water. When heated, the ammonia or baking soda produces a 'cracking' sound. The result is a crystal, which has had the hydrochloride base removed (hence the term *free basing* to describe its production).
- Its effects are more rapid and intense than cocaine's, but the 'crash' is also more intense.

Unlike heroin-dependent people, most cocaine users will get over their drug problem *without* professional help (Hammersley, 1999).

MDMA

MDMA, or 'ecstasy', is a chemical relative of amphetamine, first synthesised in 1912, and later patented as an appetite suppressant (but never marketed). It's swallowed in pill or tablet form, and sometimes taken with other mood-altering drugs. Small amounts produce a mild euphoric 'rush', which can last for up to ten hours. Self- and sexual confidence are increased. Serotonin and dopamine are the neurotransmitters affected.

Ecstasy causes extreme dehydration and hyperthermia, which induces a form of heatstroke. This can produce convulsions, collapse and death. Blood pressure also rises dangerously, which can induce a stroke and permanent brain damage. Over 50 deaths in Britain alone have been attributed to the drug (Parrott, 1997), including the much-publicised case of Leah Betts in 1995.

Most users will suffer mild side-effects. For a small minority, the side-effects can include severe depression, anxiety, paranoia, hallucinations, psychosis and panic attacks. But it's difficult in practice to establish a cause-and-effect link between ecstasy and these mental and physical reactions. The drug is taken mainly at raves and in clubs, where large numbers of sweaty people are in close proximity for hours on end. These conditions clearly make heatstroke more likely, without any drug-taking being involved. Clubbers take impure drugs and they take cocktails of drugs (which may include amphetamines: Naylor, 1988). Clubbers have been warned recently against the use of GBH (gamma hydroxybutyrate or 'liquid ecstasy'), especially when mixed with alcohol. It's not actually illegal and is relatively cheap. Overdoses are common, and it can cause convulsions and coma (Laurance, 2000).

Extreme dehydration and hyperthermia, plus MDMA, can be a lethal cocktail

Brain cells die after taking the drug, meaning that they can no longer produce serotonin. This can account for the depression that is quite commonly reported by users. Greenfield (in Ahuja, 2000) is more concerned about this long-term, irreversible, brain damage than the deaths that occur from taking ecstasy. But not everyone agrees that these brain changes necessarily constitute damage, and the drug may only induce depression (and other mental health problems) in those who already have emotional difficulties (Naylor, 1988). According to the Department of Health (1994), *tolerance* occurs, but not *physiological dependence*.

Opiates

These are derived from the unripe seed pods of the opium poppy ('plant of joy'). One constituent of opium is *morphine*, from which *codeine* and *heroin* can be extracted.

Morphine and heroin

In general, the opiates depress neural functioning and suppress physical sensations and responses to stimulation. In Europe, *morphine* was first used as an analgesic during the Franco-Prussian War (1870–71). However, it quickly became apparent that it produced physiological dependence (the 'soldier's disease'). The German Bayer Company developed *heroin* (the 'hero' that would cure the 'soldier's disease') in order to prevent this dependence, but, unfortunately, it also causes physiological dependence and has many unpleasant side-effects.

Heroin can be smoked, inhaled or injected intravenously. Puffing the heated white powder ('chasing the dragon') is now the preferred method because syringes are seen as dirty and dangerous (Khan, 2003). The immediate effects (the 'rush') are described as an overwhelming sensation of pleasure, similar to sexual orgasm but affecting the whole body. Such effects are so pleasurable that they override any thoughts of food or sex. Heroin rapidly decomposes into morphine, producing feelings of euphoria, well-being, relaxation and drowsiness.

Long-term users become more aggressive and socially isolated, as well as less physically active. Opiates in general may damage the body's immune system, leading to increased susceptibility to infection. The impurity of the heroin used, users' lack of adequate diet and the risks from contaminated needles, all increase health risks. Overdoses are common.

River Phoenix (1970–1993), victim of a cocktail of drugs

Heroin produces both *physiological* and *psychological dependence*. *Tolerance* develops quickly. *Withdrawal symptoms* initially involve flu-like symptoms, progressing to tremors, stomach cramps, and alternating chills and sweats. Rapid pulse, high blood pressure, insomnia and diarrhoea also occur. The skin often breaks out into goosebumps, where the skin resembles that of a plucked turkey (hence the term *cold turkey* to describe attempts to abstain). The legs jerk uncontrollably (hence *kicking the habit*). These symptoms last about a week, reaching a peak after about 48 hours.

Box 8.6 Heroin and endorphins

- As we saw in Chapter 4, the brain produces its own opiates (*opioid peptides* or *endorphins*).
- When we engage in important survival behaviours, endorphins are released into the fluid that bathes neurons. Endorphin molecules stimulate *opiate receptors* on some neurons, producing an intensely pleasurable effect just like that reported by heroin users.
- Regular use of opiates overloads endorphin sites in the brain, and the brain stops producing its own endorphins (Snyder, 1977). When the user abstains, neither the naturally occurring endorphins nor the opiates are available. Consequently, the internal mechanism for regulating pain is severely disrupted, producing some of the withdrawal symptoms described earlier.

Methadone

This is a synthetic opiate (or opioid) created to treat *physiological dependence* on heroin and other opiates. Methadone acts more slowly than heroin, and doesn't produce the heroin 'rush'. While heroin users may be less likely to take heroin if they're on methadone, they're likely to become at least *psychologically dependent* on it. By the early 1980s, long-term prescribing of methadone (methadone maintenance) began to be questioned, both in terms of effectiveness and the message it conveyed to users.

However, the HIV/AIDS epidemic has made harm minimisation a priority. The dispensing of injecting equipment and condoms in 'needle exchange' schemes has been combined with attempts to persuade users to substitute oral methadone for intravenous heroin. This reduces the risk of transmitting both HIV and other blood-borne viruses, such as hepatitis B (Lipsedge, 1997a).

Hallucinogens

These produce the most profound effects on consciousness. This is why they're sometimes called *psychedelics* ('mind expanding'). *Mescaline* comes from the peyote cactus, while *psilocybin* is obtained from the mushroom *psilocybe mexicana*. LSD and PCP are both chemically synthesised (see Table 8.1).

LSD

First produced in the 1940s, LSD was used during the 1960s for a variety of medical purposes, including pain relief for the terminally ill. But it became widely known during that period – and widely used – as a recreational drug. This use of LSD was largely inspired by Timothy Leary, a Harvard University psychologist, who coined the slogan 'turn on, tune in and drop out'. LSD, peace and love were central to the 1960s hippy movement ('flower power').

LSD is usually impregnated on blotting paper and swallowed. Unlike other drugs, its effects may not appear until an hour or so after being taken. These include:

- distorted sensory experiences, such as the intensification of sights and sounds, and changing form and colour; this can be pleasurable or terrifying (a 'bad trip'), depending on mood and expectations
- the dramatic slowing down of subjective time

- *synaesthesia* – the blending of different sensory experiences – for example, music may be experienced visually (see Chapter 5)
- *depersonalisation* – a state in which the body is perceived as being separate from the self; users report being able to see themselves from afar, similar to out-of-body experiences (see Chapter 6)
- *flashbacks* – some long-term users experience distorted perceptions or hallucinations days or weeks after the drug was taken; these might be psychological or physiological in origin.

Timothy Leary (1920–1996)

There's no evidence of *physiological dependence* or *withdrawal*, but *tolerance* can develop quickly. If taken repeatedly, there are few effects until a week or so after the drug was last taken. Whether LSD produces *psychological dependence* is disputed.

PCP

This was first synthesised in the 1950s for use as a surgical anaesthetic, but this was stopped once its psychoactive side-effects became apparent. It's usually combined with tobacco and smoked, producing distortions in body image and depersonalisation.

Used in small amounts, it induces euphoria, heightened awareness and a sense that all problems have disappeared. In larger quantities, it has stimulant, depressant and (not surprisingly given its original purpose) analgesic properties. Effects include violence, panic, psychotic behaviour, disrupted motor activity and chronic depression. These may persist for weeks after the drug was last taken.

Long-term use is associated with the four 'Cs' (Smith *et al.*, 1978):

1. *combativeness* – agitated or violent behaviour
2. *catatonia* – muscular rigidity of the body
3. *convulsions* – epileptic-type seizures
4. *coma* – a deep, unresponsive sleep.

Although PCP doesn't produce *physiological dependence*, users may become *psychologically dependent*.

Cannabis

This is second only to alcohol in popularity. The *cannabis sativa* plant's psychoactive ingredient is *delta-9-tetrahydrocannabinil* (THC). THC is found in the branches and leaves of the male and female plants (*marijuana*), but is highly concentrated in the resin of the female plant. *Hashish* is derived from the sticky resin and is more potent than marijuana (see Table 8.1).

Cannabis is usually smoked with tobacco, or eaten. When smoked, THC reaches the brain within seven seconds. Small amounts produce a mild, pleasurable 'high', involving relaxation, a loss of social inhibition, intoxication and a humorous mood. Speech becomes slurred and coordination is impaired. Increased heart rate, reduced concentration, enhanced appetite and impaired short-term memory are also quite common effects. Some users report fear, anxiety and confusion.

Large amounts produce hallucinogenic reactions, but these aren't full blown as with LSD. THC remains in the body for up to a month, and both male sex hormones and the female menstrual cycle can be disrupted. If used during pregnancy, the foetus may fail to grow properly, and cannabis is more dangerous to the throat and lungs than cigarettes. While tolerance is usually a sign of physiological dependence, with cannabis *reverse tolerance* has been reported: regular use leads to a *lowering* of the amount needed to produce the initial effects. This could be due to a build-up of THC, which takes a long time to be metabolised. Alternatively, users may become more efficient inhalers, and so perceive the drug's effects more quickly. *Withdrawal* effects (restlessness, irritability and insomnia) have been reported, but they seem to be associated only with continuous use of very large amounts. *Psychological dependence* almost certainly occurs in at least some people.

> *ASK YOURSELF...*
> - Do you agree with the reclassification of cannabis?
> - Do you think it should be legalised (decriminalised)?
> - Why/why not?

CRITICAL DISCUSSION 8.2: Cannabis and the drugs debate

- According to Skelton (in Naylor, 1988), coordinator of the Edinburgh drugs agency Crew 2000:

... Up until a few years ago, if anybody went to a drugs project and said they had a problem with cannabis then they wouldn't be taken seriously ... This has changed quite

a bit. People are recognising that there are side-effects, particularly for people who've got any sort of mental illness.

- Greenfield (in Ahuja, 2000) considers cannabis to be pretty potent. It takes 0.3 mg to induce the same kind of effects as 7000 mg of alcohol, primarily feelings of well-being and relaxation. This potency suggests that specific cannabis receptors exist in the brain.
- As noted earlier, cannabis was reclassified in the UK in 2004. It was 'reduced' to a Class C drug from Class B (alongside tranquillisers and steroids).
- In 2004, an estimated 3.3 million Britons (one in ten 16–59-year-olds) will have used the drug. A quarter of 15–24-year-olds used it in 2002 (Burke & Asthana, 2004).
- Research by leading British psychiatrists has pointed to a strong link between cannabis and increased risk of mental illness (as well as exacerbation of existing psychotic conditions). Research in the USA has shown that THC can induce a psychotic reaction. While these studies don't prove that cannabis is harmful for everyone, it's difficult to say that it's 'harmless'. Some experts have compared the risks to the link between smoking and lung cancer/heart disease: it's safer to abstain but vulnerable people are at greater risk. The number of people who are vulnerable to the effects of cannabis is probably tiny (Burke & Asthana, 2004).
- The debate about the 'morality' of cannabis use, its eventual legalisation, and its physical and psychological effects, goes on.

THEORIES OF DEPENDENCE

According to Lowe (1995):

> ... It is now generally agreed that addictive behaviours are multiply determined phenomena, and should be considered as biopsychosocial entities.

Similarly, Hammersley (1999) maintains that dependence is a complex behaviour that takes several years to develop. So it's unlikely that one theory or factor could account for all of it. Most researchers believe that social, personal, family and lifestyle factors are important, as well as the action of the drug itself. However, it's not yet understood fully how these work and interact. According to Hammersley (1999), theories of dependence have two dimensions. These are concerned with the extent to which dependence is:

- supposedly caused by *biological*, as opposed to *social*, factors
- the result of *abnormal/pathological* processes, as opposed to the *extreme end* of *normal* processes.

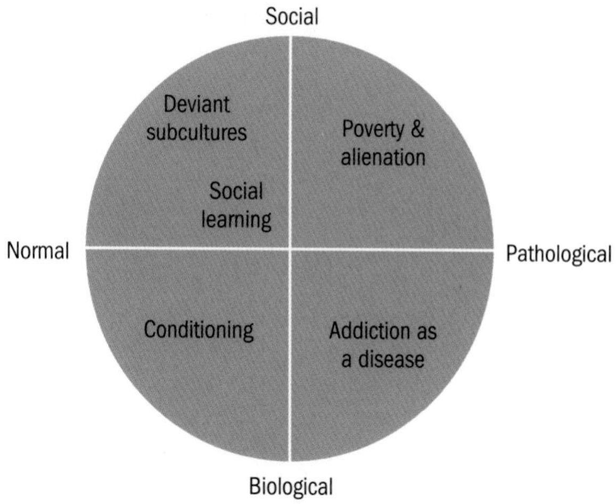

Figure 8.4 Five main theories of addiction (from Hammersley, 1999)

In the rest of this section, we shall consider one major theory (*addiction as a disease*) of one particular case of substance dependence (*alcohol dependence*).

Theories of alcohol dependence

The disease model

Rush, widely regarded as the father of American psychiatry, is commonly credited with being the first major figure to conceptualise alcoholism as a 'disease', in the early 1800s. At about the same time, the British doctor, Trotter, likened alcoholism to a mental disorder. Both men saw it as a product of a distinct biological defect or dysfunction, much like cancer, diabetes or TB (Lilienfeld, 1995).

In 1935, a doctor and former alcoholic, Smith, and Wilson (a stockbroker) founded Alcoholics Anonymous (AA) in the USA. AA assumes that certain individuals possess a physiological susceptibility to alcohol analogous to an allergy: a single drink is sufficient to trigger an unquenchable desire for more, resulting in an inevitable loss of control.

Perhaps the most influential champion of the disease model was Jellinek, a physiologist. Based on questionnaire data with AA members, Jellinek (1946, 1952) proposed that alcoholism was a biological illness with a highly characteristic and predictable course. It comprises four major stages:

1. *pre-alcoholic phase* – alcohol provides a means of reducing tension and increasing self-confidence
2. *prodromal phase* – the alcoholic begins to drink secretly and heavily, and to experience *blackouts*
3. *crucial phase* – the alcoholic begins to lose control, engage in 'benders' and to experience severe withdrawal symptoms
4. *chronic phase* – the alcoholic drinks almost constantly and neglects almost all social and occupational responsibilities.

Jellinek (1960) also distinguished five 'species' of alcoholics:

1. *alpha* – they drink to minimise tension
2. *beta* – they experience physical damage from drinking, such as cirrhosis of the liver, but aren't alcohol-dependent
3. *delta* – they're unable to abstain
4. *epsilon* – they lose control of their drinking and go on periodic benders
5. *gamma* – they lose control of their drinking, experience withdrawal symptoms, and are physically dependent.

Evaluating the disease model

According to Lilienfeld (1995), the course of alcoholism appears to be far more variable than this, and many drinkers don't fit into any of Jellinek's 'species'. Nevertheless, his research was instrumental in persuading many scientists that alcoholism is best regarded as a physiological illness with a distinctive natural history.

This was the single most influential theory for much of the twentieth century. It's still the dominant view underlying psychiatric and other medically oriented treatment programmes, but is much less influential among psychologically based programmes since the 1980s.

Peele (1989) lists six major assumptions made by the disease model.

1. alcoholics drink too much, not because they intend to, but because they can't control their drinking
2. alcoholics inherit their alcoholism, and so are born as alcoholics
3. alcoholism as a disease can strike any individual, from any socio-cultural background (it's an 'equal-opportunity destroyer')
4. alcoholism always gets worse without treatment; alcoholics can never cut back or quit on their own
5. treatment based on the AA principles (see Box 8.7) is the *only* effective treatment
6. those who reject the AA principles, or observers who reject any of the above, are in denial.

Peele argues that there's no evidence to support any of these assumptions. Regarding the second assumption, Lilienfeld (1995) observes that it implies that all individuals drink heavily for the same – or at least very similar – reasons. That is:

> ... Alcoholism is often viewed ... as a homogeneous entity resulting from a single set of causal influences...

However, Cloninger (1987) proposed that *Group 1* alcoholics are at risk of 'Type 1' alcoholism:

- they drink primarily to reduce tension, are predominantly female, are prone to anxiety and depression, and tend to have relatively late onset of problem drinking.

By contrast, *Group 2* alcoholics are at risk of 'Type 2' alcoholism:

- they drink primarily to relieve boredom, give free rein to their tendency towards risk-taking and sensation-seeking, are predominantly male, prone to antisocial and criminal behaviour, and tend to have relatively early onset of drinking behaviour.

Although the evidence for Cloninger's model is tentative and indirect, it challenges the disease model in a quite fundamental way. If he's correct, alcoholism may represent the culmination of two very different (and, in fact, essentially opposite), pathways (Lilienfeld, 1995).

Alcohol dependence syndrome (ADS: Edwards, 1986) is a later version of the disease model. It grew out of dissatisfaction with 'alcoholism' and with the traditional conception of alcoholism as disease. The term 'syndrome' adds flexibility, suggesting a group of concurrent behaviours that accompany alcohol dependence. They needn't always be observed in the same individual, nor are they observable to the same degree in everyone. For example, instead of loss of control or inability to abstain, ADS describes 'impaired control'. This implies that people drink heavily because, at certain times and for a variety of psychological and physiological reasons, they choose not to exercise control (Lowe, 1995). Lowe maintains that:

> Simple disease models have now been largely replaced by a more complex set of working hypotheses based, not on irreversible physiological processes, but on learning and conditioning, motivation and self-regulation, expectations and attributions.

(See Critical Discussion 8.1, page 124.)

Absinthe, by Degas

Treating alcohol dependence

The AA approach

According to Powell (2000), the more general concept of addiction as a 'disease of the will' has become popular. It's been broadly applied to other forms of addiction, and is adopted by the AA's 'sister' organisations, Narcotics Anonymous (NA) and Gamblers Anonymous (GA), Workaholics Anonymous (WA), Sex Addicts Anonymous (SAA), and even Survivors of Incest Anonymous.

Strictly, what AA offers isn't 'treatment' at all. Nor does it advocate any particular approach to treatment. Instead, it adopts a spiritual framework, requiring alcoholics to surrender their will to a 'higher power' (or God), confess their wrongs and try to rectify them. This requires some spiritual feeling, an acceptance of abstinence as a goal, and usually works better for those who are heavily dependent (Hammersley, 1999). The AA philosophy is embodied in its famous 12-step approach (see Box 8.7).

Box 8.7 The 12 steps of Alcoholics Anonymous

1. We admitted that we were powerless over alcohol – that our lives had become unmanageable;
2. came to believe that a Power greater than ourselves could restore us to sanity;
3. made a decision to turn our will and our lives over to the care of God as we understood Him;
4. made a searching and fearless moral inventory of ourselves;
5. admitted to God, to ourselves, and to another human being, the exact nature of our wrongs;
6. were entirely ready to have God remove all these defects of character;
7. humbly asked Him to remove our shortcomings;
8. made a list of all persons we had harmed, and became willing to make amends to them all;
9. made direct amends to such people whenever possible, except when to do so would injure them or others;
10. continued to take personal inventory and when we were wrong promptly admitted it;
11. sought through prayer and meditation to improve our conscious contact with God as we understood Him, praying only for knowledge of His will for us and the power to carry that out.
12. Having had a spiritual awakening as the result of these steps, we tried to carry the message to alcoholics, and to practise these principles in all our affairs.

At meetings, new members are introduced to the 12 steps and the 'Big Book' (of guidance and member stories). They're allocated a sponsor for one-to-one support, listen to other members' stories and tell their own. In addition to the weekly group meetings, there are professional residential programmes that use the 12-step approach (the 'Minnesota Model'). This involves progression through a very structured programme and movement through levels of seniority in a rigid hierarchy. Deviation from the rules is systematically and severely punished by, for example, 'demotion' or even expulsion. Halfway houses are also available to help the person's transition to an alcohol-free life in the community.

Evaluating the AA approach

- The 12 steps seem to work best for those who attend meetings regularly and get actively involved in the organisation. Indeed, this is part of the AA ethos (Hammersley, 1999). Extreme '12-steppers' (recovered AA members) believe that 'it's abstinence or nothing', but the basic philosophy is *neutral* about the issue of whether abstinence is for everyone. Many have benefited from AA, and there are affiliated support groups for spouses (AL-ANON) and for teenage children (AL-TEEN). However, it's certainly not the only treatment available (Hammersley, 1999).
- In recent years, several ex-members and dependence treatment professionals have accused AA of having cult-like qualities, and using brainwashing and bullying methods that weak and vulnerable people are particularly susceptible to. The anti-AA lobby is especially strong in the USA, and there's also a support group on the Internet called Recovery From 12 Steps.
- In the UK, where there are 3350 AA groups, research has found that the 12-step approach has a 70 per cent success rate (Kenny, 1998). One criticism of the approach is that members are encouraged to stay in AA *for life*: once an alcoholic, always an alcoholic. In AA, you can never move on. According to James (in Kenny, 1998):

  > ... After a year with AA, you're like a Moonie and you're probably in a relationship with another AA member ... By the end of your second year, you are definitely cured of your physical addiction, but not the underlying causes – and AA does nothing about this. It merely replaces one dependency with another...

  James describes the AA approach as authoritarian and fascistic. This is very effective when it's getting you to stop taking the drug of your choice. That's clearly the most urgent need initially – you must stop killing yourself. But at some stage – perhaps after being clean for two years – you should move on to therapy. The paternalistic structure is designed to make this break very difficult.
- The issue of complete abstinence discussed earlier is also highly contentious. For some people, this may be appropriate, while others may be able to return to drinking safely and in moderation (Kenny, 1998).

CHAPTER SUMMARY

- Drugs are **psychoactive** substances. They may be used **therapeutically** or for **pleasure**, the latter being subdivided into **recreational** and **drugs of abuse**.
- Which drugs are legal or illegal changes over time within the same society and between societies. Cigarette smoking and alcohol abuse are so widespread that they may be considered 'ordinary addictions'.

- The concept of **addiction** has been criticised for being oversimplified and for reflecting the **disease model**. The more modern view is to see drug problems as involving **substance abuse** and **dependence**. This view is adopted by DSM-IV-TR.
- Some researchers argue that the concept of addiction should be **broadened**, so as to cover forms of addictive behaviour which don't involve chemical substances at all. Examples include shopping, gambling and the Internet. Addictive behaviours may display the same components, regardless of the particular substance or activity involved.
- DSM-IV-TR defines abuse and dependence in terms of several criteria. **Dependence** can be either **psychological** or **physiological**, the latter indicated either by **tolerance** or **withdrawal**. Both types of dependence are part of the **dependence syndrome**.
- Physiologically addictive drugs, such as alcohol and heroin, typically also cause **habituation**. Most widely used recreational drugs, including cannabis, cocaine and ecstasy, produce habituation without causing physiological dependence.
- Major categories of drugs include **depressants** (**sedatives**), **stimulants**, **opiates**, **hallucinogens** (**psychedelics**) and **cannabis**.
- **Alcohol** is a depressant, although its initial effect is to stimulate the brain. With increasing amounts of alcohol, the brain generally slows down, and the breathing centres may eventually shut down.
- Alcohol can produce several life-threatening physical diseases in the drinker, as well as causing **foetal alcohol syndrome**. It also impairs **memory** function, an extreme form being **Korsakoff's syndrome**.
- Stimulants include **amphetamines**, which produce both physiological and psychological dependence, **cocaine**, which definitely causes only psychological dependence, and **MDMA** (or **ecstasy**).
- Ecstasy is associated with raves and clubbing, making it difficult to infer the drug's effect on various mental and physical reactions. While there's disagreement as to whether it causes long-term brain damage, it doesn't seem to induce physiological dependence.
- **Morphine** and **heroin** are opiates. Heroin produces both psychological and physiological dependence, and withdrawal symptoms are severe and extremely unpleasant. It's thought that regular use of opiates causes the brain to stop producing its own **endorphins**.
- **Methadone** is an orally taken synthetic opiate created to treat physiological dependence on heroin and other opiates. Users may well become psychologically dependent.
- **LSD** and **PCP** are hallucinogens, which may produce psychological dependence. Neither produces physiological dependence.
- **Cannabis** doesn't fit neatly into the other categories. It comes in different forms and can be taken in a variety of ways. There's some evidence of **reverse tolerance**, and psychological dependence is likely for some people.
- Cannabis is at the centre of a current debate regarding changes to the drug laws in the UK. While some wish to decriminalise it, others believe this would increase its use.
- **Theories of dependence** differ according to whether they see the causes as **biological** or **social**, and whether dependence is seen as **pathological** or the **extreme end** of **normal processes**.
- The single most influential theory of alcohol dependence is the **disease model**. It's an oversimplified account, assuming that everyone is dependent for the same reasons. Supporting evidence is also very limited. **Alcohol dependence syndrome** (**ADS**) is a more flexible version of the disease model.
- **Alcoholics Anonymous** (**AA**) is based on the disease model. Its '12 steps' philosophy has also been applied to other forms of 'addiction'. While it boasts a high success rate, its methods have been accused of being authoritarian and cult-like. Its core belief that alcoholics cannot be cured prevents people from becoming independent.

Links with other topics/chapters

- Substance abuse and dependence are included in DSM-IV-TR classification of *mental disorders* (Chapter 43), and there are many (non-chemical) addictions that share many of the characteristics of drug addiction, including *eating disorders* (Chapter 44).
- The disease model of addiction is one example of the more general *biomedical model* of disease. *Health psychology* represents a major challenge to the biomedical model, favouring the *biopsychosocial model* of health and illness (Chapter 12).
- Several drugs (such as amphetamines and hallucinogens) can induce *psychotic reactions* (Chapter 44), and an extreme memory disorder associated with chronic alcohol consumption is *Korsakoff's syndrome* (Chapter 17). Alcohol also suppresses *REM sleep* (Chapter 7).
- Increased alcohol consumption among younger people has been related to the trend toward 'perpetual adolescence': *puberty* starts earlier (Chapter 37), and men and women are postponing both *marriage and having children* (Chapter 38).
- The effects of long-term heroin use can be understood in terms of the brain's own *opiates* (*endorphins*) (Chapter 4).
- Cloninger's group 2 alcoholics have a *crime-prone personality* (Chapter 46).

9

MOTIVATION

INTRODUCTION AND OVERVIEW

Trying to define motivation is a little like trying to define psychology itself. Taking as a starting point the lay person's view of psychology as the study of 'what makes people tick', motivation is concerned with why people act and think the way they do. 'Why' questions – and related 'how' questions – usually imply *causes* and *underlying mechanisms or processes*.

Each of the major theoretical approaches discussed in Chapter 2 (*behaviourist, psychodynamic, humanistic, neurobiological/biogenic, cognitive, evolutionary* and *social constructionist*) tries to identify the key processes and mechanisms. This is also true of the *neurobiological/biogenic* approach (see Chapter 4). At the heart of each approach lies an image of human beings that, in essence, is a theory of the causes of human behaviour.

Motivated behaviour is *goal-directed*, purposeful behaviour. It's difficult to think of any behaviour, human or non-human, that isn't motivated in this sense. However, just how the underlying motives are conceptualised and investigated depends very much on the persuasion of the psychologist. For example:

- a *psychodynamic* psychologist will try to discover internal, *unconscious* drives and motives (see Chapter 42 for a discussion of Freud's psychoanalytic theory)
- a *behaviourist* psychologist will look for environmental *schedules of reinforcement*, which can explain the behaviour of rats and pigeons as effectively as that of human beings (see Chapter 11); as a *radical behaviourist*, Skinner rejects the claim that mental or other internal events or processes – conscious or unconscious – can influence behaviour in any way. For him, 'motivation' and other mentalistic terms are '*explanatory fictions*'
- a *humanistic* psychologist, such as Maslow, will try to understand a person's behaviour in terms of a hierarchy of motives, with *self-actualisation* at the top of the hierarchy
- for a *biopsychologist*, what's crucial are bodily events and processes taking place in the CNS, the ANS and the endocrine system, or *interactions* between these different systems (see Chapter 4); these events and processes are related to the person or animal's biological survival.

Although we shall consider a range of different motives, this chapter has a very 'biological' flavour. Maslow's *hierarchy of needs* is useful as a general framework for examining other approaches. *Homeostatic drive theories* try to explain hunger and thirst, but even in the case of such basic biological motives as these, *cognitive* and other individual factors, as well as *social*, *cultural* and other environmental factors, play a crucial role.

We shall also consider *non-homeostatic* needs and drives, including electrical self-stimulation of the brain (ES-SB), competence and cognitive motives, and some important *social* motives.

WHAT IS MOTIVATION?

According to Rubin & McNeil (1983), motives are a special kind of cause that 'energize, direct and sustain a person's behaviour (including hunger, thirst, sex and curiosity)'. Similarly:

> Motivation refers, in a general sense, to processes involved in the initiation, direction, and energization of individual behaviour ... (Geen, 1995)

The word 'motive' comes from the Latin for 'move' (*movere*), and this is captured in Miller's (1962) definition:

> The study of motivation is the study of all those pushes and prods – biological, social and psychological – that defeat our laziness and move us, either eagerly or reluctantly, to action.

As we noted in the *Introduction and overview*, different schools of thought within psychology look for the causes of behaviour in very different 'places'. These differences indicate that motives may vary with regard to a number of features or dimensions, including:

- internal or external
- innate or learned
- mechanistic or cognitive
- conscious or unconscious.

Several attempts have been made to classify different kinds of motives. For example, Rubin & McNeil (1983) classify motives into (i) survival or physiological motives, and (ii) competence or cognitive motives. Social motives represent a third category. Clearly, humans share survival motives with all other animals, as well as certain competence motives (see below). But other motives are peculiarly and uniquely human, notably *self-actualisation*, which lies at the peak of a 'hierarchy of needs' in Maslow's (1954) humanistic theory.

Maslow's hierarchy of needs

Although Maslow's theory is commonly discussed in relation to personality (see Chapter 42), its focus on needs makes it equally relevant to motivation. (The book in which he first proposed his hierarchy was called *Motivation and Personality*.) According to Maslow, we're subject to two quite different sets of motivational states or forces:

1. those that ensure survival by satisfying basic physical and psychological needs (physiological, safety, love and belongingness, and esteem), and
2. those that promote the person's self-actualisation – that is, realising one's full potential, 'becoming everything that one is capable of becoming' (Maslow, 1970), especially in the intellectual and creative domains.

As Maslow states:

> We share the need for food with all living things, the need for love with (perhaps) the higher apes, [and] the need for Self-Actualisation with [no other species].

Behaviours that relate to survival or deficiency needs (*deficiency* or *D-motives*) are engaged in because they satisfy those needs (a *means to an end*). But those that relate to self-actualisation are engaged in for their own sake, because they're intrinsically satisfying (*growth*, *being* or *B-motives*). The latter include the fulfilment of ambitions, the acquisition of admired skills, the steady increase of understanding about people, the universe or oneself, the development of creativeness in a particular field or, most important, simply the ambition to be a good human being. It's simply inaccurate to speak in such instances of tension reduction, which implies the overcoming of an annoying state, for these states aren't annoying (Maslow,

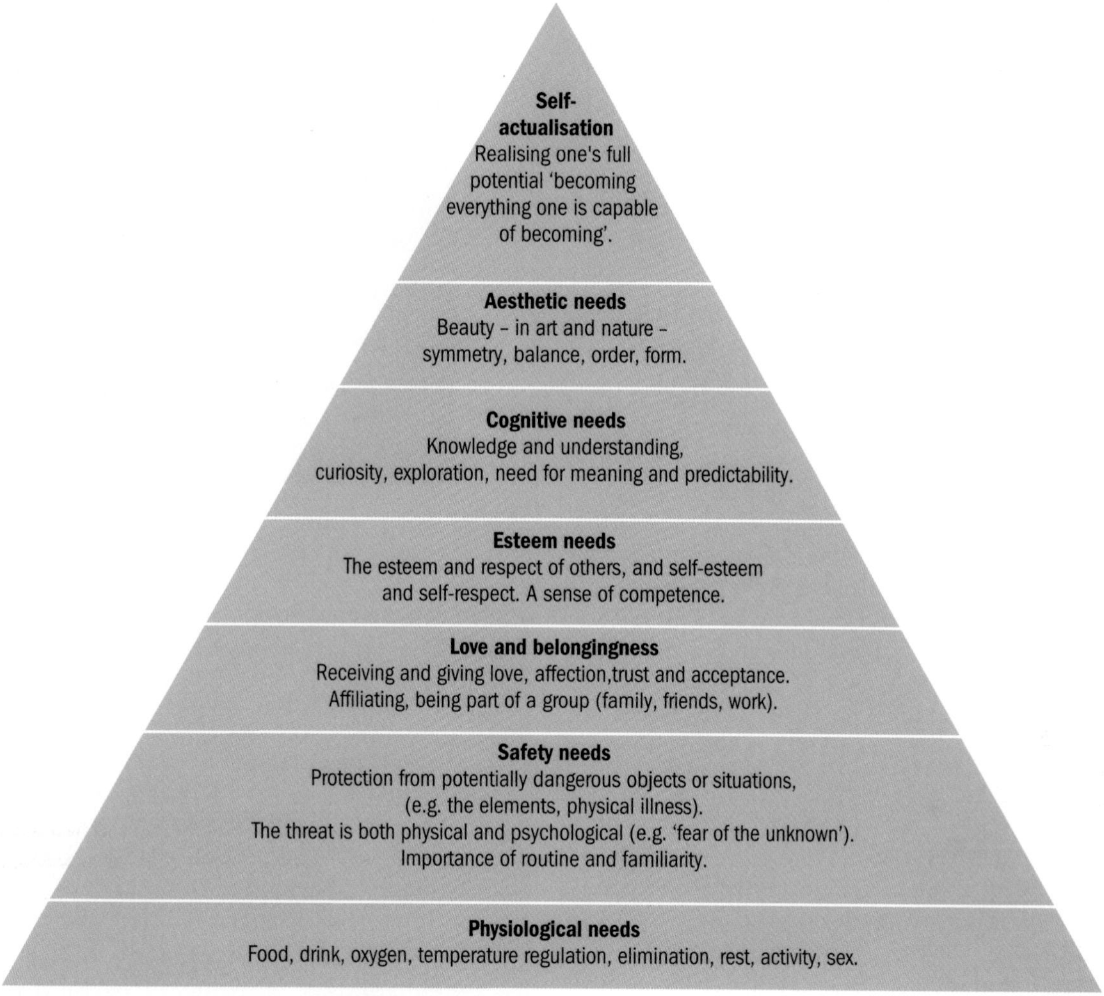

Self-actualisation
Realising one's full potential 'becoming everything one is capable of becoming'.
Aesthetic needs
Beauty - in art and nature - symmetry, balance, order, form.
Cognitive needs
Knowledge and understanding, curiosity, exploration, need for meaning and predictability.
Esteem needs
The esteem and respect of others, and self-esteem and self-respect. A sense of competence.
Love and belongingness
Receiving and giving love, affection,trust and acceptance. Affiliating, being part of a group (family, friends, work).
Safety needs
Protection from potentially dangerous objects or situations, (e.g. the elements, physical illness). The threat is both physical and psychological (e.g. 'fear of the unknown'). Importance of routine and familiarity.
Physiological needs
Food, drink, oxygen, temperature regulation, elimination, rest, activity, sex.

Figure 9.1 Maslow's hierarchy of needs (based on Maslow, 1954)

1968). (Another term for tension reduction is *drive reduction*, which is discussed below). Maslow's argument is that to reduce the full range of human motives to drives, which must be satisfied or removed, is simply mistaken.

The hierarchical nature of Maslow's theory is intended to highlight the following points.

- Needs lower down in the hierarchy must be satisfied before we can attend to needs higher up. For example, if you're reading this while your stomach is trying to tell you it's lunchtime, you probably won't absorb much about Maslow. Similarly if you're tired or in pain. Yet you can probably think of exceptions, such as the starving artist who finds inspiration despite hunger, or the mountain climber who risks his/her life for the sake of adventure (what Maslow would call a 'peak' experience – if you'll forgive the pun!).
- Higher-level needs are a later evolutionary development: in the development of the human species (*phylogenesis*), self-actualisation is a fairly recent need. This applies equally to the development of individuals (*ontogenesis*): babies are much more concerned with

'Because it's there'

their bellies than with their brains. But it's always a case of one need *predominating* at any one time, *not* excluding all other needs.

- The higher up the hierarchy we go, the more the need becomes linked to life experience, and the less 'biological' it becomes. Individuals will achieve self-actualisation in different ways, through different activities and by different routes. This is related to experience, not biology:

> A musician must make music, an artist must paint, a poet must write, if he is to be ultimately at peace with himself. What a man can be, he must be. (Maslow, 1968)

This captures nicely the *idiographic* nature of Maslow's theory – that is, the view that every individual is unique (see Chapter 42).

- The higher up the hierarchy we go, the more difficult it becomes to achieve the need. Many human goals are remote and long term, and can only be achieved in a series of steps. This pursuit of aims/goals that lie very much in the future is unique to human beings, although individuals differ in their ability to set and realise such goals.

ASK YOURSELF...

- Do you consider Maslow's hierarchy to be a useful way of thinking about human motivation? Do you think he's omitted any important motives?
- To what extent might the hierarchy reflect the culture and the historical time in which Maslow lived and wrote?

THE EARLY STUDY OF MOTIVATION

As with many other aspects of psychology, the study of motivation has its roots in philosophy (see Chapters 1 and 3). *Rationalists* saw human beings as free to choose between different courses of action. This makes the concept of motivation almost unnecessary: it's our reason that determines our behaviour. This idea of freedom and responsibility is a basic premise of both humanistic and cognitive approaches (see Chapter 49).

The seventeenth-century British philosopher Hobbes proposed the theory of *hedonism*. This maintains that all behaviour is determined by the seeking of pleasure and the avoidance of pain. These are the 'real' motives (whatever we may believe), and this idea is central to Freud's psychoanalytic theory, captured in the concept of the *pleasure principle*. Similarly, the basic principles of *positive* and *negative reinforcement* can be seen as corresponding to the seeking of pleasure and avoidance of pain, respectively, and these are central to Skinner's *operant conditioning*.

Thomas Hobbes (1588–1679)

Box 9.1 Motives as instincts

- The concept of instinct played a major role in early psychological approaches to motivation. Many psychologists, inspired by Darwin's (1859) theory of evolution (see Chapter 2), which argued that humans and animals differ only *quantitatively*, identified human instincts that would explain human behaviour.
- For example, McDougall (1908) originally proposed 12 and, by 1924, over 800 separate instincts. But to explain behaviour by labelling it is to explain nothing (e.g. 'We behave aggressively because of our aggressive instinct' is a circular statement). This, combined with the sheer proliferation of instincts, seriously undermined the whole approach.
- However, the concept of instinct – with certain important modifications – remains a central feature of the *ethological approach* to behaviour, in particular, non-human animal behaviour (see Chapter 2 and Gross *et al.*, 2000).

During the 1920s, the concept of instinct was largely replaced by the concept of *drive*. The term was first used by Woodworth (1918), who compared human behaviour with the operation of a machine: the mechanism of a machine is relatively passive and drive is the power applied to make it 'go'. The concept of drive has taken two major forms: *homeostatic drive theory* (Cannon, 1929), which is a physiological theory, and *drive reduction theory* (Hull, 1943), which is primarily a theory of learning.

HOMEOSTATIC DRIVE THEORY

The term *homeostasis* is derived from the Greek *homos* (meaning 'same') and *stasis* (meaning 'stoppage'). It was coined by Cannon (1929) to refer to the process by which an organism maintains a fairly constant internal (bodily) environment – that is, how body temperature, blood sugar level, salt concentration in the blood, and so on, are kept in a state of relative balance or equilibrium.

The basic idea is that when a state of imbalance arises (for example, through a substantial rise in body temperature), something must happen to correct the imbalance and restore equilibrium (sweating). In this case, the animal doesn't have to 'do' anything, because sweating is completely automatic and purely physiological. However, if the imbalance is caused by the body's need for food or drink (*tissue need*), the hungry or thirsty animal has to do something to obtain food or water. This is where the concept of a *homeostatic drive* becomes important. Tissue need leads to internal imbalance, which leads to homeostatic drive, which leads to appropriate behaviour, which leads to restoration of internal balance, which leads to drive reduction.

The internal environment requires a regular supply of raw materials from the external world (Green, 1980). While oxygen intake, for example, is involuntary and continuous, eating and drinking are *voluntary* and *discontinuous* (or spaced). We talk about a hunger and thirst drive, but we don't talk about an 'oxygen drive'. Because of the voluntary nature of eating and drinking, hunger and thirst are the homeostatic drives that biopsychologists have been most interested in.

Hunger and eating

Does hunger cause eating?

> ***ASK YOURSELF...***
> - What makes you eat?
> - Why do you get hungry?

If there's a common-sense theory of eating, it's that we eat because – and when – we're hungry. What could be simpler? If asked why we get hungry, most people would probably say that 'our bodies get hungry' – that is, certain events take place in our bodies when we haven't eaten for a certain period of time, and these act as the 'signal' to eat. We experience that signal as hunger.

This fits very neatly with the hunger drive outlined above. If we place the experience of hunger in between 'internal imbalance' and 'homeostatic drive', we get a nice blend of the common-sense and drive-reduction theories, with hunger towards the end of a chain of causation that results in eating.

But is hunger either a necessary or sufficient condition for eating to occur? Can eating occur in the absence of hunger, and is it possible that we might not eat despite being hungry? We've all been tempted by the look or the smell of food when not feeling hungry, and we're not usually still hungry by the time the dessert trolley comes along. In other words, we often eat simply because we like it. This suggests that *hunger isn't necessary* for eating. Conversely, people who go on diets or hunger strike aren't eating (or are eating less than they might otherwise do) despite being very hungry, suggesting that *hunger isn't sufficient*.

So, there seems to be no biological inevitability about the hunger–eating relationship. However, as Blundell & Hill (1995) point out, under many circumstances there is a close relationship between the pattern of food intake and the rhythmic fluctuation of hunger. For example, many experimental studies confirm the strong link between the intensity of experienced hunger sensations and the amount of food eaten. This fairly consistent finding has been interpreted as showing that there's a causal connection between hunger and the size of a following meal. But in reality, certain physiological mechanisms are probably producing *both* the sensations of hunger *and* the eating behaviour.

Blundell and Hill propose an *appetite control system*, in which hunger, eating and physiological mechanisms are coupled together, but the coupling isn't perfect. There will be circumstances where uncoupling can occur, as in the hunger strike example, or in cases of eating disorders (such as obesity and anorexia nervosa: see Chapter 44). So, what might some of these physiological mechanisms be? Assuming that, normally, these are 'coupled' (or correlated) with hunger, what happens when the 'body gets hungry'?

What prompts us to eat?

Carlson (1992) points out that the physiological signals that cause eating to begin aren't necessarily the ones that cause it to end. There's considerable delay between the act of eating (the *correctional mechanism*) and a change in the state of the body. So, while we may start eating because the level of nutrients has fallen below a certain point, we certainly don't stop because that level has been restored to normal. In fact, we usually stop eating long before this, since digestion takes several hours to complete. Therefore, the signals for hunger and for *satiety* (the state of no longer being hungry) are sure to be different. Probably the earliest formal theory of hunger was proposed by Cannon.

> **KEY STUDY 9.1 'Swallow a balloon if you're hungry' (Cannon & Washburn, 1912)**
> - Cannon originally believed that the hunger drive is caused by stomach contractions ('hunger pangs') and that food reduces the drive by stopping the contractions.
> - Washburn swallowed an empty balloon tied to the end of a thin tube. Then Cannon pumped some air into the balloon and connected the end of the tube to a water-filled glass U-tube, so that Washburn's stomach contractions would cause an increase in the level of water at the other end of the U-tube (see Figure 9.2). He reported a 'pang' of hunger each time a large stomach contraction was recorded.

- These results were soon confirmed by a case study (cited in Carlson, 1992) of a patient with a tube implanted through his stomach wall, just above the navel. He'd accidentally swallowed some acid, which caused the walls of his oesophagus (the muscular tube that carries food from the throat to the stomach) to fuse shut. The tube allowed him to feed himself and provided a means of observing his stomach activities.
- When there was food in his stomach, small rhythmic contractions (subsequently named peristaltic contractions/peristalsis) mixed the food and moved it along the digestive tract. When it was empty, the contractions were large and associated with the patient's reports of hunger.

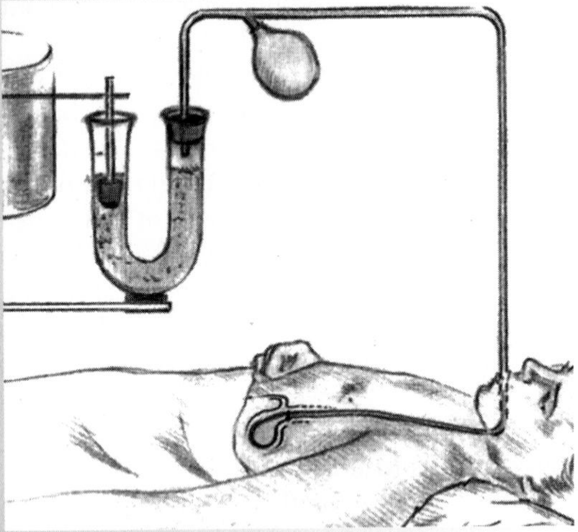

Figure 9.2 The system developed by Cannon and Washburn in 1912 for measuring stomach contractions (from Pinel, *Biopsychology* 2nd Edition, published by Allyn and Bacon, Boston, MA. Copyright © 1993 by Pearson Education. Reprinted by permission of the publisher)

An evaluation of Cannon's 'hunger pangs' theory

Sometimes patients have their stomachs removed (because of disease) and the oesophagus is 'hooked up' directly to the duodenum or small intestine (the upper portion of the intestine through which most of the glucose and amino acids are absorbed into the bloodstream: see below). They continue to report feeling hungry and satiated. Even though their stomachs are bypassed, they maintain normal body weight by eating more frequent, smaller meals (Pinel, 1993).

Similarly, cutting the neural connections between the *gastrointestinal tract* (GIT) (comprising mainly the stomach and intestine) and the brain (that is, cutting the *vagus nerve*) has little effect on food intake – either in experimental animals or human patients.

These findings suggest that Cannon exaggerated the importance of stomach contractions in causing hunger. But this doesn't mean that the stomach and the GIT play no part in hunger and satiety. If the vagus nerve is cut, signals arising from the gut can still be communicated to the brain via the circulatory system. These signals convey information about the *components* of the food that's been absorbed. Some of the nutrients whose depletion acts as a signal to start eating are fats (lipids), carbohydrates (including glucose), vitamins/mineral salts and proteins/amino acids. Fats and carbohydrates are burnt up in cellular reactions and provide the energy to fuel metabolic processes. *Metabolism* refers to all the chemical processes occurring in the body's cells and that are essential for the body's normal functioning. *Metabolic rate* refers to the amount of energy the body uses.

Also, the presence of food in the stomach (*stomach loading*) is important in the regulation of feeding: if the exit from the stomach to the duodenum is blocked off, rats will still eat normal-sized meals. It seems that information about the stretching of the stomach wall caused by the presence of food is passed to the brain (via the vagus nerve), allowing the brain's feeding centres to control meal size.

When we engage in vigorous physical activity, our muscles are fuelled by fats and carbohydrates, which are stored as energy reserves. The cells that store our fat reserves are called *adipocytes*, and they clump together as *adipose tissue* (or simply 'fat'). Carbohydrates are stored as *glycogen*. Two major accounts of why we start eating are the *glucostatic* and *lipostatic theories*.

Glucostatic theory

According to *glucostatic theory* (GT), the primary stimulus for hunger is a decrease in the level of blood glucose below a certain set point. Glucose is the body's (especially the brain's) primary fuel. The *glucostat* was assumed to be a neuron (probably in the hypothalamus), which detects the level of blood glucose in much the same way as a thermostat measures temperature.

According to Pinel (1993), Mayer's (1955) version of GT was particularly influential, because it dealt with a serious problem associated with earlier versions. He proposed that it was *glucose utilisation* (the rate at which it's used), rather than *absolute blood glucose level*, that was regulated by feeding. While these are usually highly correlated, Mayer's version could account for those few occasions where high levels are associated with *hyperphagia* (overeating). For example, people with diabetes mellitus overeat, despite high blood glucose levels. This is because their pancreas fails to produce sufficient quantities of insulin (needed for glucose to enter most body cells and to be utilised by them).

Mayer's hypothesis was supported by experiments with mice (Mayer & Marshall, 1956), which appeared to identify the location of the glucoreceptors in the *ventromedial hypothalamus* (VMH). They concluded that the VMH is a *satiety centre*. However, although a fall in blood glucose may be the most important physiological signal for hunger, it's not the only one. If animals eat a meal that's low in carbohydrate but high in fats or proteins, they still manage to eat a relatively constant amount of calories, even though their blood glucose is reduced slightly. If eating were controlled *exclusively* by blood glucose, we'd expect them to overeat and get fat (Carlson, 1992).

Lipostatic theory

According to Green (1994), *lipostatic theory* (LT) focuses on the *end product* of glucose metabolism, namely the storage of fats (lipids) in adipocytes. Body fat is normally maintained at a relatively constant level. Similarly, fluctuations in the amount of stored fats largely determine variations in body weight. According to Nisbett's (1972) version of LT, we all have a body weight set point around which our weight fluctuates within quite narrow limits; this is determined by the level of fats in the adipocytes.

The most frequently cited evidence in support of the lipostatic theory is the failure of short-term dieting programmes to produce long-term weight loss: as soon as dieting stops, the person regains the weight that's been lost. Other evidence comes from animal experiments in which lesions are made in the hypothalamus. When the *lateral hypothalamus* (LH) is damaged, rats will stop eating, even when food is readily available, to the point of death from starvation. This failure to feed is called *aphagia*. It was originally taken to indicate that the LH normally functions to *stimulate* eating (and so represents another partial answer to the question 'Why do we start eating?').

KEY STUDY 9.2 Lowering body weight before the lesion (Keesey & Powley, 1975)

- Keesey and Powley deprived rats of food, so that their body weight was lowered substantially.
- When lesions were then made in their LH, they started eating *more* food (not less). In normal rats, the lesion lowers the body weight set point, and the resulting failure to eat occurs because the animal is trying to adjust to this lower target weight.
- However, if the weight is reduced *before* the lesion is made to below the lesion-produced target, the rat now *increases* feeding (following the lesion) in order to reach the new (higher) set point.

Keesey and Powley's findings mean that damage to the LH affects feeding only *indirectly* (as Nisbett suggests), by altering the body weight set point. Feeding is aimed at attaining this new target.

Set point or settling point?

According to Pinel (1993), GT and LT are *complementary*, rather than mutually exclusive. GT was meant to account for the initiation and termination of eating (relatively *short-term* processes), while LT was proposed to explain *long-term* feeding habits and the regulation of body weight. They both assume the existence of mechanisms within the CNS that are sensitive to deviations from one or more hypothetical set points. This assumption is itself based on another, namely that homeostasis implies the existence of set-point mechanisms.

Many current biopsychological theories of eating reject these assumptions in favour of the view that body weight tends to drift around a natural *settling point* – that is, the level at which the various factors that influence it achieve balance or equilibrium. Pinel (1993) believes that earlier theorists were seduced by the analogy with the thermostat, which is a compelling set-point model. His analogy for a settling point theory is the *leaky barrel model*: the level of fat in the body, like the water level in a leaky barrel, is regulated around a natural settling point rather than a predetermined set point.

ASK YOURSELF...

- What are your two or three favourite foods (or meals)?
- What exactly is it about them that you like so much?
- How much, if at all, do you consider *social* factors play a part in your eating behaviour?

Other factors that influence eating

A settling point theory is more compatible with research findings that implicate factors other than internal energy deficits as causes of eating. As we noted earlier, hunger is neither a necessary nor a sufficient condition for eating to take place. For example, even if it were possible to explain hunger purely in terms of lowered levels of glucose and fat, we'd still need to identify other influences on eating. According to Pinel (1993):

> The modern era of feeding research has been characterized by an increasing awareness of the major role played by learning in determining when we eat, what we eat, how much we eat, and even how the food that we eat is digested and metabolised. The concept of the feeding system has changed from that of an immutable system that maintains glucose and fat levels at pre-determined set points, to that of a flexible system that operates within certain general guidelines but is 'fine-tuned' by experience ...

Eating for pleasure

Both humans and other animals are *drawn* to eat (rather than *driven* to eat) by food's *incentive properties* – that is, its anticipated pleasure-producing effects (or *palatability*). According to incentive theories, both internal and external factors influence eating in the same way, namely by changing the incentive value of available foods. Signals from the taste receptors seem to produce an immediate decline in the incentive value of *similar tasting food*, and signals associated with increased energy supply from a meal produce a general decrease in the incentive properties of *all foods*.

Support for this view comes from the discovery of LH neurons that respond to the incentive properties of food, rather than food itself (Rolls & Rolls, 1982). When monkeys were repeatedly allowed to eat one palatable foodstuff, the response of LH neurons to it declined (a form of habituation?), although not to other palatable foods. Neurons that responded to the sight of food would begin to respond to a neutral stimulus that reliably predicted the presentation of food. These findings explain very neatly the common experience of our 'mouths watering' (salivating) at the mere mention of our favourite food – or even a picture of it.

KEY STUDY 9.3 Learning to salivate (Pavlov, 1927)

- The smell of food, and the dinner bell, are *food-predicting cues* (or *classically conditioned stimuli*).
- They trigger digestive and metabolic events, such as salivation, insulin secretion and gastric secretions (*classically conditioned responses*). These digestive/metabolic events are also called *cephalic phase responses*.
- Pavlov (1927) was the first to demonstrate that a cephalic phase response can be conditioned: the sight or smell of milk produced abundant salivation in puppies raised on a milk diet, but not in those raised on a solid diet.
- Feeling hungry at those times of the day when we usually eat (whether or not we're experiencing an energy deficit) is another example of a classically conditioned response (see Chapter 11).

Knowing what to eat

If learning is involved in the way humans and other animals respond to foods that are already palatable, could learning be involved in what is found palatable in the first place?

- We have innate preferences for tastes that are associated in nature with vital nutrients. For example, sweetness detectors on the tongue are probably there because they helped our ancestors identify food that's safe to eat. Even when we're not particularly hungry, we tend to find a sweet taste pleasant, and eating something sweet tends to increase our appetite (Carlson, 1992).
- Both humans and other animals also have the ability to learn the relationship between taste and the post-ingestion consequences of eating certain food. In *taste aversion studies*, rats learn to avoid novel tastes that are followed by illness (Garcia *et al.*, 1966: see Chapter 11). Rats are also able to learn to prefer tastes that are followed by the infusion of nutrients and flavours that they smell on the breath of other rats.
- Rats and human beings have in common a metabolism that requires them to eat a variety of different foods: no single food provides all essential nutrients. We generally find a meal that consists of moderate amounts of several different foods more interesting than a huge plate of only one food, however palatable that food might be. If we have access to only one particular food, we soon become tired of it (*sensory-specific satiety*). This encourages the consumption of a varied diet.

ASK YOURSELF...
- Which would you rather eat?

- Cultural evolution helps the selection of balanced diets. For example, Mexicans increased the calcium in their diet by mixing small amounts of mineral lime into their tortillas. But in the industrialised societies of Europe and North America, we seem to prefer diets that are fundamentally detrimental to our health (see Chapter 12). Manufacturers tend to sell foods that are highly palatable and energy-dense, but that often have little nutritional value. This encourages us to overeat and, as a result, to increase fat deposits and body weight. Blundell & Hill (1995) maintain that in *evolutionary terms*, overeating makes good sense:

> ... For human beings it can be supposed that during most of the tens of thousands of years of human evolution the biggest problem facing human-kind was the scarcity of food ... the existence of an abundance of food, highly palatable and easily available, is a very recent development in evolutionary terms. Accordingly, it is unlikely that evolutionary pressure has ever led to the development of mechanisms to prevent overconsumption ...

What stops us eating?

According to Blundell & Hill (1995), *satiety* (feeling 'full up' or satisfied) is, by definition, not instantaneous but something that occurs over a considerable period of time. It's useful, therefore, to distinguish different *phases of satiety* associated with different mechanisms that, together, comprise the *satiety cascade*. Most important for understanding the suppression and subsequent control of hunger are:

- *post-ingestive effects*, which include gastric distension, the rate of gastric emptying, the release of hormones (such as CCK: see Box 9.2) and the stimulation of certain receptors along the GIT
- *post-absorptive effects*, which refer to mechanisms arising from the action of glucose, fats, amino acids (and other metabolites) after absorption across the intestine into the bloodstream.

Box 9.2 Cholecystokinin (CCK)

- After food reaches the stomach, the protein is broken down into its constituent amino acids.
- As digestion proceeds, food gradually passes into the *duodenum* (small intestine). This controls the rate of stomach emptying by secreting a peptide hormone (short chains of amino acids) called *cholecystokinin* (CCK). CCK is secreted in response to the presence of fats, detected by receptors in the walls of the duodenum.
- Many studies have found that injecting CCK into hungry rats causes them to eat smaller meals. Wolkowitz *et al.* (1990) gave people injections of a drug that blocks CCK receptors in the peripheral nervous system (but not in the brain): they reported feeling more hungry and less full after a meal than controls given a placebo.

(Source: based on Carlson, 1992)

There's currently considerable research interest in whether protein, fat and carbohydrate differ in their satiating efficiency and their capacity to reduce hunger. One clear finding is that carbohydrates are efficient appetite suppressants. Also, the fat content of food influences its texture and palatability, but it has a disproportionately weak effect on satiety (Blundell & Hill, 1995).

Although the stomach may not be very important in causing hunger (see Key Study 9.1), it does seem to be important in satiety. For example, we noted that stomach loading and stretching of the stomach wall play a part in reducing hunger. The gastric branch of the vagus nerve carries emergency signals from the stretch receptors in the stomach wall, preventing us from overeating and damaging the stomach.

The brain's control of eating

It's been known since the early 1800s that tumours of the hypothalamus can cause *hyperphagia* (excessive

The Atkins Diet advocates high fat and low carbohydrates (potatoes, bread and pasta). This goes against 'orthodox' thinking regarding healthy eating

overeating) and obesity in humans (Pinel, 1993). But not until the advent of *stereotaxic surgery* in the late 1930s (see Chapter 4) were experimenters able to assess the effects of damage to particular areas of the hypothalamus on the eating behaviour of experimental animals.

KEY STUDY 9.4 Hyperphagia in rats (Hetherington & Ranson, 1942)

- Hetherington and Ranson found that large, bilateral lesions in the lower, central portion of the hypothalamus (the *ventromedial nucleus/VMN*) cause *hyperphagia*: the rat will carry on eating until it becomes grotesquely fat, doubling or even trebling its normal body weight.
- Although several structures were damaged by such lesions, it was generally assumed that the *ventromedial hypothalamus* (VMH) was the crucial structure.
- The resulting hyperphagia was taken to indicate that the normal function of the VMH is to *inhibit* feeding when the animal is 'full'. Hence, the VMH became known as the *satiety centre*. It's been found in rats, cats, dogs, chickens and monkeys (Teitelbaum, 1967).

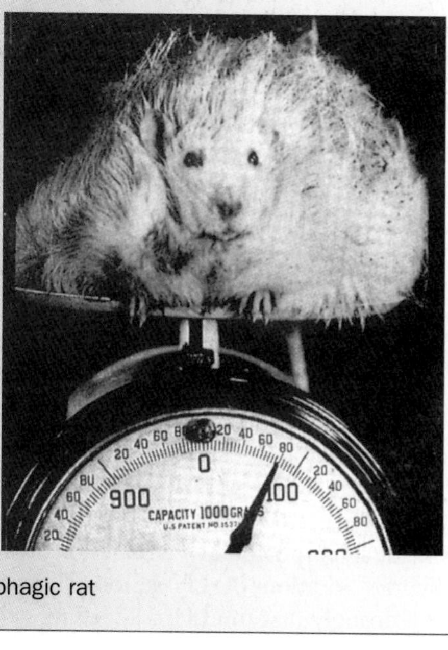

A hyperphagic rat

The VMH syndrome

Paradoxically, VMH-lesioned rats *aren't* 'hell bent' on eating – they won't eat anything and everything. The taste of food seems to be especially important in hyperphagic rats. Most animals will eat even bad-tasting food ('you'll eat anything if you're hungry enough'), but hyperphagic rats are very fussy, and will refuse their regular food if quinine is added – even if this means that they become underweight (Teitelbaum, 1955).

What about people?

One possible explanation for the 'finicky' eating of VMH-lesioned rats is that they become less sensitive to *internal* cues of satiation (such as blood glucose level and body fat content) and more responsive to *external* cues (such as taste). Schachter (1971) claims that this may also apply to overweight people. Schachter *et al.* (1968) found that normal-weight people responded to the internal cue of stomach distension ('feeling bloated') by refusing any more food. But obese people tended to go on eating. The latter seemed to be responding to the *availability* of food. However, they're *less* willing to make an effort to find food compared with normal-weight people, who'll search for food – but only if they're genuinely hungry (Schachter, 1971).

- Overweight people also tend to report that they feel hungry at prescribed eating times, even if they've eaten a short while before. Normal-weight people tend to eat only when they feel hungry, and this is relatively independent of clock time. However, this increased sensitivity to external cues isn't necessarily what causes some people to become obese – it could just as easily be an *effect* of obesity.
- Although people with hypothalamic tumours tend towards obesity, there's no evidence that the hypothalamus doesn't function properly in overweight people generally.

Differences in *basal metabolic rate* largely determine our body weight, and are probably hereditary. There's very little evidence to suggest that lack of impulse control, poor ability to delay gratification or eating too quickly contribute to overweight (Carlson, 1992). However, the role of complex psychological variables has been studied much more extensively in relation to *anorexia nervosa* and *bulimia nervosa* (see Chapter 44).

The LH syndrome

If the VMH has traditionally been regarded as a 'brake' on eating, the *lateral hypothalamus* (LH) has been seen as the 'accelerator'. Bilateral lesions to the LH cause aphagia, a refusal to eat, even to the point of death from starvation (Anand & Brobeck, 1951; Teitelbaum & Stellar, 1954). Even rats made hyperphagic by VMH lesions will become aphagic by the addition of LH lesions. These findings suggest very strongly that the LH is a feeding centre.

However, the LH syndrome also includes *adipsia* (the complete cessation of drinking). Both aphagia and adipsia are, in turn, part of a more general lack of responsiveness to sensory input. The LH itself is a relatively large, complex and ill-defined area, with many nuclei and several major nerve tracts running through it. While electrical stimulation of the LH produces eating, it also triggers drinking, gnawing, temperature changes and sexual activity. Conversely, eating can also be elicited by stimulation of other areas of the hypothalamus, the amygdala, hippocampus, thalamus and frontal cortex. For all these reasons, Pinel (1993) believes that to call the LH a 'hunger centre' is a misnomer.

Thirst and drinking

> *ASK YOURSELF...*
> - As with food, what is it exactly that you like about your favourite drinks?
> - Might social factors play a greater role here than in your eating (see Chapter 8)?

What starts us drinking?

It was thought until recently that drinking is motivated by a deficit in the body's water resources – that is, by deviation from set points, as part of a homeostatic drive mechanism. However, most drinking (like most eating) occurs in the absence of deficits. This suggests that the motivation to drink comes from anticipating its pleasurable effects (*positive incentive properties*). We tend to prefer drinks that have a pleasant taste (such as fruit juice) or pleasant pharmacological effects (such as alcohol, coffee and tea).

Positive incentive theory

Water deprivation increases the positive incentive value of almost all salt-free drinks. After 24 hours without a drink, people report that even plain water has a pleasant taste (Rolls *et al.*, 1980). If you add a little saccharine to the water of non-deprived rats, their water intake rockets. Like people, rats with unlimited access to water or other palatable fluids drink far more than they actually need. As with food, *sensory-specific satiety* has a major effect on drinking. As fond as rats are of saccharine, if saccharine solution is constantly available ('on tap'), they'll come to prefer it less than when it's only available periodically.

Dry-mouth theory

A dry mouth and throat are obvious cues to thirst (the counterpart of the stomach contraction cues to hunger: see Key Study 9.1). Although a dry mouth is one consequence of water deficiency, it's not the primary factor in thirst. For example, producing a chronic dry mouth by removal of the salivary glands doesn't substantially increase water intake, unless rats are fed dry food or kept in a very hot environment. Conversely, blocking the sensation of a dry mouth fails to decrease water intake. The most convincing evidence against the dry-mouth theory comes from *sham drinking*: water flows down the oesophagus and then out through a fistula before it can be absorbed. Despite the lack of a dry mouth, animals sham-drink continuously (Pinel, 1993).

What makes us stop drinking?

According to set-point theories, drinking brings about a return to an internal water resource set point. When this has been achieved, drinking stops. But like hunger, thirst and drinking seem to stop long before enough time has elapsed for the body to have absorbed the water from the stomach, and for the water–salt balance in the blood to have been restored.

Stomach distension probably contributes to satiety. Cold water is more thirst quenching, because it moves out of the stomach much more slowly, and so provides a clearer stomach-distension signal to the brain. The *mouth-metering mechanism* also plays a part. This gauges the amount of water being ingested, and compares the amount needed to restore the water balance.

If set-point theories were correct, we'd expect that delivering water directly to where it's needed would eliminate thirst and deprivation-induced drinking. However, if water is injected directly into a rat's stomach or bloodstream, drinking is reduced by only 30 per cent of the amount injected. Even total replenishment of an animal's water resources has only a modest inhibitory effect on deprivation-induced drinking (about 30 per cent). These findings pose difficulties for any set-point theory (Pinel, 1993).

HULL'S DRIVE-REDUCTION THEORY

As we noted earlier, Hull's motivational theory must be considered in the context of his theory of learning. Drive reduction theory was intended to explain the fundamental principle of reinforcement, both *positive* (the reduction of a drive by the *presentation* of a stimulus) and *negative* (the reduction of a drive by the *removal* or *avoidance* of a stimulus).

Hull was interested in the *primary* (physiological), *homeostatic* needs and drives of hunger, thirst, air, avoiding injury, maintaining an optimum temperature, defecation and urination, rest, sleep, activity and propagation (reproduction). He believed that all behaviour (human and animal) originates in the satisfaction of these drives.

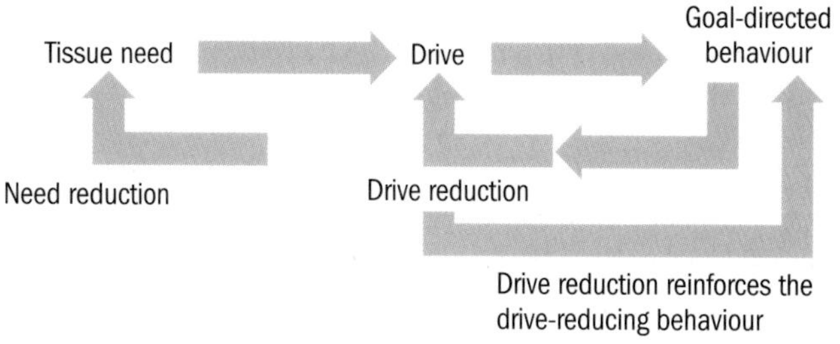

Figure 9.3 Summary of drive-reduction theory

Needs vs drives

While the terms 'need' and 'drive' are often used interchangeably, they're fundamentally different:

- *needs* are physiological and can be defined objectively (for example, in terms of hours without food or blood sugar level)
- *drives* are *psychological* (behavioural), and are *hypothetical constructs* – that is, abstract concepts that refer to processes/events believed to be taking place inside the person/animal, but that cannot be directly observed or measured.

However, Hull *operationalised* drives as hours of deprivation. He proposed a number of equations, which were meant to be testable in laboratory experiments (Walker, 1984). Perhaps the most important of these was:

$$sEr = D \times V \times K \times sHr$$

where *sEr* stands for the intensity or likelihood of any learned behaviour which can be calculated if four other factors are known, namely:

- *D* – the *drive* or *motivation*, measured by some indicator of physical need, such as hours of deprivation
- *V* – the *intensity* of the signal for the behaviour
- *K* – the *degree of incentive*, measured by the size of the reward or some other measure of its desirability
- *sHr* – *habit strength*, measured as the amount of practice given, usually in terms of the number of reinforcements.

Evaluation of drive reduction theory

ASK YOURSELF...
- Try to formulate some arguments against drive-reduction theory.

- Hull's basic premise is that animals (and, by implication, people) *always* and *only* learn through primary drive reduction. But the relationship between primary drives and needs is very unclear, as we saw earlier when discussing the eating behaviour of obese people.
- At its simplest, needs can arise without specific drives, as in learning what and how much to eat (see above). For example, we need vitamin C, but we wouldn't normally talk of a 'vitamin C drive' (in the way that we talk about a general hunger drive).
- Conversely, drives can occur in the absence of any obvious physiological need. An important example of a *non-homeostatic drive* in rats is *electrical (self-)stimulation of the brain* (ES-SB) (see Key Study 9.5).

KEY STUDY 9.5 What a rat wouldn't do for a shock (Olds & Milner, 1954)

- Olds and Milner implanted an electrode near a rat's septum (part of the limbic system), so that every time it pressed a lever, it would receive an electric shock.
- Rats made between 3000 and 7500 lever-pressing responses in a 12-hour period.
- Olds (1956) reported that one rat stimulated itself more than 2000 times per hour for 24 consecutive hours.
- Olds (1958) reported that rats, which normally press a lever 25 times per hour for food reward, will press 100 times *per minute* for a reward of ES-SB.

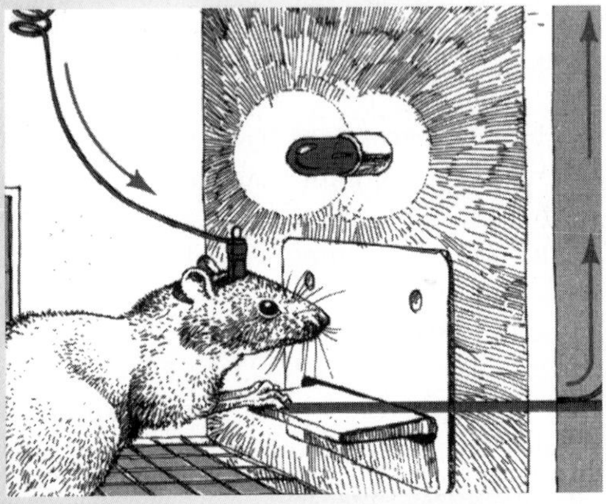

Figure 9.4 Olds (1956) implanted electrodes in the hypothalami of rats. The rats could trigger an electrical stimulus by depressing a lever. Clearly, the region where the electrode was implanted constitutes some kind of pleasure centre (adapted from J. Olds ©1956 Pleasure centres in the brain. Scientific American, Inc. All rights reserved)

Brain stimulation is such a powerful reinforcer that a male rat with an electrode in its LH will self-stimulate in preference to eating if hungry, drinking when thirsty or having access to a sexually receptive female. This effect has been found in rats, cats, monkeys and pigeons (and humans, occasionally). The main reward site for ES-SB is the *median forebrain bundle* (MFB), a fibre tract that runs from the brainstem up to the forebrain through the LH (Beaumont, 1988; Carlson, 1992). The effect seems to depend on the presence of dopamine and noradrenaline. These reward centres are generally thought of as the neural substrate of 'pleasure', so that any behaviour defined as pleasurable involves their activation (see Chapter 8). ES-SB is seen as a 'short-cut' to pleasure, eliminating the need for natural drives and reinforcers.

- Tolman's *cognitive behaviourism* challenged Skinner's theory of *operant* conditioning, because it showed that learning could take place in the absence of reinforcement (*latent learning*: see Chapter 11). By implication, Tolman showed that learning could take place in the absence of drive reduction.
- Hull's theory emphasised primary (homeostatic) drives to the exclusion of secondary (non-homeostatic) drives. Primary drives are based on primary (innate) needs, but much human (and, to a lesser extent, non-human) behaviour can be understood only in terms of secondary (acquired) drives. Several behaviourist psychologists – notably Miller (1948), Mowrer (1950), and Dollard & Miller (1950) – modified Hull's theory to include acquired drives (in particular, anxiety), which led to a great deal of research on avoidance learning in the 1950s (see Chapters 11, 32, 44 and 45).
- In Maslow's terms, drive-reduction theory deals only with survival needs, completely ignoring the self-actualisation (or 'growth') needs, which make human motivation distinctively different from that of non-humans.

NON-HOMEOSTATIC NEEDS AND DRIVES

Just as ES-SB cannot be accommodated by drive reduction when considering only non-human motivation, so non-humans seem to have other non-homeostatic drives that they share, to some degree, with humans. The rest of this chapter will be devoted to these important, and pervasive, non-homeostatic needs and drives.

ASK YOURSELF...

- When we – and non-humans – aren't eating, drinking and doing all the other things we have to do to survive, what do we do?
- Why do we do it?
- Are all our activities ultimately aimed at survival, or are even non-humans capable of doing things 'just for the sheer hell of it'?

Competence motives: motives without specific primary needs

According to White (1959), the 'master reinforcer' that keeps most of us motivated over long periods of time is the need to confirm our sense of personal competence:

our capacity to deal effectively with the environment. It's *intrinsically* rewarding and satisfying to feel that we're capable human beings, to be able to understand, predict and control our world (aims which also happen to be the major aims of science: see Chapter 3).

Unlike hunger, which comes and goes, competence seems to be a continuous, ongoing motive. We can't satisfy it and then do without it until it next appears, because it's not rooted in any specific physiological need. This is why it isn't very helpful to think of the competence motive as a drive that pushes us into seeking its reduction. While homeostatic drives involve an attempt to *reduce* something (tissue need), competence motives often involve the *search for stimulation*.

Seeking stimulation

If rats are allowed to become thoroughly familiar with a maze, and then the maze is changed in some way, they'll spend more time exploring the altered maze. This occurs even in the absence of any obvious extrinsic reward, such as food. They're displaying a *curiosity drive* (Butler, 1954). Butler (1954) and Harlow *et al.* (1950) gave monkeys mechanical puzzles to solve, such as undoing a chain, lifting a hook and opening a clasp. The monkeys did these puzzles over and over again, for hours at a time, with no other reward: they were displaying their *manipulative drive* (Harlow *et al.*, 1950).

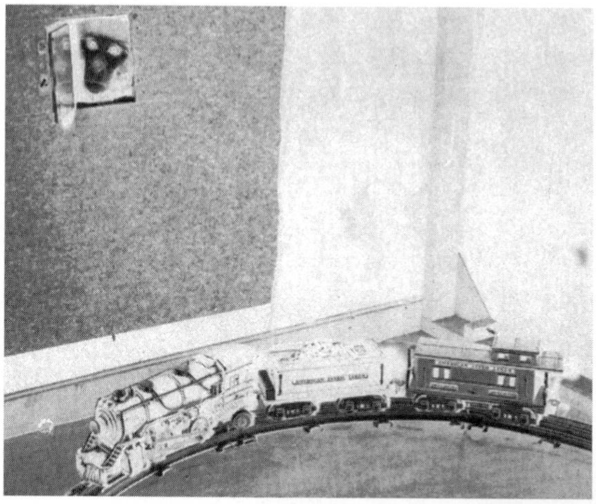

Research by Butler and Harlow has shown that animals are motivated to explore and manipulate their environments, quite unrelated to biological drives such as hunger and thirst. Monkeys will learn and work in order to open a door which allows them to view an electric train. They will also work diligently to open locks which lead to no tangible reward

Play and motivation

Much of the behaviour normally described as play can be thought of in terms of the drives for curiosity, exploration and manipulation. The purpose of play from the child's point of view is simple enjoyment. It doesn't consciously play in order to find out how things work, or to exercise its imagination, but simply because it's fun and intrinsically satisfying. Any learning that does result is quite incidental. However, for the young child there's no real distinction between 'work' and 'play' in an adult sense.

Piaget (1951) distinguishes between *play*, which is performed for its own sake, and '*intellectual activity*' or *learning*, which has an external aim or purpose. This distinction is meant to apply to all three major types of play he describes: *mastery*, *symbolic/make-believe* and *play with rules*. (Piaget's theory is discussed in detail in Chapter 34.) Nor is play confined to humans. The young of many species engage in activities that seem to have little to do with homeostatic or survival needs. However, the higher up the evolutionary scale the species, the more apparent and purposeful the play becomes, and the more the nature of play changes as the young animal develops. (Fontana, 1981a).

Play – both pleasurable and purposeful

Motivation and adaptation

Piaget saw play as essentially an *adaptive activity*. Throughout development, play helps to consolidate recently acquired abilities as well as aiding the development of additional cognitive and social skills. In the same way, the competence motives of curiosity, exploration and manipulation undoubtedly have adaptive significance for an individual and, ultimately, for the species. Investigating and exploring the environment equips an animal with 'knowledge', which can be used in times of stress or danger (Bolles, 1967).

Optimal level (or arousal) theories

According to Berlyne (1960), investigation and exploration are based on an inbuilt tendency to seek a certain 'optimum' level of stimulation or activity. Exploring the unfamiliar increases arousal, but if it's too different from what we're used to, arousal will be too high (we'll feel anxious and tense). If it's *not* different enough, arousal is too low (we'll soon become bored).

Optimum level theories are supported by *sensory deprivation experiments*. In classic experiments carried out by Hebb and his colleagues at McGill University in the 1950s (Bexton *et al.*, 1954; Heron, 1957), participants were almost completely cut off from their normal sensory stimulation, by wearing blindfolds, earmuffs, cardboard tubes on their arms and legs, and so on. They soon began to experience extreme psychological discomfort, reported hallucinations, and couldn't tolerate their confinement for usually more than three days.

Cohen & Taylor (1972) studied the psychological effects of long-term imprisonment, and found that sensory deprivation and monotony are experiences that prisoners share with explorers, space travellers and round-

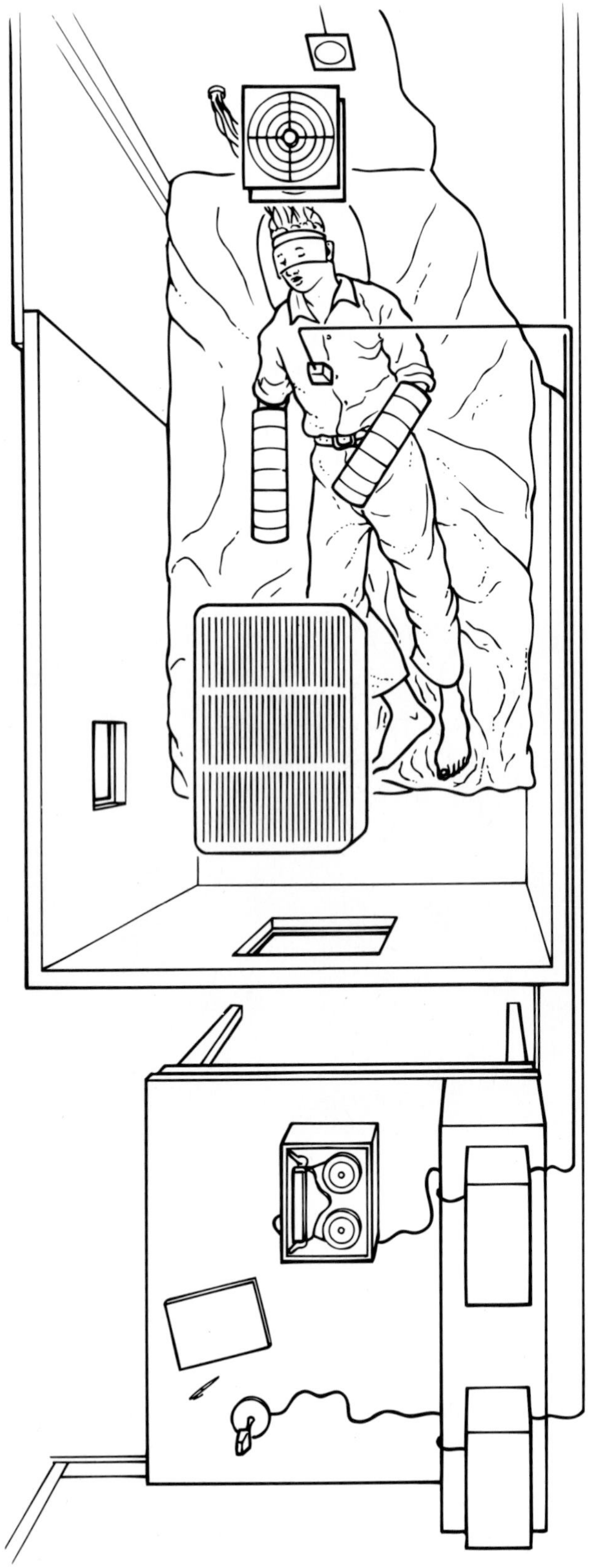

Figure 95 Sensory deprivation cubicle (Heron, 1957)

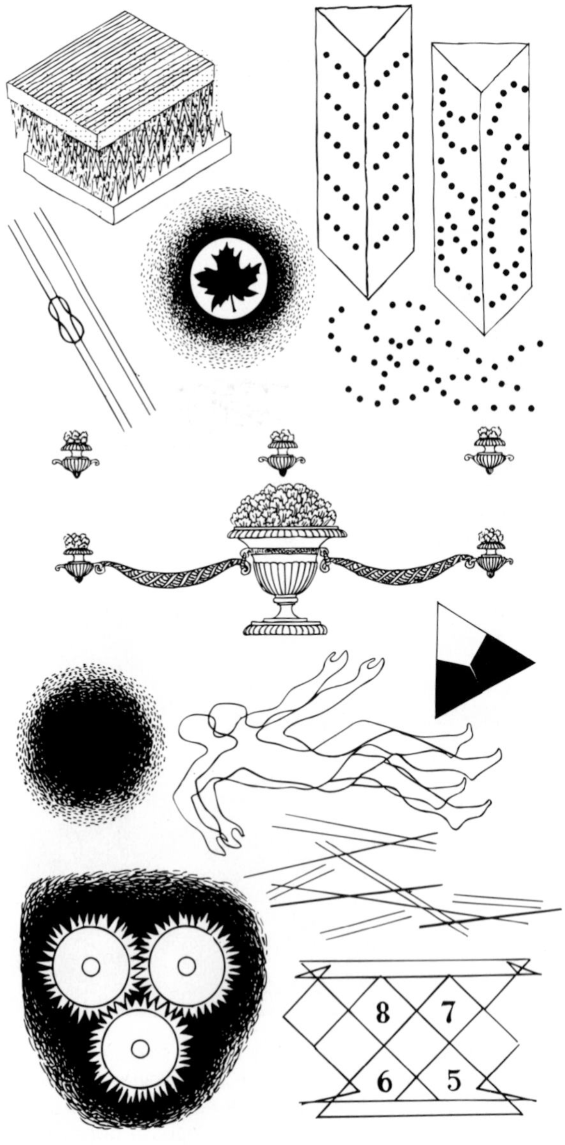

Figure 9.6 Hallucinations of sensory-deprived participants

the-world sailors. Conversely, excessive stimulation ('*sensory overload*') is also debilitating, and may be responsible for some kinds of psychological disorders in our highly urbanised society (see Chapter 12's discussion of stress).

The need for control

Another major kind of competence motive is the need to be in control of our own destiny, and not at the mercy of external forces (Rubin & McNeil, 1983). This is closely linked to the need to be free from the controls and restrictions of others, to dictate our own actions and not be dictated to. According to Brehm (1966), when our freedom is threatened, we tend to react by reasserting our freedom (*psychological reactance*: see Chapter 49).

When people initially expect to have control over the outcomes of their actions, the first experience of not doing so is likely to produce reactance, but further bad experiences are likely to result in *learned helplessness* (Seligman, 1975). Rotter's (1966) concept of *locus of control* refers to individual differences in people's beliefs about what controls events in their everyday lives (see Chapter 12).

Cognitive motives

Consistency and achievement

One of the most researched cognitive motives is the need for *cognitive consistency*, which is discussed in Chapter 24 in relation to attitudes and attitude change. Another that has generated an enormous amount of research and theorising is *achievement motivation/need for achievement* (nAch). This was one of the 20 human motives identified by Murray in 1938. He drew a sharp distinction between *psychogenic* (or psychological) needs, which are learned, and *viscerogenic* (or physiological) needs, which are innate.

Murray agreed with Freud that people express their true motives more clearly in free association than in direct self-reports (or questionnaire-type personality tests: see Chapter 42). Based on this belief, Murray (together with Morgan, 1935) devised the *Thematic Apperception Test* (TAT). This consists of a series of 20 pictures, presented one at a time, ten in each of two sessions separated by at least one day. Slightly different versions are used for men and women, boys and girls. The participant is told that the TAT is a test of imagination and asked to make up a story that describes:

- what is happening and who the people are
- what has led up to the situation
- what is being thought and what is wanted, and by whom
- what will happen, what will be done.

The pictures are sufficiently ambiguous with regard to the events depicted and the emotions of the characters to allow a wide range of interpretations. How a person interprets them reveals their own unconscious motives. Hence,

Figure 9.7 Sample TAT picture

the TAT is a major *projective test* used in motivation and personality research (see Chapter 42). A person who scores high on nAch is concerned with standards of excellence, high levels of performance, recognition from others and the pursuit of long-term goals (they're *ambitious*).

Social motives

According to Geen (1995), social motivation refers to the activation of processes involved in the initiation, direction and energisation of individual behaviour 'by situations in which other people are in close contact with the individual'. It's usually assumed that these situations don't provide specific cues for individual behaviour (they're 'weak'). He contrasts them with 'strong' situations, such as those in which there's direct social influence (as in obedience experiments: see Chapter 27). Geen gives three main examples:

1. *social facilitation* – the enhancing effect on behaviour of the mere presence of others (see Chapter 31)
2. *social presentation* – behaving in ways that attempt to present a desirable impression to others (see Chapter 22)
3. *social loafing* – the tendency for individual effort to diminish in group task situations, partly as a result of diffusion of responsibility (again, see Chapter 31).

Each of these may be thought of as a manifestation of the more general influence of *social anxiety*, a state created when a person who wishes to make a certain impression on others doubts that this impression can actually be made. But why should the fear of making a bad impression be such a powerful motive for individual behaviour?

One answer can be found at quite a low level of Maslow's hierarchy, namely love and belongingness. This includes the need for affiliation, the company of other people (especially family, friends and work colleagues), and the need to be accepted by, and included within, society. Certain kinds of conformity can be understood in terms of this basic need (a survival need in Maslow's terms: see Chapter 26). But does this need itself stem from some other, even more fundamental need?

According to Greenberg *et al.* (1986, cited in Geen 1995), human culture, which society represents, provides a buffer against facing one's own vulnerability and mortality. Society provides a 'cultural drama' that gives meaning to life and without which the individual would experience a dread of being alive. We are, therefore, motivated to play an approved role in that drama: by meeting cultural standards, the individual achieves the approval and acceptance of others, and avoids rejection and isolation. This can be seen in relation to safety needs, the second level of Maslow's hierarchy, and includes 'fear of the unknown'. The ultimate example of this is the fear of death (see Chapter 39). The general need for others (*affiliation*) and our attraction to particular others are discussed in Chapter 28 on interpersonal relationships.

Fiske (2004) argues that, from the idea that we need other people for our basic survival, it follows that over time we would have developed some *core social motives* that interact with the social situation, to help us survive in groups. We're motivated to get along with other people, because it's *adaptive* to do so. She defines core social motives as:

> ... fundamental, underlying psychological processes that impel people's thinking, feeling, and behaving in situations involving other people ...

She identifies five core social motives: *belonging* (see above), *understanding*, *controlling*, *self-enhancing*, and *trusting*. Belonging underlies the others.

CHAPTER SUMMARY

- The study of motivation is the study of the causes of behaviour. While there's general agreement that motivated behaviour is purposeful, goal-directed behaviour, different theoretical approaches see the underlying causes in very different ways.
- 'Motive' comes from the Latin for 'move' and denotes that which energises and gives direction to people's behaviour.
- Motives have been classified in various ways, but the most comprehensive classification is Maslow's **hierarchy of needs**, which distinguishes survival, deficiency or **D-motives**, and growth, being or **B-motives**.
- **Hedonism** can be seen as a central theme in both Freud's **psychoanalytic theory** and Skinner's **operant conditioning**.
- Influenced by Darwin's theory of evolution, many early psychologists tried to explain human behaviour in terms of large numbers of **instincts**. This approach was replaced by Woodworth's concept of **drive**.
- Two major forms of drive theory are Cannon's **homeostatic drive theory** and Hull's **drive reduction theory**.
- Hunger and thirst are the homeostatic drives that have been most researched by biopsychologists. The earliest formal theory of *hunger* was Cannon's theory of **stomach contractions**.
- According to the **glucostatic theory**, the primary stimulus for hunger is a decrease in the level of **blood glucose** below a certain **set point**. The **glucostat** (probably a neuron in the hypothalamus) detects the level of blood glucose in the way a thermostat measures temperature.
- The other major set-point theory is the **lipostatic theory**, which focuses on the storage of **lipids** (fats) in the **adipose tissue**. It's supported by several observations, including the finding that damage to the LH affects feeding **indirectly** by altering the body weight set point.
- The glucostatic theory was meant to account for the relatively **short-term processes** of eating initiation (and termination), while the lipostatic theory was meant to explain **long-term** feeding habits and regulation of body weight. They share the belief in predetermined set points.
- Eating, in both humans and other animals, is partly determined by food's **palatability**. Food-predicting cues elicit **cephalic phase responses**, such as salivation, through **classical conditioning**.
- **Sensory-specific satiety** encourages the consumption of a varied diet. Although humans are capable of learning which diets best meet their biological needs, people in industrialised societies seem to prefer diets that are fundamentally harmful to health, with obesity becoming increasingly common.
- Lesions in the **VMN** of the rat's hypothalamus cause **hyperphagia**, and the **VMH** became known as the '**satiety centre**'. However, the VMH syndrome also involves increased sensitivity to **external cues** of satiation. This also seems to be true of obese humans.
- Lesions to the **LH** cause **aphagia**, which suggests it's a feeding centre. However, the effects of LH lesions are much more diffuse than originally thought.
- **Drinking** has traditionally been seen as motivated by deviation from set points induced by water deprivation. Although there's some support for the **dry-mouth theory**, this isn't the primary factor in thirst.
- It's difficult for set-point theories to explain why drinking stops, whether this is water-deprived

drinking or not. Both **stomach distension** and the **mouth-metering mechanism** play a part in satiety.

- Hull's **drive-reduction theory** was intended to explain the principle of **reinforcement**. However, needs can arise without specific drives and drives can occur in the absence of any obvious tissue need, as in **ES-SB**. Brain stimulation is a very powerful reinforcer, which can override the primary drives of hunger, thirst and sex.
- **Latent learning** shows that learning can take place in the absence of reinforcement. Much behaviour can only be understood in terms of secondary (**non-homeostatic**) drives, such as anxiety and its avoidance.
- Humans and non-humans share certain non-homeostatic needs and drives, such as **curiosity**, **manipulation** and **play**. These are linked to the **search for stimulation** and the **need for competence**, important for **adaptation** to our environment.
- **Optimal level theories** can help explain why both **sensory deprivation** and **sensory overload** can be stressful and disturbing.
- **Cognitive consistency** and **need for achievement** (**nAch**) are two very important **cognitive motives**.
- Many kinds of social behaviour can be seen as a manifestation of **social anxiety**, which in turn may reflect the more fundamental need for safety and protection from our fear of death.
- **Core social motives** include **belonging**, **understanding**, **controlling**, **self-enhancing** and **trusting**.

Links with other topics/chapters

- Each *major theoretical approach* tries to identify key processes and mechanisms ('causes') underlying human behaviour (Chapters 2 and 4).
- Maslow's hierarchy of needs is commonly discussed in relation to *personality*. It represents an *idiographic* theory, seeing every individual as unique (Chapter 42).
- Many of the experiments designed to understand the mechanisms involved in eating and drinking involve surgical procedures performed on rats (including damaging parts of their brain). This raises fundamental questions about the *ethics of animal experimentation* (Chapter 48).
- The study of obesity can help identify some of the psychological variables involved in eating, but these have been explored much more extensively in relation to other *eating disorders*, in particular *anorexia nervosa* and *bulimia nervosa* (Chapter 44).
- Hull's drive-reduction theory was meant to explain the principle of *reinforcement*, and a major challenge to it (and to Skinner's *operant conditioning*) came from Tolman's *cognitive behaviourism* (Chapter 11).
- Several behaviourist psychologists modified Hull's theory by including acquired drives, especially *anxiety*, which is relevant to understanding *learning* (Chapter 11), *phobias* (and other *mental disorders*), and *behavioural treatments* for those disorders (Chapters 44 and 45).
- *Play* represents an important competence (non-homeostatic) motive, which Piaget saw as essentially an *adaptive* activity (Chapter 34).
- *Psychological reactance* is a response to threats to our freedom and the need to feel in control (Chapter 49).
- A major cognitive motive is *cognitive consistency*, which is central to certain theories of *attitude change* (Chapter 24).
- Social motives underlie many of the major areas of social psychological research. These include *social presentation/self-enhancing* (Chapter 22), *understanding* (Chapter 23), *belonging* (Chapters 26 and 27), *control* (Chapter 29), *trust* (Chapter 30), *social facilitation* and *social loafing* (Chapter 31).

10

EMOTION

INTRODUCTION AND OVERVIEW

Mr Spock in *Star Trek* often points out to Captain Kirk how much energy human beings waste through reacting emotionally to things, when a more logical and rational approach would be more productive. But would we be human at all if we didn't react in this way? This isn't to advocate 'being emotional' in the sense of losing control of our feelings or being unable to consider things in a calm and detached way, but it's the richness of our emotions, and our capacity to have feelings as well as to think things through and to reason, which makes us unique as a species. Emotions set the tone of our experience and give life its vitality. They are internal factors that can energise, direct and sustain behaviour (Rubin & McNeill, 1983).

At the same time, we often respond emotionally to events and situations that we believe make demands on us that we cannot meet – either because we don't have the necessary abilities or resources, or because they force us to make very difficult choices and decisions. We describe these negative kinds of events/situations as *stressful*, and our emotional responses to them as the experience of *stress* (see Chapter 12).

One of the key issues running through research into the nature of emotional experience is to what extent it's a *physiological* phenomenon. Related to this is the question of whether different subjective emotions (feeling angry, afraid, and so on) are also *physiologically distinct*. More recent theories have emphasised the role of *cognitive factors* in our experience of emotion, and are collectively referred to as *cognitive appraisal theories*.

WHAT IS EMOTION?

> *ASK YOURSELF...*
> - What gives emotions their 'flavour'?
> - Do different emotions share certain basic dimensions?

Wundt (1896), one of the founders of scientific psychology (see Chapters 1 and 3), believed that emotional experience can be described in terms of combinations of three dimensions – *pleasantness/unpleasantness*, *calm/excitement* and *relaxation/tension* (based on introspection). Schlosberg (1941) also identified pleasantness/unpleasantness, together with *acceptance/rejection* and *sleep/tension* (based on photographs of posed facial expressions). Osgood (1966), too, saw pleasantness as one dimension, plus activation and control, which correspond to the evaluative, activity and potency factors of the semantic differential (see Chapter 24), based on live emotional display.

Ekman *et al.* (1972) and Ekman & Friesen (1975) identified six primary emotions: surprise, fear, disgust, anger, happiness and sadness (based on photos of posed facial expressions: see Figure 10.1). These are taken to be *universal* – that is, they are expressed facially in the same way, and are recognised as such, by members of diverse cultures. This suggests very strongly that they're *innate*.

Plutchik (1980) has proposed an emotion wheel (see Figure 10.2), in which eight basic/primary emotions (composed of four pairs of opposites) are shown inside the circle, with a further eight complex emotions on the outside. The primary emotions correspond to Ekman and Friesen's six, except that 'joy' and 'sorrow' are used for 'happiness' and 'sadness', respectively, plus acceptance and expectancy. Plutchik believes that the primary emotions are both biologically and subjectively distinct.

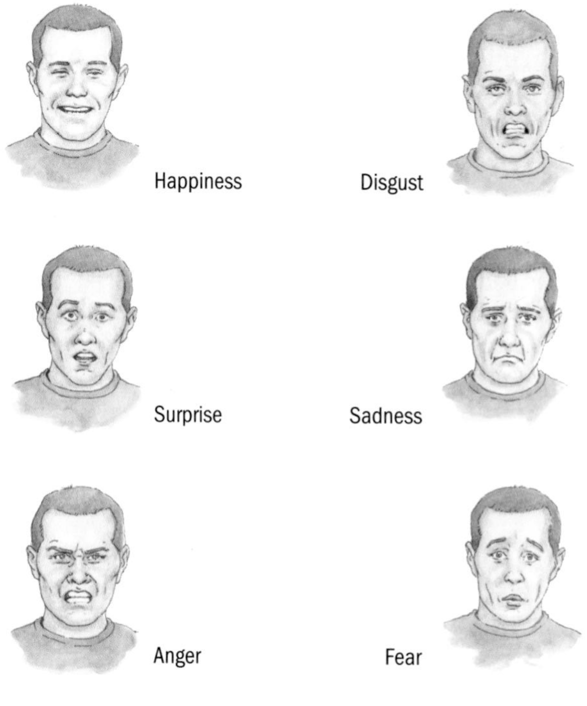

Figure 10.1 Six universal facial expressions

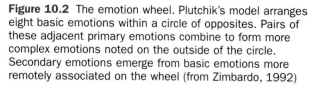

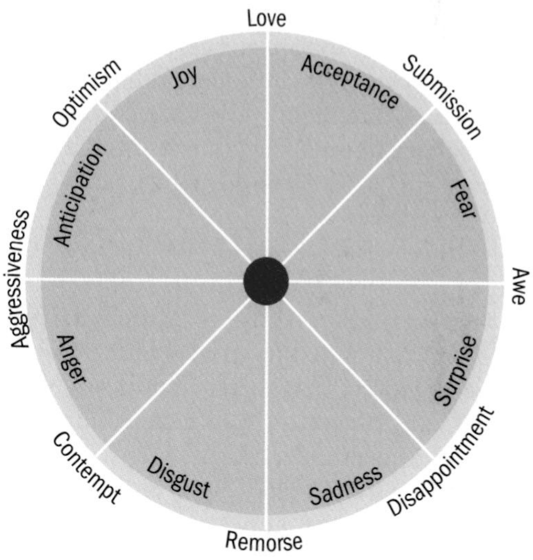

Figure 10.2 The emotion wheel. Plutchik's model arranges eight basic emotions within a circle of opposites. Pairs of these adjacent primary emotions combine to form more complex emotions noted on the outside of the circle. Secondary emotions emerge from basic emotions more remotely associated on the wheel (from Zimbardo, 1992)

'Basic' or 'primary' emotions

For Ekman (1994), 'basic' is meant to emphasise the role that *evolution* has played in shaping both the unique and the common features that emotions display, as well as their current function. Emotions evolved for their adaptive value in dealing with fundamental life tasks: they helped species to survive. Three major characteristics of emotions follow from this adaptive function.

1. there will be certain common elements in the contexts in which emotions are found to occur, despite individual and cultural differences in social learning
2. they're likely to be observable in other primates (while it's possible that there are certain emotions that are unique to humans, there's no convincing evidence that this is so)
3. they can be aroused so quickly that they start to happen before we're even aware of them:

> Quick onset is central to the adaptive value of emotions, mobilizing us quickly to respond to important events ... (Ekman, 1994)

So, emotions can occur with very rapid onset, through automatic appraisal (see below), with little awareness, and with involuntary changes in expression and physiology. Indeed, we often experience emotions as *happening to us*, rather than chosen by us.

We'll see below that there's recent evidence for distinctive patterns of autonomic nervous system (ANS) activity for various emotions. Ekman believes that these patterns are likely to have evolved because they support patterns of motor behaviour that were adaptive for each of these emotions, preparing the organism for quite different actions. For example, fighting might well have been the adaptive action in anger (which is consistent with the finding that blood flow increases to the hands when we're angry). There may also be unique patterns of CNS activity for each emotion, which aren't found in other mental activity.

Averill (1994) also recognises the influence that an evolutionary approach has had in the study of emotions, defining basic emotions as those 'that fulfil vital biological functions' (vital, that is, to the survival of the species). Like Ekman, he believes that basic emotions should be universal, be seen (at least in rudimentary form) in non-human primates, and be heritable.

However, what's considered basic also varies between cultures and within the same culture over time. For example, in the Middle Ages, hope was classified as a basic emotion, while today it's regarded as secondary (if it's considered an emotion at all) by most emotion theorists (Averill, 1994).

CRITICAL DISCUSSION 10.1: The social construction of emotions

- According to *social constructionism* (SC) (see Chapter 2), emotions are the products of culture. Human cultures influence the emotions by influencing their members' beliefs, values and social environments.
- Emotions may be understood as enmeshed within an entire system of beliefs and values, so they cannot exist independently of the culture.
- For example, *accida* is an emotion that existed in western cultures in medieval times but seems to have become extinct by about 1400. It involved a mixture of boredom with one's religious duties, attempting to put off carrying them out, sadness about one's religious failings, and a sense of loss of one's former religious enthusiasm. It disappeared during the Renaissance when values changed (Parrott, 2004).
- Today, someone facing the same religious 'crisis' is likely to feel guilt, an emotion related to a culture based on individual responsibility (rather than spiritual duty) (Harré & Finlay-Jones, 1986).
- According to Markus & Kitayama (1991), 'ego-focused' emotions (such as anger, frustration and pride) will be experienced more by people in *individualist* cultures with more *independent* selves. 'Other-focused' emotions (such as shame, belongingness and sympathy) will be more common in *collectivist* cultures with more *interdependent selves* (see Chapter 47).

Most basic of all are emotions that are *psychologically* basic: when people are asked to recount emotional episodes that evoked their 'true feelings', they typically describe incidents that reinforce or transform or enhance their sense of self (Morgan & Averill, 1992).

Components of emotion

For each distinct emotion, there are three components:

1. the *subjective experience* of happiness, sadness, anger, and so on
2. *physiological changes*, involving the autonomic nervous system (ANS) and the endocrine system, over which we have little, if any, conscious control; however, we may become aware of some of their effects (such as 'butterflies in the stomach', gooseflesh and sweating: see Chapter 4)
3. *associated behaviour* such as smiling, crying, frowning, running away and being 'frozen to the spot'.

The second and third components are sometimes categorised together as 'bodily reactions', with the former being called visceral and the latter skeletal. This distinction relates to the ANS and central nervous system (CNS) respectively. However, while running away is largely under voluntary (CNS) control, crying or sweating definitely aren't – yet in all three cases we infer another person's emotional state from this observable behaviour.

Different *theories* of emotion are distinguished by:

- how they see the relationship between the three components
- the relative emphasis given to each component
- how they see the relationship between the components and our *cognitive appraisal* or *interpretation* of the emotion-producing stimulus or situation.

Consistent with this is Parrott's (2004) definition of an emotion as;

... a reaction to personally significant events, where 'reaction' is taken to include biological, cognitive and behavioural reactions, as well as subjective feelings of pleasure or displeasure ...

THEORIES OF EMOTION

Darwin's evolutionary theory

The publication of *The Expression of Emotions in Man and Animals* (1872) represents the first formal attempt, by any scientist, to study emotion. Based largely on anecdotal evidence, Darwin argued that particular emotional responses (such as facial expressions) tend to accompany the same emotional states in humans of all races and cultures, even those who are born blind. (This claim is supported by Ekman and Friesen's research: see above). Like other human behaviours, the expression of human emotion is the product of evolution.

Darwin attempted to understand emotions by comparing them with similar behaviours in other species. Based on such comparisons, he proposed a theory of the evolution of emotional expression comprising three main ideas:

1. expressions of emotion evolve from behaviours that signal what an animal is likely to do next
2. if such behaviours benefit the animal that displays them, they'll evolve in ways that make them more effective as a form of communication, and their original function may be lost
3. opposing messages are often signalled by opposing movements or postures (the *principle of antithesis*).

Taking *threat displays* as an example:

- originally, facing one's enemies, rising up and exposing one's weapons were just the early components of animal combat
- once the enemies began to recognise these behaviours as signals of imminent aggression, those aggressors that could communicate their aggressive intent most effectively and scare off their victims without actually fighting had a distinct advantage; as a result, elaborate threat displays evolved and actual combat declined
- to be most effective, signals of aggression/submission must be clearly distinguishable, so they tended to evolve in opposite directions – for example, primates signal aggression by staring at one another, and submission by averting their gaze (Pinel, 1993).

> *ASK YOURSELF...*
> - What would you say is the 'common-sense' theory of emotion?
> - Is it 'obvious' how emotional reactions are triggered (that is, what makes us have emotional experiences)?
> - How does the experience of emotion relate to bodily/behavioural changes?
> - Draw a diagram to summarise a typical 'emotional reaction' sequence of events.

The James–Lange theory

If there is a common-sense theory of emotion, it is that something happens that produces in us a subjective emotional experience and, as a result of this, certain bodily and/or behavioural changes occur. James (originally in 1878 and then in 1890) and Lange (1885, at first quite independently of James) turned this common-sense view on its head. They argued that our emotional experience is the *result*, not the cause, of perceived bodily changes.

To give an example used by James, the common-sense view says that we meet a bear, are frightened and run. The James–Lange theory maintains that we're frightened *because* we run! Similarly, 'We feel sorry because we cry, angry because we strike, afraid because we tremble ...'. According to James (1890):

Figure 10.3 The two woodcuts from Darwin's 1872 book *The Expression of Emotions in Man and Animals*, which he used to illustrate the principle of antithesis. The aggressive posture features ears forward, back up, hair up and tail up; the submissive posture features ears back, back down, hair down and tail down

... the bodily changes follow directly the perception of the exciting fact, and ... our feeling of the same changes as they occur is the emotion.

The crucial factor in the James–Lange theory is feedback from the bodily changes (see Figure 10.4). We label our subjective state by inferring how we feel based on perception of our own bodily changes ('I'm trembling, so I must be afraid': see Chapter 18).

> *ASK YOURSELF...*
> - Do you agree with James?
> - Does the emotional experience always *precede* the associated behaviour (as common sense would have it), or can the behaviour come first (as the James–Lange theory claims)?

You may be able to think of situations in which you've reacted in a fairly automatic way (for example, you've slipped coming down the stairs), and only *after* you've grabbed the banisters do you become aware of feeling frightened (and a little shaken). It's almost as if the sudden change in your behaviour has caused the fear, quite apart from why you grabbed the banisters in the first place.

Evaluation of the James–Lange theory

The theory implies that by deliberately altering our behaviour, we can control our emotional experiences. Try smiling – do you feel any happier? A crucial test (which James admitted would be very difficult to perform) would be to examine the emotional experience of someone who's completely anaesthetised, but not intellectually or motor impaired.

In the examples that James himself gives of inferring emotion from bodily changes (such as running away from a bear), he clearly attaches much more importance to *skeletal* as opposed to *visceral* changes. Parrott (2004) calls this the 'peripheral' approach. In this respect, the James–Lange theory probably differs from other theories, which usually mean 'visceral' when they say 'physiological'. Given this emphasis on skeletal changes, there are two important studies that support the James–Lange theory.

> **KEY STUDY 10.1 Listen to your heart and smile if you want to be happy (Valins, 1966; Laird, 1974)**
> - Valins provided male participants with feedback of their heart rate while watching slides of semi-nude *Playboy* pin-ups.
> - The heart rate was in fact pre-recorded and programmed to increase in response to presentation of half the slides: participants *believed* the feedback was an indication of their true response. This is the *false feedback paradigm*.
> - The slides associated with the apparent heart rate increase were judged to be more attractive than those associated with unchanged heart rate.
> - Laird tested the *facial feedback hypothesis* by falsely informing 32 students that they were participating in an experiment to measure activity in facial muscles.
> - Bogus electrodes were attached to their faces (as if to measure physiological response), and they were instructed to raise their eyebrows, contract the muscles in their forehead, and make other facial expressions. They didn't realise the emotional significance of what they were being asked to do.
> - While this was going on, cartoon slides were projected onto a screen.
> - Regardless of their content, participants rated the slides they'd seen while 'smiling' as funnier. They also described themselves as happier when 'smiling', angrier when 'frowning', and so on.

What the Valins and Laird studies suggest is that overt behaviour may cause subjective feelings without there being any obvious physiological arousal taking place: visceral changes may not be necessary. But neither Valins nor Laird attempted to measure any accompanying visceral changes. What if smiling triggers certain physiological changes? Might these be the real cause of our feeling happy, rather than the change in our facial

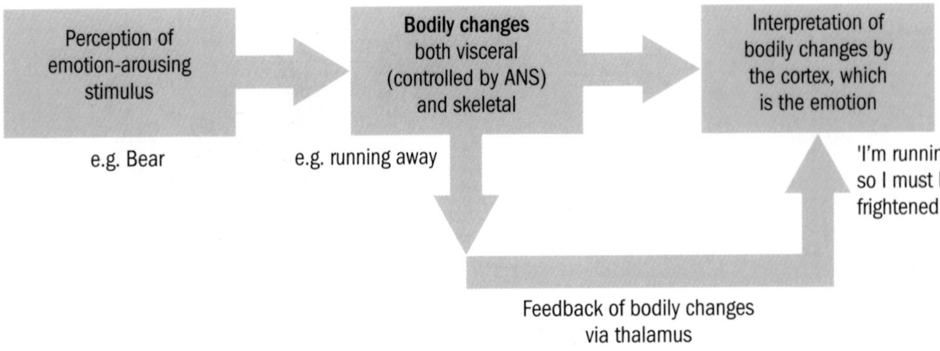

Figure 10.4 The James–Lange theory of emotion

muscles? And, if so, isn't this quite damaging to the James–Lange theory, which places so much emphasis on behavioural (skeletal) changes?

Levenson *et al.* (1990) asked participants to move particular facial muscles (to simulate the emotional expression of fear, anger, surprise, disgust, sadness and happiness). They also monitored several physiological responses controlled by the ANS while this was going on. They found that the simulated expressions *did* alter ANS activity. For example, anger increased heart rate and skin temperature, fear increased heart rate but decreased skin temperature, while happiness decreased heart rate without affecting skin temperature.

In the James–Lange theory, these bodily changes occur spontaneously, not consciously and deliberately. This makes it difficult to draw any firm conclusions from experiments like those of Valins and Laird. However, both studies strongly suggest that physiological arousal isn't sufficient to account for emotional experience. The fact that participants in the Valins study were prepared to infer emotion on the basis of (false) information about their reactions to stimuli suggests it may not even be necessary, and that cognitive factors may be sufficient (Parkinson, 1987).

According to Parrott (2004), for the body to 'know' how to respond appropriately, more than just 'perception of the exciting fact' must be involved. The event (e.g. the bear) must be interpreted or evaluated (or *appraised*) as a threat. The James–Lange theory fails to account for why the bear is seen as frightening in the first place! (We shall return to this issue below.)

Cannon's critique of the James–Lange theory

According to Cannon (1929), there are four major faults with the James–Lange theory:

1. it assumes that for each subjectively distinct emotion there's a corresponding set of physiological changes enabling us to label the emotion we're experiencing
2. even if this assumption were true, physiological arousal would still not be sufficient
3. physiological arousal may not even be necessary
4. the speed with which we often experience emotions seems to exceed the speed of response of the viscera, so how could the physiological changes be the source of sudden emotion?

Cannon argued that, 'the same visceral changes occur in very different emotional states and in non-emotional states'. In other words, the James–Lange theory was built on the (false) assumption that *different* emotional stimuli induce *different* patterns of ANS activity, and that perception of these different patterns results in different emotional experiences.

According to the Cannon–Bard theory, the ANS responds in the *same* way to all emotional stimuli: the sympathetic branch prepares the organism for flight or fight, through increased heart rate and blood pressure, pupil dilation, increased blood flow to the muscles, increased respiration and increased release of adrenaline and noradrenaline from the adrenal medulla (see Chapter 4). This means that there must be more to our emotional experience than simply physiological arousal, otherwise we wouldn't be able to tell one emotional state from another.

Evidence for physiological specificity

According to LeDoux (1994), this represents 'one of the most pesky problems in emotion research'. He points out that the emphasis of research has been on ANS activity, and this emphasis is partly due to Cannon's criticism of the James–Lange theory.

KEY STUDY 10.2 Be afraid: the Ax man's coming (Ax, 1953)

- In a famous (but ethically highly dubious) experiment, Ax measured various aspects of *electrodermal* (skin conductance), *electromyographic* (muscle action potential), *cardiovascular* and *respiratory* activity in participants who were deliberately frightened and made angry.
- They were told that they were participating in a study of *hypertension* (high blood pressure), and were asked to lie quietly on a couch while physiological measures were being taken.
- As electrodes were being attached, it was casually mentioned that the regular technician (who usually operated the technical equipment in an adjacent room) was sick, and a man who'd recently been fired for incompetence and arrogance was filling in for him. A few minutes later (after baseline measures had been recorded), either the anger condition occurred, followed by the fear condition, or vice-versa.
- In the *fear condition*, a continuous mild shock was administered to one finger (without any warning or explanation). The intensity gradually increased, until the participant complained. Then sparks were made to jump.
- In the *anger condition*, the technician (an actor) entered the room and spent five minutes checking the wiring. During this time, he jostled the participant, criticised the attending nurse and blamed the participant for causing a fault in the equipment.
- Of 14 different measures taken, Ax found that seven were significantly different between the two conditions. For example, *fear* was associated with increased heart rate, skin conduction level, muscle action potential frequency, and breathing rate (reflecting the effects of *adrenaline*). *Anger* was accompanied by increased diastolic blood pressure, frequency of spontaneous skin conduction responses and action potential size (reflecting the greater influence of *noradrenaline*).

While Ax's *methods* would be ethically unacceptable today, his findings have been confirmed by others (e.g. Frankenhaeuser, 1975). Schachter (1957) confirmed Ax's original findings that fear is influenced largely by adrenaline. But he also found that anger produces a mixed adrenaline–noradrenaline response, and pain produces a noradrenaline-like pattern. Schachter & Singer (1962) concluded that:

> Whether or not there are physiological distinctions among the various emotional states must be considered an open question. Any differences which do exist are at best rather subtle and the variety of emotion, mood and feeling states do not appear to be matched by an equal variety of visceral patterns.

This conclusion is consistent with Schachter's *cognitive labelling theory* (1964). This sees physiological arousal as necessary for emotional experience, but the nature of the arousal as irrelevant (see below, pages 162–166).

Less extreme and controversial methods than Ax's include:

- the *directed facial action method*, in which participants are instructed to make the facial expressions characteristic of various emotions while ANS activity is recorded
- the *relived emotion method*, in which participants are asked to think about previous emotional experiences while these measures are being made.

Based on a series of experiments using both kinds of method, Levenson (1994) maintains that it's a 'myth' that every emotion is autonomically different. It seems far more likely that reliable differences will only be found between emotions for which there are different associated typical behaviours, and even among this smaller set, it's quite unlikely that they won't share *some* features.

Box 10.1 The physiology of positive and negative emotions

- Levenson *et al.* (1990) compared anger, disgust, fear, sadness (*negative emotions*), plus happiness (*positive emotion*) and surprise. They identified a small number of fairly reliable differences in patterns of ANS activity, both between the negative emotions, and between the negative emotions as a group and happiness.
- For example, anger, fear and sadness all produce larger increases in heart rate than disgust, while anger produces a larger increase in finger temperature than fear does.
- These differences have been found consistently across populations differing in occupation, age (from young people to 71–90-year-olds), culture (Americans and Minangkabau males living in Western Sumatra, Indonesia) and gender, as well as across the directed facial action and relived emotion methods.
- As far as positive emotions are concerned, Levenson (1994) believes that they might not be associated with any particular pattern of behaviour or, if they are, it would be characterised by low activity, making little metabolic demand on the ANS:

  Instead of having distinctive autonomic signatures ... positive emotions might be associated with a state of physiological quiescence ... their primary function might be to 'undo' the autonomic activation produced by negative emotions ... to restore the organism to its pre-arousal state in a more efficient and rapid manner than would be the case if the negative emotions were allowed to run their natural course.

- What this implies is that, at least in our present state of knowledge, we cannot draw general conclusions about the specificity of the body's response to emotional stimuli – it depends partly on which emotion (positive or negative) we're talking about.

ASK YOURSELF...

- Given James' emphasis on skeletal, as opposed to visceral, changes, could it be argued that Cannon's first criticism is not strictly relevant?
- Since we're almost completely unaware of visceral changes, could James have claimed that 'visceral feedback' *is* the emotion?

Even if there were identifiable patterns of physiological response associated with different subjective emotions, Cannon argued that such physiological changes themselves don't necessarily produce emotional states. In other words, physiological arousal isn't sufficient. This was demonstrated by Marañon (1924). However, a study by Hohmann (1966) suggests that, although physiological changes aren't sufficient for the experience of 'full-blooded' emotions, they may still be necessary.

KEY STUDY 10.3 As if emotion were just adrenaline (Marañon, 1924)

- Marañon injected 210 people with adrenaline; 71 per cent said they experienced only physical symptoms, with no emotional overtones at all; most of the rest reported 'as if' emotions.
- The few who experienced genuine emotion had to imagine – or remember – a highly emotional event.

KEY STUDY 10.4 Real emotions need an intact ANS (Hohmann, 1966)

- Hohmann studied 25 adult males with spinal cord injuries, who suffered corresponding ANS damage.
- They reported significant changes in the nature and intensity of certain emotional experiences, especially anger, fear and sexual feelings.

- Generally, the higher the lesion in the spinal cord, the greater the disruption of visceral responses, and the greater the disturbance of normal emotional experiences.
- Like Marañon's participants, they reported 'as if' emotions – a 'mental kind of anger', for example.

According to Schachter (1964), what Marañon's and Hohmann's participants reported is precisely what would be expected from his cognitive labelling theory, which sees emotional experience as a joint function of cognitive and physiological factors (see below).

The Cannon–Bard theory

Cannon (1927) removed the sympathetic nervous system of cats, and Sherrington (1900) severed the spinal cord and vagus nerves of dogs. In both cases, feedback from the viscera to the brain was prevented, but the animals showed apparently normal emotional reactions. Cannon took these findings to mean that physiological changes may not even be necessary for emotional experience. In addition, Dana (1921) studied a patient with a spinal cord lesion: despite having no sympathetic functioning and extremely limited muscular movement, the patient showed a range of emotions, including grief, joy, displeasure and affection. Similarly, Chwalisz *et al.* (1988) found that people with spinal cord injuries (who have no sensation in much of their body) experience emotion as intensely as before the injury, as intensely as 'normal' people, and as intensely as people with spinal cord injuries that don't block bodily sensations. These findings seem to support Cannon's view.

ASK YOURSELF...

- Is it valid to generalise from the study of cats' and dogs' emotional reactions to human beings' emotional *experience*, as Cannon did?
- Is it valid to generalise from a single case, as in Dana's study? (See Chapter 42.)

So what is different about Cannon's theory (known as the Cannon–Bard theory)? As Figure 10.5 shows, the subjective emotion is quite *independent* of the physiological changes involved. The emotion-producing stimulus is processed by the thalamus. This sends impulses to the cortex, where the emotion is consciously experienced, and to the hypothalamus, which sets in motion certain autonomic physiological changes.

An evaluation of the Cannon–Bard theory

Cannon also argued that, because we often feel emotions quite rapidly, yet the viscera are quite slow to react, how could the physiological changes be the source of such sudden emotion (as required by the James–Lange theory)? However, although the viscera aren't sensitive to certain kinds of stimulation (such as burning and cutting), they provide much better feedback than Cannon suspected. Many visceral changes can occur sufficiently quickly that they *could* be the causes of feelings of emotion (Carlson, 1992).

Pinel (1993) advocates a position falling *between* the extreme views represented by the Cannon–Bard and James–Lange theories. On the one hand, the Cannon–Bard view that the ANS responds in the same way to all emotional stimuli is clearly incorrect: several differences have been well documented. On the other hand, there's insufficient evidence to make a strong case for the James–Lange view that each emotion is characterised by a different pattern of ANS activity.

Schachter's cognitive labelling theory

According to Schachter (1964), Cannon was wrong in thinking that bodily changes and the experience of emotion are independent, and the James–Lange theory was mistaken in claiming that physiological changes cause the feeling of emotion. While sharing the James–Lange belief that physiological changes *precede* the experience of emotion, Schachter argues that we have to *decide* which particular emotion we're feeling. The label we attach to our arousal depends on what we attribute that arousal to.

Schachter is saying that physiological arousal (factor 1) is *necessary* for the experience of emotion, but the nature of arousal is immaterial – what's important is how we *interpret* that arousal (factor 2). Hence, the theory is also known as the *two factor theory of emotion*. The classic experiment that demonstrates this cognitive theory of emotion is Schachter & Singer's (1962) 'adrenaline experiment' (see Key Study 10.5).

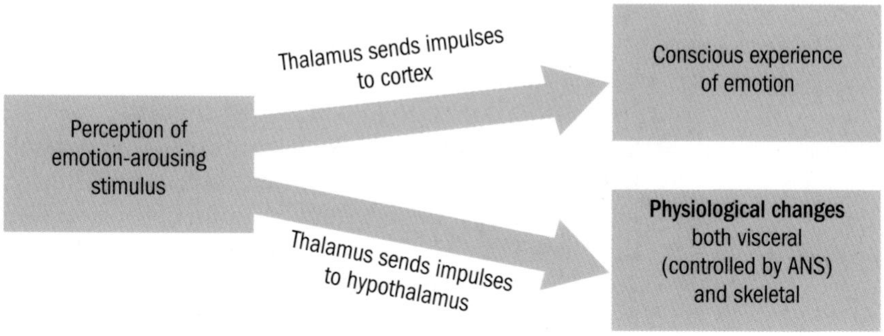

Figure 10.5 The Cannon–Bard theory of emotion

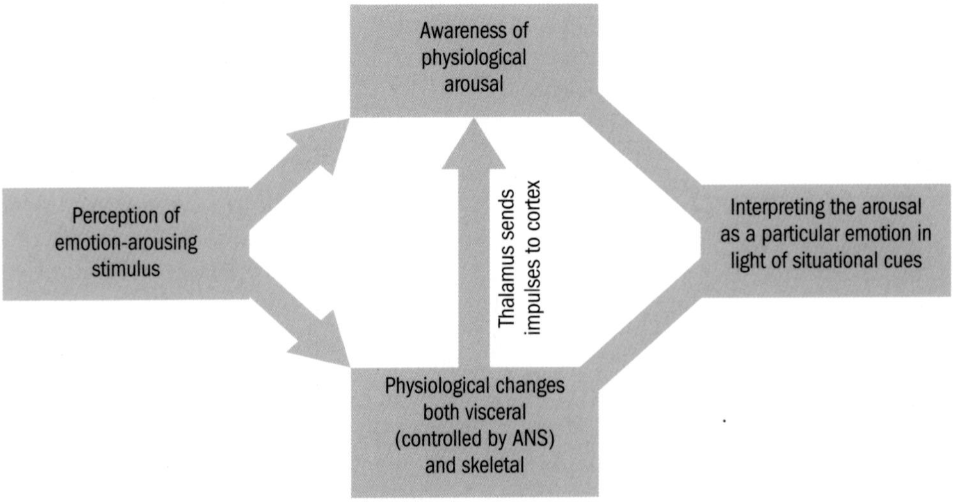

Figure 10.6 Schachter's cognitive labelling theory (or two-factor theory)

KEY STUDY 10.5 Schachter & Singer's (1962) adrenaline experiment

Participants were given what they were told was a vitamin injection, in order to see its effect on vision. In fact, it was adrenaline, and they were tested under one of four conditions.

1. *Group A* participants were given *accurate information* about the side-effects of the injection (palpitations, tightness in the throat, tremors and sweating).
2. *Group B* participants were given *false information* about the side-effects (itching and headache).
3. *Group C* participants were given *no information* about the side-effects (true or false).
4. *Group D* (control group) participants were given a saline injection (and otherwise treated like group C).

Before being given a 'vision test', each participant (one at a time) sat in a waiting room with another 'participant' (a stooge of the experimenters). For half the participants in each condition, the stooge acted *either* in a happy, frivolous way (making paper aeroplanes, laughing out loud and playing with a hula-hoop: *euphoria condition*), *or* very angrily (eventually tearing up the questionnaire which he and every participant was asked to complete: *anger condition*). (In fact, the group B condition was run only with a euphoric stooge).

Participants' emotional experience was assessed in two ways:

1. observers' ratings of the degree to which they joined in with the stooge's behaviour
2. self-report scales.

As predicted:

- groups A and D were much less likely to join in with the stooge or to report feeling euphoric or angry
- groups B and C were much *more* likely to assume the stooge's behaviour and emotional state.

ASK YOURSELF...

- Can you account for these findings in terms of Schachter's cognitive labelling/two factor theory?

Schachter and Singer were testing three inter-related hypotheses regarding the interaction between physiological and cognitive factors in the experience of emotion.

1. If we experience a state of physiological arousal for which we have no immediate explanation, we'll 'label' this state and describe it in terms of the cognitions available. So, precisely the same state of arousal could receive different labels (e.g. 'euphoria'/'anger' – groups B and C). (Physiological arousal *and* cognitive labelling are necessary.)
2. If we experience a state of physiological arousal for which we have a completely appropriate explanation (e.g. 'I've just been given an injection of adrenaline'), we'll 'label' this state accordingly (group A).
3. Given the same circumstances, we'll react emotionally or describe our feelings as emotions only to the extent that we experience a state of physiological arousal (all three groups). (Physiological arousal is necessary.)

An evaluation of cognitive labelling theory

- Schachter & Wheeler (1962) confirmed these results by injecting participants either with adrenaline or chlorpromazine (which inhibits arousal); controls were injected with a placebo. While watching a slapstick comedy, the adrenaline participants laughed more, and the chlorpromazine participants less, than the controls.

KEY STUDY 10.6 Falling in love on a suspension bridge (Dutton & Aron, 1974)

- The participants were unsuspecting males, aged 18–35, visiting the Capilano Canyon in British Columbia, Canada.
- An attractive female interviewer approached the men and asked them questions as part of a survey on the effects of scenery on creativity. One of the things they were asked to do was to invent a short story about an ambiguous picture of a woman (a picture from the Thematic Apperception Test/TAT: see Chapter 9). This was later scored for sexual content, taken to reflect the men's sexual attraction towards the interviewer.
- Some men were interviewed on an extremely unstable suspension bridge, 5 feet wide, 450 feet long, composed of wooden boards attached to wire cables, running from one side of the canyon to the other. This bridge, 230 feet above the canyon, tended to sway, tilt and wobble, giving the impression that one could fall over the side at any moment; it had only very low handrails of wire cable for support (*high arousal condition*).
- Other men were interviewed on a solid wooden bridge upstream, a mere 10 feet above a shallow rivulet, with high handrails and without any swaying or tilting (*low arousal condition*).
- As predicted, the stories of the men in the high arousal condition contained significantly more sexual imagery.
- The interviewer also invited the men to call her if they wanted more information about the research. Again in line with predictions, four times as many men from the high arousal condition called her compared with the low arousal condition.

The Capilano River bridge

- To show that arousal was the independent variable, Dutton and Aron also arranged for another group of men to be interviewed ten or more minutes *after* crossing the suspension bridge. By this time, the symptoms of their physical arousal should have been declining. These non-aroused men *didn't* show the signs of sexual arousal shown by those in the high arousal condition.

- Dutton and Aron's study confirms Schachter's claim that the autonomic arousal that accompanies all emotions is similar, and that it's our *interpretation* of that arousal that matters – even though this sometimes results in our misidentifying our emotions. Dutton and Aron's suspension bridge participants seemed to be *mislabelling* their fear as sexual attraction to the interviewer.

ASK YOURSELF...

- What do you think the outcome would have been if the interviewer had been male?

- The focus of Schachter's model is an atypical state of affairs, where the participant is unsure about the cause of arousal (groups B and C). But Schachter (1964) admitted that we usually *are* aware of a precipitating situation prior to the onset of arousal (which usually takes one to two seconds to reach consciousness). So, it's normally perfectly obvious to us what aspects of the situation have provoked the emotion. However, even here the meaning of the emotion-inducing circumstances requires *some* cognitive analysis before the emotion can be labelled.
- Schachter claims that the *quantitative* aspect of emotion can arise without cognitive mediation ('Am I in a state of emotional arousal?': as in Valins' study). But the *qualitative* aspect requires prior cognition ('What emotion is it I am experiencing?': as in Laird's study). Mandler (1984) has called Schachter's theory the *'jukebox' theory* – arousal is like the coin that gets the machine going, and cognition is the button pushed to select the emotional tune.
- According to Parkinson (1987), the view that affect (emotion) is post-cognitive is now probably the most popular attitude among emotion theorists. But even accepting the important role of cognitive factors, is our emotional experience really as labile or malleable as Schachter claims? Are environmental cues really as easily accepted as the basis for inferences about our own feelings (Fiske & Taylor, 1991)?
- Using the original Schachter and Singer paradigm, several studies (Marshall & Zimbardo, 1979; Maslach, 1979; Plutchik & Ax, 1967) have concluded that when we try to explain a state of arousal, we don't merely use others' behaviour as a guide to what we're feeling.

We call on many other sources of information as well, particularly our own past history: we search for previous occasions on which we felt this arousal state to explain why it's occurring now. While other people's behaviour might suggest – or even dictate (through conformity) – how we should *behave* in that situation, it doesn't tell us how we're *feeling*. At the very least, others' behaviour must in some way be appropriate (Weiner, 1992).

- These later studies also found that people who don't have a ready-made explanation for their adrenaline-produced arousal are more likely to attach a *negative* emotional label to it (such as unease or nervousness, similar to 'free-floating anxiety'). This suggests that emotional lability *isn't* as great as Schachter maintains: unexplained arousal has a negative, unpleasant quality about it.

The role of attribution

According to Schachter, group A participants in the adrenaline experiment could attribute their arousal to the injection (they had a ready-made explanation and so didn't need an emotional explanation). But for those in groups B and C, no such ready-made explanation was available, and so the stooge's behaviour was used as a cue for explaining their own state of arousal (as either euphoria or anger).

Taking one of James's original examples (running away from a bear), the original cause of the bodily reactions (the bear) is *irrelevant*. This is because our emotional experience is based on feedback from our bodily reactions (running away). But for Schachter, it's what we attribute our arousal to that *determines* the label we give to it. In the adrenaline experiment, the initially unexplained arousal is attributed to the (rather extreme) behaviour of the confederate, and so is labelled euphoria or anger accordingly.

Similarly, the men in Dutton and Aron's experiment who were tested on the swaying suspension bridge, were unaware of the 'real' cause of their arousal. They attributed it instead to the female interviewer. We know that arousal was the independent variable, and it's highly likely that if the attractive interviewer hadn't approached them, they'd have labelled their arousal 'fear', because it would have been attributed to a frightening stimulus (the bridge).

What all these examples show is that the cognitive labelling theory is essentially based on *attributional principles* (see Chapter 23). This represents a major form of influence that Schachter's theory has had on cognitive theories of emotion in general.

According to Weiner (1986, 1992), certain kinds of attribution produce specific emotions. For example, success produces a very general positive feeling (such as happiness), while failure produces a very general negative feeling (such as sadness). But if the outcome (either success or failure) is either very different from what's expected or has very important consequences, we try to figure out the reasons (or causes) for the outcome. These reasons will take the form of *internal* or *external* attributions, which in turn can be broken down into *controllable* or *uncontrollable*. It's the combination of internal/external and controllable/uncontrollable that will determine specific emotional responses (see Figure 10.7).

The misattribution effect

What the adrenaline and the suspension bridge experiments show is that people can make mistakes in how they attribute their arousal. This mislabelling of our feelings,

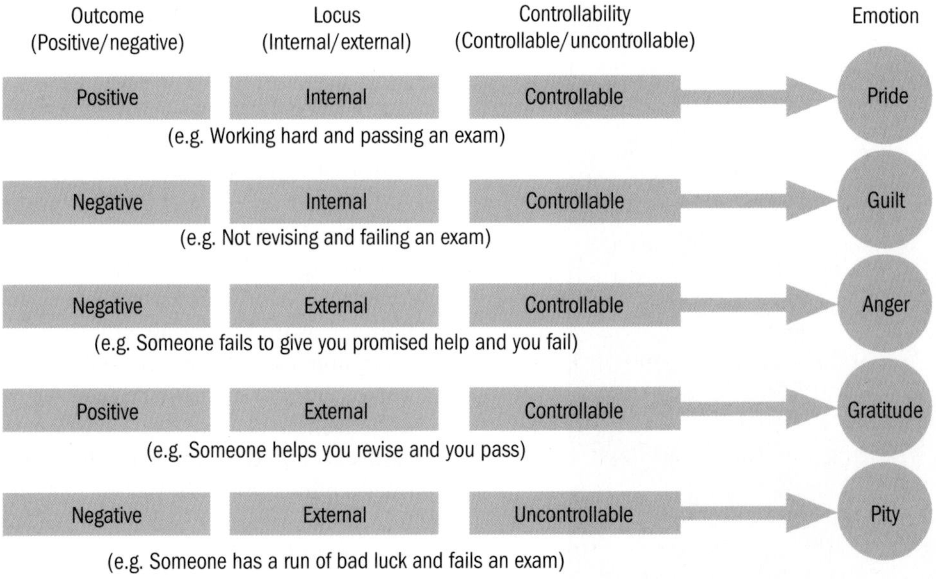

Figure 10.7 Examples of how particular kinds of attribution can produce particular emotions (based on Weiner, *Human Motivation: Metaphors, Theories and Research*. Copyright 1992, reprinted by permission of Sage Publications, Inc.)

and drawing mistaken conclusions about the causes of those feelings, is called the *misattribution effect* (Ross & Nisbett, 1991).

As part of their suspension bridge experiment, and in a later experiment, Dutton & Aron (1974, 1989) invited male students to participate in a learning experiment. After meeting an attractive female partner, half the students were frightened with the news that they would be suffering some 'quite painful' electric shocks. Before the experiment was due to begin, they were given a short questionnaire 'to get some information on your present feelings and reactions, since these often influence people on the learning task'. Asked how much they would like to date and kiss their partner, the aroused (frightened) men expressed more intense attraction than the non-frightened men.

By definition, the female partner was sexually attractive, and so it was far easier for the men to transfer their arousal to her, and to mislabel it as sexual arousal. In this way, she represented a *salient* or *credible* source of arousal (Olson & Ross, 1988). (She also represented a clear, unambiguous source of arousal.) Similarly, if female participants are shown slides of attractive male nudes, it may be easy to alter their preferences among the pictures based on false heart rate feedback, whereas this would be very difficult to achieve if the male nudes were replaced by slides of naked hippos! (This is a deliberately modified version of an example given by Taylor *et al.*, 1994.)

Cognitive appraisal or affective primacy?

When evaluating the James–Lange theory earlier, we noted that it fails to account for why a bear, say, should make us run away. In other words, it fails to take into account our *appraisal* of the emotional 'stimulus'. Appraisal is the thinking that leads to emotion (Parrott, 2004), and appraisal theory is a development of Schachter's cognitive labelling theory.

According to Lazarus (1982), some degree of cognitive processing is an essential prerequisite for an affective reaction to a stimulus to occur, and is an integral feature of all emotional states.

KEY STUDY 10.7 Subincision in the Arunta (Speisman *et al.*, 1964)

- Participants saw a film (*Subincision in the Arunta*), which shows aboriginal boys undergoing circumcision as part of a puberty rite.
- The boys are seen having their penises cut with a jagged flint knife. This usually causes high levels of stress in viewers of the film (and probably in the boys too!). The soundtrack was manipulated, so that:

  (i) the pain, jaggedness of the knife, and so on, were emphasised (*trauma*)
  (ii) the boys' anticipation of entering manhood was emphasised (*denial*)
  (iii) the emotional elements were ignored and the traditions of the aboriginal people were emphasised (*intellectualisation*)
  (iv) there was no commentary (*silent control*).

- As predicted, arousal (measured by GSR and heart rate) was highest in the trauma condition, next highest in the control condition and lowest in the other two.
- What we tell ourselves about external situations (*cognitive appraisal*) influences our level of arousal.

For Lazarus,

> ... emotion results from evaluative perception of a relationship (actual, imagined or anticipated) between a person (or animal) and the environment.

He proposes that cognitive appraisal invariably *precedes* any affective reaction, although it doesn't have to involve any conscious processing. Zajonc (1984) argues that there's generally little direct evidence of either the existence or nature of such preconscious cognitive processing (although the study of *subliminal perception* suggests otherwise: see Chapter 15). Zajonc (1980a) argues that cognition and affect operate as *independent* systems, and an emotional response *may* precede cognitive processes under certain circumstances. For example, we may meet someone very briefly and form a positive or negative impression, despite not being able to remember any detailed information about them later (such as hair or eye colour: Eysenck & Keane, 1990).

ASK YOURSELF...

- Try to formulate some arguments against Zajonc's claim that cognition and affect are separate, independent systems.

Parrott (2004) asks how it's possible to call certain emotions 'irrational' if emotions don't intrinsically entail beliefs. Also, most emotions are 'about' something – and this is cognitive. The most important problem for Zajonc is that how we think about a situation obviously influences how we feel (for example, *why* we think someone behaved as they did determines whether we feel angry or sympathetic: see Chapter 23).

Zajonc seems to overestimate the amount of cognitive processing that Lazarus and other cognitive appraisal theorists are claiming. For example, Lazarus simply argues that some minimal cognitive analysis at some level always precedes emotional experience. But this can be quite automatic, and so 'cognitive appraisal' is quite consistent with the sense of 'immediacy' that so much emotional experience has (and which Frijda (1994) sees as a characteristic of emotion).

So, what is an emotion?

Clore (1994) defines emotions as *mental states*. Neither physiological arousal nor feeling states provide the best way of trying to capture the nature of an emotion. Emotions are special kinds of feelings, namely those that we judge have an *emotional cause*. This is why feelings that are generated artificially by electrical stimulation or hormone injection (or some other non-cognitive means) *aren't* emotions. (see Key Study 10.3). For Clore, emotion terms seem to refer to something beyond feelings, to psychological states of which feelings are perhaps a necessary but not a sufficient condition.

Many of the examples Zajonc gives of emotion without cognition (*affective primacy* or 'preferences need no inferences') don't seem to describe emotional states at all. For example, when someone leaps out in front of you and shouts 'Boo!', your physiological and bodily response (including your facial expression) would be more accurately described as a *startle reflex* than fear.

"I know real men cry these days, Gerald, but not for getting soap in their eyes."

According to Scherer (1994), the classic debate between Lazarus and Zajonc, which had a major impact on the psychology of emotion during the 1980s, was mostly concerned with the level of processing involved, not whether *any* processing took place. This, in turn, revolved around the definition of 'cognition'.

What is cognition?

If 'cognition' means or includes basic sensory processing, then most, if not all, emotions will have some cognitive component. However, LeDoux (1994) and Panksepp (1994), both biologists, suggest that the brain circuitry underlying emotion and cognition are different. Cognition is seen as depending on the neocortex and hippocampus (see Chapter 4). If 'cognition' is restricted to processes involving these brain areas, then emotion *can* occur without cognition, since non-humans with extensive lesions in these structures still display emotional responses.

CONCLUSIONS

According to Davidson & Ekman (1994), the older Lazarus/Zajonc debate has advanced considerably. Most theorists now acknowledge that emotion can be elicited in the absence of conscious cognitive mediation. If a broad view of cognition is taken, most would also agree that some cognitive processing is required for most emotion. Dalgleish (1998) maintains that the view that cognition is an integral part of emotion is predominant within the psychology of emotion. The challenge is to specify more precisely the types of cognitive processing that may be critical to the emotion-generation process, and to identify the neural circuitries that underlie emotion and cognition respectively. We also need to study the *interactions* between emotion and cognition.

CHAPTER SUMMARY

- Ekman and Friesen identify six **primary**, universal emotions, which are probably innate. Plutchik's 'emotion wheel' also incorporates primary emotions, but distinguishes these from complex emotions.
- An **evolutionary** approach to understanding primary or **basic** emotions includes considering their current function. But 'basic' emotions differ between cultures and over time within the same culture. They may be **psychologically** or **culturally** basic – not biologically.
- According to **social constructionism** (SC), emotions are **culturally** and **historically relative**. They exist within a system of beliefs and values, which differs between cultures and changes over time.
- For each distinct emotion there are the **subjective experience**, **physiological changes**, **associated behaviour** and **cognitive appraisal** of the emotion-producing stimulus/situation.

- Darwin saw emotional behaviours (such as threat displays) as having evolved because they benefited those animals that used them effectively (they removed the need for actual combat).
- The **James–Lange theory** turns the common-sense theory of emotion on its head, by claiming that our emotional experience is the result of perceived bodily changes – in particular, skeletal changes.
- Studies by Valins (using the **false feedback paradigm**) and Laird (testing the **facial feedback hypothesis**) support the James–Lange theory, although they fail to take into account any visceral changes that may be taking place. They both suggest that physiological arousal isn't sufficient to account for emotional experience.
- Cannon criticised the James–Lange theory for assuming that different emotional states are associated with different patterns of ANS activity. The **Cannon–Bard theory** claims that the ANS responds in the same way to all emotional stimuli.
- Using the **directed facial action** and the **relived emotion methods**, Levenson reports physiological differences between anger, disgust, fear and sadness. Both the James–Lange and Cannon–Bard theories take too extreme a view regarding **physiological specificity**, and the truth lies somewhere in between.
- Marañon's and Hohmann's studies support Cannon's claim that physiological arousal isn't sufficient for emotional experience, although they indicate that it is necessary. However, Cannon's own study of cats, plus those of Sherrington and Dana, suggest that it might not even be necessary.
- According to Schachter's **cognitive labelling theory**, the experience of emotion depends both on **physiological changes** and the **interpretation** of those changes. Cannon, therefore, was mistaken in claiming that emotional experience and bodily changes are independent.
- Schachter and Singer's 'adrenaline experiment' demonstrates that while physiological arousal is necessary, the nature of the arousal is irrelevant. What's crucial is the **cognitive label** we give that arousal.
- Dutton and Aron's 'suspension bridge' experiment supports Schachter's theory, but also shows that how we label our arousal can be mistaken (the **misattribution effect**).
- Failure to replicate the adrenaline experiment suggests that emotional experience is much less malleable than Schachter claims, and that unexplained arousal is likely to be interpreted negatively.
- Cognitive labelling theory is essentially based on **attributional principles**. Several attributional theories of emotion have grown out of it, such as Weiner's theory.
- Lazarus's **cognitive appraisal theory** claims that some minimal cognitive analysis always precedes emotional experience, although this can be unconscious and automatic. Zajonc's **affective primacy theory** claims that emotional responses can occur without any cognition being involved.
- The basic disagreement between Lazarus and Zajonc seems to be about the **level of processing** involved, rather than whether or not any cognitive processing takes place. This, in turn, centres around the definition of 'cognition'.

Links with other topics/chapters

- The study of emotion has always been influenced by an *evolutionary approach* (Chapter 2).
- Schachter's cognitive labelling theory has had a major impact on cognitive theories of emotion in general. One major form of this influence relates to the role of *attribution*, including the *misattribution effect* (Chapter 23).
- Abramson & Martin (1981) grafted attributional principles onto Seligman's (1975) theory of *learned helplessness* (Chapter 11) in an attempt to explain *major depressive disorder/clinical depression* (Chapter 44).
- The way we account for other people's behaviour (and the resulting emotions we experience) can influence *helping behaviour/bystander intervention* (Chapter 30).
- The experience of certain kinds of negative emotions is what we commonly mean by *stress*, and Lazarus's appraisal theory is often discussed in this context (Chapter 12).

11

LEARNING AND CONDITIONING

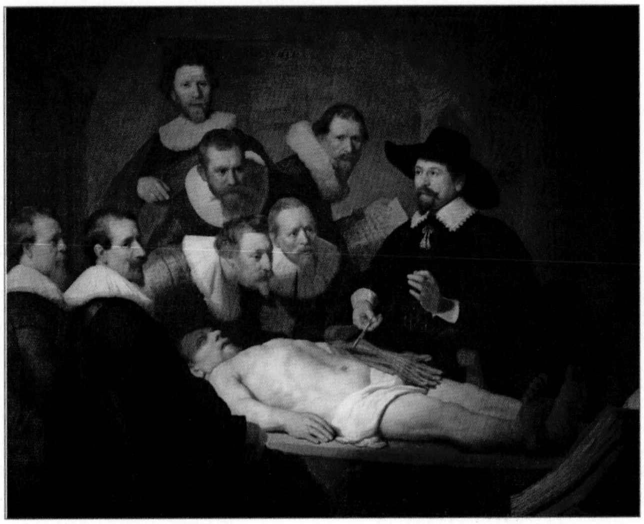

INTRODUCTION AND OVERVIEW

We've seen in earlier chapters how American psychology in particular was dominated by *behaviourism* for much of the first half of the twentieth century. Given the central role of learning in philosophical behaviourism, it's hardly surprising that the topic of learning itself should be central within psychology as a whole.

The concept of learning is a good example of the discrepancy between the everyday, common-sense use of a term and its technical, scientific use (see Chapter 1). In everyday conversation, the emphasis is usually on *what* is learned (the *end product*), such as learning to drive a car, use the Internet or speak French. But when psychologists use the term, their focus is on *how* the learning takes place (the learning *process*).

When the focus is on the end product, we generally infer that the learning is *deliberate*. For example, we pay for driving lessons that will help us, eventually, to acquire a driving licence. But, for psychologists, learning can take place without a 'teacher'. We can learn, for example, by merely *observing* others, who may not even know they're being observed, let alone trying to teach us anything. Learning can also happen without other people being involved at all, as when we observe recurring environmental events ('thunder always follows lightning').

So, the concept of learning as used by psychologists is very broad. Partly for this reason, psychologists disagree as to exactly what's involved in the learning process. Watson, the founder of behaviourism, was the first psychologist to apply Pavlov's concept of the *conditioned reflex/response* to human behaviour. A more active view of learning was taken by Thorndike, whose work formed the basis of Skinner's *operant conditioning*. Skinner's contribution, above all others, made behaviourism such a force within psychology as a whole (see Chapter 2).

WHAT IS LEARNING?

Learning is a *hypothetical construct*: it cannot be directly observed, but only inferred from observable behaviour. For example, if a person's performance on a task at time 1 differs from performance on the task at time 2, we might infer that learning has taken place. But if that change is observed just once, we may be much more hesitant about making such an inference. Learning, therefore, normally implies a fairly *permanent* change in a person's behavioural performance. Again, temporary fluctuations in behaviour can occur as a result of fatigue, drugs, temperature changes, and so on, and this is another reason for taking permanence as a minimum requirement for saying that learning has taken place.

However, permanent changes in behaviour can also result from things that have nothing to do with learning, such as the effects of brain damage on behaviour, or the changes associated with puberty and other maturational processes. So, if a change in behaviour is to be counted as learning, the change must be linked to some kind of *past experience* (regardless of whether there was any attempt to bring about that change).

For these reasons, psychologists usually define learning as 'a relatively permanent change in behaviour due to past experience' (Coon, 1983) or 'the process by which relatively permanent changes occur in behavioural potential as a result of experience' (Anderson, 1995a).

Learning versus performance

Anderson's definition has one major advantage over Coon's, namely that it implies a distinction between learning *(behavioural potential)* and performance *(actual behaviour)*.

> *ASK YOURSELF...*
> - What things have you learned to do/learned about that you're not actually doing/thinking about right now?

If you can swim, you're almost certainly not doing so as you read this chapter – but you could readily do so if faced with a pool full of water! So what you could do (potential behaviour based on learning) and what you're actually doing (current performance) are two different things. Ultimately, of course, the only proof of learning is a particular kind of performance (such as exams). Performance can fluctuate due to fatigue, drugs and emotional factors, and so is much more variable than learning, which is more permanent. (Exams come to mind again – many students have left an exam knowing what they could not demonstrate during the exam itself.)

Learning and other abilities

Howe (1980) defines learning as 'a biological device that functions to protect the human individual and to extend his capacities'. In this context, learning is neither independent of, nor entirely separate from, several other abilities, in particular memory and perception. Indeed, learning and memory may be regarded as two sides of the same coin (see Chapter 17).

According to Howe, learning is also *cumulative*: what we learn at any time is influenced by our previous learning. Developmental and learning processes are closely interlinked. Also, most instances of learning take the form of adaptive changes, whereby we increase our effectiveness in dealing with the environment. Similarly, Anderson (1995a) defines learning as 'the mechanism by which organisms can adapt to a changing and nonpredictable environment'.

Some basic questions about learning

While it's generally agreed by psychologists that learning is *relatively permanent* and *due to past experience*, there's much less agreement about exactly what changes when learning takes place, and what kinds of past experience are involved. Put another way, how do the changes occur and what mechanisms are involved? One important issue that divides psychologists is the extent to which they focus on the *overt, behavioural changes* as opposed to the *covert, cognitive changes*.

BEHAVIOURIST APPROACHES

Skinner (1938) made the crucial distinction between *respondents* (or *respondent behaviour*), which are triggered automatically by particular environmental stimuli, and *operants* (or *operant behaviour*), which are essentially voluntary. A related distinction is that between *classical* or *respondent (Pavlovian) conditioning* and *operant* or *instrumental (Skinnerian) conditioning*.

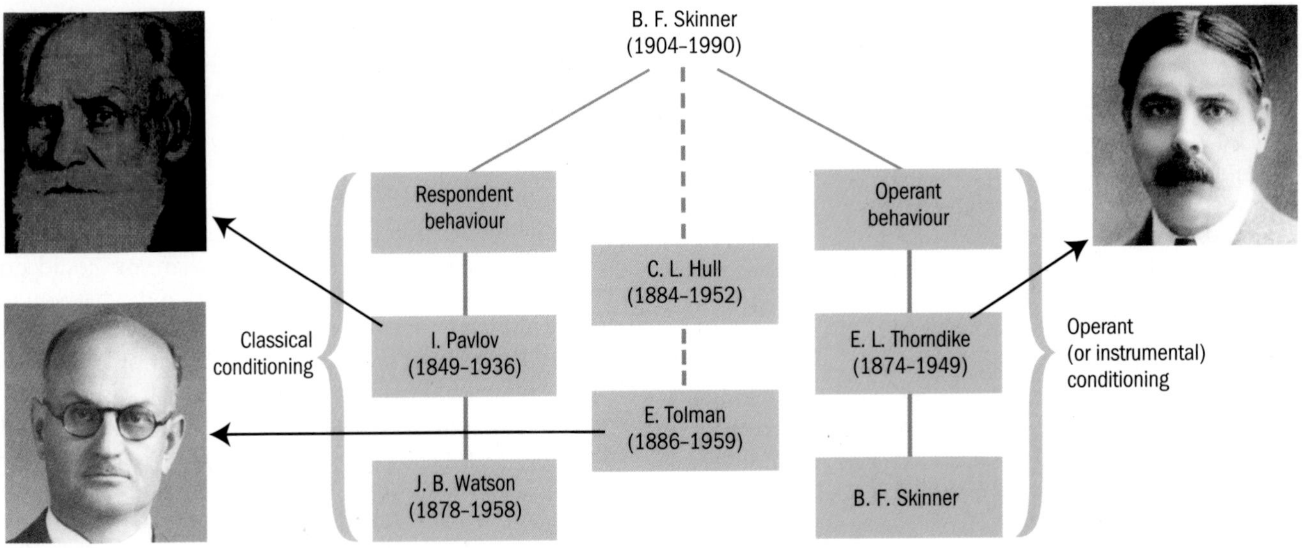

Figure 11.1 Major figures in the behaviourist (learning theory) tradition

Classical conditioning: why do dogs drool over bells?

Ivan Pavlov was a physiologist interested in the process of digestion in dogs. He was awarded the Nobel Prize in 1904 (the year Skinner was born). He developed a surgical technique for collecting a dog's salivary secretions. A tube was attached to the outside of its cheek, so the drops of saliva could easily be measured.

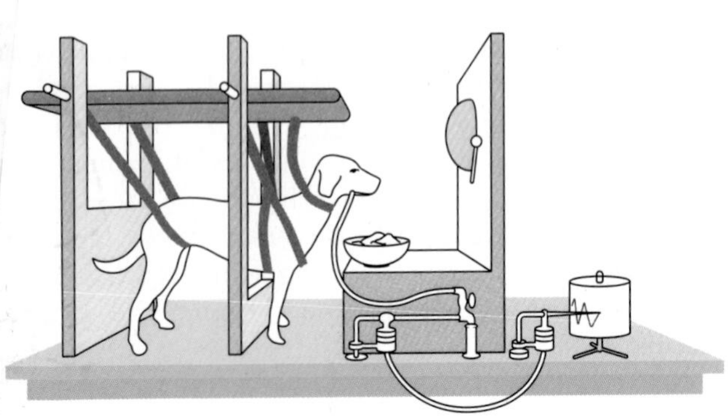

Figure 11.2 The apparatus used by Pavlov in his experiments on conditioned reflexes

Pavlov (1927) noticed that the dogs would often start salivating *before* they were given any food: when they looked at the food or saw the feeding bucket, or even when they heard the footsteps of the laboratory assistant who was coming to feed them. These observations led to the study of what's now called classical (or Pavlovian) conditioning: a stimulus (such as a bell), which wouldn't normally produce a particular response (such as salivation), eventually comes to do so by being paired with another stimulus (such as food) which *does* normally produce the response.

- *Before* conditioning, the taste of food will naturally and automatically make the dog salivate, but the sound of a bell won't. So, the food is referred to as an *unconditioned stimulus* (UCS), and the salivation is an *unconditioned*

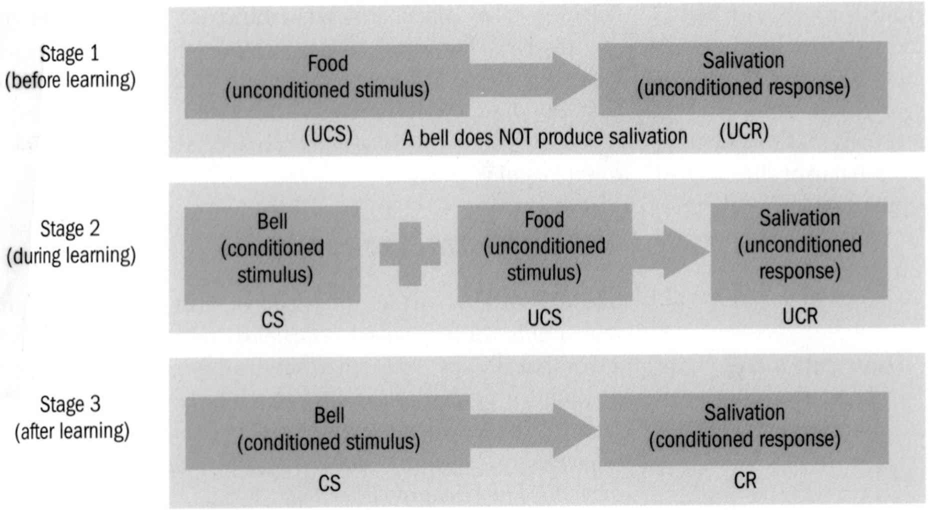

Figure 11.3 The basic procedure involved in classical conditioning

response (UCR): an automatic, reflex, biologically built-in response. The dog doesn't have to learn to salivate in response to food, because it does so naturally.

◉ *During* conditioning, the bell is paired with the food. Because the bell doesn't naturally produce salivation, it's called a *conditioned stimulus* (CS): it only produces salivation *on the condition* that it's paired with the UCS. It's also *neutral* with regard to salivation prior to conditioning.

◉ If the bell and food are paired often enough, the dog starts to salivate as soon as it hears the bell and *before* the food is presented. When this occurs, conditioning has taken place. The salivation is now referred to as a *conditioned response* (CR), because it's produced by a conditioned stimulus (CS) – the bell.

This basic procedure can be used with a variety of conditioned stimuli, such as buzzers, metronomes, lights, geometric figures, and so on. The exact relationship between the CS and the UCS can also be varied to give different kinds of conditioning. What I've described above involves *delayed/forward* conditioning (see Table 11.1).

ASK YOURSELF...
• In the basic procedure described above, the CS is presented about a half-second before the UCS. What do you think might happen if the CS is presented *after* the UCS?

Higher-order conditioning
Pavlov demonstrated that a strong CS could be used instead of food, to produce salivation in response to a new stimulus that had never been paired with food. For example, a buzzer (previously paired with food) is paired with a black square. After ten pairings (using delayed conditioning), the dog will salivate a small but significant amount at the sight of the black square before the buzzer

is sounded. Remember, the black square has never been associated with food directly, but only indirectly, through association with the buzzer. It's as if the CS were functioning as a UCS.

The buzzer and food combination is referred to as *first-order conditioning*, and the black square and buzzer pairing as *second-order conditioning*. Pavlov found with dogs that learning couldn't go beyond third- or fourth-order conditioning. Even so, conditioning is beginning to look a rather more complex process.

Generalisation and discrimination
In *generalisation*, the CR transfers spontaneously to stimuli similar to, but different from, the original CS. For example, if a dog is trained using a bell of a particular pitch and is then presented with a bell a little higher or lower in pitch, it will still salivate, although only one bell (the original CS) was actually paired with food. However, if the dog is presented with bells that are increasingly different from the original, the CR will gradually weaken and eventually stop altogether – the dog is showing *discrimination*.

CS1 (The bell used in the original conditioning procedure) → CR (salivation)

| Bells CS2, CS3 and CS4 are of increasingly lower pitch but still produce salivation through **GENERALISATION** | $\begin{cases} CS2 \rightarrow CR \\ CS3 \rightarrow CR \\ CS4 \rightarrow CR \end{cases}$ | Salivation is gradually becoming weaker as the pitch becomes lower compared with CS1 |

| Bells CS5, CS6 and CS7 fail to produce salivation because they're sufficiently different from CS1 The dog is showing **DISCRIMINATION** | $\begin{cases} CS5 \not\rightarrow CR \\ CS6 \not\rightarrow CR \\ CS7 \not\rightarrow CR \end{cases}$ | No salivation occurs |

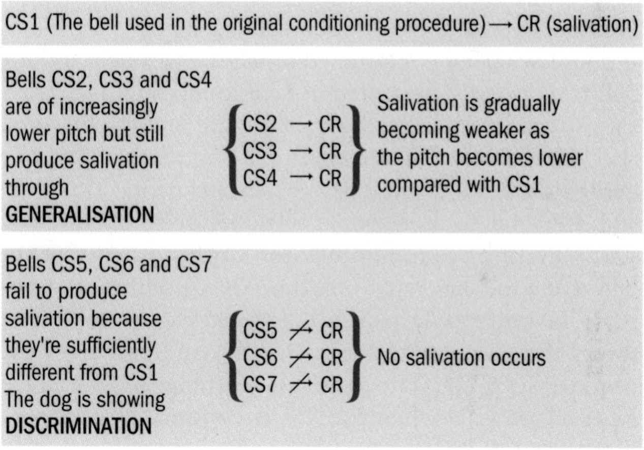

Figure 11.4 An example of discrimination occurring spontaneously as a result of generalisation stopping

Table 11.1 Four types of classical conditioning based on different CS–UCS relationships

1 Delayed or forward	The CS is presented *before* the UCS, and remains 'on' while the UCS is presented and until the UCR appears. Conditioning has occurred when the CR appears before the UCS is presented. A half-second interval produces the strongest learning. As the interval increases, learning becomes poorer. This type of conditioning is typically used in the laboratory, especially with non-humans.
2 Backward	The CS is presented *after* the UCS. Generally this produces very little, if any, learning in laboratory animals. However, much advertising uses backward conditioning (e.g. the idyllic tropical scene is set, and then the coconut bar is introduced).
3 Simultaneous	The CS and UCS are presented *together*. Conditioning has occurred when the CS on its own produces the CR. This type of conditioning often occurs in real-life situations (e.g. the sound of the dentist's drill accompanies the contact of the drill with your tooth).
4 Trace	The CS is *presented and removed* before the UCS is presented, so that only a 'memory trace' of the CS remains to be conditioned. The CR is usually weaker than in delayed or simultaneous conditioning.

Pavlov also trained dogs to discriminate in the original conditioning procedure. For example, if a high-pitched bell is paired with food but a low-pitched bell isn't, the dog will start salivating in response to the former, but not the latter (*discrimination training*). An interesting phenomenon related to discrimination is what Pavlov called *experimental neurosis*.

Box 11.1 Experimental neurosis: how to drive a dog mad

- Pavlov (1927) trained dogs to salivate to a circle but not to an ellipse, and then gradually changed the shape of the ellipse until it became almost circular.
- As this happened, the dogs started behaving in 'neurotic' ways – whining, trembling, urinating and defecating, refusing to eat, and so on.
- It was as if they didn't know how to respond: was the stimulus a circle (in which case, through generalisation, they 'ought' to salivate) or was it an ellipse (in which case, through discrimination, they 'ought not to' salivate)?

Extinction and spontaneous recovery

If dogs have been conditioned to salivate to a bell, and the bell is repeatedly presented *without* food, the CR of salivation gradually becomes weaker and eventually stops altogether *(extinction)*. However, if a dog that's undergone extinction is removed from the experimental situation, and then put back a couple of hours or so later, it will start salivating again. Although no further pairing of the bell and food has occurred, the CR of salivation reappears in response to the bell *(spontaneous recovery)*. This shows that extinction doesn't involve an 'erasing' of the original learning, but rather a learning to *inhibit* or *suppress* the CR when the CS is continually presented without a UCS.

Classical conditioning and human behaviour

There have been many laboratory demonstrations involving human participants. It's relatively easy to classically condition and extinguish CRs, such as the eye-blink and galvanic skin response (GSR). But what relevance does this have for understanding human learning and memory, let alone thinking, reasoning or problem-solving (see Chapter 20)?

In normal adults, the conditioning process can apparently be overridden by instructions: simply *telling* participants that the UCS won't occur causes *instant* loss of the CR, which would otherwise extinguish only slowly (Davey, 1983). Most participants in a conditioning experiment are aware of the experimenter's *contingencies* (the relationship between stimuli and responses), and in the absence of such awareness often fail to show evidence of conditioning (Brewer, 1974).

There are also important differences between very young children, or those with severe learning difficulties, and older children and adults, regarding their behaviour in a variety of *operant* conditioning and discrimination learning experiments. These seem largely attributable to language development (Dugdale & Lowe, 1990: see Chapter 19).

All this suggests that people have rather more efficient, language- or rule-based forms of learning at their disposal than the laborious formation of associations between a CS and UCS. Even behaviour therapy, one of the apparently more successful applications of conditioning principles to human behaviour, has given way to *cognitive-behaviour therapy* (Mackintosh, 1995: see Chapter 45).

Classical conditioning and phobias

Watson was the first psychologist to apply the principles of classical conditioning to human behaviour. He did this in what's considered to be one of the most ethically dubious psychology experiments ever conducted.

KEY STUDY 11.1 The case of Little Albert (Watson & Rayner, 1920)

- Albert B's mother was a wet-nurse in a children's hospital. Albert was described as 'healthy from birth', and 'on the whole stolid and unemotional'.
- When he was about nine months old, his reactions to various stimuli were tested – a white rat, a rabbit, a dog, a monkey, masks with and without hair, cotton wool, burning newspapers and a hammer striking a four-foot steel bar just behind his head. Only the last of these frightened him, so this was designated the UCS (and fear the UCR). The other stimuli were neutral, because they *didn't* produce fear.
- When Albert was just over 11 months old, the rat and the UCS were presented together: as Albert reached out to stroke the animal, Watson crept up behind the baby and brought the hammer crashing down on the steel bar.
- This occurred seven times in total over the next seven weeks. By this time, the rat (the CS) *on its own* frightened Albert, and the fear was now a CR. Watson and Rayner had succeeded in deliberately producing in a baby a phobia of rats.

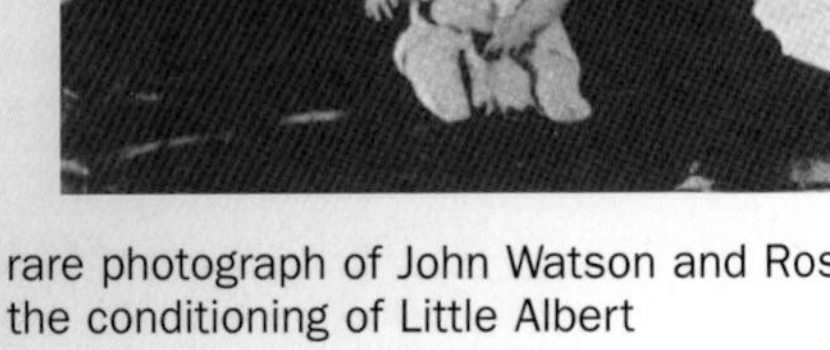

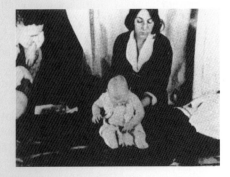

A very rare photograph of John Watson and Rosalie Rayner during the conditioning of Little Albert

- The CR transferred spontaneously to the rabbit, the dog, a sealskin fur coat, cotton wool, Watson's hair and a Santa Claus mask. But it didn't generalise to Albert's building blocks, or to the hair of two observers (so Albert was showing discrimination).
- Five days after conditioning, the CR produced by the rat persisted. After ten days it was 'much less marked', but was still evident a month later.

ASK YOURSELF...
- Why do you think Watson and Rayner's experiment is considered to be so ethically unsound?

It's unclear whether Watson and Rayner intended to remove Albert's phobia. What is certain is that his mother removed him from the hospital before this could happen. They might have attempted to remove it through the method of *direct unconditioning*, as used by Jones (1924). This is an early example of what Wolpe (1958) called *systematic desensitisation* (see Chapter 45).

KEY STUDY 11.2 The case of Little Peter (Jones, 1924)
- Peter was a two-year-old living in a charitable institution. Jones was mainly interested in those children who cried and trembled when shown an animal (such as a frog, rat or rabbit). Peter showed an extreme fear of rats, rabbits, feathers, cotton wool, fur coats, frogs and fish, although in other respects he was regarded as well adjusted. It wasn't known how these phobias had arisen.
- Jones, supervised by Watson, put a rabbit in a wire cage in front of Peter while he ate his lunch. After 40 such sessions, Peter ate his lunch with one hand and stroked the rabbit (now on his lap) with the other.
- In a series of 17 steps, the rabbit (still in the cage) had been brought a little closer each day, then let free in the room, eventually sitting on Peter's lunch tray.

Behaviour therapists, such as Eysenck, regard the Little Albert experiment as demonstrating how *all* phobias are acquired in everyday life.

ASK YOURSELF...
- How could the basic classical conditioning procedure help to explain someone's fear of the dentist?

A fear of the dentist could be learnt in the following way:

- drill hitting a nerve (UCS) ⟶ pain/fear (UCR)
- sound of drill (CS) + drill hitting nerve (UCS) ⟶ pain/fear (UCR)
- sound of the drill (CS) ⟶ fear (CR).

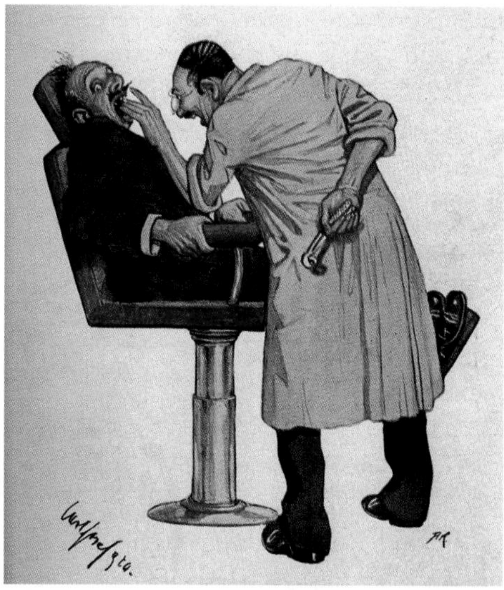

If you're looking at the dentist peering into your mouth, you may become afraid of upside-down faces. If the dentist is wearing a mask, you may acquire a fear of masks too. Also, through generalisation, you can come to fear all drill-like noises or white coats worn by medical personnel or lab technicians.

Human phobias may be perpetuated through *avoiding* the object of our fears. In other words, we don't give the fear a chance to undergo extinction (see Chapters 44 and 45). This occurs in conjunction with *operant conditioning*, whereby the avoidance behaviour becomes strengthened through negative reinforcement.

Operant conditioning: why do rats press levers?

When Skinner drew the distinction between respondent and operant behaviour, he wasn't rejecting the discoveries of Pavlov and Watson. Rather, he was arguing that most animal and human behaviour isn't triggered or elicited by specific stimuli. He was interested in how animals *operate on their environment*, and how this operant behaviour is *instrumental* in bringing about certain consequences, which then determine the probability of that behaviour being repeated. Skinner saw the learner as much more *active* than did Pavlov or Watson (see Box 11.4, page 180).

Just as Watson's ideas were based on the earlier work of Pavlov, so Skinner's study of operant conditioning grew out of the earlier work of another American, Edward Thorndike.

Thorndike's law of effect

Thorndike (1898) built puzzle-boxes for use with cats, whose task was to operate a latch that would automatically cause the door to spring open, freeing them. Each time they managed to escape from the puzzle-box, there was a piece of fish, visible from inside the puzzle-box, waiting for them. The cats were deprived of food for a considerable time before the experiments began, and so were highly motivated. After eating the fish, the cats were put straight back in, and the whole process was repeated.

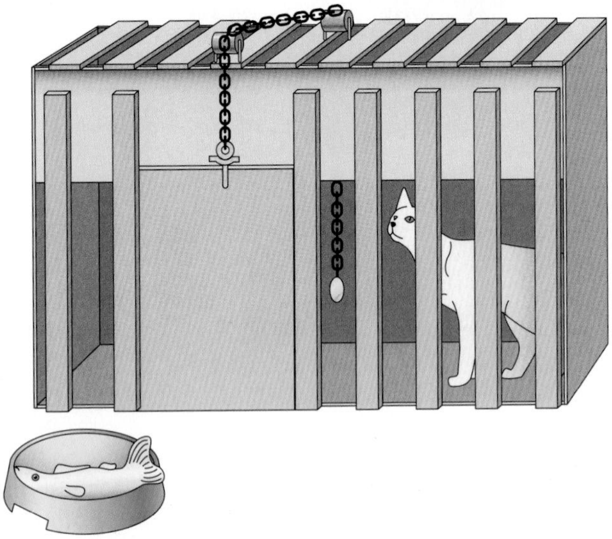

Figure 11.5 Thorndike's puzzle-box

At first the cats struggled to get out, behaving in a purely random way, and it was only by chance that the first escape was made. But each time they were returned to the puzzle-box, it took them less time to operate the latch and escape. For instance, with one of the boxes, the average time for the first escape was five minutes, but after 10–20 trials this was reduced to about five seconds.

Thorndike accounted for this by claiming that the learning was essentially random or *trial and error.* There was no sudden flash of insight into how the releasing mechanism worked, but rather a gradual reduction in the number of errors made and hence escape time (see Chapter 20). What was being learned was a connection between the stimulus (the manipulative components of the box) and the response (the behaviour that allowed the cat to escape). Further, the stimulus–response connection is 'stamped in when pleasure results from the act, and stamped out when it doesn't' *(law of effect).* This is crucially important as a way of distinguishing classical and operant conditioning, which Skinner did 40 years later.

Skinner's 'analysis of behaviour'

Skinner used a form of puzzle-box known as a *Skinner box.* This was designed for a rat or pigeon to do things in, rather than escape from. The box has a lever (in the case of rats) or illuminated discs (in the case of pigeons), under which is a food tray. The experimenter decides exactly what the relationship shall be between pressing the lever and the delivery of a food pellet, providing total *control* of the animal's environment. But it's the animal that has to do the work.

Pigeon in a Skinner box (or 'operant chamber')

Skinner used the term *strengthen* in place of Thorndike's 'stamping in', and *weaken* in place of 'stamping out'. He regarded Thorndike's terms as too mentalistic, and his own as more objective and descriptive.

Box 11.2 Skinner's analysis of behaviour (or the ABC of operant conditioning)

The *analysis of behaviour* requires an accurate but neutral representation of the relationship (or *contingencies*) between:

- ***A**ntecedents* (the stimulus conditions, such as the lever, the click of the food dispenser, a light that may go on when the lever is pressed)
- ***B**ehaviours* (or *operants*, such as pressing the lever)
- ***C**onsequences* (what happens as a result of the operant behaviour – reinforcement or punishment).

This is the ABC of operant conditioning.

According to Skinner's version of the law of effect, 'behaviour is shaped and maintained by its consequences'. The consequences of operants can be *positive reinforcement, negative reinforcement* or *punishment.*

While both positive and negative reinforcement *strengthen* behaviour (making it more probable), each works in a different way. *Positive reinforcement* involves presenting something pleasurable (such as food), while *negative reinforcement* involves the removal or avoidance of some 'aversive' (literally 'painful') state of affairs (such as electric shock). Punishment *weakens* behaviour (making it less probable), through the presentation of an aversive stimulus.

Reinforcers and reinforcement

Food itself is a reinforcer, electric shock a punisher. But the *process* whereby food is presented as a result of, say, lever-pressing is (positive) reinforcement, and when electric shock is presented instead it's called punishment.

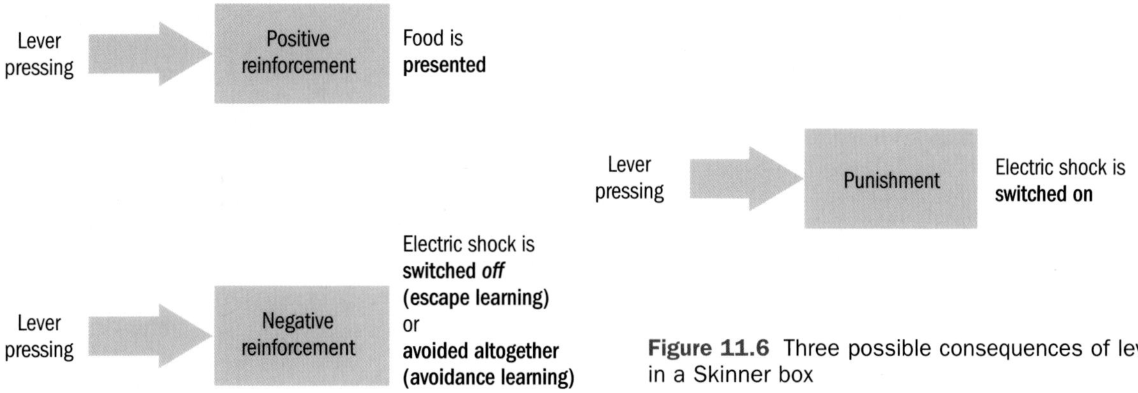

Figure 11.6 Three possible consequences of lever pressing in a Skinner box

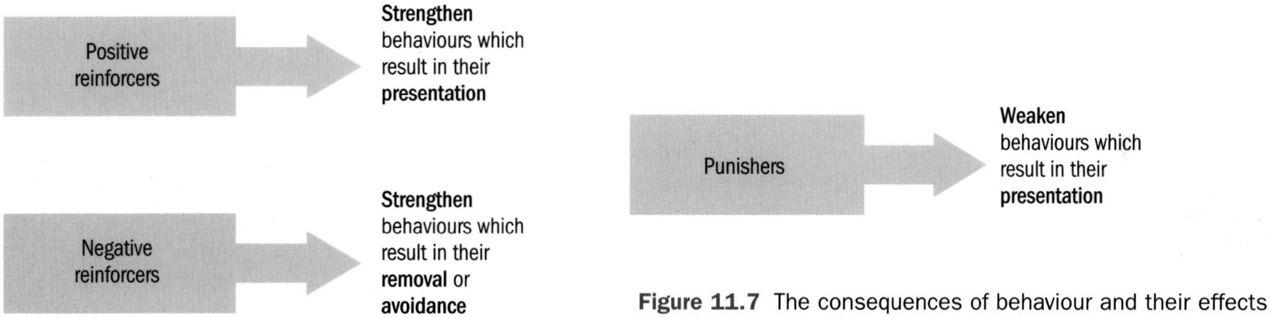

Figure 11.7 The consequences of behaviour and their effects

Skinner argues that the decision as to whether something is a reinforcer or a punisher can only be made *after* it's been made contingent on a specific behaviour on a number of occasions. So, if the behaviour is strengthened when followed by food, the food is a reinforcer, and if the shock weakens it, the shock is a punisher. Reinforcers and punishers cannot be defined *independently* of the effects they have on behaviour.

> ***ASK YOURSELF...***
> - Do you consider this to be a valid way of defining reinforcers and punishers?
> - Is it 'objective'?

Skinner's definition could be accused of circularity ('a reinforcer is whatever strengthens behaviour' and 'whatever strengthens behaviour is a reinforcer'). In practice, animals are starved for several hours before the experiments begin, to ensure they'll be motivated and find food reinforcing.

Skinner argues that his approach is *more* scientific, since the *intended* effect may not always coincide with the *actual* effect. For example, if a child who feels deprived of its parents' attention is smacked and shouted at when naughty, it's *more likely* to carry on being naughty. For a child who feels ignored, *any* attention is better than no attention at all. So, what is 'punishment' as far as the parents are concerned may be a positive reinforcement for the child. Similarly, a positive reinforcement can only loosely be called a reward, since 'reward' implies that the rewarder *expects* to strengthen some behaviour, whereas 'positive reinforcement' refers to what has been *shown* to strengthen it.

Primary and secondary reinforcers

Primary reinforcers (such as food, water, sex) are *natural* reinforcers (reinforcing in themselves). *Secondary reinforcers* acquire their reinforcing properties through association with primary reinforcers – that is, we have

Operant conditioning is the basis of most forms of dog (and other animal) training

to *learn* (through classical conditioning) to find them reinforcing. Examples of human secondary (or *conditioned*) reinforcers are money, cheques and tokens (see Chapter 45).

In a Skinner box, if a click accompanies the presentation of each pellet of food, the rat will eventually come to find the click on its own reinforcing. The click can then be used as a reinforcer for getting the rat to learn some new response. (Clickers are used in dog training, at first in conjunction with a primary reinforcer, such as a food 'treat', then on their own.) Secondary reinforcers are important, because they 'bridge the gap' between the response and the primary reinforcer, which may not be presented immediately.

Schedules of reinforcement

Another important aspect of Skinner's work is concerned with the effects on behaviour of how frequently and how regularly (or predictably) reinforcements are presented. Ferster & Skinner (1957) identified five major schedules, each of which is associated with a characteristic pattern of responding. This part of Skinner's research is largely counterintuitive (Walker, 1984).

Rats and pigeons (and probably most mammals and birds) typically 'work harder' (press the lever/peck the disc at a faster rate) for scant reward: when reinforcements are relatively infrequent and irregular or unpredictable, they'll go on working long after the reinforcement has actually been withdrawn. So, each schedule can be analysed in terms of *pattern and rate of response* and *resistance to extinction* (see Table 11.2).

The rate of response can be represented by plotting responses cumulatively as steps along a vertical axis, against the time when they're made along the horizontal axis. Skinner called this a '*cumulative record*'.

Table 11.2 Common reinforcement schedules, and associated patterns of response and resistance to extinction

Reinforcement schedule	Example	Pattern and rate of response	Resistance to extinction	Example of human behaviour
Continuous reinforcement (CRF)	Every single response is reinforced	Response rate is low but steady	Very low – the quickest way to bring about extinction	1 Receiving a high grade for every assignment 2 Receiving a tip for every customer served
Fixed interval (FI)	A reinforcement is given every 30 seconds (FI 30), provided the response occurs at least once during that time	Response rate speeds up as the next reinforcement becomes available; a pause after each reinforcement. Overall response rate fairly low	Fairly low – extinction occurs quite quickly	1 Being paid regularly (every week or month) 2 Giving yourself a 15-minute break for every hour's studying done
Variable interval (VI)	A reinforcement is given on average every 30 seconds (VI 30), but the interval varies from trial to trial. So, the interval on any one occasion is unpredictable	Response rate is very stable over long periods of time. Still some tendency to increase response rate as time elapses since the last reinforcement	Very high – extinction occurs very slowly and gradually	Many self-employed people receive payment irregularly (depending on when the customer pays for the product or service)
Fixed ratio (FR)	A reinforcement is given for a fixed number of responses, however long this may take, e.g. one reinforcement every ten responses (FR 10)	There's a pronounced pause after each reinforcement, and then a very high rate of responding leading up to the next reinforcement	As in FI	1 Piece work (the more work done, the more money earned 2 Commission (extra money for so many goods made or sales completed)
Variable ratio (VR)	A reinforcement is given on average every ten responses (VR 10), but the number varies from trial to trial. So, the number of responses required on any one occasion is unpredictable	Very high response rate – and very steady	Very high – the most resistant of all the schedules	Gambling

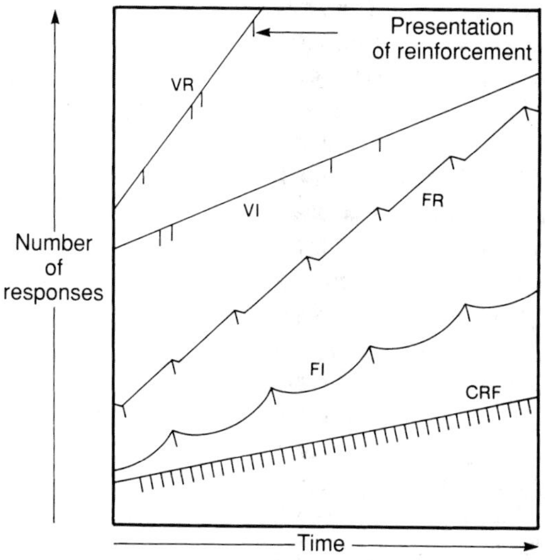

Figure 11.8 Typical cumulative records for a response (such as lever pressing) reinforced using five schedules of reinforcement

A *continuous* schedule is usually used only when some new response is being learned. Once it's being emitted regularly and reliably, it can be maintained by using one of the four *partial* or *intermittent* schedules. But this change must be gradual. If the animal is switched from a continuous schedule to, say, a VR 50, it will soon stop responding. Skinner (1938) originally used an interval schedule because a reinforcer is guaranteed, sooner or later, so long as one response is made during the interval.

Shaping: the reinforcement of successive approximations

Reinforcement can be used to build up relatively complex behaviour (not part of the animal's natural repertoire) by reinforcing closer and closer approximations to the desired behaviour *(shaping)*. First, the behaviour must be broken down into a number of small steps, each of which is reinforced in sequence. Gradually, what the animal can do is much more like what the experimenter is trying to teach it. This is what animal trainers have been doing for hundreds of years, and is the method of reinforcement Skinner used to teach pigeons to play ping-pong or turn a full (anticlockwise) circle. Most human skills are learned in this step-by-step manner.

Shaping also provides an important foundation for *behaviour modification*. This is used to teach children and adults with learning difficulties to use the toilet, feed and dress themselves, and other social skills. It's also been used to develop speech in autistic children and adult schizophrenics (see Chapter 45).

Negative reinforcement: escape and avoidance learning

Escape and avoidance learning are the two major ways in which negative reinforcement has been studied in the laboratory. *Escape learning* is relatively simple. For example, rats can learn to press a lever to turn off electric shock. *Avoidance learning* is more complex and more relevant to certain aspects of human behaviour.

Box 11.3 Avoidance learning through negative reinforcement

- Most laboratory studies use a *shuttle box*, a box divided into two compartments, sometimes with a barrier or door between them.
- Electric shocks can be delivered through the floor of either compartment independently of the other. Neither side is permanently safe, but only one is electrified at a time.
- The animal's task is to find which is the safe side on any one occasion. A *warning signal* (a light or buzzer) is given whenever the electrified side is to be changed, so the animal can always avoid being shocked if it switches sides when it hears (or sees) the signal.

According to the *two factor theory* (Mowrer, 1960) or the two process theory (Gray, 1975):

- the animal first learns to be afraid (the warning signal elicits an anticipatory emotional response of fear/anxiety through *classical conditioning*)
- it then learns a response to reduce the fear (jumping the barrier is *negatively reinforced* through avoiding the shock before it's switched on).

Miller (1948) trained rats to run out of a white room, through a small door, into a black room by giving them shocks in the white room. After pre-training, the door was closed and could only be opened by the rat turning a wheel. Even though no further shocks were given, the residual 'aversiveness' of the white room (acquired through classical conditioning) was sufficient to motivate the rats to learn quickly to turn the wheel. This allowed them to run through into the 'safe' room, thus relieving their anxiety (negative reinforcement).

This illustrates an important difference between positive and negative reinforcement in relation to extinction. If we try to teach a rat a new response in order to get it into a black box that used to contain food, it will soon stop responding (it soon 'discovers' that the food is no longer available). But if a rat successfully escapes from a white room that used to be dangerous, it may go on escaping indefinitely (it doesn't stay around long enough to 'discover' that the shock is no longer happening).

So, responses motivated by conditioned fear/anxiety should take longer to extinguish than those motivated by positive incentives. Avoidance learning prevents the learner from testing reality, and this has been found in dogs and humans (Solomon & Wynne, 1953; Turner & Solomon, 1962). This can explain both the persistence of human phobias and the use of methods to remove them based on the principle of *forced reality testing* (see Chapter 45).

Punishment

Skinner maintained that, with both humans and non-humans, positive (and, to a lesser extent, negative) reinforcement is a much more potent influence on behaviour than punishment. This is largely because punishment can only make certain responses less likely: you cannot teach anything *new* by punishment alone.

However, Campbell & Church (1969) argue that punishments are, if anything, a *stronger* influence on behaviour than the incentive effects of reinforcements (at least as far as laboratory animals are concerned). But punishment produces unpleasant side-effects, such as stress, anxiety, withdrawal and aggression.

Estes (1970) concluded that punishment merely *suppresses* lever pressing in the short term, but doesn't weaken it. Other experiments have shown that the strength and duration of the suppression effect depend on the intensity of the punishment and the degree of deprivation. However, the response is still suppressed rather than unlearned.

When alternative ways of obtaining reinforcers are available, punishment has a more powerful suppressive effect on the punished behaviour (Howe, 1980). For example, Azrin & Holz (1966) combined punishment and reinforcement, so that response A was punished while response B (incompatible with A) was positively reinforced. Skinner advocates this with human beings.

The antecedents of behaviour: stimulus control

In operant conditioning, the stimulus indicates the likely consequence of emitting a particular response: the operant behaviour is *more likely* to occur in the presence of some stimuli than others. If a rat has been reinforced for pressing the lever, it's more likely to go on emitting that response as the lever becomes associated both with reinforcement and the action of pressing (probably through classical conditioning). Technically, lever pressing has now come under the *stimulus control* of the lever. But there's still no inevitability about pressing it, only an *increased probability*. (This is why the term S–R psychology is sometimes used only to refer to classical conditioning.)

Similarly, drivers' behaviour is brought under the stimulus control of traffic signals, road signs, other vehicles, pedestrians, and so on. Much of our everyday behaviour can be seen in this way. Sitting on chairs, answering the telephone, turning on the television, and so on, are all operants that are more likely to occur in the presence of those stimuli because of the past consequences of doing so.

A special case of stimulus control is a *discriminative stimulus*. If a rat in the Skinner box is reinforced for lever pressing only when a light is on, the light soon becomes a discriminative stimulus (the rat presses only when the light is on).

A driver's behaviour (stopping the car) under the stimulus control of the (red) traffic light

ASK YOURSELF...

- What are the major similarities and differences between classical and operant conditioning?

Box 11.4 Major similarities and differences between classical and operant conditioning

Similarities

- They are both types of *associative learning*.
- *Generalisation*, *discrimination*, *extinction* and *spontaneous recovery* occur in both.

Differences

- In *classical* conditioning, the UCR or CR is *elicited* (triggered automatically) by the UCS or CS (it's essentially a reflex, involuntary response). In *operant* conditioning, behaviour is *emitted* by the organism and is essentially voluntary.
- In *classical* conditioning, the stimulus is guaranteed to produce the response, while the likelihood of a particular *operant* response being emitted is a function of the past consequences of such behaviour (it's more or less *probable*, but never certain).
- In *classical* conditioning, the UCS works in basically the same way *regardless* of whether it's pleasurable (such as food) or aversive (such as electric shock). In *operant* conditioning, responses that result in pleasurable outcomes are likely to be repeated, while those that result in aversive outcomes aren't.
- In *classical* conditioning, completely new stimulus–response connections are formed, while *operant* conditioning involves the strengthening or weakening of response tendencies already present in the animal's behavioural repertoire.
- In *classical* conditioning, the reinforcer (UCS) is presented *regardless* of what the animal does, and is presented *before* the response. In *operant* conditioning, the reinforcer is only presented if the animal emits some

specified, pre-selected behaviour, and is presented *after* the behaviour.

- In *classical* conditioning, the *strength* of conditioning is typically measured in terms of *response magnitude* (e.g. how many drops of saliva) and/or *latency* (how quickly a response is produced by a stimulus). In *operant* conditioning, strength is measured mainly as *response rate* (see Table 11.2).

Does conditioning work in the same way for all species?

The fact that many experiments involving a variety of species can all be described as classical conditioning *doesn't* in itself mean that there's only one mechanism involved, or only one explanation that applies, equally, to all species and all cases (Walker, 1984). Although *conditionability* seems to be an almost universal property of nervous systems (including those of sea snails, flatworms and fruit flies), many psychologists have argued that there can be no general laws of learning (Seligman, 1970).

If such laws do exist, one of them is likely to be the *law of contiguity*: events (or stimuli) that occur close together in time and space are likely to become associated with each other. Most of the examples of conditioning we've considered so far would appear to 'obey' the law of contiguity.

KEY STUDY 11.3 Learning to feel as sick as a rat (Garcia & Koelling, 1966; Garcia *et al.*, 1966)

- These represent an important exception to the 'law' of contiguity.
- In Garcia *et al.*'s study, rats were given a novel-tasting solution, such as saccharine-flavoured water (the CS), prior to a drug, *apomorphine* (the UCS), which has a *delayed* action, inducing severe intestinal illness (the UCR).
- In two separate experiments, the precise time lapse between tasting the solution and onset of the drug-induced nausea was either (a) 5, 6, 7, 8, 9, 10, 11, 12, 15, 16, 17, 18, 19, 20, 21 and 22 minutes, or (b) 30, 45, 75, 120 and 180 minutes.
- In (a), the rats received just four treatments (one every third day). In all cases, there was a conditioned aversive response to the solution: intestinal illness became a CR (a response to the solution alone). In some replications, just a single treatment has been required.

While rats can also be conditioned to novel smells, auditory, visual and tactile stimuli aren't so readily associated with internal illness. As for pigeons, it's impossible to deter them from water and, for other species, taste aversions are very difficult to establish, even if the animal is made very ill. In almost all species, aversions are learned more easily to new flavours than to familiar ones (saccharine solution is a novel taste for the rat).

Biological constraints on conditioning

It seems, then, that there are definite biological limitations on the ability of animals to develop a conditioned aversion. Similarly, rats typically learn very quickly to avoid shock in a shuttle box and to press a lever for food. However, they don't learn very readily to press a lever to avoid shock. Pigeons can be trained quickly to fly from one perch to another in order to avoid shock, but it's almost impossible to train them to peck a disc to avoid shock.

Findings like these have led Bolles (1980) and others to conclude that we cannot regard the basic principles of learning as applying equally to all species in all situations. We must take into account the *evolutionary history* of the species, as well as the individual organism's learning history. An important idea in this context is Seligman's concept of *preparedness* (1970). Animals are biologically prepared to learn actions that are closely related to the survival of their species (such as learned water or food aversions), and these *prepared* behaviours are learned with very little training. Equally, *contraprepared* behaviours are contrary to an animal's natural tendencies, and so are learned with great difficulty, if at all. Seligman believes that most of the behaviour studied in the laboratory falls somewhere in between these two extremes.

As far as human behaviour is concerned, much of the relevant data relates to how easily certain conditioned fear responses can be induced in the laboratory or how common certain naturally occurring phobias are compared with others. For example, Ohman *et al.* (1975a, 1975b) paired slides of snakes and spiders with a strong electric shock, and quickly established conditioned emotional responses to these slides – but *not* to slides of flowers, houses or berries.

Seligman (1972) observed that human phobias tend to fall into certain narrow categories, mostly animals or dangerous places. Most common of all were the fear of snakes, spiders, the dark, high places and closed-in places, and often there's no previous evidence for the fear actually having been conditioned (see Chapters 43 and 45). Also, classically conditioned responses extinguish faster in humans than animals. This is because the CRs are modulated by more complex human memories (Weiskrantz, 1982).

The role of cognition in conditioning

According to Mackintosh (1978), conditioning cannot be reduced to the strengthening of S–R associations by the automatic action of a process called reinforcement. It's more appropriate to think of it as a matter of detecting and learning about *relations between events*. Animals typically discover what signals or causes events that are important to them, such as food, water, danger or safety. Salivation or lever pressing are simply a convenient index of what the subject has learned, namely that certain relationships exist in its environment.

Classical conditioning

Pavlov himself described the CS as a 'signal' for the UCS, the relationship between CS and the UCS as one of 'stimulus substitution', and the CR as an 'anticipatory' response (or 'psychic secretions'), suggesting that his dogs were *expecting* the food to follow the bell. Consistent with this interpretation, Rescorla (1968) presented two groups of animals with the same number of CS–UCS pairings, but the second group also received additional presentations of the UCS on its own without the CS. The first group showed much stronger conditioning than the second, indicating that the most important factor (at least in classical conditioning) is how *predictably* the UCS follows the CS, *not* how often the CS and UCS are paired.

Blocking also supports a more cognitive interpretation (Kamin, 1969). For example, if an animal is shown a light, quickly followed by an electric shock, the light soon comes to elicit fear as a CR. If a noise is then added (noise + light + shock), then the noise should also soon become a CS, because it, too, is being paired with shock. However, this *isn't* what happens. If the noise is later presented alone, it fails to produce a CR. It seems that the noise has somehow been 'blocked' from becoming a CS because of the previous conditioning to the light. In cognitive terms, since the light already predicts shock, the noise is *irrelevant*. It provides no additional information – the animal already 'knows' that shock will follow the light.

Operant conditioning

KEY STUDY 11.4 Learned helplessness (Seligman, 1974, 1975)

- Dogs were strapped into a harness and given a series of shocks from which they couldn't escape.
- They were later required to jump a barrier in a shuttle box within 10 seconds of a warning signal, or suffer 50 seconds of painful shock.
- Control dogs (which hadn't been subjected to the inescapable shocks) learned the avoidance response very quickly.
- But about two-thirds of the experimental dogs seemed unable to do so. They seemed passively resigned to suffering the shock, and even if they did successfully avoid the shock on one trial, they were unlikely to do so on the next. Some dogs had to be pushed over the barrier 200 times or more before this learned helplessness wore off.

According to Seligman, the dogs learned that no behaviour on their part had any effect on the occurrence (or non-occurrence) of a particular event (the shock). This has been demonstrated using human participants by Miller & Norman (1979), and Maier & Seligman (1976) have tried to explain depression in humans in terms of learned helplessness (see Chapters 12 and 44).

Skinner's claim that reinforcements and punishments *automatically* strengthen and weaken behaviour has been challenged by Bandura (1977a). For Bandura:

> Reinforcements serve principally as an informative and motivational operation rather than as a mechanical response strengthener.

Reinforcement provides the learner with *information* about the likely consequences of certain behaviour under certain conditions – that is, it improves our prediction of whether a given action will lead to pleasant (reinforcement) or unpleasant (punishment) outcomes in the *future*. It also *motivates* us, by causing us to anticipate future outcomes. Our present behaviours are largely governed by the outcomes we *expect* them to have, and we're more likely to learn behaviour if we value its consequences.

This cognitive reinterpretation of reinforcement forms part of Bandura's *social learning theory* (SLT), which is discussed in more detail in relation to aggression (Chapter 29), moral and gender development (Chapters 35 and 36), and personality (Chapter 42). While not denying the role of both classical and operant conditioning, SLT focuses on *observational learning* (or *modelling*), in which cognitive factors are crucial. This is reflected in Bandura's renaming (1986, 1989) of SLT as *social cognitive theory*.

COGNITIVE APPROACHES

Tolman's cognitive behaviourism

Although he was working within the behaviourist tradition in the 1920s, 1930s and 1940s, Tolman would today be regarded as a cognitive psychologist. He explained the learning of rats in terms of inferred cognitive processes, in particular *cognitive* or *mental maps*.

KEY STUDY 11.5 Latent learning – who needs reinforcement? (Tolman & Honzik, 1930)

- *Group 1* rats were reinforced every time they found their way through a maze to the food box.
- *Group 2* rats were never reinforced.
- Group 3 rats received no reinforcement for the first 10 days of the experiment, but did so from day 11.
- Not surprisingly, Group 1 learned the maze quickly and made fewer and fewer mistakes, while Group 2 never reduced the time it took to find the food, and moved around aimlessly much of the time.
- Group 3 made no apparent progress during the first 10 days. But they then showed a sudden decrease in the time it took to reach the goal box on day 11, when they received their first reinforcement. They caught up almost immediately with Group 1.

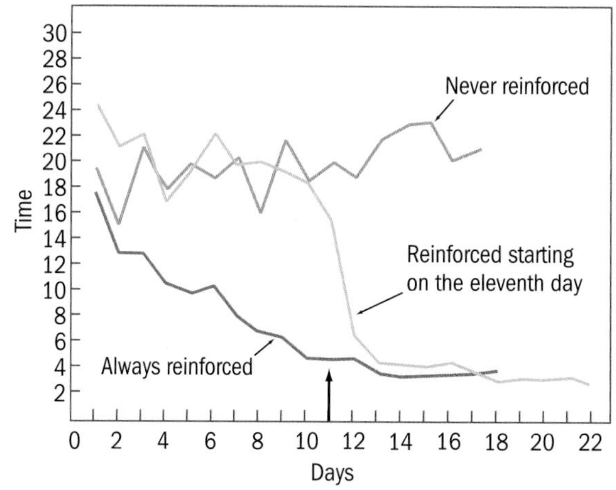

Figure 11.9 The results of Tolman and Honzik's study of latent learning in rats

> *ASK YOURSELF...*
> - How might you explain Tolman and Honzik's results?
> - Could the distinction we made earlier between learning and performance help?

Clearly, Group 3 rats had been learning their way through the maze during the first 10 days, but that learning was *latent* (hidden or 'behaviourally silent'). In other words, it didn't show up in their actual behaviour until they received the incentive of the reinforcement on day 11. Tolman and Honzik concluded that reinforcement may be important in relation to *performance* of learned behaviour, but that it *isn't* necessary for the learning itself.

Tolman's (1948) *place learning* (or *sign learning*) theory maintains that rats learn *expectations* as to which part of the maze will be followed by which other part of the maze. Tolman called these expectations *cognitive maps*, a primitive kind of perceptual map of the maze, an understanding of its spatial relationships (much like the mental map you have of familiar streets leading to home or college).

Although a cognitive map can only be *inferred* from actual behaviour, it's difficult to know how else to explain the findings that rats will take short-cuts to the food box if the old path is blocked. Similarly, if the maze were rotated, they could find the usual food location from several different starting points (Tolman *et al.*, 1946). Restle (1957) flooded a maze immediately after a group of rats had learnt to run it, and they were able to swim to the goal box with no more errors than when they'd walked. This clearly supports Tolman's interpretation.

Insight learning

Insight learning represents a view of learning as 'purely cognitive'. It stems from the Gestalt school of psychology, which is diametrically opposed to the S–R approach. The Gestalt psychologists are best known for their work on perception (see Chapter 15), and their view of learning is directly linked to their view of perception.

Table 11.3 Gagné's hierarchy of learning

1 Signal learning	Establishment of a simple connection, in which a stimulus takes on the properties of a signal (classical conditioning)
2 Stimulus–response (S–R) learning	Establishment of a connection between a stimulus and response, where the response is a voluntary movement and the connection is instrumental in satisfying a need/motive (operant conditioning)
1 and 2 are prerequisites for:	
3 Chaining	The connecting of a sequence of two/more previously learned S–R connections
4 Verbal association	The learning of chains that are specifically verbal, important for the acquisition/use of language. Enables several learned connections involving words to be emitted in a single sequence
3 and 4 are prerequisites for:	
5 Discrimination learning	Making different responses to similar stimuli. Involves more than simply making isolated S–R connections, because it's necessary to deal with the problem of interference between similar items
5 is a prerequisite for:	
6 Concept learning	Learning to make a common response to stimuli that form a class/category, but which differ in their physical characteristics. Requires representing information in memory, classifying events, and discriminating between them on the basis of abstract properties
6 is a prerequisite for:	
7 Rule learning	A rule is a chain of two/more concepts (e.g. 'if A then B')
7 is a prerequisite for:	
8 Problem solving	Involves recombining old rules into new ones, making it possible to answer questions and solve problems. Especially important for real-life human problem-solving situations

Insight learning can be defined as a *perceptual restructuring* of the elements that constitute a problem situation: a previously missing 'ingredient' is supplied, and all the parts are seen in relation to each other, forming a meaningful whole. Some of the most famous studies of insight learning were conducted by Köhler, one of the founders of Gestalt psychology, with chimps. These, and other Gestalt studies of problem-solving, are discussed in Chapter 20.

Gagné's hierarchy of learning

Koestler (1970) believes that the debate between the S–R and cognitive theorists derives to a large extent from a refusal to take seriously the notion of *ripeness*. By this, he means a person's or animal's readiness to make a discovery or solve a problem, based on relevant knowledge, skills and past experience. Rats and cats have generally been presented with tasks for which they are biologically ill-fitted, and so the resulting learning was bound to appear gradual, piecemeal and at first quite random. But Köhler set chimps problems for which they were (almost) ripe, which gave the impression that all learning is based on insight.

Gagné (1970) has proposed a way of identifying the relationship between simple and complex forms of learning. Eight major varieties of learning are related *hierarchically*, with simpler abilities constituting *prerequisites* for more complex abilities (see Table 11.3).

Learning sets and transfer of learning

According to Harlow (1949), S–R learning and insight learning are essentially two different phases of the same, continuous process. S–R learning predominates in the early stages, and insight develops out of prior S–R connections. Harlow suggests that the concept of a *learning set* (or *'learning to learn'*) represents an intervening process between S–R and insight learning. The greater the number of sets, the better equipped the learner is to adapt to a changing environment; a very large number of different sets 'may supply the raw material for human thinking'.

A learning set involves learning a general skill applicable to a whole new class of problems, a simple rule or code, based on a conceptual (not a perceptual) relationship. In experiments with monkeys, Harlow demonstrated that insightful learning is itself (at least partially) *learned* and grows out of more random, trial-and-error learning.

CONCLUSIONS: TRANSFER OF LEARNING

A learning set represents a special case of a more general phenomenon known as *transfer of learning* (or *training*). Essentially, transfer refers to the influence of earlier learning on later learning, which is an inherent feature of the learning process in general (Howe, 1980). Some kinds of transfer take the form of simple stimulus generalisation (equivalent to Gagné's signal learning), while in more complex learning situations transfer may depend on the acquisition of rules or principles that apply to a variety of different circumstances (Gagné's concept, rule learning and problem-solving). Learning sets can be viewed as intermediate between simple generalisation, and the more complex transfer phenomena involved in hierarchically organised skills (Howe, 1980).

CHAPTER SUMMARY

- **Learning** has played a major part in the development of psychology as a scientific discipline and is central to the **behaviourist** approach.
- Psychologists are interested in learning **as a process**. Theories of learning differ as to the nature of the process involved, especially the role played by **cognitive** factors.
- It's generally agreed that learning involves a relatively permanent change in behaviour due to past experience. The distinction between **learning** and **performance** refers to **potential** and **actual behaviour** respectively.
- The distinction between **respondent** and **operant** behaviour corresponds to **classical** (**respondent** or **Pavlovian**) and **operant** (**instrumental** or **Skinnerian**) **conditioning** respectively.
- In **classical conditioning**, the pairing of a **conditioned** and an **unconditioned stimulus** results in the former eliciting a response that formerly was produced only by the latter.
- **Delayed/forward**, **backward**, **simultaneous** and **trace** conditioning differ according to the relationships between the conditioned and the unconditioned stimuli.
- **Generalisation**, **discrimination**, **extinction** and **spontaneous recovery** represent conditioning phenomena, which make it more complex and versatile. Spontaneous recovery demonstrates that extinction involves a learning to **inhibit/suppress** the conditioned response.
- Watson applied classical conditioning to human behaviour for the first time by inducing fear of a rat in Little Albert. Jones removed animal phobias from Little Peter using an early form of systematic desensitisation.
- Compared with classical conditioning, **operant conditioning** sees learning as a much more **active** process. Skinner was interested in how animals operate on their environment, and how their activity is instrumental in producing certain consequences.
- Skinner's work was based on Thorndike's **law of effect**. He designed a form of puzzle-box (a **Skinner box**), and called the consequences of behaviour **positive reinforcement**, **negative reinforcement** and **punishment**.

- Reinforcement (both positive and negative) **strengthens** behaviour, while punishment **weakens** it.
- **Primary reinforcers** are **naturally** reinforcing, while **secondary**/conditioned reinforcers come to be reinforcing through association with primary reinforcers.
- Different **schedules of reinforcement** can be analysed in terms of **pattern/rate of response** and **resistance to extinction**. **Variable** schedules involve high, steady rates of response and high resistance to extinction, compared with **fixed** and **continuous** schedules.
- **Shaping** involves the reinforcement of successive approximations to the desired behaviour.
- **Escape** and **avoidance learning** are two forms of negative reinforcement. They've been explained by the **two factor theory**, according to which both classical and operant conditioning are involved. The persistence of human phobias can be understood in terms of avoidance learning.
- **Punishment** seems to involve a **suppression** of behaviour, and is most effective when combined with the reinforcement of an incompatible response.
- **Taste aversion** experiments contribute to the view that the basic principles of conditioning *don't* apply equally to all species in all situations.
- **Preparedness** helps to explain experimental findings which show that different species acquire certain conditioned responses more or less easily, and why certain human phobias are more common than others.
- Classical conditioning involves learning about relations between environmental events, rather than a simple strengthening of S–R associations. Seligman's concept of **learned helplessness** illustrates the complexity of operant conditioning and has been used to explain human depression.
- Tolman's studies of **latent learning** show that learning can take place in the absence of reinforcement. Rats learn a **cognitive map** of a maze, not the individual movements of walking or running that take them to the food box.
- **Gestalt** psychologists saw **insight learning** as involving the perceptual restructuring of the elements that constitute a problem situation.
- Insight and trial and error aren't necessarily opposed forms of learning. Gagné's **hierarchy of learning** and Harlow's concept of **learning set** show that they're related, not exclusive. A learning set represents a special case of the more general **transfer of learning**.

Links with other topics/chapters

- Learning, in the form of conditioning, lies at the heart of behaviourism (Chapter 2), one of the major theoretical approaches within psychology.
- The distinction between philosophical and methodological behaviourism is important both in the history of psychology (Chapter 1) and the debate over the scientific nature of psychology (Chapter 3).
- Learning and memory are closely inter-related processes (Chapter 17).
- The Little Albert experiment is taken by many behaviour therapists (such as Eysenck) as demonstrating how all phobias are acquired in everyday life (Chapter 44).
- The 'direct unconditioning' used in the Little Peter experiment is an early example of systematic desensitisation, a major form of behaviour therapy, used in the treatment of phobias (Chapter 45).
- Shaping provides the basis of behaviour modification, used with a range of patients, including autistic children and adult schizophrenics (Chapter 45).
- Seligman and others have drawn on the concept of learned helplessness to explain human depression (Chapter 44).
- Social learning theory has been applied to the study of aggression (Chapter 29), moral and gender development (Chapters 35 and 36).
- Gestalt psychology is best known for its principles of perceptual organisation (Chapter 15), but was also concerned with problem-solving (Chapter 20)

12

APPLICATION

HEALTH PSYCHOLOGY

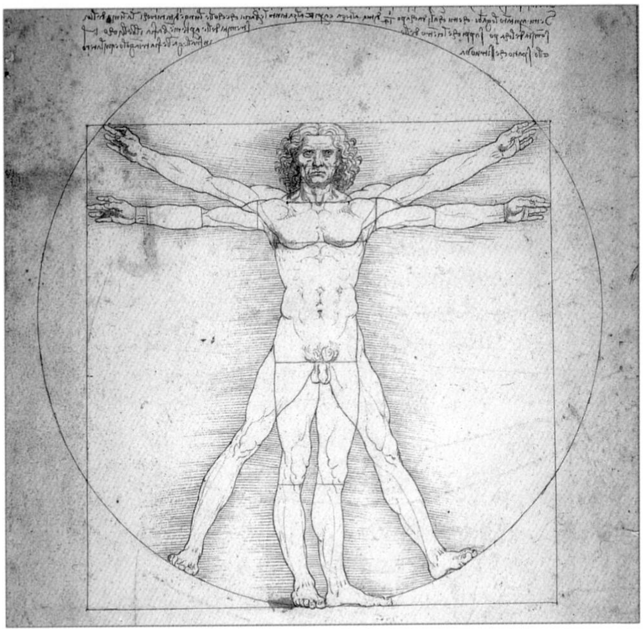

INTRODUCTION AND OVERVIEW

According to Ogden (2000), health psychology represents one of several challenges that were made during the twentieth century to the *biomedical model*. This maintains that:

- diseases either come from outside the body and invade it, causing internal physical changes, or originate as internal involuntary physical changes; such diseases can be caused by chemical imbalances, bacteria, viruses or genetic predisposition
- individuals aren't responsible for their illnesses, which arise from biological changes beyond their control; people who are ill are victims

- treatment should consist of vaccination, surgery, chemotherapy or radiotherapy, all of which aim to change the physical state of the body
- responsibility for treatment rests with the medical profession
- health and illness are qualitatively different – you're either healthy or ill, and there's no continuum between them
- mind and body function independently of each other; the abstract mind relates to feelings and thoughts, and is incapable of influencing physical matter
- illness may have psychological consequences, but *not* psychological causes.

In opposition to these ideas, health psychology maintains that human beings should be seen as complex systems. Illness is often caused by a combination of biological (e.g. viruses), psychological (e.g. behaviours and beliefs), and social (e.g. employment) factors. These assumptions reflect the *biopsychosocial model* of health and illness (Engel, 1977, 1980).

The biopsychosocial model reflects fundamental changes in the nature of illness, causes of death and overall life expectancy during the twentieth century. Average life expectancy in the USA has increased from 48 in 1900 to 76 today. This is due mainly to the virtual elimination of infectious diseases – such as pneumonia, flu, tuberculosis (TB), diphtheria, scarlet fever, measles, typhoid and polio – as causes of death. Although HIV and AIDS increased the percentage of infection-related deaths during the 1980s and early 1990s, today's major killers are cardiovascular diseases (heart disease and strokes) and cancers, the former accounting for about 40 per cent of deaths in industrialised countries (Stroebe, 2000).

In fact, there's been a small but steady decline since the 1960s in deaths due to cardiovascular disease. This is due partly to improvements in medical treatment, but also to significant changes in lifestyle, specifically reduction in serum cholesterol levels and cigarette smoking. But at the same time there's been an increase in deaths due to cancer in most industrialised countries, due almost entirely to increases in lung cancer. As Stroebe (2000) says, the influence of such non-medical factors is incompatible with the biomedical model. By conceptualising disease in purely biological terms, the model has little to offer the prevention of chronic diseases through efforts to change people's health beliefs, attitudes and behaviour.

WHAT IS HEALTH PSYCHOLOGY?

A brief history

Two of the other challenges to the biomedical model cited by Ogden (2000) are:

1. psychosomatic medicine, developed in response to Freud's analysis of the relationship between mind and body (see Chapter 43), and
2. behavioural medicine, which is concerned with health care, treatment and prevention of physical diseases/physiological dysfunction, such as hypertension, addictive behaviours and obesity.

These are historical predecessors of health psychology (Penny, 1996). As we noted earlier, cardiovascular disease and cancer (and other chronic systemic disorders, such as diabetes) are the major killers in industrialised countries. The role of social and psychological factors is much more evident in the development and treatment of these diseases. The fact that they're chronic means that people may suffer them for many years, making psychological factors more relevant (Penny, 1996).

It was gradually recognised that psychologists could make a contribution to the health field, and health psychology formally began with the founding of the Division of Health Psychology within the American Psychological Association in 1978. The journal *Health Psychology* followed in 1982. In 1984, a Health Psychology Group was established within the British Psychological Society, which became the Health Psychology Section (1987), and finally the Special Group of Health Psychology (1992). There is also a European Health Psychology Society.

It became evident in the 1970s that national health spending in western countries was getting out of control. Consequently, many countries began to explore disease *prevention*. The most powerful preventative strategy may be *health promotion*, and health psychology has made significant contributions in this area since the mid-1970s (Maes & van Elderen, 1998).

Definitions

Maes & van Elderen (1998) define health psychology as:

> ... a sub-discipline of psychology which addresses the relationship between psychological processes and behaviour on the one hand and health and illness on the other hand ... however ... health psychologists are more interested in 'normal' everyday-life behaviour and 'normal' psychological processes in relation to health and illness than in psycho-pathology or abnormal behaviour ...

From a health psychology perspective, they say, someone who avoids sex following a heart attack for fear of triggering another one is showing a normal, functional response to a dysfunctional situation, rather than an abnormal phobic response. However, Turpin & Slade (1998) maintain that within applied psychology there's a controversial debate regarding the boundaries between clinical and health psychology (see Chapter 1). They believe that health psychology is an *extension* of clinical psychology, focusing specifically on people with physical health problems and their associated psychological needs:

> ... we wish to stress the commonality of psychological approaches to mental and physical health. Indeed ... health

and well-being should not be arbitrarily separated into 'mental' and 'physical'. An approach that emphasises psychological, social and biological factors will be necessary for the understanding of all health problems … it is essential to consider all three factors when seeking to account for experiences of health and illness.

Turpin and Slade are advocating the biopsychosocial model that, as we saw earlier, is the major alternative to the biomedical model of illness.

Defining health and illness

> *ASK YOURSELF...*
> - What do you understand by the terms 'health' and 'illness'?
> - Are you healthy if you're not ill, or is health a more positive state than that?

Revisiting the biomedical model

According to the biomedical model, *disease* is a deviation from a measurable biological norm. This view, which still dominates medical thinking and practice, is based on several invalid assumptions. Most importantly, the specificity assumption maintains that understanding of an illness is greater if it can be defined at a more specific biochemical level. This *reductionist* view (see Chapter 49) originated when infectious diseases were still the major causes of death (Maes & van Elderen, 1998: see above).

According to Maes and van Elderen, traditional medicine is more focused on disease than on health:

> … It would be more appropriate to call our health care systems 'disease care systems', as the primary aim is to treat or cure people with various diseases rather that to promote health or prevent disease …

By contrast with the biomedical model's *reactive* attitude towards *illness*, the biopsychosocial model underlying health psychology adopts a more *proactive* attitude towards *health*. Many definitions of health have been proposed since the 1940s, mostly in terms of the *absence* of disease, dysfunction, pain, suffering and discomfort.

Box 12.1 Defining health and illness

- According to the World Health Organization (1946, in Maes & van Elderen, 1998), *health* is 'a complete state of physical, mental, and social well-being and not merely the absence of disease or infirmity'.
- *Disease* (which reflects the medical approach) is a 'state of the body characterised by deviations from the norm or measurable biological or somatic variables' (Maes & van Elderen, 1998).
- *Illness* is 'the state of being ill, implying that illness is a more psychological concept, which is closely related to one's own perception of a health problem (e.g. pain)' (Maes & van Elderen, 1998). Subjective psychological symptoms, such as anxiety, also play a substantial role in the construction of illness. Similarly, although illness is usually associated with evidence of medical abnormality:

  > *...it also incorporates aspects of the individual's wider functioning, self-perceptions and behaviours, and requires consideration of social context and societal norms. (Turpin & Slade, 1998)*

- The concepts of health and illness incorporate both physical, psychological and social aspects, reflecting the biopsychosocial model.

Revisiting the biopsychosocial model

In contrast with the biomedical model's reductionist view, the biopsychosocial model adopts a *holistic* approach – that is, the *person as a whole* needs to be taken into account. It maintains that both '*micro-level*' (small-scale causes, such as chemical imbalances) and '*macro-level*' (large-scale causes, such as the extent of available social support) processes interact to determine someone's health status (see Figure 12.1).

Culture and health

Culture represents one of the 'macro-level' processes referred to above (see Chapter 47). *Cross-cultural health psychology* (Berry, 1994) involves two related domains:

1. the earlier, more established study of how cultural factors influence various aspects of health

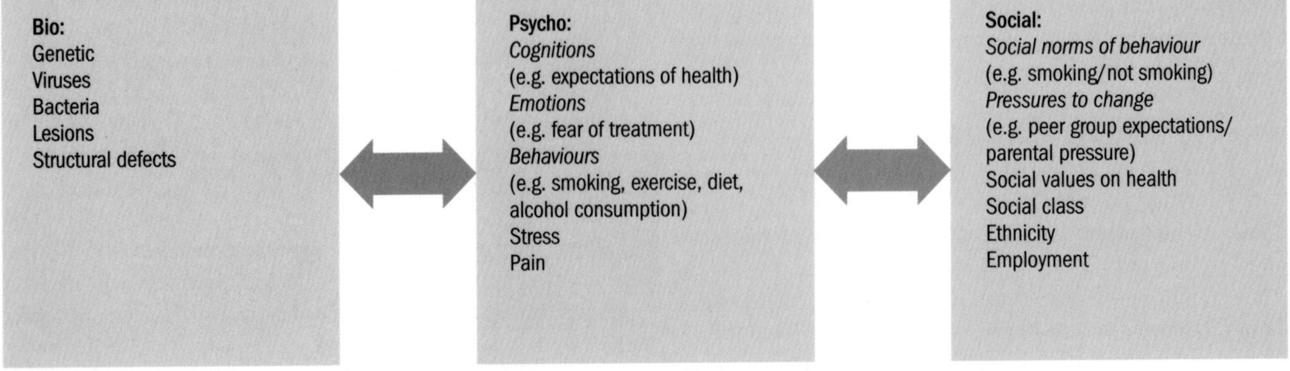

Figure 12.1 The biopsychosocial model of health and illness (adapted from Ogden, Open University Press, 2000)

2. the more recent and very active study of the health of individuals and groups as they settle into and adapt to new cultural circumstances, through migration, and of their persistence over generations as ethnic groups.

Box 12.2 Health and disease as cultural concepts

- Many studies have shown that the very concepts of health and disease are defined differently across cultures. While 'disease' may be rooted in pathological biological processes (common to all), 'illness' is now widely recognised as a culturally influenced subjective experience of suffering and discomfort (Berry, 1998: see Box 12.1).
- Recognising certain conditions as either healthy or as a disease is also linked to culture. For example, trance is seen as an important curing (health-seeking) mechanism in some cultures, but may be classified as a sign of psychiatric disorder in others. Similarly, how a condition is expressed is also linked to cultural norms, as in the tendency to express psychological problems *somatically* (in the form of bodily symptoms) in some cultures (e.g. Chinese) more than in others (see Chapter 43).

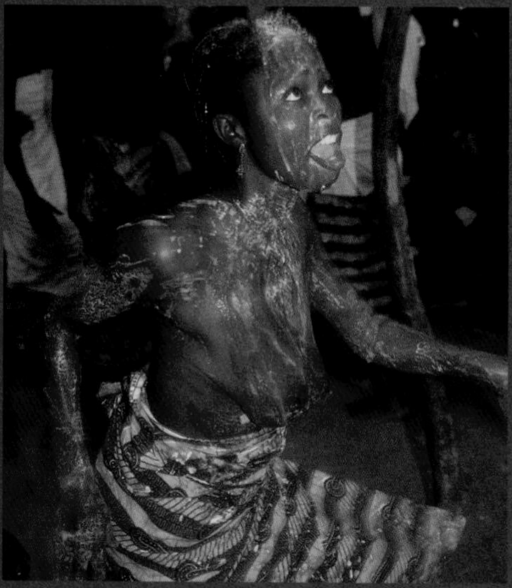

A Minah medium of the violent God Jagli, who induces trances and wild dances

- Disease and disability are highly variable. Cultural factors (such as diet, substance abuse and social relationships within the family) contribute to the prevalence of diseases including heart disease, cancer and schizophrenia (Berry, 1998).

Acculturation

Cross-cultural psychologists believe that there's a complex pattern of continuity and change in how people who've developed in one cultural context behave when they move to and live in a new cultural context. This process of adaptation to the new ('host') culture is called *acculturation*. With increasing acculturation (the longer immigrants live in the host country), health status 'migrates' to the national norm (Berry, 1998).

Was ET's near-fatal illness due to acculturation – or did he simply want to go home?

For example, coronary heart disease (CHD) among Polish immigrants to Canada increased (their rates were initially lower), while for immigrants from Australia and New Zealand the reverse was true. Data for immigrants from 26 out of 29 countries shifted their rates towards those of the Canadian-born population. Similar patterns have been found for stomach and intestinal cancer among immigrants to the USA (Berry, 1998).

ASK YOURSELF...
- How could you explain such findings?
- What is it about living in a different cultural situation that can increase or decrease your chances of developing life-threatening diseases?

One possibility is exposure to widely shared risk factors in the physical environment (e.g. climate, pollution, pathogens), over which there's little choice. Alternatively, it could be due to choosing to pursue assimilation (or possible integration) as the way to acculturate. This may expose immigrants to *cultural* risk factors, such as diet, lifestyle and substance abuse. This 'behavioural shift' interpretation would be supported if health status both improved *and* declined relative to national norms.

However, the main evidence points to a *decline*, supporting the 'acculturative stress' (or even 'psychopathology') interpretation – that is, the very process of acculturation may involve risk factors that can reduce health status. This explanation is supported by evidence that stress can lower resistance to diseases such as hypertension and diabetes (Berry, 1998: see pages 206–208).

Other aspects of the biopsychosocial model include the beliefs that:

- individuals aren't just passive victims, but are responsible for taking their medication, and changing their beliefs and behaviour

- health and illness exist on a continuum – people *aren't* either healthy or ill, but progress along the continuum, in both directions
- psychological factors contribute to the *aetiology* (causation) of illness – they're not just consequences of illness.

> *ASK YOURSELF...*
> - Can you think of examples of where being ill was (partly) caused by psychological factors, *and* where your illness affected you psychologically?

According to Ogden (2000), health psychology aims to:

- *evaluate* the role of behaviour in the aetiology of illness, such as the link between smoking, CHD, cholesterol level, lack of exercise, high blood pressure (BP) and stress
- *predict* unhealthy behaviours – for example, smoking, alcohol consumption and high-fat diets are related to beliefs, and beliefs about health and illness can be used to predict behaviour
- *understand* the role of psychological factors in the experience of illness. For example, understanding the psychological consequences of illness could help to alleviate pain, nausea, vomiting, anxiety and depression
- *evaluate* the role of psychological factors in the treatment of illness.

These aims are put into practice by:

- *promoting* health behaviour, such as changing beliefs and behaviour
- *preventing* illness – for example, by training health professionals to improve communication skills and to carry out interventions that may help prevent illness.

MODELS OF HEALTH BEHAVIOUR

A fundamentally important question for health psychology is why people adopt – or don't adopt – particular health-related behaviours. Models of health behaviour try to answer this question, and most of those discussed below belong to the family of *expectancy-value models* (Stroebe, 2000). These assume that decisions between different courses of action are based on two types of cognition:

- *subjective probabilities* that a given action will produce a set of expected outcomes
- *evaluation* of action outcomes.

Individuals will choose from among various alternative courses of action the one most likely to produce positive consequences and avoid negative ones. Different models differ in terms of the *types* of belief and attitude that should be used in predicting a particular class of behaviour. They are rational reasoning models, which assume that individuals consciously deliberate about the likely consequences of the behavioural alternatives available to them before engaging in action.

> *ASK YOURSELF...*
> - Do you agree with this view of people as rationally/consciously choosing health behaviours?
> - How would you explain your own behaviours in relation to diet, smoking, alcohol, exercise, and so on?

The health belief model (HBM)

This was originally developed by social psychologists working in the US Public Health Service (Becker, 1974; Janz & Becker, 1984). They wanted to understand why people failed to make use of disease prevention and screening tests for early detection of diseases not associated with clear-cut symptoms (at least in the early stages). It was later also applied to patients' responses to symptoms, and compliance with/adherence to prescribed medication among acutely and chronically ill patients. More recently, it's been used to predict a wide range of health-related behaviours (Ogden, 2000).

The HBM assumes that the likelihood that people will engage in a particular health behaviour is a function of:

- the extent to which they believe they're *susceptible* to the associated disease
- their perception of the *severity of the consequences* of getting the disease.

Together, these determine the *perceived threat* of the disease. Given the threat, people then consider whether or not the action will bring benefits that outweigh the costs associated with the action. In addition, *cues to action* increase the likelihood that the action will be adopted; these might include advice from others, a health problem or mass-media campaigns. Other important concepts include *general health motivation* (the individual's readiness to be concerned about health matters) and *perceived control* (for example, 'I'm confident I can give up smoking': Becker & Rosenstock, 1987).

Evaluation of the HBM

The HBM allows for demographic variables (such as age and gender) and psychological characteristics (such as ways of coping with stress and locus of control: see below) that might affect health beliefs (Forshaw, 2002). For example, young women are likely to engage in dieting behaviour. So:

> ... the HBM covers most, if not all, of the factors which, on the face of it, should be relevant in determining if a person engages in a particular behaviour ...

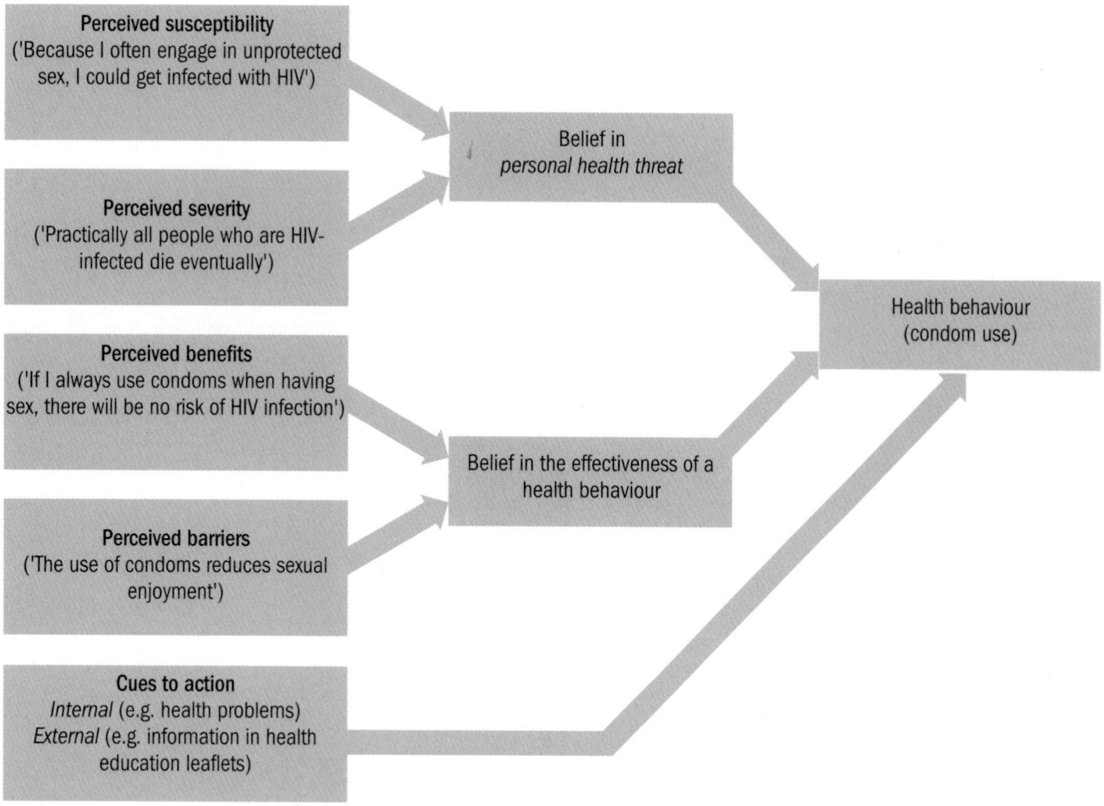

Figure 12.2 Main components of the health belief model (adapted from Stroebe, 2000, reproduced with kind permission of the Open University Press/McGraw-Hill publishing company)

There's considerable evidence supporting the HBM's predictions in relation to a wide range of behaviours. Dietary compliance, safe sex, having vaccinations, having regular dental checks, participation in regular exercise programmes, are all related to people's perception of their susceptibility to the related health problem, their belief that the problem is severe, and their perception that the benefits of preventative action outweigh the costs (e.g. Becker, 1974; Becker & Rosenstock, 1984; Becker *et al.*, 1977).

However, there's also conflicting evidence. For example, Janz & Becker (1984) found that healthy behavioural intentions are related to *low* perceived seriousness (not high, as the model predicts). Also, several studies have suggested an association between *low* susceptibility (not high) and healthy behaviour (Ogden, 2000).

The HBM has also been criticised for assuming that people's behaviour is governed by rational decision-making processes, overemphasising the individual, and ignoring emotional factors such as fear and anxiety. There's also been a lack of standardised measures used to assess the model's various components, such as perceived susceptibility (Penny, 1996). A factor that may explain the persistence of unhealthy behaviours is people's inaccurate perceptions of risk and susceptibility.

Box 12.3 Are we unrealistic optimists?

- Weinstein (1983, 1984) asked participants to examine a list of health problems and to state 'Compared with other people of your age and sex, are your chances of getting [the problem] greater than, about the same, or less than theirs?' Most believed they were *less* likely, displaying what Weinstein called *unrealistic optimism*: not everyone can be less likely to experience a particular problem! Weinstein identified four cognitive factors contributing to unrealistic optimism:

  (i) lack of personal experience with the problem
  (ii) belief that the problem is preventable by individual action
  (iii) belief that if the problem hasn't yet appeared it won't appear in the future
  (iv) belief that the problem is uncommon.

- This suggests that perception of one's own risk *isn't* a rational process. People show *selective focus*, ignoring their own risk-taking behaviour (for example, the times they've not used a condom) and concentrating primarily on their risk-reducing behaviour (the times they have used one).
- This is compounded by the tendency to ignore others' risk-reducing, and emphasise their risk-taking, behaviour. These tendencies produce unrealistic optimism.

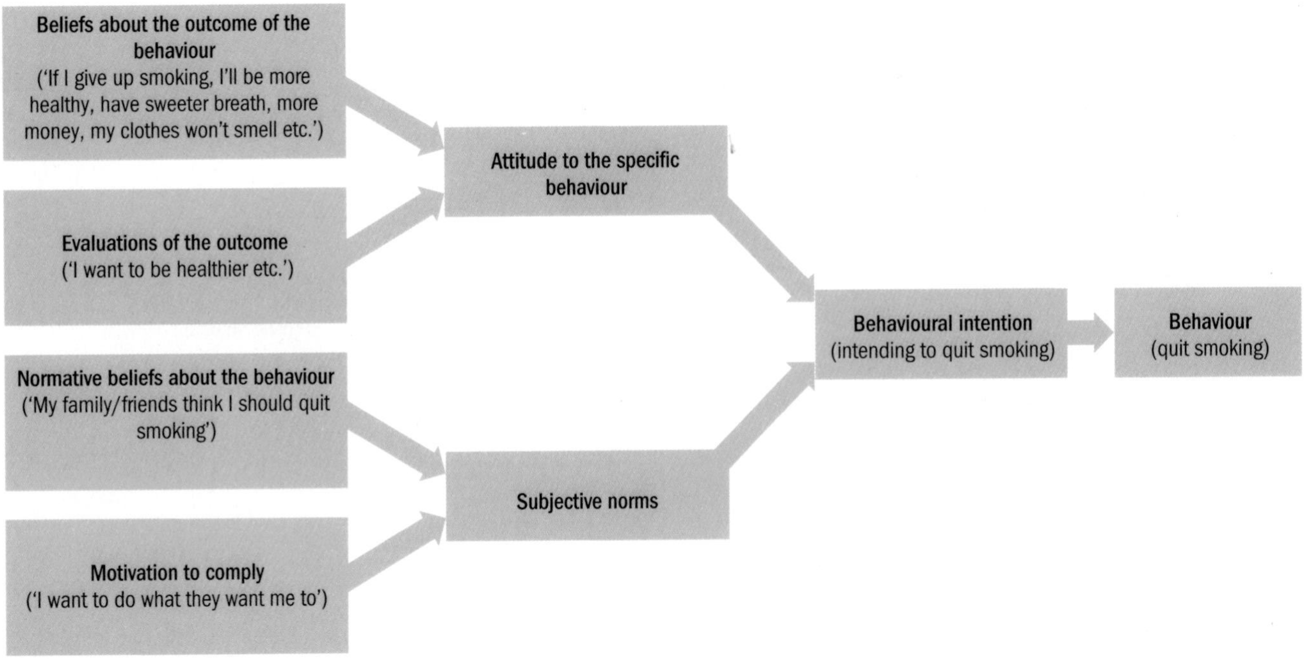

Figure 12.3 Main components of the theory of reasoned action (adapted from Penny, 1996; Maes & van Elderen, 1998)

The theory of reasoned action (TRA)

This is a more general theory than the HBM. It's been used extensively to examine predictions of behaviour and was central to the debate within social psychology regarding the relationship between attitudes and behaviour (see Chapter 24). TRA (Ajzen & Fishbein, 1970; Fishbein, 1967; Fishbein & Ajzen, 1975) assumes that behaviour is a function of the *intention* to perform that behaviour. A behavioural intention is determined by:

- a person's *attitude* to the behaviour, which is determined by (a) beliefs about the outcome of the behaviour, and (b) evaluation of the expected outcome
- subjective norms: a person's beliefs about the desirability of carrying out a certain health behaviour in the social group, society and culture s/he belongs to.

Evaluation of the TRA

The TRA has successfully predicted a wide range of behaviours, including blood donation, smoking marijuana, dental hygiene and family planning. However, attitudes and behaviour are only *weakly* related: people don't always do what they say they intend to (see Chapter 24). The model doesn't consider people's past behaviour, despite evidence that this is a good predictor of future behaviour. Nor does it account for people's irrational decisions (Penny, 1996). Similarly, Maes & van Elderen (1998) argue that:

> ... The assumption that behaviour is a function of intentions ... limits the applicability or heuristic value of the model to volitional behaviour, that is, to behaviours that are perceived to be under personal control ...

The theory of planned behaviour (TPB)

This represents a modification of the TRA. It reflects the influence of Bandura's (1977a, 1986) concept of *self-efficacy* – our belief that we can act effectively and exercise some control over events that influence our lives (see Chapter 35). Ajzen (1991) added the concept of self-efficacy to the TRA, claiming that control beliefs are important determinants of *perceived behavioural control* (PBC). This is crucial for understanding motivation: if, for example, you think you're unable to quit smoking, you probably won't try. PCB can have a *direct* effect on behaviour, bypassing behavioural intentions.

Evaluation of the TPB

The TPB has been used to assess a variety of health-related behaviours. For example, Brubaker & Wickersham (1990) examined its different components in relation to testicular self-examination: attitude, subjective norm and behavioural control (measured as self-efficacy) all correlated with the behavioural intention. Schifter & Ajzen (1985) found that weight loss was predicted by the model's components, especially perceived behavioural control.

The TPB has the advantage over the HBM (as does the TRA) of including a degree of irrationality (in the form of evaluations), and it attempts to address the problem of social and environmental factors (normative beliefs). The extra 'ingredient' of perceived behavioural control provides a role for past behaviour. For example, if you've tried several times in the past to quit smoking, you're less likely to believe you can do so successfully in the future and, therefore, you're less likely to intend to try (Ogden, 2000; Penny, 1996).

Box 12.4 Are perceived behavioural control (PBC) and self-efficacy the same thing?

- Povey *et al.* (2000) studied the TPB in relation to dieting. Their aim was partly to see if PBC and self-efficacy are separate concepts.
- They asked people about their behaviour and intentions regarding eating a low-fat diet and five portions of fruit and vegetables a day.
- They concluded that they *are* different. PBC refers to whether a person believes they can make a difference to their own behaviour, while self-efficacy is specifically related to how difficult they perceive the proposed health behaviour to be.
- *Both* factors predicted the intention to have a low-fat diet and eat five portions per day. But self-efficacy proved the stronger predictor.
- While Povey *et al.* took these findings to support the TPB, there's also evidence for the role of self-efficacy (Forshaw, 2002).

An evaluation of models of health behaviour

- A limitation shared by all the models is their failure consistently to predict behavioural intentions. Most seriously of all, they're unable to predict actual behaviour (the *intention–behaviour gap*).
- One response to these criticisms has been the concept of *implementation intentions* (Gollwitzer, 1993). Carrying out an intention involves the development of specific plans about what to do given a specific set of environmental conditions. These plans describe the 'what' and 'when' of a particular behaviour. There's some evidence that encouraging people to make implementation intentions can actually increase the correlation between intentions and behaviour for taking vitamin pills and performing breast self-examination (Ogden, 2000). Overall, though, current models are relatively poor predictors of actual behaviour (Turpin & Slade, 1998).
- Forshaw (2002) points out that our models of health behaviour are *culturally relative*: we cannot just assume that they apply universally. He cites a study by Sissons Joshi (1995) of causal beliefs about insulin-dependent diabetes in England and India. Far more Indian diabetics believed that eating too much sweet food caused their diabetes (38 per cent compared with 6 per cent of the English sample). Some people in each sample (more in the Indian sample) were reluctant to think about the causes. The reluctant English patients tended to be those who reported not having adjusted very well to the disease, but in the Indian sample adjustment *wasn't* related to causal reasoning.

Psychosocial determinants of sexual risk behaviour

Abstaining from penetrative sex is a rather unattractive option for most sexually active individuals. This is why research into strategies for reducing the risk of AIDS has mainly focused on psychosocial determinants of condom use, among both heterosexuals and gay men (Stroebe, 2000).

Heterosexuals

Sheeran *et al.* (1999) conducted a meta-analysis (a 'study of studies': see Chapter 45) of factors influencing condom use, based on 121 separate studies. They found strong support for TRA and TPB (see above). Attitudes towards condom use, social norms and intentions to use condoms were strongly related to condom use in both longitudinal and cross-sectional studies. There was also support for TPB's additional assumption that PBC is likely to increase substantially the predictability of behaviour.

Sutton *et al.* (1999) failed to find a significant effect of PBC among a national sample of 946 young people in England. However, they did report a significant influence of attitudes and subjective norms. This may have been because they all believed they had high control over condom use, regardless of the extent of their sexual experience (Stroebe, 2000).

ASK YOURSELF...
- How would the HBM account for condom use?
- Would you expect it to be more/less successful than the other models?

Sheeran *et al.* found less support for the HBM. Condom use should be determined by perceived threat of HIV infection (severity × vulnerability) and the perceived costs/benefits of condom use. But perceived threat seems to play a rather minor role. An even weaker association between vulnerability and condom use was reported in a meta-analysis of samples of heterosexuals and gay men (Gerrard *et al.*, 1996).

Stroebe (2000) suggests that one factor that might have reduced the relationship between vulnerability and condom use is that the threat of HIV has now been known for many years, and individuals who were willing and able to adopt precautionary behaviour have already done so. This may also explain why knowledge of HIV and AIDS fails to influence condom use. While health education has to be continued to maintain the current level of knowledge, especially among the most vulnerable groups (adolescents), Stroebe observes that:

> ... by now very few adult homosexual men are unaware of the health risks involved in unprotected anal intercourse. Thus the people who still engage in this high-risk activity do so knowing that it is dangerous.

The original AIDS public health warning ad: AIDS as the scary iceberg. But perceived threat seems to play a rather minor role in condom use

Sheeran *et al.* (1999) also found evidence of a strong association between (a) 'carrying a condom'/'condom availability' and (b) communication about condom use, with condom use. Neither of these two variables features in any of the models, although they could be seen as relevant to Gollwitzer's concept of *implementation intentions* (see above). Clearly, the availability of condoms is a precondition for their use, but carrying them reflects a strong intention to use them. Discussion between partners as to whether condoms should be used was strongly associated with their actual use during sex.

Gay men

This last finding is consistent with results of intervention studies, which show that training in sexual negotiation skills increases safe sex among gay men (Stroebe, 2000). Overall, findings from studies involving gay samples based on the TRA and TPB have been less consistent than those involving heterosexuals.

KEY STUDY 12.1 Partner relationship is the key to safe sex

- Stroebe cites a study which found that the ability of the TRA and TPB to predict safe sex (condom use and abstention from anal sex) depended very much on the relationship with the partner.
- With a steady partner, the intention to engage in safe sex was strongly related to attitudes, subjective norms and PBC. But with a casual partner, only PBC proved to be a significant predictor of safe-sex intentions.
- The same pattern emerged regarding the prediction of actual behaviour. TRA and TPB accounted for 64 per cent of the variance in safe-sex behaviour with steady partners, but only 21 per cent with casual partners. Stroebe concludes that:

  ... whether these homosexual men engaged in safe sex with their steady partner depended to a large extent on their intentions, but their safe sex behaviour with casual partners depended on their assertiveness and their social skills in persuading their casual partner to keep it safe ...

- Another relevant study (cited in Stroebe) found that the better the relationship with a steady partner, the more likely gay men were to take protective measures *with a casual partner*. But the relationship with the steady partner was *unrelated* to whether or not they had extra-relationship sex. These relational measures improved the prediction of behaviour, even when PBC and intentions were controlled.

Implications for interventions

According to Stroebe (2000):

- interventions that rely on epidemiological information to emphasise the severity of AIDS, and the vulnerability of the target population, are likely to fail; these factors don't appear to be a major determinant of condom use – instead communications should aim at eroticising condom use
- persuasive communications shouldn't only target beliefs, underlying attitudes, subjective norms, and PBC, but also try to persuade people to be prepared, and to discuss condom use with their prospective partners
- persuasive communications aimed at increasing condom use among gay men must differentiate clearly between condom use in steady as opposed to casual relationships. In the former, attitudes and subjective norms seem to be the crucial determinants of condom use, while in the latter it's PBC; persuasion and skills training, respectively, would probably be more effective.

Perceptions of invulnerability

According to Ogden (2000), one of the most consistent findings to emerge from the research is the perception of personal invulnerability to HIV, in both heterosexual and homosexual populations (see Box 12.3). For example, Woodcock *et al.* (1992) interviewed 125 16–25-year-olds about their sexual behaviour and examined how they evaluated their personal risk. Even though most acknowledged some degree of risk, some managed to dismiss it by claiming 'it would show by now', 'it was in the past', 'AIDS wasn't around in those days', 'it's been blown out of proportion' and 'AIDS is a risk you take in living'. The themes of being run over by a bus, and 'it couldn't happen to me', were also quite common. These are classic examples of people *rationalising* behaviour that conflicts with important aspects of self-concept (see Festinger's (1957) *cognitive dissonance theory*: Chapter 24). Most commonly, people denied they had ever put themselves at risk.

While most cognitive models, such as the HBM, TRA and TPB, emphasise people's rational decision-making, including their assessment of personal susceptibility to/being at risk from HIV:

> ... many people do not appear to believe that they are themselves at risk, which is perhaps why they do not engage in self-protective behaviour, and even when some acknowledgement of risk is made, this is often dismissed and does not appear to relate to behaviour change. (Ogden, 2000)

Exercise: doing what's good for you

Although most people, if asked, would agree that regular exercise is essential for improving health, such beliefs don't always translate into action. Even in the USA, where health consciousness appears to be far higher than in Europe, only 15 per cent of the adult population exercise regularly and intensively enough in their leisure time to meet current guidelines for fitness (three times per week for at least 20 minutes at a time). This figure changed very little during the 1990s, and we exercise less as we move from adolescence into adulthood (Stroebe, 2000).

ASK YOURSELF...
- What forms of exercise do you engage in on a fairly regular basis?
- Why do you do it?
- Why do you think people exercise less as they get older?
- How do you think exercise benefits you?

The pleasures of exercise

The benefits of exercise

Physical benefits

Like high-fat, low-fibre diets, lack of exercise is correlated with an increased risk of CHD, and people who exercise regularly seem to accumulate less body fat (Carlson *et al.*, 2000). There's strong evidence that regular, vigorous, dynamic exercise decreases the risk of hypertension, cardiovascular disease, colon cancer, non-insulin-dependent diabetes mellitus and death from all causes. It also appears to reduce symptoms of depression and anxiety, and improve mood.

Many researchers believe that *aerobic* or endurance exercise, including jogging, cycling and swimming, is superior to other forms of exercise for improving cardiovascular health. These activities involve expenditure of considerable amounts of energy, and increase blood flow and respiration, thereby stimulating and strengthening the heart and lungs, and increasing the body's efficiency in using oxygen.

Box 12.5 Do you have to sweat to benefit from exercise?

- According to the American College of Sports Medicine (1979, in Stroebe, 2000), the most effective regime for developing and maintaining cardiovascular fitness is to exercise three to five times a week for 15–60 minutes per session, at more than 60 per cent of maximum heart rate.
- However, several short exercise sessions may be just as beneficial to men at risk of heart disease as a single lengthy burst of activity.
- Research conducted for the American Heart Association (in Henderson, 2000) examined the exercise habits and medical histories of over 7300 men with an average age of 66. It found that physical activity needn't last longer than 15 minutes to reduce the risk of heart disease. The health benefits of a single lengthy exercise session were no greater than those that accrued from several short ones, provided the total amount of exercise was the same. Furthermore, men who participated in sport showed similar risks of heart disease as those who only walked or climbed stairs – provided the energy output was similar.
- However, the study also found that the *reduction in risk* of heart disease for men who jogged, swam, played tennis or did aerobics (vigorous activities) was *greater* than for those who played golf or danced (moderate activities).

Psychological benefits

The effects of exercise on mood and cognition have been investigated by sport and exercise psychologists, both in the USA and the UK (see Chapter 31). But sport psychologists aren't interested only in 'professional' sportsmen and women. Exercise appears to be beneficial for people's mental health in several ways:

- many exercisers report feeling 'high' after exercise (the 'feel-good' effect: Carlson *et al.*, 2000)

- aerobic exercise reduces heart-rate response to psychological stress, making exercisers less vulnerable to the negative effects of stress (Carlson *et al.*, 2000: see pages 204–209)
- aerobic fitness programmes, such as jogging, dancing and swimming, are now frequently prescribed as treatments for depression; there's evidence from both correlational and intervention studies that physical activity relieves the symptoms of depression and anxiety, and generally improves mood (Stroebe, 2000: see Chapter 45).

PSYCHOLOGICAL ASPECTS OF ILLNESS

The patient–practitioner relationship

Patient compliance: doing what you're told

Haynes *et al.* (1979) defined compliance as:

> ... the extent to which the patient's behaviour (in terms of taking medications, following diets or other lifestyle changes) coincides with medical or health advice.

Damrosch (1995) prefers the term adherence, since this implies a more mutual relationship between the patient and the practitioner. 'Compliance' implies that the practitioner is an authority figure, while the patient is a fairly passive recipient (see Chapter 27).

> *ASK YOURSELF...*
> - Have you ever been non-compliant? For example, have you ever failed to complete a course of antibiotics?
> - Why didn't you comply?
> - Why do you think it's important to understand non-compliance?

It's an important area of research primarily because following health professionals' recommendations is considered essential to patient recovery. According to Damrosch (1995), poor adherence is almost epidemic. Reviews of adherence research have shown 20–80 per cent non-adherence, depending on the patient population and definitions used. Patients with chronic conditions (such as hypertension and diabetes) are less adherent than those with short-term problems. According to Ogden (2000), about half these patients are non-compliant.

But even with acute conditions, adherence is problematic. Patients are notorious for prematurely discontinuing antibiotics, even if prescribed for just a few days. Remarkably, patients who've undergone renal, liver and heart transplants often fail to comply, despite good adherence prior to the transplant. Despite being informed that this can result in organ rejection and death, 34 per cent of renal patients still non-adhere. About 20 per cent of rejections and deaths in heart recipients are due to non-adherence (Damrosch, 1995). However, patients tend to overestimate their degree of compliance/adherence, because they wish to convey a socially desirable impression. Practitioners also tend to overestimate their patients' compliance. More *objective* methods of assessing compliance include pill counts, records of appointment-keeping, physical testing, measures of cholesterol (to check on diet) and electronically monitored bottle caps (which record the date/time of every bottle-opening: Damrosch, 1995).

> **Box 12.6 What makes patients comply?**
>
> According to Damrosch (1995), there's theoretical agreement regarding the importance of five factors that make patients most likely to comply:
>
> 1. they perceive the high severity of the disorder (*serious consequences*)
> 2. they believe the probability of getting the disorder is also high (personal *susceptibility*)
> 3. they have confidence in their ability to perform the behaviour prescribed to reduce the threat (*self-efficacy*)
> 4. they're also confident that the prescribed regimen will overcome the threat (*response-efficacy*)
> 5. they have the intention to perform the behaviour (*behavioural intention*).
>
> Damrosch refers to these five points as the 'double high/double efficacy/behavioural intention model'.
>
> *ASK YOURSELF...*
> - Which models of health behaviour do these five factors derive from?

Practitioner variables

Doctors' sensitivity to patients' non-verbal expression of feelings (such as tone of voice) is a good predictor of adherence. For example, Dimatteo *et al.* (1993) conducted a two-year longitudinal study of over 1800 patients with diabetes, heart disease or hypertension, and 186 doctors. The doctors' job satisfaction, willingness to answer questions, and practice of scheduling follow-up appointments, were all powerful predictors of adherence.

The way practitioners communicate their beliefs to patients also influences compliance. Misselbrook & Armstrong (2000) asked patients whether they'd accept treatment to prevent a stroke, and presented the effectiveness of this treatment in four different ways. Although the actual risk was the same in all four cases:

- 92 per cent said they'd accept the treatment if it reduced their chances of a stroke by 45 per cent (*relative risk*)
- 75 per cent if it reduced the risk from 1/400 to 1/700 (*absolute risk*)
- 71 per cent if a doctor had to treat 35 patients for 25 years to prevent one stroke (*number needed to treat*)
- 44 per cent if treatment had a 3 per cent chance of doing them good and a 97 per cent chance of doing no good/not being needed (*personal probability of benefit*).

According to Ogden (2000), these results indicate that:

> ... not only do health professionals hold their own subjective views, but ... these views may be communicated to the patient in a way that may then influence the patient's choice of treatment.

Doctor–patient communication

According to the traditional model of doctor–patient communication (the 'education' model), the doctor is an expert who communicates his/her knowledge to a naïve patient. The doctor is an authority figure, who instructs or directs the patient. Research has suggested that the communication process may be improved if a sharing, more interactive (two-way), patient-centred consulting style is used. This may produce greater patient commitment to any advice given, potentially higher levels of compliance, and greater patient satisfaction (implied by the use of 'adherence': see above).

However, a field experimental study by Savage & Armstrong (1990) of patients attending a group practice in an inner-city area of London found a preference for the education model. Patients (aged 16–75, without serious illnesses) seemed to prefer an authority figure, who offered a formal diagnosis, to a sharing doctor who asked for their views.

Patient and regimen variables

Compliance is likely to decrease over time. It's also more problematic for conditions with no obvious symptoms, especially if treatment produces unpleasant side-effects, such as reduced sex drive. Also, the more complex the regimen, the lower the adherence. For example, home monitoring of blood sugar up to ten times per day, and multiple insulin injections has been shown greatly to reduce or eliminate adherence. But this is a life-long practice, which is probably daunting to many patients (Damrosch, 1995).

According to Ley's (1981, 1989) *cognitive hypothesis model*, compliance can be predicted by a combination of:

- satisfaction with the process of consultation (see above)
- understanding of the information given
- recall of this information.

Despite some supporting evidence, Ley's model is consistent with the education model of doctor–patient communication.

Preferring a more interactive approach, Ogden and her colleagues have investigated (a) the level of agreement between patient and health professional, and (b) the impact of this agreement on patient outcome. It's important to understand the extent to which the two individuals 'speak the same language', share the same beliefs, and agree about the desired content and outcome of any consultation. This is especially relevant to general practice, where patient and health professional perspectives are most likely to coincide.

KEY STUDY 12.2 Not seeing eye to eye on depression and obesity

- Ogden *et al.* (1999) explored GPs' and patients' models of depression. They agreed about the importance of mood-related symptoms, psychological causes and non-medical treatments. But GPs had a more medical model.
- Ogden *et al.* (2001) compared GPs' and patients' views on obesity. They agreed about most psychological, behavioural and social causes, but differed consistently regarding medical causes. In particular, patients rated glandular or hormonal problems, slow metabolism and other medical causes more highly than did the GPs.
- So, compared with their patients, GPs had a *more* medical model of depression and a *less* medical model of obesity.
- It's possible that such disagreements may produce low compliance to medication and to recommended changes in behaviour, as well as low satisfaction with the consultation (Ogden, 2000).

Once a treatment is prescribed, the patient is often left to his/her own devices. Adherence then depends on his/her interpretation of the illness, treatment and symptoms. Siegel *et al.* (1999) studied middle-aged and older HIV-positive people and their drug adherence. Once taking the drugs, they'd question their efficacy and safety if they noticed any unusual symptoms. If they perceived these as side-effects of the drugs, or if the drugs seemed to be having no effect, the conditions were ripe for non-adherence. But according to Forshaw (2002):

- because a drug *seems* to be doing nothing, doesn't mean it is, and unpleasant symptoms that appear after taking the drug aren't necessarily caused by the drug
- drugs can sometimes take a while to start working, but people often expect immediate results. Also, we often think that if a problem seems to have cleared up, then it has; people commonly stop taking their antibiotics when the symptoms have eased – but the symptoms often recur because they're just the final stage of unseen bodily processes.

Forshaw recommends that:

> ... Careful education of patients as to exactly what to expect from a treatment can improve adherence, especially in cases where non-adherence stems from lack of knowledge rather than rebelliousness ...

Compliance and the placebo effect

Evidence suggests that simply adhering to medical recommendations to take pills may benefit patients recovering from a heart attack, *regardless* of whether the pills taken are active drugs or inert placebos (see Chapter 45). This has implications for understanding the mind/body relationship ('I believe I've taken my medication' is related to actually getting better: see Chapter 49), and the central role of beliefs and expectations in health and illness (Ogden, 2000).

Ogden cites data suggesting that the best predictor of mortality in men who'd survived a heart attack *wasn't* taking the lipid-lowering drug compared with a placebo, but adherence to taking *any drug at all* (active or placebo). Adherers had lower mortality after five years than non-adherers in both experimental and placebo groups. Ogden concludes by saying:

> ... 'doing as the doctor suggests' appears to be beneficial to health, but not for the traditional reasons ('the drugs are good for you') but perhaps because by taking medication, the patient expects to get better ...

Pain

What is it?

> ***ASK YOURSELF...***
> - Can you describe the experience of pain?
> - Are there different kinds of pain?
> - If so, how do they differ?
> - Is pain a purely physical, bodily phenomenon?

According to the International Association for the Study of Pain (IASP), pain is:

> ... an unpleasant sensory and emotional experience associated with actual or potential tissue damage, or described in terms of such damage ...

This definition indicates that pain is a subjective, personal experience involving both sensory (e.g. shooting, burning, aching) and emotional (e.g. frightening, annoying, sickening) qualities. Fear/anxiety can increase the perception of pain, and depression often accompanies chronic pain and is positively associated with the pain intensity ratings of chronic pain patients (Bradley, 1995).

Pain is basically a physiological phenomenon, whose biological function is to provoke special reactive patterns aimed at the removal/avoidance of the noxious stimulus. But this doesn't explain the pain *experience*, which includes both the pain sensation, and certain autonomic responses and 'associated feeling states' (Zborowski, 1952). For example, understanding the physiology of pain cannot explain the acceptance of intense pain in torture, or the strong emotional reactions of certain individuals to the slight sting of a hypodermic needle.

The IASP definition recognises that an individual needn't suffer actual tissue damage at a specific body site in order to perceive pain at that site, as in the 'phantom limb' phenomenon (see Chapter 4). In describing treatment of phantom limb pain, Ramachandran & Blakeslee (1998) maintain that:

> ... pain is an *opinion* on the organism's state of health rather than a mere reflexive response to an injury. There is no direct hotline from pain receptors to 'pain centres' in the brain. On the contrary, there is so much interaction between different brain centres, like those concerned with vision and touch, that even the mere visual appearance of an opening fist can actually feed all the way back into the patient's motor and touch pathways, allowing him to feel the fist opening, thereby killing an illusory pain in a nonexistent hand.

According to Wall (in O'Connell, 2000):

> 'Pure' pain is never detected as an isolated sensation. It's always accompanied by emotion and meaning, so that each pain is unique to the individual.

Chinese torture. The prisoner kneels on a steel chain while tied to a cross, forced to remain in that position for days

Pain and injury

Phantom limb pain is one of several examples of how it's possible to experience pain in the absence of any physical damage/injury. Others include *neuralgia* (nerve pain) and *caucalgia* (a burning pain that often follows a severe wound, such as stabbing), both of which develop *after* the wound/injury has healed. This represents the converse of phantom limb pain. People with *congenital analgesia* are incapable of feeling pain (a potentially life-threatening disorder), while those with *episodic analgesia* only experience pain minutes or even hours after the injury has occurred. This can sometimes be *life-saving*, as when soldiers suffer horrific injuries but suffer little/no pain while waiting for medical attention.

Pain as a cultural phenomenon

According to Rollman (1998), to say that pain is universal doesn't imply that it can be understood in only physiological or biochemical terms. The human pain experience comprises sensory, emotional and cognitive components. In both its expression and management, biological, psychological and social factors interact in complex ways. The influence of culture on the expression of pain almost certainly begins at birth, and extends throughout a person's lifetime.

In human society, pain acquires specific social and cultural significance. Members of different cultures may assume differing attitudes towards different types of pain. According to Zborowski (1952), two of these attitudes may be described as *pain expectancy* and *pain acceptance*:

- *pain expectancy* refers to the anticipation of pain as being unavoidable in a given situation (such as childbirth, sport or battle)
- *pain acceptance* is the willingness to experience pain, which is manifested mostly as the inevitable component of culturally accepted experiences (such as initiation rites and medical treatment).

So, labour pain is expected as part of childbirth. But in most western cultures it's not accepted (and various steps are taken to keep it to a minimum), while in others (such as Poland) it's both expected and accepted (and little or nothing is done to relieve it).

Cognitive aspects of pain

Expectancy and acceptance are as much cognitive as emotional dimensions of pain. Trusting the doctor's ability to ease your suffering (whether this takes the form of a cure or merely the relief of pain and suffering) represents part of the *cognitive appraisal* aspect of pain – that is, the belief that the illness/symptoms are controllable. If we *attribute* our symptoms to something that's controllable, this should make us feel more optimistic (see Chapter 10). The *meaning* of our illness may be a crucial factor in how we react to it, which in turn may affect the illness itself.

Box 12.7 The meaning of illness

- According to Brody (1995), the patient's health is most likely to change in a positive direction when the *meaning of the illness* has been changed for the patient in a positive way.
- For example, when Mr Smith goes to the doctor with an experience that means to him 'I might have cancer', and he leaves with an experience that means 'I have a bad case of bronchitis and it should be better in a few days if I take these antibiotics', there's the greatest likelihood that he'll feel better and breathe more easily even before the antibiotics begin to take effect.
- Although 'meaning' is hard to define, one component is giving patients an explanation (attribution) for their illness that's both understandable and as reassuring as is truthfully possible.

Treating pain

A number of methods and techniques used in the treatment of stress (see page 210) are also used for treating (mainly chronic) pain. Bradley (1995) groups these behavioural treatments into three major kinds: contingency management, biofeedback and self-management/cognitive behaviour treatment.

Contingency management

This is a form of *behaviour modification* (see Chapter 45). Its goal is to achieve sufficient control over the patient's environment so that reinforcement is withdrawn from 'pain' behaviours and made contingent on 'well' behaviours. Relatives are trained to reinforce positively the display of healthy behaviour at home, and to ignore the display of pain behaviour.

Biofeedback

This involves giving patients information (via monitors or buzzers) about certain autonomic functions (such as blood pressure, heart rate and muscle tension), enabling them to bring these functions under voluntary control. Bradley (1995) cites a study in which college students suffering from muscle-contraction headaches were given seven 50-minute sessions, twice weekly, using feedback about muscle tension (electromyograph (EMG) biofeedback). They were also urged to practise their newly learned skills at home when free of headaches, and at the first signs of a headache. Compared with a waiting-list control condition (no treatment until the study was over) and a placebo condition (which engaged in 'pseudomeditation'), the EMG biofeedback produced significant reductions in EMG and headache activity.

Biofeedback

KEY STUDY 12.3 Giving birth the EMG way (Duchene, 1990)

- Duchene used EMG biofeedback to reduce the *acute* pain associated with childbirth among 40 first-time mothers.
- They were randomly assigned to the experimental or control group, the former attending six weekly training sessions, and being loaned biofeedback machines for practice at home. The feedback was provided through both sound and a visual monitor, based on the tension of the abdominal muscles, which the women focused on relaxing when they felt a pain or contraction.
- All the women were monitored for pain perception, starting at admission, and then at various points during labour, again at delivery and once more 24 hours after delivery (to recall the overall pain intensity).
- While 14 of the 20 control-group women requested and had epidurals for pain relief, only eight of the experimental group did so (a significant difference). The experimental group's labours were also significantly shorter.

Self-management/cognitive behaviour treatment

This is based on the premise that patients' expectations influence their emotional and behavioural reactions to life events. This makes it critical that doctors help patients to believe they can acquire the necessary skills for controlling pain and other forms of disability. Self-management interventions usually involve multiple treatments, such as learning coping skills, progressive muscle relaxation training, practice in communicating effectively with family members and health-care providers, and providing positive reinforcement for displaying coping behaviour. Patients are encouraged to take responsibility for managing their pain, and to attribute their success to their own efforts. (See the discussion of cognitive behaviour therapy for stress management, page 210.)

STRESS

What is it?

ASK YOURSELF...

- What do you understand by the term 'stress'?
- Is the term used in different ways to refer to different things or processes?
- What makes you feel stressed, and how does it feel?

According to Bartlett (1998):

> ... the notion that stress is bad for you and can make you ill has become a modern cultural truism. However, there is also a significant body of research evidence which lends support to this idea ... The study of stress must ... be central to ... health psychology which concerns, at its most basic level, the role of psychosocial processes in health and disease.

Definitions of stress fall into three categories (Bartlett, 1998; Goetsch & Fuller 1995):

1. stress as a *stimulus*
2. stress as a *response*
3. stress as *interaction* between an organism and its environment.

This classification corresponds very closely to the three models of stress identified by Cox (1978), as described below.

- The *engineering model* sees external stresses giving rise to a stress reaction, or strain, in the individual. The stress is located in the stimulus characteristics of the environment: stress is what happens to a person (not what happens within a person).

The concept is derived from Hooke's law of elasticity in physics, which deals with how loads (stress) produce deformation in metals. Up to a point, stress is inevitable and can be tolerated, and moderate levels may even be beneficial (*eustress*: Selye, 1956). Complete *absence* of stress (as measured, say, by anxiety or physiological arousal) could be positively *detrimental* (for example, you're so relaxed that you fail to notice the car speeding towards you as you're crossing the road). Stress helps to keep us alert, providing some of the energy required to maintain an interest in our environment, to explore it and adapt to it (see Chapter 9). However, when we're 'stretched beyond our limits of elasticity', it becomes positively harmful.

- The *physiological model* is primarily concerned with what happens *within* the person as a result of stress (the 'response' aspects of the engineering model), in particular the physiological changes.

The impetus for this view of stress was Selye's (1956) definition that 'Stress is the non-specific response of the body to any demand made upon it'. While a medical student, Selye noticed a general malaise or syndrome associated with 'being ill', regardless of the particular illness. The syndrome was characterised by: (i) a loss of appetite; (ii) an associated loss of weight and strength; (iii) loss of ambition; and (iv) a typical facial expression associated with illness.

Further examination of extreme cases revealed major physiological changes, (confirmed by Cox, 1978). This non-specific response to illness reflected a distinct phenomenon, which Selye called the *General Adaptation Syndrome* (GAS: see below, pages 204–206)

- The *transactional model* represents a kind of blend of the first two models. It sees stress as arising from an interaction between people and their environment – in particular, when there's an imbalance between the person's perception of the demands being made of them by the situation, and their ability to meet those demands. Because it's the person's *perception* of this mismatch between demand and ability that causes stress, the model allows for important *individual differences* in what produces stress and how much stress is experienced. There are also wide differences in how people attempt to cope with stress, psychologically and behaviourally.

The *engineering model* is mainly concerned with the question 'What causes stress?', and the physiological model with the question 'What are the effects of stress?' The transactional model is concerned with both these questions, plus 'How do we cope with stress?'

What causes stress?

The causes of stress don't exist objectively, and individuals differ in what they see as a stressor in the first place (Lazarus, 1966). So, in this section we're really identifying *potential* stressors, the kinds of event or experience that most people are likely to find exceed their capacity to handle the demands that are involved.

Disruption of circadian rhythms

As we saw in Chapter 7, the word 'circadian' (meaning 'about one day') describes a particular periodicity or rhythm of a number of physiological and behavioural functions that can be seen in almost all living creatures. Many studies have shown that these rhythms persist if we suddenly reverse our activity pattern and sleep during the day and are active during the night. This indicates that these rhythms are internally controlled (*endogenous*).

However, our circadian rhythms are kept on their once-every-24-hours schedule by regular daily environmental (*exogenous*) cues called *zeitgebers* (from the German meaning 'time givers'). The most important zeitgeber is the daily cycle of light and dark. If we persist with our reversal of sleep and activity, the body's circadian rhythms will (after a period of acclimatisation) reverse and become synchronised to the new set of exogenous cues.

Individual differences and the effects of shift work

> *ASK YOURSELF...*
> - Look back at Chapter 7.
> - What is it about the disruption of circadian rhythms that could account for the effects of shift work and jet lag?

Some people take five to seven days to adjust, others take up to 14 days, and some may never achieve a complete reversal. But not all physiological functions reverse at the same time: body temperature usually reverses inside a week for most people, while the rhythms of adrenocortical hormone take much longer. During the changeover period, the body is in a state of *internal desynchronisation* (Aschoff, 1979). This is very stressful, and shift workers often report experiencing insomnia, digestive problems, irritability, fatigue, even depression, when changing work shifts. In shift work, the zeitgebers stay the same, but workers are forced to adjust their natural sleep–wake cycles in order to meet the demands of changing work schedules (Pinel, 1993).

> **KEY STUDY 12.4 Night nurses aren't all the same (Hawkins & Armstrong-Esther, 1978)**
> - Hawkins and Armstrong-Esther studied 11 nurses during the first seven nights of a period of night duty.
> - They found that performance was significantly impaired on the first night, but improved progressively on successive nights. However, body temperature hadn't fully adjusted to night working after seven nights.
> - There were significant differences between individual nurses, with some appearing relatively undisturbed by working nights, and others never really adjusting at all.

Night shift involves an enforced adjustment of sleep-wake cycles

Jet lag

Other occupational groups affected by disruption to their circadian rhythms are airline pilots and cabin crew, who experience jet lag because they cross time zones during the course of a flight. If you've ever travelled across a time zone, you'll know what it's like to have your biological rhythms 'out of sync' with your surroundings. If you arrive in Washington DC at, say, 7 pm (after an eight-hour flight from London) you may be ready to start your evening's entertainment, but as far as your body is concerned, it's time to sleep (back in London it's 1 am, the middle of the night).

Most people suffer much less jet lag when travelling in an east–west direction than a west–east direction. When going west ('chasing the sun'), the day is temporarily lengthened. Because the natural circadian rhythm cycle is 25 hours (see Chapter 7), an increase in day length is much easier to deal with than a decrease. Secretion of *melatonin* reaches a peak during the night, helping to make us sleepy. After a long flight, the cyclical release of melatonin stays locked into the day/night pattern of the home country for some days. This could account for the fatigue felt during the day and the insomnia at night. If jet-lagged volunteers are given melatonin during the evening, far fewer report feeling jet-lagged than controls who receive only a placebo (Blakemore, 1988).

Cabin crew flying across time zones had significantly raised salivary *cortisol* (one of the *glucocorticoid* stress hormones: see Figure 12.4, page 205) compared with when the same cabin crew flew short distances, and with ground crew. In a response-time test, the jet-lagged crew performed more poorly when there was a 25-second delay between presentation of the target symbol and having to recognise the symbol (but not when the delay was only one or five seconds (Cho *et al.*, 2000). De Quervain *et al.* (2000) found poorer recognition memory among non-flight crew participants given *cortisone* (another glucocorticoid). They believe that raised glucocorticoid levels may cause impairments in memory retrieval in such stressful situations as exams, job interviews, combat and courtroom testimony (see Chapter 17).

Life changes: the SRRS

Holmes & Rahe (1967) examined 5000 patient records, and made a list of 43 life events, of varying seriousness, which seemed to cluster in the months preceding the onset of their illness. Out of this grew the *Social Readjustment Rating Scale* (SRRS). Several studies have shown that people who experience many significant life changes (a score of 300 life change units (LCUs) or over) are more susceptible to physical and mental illness than those with lower scores, The range of health problems include sudden cardiac death, heart attacks (non-fatal), TB, diabetes, leukaemia, accidents and even athletics injuries.

Rank	Life event	Mean value
1	Death of spouse	100
2	Divorce	73
3	Marital separation	65
4	Jail term	63
5	Death of close family member	63
6	Personal injury or illness	53
7	Marriage	50
8	Fired at work	47
9	Marital reconciliation	45
10	Retirement	45
11	Change in health of family member	44
12	Pregnancy	40
13	Sex difficulties	39
14	Gain of new family member	39
15	Business readjustment	39
16	Change in financial state	38
17	Death of close friend	37
18	Change to different line of work	36
19	Change in number of arguments with spouse	35
20	Mortgage over $10,000	31
21	Foreclosure of mortgage or loan	30
22	Change in responsibilities at work	29
23	Son or daughter leaving home	29
24	Trouble with in-laws	29
25	Outstanding personal achievement	28
26	Wife begins or stops work	26
27	Begin or end school	26
28	Change in living conditions	25
29	Revision of personal habits	24
30	Trouble with boss	23
31	Change in work hours or conditions	20
32	Change in residence	20
33	Change in schools	20
34	Change in recreation	19
35	Change in church activities	19
36	Change in social activities	18
37	Mortgage or loan less than $10,000	17
38	Change in sleeping habits	16
39	Change in number of family get-togethers	15
40	Change in eating habits	15
41	Vacation	13
42	Christmas	12
43	Minor violations of the law	11

Table 12.1 Social Readjustment Rating Scale. The amount of life stress a person has experienced in a given period of time, say one year, is measured by the total number of life change units (LCUs). These units result from the addition of the values (shown in the right column) associated with events that the person has experienced during the target time period. The mean values (item weightings) were obtained empirically by telling 100 judges that 'marriage' had been assigned an arbitrary value of 500 and asking them to assign a number to each of the other events in terms of 'the intensity and length of time necessary to accommodate ... regardless of the desirability of the event relative to marriage'. The average of the numbers assigned each event was divided by 10 and the resulting values became the weighting of each life event (Reprinted from *Journal of Psychosomatic Research, 11*, Holmes & Rahe, 1967, The social readjustment rating scale, 213–218, © 1967, with permission from Elsevier)

Evaluation of studies using the SRRS

- While many studies may have found statistically significant correlations between LCUs and subsequent illness, they're typically too low to be of any practical value (Lazarus, 1999).
- The studies that claim to show that life change is responsible for illness are *correlational*. It's possible, therefore, that instead of life events causing illness, some life events (e.g. being fired from work, sexual difficulties, trouble with in-laws, change in sleeping habits) are themselves early manifestations of an illness that is already developing (Brown, 1986; Davison *et al.*, 2004; Penny, 1996).
- Many of these studies are also *retrospective*. People are asked to recall both the illnesses and the stressful life

events that occurred during the specified period, which is likely to produce distorted, unreliable data (see Chapter 17). For example, what people say about a past illness may be different from what the illness was actually like (Davison *et al.*, 2004).

Evaluation of the SRRS

- The SRRS assumes that *any* change, by definition, is stressful – that is, certain events are *inherently* stressful (stressful in themselves). But the *undesirable* aspects of events are at least as important as the fact that they change people's lives (Davison & Neale, 1994). A quick glance at Table 12.1 suggests that life changes have a largely *negative* feel about them (especially those in the top ten, which receive the highest LCU scores). So, the scale may be confusing 'change' and 'negativity'.
- Some of the items are *ambiguous* (e.g. those that refer to 'changes in ...' could be positive or negative changes). Others (e.g. 6 and 12) refer to states of health, so the total LCU score is already contaminated with an individual's current health status (Penny, 1996).
- The list of life events is incomplete. For example, there's no death of a child, no reference to the problems of old age, and no mention of natural or 'man-made' disasters (Lazarus, 1999).
- It fails to take individual circumstances into account. For example, the impact of the death of a spouse will be affected by the partners' age at the time, the nature of their relationship, and the cause of death (Forshaw, 2002).
- The SRRS was developed almost 40 years ago. This makes some of the original LCU scores associated with particular life events potentially out of date.
- Life changes may only be stressful if they're unexpected and, in this sense, uncontrollable. In other words, it may not be change as such that's stressful, but change we cannot prevent or reverse. Studies have shown that when people are asked to classify the undesirable life events on the SRRS as either 'controllable' or 'uncontrollable', only the latter are significantly correlated with subsequent onset of illness (Brown, 1986).

The need for control

According to Parkes (1993), the *psychosocial transitions* that are most dangerous to health are those that are sudden and allow little time for preparation. The sudden death of a relative from a heart attack, in an accident or as a result of crime are examples of the most stressful kind of life changes (see Chapter 39).

Using Rotter's (1966) *Locus of Control Scale*, and devising a new scale (the *Life Events Scale*), Johnson & Sarason (1978) found that life events stress was more closely related to psychiatric symptoms (in particular, depression and anxiety) among people rated as high on *external* locus of control, than among those rated as high on internal locus of control. In other words, people who believe that they don't have control over what happens to them are more vulnerable to the harmful effects of change than those who believe they do. This is related to Seligman's (1975) concept of *learned helplessness* (see Chapter 11).

The hassles and uplifts of everyday life

By definition, most of the 43 changes included in the SRRS aren't everyday occurrences. Kanner *et al.* (1981) designed a hassles scale (comprising 117 items), and an uplifts scale (135 items). Kanner *et al.* define hassles as:

> ... the irritating, frustrating, distressing demands that to some degree characterise everyday transactions with the environment. They include annoying practical problems, such as losing things or traffic jams and fortuitous occurrences such as inclement weather, as well as arguments, disappointments, and financial and family concerns.

Daily uplifts are:

> ... positive experiences such as the joy derived from manifestations of love, relief at hearing good news, the pleasure of a good night's rest, and so on.

In a study of 100 men and women aged 45–64 over a 12-month period, Kanner *et al.* confirmed the prediction that hassles were positively related to undesirable psychological symptoms. But the effect of uplifts was unclear, and research interest waned (Bartlett, 1998). They also found that hassles were a more powerful predictor of symptoms than life events (as measured by SRRS). 'Divorce', for example, may exert stress by any number of component hassles, such as cooking for oneself, handling money matters and having to tell people about it. So, daily hassles may intervene between major life events and health. It's the cumulative impact of these day-to-day problems that may prove detrimental to health.

Evaluation of the hassles and uplifts scales

According to Lazarus (1999), life events (as measured by the SSRS) are *distal* (remote) causes of stress. We need to know the psychological meaning a person attaches to an environmental event, the personal significance of what's happening (the *proximal* cause). This is what makes Kanner *et al.*'s scales a more valid approach. According to Lazarus (1999):

> Although daily hassles are far less dramatic than major life changes ... and what constitutes a hassle varies greatly from person to person, our research has suggested that, especially when they pile up or touch on special areas of *vulnerability* ... they can be very stressful for some people and very important for their subjective well-being and physical health ...

Bartlett (1998) claims that implicit in the concept of hassles is a stimulus-based definition of stress. This is inconsistent with the transactional approach advocated by Lazarus. This apparent contradiction stems from focusing on the hassles themselves, while simultaneously believing that it's their psychological meaning that causes stress.

Occupation-linked stressors

People working in the emergency services (police, fire, ambulance, emergency medical teams and mountain rescue) routinely encounter death, tragedy and horror. They're required to deal with people in pain and distress, and handle dead bodies. They may also face personal danger and injury.

High stress levels, an occupational hazard for those working in the emergency services

McLeod (2000) studied over 800 fire-fighters, giving them a number of standard measures of stress and coping, including the SRRS, Maslach & Jackson's (1981) *Burnout Scale*, and the *Impact of Event Scale* (Horowitz *et al.* 1979), a measure of post-traumatic stress disorder (PTSD) (see Chapter 44). McLeod found that individuals in different roles experience varying patterns of stress, and cope in different ways. For example, the highest overall stress levels were found among the day-duty fire-fighters, who live close to the station and are frequently on call. But sub-officers are the most likely to experience PTSD: they're typically first on the scene of an incident and are most intensely exposed to the suffering of fire and road traffic accident victims.

Box 12.8 Caring for others is bad for your health: nurses and stress

- In the case of nursing, intrinsic sources of stress (such as constantly having to deal with patients' pain, anxiety and death, as well as giving emotional support to patients' families) are made worse by the inadequate training received for handling such demands (Gaze, 1988).
- Those working in specialised areas or departments face additional demands. For example, nurses in intensive care units (ITUs) have to maintain high levels of concentration for long periods, are often emotionally drained by continuous close contact with a distressed and frightened family, and the process of dying may not follow a natural course: technology (such as ventilators) and drugs may prolong it (Fromant, 1988).
- Medical staff working in A&E (accident and emergency) departments are in the front line at times of major disasters, such as the 1989 Hillsborough disaster. However well prepared they may be practically, nothing can prepare them for the emotional demands placed upon them (Owen, 1990).

What are the effects of stress?

The general adaptation syndrome (GAS)

According to Selye (1956), GAS represents the body's defence against stress. The body responds in the same way to any stressor, whether it's environmental or arises from within the body itself. Selye initially observed that injecting extracts of ovarian tissue into rats produced enlargement of the adrenal glands, shrinkage of the thymus gland, and bleeding ulcers. When he used extracts of other organs (pituitary, kidney, spleen), as well as substances not derived from bodily tissue, the *same* responses were produced. He eventually found that this same 'triad' of 'non-specific' responses could be produced by such different stimuli as insulin, excessive cold or heat, X-rays, sleep and water deprivation, and electric shock. Selye (1956) defined stress as:

> ... the individual's psychophysiological response, mediated largely by the autonomic nervous system and the endocrine system, to any demands made on the individual ...

GAS comprises three stages: the *alarm reaction*, *resistance* and *exhaustion* (see Figure 12.5, page 206).

Alarm reaction

When a stimulus is perceived as a stressor, there's a brief, initial *shock phase*. Resistance to the stressor is lowered. But this is quickly followed by the *countershock* phase. The sympathetic branch of the ANS is activated, which, in turn, stimulates the *adrenal medulla* to secrete increased levels of adrenaline and noradrenaline (*catecholamines*).

These are associated with sympathetic changes, collectively referred to as the *fight or flight syndrome* (see Chapter 4). The catecholamines mimic sympathetic arousal ('*sympathomimetics*'), and noradrenaline is the transmitter at the synapses of the sympathetic branch of the ANS. Consequently, noradrenaline from the adrenals prolongs the action of noradrenaline released at synapses in the

ANS. This prolongs sympathetic arousal after the stressor's removal. This is referred to as the *ANS–adrenal–medulla system* (or *sympatho–adrenomedullary axis*).

Resistance

If the stressor isn't removed, there's a *decrease* in sympathetic activity, but an *increase* in output from the other part of the adrenal gland, the *adrenal cortex*. This is controlled by the amount of *adrenocorticotrophic hormone* (ACTH) in the blood. ACTH is released from the anterior pituitary (the 'master' endocrine gland) on instructions from the hypothalamus. The adrenal cortex is essential for the maintenance of life and its removal results in death.

The effect of ACTH is to stimulate the adrenal cortex to release *corticosteroids* (or *adrenocorticoid hormones*), one group of which is the *glucocorticoid hormones* (chiefly, corticosterone, cortisol and hydrocortisone). These control and conserve the amount of glucose in the blood (*glucogenesis*), which is to resist stress of all kinds. The glucocorticoids convert protein into glucose, make fats available for energy, increase blood flow and generally stimulate behavioural responsiveness. In this way, the *anterior pituitary–adrenal cortex*

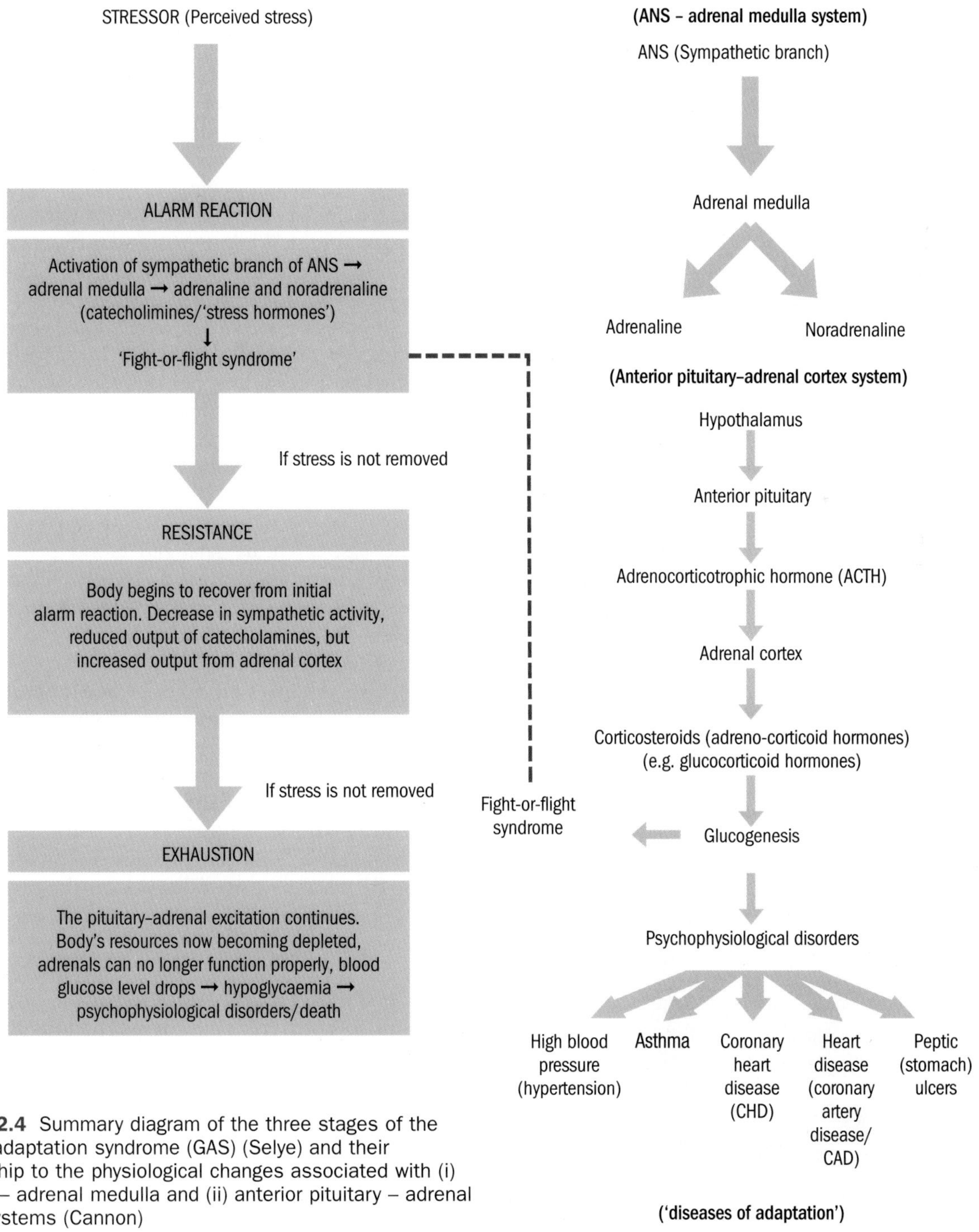

Figure 12.4 Summary diagram of the three stages of the general adaptation syndrome (GAS) (Selye) and their relationship to the physiological changes associated with (i) the ANS – adrenal medulla and (ii) anterior pituitary – adrenal cortex systems (Cannon)

system (or *hypothalamic–pituitary–adrenal axis*) contributes to the fight or flight syndrome.

Exhaustion

Once ACTH and corticosteroids are circulating in the bloodstream, they tend to inhibit the further release of ACTH from the pituitary. If the stressor is removed during the resistance stage, blood sugar levels will gradually return to normal. But when the stress situation continues, the pituitary–adrenal excitation will continue. The body's resources are now becoming depleted, the adrenals can no longer function properly, blood glucose levels drop and, in extreme cases, hypoglycaemia could result in death.

It's at this stage that *psychophysiological disorders* develop, including high blood pressure (hypertension), heart disease (coronary artery disease, CAD), coronary heart disease (CHD), asthma and peptic (stomach) ulcers. Selye called these the *diseases of adaptation*.

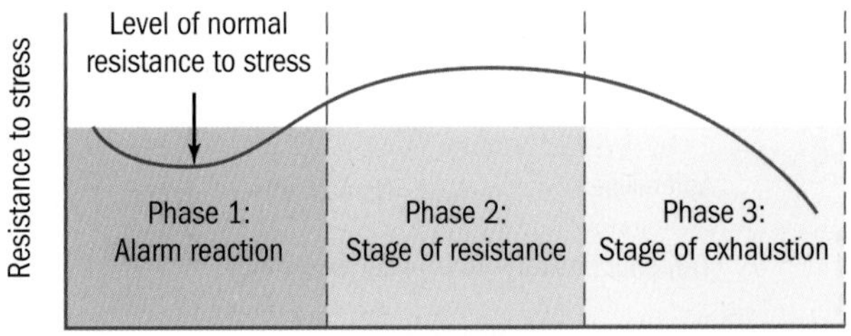

Figure 12.5 Three stages of GAS

Evaluation of GAS

Lazarus (1999) cites a study of patients dying from injury or disease. Postmortem examination showed that those who remained unconscious had normal levels of corticosteroids, while the opposite was true for those who were conscious (presumably aware they were dying).

A modern stressor

Lazarus infers from this that:

> ... some psychological awareness – akin to a conscious perception or appraisal – of the psychological significance of what is happening may be necessary to produce the adrenal cortical changes of the GAS.

While Selye helped us understand how stressors affect the body, in order to understand what makes a psychological event stressful, we must put the person into the equation. In effect, says Lazarus:

> ... it takes both the stressful stimulus conditions and a *vulnerable person* to generate a stress reaction ...

How does stress make us ill?

An evolutionary perspective

The sympathetic branch of the ANS responds as a unit, causing a state of generalised, undifferentiated arousal. This was probably of crucial importance in our evolutionary past, when our ancestors were frequently confronted by life-threatening dangers. This is precisely what the *fight-or-flight syndrome* is for. While an increase in heart rate may be necessary to supply more blood to the muscles when facing a hungry-looking bear, it may be quite irrelevant to most of the stressors we face in modern life, which involve a far higher psychological element. Most stressors *don't* pose physical threat, but our nervous and endocrine systems have evolved in such a way that we typically react to stressors as if they did. What may have been adaptive responses for our ancestors have become maladaptive today. So, what happens to all that internal activity?

- In the case of heart rate and blood pressure (BP), chronic stress will involve repeated episodes of increases in heart rate and BP which, in turn, produce increases in plaque formation within the cardiovascular system.
- Stress also produces an increase in blood cholesterol levels, through the action of adrenaline and noradrenaline on the release of free fatty acids. This produces a clumping-together of cholesterol particles, leading to clots in the blood and in the artery walls, and occlusion of the arteries. In turn, raised heart rate is related to a more rapid build-up of cholesterol on artery walls. High BP results in small lesions on the artery walls, and cholesterol tends to get trapped in these lesions (Holmes, 1994).

Stress and the immune system

The immune system is a collection of billions of cells that travel through the bloodstream and move in and out of tissues and organs, defending the body against invasion by foreign agents (such as bacteria, viruses and cancerous cells). These cells are produced mainly in the spleen, lymph nodes, thymus and bone marrow. The study of the effect of psychological factors on the immune system is called *psychoneuroimmunology* (PNI).

People often catch a cold soon after a period of stress (such as final exams), because stress seems to reduce the immune system's ability to fight off cold viruses. Goetsch & Fuller (1995) refer to studies that show decreases in the activity of *lymphocytes* among medical students during their final exams. Lymphocytes ('natural killer cells') are a particular type of white blood cell that normally fight off viruses and cancer cells. Levels of immunoglobulin A (IgA) increase immediately after an oral exam (if it appeared to go well), but *not* after written exams (suggesting that the stress isn't relieved until much later – when the results come out!) (Petit-Zeman, 2000).

Women with breast cancer who visualise their white blood cells waging war against the cancer cells, are boosting their immune system in a way that could help them fight the disease. This guided imagery was combined with progressive muscle relaxation, as well as standard surgery, chemotherapy and radiotherapy. Compared with women in a control group (given only the medical treatment), those who used the psychological techniques had higher numbers of mature T-cells, activated T-cells and cells carrying T-cell receptors (see Figure 12.6 below). These are important for attacking malignant cells. At the end of the nine-month study, these women also had higher levels of lymphokines (activated killer cells), which help prevent the disease from spreading. The women reported a better quality of life and fewer side-effects from medical treatments (Norton,

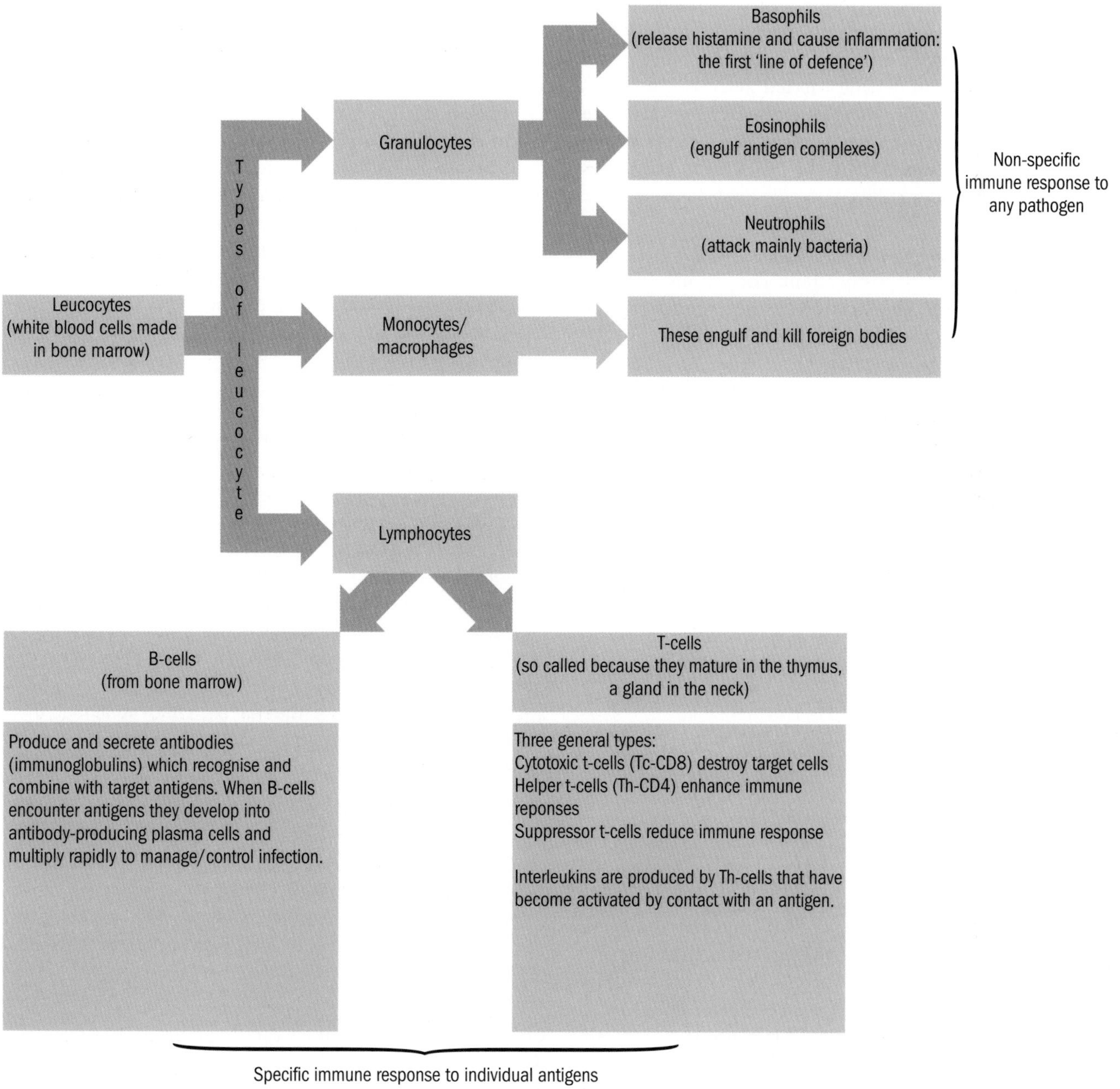

Figure 12.6 The immune system (adapted from Hayward, 1998)

2000a). While the immune system is so vital, Sternberg & Gold (1997) warn that:

> ... its responses are so powerful that they require constant regulation to ensure that they are neither excessive nor indiscriminate and yet remain effective. When the immune system escapes regulation, autoimmune and inflammatory diseases or immune deficiency syndromes result.

As we've seen, the GAS involves the release of cortisol (one of the major glucocorticoids) into the bloodstream. But the immune system, too, is capable of triggering this stream of biological events: it has a direct line to the hypothalamus. When our immune system is activated to fight an illness or infection, it sends a signal to the hypothalamus to produce its stress hormones (including cortisol). The flow of hormones, in turn, *shuts off* the immune response. This ingenious negative feedback loop allows a short burst of immune activity, but prevents the immune system from getting carried away. In this way, a little stress is 'good for you'. But *chronic* stress produces such a constant flow of cortisol, that the immune system is dampened too much. This helps explain how stress makes us ill (Sternberg, 2000).

Moderators and mediators of stress

Moderator variables are antecedent conditions (such as personality, ethnic background, and gender) that interact with exposure to stress to affect health outcome. *Mediator variables* intervene in the link between stress exposure and health outcome (for example, appraisal: Folkman & Lazarus, 1988b). If they *reduce* the impact of a stressful event, they're called 'protective' or 'buffering' variables (they soften or cushion the impact: Bartlett, 1998).

Personality

There's been an enormous amount of research into the *Type A Behaviour Pattern* (TABP). This was originally called 'Type A personality' (a stable personality trait: Friedman & Rosenman, 1974), but it's now conceptualised as a stereotypical set of behavioural responses. Typical responses are:

- *competitiveness* and *achievement orientation*
- *aggressiveness* and *hostility*
- *sense of time urgency*.

Many early studies showed that people who display TABP were at much greater risk of high BP and CHD compared with 'Type Bs'. However, these risks are only *relative*: the vast majority of Type As *don't* develop CHD, and many Type Bs do (Davison & Neale, 1994). Also, most studies have found that TABP assessed immediately following a heart attack *doesn't* predict future attacks. This suggests that TAPB *isn't* a distinct risk for CHD in those already at risk of the disorder (Penny, 1996).

Research is increasingly pointing towards *hostility* as the best single predictor of CHD. This is the non-specific dislike of others, the tendency to see the worst in others, anger and envy, and a lack of compassion. The behavioural aspect involves aggressiveness and possible bullying (Forshaw, 2002). In fact, hostility is a better predictor than the TAPB as a whole. Dembroski & Costa (1987) argue that 'potential for hostility' is a reasonably stable personality trait.

According to Temoshok (1987), *Type C personalities* are cancer-prone. The Type C personality has difficulty expressing emotion and tends to suppress or inhibit emotions, particularly negative ones such as anger. While there's no clear-cut evidence that these personality characteristics can actually cause cancer, it does seem likely that they influence the progression of cancer and, hence, the survival time of cancer patients (Weinman, 1995).

Greer & Morris (1975) found that women diagnosed with breast cancer showed significantly more emotional suppression than those with benign breast disease (especially among those under 50). This had been a characteristic for most of their lives. Cooper & Faragher (1993) reported that experiencing a major stressful event is a significant predictor of breast cancer. This was especially so in women who didn't express anger, but used denial as a form of coping.

KEY STUDY 12.5 Beating breast cancer (Greer *et al.*, 1979)

- Greer *et al.* studied women who'd had a mastectomy after being diagnosed with breast cancer.
- Those who reacted either by *denying* what had happened ('I'm being treated for a lump, but it's not serious'), or by showing '*fighting spirit*' ('This is not going to beat me'), were significantly more likely to be free of cancer five years later than women who stoically accepted it ('I feel an illness is God's will ...') or were described as 'giving up' ('Well, there's no hope with cancer, is there?').
- A follow-up at 15 years (Greer *et al.*, 1990) confirmed the improved prognosis.
- According to Hegarty (2000):

> *Such research ... appears to give scientific support to the advice ... 'to think positive' in the face of a diagnosis of cancer. It suggests the value of having psychological resources which will allow individuals to adapt to, rather than succumb to, a severe threat to their well-being. It might even be possible to teach such strategies to people who neither have nor use them.*

Other personality variables can be *protective*. For example, Kobasa and her colleagues (1979; Kobasa *et al.*, 1982) describe *hardiness*, which comprises the three Cs:

- *commitment* – a tendency to involve oneself in whatever one is doing, and to approach life with a sense of curiosity and meaningfulness
- *control* – this is related to Rotter's locus of control (see above, page 203)
- *challenge* – a tendency to believe that change, as opposed to stability, is normal in life, and to anticipate change as an incentive to personal growth and development rather than a threat to security.

According to Funk (1992), hardiness seems to moderate the stress–illness relationship by reducing cognitive appraisals of threat, and reducing the use of regressive coping (see Table 12.2, page 210).

Cultural/ethnic background

In evaluating the TABP research, Penny (1996) observes that western culture seems to encourage and value it. Competitiveness and striving for achievement are common goals in capitalist societies, but probably not in more traditional, communal ones. Similarly, the SRRS has been criticised for not taking account of cultural and ethnic differences in the kinds of potential stressors that people are exposed to.

For many years, it's been noted that both the physical and mental health of African-Americans is worse than that of whites, especially in terms of the spread of AIDS and hypertension. While this is partly due to the direct negative effects of poverty, such as poor diet, low levels of education and poor medical care, there are many psychological and social stressors involved as well. Although these are extremely difficult to measure, especially across cultures:

> ... there is little dispute that blacks in North America and Europe face a unique kind of stress – racial discrimination. (Cooper *et al.*, 1999)

> *ASK YOURSELF...*
> - Can you think of ways in which sexism might adversely affect women's health?
> - Do women have access to protective factors that men don't?

How do we cope with stress?

Primary appraisal of an event as in some way harmful or threatening is really only the beginning of the stress process, not the end. In *secondary appraisal*, we consider what can be done about the stressful situation, by evaluating our *coping options* (Lazarus, 1966, 1999). Primary appraisal doesn't necessarily come first. The difference between them is *not* timing, but *content*. They are interdependent aspects of a common process. According to Lazarus (1999):

> The more confident we are of our capacity to overcome obstacles and dangers, the more likely we are to be challenged rather than threatened and vice versa, a sense of inadequacy promotes threat ...

Cohen & Lazarus (1979) have classified all the coping strategies that a person might use into five general categories:

1. *direct action response* – the individual tries directly to change or manipulate his/her relationship to the stressful situation, such as escaping from/removing it
2. *information seeking* – the individual tries to understand the situation better, and to predict future events that are related to the stressor
3. *inhibition of action* – doing nothing; this may be the best course of action if the situation is seen as short term
4. *intrapsychic or palliative coping* – the individual reappraises the situation (for example, through the use of psychological defence mechanisms) or changes the 'internal environment' (through drugs, alcohol, relaxation or meditation)
5. turning to others for help and emotional support.

These five categories of coping overlap with the distinction between problem-focused and emotion-focused coping.

> **Box 12.9 Problem-focused and emotion-focused coping (Lazarus & Folkman, 1984)**
> - Problem-focused coping involves taking direct action in order to solve the problem, or seeking information that's relevant to a solution.
> - *Emotion-focused coping* involves trying to reduce the negative emotions that are part of the experience of stress.
> - Lazarus and Folkman argue that effective coping depends on the situation, and sometimes using *both* kinds might offer the 'best solution'.

In the *transactional model* (Cox, 1978: see above, page 200), the 'stress response' refers to both psychological and physiological means of coping. In turn, the psychological response has two components, *cognitive defence* and *behavioural response*, and the consequences of both (perceived and actual) are continuously being appraised in relation to the stressful situation.

> *ASK YOURSELF...*
> - Which of the above coping responses best describes your typical response to stressful situations?
> - How about your best friend or partner?
> - Does the way you cope depend on the nature of the stressor?

Coping and defence mechanisms

Sometimes the term 'coping response' or mechanism is used in contrast to 'defence mechanism' (e.g. Grasha, 1983; Savickas, 1995). The *ego defence mechanisms* involve some degree of distortion of reality and self-deception (see Chapter 42). While desirable in the short term, as long-term solutions to stress they're unhealthy and undesirable. *Coping mechanisms*, by contrast, are conscious attempts to adapt to stress and anxiety in a positive and constructive way. They use thoughts and behaviours to search for information, problem-solving, seeking help from others, recognising our true feelings, and establishing goals and objectives:

... In effect, coping improves fit [between the individual and the environment], whereas defence maintains misfit while reducing perceived stress (Savickas, 1995).

Table 12.2 Some major coping mechanisms and their corresponding defence mechanisms (based on Grasha, 1983)

Coping mechanism	Description	Corresponding defence
Objectivity	Separating one thought from another or our feelings from our thoughts. Allows us to obtain a better understanding of how we think/feel, and an objective evaluation of our actions	Isolation
Logical analysis	Systematically analysing our problems, in order to find explanations and make plans to solve them, based on the realities of the situation	Rationalisation
Concentration	Ability to set aside disturbing thoughts/feelings, in order to concentrate on the task in hand	Denial
Playfulness	Ability to use past feelings/ideas/behaviour appropriately to enrich the solution of problems/add enjoyment to life	Regression
Tolerance of ambiguity	Ability to function in situations where we/others cannot make clear choices, because the situation's so complicated	
Suppression	Ability consciously to forget about/hold back thoughts/feelings, until an appropriate time/place	Repression

Sublimation can be thought of as a coping mechanism and a defence mechanism. It involves channelling anxiety in socially desirable ways, and so is positive and constructive, as well as being a defence against anxiety.

Stress management

Much of what we've said about coping with stress refers to what people do in a largely *spontaneous* way. In this informal sense, we all 'manage our stress' more or less effectively. But, more formally, *stress management* refers to a range of psychological techniques used in a quite deliberate way, in a professional setting, to help people reduce their stress. These techniques may be used singly or in combination.

- In the case of *biofeedback* (discussed above in relation to pain control: see page 199), the focus is on treating the symptoms of stress rather than the stressor itself.
- The same is true for a number of procedures used to bring about a state of relaxation, in particular *progressive muscle relaxation*, meditation and hypnosis.
- *Cognitive restructuring* refers to a number of specific methods aimed at trying to change the way individuals think about their life situation and self, in order to change their emotional responses and behaviour. This approach is based largely on the work of Beck *(the treatment of automatic thoughts)* and Ellis *(rational emotive therapy)*, two major forms of *cognitive behaviour therapy* (see Chapter 45). This approach provides information to reduce uncertainty and to enhance people's sense of control.

CHAPTER SUMMARY

- While traditional medicine is based on the **biomedical model** of disease, health psychology, psychosomatic medicine and behavioural medicine all rest on the **biopsychosocial model**.
- Changes in major causes of death during the twentieth century in industrialised societies reflect changes in lifestyle. This is incompatible with the biomedical model.
- **Health psychology** focuses on normal behaviour and psychological processes in relation to health and illness, although some psychologists see it as an extension of clinical psychology. It also attempts to **promote** health behaviour and **prevent** illness.
- **Health** is more than just the absence of **disease**, which is defined in **biological/somatic** terms. By contrast, **illness** is a more **psychological** concept.
- According to **cross-cultural health psychology**, both health and disease are cultural concepts. Cultural factors contribute to the prevalence of certain diseases between cultures, and **acculturation** may expose immigrants to risk factors within the host culture.
- **Expectancy-value models** try to account for people's adoption/failure to adopt particular health behaviours. They are **rational reasoning** models.
- In the **health belief model** (**HBM**), belief in **susceptibility** to, and perception of **severity of the consequences**, of the disease, together determine the **perceived threat**.

- A factor that may explain the persistence of unhealthy behaviours is people's tendency towards **unrealistic optimism**. This suggests that perception of one's own risk *isn't* a rational process.
- The **theory of reasoned action** (**TRA**) assumes that behaviour is a function of behavioural intention, jointly determined by a person's **attitude** and **subjective norms**.
- The **theory of planned behaviour** (**TPB**) is a modification of the TRA. The extra ingredient is perceived **behavioural control**, based on Bandura's concept of **self-efficacy**.
- All the models are poor predictors of actual behaviour (the **intention–behaviour gap**). One response to this criticism is the concept of **implementation intentions**.
- The ability of the models to predict **safe sex** is limited. Overall, findings from studies involving gay samples based on the TRA/TPB are less consistent than those involving heterosexuals. In both groups, **negotiation with partners** over condom use helps predict their actual use, and perception of **personal invulnerability** is commonplace.
- **Aerobic exercise** helps decrease the risk of several life-threatening diseases, as well as increasing positive mental health. But even short exercise sessions can be beneficial.
- Research indicates that **patient non-compliance/non-adherence** is very common, although this varies depending on the particular disorder. It applies to both chronic and acute conditions, and to organ transplant patients. The **double high/double efficacy/behavioural intention model** identifies the five factors that make compliance most likely.
- Compliance is affected by both **practitioner** and **patient/regimen variables**. The former include how doctors **communicate** their beliefs to patients, and the latter include patients' **satisfaction** with the consultation, and their **understanding/recall** of the information given.
- Although **pain** is basically physiological, the pain **experience** has **emotional**, **cognitive** and **cultural** components. **Phantom limb pain** illustrates that people can feel pain in the absence of physical injury, and **congenital analgesia** illustrates the converse.
- **Treatment** of pain includes methods used to treat stress, such as **contingency management**, **EMG biofeedback** and **self-management/cognitive behaviour treatment**.
- **Stress** can be conceptualised as a **stimulus** (corresponding to the **engineering model**), a **response** (corresponding to the **physiological model**) or as an **interaction** between organism and environment (corresponding to the **transactional model**).
- The **causes** of stress include **disruption of circadian rhythms**, as in shift work and jet lag, and **occupation-linked stressors**, especially for those involved in the emergency services and health care.
- Major **life changes** have been studied using the **Social Readjustment Rating Scale** (**SRRS**). Research claiming that high scores are related to a range of health problems has been criticised on methodological grounds, as has the SRRS itself. An alternative to the SRRS is the **hassles scale**.
- Selye's **General Adaptation Syndrome** (**GAS**) represents the body's defence against stress. It comprises the **alarm reaction**, **resistance** and **exhaustion**.
- The alarm reaction involves the **fight-or-flight response**, in which the **ANS–adrenal–medulla system** is activated. In resistance, the **anterior pituitary–adrenal cortex system** is activated.
- While the fight-or-flight response may have been adaptive in our evolutionary past, it's inappropriate as a response to most 'modern' stressors. Stress can cause illness through maintaining a dangerously high level of physiological arousal.
- **Psychoneuroimmunology** studies the relationship between stress and health by assessing its effects on the **immune system**. Just as stress can make us ill by reducing the immune system's ability to fight infection, so psychological factors can enhance immune system functioning, as in fighting breast cancer.
- **Moderators** of stress include **personality** and **ethnic background**. Considerable research has investigated the link between **Type A Behaviour Pattern** (**TABP**) and coronary heart disease, and between **Type C personalities** and cancer. Unlike these, **hardiness** is a **protective** factor against the harmful effects of stress.
- **Coping** with stress involves **primary** and **secondary appraisals**, **problem-focused** and **emotion-focused** coping, and **coping mechanisms** (as distinct from **defence mechanisms**). **Stress management** involves **biofeedback**, **progressive muscle relaxation** and **cognitive restructuring**.

Links with other topics/chapters

- The biomedical model of illness is closely related to the *disease model of addiction* (Chapter 8) and the *medical model of mental disorder* (Chapter 43).
- Health psychology is closely related to *clinical psychology* (Chapter 1), although the exact relationship is controversial.
- *Culture* determines what is commonly understood by 'health' and 'illness', as well as helping to determine the prevalence of certain diseases. Pain may also be understood as a cultural phenomenon (Chapter 47).
- Models of health behaviour are culturally relative, and western culture seems to value and encourage the component response of TAPB (Chapter 47).

- *Racial discrimination* is a unique form of stress that can account for the greater susceptibility of African-Americans to certain health problems (Chapter 25).
- The TRA has been central to the debate within social psychology regarding the *relationship between attitudes and behaviour* (Chapter 24).
- The TPB is a modification of the TRA, reflecting the influence of Bandura's concept of *self-efficacy* (Chapter 35).
- Perceptions of invulnerability demonstrate how people rationalise behaviour that conflicts with aspects of their self-concept, as explained by Festinger's *cognitive dissonance theory* (Chapter 24).
- The effects of exercise on mood and cognition are part of *sport psychology* (Chapter 31).
- Patient 'compliance' implies the doctor's role as an authority figure, with the less powerful patient in a submissive (obedient) role (Chapter 27).
- Biofeedback is used in the treatment of pain and stress-related disorders, and is derived from work with rats, which demonstrated how autonomic responses could be modified using *operant conditioning* techniques (Chapter 11).
- Contingency management of pain is a form of *behaviour modification* (Chapters 11 and 45).
- Both pain and stress are also treated through cognitive behavioural techniques, including Beck's *treatment of automatic thoughts* and Ellis's *rational emotive therapy* (Chapters 44 and 45).
- The disruption of circadian rhythms is a major cause of *stress* (Chapter 7).
- People working in the emergency services are especially susceptible to *post-traumatic stress disorder* (PTSD) (Chapter 44).
- Stressors adversely affect health through their impact on the *autonomic nervous system* (ANS) and *endocrine system* (Chapter 4).
- For something to be perceived as a stressor, it first has to be appraised as potentially threatening. This also applies to *theories of emotion* (Chapter 10).
- Coping mechanisms are often contrasted with Freud's account of *defence mechanisms* (Chapter 42).

THREE

COGNITIVE PSYCHOLOGY

13

ATTENTION AND PERFORMANCE

INTRODUCTION AND OVERVIEW

According to Titchener (1903), a student of Wundt: 'The doctrine of attention is the nerve of the whole psychological system'.

However, the Gestalt psychologists believed the concept of attention was unnecessary (they believed that a stimulus array's properties were sufficient to predict the perceptual response to it: see Chapter 15). The behaviourists argued that since 'attention' was unobservable, it wasn't worthy of experimental study (see Chapters 2 and 3).

Interest in the study of attention re-emerged following the publication of Broadbent's (1958) *Perception and Communication*, which also had a great impact on the development of cognitive psychology overall. Broadbent argued that the world is composed of many more sensations than can be handled by the perceptual and cognitive capabilities of the human observer. To cope with the flood of available information, humans must selectively attend to only some information, and somehow 'tune out' the rest. Attention, therefore, is the result of a limited-capacity information-processing system. Solso (1995) calls this a 'pipeline' theory. To understand our ability to attend selectively to things, researchers study focused (or selective) attention.

Central to the information-processing approach is the computer analogy. This is arguably most evident in explanations of memory (see Chapter 17) and attention. Concepts such as buffer store and limited-capacity processor are drawn from information technology and built into the models of attention that we'll discuss in this chapter.

Almost all the early models of attention assumed *serial processing*, a step-by-step process in which each operation is carried out in turn. The first of these was Broadbent's (1958) *filter model*, followed by Treisman's (1964) *attenuation model*, and the *pertinence model* (Deutsch & Deutsch, 1963; Norman, 1969). These are all 'single-channel models' of selective attention. But early attempts to explain *divided attention*, such as Kahneman's (1973) *central capacity theory*, also assumed serial processing. In *parallel processing*, two or more operations are carried out at the same time. This is the view taken in Allport's (1980b) multi-channel theory of divided attention (doing more than one thing at a time).

Assumptions about serial or parallel processing reflect changes in the underlying computer analogy, which in turn reflect developments in computer technology. For much of the 1950s and 1960s, computers were capable of only serial processing. During the 1980s and 1990s, machines capable of massive parallel processing started to be built, and theorists have returned to an earlier belief that cognitive theories should be based more closely on the brain's neural networks (Eysenck & Keane, 1995; Jarvis, 1994; see Chapter 20). The human brain is the parallel processing machine *par excellence* (see Chapter 4).

WHAT IS ATTENTION?

> *ASK YOURSELF...*
> - What do you understand by the term 'attention'? (See Chapters 7 and 9.)

One famous definition of attention is that of William James (1890), according to whom:

> It is the taking possession by the mind, in clear and vivid form, of one out of what seem several simultaneously possible objects or trains of thought. Focalisation, concentration of consciousness are of its essence. It implies withdrawal from some things in order to deal effectively with others.

Although we cannot necessarily equate attention with consciousness (see below), James's definition underlines the selective nature of attention. This is echoed in Solso's (1995) definition: 'the concentration of mental effort on sensory or mental events'. However, this is only one of two major ways in which attention has been defined and investigated. A crucial distinction is made between:

1. the mechanisms by which certain information is registered and other information is rejected, whether or not the latter enters conscious awareness (selective or *focused attention*)
2. some upper limit to the amount of processing that can be performed on incoming information at any one time (*capacity* or *divided attention*).

As we saw in Chapters 7 and 9, the term 'attention' has also been used to refer to arousal level, vigilance, and the ability to stay alert and concentrate.

How many things can *you* do at once?

METHODS OF STUDYING ATTENTION

Selective attention

People are presented with two or more simultaneous 'messages', and are instructed to process and respond to only one of them. The most popular way of doing this is to use *shadowing*, in which one message is fed into the left ear and a different message into the right ear (through headphones). Participants have to repeat one of these messages aloud as they hear it.

The shadowing technique is really a particular form of *dichotic listening* (Broadbent, 1954). This is the simultaneous reception of two different stimulus inputs, one to each ear. Shadowing was first used by Cherry (1953), who wanted to study the *cocktail party phenomenon*, in which we manage to select one or two voices to listen to from the hubbub of conversations taking place at the same time and in the same room. The participant is asked to *select*, which can tell us something about the selection process and what happens to unattended stimuli. Most studies have looked at auditory attention.

The cocktail party phenomenon

Divided attention

In the *dual-task technique*, people are asked to attend and respond to both (or all) the messages. Whereas shadowing focuses attention on a particular message, the dual-task method deliberately *divides* people's attention. This provides useful information about a person's processing limitations, and also about attention mechanisms and their capacity.

SELECTIVE (OR FOCUSED) AUDITORY ATTENTION

Cherry's dichotic listening and shadowing research

In his initial experiments, Cherry's participants wore headphones through which pairs of spoken prose 'messages' were presented to both ears simultaneously (*binaural listening*). Cherry found that various physical differences affected a person's ability to select one of the messages to attend to, in particular voice intensity, the speaker's location, and the speaker's sex. He also found that when these differences were controlled for in the two messages (so that each message was, say, spoken in an equally intense female voice), their meaning was extremely difficult to separate. In later experiments, he used dichotic listening and shadowing. While participants were able to shadow the specified message, little of the non-shadowed message was remembered.

Box 13.1 Other research findings using shadowing

- Little of the non-shadowed message was remembered, even when the same word was presented 35 times to the non-shadowed ear (Moray, 1959).
- Also, participants didn't notice if the message was spoken in a foreign language or changed from English to a different language.
- While speech played backwards was reported as having 'something queer about it', most participants believed it to be normal speech.
- However, a pure tone of 400 cycles per second was nearly always noticed, as was a change of voice from male to female or female to male (Cherry & Taylor, 1954).

ASK YOURSELF...
- What conclusions can you draw from these findings?

These data suggested that while the *physical* properties of the message in the non-shadowed ear were 'heard', *semantic content* (its *meaning*) was completely lost.

Researchers quickly moved on from Cherry's original question about how we can attend to one conversation, and began to ask why so little seemed to be remembered about the other conversations (Hampson & Morris, 1996).

Broadbent's split-span studies

Broadbent (1954) reported the results of a series of studies using the *split-span procedure*. In this, three digits (such as 8, 2 and 1) are presented via headphones to one ear at the rate of one every half a second. Simultaneously, three different digits (such as 7, 3 and 4) are presented to the other ear. The task is to listen to the two sets of numbers and then write down as much as can be remembered.

The digits can be recalled either:

1. according to the ear of presentation (*ear-by-ear recall*: the numbers above could be recalled as either 8, 2, 1, 7, 3, 4 or 7, 3, 4, 8, 2, 1), or
2. according to their chronological order of presentation (*pair-by-pair recall*); since the digits have been presented in pairs, this would involve recalling the first pair (8, 7 or 7, 8), followed by the second pair (2, 3 or 3, 2) and finally the third pair (1, 4 or 4, 1).

When people are simply given a list of six digits at a rate of one every half a second, serial recall is typically 95 per cent accurate. However, Broadbent found that the split-span procedure produced accurate recall only 65 per cent of the time. Moreover, pair-by-pair recall was considerably poorer than ear-by-ear recall. If given a choice, people preferred ear-by-ear recall.

SINGLE-CHANNEL THEORIES OF FOCUSED AUDITORY ATTENTION

Single-channel theories propose that somewhere in information processing there's a 'bottleneck' or filter that allows some information to be passed on for further analysis, while the other information is either discarded or processed to only a limited degree. The three theories that have been proposed differ mainly over whether the filtering takes place early or late in information processing. This means that they differ in terms of the nature and extent of processing of the non-attended material.

Broadbent's early selection filter theory

Broadbent's (1958) theory was the first systematic attempt to explain both Cherry's findings and those of split-span experiments. Broadbent assumes that our ability to process information is *capacity-limited*. Information from the senses passes 'in parallel' to a short-term store. This is a temporary 'buffer system' which holds information until it can be processed further and, effectively, extends the duration of a stimulus (see Chapter 17). The various types of information (such as two or more voices) are preserved in their original form, and then passed to a selective filter. This operates on the basis of the information's physical characteristics, selecting one source for further analysis and rejecting all others.

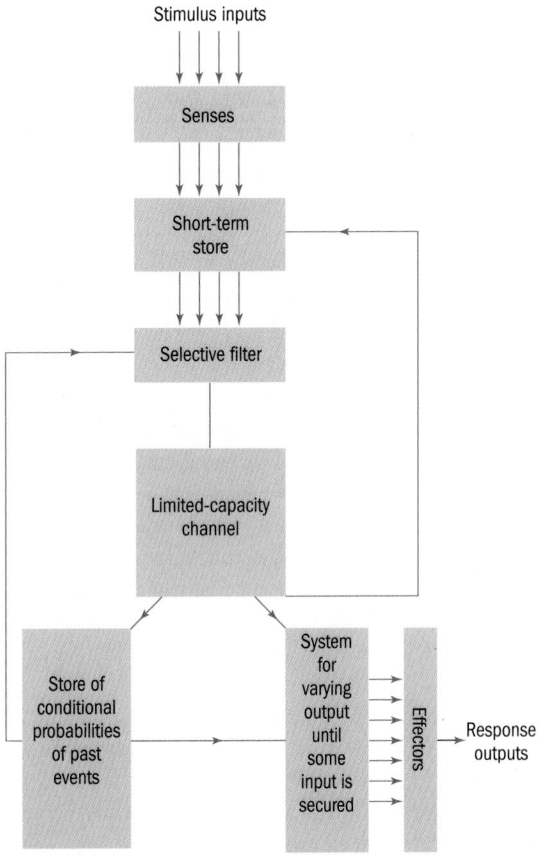

Figure 13.1 Broadbent's theory of the flow of information between stimulus and response

Information allowed through the filter reaches a limited-capacity channel (the filter is necessary precisely because the channel is capacity-limited). This corresponds to the 'span of consciousness' (James, 1890) or what we experience as happening *now*. The information allowed through the filter is analysed in that it's recognised, possibly rehearsed, and then transferred to the motor effectors (muscles), producing an appropriate response.

Broadbent considered the short-term store to be capable of holding information for a period of time before it decayed. So, two simultaneous stimuli can be processed provided the processor can get back to the store before the information in it has disappeared. Consequently, attending to one thing doesn't necessarily mean that everything else is lost. However, Broadbent maintained that processing two different pieces of information from two channels would always take longer, and be less efficient, than processing the same information from one channel. This is because switching attention between channels takes a substantial period of time.

Tests of Broadbent's theory

> *ASK YOURSELF...*
> • How can Broadbent's theory explain (a) Cherry's findings concerning the fate of the non-shadowed message, and (b) the data from the split-span experiments?

According to the filter theory, (a) the non-shadowed message isn't allowed to pass through the filter, and (b) the input to the relevant ear is the physical property on which the information is selected.

However, the theory assumes that because the non-shadowed message is filtered out according to its physical characteristics, its meaning shouldn't be subject to any sort of higher-level analysis. But when we're at a party, our attention sometimes switches from the person we're conversing with to another part of the room (if, for example, we hear our name mentioned). This was demonstrated experimentally by Moray (1959), who found that when the participant's name was presented to the non-attended (non-shadowed) ear, attention switched to that ear about one-third of the time.

KEY STUDY 13.1 Why use one ear when two will do? (Gray & Wedderburn, 1960)

- Gray and Wedderburn presented, to each ear alternately, the syllables composing a word, plus random digits. Thus, when one ear 'heard' a syllable, the other 'heard' a digit. For example, in one experiment, participants heard:
  Left ear: OB 2 TIVE
  Right ear: 6 JEC 9

- In other experiments, phrases were used in place of words, such as 'Dear Aunt Jane', 'Mice eat cheese' and 'What the hell'.

ASK YOURSELF...

- What would Broadbent have predicted about participants' responses when asked to repeat what they'd heard in one ear (or channel)?

- According to Broadbent, participants should have reported 'ob-two-tive', or 'six-jec-nine'. This, of course, is nonsense. But the filter model maintains that it's the physical nature of the auditory signal (which ear receives which input), and not meaning which determines what's attended to and, hence, what's recalled.
- What participants actually reported was 'objective' or 'Dear Aunt Jane' etc. In other words, they acted 'intelligently'. The ears don't always function as different information channels, and switching between channels is fairly easy to do.

An evaluation of Broadbent's theory

The importance of meaning

- Treisman (1960) found that if meaningful material presented to the attended ear was switched in mid-sentence to the non-attended ear, participants would occasionally change the focus of their attention to the non-attended ear, and shadow that material before changing back to the attended ear.
- Treisman (1964) discovered that if a French translation of the shadowed material was presented as non-shadowed material, some bilingual participants realised that the shadowed and non-shadowed material had the same meaning.
- Corteen & Wood (1972) conditioned participants to produce a galvanic skin response (GSR) whenever they heard a particular target word. A small electric shock was delivered immediately after the target word was heard. The target word produced a GSR when presented to the non-attended ear, as did synonyms. However, GSRs didn't occur every time the conditioned words were presented.
- Mackay (1973) presented the word 'bank' in a sentence, and participants subsequently had to recognise the sentence they'd heard. Recognition was influenced by whether the word 'river' or 'money' had been presented to the non-attended ear.

What these studies, and that of Gray and Wedderburn (see Key Study 13.1), suggest is that the meaning of the input to the non-attended ear is processed at least some of the time. Further, Underwood (1974) found that participants trained at shadowing can detect two-thirds of the material presented to the non-attended ear. This throws doubt on Broadbent's claim that the non-shadowed message is always rejected at an early stage of processing. Also, when material used is sufficiently different (such as one being auditory and the other visual), memory for the non-shadowed message is good. This indicates that it must have been processed at a higher level than proposed by Broadbent (Allport *et al.*, 1972).

Treisman's attenuation (or stimulus-analysis system) model

According to Treisman (1960, 1964), competing information is analysed for things other than its physical properties, including sounds, syllable patterns, grammatical structure and the information's meaning (Hampson & Morris, 1996). Treisman suggested that the non-shadowed message isn't filtered out early on, but that the selective filter *attenuates* it. So, a message that isn't selected on the basis of its physical properties wouldn't be rejected completely, but its 'volume' would be 'turned down'.

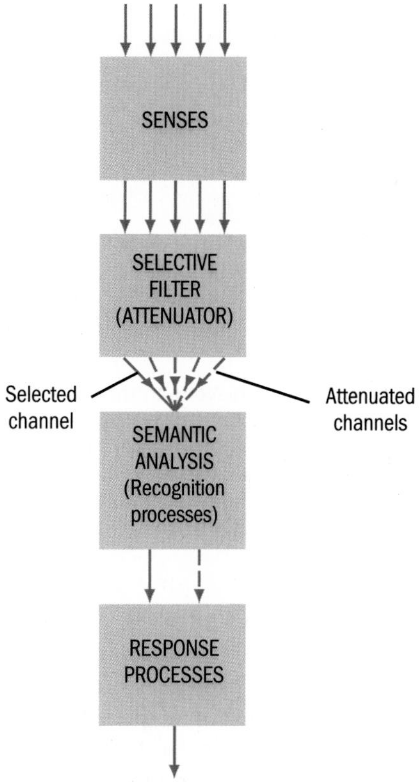

Figure 13.2 Treisman's attenuation model

Both non-attenuated and attenuated information undergoes these further analyses. This may result in an attenuated message being attended to, depending on its features.

Treisman suggested that biologically relevant and emotionally important stimuli may be 'pre-sets' to which attention is switched, irrespective of the attenuated message's content. This accounts for our ability to switch attention to a different conversation when our name is mentioned. Since it's the features of a stimulus that determine whether or not it's attended to, the concept of *probabilistic filtering* is perhaps a better way of appreciating Treisman's theory than that of attenuation (Massaro, 1989).

The Deutsch–Norman late-selection filter model

Deutsch & Deutsch (1963) and Norman (1968, 1976) completely rejected Broadbent's claim that information is filtered out early on. According to the Deutsch–Norman model, filtering or selection occurs only after all inputs have been analysed at a high level, for example after each word has been recognised by the memory system and analysed for meaning.

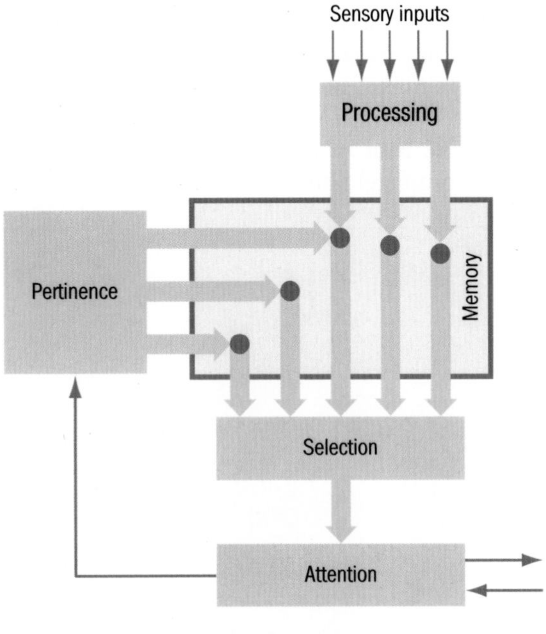

Figure 13.3 The Deutsch–Norman theory of focused attention. All sensory inputs receive perceptual processing and are recognised in the sense that they excite their representations (the green circles) in memory. The information selected is that which has the greatest pertinence (Norman, 1968)

The filter is placed nearer the *response* end of the processing system; hence, it's a 'late' selection filter. Because processing will have already been undertaken on the information that's been presented, some information will have been established as pertinent (most relevant) and have activated particular memory representations. This is why it's sometimes called the *pertinence model*. When one memory representation is selected for further processing, attention becomes selective. The model implies that we perceive everything we encounter, but are consciously aware of only some of it (Hampson & Morris, 1996).

Tests of the Treisman and the Deutsch–Norman models

Both the Treisman and the Deutsch–Norman models can account for the processing of non-shadowed material (whereas Broadbent's theory cannot). If the Deutsch–Norman model is correct, then participants should be able to identify as many target words in the non-shadowed message as in the shadowed message, since both are allegedly completely analysed for meaning. Treisman & Geffen (1967), however, found that target words were much better detected in the shadowed message (87 per cent) than the non-shadowed message (8 per cent). This is consistent with Treisman's view that the non-shadowed message is attenuated.

However, Treisman and Geffen's findings assume that the shadowed and non-shadowed messages are equally important. Deutsch & Deutsch (1967) argued that this assumption wasn't met, because participants had to indicate when they heard a target word by tapping. In other words, they had to shadow and tap in one message, but only tap in the other. This made the target words in the shadowed message more important than those in the non-shadowed message. Treisman & Riley (1969) overcame this problem by requiring participants to stop shadowing and to tap as soon as they detected a target word in either ear. Under such conditions, performance was still better for the shadowed message (76 per cent) than for the non-shadowed message (33 per cent).

This finding is consistent with Treisman's model, but inconsistent with the Deutsch–Norman claim that performance shouldn't differ (since the targets were equally pertinent irrespective of the ear they were presented to). However, the detection rate for the non-attended ear in Treisman and Riley's study (33 per cent) was much higher than that in the Treisman and Geffen study (8 per cent). This provides some support for the Deutsch–Norman model.

The Deutsch–Norman model predicts that participants asked immediately afterwards should be able to repeat back the words presented to the non-shadowed ear. However, the non-shadowed message gets into short-term memory for only a brief period and is then forgotten very quickly. Norman (1969) found that participants could remember the last couple of words presented to the non-attended ear if tested immediately, but not after a short continuation of the shadowing task. This finding was replicated by Glucksberg & Cowan (1970).

ASK YOURSELF...

- Can you think of examples where you've remembered something later that you weren't aware of hearing at the time (such as something somebody said)?
- Which of the theories of attention discussed above best accounts for these occurrences?

An evaluation of single-channel models

- Despite some support for the Deutsch–Norman model, Wilding (1982) believes that less is known about non-attended messages than it claims. However, more is known than can be explained by either Broadbent's or Treisman's models.
- The major criticism of single-channel theories is their lack of flexibility, and several more 'flexible' theories have been advanced. According to Johnston & Heinz (1978), attentional selectivity can occur at several different stages of processing, depending on the demands made by the experimental task. To minimise demands on capacity, selection is made as early as possible.
- Johnston & Heinz (1979) and Johnston & Wilson (1980) presented findings consistent with their view that processing is more flexible than predicted by single-channel theories. For example, Johnston and Wilson showed that participants processed words presented to both ears, but only when they didn't know to which ear particular target words would be presented. These data suggest that non-target words are processed only to the extent necessary to perform a task.
- Many researchers question whether any single, general purpose, limited-capacity central processor can, in principle, account for the complexities of selective attention (Allport, 1980b; Neisser, 1976; Norman & Bobrow, 1975). Much of the relevant evidence comes from dual-task studies, which are more directly concerned with processing capacity, i.e. divided attention (see below).

FOCUSED VISUAL ATTENTION

According to Driver (1996):

> The cluttered scenes of everyday life present more objects than we can respond towards simultaneously, and often more than we can perceive fully at any one time. Accordingly, mechanisms of attention are required to select objects of interest for further processing. In the case of vision, one such mechanism is provided by eye movements, which allow us to fixate particular regions so that they benefit from the greater acuity of the fovea.

The fovea (see Figure 5.2, page 81) provides maximum acuity for visual stimuli. So, when we fixate on an object, maximum visual processing is carried out on the object whose image is projected on to the fovea. The resources given to the other parts of the visual field are 'attenuated' (Anderson, 1995b).

Posner *et al.* (1978, 1980) found that when people are told to fixate on one part of the visual field, it's still possible to attend to stimuli seven or so degrees either side of the fixation point. Also, attention can be shifted more quickly when a stimulus is presented in an 'expected' rather than an 'unexpected' location. Thus, visual attention isn't confined to the part of the visual field which is processed by the fovea, but can be shifted without corresponding changes in eye movements. Indeed, such shifts in attention frequently *precede* the corresponding eye movement (Anderson, 1995b). Posner (1980) calls this *covert attention*.

The internal mental spotlight and the zoom lens

Posner likened covert attention to an internal mental spotlight that 'illuminates' any stimulus in the attended region, so that it's perceived in greater detail. It essentially duplicates the functions of eye movements *internally*, by allowing a particular region of space to be perceptually enhanced (Driver, 1996).

LaBerge (1983) required participants to judge whether the middle letter of five letters (such as LACIE) came from the beginning or end of the alphabet (*directed attention condition*). But on some occasions, a stimulus such as –7– – – was presented, and the task was to determine whether the 7 was one of two letters (T or Z). LaBerge found that the speed of judgement was a function of the distance from the centre of attention. Thus, reaction times were fastest for items at the centre of the stimulus and slower for those at its periphery, even though all items were within the fovea's region.

LaBerge concluded that visual attention is most concentrated at the centre of the internal spotlight and least at its periphery. When information beyond its centre needs to be processed, the spotlight must be shifted to ensure maximal processing. Because this takes time, participants in Posner *et al.*'s experiments took longer to judge a stimulus when it appeared in an 'unexpected' location (Eriksen & Yeh, 1987).

LaBerge also found that when participants were required to attend to the whole five-letter word string (*global attention condition*), the 'width' of the spotlight's 'beam' increased (based on the similarity of reaction times for items at the centre and periphery). These findings led Eriksen (1990) to propose the *zoom-lens model* of visual attention. This accepts the existence of an internal mental spotlight, but suggests that it has a beam which may be very narrow (in the case of LaBerge's letter task) or broad (in the case of LaBerge's word task). It's simply a variable-beam spotlight (Groome *et al.*, 1999).

An evaluation of the spotlight model

Despite evidence that little or no processing occurs beyond the spotlight (Johnston & Dark, 1986), both the spotlight and zoom-lens models have been contradicted in several studies.

KEY STUDY 13.2 Neisser & Becklen's (1975) study of selective visual attention

- Visual selective attention was studied by superimposing a film of three people playing a ball game on a film which showed two people's hands clapping (see Figure 13.4).

- The task was to follow one of the films and press a key to indicate that a 'critical event', such as the ball being thrown, had occurred.
- Adults found it difficult to follow both films simultaneously, but they were able to attend selectively to one or other of the films easily.
- This is difficult for the zoom-lens model to explain, since it proposes that the focus of attention is a given area in visual space, rather than objects within that area (Eysenck & Keane, 1995).
- Using Neisser and Becklen's methodology, it's been shown that infants as young as four months can selectively follow one of the two films. This suggests that selective visual attention is innate rather than learned (Bahrick *et al.*, 1981: see Chapter 16).

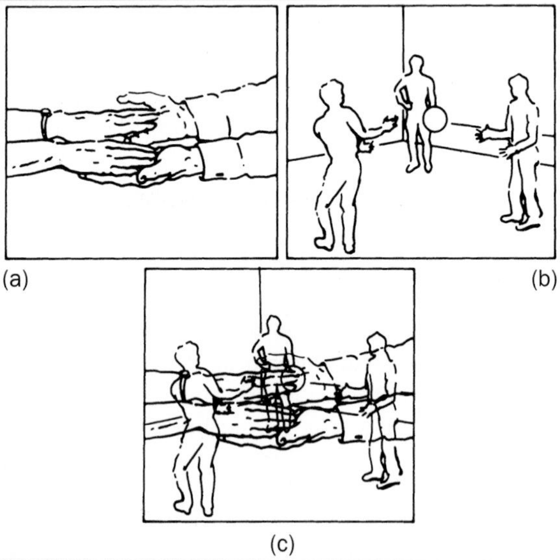

Figure 13.4 A film of two people clapping hands (a), and three people playing a ball game (b), which have been superimposed (c)

The fate of unattended visual stimuli

For Johnston & Dark (1986), stimuli beyond the focus of visual attention are subject to no, or virtually no, semantic processing. Any such processing is limited to mainly simple physical features. However, Driver (1996) disagrees. For example, when a picture is shown as the unattended stimulus on one trial, it slows the processing of an attended word with an identical or similar meaning on the next trial (*negative priming*). The fact that processing of the attended stimulus is reduced suggests that the meaning of the unattended stimulus must have been subject to some sort of processing (Tipper & Driver, 1988).

Treisman's feature-integration theory

Treisman's (1988) theory was developed on the basis of findings using the visual search procedure. Participants are presented with an array of visual material in which a target item is embedded on some trials but absent on others, and the 'distractor' items can be varied so that they're similar to the target letter, or different from it. The participant's task is to decide if the target is present or absent.

X	P	T	L	A	B	N	T
A	R	H	N	J	I	F	R
E	W	R	N	P	A	Z	X
A	H	Y	5	Y	T	E	S
A	N	H	C	E	S	T	I
G	D	T	K	D	Y	U	I

Figure 13.5 A visual search array. The task is to find the number five amongst the letters

Neisser (1967) argued that when people perform a visual search task, they process many items simultaneously, without being fully 'aware' of the exact nature of the distractor items. Visual information processing might occur pre-attentively, depending on the nature of the stimuli (such as whether they have angular or curved features when the task is to detect a particular letter).

However, Treisman argues that attention must be focused on a stimulus before its features can be synthesised into a pattern. In one of Treisman & Gelade's (1980) experiments, participants were required to detect the presence of the letter T amongst an array of Is and Ys. Because the horizontal bar at the top of a T distinguishes it from an I and a Y, this could be done fairly easily just by looking for the horizontal bar. Participants took around 800 milliseconds to detect the T, and the detection time wasn't affected by the size of the array (that is, the number of Is and Ys).

In another experiment, the T was embedded in an array of Is and Zs. Here, looking for a horizontal bar on its own doesn't aid detection, since the letter Z also has a horizontal bar on top of it. To detect a T, participants needed to look for the conjunction of a horizontal and vertical line. This took around 1200 milliseconds. Moreover, detection time was longer when the size of the array was increased. On the basis of these (and other) findings, Treisman proposed her *feature-integration theory*.

Box 13.2 Treisman's feature-integration theory (FIT)

- According to Treisman, it's possible to distinguish between objects (such as a strawberry) and their features (such as being red, possessing curves and being of a particular size).
- In the *first stage* of visual processing, we process the features of stimuli in the visual environment rapidly and in parallel, without attention being required.

- Next, the features are combined to form objects (such as a small, red curved object). This *second stage* of processing is a slow and serial process.
- Focusing attention on an object's location provides the 'glue' that allows meaningless features to be formed into objects. But features can also be combined on the basis of knowledge stored in memory (such as the knowledge that strawberries are typically red).
- When relevant stored knowledge isn't available or focused attention is absent, feature combination occurs in a random way. This can produce *illusory conjunctions* (for example, a blue banana) or odd combinations of features.

(Source: based on Anderson, 1995b, and Eysenck & Keane, 1995)

An evaluation of Treisman's theory

- Treisman has claimed evidence for the occurrence of illusory conjunctions in her visual search experiments. Treisman & Schmidt (1982), for example, required participants to identify two black digits flashed in one part of the visual field. In another part, letters in various colours were presented (such as a blue T or a red S). After reporting the digits, participants were asked what letters they'd seen and their colour. Most reported seeing illusory conjunctions (such as a blue S) almost as frequently as correct conjunctions. This supports the view that accurate perception occurs only when attention is focused on an object. When it's not, the features of objects are processed but not always combined accurately.
- However, results from experiments in which moving items are intermingled with static items challenge Treisman's theory.

KEY STUDY 13.3 The moving target experiment (McLeod *et al.*, 1991)

- Participants were asked to search for the presence or absence of a single moving X amongst static Xs and moving Os.
- The target is defined only by its specific conjunction of form and movement, since its shape is shared with the static Xs and its movement with the Os.
- Treisman's theory would predict that serial attention was necessary for each item when searching for the target, so that decision times would increase with an increasing number of distractors.
- In fact, the target was found easily regardless of the display's size.
- This implies a *parallel process*, and in other experiments McLeod *et al.* showed that the parallel search arose because attention could be restricted to just the group of items with common motion to the exclusion of the static items. Because the target has a unique shape, it can be detected in parallel.

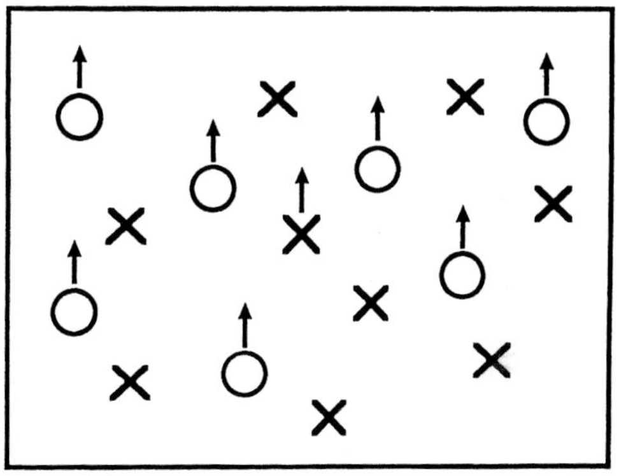

Figure 13.6 A schematic representation of the display used by McLeod *et al.* (1991). The arrows indicate motion, and the task is to search for a single moving X among moving Os and intermingled static Xs

Visual attention and brain damage

Many researchers are interested in the brain regions involved in attention (e.g. Muller & Maxwell, 1994; Halligan, 1995; Driver, 1996). People who've suffered a right-hemisphere stroke involving the *parietal lobe* may completely ignore stimuli occurring on the *left side* (see Chapter 4). For example, they may fail to eat food from the left side of their plate, and be unaware of their body on that side. The fascinating thing about this *unilateral visual neglect* is that these effects occur even though the pathways from the receptors to the central nervous system for the neglected information remain intact.

According to Posner & Petersen (1990), the parietal lobe is responsible for disengaging attention from its present focus, and patients with damage to the *pulvinar nucleus* (part of the thalami) have difficulty in shifting attention to a new target (Rafal & Posner, 1987).

Interestingly, among four- to ten-year-old children, those who took less time to switch attention in a specially devised computer game were more likely to show awareness of traffic as they approached a busy road (Dunbar *et al.*, 1999).

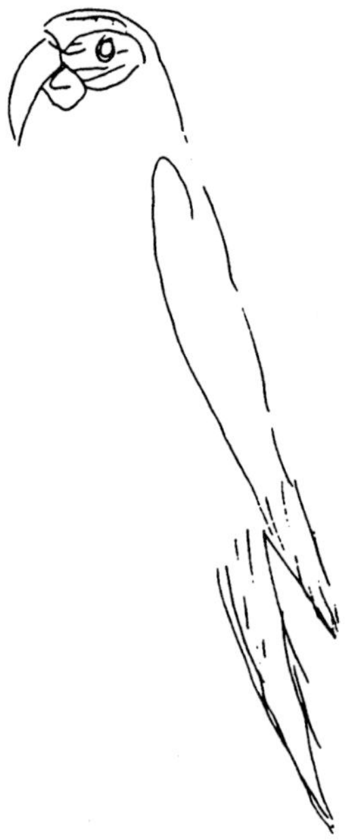

Figure 13.7 Drawing of a parrot by a person with left-side neglect

DIVIDED ATTENTION

> *ASK YOURSELF...*
> - What are you doing now, apart from reading this sentence?
> - What other examples can you give of being able to do more than one thing at a time?
> - How can you explain this ability?

Some demonstrations of dual-task performance

Allport *et al.* (1972) showed that skilled pianists were able to read music successfully while shadowing speech. Later, Shaffer (1975) reported the case of an expert typist who could type accurately from sight while shadowing speech. But perhaps the most striking example of dual-task performance comes from Spelke *et al.* (1976), who had two students spend five hours a week training at performing two tasks simultaneously.

Initially, the students were required to read short stories while writing down dictated words. At first they found this difficult, and both their comprehension and writing suffered. But after six weeks of training, they could read as quickly, and comprehend as much of what they read, when reading with dictation as when reading without it. Interestingly, though, they could remember very little of what they'd written down, even though thousands of words had been dictated to them over the course of the experiment.

At this point, the task was altered and the students had to write down the category a word belonged to (requiring more processing of the words), while simultaneously reading the short stories. Although the task was again difficult initially, they eventually performed it without any reduction in their comprehension of the stories.

Factors affecting dual-task performance

According to Hampson (1989), factors that make one task easier also tend to make the other easier because:

> Anything which minimises interference between processes or keeps them 'further apart' will allow them to be dealt with more readily either selectively or together.

Eysenck & Keane (1995) identify three factors which affect our ability to perform two tasks at once. These are *difficulty*, *practice* and *similarity*.

> **Box 13.3 The effects of difficulty, practice and similarity on dual-task performance**
>
> **Difficulty**: Generally, the more difficult the task, the less successful dual-task performance is. However, it's hard to define task difficulty objectively, since a task that's difficult for one person might not be for another (and this relates to practice: see below). Also, the demands made by two tasks individually aren't necessarily the same as when they're performed concurrently. Thus, performing two tasks together may introduce fresh demands and the risk of interference.
>
> **Practice**: As we've seen, practice improves dual-task performance. This could be because people develop new strategies for performing each task, minimising interference between them. Another possibility is that practice reduces a task's attentional demands. Finally, practice may produce a more economical way of functioning that uses fewer resources (see pages 226–228).
>
> **Similarity**: Allport *et al.* (1972) showed that when people are required to shadow one message and learn pictorial information, both tasks can be performed successfully. This is presumably because they don't involve the same stimulus modality. Two tasks also disrupt performance when both rely on related memory codes (such as visual memory), make use of the same stages of processing (such as the input stage), or require similar responses to be made.
>
> (Source: based on Eysenck and Keane, 1995)

Theories of divided attention

As we noted earlier, models of selective attention assume the existence of a limited-capacity filter capable of dealing with one information channel at a time. As Hampson & Morris (1996) have observed, these theories:

> ... imply a series of stages of processing, starting with superficial, physical analysis, and working 'upwards' towards the 'higher' cognitive analyses for meaning.

In Hampson and Morris's view, these processes are better thought of as an integrated mechanism, with the high and low levels interacting and combining in the recognition of stimuli. Accordingly, it's better to look at the system's overall processing.

Limited-capacity theories

Kahneman's theory

According to Kahneman (1973), humans have a limited amount of processing capacity, and whether or not tasks can be performed successfully depends on how much demand they make on the limited-capacity processor. Some tasks require little processing capacity, leaving plenty available for performing another task simultaneously. Others require much more, leaving little 'spare'.

The process of determining how much capacity is available ('effort') is related to the allocation of that capacity. How much capacity a task requires depends on things like its difficulty and a person's experience of it. How capacity is allocated depends on *enduring dispositions*, *momentary intentions*, and the *evaluation of the attentional demands* (see Figure 13.8, below). The central processor is responsible for the allocation policy, and constantly evaluates the level of demand. When demand is too high, the central processor must decide how available attention should be allocated.

Kahneman sees arousal as playing an important part in determining how much capacity is available. Generally, more attentional resources are available when we're aroused and alert than when we're tired and lethargic. Attention can be divided between tasks provided the total available capacity isn't exceeded. This explains the findings of the dichotic listening tasks discussed earlier: shadowing requires almost all of the capacity available, leaving the non-shadowed message insufficient capacity. Kahneman's theory also predicts that as skill at carrying out a task increases, so less capacity is needed for it and more becomes available for other tasks. Thus, when people are trained at shadowing, they become able to shadow and to attend to the non-shadowed message (Underwood, 1974).

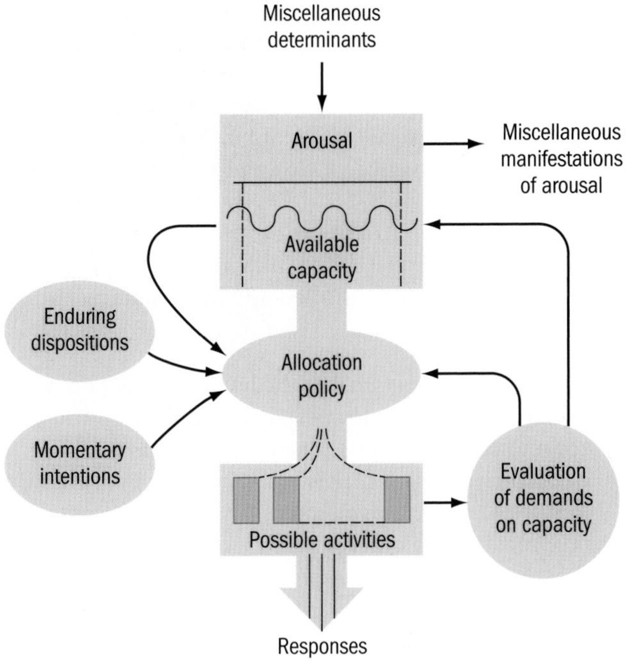

Figure 13.8 Kahneman's theory of attention. Enduring dispositions are the rules for allocating capacity which are outside voluntary control. These include allocating capacity to novel stimuli and hearing one's own name used in a different conversation. Momentary intentions are voluntary shifts in attention such as listening to a message in a dichotic listening task. Evaluation of demands on capacity include rules for overload on the system, such as deciding to complete one task rather than failing to complete two

Evaluation of Kahneman's theory

Kahneman's theory portrays attention as a much more flexible and dynamic system than do the models of focused attention. However, it doesn't address the issue of how decisions to channel attention are made. The difficulty in defining the general limits of capacity has led some researchers to suggest that the concept of a limited capacity should be abandoned (Hampson & Morris, 1996).

Norman and Bobrow's theory

Following on from Kahneman, Norman & Bobrow (1975) have offered a *central capacity interference account* of attentional phenomena.

Box 13.4 Norman & Bobrow's (1975) central capacity interference theory (CCIT)

- This theory's central feature is its distinction between *resource-limited* and *data-limited* processes.
- On a complex task, performance is related to the amount of resources devoted to it. As more resources are allocated, so task performance improves *up to some point*. Performance is thus resource-limited.
- But on some tasks, applying more resources doesn't lead to improved performance because of external influences (as when participants are required to identify a quiet tone amongst loud, masking 'white' noise). This sort of task is data-limited, because performance can be improved only by altering the stimuli (such as by making the tone louder and/or the masking noise quieter).

Evaluation of Norman and Bobrow's theory

This distinction between resource- and data-limited processes can explain findings from both focused and divided attention research. For example, Treisman & Geffen (1967: see page 220) found that participants shadowing words in one ear had difficulty recognising target words presented simultaneously to the other ear. Lawson (1966), however, found that under similar conditions participants could detect target tones presented in the non-attended ear. This finding can be explained by proposing that the tone-detection process becomes data-limited much sooner than the word-recognition process.

However, the theory's biggest weakness is its inability to predict beforehand the results an experiment is likely to produce. Because it allows for differential allocation of resources to tasks, an experimenter can never know the level of resources allocated to a particular task. Any results can therefore be interpreted in a way consistent with the theory, and no results can ever be taken as negative evidence.

Multi-channel theories

Supporters of limited-capacity models defend their approach by pointing out that the attentional system breaks down as more and more is demanded of it. Also, if data from divided-attention studies are considered carefully it's not true that two tasks can be performed together with no disruption at all (Broadbent, 1982). Nevertheless, several researchers have rejected the concept of a general-purpose, limited-capacity processor completely. For Allport (1980b, 1989, 1993), the concept of attention is often used synonymously with 'consciousness', with no specification of how it operates. This has done little to increase our understanding of the very problems it's meant to explain.

Modules and multiple resources

According to Allport, it's difficult to see how the neurology of the brain could produce a system of processing capacity that was completely open to any of the tasks that might be presented to it (Hampson & Morris, 1996). It's much more profitable to view the data in terms of tasks competing for the same specialised processing mechanisms or modules, each of which has a limited capacity but none of which is uniquely 'central'.

When two tasks are highly similar, they compete for the same modules, and this leads to performance impairments. However, because dissimilar tasks use different modules, both can be performed simultaneously. A virtually identical theoretical account has been proposed by Navon & Gopher (1979) and Wickens (1992) in their *multiple-resource theory*. Certainly, the findings of dual-task studies (e.g. Allport *et al.*, 1972) are consistent with the idea of different processing mechanisms handling the requirements of different tasks.

However, this approach is also non-falsifiable, since any pattern of data can be explained by proposing the existence of a particular pattern of modules (Navon, 1984). If multiple resources do operate in parallel, they must do so in a highly integrated way, since our behaviour is typically coherent (Eysenck & Keane, 1995).

Attempts at synthesising capacity and module accounts

According to Eysenck (1982, 1984, 1997a) and Baddeley (1986), a much better way of accommodating the data from divided-attention studies is to see capacity and module accounts as being complementary rather than competitive. *Synthesis models* propose the existence of a *modality-free central capacity processor*, which is involved in the coordination and control of behaviour, and *specific processing systems*. In Baddeley's (1986) *working memory model*, for example, there are two independently operating and specific systems, an *articulatory/phonological loop* and a *visuo-spatial scratch pad*. These systems can explain why overt repetition of an overlearned sequence of digits doesn't interfere with verbal reasoning, since the former uses an articulatory loop and the latter a central processor (see Chapter 17, pages 292–294).

> *ASK YOURSELF...*
> - Thinking of a skill you possess (such as driving a car or playing a musical instrument), how did demands on your attention and concentration change during the course of acquiring it?
> - Can you now do things at the same time as performing these skills that you couldn't have done while learning them?

Automatic vs controlled processing

As we've seen, both laboratory evidence and everyday experience indicate that we can learn to perform two tasks simultaneously and highly efficiently. For some researchers, this is because many processes become *automatic*, that is, they make no attentional demands, if they're used/practised often enough. Two important theoretical contributions are those of Schneider & Shiffrin (1977) and Norman & Shallice (1986).

Schneider and Shiffrin's automaticity model

Schneider & Shiffrin (1977; Shiffrin & Schneider, 1977) distinguish between controlled and automatic attentional processing as follows:

- *controlled processing* makes heavy demands on attentional resources, is slow, capacity-limited, and involves consciously directing attention towards a task
- *automatic processing* makes no demands on attentional resources, is fast, unaffected by capacity limitations, unavoidable and difficult to modify (it always occurs in the presence of an appropriate stimulus), and isn't subject to conscious awareness.

The results of several studies (e.g. Schneider & Fisk, 1982) are consistent with Schneider and Shiffrin's view. If people are given practice at a task, they can perform it quickly and accurately, but their performance is resistant to change. An example of apparent automaticity in real life occurs when we learn to drive a car. At first, focused attention is required for each component of driving, and any distraction can disrupt performance. Once we've learned to drive, and as we become more experienced, our ability to attend simultaneously to other things increases.

At first, learning to drive a car, like other psychomotor skills, requires focused attention. The experienced driver, however, displays automaticity

Logan (1988) suggests that automaticity develops through practice, because automatic responses involve an almost effortless retrieval of an appropriate and well-learned response from memory. This doesn't involve conscious memory, because no thought processes intervene between the presentation of a stimulus and the production of an appropriate response. In Logan's view, then, automaticity occurs when stored information about the sequence of responses necessary to perform a task can be accessed and retrieved rapidly.

An evaluation of Schneider and Shiffrin's model

Despite its intuitive appeal, it's unclear whether automaticity results from a speeding up of the processes involved in a task, or a change in the nature of the processes themselves. Also, the view that automatic processing makes no demands on attention has been challenged by findings indicating that allegedly automatic tasks do influence the performance of simultaneously performed tasks (e.g. Hampson, 1989). Additional problems occur with the Stroop effect.

KEY STUDY 13.4 The Stroop effect

- Stroop (1935) showed that if a colour word (such as 'blue') is written in a conflicting colour (such as 'blue' being written in red), participants find it difficult to name the colour the word's been written in.

RED	BLACK
BLUE	YELLOW
GREEN	BLACK
YELLOW	GREEN
BLUE	RED

- Because reading is such a well-learned, unavoidable and automatic activity, the word interferes with the requirement to name the colour.

ASK YOURSELF...

An analogue of the Stroop effect can be tried here.

- Say as quickly as you can the number of characters in each of the rows below.

5 5 5
1 1 1 1
2
3 3 3 3 3
4 4
5 5 5
4 4 4 4 4
5 5 5 5
3
4 4 4
2 2 2 2
3 3
4 4 4
1 1 1 1
3
2 2 2

- Flowers *et al.* (1979) found that people have difficulty resisting saying the numbers that make up each row rather than counting the numbers, because number recognition is much more automatic compared with number counting. But automatic responses aren't always unavoidable (Eysenck, 1993).

Norman and Shallice's SAS model

To overcome what Eysenck (1993) calls the 'unavoidability criterion', Norman & Shallice (1986) proposed that processing involves two separate control systems: *contention scheduling* and the *supervisory attentional system* (SAS). Some behaviours involve *fully automatic processing*, which occurs with little conscious awareness of the processes involved, and is controlled by *schemas* (organised plans for behaviour: see below, and Chapter 21, pages 356–358).

However, such processes are capable of disrupting behaviour, and so contention scheduling occurs as a way of resolving conflicts among schemas. This produces *partially automatic processing*, which generally involves more conscious awareness than fully automatic processing, but doesn't require deliberate direction or conscious control. *Deliberate control* involves the SAS and occurs in decision-making and trouble-shooting, allowing flexible responding to occur in novel situations. Baddeley (1997) claims that the SAS is like the operation of free will, while contention scheduling leaves no place for free will (see Chapter 49).

An evaluation of Norman and Shallice's model

According to Eysenck & Keane (1995), Norman and Shallice's model is superior to Schneider and Shiffrin's because it:

... provides a more natural explanation for the fact that some processes are fully automatic whereas others are only partially automatic.

Their SAS model isn't worked out in the same degree of detail, nor empirically tested as extensively as Schneider and Shiffrin's automaticity model. But it provides a very useful basis for conceptualising the central executive of Baddeley & Hitch's (1974) working-memory model (Baddeley, 1997: see Chapter 17, pages 292–294).

Action slips

ASK YOURSELF...

- Have you ever done something you didn't intend to do or, conversely, failed to do something you *did* intend to do?
- How might you explain these 'lapses' in terms of attentional processes?

Action slips have been defined as the performance of unintended actions, or actions which deviate from the actor's intentions, and have been extensively researched by Reason (1979, 1992). Reason originally asked 36 participants to keep a diary record of the action slips they made over a four-week period; they recorded 433 action slips between them. Reason was able to place 94 per cent of these into one of five categories.

Box 13.5 Reason's five categories of action slips

Storage failures: repeating an action that's already been completed. For example, pouring a second kettle of boiling water into a teapot of freshly made tea without any recognition of having made the tea already. These were the most common, accounting for 40 per cent of those recorded.
Test failures (20 per cent): forgetting the goal of a particular sequence of actions and switching to a different goal. For example, intending to turn on the radio but walking past it and picking up the telephone instead. These occur, presumably, because a planned sequence of actions isn't monitored sufficiently at some crucial point in the sequence.
Sub-routine failures (18 per cent): either omitting or re-ordering the stages in a sequence of behaviour. For example, making a pot of tea but failing to put any tea bags in it.
Discrimination failures (11 per cent): failing to discriminate between two objects involved in different actions. For example, mistaking toothpaste for shaving cream.
Programme assembly failures (5 per cent): incorrectly combining actions, as in unwrapping a sweet, putting the paper in your mouth and throwing the sweet in the waste-paper bin.

(Source: based on Reason, 1992, and Eysenck, 1997b)

Explaining action slips

Closed- and open-loop control

Paradoxically, action slips seem to occur with highly practised and over-learned actions (which should, therefore, be least subject to errors). Reason (1992) proposes that when we first learn to perform a behaviour, our actions are subject to *closed-loop control* (Adams, 1976). In this, a central processor or attentional system guides and controls a behaviour from start to finish. When we're skilled at a behaviour, it's under *open-loop control*, controlled by motor programmes or other automatic processes.

Closed-loop control is slow and effortful, whereas open-loop control is fast and allows attentional resources to be given over to other activities. However, closed-loop control is less prone to error and responds more flexibly to environmental demands than open-loop control. As a result, action slips occur because of an over-reliance on open-loop control when closed-loop control (selectively attending to the task) should be occurring.

As we saw in studies of focused attention, material not attended to is typically poorly remembered because it doesn't get stored in long-term memory. So, storage failures, the most common type of action slip, can be explained in terms of open-loop induced attentional failures leading to a failure to store (and hence recall) previous actions. As a result, an action may be repeated. Other slips also seem amenable to explanation in terms of open-loop control (Eysenck, 1997b).

Schema theory

An alternative theoretical account has been advanced by Norman (1981) and elaborated by Sellen & Norman (1992). Their theory is based on the concept of the schema, first proposed by Bartlett (1932). Briefly, a schema is an organised mental representation of everything we understand by a given object, concept or event, based on past experience.

Box 13.6 Sellen & Norman's (1992) schema theory of action slips

- *Parent schemas* are the highest-level schemas, corresponding to an overall intention or goal (such as going to a football match).
- At a lower level are *child schemas*, which correspond to the actions involved in accomplishing the overall intention or goal (such as driving the car to the football ground, buying a ticket, and so on).
- Each schema has a particular *activation level*, and a behaviour occurs when the activation level is reached (which depends on the current situation and current intentions) and when appropriate 'triggering' conditions exist. If:

(a) there's an error in the formation of an intention;
(b) an incorrect schema is activated;

(c) activation of the correct schema is lost; or
(d) there's faulty triggering of an active schema,
(e) then an action slip occurs.

Reason & Mycielska (1982) believe that a thorough understanding of the nature of action slips is necessary to avoid potential disaster occurring in the real world. Eysenck (1995) maintains that action slips would be eliminated if we were to use closed-loop control for all behaviours, but this would be a waste of valuable attentional resources! The frequency of action slips reported by Reason's (1979) participants (an average of about one per day) suggests that people alternate between closed-loop and open-loop control as the circumstances dictate. For Eysenck (1995):

> The very occasional action slip is a price which is generally worth paying in order to free the attentional system from the task of constant monitoring of our habitual actions.

Action slips represent the minor errors of an action system that typically functions very well indeed (Eysenck, 1997b). Similarly:

> Absent-minded errors demonstrate misapplied competence rather than incompetence. (Reason, 1984)

Each type of action slip might require its own explanation. While the mechanisms underlying them may appear similar, they might actually be very different (Eysenck & Keane, 1995). Additionally, any theoretical account depends on the validity of the data it attempts to explain. The diary method used by Reason may supply weak data, because participants might not have detected some of their action slips or remembered to record them when they did (Eysenck, 1997b). As a result, the percentages reported by Reason may be inaccurate.

Box 13.7 Reason's (1992) 'oak–yolk effect' experiment

ASK YOURSELF...

- Answer the following series of questions as quickly as possible:
  - Q What do we call the tree that grows from acorns?
  - A Oak
  - Q What do we call a funny story?
  - A Joke
  - Q What sound does a frog make?
  - A Croak
  - Q What is Pepsi's major competitor?
  - A Coke
  - Q What's another word for cape?
  - A Cloak
  - Q What do you call the white of an egg?
  - A Yolk

'Yolk' is, in fact, the *wrong* answer (correct answer = albumen). Reason found that 85 per cent of his participants made this error, compared with only 5 per cent of a control group given just the final question. However, are such trick-induced action slips comparable to those that occur spontaneously in everyday life? According to Sellen & Norman (1992), the laboratory environment is the least likely place to see truly spontaneous absent-minded errors.

Finally, in Eysenck & Keane's (1995) words:

> The number of occurrences of any particular kind of action slip is meaningful only when we know the number of occasions on which the slip might have occurred but did not. Thus, the small number of discrimination failures [reported by Reason] may reflect either good discrimination or a relative lack of situations requiring anything approaching a fine discrimination.

CONCLUSIONS

It's sometimes possible to divide attention between two different tasks, although how this is achieved hasn't yet been satisfactorily explained. Two broad types of explanation are those that propose a general purpose limited-capacity processor, and those that identify modules, each with a limited capacity but none of which is central. The idea that many processes become automatic and make no demands on attention has some support, and helps explain why we sometimes perform behaviours we didn't intend. Action slips involve behaviours that are highly practised, and are the price we pay for not having continuously to monitor our actions.

CHAPTER SUMMARY

- According to Broadbent, who was trying to account for Cherry's **cocktail party phenomenon**, humans must **selectively attend** to some information and 'tune out' the rest.
- Using **binaural listening**, Cherry identified several physical differences affecting selective attention to one of two messages. He also used **dichotic listening**, in which participants had to **shadow** one of the messages. They could do this, but remembered little, if anything, of the non-shadowed message, whose meaning was completely lost.
- Three **single-channel models** share the belief in a 'bottleneck' or **filter** which allows some information to be passed on for further processing, either discarding the rest or processing it only to a limited degree. They differ mainly in terms of how early or late the filtering takes place.
- Broadbent's **early selection filter theory** accounts for Cherry's findings and his own **split-span** data. But people's ability to switch attention to the non-attended ear when their name is spoken, together with other research findings relating to the processing of **meaning**, are inconsistent with Broadbent's account.

- According to Treisman's **attenuation model**, competing information is analysed for its physical properties, *and* for sounds, syllable patterns, grammatical structures and meaning. The selective filter 'turns down' the non-shadowed message. If this includes biological 'pre-sets', our attention will switch to the non-shadowed message.
- The Deutsch–Norman **late-selection filter theory/pertinence model** sees selection as occurring only after all inputs have been analysed at a high level. The filter is nearer the response end of the processing system.
- Mechanisms involved in **focused visual attention** include eye movements that allow us to fixate specific regions of the visual field. But visual attention *isn't* confined to the part of the visual field processed by the fovea, as demonstrated by **covert attention**. This is like an **internal mental spotlight**.
- According to Eriksen's **zoom-lens model**, the internal spotlight has a beam which may be very narrow or very broad.
- According to Treisman's **feature-integration theory** (FIT), focusing attention on their location allows unitary **features** to be formed into their various **objects**. **Illusory conjunctions** can arise in the absence of relevant stored knowledge or focused attention.
- Researchers interested in **divided attention** typically measure **dual-task performance**. Three factors affecting dual-task performance are **task difficulty**, **practice** and **similarity**.
- According to Kahneman, humans have only a limited processing capacity. Different tasks require different amounts of processing capacity, leaving more or less available for performing other tasks.
- The **central processor** controls the allocation policy and constantly evaluates demand level. **Arousal** is important for determining the amount of available capacity, and the more skilled we are at a particular task, the less capacity is needed.
- Norman and Bobrow's **central capacity interference theory** (CCIT) distinguishes between **resource-limited** and **data-limited performance**.
- Several researchers have rejected the concept of a general purpose, limited-capacity processor. The most useful way of interpreting the data is in terms of tasks competing for the same **modules**, each of which has a limited capacity but none of which is uniquely 'central'.
- Two highly similar tasks compete for the same modules, leading to performance deficits, while dissimilar tasks use different modules and thus don't compete. This view is also taken by **multiple-resource theory**.
- **Synthesis models** propose the existence of a modality-free central capacity processor, plus specific independent processing systems, such as Baddeley's **articulatory/phonological loop** and **visuo-spatial scratch pad**.
- Schneider and Shiffrin distinguish between **controlled** and **automatic processing**. The '**Stroop effect**' shows that well-learned, unavoidable and automatic skills (such as reading) can interfere with other tasks (such as naming the colour of a written word).
- **Contention scheduling** is used to resolve conflicts among **schemas**, which control **fully automatic processing** and produces **partially automatic processing**. The **supervisory attentional system** (SAS) is involved in **deliberate control**, which allows flexible responses in novel situations.
- The most common types of **action slips** are **storage failures**. Other categories include **test**, **sub-routine**, **discrimination** and **programme assembly failures**.
- Action slips seem to involve actions that are highly practised or over-learned. Action slips reflect an over-reliance on **open-loop control** when **closed-loop control** (focused attention) is needed. Different types of action slip may require their own explanations.

Links with other topics/chapters

- The concept of attention has been defined in more *biological/physiological* ways, as referring to *arousal level, vigilance* and *alertness* (*consciousness*) (Chapters 7 and 9), and more *cognitively*. It features prominently in the cognitive revolution (Chapters 1, 2 and 3), in which *information processing* and the *computer analogy* are central (Chapter 20).
- The dependent variable (DV) in many experimental studies of both selective and divided attention is operationalised in terms of *recall* and other forms of *remembering* (Chapter 17).
- Explanations of focused visual attention go beyond what's known about the sensitivity of the *fovea* (Chapter 5).
- A person who suffers damage to the right *parietal lobe* will suffer left-sided unilateral visual neglect (Chapter 4).
- Controlled processing and deliberate control (which involves the supervisory attentional system/SAS) can be seen in terms of *free will*, while automatic processing and contention scheduling leave no room for free will (Chapter 49).
- Baddeley and Hitch's *working memory model* (of *short-term* memory) is essentially a synthesis model of divided attention: a *central executive* has overall control of two major 'slave systems', *an articulatory/phonological loop* and a *visuo-spatial scratch* (or *sketch*) *pad*. (Chapter 17).
- Norman and Shallice's SAS provides a useful basis for conceptualising the *central executive* (Chapter 17).
- Sellen and Norman's *schema* theory of action slips stems from Bartlett's research into *reconstructive memory* and the more general *schema theory* of everyday memory (Chapter 21).

14

PATTERN RECOGNITION

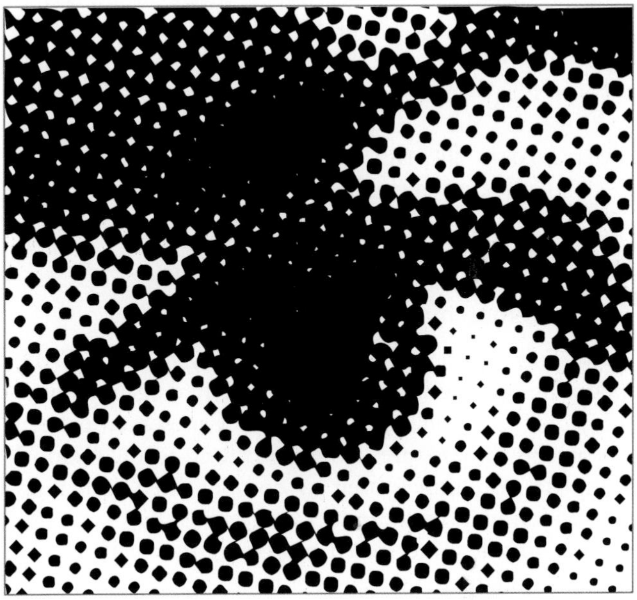

INTRODUCTION AND OVERVIEW

Pattern recognition is the process by which we assign meaning to visual input by identifying the objects in the visual field (Eysenck, 1993). Although our ability to recognise, identify and categorise objects seems effortless, it actually comprises several remarkably complex achievements. While we're usually aware only of structured, coherent objects:

> Our visual systems have to 'decide' which edges, surfaces, corners and so on go together to form units or wholes. (Roth, 1995)

As Roth says, what theories of pattern recognition must do is explain the complexity of a process which 'is so ingrained in our experience that we rarely even notice that we do it' (Houston *et al.*, 1991). A way of illustrating this challenge is to consider the ease with which we're able to recognise the letter 'T', whether it's printed on paper, handwritten or spoken.

T T T T T T T T T T T T T T T T T T T T T T T

A major contribution to our understanding of this process comes in the form of the Gestalt laws of perception, which are discussed in Chapter 15. Pattern (or object) recognition can be regarded as the central problem of perception and, indeed, the terms are almost synonymous. To this extent, all the theories of perception discussed in Chapter 15 can be thought of as trying to account for pattern recognition (PR).

However, the theories discussed here are usually referred to as theories of PR (rather than perceptual theories). *Face recognition* is a special case of PR.

THEORIES OF PR

Template-matching hypothesis

According to the *template-matching hypothesis* (TMH), incoming sensory information is matched against miniature copies (or *templates*) of previously presented patterns or objects. These are stored in long-term memory. Template matching is used by computerised cash registers, which identify a product and its cost by matching a bar code with some stored representation of that code. Every product has a unique bar code.

7 33809 00031 4

Figure 14.1 The bar codes on the goods we buy identify them. When the bar code is read by a computerised cash register (scanned), the computer supplies the price, which is then entered on the cash register tape. The code is read by template-matching on the basis of the positions, widths and spacing of the lines

An evaluation of TMH

Given the complexity of the environment, we'd need an incredibly large number of templates, each corresponding to a specific visual input. Even if we were able to use a wheelbarrow to carry around the cerebrum needed for this, the time needed to search for a specific template would be inordinately long, and we'd never recognise unfamiliar patterns (Solso, 1995).

> *ASK YOURSELF...*
> - How would you describe (a) a cup, (b) a torch, (c) a penguin?
> - What kinds of basic components could they be broken down into?

Biederman's geon theory

Biederman's (1987) *geon theory* of PR ('geon' stands for 'geometrical icon'), or *recognition-by-components model*, is intended to overcome TMH's limitations. Biederman's starting point is the everyday observation that if we're asked to describe an object, familiar or unfamiliar, we tend to use the same basic strategy. We almost certainly divide it into parts or components (*parsing/segmentation*), comprising various three-dimensional-shape concepts (*volumetric concepts* or *geons*), such as 'block', 'cylinder', 'funnel' and 'wedge'.

The regions of the object used to divide it up are probably the regions of greatest *concavity* (where one part makes a sharp angle with another part). According to geon theory, a very large range of different objects can be described by combining geons in various ways. Geons (simple geometric 'primitives') can be combined to produce more complex ones.

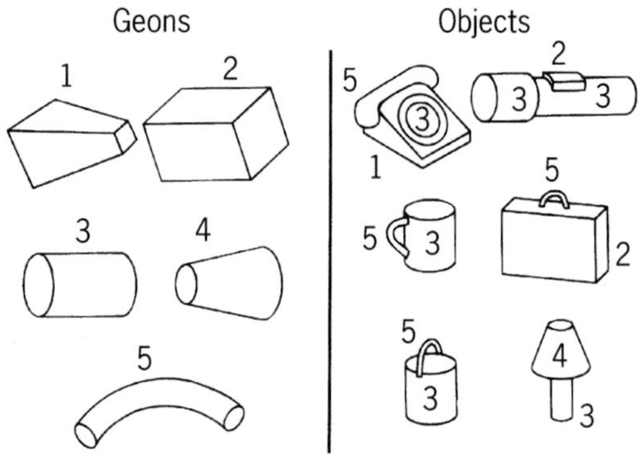

Figure 14.2 Biederman's geons (left) and some of the objects they can combine to make (right)

Component- or geon-based information extracted from the visual object is matched in parallel against stored representations of 36 geons that make up the basic set. The identification of any visual object is determined by whichever stored representation provides the best fit. But for a complete object to be recognised, there must also be a store of *complete* object descriptions, in which both the characteristic geon set and *relationships* amongst it are specified (Roth, 1995).

Tests of geon theory

According to Roth (1995), Biederman's theory was designed to:

- provide an intuitively plausible account of how we recognise objects in terms of their obvious components
- explain the fact that this recognition is both rapid and accurate, despite variations in angle of viewing and the 'degraded' information available (such as poor lighting, one object obscuring another, and so on).

One general prediction is that since an appropriate arrangement of geons provides a very powerful cue for object recognition, this recognition will occur even when an object's full complement of geons is absent.

KEY STUDY 14.1 Geons can be so degrading (Biederman, 1987)

- Biederman produced line drawings of 36 common objects, differing in complexity (the number of basic geon components needed to draw them ranged from two to nine).
- For each drawing, there were 'partial' versions (one or more geons were missing), and each stimulus was presented for 100 m/secs via a tachistoscope. Participants had to name the object aloud as quickly as possible.

Figure 14.3 Complete and partial versions of objects used in Biederman's experiment

- Error rates for 'partial' objects were extremely low, with 90 per cent accuracy even for complex objects with two-thirds of their components missing.
- So, even the simplest line drawings can be readily and correctly identified, provided the relevant geons are present. These findings are consistent with geon theory.
- Also, response times were almost as fast for partial as for complete objects, although complex complete objects were identified slightly more quickly than simple ones. This, too, is consistent with the theory: if an object's geons are simultaneously matched with stored geon descriptions, then the greater the number of such geons available, the faster the critical level needed for a 'match' will be reached.

A more stringent test is participants' ability to identify degraded versions of objects, in which the normal contours are disrupted. In a second experiment (using the same basic procedure as the first), Biederman presented stimulus objects like those shown in Figure 14.4.

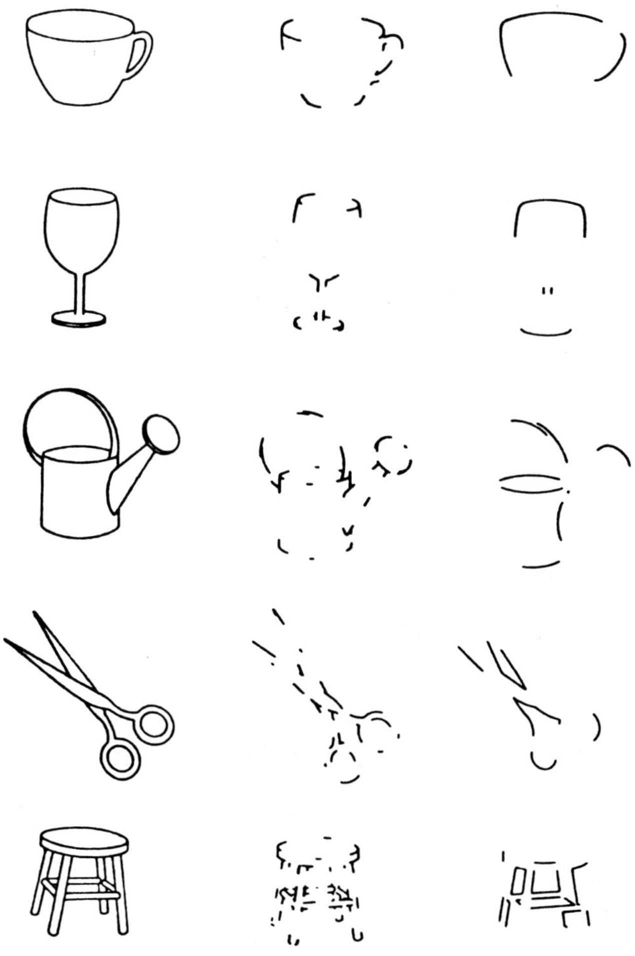

Figure 14.4 The middle column shows degraded but 'recognisable' versions; the right-hand column shows 'non-recognisable' versions

In the right-hand column, the contours have been deleted at regions of concavity. These stimuli were presented for 100, 200 or 750 m/secs, with 25, 45 or 65 per cent of their contours removed. Once again, results supported the theory.

An evaluation of geon theory

Roth (1995) believes that geons are intuitively appealing, and that they also offer a relatively flexible and comprehensive system for describing objects. Geons include a range of different shapes that can be applied not only to artefacts such as chairs, tables and houses, but also to mammals and other animals.

Although the theory makes clear predictions that can be experimentally tested (see Key Study 14.1), identification of the 36 geons and structural relationships is based more on 'hunch' than empirical evidence. There have been *no* tests to determine whether it's *these* geons that are used in object recognition, rather than other components.

Prototype theories of PR

Prototype theories propose that instead of storing templates, we store a smaller number of *prototypes* ('abstract forms representing the basic elements of a set of stimuli': Eysenck, 1993). Whereas TMH treats each stimulus as a separate entity, prototype theories maintain that similarities between related stimuli play an important part in PR. So, each stimulus is a member of a *category* of stimuli and shares basic properties with other members of the category.

An evaluation of prototype theories

The main weakness of this approach is its inability to explain how PR is affected by the *context*, as well as by the stimulus itself (Eysenck, 1993). Knowing just what properties are shared by a category of stimuli is important, but not specified by the theories. What, for example, is an 'idealised' letter 'T' and what is the 'best representation of the pattern'? This question has been addressed by *feature-detection theories*.

Feature-detection theories

Feature-detection theories form the most influential approach to PR, maintaining that every stimulus can be thought of as a configuration of elementary features. Gibson *et al.* (1968) argue that the letters of the alphabet, for example, are composed of combinations of 12 basic features (such as vertical lines, horizontal lines and closed curves).

In *visual scanning tasks*, participants search lists of letters as quickly as possible to find a randomly placed target letter. Since finding a target letter entails detecting its elementary features, the task should be more difficult when the target and non-target letters have more features in common. This is exactly what researchers (e.g. Rabbitt, 1967) have found. Additional support comes from studies of eye movements and fixation. Presumably, the more a feature in a pattern is looked at, the more information is being extracted from it. The perception of features within complex patterns depends on higher cognitive processes (such as attention and purpose), as well as the nature of the physical stimuli being looked at.

It's also well established that the visual systems of some vertebrates contain both peripheral (retinal) and central (cortical) cells that respond only to particular features of visual stimuli. In their pioneering research, Hubel & Wiesel (1968) identified three kinds of cortical cell ('simple', 'complex' and 'hypercomplex', referring to the types of stimuli the cells respond to: see Box 5.9, page 86). More recently, it's been claimed that there are face-specific cells in the infero–temporal cortex of the monkey (Ono *et al.*, 1993: see below, page 241).

In humans, Perrett (cited in Messer, 1995) has identified cells that respond to specific aspects of a face or to a set of features. There may also be cells that respond to many different views of a face, 'summing' inputs from a variety of sources.

KEY STUDY 14.2 Eye movements reflect what you're looking for (Yarbus, 1967)

Yarbus found that when participants were shown the scene in Figure 14.5, different patterns of eye movements were recorded depending on whether they were asked to:

- examine the picture at will
- estimate the economic status of the people shown
- judge their ages
- query what they had been doing prior to the arrival of the visitor
- remember their clothing
- remember their positions (and objects in the room), or
- estimate how long since the visitor had last seen the family.

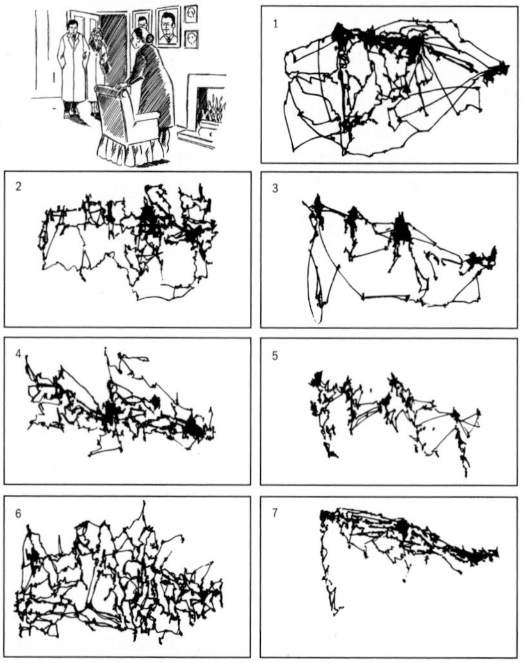

Figure 14.5 Different patterns of eye movements corresponding to different instructions

An evaluation of feature-detection theories

Whether such cells constitute the feature detectors proposed by feature-detection theories is unclear. These neurological detectors may be a necessary pre-condition for higher-level (or cognitive) pattern task analysis. However, feature-detection theories typically assume a *serial* form of processing, with feature extraction being followed by feature combination, which itself is then followed by PR (Eysenck, 1993). For example, Hubel and Wiesel saw the sequence of simple, complex and hypercomplex cells representing a serial flow of information, whereby only particular information is processed at any one time before being passed on to the next level upwards, and so on.

The alternative and widely held view is that considerable *parallel* processing takes place in the visual cortex, and that the relationship between different kinds of cortical cell is more complex than originally believed. An early example of a non-serial processing computer program is Selfridge's (1959) *Pandemonium model.*

Box 14.1 Selfridge's (1959) Pandemonium model

Selfridge's computer program was designed to recognise Morse code and a small set of handwritten letters. The components of the model are known as *demons*, of which there are four kinds:

1. *image demons* simply copy the pattern presented (and these are analogous to the retina)
2. *feature demons* analyse the information from the image demons in terms of combinations of features
3. *cognitive demons* are specialised for particular letters and 'scream' according to how much the input from the feature demons matches their special letter
4. finally, a *decision demon* chooses the 'loudest scream' and identifies the letter (see Figure 14.6).

Although Pandemonium was never intended as a model of human perception, Groome *et al.* (1999) ask what assumptions about human perception would need to be made if it were modelled. These could then be tested against human data. One such assumption is that context would have minimal effect on PR. Feature-detection theories in general have been criticised for not taking sufficient account of the role played by *context* and *perceiver characteristics* (such as *expectations*: see Box 15.4, page 256). An ambiguous feature can produce *different* patterns, and different features can produce the *same* pattern, depending on the context.

Context can tell us what patterns are likely to be present and, hence, what to expect. Sometimes we may fail to notice the absence of something (such as a typing or printing error) because of its high predictability. The influence of context and expectation illustrates *top-down/conceptually driven processing*, while most feature-detection theories are *bottom-up/data-driven* (see theories of perception in Chapter 15). PR involves selectively attending to some aspects of the presented stimuli but not to others, aided by context. PR and selective attention are therefore closely related (Solso, 1995: see Chapter 13).

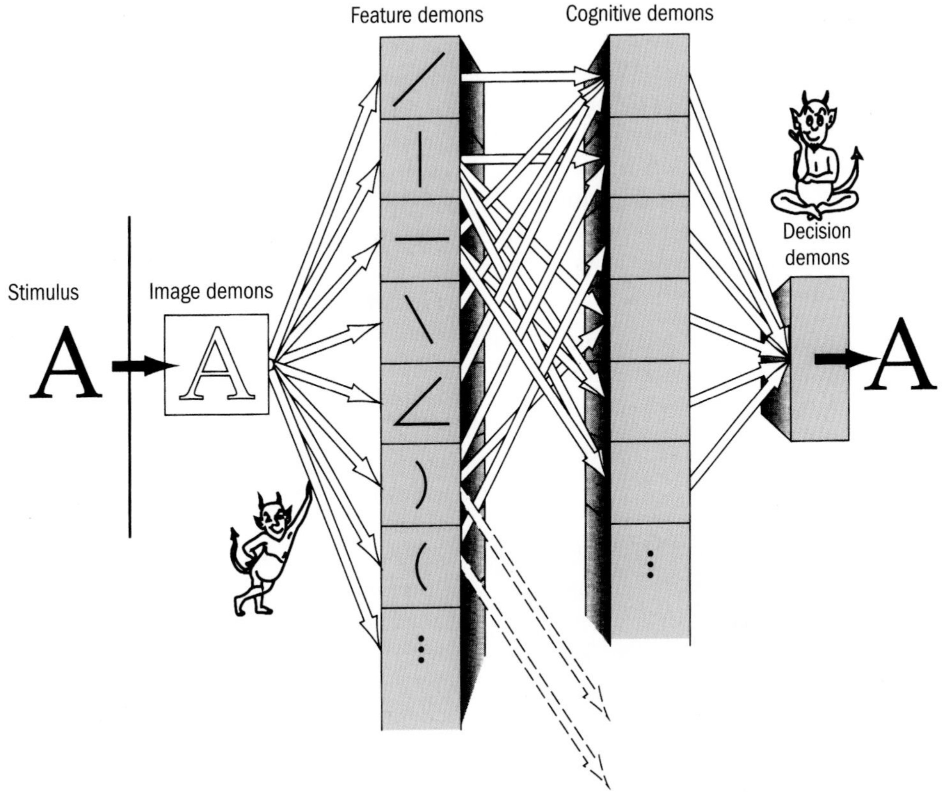

Figure 14.6 A representation of Selfridge's Pandemonium model of pattern recognition (based on Ruch, 1984)

Just as we can identify different categories of dogs or chairs, so we can identify 'baby's face', 'man's face' or, say, 'Japanese face'. We also have some ability to identify individual dogs or chairs, but in the case of human faces this ability to identify individuals is of paramount importance (Bruce, 1995). Recognising faces is probably one of the most demanding tasks that we set our visual systems. Unlike most other cases of object identification, the task is to identify one specific instance of the class of objects known as faces (Groome *et al.*, 1999).

Strictly, *face recognition* (using the face to identify an individual) is part of the broader process of *face perception* (the whole range of activities where information is derived from the face, such as inferring emotional states from facial expressions). According to Eysenck & Keane (1995), substantial recent research has provided greater knowledge about the processes involved in face recognition than about those involved in most other forms of PR.

Are faces more than the sum of their parts?

> *ASK YOURSELF...*
> - Choose a familiar face (friend, lecturer, film star) and describe it.
> - What makes this face unique – that is, what enables you to recognise it as that specific face?
> - What do all faces have in common?

Based on theories of basic-level PR (such as Biederman's geon theory), faces could be described as a set of parts (the features) and their spatial arrangement. When we're asked to describe a face, or speculate about how individual faces are represented in memory, we're likely to think in terms of separate features. This tendency is undoubtedly created partly by our language, which has discrete terms for the different functional parts of the face. But the *visual system* may not describe faces in this way. According to Bruce & Young (1998):

> ... there is a good deal of evidence that face patterns are treated more as wholes or as interrelationships between different features, than simply as a list of their features ...

In other words, it seems more valid to describe faces in a more *configural* way (Bruce, 1995).

Box 14.2 The meanings of 'configural'

According to Bruce (1995), although psychologists tend to agree that a face is greater than the sum of its parts, studies of face perception haven't always made explicit which sense of 'configural' is being investigated. She identifies three meanings.

1. The *spatial relationships* between features are as important as the features themselves.
2. Facial features *interact* with one another (for example, perception of mouth shape is affected by the shape of the nose).
3. Faces are processed *holistically* (they aren't analysed into separable features at all).

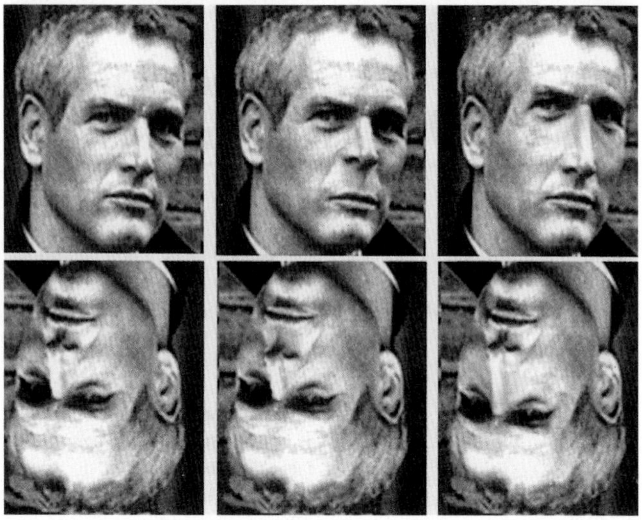

You should find it easy to detect which image shows the real Paul Newman, though the distortions are much easier to see in the upright than in the inverted images (from Bruce & Young 1998)

However, early research into face recognition implicitly assumed that a part-based description *might* be appropriate, comprising a list of features each with different specific values. Many psychologists during the 1970s used *artificially constructed faces*, such as Bradshaw & Wallace's (1971) use of Identikit (Figure 14.7). This refers to a set of varying line-drawn features used by the police to construct a criminal/suspect's face, based on a witness's description (see Chapter 21).

Bradshaw and Wallace presented pairs of faces to see how quickly participants decided that two faces in a pair were different as a function of the number of features that differed. They found that the *more* differences between the two faces, the *faster* participants responded. They concluded that facial features are processed *independently* and *in sequence*. Sergent (1984) reviewed several other studies that reached similar conclusions.

However, Sergent also noted that faces that differed in several features also differed more in terms of overall configuration than those differing only in a few. If features really are processed independently, the number of feature differences shouldn't affect how quickly a 'difference' judgement is made (the judgement can be made as soon as any one feature difference is spotted). Accordingly, Sergent constructed eight slightly different faces from the same 'kit' of face features, but each had one of two different *chins*, *eye colours* and arrangements of internal features (*internal space*). 'Different' pairs (one, two or three feature differences) were intermixed with pairs

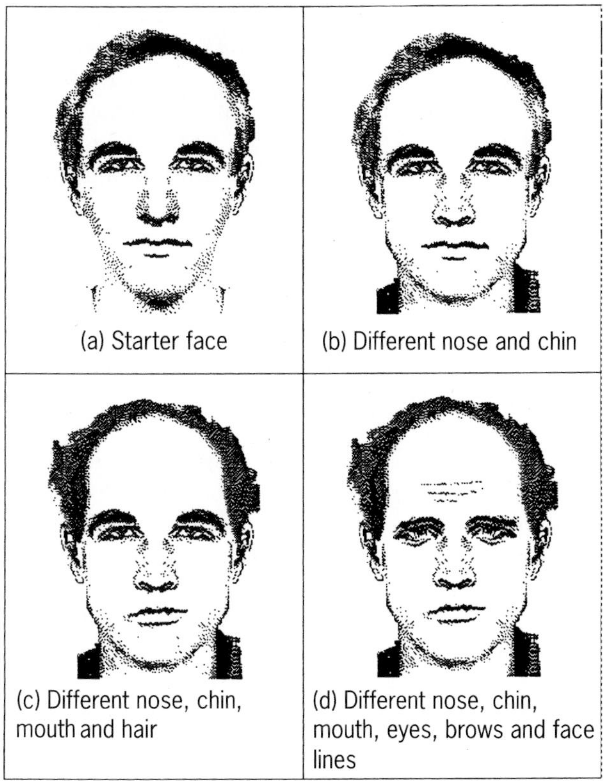

Figure 14.7 Examples of Identikit faces used in Bradshaw & Wallace's (1971) experiment

of identical faces, and participants were asked to decide whether the 'different' pairs were the same or different.

Sergent confirmed Bradshaw and Wallace's finding that the more features that differed, the faster a 'difference' decision was made. However, when only a single feature differed, 'difference' decisions were faster when this involved *chins* (and this was true for all participants). When something *in addition* to chins differed, the decisions were even faster. This latter finding suggests that there's *interactive processing* of different dimensions of facial appearance: a configuration emerges from a set of features that's more than the sum of its parts (see Box 14.2).

Are upright and inverted faces processed differently?

ASK YOURSELF...
- Before reading on, look at the photographs of Margaret Thatcher (in Box 14.3).
- Describe what you see.

An interesting additional finding from Sergent's study was that when she repeated the experiment using *inverted* face images, the results supported the view that the face is processed as a set of *independent* features. Several other studies have confirmed this finding.

According to Bartlett & Searcy (1993), the most likely explanation of the Thatcher illusion is what they call the *configural processing hypothesis*. The relationship between the features is more difficult to perceive when the face is inverted (so the features are processed independently), and the strangeness of the grotesque face cannot be seen (since it arises from the relationship between the features).

Box 14.3 Evidence relating to differential processing of upright and inverted faces

- Tanaka & Farah (1993) found that facial features learned in the context of an *upright* normal face were more likely to be identified correctly in the context of that face (as opposed to being tested in isolation). However, this advantage wasn't found for inverted faces. They concluded that the representation of whole faces is based on a holistic description, while inverted faces (as well as houses and scrambled faces: see Chapter 16) are represented as a set of independent components.
- According to Yin (1969), while upright faces are recognised more accurately than physical objects, the reverse is true for inverted faces. Somehow, the different features in inverted faces cannot be integrated to give a coherent impression. This is one of the best established findings in the field of face recognition (Bruce, 1995).
- Young *et al.* (1987) took pictures of well-known faces and sliced them horizontally to form separate upper and lower face halves. They then paired the upper half with a 'wrong' lower half. Participants were asked to name the top halves of faces presented either in isolation or when paired with the 'wrong' lower halves. The top halves were much harder to name when combined with the wrong lower halves than when shown alone, or when the two correct halves were misaligned. Young *et al.*'s explanation was that combining the two halves produced a 'new' configuration (see the 'Gazzaker' images, page 238). Significantly, when composite faces were inverted, participants named them *more accurately* than when they were presented upright.
- In Thompson's (1980) Thatcher illusion, the eyes and mouth are cut out and inverted within the face. When viewed upright, this produces a grotesque appearance, but when inverted, it looks quite similar to the 'normal' version.

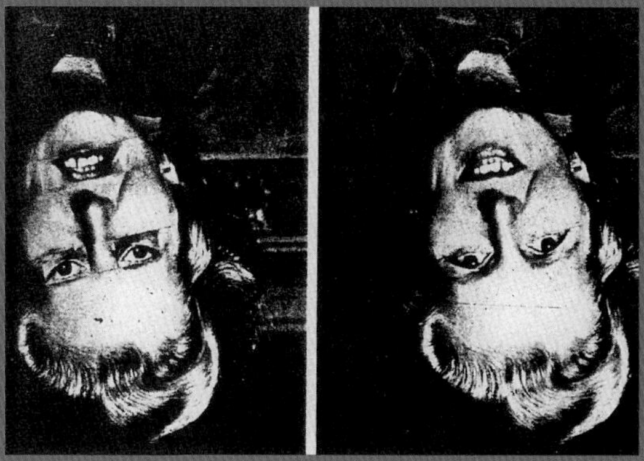

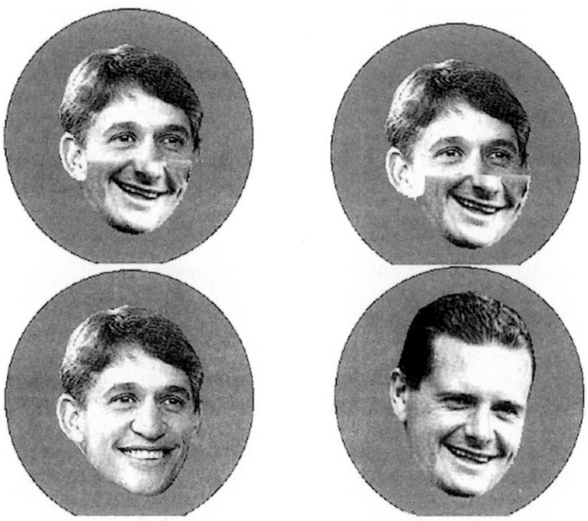

Who can you see?

If Bartlett and Searcy are correct, does this necessarily mean there's something special about face recognition? A study by Diamond & Carey (1986) of dog breeders and judges suggests that expertise may be the crucial variable. These dog experts were just as affected by the inversion of dog pictures as non-experts were by the inversion of human faces. So, configural processing might enable experts to make fine discriminations within a particular category, in which all the members share the same overall structure. When it comes to human face recognition, we all appear to be experts.

Disorders of face processing

While we might all be experts at face recognition, there are rare but dramatic cases of people who are unable to recognise familiar faces, including those of their spouses, other relatives and friends. The most common such disorder is *prosopagnosia*.

Prosopagnosia

CASE STUDY 14.1 W.J. (McNeil & Warrington, 1993)

- W.J. was a 51-year-old man who suffered a series of strokes, causing lesions in his left occipital, frontal and temporal lobes (see Chapter 4)
- When shown a set of three photographs (one famous and two unfamiliar faces), he couldn't select the famous one. However, if he was asked 'Which one is ...?', his performance improved significantly (*covert recognition*).
- Following the onset of his *prosopagnosia*, he acquired a flock of sheep which he photographed. He knew them by number and could recognise at least 8 of the 16 pictures. This represents remarkable evidence of an ability to learn to recognise individual sheep, while still being profoundly prosopagnosic for human faces (Groome *et al.*, 1999).

The case of W.J. demonstrates that prosopagnosia appears to be a face-specific deficit. Several other case studies show that patients can still identify personal possessions (including non-human animals), and can recognise faces if tested indirectly (unconscious or covert recognition: Groome *et al.*, 1999). Covert recognition suggests that prosopagnosia *isn't* a memory deficiency.

Some of these patients can derive particular kinds of *meaning* from faces (including emotional expression), despite being unable to recognise them. Conversely, some patients with a form of dementia find it difficult to recognise emotional expressions, while still being able to classify famous faces according to occupation (which requires knowledge of personal identity: Kurucz & Feldmar, 1979). The task of recognising individual identity from a face, therefore, seems to be quite separate from that of recognising an emotional expression. While the former requires recognition of an individual regardless of the expression, the latter requires recognising emotion irrespective of other aspects of facial appearance. Experiments with normal adults have shown that identity seems to be ignored when identifying emotional expressions, and expressions are identified no more quickly from familiar than from unfamiliar faces.

Unilateral neglect

We saw in Chapter 13 that people who suffer a stroke in their right parietal lobe display *left-sided neglect* (*unilateral neglect*). This usually affects perception of a wide range of objects, but in rare cases it may present as *face-specific* (as in the case of Keith: Young *et al.*, 1990). The parietal lobe is involved in attention, perception of the world's spatial layout, and especially in the visual abilities we need to control our actions (Milner & Goodale, 1996).

In evolutionary terms, the key task of vision is to construct a representation of the external environment that will permit effective actions. Many parts of the visual system are highly integrated with the mechanisms that control our movements (Bruce & Young, 1998). Unilateral neglect involves a deficit in a specific form of motor activity, namely *eye movements* (see Chapter 5). When people with left-sided neglect are shown a *chimeric*, comprising halves of two different photographs of faces joined at the midline, they often identify only the half-face falling to their *right*.

Robert (Walker *et al.*, 1996), who suffered a right-hemisphere stroke, was shown a photograph of Gorbachev (ex-President of the former USSR), and the chimeric of Anna Ford and Terry Wogan (see page 239). The white squares represent the initial fixation position on the midline before the face was actually presented. Robert's saccades went from the midline to the *right* side of each image, but after that *only* the right side was explored. Despite being warned that the stimuli would be composed of two faces joined together, he identified only Terry Wogan.

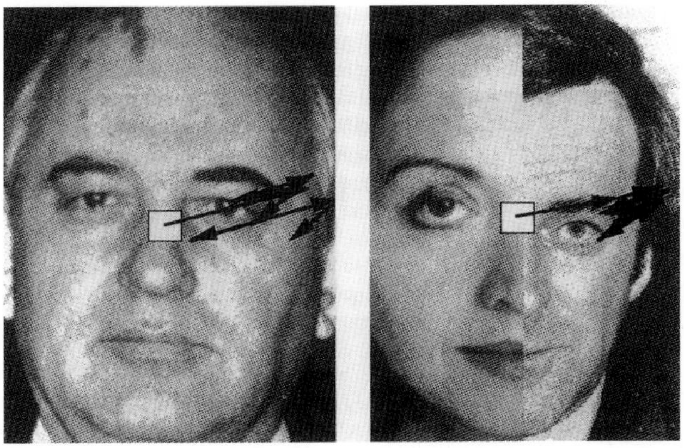

Neglect *doesn't* appear to be caused by an inability to scan the left side, but exactly what does cause this is still unclear. It most likely involves some kind of difficulty in forming an adequate representation of the face's left side, or an inability or disinclination to attend properly to it. Interestingly, neurologically normal people tend to overestimate the importance of information from the *left* side of the face (Bruce & Young, 1998).

Capgras' delusion/syndrome

Once thought to be extremely rare, *Capgras' syndrome* has been increasingly recognised and reported in recent years. Some studies suggest that it may be present in up to 4 per cent of psychotic patients (see Chapter 44), and up to a third of Alzheimer's patients may display the syndrome at some point during their illness (see Chapter 39) (Enoch & Ball, 2001). It is one of the most extensively studied forms of *delusional misidentification.*

It involves the belief that one or more close relatives have been replaced by near-identical imposters. Cases have been found in many cultures, and show a consistent pattern. Patients can be otherwise rational and lucid, and able to appreciate that they're making an extraordinary claim (Bruce & Young, 1998).

CASE STUDY 14.2 Arthur (Ramachandran, 1998)

- Arthur had been in a near-fatal car accident and lay in a coma for three weeks. When he finally awoke, he seemed restored to his former self, except for this one incredible delusion about his parents – they were imposters. Nothing could convince him otherwise.
- Ramachandran asked him, 'Arthur, who brought you to the hospital?'

  'That guy in the waiting room,' Arthur replied. 'He's the old gentleman who's been taking care of me.'

  'You mean your father?'

  'No, no, doctor. That guy isn't my father. He just looks like him. But I don't think he means any harm.'

  'Arthur, why do you think he's an imposter? What gives you that impression?'

  '... Maybe my real father employed him to take care of me, paid him some money so that he could pay my bills.'
- Arthur's parents revealed that he didn't treat them as imposters when they spoke to him on the phone, but only in face-to-face encounters. This implied that Arthur wasn't amnesic regarding his parents, and that he wasn't simply 'crazy'.

It was originally thought that Capgras' syndrome was based on prosopagnosia – either alone or in combination with a psychotic state. But patients with prosopagnosia don't become deluded over their disorder (they recognise their problem), and they search for similarities, while Capgras patients look for dissimilarities. The key difference is that Capgras can occur in a person who is blind (Enoch & Ball, 2001).

Models of face recognition

According to Bruce (1995), the complete identification of a known face requires not just that we recognise the pattern of the face as a familiar one, but that we know the context in which we've encountered the person and can retrieve his/her name. Studies of both normal and brain-damaged people suggest that there's a sequence of distinct stages involved in retrieving someone's identity. Failures at each stage are characterised by different problems of identification.

Hay & Young (1982) were the first to outline a stage model, which was supported by the pattern of errors reported by Young *et al.* (1985) in their diary study of everyday failures in person identification. On the basis of their data, Young *et al.* proposed a model of the functional components involved in person identification.

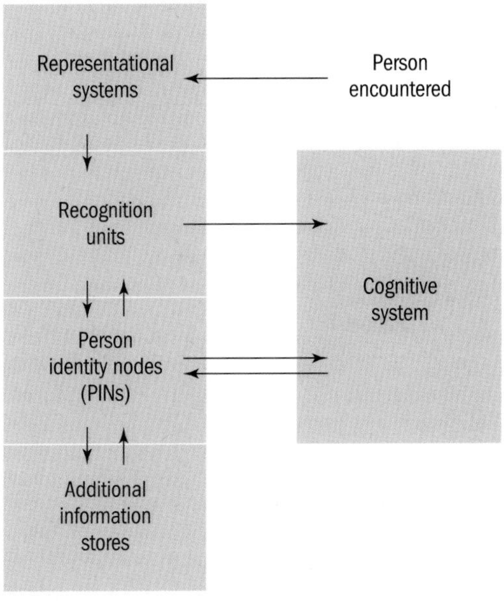

Figure 14.8 Young *et al.*'s (1985) model of the functional components involved in person identification

After representational processing, information about the face of the person encountered is processed by *recognition units*. These contain stored representations of known faces. If the currently viewed face matches one of these representations, information about the resemblance is signalled to *person identity nodes* (PINs). Basic information about personal identity is stored in the PINs, via which names and other details are accessed (from the *additional information stores*). Decisions as to whether or not a particular face is familiar, or about the person's identity, are made as a result of communication between these levels and the *cognitive system*.

This model was revised by Bruce & Young (1986). The stages of person identification are now put into the broader context of their relationship with the other uses made of facial information. The model comprises several different processing 'modules' linked in sequence or in parallel.

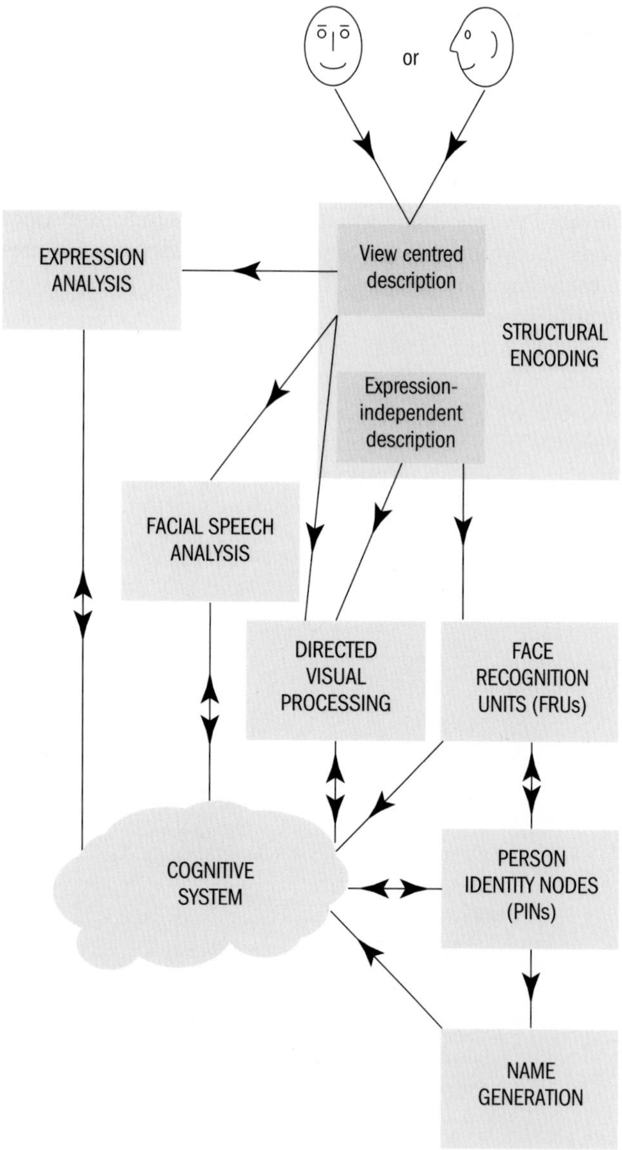

Figure 14.9 Bruce & Young's (1986) functional model for face recognition

Independent routes are drawn for the processing of emotional expressions, lip-reading ('facial speech') and identification, thus allowing the processing of information from both familiar and unfamiliar faces. *Directed visual processing* allows for certain kinds of operation to be performed on faces without accessing their identities (such as looking out for white-haired people when meeting your grandmother at the station). The route by which familiar faces are identified involves separate stages of representation of the face image (*structural encodings*), access of stored structural descriptions of known faces (*face recognition units*/FRUs), access of information about personal identity (via PINs) and, finally, retrieval of proper names.

An evaluation of the Bruce & Young (1986) model

According to Groome *et al.* (1999), the *dissociation* between processing of emotional expression and person identification makes good sense. We need to be able to recognise a face irrespective of its expression, and vice versa. Despite the fact that the model is broad, Bruce (1995) believes that it has the strength of being falsifiable.

Some relevant experimental evidence comes in the form of the *tip-of-the-tongue* (TOT) *phenomenon* for people's names (see Key Study 17.10, page 301). Brennen *et al.* (1990) wanted to know if participants in a TOT state, after being asked to identify someone from a description, could be helped to retrieve the name by viewing a picture of the person or by being given the initials of the missing name. Providing the initials allowed about half the missing names to be retrieved, but pictures produced just as little success as simply repeating the questions. These results are consistent with Bruce and Young's model. In a TOT state, participants must be at the stage of PINs, but are unable to reach the next stage of name retrieval. Seeing the face shouldn't help, since there's no direct link between faces and names; but the initials provide partial cues to help name retrieval.

However, evidence of *covert recognition* in prosopagnosic patients (see Case Study 14.1) are difficult for the model to explain. Familiarity judgements are supposedly made on the basis of activation levels at FRUs, forming an early stage in the sequence of establishing the person's full identity. If patients consistently fail to make familiarity judgements at better than chance levels, they should be unable to access information from later ('deeper') levels (stages) in the system. Yet this is exactly what covert recognition entails. Partly as an attempt to overcome these difficulties, the model was revised and extended by Burton *et al.* (1990) and Bruce (1992: see Bruce, 1995).

Face recognition and the brain

Given that face perception is such a demanding perceptual task, it's not surprising that brain damage can result in deficits in face processing, such as prosopagnosia (Groome *et al.*, 1999). According to Young & Bruce (1998):

Because faces are of such fundamental social importance to a creature that lives in a complex society, extensive areas of the brain are involved in their perception.

The functions of these areas are being revealed in studies of the effects of different types of brain injury, and using modern neuro-imaging techniques to study face processing in the normal brain (see Chapter 4). The brain seems to 'farm out' different aspects of the task to different specialised areas. For example, some regions are more closely involved in determining an individual's identity from their facial appearance, and others in interpretation of facial expressions of emotion (Young *et al.*, 1993).

According to Ellis & Young (1990), when we look at the faces of people we know, we recognise who they are and parts of our brains set up preparatory emotional responses for the types of interaction that are likely to follow (the *orienting response*). Recognising *who* it is, and preparing for *what* you're likely to do (the orienting response) involve *separate* neurological pathways. If the pathway responsible for the orienting response is damaged, and the orienting response is impaired, faces that can still be recognised (and so look familiar) can somehow seem strange (because they don't elicit the usual reactions).

The *temporal lobes* contain regions that specialise in face and object recognition (the '*what pathway*'). Normally, these face recognition areas relay information to the *limbic system* (specifically, the *amygdala*), which then helps to generate emotional responses to particular faces. For example, our GSR increases when we see someone familiar (or just see their photograph), but we'd expect this *not* to happen in the case of Capgras' patients. This was confirmed by Ramachandran (1998) in the case of Arthur (see Case Study 14.2). The discrepancy between recognition and the emotional response (there is none) produces a highly disturbing sense of strangeness. The belief that parents, say, are imposters (the delusion) might simply be a *rationalisation* of that disturbing experience (Bruce & Young, 1998; Young & Bruce, 1998).

CHAPTER SUMMARY

- **Pattern recognition** (PR) is the process of assigning meaning to visual input by identifying the objects in the visual field. Like perception, with which it's almost synonymous, PR is a deceptively simple process.
- According to the **template matching hypothesis** (TMH), incoming sensory information is matched against miniature copies (or templates) of patterns/objects stored in long-term memory. However, TMH fails to account for our ability to recognise unfamiliar patterns.
- Biederman's **geon theory** (or **recognition-by-components model**) tries to overcome TMH's limitations. Descriptions of objects usually divide them into **volumetric concepts** or **geons**, and the regions used to divide them up are probably those of greatest **concavity**.
- Geon theory has been supported by experiments using 'partial' objects. A more stringent test involves the use of 'degraded' versions of objects. Again, the results tend to support the theory. While geons are intuitively appealing, there's little empirical support for the specific geons Biederman identifies.
- **Prototype theories** claim that what's stored is a small number of prototypes. Instead of treating every stimulus as a separate entity, prototype theories regard each stimulus as belonging to a **category** of stimuli. This approach fails to take account of **context**.
- **Feature-detection theories** are the most influential approach to PR. Every stimulus can be regarded as a configuration of elementary features. **Visual scanning tasks** and studies of **eye movements/fixations** support feature-detection theories. The latter also show that the perception of features within complex patterns depends on attention and purpose.
- Hubel and Wiesel identified three kinds of **cortical cell**, which may or may not be the feature detectors proposed by feature-detection theories. There may be face-specific cells in the monkey cortex, and there also appear to be cells in the human cortex that respond to specific aspects of faces.
- While feature-detection theories typically assume a **serial** form of processing, it's widely believed that the visual cortex involves considerable **parallel** processing.
- Selfridge's **Pandemonium** computer program used parallel processing. Although not intended as a model of human perception, Pandemonium shares with other feature-detection theories the neglect of **context** and **perceiver characteristics** as influences on PR.
- Most feature-detection theories are **bottom-up/data-driven**, while the influence of context and expectations illustrates **top-down/conceptually driven processing**.
- **Face recognition** involves the identification of individual faces. It's part of face perception, which includes inferring emotional states and other information from the face. Probably more is understood about face recognition than about any other aspect of PR.
- Although faces could be described in terms of basic components, it seems more valid to describe them in a more **configural** way. However, this can refer to different things, including the **interaction** between features and the **holistic** processing of the whole face.
- Early research often used **artificially constructed faces**, such as Identikit faces, and indicated that facial features are processed independently and in sequence. However, some features (such as chins) seemed to influence facial judgements more than others, and there was evidence of **interactive processing**.

- According to the **configural processing hypothesis**, the relationship between the features is more difficult to perceive when the face is **inverted** (they are processed **independently**). In a normal upright face, the configuration of the features is crucial.
- Patients with **prosopagnosia** are unable to recognise familiar faces, despite an otherwise normal capacity for recognising individual objects or animals. However, they often display **covert** (unconscious) **recognition**.
- Studies involving prosopagnosics, patients with other face-perception disorders, and normal adults also suggest that recognising individual identity is quite separate from recognising emotional expression.
- In Bruce and Young's **model of face recognition**, several different processing 'modules' are linked in sequence or in parallel, including **face recognition units** (FRUs) and **person identity nodes** (PINs).
- While there's experimental support for this model (such as the TOT phenomenon for people's faces), it has difficulty explaining covert recognition in prosopagnosic patients.
- Studies of brain damage, and neuro-imaging studies of the normal brain, suggest that different areas of the brain are specialised for different aspects of face recognition. In **Capgras' delusion**, the normal integration of face recognition and orienting response appears to be impaired.

Links with other topics/chapters

- PR is almost synonymous with *perception*, and theories of perception can be thought of as trying to account for PR (Chapter 15).
- The three kinds of *cortical cell* that respond to different features of *visual stimuli* (identified by Hubel and Wiesel) may be the feature detectors proposed by feature-detection theories (Chapter 5).
- The *serial processing* proposed by feature-detection theories contrasts with the *parallel processing* thought to take place in the visual cortex. This distinction is also relevant to the debate about *artificial intelligence* (AI) (Chapter 20).
- A major limitation of feature-detection theories in general is their failure to take account of the role of *context*, and *perceiver characteristics* (such as *expectations*) (Chapter 15).
- Early research into face recognition assumed that faces could be analysed into individual features, as in Bradshaw and Wallace's *Identikit*, used by the police to construct a suspect's face based on witnesses' descriptions (Chapter 21).
- People who suffer strokes in the right parietal lobe display left-sided neglect (*unilateral neglect*) (Chapter 13), which involves a deficit in *eye movements* (which normally ensure that we scan the whole picture) (Chapter 5).
- Capgras' syndrome is found in about 4 per cent of *psychotics* (Chapter 44) and up to a third of *Alzheimer's patients* (Chapter 39).
- In Capgras' syndrome there seems to be a breakdown in communication between areas in the *temporal lobe* (concerned with object/face recognition) and the *amygdala* (part of the limbic system), which helps generate emotional responses (Chapter 4).
- Relevant to evaluating Bruce and Young's functional model of face recognition is the *tip-of-the-tongue* (TOT) *phenomenon* (Chapter 17).

15

PERCEPTION: PROCESSES AND THEORIES

INTRODUCTION AND OVERVIEW

When we compare our experience of the world (in which objects remain stable and constant) with what our sense organs receive in the form of physical stimulation (a state of near-continuous flux), it's almost as if there are two entirely different 'worlds'. Psychologists call these *sensation* and *perception* respectively. Sensations are the experiences that physical stimuli elicit in the sense organs (see Chapter 5). Perception is the organisation and interpretation of incoming sensory information to form inner representations of the external world.

This chapter begins by looking at some basic visual perceptual phenomena, namely, form and depth perception, perceptual constancy and visual illusions. Many of the principles that govern human visual perception were first identified by the German 'school' of Gestalt psychology. As Dodwell (1995) has observed:

> To perceive seems effortless. To understand perception is nevertheless a great challenge.

One response to this challenge claims that our perception of the world is the end result of a process which also involves making inferences about what things are like. Those who subscribe to this 'end result' view, such as Bruner (1957), Neisser (1967) and Gregory (1972, 1980), are called *top-down* (or *conceptually driven*) *perceptual processing* theorists. Making inferences about what things are like means that we perceive them *indirectly*, drawing on our knowledge and expectations of the world. Others argue that our perception of the world is essentially determined by the information presented to the sensory receptors, so that things are perceived in a fairly direct way. The most influential of these *bottom-up* (or *data-driven*) *perceptual processing* theorists is Gibson (1966, 1979). Others still, notably Marr (1982), display elements of both approaches.

GESTALT PSYCHOLOGY AND PERCEPTUAL ORGANISATION

Ehrenfels (1890) claimed that many groups of stimuli acquire a pattern quality that is greater than the sum of their parts. A square, for example, is more than a simple assembly of lines – it has 'squareness'. Ehrenfels called this 'emergent property' *Gestalt qualität* (or form quality). In the early 1900s, Gestalt psychologists (notably Wertheimer, Koffka and Köhler) attempted to discover the principles through which sensory information is interpreted. They argued that as well as creating a coherent perceptual experience that's more than the sum of its parts, the brain does this in regular and predictable ways. They believed that these organisational principles are largely *innate* (see Chapter 16).

Form perception

In order to structure incoming sensory information, we must perceive objects as being separate from other stimuli and as having meaningful form.

Figure and ground

ASK YOURSELF...
- What do you see in Figure 15.1?
- Although it's visually quite simple, can you suggest how it might illustrate a basic principle of how we see things?

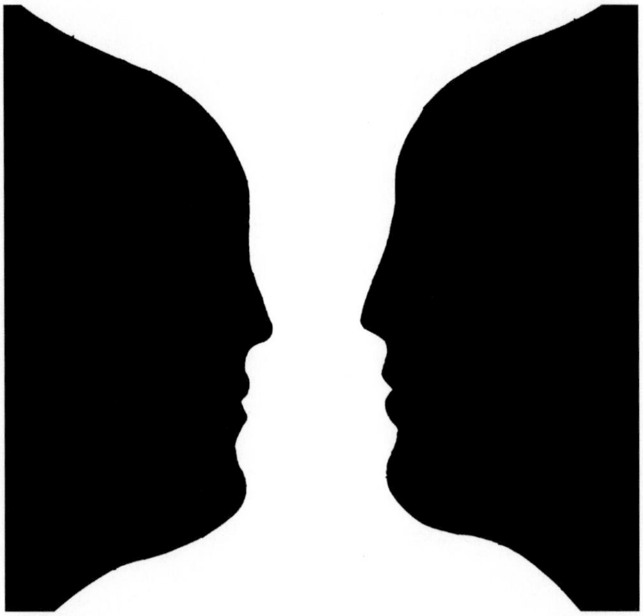

Figure 15.1

The first perceptual task when confronted with an object (or *figure*) is to recognise it (see Chapter 14). To do this, we must perceive the figure as being distinct from its surroundings (or *ground*). A figure's familiarity can help determine whether it's perceived as figure or ground, but unfamiliar and even meaningless 'blobs' are also seen as figures. One of the strongest determinants of figure and ground is *surroundedness*. Areas enclosed by a contour are generally seen as figures, whereas the surrounding area is generally seen as ground. Size, orientation and symmetry also play a role in figure–ground separation.

Sometimes, though, there may not be enough information in a pattern to allow us to distinguish easily between figure and ground. A good example of this is shown in Figure 15.2 (see below), which illustrates the principle underlying camouflage.

Figure 15.2 The dalmatian dog (the figure) is difficult to distinguish from the ground because it has few visible contours of its own

In *figure–ground reversal*, a figure may have clear contours, but is capable of being perceived in two very different ways: it's unclear which part of it is the figure and which the ground. A famous example is Figure 15.1, usually called Rubin's vase (Rubin, 1915). Here, the figure–ground relationship continually reverses, so that it's perceived as either a white vase with a black background, or two black profiles on a white background. However, the stimulus is always organised into a figure seen against a ground, and the reversal indicates that the same stimulus can trigger more than one perception.

The picture at the beginning of this chapter (page 243) shows how the artist Escher used figure–ground reversal.

> *ASK YOURSELF...*
> - Can you think of some 'everyday' examples of figure–ground (reversible or not)?
> - Can you think of some non-visual examples?

A map is another example. We normally see the land as figure and the sea as (back)ground, because we're more familiar with the shape of Africa, say, than with the shape of the Atlantic ocean. An auditory example is the *cocktail party phenomenon* (see Chapter 13). Here's another: try repeating 'over-run' out loud and you'll find the two words alternating as figure and ground.

Grouping

Once we've discriminated figure from ground, the figure can be organised into a meaningful form. Gestalt psychologists believed that objects are perceived as *Gestalten* ('organised wholes', 'configurations' or 'patterns') rather than combinations of isolated sensations. They identified several 'laws' of perceptual organisation or grouping, which illustrate their view that the perceived whole of an object is more than the sum of its parts.

These laws can be summarised under one heading, the *law of prägnanz* ('precision'), according to which:

> Psychological organisation will always be as good as the prevailing conditions allow. In this definition, 'good' is undefined. (Koffka, 1935)

'Good' can be defined as possessing a high degree of *internal redundancy*, that is, the structure of an unseen part is highly predictable from the visible parts (Attneave, 1954). Similarly, according to Hochberg's (1978) *minimum principle*, if there's more than one way of organising a given visual stimulus, we're most likely to perceive the one requiring the least amount of information to perceive it.

In practice, the 'best' way of perceiving is to see things as symmetrical, uniform and stable, and this is achieved by following the laws of prägnanz.

Box 15.1 Gestalt laws of perception

Proximity: Elements appearing close together in space or time tend to be perceived together, so that different spacings of dots produce four vertical lines or four horizontal lines:

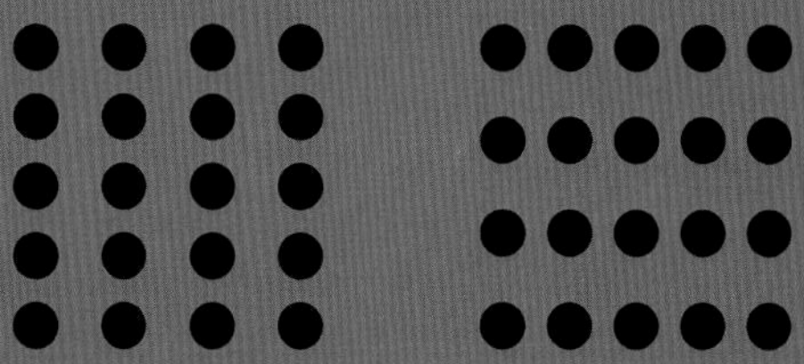

An auditory example would be the perception of a series of musical notes as a melody, because they occur soon after one another in time.

Similarity: Similar figures tend to be grouped together. So, the triangles and circles below are seen as columns of similar shapes rather than rows of dissimilar shapes.

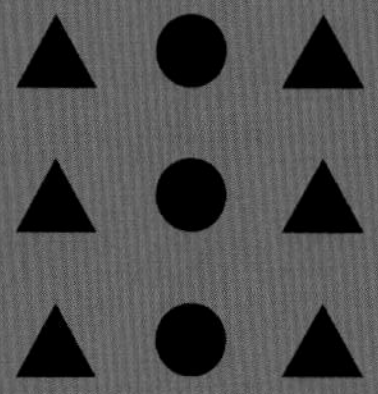

Hearing all the separate voices in a choir as an entity illustrates the principle of similarity.

Continuity: We tend to perceive smooth, continuous patterns rather than discontinuous ones. The pattern below could be seen as a series of alternating semi-circles, but tends to be perceived as a wavy line and a straight line.

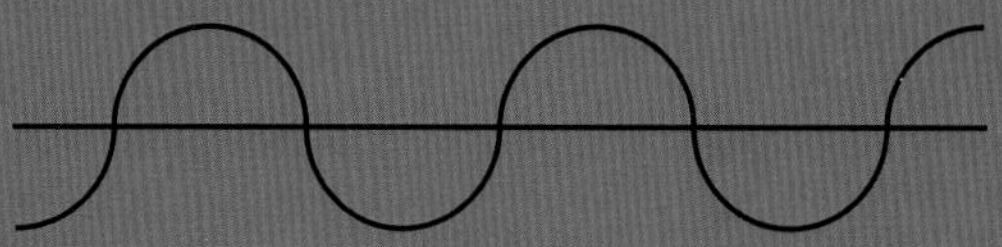

Music and speech are perceived as continuous, rather than a series of separate sounds.

Closure: Closed figures are perceived more easily than open/incomplete ones. So, we often supply missing information to close a figure and separate it from its background. By filling in the gaps, the illustrations below are seen as a triangle and a seashell.

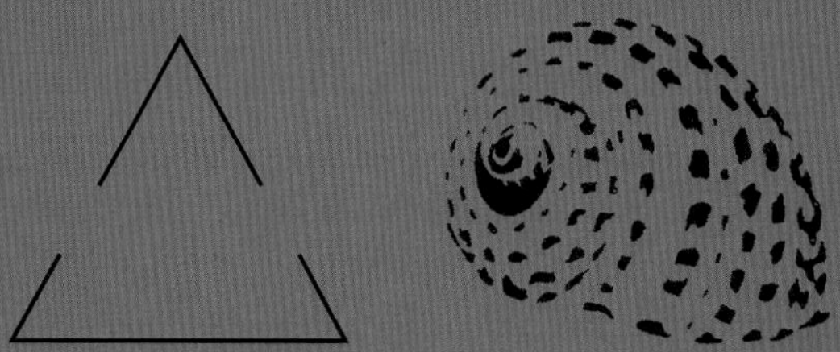

Part–whole relationship: As well as illustrating continuity and proximity, the three figures below illustrate the principle that 'the whole is greater than the sum of its parts'.

Despite the similarity of the parts (each pattern is composed of twelve crosses), the Gestalten are different.

The same melody can be recognised when hummed, whistled or played with different instruments and in different keys.

Common fate: Elements seen moving together are perceived as belonging together. This is why a group of people running in the same direction appear to be unified in their purpose.

An evaluation of the Gestalt contribution

A major philosophical influence on Gestalt psychology was *phenomenology*. This sees the world as we ordinarily experience it as being of central concern. Koffka, for example, believed that the most important question for perceptual psychologists was 'Why do things look as they do?', and for Köhler:

> There seems to be a single starting point for psychology, exactly as for all the other sciences: the world as we find it, naïvely and uncritically.

The most comprehensive account of perceptual grouping is still that provided by the Gestaltist psychologists (Roth, 1986), and in Gordon's (1989) view, Gestalt psychology's discoveries 'are now part of our permanent knowledge of perception'.

However, many contemporary researchers (e.g. Greene, 1990) have argued that, as originally expressed, the various Gestalt 'laws' are at best only descriptive and at worst extremely imprecise and difficult to measure. Several studies have attempted to address the various criticisms made of the Gestalt laws.

KEY STUDY 15.1 Trying to ignore what comes naturally (Pomerantz & Garner, 1973)

- One objective measure of grouping is how quickly participants can sort/classify one element presented with others they must try to ignore.
- Pomerantz and Garner used a pile of cards, each with a pair of brackets printed on it. Participants had to sort the cards into two piles according to whether the *left-hand bracket* looked like '(' or ')', and were told to ignore the right-hand bracket completely.
- In one condition, the pairs of brackets were identified as *groupable*, in the other condition, as *non-groupable*. (As Figure 15.3 shows, there was an experimental and a control pack in each condition.)
- Pomerantz and Garner predicted that reaction times for the groupable cards would be *longer* than for the non-groupable, and this is what they found. Participants were having to select out one element of the pair, and this takes time.
- Pomerantz & Schwaitzberg (1975) systematically manipulated proximity by using cards with brackets drawn further and further apart. Given a suitable distance between the brackets, grouping effects disappeared: there was no longer a difference in sorting times between the control and experimental packs of 'groupable' stimuli.

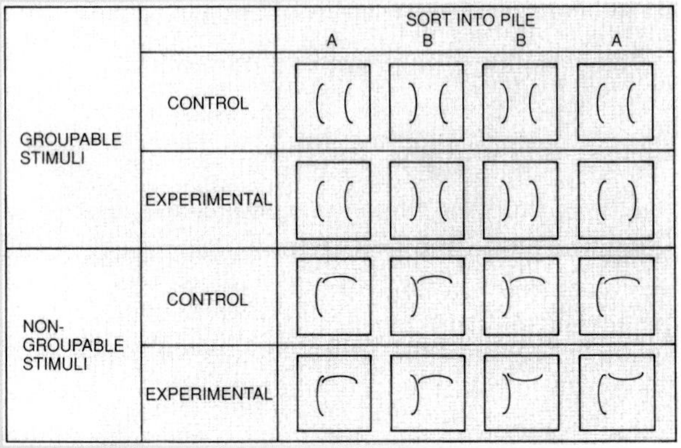

Figure 15.3 Pomerantz & Garner's (1973) experimental test of Gestalt laws

Navon (1977) tested the idea that the whole is perceived before the parts that make it up by presenting participants with various stimuli, as shown in Figure 15.4.

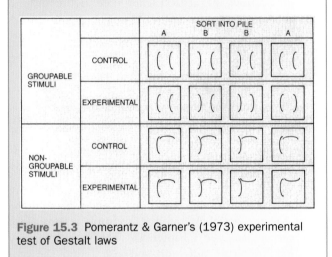

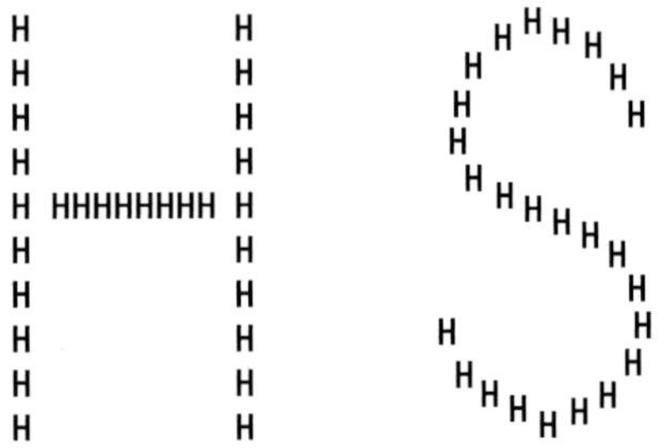

Figure 15.4

Navon distinguished between the global (or 'whole-like' features of a stimulus) and the local (or more specific and 'part-like' features). Each stimulus consisted of a large (global) letter made up of many small (local) letters. In some cases, the global and local letters matched (as shown in the stimulus on the left), and in some cases they didn't (as shown on the right).

Participants had to identify either the large or the small letter as quickly as possible. Navon found that the time taken to identify the large letter was unaffected by whether the small letters matched or not. However, the time taken to identify the small letters was affected by whether the large letter matched or not: when the large letter was different, response times were longer. This suggests that it's difficult to avoid processing the whole, and that global processing necessarily occurs before any more detailed perceptual analysis.

Table 15.1 Decision time for global and local letters under match or mismatch conditions (based on Navon, 1977)
Time in m/secs to respond to 'global' and 'local'

Condition	Match	Mismatch
Global	471	477
Local	581	664

Does the global always predominate?

The findings from Pomerantz and Garner's, and Navon's experiments clearly support Gestalt laws. But these are difficult to apply to the perception of solid (three-dimensional/3-D) objects (as opposed to two-dimensional/2-D drawings). Our eyes evolved to see 3-D objects, and when 3-D arrays have been studied, Gestalt laws haven't been consistently upheld (Eysenck, 1993). The world around us comprises 'whole' scenes, in which single objects are but 'parts' (Humphreys & Riddoch, 1987). Because many of the Gestalt displays involve single objects, they have very low ecological validity, that is, they're not representative of 'the objects and events which organisms must deal with in order to survive' (Gordon, 1989).

Factors such as the sizes of the local and global features, the viewing conditions, and the nature of the observer's task are all likely to play a part in determining the role played by individual features in pattern recognition (Eysenck & Keane, 1990). In everyday life, it's obviously easier sometimes to process 'forests' and sometimes easier to process 'trees' (Roth, 1986).

Some theorists (e.g. Palmer, 1975) have suggested that under most circumstances, the interpretation of parts and wholes takes place in top-down and bottom-up directions simultaneously, such as in the recognition of parts of a face with and without context. As shown in Figure 15.5, the features that can easily be recognised in context are somewhat ambiguous when seen alone (out of context). But they're recognisable when more detail is provided.

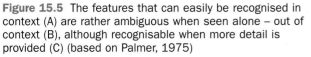

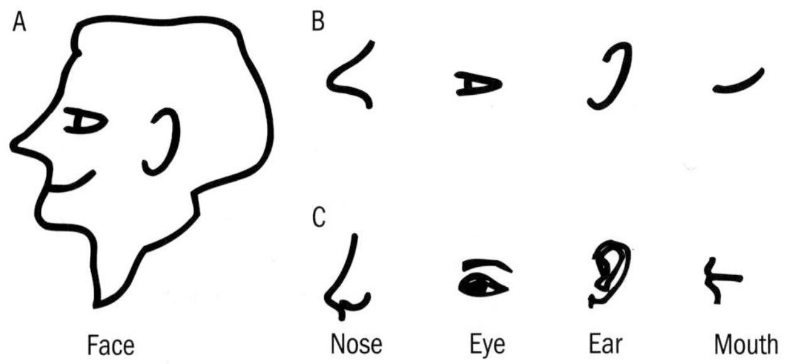

Figure 15.5 The features that can easily be recognised in context (A) are rather ambiguous when seen alone – out of context (B), although recognisable when more detail is provided (C) (based on Palmer, 1975)

(Compare Palmer's approach with that of Neisser's analysis-by-synthesis model: see Box 15.5, page 259.)

Marr (1976) found the Gestalt principles useful in achieving accurate *segmentation*, that is, how visual information is used to decide which regions of a visual scene belong together and form coherent structures. He devised a computer program aimed at achieving segmentation (of a teddy bear, for example) using the Gestalt principles. He succeeded in obtaining appropriate segmentation of the teddy's outline, eyes and nose. But some scenes are ambiguous and require using knowledge about objects in order to achieve segmentation (such as two leaves overlapping substantially in a bowl of flowers: Marr, 1982).

DEPTH PERCEPTION

From the 2-D images that fall on our retinas, we manage to organise 3-D perceptions. This ability is called *depth perception*, and it allows us to estimate an object's distance from us. Some of the cues used to transform 2-D retinal images into 3-D perceptions involve both eyes and rely on their working together. These are called *binocular cues*. *Monocular cues* are available to each eye separately.

> *ASK YOURSELF...*
> - How do we judge the distance of objects from us?
> - Is it always done unconsciously, or do we sometimes try to 'work it out' consciously?

Non-pictorial (primary) cues

Most preyed-upon non-humans (such as rabbits) have their eyes on the sides of the head, allowing them to see danger approaching over a wide area. Most predators (such as lions) have their eyes set close together on the front of the head, equipping them with binocular vision, which helps in hunting prey. Like non-human predators, humans have predatory vision, which influences the way we perceive the world. Four important non-pictorial cues are *retinal disparity*, *stereopsis*, *accommodation* and *convergence*. These are all binocular, except accommodation.

- Because our eyes are nearly three inches apart, each retina receives a slightly different image of the world. The amount of *retinal disparity* (the difference between the two images) detected by the brain provides an important cue to distance.

> *ASK YOURSELF...*
> - Hold your finger directly in front of your nose.
> - The difference between the two retinal images is large (and this can be shown by looking at your finger first with the left eye closed and then with the right eye closed).
> - When the finger is held at arm's length, retinal disparity is much smaller.

- Ordinarily, we don't see double images, because the brain combines the two images in a process called *stereopsis* (literally, 'solid vision': Harris, 1998). This allows us to experience one 3-D sensation, rather than two different images.
- In *accommodation*, which is a muscular cue, the lens of the eye changes shape when we focus on an object, thickening for nearby objects and flattening for distant objects (see Figure 5.3, page 81).
- *Convergence*, another muscular cue to distance, is the process by which the eyes point more and more inward as an object gets closer. By noting the angle of convergence, the brain provides us with depth information over distances from about 6 to 20 feet (Hochberg, 1971).

Pictorial (secondary) cues

Except with relatively near objects, each eye receives a very similar retinal image when looking ahead. At greater distances, we depend on pictorial cues. These refer to features of the visual field itself (rather than to the eyes), and are all also monocular (see Table 15.2).

Table 15.2 Some pictorial depth cues

Depth cue	Description
Relative size	In an array of different sized objects, smaller ones are usually seen as more distant (especially if they're known to have a constant size).
Relative brightness	Brighter objects normally appear to be nearer.
Superimposition (or overlap)	An object which blocks the view of another is seen as being nearer.
Linear perspective	Parallel lines (e.g. railway tracks) appear to converge as they recede into the distance.
Aerial perspective	Objects at a great distance appear to have a different colour (e.g. the hazy, bluish, tint of distant mountains).
Height in the horizontal plane	When looking across a flat expanse (e.g. the sea), objects that are more distant seem higher (closer to the horizon) than nearer objects, which seem lower (closer to the ground).
Light and shadow	3-D objects produce variations in light and shade (for example, we normally assume that light comes from above).
Texture gradient	Textured surfaces (e.g. sand) look rougher close up than from a distance. A stretch of beach looks more smooth and uniform.
Motion parallax	This is the major *dynamic* depth cue (pictorial/non-pictorial). Objects nearer to us seem to move faster than more distant objects (e.g. telegraph poles seen from a (moving) train window flash by when close to the track).

Linear perspective

PERCEPTUAL CONSTANCY

Having perceived an object as a coherent form and located it in space, we must next recognise the object without being 'fooled' by changes in its size, shape, location, brightness and colour. The ability to perceive an object as unchanging, despite changes in the sensory information that reaches our eyes, is called *perceptual constancy*.

Size constancy

The image on the retina of an average-height person would be the same size for a dwarf seen from close up or a giant viewed from a distance (Ramachandran & Rogers-Ramachandran, 2004). *Size constancy* occurs because the perceptual system takes into account an object's distance from the perceiver. So, perceived size is equal to retinal image size taking distance into account.

The perception of an *after-image* demonstrates how distance can be varied without changing the retinal image's size.

> *ASK YOURSELF...*
> - Stare at a bright light for a few seconds, and then look away.
> - You'll experience an after-image. This has a fixed size, shape and position on the retina.
> - Now quickly look at a nearby object, and then an object further away.
> - The after-image seems to shrink and swell, appearing to be largest when you look at a more distant object.

Real objects cast smaller images the further away they are, and to maintain perceptual constancy the brain 'scales up' the image (*constancy scaling*). The same constancy scaling is applied to an after-image, producing changes in its apparent size.

Shape constancy

We often view objects from angles at which their 'true' shapes aren't reflected in the retinal image they project. For example, rectangular doors often project trapezoid shapes and round cups often project elliptical-shaped images. Just as with size constancy, the perceptual system maintains constancy in terms of shape.

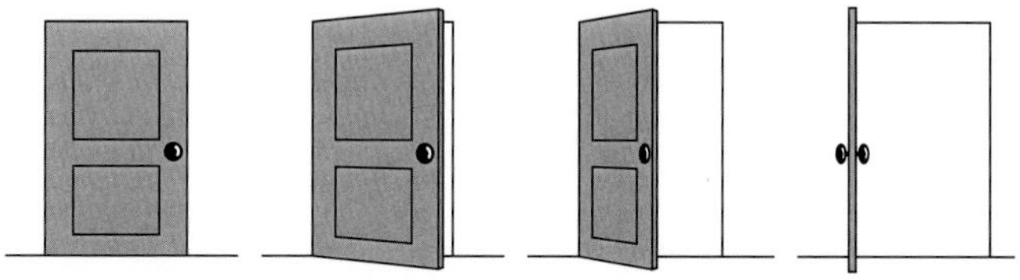

Figure 15.6 No matter what angle a door is viewed from, it remains a door

However, shape and size constancy don't always work. When we look down at people from the top of a very tall building, they do look more like ants to us, even though we *know* they're people.

Location constancy

Moving our heads around produces a constantly changing pattern of retinal images. However, we don't perceive the world as spinning around. This is because *kinaesthetic feedback* from the muscles and balance organs in the ear are integrated with the changing retinal stimulation in the brain to inhibit perception of movement (see Chapter 5). To keep the world from moving crazily every time we move our eyes, the brain subtracts the eye-movement commands from the resulting changes on the retina. This helps to keep objects in a constant location.

Brightness constancy

We see objects as having a more or less constant brightness, even though the amount of light they reflect changes according to the level of illumination. For example, white paper reflects 90 per cent of light falling on it, whereas black paper reflects only 10 per cent. But in bright sunlight black paper still looks black, even though it may reflect 100 times more light than does white paper indoors. Perceived brightness depends on how much light an object reflects relative to its surroundings (*relative luminance*).

ASK YOURSELF...
- View sunlit black paper through a narrow tube, so that nothing else is visible.
- It will appear greyish, because in bright sunlight it reflects a fair amount of light.
- Now view it without the tube.
- It appears black again, because it reflects much less light than the colourful objects around it.

Colour constancy

Familiar objects retain their colour (or, more correctly, their hue) under a variety of lighting conditions (including night light), provided there's sufficient contrast and shadow (see Chapter 5, page 89). However, when we don't already know an object's colour, colour constancy is less effective. If you've bought new clothes under fluorescent light without viewing them in ordinary lighting conditions, you'll probably agree.

ILLUSIONS

Although perception is usually reliable, our perceptions sometimes misrepresent the world. When our perception of an object doesn't match its true physical characteristics, we've experienced an illusion. Some illusions are due to the physical distortion of stimuli, whereas others are due to our misperception of stimuli (Coren & Girgus, 1978). An example of a physical illusion is the bent appearance of a stick when placed in water. Gregory (1983) identifies four types of perceptual illusion:

1. *distortions* (or *geometric illusions*)
2. *ambiguous* (or *reversible*) *figures*
3. *paradoxical figures* (or *impossible objects*)
4. *fictions*.

Distortions

Figure 15.7 shows several examples of distortions. The Poggendorf illusion (Figure 15.7b) is accentuated when the diagonal line is more steeply slanted and when the parallel bars are more separated. As the line is brought closer to the horizontal, the illusion disappears (MacKay & Newbigging, 1977). The horizontal–vertical illusion (Figure 15.7d) illustrates our tendency to overestimate the size of vertical objects. This helps to explain why a small tree we've chopped down looks shorter than it did when it was standing (Coren & Girgus, 1978).

Ambiguous figures

In addition to Rubin's vase (see page 244), three other well-known reversible figures are shown in Figure 15.8 (a–c). In the Necker cube (Figure 15.8a), the figure undergoes a *depth reversal*. The cube can be perceived with the crosses being drawn either on the back side of the cube or on the top side looking down. Although our perceptual system interprets this 2-D line drawing as a 3-D object, it seems unsure as to which of the two orientations should be perceived. Hence, the cube spontaneously reverses in depth orientation if looked at for about 30 seconds.

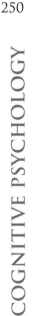

Figure 15.8b shows Boring's 'Old/Young Woman'. These two are examples of reversible figures in which the change in perception illustrates object reversal. The figure can be perceived as the profile of a young woman's face with the tip of her nose just visible, or the young woman's chin can be perceived as the (very large) nose of a much older woman (who also has a very long chin).

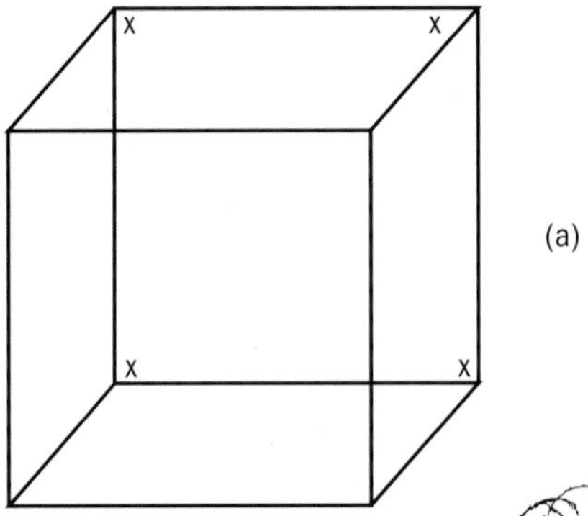

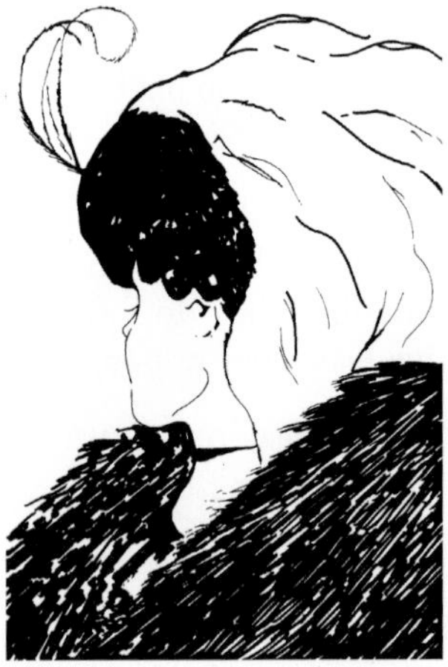

Figure 15.8 Two ambiguous/reversible figures: (a) the Necker cube; and (b) Boring's 'Old/Young Woman'

Paradoxical figures

While paradoxical figures look ordinary enough at first, on closer inspection we realise they cannot exist in reality (hence 'paradoxical'). Figure 15.9 (a–d) illustrates four such paradoxical figures.

According to Hochberg (1970), it takes us a few seconds to realise that a figure is impossible. This is because we need time to examine it fully or scan it and

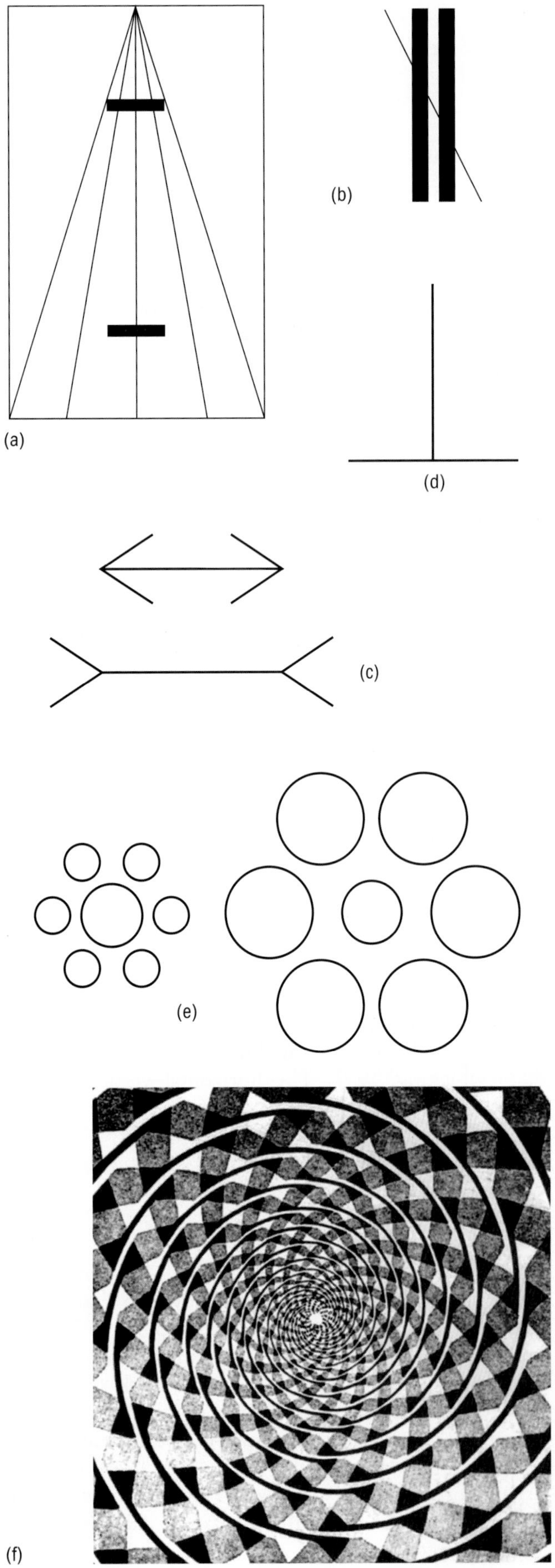

Figure 15.7 Distortions (or geometric illusions). In the Ponzo illusion (a), the horizontal bar at the top is seen as being longer than the horizontal line at the bottom, even though they're both the same length. The Poggendorf illusion (b) suggests that the segments of the diagonal line are offset, even though they're not. The line with the outgoing fins in the Müller–Lyer illusion (c) appears to be longer than the line with the ingoing fins, but in fact they're the same length. In the horizontal–vertical illusion (d), the vertical line is seen as being longer, although it is the same as the horizontal line. In Titchener's circles (e), the central circle in the left-hand group is seen as being larger than the central circle of the right-hand group, but they're both the same size. Finally, in the twisted card illusion (f), the twisted cards appear to be a spiral pattern, but the circles are, in fact, concentric

organise its parts into a meaningful whole. When we look at a figure, our eyes move from place to place at the rate of about three changes per second (Yarbus, 1967: see Key Study 14.2, page 234). So, when we look at an impossible figure, it takes time for us to scan it and perceive its form, and only after this scanning can we appreciate its impossible nature.

Fictions

Fictions help explain how we perceive that objects possess specific shapes. The idea that shape is determined by the physical contours of an object (which cause edge-detector cells in the visual system to fire: see Chapter 5) has been challenged by the existence of *subjective contours*. These are the boundaries of a shape perceived in the absence of physical contours (Kanizsa, 1976).

In Figure 15.10a, there's no white triangular contour physically present. But we perceive the shape of a white triangle, which appears to be opaque and lighter than the background. There are some contours that are physically present (the overlap of the triangle and the disc), which might cause enough edge-detector cells to fire. However, this explanation cannot account for the fact that in Figure 15.10b, the partial and straight physical contours give rise to a curved triangle. Nor can it explain the subjective contour in Figure 15.10c, which is marked by lines in a totally different orientation (Krebs & Blackman, 1988).

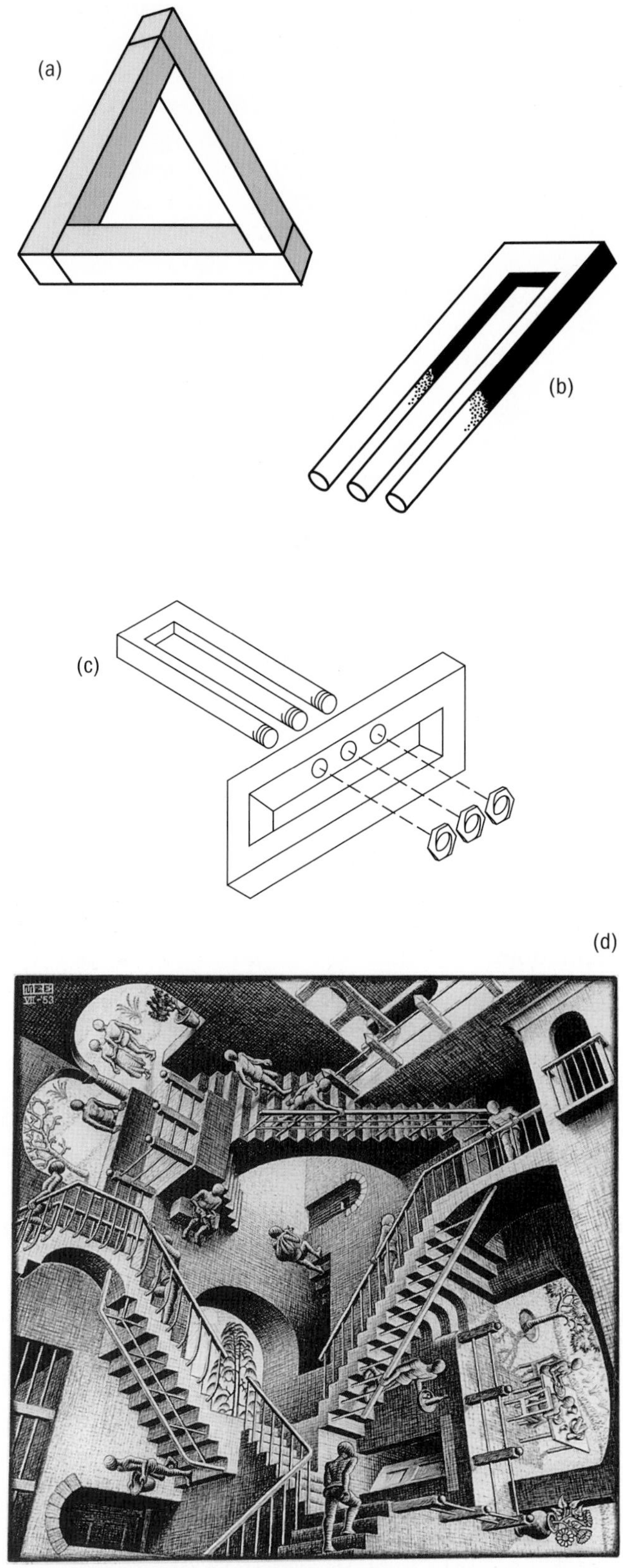

Figure 15.9 Four paradoxical objects. (a) is the Penrose impossible triangle and (b) is variously known as 'Trident' and 'The Devil's Pitchfork'. In (c), Trident has been combined with another impossible object. (d) is M.C. Escher's *Relativity*. Although working in two dimensions, Escher has used perceptual cues in such a way as to encourage the viewer to perceive a three-dimensional figure

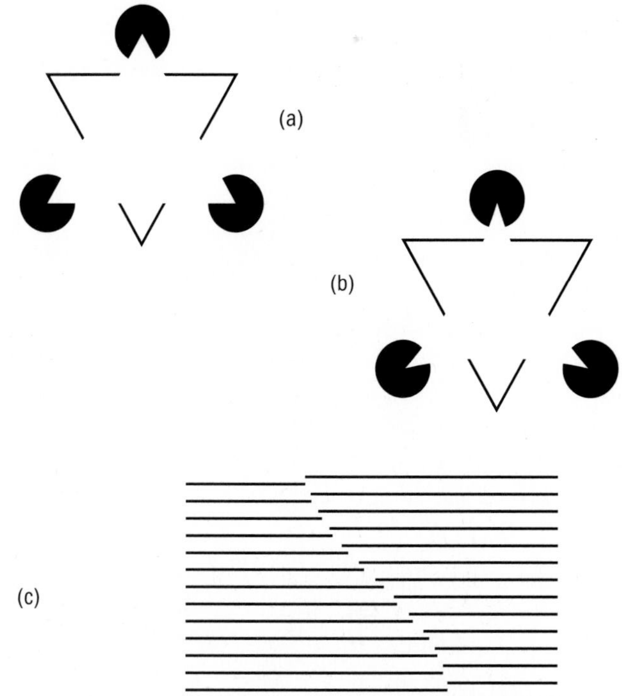

Figure 15.10 Three fictions. In (a), the 'white triangle' is banded by a subjective contour, rather than a continuous physical one. In (b), the subjective contours are curved. In (c), lines of different orientation produce a subjective contour

It's the *relationship between its parts* that defines a shape, rather than its physical contours (Rock, 1984). Physical contours are, of course, usually indicative of the location of an object's parts. But the location of the parts can also be determined by subjective contours. As a result, the perception of shape must involve more than simply detecting the elements of a pattern (Krebs & Blackman, 1988).

> *ASK YOURSELF...*
> - Can you think of any 'real-life' illusions – that is, illusions that haven't been deliberately created by psychologists (or artists) to study perception?

Illusions of movement

We're surrounded by illusions in our everyday life. The use of perspective cues by artists leads us to infer depth and distance, that is, we add something to a picture which isn't physically present, just as we do to the images projected on our television screens. Television pictures also use the illusion of movement. Just as it's possible for changes in patterns of retinal stimulation not to be accompanied by the perception of movement, so it's possible to perceive movement without a successive pattern of retinal stimulation (Ramachandran & Anstis, 1986). This is called *apparent movement*.

> **Box 15.2 Some examples of apparent movement**
>
> **The autokinetic effect:** If you look at a stationary spot of light in an otherwise completely dark room, the light will appear to move. According to Gregory (1973), this illusion is produced by small and uncontrollable eye movements. Another explanation suggests that it's caused by the absence of a stimulating background to provide a frame of reference for measuring movement. This is supported by the fact that the autokinetic effect disappears if other lights are introduced (see also Key Study 26.1, pages 442–443).
>
> **Stroboscopic motion:** The illusion of movement is created by the rapid succession of slightly different stationary images. If these are presented sufficiently quickly (around 16 to 22 frames per second), an illusory impression of continuous movement is produced. This is the mechanism by which moving pictures operate. With fewer than 16 frames per second, the moving picture looks jumpy and unnatural. Smooth slow motion is achieved by filming at a rate of 100 or more frames per second, and then playing back at about 20 frames per second.
>
> **The phi phenomenon:** This is a simpler form of stroboscopic motion, in which a number of separate lights are turned on and off in quick succession. This gives the impression of a single light moving from one position to another. Both stroboscopic motion and the phi phenomenon can be explained by the law of continuity (see Box 15.1, page 245).
>
> **Induced movement:** This occurs when we perceive an object to be moving, although in reality it's stationary and the surroundings are moving. Movie stars, for example, are often filmed in a stationary car with a projection of a moving background behind them. Similarly, when the moon is seen through a thin cover of moving clouds, we sometimes perceive it to be moving very quickly. Another example is the experience of sitting in a car at traffic lights and noticing that we are 'moving backwards', when in fact the car at our side is moving forwards.
>
> **Motion after-effects:** People who work on inspection belts in factories experience movement after-effects when the belt suddenly stops but is then perceived as moving backwards. Similarly, if you stare at a waterfall and then switch your gaze to the ground surrounding it, the ground appears to be moving in the opposite direction.

At least some examples of apparent movement can be termed *intelligent errors*, because they result from perceptual strategies that work most of the time (Rock, 1983). Motion after-effects, however, can be more easily explained in physiological terms.

Illusions of shading

According to Ramachandran & Rogers-Rachamandran (2004), the visual image is inherently ambiguous. Perception is partly a matter of using certain assumptions about the world in order to resolve such ambiguities, and illusions can help uncover the brain's hidden rules and assumptions.

> *ASK YOURSELF...*
> - How would you describe the group of disks on the left in Figure 15.11?
> - How would you describe those on the right?
> - Can you try to explain the different perceptions?

In Figure 15.11, the disks on the left are usually seen as eggs, while those on the right are seen as cavities. The eggs are light on the top, and the cavities are light on the bottom. According to Ramachandran and Rogers-Ramachandran, this reveals an assumption made by the visual system, namely that it expects light to shine from *above*.

> *ASK YOURSELF...*
> - Turn the page upside down.
> - All the eggs and cavities instantly switch places.
> - Ask a friend to hold the page right side up for you. Then bend down and look between your legs at the page (which is now behind you).
> - Again, the switch occurs, 'as if the sun is stuck to your head and shining upward from the floor' (Ramachandran & Rogers-Ramachandran, 2004).

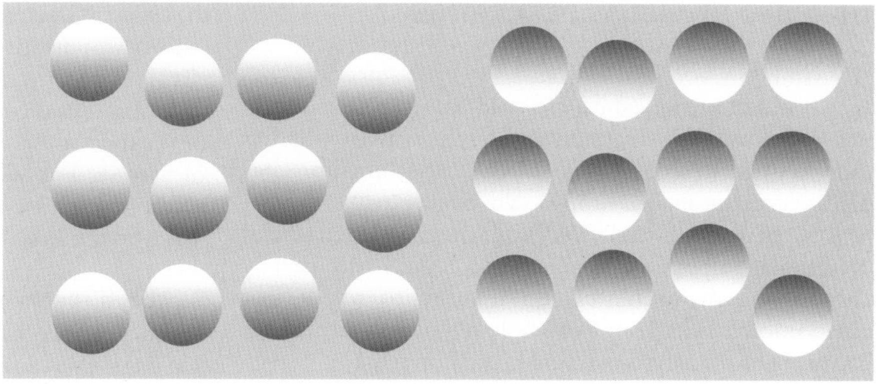

Figure 15.11 From Ramachandran & Rogers-Ramachandran (2004)

PERCEPTION OF REAL MOVEMENT

The importance of eye movements

To perceive real (actual) movement, there must be changes in the retinal image. Indeed, it seems that the receptors respond only to changes in the environment. As we saw in Chapter 5, the eyes are constantly making minute, oscillatory movements which keep the receptors stimulated. A device for stabilising the retinal image (Cornsweet, 1970) shows that these movements are necessary for seeing things at all. A tiny slide projector, mounted on a contact lens, is attached to the cornea and a slide projected on to a screen. Since the lens and the projector move with the eye, the retinal image is stabilised. In other words, eye movements and the movement of the image on the screen 'cancel each other out', so the retinal image stays in the same place. After initially seeing the picture with normal acuity, it begins to fade within a few seconds, and after a minute disappears altogether.

If you turn your head slowly around with your eyes open, or you scan a stationary scene, you'll create a succession of different retinal images. But you won't perceive movement (location constancy 'kicks in'). So, changes in the retinal image cannot be a sufficient basis for the perception of movement. Conversely, when an object moves across your visual field and you follow it with your eyes, the retinal image remains the same, but you do perceive movement.

Configurational change

Objects moving in the environment usually do so against a background of stationary (or differently moving) objects. Also, the nose and other anatomical borders to the visual field provide stationary reference points against which to judge movement. This causes a *configuration change*, or change in the overall pattern and interrelationship between objects. However, although in practice this is often an important source of information, it may not be a necessary one. If a lighted cigarette is moved about in a dark room it will be perceived as moving, even though there are no background cues or frames of reference (Gregory, 1973). (This shouldn't be confused with the autokinetic effect: see Box 15.2.)

So how does the brain do it?

It seems that the brain is capable of distinguishing between eye movements which do signal movement of objects (real movement), and those (and head movements) which don't. Probably the *superior colliculus* plays an important role in making this distinction (see Chapter 5). Gregory (1973) describes two systems:

1. the *image–retina system*, which responds to changes in the visual field that produce changes in the retinal image
2. the *eye–head system*, which responds to movements of the head and eyes.

The perception of movement is the product of an interplay between the two systems.

According to Braddick (1974), the human visual system seems to have two separate systems for measuring the speed and direction of individual features moving in the retinal image:

1. a long-range, *feature-tracking* system seems to infer motion from one instant to the next, which underpins our conscious impression of motion in films and television
2. a short-range, *motion-sensing* system seems to measure motion more directly by signalling changes in the image content over time.

Although neither system is fully understood, the basic requirements are in place even at the retina. P-type ganglion cells respond to abrupt *spatial* changes in the image, while *M-type* ganglion cells may respond to abrupt *temporal* (time-related) changes (see Chapter 5, page 84). Additionally, the temporal cortex contains many cells selective for different types of motion, and most visual cortical cells prefer moving to stationary stimuli (Harris, 1998).

Classifying theories

As we noted in the *Introduction and overview*, one way in which theories of perception differ is in terms of whether they regard perception as a *direct* (bottom-up/data-driven), or an *indirect* (top-down/conceptually driven) process. Bruce & Green (1990) call these 'ecological' and 'traditional' respectively. The term 'ecological' was used by Gibson, the major bottom-up theorist, to imply that visual information from the whole physical environment is available for analysis by retinal receptor cells.

Another issue which divides theories relates to the *nature–nurture debate* (see Chapter 50). *Empiricists* regard perception as primarily the result of learning and experience, while *nativists* believe it's essentially an innate ability, requiring little, if any, learning. All the top-down theorists are also empiricists, and the major nativists are the Gestalt psychologists (see pages 244–247). Gibson was influenced by the Gestalt school, but he's generally regarded as an empiricist. Finally, Marr's theory has both top-down and bottom-up components, and he too was influenced by some of the Gestalt laws.

Table 15.3 A classification of theories of perception

	Direct (bottom-up/ecological)	**Indirect (top-down/traditional)**
Empiricist	Gibson (1966, 1979)	Gregory (1972, 1980)
		Bruner (1957)
	Neisser (1967)	
	Marr (1982)	
Nativist	Gestalt	

Gregory's constructivist theory

According to Gregory (1966):

> Perception is not determined simply by stimulus patterns. Rather, it is a dynamic searching for the best interpretation of the available data ... [which] involves going beyond the immediately given evidence of the senses.

To avoid sensory overload, we need to *select* from all the sensory stimulation which surrounds us. Also, we often need to *supplement* sensory information, because the total information we need might not be directly available to the senses. This is what Gregory means by 'going beyond the immediately given evidence of the senses', and it's why his theory is known as *constructivist*. For Gregory, we make inferences about the information the senses receive (based on Helmholtz's nineteenth-century view of perception as consisting of *unconscious inferences*).

Gregory's theory and perceptual constancies

Perceptual constancies (see pages 248–249) tell us that visual information from the retinal image is sketchy and incomplete, and that the visual system has to 'go beyond' the retinal image in order to test hypotheses which fill in the 'gaps' (Greene, 1990). To make sense of the various sensory inputs to the retina (*low-level information*), the visual system must draw on all kinds of evidence, including distance cues, information from other senses, and expectations based on past experience (*high-level knowledge*). For all these reasons, Gregory argues that perception must be an indirect process involving a construction based on physical sources of energy.

Gregory's theory and illusions

Gregory argues that when we experience a visual illusion (see pages 249–252), what we perceive may not be physically present in the stimulus (and hence not present in the retinal image). Essentially, an illusion can be explained in terms of a perceptual hypothesis which isn't confirmed by the data: our attempt to interpret the stimulus figure turns out to be inappropriate. In other words, an illusion occurs when we attempt unsuccessfully to construe the stimulus in keeping with how we normally construe the world.

Box 15.3 Explaining the Ponzo illusion

In the Ponzo illusion (see Figure 15.7a, page 250), our system can *either*:

- accept the equal lengths of the two central bars as drawn on a flat 2-D surface (which would involve assuming that the bars are equidistant from us), or
- 'read' the whole figure as a railway track converging into the distance (so that the two horizontal bars represent sleepers, the top one of which would be further away from us but appears longer, since it 'must' be longer in order to produce the same length image on the retina).

The second interpretation is clearly inappropriate, since the figure is drawn on a flat piece of paper with no actual distance differences. As a result, we experience an illusion.

All illusions illustrate how the perceptual system normally operates by forming a 'best guess', which is then tested against sensory inputs. For Gregory (1966), illusions show that perception is an active process of using information to suggest and test hypotheses. What we perceive aren't the data, but an interpretation of them, so that:

> A perceived object is a hypothesis, suggested and tested by sensory data.

As Gregory (1996) has noted, 'this makes the basis of knowledge indirect and inherently doubtful'.

Gregory argues that when we view a 3-D scene with many distance cues, the perceptual system can quickly select the hypothesis that best interprets the sensory data. However, reversible figures supply few distance cues to guide the system. For example, the spontaneous reversal of the Necker cube (see page 250) occurs because the perceptual system continually tests two equally plausible hypotheses about the nature of the object represented.

One striking illusion is the *rotating hollow mask* (Gregory, 1970). There's sufficient information for us to see the mask as hollow, but it's impossible not to see it as a normal face. The perceptual system dismisses the hypothesis that the mask is an inside-out face, because it's so improbable. The hypothesis we select is strongly influenced by our past experiences of faces (Gregory, 1970).

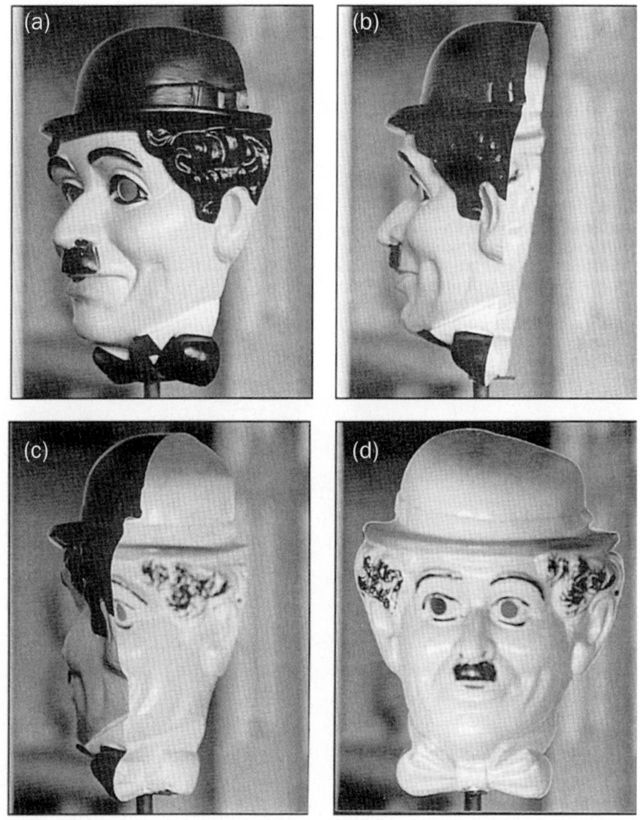

Figure 15.12 The rotating hollow mask. (a) shows the normal face which is rotated to (d), which is a hollow face. However, (d) appears like a normal face rotating in the opposite direction

With the impossible triangle (see Figure 15.9a), our perceptual system makes reasonable, but actually incorrect, judgements about the distance of different parts of the triangle.

> **ASK YOURSELF...**
> - Knowing what you do about Gregory's theory, how do you think he might try to explain the Müller–Lyer illusion (see Figure 15.7c)? You may find Box 15.3 (page 254) helpful.

Misapplied size constancy theory

According to Gregory, the Müller–Lyer illusion can be explained as follows.

- The arrow with the ingoing fins provides linear perspective cues, suggesting that it could be the outside corner of a building. Hence, the fins are seen as walls receding away from us, making the shaft look closer to us.
- In the arrow with the outgoing fins, the cues suggest that it could be the inside corner of a room, and the outgoing fins as walls coming towards us. This would make the shaft appear 'distant'.

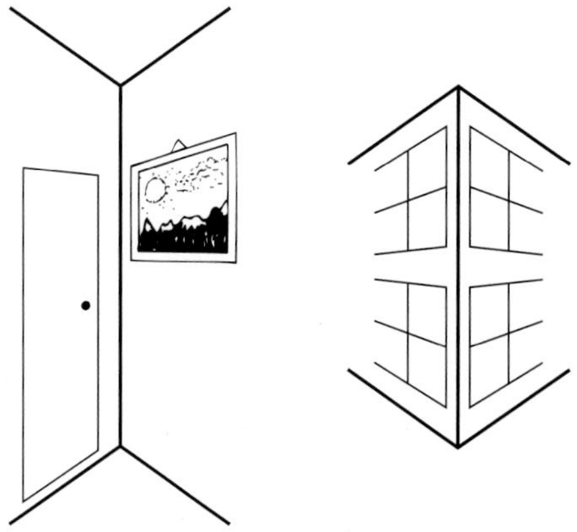

Figure 15.13 A representation of the Müller–Lyer illusion as suggested by Gregory's misapplied size constancy theory

- The retinal images produced by the arrows are actually equal and, according to size constancy, if equally sized images are produced by two lines, one of which is further away from us than the other, then the line which is furthest from us must be longer! Because this interpretation is taking place unconsciously and quickly, we immediately perceive the illusion.

However, if the perspective cues are removed, the illusion remains, suggesting that the misapplied size constancy theory is itself misapplied (see Figure 15.14). Alternatively, the apparent distance of the arrow could be caused by the apparent size of the arrows rather than, as Gregory claims, the other way around (Robinson, 1972).

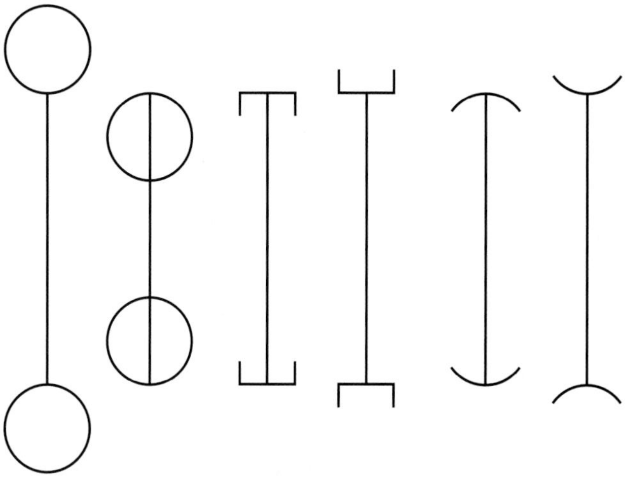

Figure 15.14 The Müller–Lyer illusion with the depth cues removed (after Delboeuf, 1892)

In a variation of the original Müller–Lyer illusion, Morgan (1969) placed a dot mid-way along the arrow (see Figure 15.15). The dot appears to be nearer the left-hand end, and the only way this can be explained by Gregory is to claim that the fins make the arrow appear to slope away from us, providing a rather odd perspective interpretation of the figure. According to Gregory (1972), such a slope can be demonstrated, although this claim has been disputed (Eysenck & Keane, 1995).

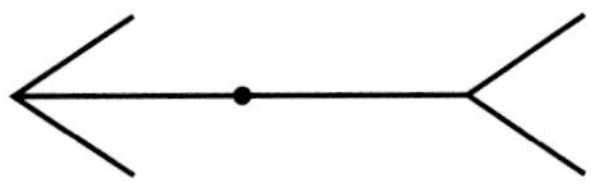

Figure 15.15 Morgan's (1969) modified Müller–Lyer illusion

In the Müller–Lyer illusion, we know the arrows are the same length, yet we still experience the illusion. Our knowledge should enable us to modify our hypotheses in an adaptive way. While some illusions can be explained in terms of the same unconscious processes occurring (an example being size constancy), not all illusions are amenable to explanation in the way Gregory proposes (Robinson, 1972).

Gregory's theory and perceptual set

Perceptual set is directly relevant to Gregory's view that perception is an active process involving selection, inference and interpretation. Allport (1955) describes perceptual set as:

> ... a perceptual bias or predisposition or readiness to perceive particular features of a stimulus.

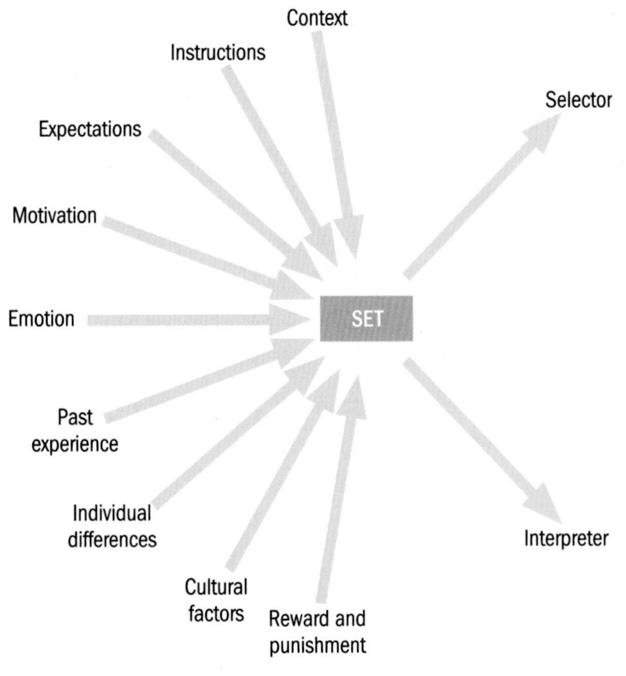

Figure 15.16 The indirect influence of perceiver and stimulus variables on perception through their direct influence on set

It refers to the tendency to perceive or notice some aspects of available sense data and ignore others. According to Vernon (1955), set acts as:

- a *selector* – the perceiver has certain expectations which help focus attention on particular aspects of the incoming sensory information, and
- an *interpreter* – the perceiver knows how to deal with the selected data, how to classify, understand and name them, and what inferences to draw from them.

Several factors can influence or induce set, most of them being *perceiver* (or *organismic*) variables. But some relate to the nature of the stimulus or the conditions under which it's perceived (*stimulus* or *situational variables*). Both types of variable influence perception indirectly, through directly influencing set which, as such, is a perceiver variable or characteristic.

Box 15.4 Some findings relating to perceptual set

Motivation: People with some particular need (such as hunger) are more likely to perceive vague or ambiguous pictures as relating to that need (Sanford, 1937; McClelland & Atkinson, 1948).
Emotion: '*Perceptual defence*' refers to the findings from laboratory experiments that *subliminally perceived* words (below the threshold of conscious awareness) which evoke unpleasant emotions take longer to perceive at a conscious level than neutral words (McGinnies, 1949).
Values: Lambert *et al.* (1949) found that when children were taught to value something more highly than they'd previously done, they perceived the valued thing as being larger (*perceptual accentuation*).
Beliefs: The beliefs we hold about the world can affect our interpretation of ambiguous sensory signals. A person who believes in UFOs is likely to perceive an ambiguous object in the sky differently from a person who doesn't share that belief (Wade & Tavris, 1993).
Cognitive style: The way we deal with our environment appears to affect our perception of it. Some people perceive the environment as a whole and don't clearly differentiate the shape, colour and so on of individual items. Others perceive the elements of the environment as separate and distinct (Witkin *et al.*, 1962).
Context and expectations: The interaction between context and expectations was demonstrated by Bruner & Postman (1949) and Bruner *et al.* (1952). When participants are asked to copy a briefly presented stimulus such as:

PARIS IN THE THE SPRING	ONCE IN A A LIFETIME	A BIRD IN THE THE HAND

it's typically copied as PARIS IN THE SPRING/ONCE IN A LIFETIME/A BIRD IN THE HAND. One reason eyewitness testimony is so unreliable is that our general expectation of people is that they'll be of 'average height and weight', and this is what almost all eyewitness accounts describe people as being (Loftus, 1980: see Chapter 21).

An evaluation of Gregory's theory of perception

- Gregory's theory raises many important questions which have yet to be answered satisfactorily (Gordon, 1989). For example, if perception is essentially constructive, then we need to know how it gets started and why there's such common experience among different people, all of whom have had to construct their own idiosyncratic perceptual worlds. Also, given that perception is typically accurate (and our hypotheses are usually correct), it seems unlikely that our retinal images are really as ambiguous and lacking in detail as Gregory suggests.
- Gregory has been much more successful in explaining at least some types of illusion than in explaining perception as a whole (Eysenck & Keane, 1995). His theory may be most relevant when stimuli are ambiguous or incomplete, presented very briefly, or their processing interrupted (Groome *et al.*, 1999). In Gordon's (1989) view, constructivist theories have underestimated the richness of sensory evidence in the real world. For Gordon:

> It is possible that we perceive constructively only at certain times and in certain situations. Whenever we move under our own power on the surface of the natural world and in good light, the necessary perceptions of size, texture, distance, continuity, motion and so on, may all occur directly and reflexively.

Gibson's theory of direct perception

Constructivists use the retinal image as their starting point for explaining perception. According to Gibson (1966), this approach mistakenly describes the input for a perceiver in the same terms as that for a single photoreceptor, namely a stream of photons. For Gibson, it's better to begin by considering the input as a pattern of light extended over time and space (an *optic array* containing all the visual information from the environment striking the eye of a stationary perceiver).

The optic array provides unambiguous, invariant information about the layout and relevant properties of objects in space. This information takes three main forms: *optic flow patterns*, *texture gradient*, and *affordances*. Perception essentially involves 'picking up' the rich information provided by the optic array in a direct way, which involves little or no (unconscious) information processing, computations, or internal representations (Harris, 1998).

Optic flow patterns

During the Second World War, Gibson prepared training films describing the problems pilots experience when taking off and landing. He called the information available to pilots *optic flow patterns* (OFPs). As shown in Figure 15.17, the point to which a pilot moves appears motionless, with the rest of the visual environment apparently moving away from that point. Thus, all around the point there's an apparent radial expansion of textures flowing around the pilot's head.

Figure 15.17 The optic flow patterns as a pilot approaches the landing strip (from Gibson, 1950)

The lack of apparent movement of the point towards which the pilot moves is an invariant, unchanging feature of the optic array. Such OFPs provide unambiguous information about direction, speed and altitude. OFPs in general refer to changes in the optic array as the perceiver moves about.

Texture gradients

Textures expand as we approach them and contract as they pass beyond our heads. This happens whenever we move toward something, so that over and above the behaviour of each texture element, there's a 'higher-order' pattern or structure available as a source of information about the environment (and so the flow of the texture is invariant). Texture gradients (or *gradients of texture density*) are important depth cues perceived directly without the need for any inferences. The depth cues described in Table 15.2 are all examples of directly perceived, invariant, higher-order features of the optic array. For Gibson, then, the third dimension (depth) is available to the senses as directly as the other two dimensions, automatically processed by the sense receptors, and automatically producing the perceptual experience of depth.

Affordances

The environment contains invariant information, the detection of which has survival value for the perceiver. *Affordances* are directly perceivable, potential uses of objects, such as surfaces that are stand-on-able or sit-on-able, objects that are graspable or throwable, or that afford eating (are 'edible'). In other words, affordances are the *meanings* that an environment has for an animal, and the relationship between perceiver and environment is vitally important.

An evaluation of Gibson's theory

- Gibson was concerned with the problem of how we obtain constant perception in everyday life, based on continually changing sensations. According to Marr (1982), this indicated that he correctly regarded the problem of perception as that of recovering from sensory information 'valid properties of the external world'.
- However, as Marr points out, Gibson failed to recognise two equally critical things:

> First, the detection of physical invariants, like image surfaces, is exactly and precisely an information-processing problem ... Second, he vastly underrated the sheer difficulty of such detection.

- An interesting study by Lee & Lishman (1975) tends to support Gibson's belief in the importance of movement in perception, and the artificiality of separating sensory and motor aspects of behaviour (see Key Study 15.2).
- Gibson's concept of affordances is part of his attempt to show that all the information needed to make sense of the visual environment is directly available in the visual input (a purely 'bottom-up' approach to perception). Bruce & Green (1990) argue that this concept is most powerful and useful in the context of *visually guided* behaviour, as in insects. Here, it makes sense to speak of an organism detecting information available in the light needed to organise its activities, and the idea of it needing a conceptual representation of its environment seems redundant.

KEY STUDY 15.2 If the room sways, there may be an experiment going on (Lee & Lishman, 1975)

- Lee and Lishman used a specially built swaying room (suspended above the floor), designed to bring texture flow under experimental control.
- As the room sways (so changing the texture flow), adults typically make slight unconscious adjustments, and children tend to fall over. Normally, the brain is very skilled at establishing correlations between changes in the optic flow, signals to the muscles, and staying upright.
- Arguably, the most important reason for having a visual system is to be able to anticipate when contact with an approaching object is going to be made. Lee and Lishman believe that estimating 'time to contact' is crucial for actions such as avoidance of objects and grasping them, and thus represents extremely important ecological information. This can be expressed as a formula:

$$\text{Time to contact} = \frac{\text{Size of retinal image}}{\text{Rate of expansion of retinal image}}$$

- This is a property shared by all objects, and so is another invariant, demonstrating the unambiguous nature of the retinal image.
- Measures of optic flow have also provided some understanding of how skilled long-jumpers control their approaches to the take-off position (Gordon, 1989).

- However, humans act in a *cultural* as well as physical environment. It's inconceivable that we don't need any knowledge of writing or the postal system in order to detect that a pen affords writing or a postbox affords posting a letter, and that these are directly perceived invariants. People see objects and events as what they are in terms of a culturally given conceptual representation of the world, and Gibson's theory says much more about '*seeing*' than about '*seeing as*'.

'Seeing' and 'seeing as'

According to Fodor & Pylyshyn (1981):

> What you see when you see a thing depends upon what the thing you see is. But what you see the thing as depends upon what you know about what you are seeing.

This view of perception as 'seeing as' is the fundamental principle of *transactionalism*. Transactionalists (such as Ames, cited in Ittelson, 1952) argue that because sensory input is always ambiguous, the interpretation selected is the one most likely to be true given what's been perceived in the past.

In the Ames distorted room (see Figure 15.18), the perceiver has to choose between two different beliefs about the world built up through past experience. The first is that rooms are rectangular, consist of right angles, and so on. The second is that people are usually of 'average' height. Most observers choose the first, and so judge the people to be an odd size. However, a woman who saw her husband in the room and judged the room to be odd, shows that particularly salient past experiences can override more generalised beliefs about the world.

The Ames room is another example of a visual illusion, and the inability of Gibson's theory to explain mistaken perception is perhaps its greatest single weakness. Gibson argues that most 'mistaken perceptions' occur in situations very different from those which prevail in the natural environment. However, to suggest that illusions are nothing but laboratory tricks designed to baffle ordinary people isn't true, since at least some produce effects similar to those found in normal perception. A striking example is the 'hollow mask' illusion (Bruce & Green, 1990: see Figure 15.12).

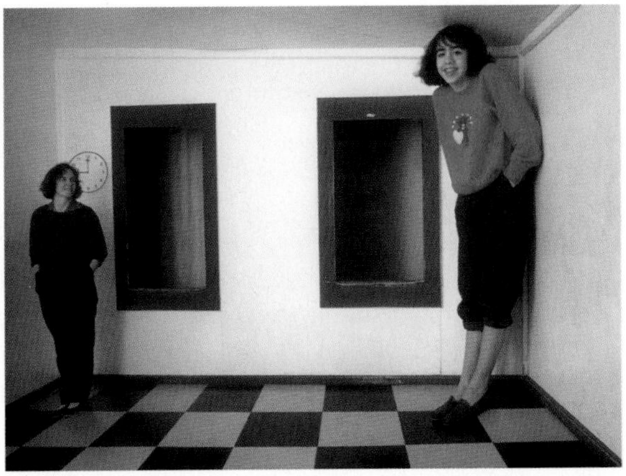

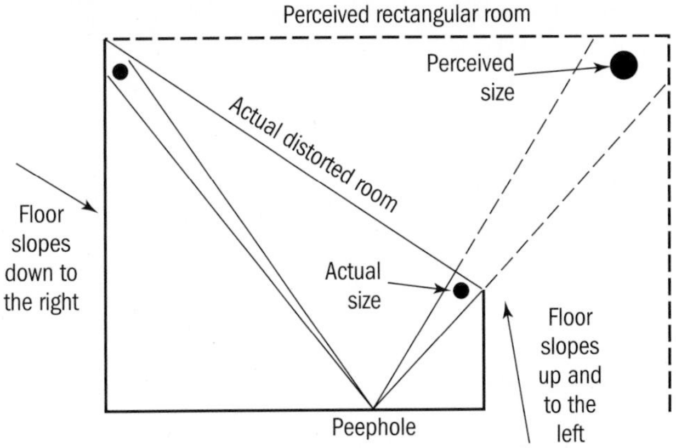

Figure 15.18 The Ames room and a schematic representation of its 'secret'. The room is constructed in such a way that, when viewed with one eye through a peephole, a person at one end may appear very small and the person at the other end very tall. When they cross the room, they appear to change size. The room itself appears perfectly normal and regular to an observer

A possible synthesis of Gregory's and Gibson's theories

Despite the important differences between Gibson's and Gregory's theories, they also agree on certain points.

Similarities

- Visual perception is mediated by light reflected from surfaces and objects.
- Some kind of physiological system is needed to perceive.
- Perception is an active process. (In Gibson's, 1966, view, 'a perceiving organism is more like a map-reader than a camera').
- Perceptual experience can be influenced by learning.

Differences

- Gregory believes that meaningless sensory cues must be supplemented by memory, habit, experience and so on, in order to construct a meaningful world. Gibson argues that the environment (initially the optic array) provides us with all the information we need for living in the world. Perceptual learning consists not in 'gluing' together sensory 'atoms', but in coming to differentiate and discriminate between the features of the environment as presented in the optic array.
- To the extent that Gibson acknowledges the role of learning (albeit a different kind of learning from Gregory), he may be considered an *empiricist* (see above), together with his emphasis on what's provided by the physical world. In other respects, though, Gibson can be considered a *nativist*. As we noted earlier, he was very much influenced by the Gestalt psychologists, stressing the organised quality of perception. However, while for Gibson this organised quality is part of the physical structure of the light impinging on the observer's eye, for Gestaltists it's a function of how the brain is organised.

Eysenck & Keane (1995) argue that the relative importance of bottom-up and top-down processes is affected by several factors. When viewing conditions are good, bottom-up processing may be crucial. However, with brief and/or ambiguous stimuli, top-down processing becomes increasingly important. Gibson seems to have been more concerned with optimal viewing conditions, while Gregory and other constructivists have tended to concentrate on sub-optimal conditions (Eysenck, 1993). In most circumstances, both bottom-up and top-down processes are probably needed, as claimed by Neisser (1976).

Box 15.5 Neisser's (1976) analysis-by-synthesis model

- Neisser assumes the existence of a *perceptual cycle* involving *schemata*, *perceptual exploration*, and *stimulus environment*.
- Schemata contain collections of knowledge based on past experience (see Chapter 21), and these direct perceptual exploration towards relevant environmental stimulation. Such exploration often involves moving around the environment, leading the perceiver actively to sample the available stimulus information. If this fails to match the information in the relevant schema, then the hypothesis is modified accordingly.
- An initial *analysis* of the sensory cues/features (a *bottom-up* process) might suggest the hypothesis that the object being viewed is, say, a chair.
- This initiates a search for the expected features (such as four legs and a back), which is based on our schema of a chair (and this *synthesis* is a *top-down* process).
- But if the environmental features disconfirm the original hypothesis (the 'chair' has only three legs and no back), then a new hypothesis must be generated and tested (it might be a stool), and the appropriate schema activated.
- Neisser argues that perception never occurs in a vacuum: our sampling of sensory features of the environment is

always guided by our knowledge and past experience. Perception is an interactive process, involving both bottom-up feature analysis and top-down expectations.

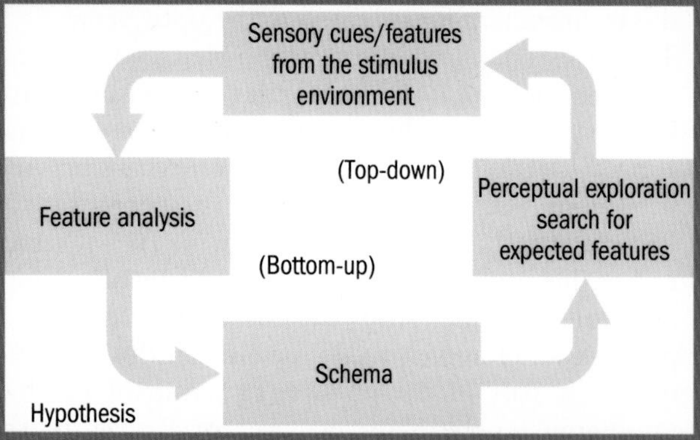

Figure 15.19 Neisser's analysis-by-synthesis model of perception

Marr's computational theory of vision

According to Marr (1982), the central 'problem' of perception is identifying the precise mechanisms and computations by which useful information about a scene is extracted from that scene ('useful information' being what will guide the thoughts or actions of the total system of which the visual system is part). Marr's theory begins by asking 'What is the visual system for?', because only by answering this can we understand how it works.

For Marr, there are three levels at which any process must be understood:

- The *computational theory level* is a theoretical analysis of the tasks performed by a system (in this case, the visual system), and the methods needed to perform them.
- The *algorithmic level* is concerned with identifying the actual operations by which perceptual tasks (processes and representations) are achieved.
- The *hardware or implementation level* is concerned with the mechanisms underlying the system's operation. In the case of a biological visual system, these are neuronal or nervous system structures.

Marr argues that vision's main 'job' is to derive a representation of the shape of objects from information contained in the retinal image. This happens via four successive stages, which constitute individual *modules*. Each stage or module takes as its input the information it receives from the previous stage/module, converting it into a more complex description/representation. By taking the image as the starting point, Marr's approach is strictly bottom-up (Roth, 1995). But as we'll see later, there are also top-down aspects.

Box 15.6 The four stages, or modules, of Marr's computational theory of vision

The image (or grey-level description): This represents the intensity of light at each point in the retinal image, so as to discover regions in the image and their boundaries. Regions and boundaries are parts of images, not parts of things in the world, so this represents the starting point of seeing.
The primal sketch: Useful attributes of a 3-D scene (such as object boundaries and shadows) can be recovered from the image by locating and describing the places where the image intensity changes relatively abruptly from place to place.

- The function of the *raw primal sketch* is to describe potentially significant regions, which may correspond in the real world to the boundaries between overlapping objects, their edges, and texture.
- The *full primal sketch* provides information about how these regions 'go together' to form structures (it provides a functional explanation of the Gestalt grouping principles: see Box 15.1). Grouping is necessary, since in complex scenes the images of different objects may *occlude* (overlap) each other. Overall, it provides a more useful and less cluttered description of the image (hence 'sketch').

2½-D sketch: Its function is to make explicit the orientation and depth of visible surfaces, as if a 'picture' of the world is beginning to emerge. It's no longer an image, because it contains information about things in the world which provide the image. But it describes only the visible parts of the scene, and so isn't fully three-dimensional.

- Object recognition requires that the input representation of the object is mapped against a representation stored in memory, so that non-visible parts are taken into account (which is essentially what perceptual constancy involves: see pages 248–249).
- The sketch changes relative to the observer's perspective (it's viewpoint-dependent).

3-D model representation: Its function is to make shapes and their spatial organisation explicit as belonging to particular 3-D objects, independently of any particular position or orientation. The observer now has a model of the external world. Knowledge of the nature and construction of the object is now used (*top-down processing*). It can be thought of as *object recognition*.

These four stages are summarised in Figure 15.20.

3-D model representation and object recognition

Since the 3-D model representation involves top-down processes, Marr claimed that in many cases 3-D structures can be derived from the 2½-D sketch using only general principles of the kind used in the earlier stages. This view is based on the observation that stick-figure representations (especially of animals and plants) are easy to recognise (Garnham, 1991). The brain automatically transposes the contours derived from the 2½-D sketch on

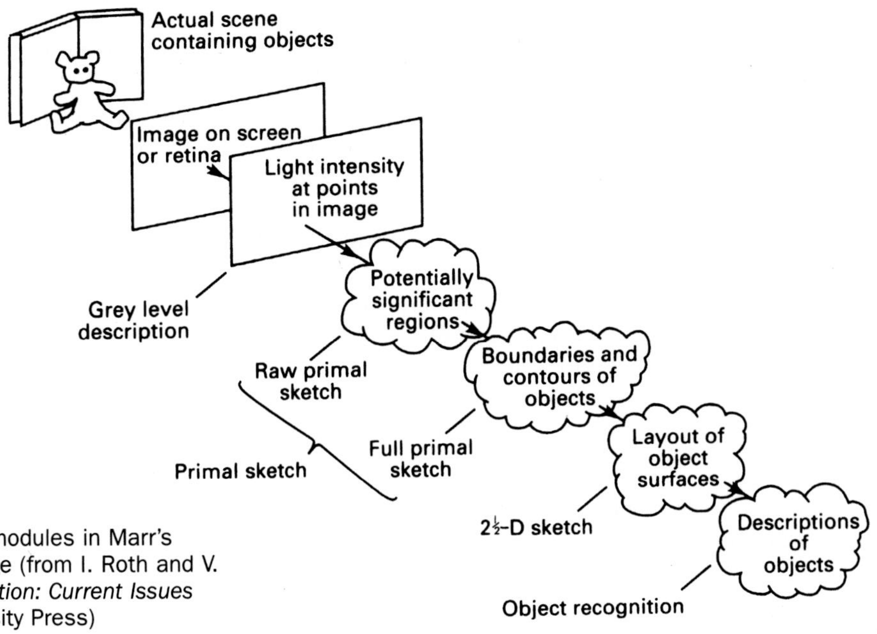

Figure 15.20 The four basic stages or modules in Marr's model of the processing of a visual image (from I. Roth and V. Bruce (1995) *Perception and Representation: Current Issues* (2nd edition). Buckingham: Open University Press)

to axes of symmetry which resemble stick figures composed of pipe cleaners.

Marr & Nishihara (1978) argued that the parts of the body can be represented as jointed cylinders or generalised cylinders which change their size along their length (see Figure 15.21). They then showed that the cylinders which compose an object can be computed from the 2½-D sketch: the lines running down the centre of these cylinders (important in the recognition process) make up the stick figures. Once a generalised cylinder representation of objects in a scene has been computed, it can be compared with stored representations of objects in a catalogue of 3-D models, where objects are represented in 'standard' orientations (Garnham, 1991).

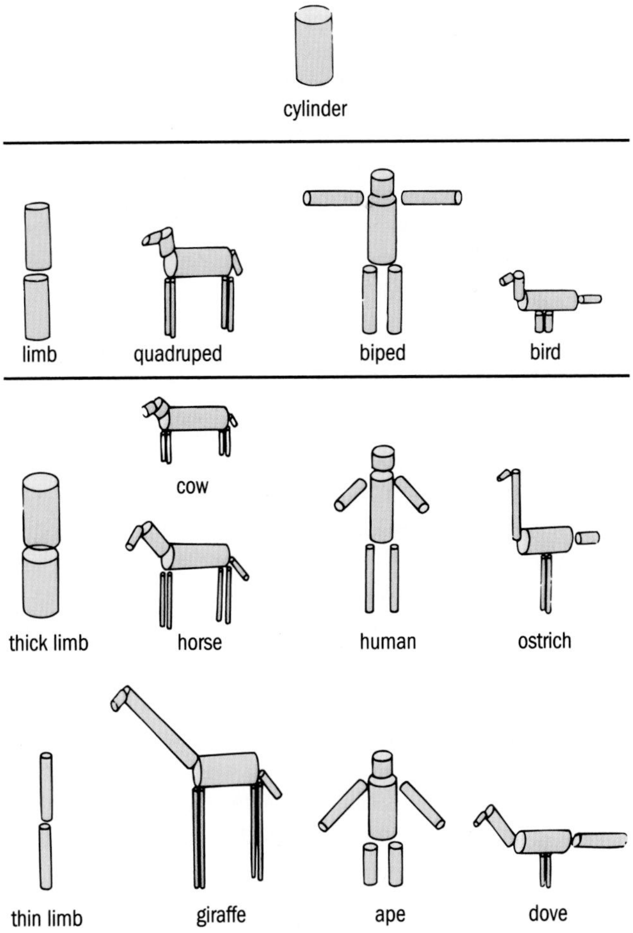

Figure 15.21 Cylinders of various sizes can be combined to represent the shapes of various (parts of) objects (from Marr & Nishihara, 1978)

Evaluation of Marr's theory

- According to Harris & Humphreys (1995), Marr was the first to popularise the computational approach, and his framework remains the widest-ranging computational account of visual object recognition. Marr's work is regarded by many as the most important development in perception theory in recent years (Gordon, 1989).
- Marr & Hildreth (1980) have shown that Marr's model does what it claims to do, broadly speaking. But this doesn't mean that biological vision systems necessarily work in the same way (Roth, 1995). The main evidence supporting the relevance of Marr's model to biological vision comes from the neurophysiological studies of Hubel and Wiesel (see Chapter 5).
- The general claim that the early stage of vision consists of a representation of simple components, such as edge segments, is generally accepted (Roth, 1995). But the least well supported stage is the 3-D model, since the

early stages make only very general assumptions about the structure of the external world and don't require knowledge of specific objects. Although a bottom-up approach isn't an inevitable consequence of the computational approach, it has dominated recent research. This is partly because it's easier to derive computational theories from the early stages of perception, where the relationships between the stimulus and the world are much easier to specify (Harris & Humphreys, 1995).

- Gardner (1985), too, has argued that most of Marr's theory focuses on the steps prior to recognition of real objects in the real world ('the most central part of perception'):

> ... the procedures [Marr] outlined for object recognition may prove applicable chiefly to the perception of figures of a certain sort, for example, the mammalian body, which lends itself to decomposition in terms of generalised cylindrical forms.

- Researchers are beginning to reconsider whether top-down, domain-specific knowledge might be used. This trend has been encouraged by *connectionist models of visual perception* (see Chapter 20) and Biederman's (1987) *recognition-by-components theory* (see Chapter 14). Marr's general approach to perception, and his argument for computational theories, is, according to Harris & Humphreys (1995):

> ... likely to remain as one of the most important contributions of research in artificial intelligence to psychological theory. Such theories are able to guide empirical and theoretical research, even if the detailed models specified at any one time later turn out to be wrong.

CONCLUSIONS

Form and depth perception, perceptual constancy and visual illusions are all concerned with perceptual organisation, and many of the principles governing perceptual organisation are commonly referred to as Gestalt laws.

While Gregory's constructivist ('top-down') and Gibson's direct ('bottom-up') approaches may appear to contradict each other, it's possible to see them as complementary. According to Harris (1998):

> Perception is not just a single task but ... contributes in many different ways to everyday life ... Some of these ... are obviously more difficult than others and it seems likely that some can be accomplished directly, as Gibson maintained, whilst others may require sophisticated internal knowledge and are thus better described by the indirect approach.

CHAPTER SUMMARY

- **Sensation** involves physical stimulation of the sense organs, while **perception** is the **organisation** and **interpretation** of incoming sensory information.
- **Gestalt psychologists** identified innately determined principles through which sensory information is interpreted and organised. The most basic of these is **form perception**, which organises incoming sensory information into **figure and ground**.
- Laws for **grouping** stimuli together all rest on the belief that 'the whole is greater than the sum of its parts'. These laws can be summarised under Koffka's **law of prägnanz**. Major Gestalt laws of perception include **proximity**, **similarity**, **continuity**, **closure**, **part–whole relationship**, **simplicity**, and **common fate**.
- The various 'laws' are merely descriptive and often imprecise and difficult to measure. Despite empirical support, Gestalt laws are difficult to apply to 3-D perception and to whole scenes (they lack **ecological validity**).
- **Depth perception** allows us to estimate the distance of objects from us. **Pictorial cues** refer to aspects of the visual field, and are **monocular**. **Non-pictorial cues** include **convergence** and **retinal disparity**, which are **binocular**.
- **Perceptual constancy** refers to the ability to recognise an object as unchanging despite changes in its **size**, **shape**, **location**, **brightness** and **colour**.
- Four main kinds of **perceptual illusion** are **distortions/geometric illusions**, **ambiguous/reversible figures**, **paradoxical figures** and **fictions**. Other illusions include those involving **apparent movement** and **shading**.
- According to **top-down** (**conceptually driven**) perceptual processing theorists, perception is the end result of an indirect process that involves making inferences about the world, based on knowledge and expectations. **Bottom-up** (**data-driven**) theorists argue that perception is a **direct** process, determined by the information presented to the sensory receptors.
- According to **Gregory's constructivist theory**, we often **supplement** perception with **unconscious inferences**. His **misapplied size constancy theory** claims that we interpret the ingoing and outgoing fins of the arrows in the Müller–Lyer illusion as providing perspective cues to distance.
- **Perceptual set** acts as a **selector** and **interpreter**, and can be induced by **perceiver/organismic** and **stimulus/situational variables**. Perceiver variables include expectations, which often interact with context.
- According to **Gibson**, the **optic array** provides information about the layout and properties of objects in space requiring little or no (unconscious) information

processing, computations or internal representations. **Optic flow patterns**, **texture gradients** and **affordances** are all **invariant**, unchanging and 'higher-order' features of the optic array.

- Gibson overlooked the role of **culturally determined knowledge** in perception. He also failed to distinguish between **seeing** and **seeing as**, the latter forming the basic principle of **transactionalism**.
- Both Gibson and Gregory agree that perception is an active process, influenced by learning (making them **empiricists**), although they propose different kinds of learning. Gibson is also a **nativist** in certain respects and was influenced by the Gestalt psychologists.
- Bottom-up processing (Gibson) may be crucial under **optimal viewing conditions**, but under **sub-optimal conditions**, top-down processing (Gregory) becomes increasingly important.
- According to **Neisser's analysis-by-synthesis model**, perception is an **interactive** process, involving both bottom-up feature analysis and top-down expectations (appearing at different stages of a perceptual cycle).
- **Marr's computational theory** states that vision's main function is to derive a representation of object **shape** from information in the retinal image. This is achieved via a series of four increasingly complex stages/modules: the **image/grey-level description**, the **primal sketch**, the **2½-D sketch**, and the **3-D model representation/object recognition**.
- 3-D descriptions are often derived from the 2½-D sketch, using stick-figure representations composed of the lines running down the centre of jointed or generalised cylinders.
- It's easier to derive computational theories from the early (bottom-up) stages of perception, and the 3-D model representation (which involves top-down processes) is the least well supported.

Links with other topics/chapters

- Although perception may require *sensation*, it's commonly distinguished from it. However, there are some important areas of overlap, as in *non-pictorial depth cues*, *colour* and *brightness constancy*, and the importance of *eye movements* (Chapter 5).
- All the major theories of perception, and in particular the Gestalt principles of perceptual organisation, can be seen as concerned with *pattern recognition* (Chapter 14).
- Most theories of perception can be classified as *empiricist*, the main exception being the Gestalt theory, which is *nativist* (Chapter 50).
- The Gestalt psychologists contributed to early research into *problem-solving* (Chapter 20).
- Gestalt principles have also had a considerable impact on many aspects of *social psychology*, in particular *social perception* (interpersonal perception/the perception of other people: Chapter 22), *attribution theory* (Chapter 23) and *theories of attitude change* (Chapter 24).

16

THE DEVELOPMENT OF PERCEPTUAL ABILITIES

INTRODUCTION AND OVERVIEW

Chapters 5 and 15 showed that visual perception is a complex set of interconnected and overlapping abilities, including perception of depth, shape and movement. Whether these are present at birth or develop through experience has been one of psychology's most enduring debates. This chapter examines the evidence concerning the development of visual perception.

In Chapter 15, we distinguished between *nativists* and *empiricists*. While these terms originally denoted philosophical schools of thought (see Chapters 1 and 3), they're still used in the context of psychological debates regarding the origins of human abilities, such as language (see Chapter 19) and perception. Nativists are 'naturists', who believe that we're born with certain capacities to perceive the world in particular ways. These abilities may take time to appear, but they do so through the genetically determined process of maturation, with little or no learning being involved (see Chapter 50). Empiricists, by contrast, are 'nurturists', maintaining that all our knowledge and abilities are acquired through experience; that is, they're learned. For Locke (1690), the mind at birth is a blank slate (or *tabula rasa*) on which experience 'writes'. Locke's belief was supported by James (1890), according to whom:

> The baby, assailed by eyes, ears, nose, skin and entrails at once, feels it all as one great booming, buzzing confusion.

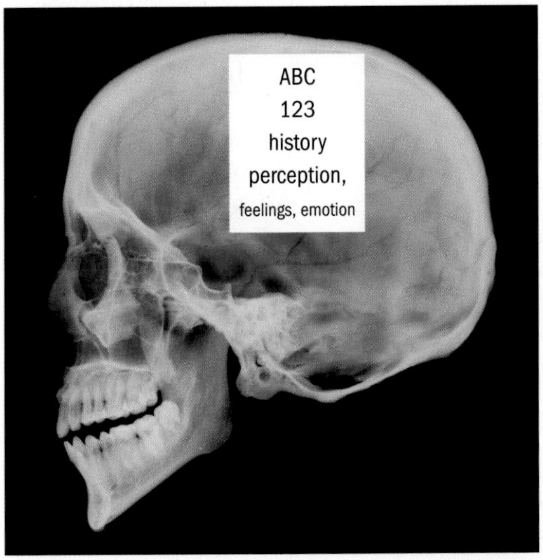

Nativist

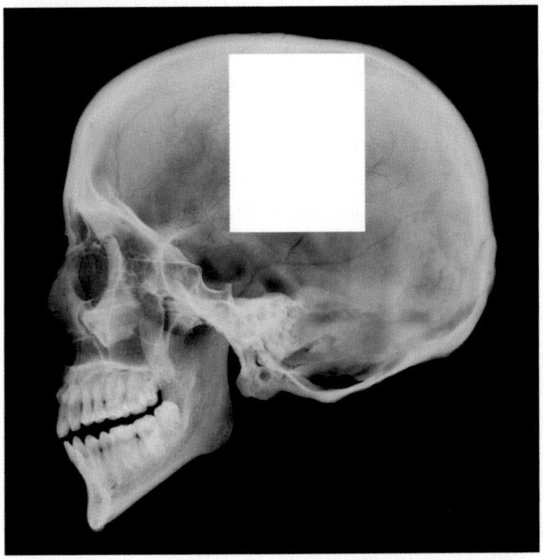

Empiricist

Most present-day psychologists wouldn't take such extreme views. They'd probably consider themselves to be *interactionists*, believing that while we may be born with certain capacities, environmental influences are crucial for determining how – and even whether – these capacities actually develop. Although particular abilities may be more affected by genetic or environmental influences, *all* abilities are the product of an interaction between both sets of factors.

In a different sense, empiricists are also interactionists. Segall (1994) says that every perception is the result of an interaction between a stimulus and a perceiver, shaped by prior experience. This is essentially a 'top-down' view consistent with Gregory's theory (see Chapter 15). But it also helps to underline an important, but rarely acknowledged, similarity between those who favour the nativist or empiricist approaches: the perceiver isn't a passive responder to external stimuli, but in some way contributes to, and influences, the perceptual experience.

OVERVIEW OF THE RESEARCH

ASK YOURSELF...

- What do you consider might be the main advantage and disadvantage of studying (a) newborn babies and (b) non-human animals in trying to understand the development of perceptual abilities?

An evaluation of the research methods

- Investigating the perceptual abilities of newborn babies (or *neonates*) represents the most direct way of investigating the nature–nurture issue. In general, the earlier a particular ability appears, the more likely it is to be under the influence of genetic factors. But the fact that it develops some time after birth doesn't necessarily mean it's been learnt: it could take time to mature. However, there are other special difficulties involved in studying speechless participants.
- *Non-human animal experiments* often involve depriving animals of normal sensory and perceptual stimulation, and recording the long-term effects on their sensory and perceptual abilities. Others study how animals' brains control perceptual abilities. From a research point of view, the main advantage of studying animals is that we can manipulate their environments in ways that aren't permissible with humans. Deprivation studies can tell us how much and what kinds of early experience are necessary for normal perceptual development in those species being studied. But we must be very cautious about generalising these findings to humans. We must also be aware of the ethical objections to such research (see Chapter 48).
- Studies of *human cataract patients* represent the human counterpart to non-human deprivation experiments. These patients have been deprived of normal visual

experience through a physical defect, rather than through experimental manipulation/interference, and constitute a kind of 'natural experimental group'. Their vision is restored through surgical removal of the cataract, and the abilities that are evident immediately after removal of the bandages are normally taken to be unlearned. However, generalising from 'unusual' adults can be misleading.

- In studies of *perceptual adaptation/readjustment*, human volunteers wear special goggles which distort the visual world in various ways. If they can adapt to such a distorted-looking world, then human 'perceptual habits' cannot be as fixed or rigid as they would be if they were under genetic control. However, the adaptation involved may be motor, rather than perceptual, that is, learning to move about successfully in a very different-looking environment. If this is the case, then we cannot be sure that our perceptual 'habits' are habits at all (learned in the first place), but only that we're good at changing our body movements to 'match' what we see.
- *Cross-cultural studies* attempt to test whether or not the way that people in western culture perceive things is universal, that is, perceived in the same way by people who live in cultures very different from our own. The most common method of testing is to present members of different cultural groups with the same stimulus material, usually visual illusions. Cross-cultural studies prevent us from generalising from a comparatively small sample of the earth's population (Price-Williams, 1966: see Chapter 47). Consistent differences between different cultural groups are usually attributed to environmental factors of some kind. Such studies, therefore, enable us to discover the extent to which perceiving is structured by the nervous system (and so common to all human beings), and to what extent by experience. But, as we'll see, psychologists cannot agree as to the key features of such cultural experience.

What general conclusions can we draw?

As we noted in the *Introduction and overview*, most psychologists are interactionists. However, some attempts have been made to test directly the merits of the nativist and empiricist positions, particularly in relation to neonates and infants. Most of the evidence supporting the nativist view derives from infant studies. Recall that the earlier a particular ability appears, the less likely it is to have been learned, and so the more likely it is to be under genetic control.

Although the bulk of the evidence supports the interactionist position, there are grounds for concluding that relatively simple perceptual abilities are controlled more by genes and less susceptible to environmental influence. The reverse is true for more complex abilities. The most clear-cut demonstration of this comes from human cataract patients, and this is where we'll begin.

> *ASK YOURSELF...*
> - Looking back at Chapters 5 and 15, identify some examples of what you think may count as simple and complex visual abilities.
> - What determined your choice; in other words, what makes them simple or complex?

STUDIES OF HUMAN CATARACT PATIENTS

Most of the evidence comes from the work of von Senden (1932), a German doctor, who reported on 65 cases of people who'd undergone cataract-removal surgery between 1700 and 1928. A cataract is a film over the lens of the eye, which prevents normal (patterned) light from entering the eye. Cataracts can be present at birth or develop any time afterwards, and their removal 'restores' vision.

Hebb (1949) re-analysed von Senden's data in terms of:

- *figural unity*, the ability to detect the presence of a figure or stimulus, and
- *figural identity*, being able to name or in some other way identify the object, to 'say' what it is.

Initially, cataract patients are bewildered by an array of visual stimuli (rather like the 'booming, buzzing confusion' which James believed was the perceptual experience of newborn babies). However, they can distinguish *figure from ground* (see Chapter 15), *fixate* and *scan* objects, and follow moving objects with their eyes. But they cannot identify by sight alone those objects already familiar through touch (including faces), distinguish between various geometrical shapes without counting the corners or tracing the outline with their fingers, or say which of two sticks is longer without feeling them (although they can tell there's a difference).

They also fail to show *perceptual constancy*. For example, even after recognising by sight alone a sugar lump held in someone's hand, patients may be unable to identify it correctly if it's suspended from a piece of string. This is contradicted by Bower's research with neonates, which suggests that size and shape constancy are innate: see pages 275–276.

So, the more simple ability of figural unity is available very soon after cataract removal and doesn't seem to depend on prior visual experience. But the more complex figural identity seems to require learning. Hebb believes that this is how these two aspects of perception normally develop. Further evidence comes from the case of S.B.

> **CASE STUDY 16.1:** S.B. (Gregory & Wallace, 1963)
> - S.B. was 52 when he received his sight after a corneal graft operation.
> - His judgement of size and distance was good, provided he was familiar with the objects in question.

- Unlike most of the cases studied by Hebb, he could recognise objects visually if he was already familiar with them through touch (he displayed good *cross-modal transfer*).
- However, he seemed to have great difficulty in identifying objects visually if he wasn't already familiar with them in this way. A year after his operation, he still couldn't draw the front of a bus although the rest of the drawing was very well executed (see Figure 16.1).
- As the months passed, it became clear that S.B. was in some ways like a newborn baby when it came to recognising objects and events by sight alone. For instance, he found it impossible to judge distances by sight alone. He knew what windows were, from touching them both from inside a room and from outside (while standing on the ground). But, of course, he'd never been able to look out from a top-floor window, and he thought 'he would be able to touch the ground below the window with his feet if he lowered himself by his hands'. The window in question was the one in his hospital room – 40 feet above the ground!
- He never learnt to interpret facial expressions such as smiles and frowns, although he could infer a person's mood from the sound of their voice. He preferred to sit in the dark all evening, instead of putting on the light.

Figure 16.1 This was drawn after S.B. had had some experience of sighted travel. Basically it shows the parts he knew by touch but clearly he had also, by this time, noticed the bright advertisement for Typhoo Tea on the side of the bus

Evaluation of cataract patient studies

- Adult patients aren't the same as babies. While infants' sensory systems are all relatively immature (see page 271), adults have other well-developed sensory modalities which tend to compensate for the lack of vision (especially touch and hearing). These other channels may actually hinder visual learning, because the patient may have to 'unlearn' previous experience. For example, S.B.'s continued preference for touch over vision may reflect a tendency to stick with what's familiar, rather than experiment with the unknown. This may be a safer conclusion to draw than Hebb's, which is that figural identity is (normally) learned.
- Traditionally, cataract patients haven't been adequately prepared for their 'new world of vision'. The resulting confusion and general emotional distress following the operation may make it difficult to be sure just what they can and cannot see. When blind, S.B. would cross the street on his own. But once he could *see* the traffic, it frightened him so much that he refused to cross on his own. In fact, he died three years after his operation, at least partially from depression. Depression was also common amongst von Senden's cases.
- Some physical deterioration of the visual system may have occurred during the years of blindness. This could account for the absence of figural identity, rather than lack of visual stimulation and learning (as Hebb maintains).
- The reliability of the case histories themselves is open to doubt. There's great variability in the ages of the patients, when they underwent surgery, and when their cataracts first appeared, and hence in the amount of their previous visual experience.

NON-HUMAN ANIMAL EXPERIMENTS

Riesen (1947) deprived one group of chimps of light by raising them in darkness, except for several 45-second periods of exposure to light while they were being fed. This continued until they were 16 months old, when they were compared with a group of normally reared chimps. The deprived group showed pupil constriction to light, and were startled by sudden, intense illumination. But they didn't blink in response to threatening movements made towards their faces, or show any interest in their toys unless they accidentally touched them.

Weiskrantz (1956) pointed out that the deprived group's visual deficiencies were probably due to failure of the retinas to develop properly, as a result of insufficient light stimulation. Riesen's experiment, therefore, may show only that a certain amount of light is physically necessary to maintain the visual system and allow it to mature normally.

In response to these criticisms, Riesen (1965) reared three chimps from birth to seven months of age, under three different conditions:

- Debi spent the whole time in darkness
- Kova spent 1½ hours per day exposed to *diffuse* (or unpatterned) light by wearing translucent goggles; the rest of the time was spent in darkness.
- Lad was raised in normal lighting conditions.

ASK YOURSELF...

- What do you think the outcome of this experiment was?
- For example, which chimp suffered retinal damage, and what effects might exposure to unpatterned light have had?

As expected, only Debi suffered retinal damage. Lad was no different, perceptually, from any other normally reared chimp. It was Kova who was of special interest, because she was only exposed to unpatterned light (patches of different colours and brightnesses – not distinguishable shapes or patterns), but without suffering any retinal damage. Her perceptual development was noticeably retarded.

These, and similar experiments with monkeys, chimps and kittens, suggest that:

- light is necessary for normal physical development of the visual system (at least in chimps, some monkeys and kittens)

KEY STUDY 16.1 Kitten carousel experiment (Held & Hein, 1963)

- Held and Hein used a kitten carousel to study kittens' ability to guide their movements using vision (see Figure 16.2).
- For their first eight weeks, kittens were kept in darkness. They then spent three hours each day in the carousel, the rest of the time being spent in darkness.
- The 'active' kitten could move itself around (its legs were free), and its movements were transmitted to the 'passive' kitten via a series of pulleys. Every time the active kitten moved, the passive kitten moved the same distance, at the same speed. Since the visual environment was constant, both kittens had exactly the same visual experience.

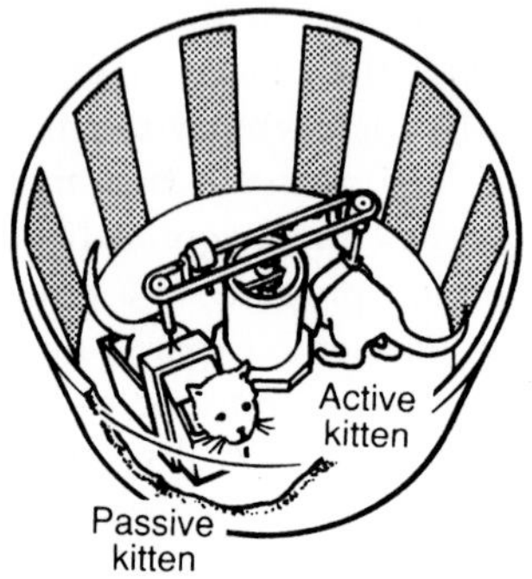

Figure 16.2 The kitten carousel (from Held, 1965)

- When paw–eye coordination was tested several weeks later, the passive kittens were markedly inferior. For example, they showed no evidence of depth perception when placed on the deep side of the visual cliff apparatus (see text below and Figure 16.9).
- However, the passive kittens soon learned the normal avoidance responses on the deep side of the cliff when allowed to run around in a lighted environment.
- This suggests that what they'd failed to learn were the correct motor responses associated with depth perception (sensorimotor coordination), rather that depth perception as such (see the section on perceptual readjustment studies below).

- patterned light is also necessary for the normal development of more complex visual abilities (in those species), such as following a moving object, differentiating between geometrical shapes, perceiving depth and distinguishing a moving from a stationary object.

Other animal experiments have also shown the impact of early experience on perceptual abilities.

Blakemore & Cooper (1970) raised kittens from birth in darkness, except for a five-hour period each day when they were placed in a large round chamber. This had either vertical or horizontal stripes painted on the inside, and a glass floor which reflected the pattern of stripes. The kittens wore special collars which prevented them from seeing their own bodies, and the stripes were the only visual stimuli they encountered.

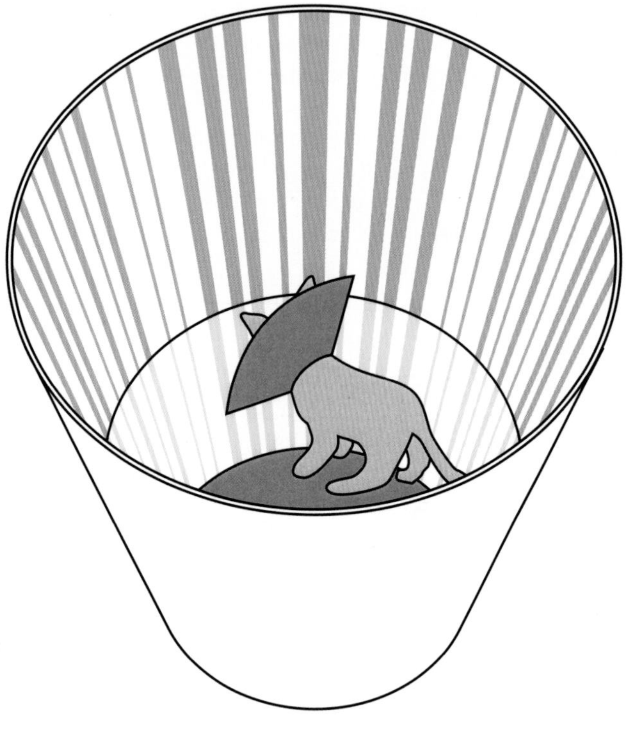

Figure 16.3 The 'vertical' world used in Blakemore & Cooper's (1970) experiment

At five months old, the kittens were tested for line recognition by being presented with a moving pointer held either vertically or horizontally. Those reared in the 'vertical world' would reach out only to a vertical pointer, while those raised in the 'horizontal world' reached only for a horizontal pointer. Depending on their early visual experience, the kittens acted as if they were blind in the presence of the other kind of visual stimulus.

This 'behavioural blindness' mirrored 'physiological blindness'. By placing microelectrodes into individual cells in the visual cortex, Blakemore and Cooper found that the 'vertical' kittens didn't possess cells that were responsive to bars of light moved horizontally, and the reverse was true for the 'horizontal' kittens. The only receptive fields to have developed were those which reflected the kittens' early visual experience (see Chapter 5).

However, this doesn't show conclusively that responding to lines at different angles develops solely through environmental influence. It's possible that receptive fields for all angles are present at birth, but that where a kitten sees only vertical lines, those fields which would otherwise have responded to horizontal lines are 'taken over' by vertical fields. Nevertheless, these findings suggest very strongly that the environment is important in the development of at least certain kinds of perceptual ability in some species: in kittens, perception does seem to be at least partly learned.

Evaluation of non-human animal experiments

- A general problem with non-human animal studies (as with studies of human infants) is that we can only *infer* their perceptual experiences through observing their behaviour or their physiological responses. They're unable to tell us more directly what they can or cannot see.
- We cannot be certain that animals deprived in particular ways don't perceive particular stimuli, only that they don't *behave* as if they do. It's possible that certain perceptual abilities have developed, but if they've not become linked to the animal's behaviour, we may have no way of knowing.

ASK YOURSELF...

- Do you consider the experiments by Riesen, Held and Hein, and Blakemore and Cooper to be ethically acceptable?
- What kinds of scientific justification could be made in their defence?

PERCEPTUAL ADAPTATION/READJUSTMENT STUDIES

If it can be shown that people are capable of perceiving the world in a different way from normal, and adjusting to this altered perception, then perception is probably learned. The greater the degree of adaptation, the more significant the role of learning is taken to be. Neither salamanders (Sperry, 1943) nor chickens (Hess, 1956) show any evidence of being able to adapt to distorted perceptions, suggesting that genetic factors largely control their perceptual abilities.

One of the earliest recorded human studies was that of Stratton. (See Key Study 16.2.)

KEY STUDY 16.2 Turning the world upside down (Stratton, 1896)

- Stratton fitted himself with a telescope on one eye which 'turned the world upside down'. The other eye was kept covered.
- He wore the telescope for a total of 87 hours over an eight-day period, wearing blindfolds at night and at other times when not wearing the inverting lens.
- As far as possible, Stratton went about his normal routine.
- For the first three days, he was aware that part of his environment – the part not in his immediate field of vision but on the periphery – was in a different orientation.
- But by day four, he was beginning to imagine unseen parts as also being inverted, and by day five he had to make a conscious effort to remember that he actually had the telescope on. He could walk round the house without bumping into furniture, and when he moved his surroundings looked 'normal'.
- However, when he concentrated hard and remained still, things still appeared upside down.
- By day eight, everything seemed 'harmonious'; he began to 'feel' inverted, but this was quite normal and natural to him.

When Stratton removed the telescope, he immediately recognised the visual orientation as the one that existed before the experiment began. He found it surprisingly bewildering, although definitely *not* upside-down. This absence of an inverted after-image/after-effect means that Stratton hadn't actually learnt to see the world in an upside-down fashion. If he had, removal of the telescope would have caused the now normal (right-way-up) world to look upside-down again! Instead, it suggests that the adaptation took the form of learning the appropriate *motor responses* in an upside-down-looking world. (Compare this with the question of depth perception in Held and Hein's kittens: see Key Study 16.1.) But Stratton did experience an after-effect which caused things before him to 'swing and sweep' as he moved his eyes, showing that *location constancy* had been disrupted.

In another experiment, Stratton made goggles which visually displaced his body, so that he always appeared

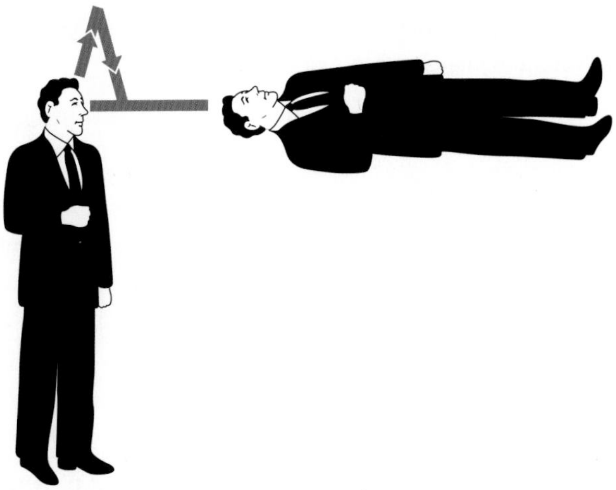

Figure 16.4 One of Stratton's experiments in which goggles displaced the wearer's body image at right angles

horizontally in front of himself (see Figure 16.4). Wherever he walked, he 'followed' his own body image, which was suspended at right angles to his actual body. When he lay down, his body would appear above him, vertically, again at right angles. After three days, he was able to go out for a walk on his own – and lived to tell the tale!

Gilling & Brightwell (1982) replicated Stratton's inverted goggles experiment.

CASE STUDY 16.2: Susannah Fienues (Gilling & Brightwell, 1982)

Susannah Fienues, a young art student, wore inverted goggles for a period of seven days. After first putting them on she reported:

> The cars are going upside down. They're going the wrong way. It's all going completely the wrong way to what you'd expect. It's really strange.

After one hour, she reported:

> In fact, looking at people in cars was quite normal, I didn't think they were upside down, and I just got adjusted to it, I think. But the difficult thing is just walking and being very disorientated, because how you feel is completely different to what you're doing ... As for things being upside down, it just doesn't feel like that at all because I know very well that I'm sitting here and so I think my brain still knows that, so it's all right.

Like Stratton, she at first had great difficulty in pouring milk from a jug into a glass. By the fourth day, she could walk without difficulty, from the bedroom to the sitting room. And she could now pour the milk! She felt 'Just fine ... I don't notice that things are upside down at all.' She could write her name normally, but only if she closed her eyes and didn't see her hand as she wrote it. With her eyes open, she could write it so that it appeared normal to her but inverted to anyone else!

By day seven her early problems seemed to have vanished – she could ride her bike, walk, run, climb stairs, turn corners, make coffee and put records on.

> The only thing that's still quite difficult is eating and using a knife and fork.

Again:

> It's become more and more difficult to imagine myself standing upright or sitting down normally. I almost want to sit upside down because I can't quite imagine myself sitting normally.

This account supports the view of vision as an active process, enabling us to deal with the world. When Susannah removed the goggles, she was annoyed that nothing seemed any different! She reverted to normal vision within a few minutes, very relieved that the experiment was over. Like Stratton, she learnt to match her vision with signals reported by the rest of her body. According to Gilling and Brightwell:

> She was not just seeing, but sampling the world as a whole with her senses, and organising them so that they told stories which could be sensibly related to each other. She saw with her whole body, the whole apparatus of her senses, as it were, and not just with her eyes ...

Snyder & Pronko (1952) made goggles which inverted and reversed the visual world. Their volunteers wore them continually for 30 days and adapted to the changes. Two years after the experiment, these participants coped just as well when refitted with the goggles as first-time participants at the end of the 30-day period. This shows that motor adaptations are extremely resistant to forgetting.

ASK YOURSELF...

- What conclusions can you draw from adaptation studies?

Evaluation of adaptation studies

- When volunteers adapt to a distorted perceptual world, they're not, for the most part, actually learning to see 'normally', but are developing the appropriate *motor behaviour* which helps them to get around and function efficiently in their environment. What's learnt is not a new way of perceiving the world, but a new set of body movements.
- The visual system, at least in adults, is extremely *flexible*, and can adjust to distorted conditions. This strongly suggests that learning plays an important role in perceptual development, since a totally or largely innate system wouldn't allow such adaptation to occur.
- The volunteers are adults, who've already undergone a great deal of learning and in whom maturation has already taken place. This makes it difficult to generalise from these studies to how babies develop under normal circumstances.

STUDYING NEONATE AND INFANT VISUAL PERCEPTION

Before looking at the perceptual world of the human neonate, we need to be familiar with some of the methods that have been used in this area.

Box 16.1 Some methods used to study neonate and infant perception

Spontaneous visual preference technique (or **preferential looking**)**:** Two stimuli are presented simultaneously to the neonate. If more time is spent looking at one, it can reasonably be assumed that (a) the difference between the stimuli can be perceived, and (b) the stimulus which is looked at longer is preferred.

Sucking rate: A dummy (or pacifier) is used and the sucking rate in response to different stimuli is measured. First, a baseline sucking rate is established, and then a stimulus introduced. The stimulus may produce an increase or decrease in sucking rate but, eventually, *habituation* will occur, and the baby will stop responding. If the stimulus is changed and another increase or decrease in sucking rate occurs, it can be inferred that the baby has responded to the change as a novel stimulus, and hence can tell the difference between the two stimuli.

Habituation: This is used as a method in its own right. If an external stimulus and a baby's representation of it match, then the baby presumably recognises the stimulus. This will be reflected by the baby ignoring it. Mismatches will maintain the baby's attention, so that a novel (and discriminable) stimulus presented after habituation to a familiar stimulus re-excites attention (the baby starts responding again).

Conditioned head rotation: The infant is *operantly conditioned* (see Chapter 11) to turn its head in response to a stimulus. The stimulus can then be presented in a different orientation, and the presence or absence of the conditioned response recorded. It's been used to test for *shape constancy* (see page 276) and in *auditory perception* (Bornstein, 1988).

Physiological measures: If a physiological change (such as heart rate or breathing rate) occurs when a new stimulus is presented, it can be inferred that the infant can discriminate between the old and new stimuli.

Measures of electrical activity in the brain: By using electrodes attached to the scalp, researchers can look for visually evoked potentials (VEPs) occurring in response to particular stimuli. If different stimuli produce different VEPs, the infant can presumably distinguish between those stimuli. A recent piece of equipment used for doing this is the 'geodesic hair-net' (see Chapter 4, page 61).

The perceptual equipment of babies

At birth, the whole nervous system is immature. The optic nerve is thinner and shorter than in adults, and the myelin sheath won't be fully developed until about four months. As a result, visual information is transmitted less effectively to the immature cortex. Also, at birth a baby's eye is about half the size and weight of an adult's, and the eyeball is shorter. This reduces the distance between the retina and lens, making vision less efficient. So, although the new-born's eyeball is anatomically identical to an adult's, the relationship between the parts is different, and they don't develop at the same rate (see Chapter 5, pages 80–82).

Box 16.2 What can babies see?

Colour perception: The retina, rods and cones are reasonably well developed at birth. Using habituation, Bornstein (1976) found that in the absence of brightness cues, three-month-old babies could discriminate blue-green from white, and yellow from green (tests which are typically failed by those who are red–green colour blind). Most babies possess largely normal colour vision at two months, and some as early as one month (Bornstein, 1988).

Brightness: The fovea is also reasonably well developed at birth. The developing foetus reacts to bright light, and the pupillary reflex is present even in premature babies, with the blink reflex present at birth. These findings suggest that a baby's sensitivity to brightness is reasonably similar to an adult's.

Movement: The *optokinetic reflex* (or *optic nystagmus*), which enables us to follow a moving object, is present within two days of birth. While less efficient than an adult's, it improves rapidly in the first three months. Horizontal movement is better tracked than vertical movement, but is still 'jerky'. This may be because convergence (essential for fixation and depth perception) is absent at birth, although fully developed by two to three months. *Accommodation* reaches adult standards by about four months, probably due to maturation (see Chapter 15, page 248).

Visual acuity: The threshold of visual acuity (the ability to discriminate fine detail) is about 30 times poorer than in adults and, at birth, everything beyond 20 centimetres is seen as a blur (Gwiazda *et al.*, 1980). However, babies aged one to three months will learn to suck on a nipple connected to the focus on a projector to bring a blurred picture into focus (Kalnins and Bruner, 1973). Between 6 and 12 months, visual acuity comes within adult range (20/20 vision: Haith, 1990; Slater, 1994).

The perceptual abilities of babies

According to Schaffer (2004), any deficiencies that exist in the newborn's visual system are soon made up as a result of visual experience ('Looking ... is improved by looking'). But babies aren't merely passive recipients of stimulation:

> ... from a very early age on they can be observed actively to explore their environment with their eyes, looking for interesting sights and in this way supplying their own stimulation ... (Schaffer, 2004)

Pattern (or form) perception

Using the preferential looking technique, Fantz (1961) presented one- to 15-week-old babies with pairs of stimuli (see Figure 16.5). The stimuli were presented at weekly intervals, and Fantz measured how long the babies spent looking at each. There was a distinct preference for more complex stimuli; that is, stimuli which contain more information and in which there's more 'going on'. According to Fantz:

> The relative attractiveness of the two members of a pair depended on the presence of a pattern difference. There were strong preferences between stripes and bull's-eyes and between checkerboard and square. Neither the cross and circle nor the two triangles aroused a significant differential interest. The differential response to pattern was shown at all ages tested, indicating that it was not the result of a learning process.

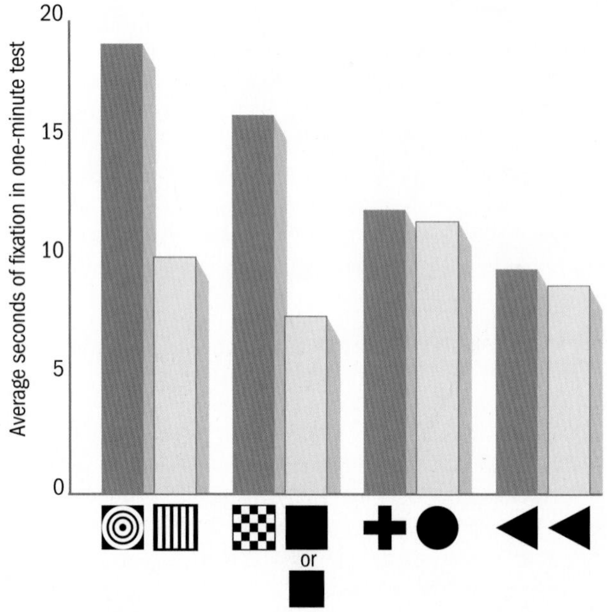

Figure 16.5 Average time spent looking at various pairs of stimulus patterns in babies aged one to 15 weeks. (From Fantz, 1961)

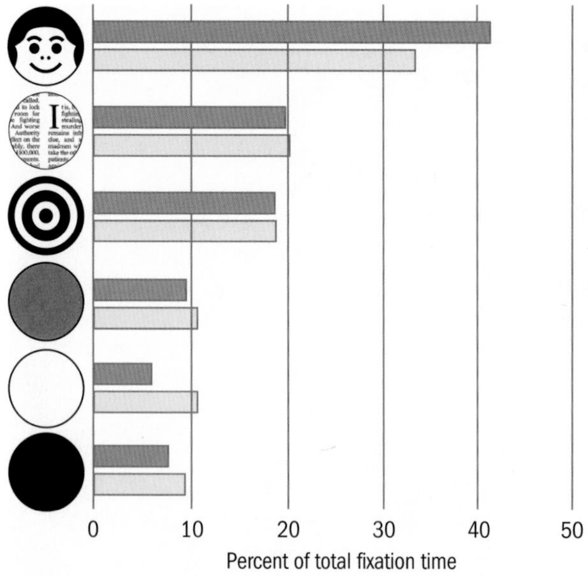

Figure 16.6 Preference for complex stimuli over simple stimuli. The dark green bars show the percentage of fixation time for two- to three-month-olds. The light green bars show the percentage of fixation time for four-month-olds (from Fantz, 1961)

This preference for complexity is apparently a function of age. The babies tested at weekly intervals could discriminate between stimuli with progressively narrower stripes. Later, Fantz showed that two- to four-month-old babies prefer patterns to colour or brightness, as shown in Figure 16.6.

The preference for increasing complexity suggests that the baby's capacity for differentiation steadily improves. Possibly this is because its ability to scan becomes more efficient and thorough. Support for this comes from studies showing that very young infants confine their scanning to one corner of a triangle, suggesting a preference for areas of greatest contrast (Salapatek, 1975). Only later does the baby begin to explore all around the stimulus and inside it, and attend to the whole pattern and not just specific parts. Before two months of age, neonates probably discriminate between shapes on the basis of *lower-order variables*, such as orientation and contrast (Slater & Morison, 1985). But after two months, 'true form perception' begins (Slater, 1989), and babies respond to *higher-order variables* (such as configurational invariance and form categories).

The perception of human faces

> ***ASK YOURSELF...***
> - Can you think of any reasons why it would be a 'good idea' for babies to have an inborn knowledge of/preference for faces?
> - What is it about faces that babies are likely to find particularly attractive?

Eye movements already occur in the womb and in the dark, so they aren't just a reaction to being stimulated. Rather, they're a sign that babies are born prepared to explore their visual world. This exploration is far from being a random process. Babies have quite specific attentional preferences and will scan their surroundings in an active search for those features of their visual world that matter to them. This is best illustrated by their interest in the human face (Schaffer, 2004).

The human face is three-dimensional, contains high-contrast information (especially the eyes, mouth and hairline), constantly moves (the eyes, mouth and head), is a source of auditory information (the voice), and regulates its behaviour according to the baby's own activities. Thus, the human face combines complexity, pattern and movement (it's a *supernormal stimulus*: Rheingold, 1961), all of which babies appear innately to prefer. As Schaffer (2004) says:

> ... It is as though nature has ensured that babies are preadapted to attend to that aspect of their environment that is most important to their survival and welfare, namely, other people ...

A crucial question is whether preference for faces occurs because of this combination of factors, or whether there's an innate perceptual knowledge of a face *as a face*.

Fantz (1961) presented babies aged between four days and six months with all possible pairs of the three stimuli shown in Figure 16.7. The stimuli were coloured black, presented against a pink background, and of the approximate shape and size of an adult's head.

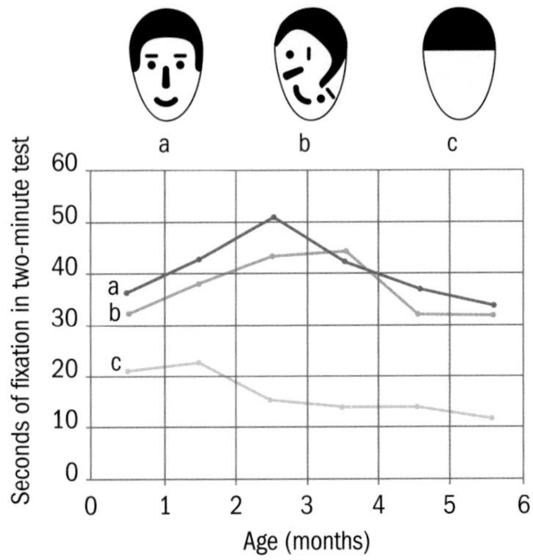

Figure 16.7 Looking times for each of the stimuli used in Fantz's study of the perception of faces (from Fantz, 1961)

Irrespective of age, the babies preferred to look at the schematic representation of a face (a) more than the 'scrambled' face (b). The control stimulus (c) was largely ignored. Even though the difference between (a) and (b) was small, Fantz concluded that 'there is an unlearned, primitive meaning in the form perception of infants', and that babies have an innate preference for 'facedness'.

But according to Bremner (2003), (a) contained more information around the *edge* of the stimulus. This is important, because, as we noted earlier, young infants tend to scan around the *periphery* of complex stimuli. This alone could explain their preference for (a). Hershenson *et al.* (1965) argued that both (a) and (b) were more complex than (c), and this might account for Fantz's findings, rather than a preference for looking at human faces. So they presented neonates with all possible pairs of three *equally complex* stimuli:

- a real female face
- a distorted picture, which retained the outline of head and hair but altered the position of the other features
- a scrambled face (stimulus (b) in Fantz's experiment).

They found no preference for any of the three stimuli, and concluded that a preference for real faces isn't innate, and doesn't appear until about four months of age.

KEY STUDY 16.3 Early evidence of face preference (Johnson *et al.*, 1991)

- Lying on their backs, neonates (with an average age of 43 minutes) saw one of four patterned boards moved in an arc in front of their faces.
- Their eyes followed the most face-like pattern longer than the un-face-like patterns.
- Even the most face-like board was only a schematic representation, with only moderate realism. But it still contains intensity changes, which approximate (or even exaggerate) those of real faces, and for an innate mechanism, that's all that is needed (Bruce & Young, 1998).

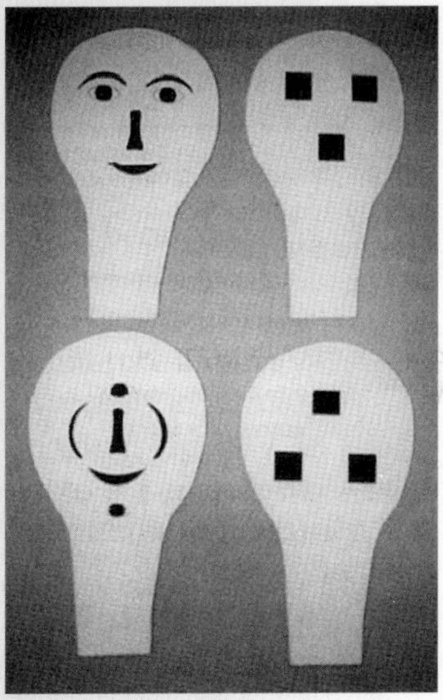

Figure 16.8 Four face-like boards

Perception of real faces

Since Hershenson *et al.*'s study, several studies have found that young babies can discriminate between their mother's face and that of a female stranger (e.g. Carpenter, 1974; Maurer & Salapatek, 1976). Even newborns with only a few hours' contact with their mother show this preference (Bushnell, 2001; Field *et al.*, 1984).

But a possible confounding variable is the infant's ability to recognise the mother through *smell*. Bushnell *et al.* (1989) controlled for this by using a strong-smelling perfume to act as an olfactory mask, and they still found the same preference for the mother among babies as young as 12–36 hours. So far, there's no evidence of a preference for their father's face over a male stranger's, even when he has spent more time with the baby than the mother has. There's no obvious explanation for this (Bee, 2000).

Meltzoff & Moore (1977) found that two- to three-week-old babies, and even newborns (1983) can imitate facial expressions, including sticking out their tongues, opening their mouths and protruding their lips. To achieve this, infants must be able to perceive the *internal* parts of the face making the gestures, and be able to match this to the equivalent parts of their own face (Bremner, 2003).

Baby imitating facial expressions

This perception of the internal features could also explain the very early recognition of the mother's face. Bremner claims that it's distinctly possible that even newborns can discriminate on the basis of *configurational differences* (such as differences in spacing of the eyes, the relationship between eyes and nose, and so on). But this seems to conflict with the finding that young babies only scan the *outside* of a stimulus (see above) – and they would have to be exceptionally fast learners!

According to Slater (1994), the evidence indicates that:

> Some knowledge about faces is present at birth, suggesting that babies come into the world with some innate, genetically determined knowledge about faces.

Depth perception

Perhaps the most famous way of investigating infants' depth perception is Gibson & Walk's (1960) *visual cliff apparatus* (see Figure 16.9). This consists of a central platform, on the *shallow* side of which is a sheet of plexiglass. Immediately below this is a black-and-white checkerboard pattern. On the *deep* side is another sheet of plexiglass, this time with the checkerboard pattern placed on the floor, at a distance of about four feet. This gives the appearance of a 'drop' or 'cliff'. The baby is placed on the central platform, and its mother calls and beckons to it, first from one side and then the other.

Gibson and Walk found that most babies aged between 6 and 14 months wouldn't crawl on to the 'deep' side when beckoned by their mothers. This was interpreted as indicating that neonates have the innate ability to perceive depth. Those babies who did venture onto the deep side did so 'accidentally', either by backing on to it or resting

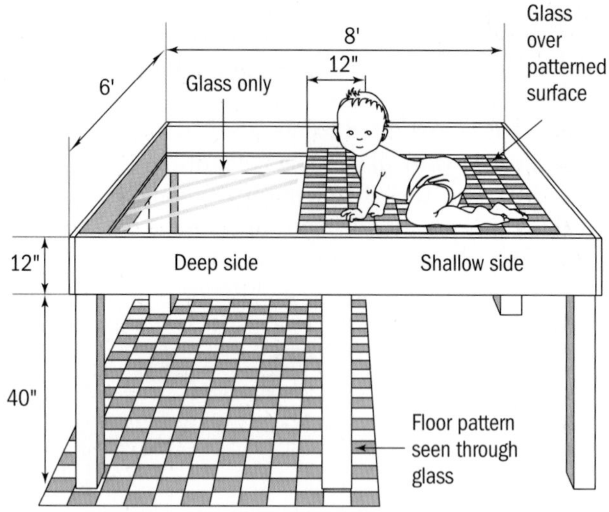

Figure 16.9 The visual cliff (from Dworetzky, 1981)

on it. It's likely that their poor motor control was responsible for this, rather than their inability to perceive depth.

> *ASK YOURSELF...*
> - Can you think of an alternative interpretation of Gibson and Walk's findings?

The visual cliff apparatus required the use of babies who could crawl, the youngest being six months old. By that age, the babies might have *learned* to perceive depth. Gibson and Walk subsequently tested a number of members of *precocial species* (capable of moving about independently at or shortly after birth), namely chicks, goat kids, lambs, and rats with their sensitive whiskers removed. None would venture on to the deep side. If forcibly placed on the deep side, they invariably 'froze'.

KEY STUDY 16.4 Using heart rate to measure depth perception (Campos *et al.*, 1970)

- In an ingenious way of assessing babies younger than six months, Campos *et al.* used heart rate as an index of depth perception.
- Babies of various ages had their heart rates monitored while they were on the visual cliff.
- Older babies (nine months) showed an *increased* heart rate, a response presumably indicating fear.
- The youngest (two months) showed a *decreased* heart rate when placed on the 'deep' side. They were *less* likely to cry, *more* attentive to what was underneath them, and clearly *not* frightened by what they saw. No such changes were observed when the infants were placed on the 'shallow' side.
- It seems that even two-month-old babies can perceive depth, and that avoidance behaviour is probably learnt (perhaps after having a few experiences of falling).

Depth perception has also been studied by looking at how neonates react when an object approaches their faces from a distance. For example, if a large box is moved towards a 20-day-old neonate's face, it shows an *integrated avoidance response*, throwing back its head, shielding its face with its hands, and even crying (Bower *et al.*, 1970). This suggests that the baby understands that the box is getting closer and, because it's potentially harmful, some sort of protective reaction is needed. Interestingly, this response occurs even with one eye closed, but not when equivalent pictures are shown on a screen. This indicates that *motion parallax* is the critical cue for distance (see Table 15.2, page 248).

The perception of 3-D objects

The integrated avoidance response suggests that as well as perceiving depth, neonates see boxes as solid, 3-D objects. To explore this, Bower (1979) devised a piece of apparatus that creates illusions of 3-D objects (see Figure 16.10). Babies aged 16 to 24 weeks were put in front of a screen. A plastic, translucent object was suspended between lights and the screen, casting a double shadow on the back. When the screen is viewed from the front and the baby wears polarising goggles, the double shadows merge to form the image of a solid 3-D object.

Figure 16.10 Trying to grasp a 'virtual object' produces surprise in a four- to six-month-old baby

Bower found that none of the babies showed any surprise when they grasped a real and solid object. But when they reached for the apparent object, and discovered there was nothing solid to get hold of, they all expressed surprise and some were even distressed. This indicates that they expected to be able to touch what they could 'see', an ability Bower believes to be innate.

Perceptual organisation: constancies and Gestalt principles

Size constancy

Despite a newborn's vision being much poorer than an adult's, its visual world is highly organised (Slater, 1994). According to *empiricists*, constancy is learned, and so neonates are likely to be 'tricked' by the appearance of things (for example, if something *looks* smaller – projects a smaller retinal image – then it *is* smaller). *Nativists*, however, would argue that neonates are innately able to judge the size of an object regardless of retinal image.

KEY STUDY 16.5 'Peek-a-boo' and size constancy too (Bower, 1966)

- To assess nativist and empiricist claims, Bower initially conditioned two-month-old babies to turn their heads whenever they saw a 30-centimetre cube at a distance of one metre (an adult popping up in front of the baby whenever it performed the desired behaviour served as a powerful reinforcer).
- Once the response was conditioned, the cube was replaced by one of three different cubes:

(a) a 30-centimetre cube at a distance of three metres (producing a retinal image *one-third* of the size of the original)
(b) a 90-centimetre cube at a distance of one metre (producing a retinal image *three times* the size of the original)
(c) a 90-centimetre cube at a distance of three metres (producing exactly the *same-sized* retinal image as the original).

(See Figure 16.11.)

Bower recorded the number of times each stimulus produced the conditioned response (CR), and used this as a measure of how similar the neonate considered the stimulus to be to the original. The original stimulus

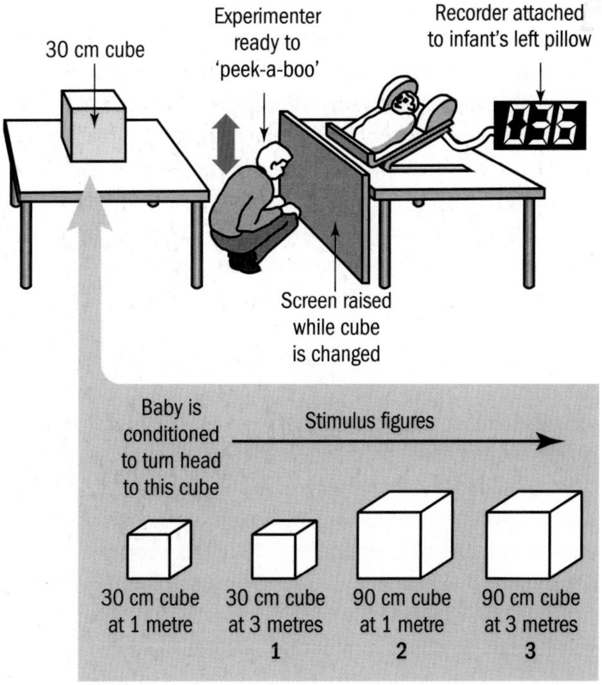

Figure 16.11 The experimental set-up in Bower's study of size constancy

produced a total of 98 CRs, while (a) produced 58, (b) 54 and (c) 22. The finding that most CRs occurred in response to (a) indicates that the baby was responding to the *actual size* of the cube, irrespective of its distance. This suggests the presence of size constancy, and supports the nativist view that this constancy is inbuilt.

The nativist position is further strengthened by the finding that fewest CRs occurred in response to (c). If size constancy was absent, as predicted by empiricists, neonates would 'compare' retinal images and base their perception of similarity on these regardless of distance. Empiricists, then, would have expected (c) to produce the most CRs. Bower's findings have been replicated with two-day-old babies by Slater *et al.* (1990). Although these findings demonstrate that size constancy is an organising feature of perception present at birth, learning still plays some part (Slater, 1994). For example, in the Slater *et al.* study, the procedure depends on infants learning the characteristics of the cubes in the early 'familiarisation trials'.

Shape constancy

According to Slater (1989), neonates can extract the constant real shape of an object that's rotated in the third dimension, that is, they're capable of recognising an object's form independently of (transformations in) its spatial orientation. For example, Bower (1966) found that if a two-month-old infant was conditioned to turn its head to look at a rectangle, it would continue to make the CR when the rectangle was turned slightly to produce a trapezoid retinal image.

Feature, identity and existence constancy

- *Feature constancy* is the ability to recognise the invariant features of a stimulus, despite some detectable but irrelevant transformation. If a neonate has been habituated to a moving stimulus, it will display a novelty preference when shown the same stimulus paired with a novel shape, both of which are stationary. This indicates that the neonate perceives the familiar stationary stimulus as the same stimulus that was moving, and that feature constancy is present at birth.
- Feature constancy is a prerequisite for *identity constancy:* the ability to recognise a particular object as being exactly the same object despite some transformation made to it. Distinguishing between feature and identity constancy is extremely difficult. In Bower's (1971) study, babies younger or older than 20 weeks were seated in front of mirrors which could produce several images of the mother. Babies younger than 20 weeks smiled, cooed and waved their arms to each of the 'multiple mothers', whereas older babies became upset. This suggests that only the older babies, who are aware that they have just one mother, possess identity constancy.
- *Existence constancy* refers to the belief that objects continue to exist even when they're no longer available to the senses (what Piaget calls object permanence: see Chapter 34). Together, existence and identity constancy comprise the *object concept*, which typically appears around six months of age.

Gestalt principles

Bower has also looked at how neonate perception is organised in terms of certain Gestalt principles (see Chapter 15). Bower wanted to discover if *closure* (or *occlusion*) is, as Gestalt psychologists claim, an inborn characteristic.

KEY STUDY 16.6 Closure (Bower, 1977)

- Two-month-old babies were conditioned to respond to a black wire triangle with a black iron bar across it (Figure 16.12, top).
- Then various stimuli (Figure 16.12, bottom) were presented.

ASK YOURSELF...
- If nativists are correct, and closure is an inborn ability, to which of A, B, C and D should the conditioned response generalise?

- Bower found that the CR was generalised to the complete triangle (A), suggesting that the babies perceived an unbroken triangle to lie behind the black iron bar.
- Given that they were unlikely to have encountered many triangles, Bower concluded that closure is almost certainly an inborn feature of neonate perceptual ability.

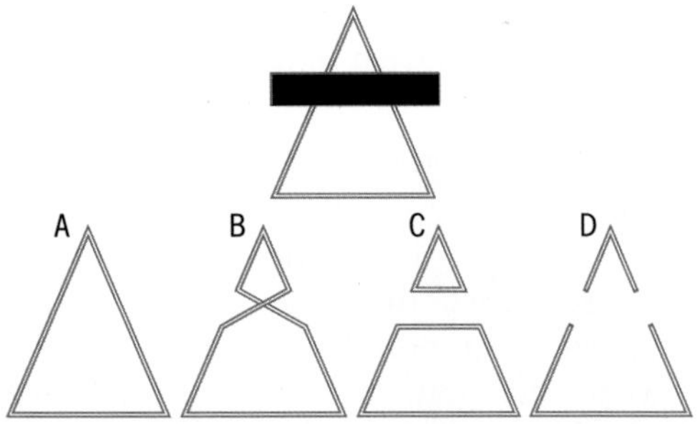

Figure 16.12 The stimulus figures used in Bower's study of closure

Bruce & Young (1998) sum up like this:

> These studies of infants allow us to glimpse the intricate interplay between the innate organisation of the brain and its astonishing capacity for perceptual-learning ... the infant's brain is highly plastic – ready to be moulded by the experiences it encounters. But it also contains crafty mechanisms (such as attention-capturing properties for face-like stimuli) which keep

the odds high that these experiences will be optimal for what the baby will need to learn.

CROSS-CULTURAL STUDIES

ASK YOURSELF...

- We noted earlier that if we find consistent perceptual differences between different cultural groups, then we're likely to attribute them to environmental factors. In what ways do cultures differ that could suggest what these environmental factors might be?

Studies using visual illusions

There's a long history of cross-cultural research into perceptual development using visual illusions.

Box 16.3 Some early research into cross-cultural differences using visual illusions

- Rivers (1901) compared English adults and children with adult and child Murray Islanders (a group of islands between New Guinea and Australia) using the Müller–Lyer and the horizontal–vertical illusions. The Murray Islanders were less susceptible to the Müller–Lyer illusion than their English counterparts, but more susceptible to the horizontal–vertical illusion.
- Allport & Pettigrew (1957) used the rotating trapezoid illusion. This is a trapezoid with horizontal and vertical bars attached to it to give the impression of a window.

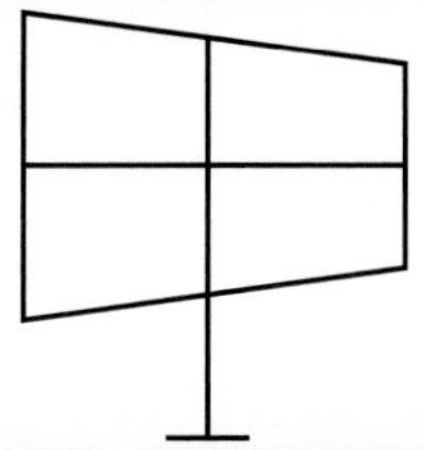

When attached to a motor and revolved in a circle, most western observers report seeing a rectangle oscillating backwards and forwards, rather than a trapezoid rotating through 360° (which it actually is). Allport and Pettigrew reasoned that for people unfamiliar with windows (at least as people from western cultures know them), the illusion wouldn't be perceived. When the trapezoid was viewed with both eyes and from a short distance, Zulus (who live in a rather 'circular environment') were less likely than either urban Zulus or Europeans to perceive an oscillating rectangle, and more likely to perceive a rotating trapezoid.

- Segall *et al.* (1963) used the Müller–Lyer illusion with members of African and Filipino cultures. Compared with white South Africans and Americans, the Africans and Filipinos were much less susceptible to the illusion. But on the horizontal–vertical illusion, members of two African cultures (the Batoro and the Bayankole) were most susceptible. People of these cultures live in high, open country where vertical objects are important focal points used to estimate distances. For example, when a tree or pole falls away from you, it seems to grow shorter (foreshortening), but when it falls to the left or right across your field of vision its length doesn't appear to change (Price & Crapo, 1999). The Bete, who live in a dense jungle environment, were least likely of all groups tested to see the illusion. The white South Africans and Americans fell between the extremes of the three African cultures.
- Stewart (1973) used the Ames distorted room (see Figure 15.17, page 259) with rural and urban Tongan children. The rural children were less likely to see the illusion than those living in urban environments and European children. This was also true for other illusions, including the Müller–Lyer.

The carpentered world hypothesis

According to Segall *et al.*'s (1963) *carpentered world hypothesis* (CWH), people in western cultures:

> ... live in a culture in which straight lines abound and in which perhaps 90 per cent of the acute and obtuse angles formed on [the] retina by the straight lines of [the] visual field are realistically interpretable as right angles extended in space.

Segall *et al.*, therefore, believe that we tend to interpret illusions, which are 2-D drawings, in terms of our past experiences. In the 'carpentered world' of western societies, we add a third dimension (depth), which isn't actually present in the drawing, and this leads to the illusion experience (cf. Gregory's account of visual illusions: see Chapter 15, pages 254–256).

Jahoda (1966) compared the Lobi and Dagomba tribes of Ghana, who live in open parkland in round huts, with the Ashanti, who live in dense forest in roughly rectangular huts. The prediction that the Lobi and Dagomba would be significantly more susceptible to the horizontal–vertical illusion, while the Ashanti would be significantly more susceptible to the Müller–Lyer, wasn't supported. Similarly, Gregor & McPherson (1965) found no significant differences between two groups of Australian aborigines on the two illusions, despite one group living in a relatively urbanised, carpentered environment and the other living primitively out of doors. However, both groups were significantly less prone to the Müller–Lyer than Europeans and more prone to the horizontal–vertical.

Despite some inconsistent evidence regarding illusion susceptibility and its interpretation, Segall *et al.* (1999) conclude their review by stating:

> ... people perceive in ways that are shaped by the inferences they have learned to make in order to function most effectively in the particular ecological settings in which they live ...

we learn to perceive in the ways that we need to perceive. In that sense, environment and culture shape our perceptual habits.

Studies of other perceptual phenomena

In various African cultures, children and adults find it difficult to perceive depth in both pictorial material and under certain conditions, in the real world too.

> **CASE STUDY 16.3: Confusing your buffalo with your insects (Turnbull, 1961)**
>
> - The BaMbuti pygmies live in the dense rainforests of the Congo, a closed-in world without open spaces.
> - When a BaMbuti archer was taken to a vast plain and shown a herd of buffalo grazing in the distance, he claimed he'd never seen such insects before. When informed that the 'insects' were buffalo, the archer was offended.
> - They then rode in a jeep towards the buffalo. The sight of the buffalo in the distance was so far removed from the archer's experience that he was convinced Turnbull was using magic to deceive him. The archer lacked experience with distance cues, preventing him from relating distance to size (Price & Crapo, 1999).

'Reading' pictures

Hudson (1960) showed people from various African cultures a series of pictures depicting hunting scenes (see Figure 16.13). Participants were first asked to name all the objects in the scene, then they were asked about the relationship between them, such as 'Which is closer to the man?' If the 'correct' interpretation was made, and depth cues were taken into account, respondents were classified as having 3-D vision. If such cues were ignored, they were classified as having 2-D vision. Hudson reported that both children and adults found it difficult to perceive depth in the pictorial material.

Deregowski (1972) refers to a description given of an African woman slowly discovering that a picture she was looking at portrayed a human head in profile:

> She discovered in turn the nose, the mouth, the eye, but where was the other eye? I tried turning my profile to explain why she could see only one eye, but she hopped round to my other side to point out that I possessed a second eye which the other lacked.

The woman treated the picture as an object, rather than a 2-D representation of an object, that is, she didn't 'infer' depth in the picture. What she believed to be an 'object' turned out to have only two dimensions, and this is what the woman found bewildering. But when familiar pictorial stimulus material is used, recognition tends to be better (Serpell, 1976). Thus, some (but not all) of the Me'en of Ethiopia found it much easier to recognise material when it was presented in the form of pictures

Figure 16.13 Hudson (1960) found that when shown the top picture and asked which animal the hunter is trying to spear, members of some cultures reply 'the elephant'. This shows that some cultures don't use cues to depth (such as overlap and known size of objects). The second picture shows the hunter, elephant and antelope in true size ratios when all are the same distance from the observer

painted on cloth (which is both familiar to them and free of distracting cues such as a border) than line drawings on paper (Deregowski, 1972).

> *ASK YOURSELF...*
>
> - In Hudson's pictures (Figure 16.13), which depth cues are used (see Table 15.2, page 248)?
> - Which cues *aren't* used, that you think could be important to people living in open terrain?

Are Hudson's pictures biased?

Hudson's pictures use *relative size* and *overlap/superimposition*, but *texture gradient*, *binocular disparity* and *motion parallax* are all missing. When the pictures were redrawn to show texture gradients (by, for example, adding grass to open terrain), more Zambian children gave 3-D answers than in Hudson's original study (Kingsley *et al.*, cited in Serpell, 1976). Research summarised by Berry *et al.* (1992) indicates that the absence of certain depth cues in pictorial material makes the perception of depth difficult for non-western peoples (see Gross, 2003a).

CONCLUSIONS: NATURE, NURTURE OR AN INTERACTION?

According to Bee (2000), as researchers have become increasingly ingenious in devising ways of testing infants' perceptual skills, they've found more and more skills already present in neonates and very young infants. There's growing evidence to support Kagan's (1971) claim that:

> Nature has apparently equipped the newborn with an initial bias in the processing of experience. He does not ... have to learn what he should examine.

Slater (1994) is a little more cautious. Auditory perception and learning about the auditory world (not dealt with in this chapter) are well advanced even in very young babies, and a nativist view is closest to the truth. But in the case of vision, the truth lies somewhere in-between a nativist and empiricist view. Evidence suggests that the newborn infant:

> ... comes into the world with a remarkable range of visual abilities ... Some rudimentary knowledge and understanding of important stimuli such as objects and faces is present at birth, and experience builds on this genetically or evolutionarily provided range of abilities. (Slater, 1994)

Some of the strongest evidence in support of the role of nurture comes from cross-cultural studies, deprivation studies using non-humans, and studies of human cataract patients. However, nature and nurture are never entirely separable. For example, the neonate's ability to discriminate between the mother's face and that of a similar-looking female must be the result of experience, but the capacity to make the distinction must be built in. As Bee (2000) says, whenever there's a dispute between nativists and empiricists:

> Both sides are correct. Both nature and nurture are involved.

CHAPTER SUMMARY

- **Nativists** argue that we're born able to perceive the world in particular ways, with little or no learning necessary. **Empiricists** believe that our perceptual abilities develop through learning and experience. Most psychologists reject these extreme viewpoints in favour of an **interactionist** position.
- Studying **neonates** represents the most **direct** source of evidence, but we can only **infer** what their perceptual experience is.
- **Non-human animal experiments** usually involve **deprivation** of normal sensory experience, raising serious **ethical questions**. There's also the problem of generalising the results of such studies to humans.
- Studies of **human cataract patients** represent the human counterpart to non-human animal experiments. Problems in interpretation of the research findings include possible physical deterioration of the visual system and dubious reliability of the case histories.
- Studies of **perceptual adaptation/readjustment** demonstrate the **flexibility** of human perception, but caution is needed in deciding whether **perceptual** or **motor adaptation** is involved.
- **Cross-cultural studies** help to identify the influences on perceptual development, in particular the role of **learning** and **experience**. But psychologists disagree as to the key features of cultural learning.
- When analysing data from cataract patients, Hebb distinguished between **figural unity**, which he believed is largely innate, and **figural identity** which is largely learnt.
- Deprivation experiments suggest that light is necessary for normal physical development of the visual system, and that **patterned light** is necessary for the normal development of more complex abilities in chimps, cats and monkeys.
- Perceptual adaptation/readjustment studies illustrate the enormous adaptability of the human visual system, but this seems to involve learning appropriate **motor behaviour**.
- Methods used to study **neonate perception** include **spontaneous visual preference/preferential looking, sucking rate**, **habituation**, **conditioned head rotation**, **physiological measures** and **measures of electrical brain activity**.
- Babies show a preference for **complexity**, which is a function of age. This is probably related to improvement in the ability to scan the whole pattern, rather than just areas of greatest contrast.
- One aspect of **form perception** that has been extensively investigated is 'facedness'. Evidence that babies quickly learn to prefer their mothers' faces (and voices) is contributing to the view that the human face has **species-specific** significance from birth onwards.
- **Depth perception** has been studied using the **visual cliff apparatus**. Heart rate measures support Gibson and Walk's original claim (based on crawling) that depth perception is probably innate.
- Bower believes that babies have an inborn understanding of the solidity of 3-D objects, as well as **size** and **shape constancy** and the Gestalt principle of **closure**.
- Cross-cultural studies involve giving members of different cultural groups the same test materials, usually **visual illusions**, including the Müller–Lyer, horizontal–vertical, and the rotating trapezoid.
- Segall *et al.* proposed the **carpentered world hypothesis** (CWH) to explain why different cultural groups are more/less susceptible to different illusions. This stresses the role of the **physical environment** on perception.
- Evidence that contradicts the carpentered world hypothesis has led to the proposal that exposure to western **cultural variables** may be more important, such as 2-D drawings and photographs.

- The generally accepted conclusion is that some perceptual abilities are present at birth, while others develop later. Perceptual development after birth involves a complex interaction between genetic/maturational and environmental/experiential influences.

Links with other topics/chapters

- The continuing debate within psychology about the *relative influence of nature and nurture* (Chapter 50) partly reflects its *philosophical roots* (Chapters 1 and 3).
- Vision consists of a large number of abilities, some more simple, others more complex (Chapter 15), and it's likely that the relative contributions of genetic and environmental factors vary between different abilities.
- The experimental study of non-human animals, especially those involving deprivation or any kind of pain or suffering, raise fundamental *ethical issues* (Chapter 48).
- *Cross-cultural psychology* helps to question the universality of the theories and research findings reported using western-only populations. But it's still mainly western psychologists that conduct this cross-cultural research, using methods and instruments designed in the West (Chapter 47).
- Cross-cultural studies have made considerable use of *visual illusions* (Chapter 15).
- An inborn attraction to human faces makes the baby interested in its caregivers, which, in turn, encourages them to provide the care the baby needs. The very rapid learning to recognise the mother could be seen as *evolutionarily determined attachment behaviour* (Chapters 2 and 32).

17

MEMORY AND FORGETTING

INTRODUCTION AND OVERVIEW

As we noted in Chapter 11, learning and memory represent two sides of the same coin: learning depends on memory for its 'permanence', and memory would have no 'content' without learning. Hence, we could define memory as the retention of learning and experience. As Blakemore (1988) says:

> In the broadest sense, learning is the acquisition of knowledge and memory is the storage of an internal representation of that knowledge …

Blakemore expresses the fundamental importance of memory like this:

> ... without the capacity to remember and to learn, it is difficult to imagine what life would be like, whether it could be called living at all. Without memory, we would be servants of the moment, with nothing but our innate reflexes to help us deal with the world. There could be no language, no art, no science, no culture. Civilisation itself is the distillation of human memory ...

Both learning and memory featured prominently in the early years of psychology as a science (see Chapters 1, 3 and 11). William James, one of the pioneers of psychology, was arguably the first to make a formal distinction between *primary* and *secondary memory*, which correspond to *short-term* and *long-term memory* respectively. This distinction is central to Atkinson and Shiffrin's (1968, 1971) very influential *multi-store model*.

As with other cognitive processes, memory remained a largely unacceptable area for psychological research until the cognitive revolution of the mid-1950s, reflecting the dominance of behaviourism up until this time. However, some behaviourists, especially in the USA, studied 'verbal behaviour' using paired–associate learning. This associationist approach was (and remains) most apparent in *interference theory*, an attempt to explain forgetting. Other theories of forgetting include *trace decay*, *displacement*, *cue-dependent forgetting* and *repression*.

Several major accounts of memory have emerged from criticisms of the limitations of the multi-store model. These include Craik and Lockhart's *levels-of-processing approach*, Baddeley and Hitch's *working-memory model*, and attempts to identify different types of long-term memory (e.g. Tulving, 1972). Psychologists are increasingly interested in *everyday memory*, rather than studying it merely as a laboratory phenomenon.

THE MEANINGS OF 'MEMORY'

Memory, like learning, is a hypothetical construct denoting three distinguishable but interrelated processes:

- *registration* (or *encoding*) – the *transformation* of sensory input (such as a sound or visual image) into a form which allows it to be entered into (or registered in) memory. With a computer, for example, information can only be encoded if it's presented in a format the computer recognises
- *storage* – the operation of *holding* or *retaining* information in memory. Computers store information by means of changes in the system's electrical circuitry; with people, the changes occurring in the brain allow information to be stored, though exactly what these changes involve is unclear
- *retrieval* – the process by which stored information is *extracted* from memory.

Registration can be thought of as a necessary condition for storage to take place, but not everything which registers on the senses is stored. Similarly, storage is a necessary, but not sufficient, condition for retrieval: we cannot recover information which hasn't been stored, but the fact that we know it is no guarantee that we'll remember it on any particular occasion. This is the crucial distinction between *availability* (whether or not the information has been stored) and *accessibility* (whether or not it can be retrieved), which is especially relevant to theories of forgetting (see pages 299–304).

STORAGE

> *ASK YOURSELF...*
> - Can saying 'I can't remember' mean different things?
> - Do you consider yourself to have a 'good'/'poor' memory? What criteria do you apply in making that assessment?

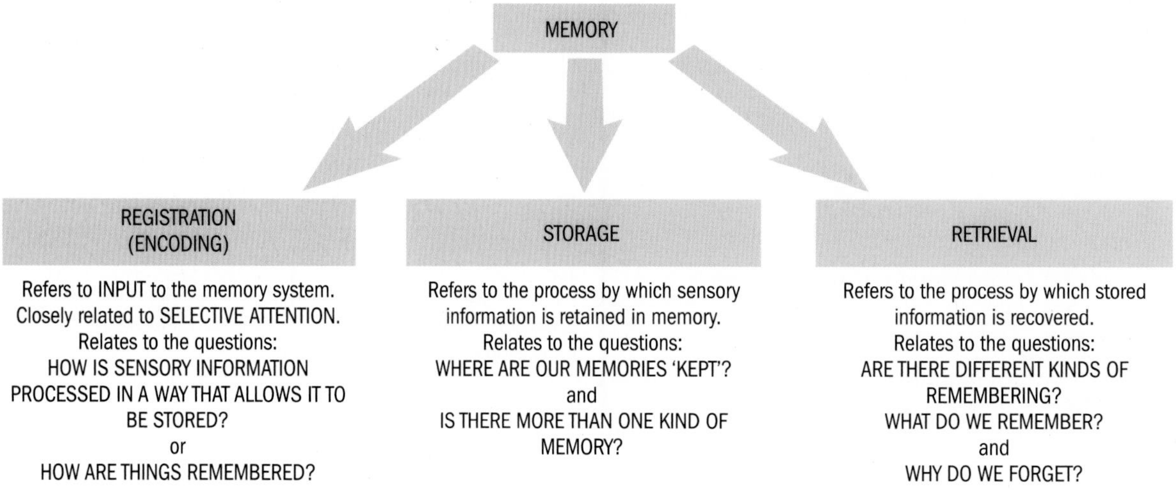

Figure 17.1 The three processes of memory

In practice, storage is studied through testing people's ability to retrieve. This is equivalent to the distinction between learning and performance: learning corresponds to storage, while performance corresponds to retrieval (see Chapter 11). But there are several kinds of retrieval (see below). So, if we're tested by recall it may look as though we haven't learnt something, but a test of recognition may show that we have. For these reasons, it's useful to distinguish between *memory as storage* and *memory as retrieval*. When people complain about having a 'poor memory', they might mean storage or retrieval, but they're unlikely to make the distinction (they'd simply say 'I can't remember').

As we noted earlier, it was James who first distinguished between primary and secondary memory. Ebbinghaus (1885), the pioneer of memory research, would have accepted it. Many psychologists since James have also made the distinction, including Hebb (1949), Broadbent (1958), and Waugh & Norman (1965). In Atkinson & Shiffrin's (1968, 1971) multi-store model, they're called short-term memory (STM) and long-term memory (LTM) respectively. Strictly, STM and LTM refer to experimental procedures for investigating short-term and long-term storage respectively.

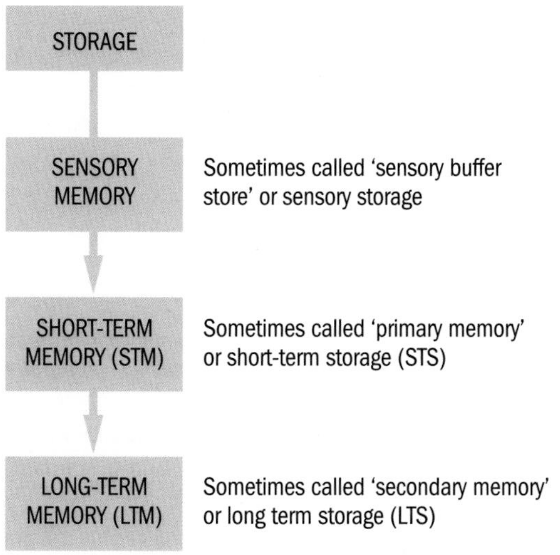

Figure 17.2 The three forms of storage

Sensory memory

Sensory memory gives us an accurate account of the environment as experienced by the sensory system. We retain a 'literal copy' of the stimulus long enough for us to decide whether it's worthy of further processing. Any information we don't attend to or process further is forgotten. It's probably more useful to think of sensory memory as an aspect of perception and as a necessary requirement for storage proper (that is, STM).

The storage (such as it is) occurs within the sensory system that receives the information (it's *modality-specific*). Additional information entering the same sensory channel immediately disrupts the storage. For example, if two visual stimuli are presented within quick succession, memory of the first stimulus may be lost. But if the second stimulus is a sound or smell, it won't interfere with memory of the visual stimulus. Although it's likely that a sensory memory exists for each of our sensory systems (see Chapter 5), most research has concentrated on:

- *iconic memory* (an icon is an image) stores visual images for about half a second
- *echoic memory* stores sounds for up to two seconds.

We're usually unaware of sensory memory, but if you watch someone wave a lighted cigarette in a darkened room, you'll see a streak rather than a series of points (Woodworth, 1938). If we had no iconic memory, we'd perceive a film as a series of still images interspersed with blank intervals, rather than as a continuously moving scene. Without echoic memory, instead of hearing speech as such we'd hear a series of unrelated sounds (Baddeley, 1995).

> *ASK YOURSELF...*
> - Can you relate these examples to any of the Gestalt laws of perception discussed in Chapter 15?

KEY STUDY 17.1 Iconic memory (Sperling, 1960, 1963)

Sperling used a tachistoscope to flash visual displays for very brief intervals (50 milliseconds or 1/20 of a second). The display comprised three rows of four letters in a 4×3 matrix.

- In the **whole report condition** (or span of apprehension), participants were asked to recall as many as possible from the whole matrix. On average, they recalled 4.32 letters (out of 12), although they commonly reported having seen more than they could actually remember.
- In the **partial report condition**, participants were required to recall the top, middle or bottom row, depending on whether they heard a high-, medium- or low-pitched tone following the presentation. Although they couldn't know in advance which tone would be heard, they succeeded in recalling an average of 3.04 of the letters from each row. This meant that between nine and ten words were available immediately after presentation.

In the first condition, approximately five words must have been lost during the time it took to recall the whole array. This was supported by the finding that the advantage of partial reports was lost if the tone was delayed for a second or so.

Similar effects have been reported for the echoic store by Broadbent (1958) and Treisman (1964). Broadbent's filter model of selective attention was in many ways the main precursor of the multi-store approach to memory, and there's a definite resemblance between sensory memory (or storage) and Broadbent's sensory 'buffer' store (Eysenck & Keane, 1990: see Chapter 13).

Short-term memory (STM)

Probably less than one-hundredth of all the sensory information that impinges on the human senses every second reaches consciousness. Of this, only about 5 per cent is stored permanently (Lloyd *et al.*, 1984). Clearly, if we possessed only sensory memory, our capacity for retaining information about the world would be extremely limited. However, according to models of memory such as Atkinson and Shiffrin's multi-store model (1968, 1971), some information from sensory memory is successfully passed on to STM.

STM (and LTM) can be analysed in terms of:

- *capacity* – how much information can be stored
- *duration* – how long the information can be held in storage
- *coding* – how sensory input is represented by the memory system.

Capacity

Ebbinghaus (1885) and Wundt (in the 1860s) were two of the first psychologists to maintain that STM is limited to six or seven bits of information. But the most famous account is given by Miller (1956) in his article 'The magical number seven, plus or minus two'. Miller showed how *chunking* can be used to expand the limited capacity of STM by using already established memory stores to categorise or encode new information.

If we think of STM's capacity as seven 'slots', with each slot being able to accommodate one bit or unit of information, then seven individual letters would each fill a slot and there'd be no 'room' left for any additional letters. But if the letters are chunked into a word, then the word would constitute one unit of information, leaving six free slots. In the example below, the 25 bits of information can be chunked into (or reduced to) six words, which could quite easily be reduced further to one 'bit' (or chunk) based on prior familiarity with the words:

S	A	V	A	O
R	E	E	E	G
U	R	S	Y	A
O	O	D	N	S
F	C	N	E	R

To be able to chunk, you have to know the 'rule' or the 'code', which in this case is: starting with F (bottom left-hand corner) read upwards until you get to S and then drop down to C and read upwards until you get to A, then go to N and read upwards and so on. This should give you 'four score and seven years ago'.

Chunking is involved whenever we reduce a larger amount of information to a smaller amount. This (a) increases the capacity of STM, and (b) represents a form of encoding information, by imposing a meaning on otherwise meaningless material. For example:

- arranging letters into words, words into phrases, phrases into sentences
- converting 1066 (four bits of information) into a date (one chunk), so a string of 28 numbers could be reduced to seven dates
- using a rule to organise information: the series 149162536496481100121 (21 bits) is generated by the rule by which $1^1 = 1$, $2^2 = 4$, $3^3 = 9$, and so on. The rule represents a single chunk, and that's all that has to be remembered.

These examples demonstrate how chunking allows us to bypass the seven-bit 'bottleneck'. Although the amount of information contained in any one chunk may be unlimited (e.g. the rule above can generate an infinitely long set of digits), the number of chunks which can be held in STM is still limited to seven plus or minus two.

Duration

A way of studying 'pure' STM was devised by Brown (1958) and Peterson & Peterson (1959), and is called the Brown–Peterson technique. By repeating something that has to be remembered (maintenance rehearsal), information can be held in STM almost indefinitely. The *Brown–Peterson technique* overcomes this problem.

KEY STUDY 17.2 The Brown–Peterson technique (Peterson & Peterson, 1959)

- In the Brown–Peterson technique, participants hear various trigrams (such as XPJ). Only one trigram is presented on each trial.
- Immediately afterwards, they're instructed to recall what they heard or to count backwards, in threes, out loud, from some specified number for 3, 6, 9, 12, 15 or 18 seconds (the retention interval). The function of this distractor task is to prevent rehearsal.
- At the end of the time period, participants try to recall the trigram.
- Peterson and Peterson found that the average percentage of correctly recalled trigrams was high with short delays, but decreased as the delay interval increased. Nearly 70 per cent was forgotten after only a nine-second delay, and 90 per cent after 18 seconds.
- In the absence of rehearsal, then, STM's duration is very short, even with very small amounts of information. If a more difficult distractor task is used, it can be made even shorter.

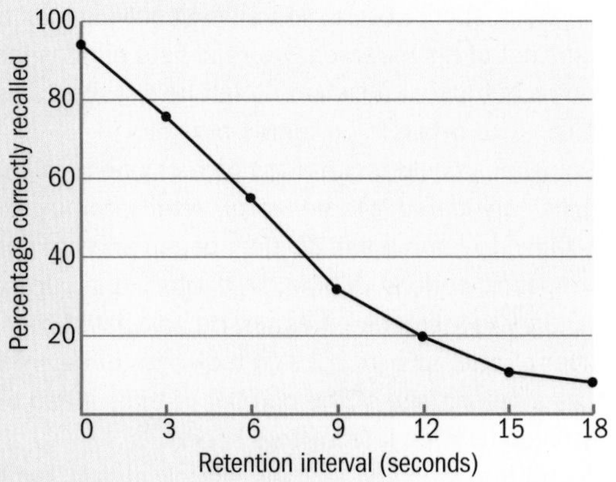

Figure 17.3 The data reported by Peterson and Peterson in their experiment on the duration of STM

Coding

Conrad (1964) presented participants visually with a list of six consonants (such as BKSJLR), each of which was seen for about three-quarters of a second. They were then instructed to write down the consonants. Mistakes tended to be related to a letter's *sound*. For example, there were 62 instances of B being mistaken for P, 83 instances of V being mistaken for P, but only two instances of S being mistaken for P. These *acoustic confusion errors* suggested to Conrad that STM must code information according to its sound. Even when information is presented *visually*, it must somehow be *transformed* into its acoustic code (see also Baddeley's, 1966, study below).

Other forms of coding in STM

Shulman (1970) showed participants lists of ten words. Recognition of the words was then tested using a visually presented 'probe word', which was either:

- a *homonym* of one of the words on the list (such as 'bawl' for 'ball')
- a *synonym* (such as 'talk' for 'speak'), or
- identical to it.

> *ASK YOURSELF...*
> - Shulman found that homonym and synonym probes produced similar error rates.
> - What does this tell us about the types of coding used in STM?

Shulman's results imply that some *semantic coding* (coding for *meaning*) had taken place in STM. If an error was made on a synonym probe, some matching for meaning must have taken place.

Visual images (such as abstract pictures, which would be difficult to store using an acoustic code) can also be maintained in STM, if only briefly.

Long-term memory (LTM)

Capacity and duration

It's generally accepted that LTM has unlimited capacity. It can be thought of as a vast storehouse of all the information, skills, abilities and so on, which aren't being currently used, but which are potentially retrievable. According to Bower (1975), some of the kinds of information contained in LTM include:

- a spatial model of the world around us
- knowledge of the physical world, physical laws and properties of objects
- beliefs about people, ourselves, social norms, values and goals
- motor skills, problem-solving skills, and plans for achieving various things
- perceptual skills in understanding language, interpreting music, and so on.

Many of these are included in what Tulving (1972) calls *semantic memory* (see below).

Information can be held for between a few minutes and several years (and may in fact span the individual's entire lifetime).

Coding

With verbal material, coding in LTM appears to be mainly *semantic*. For example, Baddeley (1966) presented participants with words which were either:

- *acoustically similar* (e.g. 'caught', 'short', 'taut', 'nought')
- *semantically similar* (e.g. 'huge', 'great', 'big', 'wide')
- *acoustically dissimilar* (e.g. 'foul', 'old' and 'deep'), or
- *semantically dissimilar* (e.g. 'pen', 'day', 'ring').

When recall from STM was tested, acoustically similar words were recalled less well than acoustically dissimilar words. This supports the claim that acoustic coding occurs in STM. There was a small difference between the number of semantically similar and semantically dissimilar words recalled (64 and 71 per cent respectively). This suggests that while some semantic coding occurs in STM, it's not dominant. When an equivalent study was conducted on LTM, fewer semantically similar words were recalled, while acoustically similar words had no effect on LTM recall. This suggests that LTM's *dominant* code is semantic. Similarly, Baddeley found that immediate recall of the order of short lists of unrelated words was seriously impeded if the words were acoustically similar, but not if they were semantically similar. After a delay, however, exactly the opposite effect occurred.

Does LTM use only semantic coding?

Findings such as Baddeley's don't imply that LTM uses only a semantic code (Baddeley, 1976). Our ability to picture a place we visited on holiday indicates that at least some information is stored or coded visually. Also, some types of information in LTM (such as songs) are coded acoustically. Smells and tastes are also stored in LTM, suggesting that it's a very flexible system, as well as being large and long-lasting.

Long-term memory of this scene requires the use of a visual code

Table 17.1 Summary of main differences between STM and LTM

	Capacity	Duration	Coding
STM	Seven bits of (unrelated) information. Can be increased through chunking	15–30 seconds (unaided). Can be increased by (maintenance) rehearsal	Mainly acoustic. Some semantic. Visual is also possible
LTM	Unlimited	From a few seconds to several years (perhaps permanently)	Semantic, visual, acoustic, and also olfactory (smells) and gustatory (tastes). Very flexible

RETRIEVAL

There are many different ways of recovering or locating information which has been stored; that is, 'remembering' can take many different forms. Likewise, there are also different ways of measuring memory in the laboratory.

How is memory measured?

The systematic scientific investigation of memory began with Ebbinghaus (1885).

KEY STUDY 17.3 Pure memory (Ebbinghaus, 1885)

- To study memory in its 'purest' form, Ebbinghaus invented three-letter nonsense syllables (a consonant followed by a vowel followed by another consonant, such as XUT and JEQ).
- Ebbinghaus spent several years using only himself as the subject of his research. He read lists of nonsense syllables out loud, and when he felt he'd recited a list sufficiently to retain it, he tested himself.
- If Ebbinghaus could recite a list correctly twice in succession, he considered it to be learnt. After recording the time taken to learn a list, he then began another one.
- After specific periods of time, he'd return to a particular list and try to memorise it again. He calculated the number of attempts (or *trials*) it took him to *relearn* the list, as a percentage of the number of trials it had originally taken to learn it (a *savings score*).
- He found that memory declines sharply at first, but then levels off. For example, in one set of experiments involving a series of eight different lists of 13 nonsense syllables, he found savings scores of:
  - 58 per cent, 20 minutes after training
  - 44 per cent, 60 minutes after training
  - 34 per cent, 24 hours after training
  - 21 per cent, 31 days after training.

... Thus, most of the memory loss occurred within the first minutes after training; once the memory had survived this hurdle it seemed much more stable ... (Rose, 2003)

This finding has subsequently been replicated many times.

Other techniques for measuring memory include the following:

- *Recognition*: This involves deciding whether or not a particular piece of information has been encountered before (as in a multiple-choice test, where the correct answer is presented along with incorrect ones). The *sensitivity* of recognition as a form of retrieval is demonstrated by Standing (1973).

KEY STUDY 17.4 Recognising how to ask people to remember (Standing, 1973)

- Participants were shown series of either pictures or words (20 or so per series), each slide for five seconds, and each series at three-minute intervals.
- Two days later they were shown further series of slides using a double projector. Thus they saw two pictures side by side, one taken from the original series, the other being new. They had to indicate which looked more familiar.
- Amazingly, as Standing went on increasing the number of images up to 10,000, the error rate continued to stay very low, and didn't seem to increase at all with the number of items to be remembered.
- Standing concluded that, for all practical purposes, there's no upper limit to memory capacity.
- Contrary to the evidence that there are limits to what's transferred from STM to LTM (see text below), it seems that some accessible trace of each item must have been

left – enough to enable a new item to be compared with the trace and classified as familiar or unfamiliar. According to Rose (2003):

> *... On this basis, it could be argued that nothing is forgotten, provided we know how to ask if it is remembered ...*

- *Recall*: This involves participants actively searching their memory stores in order to retrieve particular information (as in timed essays). Retrieval cues are missing or very sparse. The material can be recalled either in the order in which it was presented (*serial recall*) or in any order at all (*free recall*).
- *Memory-span procedure*: This is a version of serial recall, in which a person is given a list of unrelated digits or letters, and then required to repeat them back immediately in the order in which they were heard. The number of items on the list is successively increased until an error is made. The maximum number of items that can consistently be recalled correctly is a measure of *immediate memory span*.
- *Paired-associates recall*: Participants are required to learn a list of paired items (such as 'chair' and 'elephant'). When one of the words (e.g. 'chair') is re-presented, the participant must recall the paired word ('elephant').

THE MULTI-STORE MODEL (MSM)

Atkinson & Shiffrin's (1968, 1971) *multi-store model* (MSM) (sometimes called the *dual-memory model* because of the emphasis on STM and LTM) was an attempt to explain how information flows from one storage system to another. The model sees sensory memory, STM and LTM as *permanent structural components* of the memory system (built-in features of the human information-processing system). In addition to these structural components, the memory system comprises more *transient control processes*. *Rehearsal* is a key control process, serving two main functions:

1. to act as a *buffer* between sensory memory and LTM by maintaining incoming information within STM
2. to transfer information to LTM.

Information from sensory memory is scanned and matched with information in LTM, and if a match (i.e. pattern recognition) occurs, then it might be fed into STM along with a verbal label from LTM.

Evidence for the MSM

Three kinds of evidence are relevant here:

1. experimental studies of STM and LTM (sometimes referred to as two-component tasks)
2. studies of coding
3. studies of brain-damaged patients.

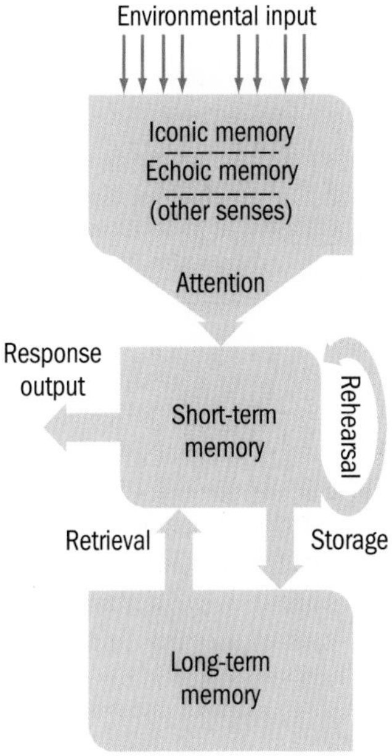

Figure 17.4 The multi-store/dual-memory model of memory proposed by Atkinson and Shiffrin

Experimental studies of STM and LTM

The serial position effect

Murdock (1962) presented participants with a list of words at a rate of about one per second. They were required to free-recall as many of these as they could. Murdock found that the probability of recalling any word depended on its position in the list (its *serial position*: hence the graph shown in Figure 17.5 is a *serial position curve*). Participants typically recalled those items from the end of the list first, and got more of these correct than earlier items (the *recency effect*). Items from the beginning of the list were recalled quite well relative to those in the middle (the *primacy effect*), but not as well as those at the end. Poorest recall is for items in the middle. The serial position effect holds regardless of the length of the list (Murdock, 1962).

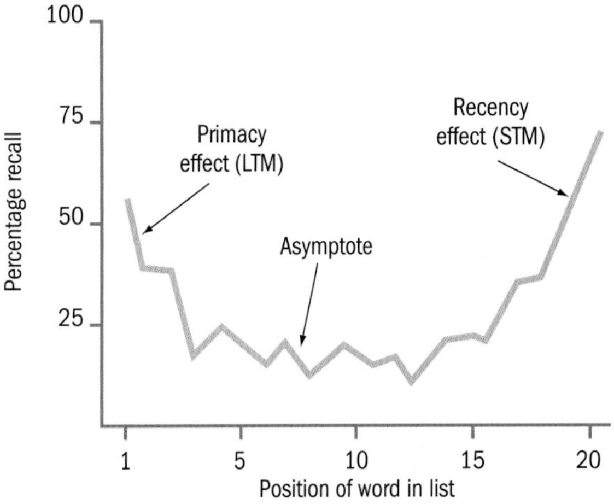

Figure 17.5 A typical serial position curve (Reprinted from *Journal of Verbal Learning & Verbal Behaviour, 5*, Glanzer & Cunitz, 1966, Two storage mechanisms in free recall, 928–935, © 1966, with permission from Elsevier.)

> *ASK YOURSELF...*
> - Using what you already know about STM, LTM and rehearsal, try to explain:
>   (a) the primacy and recency effects
>   (b) why words in the middle of the list are the least well remembered.

The primacy effect occurs because the items at the beginning of the list have (presumably) been rehearsed and transferred to LTM, from where they're recalled. The recency effect presumably occurs because items currently in STM are recalled from there. Because STM's capacity is limited and can hold items for only a brief period of time, words in the middle are either lost from the system completely, or are otherwise unavailable for recall. The last items are remembered only if recalled first and tested immediately, as demonstrated by Glanzer & Cunitz (1966) in a variation of Murdock's study.

KEY STUDY 17.5 Removing the recency effect (Glanzer & Cunitz, 1966)

- Glanzer and Cunitz presented two groups of participants with the same list of words.
- One group recalled the material immediately after presentation, while the other group recalled after 30 seconds. They had to count backwards in threes (the Brown–Peterson technique), which prevented rehearsal and caused the recency effect to disappear.
- The primacy effect was largely unaffected.

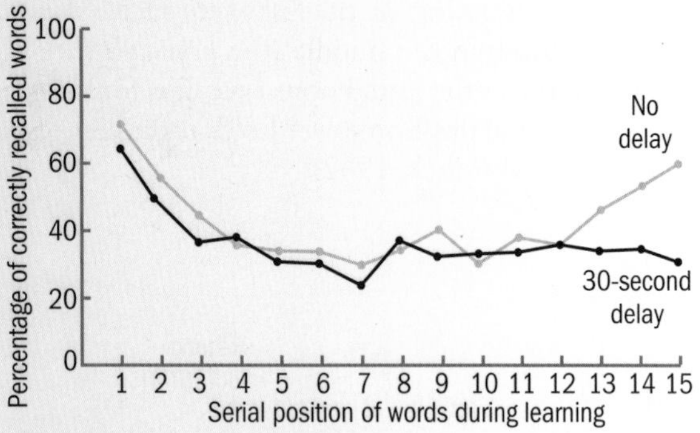

Figure 17.6 Data from Glanzer and Cunitz's study showing serial position curves after no delay and after a delay of 30 seconds

> *ASK YOURSELF...*
> - Try to account for Glanzer and Cunitz's findings.

It's likely that the earlier words had been transferred to LTM (from where they were recalled), while the most recent words were 'vulnerable' to the counting task (Eysenck, 1993).

Brown–Peterson technique and rehearsal

When discussing the characteristics of STM earlier (see page 284), we noted the rapid loss of information from memory when rehearsal is prevented using the Brown–Peterson technique. This is usually taken as evidence for the existence of a STM with rapid forgetting (see below, page 299). But the concept of rehearsal itself has been criticised as both unnecessary and too general.

KEY STUDY 17.6 Maintenance vs elaborative rehearsal (Craik & Watkins, 1973)

- Craik and Watkins asked participants to remember only certain 'critical' words (those beginning with a particular letter) from lists presented either rapidly or slowly.
- The position of the critical words relative to the others determined the amount of time a particular word spent in STM, and the number of potential rehearsals it could receive.
- Craik and Watkins found that long-term remembering was unrelated to either how long a word had spent in STM, or the number of explicit or implicit rehearsals it received.
- Based on this and later findings, Craik and Watkins distinguished between:

  (a) **maintenance rehearsal**, where material is rehearsed in the form in which it was presented ('rote'), and
  (b) **elaborative rehearsal** (or **elaboration of encoding**), which elaborates the material in some way (such as by giving it a meaning, or linking it with pre-existing knowledge stored in LTM).

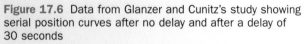

Elaborative rehearsal is much more like the rehearsal involved in a play than is maintenance rehearsal

An earlier study by Glanzer & Meinzer (1967) found that participants required to repeat items aloud recalled fewer of them than those allowed an equal period of silent rehearsal. Perhaps in silent rehearsal the material isn't being merely repeated, but recoded into a different form which enhances recall.

It seems, then, that what's important is the *kind* of rehearsal or processing, rather than how much. This has been investigated in particular by Craik & Lockhart (1972), in the form of the levels-of-processing approach (see pages 294–296).

Studies of coding

Table 17.1 (page 286) indicates that the major form of coding used in STM is acoustic, while LTM is much more flexible and varied in how it encodes information. It also suggests that semantic coding is used primarily by LTM. This is usually taken to support the multi-store model. However, not everyone accepts this view.

Chunking, STM and LTM

When discussing the characteristics of STM (pages 284–285), we saw that chunking increases STM's capacity by imposing meaning on otherwise meaningless material. According to Miller (1956), chunking represents a *linguistic recoding* which seems to be the 'very lifeblood of the thought process'. But this cannot occur until certain information in LTM is activated, and a match made between the incoming items and their representation in LTM.

Miller & Selfridge (1950) gave participants 'sentences' of varying lengths, which resembled (or approximated to) true English to different degrees, and asked them to recall the words in their correct order. The closer a 'sentence' approximated normal English, the better it was recalled. This suggests that knowledge of semantic and grammatical structure (presumably stored in LTM) is used to aid recall from STM.

In a similar study, Bower & Springston (1970) presented one group of American college students with letters that formed familiar acronyms (e.g. fbi, phd, twa, ibm). A second group was presented with the same letters, but in a way that didn't form those acronyms (e.g. fb, iph, dtw, aib, m). The first group recalled many more letters than the second group. The pause after 'fbi', and so on, allowed the students to 'look up' the material in their mental dictionaries and so encode the letters in one chunk.

Clearly, an acoustic code isn't the only one used in STM. According to Wickelgren (1973), the kind of coding might reflect the processing which has occurred in a given context, rather than being a property of the memory store itself (see pages 294–296).

The study of brain-damaged patients

Anterograde amnesia and the amnesic syndrome

If STM and LTM really are distinct, then there should be certain kinds of brain damage which impair one without affecting the other. One such form of brain damage is *anterograde amnesia*.

CASE STUDY 17.1 H.M. (Milner *et al.*, 1968)

- H.M. is probably the single most studied amnesic patient in the history of neuropsychology (Rose, 2003).
- He'd been suffering epileptic fits of devastating frequency since the age of 16. In 1953 (aged 27), he underwent surgery aimed at alleviating his epilepsy. The anterior two-thirds of his hippocampus and amygdala, plus part of the temporal lobe (on both sides of his brain) were removed (see Chapter 4).
- While this was fairly successful in curing his epilepsy, at the time the role of these brain structures in memory was unknown, and he was left with severe *anterograde amnesia*, that is he has near normal memory for anything learned *before* the surgery, but severe memory deficits for events that occurred afterwards.
- His STM is generally normal. He can retain verbal information for about 15 seconds without rehearsal, and for much longer with rehearsal. But he cannot transfer information into LTM or, if he can, is unable to retrieve it. He seems entirely incapable of remembering any new fact or event.
- He has almost no knowledge of current affairs, because he forgets all the news almost as soon as he's read about it. He has no idea what time of day it is unless he's just looked at the clock, he cannot remember that his father has died or that his family has moved house, and he rereads the same magazine without realising he's already read it.
- People he met after the operation remain, in effect, total strangers to him, and he has to 'get to know them' afresh each time they come into his house. Brenda Milner has known him for 25 years, yet she's a stranger to him each time they meet.
- He's able to learn and remember perceptual and motor skills, although he has to be reminded each day just what skills he has. However:

> *... new events, faces, phone numbers, places, now settle in his mind for just a few seconds or minutes before they slip, like water through a sieve, and are lost from his consciousness. (Blakemore, 1988)*

An equally dramatic, but in many ways more tragic case is that of Clive Wearing.

CASE STUDY 17.2 Clive Wearing (based on Baddeley, 1990; Blakemore, 1988)

- Clive Wearing was the chorus master of the London Sinfonietta and a world expert on Renaissance music, as well as a BBC radio producer.

- In March 1985 he suffered a rare brain infection caused by the cold sore virus (Herpes simplex). The virus attacked and destroyed his hippocampus, along with parts of his cortex.
- Like H.M., he lives in a snapshot of time, constantly believing that he's just awoken from years of unconsciousness. For example, when his wife, Deborah, enters his hospital room for the third time in a single morning, he embraces her as if they'd been parted for years, saying, 'I'm conscious for the first time' and 'It's the first time I've seen anybody at all'.
- At first his confusion was total and very frightening to him. Once he held a chocolate in the palm of one hand, covered it with the other for a few seconds until its image disappeared from his memory. When he uncovered it, he thought he'd performed a magic trick, conjuring it up from nowhere. He repeated it again and again, with total astonishment and growing fear each time.
- Like H.M., he can still speak and walk, as well as read music, play the organ and conduct. In fact, his musical ability is remarkably well preserved.
- Also like H.M, he can learn new skills (e.g. mirror-reading). Over the course of a few days of testing, the speed of reading such words doubles, and it can be done just as well three months later. Yet for Clive, it's new every time.
- But unlike H.M., his capacity for remembering his earlier life is extremely patchy. For example, when shown pictures of Cambridge (where he'd spent four years as an undergraduate and had often visited subsequently) he only recognised King's College Chapel – the most distinctive Cambridge building – but not his own college. He couldn't remember who wrote *Romeo and Juliet,* and he thought the Queen and the Duke of Edinburgh were singers he'd known from a Catholic church.
- According to Deborah, 'without consciousness he's in many senses dead'. In his own words, his life is 'Hell on earth – it's like being dead – all the bloody time'.

ASK YOURSELF...
- In what ways do the cases of H.M. and Clive Wearing support the multi-store model?
- In what ways do they challenge it?

Atkinson and Shiffrin regard the kind of memory deficits displayed by H.M. and Clive Wearing as 'perhaps the single most convincing demonstration of a dichotomy in the memory system'. According to Parkin (1987), the *amnesic syndrome* isn't a general deterioration of memory function, but a selective impairment in which some functions (such as learning novel information) are severely impaired, while others (including memory span and language) remain intact.

If amnesics do have an intact STM, they should show a similar recency effect (based on STM) but a poorer primacy effect (based on LTM) compared with normal controls. This is exactly what's found (e.g. Baddeley & Warrington, 1970). These results have led most psychologists to accept that in the amnesic syndrome, STM function is preserved but LTM function is impaired.

However, this difference in STM and LTM functioning could mean that:

- the problem for amnesics is one of transfer from STM to LTM, which is perfectly consistent with the MSM, or, alternatively
- amnesics have difficulties in retrieval from LTM (Warrington & Weiskrantz, 1968, 1970); this interpretation is more consistent with Craik & Lockhart's (1972) levels-of-processing approach.

Another major implication of cases such as those of H.M. and Clive Wearing is that the multi-store model's 'unitary' LTM is a gross oversimplification (see the next section).

Retrograde amnesia

In retrograde amnesia, a patient fails to remember what happened *before* the surgery or accident that caused the amnesia. It can be caused by head injuries, electroconvulsive therapy (ECT: see Chapter 45), carbon monoxide poisoning, and extreme stress (see Chapter 12). As in anterograde amnesia, there's typically little or no disruption of STM, and the period of time for which the person has no memories may be minutes, days or even years. When retrograde amnesia is caused by brain damage, it's usually accompanied by anterograde amnesia. Similarly, patients with Korsakoff's syndrome (caused by severe, chronic alcoholism involving damage to the hippocampus) usually experience both kinds of amnesia.

Retrograde amnesia seems to involve a disruption of *consolidation* whereby, once new information has entered LTM, time is needed for it to become firmly established physically in the brain (see the discussion of forgetting, pages 299–304).

ALTERNATIVES TO THE MSM

Multiple forms of LTM

Episodic and semantic memory

Despite their brain damage, H.M. and Clive Wearing retained many skills, both general and specific (such as talking, reading, walking, playing the organ). They were also capable of acquiring (and retaining) new skills – although they didn't know that they had them! This suggests very strongly that there are different kinds of LTM. But as far as the MSM is concerned, there's only 'LTM' (LTM is *unitary*).

Box 17.1 Episodic and semantic memory (Tulving, 1972)

- **Episodic memory** (EM) is an 'autobiographical' memory responsible for storing a record of our past experiences – the events, people, objects and so on which we've personally encountered.
- EM usually includes details about the particular time and place in which objects and events were experienced (they have a spatio-temporal context: e.g. 'Where did you go on your holiday last year?' and 'What did you have for breakfast this morning?'). They have a subjective (self-focused) reality, but most could, in principle, be verified by others.
- **Semantic memory** (SM) is our store of general, factual knowledge about the world, including concepts, rules and language, 'a mental thesaurus, organised knowledge a person possesses about words and other verbal symbols, their meanings and referents' (Tulving, 1972).
- SM can be used without reference to where and when that knowledge was originally acquired. For example, we don't remember 'learning to speak' – we just 'know English' (or whatever our native language happens to be). But SM can also store information about ourselves. For example, if we're asked how many brothers and sisters we have, or how much we like psychology, we don't have to remember specific past experiences in order to answer.

Our 'general' knowledge about, say, computers (part of our SM) is built up from past experiences with particular computers (part of EM), through abstraction and generalisation. This suggests that, instead of regarding EM and SM as two quite distinct systems within the brain (which is what Tulving originally intended), it might be more valid to see SM as made up from multiple EMs (Baddeley, 1995).

Autobiographical vs experimental EM

Tulving maintained that EM is synonymous with *autobiographical memory* (AM). For example, the forgetting of words in a free-recall task can be thought of as a failure in our EM. Clearly, we already know the words as part of our SM, but we've failed to remember that they appeared *in that particular list* just presented to us. However, Cohen (1993) argues that learning word lists isn't what most people understand by AM. Instead, AM is a special kind of EM, concerned with specific life events that have personal significance. Accordingly, she distinguishes between autobiographical EM and *experimental* EM; taking part in an experiment in which we're required to learn lists of words is an example of the latter.

Flashbulb memories

Flashbulb memories are a special kind of EM, in which we can give vivid and detailed recollections of where we were and what we were doing when we first heard about some major public national or international event (Brown & Kulik, 1977).

ASK YOURSELF...

- Where were you, and what were you doing, at the time of the total eclipse of the sun in the summer of 1999?

According to Brown & Kulik (1982), a neural mechanism is triggered by events that are emotionally arousing, unexpected or extremely important, with the result that the whole scene becomes 'printed' on the memory. However, Neisser (1982) argued that the durability of flashbulb memories stems from their frequent rehearsal and reconsideration after the event. Also, the detail and vividness of people's memories aren't necessarily signs of their accuracy – we can be very confident about something and still be mistaken!

Procedural vs declarative memory

Procedural memory (PM) refers to information from LTM which cannot be inspected consciously (Anderson, 1985; Tulving, 1985). For example, riding a bike is a complex skill which is even more difficult to describe. In the same way, native speakers of a language cannot usually describe the complex grammatical rules by which they speak correctly (perhaps because they weren't learnt consciously in the first place: see Chapter 19). By contrast, EM and SM are both amenable to being inspected consciously, and the content of both can be described to another person.

Cohen & Squire (1980) distinguish between PM and *declarative memory*, which corresponds to Ryle's (1949) distinction between *knowing how* and *knowing that* respectively (see Figure 17.7). Anderson (1983) argues that when we initially learn something, it's learned and encoded declaratively, but with practice it becomes compiled into a procedural form of knowledge. (This is similar to the distinction between controlled/automatic processing discussed in Chapter 13.)

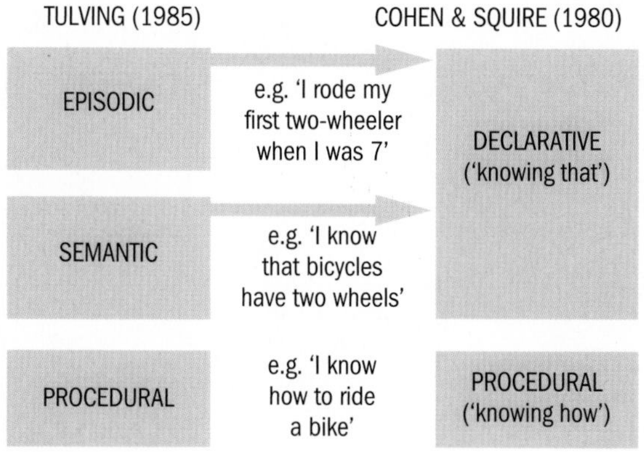

Figure 17.7 Distinctions between different kinds of LTM

> *ASK YOURSELF...*
> - How do these different types of LTM help us understand the memory deficits of H.M. and Clive Wearing?

Most aspects of their PMs seemed to be intact, but both their EM and SM were partially impaired. For instance, H.M. was given extensive training (by Gabrieli *et al.*, 1983) in the task of learning the meaning of unfamiliar words which had come into popular use since his operation. He made very little progress, despite extensive practice every day for ten days.

Most other amnesics similarly fail to update their SMs to take account of changes in the world since onset of their dysfunction (Eysenck & Keane, 1990). For example, many don't know the name of the current Prime Minister or President, and have very poor recognition for faces of people who've become famous only quite recently (Baddeley, 1984).

The major problem seems to involve recent *declarative* memory. We saw earlier that Clive Wearing denied all knowledge of having learnt to mirror-read. Similarly, H.M. was trained to solve the Tower of Hanoi problem (see Chapter 20) over several days, but each time he was presented with it he denied ever having seen it before. Yet their performance on these two tasks steadily improved. As Rose (2003) puts it:

> ... procedural memory continued to testify to the truth of what declarative memory denied.

PM involves more automatic processes, and allows patients to demonstrate learning without the need for conscious recollection of the learning process. But declarative learning/memory involves conscious recollection of the past. Damage to a number of cortical and subcortical areas (including the temporal lobes, hippocampus and mamillary bodies) seriously impairs declarative memory in amnesic patients. PM doesn't appear to be impaired by damage to these areas (Baddeley, 1995).

The working-memory (WM) model: rethinking STM

In their MSM, Atkinson and Shiffrin saw STM as a system for temporarily holding and manipulating information. However, Baddeley & Hitch (1974) criticised the model's concept of a *unitary* STM. While accepting that STM rehearses incoming information for transfer to LTM, they argued that it was much more complex and versatile than a mere 'stopping-off station' for information.

> *ASK YOURSELF...*
> - How does Miller & Selfridge's (1950) experiment (see page 289) demonstrate the two-way flow of information between STM and LTM?

Box 17.2 The two-way flow of information between STM and LTM

- It's highly unlikely that STM contains only new information, and more likely that information is retrieved from LTM for use in STM.
- For example, the string of numbers 18561939 may appear to be unrelated. However, they can be 'chunked' into one unit according to the rule 'the years in which Sigmund Freud was born and died'.
- If we can impose meaning on a string of digits, we must have learned this meaning previously, the previously learned rule presumably being stored in LTM. Information has flowed not only from STM to LTM, but also in the opposite direction.
- A vivid illustration of this comes from studies of people who are experts in some particular field. De Groot (1966), for example, showed that expert chess players had phenomenal STMs for the positions of chess pieces on a board, provided they were organised according to the rules of chess. When the pieces were arranged randomly, recall was no better than that of non-chess players. Chess experts use information about the rules of chess, stored in LTM, to aid recall from STM.

Other examples of how 'expertise' can increase STM capacity for information include the observation that avid football supporters can remember match scores more accurately than more casual fans (Morris *et al.*, 1985). Also, experienced burglars can remember details of houses seen in photographs a few moments before better than police officers or householders can (Logie *et al.*, 1992).

These examples show that STM is an active store used to hold information which is being manipulated. According to Groome *et al.* (1999), working memory (WM) is like the computer screen, a kind of mental workspace where various operations are performed on current data. By contrast, LTM resembles the computer's memory ('storage memory'), which holds large amounts of information in a fairly passive state for possible future retrieval. WM is a cognitive function that:

While some card games are largely a matter of chance, others require considerable expertise

- helps us keep track of what we're doing or where we are from moment to moment
- holds information long enough to allow us to make a decision, dial a telephone number, or repeat a strange foreign word that we've just heard.

Instead of a single, simple STM, Baddeley & Hitch (1974) proposed a more complex, multi-component WM. This comprises a *central executive*, which is in overall charge, plus sub- or *slave systems*, whose activities are controlled by the central executive. These are the *articulatory* (or *phonological*) loop and the *visuospatial scratch* (or *sketch*) pad.

The central executive

This is thought to be involved in many higher mental processes, such as decision-making, problem-solving and making plans (see Chapter 20). More specifically, it may coordinate performance on two separate tasks, and attend selectively to one input while inhibiting others (Baddeley, 1996). Although capacity-limited, it's very flexible and can process information in any sense modality (it's *modality-free*). It resembles a *pure attentional system* (Baddeley, 1981: see Chapter 13).

The articulatory (or phonological) loop

This is probably the most extensively studied component of the model. It was intended to explain the extensive evidence for acoustic coding in STM (Baddeley, 1997). It can be thought of as a verbal rehearsal loop used when, for example, we try to remember a telephone number for a few seconds by saying it silently to ourselves. It's also used to hold words we're preparing to speak aloud. It uses an articulatory/phonological code, in which information is represented as it would be spoken. For this reason, it's been called the *inner voice*.

Its name derives from the finding that its capacity isn't limited by the number of items it can hold, but by the length of time taken to recite them (Baddeley *et al.*, 1975). This is similar to the way that the faster you recite something into a microphone, the more words you can record on a short loop of recording tape (Groome *et al.*, 1999).

The articulatory loop has two components:

1. a phonological store capable of holding speech-based information, and
2. an articulatory control process based on inner speech.

While memory traces within the store fade after about two seconds, the control process feeds it back into the store (the process underlying silent rehearsal). The control process is also able to convert written material into a phonological code, which is then transferred to the phonological store (Baddeley, 1997).

The visuospatial scratch, or sketch, pad

This can also rehearse information, but deals with visual and/or spatial information as, for example, when we drive along a familiar road, approach a bend, and think about the road's spatial layout beyond the bend (Eysenck, 1986). It uses a visual code, representing information in the form of its visual features such as size, shape and colour. For this reason, it's been called the *inner eye*.

The scratch pad appears to contain separate visual and spatial components. The more active spatial component is involved in movement perception and control of physical actions, while the more passive visual component is involved in visual pattern recognition (Logie, 1995).

Figure 17.8 The visuospatial scratch pad is where we store information about familiar roads, so we know what's round the bend

ASK YOURSELF...

- One way of understanding how WM operates can be gained from trying to calculate the number of windows in your house (Baddeley, 1995). Most of us do this by forming a visual image and then either 'looking' at the house from the outside, or taking a 'mental journey' through its various rooms.
- Complete the following sentences:

To set up and manipulate the image, we need the _______ ________, and to sub-vocally count the number of windows we need the _____ ______. The whole operation is organised and run by the _________ ________.

(Answers can be found on page 305.)

Research into WM has often used the *concurrent- (interference- or dual-) task* method, in which participants perform two tasks at the same time. Assuming that each slave system's capacity is limited:

- with two tasks making use of the *same* slave system(s), performance on one or both should be worse when they're performed together than when they're performed separately (Baddeley *et al.*, 1975)
- if two tasks require *different* slave systems, it should be possible to perform them as well together as separately.

Some researchers have used *articulatory suppression*, in which the participant rapidly repeats out loud something meaningless (such as 'hi-ya' or 'the').

ASK YOURSELF...

- Explain the reasoning behind the use of articulatory suppression.
- If this method produces poorer performance on another simultaneous task, what can we infer about the slave system involved in the first task?

Articulatory suppression uses up the articulatory loop's resources, so it cannot be used for anything else. If articulatory suppression produces poorer performance on another simultaneous task, then we can infer that this task also uses the articulatory loop (Eysenck & Keane, 1995).

An evaluation of the WM model

- It's generally accepted that (a) STM is better seen as a number of relatively independent processing mechanisms than as the MSM's single unitary store, and (b) attentional processes and STM are part of the same system (they're probably used together much of the time in everyday life).
- The idea that any one slave system (such as the phonological loop) may be involved in the performance of apparently very different tasks (such as memory span, mental arithmetic, verbal reasoning, and reading) is a valuable insight.
- It has practical applications which extend beyond its theoretical importance (Gilhooly, 1996; Logie, 1999: see Box 17.3).
- One weakness of the WM model is that least is known about the most important component, namely the central executive (Hampson & Morris, 1996). It can apparently carry out an enormous variety of processing activities in different conditions. This makes it difficult to describe its precise function, and the idea of a single central executive might be as inappropriate as that of a unitary STM (Eysenck, 1986).

Box 17.3 Working memory and learning to read

- One of the most striking features of children with specific problems in learning to read (despite normal intelligence and a supportive family) is their impaired memory span (Gathercole & Baddeley, 1990).
- They also tend to do rather poorly on tasks which don't test memory directly, such as judging whether words rhyme.
- These children show some form of phonological deficit that seems to prevent them from learning to read (and which is detectable before they have started to learn). This deficit might be related to the phonological loop (see Chapter 40, pages 699–700).

The levels of processing (LOP) model

Rehearsal and the MSM

As we noted above, the MSM sees rehearsal as a key control process which helps to transfer information from STM to LTM. There's also only one type of rehearsal as far as the model is concerned, what Craik & Watkins (1973) call *maintenance* (as opposed to *elaborative*) rehearsal (see Key Study 17.6). This means that what matters is how much rehearsal occurs. But maintenance rehearsal may not even be necessary for storage. Jenkins (1974) found that participants could remember material even though they weren't expecting to be tested – and so were unlikely to have rehearsed the material. This is called *incidental learning*.

According to Craik & Lockhart (1972), it's the *kind* of rehearsal or processing that's important. Craik and Lockhart also considered that the MSM's view of the relationship between structural components and control processes was, essentially, the wrong way round.

ASK YOURSELF...

- How does the MSM see the relationship between structural components and control processes?

According to the MSM, the structural components (sensory memory, STM and LTM) are fixed, while control processes (such as rehearsal) are less permanent. Craik and Lockhart's *levels-of-processing* (LOP) model begins with the proposed control processes. The structural components (the memory system) are what results from the operation of these processes. In other words, memory is a *by-product of perceptual analysis*. This is controlled by the central processor, which can analyse a stimulus (such as a word) on various levels:

- at a superficial (or *shallow*) level, the surface features of a stimulus (such as whether the word is in small or capital letters) are processed
- at an intermediate (*phonemic* or *phonetic*) level, the word is analysed for its sound
- at a deep (or *semantic*) level, the word's meaning is analysed.

The level at which a stimulus is processed depends on both its nature and the processing time available. The more deeply information is processed, the more likely it is to be retained.

KEY STUDY 17.7 Does 'chicken' rhyme with 'wait'? (Craik & Tulving, 1975)

- Craik and Tulving presented participants with a list of words via a tachistoscope. Following each word, participants were asked one of four questions, to which they had to answer 'yes' or 'no'. The four questions were:

  1. Is the word (e.g. TABLE/table) in capital letters? (This corresponds to *shallow* processing.)
  2. Does the word (e.g. hate/chicken) rhyme with 'wait'? (This corresponds to *phonemic* processing.)
  3. Is the word (e.g. cheese/steel) a type of food? (This corresponds to *semantic* processing.)
  4. Would the word (e.g. ball/rain) fit in the sentence 'He kicked the ... into the tree'? (This also corresponds to *semantic* processing.)

- Later, participants were unexpectedly given a recognition test, in which they had to identify the previously presented words which appeared amongst words they hadn't seen.
- There was significantly better recognition of words that had been processed at the deepest (semantic) level (questions 3 and 4). Also, recognition was superior when the answer was 'yes' rather than 'no'.

Elaboration vs distinctiveness

Elaboration (the amount of processing of a particular kind at a particular level) is also important in determining whether material is stored or not. For example, Craik & Tulving (1975) asked participants to decide if a particular (target) word would be appropriate in simple sentences (such as 'She cooked the ...') or complex sentences (such as 'The great bird swooped down and carried off the struggling ...'). When participants were later given a *cued recall test* (the original sentences were again presented but without the target words), recall was much better for those that fitted into the *complex* sentences.

More important than elaboration is *distinctiveness*, which relates to the nature of processing. For example, 'A mosquito is like a doctor because they both draw blood' is more distinctive than 'A mosquito is like a racoon because they both have hands, legs and jaws'. Although the former involves less elaboration, it was more likely to be remembered (Bransford *et al.*, 1979). However, because LOP, elaboration and distinctiveness can occur together, it's often difficult to choose between them, and all three may contribute to remembering.

Evaluation of the LOP model

- The model was proposed as a new way of interpreting existing data, and to provide a conceptual framework for memory research. Prior to 1972, it was assumed that the same stimulus would typically be processed in a very similar way by all participants on all occasions. The LOP model proposed that perception, attention and memory are interrelated processes.
- It's mainly descriptive rather than explanatory (Eysenck & Keane, 1995). In particular, it fails to explain why deeper processing leads to better recall.
- It's difficult to define/measure depth *independently* of a person's actual retention score. So, if 'depth' is defined as 'the number of words remembered', and 'the number of words remembered' is taken as a measure of 'depth', this definition of depth is circular (what's being defined is part of the definition!). There's no generally accepted way of independently assessing depth, which 'places major limits on the power of the levels-of-processing approach' (Baddeley, 1990).
- Some studies have directly contradicted the model. For example, Morris *et al.* (1977) predicted that stored information (deep or shallow) would be remembered only to the extent that it was relevant to the memory test used. So, deep or semantic information would be of little use if the memory test involved learning a list of words and later selecting those that rhymed with the stored words – but shallow rhyme information would be very relevant. The prediction was supported.
- According to Parkin (1993), different orienting tasks vary in the extent to which they require participants to treat the stimulus as a word (e.g. 'Is 'tiger' a mammal?' compared with 'Does 'tiger' have two syllables?'). Yet retention tests *always* require participants to remember words. Since semantic tasks, by definition, always require attention to be paid to stimuli as words, the superior retention they produce

could reflect the bias of the retention test towards the type of information being encoded. In other words, the orienting task and the retention test are both concerned with the same type of information, which isn't the case when other kinds of task are used.

MEMORY AND THE REPRESENTATION OF KNOWLEDGE

What psychologists have traditionally called knowledge is information that's represented mentally in a particular format and structured or organised in some way (Eysenck & Keane, 1990). This leads to two inter-related questions about the nature of knowledge.

- What format do mental representations take?
- How are these mental representations organised?

This area was neglected until quite recently, when attempts to provide a knowledge base for computer systems stimulated an interest in how 'this enormously important but complex facility operates in people' (Baddeley, 1990).

The organised nature of memory

As we've seen, chunking is a way of increasing STM's limited capacity by imposing a meaning on unrelated items of information. We do this by organising it, giving it a structure that it doesn't otherwise have. As Baddeley (1995) says:

> The secret of a good memory, as of a good library, is that of organisation; good learning typically goes with the systematic encoding of incoming material, integrating and relating it to what is already known.

Organisation can be either imposed by the experimenter (EO) or spontaneously by the participant ('subjective organisation' (SO): Tulving, 1962). Mandler (1967) found that instructions to organise will facilitate learning, even though the participant isn't trying to remember the material. A classic study of organisation is that of Bower *et al.* (1969).

KEY STUDY 17.8 Helpful hierarchies (Bower *et al.*, 1969)

- Bower *et al.* gave participants the task of learning a list of 112 words arranged into conceptual hierarchies.
- For the experimental group, the words were presented as a hierarchy (28 on each of four trials: see Figure 17.9, below), while the control group was shown 28 words on each of four trials presented randomly.
- The former recalled an average of 73 words correctly, while the latter recalled an average of only 21. Clearly, organisation can facilitate retention.

Imagery as a form of organisation

According to Paivio (1969), probably the most powerful predictor of the ease with which words will be learned is their 'concreteness'; that is, how easily a word evokes a mental image. Richardson (1974) tested free recall of a series of 'concrete' and 'abstract' words. By varying the interval between presenting the stimulus and recalling it, he concluded that the 'effect of imageability lies in secondary memory'; in other words, 'concrete' words were recalled significantly more efficiently from LTM (compared with 'abstract' words), whereas there was no difference with recall from STM.

Bower (1972) showed that asking participants to form a mental image of pairs of unrelated nouns (e.g. 'dog' and 'bicycle'), where the two words were interacting in some way, resulted in significantly better recall than when they were instructed merely to memorise the words. Bower considers that the more bizarre the details of the image, the better (for example, a dog riding a bicycle).

Wollen *et al.* (1972) studied the relative contribution of concreteness/interactiveness and bizarreness by giving pictures to participants to help them learn paired associates, such as 'piano–cigar'. Figure 17.10 (page 296) shows all four combinations of these two dimensions. Wollen *et al.* found a large effect of interaction, but not of bizarreness, which suggests that interaction promotes elaborative encoding that aids later recall. However, the study used an unrelated design, and when related designs are used, bizarre images stand out from the rest as the most distinctive, producing the best recall (Anderson, 1995a).

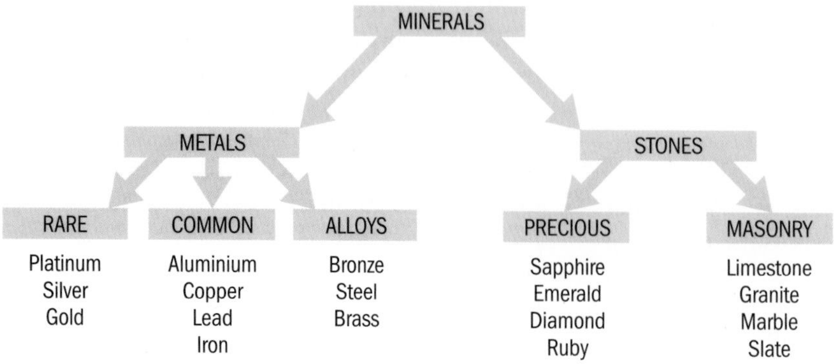

Figure 17.9 An example of a conceptual hierarchy used in Bower *et al.*'s (1969) experiment

According to Paivio's (1986) *dual-coding hypothesis*, mental activity involves interaction between two interconnected but functionally independent sub-systems:

1. a *non-verbal imagery system*, which processes information about objects and events in the form of *imagens*, and
2. a *verbal system*, specialised for handling speech and writing. Each known word is represented by a *logogen*.

The two systems are connected via *referential links*, which allow a word to be associated with its relevant image and vice versa. This can help explain the better learning of concrete words: they activate both verbal and non-verbal codes, while abstract words activate only a verbal code. Similarly, pictures are easier to memorise than words representing those pictures: a picture is more likely to activate a verbal code as well as an imaginal one, while words are less likely to evoke a picture (especially if they're abstract) (Parkin, 1993).

A dramatic illustration of the role of imagery is the man with the exceptional memory documented by Luria (1968).

CASE STUDY 17.3: The mind of a mnemonist (Luria, 1968)

- 'S.' was a reporter for a Moscow newspaper in the early 1920s. His astounding ability to produce reports, rich in the minutest factual detail, without ever taking notes, so amazed the editor that he sent him to Luria for psychological evaluation.
- There seemed to be no limit either to his memory's capacity or durability. He could commit to memory, in a few minutes, long lists of numbers and recall them perfectly, hours, days or weeks later. Luria tested him 30 years after they first met, and S. could still remember perfectly the numbers of tables he'd previously learned!
- He seemed to have spontaneously developed *mnemonic tricks*. For example, he would associate, in his mind's eye, lists of objects he wished to remember with familiar features of a street or some other familiar place. He mentally placed each object at some point on the scene; all he had to do to remember the list was to recall the mental image of the scene and locate each object on display. He would imagine himself walking along a Moscow street looking in each hiding place for the object he'd put there (this is the method of loci).
- His recall was accompanied by extreme *synaesthesia*, in which sensory information from one modality evokes a sensation in another. For example, colours are associated with tastes. He once said to Luria, 'What a crumbly yellow voice you have'. (See Chapter 5.)
- His peculiar problem was his apparent *inability to forget*. He couldn't hold down an ordinary job, and ended up as a professional memory man (Rose, 2003).

Knowledge and semantic memory

The hierarchical network model

The *hierarchical network model* of SM (Collins & Quillian, 1969, 1972) is concerned with our memory for words and their meanings. As shown in Figure 17.11, SM is

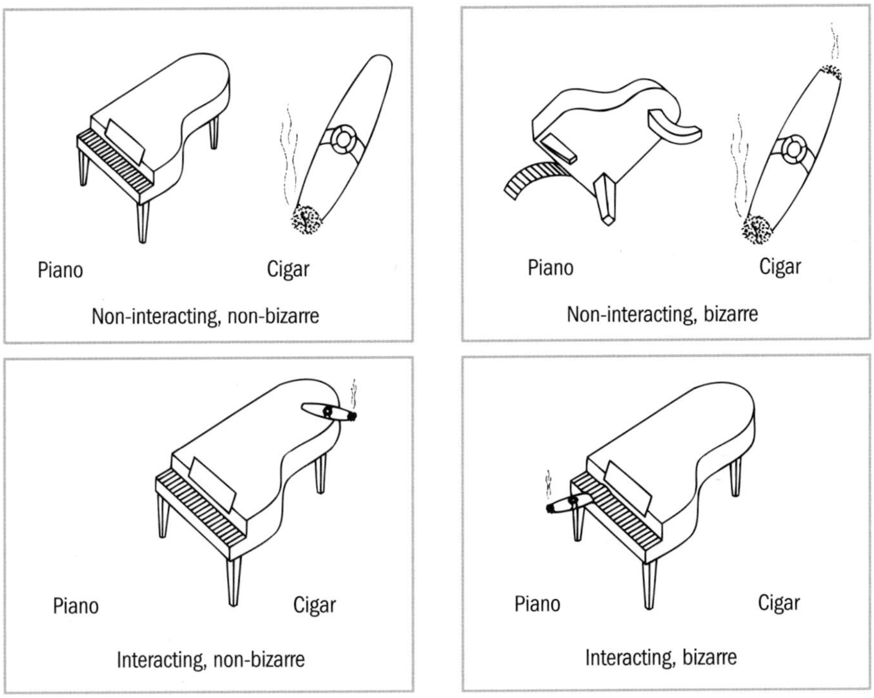

Figure 17.10 Examples of pictures used to associate piano and cigar in the Wollen *et al.* (1972) study of image bizarreness. From Wollen, K.A., Weber, A. & Lowry, D.H., *Cognitive Psychology*, Volume 3. Copyright © 1972 Academic Press

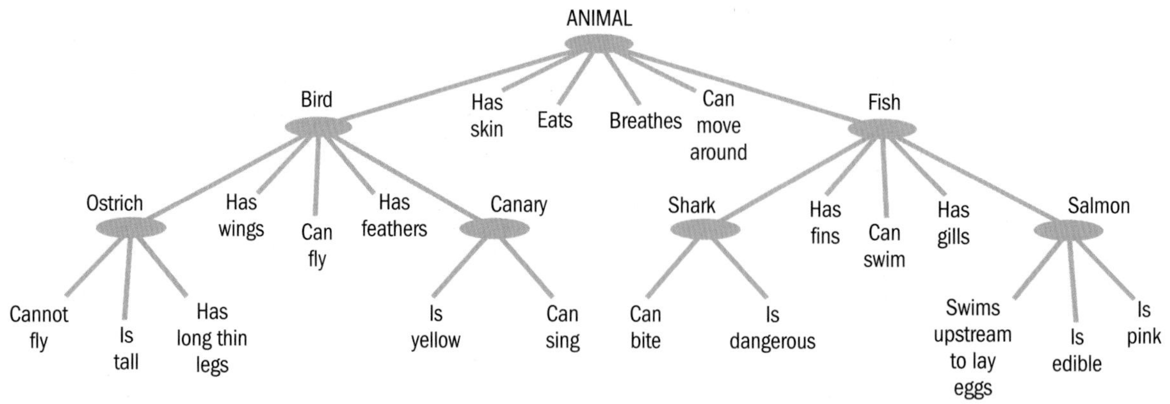

Figure 17.11 Part of the semantic memory network for a three-level hierarchy (from Collins & Quillian, 1969)

portrayed as a network of concepts connected with other concepts by pointers. Each word or concept is represented by a particular node in the network. The meaning of a particular word is given by the configuration of pointers that connect that word with other words.

If we were asked whether the statement 'A canary can sing' is true, we'd need only to find the word 'canary' and retrieve the properties stored with that word. But to verify 'A canary can fly' we'd first have to find 'canary', and then move up one level to 'bird' before retrieving the property 'can fly'. Assuming that it takes time to move from one level to another, it should take longer to verify 'A canary can fly' than to verify 'A canary can sing', and it would take even longer to verify 'A canary has skin'. The model assumes that the various properties stored with each word are scanned simultaneously.

Collins and Quillian presented participants with various sentences, including the examples given above, which they had to judge as true or false by pressing an appropriate button as quickly as possible (reaction time was used as a measure of difficulty). The main finding was that the time taken to decide that a statement is true increased as a function of the number of levels that had to be worked through to verify it. So, as the model predicts, more time was needed to verify 'A canary is an animal' than 'A canary is a bird'.

An evaluation of Collins and Quillian's model

- It takes longer to verify 'A canary is an animal' because there are more animals than birds. So Collins and Quillian's findings could be explained in terms of the relationship between category size and reaction time.
- Some members of a category are more typical than others. Participants respond faster to typical instances ('A canary is a bird') than to atypical ones ('An ostrich is a bird'). That shouldn't happen according to the hierarchical model, since presumably the same distance has to be travelled in both cases (Baddeley, 1990).
- Rips *et al.* (1973) found that it took longer to verify 'A bear is a mammal' than 'A bear is an animal'. This is the *opposite* of what the hierarchical model predicts, since 'animal' is higher up in the hierarchy than 'mammal'.

ASK YOURSELF...
- Could the model be criticised in terms of research into imagery?

- The findings could be explained in terms of how easy (or difficult) it is to imagine concepts at different levels. The higher up the hierarchy you go, the more abstract the category becomes, and the more difficult it becomes to form a mental image of it (it's easier to picture a canary than 'an animal').

The spreading-activation model

In the light of these criticisms, Collins & Loftus (1975) proposed a revised network model. The major changes include the following:

- The network is no longer hierarchically organised, making it more flexible.
- The new concept of *semantic distance* denotes that highly related concepts are located close together, and distance reflects how easily 'excitation' can flow from one node to the next (see Figure 17.12, page 299).
- A range of different types of link is introduced, including *class membership associations* (or 'is a' links – 'A dog is a mammal', including some negative instances, such as 'A dolphin is not a fish'), 'has' links ('An animal has skin'), 'can' links ('A bird can fly'), and 'cannot' links ('An ostrich cannot fly').
- It no longer sees the memory network in terms of logical, hierarchical relationships. Human memory may simply not be as logical and systematic as originally proposed, and it allows for an individual's personal experience and the structure of the environment to act

as at least partial influences on the relationship between concepts.

- The concept of *spreading activation* implies that when two concepts are stimulated, an activation from each spreads throughout the network until they're linked. This takes time, because semantically related concepts are closer together than semantically unrelated concepts.

An evaluation of the spreading-activation model

- Johnson-Laird *et al.* (1984) believe that there are many examples where the interpretation offered by the network will tend, in actual discourse, to be overridden by the constraints of real-world knowledge.
- Take, for instance, 'The ham sandwich was eaten by the soup'. This would appear to be nonsensical until you put it into the context of a restaurant, where waiters/waitresses sometimes label customers in terms of their orders. Johnson-Laird *et al.* call this failure to 'escape from the maze of symbols into the world' the *symbolic fallacy*: you have to know the relationship between symbols and what they refer to.

Schema theory and everyday memory

According to Baddeley (1990), it became increasingly obvious during the 1970s that SM must contain structures considerably larger than the simple concepts involved in network models such as those of Collins and Quillian, and Collins and Loftus. This 'larger unit' of SM is the *schema*, a concept first used by Bartlett (1932) in his research into *reconstructive memory*. Because of the importance of reconstructive memory to eyewitness testimony, I shall postpone discussion of schema theory to Chapter 21.

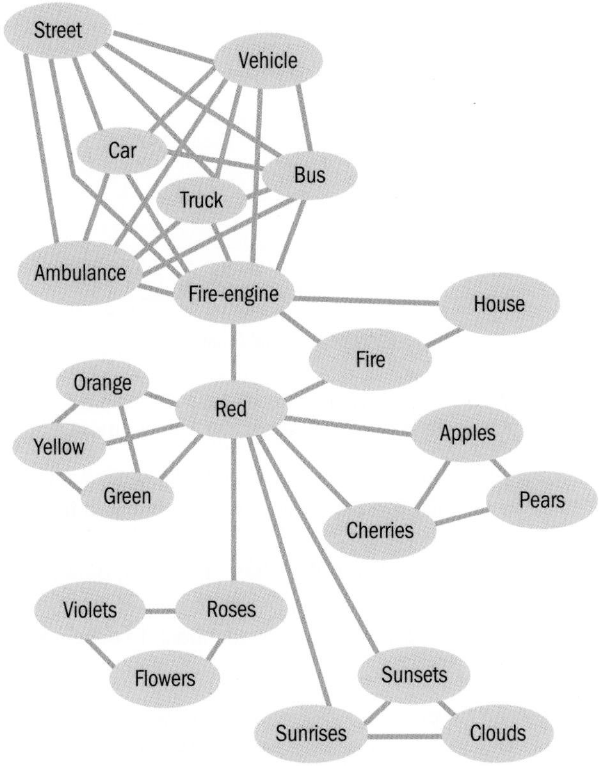

Figure 17.12 An example of a spreading-activation model. The length of each line (or link) represents the degree of association between particular concepts (based on Collins & Loftus, 1975)

THEORIES OF FORGETTING

To understand why we forget, we must recall the distinction between *availability* (whether or not material has been stored) and *accessibility* (being able to retrieve what's been stored). In terms of the MSM, since information must be transferred from STM to LTM for permanent storage:

- availability mainly concerns STM and the transfer of information from STM into LTM
- accessibility has to do mainly with LTM.

Forgetting can occur at the encoding, storage or retrieval stages.

One way of looking at forgetting is to ask what prevents information staying in STM long enough to be transferred to LTM (some answers are provided by *decay* and *displacement theories*). Some answers to the question about what prevents us from locating the information that's already in LTM include those offered by *interference theory*, *cue-dependent forgetting* and *motivated forgetting* (or *repression*: this is discussed in Chapter 21).

Decay theory

Decay (or *trace decay*) theory tries to explain why forgetting increases with time. Clearly, memories must be stored somewhere, the most obvious place being the brain. Presumably, some sort of structural change (the *engram*) occurs when learning takes place. According to decay theory, metabolic processes occur over time which cause the engram to degrade/break down, unless it's maintained by repetition and rehearsal. This results in the memory contained within it becoming unavailable.

Hebb (1949) argued that while learning is taking place, the engram which will eventually be formed is very delicate and liable to disruption (the *active trace*). With learning, it grows stronger until a permanent engram is formed (the *structural trace*) through neurochemical and neuroanatomical changes.

Decay in STM and LTM

The active trace corresponds roughly to STM, and, according to decay theory, forgetting from STM is due to disruption of the active trace. Although Hebb didn't apply the idea of decay to LTM, other researchers have argued that it can explain LTM forgetting if it's assumed that decay occurs through disuse (hence, *decay-through-disuse theory*). So, if certain knowledge or skills aren't

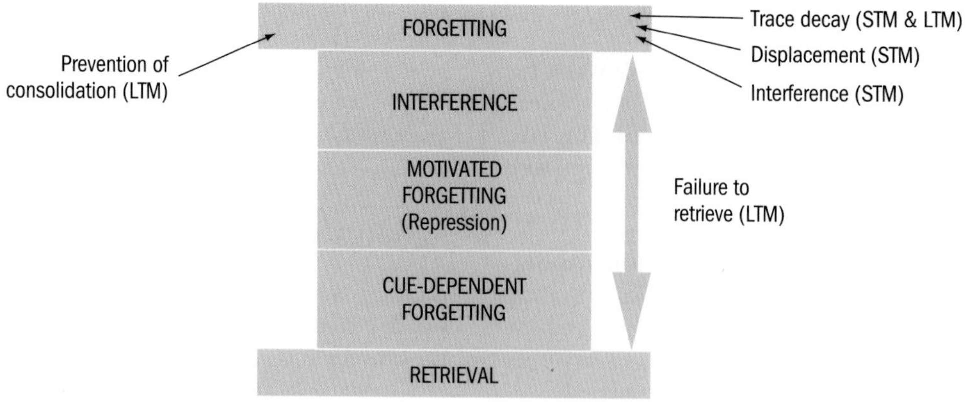

Figure 17.13 Different theories of forgetting, including retrieval failure

used or practised for long periods of time, the corresponding engram will eventually decay away (Loftus & Loftus, 1980).

> *ASK YOURSELF...*
> • Try to think of skills/knowledge that, contrary to decay-through-disuse theory, *aren't* lost even after long periods of not being used/practised.

Is forgetting just a matter of time?

Peterson & Peterson's (1959) experiment (see Key Study 17.2) has been taken as evidence for the role of decay in STM forgetting. If decay did occur, then we'd expect poorer recall of information with the passage of time, which is exactly what the Petersons reported.

The difficulty with the Petersons' study in particular, and decay theory in general, is that other possible effects need to be excluded before a decay-based account can be accepted. The ideal way to study the role of decay in forgetting would be to have people receive information and then do nothing, physical or mental, for a period of time. If recall was poorer with the passage of time, it would be reasonable to suggest that decay had occurred. Such an experiment is, of course, impossible. However, Jenkins & Dallenbach (1924) were the first to attempt an approximation to it.

KEY STUDY 17.9 If you want to remember, sleep on it (Jenkins & Dallenbach, 1924)

- Participants learnt a list of ten nonsense syllables. Some then went to sleep immediately (approximating the ideal 'do nothing' state), while the others continued with their normal activities.
- After intervals of one, two, four or eight hours, all participants were tested for their recall of the syllables.
- While there was a fairly steady increase in forgetting as the retention interval increased for the 'waking' participants, this wasn't true for the sleeping participants (see Figure 17.14).

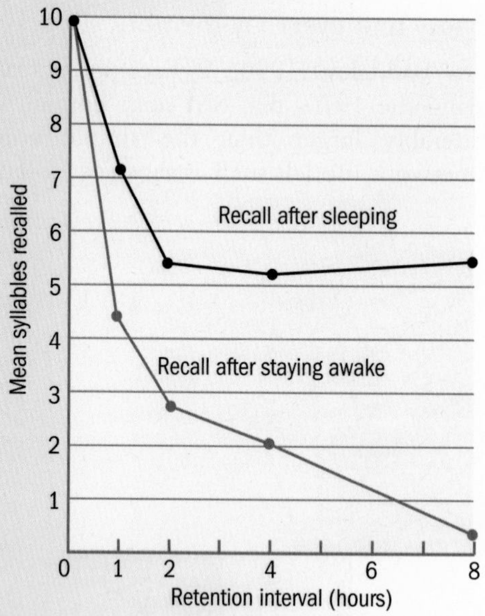

Figure 17.14 Mean number of syllables recalled by participants in Jenkins and Dallenbach's experiment

- If decay is a natural result of the passage of time alone, then we should have expected equal forgetting in both groups.
- The results suggest that it's what happens in between learning and recall that determines forgetting, not time as such. This led Jenkins and Dallenbach to conclude that:

> *Forgetting is not so much a matter of decay of old impressions and associations as it is a matter of interference, inhibition or obliteration of the old by the new.*

Interference theory is discussed on pages 302–304.

Although some data exist suggesting that neurological breakdown occurs with age and disease (such as Alzheimer's disease), there's no evidence that the major cause of forgetting from LTM is neurological decay (Solso, 1995).

Displacement theory

In a limited-capacity STM system, forgetting might occur through *displacement*. When the system is 'full', the oldest material in it would be displaced ('pushed out') by incoming new material. This possibility was explored by Waugh & Norman (1965) using the *serial probe task*. Participants were presented with 16 digits at the rate of either one or four per second. One of the digits (the 'probe') was then repeated, and participants had to say which digit followed the probe. Presumably:

- if the probe was one of the digits at the beginning of the list, the probability of recalling the digit that followed would be small, because later digits would have displaced earlier ones from the system
- if the probe was presented towards the end of the list, the probability of recalling the digit that followed would be high, since the last digits to be presented would still be available in STM.

When the number of digits following the probe was small, recall was good, but when it was large, recall was poor. This is consistent with the idea that the earlier digits are replaced by later ones.

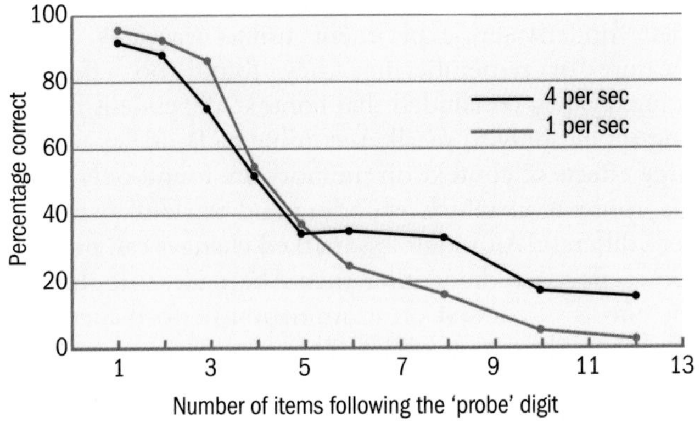

Figure 17.15 Data from Waugh and Norman's serial probe experiment

> *ASK YOURSELF...*
> - Waugh and Norman also found that recall was generally better with the faster (4 per second) presentation rate. How does this support decay theory?

Since less time had elapsed between presentation of the digits and the probe in the four-per-second condition, there would have been less opportunity for those digits to have decayed away. This makes it unclear whether displacement is a process distinct from decay.

Retrieval-failure theory and cue-dependent forgetting

According to *retrieval-failure theory*, memories cannot be recalled because the correct retrieval cues aren't being used. The role of retrieval cues is demonstrated by the *tip-of-the-tongue phenomenon* (TOT), in which we know that we know something but cannot retrieve it at that particular moment in time (Brown & McNeill, 1966).

> **KEY STUDY 17.10 It's on the tip of my tongue (Brown & McNeill, 1966)**
> - Brown and McNeill gave participants dictionary definitions of unfamiliar words, and asked them to provide the words themselves. Most participants either knew the word or knew that they didn't know it.
> - Some, however, were sure they knew the word but couldn't recall it (it was on the tip of their tongue). About half could give the word's first letter and the number of syllables, and often offered words which sounded like the word or had a similar meaning. This suggests that the required words were in memory, but the absence of a correct retrieval cue prevented them from being recalled.
> - Examples of definitions used by Brown and McNeill:
>
> 1. A small boat used in the harbours and rivers of Japan and China, rowed with a scull from the stern, and often having a sail
> 2. Favouritism, especially governmental patronage extended to relatives
> 3. The common cavity into which the various ducts of the body open in certain fish, reptiles, birds and mammals.
>
> **Answers:** sampan; nepotism; cloaca

Tulving & Pearlstone (1966) read participants lists of varying numbers of words (12, 24 or 48) consisting of categories (e.g. animals) of one, two or four *exemplars* (e.g. dog) per list, plus the category name. Participants were instructed to try to remember only the exemplars. Half the participants (group 2) free-recalled the words and wrote them down on blank pieces of paper. The other half (group 1) was given the category names. Group 1 recalled significantly more words, especially on the 48-item list. However, when group 2 was given the category names, recall improved (see Figure 17.16).

This illustrates very well the availability/accessibility distinction. The category name acted as a contextual cue, helping to make accessible what was available. Group 2 participants knew more than they could actually retrieve under the cue-less conditions.

Tulving (1968) showed participants a list of words, and then asked them to write down as many as they could remember in any order. Later, and without being

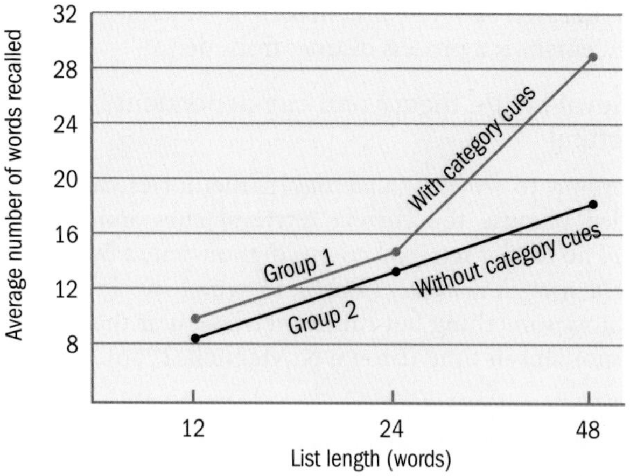

Figure 17.16 Average number of words recalled with and without cues in Tulving & Pearlstone's (1966) experiment

presented with the list again or seeing the words they'd written down previously, participants were asked to recall them. Later still, they were asked a third time to recall the words on the original list.

Table 17.2 Typical results from Tulving's experiment

Trial 1	Trial 2	Trial 3
Table	Table	Table
Driver	Escalator	Driver
Escalator	Apple	Escalator
Apple	Railway	Apple
Railway	Pen	Pen
Pen		Fountain

ASK YOURSELF...

- As Table 17.2 shows, the same words weren't recalled across the three trials. Why is this finding difficult for decay theory to explain?

Decay theory wouldn't predict the recall of a word on trial 3 if it wasn't recalled on trials 1 or 2. For it to be recalled on a later trial, it couldn't have decayed away on the earlier trials. But retrieval-failure theory can explain these findings by arguing that different retrieval cues were involved in the three trials.

According to Tulving's (1983) *encoding-specificity principle* (ESP), recall improves if the same cues are present during recall as during the original learning. In Tulving and Pearlstone's experiment, the category names were presented together with the exemplars for group 1. Presumably, they were encoded at the time of learning. The ESP explains why recall is sometimes superior to recognition (even though recognition is generally considered to be easier than recall: see pages 286–287).

Tulving (1974) used the term *cue-dependent forgetting* to refer jointly to *context-dependent* and *state-dependent forgetting*.

Table 17.3 Cue-dependent forgetting

Context-dependent forgetting	State-dependent forgetting
Occurs in absence of relevant environmental or contextual variables. These represent *external* cues.	Occurs in absence of relevant psychological or physiological variables. These represent *internal* cues.
Abernathy (1940): One group had to learn and then recall material in the same room, while a second group learned and recalled in different rooms. The first group's recall was superior.	Clark *et al.* (1987): Victims' inabilities to recall details of a violent crime may be due at least partly to the fact that recall occurs in a less emotionally aroused state. (See Chapter 21.)
Godden & Baddeley (1975): Divers learned lists of words either on land or 15 ft under water. Recall was then tested in the same or a different context. Those who learned and recalled in different contexts showed a 30% deficit compared with those who learned and recalled in the same context.	McCormick & Mayer (1991): The important link may be between mood and the sort of material being remembered. So we're more likely to remember happy events when we're feeling happy rather than sad.

Interestingly, when Godden & Baddeley (1980) repeated their 'underwater' experiment using *recognition* as the measure of remembering, they found no effect of context. They concluded that context-dependent forgetting applies only to recall. According to Baddeley (1995), large effects of context on memory are found only when the contexts in which encoding and retrieval occur are very different. Although less marked changes can produce some effects, studies (other than Abernathy's) looking at the effects of context on examination performance have tended to show few effects. This may be because when we're learning, our surroundings aren't a particularly salient feature of the situation, unlike our internal state (such as our emotional state).

Interference theory

According to *interference theory*, forgetting is influenced more by what we do before or after learning than by the mere passage of time (see Key Study 17.9).

- In *retroactive interference/inhibition* (RI), later learning interferes with the recall of earlier learning. For example, if you originally learned to drive in a manual car, then learned to drive an automatic car, when returning to a manual, you might try to drive it as though it was an automatic.

- In *proactive interference/inhibition* (PI), earlier learning interferes with the recall of later learning. For example, say you learned to drive a car in which the indicator lights are turned on by using the stalk on the left of the steering wheel, and the windscreen wipers by the stalk on the right. After passing your driving test, you buy a car in which this arrangement is reversed. When you're about to turn left or right, you activate the windscreen wipers!

Interference theory has been extensively studied in the laboratory using paired-associate lists (see page 287). The usual procedure for studying interference effects is shown in Figure 17.17.

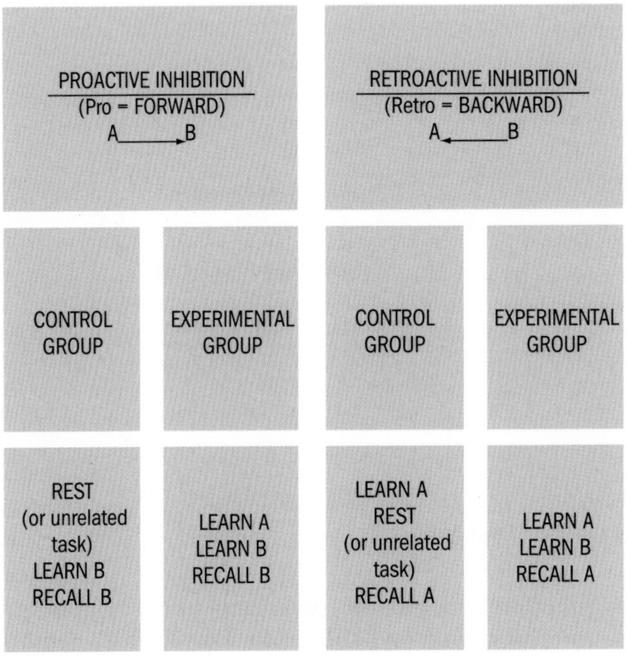

Figure 17.17 Experimental procedure for investigating retroactive and proactive interference

Usually, the first member of each pair in list A is the same as in list B, but the second member of each pair is different in the two lists.

- In RI, the learning of the second list interferes with recall of the first list (the interference works *backwards* in time).
- In PI, the learning of the first list interferes with recall of the second list (the interference works *forwards* in time).

Interference theory offers an alternative explanation of Peterson & Peterson's (1959) data (see Key Study 17.2). Keppel & Underwood (1962) noted that the Petersons gave two practice trials, and were interested in how these practice trials affected those in the actual experiment. While there was no evidence of forgetting on the first trial, there was some on the second and even more on the third.

Although forgetting can occur on the first trial (supporting decay theory), Keppel and Underwood's finding that performance didn't decline until the second trial suggests that PI was occurring in the Petersons' experiment.

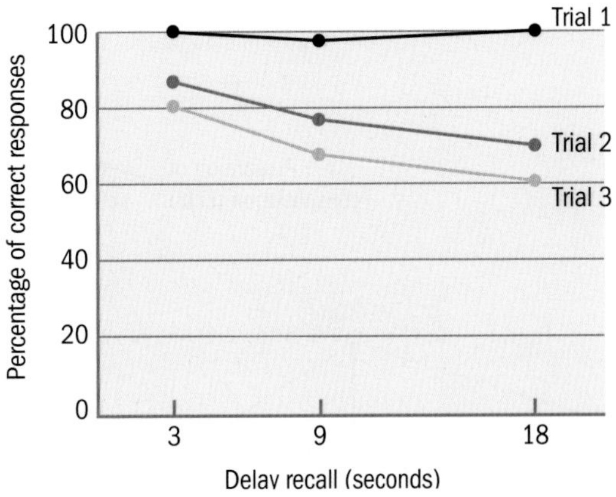

Figure 17.18 Mean percentage of items correctly recalled on trials 1, 2 and 3 for various delay times (based on Keppel & Underwood, 1962)

Like Keppel and Underwood, Wickens (1972) found that participants became increasingly poor at retaining information in STM on successive trials. However, when the category of information was changed, they performed just as well as on the first list. So performance with lists of numbers became poorer over trials, but if the task was changed to lists of letters, it improved. This is called *release from proactive inhibition.*

Limitations of laboratory studies of interference theory

The strongest support for interference theory comes from laboratory studies. However, the following points should be borne in mind:

- Learning in such studies doesn't occur in the same way as it does in the real world, where learning of potentially interfering material is spaced out over time. In the laboratory, learning is artificially compressed in time, which maximises the likelihood that interference will occur (Baddeley, 1990). Such studies therefore lack ecological validity.
- Laboratory studies tend to use nonsense syllables as the stimulus material. When meaningful material is used, interference is more difficult to demonstrate (Solso, 1995).
- When people have to learn, say, the response 'bell' to the stimulus 'woj', the word 'bell' isn't actually learned in the laboratory, since it's already part of SM. What's being learned (a specific response to a specific stimulus in a specific laboratory situation) is stored in EM. SM is much more stable and structured than EM, and so is much more resistant to interference effects. No

amount of new information will cause someone to forget the things they know that are stored in their SM (Solso, 1995).

- However, in support of interference theory, it's generally agreed that if students have to study more than one subject in the same time-frame, these should be as *dissimilar* as possible.

> ***ASK YOURSELF...***
> - Think of examples of subjects that (a) should definitely *not* be studied together in the same time-frame, and (b) *could* be studied together without much risk of interference.

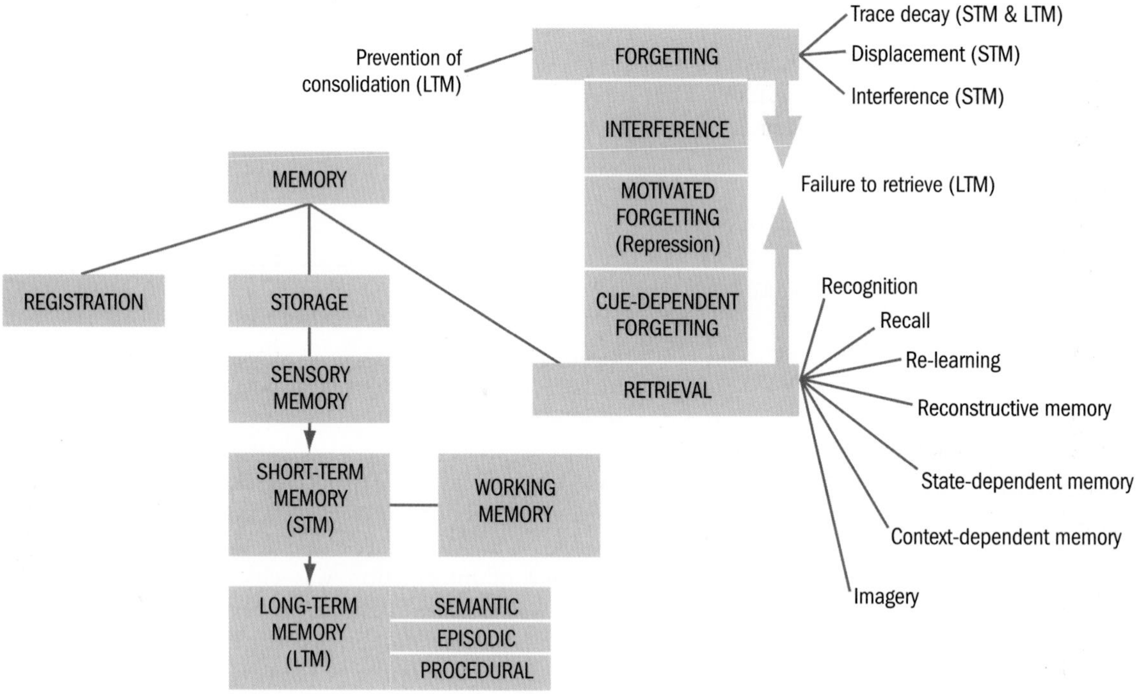

Figure 17.19 A summary of the three components of memory and theories of forgetting

CONCLUSIONS

In the *Introduction and overview*, I quoted Blakemore, who claims that, without memory, there'd be no language, art, science or culture. He also describes what it would be like for an individual with no memory. In a similar fashion, Rose (2003) argues that:

> ... Memory defines who we are and shapes the way we act more closely than any other single aspect of our personhood ...

Whatever happens to us (including losing a limb), we're still, in an important sense, recognisably ourselves provided our memories are intact. However:

> ... Lose your memory and you, as you, cease to exist ... (Rose, 2003)

CHAPTER SUMMARY

- Memory can be defined as the **retention of learning** or **experience**. Learning and memory are **interdependent** processes.
- Ebbinghaus began the systematic study of memory, using **nonsense syllables**. He showed that memory declined very rapidly at first, then levelled off.
- Memory is now studied largely from an **information-processing approach**, which focuses on **registration/encoding**, **storage**, and **retrieval**. Storage corresponds to **availability**, retrieval to **accessibility**.
- Techniques for measuring memory include **recognition**, **recall** (**serial** or **free**), **paired associates recall**, and the **memory-span procedure**.
- James's distinction between **primary** and **secondary memory** corresponds to that between short-term memory (STM) and long-term memory (LTM).
- **Sensory memory** is modality-specific and works in a similar way to the sensory buffer store in Broadbent's filter model of attention.
- The limited capacity of STM can be increased by **chunking**, which draws on LTM to encode new information in a meaningful way. **Rehearsal** is a way of holding information in STM almost indefinitely, and the primary code used by STM is **acoustic**. But semantic and visual coding are also used.

- LTM probably has an **unlimited capacity**, and information is stored in a **relatively permanent** way. Coding is mainly **semantic**, but information may also be coded visually, acoustically and in other ways.
- Atkinson and Shiffrin's **multi-store model** (MSM) sees sensory memory, STM and LTM as **permanent structural components** of the memory system. Rehearsal is a **control process**, which acts as a **buffer** between sensory memory and LTM, and helps the **transfer** of information to LTM.
- The **primacy effect** reflects recall from LTM, while the **recency effect** reflects recall from STM. Together they comprise the **serial position effect**.
- Studies of **brain-damaged, amnesic patients** appear to support the STM–LTM distinction. While STM continues to function fairly normally, certain aspects of LTM functioning are impaired.
- LTM isn't unitary, but comprises **semantic**, **episodic**, and **procedural memory**. **Autobiographical memory** and **flashbulb memories** are two kinds of episodic memory. An overlapping distinction is that between procedural and **declarative** memory/learning.
- Baddeley and Hitch's **working-memory** (WM) model rejected the MSM's view of STM as unitary. Instead, STM is seen as comprising a **central executive**, which controls the activities of the **phonological loop** (inner voice), and **visuospatial scratch pad** (inner eye).
- Craik and Watkins' distinction between **maintenance** and **elaborative rehearsal** implies that it's not the amount but the **kind** of rehearsal or processing that matters.
- According to Craik and Lockhart's **levels-of-processing** (LOP) model, memory is a **by-product of perceptual analysis**, such that STM and LTM are the consequences of the operation of control processes.
- The more deeply information is processed, the more likely it is to be retained. **Semantic processing** represents the **deepest** level. **Distinctiveness** is probably more important than **elaboration**.
- Both chunking and **imagery** are forms of organising information, making it easier both to store and to retrieve.
- The **hierarchical network model** of SM sees the memory network in terms of logical, hierarchical relationships between words and concepts. This has been modified to include **semantic distance** and **spreading activation**, making it more flexible and realistic.
- **Decay/trace decay theory** attempts to explain why forgetting increases over time. STM forgetting is due to disruption of the **active trace**, and **decay through disuse** explains LTM forgetting.
- **Displacement theory** is supported by data from Waugh and Norman's **serial probe task**. However, displacement may not be distinct from decay.
- According to **retrieval-failure theory**, memories cannot be recalled because the correct **retrieval cues** are missing. This is demonstrated by the **tip-of-the-tongue** (TOT) phenomenon, and the provision of **category names**. Unlike decay theory, retrieval-failure theory can explain our ability to recall different items on different occasions.
- **Cue-dependent forgetting** comprises **context-dependent** and **state-dependent** forgetting, which refer to **external** and **internal** cues respectively.
- According to **interference theory**, forgetting is influenced more by what we do before/after learning than by the mere passage of time. **Retroactive interference/inhibition** (RI) works **backwards** in time, while **proactive interference/inhibition** (PI) works **forwards** in time.
- Laboratory studies of interference lack **ecological validity**, and interference is more difficult to demonstrate when material other than nonsense syllables is used. Some types of LTM (such as episodic) are more vulnerable to interference effects than others (such as semantic).

Links with other topics/chapters

- Broadbent's *filter model of selective attention* was in many ways the precursor to Atkinson and Shiffrin's MSM, and sensory memory is very similar to Broadbent's concept of a sensory 'buffer' store (Chapter 13).
- The *case study* is a method that, in practice at least, often involves unusual or abnormal behaviour. While this can shed light on 'normal' behaviour, critics argue that we cannot generalise from such cases, making it *unscientific* (Chapter 3). Traditional science adopts a *nomothetic* ('law-like') approach, while the case study is central to the *idiographic* ('uniqueness') approach (Chapter 42). But these aren't necessarily mutually exclusive, as demonstrated by Freud's *psychoanalytic theory* (Chapters 2, 35, 36, 42, 45, 49 and 50). Rose (2003) argues that cases like those of H.M. and Clive Wearing involve brain damage that is clinically unique, making it impossible to generalise as can be done from patients with Korsakoff's syndrome or *Alzheimer's disease* (Chapter 39).
- The distinction between PM and declarative memory is similar to that between *controlled* and *automatic processing* (Chapter 13).
- Chess masters' phenomenal STM only for non-random board positions demonstrates an important difference between how people and *computers* 'think' and solve problems (Chapter 20).

Answers to questions on page 294

visuospatial scratchpad; articulatory loop; central executive

18

LANGUAGE, THOUGHT AND CULTURE

INTRODUCTION AND OVERVIEW

The relationship between language and thought is one of the most fascinating and complex issues within psychology, and it's been debated by philosophers for over 2000 years. Our thinking often takes the form of imagery, and our thoughts and feelings are often expressed (unconsciously) through gestures and facial expressions. Artists 'think' non-linguistically. Knowing what we want to say, but being unable to 'put it into words', is one of several examples of thought taking place without language (Weiskrantz, 1988).

However, the exact relationship between language and thought has been the subject of much debate amongst philosophers and psychologists. Views fall into four main categories.

1. *Thought is dependent on, or caused by, language.* This view is taken by people working in a variety of disciplines, including psychology, sociology, linguistics and anthropology. Sapir (a linguist and anthropologist) and Whorf (a linguist) were both interested in comparing languages, which they saw as a major feature of a culture. Language is shared by all members of a culture, or sub-cultures within it, and this makes it a determining influence on how individuals think. Bernstein (a sociologist) focused on sub-cultural (social class) differences in language *codes*, which he saw as a major influence on intelligence and educational attainment. *Social constructionists* (e.g. Gergen) regard language as providing a basis for all our thought, a system of categories for dividing up experience and giving it meaning (see Chapter 2).
2. *Language is dependent on, and reflects, thought.* Probably the most extreme version of this view is Piaget's, according to whom language reflects the individual's level of cognitive development. Piaget's theory is discussed in detail in Chapter 34.
3. *Thought and language are initially quite separate activities*, which then come together and interact at a later point in development (about age two). This view is associated with the Russian psychologist, Vygotsky, whose developmental theory is also discussed in Chapter 34.
4. *Language and thought are one and the same.* This rather extreme view is associated mainly with Watson, the founder of behaviourism.

The focus of this chapter is the various versions of the first of these viewpoints.

LANGUAGE AND THOUGHT ARE THE SAME

Watson's 'peripheralist' approach

The earliest psychological theory of the relationship between language and thought was proposed by Watson (1913). In his view, thought processes are really no more than the sensations produced by tiny movements of the speech organs too small to produce audible sounds. Essentially, then, thought is talking to oneself very quietly. Part of Watson's rejection of 'mind' was his denial of mentalistic concepts such as 'thought' (see Chapter 3), and hence his reduction of it to 'silent speech' (see Chapter 49).

Watson's theory is called *peripheralism,* because it sees 'thinking' occurring peripherally in the larynx, rather than centrally in the brain. Movements of the larynx do occur when 'thought' is taking place. But this indicates only that such movements may *accompany* thinking, not that the movements *are* thoughts or that they're necessary for thinking to occur.

> *ASK YOURSELF...*
> • Can you think of any ways in which you might test Watson's theory?

Smith (*et al.*, 1947) attempted to test Watson's theory by giving himself an injection of curare, a drug that causes total paralysis of the skeletal muscles without affecting consciousness. The muscles of the speech organs and the respiratory system are paralysed, and so Smith had to be kept breathing artificially. When the drug's effects had worn off, he was able to report on his thoughts and perceptions during the paralysis.

Additionally, Furth (1966) has shown that people born deaf and mute, and who don't learn sign language, can also think in much the same way as hearing and speaking people. For Watson, deaf and mute individuals should be incapable of thought, because of the absence of movement in the speech organs.

THOUGHT IS DEPENDENT ON, OR CAUSED BY, LANGUAGE

Bruner (1983) has argued that language is essential if thought and knowledge aren't to be limited to what can be learned through our actions (the *enactive mode of representation*) or images (the *iconic mode*). If the *symbolic mode* (going beyond the immediate context) is to develop, then language is crucial (see Chapter 34).

Social constructionists (e.g. Gergen, 1973) have argued that our ways of understanding the world derive from other people (past and present), rather than from objective reality. We're born into a world where the conceptual frameworks and categories used by people in our culture already exist. Indeed, these frameworks and categories are an essential part of our culture, since they provide meaning, a way of structuring experience of both ourselves and the world of other people. Language is of fundamental importance in this process. This view has much in common with the 'strong' version of the *linguistic relativity hypothesis,* the most extensively researched of the theories arguing that thought is dependent on, or caused by, language.

> *ASK YOURSELF...*
> • What would you say are some of the fundamental categories that exist in contemporary Britain, taken-for-granted ways of thinking and perceiving, which we may/may not share with other western cultures?

The linguistic relativity hypothesis (LRH)

According to the philosopher Wittgenstein (1921), 'The limits of my language mean the limits of my world'. By this he meant that people can only think about and understand the world through language, and that if a particular language doesn't possess certain ideas or concepts, these couldn't exist for its native speakers.

The view that language determines how we think about objects and events, or even what we think (our ideas, thoughts and perceptions), can be traced to the writings of Sapir (1929) and Whorf (1956), a student of Sapir. Their perspective is often called the *Sapir–Whorf linguistic relativity hypothesis* (LRH), and is sometimes referred to as the *Whorfian hypothesis* in acknowledgement of the greater contribution made by Whorf. For Whorf (1956):

> We dissect nature along the lines laid down by our native languages. The categories and types that we isolate from the world of phenomena we do not find there because they stare every observer in the face; on the contrary, the world is presented in a kaleidoscopic flux of impressions that has to be organised by our minds – and this means largely by the linguistic systems in our minds. We cut nature up, organise it into concepts and ascribe significance as we do, largely because we are parties to an agreement to organise it this way – an agreement that holds throughout our speech community and is codified in patterns of our language.

According to Whorf's *linguistic determinism,* language determines our concepts, and we can think only through the use of concepts. So acquiring a language involves acquiring a 'world view' (or *Weltanschauung*). People who speak different languages have different world views (hence linguistic 'relativity').

ASK YOURSELF...

- In a general sense, do you agree with the claims of linguistic determinism? Is language really that 'powerful'? Have another read of this chapter's *Introduction and overview.*
- If people who speak different (native) languages really do have different world views, what would that imply for communication between them?

What was Whorf's evidence?

Whorf compared standard average European (SAE) languages, such as English, French and Italian (Indo-European), with Native American languages, particularly Hopi. While in English we have a single word for snow, the Inuit Eskimos have approximately 20 (including one for fluffy snow, one for drifting snow, another for packed snow, and so on). The Hopi Indians have only one word for 'insect', 'aeroplane' and 'pilot' and the Zuni Indians don't distinguish, verbally, between yellow and orange.

Whorf also saw a language's grammar as determining an individual's thought and perception. In the Hopi language, for example, no distinction is made between past, present and future which, compared with English, makes it a 'timeless language'. In European languages, 'time' is treated as an objective entity, with a clear demarcation between past, present and future. Although the Hopi language recognises duration, Hopis talk about time only as it appears subjectively to the observer. For example, rather than saying 'I stayed for ten days', Hopis say 'I stayed until the tenth day' or 'I left on the tenth day'.

According to Whorf, the fact that Inuit Eskimos have 20 different words for snow means that they literally perceive more varieties of snow than native English speakers who have only one or two words

In English, nouns denote objects and events, and verbs denote actions. But in the Hopi language, 'lightning', 'wave', 'flame', 'meteor', 'puff of smoke' and 'pulsation' are all verbs, since events of necessarily brief duration must be verbs. As a result, a Hopi would say 'it lightninged', 'it smoked' and 'it flamed'.

ASK YOURSELF...

- Does the finding that Inuit Eskimos have 20 words for snow (if true) necessarily mean that native speakers of Inuit actually *perceive* more varieties of snow than speakers of English?
- Did Whorf show that the Hopi Indians cannot discriminate between past, present and future in essentially the same way as SAE speakers?

Greene (1975) asks us to imagine a Hopi linguist applying a Whorfian analysis to English. Would s/he think that we have 'primitive' beliefs that ships are really female or that mountains have feet, or that 'driving a car', 'driving off in golf' and 'driving a hard bargain' all involve the same activity? Of course not. (See 'Evaluation of the LRH', pages 312–313.)

Testing the LRH

Miller & McNeill (1969) distinguish between three different versions of the LRH, all of which are consistent with it but vary in the strength of claim they make:

Do mountains really have feet?

- the *strong* version claims that *language determines thought*
- the *weak* version claims that *language affects perception*
- the *weakest* version claims that *language influences memory* – information that's more easily described in a particular language will be better remembered than information that's more difficult to describe.

The questions and criticisms that we considered above relate mainly to the strong version, But almost all the research has focused on the weak and weakest versions. One of the few attempts to test the strong version was a study by Carroll & Casagrande (1958).

KEY STUDY 18.1 How Navaho children shape up on cognitive development (Carroll & Casagrande, 1958)

- Carroll and Casagrande compared Navaho Indian children who spoke only either Navaho (*Navaho–Navaho*) or English and Navaho (*English–Navaho*) with American children of European descent who spoke *only English*.
- The children were tested on the development of form or shape recognition.
- The Navaho language stresses the importance of form, such that 'handling' verbs involve different words depending on what's being handled. For example, long and flexible objects (such as string) have one word form, whereas long and rigid objects (such as sticks) have another.
- American children of European descent develop object recognition in the order: size, colour, and form or shape.
- If, as the strong version of the LRH claims, language influences cognitive development, then the developmental sequence of the Navaho children should differ from the English-only American children, and their form or shape recognition abilities should be superior.
- This is what Carroll and Casagrande found, thus supporting the strong version of the LRH.
- However, they also found that the *English–Navaho* group showed form recognition *later* than the English-only American children, which doesn't support the LRH strong version.
- Carroll and Casagrande attributed the superior performance of the English-only children to the fact that they'd had a great deal of experience of shape classification at nursery school. This made them an atypical sample.

Attempts at testing the 'weak' and 'weakest' versions of the LRH have typically involved the *perception and memory of colour*. The Jalé (New Guinea) only have terms for black and white, while the Dani (New Guinea) use 'mola' for bright, warm hues, and 'mili' for dark, cold hues. The Shona people (Zimbabwe) have three colour words, and members of the Ibibio culture (Nigeria) have terms for black, white, red and green.

ASK YOURSELF...

- Would the Jalé or the Ibibio find tests of colour perception and memory more difficult, according to the weak and weakest versions of the LRH?

According to the weaker versions of the LRH, tests of colour perception and memory should be more difficult for the Jalé than the Ibibio. Since the Ibibio word for green encompasses the English green, blue and yellow, the Ibibio should find colour perception and memory tasks more difficult than English speakers. Taking a previous example, since the Zuni language doesn't distinguish between yellow and orange, Zuni speakers should be unable to discriminate them (they should be 'blind' for these two colours).

Brown & Lenneberg (1954) found that Zuni Indians *did* make more mistakes than English speakers in recognising these colours. But Lenneberg & Roberts (1956) found that the number of errors made by *bilingual* Zuni–English speakers in distinguishing orange and yellow fell *midway* between that of monolingual Zuni and monolingual English speakers. This suggests that the two languages don't determine two different sets of conflicting perceptions, but rather two sets of *labels* for essentially the same colour perceptions. Language serves to draw attention to differences in the environment and acts as a label to help store these differences in memory. Sometimes the label we apply to what we see may *distort* our recall of what was seen, since the label determines how we code our experiences into memory storage (see Chapter 17).

KEY STUDY 18.2 Drawing different conclusions (Carmichael *et al.*, 1932)

- Two separate groups of participants were given identical stimulus figures, but two different sets of labels.
- After a period of time, both groups were asked to reproduce the figures.
- The drawings of both groups were distorted in comparison with the original stimulus according to which label had been presented. (See Figure 18.1.)

So, while there's very little direct evidence to support the strong form of the LRH, there's rather more support for the weaker versions. Language merely predisposes people to think or perceive in certain ways or about certain things (Brown, 1958). However, Brown & Lenneberg's (1954) results (and those of other researchers using a similar methodology) have been challenged in a way that throws doubt even on the weaker versions.

The *Tower of Babel* by Breughel. From the Old Testament story of Babel, the word 'babble' is derived

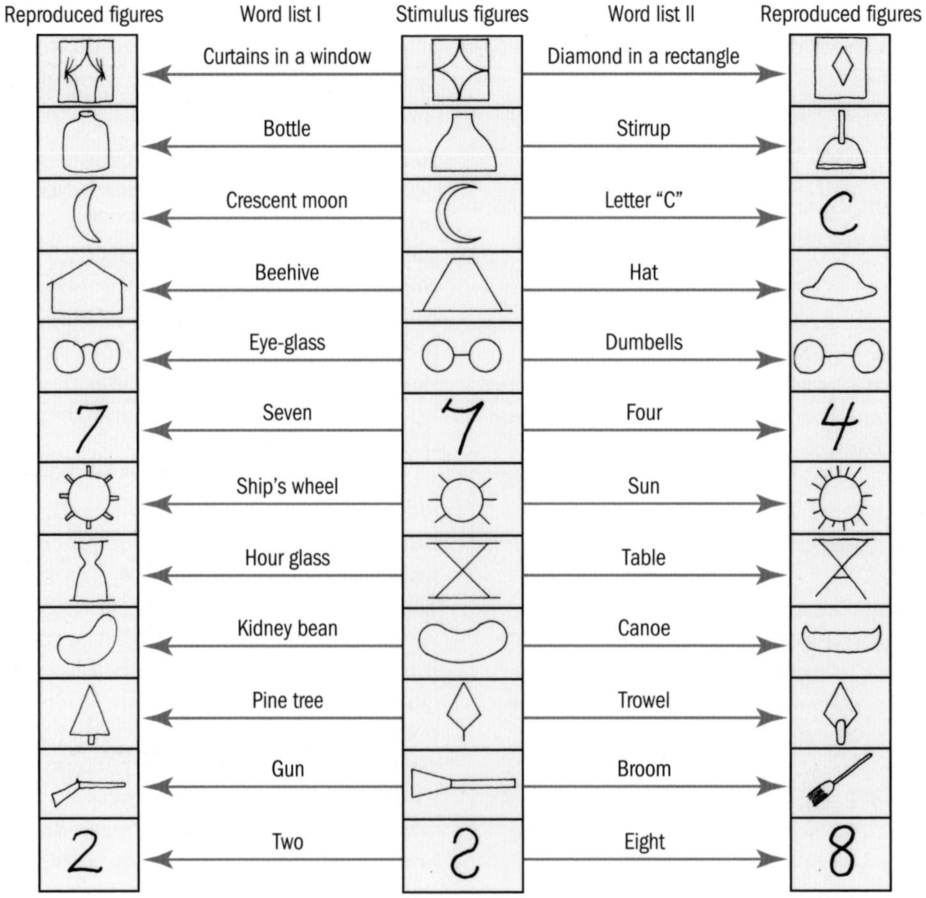

Figure 18.1 Stimulus figures, word lists and reproduced figures (from the experiment by Carmichael *et al.*, 1932)

Perceiving focal colours

Berlin & Kay (1969) used a chart with an array of 329 small coloured chips, comprising virtually all the hues that the human eye can discriminate. They asked native speakers of 20 languages (other than English) (a) to trace the boundaries of each of their native language's basic colour terms, and (b) to point to the chip which was the best example of each basic colour term. A basic or focal colour was defined by a list of linguistic criteria, including:

- a term should consist of only a single unit of meaning (e.g. 'red' as opposed to 'dark red'), and
- it should name only colours and not objects (e.g. 'purple' as opposed to 'wine').

As expected from anthropological research, there was considerable variation in the placement of boundaries. But the choice of best examples was surprisingly similar. The largest clusters were for black and white and red, for which all the 20 languages have colour terms, then 19 for green, 18 yellow, 16 blue, 15 brown and purple, 14 grey, and 11 pink and orange. Berlin and Kay concluded that 'colour categorisation is not random and the foci of basic colour terms are similar in all languages'.

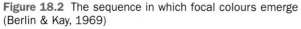

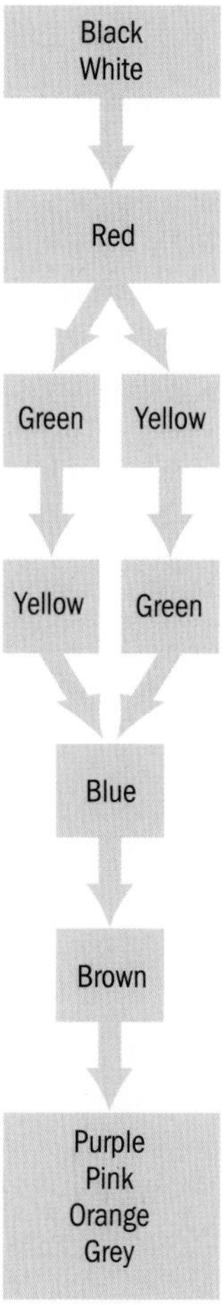

Figure 18.2 The sequence in which focal colours emerge (Berlin & Kay, 1969)

So, while cultures may differ in the number of basic colour terms they use, all cultures draw their focal terms from only 11 colours: black, white, red, green, yellow, blue, brown, purple, pink, orange and grey. Moreover, the colour terms emerge in a particular sequence in the history of languages.

For cultures with only two colours, these will always be black and white, whereas in cultures with three colours, these will always be black, white and red (Newstead, 1995). As Newstead has observed:

> This, then, gives a rather different perspective on the use of colour terms. It had been assumed that verbal labels were chosen more or less arbitrarily, and that those chosen influenced the way in which colour was perceived. Berlin and Kay's findings suggest that there are certain focal colours which will always be labelled if colour terms are used at all. This suggests an alternative explanation for Brown and Lenneberg's findings: that the colours which participants in their study had found easier to learn were the focal colours and these were easy to remember not because they had verbal labels but because they were the most basic colours.

A study which supports Berlin and Kay's findings was conducted by Heider & Oliver (1972).

KEY STUDY 18.3 Colour naming among the Dani (Heider & Oliver, 1972)

- As we noted earlier, the Dani (a Stone-Age agricultural people of Indonesian New Guinea) have only two words for colours, whereas native English speakers have words for 11 basic colours.
- Heider and Oliver gave both Dani and English-speaking participants a coloured chip which they were allowed to look at for five seconds. After a 30-second delay, participants were asked to pick out a chip of the same colour among a set of 40 different-coloured chips.
- On the *weakest* version of the LRH, the Dani's colour vocabulary should have influenced their memory for colours, and on the *weak* version they should have had difficulty discriminating similar colours of a slightly different hue that they'd labelled with the same name.
- Both the Dani-speaking and English-speaking participants made many mistakes. But there were *no* significant differences between them in their rate of confusion of similar colours, despite the differences in their colour vocabularies.
- In other research, Heider showed that both Dani and English speakers were better at recognising focal colours than non-focal colours, and that the Dani found it much easier to learn labels for focal than non-focal colours.

Heider (1972) concluded that:

> Far from being a domain well suited to the study of the effects of language on thought, the colour-space would seem a prime

example of the influence of underlying perceptual–cognitive factors on the formation and reference of linguistic categories.

By this, Heider (sometimes referred to as Rosch – her married name) means that her data are better explained in terms of physiological factors underlying colour vision, rather than linguistic factors. Thus, people are sensitive to focal colours because the human visual system processes reality in a certain way (Lakoff, 1987). Indeed, evidence suggests that focal colours can be discriminated before any verbal labels for them have been learned. Bornstein (1988), for example, has argued that preverbal infants categorise the visible spectrum in a similar way to adults, namely, on the basis of the relatively discrete hues of blue, green, yellow and red.

However, Kay (in Ross, 2004) denies that there's any evidence to support a physiological explanation. In addition, a study of another New Guinea people, the Berinmo, casts doubt on Heider's interpretation, and seems to support the weakest and weak versions of the LRH.

KEY STUDY 18.4 Colour naming among the Berinmo

- Robertson *et al.* (cited in Hanlon, 1999b) studied the Berinmo people of New Guinea, who live a simple hunter-gatherer lifestyle in remote forests.
- They have five colour names: one for green, blue and purple, another for yellow, orange and brown, a third for all dark colours, a fourth for white and all light colours; and a fifth for all shades of red and pink.
- Using a procedure similar to Heider & Oliver's (1972), Robertson *et al.* found that the Berinmo could remember only those colours which matched their colour names, and that they were unable to discriminate between colours which their language didn't discriminate (for example, green and blue).
- Although all the focal colours were 'represented' by the Berinmos' five colour names, the fact that green, blue and purple were lumped together, as were yellow, orange and brown, and also red and pink, seems inconsistent with the claim that colour terms emerge in a particular order in the history of languages (see Figure 18.2):

While it has been assumed that a lot of low-level things like colour perception have taken place at a low, almost a genetic level, we found that even something as simple as colour is affected by culture. (Robertson, cited in Hanlon, 1999b)

Evaluation of the LRH

- Berry *et al.* (1992) and Jackendoff (1993) have argued that Whorf's evidence was anecdotal rather than empirical, and that he exaggerated the differences between Hopi and other languages. Moreover, far from having 'over 20' words for 'snow', the Inuit Eskimos have relatively few such words (Newstead, 1995), and no more than do English speakers (Pinker, 1997a). According to Pagel (1995), Whorf simply got his facts wrong.
- There's an important difference between a language's grammar and our perceptual experience. The fact that Hopi can be translated into English (and vice versa) implies a universally shared knowledge of the world that's independent of the particular language in which it's expressed (Pagel, 1995).
- A crucial question that Whorf seems to have overlooked is *why* Eskimos have so many names for snow (if, indeed, they do) and SAE languages so few. One answer is that the more significant an experience or some feature of our environment is for us, the greater the number of ways of expressing it in the language. In other words, while Whorf argued that language structures the Eskimo's world, it could equally well be argued that the Eskimo's language develops *as a result of* his/her different perception of the world (Baddeley, 1999). According to Solso (1995):

> The development of specific language codes ... is dependent on cultural needs; the learning of these codes by members of a language group also involves the learning of significant values of the culture, some of which must be related to survival ...

- Solso's view is supported by the fact that English-speaking skiers learn to discriminate between varied snow conditions and invent a vocabulary to describe these differences. Such terms include 'sticky snow', 'powder', 'corn' and 'boilerplate' (or ice: Crooks & Stein, 1991). Similarly, the Hanunoo people of the Philippines have modified their language in response to environmental conditions. For example, women have developed a more complex vocabulary for shades of blue to distinguish the colours of dyed textiles that have been introduced into their society (Price & Crapo, 1999).
- It's now widely accepted that Whorf overestimated the importance of language differences. As Berry *et al.* (1992) have observed:

> Language as an instrument for thinking has many cross-culturally variant properties. As humans, we may not all be sharing the same thoughts, but our respective languages do not seem to predestine us to different kinds of thinking.

- What language may do, though, is to affect the ease of information processing. Newstead (1995), for example, describes research conducted by Hunt & Agnoli (1991) which supports this view. The English word 'seven' has two syllables, whereas the equivalent French word ('sept') has only one. The English word 'eleven' has three syllables, whereas the French word 'onze' has one. Hunt and Agnoli argue that when a name is shorter, information is processed more quickly, and so French speakers would have an advantage over English speakers when performing mental arithmetic involving these numbers, at least in processing terms.

- According to Price & Crapo (1999), the study of semantic domains (such as colour naming) helps us to discover what's important in the daily lives of different cultural groups, as well as the changing cultural history of a society. Similarly, Kay (in Ross, 2004) argues that the degree to which the world is *man-made* seems to explain the variation in the number of colour words. Hunter-gatherers need fewer, because colour data rarely provide much crucially distinguishing information about a natural scene or object. But industrialised societies get a bigger 'information pay-off' for colour words.
- Kay (in Ross, 2004) claims that his research into focal colours has been interpreted by some as undermining the LRH as a whole. But he and Berlin were concerned with one restricted domain, namely colour. Even if it's accepted that the colour perception research doesn't support the LRH, there's no reason to rule it out in relation to other domains.

KEY STUDY 18.5 'There's a fly to the north of your nose'

- Ross (2004) cites a study of speakers of Guugu Yimithirr (a language of Australia). Like several world languages, this lacks subjective terms equivalent to 'left' and 'right', and instead uses absolute directions akin to 'north' and 'south'. In such a language, you might say 'There's a fly to the north of your nose.'
- If Guugu speakers are presented with an arrow pointing to their *left*, they'll later draw it pointing to the left only if they're still facing in the direction in which they saw the arrow originally.
- But if they turn round, they'll draw it pointing to the *right* – that is, in the same *absolute* direction as the original arrow.
- This illustrates quite strikingly how linguistic categories can mould thought and behaviour (Ross, 2004).

While this shows that the LRH may be correct:

> ... it is unlikely that the various languages of the world are so different from one another, in underlying conceptual structure, that the ways their speakers think are incommensurable ... (Kay, in Ross, 2004)

The LRH, social class and race

Social-class differences in language and thought

Stones (1971) gives examples of imaginary conversations on a bus between a mother and child:

1

Mother: Hold on tight.
Child: Why?
Mother: Hold on tight.
Child: Why?
Mother: You'll fall.
Child: Why?
Mother: I told you to hold on tight, didn't I?

2

Mother: Hold on tight, darling.
Child: Why?
Mother: If you don't you'll be thrown forward and you'll fall.
Child: Why?
Mother: Because if the bus suddenly stops, you'll jerk forward on to the seat in front.
Child: Why?
Mother: Now, darling, hold on tightly and don't make such a fuss.

ASK YOURSELF...

- How would you characterise the differences between these two conversations?

Restricted and elaborated codes

Bernstein (1961) was interested in language's role as a social (rather than individual) phenomenon, especially its relation to cultural deprivation. He showed that there were generally no differences between the verbal and non-verbal intelligence test performance of boys from public schools, and boys from lower-working-class homes. But the latter often showed considerable inconsistencies, with non-verbal performance sometimes being as much as 26 points better than verbal performance. Bernstein argued that working- and middle-class children speak two different kinds (or *codes*) of language, which he called *restricted* code and *elaborated* code respectively (see Table 18.1).

Bernstein saw the relationship between potential and actual intelligence as being mediated through language; consequently, the lack of an elaborated code would prevent working-class children from developing their full intellectual potential. The different language codes underlie the whole pattern of relationships (to objects and people) experienced by members of different classes, as well as the patterns of learning which their children bring with them to school.

In support of Bernstein's views, Hess & Shipman (1965) found that social-class differences influence children's intellectual development. In particular, there was a lack of meaning in the mother–child communication system for low-status families. Language was used much less to convey *meaning* (to describe, explain, express and so on), and much more to give orders and commands to

Table 18.1 Characteristics of restricted and elaborated codes (Bernstein, 1961)

Restricted code		Elaborated code	
1	Grammatically crude, repetitive and rigid, limited use of adjectives and adverbs, greater use of pronouns than nouns. Sentences often short, grammatically simple and incomplete	1	Grammatically more complex and flexible. Uses a range of subordinate clauses, conjunctions, prepositions, adjectives and adverbs. Uses more nouns than pronouns. Sentences are longer and more complex
2	Context-bound: the meaning isn't made explicit but assumes the listener's familiarity with the situation being described, e.g. 'He gave me it'; listener cannot be expected to know what 'he' or 'it' refers to	2	Context-independent: the meaning is made explicit, e.g.'John gave me this book'
3	'I' very rarely used; much of the meaning conveyed non-verbally	3	'I' often used, making clear the speaker's intentions, as well as emphasising the precise description of experiences and feelings
4	Frequent use of uninformative but emotionally reinforcing phrases, such as 'you know', 'don't I'	4	Relatively little use of emotionally reinforcing phrases
5	Tends to stress the present, the here-and-now	5	Tends to stress the past and future
6	Doesn't allow expression of abstract/hypothetical thought	6	Allows expression of abstract/hypothetical thought

The mother's description of pictures illustrates the use of meaning in the mother–child communication, as opposed to using language to give orders or commands

the child (see the two mother–child conversations above).

However, instead of seeing 'restricted' and 'elaborated' as distinct types of language code, they're better thought of as two ends of a continuum. Also, the terms 'restricted' and 'elaborated' imply a value judgement of middle-class speech as being superior to working-class speech (closer to 'standard' or 'the Queen's' English). The lack of objectivity makes this judgement difficult to defend.

Black English

A version of English spoken by segments of the African-American community is called 'Black English'. For example, when asked to repeat the sentence 'I asked him if he did it, and he said he didn't do it', one five-year-old girl repeated the sentence like this: 'I asks him if he did it, and he says he didn't did it, but I knows he did' (Labov, 1973). Bernstein argued that Black English is a restricted code, and that this makes the thinking of Black English speakers less logical than that of their white elaborated-code counterparts.

One major difference between Black and standard English relates to the use of verbs (Rebok, 1987). In particular, Black English speakers often omit the present tense copula (the verb 'to be'). So, 'he be gone' indicates standard English 'he's been gone for a long time' and 'he gone' signifies that 'he's just gone'. Black English is often termed *sub-standard* and regarded as illogical rather than *non-standard* (Bereiter & Engelman, 1966). According to Labov (1970), Black English is just one dialect of English, and speakers of both dialects are expressing the same ideas equally well.

Black English and prejudice

While the grammatical rules of Black English differ from those of standard English, Black English possesses consistent rules which allow the expression of thoughts as complex as those permitted by standard English (Labov, 1973). Several other languages, such as Russian and Arabic, also omit the present-tense verb 'to be', and yet we don't call them 'illogical'. This suggests that black dialects are considered sub-standard as a matter of convention or prejudice, and not because they're poorer vehicles for expressing meaning and logical thinking. However, because the structure of Black English does differ in important ways from standard English, and since intelligence tests are written in standard English, Black English speakers are at a linguistic disadvantage (as, indeed, are white working-class children: see Chapters 41 and 47).

Language in context

Labov also showed that the social situation can be a powerful determinant of verbal behaviour. A young boy called Leon was shown a toy by a white interviewer and asked to tell him everything he could about it. Leon said very little and was silent for much of the time, even when a black interviewer took over. However, when Leon sat on the floor and shared a packet of crisps with his best friend and with the same black interviewer introducing topics in a local black dialect, Leon became a lively conversationalist. Had he been assessed with the white or black interviewers on their own, Leon might have been labelled 'non-verbal' or 'linguistically retarded'.

Black children may actually be *bilingual*. In their home environments, the school playground and their neighbourhoods, they speak the accepted vernacular. In the classroom, however, and when talking to anyone in authority, they must adopt standard English with which they're unfamiliar. This results in short sentences, simple grammar and strange intonation. But out of school, their natural language is easy, fluent, creative and often gifted. So, while Black English is certainly *non-standard*, it's another language with its own grammar which is certainly *not* sub-standard.

CRITICAL DISCUSSION 18.1 'Ebonics': an ongoing debate

- Ebonics is a fusion of the words 'ebony' and 'phonics' and was coined in 1975 as an alternative to the term 'Black English'. In 1996, Ebonics (or African-American Vernacular English/AAVE) was officially recognised by the Oakland public school board in California, and schools were ordered to teach 28,000 black children in their own 'tongue'. The board claimed that Ebonics was a separate language, genetically rooted in the West-African and Niger–Congo language system, rather than a dialect of standard American English (Hiscock, 1996; Whittell, 1996).
- In early 1997, the school board edited its statement so that the word 'genetically' referred to linguists' use of the word for the roots of a language rather than to a gene pool. They also indicated that it wasn't the intent to teach in Ebonics, but rather to have teachers use the vernacular to be able to understand their children (Zinberg, 1997).
- Both conservatives and liberals in America claim that the decision to require Ebonics to be taught would be 'political correctness run amok' (Cornwell, 1997).
- Educationalists such as Zinberg disagree. In her view, many students are:

  ... bewildered, then angered and finally alienated from the schools where their language and self-esteem are belittled by a seemingly insensitive system.

- Although regional dialects in the USA are diverging, there's no evidence of convergence between black and white vernaculars (Hawkes, 1998).
- By contrast, British blacks and whites still speak the same language, partly because there's no segregation in housing in Britain as there is in the USA (Labov, in Hawkes, 1998).

LANGUAGE IS DEPENDENT ON, AND REFLECTS, THOUGHT

According to Piaget (1950), children begin life with some understanding of the world and try to find linguistic ways of expressing their knowledge. As language develops, it 'maps' onto previously acquired cognitive structures, and so language is dependent upon thought (Piaget & Inhelder, 1969). For example, a child should begin talking about objects that aren't present in its immediate surroundings only after *object permanence* has developed (see Box 19.4, page 324). Similarly, children who could *conserve* liquid quantity (see Chapter 34, page 586) understood the meaning of phrases and words such as 'as much as', 'bigger' and 'more'. However, children who couldn't conserve didn't improve their performance of the correct use of these words after receiving linguistic training (Sinclair-de-Zwart, 1969).

In Piaget's view, children can be taught words, but they won't understand them until they've mastered certain intellectual skills during the process of cognitive growth. So, language can exist without thought, but only in the sense that a parrot can 'speak'. Thought, then, is a necessary forerunner to language if language is to be used properly.

Contrary to Piaget's view that thought structures language, Luria & Yudovich (1971) suggest that language plays a central role in cognitive development.

CASE STUDY 18.1: The Russian twins (Luria & Yudovich, 1971)

- Luria and Yudovich studied five-year-old twin boys whose home environment was unstimulating. They played almost exclusively together and had only a very primitive level of speech. The boys received little adult encouragement to speak, and made little progress towards the symbolic use of words. Essentially, their speech was *synpraxic*, a primitive form in which words cannot be detached from the action or object they denote.
- The twins hardly ever used speech to describe objects or events or to help them plan their actions. They couldn't understand other people's speech, and their own constituted a kind of *signalling* rather than symbolic system.
- Although they never played with other children, and played with each other in a primitive and repetitive way, they were otherwise normal.

- After being separated, one twin was given special remedial treatment for his language deficiency, but the other wasn't. The former made rapid progress and, ten months later, was ahead of his brother. However, both made progress, and their synpraxic speech died away. For Luria and Yudovich:

The whole structure of the mental life of both twins was simultaneously and sharply changed. Once they acquired an objective language system, [they] were able to formulate the aims of their activity verbally, and after only three months we observed the beginnings of meaningful play.

THOUGHT AND LANGUAGE AS INITIALLY SEPARATE ACTIVITIES

For Vygotsky (1981), language is by far the most important psychological tool the human species possesses, capable of transforming how we think about the world and altering 'the entire flow and structure of mental functions'. So, while for Piaget thought is prior to language (the development of representational thinking enables the child to use words), Vygotsky sees language as prior to thought (developing the ability to use words makes representational thought possible) (Schaffer, 2004).

According to Vygotsky (1962), language and thought begin as separate and independent activities. Early on, thinking occurs without language (consisting primarily of images) and language occurs without thought (as when babies cry or make other sounds to express feelings, attract attention or fulfil some other social aim). But at about age two, *prelinguistic thought* and *pre-intellectual language:*

... meet and join to initiate a new kind of behaviour [in which] thought becomes verbal and speech rational. (Vygotsky, 1962)

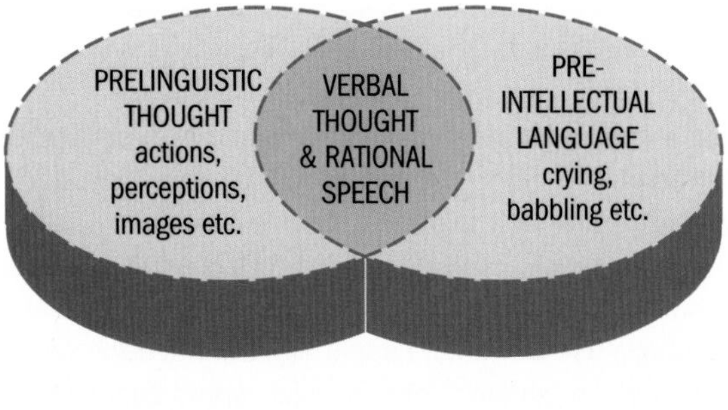

Figure 18.3 A diagrammatic representation of Vygotsky's views on the relationship between language and thought

Vygotsky believed that between ages two and seven, language performs two functions:

1. an *internal* function, which enables internal thought to be monitored and directed
2. an *external* function, which enables the results of thinking to be communicated to others.

However, children cannot yet distinguish between the two functions and, as a result, their speech is *egocentric:* they talk out loud about their plans and actions, and can neither think privately nor communicate publicly to others. Instead, they're caught somewhere between the two, and cannot distinguish between 'speech for self' (what Piaget calls *autistic speech*) and 'speech for others' (*socialised speech*).

Vygotsky believed that around age seven (when children typically enter Piaget's *concrete operational stage* of cognitive development: see Chapter 34), overt language begins to be restricted to communication, while the thought function of language becomes internalised as *internal speech* (*verbal thought*). For Piaget, egocentric speech is a kind of 'running commentary' on the child's behaviour. At about age seven, it simply fades away and is replaced by socialised (or communicative) speech.

Box 18.1 The function of egocentric speech

- When six- or seven-year-olds are trying to solve a problem and something goes wrong (such as a pencil breaking) which requires them to revise their thinking, they often revert to overt verbalisation (Vygotsky, 1962).
- Adults sometimes do the same in similar situations, especially when they believe no one can hear them. For example, we'll often retrace our steps out loud (such as 'Now, I know I didn't have it when I went in the room, so what did I do before that?').
- Vygotsky concluded that the function of egocentric speech was similar to that of inner speech. It doesn't merely accompany the child's activity but:

... serves mental orientation, conscious understanding; it helps in overcoming difficulties, it is speech for oneself, intimately and usefully connected with the child's thinking. In the end it becomes inner speech ... [see Figure 18.4]

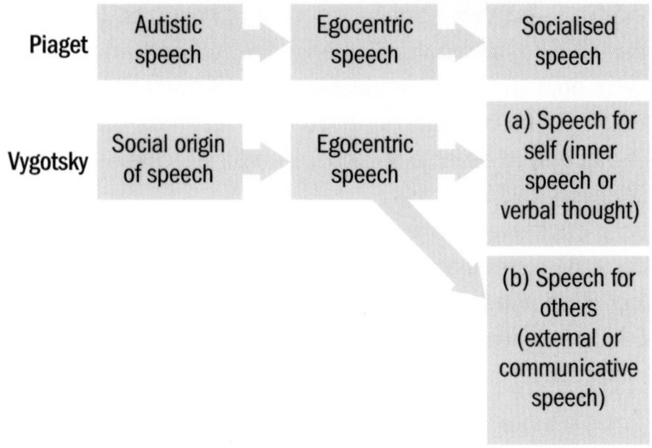

Figure 18.4 The difference between Piaget and Vygotsky with respect to egocentric speech

An evaluation of Vygotsky's position

- A considerable body of research into inner speech has largely supported Vygotsky's account, demonstrating how closely language and thought become intertwined during development (Schaffer, 2004).
- Egocentric speech commonly accompanies problem-solving, even in young children. But with age, it becomes less and less audible, and eventually becomes silent.
- For example, Bivens & Berk (1990) observed six- to seven-year-olds as they worked on maths problems. This was repeated one to two years later. The overall incidence of egocentric speech was extremely high and remained high over the three years of observation. But task-relevant speech increased greatly, and the *nature* of the speech changed – there was more inaudible muttering and lip movements. These changes were paralleled by the children's greater ability to inhibit extraneous movements and restlessness, and to pay closer attention to the task. This is consistent with Vygotsky's belief that inner speech is used increasingly to aid the child's *self-regulation/self-control* (Schaffer, 2004).

Box 18.2 Language and self-regulation

- According to Luria (1961), a colleague and supporter of Vygotsky, there are three stages in children's ability to use language for directing their behaviour.
  1. Up to about three, another person's verbal instructions can trigger an action, but not inhibit it. For example, given a rubber bulb to squeeze, children will correctly squeeze in response to 'Squeeze', but 'Stop' will simply make them squeeze again.
  2. Between four and five, they respond to instructions in an impulsive way: told to squeeze when a light comes on, they'll squeeze repeatedly. They're responding more to the energising quality of speech than to its content (the louder the instructions, the more often they squeeze).
  3. After about five, they respond to the contents of speech and become capable of using it to inhibit or activate their behaviour.

- Both inner speech and egocentric speech differ from speech for others in that they don't have to satisfy grammatical conventions. Thus, both are abbreviated, incomplete and concerned more with the essential meaning rather than how it's expressed. For Vygotsky, inner speech is a 'dynamic, shifting and unstable thing which "flutters" between word and thought' (see Figure 18.3).
- Overt speech can sometimes resemble inner speech in its abbreviated nature, long after egocentric speech has been replaced. For example, people who know each other well may talk in an abbreviated form that wouldn't be used with strangers. Understanding occurs because the more familiar we are with others, and the more experiences we have in common, the less explicit our speech has to be. 'Coffee?', for example, asked with a rising inflection and in a particular context, would be interpreted as 'Would you like a cup of coffee?' This is similar to how adults interpret the holophrastic speech of young children (see Box 19.2, page 323). In Bernstein's terms, we use restricted code when talking in familiar surroundings to familiar others, whose view of the world we assume is similar to our own.

CONCLUSIONS

While there are many examples indicating that thought can occur without language, the exact relationship between thought and language remains unclear. What is certain, however, is that no one account of this relationship is true and all others false; several theoretical perspectives can claim some support from the experimental literature. However, since language represents such a central feature of culture, both shaping it and being shaped by it, any theory which fails to take account of cultural factors is likely to be inadequate.

CHAPTER SUMMARY

- According to Watson's **peripheralism**, thought is no more than sensations produced by tiny movements of the larynx, too small to produce audible sounds. While these movements accompany thought, they're not necessary for thinking to occur.
- Contrary to Watson's view, thinking can occur despite complete paralysis, and people born deaf and mute are also capable of thinking.
- Bruner argues that language is essential for thought and knowledge to progress beyond the **enactive** and **iconic modes of representation** to the **symbolic mode**.
- **Social constructionists** claim that conceptual frameworks and categories provide meaning within a culture, a way of structuring our experience of ourselves and the world.
- According to the **Sapir–Whorf linguistic relativity hypothesis** (LRH), language determines how we think about objects and events, and even what we think. This is related to **linguistic determinism**.
- The '**weak**' and '**weakest**' versions of the LRH have typically been tested through perception and memory of **colour**. The fewer colour words there are in a language, the more difficult native speakers should find tests of colour perception and memory.
- Early studies seemed to support these two versions. But while cultures may differ in the number of basic colour terms they use, all cultures draw their colour terms from only eleven **focal colours**, which emerge in a particular sequence in the history of languages.

- Whorf's evidence was anecdotal rather than empirical, and he exaggerated the differences between Hopi and other languages. Also, he mistakenly equated language's grammar with perceptual experience. Translation between languages implies a universally shared knowledge of the world independent of any particular language.
- Bernstein claimed that working-class children speak a **restricted code** and middle class children an **elaborated code**. The relationship between actual and potential intelligence is mediated through language, so working-class children are prevented from developing their full intellectual potential.
- Differences between standard and **Black English** have resulted in the latter being called **sub-standard**, rather than **non-standard**. According to Labov, this is an expression of prejudice.
- Black children may be **bilingual**, using the accepted register fluently at home and with their peers, but adopting unfamiliar standard English in the classroom.
- According to Piaget, language 'maps' on to previously acquired cognitive structures, so that **language is dependent on thought**. Words can be understood only if certain intellectual skills (such as **object permanence** and **conservation**) have already been mastered.
- For Vygotsky, **language and thought are initially separate and independent** activities. At around age two, **pre-linguistic thought** and **pre-intellectual language** begin to interact to form **verbal thought** and **rational speech**.
- Between the ages of two and seven, language performs both internal and external functions. The child's failure to distinguish between them results in **egocentric speech**. For Vygotsky, this indicates the separation of the two functions.
- According to both Vygotsky and Luria, language plays a vital role in **self-regulation/self-control**.

Links with other topics/chapters

- Watson's peripheralism demonstrates both his *behaviourist* rejection of mentalistic terms (Chapters 2 and 3), and the *reductionist* approach of behaviourism (Chapter 49).
- *Social constructionism* (SC) is a theoretical orientation that lies behind a number of recent alternative approaches to the study of human beings as social animals, including *critical psychology, discourse analysis* and *feminist psychology* (Chapters 2, 3 and 47).
- The weak version of the LRH claims that language affects *perception* (Chapter 15), while the weakest version claims that language influences *memory* (Chapter 17).
- Regarding Black English as sub-standard (rather than non-standard) is an expression of *prejudice* (Chapter 25).
- Since standard *intelligence (IQ) tests* are written in standard English, Black English speakers are at a linguistic disadvantage, as are white working-class children (Chapters 41 and 47).
- Bruner's, Piaget's and Vygotsky's accounts of the relationship between language and thought are part of their more general theories of *cognitive development* (Chapter 34).

19

LANGUAGE ACQUISITION

INTRODUCTION AND OVERVIEW

Since our brains seem specially designed to enable us to use speech (see Chapter 4), it's hardly surprising that language is so crucial to most human activities. Many psychologists and philosophers have claimed that language is what makes us unique as a species.

Until quite recently, the study of language was largely the domain of linguistics, which is concerned primarily with the structure of language (its grammar). According to Durkin (1995), while developmental psychologists have always been interested in language, during the mid-twentieth century it became marginalised as an area of psychological research. As we noted in Chapter 18, Piaget saw language as merely reflecting cognitive structures – a lens through which to inspect the child's thought. This seemed to reinforce the behaviourists' earlier rejection of anything 'mental' (such as grammar and meaning).

However, there's been a revival of interest in language since the 1960s, inspired largely by Chomsky's (1959) theory of an innate *language acquisition device* (LAD). This is probably the most extreme *nativist* theory in the whole of psychology (see Chapter 50). The 'marriage' between psychology and linguistics (Chomsky is a linguist) is called *psycholinguistics,* which studies the perception, understanding and production of language, together with their development.

According to *learning theory,* associated with Skinner and Bandura, language development can be attributed primarily to environmental input and learning. But Chomsky's nativist approach argues that, although the environment may supply the content of language, grammar is an inherent, biologically determined capacity of human beings. Hence, the process of language development is essentially one of *acquisition* (as distinct from *learning*). Attempts to teach language to non-humans have major implications for Chomsky's claim that language is a uniquely human ability.

Graham Rawle's LOST CONSONANTS
MAGNIFICENT! I AM SURELY THE GREATEST ARCHITECT OF MY GENERATION
672 Nicholas was building things with his ego

A single missing letter can totally change a word's meaning – and with it, the meaning of the entire sentence

WHAT IS LANGUAGE?

According to Brown (1965), language is a set of arbitrary symbols:

> ... which, taken together, make it possible for a creature with limited powers of discrimination and a limited memory to transmit and understand an infinite variety of messages and to do this in spite of noise and distraction.

This 'infinite variety of messages' is called *productivity,* which Kuczaj & Hill (2003) describe as the most important characteristic of human language.

While other species are able to communicate with each other, they can do so only in limited ways, and it's perhaps the 'infinite variety of messages' part of Brown's definition that sets humans apart from non-humans. For example, wild chimpanzees use over 30 different vocalisations to convey a large number of meanings, and repeat sounds in order to intensify their meaning. However, they don't string these sounds together to make new 'words' (Calvin, 1994). The claim that chimpanzees are capable of using language is based largely, and until recently, on deliberate training (see below, pages 331–335). Human language is mastered spontaneously and quite easily within the first five years of life.

What makes productivity possible is that humans acquire a *rule system*. This rule system is called *grammar* (or *mental grammar*). However, for psycholinguists, grammar is much more than the parts of speech we learn about in school. It's concerned with the description of language, the rules that determine how a language 'works', and what governs patterns of speech (Jackendoff, 1993).

THE MAJOR COMPONENTS OF GRAMMAR

Grammar consists of *phonology, semantics* and *syntax* (see Figure 19.1, page 321).

Phonology

Phonologists are concerned with a language's *sound system* – what counts as a sound and what constitutes an acceptable sequence of sounds. Basic speech sounds are called *phones* (or *phonetic segments*), and are represented by enclosing symbols inside square brackets. For example, [p] is the initial phone in the word 'pin'. Some languages have as few as 15 distinguishable sounds, and others as many as 85. The English language has 46 phones (Solso, 1995).

The phones that matter are those that affect the *meaning* of what's being said. For example, the difference between [p] and [d] matters because it can lead to two words with different meanings (such as 'pin' and 'din'). Because [p] and [d] cannot be interchanged without altering a word's meaning, they belong to different functional classes of phones called *phonemes* (*phonological segments*). Languages differ in their number of phonemes. *Phonological rules* constrain the permitted sequence of phonemes, which correspond roughly to the vowels and consonants of a language's alphabet. However, languages (including English) can have more phonemes than letters in the alphabet. This is because some letters, such as 'o', can be pronounced differently (as in 'hop' and 'hope').

The development of speech sounds continues for several years after birth, and most children recognise sounds in adult speech before they can produce them. So, in response to the instruction: 'I am going to say a word two times and you tell me which time I say it right and which time I say it wrong: rabbit, wabbit', a child might reply: 'Wabbit is wight and wabbit is wong', indicating that the 'r' sound can be recognised but not yet produced (Dale, 1976).

Semantics

Semantics is the study of the *meaning* of language, and can be analysed at the level of *morphemes* and *sentences*. Morphemes are a language's basic units of meaning and consist mainly of words. Other morphemes are prefixes (letters attached to the beginning of a word, such as 'pre' and 're') and suffixes (word-endings, such as 's' to make a plural). Some morphemes, such as the plural 's', are 'bound' (they only take on meaning when attached to other morphemes), but most morphemes are 'free' (they have meaning when they stand alone, as most words have). But single words have only a limited meaning, and are usually combined into longer strings of phrases and sentences, the other level of semantic analysis.

Syntax

Syntax refers to the rules for combining words into phrases and sentences. One example of a *syntactic rule* is word order. This is crucial for understanding language development. Clearly, the sentences 'The dog bit the postman' and 'The postman bit the dog' have very different meanings!

'Then you should say what you mean', the March Hare went on. 'I do', Alice hastily replied; 'at least – at least I mean what I say – that's the same thing, you know'. 'Not the same thing a bit!' said the Hatter. 'Why, you might just as well say that 'I see what I eat' is the same thing as 'I eat what I see'!'

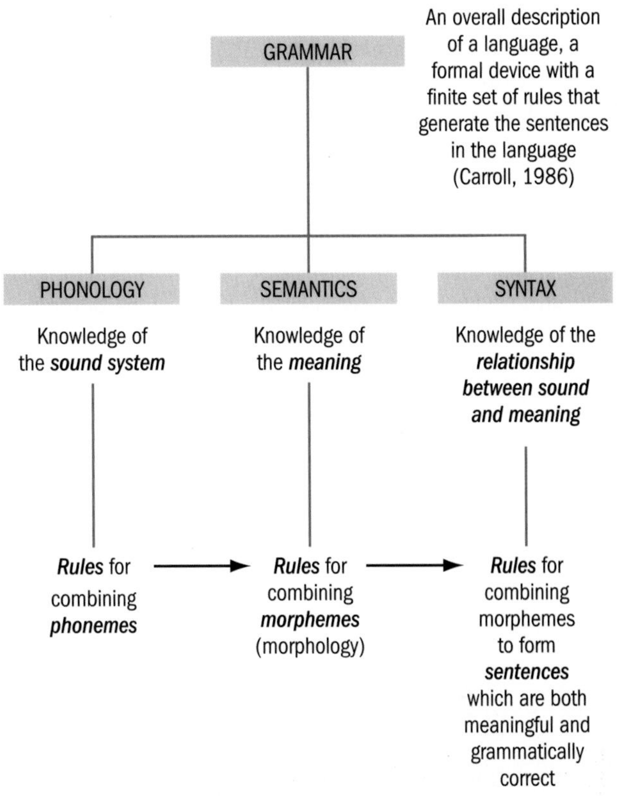

Figure 19.1 The major components of grammar

Another example of a syntactic rule occurs in the sentence 'The dog chased the …'. In English, only a noun can complete this sentence. Some sentences may be syntactically correct but lack meaning. For example, 'The player scored a goal' and 'The goal post scored a banana' are both syntactically correct, but one has much more meaning than the other. While sentences have sounds and meanings, syntax refers to the structures which relate the two.

STAGES IN LANGUAGE DEVELOPMENT

It's generally agreed that language development follows a universal timetable – that is, regardless of their language or culture, all children pass through the same sequence of stages at approximately the same ages (although children may vary with respect to their rate of development). While this belief implies the role of *maturation,* children can come to speak a language only if they're exposed to it.

It's also generally agreed that there are three major stages in language development. These are the *prelinguistic stage* (0–12 months), the *one-word stage* (12–18 months), and the *stage of two-word sentences.* This third stage is divided into two sub-stages*: stage 1 grammar* (18–30 months) and *stage 2 grammar* (30 months and beyond).

The prelinguistic stage (0–12 months)

In their first year, babies are essentially *prelinguistic*. They make various sounds with their vocal organs (including crying) long before they can talk. Crying tends to dominate in the first month, with parents gradually learning to discriminate between the various cries (Gustafson & Harris, 1990). By one month, babies are able to distinguish between phonemes (such as 'ba' and 'pa') and other sounds, even though these may be physically and acoustically almost identical (Aslin *et al.*, 1983). This perceptual ability (*categorical speech perception*) is probably innate (see Box 19.7, page 328).

At about six weeks, *cooing* begins. This is associated with pleasurable states and doesn't occur when babies are hungry, tired or in pain. Although vowel sounds may be produced at this age, they're different from those that will be made later and from which the first words will be formed. This is because the baby's oral cavity and nervous system aren't sufficiently mature to enable it to produce the sounds necessary for speech.

Box 19.1 The development of babbling

- This is the major development in the first year of life, and usually begins between six and nine months. Phonemes are produced and take the form of combinations of consonants and vowels (such as *ma* and *da*). These may be repeated to produce *reduplicated monosyllables* (such as *mama* and *dada*). Although these are very different from the earlier cooing sounds, they have no meaning.
- Babbling and pre-babbling vocalisations differ in two main ways:

  1. babies spend more time making noises, especially when alone in their cots (*spontaneous babbling*), and they seem to enjoy exercising their voices for the sake of it
  2. babbling has *intonational patterns*, just like speech, with rising inflections and speech-like rhythms; by one year, syllables are often produced over and over again (as in *dadadada*), a phenomenon called *echolalia*.

- Babbling occurs at around the same age in all babies regardless of culture, and even deaf babies of deaf–mute parents show a kind of 'sign-babbling' (Petitto, 1988). These findings suggest that the onset of babbling is based on maturation.

Babies initially produce only a few phonemes, but soon almost every available phoneme is produced, whether or not it belongs in what will become the baby's native language (*phonemic expansion*). At around 9–10 months, *phonemic contraction* begins: phoneme production is now restricted to those used in the baby's native language. At this stage, babies of different 'native tongues' can already be distinguished by the sounds they produce. Additionally, deaf babies usually stop babbling at around this time, presumably because of the lack of feedback from their own voices. By two and a half years, still only about 60 per cent of the phonemes used in English are mastered, and complete mastery won't be achieved until around age seven.

One-word stage

ASK YOURSELF...

- How do words differ from a baby's babbling?
- When people ask parents 'Is your baby talking yet?', what do they mean?

Typically, a child produces its first word at around one year, although there's considerable variability in this (Rice, 1989). Babies don't, of course, suddenly switch from babbling to the production of words, and non-words (*jargon*) continue to be produced for up to another six months. Their first words (or *articulate sounds*) are often invented, quite unlike 'adult words', phonologically the easiest (most similar to their babbling). This also explains why the words for mother and father are so similar across a wide range of different languages (Siegler, 1998).

Scollon (1976) has defined a word as 'a systematic matching of form and meaning'. On this definition, 'da' is a word if it's consistently used to refer to a doll, since the same sound is being used to label the same thing or kind of thing, and there's a clear intention to communicate.

However, an infant's earliest words are usually *context-bound*, produced in only very limited and specific situations or contexts in which particular actions or events occur (Barrett, 1989). For example, one infant, at least initially, only produced the word 'duck' while hitting a toy duck off the edge of a bath. The word was never used in any other context. Barrett argues that an infant's first words often *don't* serve a communicative purpose as such. Rather, because they typically occur as accompaniments to particular actions or events (as in the case above), they function as '*performatives*'. Some words may be more like the performance of a ritualised action than the expression of a lexical meaning to another person. However, words seem to have either:

- an *expressive function* – they communicate internal states (such as pleasure and surprise) to others, or
- a *directive function* – the behaviour of others is directed (by, for example, requesting or obtaining and directing attention).

Box 19.2 Holophrases: making a sentence out of a word

- The one-word stage is also characterised by the use of *holophrases*.
- In holophrastic speech, a single word (such as 'milk') is used to convey a much more complex message (such as 'I want some more milk' or 'I have spilt my milk').
- Because holophrases are accompanied by gestures and tone of voice to add full meaning to an individual word, they may be seen as precursors of later, more complex sentences (Greenfield & Smith, 1976). They represent 'two-word meanings' (word plus gesture) before two words are actually used together in speech (Bates *et al.*, 1987). But they depend on the recipient of the holophrase making the 'correct' interpretation.

Nelson (1973) identified six categories of words, and calculated the percentage of children's first 50 words (typically acquired by 19 to 20 months) that fell into each category.

Table 19.1 Nelson's six categories and the percentage of children's first 50 words falling into each of them

1	**Specific nominals:**	names for unique objects, people or animals (14 per cent)
2	**General nominals:**	names for classes of objects, people or animals, e.g. 'ball', 'car', 'milk', 'doggie', 'girl', 'he', 'that' (51 per cent)
3	**Action words:**	describe or accompany actions or express or demand attention, e.g. 'bye-bye', 'up', 'look', 'hi' (13 per cent)
4	**Modifiers:**	refer to properties or qualities of things, e.g. 'big', 'red', 'pretty', 'hot', 'all gone', 'there', 'mine' (9 per cent)
5	**Personal–social words:**	say something about a child's feelings or social relationships, e.g. 'ouch', 'please', 'no', 'yes', 'want' (8 per cent)
6	**Function words:**	have only a grammatical function, e.g. 'what', 'is', 'to', 'for' (4 per cent)

Nelson argued that it's not just the amount of exposure to objects and words that's important in word acquisition. Rather, given that specific and general nominals and action words make up the vast majority of those produced (78 per cent), it's the child's *active involvement* with its environment that determines many of its first words.

The kinds of things that first words refer to are similar the world over. They're the things that matter to a one-year-old: parents, siblings, pets, toys, clothes and food. Things that *move* are also more likely to be named (e.g. a bus rather than the road) (Schaffer, 2004).

Children understand more words than they can produce. For example, a child who uses 'bow-wow' to refer to all small animals will nonetheless pick a picture of a dog, rather than any other animal, when asked to select a 'bow-wow' (Gruendel, 1977). The child's *receptive vocabulary* (the words it can understand) is therefore much bigger than its *expressive vocabulary* (the words it uses in speech).

Even before age two, children begin acquiring words at the rate of about 20 per day (Miller, 1978). While some of these are context-bound, they gradually become more *decontextualised*. Other words are used from the start in a decontextualised way (Barrett, 1989). As the one-word stage progresses, the child becomes able to ask and answer questions, and provide comments on people and objects in the immediate environment. These abilities enable the child to participate in very simple conversations with other people.

Stage of two-word sentences

Like the one-word stage, the *two-word stage* is universal (although individual differences become more marked). Also, like the transition from babbling to the one-word stage, the transition to the two-word stage is gradual (Slobin, 1979). As well as continued vocabulary development, the understanding of grammar grows. Brown (1973) divides this stage into *stage 1* and *stage 2 grammar.*

Stage 1 grammar (18–30 months)

Here, the child's speech is essentially *telegraphic* (Brown, 1973); that is, only those words which convey the most information (*contentives*) are used. Purely grammatical terms (*functors*), such as the verb 'to be', plurals and possessives, are left out. For example, children will say 'There cow' to convey the underlying message 'There is a cow'. It seems that irrespective of culture, children express basic facts about their environment (Brown, 1973).

Telegraphic speech has a *rigid word order,* which seems to preserve a sentence's meaning. For example, if asked 'Does John want some milk?', the child might reply 'John milk' (or, later on, 'John want milk'). Adult speech, by contrast, doesn't rely exclusively on word order to preserve meaning, as in the passive form of a sentence. So, 'John drank the milk' and 'The milk was drunk by John' both convey the same meaning, even though the word order is different.

Children's imitations of adult sentences are also simple and retain the original sentence's word order. For example, 'John is playing with the dog' is imitated as 'Play dog' (*imitation by reduction:* Brown, 1965). Complementary to this is *imitation with expansion,* in which the adult imitates the child's utterances by inserting the 'missing' functors. The rigid order of the child's utterances makes it easier to interpret their meaning, but gestures and context still provide important clues (as with the one-word stage).

ASK YOURSELF...

- How would you adapt your speech when talking to a young child compared with how you talk to other adults?

Box 19.3 Motherese

- Babies are exposed to an undifferentiated series of speech sounds (*speech stream*: Jusczyk, 1997), but they need to separate this into individual sounds and sound combinations in order to learn the relevant sounds of their language (phonemes and morphemes). For example, the way an adult might ask a seven-year-old a question could be represented as 'Wheredidyougowithgrandpa?' (the words are joined when they're being spoken). But long before the child learns to read (where the words are spaced), how does it learn to *hear* 'Where did you go with grandpa?' (Slobin, 1979)?
- Part of the answer is *motherese* (or *infant-directed speech*).
- Compared with talking to one another, adults talking to children tend to use much shorter sentences and simpler syntax, raise the pitch of their voice for emphasis, use their voice more rhythmically, and repeat or paraphrase much of what the child says.
- This helps to achieve a mutual understanding with children who haven't yet mastered the full complexity of language. Sensitivity to the child's vocabulary and its intellectual and social knowledge is an example of a *pragmatic rule* for ensuring a degree of shared understanding (Greene, 1990).
- It also supports a *social interaction approach* to language acquisition (see page 330).

Children's two-word utterances aren't just random word combinations, but are based on rules. They focus on certain types of words, and put them together in particular orders. However, not all children seem to use exactly the same rules (Braine, 1976), and children convey many different meanings with exactly the same sentence forms.

Table 19.2 Some of the different meanings children appear to express in Stage 1 Grammar (Maratsos, 1983)

Meaning	Examples
agent–action	Sarah eat; Daddy jump
action–object	eat cookie; read book
possessor–possessed object	Mommy sock; Timothy lunch
action–location	come here, play outside
located object–location	sweater chair; juice table
attribute–modified object	big book; red house
nomination	that cookie; it dog
recurrence	more juice; other book

For example, young children often use a sentence composed of two nouns, such as 'Mommy sock' or 'sweater chair' (Bloom, 1973). We might conclude from this that a 'two-noun' form is a basic grammatical characteristic of early language – but this would miss its complexity (Bee, 1989). For example, the child in Bloom's study said 'Mommy sock' when she picked up her mother's sock, and again when the Mother put the child's own sock on the child's foot. In the first case 'Mommy sock' seems to mean 'Mommy's sock' (a *possessive* relationship), while in the second instance, it conveys 'Mommy's putting the sock on me' (an *agent–object* relationship).

Box 19.4 Cromer's (1974) cognition hypothesis

- Word order in two-word utterances seems to reflect the child's *prelinguistic knowledge*.
- According to Cromer's *cognition hypothesis*, language structures can be used correctly only when permitted by our cognitive structures. Children form *schemata* to understand the world and then talk about it.
- A good example is *object permanence*, which is a prerequisite for understanding that words can represent things. If a child didn't already understand the relationships between objects, people and events in the real world, its first words would be like random unconnected lists.
- These are important concepts in Piaget's developmental theory (see Chapter 34), and are consistent with his view of language development reflecting the child's stage of cognitive development (see Chapter 18).

Stage 2 grammar (from about 30 months)

This lasts until around age four or five, and while it may be different for different languages, the rule-governed nature of language development is universal. The child's vocabulary grows rapidly, and sentences become longer and more complex. *Mean length of utterance* (MLU) is the number of words in a sentence divided by the total number of sentences produced. So, a child who produced 100 sentences with 300 words would have an MLU of 3.00.

The increase in MLU shown in Figure 19.2 is due largely to the inclusion of the functors that are omitted from the telegraphic speech of stage 1 grammar. For example, 'Daddy hat' may become 'Daddy wear hat' and finally 'Daddy is wearing a hat'. Sentences also become longer because conjunctions (such as 'and' and 'so') are used to form compound sentences like 'You play with the doll and I play with the ball'. Stage 2 grammar, then, really begins with the first use of purely grammatical words. While most children up to 20 months still use one- or two-word sentences, by 24 months the longest sentences include four to five words. By 30 months, this has risen to between eight and ten. This is strongly linked to vocabulary development (Fenson *et al.*, 1994).

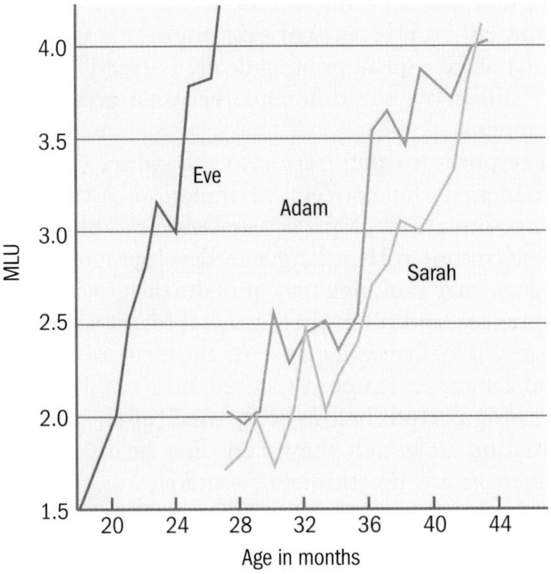

Figure 19.2 Mean length of utterance (MLU) plotted against age in months for three children (based on Brown, 1973)

Brown (1973) found a distinct regularity among English-speaking children in terms of the order in the addition of grammatical complexities. Similarly, de Villiers & de Villiers (1979) found that, irrespective of culture, children acquire functional words in the same general order but at different rates. Each function word corresponds to a syntactic rule. Several studies show that when children begin to apply these rules (such as the rule for forming plurals), they're not just imitating other people.

KEY STUDY 19.1 Wugs rule OK (Berko, 1958)

- Berko showed children a picture of a fictitious creature called a wug and told them 'This is a wug'.

This is a wug

- They were then shown a second picture in which there were two of the creatures and told 'Now there is another one. There are two of them'.

Now there is another one.
There are two of them.
There are two ______

- The children were asked to complete the sentence 'There are two ...'.
- Three- and four-year-olds answered 'wugs' despite never having seen a 'wug' before.
- Although the children couldn't have been imitating anybody else's speech, and hadn't been told about the rule for forming plurals, they were able to apply this rule. Significantly, they weren't consciously aware of having acquired the rule for forming a plural, and couldn't say what the rule was.

ASK YOURSELF...

- Can you think of any other examples of grammatical rules that children of this age display (including their speech errors)?

The rule-governed nature of language is also shown in children's grammatical mistakes. For example, while the rule 'add an 's' to a word to form a plural' usually works, there are exceptions to it (such as 'sheep' rather than 'sheeps' and 'geese' rather than 'gooses'). Similarly, the rule 'add 'ed' to form the past tense' usually works, but not in the case of 'cost' and 'go'. The observation that children use words like 'costed' and 'goed', without ever having heard others use them, suggests that they're applying a rule rather than just imitating. But the rule is being *overgeneralised* or the language *over-regularised*. It also shows that children are actively and quite spontaneously involved in rule learning, and that they're trying to make sense of the whole business of how to talk (Schaffer, 2004).

By age four or five, basic grammatical rules have been acquired, but a typical five-year-old will have difficulty understanding passive sentences. There are also many irregular words still to be learned, and this aspect of grammatical development will take several more years.

By age 13, most English-speaking children have a vocabulary of 20,000 words, and by age 20, this will have risen to 50,000 or more (Aitchison, 1996). This vocabulary is acquired at an average rate of 10 words per day (Pinker, 1994).

THEORIES OF LANGUAGE DEVELOPMENT

Learning theory: operant conditioning

According to Skinner (1985):

> Verbal behaviour evidently came into existence when, through a critical step in the evolution of the human species, the vocal musculature became susceptible to operant conditioning.

ASK YOURSELF...

- Given what you know about operant conditioning (see Chapter 11), how do you think Skinner might have tried to explain language development?

Skinner (1957) first applied operant conditioning principles to explain language development when he argued that:

> A child acquires verbal behaviour when relatively unplanned vocalisations, selectively reinforced, assume forms which produce appropriate consequences in a given verbal community.

While Skinner accepted that prelinguistic vocalisations, such as cooing and babbling, were probably inborn, he argued that adults *shape* the baby's sounds into words by reinforcing those which approximate the form of real words. Through *selective reinforcement,* words are shaped into sentences with correct grammar being reinforced and incorrect grammar ignored.

One form of positive reinforcement is the child getting what it asks for (*mands*). For example, 'May I have some water?' produces a drink that reinforces that form of words. Reinforcement may also be given by parents becoming excited and poking, touching, patting and feeding children when they vocalise. The mother's delight on hearing her child's first real word is exciting for the child, and so acquiring language becomes reinforcing in itself.

Skinner also believed that *imitation* (emitting *echoic responses*) plays an important role. When children imitate verbal labels (*tacts*), they receive immediate reinforcement in the form of parental approval to the extent that the imitations resemble correct words. As children continue to learn new words and phrases through imitation, so their language becomes progressively more like that of adults (Moerk & Moerk, 1979).

ASK YOURSELF...

- How easily can operant conditioning explain the stages of language development described on pages 322–325?

An evaluation of Skinner's theory

- While imitation must be involved in the learning of accent and vocabulary, its role in complex aspects of language (syntax and semantics) is less obvious. As we saw earlier, when children do imitate adult sentences, they tend to convert them to their own currently operating grammar. So, between 18 and 30 months, the child's imitations are as telegraphic as its own spontaneous speech. However, a child is more likely to imitate a correct grammatical form after an adult has *recast* the child's own sentences than when the adult uses the same grammatical form spontaneously in normal conversation (Farrar, 1992; Nelson, 1977). Recasting, though, is relatively rare (or sometimes non-existent) in normal toddler–parent conversations, yet children still acquire a complex grammar (Bee, 2000). Since at least some adult language is ungrammatical, imitation alone cannot explain how children ever learn 'correct language'. Even if we don't always speak grammatically correctly ourselves, we still know the difference between good and bad grammar.
- In response to these criticisms, Bandura (1977a) has broadened the concept of imitation. Although the exact imitation of particular sentences plays a relatively minor role in language development, Bandura argues that children may imitate the *general form* of sentences, and fill in these general forms with various words. *Deferred imitations* are those word sequences and language structures stored in a child's memory for long periods before being used (often in the same situation in which they were first heard). *Expanded imitations* are repetitions of sentences or phrases not present in the original form (Snow, 1983). Children's language production sometimes exceeds their competence in that they imitate forms of language they don't understand. By storing examples of adult language in memory, children have a sort of 'delayed replay' facility that enables them to produce language forms after they've been acquired.
- Operant conditioning cannot explain the *productivity* (or *creativity*) of language. As Chomsky (1968) states:

  > The normal use of language is innovative, in the sense that much of what we say in the course of normal language use is entirely new [and] not a repetition of anything that we have heard before.

- Operant conditioning cannot explain children's spontaneous use of grammatical rules which they've never heard or been taught, and especially the overgeneralisation of these rules (see Box 19.5).
- Operant conditioning cannot account for children's ability to understand sentence as opposed to word meaning. A sentence's meaning is not simply the sum of the meanings of the individual words. The structure of language is comparable to the structure of perception as described by the Gestalt psychologists (Neisser, 1967: see Chapter 15).
- Brodbeck & Irwin (1946) found that, compared with institutionalised children who received less attention, children whose parents reinforced their early attempts at meaningful sounds tended to vocalise more. Parents often reinforce children when they imitate adult language, and, using behaviour modification, Lovaas (1987) has shown that selective reinforcement can be used successfully to teach language to emotionally disturbed or developmentally delayed children (see Chapter 45). However, Skinner's views have been challenged by a number of researchers.

Box 19.5 Does selective reinforcement have any influence on children's grammar?

- Mothers respond to the 'truth value', or presumed meaning of their children's language, rather than to its grammatical correctness or complexity. Mothers extract meaning from, and interpret, their children's incomplete and sometimes primitive sentences (Brown *et al.*, 1969).
- Tizard *et al.* (1972) argue that attempts to correct grammatical mistakes or teach grammar have very little effect. Indeed, vocabulary develops more slowly in children of mothers who systematically correct poor word pronunciation and reward good pronunciation (Nelson, 1973).
- Slobin (1975) found that children learn grammatical rules *despite* their parents, who usually pay little attention to the grammatical structure of their children's speech and often reinforce incorrect grammar. According to Slobin:

  A mother is too engaged in interacting with her child to pay attention to the linguistic form of [its] utterances.

Chomsky's LAD and the biological approach

Although language cannot develop without some form of environmental input, Chomsky (1957, 1965, 1968), Lenneberg (1967) and McNeill (1970) believe that environmental factors could never explain language development adequately. Chomsky proposed the existence of an innate *language acquisition device* (LAD), whereby children are born already programmed to formulate and understand all types of sentences even though they've never heard them before.

Chomsky (1957) argued that language is much more complex and much less predictable than Skinner believed. Central to his theory of *transformational grammar* (TG) are *phrase-structure rules,* which specify what are

Noam Chomsky (born 1928)

Rule (1) An S (sentence) consists of (or can be broken down into) NP (noun phrase) and VP (verb phrase)

Rule (2) NP ⟶ Article + (Adjective) + Noun

(The brackets denote 'optional')

Rule (3) VP ⟶ Verb + NP

Rule (4) Article ⟶ a(n), the

Rule (5) Adjective ⟶ big, small, red etc.

Rule (6) Noun ⟶ boy, girl, stone etc.

Rule (7) Verb ⟶ hit, threw, helped etc.

These are *lexical rewrite rules.*

The commas imply that only *one* word should be selected from the list

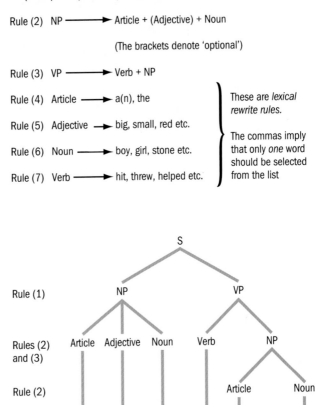

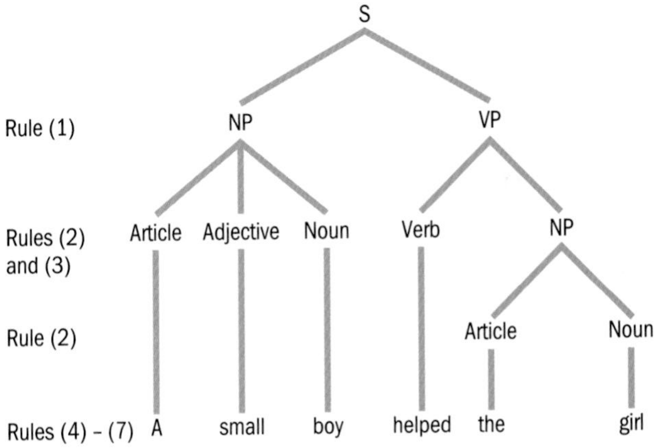

Figure 19.3 Some of Chomsky's phrase-structure rules and an example of a sentence produced by using them

acceptable/unacceptable utterances in a speaker's native language. When applied systematically, these rules generate sentences in English (or any other language).

While phrase-structure rules specify some important aspects of language, they don't specify them all (Chomsky, 1957).

Box 19.6 Deep and surface structure, and TG

- A sentence's *surface structure* refers to the actual words or phrases used in the sentence (its *syntactical structure*), while its *deep structure* more or less corresponds to the *meaning*.
- Chomsky argues that when we hear a spoken sentence, we don't 'process' or retain its surface structure, but transform it into its deep structure.
- Transformational grammar (TG) is knowing how to transform a sentence's meaning into the words that make it up (and vice versa). This knowledge is an innate LAD, and is what enables us to produce an infinite number of meaningful sentences.

- A *single* surface structure may have *more than one* deep structure, as in the sentence 'The missionary was ready to eat'. This could be interpreted either as 'The missionary is ready to consume a meal' or 'The missionary has been prepared for consumption by others'.
- Conversely, *different* surface structures can have the *same* deep structure (as in the sentences 'A small boy helped the girl' and 'The girl was helped by a small boy').

ASK YOURSELF...

- Try a Chomsky-type analysis on the following.
  - Cleaning ladies can be delightful.
  - Shaving men can be dangerous.

For Chomsky, children are equipped with the ability to learn the rules for transforming deep structure into various surface structures. They do this by looking for certain kinds of linguistic features common to all languages, such as the use of consonants and vowels, syllables, modifiers and so on. Collectively, these linguistic features (*linguistic universals*) provide the deep structure. They must be universal, because all children can learn with equal ease any language to which they're exposed. So, a child born in England of English parents who went to live in China soon after its birth would learn Chinese, if brought up by a Chinese-speaking family, just as easily as a native-born Chinese child. Chomsky argues that only some kind of LAD can account for children's learning and knowledge of grammatical rules in view of the often ungrammatical and incomplete samples of speech they hear.

Chomsky didn't suggest that we go through the procedures of phrase structure and TG each time we prepare to speak a sentence (Hampson & Morris, 1996). A language's grammar is an idealised description of the *linguistic competence* of its native speakers. Any model of how this competence is applied in actual performance must acknowledge certain psychologically relevant factors, such as memory, attention, the workings of the nervous system, and so on (Lyons, 1970).

Box 19.7 Some evidence supporting Chomsky's theory

- The human vocal organs, breathing apparatus, auditory system, and brain are all specialised for spoken communication.
- Babies as young as two days old can discriminate between 'ba' and 'pa' sounds (Eimas, 1975). According to Chomsky, these phonetic discriminations can be thought of as the first linguistic universals the baby discovers.
- All adult languages appear to have certain linguistic universals. TG is acquired in some form by all people (unless brain-damaged or reared in isolation), irrespective of culture and general intelligence. For Lenneberg (1967), this shows that language acquisition must be controlled by genetic factors that are (at least partially) independent of those controlling general intelligence.
- Studies of congenitally deaf children have shown the emergence of 'gestural language', even though the children received no encouragement or training from their parents (Gerrard, 1997; Goldin-Meadow & Feldman, 1977). These languages have the characteristics of ordinary languages (such as verbs, nouns and syntax), supporting the view that knowledge of syntax is innate. These findings also demonstrate that language is very difficult to suppress even in adverse environmental circumstances. As Bee (2000) says:

  The baby is somehow primed to learn 'language' in some form, be it spoken or gestural.

Is there a critical period for language?

Lenneberg has argued that the years leading to puberty constitute a *critical period* for language development, based on the still-developing brain's relative lack of specialisation. Children born brain-damaged or who lose their language abilities, can relearn at least some of them because other, non-damaged, parts of the brain seem to take over. But adolescents or adults who experience an equivalent amount of damage are unable to regain abilities corresponding to the site of the injury, because the brain is now specialised (or 'committed') and no longer 'plastic' (see Chapter 4).

According to Locke (1993), there are four main sources of relevant data.

1. *Second-language learning* – Johnson & Newport (1989) tested Chinese and Korean immigrants to the USA for English competence. Their knowledge of grammar was closely related to the age at which they'd begun to learn English. Before seven, they were just as proficient as native speakers; after 15, they showed considerable deficiencies (even after living in the USA for as long as the younger learners). But there's no indication that there's a definite cut-off point for learning a second language (Schaffer, 2004).
2. *Late exposure to language in deaf children* – some deaf children aren't given the opportunity to acquire a formal language (oral or manual) until relatively late on in childhood. Newport (1990) found similar results to Johnson and Newport: the later that deaf children are first exposed, the more difficulty they have – but again there's no specific cut-off point.
3. *Effects of brain damage at different ages* – this relates to Lenneberg's observations above.
4. *Children reared in isolation* – see Case Study 19.1.

CASE STUDY 19.1: Genie (Curtiss, 1977)

- Genie was an American child raised in conditions of extreme (de)privation until her discovery (in 1970) at the age of 13 years and seven months.
- Among other appalling treatment, Genie was beaten if she made any noise, and had learned to suppress almost all vocalisations except for a whimper. According to Curtiss, 'Genie was unsocialised, primitive, hardly human'.
- Genie could understand a handful of words (including 'rattle', 'bunny' and 'red'), but always responded to them in the same way. Essentially, then, she had to learn language at the age of nearly 14.
- She never developed normal language skills, and by age 18 could produce only short sentences that lacked important aspects of grammar (such as the use of pronouns).
- Her vocabulary expanded and she could hold a conversation, but her use of intonation was poor and only those who knew her well could understand much of what she said. Genie herself had great difficulty in understanding complex syntax.

The fact that Genie was capable of learning any language at all weakens Lenneberg's claim for a critical period. However, her obvious linguistic retardation is consistent with the existence of a *sensitive period* for language development. According to Schaffer (2004), the 'safe and not very startling conclusion' is that:

> ... childhood is the optimal period for language learning. There is, however, some flexibility in the precise age when children need to start on this task, and there is also no definite indication supporting Lenneberg's contention that puberty is the point beyond which any further learning becomes possible.

An evaluation of Chomsky's theory

- Aitchison (1983) agrees with Chomsky's claim that children are 'wired' with the knowledge that language is rule-governed, and that they make a succession of hypotheses about the rules underlying speech. However, she disputes the claim that the LAD also consists of TG (what she calls 'Content Cuthbert'). Aitchison prefers a *process* approach, in which children are seen as having inbuilt puzzle-solving equipment that enables them to process linguistic data along with other sorts of data ('Process Peggy').
- By contrast, Chomsky (1979) argues that an innate language ability exists *independently* of other innate abilities, because the mind is constructed of 'mental organs' which are:

  > ... just as specialised and differentiated as those of the body ... and ... language is a system easy to isolate among the various mental faculties.

- According to Chapman (2000), belief in some kind of LAD has persisted despite evidence that language structure is acquired piecemeal, occurs over a period of many years, and that there are wide variations in how quickly children acquire language. Also, language input to young children is well-formed, responsive to the child's communicative attempts, well-adapted to the child's current focus of attention and understanding. This suggests that language development needs to be understood within the context of the child's social interactions, rather than by focusing almost exclusively on what the child possesses in the form of a LAD.
- Kuczaj & Hill (2003) believe that the data relating to parents' influence on children's syntactic development (see Box 19.5) support Chomsky's claim that parents' role isn't significant. However:

  > ... they do in fact learn the language that they have heard their parents speak ...

  Parents do a much better job of providing children with good examples of grammatical sentences than Chomsky gives them credit for.
- But Chomsky insists that, however grammatically correct parents' speech might be, and however much they might adapt their speech to children's needs and abilities (see Box 19.3), it still consists only of *surface structure*. The only source of *deep structure,* he says, is an innate LAD. But Kuczaj & Hill (2003) draw a distinction between a *predisposition* to learn language (which is relatively uncontroversial and widely accepted) and *innate knowledge* of language (Chomsky's much more controversial claim that is accepted by very few).

Some alternatives to learning theory and biological approaches

Recently, there's been a growing acceptance that neither operant conditioning nor nativist approaches offers a complete account of language development. Instead, an *integrated view* maintains that:

- children cannot acquire language until an appropriate maturational level has been reached, but that
- language development is more closely related to environmental input and cognitive development than Chomsky proposes.

Maratsos (1983) has identified several assumptions made by *integrative theorists*.

Box 19.8 Some assumptions made by integrative theorists

- Children are highly motivated to communicate, and therefore are active language learners.
- Children can learn the major aspects of grammar because they've already acquired important concepts on which grammar is based (namely that events involve agents, actions, objects of actions, and so on). For this

reason, learning a grammar doesn't require much information-processing.
- Other aspects of language can be explained by the language parents use to talk to children.
- Those grammatical rules that don't fit in with children's natural cognitive processes, and aren't conveyed adequately through parental input, are unnatural and difficult for the child. They're also acquired very late (such as the passive voice in English).

ASK YOURSELF...
- What aspects of the interaction between a baby and its caregiver might be important for the baby's future language development? Think of this from the perspective of *both* partners.

The language and social-interaction approach

One alternative explanation to Chomsky's of the rule-bound nature of children's speech, is that it arises from the child's *prelinguistic knowledge* (see Box 19.4). During the 1970s, psychologists began to look at language development in the first 12 to 18 months of life, because the basic skills acquired then contribute substantially to the syntactic skills characteristic of adult language.

A purely syntactic analysis of language cannot explain how children 'discover' their language; that is, how they learn that there's such a thing as language which can be used for communicating, categorising, problem-solving and so on. However, Smith *et al.*'s (1998) *language and social-interaction approach* sees language as being used to communicate needs and intentions, and as an enjoyable means of entering into a community.

Several studies have indicated how babies initially master a social world on to which they later 'map' language. Snow (1977), for example, notes that adults tend to attach meaning to a baby's sounds and utterances. As a result, burps, grunts, giggles and so on are interpreted as expressions of intent and feeling, as are non-verbal communications (such as smiling and eye contact). Snow sees this as a kind of primitive conversation (or *proto-conversation*). This has a rather one-sided quality, in that it requires a 'generous' adult attributing some kind of intended meaning to the baby's sounds and non-verbal behaviours. From this perspective, the infant is an inadequate conversational partner.

Box 19.9 Visual co-orientation, formats and turn-taking: two-way interaction

- *Visual co-orientation* (or *joint attention*) and *formats* (Collis & Schaffer, 1975) are exchanges that are far more two-way than proto-conversations.
- Visual co-orientation involves two individuals coming to focus on some common object. This puts an infant's environmental explorations into a social context, so that an infant–object situation is converted into an infant–object–mother situation (Schaffer, 1989).
- This entails joint attention, which provides opportunities for learning how to do things. So, as parents and children develop their mutual patterns of interaction and share attention to objects, some activities recur, as happens, for instance, in joint picture-book reading.
- Bruner (1975, 1978) uses 'formats' to refer to rule-bound activity routines, in which the infant has many opportunities to relate language to familiar play (as when the mother inserts name labels into a game or activity), initially in *indicating* formats and later in *requesting* them (see Box 19.10).
- These ritualised exchanges stress the need for *turn-taking* (which occurs in games such as peek-a-boo, and give-and-take), and so help the baby to discover the social function of communication. As a result, the infant can learn about the structures and demands of social interaction, and prepare and rehearse the skills that will eventually become essential to successful interchanges such as conversation.
- As Schaffer (2004) says:

... the acquisition of language is very much a social interactive process and ... any attempt to understand it in terms of the activities of the learner alone is doomed to failure ...

Peek-a-boo: the fun of turn-taking

LASS: the active adult

According to Bruner (1983), formats comprise the *language acquisition support system* (LASS). He's concerned with the *pragmatics* and *functions* of language (what language is for). In Bruner's view:

Entry into language is entry into discourse that requires both members of a dialogue pair to interpret a communication and its intent. Learning a language ... consists of learning not only the grammar of a particular language, but also learning how to realise one's intentions by the appropriate use of that grammar.

The emphasis on intent requires a far more active role on the adult's part in helping a child's language acquisition than just being a 'model', or providing the input for the child's LAD. According to Moerk (1989), 'the LAD was a lady', that is, the lady who does most of the talking to the child (namely its mother). Mothers simplify linguistic input and break it down into helpful, illustrative segments for the child to practise and build on (see Box 19.3). This view sees language development as a very sophisticated extension of the processes of meaningful interaction that the caregiver and child have constructed over several months (Durkin, 1995).

The active child

Another way of looking at the 'partnership' is to see the infant as being the more 'active' partner. The view of language as a *cause–effect analytic device* has been summarised by Gauker (1990), for whom:

The fundamental function of words is to bring about changes in the speaker's environment ... Linguistic understanding consists of a grasp of these causal relations.

Box 19.10 The emergence of communicative intentionality

- According to Gauker (1990), language comprises a set of symbols whose use results in a change of behaviour in the listener. The use of words as communicative tools is shown in the emergence of *communicative intentionality*.
- During the prelinguistic stage, children have no awareness that they can gain a desired effect indirectly by changing somebody else's behaviour. So, they may cry and reach for something, but not direct the cry towards the caregiver or look back at the caregiver. The cry merely expresses frustration, and isn't a communicative signal designed to affect the other's behaviour. This 'analysis' of means–ends relationships (what causes what) solely as a product of one's own actions, is called *first-order causality*.
- The emergence of communicative intentionality involves *second-order causality*, the awareness that it's possible to bring about a desired goal by using another person as a tool. Pointing gestures and glances now rapidly increase as a means of asking others to look at or act upon an object.
- According to Savage-Rumbaugh (1990), the child is beginning to understand in a general sense:

  ... that it is possible to 'cause' others to engage in desired actions through the mechanism of communication about those actions.

However, it's easier to analyse language *production* than language *comprehension* in terms of a cause–effect analysis: what do we cause to happen when we understand things that have been said to us? Based on her work with chimpanzees, Savage-Rumbaugh (1990) concludes that language comprehension is clearly the driving force underlying the language acquisition process: under normal circumstances, language production is just one outcome of the development of language comprehension (see below, pages 334–335).

TEACHING LANGUAGE TO NON-HUMAN ANIMALS

As we've seen, Chomsky believes that language is unique to human beings. Similarly, Lenneberg claims that it represents a *species-specific* behaviour, common to all humans and found only in humans. But if non-humans can be taught to use language, then they must have the capacity for language. The obvious subjects for such language training are our closest evolutionary relatives, chimpanzees and gorillas (the non-human primates).

Criteria for language

We need to define language in a way that will enable us to evaluate the results of studies where humans have tried to teach it to speechless non-humans. Hockett (1960) proposed 13 'design features' of language (see Figure 19.4). Based on these, Aitchison (1983) proposed that ten criteria should be sufficient (not all of these are included in Hockett's list). These are shown in Table 19.3.

By analysing human and non-human animal language in terms of all ten criteria, Aitchison concludes that four are unique to humans. These are highlighted in Table 19.3. It's in terms of these criteria that attempts to teach language to non-human primates have been evaluated.

Early studies

Early attempts to teach chimpanzees to speak were almost totally unsuccessful. Kellogg & Kellogg (1933) raised Gua with their own child and treated them exactly alike. Although Gua could understand a total of 70 words or commands, she failed to utter a single word. Hayes & Hayes (1951) used operant conditioning in what was the first deliberate attempt to teach human language to a non-human – Viki, a baby chimp. By age three, she could say 'up' and 'cup' and (less convincingly) 'mama' and 'papa'. It became obvious that the vocal apparatus of a chimp is unsuited to making English speech sounds.

However, this doesn't rule out the possibility that chimps may still be capable of learning language in some non-spoken form. This is precisely what several psychologists have tried to demonstrate since the 1960s in what have come to be called *production-based training* (see Gross, 2003a; Gross *et al.*, 2000).

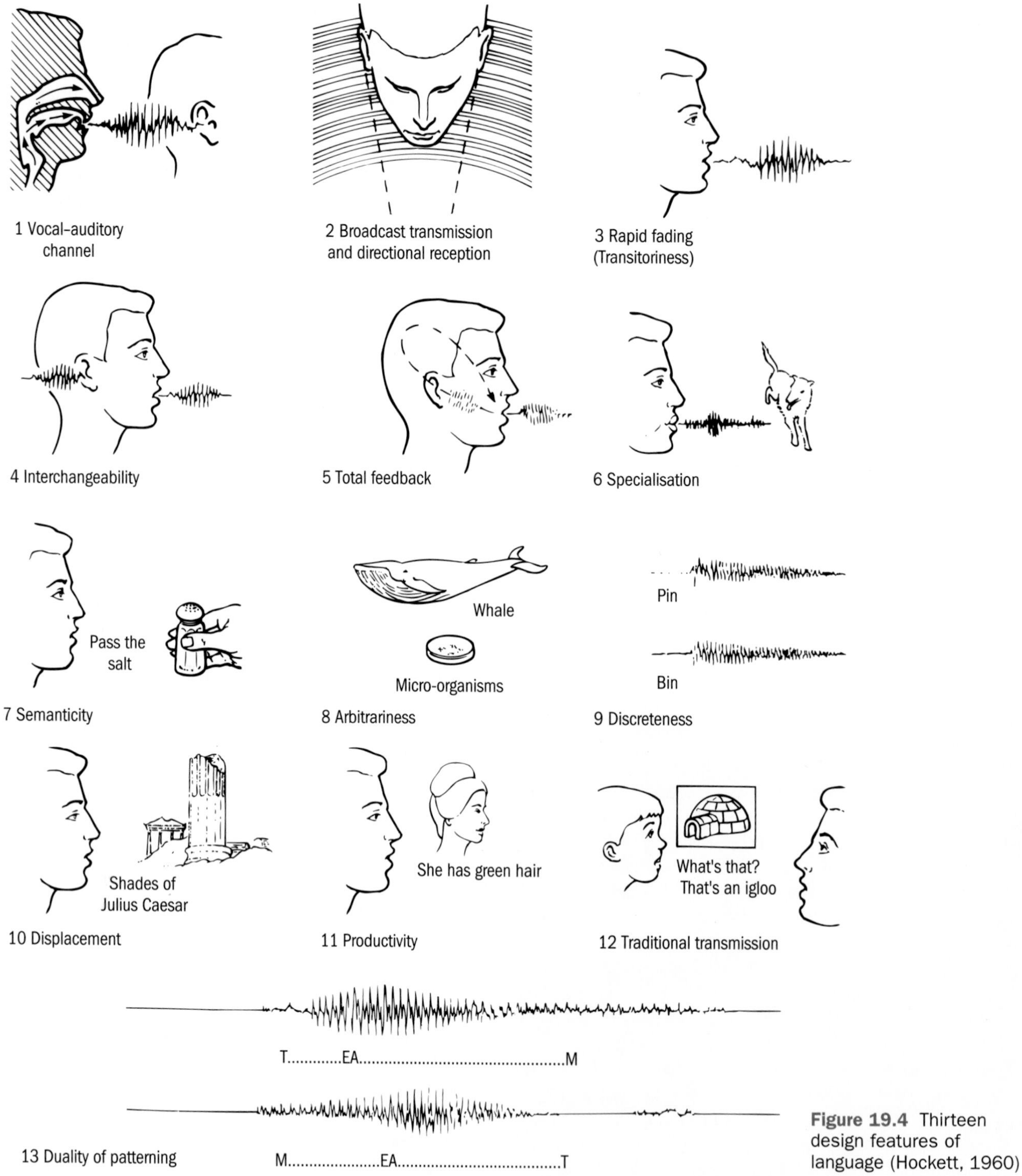

Figure 19.4 Thirteen design features of language (Hockett, 1960)

> *ASK YOURSELF...*
> - Why do we need to know if non-human primates are capable of language?
> - Has this research any potential practical implications for the subjects?
> - Does it have implications for how we see ourselves as a species?

Evaluating production-based studies

One way of evaluating the studies summarised in Table 19.4 (production-based training) is to ask whether the languages of children and chimps are qualitatively different.

As far as *semanticity* is concerned, is the correct use of signs to refer to things a sufficient criterion? Savage-Rumbaugh *et al.* (1980) seriously doubt whether any of the apes (including their own, Lana) used the individual

Table 19.3 Ten criteria for language (Aitchison, 1983, based on Hockett, 1960)

1	Use of the vocal–auditory channel	**6**	Turn-taking (conversation is a two-way process)
2	Arbitrariness (use of neutral symbols – words – to denote objects, actions etc.)	**7**	Duality (organisation into basic sounds plus combinations/sequences of sounds)
3	**Semanticity** (use of symbols to mean or refer to objects, actions etc).	**8**	**Displacement** (reference to things not present in time or space)
4	Cultural transmission (handing down the language from generation to generation)	**9**	**Structure dependence** (the patterned nature of language/use of 'structured chunks', e.g. word order)
5	Spontaneous usage (freely initiating speech)	**10**	**Creativity** (what Brown calls productivity: the ability to produce/understand an infinite number of novel utterances.

N.B. Items in bold are criteria unique to humans

elements of their vocabularies as words. Terrace (1987) argues that the deceptively simple ability to use a symbol as a name required a cognitive advance in the evolution of human intelligence at least as significant as the advances that led to grammatical competence.

The function of much of a child's initial vocabulary of names is to inform another person (usually an adult) that it has noticed something (MacNamara, 1982). A child often refers to the object spontaneously, showing obvious delight from the sheer act of naming. This *hasn't* been observed in apes. MacNamara believes that no amount of training could produce an ape with such an ability, for the simple reason that the act of referring isn't learnt but is a 'primitive of cognitive psychology' (and is a necessary precursor of naming). Instead, a chimp usually tries to 'acquire' an object (approach it, explore it, eat it), and shows no sign of trying to communicate the fact that it has noticed an object as an end in itself (Terrace, 1987).

Several critics have claimed that the linguistic abilities of chimps amount to a wholly 'instrumental use' of symbols. Referring to Savage-Rumbaugh's work with Kanzi (see below), Seidenberg & Petitto (1987) claim that Kanzi 'may not know what the symbols mean' but only 'how to produce behaviours that others can interpret'. However, Gauker (1990) argues that:

> ... we might do well to view 'knowing what symbols mean' as nothing other than an understanding of more or less sophisticated instrumental uses of symbols... even in human beings linguistic understanding consists in a grasp of the causal relations into which linguistic signs may enter ...

This relates to what we said earlier about the 'emergence of communicative intentionality' (see Box 19.10).

Table 19.4 The major studies which have attempted to teach language to non-human primates

Study	Subject	Method of language training
Gardner & Gardner (1969)	Washoe (female chimp)	American sign language (ASL or Ameslan). Based on a series of gestures, each corresponding to a word. Many gestures visually represent aspects of the word's meaning
Premack (1971)	Sarah (female chimp)	Small plastic symbols of various shapes and colours, each symbol standing for a word; they could be arranged on a special magnetised board. e.g. a mauve △ = 'apple'; a pale blue ✧ = 'insert'; a red □ = 'banana'
Rumbaugh *et al.* (1977)/Savage-Rumbaugh *et al.* (1980)	Lana (female chimp)	Special typewriter controlled by a computer. Machine had 50 keys each displaying a geometric pattern representing a word in a specially devised language ('Yerkish'). When Lana typed, the pattern appeared on the screen in front of her 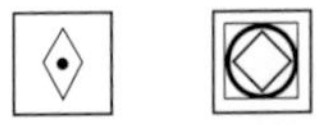
Patterson (1978, 1980)	Koko (female gorilla)	American sign language
Terrace (1979)	Nim Chimpsky (male chimp)	American sign language

Operant conditioning is used in all these studies when signs etc. are correctly used.

Helping chimps be more like children

Since the 1980s, Savage-Rumbaugh, at the Yerkes Primate Centre and Georgia State University, has been working with chimps in a way which is much more like how children acquire language (and in certain respects more like that of the pioneers in this field, the Kelloggs' and the Hayes'). Instead of putting the chimps through rote learning of symbols, gradually building up a vocabulary a symbol at a time, Savage-Rumbaugh aimed to use a large vocabulary of symbols from the start, using them as language is used around human children. This represents a move away from an emphasis on grammatical structure (at least in the beginning) and towards *comprehension:*

> It seemed reasonable to me – obvious even – that comprehension was an important element of language, that language is first acquired through comprehension, and that production flows from that. (Savage-Rumbaugh, quoted in Lewin, 1991)

This new approach was applied on a limited scale with Austin and Sherman, two common chimps. But it really got going with some pygmy chimps (*bonobos*), which are slightly smaller than common chimps, and more vocal and communicative through facial expressions and gestures. In 1981, work began with Matata, who six months earlier had kidnapped a newborn infant, Kanzi, and kept him as her own. Instead of ASL, Savage-Rumbaugh used an extensive 'lexigram', a matrix of 256 geometrical shapes on a board (see the photograph in the *Introduction and overview*). Instructors touch the symbols, which represent verbs and nouns, to create simple requests or commands. At the same time, the sentence is spoken, with the aim of testing comprehension of spoken English. When the chimpanzee presses a symbol, a synthesised voice from the computer 'speaks' the word.

Although clearly intelligent in many ways, Matata was a poor learner and used only about six symbols. However, despite no attempt to teach Kanzi anything, he picked up the symbols Matata knew, as naturally as human children do. From that point onwards, an even greater effort was made to place language learning in a naturalistic context. Kanzi acquired a sister, Mulika, when he was two and a half years old and they grew up together.

CASE STUDY 19.2: Kanzi

- By age ten (1991), Kanzi had a vocabulary of some 200 words. But it's not so much the size of his vocabulary that's impressive, rather what the words apparently mean to him.
- He was given spoken requests to do things, in sentence form, by someone out of his sight. Savage-Rumbaugh's assistants in the same room with Kanzi wore earphones, so they couldn't hear the instructions and thereby cue Kanzi, even unconsciously. None of the sentences was practised and each one was different. 'Can you put the raisins in the bowl?' and 'Can you give the cereal to Karen?' posed no problems for Kanzi. Nor did 'Can you go to the colony room and get the telephone?' (there were four or five objects in the colony room, which weren't normally there).
- More testing still was the instruction 'Go to the colony room and get the orange' when there was an orange in front of Kanzi. This caused him confusion about 90 per cent of the time. But if asked to 'Get the orange that's in the colony room', he did so without hesitation, suggesting that the syntactically more complex phrase is producing better comprehension than the simple one (Savage-Rumbaugh, in Lewin, 1991).
- Kanzi showed this level of comprehension when he was nine years old, but not when he was younger than six. He also showed understanding of the syntactic rule that in two-word utterances, action precedes object and, significantly, he went from a random ordering initially to a clear, consistent preference.
- Now well over 20, Kanzi's grammatical comprehension has been officially assessed as exceeding that of a two-and-a-half-year-old child, and he understands about 2000 words. His 15-year-old sister, Panbanisha, has a vocabulary of at least 3000 words, and Nyota, Panbanisha's son, is learning faster than her mother and uncle. It seems that the researchers' expectations were higher for those who came after Kanzi (Cohen, 2000).

According to Savage-Rumbaugh (1990), production-based language training can be said to disrupt the 'normal course' of language acquisition in the ape:

> When the environment is structured in a way that makes it possible for the chimpanzee to acquire language much as does the normal child, by coming to understand what is said to it before it elects to produce utterances, the perspective of language acquisition and function that emerges is very different from that seen by Sherman and Austin.

Kanzi was the first to demonstrate that *observational exposure* is sufficient for the acquisition of lexical and vocal symbols. Three other chimps (two pygmy and one common) have also learned symbols without training (so Kanzi's ability is unique neither to him nor to his species). According to Savage-Rumbaugh (1990), chimps learn where one word ends and the next begins, that is, what the units are, through the learning of routines which emerge out of daily life that has been constructed for the chimpanzees.

Panbanisha and Panzee using the lexigram keyboard

Box 19.11 A day in the life of a chimp exposed to language

- A typical day is like a field-based preschool for apes. Food can be found throughout a 50-acre forest. They have time off for social play with different companions, interesting places to visit, plus time devoted to structured testing, during which the chimps are asked to sit quietly and apply themselves as fully as possible.
- Caretakers' only instructions are to communicate with them much as one would with very young children, except that they must accompany their speech with pointing to lexical symbols.
- They talk about things which are concrete and immediate (such as where they're going, and what just happened to them), and clarify their intent with gestures and actions. 'Conversations' move from topic to topic with the natural flow of the day, and routines include nappy changing, getting ready to go outside, bathing, riding in the car, looking at a book, blowing bubbles, putting things in the backpack, visiting other apes, playing games of tickle, and travelling down various forest trails.

At first, a symbol is understood only within an established routine; later it will be understood and used beyond the routine itself. The driving force that moves the ape from symbol comprehension to symbol production is the desire to exert some control over what happens next (Savage-Rumbaugh, 1990).

ASK YOURSELF...

- Is it ethically acceptable to use chimps and other apes for this kind of research?
- Is it right that they're treated as if they were human when they're not? (See Chapter 48.)

Is language uniquely human?

According to Aitchison (1983), the apparent ease with which children acquire language, compared with apes, supports the suggestion that they're innately programmed to do so. Similarly, although these chimps have grasped some of the rudiments of human language, what they've learned and the speed at which they learn it are *qualitatively different* from those of human beings (Carroll, 1986).

Aitchison and Carroll seem to be talking for a majority of psychologists. However, the criticisms of ape studies and the conclusions that have been drawn from them are based on the production-based studies (as summarised in Table 19.4). Savage-Rumbaugh believes there's only a *quantitative difference* (one of degree) between ape and human language. Responding to criticisms by Terrace that Kanzi still uses his symbols only in order to get things done, to ask for things, rather than to share his perception of the world, Savage-Rumbaugh observes that so do young children. In fact, the predominant symbol use of normal children is 'requesting'.

Kanzi's capacity for comprehension far outstrips his capacity for producing language using the lexigram. This makes him extremely frustrated, at which times he often becomes very vocal, making high-pitched squeaks. Is he trying to speak? If Kanzi were to talk, maybe the first thing he'd say is that he's fed up with Terrace claiming that apes don't have language (Lewin, 1991).

CONCLUSIONS

Many psychologists believe that there's a biologically determined 'timetable' for language development, while others emphasise the role of conditioning. Although the evidence suggests that biologically based accounts are probably closer to the truth, it's unlikely that they offer a complete account of language development. According to Bee (2000):

> The fact that children learn complex and varied use of their native tongue within a few years remains both miraculous and largely mysterious.

For Chapman (2000):

> The study of child language development is at an exciting moment, one in which new advances in research methods and multiple theoretical perspectives – psychological, linguistic, social, cognitive, anthropological, neurobiological – are converging on a new understanding of how children learn to talk. The older debates of the importance of nature vs nurture in explanations of language acquisition are giving way to interactionist perspectives ...

According to Kuczaj & Hill (2003):

> ... A true explanation of language development will require a combination of innate and environmental factors, and so researchers need to look beyond their 'favourite' theories and consider all possible explanations. As this occurs more and more frequently, we will move that much closer to understanding the incredible feats that characterize language development.

As for language being unique to human beings, opinions are still divided. But what's indisputable is that attempts to teach language to non-human primates have raised some fundamental ethical issues. Wise, an American lawyer, argues that bonobos and other chimps deserve basic legal rights. He rejects the idea of human superiority (Cohen, 2000).

CHAPTER SUMMARY

- Language involves the acquisition of a rule system (**grammar/mental grammar**), which consists of **phonology**, **semantics**, and **syntax**.
- During the **prelinguistic stage**, babies make various non-speech sounds including crying and cooing. But **babbling** involves the production of **phonemes**. **Phonemic expansion** is replaced at around 9–10 months by **phonemic contraction.**
- The child's first **words** are often invented and **context-bound**, denoting specific actions, events or objects. They serve less of a communicative function and more of a **performative function**.
- The full meaning of **holophrases** is provided by accompanying gestures and tones of voice. They can be thought of as precursors of later, more complex sentences.
- Language in **stage 1 grammar** is **telegraphic**, consisting of **contentives** but no **functors**, and involving a **rigid word order**. The child's **imitation by reduction** is complemented by the adult's **imitation with expansion**.
- Word order seems to reflect the child's **prelinguistic knowledge**, as claimed by Cromer's **cognition hypothesis**. Similarly, Piaget believes that language development reflects the child's stage of cognitive development.
- In **stage 2 grammar**, sentences become longer and more complex, as measured by the **mean length of utterance** (MLU). MLU increase is due largely to the inclusion of functors missing from stage 1 telegraphic speech.
- Each functor corresponds to a **syntactic rule**. The rule-governed nature of language is also illustrated in children's grammatical mistakes, which often involve the **overgeneralised/over-regularised** application of a rule.
- According to Skinner, verbal behaviour is acquired through **operant conditioning**. Cooing and babbling are **shaped** by adults into words, and selective reinforcement shapes words into grammatically correct sentences.
- Operant conditioning cannot explain the **culturally universal** and **invariant sequence** in the stages of language development. It also fails to explain the **creativity** of language.
- According to Chomsky, children are innately equipped with a **language acquisition device** (LAD), which consists essentially of **transformational grammar** (TG). TG enables us to transform **surface** into **deep structure** and vice versa.
- LAD is used to look for **linguistic universals**, which collectively provide the deep structure. Children can learn any language they're exposed to with equal ease.
- According to **integrative theorists**, children are **active** learners of language whose learning of grammar is based on important already acquired concepts. The **language and social-interaction approach** emphasises children's prelinguistic knowledge.
- The emergence of **communicative intentionality** parallels the use of physical tools, an important feature of Piaget's **sensorimotor intelligence**.
- Early attempts to teach chimps to speak failed because their vocal apparatus is unsuited to making speech sounds. **Production-based training** studies have found that, compared with children, chimps show little spontaneous naming of objects, and they seem to use symbols in a purely **instrumental** way.
- Since the 1980s, Savage-Rumbaugh has been using a **comprehension-based** approach, with Kanzi and other bonobos. This structures the environment in a way that allows the chimp to acquire language through **observational learning**, much like a child, by exposing it to language in the course of daily life routines.
- Data from comprehension-based studies suggest that there's only a **quantitative difference** between ape and human language. Rejection of the claim that chimps are capable of language has arisen from the earlier, production-based studies.

Links with other topics/chapters

- Cromer's cognition hypothesis sees word order in two-word utterances as dependent on the child's prelinguistic knowledge, in particular Piaget's concept of *object permanence* (Chapter 34). This is consistent with Piaget's view of the *relationship between language and thought* (Chapter 18).
- This use of animate tools (other people) in communicative intentionality (second-order causality) parallels the use of inanimate tools (physical objects). This is an important feature of *sensorimotor intelligence,* the first stage in Piaget's theory of cognitive development Chapter 34).
- Skinner's theory of language development is based on the same principles of *operant conditioning* that are applied to all other (*voluntary*) behaviours (Chapters 2, 11 and 49), but he also sees *imitation* as playing an important role, which is more a feature of *social learning theory* (Chapters 35 and 36).
- Some support for Skinner comes from the use of *behaviour modification* to teach language to emotionally disturbed/developmentally delayed children (Chapter 45).

- Language (like perception: Chapter 16) is one of the major arenas for the *nature–nurture debate* in psychology, and Chomsky's LAD represents one of the major *nativist* theories within psychology as a whole – past or present (Chapter 50).
- Attempts to teach language to bonobos and other chimps raise fundamental philosophical, scientific and *ethical* issues (Chapter 48).

20

PROBLEM-SOLVING, DECISION-MAKING AND ARTIFICIAL INTELLIGENCE

INTRODUCTION AND OVERVIEW

The basic cognitive processes we've considered in the previous chapters are all aspects of 'thought'. However, there's more to thinking than perception, attention and language. Two closely related aspects of thinking of interest to cognitive psychologists are *problem-solving* (PS) and *decision-making* (DM). DM is a special case of PS, in which we already know the possible solutions (or options). A problem can be defined as arising whenever a path to a desired goal is blocked.

In another sense:

> ... all thinking involves problem-solving, no matter how simple, immediate and effortless it may appear ... (Boden, 1987a)

A good example of what Boden means is perception. As we noted in Chapter 15, the effortless and (usually) accurate nature of perception suggests that there's no problem-solving involved (no 'vision problem'). But that's not how psychologists – and other researchers – see it. For example, Marr (1982) considered that to understand vision, we must explain how useful information about a scene can be extracted from images of that scene. Specifically, we must define what computations must be performed.

Much of the work of computer simulation and artificial intelligence (AI) has been concerned with PS. If we can create computer programs that will solve 'human' problems, we might understand better how *we* solve them. This research is based on the argument that both computers and human problem-solvers are *information-processing machines* (Greene, 1987).

Significantly, some early research into human PS was going on during the 1920s and 1930s in Germany and elsewhere in Europe, where the impact of American behaviourism was minimal. It wasn't until the mid-1950s that behaviourism's domination of American psychology gave way to cognitive psychology. The new information-processing approach to PS was quite different from early PS research, being largely inspired by computer scientists, including those working within AI.

THE NATURE OF PROBLEMS

Stages in problem-solving (PS)

A problem is a situation in which there's a discrepancy between a present state and some goal state, with no obvious way of reducing it. PS is an attempt to reduce the discrepancy and achieve the goal state, and can be seen as progressing through a series of logical stages (Bourne *et al.*, 1979). These are:

- *defining or representing the problem*
- *generating possible solutions*
- *evaluating possible solutions.*

Some researchers have claimed that there's also an *incubation stage* (in which no attempt is made to solve the problem), which occurs between the generating and evaluating stages.

Classifying problems

Garnham (1988) distinguishes between two broad classes of problem, *adversary* and *non-adversary*.

Adversary problems

Adversary problems involve two or more people pitting their wits against each other, as in chess. Garnham says that game-playing is a special kind of PS, in which the problem is to find a winning strategy or the best current move. The focus of AI research here has been on two-player games, in which each player always has complete information about the state of play, and in which there's no element of chance. Apart from chess, games used include noughts and crosses (tic-tac-toe) and draughts (checkers).

Non-adversary problems

Most problems fall into the *non-adversary* category, in which another person is only involved as the problem setter. Some of the most commonly used include the following.

- **The eight-puzzle**: a 3 × 3 matrix containing the numbers one to eight, with one vacant square, must be moved until the numbers are in order.

5	4	8
7	2	6
3	■	1

Figure 20.1 The eight-puzzle

- **The missionaries and cannibals** (or '**hobbits and orcs**') **problem**: the three missionaries and three cannibals must be transported across the river in a single boat, which can hold only two people but needs at least one to get it across the river. The cannibals must never outnumber the missionaries on either bank (or they'll be eaten).

Left bank River Right bank

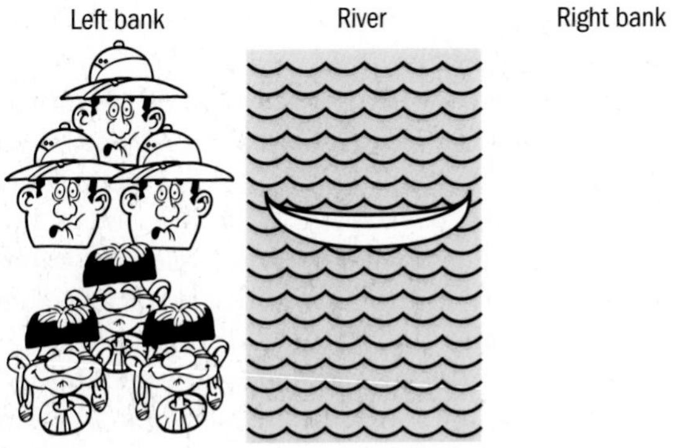

Figure 20.2 The missionaries and cannibals problem

- **The Tower of Hanoi problem**: there are three vertical pegs with four (or more) discs of increasing size stacked on one peg. The problem is to transfer the discs to the second peg, moving only one at a time and never placing a larger disc on top of a smaller one.

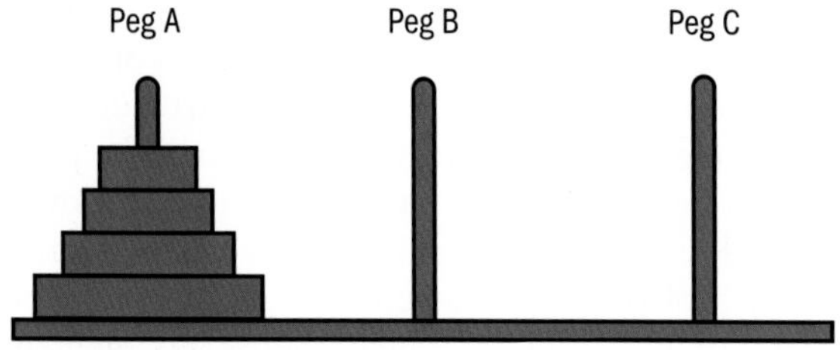

Figure 20.3 The Tower of Hanoi problem

- **Cryptarithmetic** (Bartlett, 1958): given that D = 5 and each letter stands for a digit (0–9), find the digits which make the sum correct.

```
   GERALD
 + DONALD
 --------
   ROBERT
```

> *ASK YOURSELF...*
> - Have a go at solving these puzzles, trying to monitor the *strategies* you adopt as you do so.

EXPLAINING PS

The Gestalt approach

According to *behaviourists,* PS is essentially a matter of *trial-and-error* and *accidental success* (Thorndike, 1911: see Chapter 11). Behaviourists argued that as acquired habits are learned, so PS (essentially a chain of stimulus–response associations) improves. While trial-and-error can be effective in solving some problems, the behaviourist approach was challenged by Gestalt psychologists. Rather than being 'senseless drill and arbitrary associations' (Katona, 1940), Gestalt psychologists saw PS as involving the *perceptual restructuring* of the problem, resulting in *insight* (see Chapter 15).

Functional fixedness

Functional fixedness (or '*fixity*') is a type of *mental set* (see below), in which we fail to see that an object may have functions (or uses) other than its normal ones. Duncker (1926, 1945) gave participants a candle and a box of drawing pins, and instructed them to attach the candle to a wall over a table so that it would stay upright and not drip on to the table underneath. Most tried to tack the candle directly to the wall, or glue it by melting it. Few thought of using the inside of the tack-box as a candle-holder and tacking that to the wall. Participants were 'fixated' on the box's normal function, and they needed to reconceptualise it (to use *lateral thinking:* de Bono, 1967). Their past experience was leading them away from the solution. When people are shown an empty box and the drawing pins are scattered on a table, the box is much more likely to be used as a candle-holder (Glucksberg & Weisberg, 1966).

Similar is Scheerer's (1963) nine-dot problem (see Figure 20.4). The problem is to draw four continuous straight lines, connecting all the dots, without lifting the pencil from the paper. Most people fail, because they assume that the lines must stay within the square formed by the dots – they 'fixate' on the shape of the dots. (The solution can be found on page 354.)

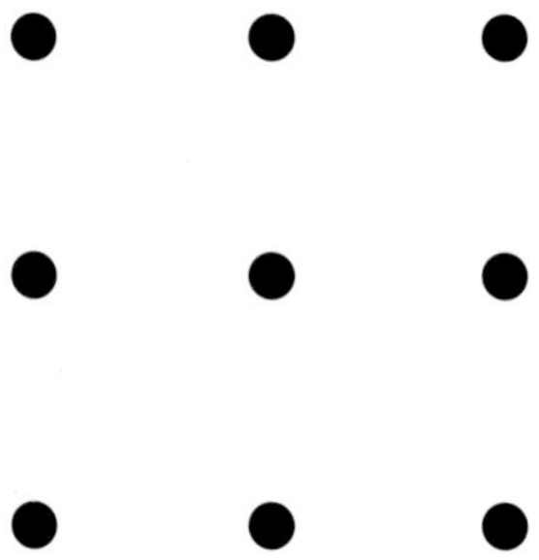

Figure 20.4 Scheerer's nine-dot problem

Mental set

Mental (or *problem-solving*) *set* is a form of functional fixedness, in which we tend to continue using a previously successful strategy to solve new problems, even when more efficient strategies exist. Luchins (1942) and Luchins & Luchins (1959) asked people to imagine they had three different containers, each of a different size. The task was to use the containers to obtain a specific volume of liquid. Once this problem had been solved, the task was repeated, but participants had to imagine a different set of three containers.

Table 20.1 The water container problems used by Luchins & Luchins (1959)

	Containers with capacity in fluid ounces			Obtain exactly these amounts of water
Problem no.	**Container A**	**Container B**	**Container C**	
1	21	127	3	100
2	14	163	25	99
3	18	43	10	5
4	9	42	6	21
5	20	59	4	31
6	23	49	3	20
7	10	36	7	3

Problems 1–5 can be solved using the formula B–2C–A (that is, fill container B, pour its contents into container C twice, and then pour what remains in container B into container A to leave the desired amount in container B). While problem 6 can also be solved using this formula, there's a more direct solution, namely A–C. Problem 7 *cannot* be solved using the formula B–2C–A, but can be solved using the formula A–C.

Once people discovered a solution to the first problem, they continued to use it even when (in the case of problem 6) it was less efficient, or (in the case of problem 7) it didn't apply. In Gestalt terms, mental set produces *reproductive thinking,* when in fact a problem calls for *productive thinking* (Maier, 1931; Scheerer, 1963). In productive thinking, problems are solved by the principle of *reorganisation,* or solving a problem by perceiving new relationships among its elements.

Consider, for example, trying to arrange six matchsticks into four equilateral triangles with each side equal to one stick. If you try to arrange the matchsticks by pushing them around on a table, the problem cannot be solved. But through reorganisation, and realisation that the matchsticks don't have to be arranged in two dimensions, the problem can be solved (as shown on page 354). The principle of reorganisation is similar to what Köhler (1925) called insight in his studies of PS in chimpanzees.

KEY STUDY 20.1 Sultan and the banana (Köhler, 1925)

- Köhler suspended, out of reach, a bunch of bananas from the ceiling of the cage of a chimpanzee called Sultan. In the cage were several items that could be used to reach the bananas (such as sticks of different lengths), although none on its own was sufficient. Eventually, Sultan solved the problem by placing empty boxes beneath the bananas and climbing on the boxes.

- Later, Köhler allowed Sultan to see a box being placed in the corridor leading to his cage. Sultan was then taken to his cage where, again, bananas were suspended from the ceiling. Sultan's first strategy was to remove a long bolt from the open cage's door. Quite suddenly, though, he stopped, ran down the corridor, and returned with the box which was again used to retrieve the bananas.
- For Köhler, Sultan's behaviour was a result of sudden perceptual reorganisation or insight, which was different from trial-and-error learning.
- Other experiments showed that Sultan's perceptual reorganisation was maintained as a plan of action. So, when the bananas were placed outside the cage, Sultan still built several boxes. Experience can sometimes be an obstacle to PS!

An evaluation of the Gestalt approach

- Gestalt psychologists made a significant contribution to our understanding of the processes involved in solving certain types of problem, but they didn't develop a theory that applies to all aspects of PS.
- The concepts of 'insight' and 'restructuring' are attractive, because they're easily understood (especially when accompanied by perceptual demonstrations). But they're extremely vague and ill-defined as theoretical constructs: it's very unclear under what conditions they occur and exactly what insight involves (Eysenck & Keane, 1995).
- However, in many ways the spirit of Gestalt research, with its emphasis on the goal-directed and non-associationist nature of thinking, provides a basis for the information-processing approach.
- It also left a large body of experimental problems and evidence, which any later theory had to be able to account for; 'the legacy of the school was, therefore, substantial' (Eysenck & Keane, 1995).

The information-processing approach

Information-processing approaches analyse cognitive processes in terms of a series of separate stages. In the case of PS, the stages are those mentioned earlier; that is, representing the problem, generating possible solutions, and evaluating those solutions.

Algorithms

An *algorithm* is a systematic exploration of every possible solution until the correct one is found. For example, to solve the anagram YABB, we could list all the possible combinations of letters, checking each time to see whether the result is a real word. So, we might generate BBAY (non-word), BYAB (non-word) and so on, until we eventually arrive at BABY. Algorithms guarantee a solution to a problem, and are effective when the number of possible solutions is small (as in the above example). But when there's a very large number of possible solutions, algorithms are time-consuming (unless we're fortunate enough to find the solution early).

Heuristics

Heuristics are 'rules of thumb':

> ... guidelines for selecting actions that are most likely to lead a solver towards a goal, but may not always do so. (Greene, 1987)

So, while not guaranteeing a solution to a problem, heuristics can result in solutions being reached more quickly (Newell *et al.*, 1958). These 'fuzzy' procedures are based on intuition, past experience, and any other relevant information. With solving anagrams, for example, a heuristic approach would involve looking for letter combinations that are/are not permitted in the English language. BB isn't a permitted combination of letters at the beginning of a word, and so this would immediately exclude BBAY as a solution to the example above. Although less likely with four-letter anagrams, heuristic devices applied to longer anagrams might not be successful, and we might miss a solution based on a lack of intuition, past experience, and other relevant factors. Heuristic devices include *means–end analysis* (Newell & Simon, 1972).

Means–end analysis (MEA)

In *MEA* (or *working backwards*), the search for a solution begins at the goal (or end) and works backwards to the original state (the means being the steps that must be taken to get from the present state – the problem – to the goal of solving the problem).

However, it's often not possible to achieve the main goal all in one step. So, another important characteristic of MEA is to break down the main goal into sub-goals (or a problem into subproblems), each of which has to be solved before the final (main) goal can be reached.

> ***ASK YOURSELF...***
> - Try to think of some examples of real-life/everyday problems that can be achieved only by being broken down into sub-goals.

This form of MEA is called *problem-reduction representation* (a 'divide and conquer' approach: Garnham, 1991). As each of the sub-problems is solved, so the distance between the original state and the goal state decreases (Newell & Simon, 1972).

For example, in the Tower of Hanoi (see pages 339–340), the overall goal is to move four discs from A to B, moving one disc at a time and never placing a larger disc on top of a smaller one. This overall goal can be subdivided into three sub-goals:

1. transfer the three smaller discs from A to C
2. transfer the largest disc from A to B
3. transfer the three smaller discs from C to B.

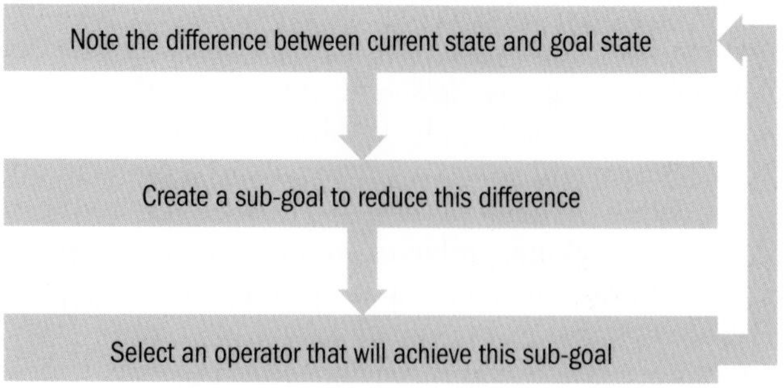

Figure 20.5 Outline of major steps involved in subgoal MEA

(1) and (3) can be reduced further. (2) can be achieved directly, assuming that (1) has been achieved. Complete reduction analyses the problem into moves of single discs whose preconditions are met; they correspond to the rules (*control strategies*) about moving only one disc at a time and only smaller discs being placed on a larger one (not vice versa). But is it always this clear just what the sub-goals are?

> **Box 20.1 Limitations of MEA**
> - The missionaries and cannibals problem is a good example of how the final goal may be obvious enough, while the subgoals may be far less obvious.
> - Indeed, many puzzles are chosen for experiments precisely because the basis for selecting the shortest set of moves to reach the final goal is obscure. So how do you measure progress towards the final goal in such problems?
> - It cannot be measured simply by the total number of people transported from the left to the right, because if there are too many cannibals the missionaries will get eaten!
> - While it's possible for a computer to work out a sequence of all possible moves and then to plot the quickest path of moves towards a solution, people cannot hold this type of structure in their limited-capacity working memories (see Chapter 17).
> - The water-jug problem poses the same difficulties for human solvers. (If a computer program systematically checked every possible move until the goal were reached, it would be using a 'check-every-move' algorithm.)

A further problem with MEA as a heuristic for PS is that it's sometimes necessary to move *further away* from a goal in order to achieve a solution. One reason the missionaries and cannibals problem is so difficult is that at one point it becomes necessary to take a missionary and a cannibal back to the left bank from where they started. This apparently increases the distance from the final goal of getting them all over to the right bank (Greene, 1987).

Well-defined and ill-defined problems

Garnham (1988) believes that in everyday problems, and those requiring a high degree of creative thinking, one or more of: (i) the initial state; (ii) the goal state; or (iii) the operators are typically *ill-defined* (not made explicit). This makes it difficult to write AI programs designed to solve such problems. But in the missionaries and cannibals problem, Tower of Hanoi, and other puzzle problems, all three are clearly specified (they're *well-defined* problems) and AI programs are relatively successful in solving them. According to Greene (1987), there are two major differences between puzzle problems and real-life problems.

1. Puzzle problems are unfamiliar problems about which the solver has little knowledge, whereas many everyday problems require considerable amounts of knowledge. The knowledge which is relevant in puzzle problems is called *general-purpose* (or *domain-independent heuristic*) knowledge. For example, MEA can be applied in a wide range of different situations (domains). By contrast, everyday problems require substantial *domain-specific* knowledge. Substantial domain-specific knowledge is also required in adversary problems, such as chess (see below).
2. The knowledge required to solve puzzles is present in the statement of the problem, whereas much of the difficulty with everyday problems is finding the relevant information needed to solve them.

Solving adversary problems: the case of chess

According to Ginsberg (1998):

> The world watched with considerable amazement in May 1997 as IBM's chess computer, Deep Blue, beat Garry Kasparov, the world champion, in a six-game match. With a machine's victory in this most cerebral of games, it seemed that a line had been crossed, that our measurements of ourselves might need tailoring.

However, the contest was very close (two wins, one defeat and three ties), and Kasparov clearly wasn't on top form. Although Deep Blue and other recent chess-playing programs generally play well, Ginsberg observes that:

> As an element of artificial intelligence, game-playing software highlights the key differences between the brute-force calculation of machines and the often intuitive, pattern-matching abilities of humans.

The number of possible sequences of moves in a game of chess is frighteningly large (there are an estimated 10^{20} possible games of chess, compared with a mere 10^{12} microseconds per century: Garnham, 1988). Human players will consider tens (or perhaps hundreds) of positions when selecting a move, which represents a tiny fraction of the potential moves, and only rarely can they think through to a win, lose or stalemate situation. Chess-playing computer programs used to be like human players. They selected a small number of moves to follow up, then used the *minimax procedure* (*minimising* the *maximum* loss that can be inflicted by the opponent) to analyse these in detail. Programs run on small computers still operate in this way.

But top programmers have access to the most powerful machines available, and they often revert to a more algorithmic method; for example, examining every possible position that can be reached in the next five moves by each player (which involves comparing hundreds of thousands of positions). While modern computers can perform many millions of operations per second (through 'brute-force' methods), this provides few insights for cognitive scientists, since it bears no relationship to the way that people solve difficult problems (Garnham, 1991).

Box 20.2 Key differences between human and computer chess masters

- Considering the far superior computational capacity of computers, it might seem unlikely that humans could ever win. But although people look at a mere handful of successive positions, they tend to look at the right handful. They identify the best positions to consider through *pattern matching* (or PR: see Chapter 14). Chess experts compare a given board position with the vast number of such positions they've seen during their career, using lessons learned from analysing those other positions to identify good moves in the current game. For Deep Blue, however, there are no pre-existing lists of positions it can use to evaluate the current game. As Boden (1987b) puts it:

  Master chess players develop global perceptual schemata in terms of which they can see threats and oppositions on the board much as a lesser mortal can see complex emotional response in a cartoon face ...

- Pattern matching is a *parallel process*, while the computer's capacity for searching through vast numbers of possibilities is a *serial process*. Since the brain is a massively parallel structure, it's far superior to computers at recognising patterns.

According to Boden (1987b):

> Like problem-solving in other ... domains ... chess playing needs more than quick thinking and a retentive memory: it requires an appreciation of the overall structure of the problem, so that intelligent action can be economically planned ...

De Groot (1965, 1966) compared the performance of five grand masters and five expert players on choosing a move from a particular board position. He asked participants to think aloud, and then determined the number and type of different moves they'd considered. Grand masters didn't consider more alternative moves or search any deeper than experts, and yet they took slightly less time to make a move. Independent raters judged the final moves of the masters to be superior to those of the experts.

De Groot's initial explanation for these differences was in terms of knowledge of different board positions stored in LTM. When participants were given a five-second presentation of board positions from actual games and asked to reconstruct them from memory, the masters were correct 91 per cent of the time compared with 41 per cent for the experts. Clearly, the masters could recognise and encode the various configurations of pieces using prior knowledge. When pieces were *randomly* arranged on the board, both groups did equally badly.

Chess experts are only better at remembering the position of chess pieces when they're positioned as they might be during a game. If the pieces are placed randomly, the experts are no better than non-experts at memorising their positions (de Groot, 1966)

Experts and domain-specific knowledge

According to Sternberg (1990):

> ... intelligent systems rely to a great extent on stored problem patterns when they face a familiar task. Instead of creating solutions from scratch for every problem situation, they make use of previously stored information in such a way that it facilitates their coping with the current problem.

Studies of experts and novices have revealed many important differences between them. These don't necessarily occur because experts are faster thinkers, have better memories, or are cleverer than non-experts (Hampson & Morris, 1996). The gain from being an expert seems to be that it places less strain on *working memory* (see Chapter 17). Since PS strategies depend on knowledge which is already available, 'the more you know, the less you have to think' (Greene, 1987).

According to Greene (1987), what's missing from AI accounts of human PS are the different experiences people bring to different tasks. For example, MEA is meant to be typical of all PS by all problem-solvers. It was originally presented as a general characteristic of human thinking which can, in principle, be applied to any problem. However, the ability to implement a particular PS strategy depends on knowledge. Thinking mechanisms may be universal, but solvers are categorised as experts or novices in relation to different problem situations. Expertise is more far-reaching than simple knowledge of the rules which apply to a particular problem (otherwise we'd all be chess masters!).

Expert systems

Expert systems (ESs or *intelligent knowledge-based systems*) promise to be the first major application of AI research (Garnham, 1991). Basically, an ES is a computer program that embodies (some of) the knowledge of a human expert in a domain in which expertise comes with experience (Garnham, 1988).

In fields such as medicine, it's difficult to formulate an expert's knowledge explicitly – otherwise human experts would be easier to train. ESs are intended to do (some of) the work of human experts. So, for a problem to be tackled by an ES, there must first be recognised experts in solving it, and their performance should be demonstrably better than that of non-experts (e.g. a medical consultant compared with both the layperson and non-specialist GPs). The case of medical diagnosis illustrates certain other features a problem should have.

- There's no simple set of rules a medical expert can follow in diagnosing illness. If there were, diagnosis could be performed by non-intelligent programs (and there would probably be no experts). Instead, consultants draw on wide experience of the connection between manifestations of illnesses and underlying causes.
- A single manifestation (symptom, sign, test result) may indicate one of a number of different diseases, but it's unlikely to be associated with any one of them in every case. Further, some of the data that diagnosis is based on may be misleading, irrelevant or incorrect: reasoning about diagnosis is, in some sense, *probabilistic* (it's never *certain*).
- Diagnosis doesn't depend on general knowledge, but requires a large but manageable amount of domain-specific knowledge.

Apart from the primary goal of solving domain-specific problems (e.g. medical diagnosis), ESs should be able to explain how they reached a particular conclusion. They usually interact with people in solving problems, and those users often need to know how a decision has been reached.

How is ES knowledge obtained?

The process of encoding knowledge into the system is called *transfer of expertise.* However, experts cannot always formulate explicitly the knowledge they use, nor can they say how they combine different items of information to make a judgement about a particular case. Lengthy interviews may need to be conducted, in which experts are asked to give their opinions on sample cases. These data may have to be supplemented by survey data, such as correlating patterns of medical symptoms and test results with eventual diagnosis. This makes the writing of ESs difficult and time-consuming.

Box 20.3 Some examples of ESs – MYCIN and GUESSING

- MYCIN diagnoses bacterial infections requiring antibiotics, and is intended for use in situations where drugs must be prescribed before the micro-organism responsible for the infection has been properly identified (a laboratory culture may take up to two days to grow).
- A chronically sick patient needs earlier treatment, so drugs have to be prescribed on the basis of symptoms and the results of quick tests. MYCIN interacts with a medical expert, requesting information and suggesting treatments. It asks specific questions related only to the hypothesis it's currently considering.
- While ESs have now been used in medicine for over 30 years, they've only fairly recently appeared in nursing. One example is the Glasgow University Expert Systems in Nursing Group (GUESSING), which has designed experiments to discover the cognitive skills of clinically excellent nurses in the area of pressure sore risk and preventative care planning. These were then formalised into a computer program, which can be used both as a decision support and a tutoring tool (Jones *et al.*, 1989, in Eaton, 1991).

An evaluation of ESs

According to Boden (1987a), ESs are much less flexible than their human counterparts and most in actual use are considerably less complex than MYCIN, which was one of the prototypes and took many work-years to create. In Boden's view:

> In almost every case, their 'explanations' are merely recapitulations of the previous firing of if–then rules ... for they still have no higher-level representations of the knowledge domain, their own problem-solving activity, or the knowledge of their human user.

Some researchers are trying to provide ESs with causal reasoning, so that they not only arrive at a conclusion but can also explain the reason to the user. Boden claims that ESs cannot integrate knowledge from distinct domains, using concepts and patterns of inference from one domain to reason (by analogy) in another. Genuine expertise requires both high-level knowledge and *analogical thinking.*

DECISION-MAKING

Decision-making (DM) is a special case of PS, in which we already know the possible solutions (or choices). Some decisions we have to make are relatively trivial. Others are more important, such as deciding which university to study at, or whether or not to have children. In DM, then, we're faced with various alternative choices from which one must be selected and the others rejected.

ASK YOURSELF...

- Think of a situation in which you had to choose between various options (e.g. which college or university to go to, or which subjects to study).
- How did you make your decision?

Compensatory and non-compensatory models of DM

Compensatory models

If we were completely logical in our DM, we'd evaluate how *all* the desirable potential outcomes of a particular decision might compensate for all the undesirable potential outcomes. According to the *additive compensatory model,* we start the DM process by listing common features of various alternatives, and assigning arbitrary weights that reflect their value to us. The weights are then added up to arrive at a separate score for each alternative. Provided the criteria have been properly weighted and each criterion has been correctly rated, the alternative with the highest score is the most rational choice given the available information.

Another compensatory model is the *utility–probability model.* This proposes that important decisions are made by weighting the desirability of each potential outcome according to its *utility* (the value placed on potential positive or negative outcomes) and *probability* (the likelihood that the choice will actually produce the potential outcome).

Non-compensatory models

Evidence suggests that we actually use various, and less precise, non-compensatory models. In these, we may not consider every feature of each alternative, and features don't compensate for each other. There are at least four such models.

Box 20.4 Some non-compensatory DM models

Elimination by aspects: When faced with complex decisions, we eliminate various options if they don't meet particular criteria, irrespective of their quality on other criteria (Tversky, 1972). This assumes that we begin with a maximum criterion and use it to test the various options. If, after applying this criterion, more than one alternative remains, the second most important criterion is used. The procedure continues until just one option remains. This is the chosen option.

Maximax strategy: After comparing the various options according to their best features, we then select the one with the strongest best feature.

Minimax strategy: After considering the weakest feature of each option, we select the option whose weakest feature is most highly rated.

Conjunctive strategy: This involves setting a 'minimum' acceptable value on each option. The next step is to discard any option which doesn't meet, or exceed, this value as the criteria are considered from most to least important. The chosen option is the one that meets or exceeds the minimum acceptable value on each criterion.

Heuristics in DM

Clearly, important decisions should be approached rationally and systematically. But it's not always easy to make rational decisions, even in important matters, because of the absence of information about the various alternatives. Moreover, with all the decisions we have to make daily, there isn't time to engage in the rational processes described above. We also have only a limited capacity for reasoning according to formal logic and probability theory (Evans & Over, 1996). As a result, we often rely on heuristics. Two of these are the *availability heuristic* (or *bias*) and the *representativeness heuristic* (or *bias:* Tversky & Kahneman, 1973).

Availability heuristic (or bias)

Sometimes, decisions must be made on the basis of whatever information is most readily available in LTM. The availability heuristic is based on the assumption that an event's probability is directly related to the frequency with which it's occurred in the past, and that more frequent events are usually easier to remember than less frequent events.

A statistically very rare – but newsworthy – event

ASK YOURSELF...

- Does the letter K appear more often as the *first* letter of a word or as the *third* letter?

Most people say the former. In fact, 'K' is three times more likely to appear as the third letter, but because words beginning with 'K' come to mind more easily, we assume they're more commonplace (Hastie & Park, 1986).

The availability heuristic also plays a role in our tendency to overestimate the chances of being the victim of a violent crime or a plane crash (Tyler & Cook, 1984). This is because the extensive media coverage of these statistically very rare events brings vivid examples of them to mind very readily.

Representativeness heuristic (or bias)

ASK YOURSELF...

Steve is very shy and withdrawn, invariably helpful, but with little interest in people, or in the world of reality. A meek and tidy soul, he has a need for order and structure, and a passion for detail.

- Try to guess Steve's occupation: is he a musician, pilot, physician, salesman or librarian?
- Why did you choose that one?

Tversky & Kahneman (1973) found that most of their participants chose librarian, presumably because his personality characteristics matched certain *stereotypes* of librarians (see Chapter 22, pages 384–389). Whenever we judge the likelihood of something by intuitively comparing it with our preconceived ideas of a few characteristics we believe represent a category, we're using the representativeness heuristic. It can also explain the *gambler's fallacy* (see Box 20.5) and the *base rate fallacy.*

Box 20.5 The gambler's fallacy

ASK YOURSELF...

- Consider the following possible outcomes of tossing a coin six times: HHHHHH, TTTHHH and HTTHTH.
- Which of these is the *least*, and which the *most*, likely?

- Most people believe the *first* outcome is the *least* likely of the three, and the *third* the *most* likely.
- In fact, the probability of the three sequences is *identical*.
- Our assumption that coin tossing produces a random sequence of heads and tails leads us to decide that the third is the most likely (it looks the most random).

- Indeed, if people observe five consecutive heads, and are then asked to estimate the probability of the next toss being a head, they tend to say that a *tail* is the more likely outcome – even though the probability of *either* heads *or* tails is actually 0.5! This tendency is called the *gambler's fallacy*.

In the *base rate fallacy,* we ignore important information about base rates (the relative frequency of different objects/events in the world). For example, Tversky & Kahneman (1973) asked participants to decide whether a student who could be described as 'neat and tidy', 'dull and mechanical' and 'a poor writer' was a computer-science student or a humanities student. Over 95 per cent decided the student studied computing. Even after they were told that over 80 per cent of students at their school were studying humanities, their estimates remained virtually unchanged. So, even when we know the relative frequency of two things, we tend to ignore this information and base a decision on how well something matches our stereotype; that is, how representative it is.

However, if prior odds are the only relevant information (base rates without the description of the student), then participants will estimate correctly. People may also be more inclined to take account of base rate information when it seems to be *causally* relevant (Tversky & Kahneman, 1980).

Box 20.6 Some other influences on DM

Belief perseverance: This is the tendency to cling to a belief even in the face of contrary evidence (Lord *et al.*, 1979). It can be overcome by considering the *opposite*. But some false beliefs, such as stereotypes, are difficult to remove even when information exists which clearly discredits them.
Entrapment: When we make costly investments in something that goes wrong (such as a relationship: see Chapter 28), we may come to feel we've no choice but to continue, because withdrawal cannot justify the costs already incurred (Brockner & Rubin, 1985). For example, industrial disputes often continue beyond the stage where either side can hope to achieve any gains (Baron, 1989).
Over-confidence: This is the tendency to overestimate the accuracy of our current knowledge, because it's generally easier for us to remember successful decisions or judgements than unsuccessful ones. So, using the availability heuristic, we overestimate our success at particular tasks. Over-confidence can be overcome by providing feedback about the accuracy of decisions and judgements.
Loss aversion and costs against losses: Typically, we tend to reject riskier, though potentially more rewarding, decisions in favour of a certain gain unless taking a risk is a way to avoid loss (Tversky & Kahneman, 1986). We also tend to see losses as being more acceptable if we label them as 'costs' rather than 'losses' (although the evaluation of a cost depends on the context: Kahneman & Tversky, 1984).
Expectations: Expectations can affect both our perception of the world (see Box 15.4, page 256) and what's done with the perceived information. For example, the shooting down of an ascending Iranian airliner by an American warship occurred as a result of initial, but later corrected, computer information that the plane was a descending F14 fighter jet. The expectation of an attack led the ship's captain to pay more attention to his crew's reports of an emergency than to the new computer information (Wade & Tavris, 1993).
Hindsight: *Hindsight bias* refers to our tendency, in retrospect, to overestimate the probability that something would have happened, as if we'd known this all along (Hawkins & Hastie, 1990).
Framing: When the same issue is presented (or framed) in two different but equivalent ways, we tend to make different judgements about it. For example, people respond more positively to minced beef if it's described as '75 per cent lean' rather than '25 per cent fat'. Also, medical treatments are seen as being more successful if framed as having a '50 per cent success rate' rather than a '50 per cent failure rate' (Levin & Gaeth, 1988: see Chapter 12 page 196).

Neville Chamberlain, the British Prime Minister, returned home in September 1938 from seeing Hitler in Munich with a pledge of non-aggression. He over-confidently declared 'I believe it is peace in our time'

Gambling and risk-taking

Many laboratory studies have used gambling as a model of risk-taking behaviour, despite the fact that it isn't typical of the risks we take in everyday life (Jones, 1998). However, the heuristics discussed above (which are based largely on laboratory studies) can help explain an increasingly common case of real-life gambling, namely, playing the National Lottery. Although the odds against winning the jackpot are 14 million to one (far greater than any other form of average gambling return), 90 per cent of the population are estimated to have bought at least one ticket, and 65 per cent claim to play regularly (Hill & Williamson, 1998). Given these odds, it's likely that the ordinary 'social gambler' doesn't think about the actual probability of winning, but relies on heuristic strategies for handling the available information (Griffiths, 1997b).

The fact that there are so many heuristics and biases, and that several can be applied to any one particular situation, gives them little predictive value (Griffiths, 1997b; Wagenaar, 1988). However, the availability bias, illusory correlations, and illusion of control can help explain the persistence of gambling (Griffiths, 1997b; Hill & Williamson, 1998). Uncovering the false beliefs underlying people's mistakes when becoming involved in a risk situation can help to reduce the irrational thinking of a potential gambler (Griffiths, 1990; Walker, 1992).

ASK YOURSELF...
- Try to relate these heuristics and biases to explanations of risky *health* behaviours (see Chapter 12) and *addictive* behaviours (see Chapter 8).

ARTIFICIAL INTELLIGENCE (AI)

Throughout the chapter so far, we've talked about computers as problem-solvers and have looked at some of the important differences between them and human problem-solvers. Also, we've discussed mainly puzzle problems. But what about the kind of 'problem' referred to in the *Introduction and overview,* such as vision and language understanding, which humans are 'designed' for? Can computers be programmed to mimic these basic human abilities and, if so, what can we learn about the way we use them?

Defining AI

According to Garnham (1988), AI is 'the science of thinking machines' and, again:

Table 20.2 Heuristic strategies and biases that might be used by lottery players

Heuristic	Application to lottery participation
Availability bias (see page 346)	Wide publicity concerning winners, and pleasant memories of an occasional small prize, make winning more salient than losing
Randomness bias: not expecting a random sequence to have any apparent biases and regularities (Teigen, 1994)	Despite the mechanical and random nature of the draw, many people seem to be trying to predict which numbers will be drawn (Haigh, 1995). So, there's difficulty in choosing six random numbers from 49
Representativeness bias: equating a 'random' sample with a 'representative' sample (Tversky & Kahneman, 1971; see also page 346)	A tendency to choose numbers that appear 'random' (irregular, no pattern), and avoid those which appear less random (adjacent numbers and repeating digits)
Gambler's fallacy: the belief that subsequent events will cancel out previous events to produce a representative sequence (Holtgraves & Skeel, 1992), and that the probability of winning will increase with the length of an ongoing run of losses (Wagenaar, 1988: see also Box 20.5, page 346)	Choosing numbers which have been least drawn (they're therefore 'due'), and overestimating the chances of winning
Illusory correlations: the use of superstitious behaviour when it's believed variables correlate when they don't (Wagenaar, 1988: see also Chapter 22, page 388)	Choosing 'lucky numbers' – birthdays, house numbers etc. – which causes players to discard statistical probabilities
Flexible attribution: tendency to attribute success to personal skill and failures to some external influence (Wagenaar, 1988: see Chapter 23)	Preference for choosing own numbers rather than buying 'lucky dips', so that any win is due to player's own skill (game of luck), whereas losses are due to features of the game (game of chance)
Illusion of control: an expectancy of success which is greater than the objective probability warrants (Langer, 1975)	Being able to choose own numbers induces skill orientations, which cause players to feel inappropriately confident
Sunk cost bias: continuing an endeavour once an investment has been made (Arkes & Blumer, 1985)	Continuing to buy lottery tickets while experiencing losses. The more money that's spent, the more likely people are to continue 'investing', and to inflate their estimations of winning

(Based on Griffiths, 1997b, and Hill & Williamson, 1998)

... an approach to understanding behaviour based on the assumption that intelligence can best be analysed by trying to reproduce it. In practice, reproduction means simulation by computer. AI is, therefore, part of computer science ...

Garnham observes that most contemporary AI research is influenced more or less by consideration of how people behave. Very few researchers simply try to build clever machines disregarding the principles underlying its behaviour, and many still have the explicit goal of writing a program which works in the way people do (such as Marr's computational theory of vision: see Chapter 15). So, cognitive psychologists and workers in AI share an interest in the scientific understanding of cognitive abilities.

Abilities such as vision, language, PS, and DM are all part of 'intelligence' in the broadest sense of that term, and intelligence has always been a central concern of psychologists (see Chapters 34 and 41). As we saw in Chapter 1, since the late 1970s cognitive psychology and AI have both become component disciplines of cognitive science. By the late 1970s, cognitive psychologists had more in common with AI researchers than with other psychologists, and AI researchers had more in common with cognitive psychologists than with other computer scientists (Garnham, 1988).

Boden (1987b) defines AI as '... the science of making machines do the sorts of things that are done by human minds ...'. The 'machines' in question are, typically, digital computers. But she's at pains to make clear that AI isn't the study of computers but the study of intelligence in thought and action. Computers are its tools, because its theories are expressed as computer programs which are tested by being run on a machine.

What is a computer?

The initial concept of the 'computer', and the first attempts to build the modern digital computer, were made by the Cambridge mathematician, Charles Babbage (1792–1871).

Charles Babbage (1792–1871)

Box 20.7 Turing machines

- Turing (1936) described an abstract computing device (a Turing machine), which performs its calculations with the help of a tape divided into squares, each with a symbol printed on it.
- Its basic operations comprise reading and writing symbols on the tape and shifting the tape to the left or right. It uses a finite vocabulary of symbols, but the tape is indefinitely long.
- A *universal Turing machine* can mimic the operation of any other Turing machine. To do this, it must be given a description of how that machine works, which can be written on to its tape in standard Turing machine format.
- Every general-purpose digital computer is an approximation to the universal Turing machine (since no real machine has an indefinitely large memory). When it runs a program, it behaves as if it were a machine for performing just the task the program performs.

Alan Turing (1912–1954)

A digital computer's memory consists of chips (silicon wafers with transistors engraved on them), which store data in the form of a *binary code* – that is, each unit can exist in one of two states (on/off, represented by the symbols 0/1) (Rose, 2003). These two states can symbolise an indefinitely large number of things (as can the 26 letters of the alphabet), because they can be grouped together in indefinitely numerous ways. As described by Turing, they are machines that change according to the problem to be solved (based on the particular instructions contained within the program). 'Digital' refers to the finger, and the fingers can be used as a kind of abacus, a simple form of computing machine. Computers are, in essence, *autonomous abaci* – working without continuous human intervention (Gregory, 1981).

Although originally designed as calculating machines ('compute' means to 'calculate'), computers aren't mere 'number crunchers' or supercalculating arithmetic machines. Digital computers are, in fact, *general-purpose symbol manipulating machines.* It's up to the programmer to decide what interpretations can sensibly (consistently) be made of the symbols of machine and programming languages, which, in themselves, are meaningless (Boden, 1987a).

Strong and weak AI, and the computational theory of mind

> *ASK YOURSELF...*
> - Do you believe that computers literally think/behave intelligently (that is, are *reproducing/duplicating* the equivalent human thinking/behaviour) or are they merely *simulating* (mimicking) human thought/intelligence?

This distinction corresponds to the one made by Searle (1980) between *strong* and *weak* AI, respectively:

> According to weak AI, the main value of the computer in the study of the mind is that it gives us a very powerful tool, e.g. it enables us to formulate and test hypotheses in a more rigorous and precise fashion than before. But according to strong AI the computer is not merely a tool; rather, the appropriately programmed computer really is a mind in the sense that computers given the right program can be literally said to understand and have other cognitive states. Further, because the programmed computer has cognitive states, the programs are not mere tools that enable us to test psychological explanations but the programs are themselves explanations ...

Searle is very critical of strong AI, a view advocated by computer scientists such as Minsky (1975), who defines AI as '... the science of making machines do things that would require intelligence if done by men'. The implication of such a definition is that machines must be intelligent if they can do what humans can do (although this rather begs the question as to what it means to display intelligence). Underlying strong AI is the *computational theory of mind* (CTM), one supporter of whom is Boden (1987a):

> Intelligence may be defined as the ability creatively to manipulate symbols, or process information, given the requirements of the task in hand. If the task is mathematical, then numerical information may need to be processed. But if the task is non-numerical (or 'semantic') in nature ... then the information that is coded and processed must be semantic information, irrespective of the superficial form of the symbols used in the information code ...

Symbols have no inherent similarity to what they symbolise, and represent something in a purely formal way. Computer programs comprise formal systems, 'a set of basic elements or pieces and a set of rules for forming and transforming the elements or pieces' (Flanagan, 1984). In computer languages, symbols stand for whatever objects, relations or processes we wish. The computer manipulates the symbols, not their meaning. Programs consist of rules for manipulating symbols, and don't refer to anything in the world.

However, CTM defines all intelligent systems as symbol manipulators which, of course, include human minds. If symbols are meaningless to a computer, it follows that they're also meaningless to a human mind. But in that case, what's the 'meaning' which, according to Boden, the human programmer attaches to the meaningless symbols? Searle's attack on strong AI and CTM takes the form of a *Gedanken* experiment ('thought experiment') called the Chinese room.

Box 20.8 The Chinese room (Searle, 1980)

- Suppose that I am locked in a room and am given a large batch of Chinese writing. Suppose that I know no Chinese, either written or spoken ...
- After this first batch of Chinese writing, I am given a second batch together with a set of rules for correlating the second batch with the first batch. The rules are in English and I understand them as well as any other English native speaker. They enable me to correlate one set of formal symbols with another set of formal symbols and all that 'formal' means here is that I can identify the symbols entirely by their shapes.
- I am then given a third batch of Chinese symbols together with some instructions, again in English, which enable me to correlate elements of this third batch with the first two batches and these rules instruct me how to give back certain Chinese symbols with certain sorts of shapes in response to certain sorts of shapes provided by the third batch.
- Unknown to me, the people giving me all these symbols call the first batch a 'script', the second batch a 'story', the third batch 'questions', the symbols I give back in response to the third batch, 'answers to the questions' and the set of English rules 'the program' ...
- After a while I get so good at following the instructions for manipulating the Chinese symbols and the programmers get so good at writing the program that, from the point of view of somebody outside the room, my answers are indistinguishable from those of native Chinese speakers ... However ... I am manipulating uninterpreted formal symbols and in this respect I am simply behaving like a computer, i.e. performing computational operations on formally specified elements ... I am simply a realisation of the computer program.

The Chinese room and the Turing test

Searle believes the Chinese room demonstrates quite conclusively that there's more to intelligence and understanding than mere manipulation of symbols. In particular, he's trying to show that the *Turing test* (or *imitation game*) isn't the ultimate test of machine intelligence that supporters of strong AI have traditionally claimed it is.

Box 20.9 The Turing test (Turing, 1950)

- Turing suggested that a suitable test for success in AI would be an 'imitation game', in which a human judge would hold a three-way conversation with a computer and another human, and try to tell them apart.
- The judge would be free to turn the conversation to any topic, and the successful machine would be able to chat about it as convincingly as the human.
- This would require the machine participant to understand language and conversational conventions, and to have a general ability to reason.
- If the judge couldn't tell the difference after some reasonable amount of time, the machine would pass the test: it would seem human to a human.

I believe that in about 50 years time it will be possible to program computers ... to make them play the imitation game so well that, on average, the interrogator will not have more than a 70 per cent chance of making the right identification after five minutes of questioning. When this occurs, there is no contradiction in the idea of thinking machines. (Turing, 1950)

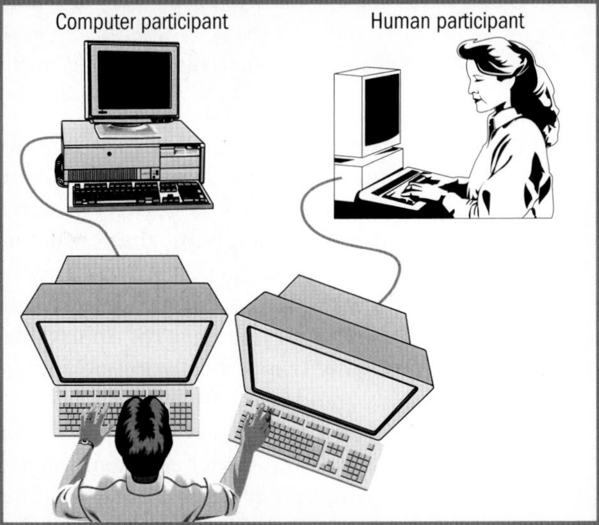

Figure 20.6 The Turing test for artificial intelligence

Both the Chinese room and the Turing test have been criticised. Gregory (1987b) argues that, because it's such a highly restricted and artificial environment:

> The Chinese room parable does not show that computer-based robots cannot be as intelligent as we are – because we wouldn't be intelligent from this school either.

Boden (1993) contends that a functioning program is comparable to Searle-in-the-Chinese-room's understanding of English (not Chinese). A word in a language one understands is a mini-program, which causes certain processes to be run in one's mind. Clearly, this doesn't happen with the Chinese words, because Searle-in-the-Chinese-room doesn't understand Chinese.

The real aims of AI

According to Ford & Hayes (1998), the central defect of the Turing test is that it is *species-centred*. In other words, it assumes that human thought is the ultimate, highest form of thinking against which all others must be judged. Most contemporary AI researchers explicitly reject the goal of the Turing test. Instead, Ford and Hayes maintain that:

> The scientific aim of AI research is to understand intelligence as computation, and its engineering aim is to build machines that surpass or extend human mental abilities in some useful way. Trying to imitate a human conversation (however 'intellectual' it may be) contributes little to either ambition.

Ford and Hayes draw an analogy between AI and artificial flight. They argue that the traditional view of (strong) AI's goal – to create a machine that can successfully imitate human thought – is mistaken. The Turing test should be relegated to the history of science, in the same way that the aim of imitating a bird was eventually abandoned by the pioneers of flight. The development of aircraft succeeded only when people stopped trying to imitate birds:

> In some ways, aircraft may never match the elegant precision of birds. But in other ways, they outperform them dramatically. Aircraft do not land in trees, scoop fish from the ocean or use the natural breeze to hover motionless above the countryside. But no bird can fly at 45,000 feet or faster than sound.

Rather than limiting the scope of AI to the study of how to mimic (or reproduce) human behaviour, Ford and Hayes argue that:

> ... the proper aim of AI is ... to create a computational science of intelligence itself, whether human, animal or machine ...

This brings us back to the CTM.

Do we need brains to be brainy?

For supporters of strong AI, our bodies – including our brains – are in no way necessary to our intelligence. In Boden's terms 'You don't need brains to be brainy' (in Rose, 2003). What she means by this is that you can model mind processes using the latest and most powerful computer systems, without paying attention to the underlying biology. Putting it another way, what matters is the program (software): the brain (hardware) is incidental. Strong AI claims that any physical system capable of carrying out the necessary computational processes can be described as intelligent, even if it's 'made of old

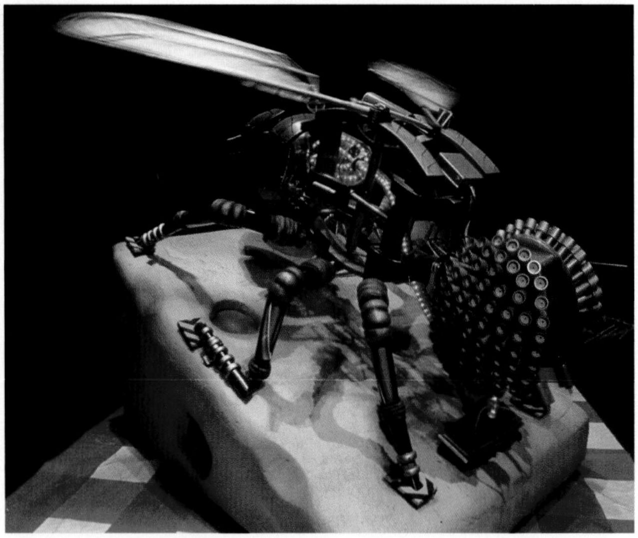

Giant robotic fly, designed to teach people about the structure and habits of this insect

beer cans' (in Searle's words). But many, as noted below, have argued that our brains *are* necessary.

- Flanagan (1984) finds it highly unlikely that our evolutionary history, genes, biochemistry, anatomy, and neurophysiology have nothing essential to do with our defining features (even though it remains logically possible).
- Searle (1987) believes that mental states and processes are real biological phenomena in the world, as real as digestion, photosynthesis, lactation, and so on (they are 'caused by processes going on in the brain').
- Penrose (1987) agrees that there's more to understanding than just carrying out some appropriate program, and that the actual physical construction of the brain is also important. He argues that a computer designed to follow the logical operations of every detail of the workings of the human brain would itself not achieve 'understanding', even though the person whose brain is being considered would claim to understand.
- The earlier generations of computers were essentially *serial processors.* They could perform – although admittedly incredibly quickly – only one operation at a time in sequence (in a *linear* fashion). AI researchers became convinced that real (biological) brains *don't* work like this at all, but instead carry out many operations in *parallel* and in a *distributed* manner. In other words, many parts of a network of cells are involved in any single function, and no single cell is uniquely involved in any. These considerations caused an explosion of interest in new computer designs based on *parallel distributed processing* (PDP) *principles,* promising new generations of machines.
- The central principle of this new brain-modelling approach is *connectionism,* based on the idea that the brain is composed of neural networks with multiple connections between them (see Chapter 4). If the aim of AI is to construct models which offer insights into human cognition, then it was necessary to look much more closely at the microstructure of the brain itself, to see if insights into the power of this natural information-processing engine might help develop a more realistic modelling system. Most PDP researchers were interested in how individual components (neurons) might operate collectively to produce the brain's information-processing capacity.
- According to Rose (2003), strong AI's separation of the mind from the brain is a form of mind–body dualism (see Chapter 49). But equally:

> ... the insistence on treating the brain as a sort of black box whose internal biological mechanisms and processes are irrelevant and all that matters is to match input to output, is reminiscent of the behaviourist programme in psychology ...

Can computers ever be like brains?

- According to Rose (2003), the very concept of AI implies that intelligence is simply a property of the machine itself. However, the neuronal system of brains, unlike computers, is radically indeterminate:

> ... brains and the organisms they inhabit, above all human brains and human beings, are not closed systems, like the molecules of a gas inside a sealed jar. Instead they are open systems, formed by their own past history and continually in interaction with the natural and social worlds outside, both changing them and being changed in their turn ...

- This openness creates a further level of indeterminacy to the functioning of both brain and behaviour. Unlike computers, brains aren't error-free machines. Yet brains are capable of modifying their structural, chemical and physical output in response to environmental events (they're highly *plastic*). They're also extraordinarily resilient in the face of injury, with undamaged parts taking over the function of damaged areas (they're highly *redundant*).
- Rose argues that brains process and remember information based on its *meaning,* which *isn't* equivalent to information in a computer sense. An essential difference between human and computer memory is that:

> ... each time we remember, we in some sense do work on and transform our memories, they are not simply being called up from store and, once consulted, replaced unmodified. Our memories are re-created each time we remember ... (Rose, 2003)

- At least for the foreseeable future, it seems that brains will continue to outperform computers when doing the kinds of things that they were naturally designed to do.

One of these might be consciousness (see Chapters 4 and 7). Currently, we simply don't know what makes the brain conscious, and so we cannot design a conscious machine. But since the brain is a physical entity and is conscious, it must have some design features (presumably physical) which make it conscious (McGinn, 1987). This doesn't mean that a machine *couldn't* be conscious, only that it would have to be the same kind of machine the brain is. Agreeing with Searle, Teichman (1988) states that, while we know that the computer hardware doesn't produce (initiate) the program, it's highly probable that the brain *does* help to produce mental states (see Chapter 49).

CHAPTER SUMMARY

- According to an **information-processing approach**, PS progresses through a series of logical stages: **defining/representing the problem**, **generating possible solutions** and **evaluating possible solutions**.
- The **behaviourist** view of PS as **trial-and-error** and **accidental success** was challenged by the **Gestalt** psychologists, who looked at how we impose **structure** on a problem.
- **Algorithms** and **heuristics** are two ways of generating possible solutions to a problem. Algorithms **guarantee** a solution, but can be time-consuming. Heuristics don't guarantee a solution, but can help produce solutions more quickly, as in **means–end analysis** (MEA).
- **Mental set/rigidity** and **functional fixedness/fixity** are ways in which past experience can hinder PS. Functional fixedness is a type of mental set, in which we fail to see that an object may have functions/uses other than its normal ones.
- Chess experts are only better at remembering board positions that could appear in an actual game, as opposed to random positions. Chess masters develop **global perceptual schemata** which allow them to see possible threats.
- **Expertise** reduces the strain on working memory (WM) by enabling the expert to draw on already available, **domain-specific knowledge** stored in long-term memory (LTM).
- **Expert systems** (ESs) apply knowledge in specific areas (such as medical diagnosis), enabling a computer to function as effectively as a human expert. But human experts cannot always say explicitly how they solve particular problems or make particular decisions.
- **DM** is a special case of PS, in which we already know the possible solutions or choices. According to **compensatory models**, we evaluate how all desirable potential outcomes might compensate for undesirable ones.
- **Non-compensatory models** are less precise but more commonly used approaches, in which not all features of each alternative are considered, and features don't compensate for each other.
- Because of the absence of information and time, rational decisions cannot always be made. So, we often resort to the **availability** and **representativeness heuristics**.
- Gambling is a form of **risk-taking** behaviour. Playing the National Lottery can be explained in terms of several heuristic strategies and biases, including the representativeness bias (which can explain the **gambler's fallacy**) and availability bias, **randomness bias**, **illusory correlation**, **flexible attribution**, **illusion of control** and **sunk cost bias**.
- Every general-purpose digital computer is an approximation to a **universal Turing machine**. Although originally designed as powerful calculators, computers are **general-purpose**, **symbol-manipulating machines**.
- According to **weak AI**, computers merely **simulate/mimic** thought or intelligence, while according to **strong AI**, they literally **reproduce/duplicate** thinking and intelligence.
- Underlying strong AI is the **computational theory of mind** (CTM), according to which intelligence is the ability to manipulate symbols. This is as true of a human mind as it is of a computer.
- Searle's **Chinese room thought experiment** is meant to show that the **Turing test** isn't the ultimate test of machine intelligence. But both have been criticised, and human intelligence shouldn't be regarded as the only or truest form of intelligence.
- According to CTM, the possession of a brain/the structure and mode of operation of the human brain are irrelevant. But many biologists, psychologists and others believe that there must be certain design features of the brain that have evolved to make it conscious.
- While digital computers process information in a **serial** fashion, brains operate in a **parallel** and also in a **distributed** manner. These considerations led to the development of **parallel distributed processing** (PDP).
- Brains and human beings are **open systems**, constantly interacting with the natural and social world. Brains may not be error-free machines, but they can perform certain tasks that are currently beyond the capability of any computer.

Links with other topics/chapters

- The Gestalt approach to PS is directly related to *Gestalt principles of perceptual organisation* (Chapter 15).
- The behaviourist emphasis on *trial-and-error learning of stimulus-response associations* (Chapter 11) is a *reductionist* account, while the Gestalt emphasis on the relationship between all the elements is a *holistic* approach (Chapter 49).

- Chess experts have phenomenal *short-term memory* for board positions – provided they're arranged non-randomly (according to the rules of chess). Knowledge of chess is stored in *long-term memory* (Chapter 17).
- The way that doctors frame the risks involved have been shown to influence patients' *compliance* with *medical advice and treatment* (Chapter 12).
- The illusory correlation can help explain the formation of *negative stereotypes* of racial and other minority groups (Chapter 22).
- Flexible attribution combines elements of the *actor-observer effect* (AOE) and the *self-serving bias* (SSB) (Chapter 23).
- According to Rose (2003), the PDP approach is *reductionist*. It takes the neuron as the unit of functioning and tries to simulate some of the brain's known properties using a new generation of supercomputers that perform parallel processing. By contrast, the CMT approach (which attempts to model *minds* rather than brains) is *holistic* (Chapter 49).
- Rose's (2003) claim that human memories (unlike a computer's) are re-created each time we remember is closely related to Bartlett's theory of *reconstructive memory,* which has had a major influence on research into *eyewitness testimony* (EWT) (Chapter 21).

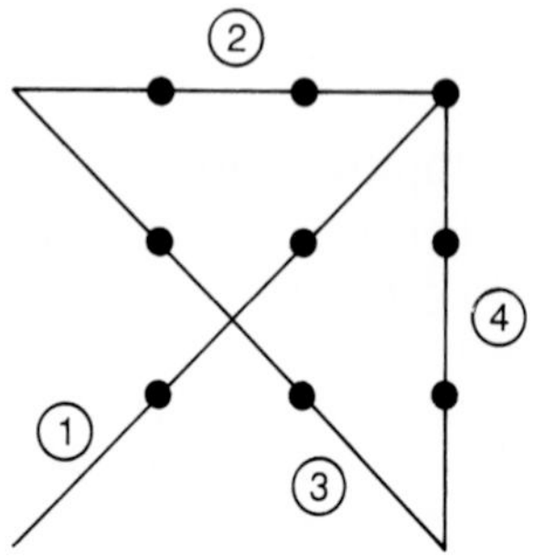

Solution to the nine-dot problem

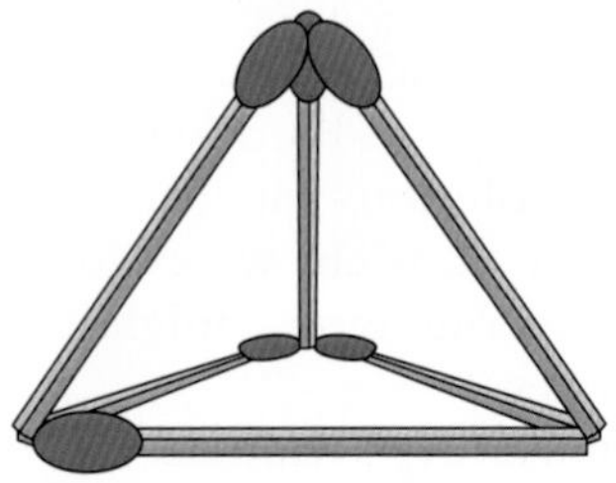
Solution to the matchsticks problem

21 APPLICATION COGNITION AND THE LAW

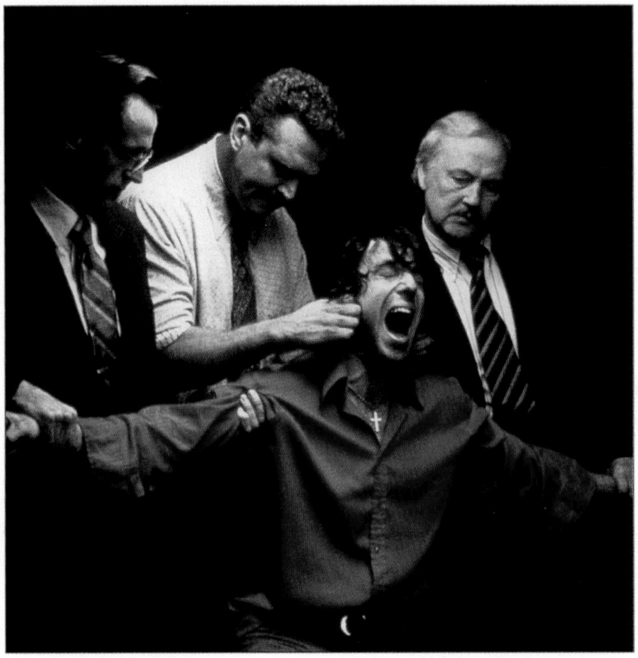

INTRODUCTION AND OVERVIEW

This chapter is concerned mainly with *memory* and *forgetting*. But unlike Chapter 17, we'll be focusing on these crucially important cognitive processes from an *applied* perspective. Specifically, how has psychological research into memory and forgetting helped us understand and deal with certain situations that arise within our legal system, in particular, the issue of *eyewitness testimony* (EWT) and the controversy surrounding the *recovery of repressed memories* (sometimes referred to as the *false-memory debate*).

In 1973, the Devlin Committee was set up to look at over 2000 legal cases in England and Wales that had involved identification parades (or line-ups). In 45 per cent of cases, suspects were picked out, and of those people prosecuted after being picked out, 82 per cent were subsequently convicted. Of the 347 cases in which prosecution occurred when EWT was the *only* evidence against the defendant, 74 per cent were convicted (Devlin, 1976). This indicates the overwhelming weight given to EWT (Baddeley, 1999).

Nevertheless, the *reconstructive* nature of memory has led some researchers to question the accuracy of EWT (e.g. Wells, 1993). The view of memory as reconstructive stems from the work of Bartlett (1932), and central to his theory is the concept of a *schema*. Bartlett has had an enormous impact on Loftus's research into EWT.

Since the early 1990s, considerable publicity has been given to court cases in the USA, where parents are being sued for damages by their teenage or adult children, who accuse them of child sexual abuse (CSA). This has been remembered during the course of psychotherapy. It's assumed that these *recovered memories* had been repressed since the alleged CSA happened, and that the safety and support provided by the therapist allow them to become conscious many years later.

However, accused parents, and retractors (people who had recovered memories of CSA, accused their parents, then later withdrew the accusations) have also sued therapists and hospitals for implanting false memories in the children's minds. The False Memory Syndrome Foundation was set up in the USA in 1992, and in 1993 the British False Memory Society was founded, with 1000 families on its books by 1998 (Showalter, 1998). *Repression* is a theory of forgetting originally proposed by Freud, who's also regarded by many as at least partly responsible for the phenomenon of *false-memory syndrome*.

SCHEMA THEORY AND EVERYDAY MEMORY

When discussing semantic memory (SM) in Chapter 17, we noted that it became increasingly obvious during the 1970s that SM must contain structures considerably larger than the simple concepts involved in Collins & Quillian's (1969) *hierarchical network model* and Collins & Loftus's (1975) *spreading-activation model*. This 'larger unit' of SM is the *schema,* a concept first used by Bartlett (1932) as part of his theory of reconstructive memory (see below, pages 358–360).

At the core of *schema theory* is the belief that what we remember is influenced by what we already know, and that our use of past experience to deal with new experience is a fundamental feature of the way the human mind works. Our knowledge is stored in memory as a set of schemas, simplified, generalised mental representations of everything we understand by a given type of object or event based on our past experience. Schemas operate in a 'top-down' way to help us interpret the 'bottom-up' flood of information reaching our senses from the outside world.

Two major modern schema theories are those of Rumelhart (1975), and Schank (1975) and Schank & Abelson (1977). There's a good deal of overlap between them, and the broad characteristics they share are summarised by Rumelhart & Norman (1983, 1985), as follows:

- A schema is a packet of information comprising a *fixed/compulsory value* plus a *variable/optional value.* For example, a schema for buying something in a shop would have relatively fixed slots for the exchange of money and goods, while the variable values would be the amount of money and the nature of the goods. In particular cases, a slot may be left unspecified, and can often be filled with a 'default' value (a best guess given the available information).
- *Schemas can be related together to form systems.* They aren't mutually exclusive packets of information, but can overlap. For example, a schema for a picnic may be part of a larger system of schemas including 'meals', 'outings' and 'parties'.
- *Schemas represent knowledge at all levels of abstraction.* They can relate to abstract ideologies, abstract concepts (e.g. justice), or concrete objects (e.g. the appearance of a face).
- *Schemas represent knowledge rather than definitions.* They embody knowledge and experience of the world, rather than abstract rules.
- *Schemas are active recognition devices.* This is very similar to Bartlett's 'effort after meaning', whereby we try to make sense of ambiguous and unfamiliar information in terms of our existing knowledge and understanding (see below).

According to Schank (1975) and Schank & Abelson (1977), schemas or *scripts* represent commonly experienced social events, such as catching a bus and going to a restaurant. These allow us to fill in much of the detail not specified in any text that we might read. For example:

> We had a tandoori chicken at the Taj Mahal last night. The service was slow and we almost missed the start of the play ...

can only be interpreted by bringing in a great deal of additional information (Baddeley, 1990). We need schemas that predict what would happen next and fill in those aspects of the event which are left implicit in the text. Scripts are essential ways of summarising common cultural assumptions, which not only help us to understand text and discourse but also predict future events and behave appropriately in given social situations. Scripts contain the sequences of actions we go through when taking part in familiar events, including the sorts of objects and actors we're likely to encounter.

> *ASK YOURSELF...*
> - Try writing a script for going to a restaurant, i.e. what sequence of events typically occurs when you go out for a meal, and who's involved at different times?

Table 21.1 A simplified version of Schank & Abelson's (1977) schematic representation of activities involved in going to a restaurant (from Bower *et al.*, 1979)

Name:	Restaurant
Props:	Tables
	Menu
	Food
	Bill
	Money
	Tip
Roles:	Customer
	Waiter
	Cook
	Cashier
	Owner
Entry conditions:	Customer is hungry
	Customer has money
Results:	Customer has less money
	Owner has more money
	Customer is not hungry
Scene 1:	Entering
	Customer enters restaurant
	Customer looks for table
	Customer decides where to sit
	Customer goes to table
	Customer sits down
Scene 2:	Ordering
	Customer picks up menu
	Customer looks at menu
	Customer decides on food
	Customer signals to waitress
	Waitress comes to table
	Customer orders food
	Waitress goes to cook
	Waitress gives food order to cook
	Cook prepares food
Scene 3:	Eating
	Cook gives food to customer
	Customer eats food
Scene 4:	Exiting
	Waitress writes bill
	Waitress goes over to customer
	Waitress gives bill to customer
	Customer gives tip to waitress
	Customer goes to cashier
	Customer gives money to cashier
	Customer leaves restaurant

An evaluation of schema theory

- Bower *et al.* (1979) asked people to list about 20 actions or events, in order, which commonly occur while eating at a restaurant, and found considerable agreement. For example, at least 73 per cent mentioned sitting down, looking at the menu, ordering, eating, paying the bill and leaving. Also, at least 48 per cent included entering, giving the reservation name, ordering drinks, discussing the menu, talking, consuming salad or soup, and ordering dessert, eating dessert and leaving a tip. So there were at least 15 events which formed part of many people's knowledge of what's involved in going to a restaurant. These findings broadly agreed with Schank and Abelson's restaurant script.
- When such events were incorporated into stories, people mistakenly tended to recall aspects of the passage which weren't explicitly included, but which were consistent with the script (that is, which could well have happened). The order of events was also changed to fit what would 'normally' happen. This is exactly what Bartlett would have predicted (see below).
- According to Cohen (1993):
  1. the whole idea of a schema is too vague to be useful
  2. there's an overemphasis on the inaccuracies of memory, overlooking the fact that complex events are sometimes remembered very precisely and accurately (especially the unexpected, unusual aspects)
  3. it's unclear how schemas are acquired in the first place; there seems to be a 'Catch-22' involved, since without schemas we cannot interpret new experiences, but we need new experiences to build up our schemas.

> *ASK YOURSELF...*
> - Can you apply this last criticism to Gregory's top-down theory of perception? (See Chapter 15.)

- Schank's (1982) *dynamic-memory theory* attempts (as the name implies) to take account of the more dynamic aspects of memory, and is a more elaborate and flexible model. It tries to clarify the relationship between general knowledge schemas and memory for specific episodes, based on a more hierarchical arrangement of memory representations. *Memory organisation packets* (MOPs) are at the bottom of the hierarchy, storing specific details about particular events. At higher levels, the representations become more and more general and schema-like. MOPs aren't usually stored for very long, becoming absorbed into the event schemas which store those features that are common to repeated experience. However, details of unusual or atypical events are retained (Cohen, 1993).

RECONSTRUCTIVE MEMORY

The Bartlett 'approach'

As we saw in Chapter 17, Ebbinghaus was the first to study memory systematically, using nonsense syllables. Although this 'tradition' is still popular with today's memory researchers, Bartlett (1932) argued that:

- Ebbinghaus's use of nonsense syllables excluded 'all that is most central to human memory'
- the study of 'repetition habits' had very little to do with memory in everyday life
- research should examine people's *active search for meaning,* rather than their passive responses to meaningless stimuli presented by an experimenter.

Although meaningful material is more complex than meaningless material, Bartlett argued that it too could be studied experimentally. As we saw earlier, Bartlett's concept of a schema is central to theories which attempt to explain the structure and organisation of knowledge in SM (a major part of LTM). Because of the large amount of work on the organisational aspects of memory (see Chapter 17), and because of the growing recognition of the need to study meaningful material (as opposed to lists of unrelated words, numbers, and so on), there has been a 'rediscovery' of Bartlett's work.

Serial reproduction and 'The War of the Ghosts'

One method used by Bartlett was *serial reproduction,* in which one person reproduces some material, a second person has to reproduce the first reproduction, a third has to reproduce the second reproduction and so on, until six or seven reproductions have been made. The method is meant to duplicate, to some extent, the process by which gossip or rumours are spread, or legends passed from generation to generation (and may be more familiar as 'Chinese whispers'). One of the most famous pieces of material Bartlett used was 'The War of the Ghosts', a North American folk tale.

Box 21.1 'The War of the Ghosts'

The title of this story is 'The War of the Ghosts'. One night two young men from Egulac went down to the river to hunt seals and while they were there it became foggy and calm. Then they heard war-cries and they thought: 'Maybe this is a war party'. They escaped to the shore and hid behind a log. Now canoes came up and they heard the noise of paddles and saw one canoe coming up to them. There were five men in the canoe and they said: 'What do you think? We wish to take you along. We are going up the river to make war on the people'. One of the young men said 'I have no arrows'. 'Arrows are in the canoe', they said. 'I will not go along. I might be killed. My relatives do not know where I have gone. But you', he said, turning to the other, 'may go with them'. So one of the young men went but the other returned home. And the warriors went on up the river to a town on the other side of Kalama. The people came down to the water and they began to fight and many were killed. But presently the young man heard one of the warriors say: 'Quick, let us go home; that Indian has been hit'. Now he thought: 'Oh, they are ghosts'. He did not feel sick but they said he had been shot. So the canoes went back to Egulac and the young man went ashore to his house and made a fire. And he told everybody and said: 'Behold I accompanied the ghosts and we went to fight. Many of our fellows were killed and many of those who attacked us were killed. They said I was hit and I did not feel sick'. He told it all and then he became quiet. When the sun rose he fell down. Something black came out of his mouth. His face became contorted. The people jumped up and cried. He was dead.

Frederic Bartlett (1886–1969)

When used with English participants, who were unfamiliar with its style and content, the story changed in certain characteristic ways (as noted below) as it was re-told.

- The story became noticeably *shorter*. Bartlett found that after six or seven reproductions, it shrank from 330 to 180 words.
- Despite becoming shorter, and details being omitted, the story became *more coherent*. No matter how distorted it became, it remained a story: the participants were interpreting the story as a whole, both listening to it and retelling it.
- It also became *more conventional*, retaining only those details which could be easily assimilated to the participants' shared past experiences and cultural backgrounds.
- It became *more clichéd* – any peculiar or individual interpretations tended to be dropped.

Replications of Bartlett's findings

Hunter (1964) used '*The War of the Ghosts*' and the serial reproduction method. He found similar changes to those originally reported by Bartlett. But the use of this folk tale has been criticised, because it's written in an unusual style, making it difficult for western participants to find connections between different parts of the story.

Another method used by Bartlett, *repeated reproduction*, involves the same participants recalling the story on different occasions. This produced similar results to those obtained with serial reproduction. Wynn & Logie (1998) used this alternative method, but instead of '*The War of the Ghosts*', they used a real-life event, namely first-year undergraduates' recollections of details of their first week at university. They were asked to recall this information in November, January, March and May (the students being unaware that this would happen).

Contrary to Bartlett's findings, Wynn and Logie found that the accuracy of the descriptions was maintained across the different intervals and regardless of the number of repeated recalls. This suggests that memories for distinctive events can be relatively resistant to change over time, even when repeatedly reproduced.

CROSS-CULTURAL STUDY 21.1

Remembering as a cultural activity

- An important implication of Bartlett's work is that memory is a *social phenomenon* that cannot be studied as a 'pure' process. Because he emphasised the influence of previous knowledge and background experience, Bartlett found that remembering is integrally related to the social and cultural contexts in which it's practised.
- When members of western and non-western cultures are compared on tasks devised in psychology laboratories, such as free-recalling lists of unrelated words, the former do better; this seems to reflect the meaninglessness of such tasks for the latter (see Chapter 17).
- According to Mistry & Rogoff (1994), culture and memory are enmeshed skills, and 'remembering' is an activity with goals whose function is determined by the social and cultural contexts in which it takes place.
- This helps to explain the phenomenal memory for lines of descent and history of Itamul elders in New Guinea, needed to resolve disputes over claims to property by conflicting clans.
- Bartlett himself described the prodigious ability of Swazi herdsmen to recall individual characteristics of their cattle. But since Swazi culture revolves around the possession and care of cattle, this ability isn't so surprising.
- What these examples show is that remembering is a means of achieving a culturally important goal, rather than the goal itself (Mistry & Rogoff, 1994).

Schemas and reconstructive memory

Bartlett concluded from his findings that *interpretation* plays a major role in the remembering of stories and past events. Learning and remembering are both active processes involving 'effort after meaning'; that is, trying to make the past more logical, coherent and generally 'sensible'. This involves making inferences or deductions about what could or should have happened. We reconstruct the past by trying to fit it into our existing understanding of the world. Unlike a computer's memory, where the output exactly matches the input, human memory is an 'imaginative reconstruction' of experience (see Chapter 20, page 352).

Bartlett called this existing understanding of the world a *schema*. Schemas (or schemata):

- provide us with ready-made expectations, which help to interpret the flow of information reaching the senses
- help to make the world more predictable
- allow us to 'fill in the gaps' when our memories are incomplete
- can produce significant distortions in memory processes, because they have a powerful effect on the way in which memories for events are encoded; this happens when new information conflicts with existing schemas (or schemata).

For example, Allport & Postman (1947) showed white participants a picture of two men evidently engaged in an argument (see Figure 21.1).

After looking briefly at the picture, participants were asked to describe the scene to someone who hadn't seen it. This person was then required to describe the scene to another person, and so on. As this happened, details changed. The most significant change was that the cut-throat razor was reported as being held by the black man.

Figure 21.1 The stimulus material used by Allport & Postman (1947). The two men are engaged in an argument. The better-dressed man is black, and the white man has a cut-throat razor in his hand

> *ASK YOURSELF...*
> - What method was involved in Allport and Postman's experiment?
> - What can you infer about the schema that the participants were using, which helps account for the distortion that took place?
> - If the participants had been black, would you expect a similar distortion to have taken place?
> - Are these results consistent with Bartlett's theory of reconstructive memory? Explain your answer.

Allport and Postman used serial reproduction, as Bartlett had done in his study using '*The War of the Ghosts*'. Presumably, the white participants used a schema which included the belief that black men are prone to violence. Black participants would be expected to have a rather different schema of black men, making them less likely to distort the details in the picture. Allport and Postman's findings are consistent with Bartlett's theory of reconstructive memory.

EYEWITNESS TESTIMONY (EWT)

Loftus's research

Bartlett's view of memory as reconstructive is also taken by Loftus, who has investigated it mainly in relation to *eyewitness testimony* (EWT). Loftus argues that the evidence given by witnesses in court cases is highly unreliable, and this is explained largely by the kind of misleading questions that witnesses are asked. Lawyers are skilled in asking such questions deliberately, as are the police when interrogating suspects and witnesses to a crime or accident.

Loftus has tried to answer the following questions:

- Is EWT influenced by people's tendency to reconstruct their memories of events to fit their schemas?
- Can subtle differences in the wording of a question cause witnesses to remember events differently?
- Can witnesses be misled into 'remembering' things that didn't actually occur?

How useful are identification parades?

The Devlin Committee (see *Introduction and overview*) recommended that the trial judge be required to instruct the jury that it isn't safe to convict on a single eyewitness's testimony alone, except in exceptional circumstances (such as where the witness is a close friend or relative of the accused, or where there's substantial corroborative evidence).

This recommendation is underlined by a famous case of misidentification involving an Australian psychologist. The psychologist in question had appeared in a TV discussion on EWT, and was later picked out in an identity parade by a very distraught woman who claimed that he'd raped her. The rape had in fact occurred while the victim was watching the psychologist on TV. She correctly recognised his face, but not the circumstances!

EWT, episodic memory (EM) and SM

According to Fiske & Taylor (1991), it's easy to see how a witness could confuse the mention of something in a question with its actual presence at the scene of the crime, if that something is commonly found in such situations. For example, a 'leading' question might refer to things that weren't actually present at the scene of the crime (stored in EM), but which might well have been (based on our schemas and stereotyped beliefs about the world stored in SM).

Similarly, a witness who examines a preliminary identification parade may later remember having seen one of the suspects before, but fail to distinguish between the identification parade and the scene of the crime – the innocent suspect may be misidentified as the criminal because s/he is *familiar.* This can be taken one stage further back. Several studies have shown that when witnesses view a line-up after having looked at mugshots, they're more likely to identify one of those depicted (regardless of whether that person actually committed the crime) than people who aren't shown the mugshot (Memon & Wright, 1999).

These (and the case of the Australian psychologist above) are examples of *source confusion* (or *source misattribution:* see page 363) – you recognise someone, but you're mistaken about where you know them from. This can have very serious consequences for the person who is misidentified!

Is a mistaken eyewitness better than none?

Using a fictitious case, Loftus (1974) asked students to judge the guilt or innocence of a man accused of robbing a grocer's and murdering the owner and his five-year-old granddaughter. On the evidence presented, only nine of the 50 students considered the man to be guilty. Other students were presented with the same case, but were also told that one of the shop assistants had testified that the accused was the man who had committed the crimes. Thirty-six of these 50 students judged him to be guilty.

A third group of 50 students was presented with the original evidence and the assistant's EWT. However, they were also told that the defence lawyer had discredited the assistant: he was shortsighted, hadn't been wearing his glasses when the crime occurred, and so couldn't possibly have seen the accused's face from where he was standing at the time.

> *ASK YOURSELF...*
> - How many students in the third group do you think judged the accused to be guilty?
> - Explain your answer and say what this tells us about the importance of EWT.

In fact, 34 out of 50 thought he was guilty! So, a mistaken witness does seem to be 'better' than no witness. Moreover, confident witnesses are more likely to be seen as credible (i.e. accurate) compared with anxious witnesses, even though actual accuracy may not differ (Nolan & Markham, 1998).

Factors influencing EWT

- **Race:** Errors are more likely to occur when the suspect and witness are racially different (Brigham & Malpass, 1985). So, we're much better at recognising members of our own racial groups than members of other racial groups. This is reflected in the comment that 'They all look the same to me' when referring to members of different races (*the illusion of outgroup homogeneity:* see Chapter 22, page 388).
- **Clothing:** Witnesses pay more attention to a suspect's clothing than to more stable characteristics, such as height and facial features. It seems that criminals are aware of this, since they change what they wear prior to appearing in a line-up (Brigham & Malpass, 1985).
- **Social influence:** One source of social influence (see Chapter 26) is contact and exchange of information among witnesses. For example, Memon & Wright (1999) describe a study in which participants were asked in pairs whether they'd seen several cars in a previous phase of the study. When responding second, people were influenced by the first person's answers. If the first person said s/he did see the car previously, the second person was more likely to say the same, irrespective of whether the car really was previously seen.
- **Violence:** Does extreme emotion brand the experience indelibly on the victim's memory, or does it reduce the capacity for recollection, perhaps through repression (Baddeley, 1999: see below)? The usual method for investigating this is to expose participants to a film or a staged incident, in which some crucial violent event occurs (such as the apparent shooting of a child). Overall, the evidence suggests that memory for violent events is stronger than for a neutral event, but that recollection of associated detail is poorer. For example, there appears to be a 'weapons focus', whereby victims may concentrate their attention on the weapon itself, rather than the attacker's appearance. So:

> ... fear may put a crucial feature of a situation into sharp focus, but may reduce the reliability of the witness's account of peripheral features. (Baddeley, 1999)

- **Misleading questions and suggestibility:** It seems that both adults and children are subject to reconstructive errors in recall, particularly when presented with misleading information. In other words, a witness can be highly suggestible. Different types of misleading question include:
  1. *leading questions,* as illustrated by Loftus & Palmer's (1974) experiment (see Key Study 21.1)
  2. questions which introduce *after-the-fact information,* as illustrated by Loftus (1975: see Key Study 21.2).

> **KEY STUDY 21.1 The effect of leading questions (Loftus & Palmer, 1974)**
> - Loftus and Palmer tested the effect of changing single words in certain critical questions on the judgement of speed.
> - Participants were shown a 30-second videotape of two cars colliding, and were then asked several questions about the collision.
> - One group was asked 'About how fast were the cars going when they *hit*?' For others, the word 'hit' was replaced by 'smashed', 'collided', 'bumped' or 'contacted'.
> - These words have very different connotations regarding the speed and force of impact, and this was reflected in the judgements given.
> - Those who heard the word 'hit' produced an average speed estimate of 34.0 mph. For 'smashed', 'collided', 'bumped' and 'contacted', the average estimates were 40.8, 39.3, 38.1 and 31.8 mph respectively (see Figure 21.2).

What do leading questions actually do?

Loftus and Palmer wanted to know if memory for events actually *changes* as a result of misleading questions, or whether the existing memory is merely *supplemented.*

Memory as reconstruction implies that memory itself is transformed at the point of retrieval, so that what was originally encoded changes when it's recalled.

To test this, Loftus & Palmer's (1974) study included a follow-up experiment. A week after the original experiment, those participants who'd heard the word 'smashed' or 'hit' were asked further questions, one of which was whether they remembered seeing any broken glass (even though there was none in the film). If 'smashed' really had influenced participants' memory of the accident as being more serious than it was, then they might also 'remember' details they didn't actually see, but which are consistent with an accident occurring at high speed (such as broken glass).

Of the 50 'smashed' participants, 16 (32 per cent) reported seeing broken glass. Only seven (14 per cent) of the 50 'hit' participants did so. These results appear to support the memory-as-reconstruction explanation.

Similarly, Loftus & Zanni (1975) showed participants a short film of a car accident, after which they answered questions about what they'd witnessed. Some were asked if they'd seen *a* broken headlight, while others were asked if they'd seen *the* broken headlight. Those asked about *the* headlight were far more likely to say 'yes' than those asked about a headlight.

Figure 21.2 Assessments of speeds of crashing vehicles can be influenced by the verb used to describe the impact. While (a) represents 'two cars hitting', (b) represents 'two cars smashing'. Which word is used in a question can influence people's estimates of how fast the cars were travelling at the time of impact

KEY STUDY 21.2 The effect of 'after-the-event' information (Loftus, 1975)

- Participants watched a short film of a car travelling through the countryside. They were all asked the same ten questions about the film, except for one critical question.
  - (a) Group A was asked 'How fast was the white sports car going when it passed the 'Stop' sign while travelling along the country road?' (There *was* a 'Stop' sign in the film.)
  - (b) Group B was asked 'How fast was the white sports car going when it passed the barn while travelling along the country road?' (There was *no* barn.)
- 'The' barn implies that there actually was a barn in the film, which is what makes it misleading.
- A week later, all the participants were asked ten new questions about the film. The final question was 'Did you see a barn?' Of group A participants, only 2.7 per cent said 'yes', while 17.3 per cent of group B participants said 'yes'.

Memory as reconstruction sees questions that provide misleading new information about an event (as with leading questions) becoming integrated with how the event is already represented in memory.

Suggestibility and source misattribution

As the Loftus studies show, witnesses may come to believe that they actually remember seeing items in an event that in fact have been (falsely) suggested to them. Currently, the most popular explanation for suggestibility effects is *source misattribution*. Witnesses are confusing information obtained outside the context of the witnessed event (*post-event information*) with the witnessed event itself (Memon & Wright, 1999). Memories of details from various sources can be combined with memories of that event (*memory blending*).

An evaluation of Loftus's research

While the evidence described above suggests that eyewitnesses are unreliable, are they really as unreliable as Loftus believes?

- Bekerian & Bowers (1983) have argued that Loftus questions her witnesses in a rather unstructured way. If questions followed the order of events in strict sequence, then witnesses weren't influenced by the biasing effect of subsequent questions. Despite some failures to replicate these findings (e.g. McCloskey & Zaragoza, 1985), an important practical consequence of Bekerian and Bower's research is the *cognitive interview* (see Box 21.2).

- Contrary to the memory-as-reconstruction interpretation, Baddeley (1995) believes that 'the Loftus effect is not due to destruction of the memory trace but is due to interfering with its retrieval' (see Chapter 17).
- Stephenson (1988) points out that the bulk of the work on EWT has been carried out in laboratories, and has concentrated on eyewitness identification of people seen under fairly non-threatening conditions, or even people seen on films. In sharp contrast were the participants of a study by Yuille & Cutshall (1986): see Case Study 21.1.
- Loftus herself acknowledges that when misleading information is 'blatantly incorrect', it has no effects on a witness's memory. For example, Loftus (1979) showed participants colour slides of a man stealing a red purse from a woman's bag. 98 per cent correctly identified the purse's colour, and when they read a description of the event which referred to a 'brown purse', all but 2 per cent continued to remember it as red. This suggests that our memory for obviously important information accurately perceived at the time isn't easily distorted, as shown by Yuille & Cutshall's (1986) study.
- According to Cohen (1993), people are more likely to be misled if:
  (a) the false information they're given concerns insignificant details that aren't central to the main event
  (b) the false information is given after a delay (when the memory of the event has had time to fade)
  (c) they have no reason to distrust it.

CASE STUDY 21.1 Eyewitness memory of a crime (Yuille & Cutshall, 1986)

- The incident involved a shooting which occurred outside a gun shop in full view of several witnesses (in Vancouver, Canada).
- A thief had entered the gun shop, tied up the proprietor, and stolen some money and a number of guns. The store-owner freed himself, picked up a revolver and went outside to take the thief's licence number. But the thief hadn't yet entered his car, and in a face-to-face encounter on the street, separated by six feet, the thief fired two shots at the store-owner.
- After a slight pause the store-owner discharged all six shots from his revolver. The thief was killed, but the store-owner recovered from serious injury.
- Witnesses viewed the incident from various vantage points along the street, from adjacent buildings or from passing automobiles.
- Twenty-one of the witnesses were interviewed by the police shortly after the event, and 13 of them agreed to take part in a research interview four to five months later. In both sets of interviews (police and research), verbatim accounts of the incident were obtained and follow-up questions were asked in order to clarify points of detail. Also Yuille and Cutshall asked two misleading questions based on Loftus's 'a broken headlight'/'the broken headlight' technique.
- The sheer volume of accurate detail produced in both sets of interviews is truly impressive. The researchers obtained much more detail than did the police, because they were concerned with memory for details which had no immediate forensic value. Witnesses who were central to the event gave more details than did peripheral witnesses, but there was no overall difference in accuracy between the two groups.
- Significantly, the wording of the misleading questions had no effect, and those who were most deeply distressed by the incident were the most accurate of the witnesses.

The cognitive interview

An increasing number of police forces are using the *cognitive interview* (CI). Traditionally, police officers and lawyers have used the standard interview procedure, which involves a period of free recall about the event, followed by specific questions about details that emerge from the free recall. The CI draws on Tulving's research concerning the relationship between encoding and retrieval cues (see Chapter 17, pages 301–302).

Box 21.2 The cognitive interview (Geiselman *et al.*, 1985)

- **Reinstating the context:** The interviewer and interviewee try to recreate the context in which the incident occurred (the surroundings, such as the temperature, smells, sounds, the witness's feelings) before any attempt is made to recall the events themselves.
- **Reporting the event:** The interviewee is asked to report absolutely everything, regardless of how unimportant/irrelevant it may seem.
- **Recalling the event in several orders:** This includes reporting the event in reverse order.
- **Reporting the event from multiple perspectives:** The interviewee is asked to recall the event from, say, the perspective of the cashier in the case of a bank robbery.

The first two 'stages' are based on the concept of *encoding specificity,* that is, trying to provide maximum overlap between the context in which the crime was committed and the context in which the recall attempt is made. The second two try to capitalise on the idea that material can be retrieved using a number of different routes that may produce information about rather different aspects of the original event (Baddeley, 1999).

The initial test of the CI (Geiselman *et al.*, 1985) used a police training film of a violent crime. Participants were interviewed 48 hours later, using either the new CI, or the standard Los Angeles police interview, or hypnosis prior to being asked to recall the incident using the standard procedure. Although the three methods didn't differ in the amount of false information they produced, the standard interview produced the least overall amount of information (an average of 29.4 items). The CI produced the most (41.2 items).

A second experiment introduced misleading information during the interview: 'Was the guy with the green backpack nervous?' (it wasn't green). Those tested with the CI were the *least likely* to be misled by false information.

Fisher & Geiselman (1988) have continued to develop the CI, using hints obtained from watching 'good' and 'poor' interviewers. These include the greater use of *open-ended questions,* and attempts to fit the *order of questioning* to the witness's order of experience. This has increased accurate reporting from 40 to 60 per cent. Bekerian & Dennett (1993) reviewed 27 experiments comparing the effects of the CI with more standard techniques. The CI proved superior in all cases: on average, about 30 per cent more information is accurately reported, with false information being slightly less common.

Harrower (1998) maintains that the CI procedure may be particularly beneficial for those interviewing *child witnesses,* especially those who may have been the victims of physical or sexual abuse. However, the interviewer must be trained in assessing the linguistic and cognitive competence of each child interviewee, and adapt the interview accordingly.

ASK YOURSELF...

- Without looking back at the photograph on page 358 of two men involved in a violent incident, try to answer the following questions.
  1. What are the two men doing?
  2. In which hand is one of the men holding a knife?
  3. Are both men clean-shaven?
  4. Is there anyone else in the picture?
  5. How would you describe the man who isn't holding the knife?

Now look back at the photograph and check your answers.

Recognising faces

While the face isn't the only route to person identification, it's probably the most reliable (Bruce & Young, 1998). Laboratory experiments have shown that people are remarkably accurate at remembering briefly viewed, previously unfamiliar faces, typically scoring over 90 per cent correct when asked to decide which of a large set of faces were previously presented. But this may seem to be at odds with our sometimes embarrassing failure to recognise or identify faces in everyday life (e.g. Young *et al.*'s 1985 diary study). Bruce and Young suggest two main reasons for this discrepancy.

1. Laboratory experiments tend to test memory for identical pictures of faces, thereby confounding picture memory with true face memory. If memory for faces is tested with different pictures of the same face, accuracy drops dramatically (to 60 per cent: Bruce, 1982).
2. Recognition can be affected by changes in context between where the face was originally encountered and where memory for it is subsequently tested. Context is broadly defined to include expectations (consistent with reconstructive memory; see also Chapter 15), clothing, head shape and hairstyle. Most criminals disguise themselves in some way when committing a crime, which suggests their implicit understanding of the importance of context for later recognition. With familiar people, head shape/hairstyle become less dominant, and internal facial features become more important for recognition.

ASK YOURSELF...

- How could you account for this difference between familiar and unfamiliar faces?

Bill Clinton and Al Gore? Same face, different hair

Helping people to remember faces

Two major techniques used to probe witnesses' memory for faces are *reconstruction* and *identification.*

Reconstruction

Reconstruction involves producing, from the witness's description, an image of the criminal for circulation to other police forces or for the general public. Typically, the witness, with or without a trained operator, tries to construct a target face using a 'kit' of isolated facial features. Identification involves looking through photographs in an album of 'mug shots', or looking at a live 'line-up'/identity parade of potential offenders.

Performance using *Photofit* (and other similar 'kits') is generally very poor (e.g. Ellis *et al.*, 1978). One problem is that kits assume that a face can be deconstructed into its component parts. But facial identity may be more *holistic* than this, and relationships between features are at least as important as the features themselves (see Chapter 14, pages 236–238). *Photofit* offers only limited opportunities for the manipulation of such factors. There's a small number of 'cardinal' features, which people use regularly and reliably to describe and categorise faces (such as face shape, hair and age), but these are difficult to manipulate directly using *Photofit* (Bruce & Young, 1998).

The rapid development of powerful computer graphics at relatively low cost has made it possible to develop more interactive systems. *E-fit,* for example, although still based around a basic 'kit' of photographic face parts, provides much greater opportunity for the blending and elaboration of these parts. This results in much more realistic images (Bruce & Young, 1998). Currently, as a witness gives a description of, say, the eyes, the computer chooses the best set of eyes for you. The witness doesn't see the face until it's completed. But a modified 'jigsaw' *E-fit,* being pioneered by the UK Face Processing Research Group, allows the witness to watch the face being built up. But because it's important that the features are always seen as part of a face, a cartoon outline and features are used to replace those elements that haven't yet been described (Greenhaigh, 2000).

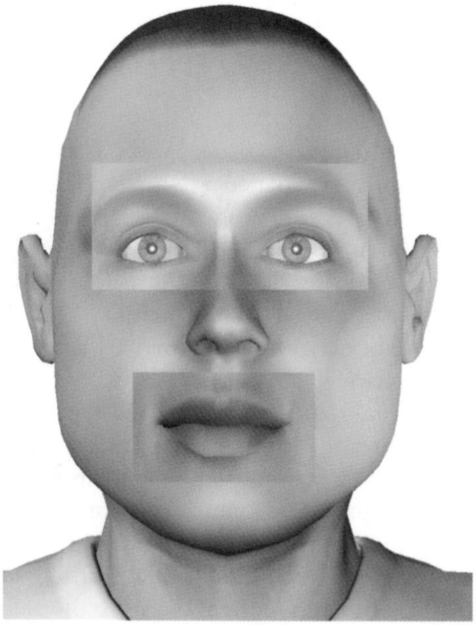

Figure 21.3 An E-fit face

Identification

It's essential that the other members of a line-up/ID parade (the non-suspects or 'distractors') aren't obviously different from the suspect. For example, in one extreme case, the suspect was known to be Asian, and the line-up included only one Asian (Baddeley, 1999)! More subtle problems include:

- showing a photograph of the accused to a witness before the line-up; this could cause false identification based on *source confusion* (see above); this should clearly be avoided (Baddeley, 1999)
- there's often an assumption (usually implicit, but occasionally explicit) that the line-up actually includes the criminal. This reinforces a bias towards making a positive identification: witnesses are already highly motivated to do so and know the police don't go the trouble of arranging a line-up unless they have a suspect (Baddeley, 1999; Bruce & Young, 1998).

Video-witness testimony: a special case of EWT

Now that closed-circuit television (CCTV) is commonplace in shops, banks and so on, there's an increased chance that an image of a criminal will be captured on videotape. This would seem to side-step neatly the problems with human face memory. Once a suspect has been apprehended (using some combination of eyewitness and other forensic evidence), the person's identity can be readily confirmed by comparison with the videotape. But things are rather more complicated than this (Bruce, 1998).

A violent crime caught on CCTV

Cameras may be set to scan large public areas, so that images obtained of any individual may be of very poor resolution. Bruce cites the example of a prosecution case based entirely on the evidence of a CCTV image, which showed a young black man robbing a building society. The defence used an expert witness, who helped get the evidence thrown out. Clearly, a CCTV image alone might prove very little about a suspect's precise identity.

Bruce has investigated face recognition and memory for over 25 years. She'd always assumed that people's difficulties in matching two different views, expressions, or lightings were due to major changes along these dimensions. Evidence now suggests that rather subtle pictorial differences are difficult for human vision to deal with. Even the more successful computer systems for face recognition have the same difficulties.

The quality of CCTV images can vary considerably:

- camera and lighting angles may provide only a poorly lit, messy image of the top or back of someone's head
- images may be blurred, and black-and-white images cast lots of shadows
- even when the image quality is reasonably high, judging different images as being of the same individual may be remarkably prone to error
- CCTV images may be most helpful in identifying criminals when the faces captured on tape are of someone known to a witness. People who are highly familiar are easily identified from CCTV images of a quality that would make identification of an unfamiliar face extremely difficult.

KEY STUDY 21.3 Make sure you know the offender (Burton *et al.*, 1999)

Bruce and her colleagues at Stirling and Glasgow Universities conducted two experiments, in which they manipulated familiarity.

- Male and female psychology lecturers were caught on security cameras at the entrance to the psychology department. This video footage was shown to both psychology and non-psychology students, and experienced police officers, who were then asked to indicate which of the people in a set of high-quality photographs they'd seen on tape.
- The psychology students made the most correct identifications, suggesting that previous familiarity with the target helps with recognition.
- The same video footage was used, but this time the head, body or gait was obscured. Participants performed quite poorly when the gait or body were obscured, but they did significantly worse when the head was obscured.
- Thus, the advantage of familiarity seems to be due to recognition of facial features, rather than body shape or how people walk. But unusual gait or body shape might produce different results.

Consistent with these findings are those of a study by Davies & Thasen (2000). When participants were asked to match unfamiliar faces seen on videotape to one of a series of 'mugshots', they found very low rates of correct identification, even when a close-up still of the target face was in constant view. Whether the video images were in colour or black and white made no difference.

ASK YOURSELF...

- According to Harrower (1998), research clearly shows that most people remember faces poorly and recall details not from memory, but in terms of what they believe criminals *should* look like. How can this finding be explained?

This is another example of how schemas are used to fill the gaps in memory. It represents another demonstration of reconstructive memory.

REPRESSION AND THE FALSE-MEMORY DEBATE

Motivated-forgetting theory (repression)

According to Freud (1901), forgetting is motivated, rather than the result of a failure to learn or other processes. Memories which are likely to induce guilt, embarrassment, shame or anxiety are actively, but unconsciously, pushed out of consciousness as a form of *ego defence* (see Chapters 12 and 42):

> The essence of repression lies simply in turning something away, and keeping it at a distance, from the conscious ... (Freud, 1915)

Unconscious or repressed memories are exceedingly difficult to retrieve (they're *inaccessible*) but remain *available* ('in storage': see Chapter 17). They continue to exert a great influence over us, even though we have no awareness of them.

Evidence for repression

Clinical evidence

As far as clinical evidence is concerned, it's widely accepted that repression plays a crucial role in different types of *psychogenic* (or *functional*) amnesia such as fugue and multiple personality disorder (see Gross, 2003a). These disorders involve a loss of memory associated with a traumatic experience (as opposed to brain injury or surgery). A relatively common form of psychogenic amnesia is *event-specific amnesia:* loss of memory for a fairly specific period of time. For instance, some violent criminals claim they cannot remember carrying out their crimes (see Chapter 46). Even when we have ruled out both malingering and the effects of intoxication at the time the crime was committed, there's still a substantial number of criminals whose memories of their crimes seem to have been repressed (Parkin, 1993). This is especially likely when murder victims are close relatives or lovers of the murderer killed in a crime of passion (Taylor & Kopelman, 1984).

Ian Brady (convicted along with Myra Hindley of the so-called Moors Murders) repressed memories of his hideous crimes for many years before finally remembering where he'd buried his victims (Parkin, 2000). However, in a study of children who'd seen a parent killed, none showed evidence of repression; on the contrary, the experience tended to be recalled all too frequently (Baddeley, 1999). This, and the observation that psychogenic amnesia can disappear as suddenly as it appeared, are difficult for motivated-forgetting theory to explain.

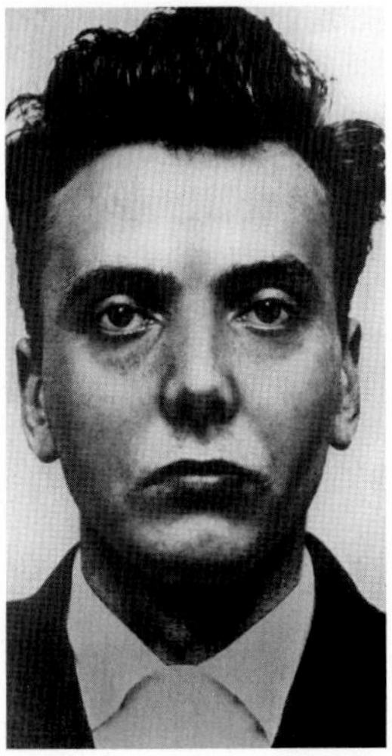

Ian Brady (born 1938)

Parkin (1993) also cites evidence that repressive mechanisms may play a beneficial role in enabling people with *post-traumatic stress disorder* to adjust (see Chapters 12 and 44). For example, survivors of the Holocaust judged to be better adjusted were significantly less able to recall their dreams when woken from REM sleep (see Chapter 7) than less well-adjusted survivors (Kaminer & Lavie, 1991).

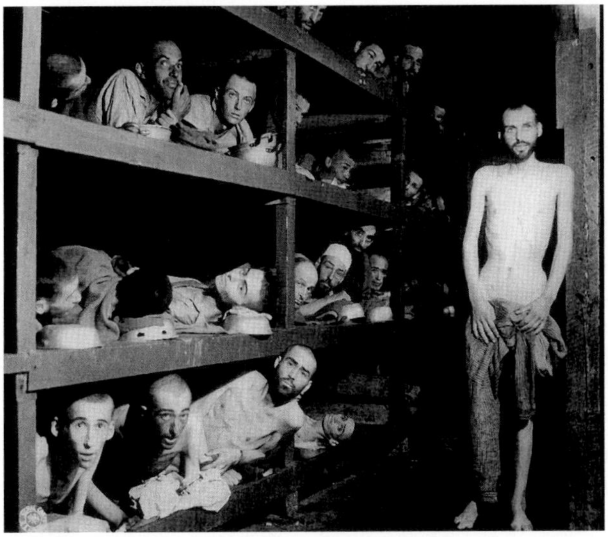

For those who endured them, are these horrors best forgotten?

However, 'repression' doesn't necessarily imply a strictly Freudian interpretation. When the concept is considered more broadly than Freud intended, that is, in the general sense that our memory systems can in some way block particular forms of memory, it deserves to be taken seriously (Parkin, 2000). This is also the view taken by the British Psychological Survey on 'Recovered Memories' (BPS, 1995: see below). Similarly, although traumatic experiences can undoubtedly produce memory disturbances, there's greater doubt as to whether Freud's explanation is the best one (Anderson, 1995a).

Experimental evidence

KEY STUDY 21.4 Testing Freud's repression hypothesis (Levinger & Clark, 1961)

- Levinger and Clark looked at the retention of associations to negatively charged words (such as 'quarrel', 'angry', 'fear') compared with those for neutral words (such as 'window', 'cow', 'tree').
- When participants were asked to give immediate free associations to the words (to say exactly what came into their minds), it took them longer to respond to the emotional words. These words also produced higher galvanic skin responses (GSR – a measure of emotional arousal).
- Immediately after the word association tests had been completed, participants were given the cue words again and asked to try to recall their associations.
- They had particular trouble remembering the associations to the emotionally charged words.
- This is exactly what Freud's repression hypothesis predicted, and for some years the study stood as the best experimental demonstration of repression (Parkin, 1993).

However, other studies show that, while highly arousing words tend to be poorly recalled when tested immediately, the effect *reverses* after a delay (Eysenck & Wilson, 1973). If the words are being repressed, this shouldn't happen (they should stay repressed), suggesting that *arousal* was the crucial factor.

ASK YOURSELF...

- If you were to repeat the Levinger and Clark experiment, what change would you introduce in order to test the 'arousal hypothesis'?

Parkin *et al.* (1982) replicated the original study, but added a *delayed recall* condition: participants were asked to recall their associations seven days after the original test. The results supported Eysenck and Wilson's interpretation – higher arousal levels inhibit immediate recall but increase longer-term recall.

In a later replication, Bradley & Baddeley (1990) used an immediate and a 28-day delayed condition. They found clear support for the arousal hypothesis. But later research hasn't always supported the arousal interpretation, and the question of emotional inhibition remains open (Parkin, 1993).

Recovered memories and the false-memory debate

As noted in the *Introduction and overview*, the False Memory Syndrome Foundation (in the USA) and the British False Memory Society (BFMS) were founded in the early 1990s, largely by parents accused by their grown-up children of having sexually abused them when they were children. The accusing children discovered repressed memories of child sexual abuse (CSA) during the course of psychotherapy; hence, from their and their therapists' perspectives, these are *recovered memories* (RMs).

However, from the perspective of the accused parents, these are *false memories* (FMs), implanted by therapists into the minds of their emotionally vulnerable patients/clients. These unethical, unscrupulous therapists are, in turn, accused by parents of practising *recovered-memory therapy,* which induces *false-memory syndrome* (FMS).

This brief account of the false-memory debate raises several, interrelated issues, spanning the psychology of memory and forgetting, the nature of psychotherapy (in particular, Freudian psychoanalysis), and the ethics of psychotherapy in general. When children sue their parents over alleged CSA, the family is inevitably torn apart and individual lives can be ruined. Hence, the need for support groups such as the BFMS. But the false memory debate has also caused division amongst psychologists, as well as between psychologists and psychiatrists. The key questions that we'll concentrate on in the remainder of this chapter are: do RMs exist, do FMs exist and, if so, how might they be created?

Do recovered memories exist?

The answer to this question depends very largely on how the concept of repression is understood. If these memories have been repressed, and are now retrieved from the unconscious during the course of therapy, then there must first be sound evidence for the existence of repression. This is the process which is supposed to keep recollections of the CSA hidden from the victim in the first place, until many years later, as an adult in therapy, the unconscious is 'unlocked'.

When discussing repression above, we saw that the strongest evidence is clinical, but that this is far from conclusive. We also need to take a closer look at Freud's view of memory.

Box 21.3 Freud and screen memories

- According to Mollon (2000), it's sometimes asserted that Freud believed that the events of a person's life are all recorded accurately somewhere in the mind, like video recordings. They're supposedly preserved in their original form, available but made inaccessible by repression.
- However, in a paper on *Screen Memories* (1899), Freud argued that memories, especially of events of long ago, may be constructed like dreams. A 'screen memory' is one that's apparently emotionally insignificant, but is actually a substitute for a more troubling memory with which it's become associated. But he argued that the distinction between screen memories and other memories from childhood is unclear:

> It may indeed be *questioned whether we have any memories at all from our childhood: memories relating to our childhood may be all that we possess. Our childhood memories show us our earliest years not as they were but as they appeared at the later periods when the memories were aroused. In these periods of arousal, the childhood memories did not, as people are accustomed to say, emerge; they were found at that time. And a number of motives, with no concern for historical accuracy, had a part in forming them, as well as in the selection of the* memories themselves. (Freud, 1899)

- Thus, Freud argued that memories of childhood may not be what they seem. The subjective sense of remembering doesn't mean that the memory is literally true. Memories are like dreams or works of fiction, constructed out of psychodynamic conflict, serving wish-fulfilment and self-deception (see Chapter 45). True memories of childhood may simply be unobtainable. Our apparent memories may be fabrications created later (Mollon, 2000).

If Freud is right, then RMs can no longer be memories of actual CSA, but phantasies of abuse. This reflects Freud's rejection of the *seduction theory* in favour of the Oedipal theory (see Chapter 35). Essentially, these correspond to actual abuse and phantasised abuse respectively as causes of adult neurosis. But, rightly or wrongly:

> ... that adult emotional disorders originate from repression of memories of experiences in early childhood which can be 'uncovered' by psychoanalysis ... [is] ... part and parcel of Freud's heritage. ... [it is an] essential element ... in the recovered memory therapist's armoury. (Esterson, 2000: personal communication)

Freud appears to be in a no-win situation. Esterson is claiming that Freud's theory of repression and his therapeutic methods are the basic tools of RM therapists, which makes Freud the arch-enemy of accused parents and the BFMS. But if it's pointed out that RM therapists have misunderstood Freud's theory of repression and the nature of childhood memories, this also seems to play into the hands of Freud's accusers. In other words, if memories are essentially *constructed,* rather than 'discovered' or 'recovered' ('unearthed' to use an archaeological analogy which Freud himself used), it becomes easier to understand how FMS occurs: vulnerable patients can easily be 'persuaded' that a constructed memory (a phantasy that CSA took place) is, in fact, an objectively true, historically verifiable event (the CSA actually happened).

In defence of Freud, Ofshe (in Jaroff, 1993) contends that RM therapists have invented a mental mechanism ('robust' repression) that supposedly causes a child's awareness of sexual abuse to be driven entirely from consciousness. There's no limit to the number of traumatic events that can be repressed, or to the length of time over which the series of events can occur.

According to Loftus (in Jaroff, 1993):

> If repression is the avoidance in your conscious awareness of unpleasant experiences that come back to you, yes, I believe in repression. But if it is a blocking out of an endless stream of traumas that occur over and over that leave a person with absolutely no awareness that these things happen ... and re-emerge decades later in some reliable form, I don't see any evidence for it. It flies in the face of everything we know about memory.

Many practising psychotherapists would agree with Loftus. A report published in the British Journal of Psychiatry (Brandon *et al.*, 1998) distinguishes between (a) CSA that's reported in childhood or kept secret although unforgotten, and (b) RMs of CSA, previously completely forgotten, that emerge in adulthood during therapy, usually in women in their thirties or forties. For some patients, RMs can escalate into FMS, in which a person's identity comes to centre around the:

> ... memory of a traumatic experience which is objectively false but in which the person strongly believes ... The individual avoids confrontation with any evidence that might challenge the memory ...

Brandon *et al.* summarise the findings of studies that have compared these two kinds of CSA:

- 90 per cent of RM patients are women, while in documented abuse cases the sex ratio is close to 50:50
- while only 3 per cent of RM accusations are made against stepfathers, they are much more likely to be involved in documented childhood cases
- while documented abuse usually involves older children or adolescents, RM cases recall abuse before the age of four, or even in infancy.

> *ASK YOURSELF...*
> - What conclusions can you draw from these reported differences about the validity of RMs?
> - Do you find it plausible that we can recall events that happened to us as infants?
> - What's your earliest childhood memory?

Do false memories exist?

According to the 1995 British Psychological Society (BPS) report on RMs, CSA which is alleged to have occurred before four years of age and which doesn't continue beyond that age, might not be retrievable in adulthood in a *narrative* form (*describable in words*). Very early memories are *implicit* rather than explicit, and are reflected in behaviour, outside conscious awareness. This means that we don't need the concept of repression in order to explain the 'forgetting' of childhood experiences, but it also implies that some RMs *could* be false (or at the very least inaccurate).

In a survey of 810 chartered psychologists, about 90 per cent believed that RMs are sometimes or usually 'essentially correct', a negligible number believed they're always correct, about 66 per cent believed they're possible, and over 14 per cent believed that one of their own clients has experienced FMs (BPS, 1995).

How might FMs be created?

The role of suggestion

According to Loftus (1997), false memories can be constructed by combining actual memories with the content of *suggestions* from others. This may result in source confusion (see above, page 363). Consistent with the role of suggestion is the fact that RMs began to be reported more frequently after the publication of *The Courage to Heal* (Bass & Davis, 1993) in the USA. This book claimed that virtually every behavioural or emotional disorder is caused by CSA, and could be cured by recovering repressed memories of that abuse. It was largely responsible for the RM 'movement' in psychotherapy. Many therapists began to introduce 'memory work', which usually involved the use of hypnosis, under the false assumption that hypnosis can unlock forgotten memories (Parkin, 2000).

While there have been many experimental studies of FMs (see Loftus, 1997), their generalisability to the therapeutic setting may be limited (Lyddy, 1999). But the findings of a recent study by Loftus and her colleagues have serious implications for therapeutic practice. They simulated the kinds of activities that go on in psychotherapy, and examined how they affected a client's autobiographical memory (AM).

> **KEY STUDY 21.5 Changing beliefs and memories through dream interpretation (Mazzoni *et al.*, 1999)**
> - Participants were selected from a sample who completed a life events inventory (LEI) and reported not having experienced specific important childhood events (such as being bullied or lost in a crowd).
> - Two weeks following the initial LEI, those in the experimental group completed what they thought was an unrelated dream survey. In a 30-minute session, they received information about the content of their reported dreams that suggested they'd either been bullied or lost before age three. Their attitudes towards dream interpretation were also probed.
> - Controls received no such suggestion, but completed unrelated filler tasks or participated in a non-suggestive dream session.

- Two weeks later, participants completed another LEI. They were all fully debriefed, and a final sub-set of dream participants completed a questionnaire stating their post-experimental beliefs about their memories.
- The mean LEI change showed that half of the experimental group participants were now confident that the critical event had occurred. Some also produced concrete, specific memories of the events, and denied a link between the dream and childhood event sessions.
- In addition, a strong prior belief in the value of dream interpretation was associated with increased confidence in the target event. No such changes occurred in the controls.

The role of imagination

A survey of psychotherapists in the USA and UK (Poole *et al.*, 1995) found that over 20 per cent reported using instructions to give free rein to imagination as a memory recovery technique with patients who couldn't explicitly remember childhood abuse. Loftus and her colleagues asked what effect such imaginative activity would have with people who hadn't had the experience in the first place.

Garry *et al.* (1996) found that a one-minute period of imagination (regarding childhood incidents such as 'breaking a window with your hand') led a significant minority of participants to claim the event was more likely to have occurred, compared with controls who weren't asked to imagine the incident. (The experimental participants had previously said the incident was unlikely to have occurred.)

This demonstrates what Loftus (2001) calls *imagination inflation,* 'the phenomenon that imagining an event increases subjective confidence that the event actually happened'. Other investigators have replicated the basic finding and have helped to answer some key questions, such as those listed below.

- How does imagination inflation work?
- Does imagination inflation produce false beliefs, or does it merely act as a retrieval cue to dredge up true beliefs?
- Does imagination inflation change a person's beliefs about the past, or does it act to produce specific pseudo-memories?
- Are particular kinds of individuals particularly susceptible to imagination inflation?

Based on a review of relevant research, Loftus (2001) maintains that:

> ... imagination can influence memory for a complex event that occurred only a few minutes before the imagination activity. In less time than it takes to make an omelette, people can be led to report that they witnessed events that would have constituted criminal activity in real life.

And again:

> ... Imagination supplies pieces of detail. Subsequent repetition of that detail (overtly or covertly) can turn those pieces into autobiographical memory facts.

CONCLUSIONS

The fact that FMs can be created doesn't mean that all RMs are false (Loftus, 1997). The BPS has published a draft set of new guidelines for psychologists working with clients in contexts in which issues related to RMs may arise. The preamble states that:

> ... there can be no doubt for psychologists of the existence of ... (CSA) as a serious social and individual problem with long-lasting effects. In addition, there can be little doubt that at least some recovered memories of CSA are recollections of historical events. However, there is a genuine cause for concern that some interventions may foster in clients false beliefs concerning CSA or can lead them to develop illusory memories. (Frankland & Cohen, 1999)

CHAPTER SUMMARY

- **Schema theory** sees schemas as the 'units' of SM, rather than simple concepts. Our knowledge is stored in memory as simplified mental representations of objects and events, which we use to interpret new experiences. One influential form of schema theory is the notion of **scripts**.
- Bartlett introduced the concept of **schema** to help explain how we remember **meaningful material**, such as stories. Memory isn't a 'pure' process that can be studied outside the **social/cultural contexts** in which it takes place.
- Bartlett used **serial reproduction** to study **reconstructive memory**, which uses schemas (schemata) to interpret new information. While schemas help to make the world more **predictable**, they can also **distort** our memories.
- Loftus has applied Bartlett's view of memory as reconstructive to the study of **eyewitness testimony** (EWT). The Devlin Committee recommended that convictions shouldn't be based on a single EWT alone (except in exceptional circumstances).
- Source **confusion/misattribution** can account for why suspects may be mistakenly selected from identification parades. EWT appears to be a persuasive source of evidence, even if the witness is discredited by the defence lawyer.
- **Misleading questions** can take the form of either **leading questions** or those which introduce **after-the-fact information**. Both types can induce **reconstructive errors**.
- Loftus believes that leading questions actually **change** the memory for events, rather than merely **supplementing** the existing memory. But the influence of

misleading questions may be reduced if witnesses are interviewed in a structured way (as in the **cognitive interview**), and the 'Loftus effect' may relate to the **retrieval** of the original memory.

- Blatantly incorrect information has no effect on EWT. People are more likely to be misled if the false information is insignificant, presented after a delay, and believable.
- The use of CCTV hasn't removed the problem of misidentification of suspects. Both humans and computer systems have difficulty dealing with subtle pictorial differences, and the quality of CCTV images can vary considerably. Highly **familiar** faces are identified most reliably.
- According to Freud's **motivated-forgetting** theory, unacceptable memories are made inaccessible through **repression**.
- While cases of **psychogenic amnesia** are consistent with Freud's theory, a strictly Freudian interpretation may not be necessary, and experimental support for the repression hypothesis is inconclusive.
- There is currently great controversy over **recovered memories** (RMs) of CSA and **false-memory syndrome**. RM therapists are accused of implanting false memories of CSA into patients, while patients accuse their parents of the abuse.
- There is experimental evidence that implicates both **suggestions** from others (including therapists) and the use of **imagination** (often encouraged by therapists) in the creation of FMs.
- Most psychologists and psychiatrists seem to accept the **possibility** of FMs, but this doesn't mean that all RMs of CSA are false.

Links with other topics/chapters

- The term 'schema' was borrowed from the neurologist Henry Head, who used it to represent a person's concept of the location of limbs and body: see Penfield's *homunculus* (Chapter 4).
- Schemas as the basic unit of *semantic memory* are much more widely accepted than the simple concepts involved in Collins and Loftus's *hierarchical network model* or Collins and Quillian's *spreading activation model* (Chapter 17).
- Schank and Abelson (1977) built their scripts into a *computer program* (SAM), which they claim is capable of answering questions about restaurants and understanding stories about restaurants (see Chapter 20).
- *Stereotypes* are a type of schema that help to explain Allport and Postman's findings, as well as other evidence relating to *selective remembering* (Chapter 22).
- While Loftus believes that misleading questions actually change the *memory trace* for events, Baddeley claims that they merely interfere with its *retrieval* (Chapter 17).
- The cognitive interview draws on Tulving's research into the relationship between *encoding* and *retrieval cues* (Chapter 17).
- *Photofit,* and other similar means of helping witnesses remember the face of a suspect, are based on the assumption that faces can be deconstructed into their *component parts.* But facial identity is much more *holistic* than this – it's the *relationship* between the features that's crucial (Chapter 14).
- Some of the *clinical* support for Freud's theory of repression comes from the *event-specific amnesia* of *violent criminals* for their crimes (Chapter 46).
- The FM debate raises fundamental questions regarding the very nature of our memories of childhood, as well as the nature of psychotherapy (Chapter 45). It also highlights some of the *ethical* issues relating to psychotherapy, including the *power* of the therapist and the *vulnerability* of the patient (Chapter 48).

FOUR

SOCIAL PSYCHOLOGY

22

SOCIAL PERCEPTION

INTRODUCTION AND OVERVIEW

Social (or person) perception refers to the perception of people (as opposed to physical objects: see Figure 22.1). The focus of this chapter is on *interpersonal perception* or *ordinary personology*, the process by which

> ordinary people come to know about each others' temporary states (such as emotions, intentions, and desires) and enduring dispositions (such as beliefs, traits, and abilities) from their actions ... (Gilbert, 1998)

This is included in what Fiske & Taylor (1991) call *social cognition* ('the process by which people think about and make sense of other people, themselves, and social situations'). According to Fiske (2004), social cognition builds on *attribution theory*, which is discussed in Chapter 23.

This area of research illustrates the unique nature of psychology as a whole. Psychologists are, effectively, studying 'themselves': they're part of the subject matter. In order to study human behaviour, they must utilise the very same processes they're trying to explain – in this case, perception.

The impression-formation research represents some of the earliest research conducted in social psychology, and it flourished during the 1950s, 1960s and 1970s. It was carried out largely from the perspective of *the perceiver* and looked at *central vs peripheral traits*, the *primacy–recency effect*, *implicit personality theory* and *stereotyping*. But we'll also discuss it from *the actor's* point of view (that is, the person being perceived), by considering some of the ways in which we try to influence others' impressions of us (*impression management/self-presentation*).

Since the 1980s, these traditional perspectives of person perception have largely been replaced by that of *social cognition*. This differs from the earlier research more in terms of the overall approach than the phenomena being investigated. The study of impression formation was very 'cognitive', in that it was concerned with the content of our thoughts about others. But social cognition reflected the *information-processing approach*, which has become psychology's dominant paradigm since the 1950s (see Chapters 2 and 3). This is concerned less with the content and more with the, often unconscious, automatic processes that underlie our (usually) conscious impressions of others.

PERCEIVING OBJECTS AND PERCEIVING PEOPLE

According to Fiske (2004), when we form impressions of other people it seems to happen *immediately* ('automatically'). But in fact we:

> ... search the social horizon unaware that [we] are using mental binoculars and that things are much farther away than they appear. All our experience ... is actually *mediated* or filtered through a psychological lens, our perceiving apparatus. Although we experience the world as if we take in a literal, unfiltered copy, each person passes reality through a different lens...

We're aware only of the *end product* of this process, which is our experience of the person. Part of Heider's (1958) common-sense psychology (equivalent to ordinary personology) is this direct experience of the world, which he contrasts with the *scientific* analysis of how people perceive it (see Chapter 23).

As we saw in Chapter 15, this applies equally to perception of objects. As Figure 22.1 shows, both social (or person) and object perception involve *selection, organisation* and *inference*. As applied to perceiving people, this might mean:

- focusing on people's physical appearance or on just one particular aspect of their behaviour (*selection*)
- trying to form a complete, coherent impression of a person (*organisation*)
- attributing characteristics to someone for which there's no direct or immediate evidence, as in stereotyping (*inference*).

ASK YOURSELF...
- In what ways does perceiving people differ from perceiving objects?

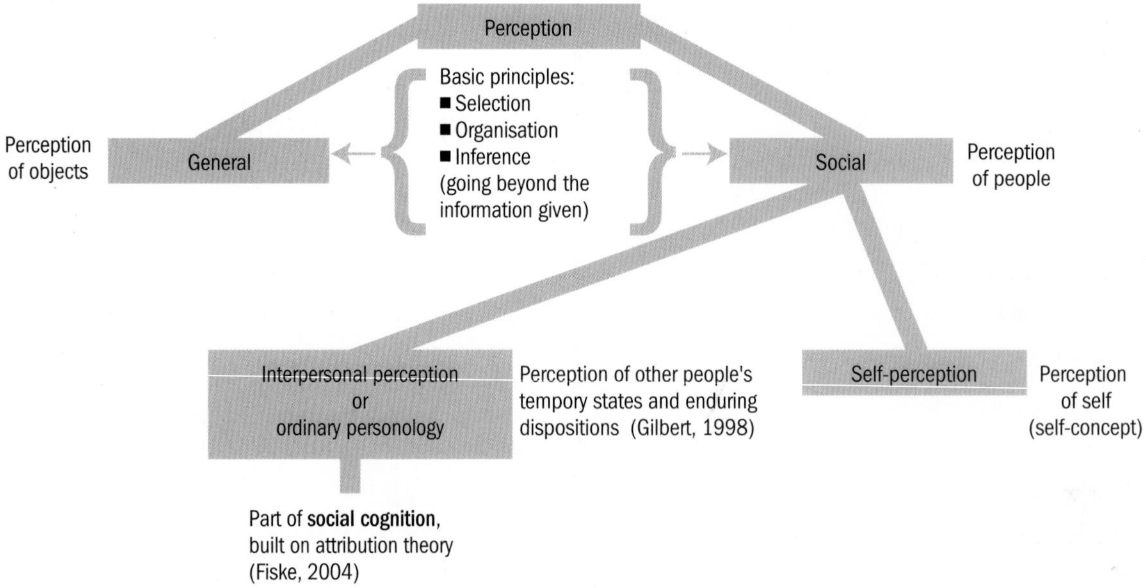

Figure 22.1 Relationship between general and social perception

- People *behave* (but objects don't). It's often behaviour which provides the data for making inferences about what people are like.
- People are *causal agents* – that is, they intend to act on their environment (Fiske & Taylor, 1991).
- People *interact* with other people (but they don't interact with objects or objects with each other). One person's behaviour can influence another's, so that behaviour is *mutually influential*.
- People anticipate being observed, and this is related to *self-presentation* (Fiske & Taylor, 1991: see below).
- People are generally more *changeable* than objects, and it's harder to verify the *accuracy* of observations about people (what they're 'really' like) (Fiske & Taylor, 1991: see Chapter 42).
- People *perceive* and *experience* (but objects cannot). One person's perception can influence the other's (especially his/her non-verbal behaviour), so that each person's perception of the other is at least partly a product of the other's perception of him/her. As Fiske & Taylor (1991) put it, social perception is *mutual perception*.

Phenomenological psychologists regard experience as the major source of 'data' (as opposed to behaviour) in social interaction (see Chapter 2). For example, Laing (1967) argued that the task of *social phenomenology* is to relate 'my experience of your behaviour to your experience of my behaviour'. In other words, it studies the relationship between experience and experience.

In his book *Knots* (1972), Laing dramatically (and often humorously) demonstrates the kinds of tangles that human relationships can get into. He does this in the form of short prose poems and diagrammatic poems. Here are two of the shorter and more straightforward examples.

1. Jack frightens Jill that he will leave her because he is frightened she will leave him.
2. Jack: 'You are a pain in the neck.
   To stop you giving me a pain in the neck
   I protect my neck by tightening my neck muscles,
   Which gives me the pain in the neck you are.'
   Jill: 'My head aches through trying to stop you giving me a headache.'

For Laing, 'knots' like these illustrate how 'my experience of another is a function of the other's experience of me', and vice versa.

ARE WE ALL PSYCHOLOGISTS?

> *ASK YOURSELF...*
> • In what ways can we all be considered psychologists?

As we noted earlier, everyone tries to 'figure people out', explain, predict and, very often, control others' behaviour, as part of their everyday living in a social world. These also happen to be the three traditionally accepted aims of science, including psychology (see Chapter 3). Gahagan (1984) defines interpersonal perception as 'the study of how the layperson uses theory and data in understanding people'. She breaks this definition down further into three main components:

1. The study of how people perceive others as *physical objects* and form impressions of their physical appearance, actions and the social categories to which they can be assigned. Often the first thing we notice about other people is some aspect of their appearance (such as their clothes or hair: see Chapter 21), and to this extent we're treating them as no more than 'things'. This is usually the first step involved in stereotyping, since we usually categorise people on the basis of physical appearance.
2. The study of how people perceive others as *psychological entities*. We form impressions of what kind of person they are, or we infer what their feelings, motives, personality traits, and so on might be (having already categorised them).
3. The study of the *lay person as a psychologist*. According to Nisbett & Ross (1980):

> We are all psychologists. In attempting to understand other people and ourselves, we are informal scientists who construct our own intuitive theories of human behaviour. In doing so, we face the same basic tasks as the formal scientist ...

'Intuitive theories' is another way of referring to 'implicit personality theories' (see below, pages 383–384).

Box 22.1 Some important differences between the psychologist and the lay person

- The lay person uses his/her theories for *pragmatic* (or *practical*) and immediate purposes, as opposed to gaining knowledge for its own sake.
- The lay person is rarely a disinterested observer of another's behaviour. We usually have a vested interest in what's going on, and are emotionally involved to some extent. The professional, as a scientist, has to be 'detached' and objective (although complete detachment is impossible: see Chapter 3).
- The lay person may be completely unaware of the reasoning s/he has followed when making inferences about others, and this reasoning may change from one situation to another. (This relates to the apparently automatic nature of our perceptions: see above). So, the lay person's 'theories' aren't spelled out or articulated (hence 'implicit' personality theories) and may not be consistent. But psychologists must try to be consistent and make their reasoning explicit, so that other psychologists can examine it.

(Based on Gahagan, 1984, 1991)

'I spy, with my little eye...'

THE PERSON AS THINKER

We've already noted that social psychology has always been strongly cognitive. People are thinking organisms (as opposed to emotional organisms or mindless automatons) who 'reside' between stimulus and response (a S–O–R model as opposed to an S–R model: see Chapters 2 and 11). We've also seen that social cognition represents a fairly recent way of looking at the thinking involved in our social interactions.

According to Fiske & Taylor (1991), there are four guises that the cognitive tradition has assumed. They see the thinker, respectively, as follows:

1. *Consistency seeker.* This refers to the principle of *cognitive consistency,* around which a number of theories of attitude change were built in the 1950s, the most influential being Festinger's *cognitive dissonance theory* (see Chapter 24). All the theories claimed that cognitive inconsistency produces a strong motivation to reduce the inconsistency.
2. *Naïve scientist.* Attribution theories are central to the view that, by trying to infer unobservable causes from observable behaviour, we all operate as amateur scientists (see above). This view was first proposed by Heider, the 'father of attribution theory', in 1958, but most attribution theories were formulated between the mid-1960s and early 1970s. They attempted to account for how people *ought* to attribute causes to behaviour under 'ideal' conditions (they're *normative*). They also took the 'naïve scientist' model too far, by seeing ordinary people as completely logical and systematic in their thinking (see Chapter 23).
3. *Cognitive miser.* Partly as a reaction against normative attribution theories, Nisbett and Ross (1980), Taylor (1981) and others introduced the term 'cognitive miser' to convey the idea that people are limited in their capacity to process information. They take shortcuts whenever they can, adopting strategies that simplify complex problems. This might lead them to draw biased and hence inaccurate conclusions (relative to what the normative theories predict), but seeing people as fallible thinkers represents a much more *descriptively accurate* account of how people actually think about behaviour. This is reflected in studies of error and bias in the attribution process, but also, more generally, in *heuristics* (Tversky & Kahneman, 1974) or 'rules of thumb' (see Chapter 20). Some examples are given in Table 22.1.
4. *Motivated tactician.* This refers to a development of the cognitive miser view, 'putting back' the motivational and emotional variables that were removed from the original cognitive consistency model. The motivated tactician is a:

> ... fully engaged thinker who has multiple cognitive strategies available and chooses among them based on goals, motives, and needs ... (Fiske & Taylor, 1991)

This corresponds to what Leyens & Codol (1988) call the 'cognitive–affective human being'.

Table 22.1 Some examples of heuristics used in uncertain or ambiguous situations

Availability: We judge the frequency/probability of an event according to the number of instances of it that can readily be brought to mind (remembered), and so which are cognitively available. For example, being able to think of several friends who are studying psychology in other colleges/universities leads you to believe that psychology is nationally one of the most popular subjects (which, in fact, it is!).
Representativeness: We decide whether a particular person/event is an example of a particular category. For example, if X has long hair, is wearing a skirt, has a high-pitched voice, and is called Jo, then there's a good chance X is female – but not necessarily! It's a safe bet, because there's a match between the person in front of you and your stereotyped belief (or prototype) of what females are like.
Simulation: Judging what's likely to be/have been the outcome of some event/incident, according to how easily different outcomes can be brought to mind. For example, we're often much more angry and upset by 'near misses' than when we 'missed it by a mile' – we can imagine 'If only I'd ...', or 'If only that man in front of me ...' much more easily in the former than in the latter.
Anchoring: When we have no information about a particular event, we may draw on information about a similar event as a reference point or 'anchor'. For example, if asked to estimate how many hours per week a fellow psychology student studies, in the absence of any specific knowledge you may base your answer on how many (or few!) hours you yourself put in.

Evaluation of social cognition: what's happened to the 'social'?

Critics of social cognition (e.g. Moscovici, 1982; Zajonc, 1989) have argued that it may have taken social psychology too far towards cognitive psychology, so that there may not be any 'social' in social cognition. Many of the cognitive processes and structures that have been proposed seem to be unaffected by social context: they seem to be taking place within an apparently isolated person who (just happens to be) thinking about social objects. But this isn't what's meant by 'social cognition'. Instead, we should be focusing on the link between people and the social object. This is truly social, because it's concerned with how cognition is socially constructed, shared and maintained by different members of a given social group, or even a whole society. To study 'social' cognition by studying what's going on inside the head of individuals is *reductionist* (see Chapter 49).

Stereotypes illustrate the shared nature of cognition, but perhaps the best example of how cultural knowledge may be constructed and transmitted is Moscovici's (1961, 1981) theory of *social representations* (see Chapter 2, pages 29–30).

Social representations (SRs)

According to Moscovici (1981), social representations are:

> ... a set of concepts, statements and explanations originating in daily life in the course of inter-individual communications. They are the equivalent, in our society, of the myths and belief systems in traditional societies; they might even be said to be the contemporary version of common sense ...

Characteristics of SRs

- Moscovici (1961) showed that people have simplified (and often mistaken) ideas about Freud's psychoanalytic theory. Many people have heard of Freud, just as they've heard of Einstein or Stephen Hawking, but most will have only the vaguest knowledge of their respective ideas and theories. This illustrates the *personification* of new and complex ideas, that is, linking them with a person.
- Complex ideas are also often converted into the form of visual images, as in a cartoon where the darker side of a person's nature is portrayed as a devil (in one balloon) and his/her conscience as an angel (in another). This kind of *figuration* is sometimes used to convey Freud's concepts of the id and superego respectively (with the person him/herself being the ego).
- Both personification and figuration are examples of *objectification,* that is, the need to make the abstract concrete (Moscovici & Hewstone, 1983). For example, thinking of God as 'a father' gives some sort of reality to a supernatural concept. We also need to *anchor* new and unfamiliar ideas into some pre-existing system (see Table 22.1).

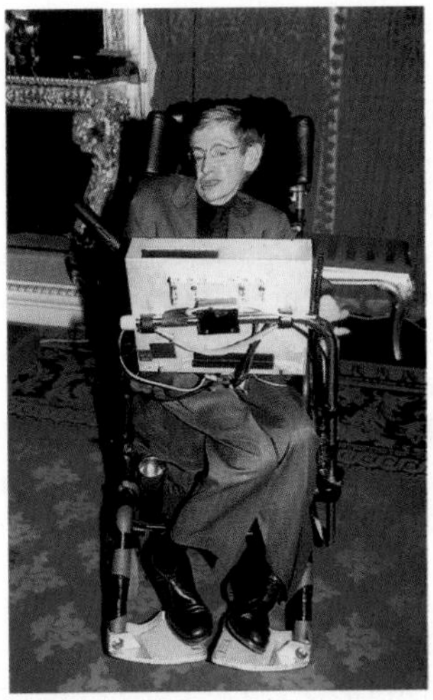

Stephen Hawking (born 1942). You don't have to be a cosmologist, physicist or mathematician to have heard of him, or even to have read one of his books

An example of anchoring is given in Jodelet's (1980) study of the re-housing of ex-psychiatric hospital patients in a French village. They were immediately labelled '*bredins*' (a local term for vagrants or 'half-wits'). Despite the term's almost total inaccuracy, it served to reduce something totally unknown and alien to something familiar.

Figure 22.2 A representation of Freud's concept of the id, ego, and superego, using figuration

The functions of SRs

- They facilitate communication between individuals and groups by establishing a shared 'social reality'.
- They also guide social action: individuals will interpret their own and others' behaviour in the light of this shared knowledge.

- Through socialisation, shared SRs are impressed on the child, infiltrating to the 'core of the personality', and imposing limits to perceptions and attitudes (Moscovici & Hewstone, 1983).
- In a way, the study of SRs is the study of the transformation from knowledge to common sense (Moscovici & Hewstone, 1983) or 'popular consciousness', and the theory of SRs 'explains how the strange and the unfamiliar become, in time, the familiar' (Farr & Moscovici, 1984). It's the study of how SRs evolve and are communicated between groups and individuals that makes this true social cognition.

> ***ASK YOURSELF...***
> - Can you think of any other examples of SRs?
> - Where do you think they come from?

SRs provide an evolving framework for making sense of the world, deriving from the mass media, scientific and religious movements, and intergroup relations (Moscovici, 1984). They also have important consequences for how we deal with one another, and how society responds to particular individuals and groups. For example, whether abnormal behaviour is conceptualised in moral, biological, religious, or social terms will determine how social policy-makers, the government, as well as the general public, will respond to it (see Chapter 43). When the Yorkshire Ripper was convicted for multiple rapes and murders, he was held to be criminally responsible (despite his schizophrenia). As Hogg & Abrams (2000) point out:

> Such distinctions are dependent more on society's current social representations of good and evil, sanity and insanity, than they are on objectively measurable criteria.

Whenever people engage in conversation or debate controversial issues, such as 'what to do with paedophiles', whether homosexuals should be allowed to become foster/adoptive parents, whether cannabis should be legalised, or whether we should pay higher taxes to fund public services like the NHS, SRs become apparent.

SRs, prejudice and discrimination

According to Horton (1999), underlying much racist talk or discourse is a hidden core, which consists of:

> ... a social representation of human nature, including the belief in a hereditary factor in natural character. Biological, psychological and religious images and ideas make up this inner core. Racialism corresponds to a social representation which gives replies to questions such as 'What is man?', 'What are his origins?' and 'Why are people different?'

Billig's (1978) participant observational study of the National Front (now the British National Party/BNP) revealed that beneath black stereotypes and active hostility towards blacks lay a complex set of ideas. These included the need for racial cleansing and belief in a Zionist conspiracy.

Residents campaigning against the planned move of a convicted paedophile into their neighbourhood on his release from prison. The belief that they cannot help but reoffend is part of the Social Representation of paedophiles

> By offering scapegoats instead of a rational analysis of the situation, the Nazis gave hope to the German people by attributing the crisis to a cause that was relatively easily controllable by elimination – the Jews ... (Horton, 1999)

For Horton, SR theory, by providing a lay theory of causality:

> ... offers a social psychological explanation of 'prejudice' that takes into full account the phenomena of active hostility towards, and persecution and elimination of, outgroups, which experimental social psychology has not been able to offer.

Scapegoating and other theories of prejudice and discrimination are discussed in Chapter 25.

Box 22.2 The social representation of AIDS

- According to Joffe (1996), the early representation of AIDS in the West, by both the scientific and lay communities, was in terms of *outgroups*, namely, homosexuals and/or Africans. This anchoring acts as a form of identity-protection, and has operated throughout the ages.
- Joffe gives the example of syphilis as it swept through Europe in the fifteenth century. It became associated with foreigners and outgroups: the English called it the 'French pox', and for the Japanese it was the 'Chinese disease'. This applied also to typhus, leprosy, polio and cholera (the pandemic diseases).

- 'Blaming the foreigner' is necessary in order to punish the perceived cause of the crime and prevent its return. This *scapegoating* is vital for maintenance of the social order, and the greater the potential threat, the greater the need to exterminate the 'demons' (Poliakov, 1980, in Horton, 1999).

FORMING GLOBAL IMPRESSIONS OF PEOPLE

Central versus peripheral traits

Certain information we have about a person (certain traits we believe they possess) may be more important in determining our overall impression of that person than other information. This was demonstrated in Asch's (1946) classic study.

KEY STUDY 22.1 Building our impressions around something warm or cold (Asch, 1946)

- Asch presented participants with a stimulus list of adjectives describing a fictitious person. For one group, the adjectives were: intelligent, skilful, industrious, warm, determined, practical and cautious. A second group had the same list, except that the word 'cold' replaced the word 'warm'.
- Both groups were then presented with a response list of 18 different adjectives and were asked to underline those which described the target person.
- The two groups chose significantly and consistently different words from the response list. For example, the 'warm' group saw the character as generous, humorous, sociable and popular, while the 'cold' group saw him as having the opposite traits. There were also certain qualities attributed to him equally by both groups (reliable, good-looking, persistent, serious, restrained, strong and honest).
- When 'polite' and 'blunt' were used instead of 'warm' and 'cold', participants underlined almost identical words in the response list.
- Asch concluded that 'warm–cold' represented a *central trait* or *dimension*, while 'polite–blunt' represented a *peripheral trait* or *dimension*.
- The central traits which seem to influence our global perception in this way are implicitly *evaluative;* they're to do with whether the person is likeable or unlikeable, popular or unpopular, friendly or unfriendly, kind or cruel, and so on.

Kelley (1950) wanted to see whether the description of the target person as 'warm' or 'cold' would influence participants' behaviour towards a *real* (as opposed to hypothetical) person.

KEY STUDY 22.2 The 'warm–cold' variable in a naturalistic setting (Kelley, 1950)

- Students were told that their regular teacher wouldn't be coming, that they'd be having Mr X instead, and that they'd be asked to assess him at the end of the session. Mr. X was a male member of staff not known to the students.
- Before he arrived, the students were given some biographical notes about Mr X. For half the students, these included the description 'rather warm' and for the other half 'rather cold'; otherwise the biographies were identical.
- There then followed a 20-minute discussion between the teacher and the students, during which Kelley recorded how often each student attempted to interact with the teacher. After he left the room, students assessed him on 15 rating scales (e.g. 'knows his stuff–doesn't know his stuff', 'good-natured–irritable').
- Those given the 'warm' description consistently responded more favourably to him than those given the 'cold' description. The two groups also responded differently when asked to write a free description.
- In addition, 56 per cent of the 'warm' group participated in the discussion, compared with 32 per cent of the 'cold' group.

What makes central traits central?

For Asch, a set of traits produces a coherent impression or configuration (a Gestalt: see Chapter 15), in which the meaning of one trait has been influenced by the others. The principle of coherence makes all the traits fit together into a well-integrated portrait (Fiske, 2004). Central traits exert a major organising influence, and can generate inferences about additional traits not given in the set, while peripheral traits have little or no influence. However:

- according to Anderson's (1974) *averaging/algebraic model,* people extract the evaluative element from each component of the impression (that is, each trait's inherent likeability). They then average the separate evaluations into an overall evaluation – this is an explicitly *piecemeal, elemental* account, which sees traits as completely independent of each other and having no influence on each other (Fiske, 2004)
- Bruner & Tagiuri (1954) argued that both general impressions and inferences about additional traits are due to people's *implicit personality theories* (IPTs: see below)
- Wishner (1960) found that the impact of the traits 'warm' and 'cold' on inferences about other traits depends on their prior associations with those traits; so 'warm' and 'cold' affect inferences of traits like 'generous' and 'popular' because they're all (already)

associated in people's IPTs, but they *aren't* associated with other traits (such as 'reliable' and 'honest'). This suggests that central traits *don't* need to be incorporated into different Gestalten as Asch claimed; indeed, Asch found only negligible differences in the traits inferred when 'warm' and 'cold' were presented alone, and when they were presented as described in Key Study 22.1

- the *meaning* of various traits may nevertheless be altered by the context in which they appear, as Asch originally suggested. For example, if someone is described as 'proud', this is rated as closer to 'confident' when it appears in the context of positive traits, but as closer to 'conceited' when presented in the context of negative traits (Zebrowitz, 1990)
- Wishner also showed that whether or not a trait is central depends on what else is known about the person (it's *relative*). For example, in Asch's study, 'warm–cold' was central in relation to generous/humorous/sociable/popular, but peripheral (or at least neutral) in relation to reliable/good-looking/persistent/serious/restrained/strong/honest. This suggests that traits are neither central nor peripheral in themselves; rather, it depends on the pattern of correlations with other traits in any particular study.

The primacy–recency effect

ASK YOURSELF...
- Do you believe that first impressions are more influential than later impressions? If so, why?
- Does it make a difference if the person is a potential sexual partner (i.e. does the element of potential sexual attraction affect the impact of initial impressions)?

The other major explanation of global perception concentrates on the *order* in which we learn things about a person:

- the *primacy effect* refers to the greater impact of what we learn first about someone ('first impressions count')
- the *recency effect* refers to the greater impact of what we learn later on.

Initial support for a primacy effect came in another study by Asch (1946). He used two lists of adjectives describing a hypothetical person, one in the order: intelligent, industrious, impulsive, critical, stubborn and envious, and the other in the reverse order. Participants given the first list formed a favourable overall impression, while those given the second list formed an unfavourable overall impression.

ASK YOURSELF...
- How might you account for Asch's findings?

KEY STUDY 22.3 Forming an impression of Jim (Luchins, 1957)

Participants were allocated to one of four groups.

- Group 1 heard a description of an extrovert character called Jim.
- Group 2 heard an introvert description.
- Group 3 heard the first half of the extrovert description, followed by the second half of the introvert description.
- Group 4 heard the reverse of the list of group 3.

Groups 1 and 2 were control groups used to establish that participants could accurately identify extroverts and introverts.

- All the participants were then asked to rate Jim in terms of introversion–extroversion. Group 1 judged him to be the most extroverted and group 2 the most introverted (as you'd expect). Although the judgements of groups 3 and 4 were less extreme, group 3 rated Jim as being more extrovert than group 4.
- Remember, groups 3 and 4 received the same information about Jim, only the *order* was different. Luchins concluded that the *earlier* elements of the description had a *greater impact* than the later elements.

Both the Luchins and Asch studies involved hypothetical people. In a study by Jones *et al.* (1968), participants watched a student (a stooge of the experimenters) trying to solve a series of difficult multiple-choice problems. They were then asked to assess his intelligence. The student always solved 15 out of 30 correctly, but one group saw him get most of the right answers towards the beginning, while another group saw him get most of the right answers towards the end.

ASK YOURSELF...
- Which group do you think assessed him as more intelligent?
- According to common sense, which group would judge him to be more intelligent?

The common-sense prediction would be that when the student got most right towards the *end,* he'd be judged as *more* intelligent: he'd seem to be learning as he went along. When he got most right towards the beginning, his early successes could be attributed to guesswork or 'beginner's luck'. Jones *et al.* in fact made the common-sense prediction that there'd be a *recency* effect. But what they found was a *primacy effect.* Significantly, when asked to recall how many problems the student had solved correctly, those who'd seen the 15 bunched at the beginning said 20.6 (on average), while those who'd seen them bunched at the end said 12.5 (on average). These memory distortions (over- and underestimations) also reflected the impact of the primacy effect.

Explaining the primacy effect

- Luchins says that when later information is discrepant with earlier information, people tend to regard the first information as revealing the 'real' person. The later information is discounted, because it contradicts what came first.
- Anderson (1974) maintains that people pay more attention to information presented when they're first trying to form an impression about someone. Having formed some initial impression, they pay less attention to any subsequent information.
- Asch's explanation is that the first bit of information affects the meaning of later information, which is made consistent with the former. For example, if you initially find out that someone is courageous and frank, and you later learn that he's also undecided, you may take that to mean 'open-minded' rather than 'wishy-washy' (Zebrowitz, 1990).

But does the primacy effect always prove more powerful than the recency effect? The answer seems to be yes, generally, but there are certain conditions.

- Luchins reasoned that if the primacy effect is due to decreased attention to later information, then it should be possible to prevent it by warning people against making snap judgements. He found this to be particularly effective if it was given between the presentation of the two inconsistent pieces of information about the same individual. Similarly, Hendrick & Constanini (1970) found that primacy seems to prevail unless participants are specifically instructed to attend closely to all the information.
- A negative first impression appears to be more resistant to change than a positive one. One explanation is that negative information carries more weight, because it's likely to reflect socially undesirable traits or behaviour and, therefore, the observer can be more confident in attributing the trait or behaviour to the person's 'real' nature. (This is relevant to Jones and Davis's attribution theory: see Chapter 23, pages 396–398.) It may be more adaptive for us to be aware of negative traits than positive ones, since the former are potentially harmful or dangerous.
- Luchins found that, although the primacy effect may be important in relation to strangers, as far as friends and other people whom we know well are concerned, the recency effect seems to be stronger. For example, we may discover something about a friend's childhood or something that happened to them before we knew them, which might change our whole perception of them. 'How well do we (or can we) know anybody?'

> ***ASK YOURSELF...***
> - Can you think of any experiences like this that you have had?

The halo effect

Asch's original finding that the inclusion of 'warm' produces a more positive impression compared with the same list including 'cold' demonstrates the *halo effect*. If we're told a person is warm, then we tend to attribute them with other favourable characteristics (a positive halo). The reverse is true if we're told the person is 'cold' – we attribute them with a *negative halo*. The halo effect seems to illustrate very well two basic principles of perception (see Figure 22.1):

- we like to see people in as *consistent* (or organised) a way as possible. It's easier to regard someone as having either all good or all bad qualities than a mixture of good and bad. Two quite extreme examples of this are when lovers regard each other as perfect and faultless ('love is blind': see Chapter 28) and the '*mirror-image phenomenon*', where enemies see each other as all bad (see Chapter 25)
- the halo effect is a very general form of implicit personality theory (IPT). These theories enable us to infer what people are like when we have only very limited information about them.

Implicit personality theories (IPTs)

As we saw earlier, we all have 'implicit' theories about what makes people 'tick'. One kind of implicit theory is to do with how personality is structured and what traits tend to go together or cluster. Zebrowitz (1990) refers to these as 'person type' IPTs.

The importance of names

Our names are part of the central core of our self-image (see Chapter 33), and they can sometimes form the basis for others' expectations. Harari & McDavid (1973) pointed out that first names, like surnames, are often associated with particular characteristics, partly determined by the media (for example, in American movies the hero and heroine are often called Stephen and Elizabeth, and the villains and fall-guys Elmer and Bertha). They asked experienced teachers to evaluate a set of short essays written by 11-year-olds who were identified by first name only. Some essays were randomly associated with four names stereotyped by other teachers as attractive and favourable (David, Michael, Karen and Lisa) and four stereotyped as unattractive and unfavourable (Elmer, Hubert, Bertha and Adelle). So, the *same* essays were associated with *different* names for *different* teachers. Those written by 'attractive' names were graded a full letter grade higher than those by 'unattractive' names and, significantly, the effect was stronger with boys' names than with girls'.

KEY STUDY 22.4 Names and psychiatric diagnosis (Birmingham, in Adler, 2000)

- Birmingham, a forensic psychiatrist at Southampton University, asked 464 British psychiatrists to provide a diagnosis based on a one-page description of a 24-year-old who'd assaulted a train conductor.
- When they were asked to assess 'Matthew', over 75 per cent gave him a sympathetic hearing, proposing that he was suffering from schizophrenia and in need of medical help.
- But when renamed 'Wayne', psychiatrists gave him a more sinister character: he was twice as likely as Matthew to be diagnosed as a malingerer, a drug abuser, or suffering from a personality disorder (see Chapter 43).

The importance of physical appearance

Another kind of IPT involves inferring what somebody is like psychologically from certain aspects of their physical appearance. Allport (1954) gave examples of widely held, but totally unfounded, beliefs that fat people are jolly, high foreheads are a sign of superior intelligence, eyes too close together are a sign of untrustworthiness, and redheads have fiery tempers.

A number of studies have demonstrated the 'attractiveness stereotype'; that is, the tendency to infer that physically attractive people also have more attractive personalities (see Chapter 28).

Stereotypes and stereotyping

Stereotypes can be thought of as a special kind of IPT that relates to an entire social group. The term was introduced into social science by Lippman (1922), who defined stereotypes as 'pictures in our heads'. Table 22.2 gives some other definitions.

Table 22.2 Some definitions of stereotypes and stereotyping

'... the general inclination to place a person in categories according to some easily and quickly identifiable characteristic such as age, sex, ethnic membership, nationality or occupation, and then to attribute to him qualities believed to be typical to members of that category ...' (Tagiuri, 1969)
'... a shared conception of the character of a group ...' (Brown, 1986)
'... the process of ascribing characteristics to people on the basis of their group memberships ...' (Oakes *et al.*, 1994)
'... widely shared assumptions about the personalities, attitudes and behaviour of people based on group membership, for example ethnicity, nationality, sex, race and class ...' (Hogg & Vaughan, 1995)
'... applying to an individual one's cognitive expectancies and associations about the group. As such, stereotypes represent one specific kind of schema ...' (Fiske, 2004)

The *process of stereotyping* involves the following reasoning:

- we assign someone to a particular group (for example, on the basis of their physical appearance)
- we bring into play the belief that all members of the group share certain characteristics (the stereotype), and
- we infer that this particular individual must possess these characteristics.

The basic method of studying ethnic stereotypes is that used by Katz & Braly (1933) in one of the earliest studies of its kind.

KEY STUDY 22.5 Studying stereotypes at Princeton (Katz & Braly, 1933)

- One hundred undergraduates at Princeton University, USA, were presented with a list of ethnic groups (Americans, Jews, Negroes, Turks, Germans, Chinese, Irish, English, Italians and Japanese) and 84 words describing personality.
- They were asked to list, for each ethnic group, the five or six traits that were 'typical' of that group.
- The aim was to find out whether traditional social stereotypes (as typically portrayed in newspapers and magazines) were actually held by Princeton students.
- In fact, they showed considerable agreement, especially about negative traits.
- Rather disturbingly, most of the students had had no personal contact with any members of most of the ethnic groups they had to rate. Presumably, they'd absorbed the images of those groups prevalent in the media.

Gilbert (1951) studied another sample of Princeton students, and this time found less uniformity of agreement (especially about unfavourable traits) than in the 1933 study. Many expressed great irritation at being asked to make generalisations at all. In 1967, Karlins *et al.* repeated the study (but reported their findings in 1969). Many students again objected to doing the task, but there was greater agreement compared with the 1951 study. There seemed to be a re-emergence of social stereotyping, but towards more favourable stereotypical images.

ASK YOURSELF...

- Do you think that stereotypes/stereotyping are inherently bad/wrong?
- Give reasons for your answer.

The traditional view of stereotypes: are they inherently bad?

For most of the time that psychologists have been studying stereotypes and stereotyping, they've condemned them for being both false and illogical, and dangerous, and people who use them have been seen as prejudiced and even pathological (see Chapter 25).

Table 22.3 The five traits most frequently assigned to four ethnic groups by three generations of Princeton students (from Brown, 1986)

Group	1933	1951	1967
Americans	industrious	materialistic	materialistic
	intelligent	intelligent	ambitious
	materialistic	industrious	pleasure-loving
	ambitious	pleasure-loving	industrious
	progressive	individualistic	conventional
Japanese	intelligent	imitative	industrious
	industrious	sly	ambitious
	progressive	extremely nationalistic	efficient
	shrewd	treacherous	intelligent
	sly		progressive
Jews	shrewd	shrewd	ambitious
	mercenary	intelligent	materialistic
	industrious	industrious	intelligent
	grasping	mercenary	industrious
	intelligent	ambitious	shrewd
Negroes	superstitious	superstitious	musical
	lazy	musical	happy-go-lucky
	happy-go-lucky	lazy	lazy
	ignorant	ignorant	pleasure-loving
	musical	pleasure-loving	ostentatious

Lippman (1922), for example, described stereotypes as selective, self-fulfilling and ethnocentric, constituting a 'very partial and inadequate way of representing the world'. The research started by Katz & Braly (1933) was intended to trace the link between stereotypes and prejudice: stereotypes are public fictions arising from prejudicial influences 'with scarcely any factual basis'. So, should they be dismissed as completely unacceptable?

According to Allport (1954), most stereotypes do contain a 'kernel of truth', and Lippman had recognised the categorisation processes involved in stereotyping as an important aspect of general cognitive functioning. Allport built on these ideas, arguing that 'The human mind must think with the aid of categories ...'. However, he also believed that prejudiced people tend to make extremely simple *dichotomous* (either/or) judgements compared with tolerant, non-prejudiced people.

Asch (1952) also rejected the view of stereotyping as 'faulty processing'. In a great many situations, the behaviour of individuals (for example, members of audiences, committees, families, football teams, armies) is determined by their group membership. So, representing people in terms of these group memberships (stereotyping) could be seen as an important way of representing social reality. In keeping with his belief in Gestalt principles, Asch argued that groups have distinct psychological properties which cannot be reduced to the characteristics of the individual members (see Chapter 15).

Sherif (1967) also argued that stereotypes aren't in themselves deficient, but serve to reflect the reality of intergroup relations. Instead of asking if they are objectively true or accurate, we need to understand stereotypes in this *intergroup* context. To this extent, they are highly flexible, since changes in the relationship with other groups will result in changes to the stereotyped images of those groups (see Chapter 25). But according to Operario & Fiske (2004), it's precisely this broader context of stereotypes, reflected in social hierarchy and history, that defines their truly insidious nature.

CRITICAL DISCUSSION 22.1 : Do stereotypes reflect social power inequalities?

- The nature of social power dynamics and group hierarchy make stereotypes particularly oppressive for certain individuals and groups (Operario *et al.*, 1998). In particular:

  ... individuals whose outcomes are controlled by others, and groups low in the social hierarchy, are vulnerable to the demeaning content of their stereotypes. Conversely, individuals who control others' outcomes, and groups near the top of the social hierarchy, are more likely to employ stereotypes about others ... (Fiske, 1993)

- Because of their dependence on the powerful, the powerless direct their attention up the hierarchy and don't categorise those with power. But the powerful themselves are too busy, too unconcerned with accuracy, or too dominance-oriented to pay any attention to the powerless. They, therefore, tend to categorise and form highly stereotypical impressions of those over whom they can exert power (Oakes, 2004).
- Powerful people simply pay less individuating attention to their subordinates – that is, they treat them less as individuals, while the reverse is true for subordinate individuals and groups. According to Operario & Fiske (2004):

  ... Not only does power perpetuate beliefs associated with social subordinates and minority groups, it also enables people to act upon stereotypical beliefs through legislation, economic policies, and institutional practices ...

- A counterintuitive finding is the tendency for the powerless and disadvantaged to show biases that justify and maintain their group's low status (that is, they accept the status quo). This helps explain why social injustice can endure within cultural contexts that outwardly endorse egalitarianism and equality.
- But this isn't necessarily the same as *internalising* negative stereotypes. Members of low-status groups tend to acknowledge their group's disadvantaged status, but minimise perceptions of *personal* vulnerability to discrimination. In this way, they can maintain their self-esteem and personal control, and avoid feeling personally victimised (Operario & Fiske, 2004).

The changing face of stereotypes: are they 'normal' after all?

Almost all the researchers whose views of stereotyping we've discussed so far are American. According to Taylor & Porter (1994), there are compelling reasons why American psychologists should condemn stereotyping and wish to rid society of this evil. One of these is the political ideology, according to which everyone who lives in America is first and foremost 'American' regardless of the country they might have come from or their ethnic/cultural origins. This is the 'melting pot' idea, whereby differences are 'boiled away', leaving just one culture.

Rioting English soccer fans displaying stereotypical behaviour in Charleroi, Belgium, during Euro 2000

By contrast, European social psychologists, notably Tajfel, had been brought up in contexts where it was normal to categorise people into groups, where they expected society to be culturally diverse, and where people were proud of their cultural identities. From this personal experience, Tajfel and others mounted a challenge to the American view of stereotyping. Tajfel (1969), for example, reconceptualised stereotyping as the product of quite normal cognitive processes common to all (non-prejudiced) individuals. Specifically, it's a special case of *categorisation,* which involves an exaggeration of similarities within groups and of differences between groups (the *accentuation principle*). According to Oakes *et al.* (1994), Tajfel's contribution is widely seen as having been revolutionary. One effect of his ideas was to move researchers away from studying the *content* of stereotypes and towards the study of the *process of stereotyping* in its own right.

Stereotyping as a normal cognitive process

According to Brislin (1993):

> Stereotypes should not be viewed as a sign of abnormality. Rather, they reflect people's need to organise, remember, and retrieve information that might be useful to them as they attempt to achieve their goals and to meet life's demands ...

Stereotypes are 'categories about people' (Allport, 1954; Brislin, 1981), and categories in general, and stereotypes in particular, are shortcuts to thinking. From a purely cognitive point of view, there's nothing unique about stereotypes. They're universal and inevitable, 'an intrinsic, essential and primitive aspect of cognition' (Brown, 1986).

Lippmann (1922) himself argued that stereotypes serve a crucially important *practical* function:

> ... the real environment is altogether too big, too complex and too fleeting for direct acquaintance. We are not equipped to deal with so much subtlety, so much variety, so many permutations and combinations, And although we have to act in that environment, we have to reconstruct it on a simpler model before we can manage it.

> ***ASK YOURSELF...***
> - How does this view of stereotyping relate to the view of the person as thinker (Fiske & Taylor, 1991: see above, page 378)?

According to the *cognitive miser* perspective, stereotypes are resource-saving devices. They simplify the processing of information about other people. As Fiske (2004) says:

> ... under the busy conditions of ordinary interaction, people can save cognitive resources by using stereotype-consistent information ...

This is a good example of the *selective* nature of person perception.

The accuracy of stereotypes

Definitions claim that stereotypes are *exceptionless generalisations* (see Table 22.2). But, clearly, the degree of generalisation involved is too great to make a stereotype factually true: no group is completely homogeneous, and individual differences are the norm. Yet in Katz and Braly's study, the instruction to list the traits typical of each ethnic/national group was taken to mean 'true of all members of each group' (Brown, 1986). However, the early studies never actually found out what participants understood by 'typical'. McCauley & Stitt (1978) attempted to rectify this.

> **KEY STUDY 22.6 What does the 'typical' mean in 'stereotypical'? (McCauley & Stitt, 1978)**
> - McCauley and Stitt chose Germans as the target group, plus three 'typical' traits (efficient/extremely nationalistic/scientifically minded), and two 'atypical' traits (pleasure-loving/superstitious).
> - Junior college students were told they'd be asked a series of questions which they wouldn't be able to

answer exactly (e.g. 'What percentage of American cars are Chevrolets?'). Intermixed with these were critical questions about Germans – 'What percentage of Germans are efficient/extremely nationalistic/scientifically minded/pleasure-loving/superstitious?' and, corresponding to these, 'What percentage of people in the world generally are efficient/extremely nationalistic/scientifically minded/pleasure-loving/superstitious?'.

- The *diagnostic ratio* was calculated simply by dividing the percentage for Germans by the percentage for people in the world: anything over 1.00 represents a trait which belongs to the stereotype; anything below 1.00 represents a trait which doesn't.
- None of these values is even close to 100 per cent, so clearly 'typical' *doesn't* mean 'true of all'. 'Scientifically minded' isn't even attributed to a majority of Germans.

Table 22.4

Trait	% People in the world	% Germans	Diagnostic ratio
Efficient	49.8	63.4	1.27
Extremely nationalistic	35.4	56.3	1.59
Scientifically minded	32.6	43.1	1.32
Pleasure-loving	82.2	72.8	0.89
Superstitious	42.1	30.4	0.72

ASK YOURSELF...

- What do McCauley and Stitt's results tell us about the meaning of 'typical'?

What 'typical' seems to mean is *characteristic,* that is, true of a higher percentage of the group in question than of people in general (Brown, 1986). Stereotypes, then, seem to be *schemas* about what particular groups are like relative to 'people in general'. They *aren't* exceptionless generalisations. Perhaps this is how we should understand Allport's claim that stereotypes do contain a 'kernel of truth'.

Consistent with this conclusion, Operario & Fiske (2004) claim that stereotypes are more *ambivalent* than is commonly recognised: they comprise both positive and negative attributes about social groups. This makes their potency largely dependent on the social contexts in which they arise. This ambivalence is illustrated by the stereotypes of 'Negroes' in the Katz & Braly (1933) study (see Table 22.3). The blend of traits reflects an overall disparagement – but *not* utter repugnance.

Operario and Fiske claim that minority groups tend to be viewed as either (a) highly competent but not nice, or (b) extremely incompetent but nice, and stereotype content reflects this pattern.

ASK YOURSELF...

- Based on Operario and Fiske's distinction, which of the following groups would you classify as 'nice but incompetent' or 'not nice but competent': Jews, the mentally retarded, feminists, the blind, black professionals, housewives, business women, the elderly, Asians, the physically disabled?

According to Operario & Fiske (2004) you're likely to have answered as follows:

- 'nice but incompetent': the mentally retarded, housewives, the elderly, the physically disabled, the blind
- 'not nice but competent': feminists, business women, black professionals, Asians, Jews.

The beliefs associated with these two clusters reflect the particular group's relationship with the dominant majority (white, male, middle class, able-bodied). The first cluster presents no threat to the majority, while the second cluster poses a significant threat. However, research participants have become much more reluctant to engage in stereotyping over the past 80 years (Fiske, 2004), and stereotypes do *change.* For example, the most negatively rated groups in Katz & Braly's (1933) study (Negroes, Turks, Chinese) are now neutral or even slightly more positive than the most positively rated (Americans), who are rated less positively than they were (Leslie *et al.*, 2003).

Stereotypes, ingroups and outgroups

Instead of seeing comments such as 'They're all the same' as simply bigoted and discriminatory, research has shown that such statements may stem from the *outgroup homogeneity effect* (Quattrone, 1986). People tend to perceive members of an outgroup as highly similar to each other (stereotype), whereas they tend to see all kinds of individual differences among members of their own groups (the *ingroup differentiation hypothesis:* Linville *et al.*, 1989). These are consequences of the act of categorisation, and could be seen as an extension of Tajfel's accentuation principle (see above).

This differential perception of ingroup and outgroup members isn't necessarily indicative of outgroup prejudice, but is the natural outcome of social interaction patterns. We tend to interact with members of our own groups and therefore perceive differences within them. We may have limited interaction with other social groups, and this encourages a simplified social representation of these groups. In this context, it's both necessary and useful to see all outgroup members as similar. Ironically, study of the processes involved in stereotyping has suggested that it's the content that should – and can – be modified: the process itself may be 'hard-wired' as an element of human cognition, so that there's nothing we can do about it (Taylor & Porter, 1994).

Box 22.3 Stereotyping and the brain

- Adler (2000) cites research using EEG recordings to see what happens in people's brains when stereotypes are activated.
- He found that sentences in which gender stereotypes are violated (such as 'The surgeon prepared herself for the operation') provoke the same surge of electrical activity as sentences that don't make grammatical sense (such as 'The cat won't eating'). The telltale signal is a strong positive brainwave (the P600), which is often associated with surprise (see Chapter 7).
- The brains of men and women showed this reaction, even if they consciously found the sentence completely acceptable. Their brains seemed to be 'saying' one thing, and their overt responses something quite different.
- Other researchers have used MRI scans to measure the differing reactions in the amygdala of white participants to black and white faces. The amygdala is thought to act like a spotlight, focusing attention on frightening or other emotionally charged events (see Chapter 4). There's greater amygdala activity in response to black faces or race-related words and images.
- This dissociation between conscious beliefs and unconscious reactions supports the view that racial evaluations have a subtle influence on people's behaviour (Adler, 2000).

Figure 22.3 One of the drawings used by Buckhout (1974)

The *illusory correlation* (Chapman, 1967; Hamilton & Gifford, 1976) refers to the tendency to regard two variables that are unusual or distinct in some way, and which happen to become linked on one occasion, as always linked in that way (see Table 20.2, page 348). For example, if a member of a minority ethnic group is involved in a serious crime, majority group members are likely to associate the two, such that 'muggers are likely to be ...' becomes part of the negative stereotype of that group.

Stereotypes, expectations and memory

Buckhout (1974) gave participants a series of drawings in which some stereotypical pattern was violated. One drawing (based on Allport & Postman's (1947) experiment: see Chapter 21, page 360) showed a casually dressed white man threatening a well-dressed black man on a subway train, with the white man holding a razor. After seeing the picture briefly, approximately half the (white) participants 'remembered' seeing a black man holding a razor.

Similarly, Rothbart *et al.* (1979) found that people often recall better those facts that support their stereotypes (*selective remembering*), and Howard & Rothbart (1980) found that people have better recall of facts which are critical of the minority group than facts which are favourable (*negative memory bias*).

Duncan (1976) showed white participants a video of a discussion between two males, and told them it was a 'live' interaction over CCTV. At one point, the discussion became heated, and one actor gave the other a shove – the screen then went blank. Participants were asked to classify the shove as 'playing around', 'dramatising', 'aggressive behaviour' or 'violent behaviour'. Different participants saw different versions of the video, which differed only in the race of the two actors – two whites, two blacks, a white who shoved a black, or a black who shoved a white.

ASK YOURSELF...

- How do you think participants classified the shove under different conditions?
- How could you explain the results?
- What relevance do all the above studies have for eyewitness testimony (EWT) (see Chapter 21)?

Duncan found that many more participants classified the black man's shove as violent behaviour, especially if he shoved a white man.

Stereotypes, expectations and behaviour

Our expectations of people's personalities or capabilities may influence the way we actually treat them, which in turn may influence their behaviour in such a way that confirms our expectation (the *self-fulfilling prophecy*). This illustrates how stereotypes can (unwittingly) influence our behaviour towards others, and not just our perception and memory of them.

Stereotypes also affect our expectations of ourselves, which, in turn, can influence our behaviour. This may take place under naturalistic conditions and over a substantial period of time, as when members of minority groups internalise the negative stereotypes of them prevalent in the majority culture (see Chapter 25). But it can also happen under more artificial, experimental conditions in the short term.

KEY STUDY 22.7 How stereotypes can slow you down (Bargh *et al.*, 1996)

- College students were asked to unscramble sentences scattered with negative age-related words.
- Students who'd sorted sentences containing negative words walked down the corridor at the end of the experiment significantly more slowly, and remembered less about the experiment, than students who'd sorted neutral words.
- In an extension of Bargh *et al.*'s study, Dijksterhuis *et al.* (in Hogg & Abrams, 2000) asked participants to unscramble sentences containing words associated with negative stereotypes of the elderly. This primed the elderly stereotype, by making attributes of the elderly more accessible in participants' minds.
- Half were asked to make judgements about Princess Julianna (the 89-year-old Dutch Queen Mother). All the participants were then shown to the lifts, situated at the end of the corridor, and the time taken to reach them was recorded.
- Those who'd been primed with Princess Julianna walked significantly *faster*.

ASK YOURSELF...

- Try to explain the findings described in Key Study 22.7

The studies illustrate that when general stereotypes are activated, we may automatically adopt some of those characteristics ourselves. But when images of specific extreme individuals (exemplars) are activated, we automatically make a contrast between ourselves and the exemplar. This makes us react in the *opposite* way to how we think that person would react (Hogg & Abrams, 2000).

So, it's not stereotypes themselves which are dangerous or objectionable, but how they affect behaviour. While the experiments described above show that anyone can be affected by negative stereotypes, under normal circumstances it's the elderly who are affected by negative stereotypes of the elderly (see Chapter 39). The same applies, of course, to ethnic minority groups and race stereotypes, and to women and gender stereotypes (see Chapters 25 and 36). According to Operario & Fiske (2004):

> ... stereotypes are both (a) basic human tendencies inherent within our mental architecture; and (b) potentially damaging belief systems, depending on the power of the situation ...

INFLUENCING HOW OTHERS SEE US

Impression management

It's difficult to think of a social situation in which we're not trying (consciously or otherwise) to manipulate how others perceive us. This fundamental aspect of social interaction is referred to as *impression management* (or *self-presentation*) (Baumeister, 1982; Leary & Kowalski, 1990), which Turner (1991) defines as 'the process of presenting a public image of the self to others'. Sometimes we may be trying to influence particular people on a particular occasion, such as in a job interview, or we may be trying to maintain an image of ourselves (as a caring or competent person, for example).

According to Leary & Kowalski (1990), impression management can increase our subjective wellbeing by meeting three primary motivations:

1. maximising the reward of social relationships (*belonging:* its major function)
2. enhancing self-esteem (*self-enhancement*)
3. establishing desired identities (*self-understanding*).

It's widely agreed that we usually try to influence others in a positive way – that is, we want them to have a favourable impression of us (Schlenker, 1980; Turner, 1991).

In books such as *The Presentation of Self in Everyday Life* (1971), Goffman, the Canadian sociologist, offers a 'dramaturgical' analysis of social interaction. To create a successful impression requires the right setting, props (e.g. the way you're dressed), skills, and a shared understanding of what counts as 'backstage'. For example, the person who takes *self-disclosure* too far (see below), may be regarded as bringing on to stage what should be kept 'backstage', and so creates an unfavourable impression.

Woody Allen (in *Manhattan*) typically plays a character who's unlucky in love. This is partly due to his inappropriate self-disclosure

How is impression management carried out?

Impression management requires us to 'take the role of the other' (see Cooley and Mead's theories of self: Chapter 33). We must be able, psychologically, to step into someone else's shoes to see how we look from their viewpoint, and to adjust our behaviour accordingly. Fiske & Taylor (1991)

and Fiske (2004) identify several components of impression management, ways of adjusting our behaviour to take into account other people's viewpoints (see Table 22.5).

Table 22.5 Major components involved in impression management (based on Fiske & Taylor, 1991; Fiske, 2004)

In **behaviour matching**, we try to match the target person's behaviour. For example, if the other person is self-disclosing, we'll tend to do so to a comparable degree.
When we **conform to situational norms**, we use our knowledge of what's appropriate behaviour in a particular situation to adopt that behaviour ourselves. For every social setting, there's a pattern of social interaction which conveys the best identity for that setting (the 'situated identity'). **High self-monitors** (see text below) are more likely to make a favourable impression.
Appreciating or flattering others (**ingratiation**) can sometimes produce a favourable response from the target person, especially if it's done sincerely. But if seen for what it is, flattery (or laughing at their jokes etc.) can backfire on the flatterer, who'll be seen as deliberately trying to achieve his/her own ends (a hypocrite or sycophant: an 'arse-licker' in popular terminology).
If we show **consistency** among our beliefs, or between our beliefs and behaviour, we're more likely to impress other people favourably. Inconsistency is usually seen as a sign of weakness.
Our **verbal and non-verbal behaviours** should match, which they usually do if we're sincere. But if we're flattering, or in some other way being dishonest, the non-verbal channel will often 'leak', giving away our true feelings. When people perceive an inconsistency between what someone says and what they're trying to convey with their body, the latter is usually taken as revealing the 'true' message (Argyle *et al.*, 1972; Mehrabian, 1972).
Self-promotion is an attempt to be seen as *competent,* but this can conflict with the wish to be **liked**. Also, there's the danger of being seen as conceited and, at worst, a fraud.
Intimidation is meant to convey the impression of being **dangerous** ('don't mess with me'). But empty threats can produce a loss of credibility (as with parents and children).
In **exemplification**, the person wants to be seen as **worthy**, **moral** and **saintly**. The downside is being seen as sanctimonious, 'holier than thou' (a 'pain').
Supplication is the strategy of last resort. The aim is to be seen as **helpless** ('strategic incompetence'), but the downside is being perceived as lazy, calculating and manipulative.

Are some positive impressions more positive than others?

> *ASK YOURSELF...*
> - Can you think of any exceptions to the rule that we always try to create favourable impressions in others?
> - Do we sometimes go about creating negative impressions in a defensive, self-protective way?

It isn't surprising that we're usually – and predominantly – motivated to be evaluated positively by others. After all, being regarded favourably by others is a prerequisite for many positive life outcomes (such as respect, friendship, romantic relationships and job success) (Leary, 2004). Sometimes, however, people believe that their interests will be best served by projecting an *unfavourable* impression, leading to a negative evaluation.

- If we're seen as emotionally unstable, this will reduce the demands others make on us. Similarly, if others see us as threatening or hostile, we'll more easily be able to coerce them into behaving in ways that we want (see Table 22.5).
- We may feel constrained by the impressions others already have of us, and we act in order to 'muddy the waters'. For example, if you're continually being told how good a son or daughter you are, the responsibility this places on you might encourage you to behave in the opposite fashion, so that you 'free yourself' from the expectation that you'll go on behaving dutifully and respectfully.
- You might protect yourself from anticipated failure by engaging in behaviours that will produce insurmountable obstacles to success. So, when the inevitable failure happens, you've a ready-made excuse (*behavioural self-handicapping*).
- Alternatively, you may blame, in advance, things about yourself that could explain the failure (apart from your lack of competence). For example, lecturers at exam time get quite used to students telling them how badly they're going to do because of lack of sleep, not having been well, having been unable to revise, always getting anxious about exams, and so on (*self-reported handicaps*).

One way of thinking about self-handicapping is to see it as an attempt to influence the kind of *attribution* other people make about our behaviour. We want them to see our failures as caused by factors 'beyond our control' and that don't, therefore, threaten the positive impression they have of us (and that we have of ourselves). Making excuses for, as well as confessing, our socially undesirable behaviour after it's occurred can also be explained in attributional terms (Weiner, 1992: see Chapter 23).

Self-monitoring

While people in general are concerned with the impressions they make on others, individuals differ in the extent to which they can and do exercise intentional control over their self-presentation. Although social psychology as a whole isn't concerned with individual differences, *self-monitoring* is profoundly social psychological. It refers to how much people attend to the social situation as guides for their behaviour, as opposed to their own internal states (Snyder, 1974, 1987). *High self-monitors* are particularly talented in this way compared with *low self-monitors* (Snyder, 1995).

- *High self-monitors* are concerned with behaving in a socially appropriate manner, and so are more likely to monitor the situation (rather than themselves), looking for subtle cues as to 'how to behave'. They're more skilled in using facial expressions and their voices to convey particular emotions, and can interpret others' non-verbal communication more accurately compared with low self-monitors (Ickes & Barnes, 1977; Snyder, 1979). But carried to an extreme, their perceptiveness and social sensitivity can make them look like self-interested opportunists who change themselves and their opinions to suit the situation (Snyder, 1987). Their behaviour shows greater *cross-situational inconsistency* – they behave differently in different situations.
- *Low self-monitors* remain 'themselves' regardless of the situation, rarely adapting to the norms of the social setting. They monitor their behaviour in relation to their own enduring needs and values. Carried to an extreme, they can be seen as insensitive, inflexible and uncompromising (Snyder, 1987). They show greater *cross-situational consistency.*

Snyder (1987) has developed a pencil and paper test (the Self-Monitoring Scale), which comprises a number of statements with which the respondent has to agree or disagree. Some examples are given in Table 22.6.

Table 22.6 Some sample items from the self-monitoring scale (Snyder, 1987, in Snyder, 1995)

High scorers will tend to agree with the following:
• I would probably make a good actor.
• I'm not always the person I appear to be.
• In different situations and with different people, I often act like very different persons.
Low scorers will tend to agree with the following:
• I have trouble changing my behaviour to suit different people and different situations.
• I can only argue for ideas which I already believe.
• I would not change my opinions (or the way I do things) in order to please someone else or win their favour.

According to Fiske (2004):

> Both levels of self-monitoring can be useful in the social world. Groups need people who are sensitive to norms and flexible about adjusting to them, and groups also need people who stand up for enduring principles, so a mix of high and low self-monitors is arguably good for group survival.

Self-disclosure

How accurately others perceive us is determined partly by how much we reveal to them about ourselves (*self-disclosure*). Wiemann & Giles (1988) define it as 'the voluntary making available of information about one's self that would not ordinarily be accessible to the other at that moment'.

According to Jourard (1971), we disclose ourselves through what we say and do (as well as what we omit to say and do). This means that we have greater control over some aspects of self-disclosure than others since, generally, we have greater control over verbal than non-verbal behaviour. However, Jourard believes that the decision to self-disclose (or to become 'transparent') is one taken freely, and the aim in disclosing ourselves is to 'be known, to be perceived by the other as the one I know myself to be'. Jourard believes that we can learn a great deal about ourselves through mutual self-disclosure, and our intimacy with others can be enhanced. It's a way of both achieving and maintaining a healthy personality, but only if the self-disclosure meets the criterion of *authenticity* (or honesty).

> ***ASK YOURSELF...***
> - Think of your various relationships. What determines the nature and extent of what you disclose to other people?

Factors influencing disclosure

- *Reciprocity:* The more personal the information we disclose to someone, the more personal the information they're likely to disclose to us. This relates to the *norm of reciprocity* (Gouldner, 1960), according to which our social behaviours 'demand' an equivalent response from our partners. We might sometimes feel the other person is giving too much away (or doing so too quickly), but we're still likely to reveal more about ourselves than we otherwise would.
- *Norms:* The situation we're in often determines how much (or what kind of) disclosure is appropriate. For instance, it's acceptable for someone we meet at a party to tell us about their job, but not to reveal details about medical problems or political beliefs.
- *Trust:* Generally, the more we trust someone, the more prepared we are to self-disclose to them.
- *Quality of relationships:* Altman & Taylor's (1973) *social penetration theory* maintains that the more intimate we are with somebody, the greater the range of topics we disclose to them and the more deeply we discuss any particular topic. Equally, a high degree of mutual self-disclosure can enhance the intimacy of the relationship, and is an excellent predictor of whether couples stay together over a four-year period (see Chapter 28).

- *Gender:* Women generally disclose more than men, and Jourard (1971) argues that men's limited self-disclosure prevents healthy self-expression and adds stress to their lives.

CONCLUSIONS

It would be quite appropriate to begin a textbook on psychology with a chapter on social perception. Since most of us are, by definition, neither psychologists nor any other kind of scientist in a literal sense, the person-as-psychologist is a metaphor. However, it combines two essential truths about human beings:

1. science (including psychology) is conducted by people and, as far as we know, is uniquely human
2. observing, explaining, predicting, and trying to control others' behaviour are activities shared by professional psychologists and all other human beings.

CHAPTER SUMMARY

- **Interpersonal perception** refers to how we all attempt to explain, predict and to some degree control the behaviour of other people. In these ways, we can all be thought of as psychologists.
- Although social psychology in general, and interpersonal perception in particular, has always been concerned with the content of people's thoughts about others, **social cognition** emphasises the **information-processing approach**.
- Both object and person perception involve **selection**, **organisation** and **inference**. But only people behave, interact with each other, perceive and experience.
- **Social phenomenologists** regard **experience**, rather than behaviour, as the major source of 'data' in social interaction.
- Four views of people as thinking organisms have been identified, seeing us as **consistency seekers**, **naïve scientists**, **cognitive misers** and **motivated tacticians**.
- As cognitive misers, we use **heuristics** as shortcuts to thinking, including **availability**, **representativeness**, **simulation** and **anchoring**.
- **Social representations** (SRs) refer to 'common sense', simplified, widely shared understanding of complex theories and ideas, and involve **personification** and **figuration**.
- **Central traits** exert a major organising influence on our overall impression of a person, while **peripheral traits** have little or no influence. An alternative, but not contradictory explanation, is that overall impressions and inferences about additional traits reflect our **implicit personality theories** (IPTs).
- While most of the evidence supports a **primacy effect** with regard to strangers, a **recency effect** may be more powerful with regard to people we know well.
- The **halo effect** is one kind of IPT, which enables us to infer what people are like when we have only limited information about them. IPTs may be based on people's names, and their physical attractiveness.
- **Stereotypes** represent a special kind of IPT, and they characterise entire **groups**. Traditionally, American researchers studied stereotypes in relation to prejudice, and regarded them as false, illogical **overgeneralisations**.
- European psychologists saw the **categorisation** of people as normal and expected. From a cognitive point of view, stereotyping is a normal mental shortcut.
- The act of categorising people produces the **accentuation principle**, the **outgroup homogeneity effect**, and the **ingroup differentiation hypothesis**. The **illusory correlation** can help explain the formation of negative stereotypes of minority groups.
- **Stereotyping** affects **attention**, **perception** and **memory**. Stereotypes may also influence people's **behaviour** towards members of outgroups, as well as the behaviour of outgroup members themselves through the **self-fulfilling prophecy**.
- We try actively to influence the impression that others form of us through **impression management/self-presentation**. Strategies used to create favourable impressions include **behaviour matching**, **appreciating/flattering others**, **showing consistency among our beliefs**, and **matching our verbal and non-verbal behaviours**.
- **High self-monitors** try to match their behaviour to the situation, while **low self-monitors** are more likely to 'be themselves'.
- Important factors that influence **self-disclosure** include **reciprocity**, **norms**, **trust**, **quality of relationship**, and **gender**.

Links with other topics/chapters

- Perception of people has much in common with *object perception* (Chapter 15).
- Social cognition is built on *attribution theories,* which originated with Heider's (1958) account of the *naïve scientist* (Chapter 23).
- Consistency is a concept central to many *theories of attitude change* (Chapter 24) and *minority influence* (Chapter 26).
- Social representations (SRs) are the basis of much *racist talk/discourse* (Chapter 25). Social representation theory is also a major *social constructionist* approach (Chapter 2)
- Asch's research into impression formation was heavily influenced by the *Gestalt principles of perceptual organisation* (Chapter 15).
- Stereotypes represent the *cognitive component of attitudes* (Chapter 24), and *prejudice* may be thought of as an *extreme attitude* (Chapter 25).

- Stereotypes can help explain *selective remembering* and the *negative memory bias* (Chapter 17).
- Impression management/self-presentation is relevant to *interpersonal attraction:* instead of simply sitting back and letting others be impressed (or not), we can take an active role in making ourselves likeable to others (Duck, 1988: Chapter 28).
- According to Turner (1991), several studies suggest that concerns with self-presentation may underlie a whole range of phenomena, including *bystander intervention* (Chapter 30), *aggression and deindividuation* (Chapter 29), *conformity* (Chapter 26) and *cognitive dissonance* (Chapter 24).

23

ATTRIBUTION

INTRODUCTION AND OVERVIEW

As we noted at the beginning of Chapter 22, attribution is an important aspect of social perception, theories of which flourished during the 1950s to the 1970s. Most of our impressions of others are based on their overt behaviour, and the setting in which it occurs. How we judge the causes of someone's behaviour (the 'actor') will have a major influence on the impression we form about them. Was their behaviour something to do with them 'as a person', such as their motives, intentions or personality (an *internal* cause)? Or was it something to do with the situation, including some other person or some physical feature of the environment (an *external* cause)?

Unless we can make this sort of judgement, we cannot really use the person's behaviour as a basis for forming an impression of them. Although we might mistakenly attribute the cause to the person instead of the situation, an attribution still has to be made.

Attribution theory deals with the general principles governing how we select and use information to arrive at causal explanations for behaviour. *Theories of attribution* draw on the principles of attribution theory, and predict how people will respond in particular situations (or *life domains:* Fiske & Taylor, 1991).

Rather than being a single body of ideas and research, attribution theory is a collection of diverse theoretical and empirical contributions sharing several common concerns (or mini-theories: Antaki, 1984). Six different traditions form the 'backbone' of attribution theory (Fiske & Taylor, 1991). These are: Heider's (1958) *'common-sense' psychology,* Jones & Davis's (1965) *correspondent inference theory,* Kelley's (1967, 1972, 1983) *covariation* and *configuration models,* Schachter's (1964) *cognitive labelling theory* (of emotion: see Chapter 10), Bem's (1967, 1972) *self-perception theory* (of attitude change: see Chapter 24), and Weiner's (1986) *attributional theory of motivation.*

The models and theories of Heider, Jones and Davis, and Kelley see people as being logical and systematic in their explanations of behaviour. In practice, however, people tend to make attributions quickly, based often on very little information, and show clear tendencies to offer certain types of explanation for particular behaviours (Hewstone & Fincham, 1996). As Fiske (2004) says:

> ... Using an intuitive and relatively automatic process, people do not think about making attributions; they just do it. People are experts at understanding other people – at least we all think we are – but we do not actually understand how we do it until we reflect on it. And attribution theory is one way of systematically reflecting on it.

ATTRIBUTION AND THE NAÏVE SCIENTIST

The process by which we make judgements about internal/external causes is called the *attribution process,* which was first investigated by Heider (1958). In a famous study, Heider & Simmel (1944) demonstrated the strength of the human tendency to explain people's behaviour in terms of intentions, by showing that we sometimes attribute intentions to inanimate objects!

KEY STUDY 23.1 Even geometrical figures have intentions (Heider & Simmel, 1944)

- Heider and Simmel showed animated cartoons of three geometrical figures (a large triangle, a smaller triangle and a disc) moving around, in and out of a large square.
- Participants tended to see them as having human characteristics and, in particular, as having intentions towards each other.
- A common perception was to see the two triangles as two men in rivalry for a girl (the disc), with the larger triangle being seen as aggressive and a bully, the smaller triangle as defiant and heroic, and the disc as timid. (Compare this with what Piaget calls *animism* in the child: see Chapter 34.)

We noted in Chapter 22 that there's a sense in which we're all psychologists. Perhaps this is most apparent in the case of attribution theory, which promises to:

> ... uncover the way in which we, as ordinary men and women, act as scientists in tracking down the causes of behaviour; it promises to treat ordinary people, in fact, as if they were psychologists ... (Antaki, 1984)

Heider's 'common-sense' psychology

Heider (1958) argued that the starting point for studying how we understand the social world is the 'ordinary' person. He asked 'How do people usually think about and infer meaning from what goes on around them?' and 'How do they make sense of their own and other people's behaviours?' These questions relate to what he called 'common-sense' psychology. In Heider's view, the 'ordinary' person is a naïve scientist who links observable behaviour to unobservable causes, and these *causes* (rather than the behaviour itself) provide the meaning of what people do.

What interested Heider was the fact that members of a culture share certain basic assumptions about behaviour. These assumptions belong to the belief system that forms part of the culture as a whole, and distinguishes one culture from another. As Bennett (1993) has observed:

> It is important that we do subscribe to a common psychology, since doing this provides an orienting context in which we can understand, and be understood by, others. Imagine a world in which your version of everyday psychology was fundamentally at odds with that of your friends – without a shared 'code' for making sense of behaviour, social life would hardly be possible.

ASK YOURSELF...

- Can you see any parallels between Heider's common-sense psychology and Moscovici's social representations? (See Chapter 22.)

As we noted in the *Introduction and overview,* we explain people's behaviour in terms of *dispositional* (or personal/internal) factors, such as ability or effort, and *situational* (or environmental/external) factors, such as circumstances or luck. When we observe somebody's behaviour, we're inclined to attribute its cause to one or other of these two general sources. This represents one of these culturally shared beliefs about behaviour that forms part of common-sense psychology.

Fritz Heider (1896–1988)

Although Heider didn't formulate his own theory of attribution, he inspired other psychologists to pursue his original ideas. As well as his insight relating to personal and situational factors as causes of behaviour, three other ideas have been particularly influential (Ross & Fletcher, 1985):

1. when we observe others, we tend to search for enduring, unchanging, and dispositional characteristics
2. we distinguish between intentional and unintentional behaviours
3. we're inclined to attribute behaviours to events (causes) that are present when the outcome is present, and absent when the outcome is absent.

JONES AND DAVIS'S CORRESPONDENT INFERENCE THEORY (CIT)

Correspondent inferences and intentionality

Jones & Davis (1965) were very much influenced by Heider. They argued that the goal of the attribution process is to be able to make *correspondent inferences.* We need to be able to infer that both the behaviour and the intention that produced it correspond to some underlying, stable feature of the person (a *disposition*). An inference is 'correspondent' when the disposition attributed to an actor 'corresponds' to the behaviour from which the disposition is inferred. For instance, if someone gives up his seat on the bus to allow a pregnant woman to sit down, we'd probably infer that he's 'kind and unselfish'. This is a correspondent inference, because both the behaviour and the disposition can be labelled in a similar way ('kind and unselfish'). But if we attribute the behaviour to compliance with someone else's demands ('he' is a husband whose wife has told him to give up his seat), then we wouldn't be making a correspondent inference.

According to Jones and Davis, a precondition for a correspondent inference is the attribution of *intentionality,* and they specify two criteria or conditions for this. We have to be confident that the actor:

- is capable of having produced the observed effects, and
- knew the effects the behaviour would produce.

The analysis of uncommon effects

Having made these preliminary decisions, how do we then proceed to infer that the intended behaviour is related to some underlying disposition? One answer is the *analysis of uncommon effects.* When more than one course of action is open to a person, a way of understanding why s/he chose one course rather than another is to compare the consequences of the chosen option with the consequences of those that weren't. In other words, what's *distinctive* (or *uncommon*) about the effects of the choice that's made?

For example, you've a strong preference for one particular university, even though there are several that are similar with regard to size, reputation, type of course and so on. The fact that all the others require you to be in residence during your first year suggests that you've a strong preference for being independent and looking after yourself.

Generally, the fewer differences between the chosen and the unchosen alternatives, the more confidently we can infer dispositions. Also, the more negative elements involved in the chosen alternative, the more confident still we can be of the importance of the distinctive consequence. (If living out of residence means a lot of extra travelling, or is more expensive, then the desire to be self-sufficient assumes even greater significance.)

Other factors affecting dispositional attributions

Because the analysis of uncommon effects can lead to ambiguous conclusions, other cues must also be used.

- *Choice* is self-explanatory: is the actor's behaviour influenced by situational factors, or a result of free will?
- *Social desirability* relates to the norms associated with different situations. Because most of us conform most of the time, the need to explain other people's behaviour doesn't often arise. We base our impressions of others more on behaviour which is in some way unusual, novel, bizarre, or antisocial, than on behaviour that's expected or conventional.

> ***ASK YOURSELF...***
> - Do you agree with this account of social desirability?
> - Give your reasons.
> - Can you think of an example from your own experience, or something in the media, that is consistent with Jones and Davis's account?

'Deviant' behaviour seems to provide more information about what the person is like, largely because when we behave unconventionally we're more likely to be ostracised, shunned or disapproved of (which, presumably, people don't want).

For example, at a funeral people are expected to dress soberly, look sad and talk respectfully of the deceased. So, when we observe such behaviour, we can easily attribute it to the situation ('That's how one acts at funerals'). But if somebody arrives in brightly coloured clothes, making jokes, and talking disrespectfully of the deceased, s/he is 'breaking the rules'. His/her behaviour needs explaining, and we're likely to attribute it to personal/dispositional characteristics. This was demonstrated in an experiment by Jones *et al.* (1961).

KEY STUDY 23.2 If you want to be an astronaut, be a loner (Jones *et al.*, 1961)

- Participants heard a tape-recording of a job interview, where the applicant was, supposedly, applying to be an astronaut or a submariner.
- Prior to hearing the tape, participants were informed of the ideal qualities for the job: astronauts should be inner-directed and able to exist without social interaction, while submariners should be other-directed and gregarious.
- The participants believed the candidates also understood these ideal qualities.
- The tape presented the candidate as either displaying these qualities or behaving in the opposite way, and participants had to give their impressions of the candidate.
- When the candidate behaved in the *opposite* way, participants more confidently rated him as actually being like that, compared with those who heard a 'conforming' candidate.

Social desirability can also be explained in terms of the *positivity bias.*

Box 23.1 The positivity bias, vigilance and the 'Pollyanna principle'

- We usually see people as 'good', trustworthy, and so on (the *positivity bias*) (Fiske, 2004).
- According to the 'Pollyanna principle' (Matlin & Stang, 1978), people seek the pleasant and avoid the unpleasant, communicate good news more often than bad, judge pleasant events as more likely than unpleasant events, recall pleasant life experiences more accurately than unpleasant experiences, rate themselves better than the average and as more happy than not, and evaluate each other positively.
- Also, desirable traits are perceived as more common than undesirable traits (Rothbart & Park, 1986).
- North Americans, at least, view their future as unequivocally positive (Ross & Newby-Clark, 1998), and positive words even outnumber negative words in most languages (Zajonc, 1998).

... The positivity assumption, then, is widespread in people's expectations about life experiences, but people expect positive outcomes from other people even more than from events in general ... positivity implies approach rather than avoidance, so it encourages interaction with other people and the environment ... (Fiske, 2004)

- Positivity is offset by *vigilance:* unexpected bad behaviour grabs people's attention. Why is this?
- According to Fiske: (a) if negative events are perceived as rare, they should provide more information about the individual – they set the person apart from the norm; (b) negative events might also be more diagnostic – that is, allow more confident categorisation of the person as a particular kind or other, regardless of the norm.

◎ *Roles* refer to another kind of conformity. When people in well-defined roles behave as they're expected to, this tells us relatively little about their underlying dispositions (they're 'just doing their job'). But when they display out-of-role behaviour, we can use their actions to infer 'what they're really like'. This is similar to the effects of social desirability, except that the norms are associated with particular social positions within an overall social context, rather than with the context or situation itself.

Pope damns paedophile priests

The Pope addresses American cardinals in his private library in the Vatican yesterday after calling them to Rome to discuss the problem of paedophile priests. He told them there was no place for child molesters in the Church

By David Rennie in Washington and Bruce Johnston in Rome

THE Pope said yesterday that there was no place in the Church for priests who abused children as he acknowledged for the first time the gravity of the crisis engulfing the Catholic Church.

Addressing an unprecedented emergency gathering of American cardinals in the Vatican, he said that the molestation of children by priests was "an appalling sin in the eyes of God".

The Pope added: "People need to know that there is no place in the priesthood and religious life for those who would harm the young."

His remarks were directed at the scandal sweeping the Church in America. The most powerful of its 13 cardinals, Bernard Law, Archbishop of Boston, faces calls for his resignation. This follows disclosure of church documents showing that his archdiocese shuffled a known paedophile, Paul Shanley, from parish to parish over 20 years, despite receiving a string of complaints.

A series of recent court actions in Boston and elsewhere has uncovered previously secret settlements paid by the American church to hundreds of boys after they were abused and raped by priests.

In most cases, victims had to sign legally binding gagging clauses in return for their settlements, which ranged from tens of thousands to hundreds of thousands of pounds.

Scandals have also emerged in Canada, Germany, Australia, and Britain, and in countries traditionally seen as strongholds of the Catholic faith, including France, Ireland, Poland and Mexico.

The Pope's strong comments yesterday led Cardinal Roger Mahoney, Archbishop of Los Angeles, to say there was a new policy of "zero tolerance" towards abusive priests. However, Cardinal Francis George, Archbishop of Chicago, said the issue remained unclear, as the Pope had spoken of the power of "Christian conversion" to work "extraordinary changes", implying that priests could take a "radical decision to turn away from sin and towards God".

As the cardinals flew to Rome, one, speaking anonymously, said that he had been asked by senior colleagues to seek Vatican help in forcing Cardinal Law to step down. He said the American Bishops Conference had developed an almost unanimous stand against him.

Cardinal George said that the subject of Cardinal Law's resignation had not been raised yesterday, nor during a private meeting of cardinals the night before. But Cardinal Law had admitted to his col leagues that "if he hadn't mad some terrible mistakes, we proba bly all wouldn't be here".

In his address, the Pope vowe that the Church would not be over come by the scandal. "A great wor of art may be blemished, but it beauty remains. That is a trut which all intellectual honesty mus acknowledge," he said.

He said that he understoo

Continued on Page 4

Church scandal in US: Page 4

◎ *Prior expectations* are based on past experiences with the same actor. The better we know someone, the better placed we are to decide whether his/her behaviour on a particular occasion is 'typical'. If it's 'atypical', we're more likely to dismiss it, or play down its significance, or explain it in terms of situational factors.

An evaluation of Jones and Davis's CIT

While there are data consistent with Jones and Davis's theory, several weaknesses have been identified.

- Eiser (1983) has argued that intentions aren't a precondition for correspondent inferences. When someone is called 'clumsy', that dispositional attribution doesn't imply that the behaviour was intentional. In Eiser's view, behaviours which are unintended or accidental are beyond the scope of Jones and Davis's theory.
- Also, it isn't just undesirable or unexpected behaviour that's informative. 'Conforming' behaviour can also be informative, as when behaviour confirms a stereotype (Hewstone & Fincham, 1996: see Chapter 22, page 388).
- Although CIT continues to attract interest, most of the studies supporting it didn't measure causal attributions (Gilbert, 1995). Indeed, the model focuses on the covariation (correlation) of actions and their *consequences* as the key to attribution (Fiske, 2004). Inferring a disposition isn't the same as inferring a cause, and each appears to reflect different underlying processes (Hewstone & Fincham, 1996).
- Both of Kelley's models discussed next are concerned with the processes that determine whether an internal or external attribution is made for a behaviour's cause. Focusing on the covariation of actions and their potential causes is *complementary* to CIT (Fiske, 2004).

KELLEY'S COVARIATION AND CONFIGURATION MODELS

ASK YOURSELF...

- One of your fellow students (let's call her Sally) is late for psychology class one morning. How might you explain her late arrival?
- What kinds of information would you need in order to make a causal attribution?

The covariation model

Kelley's *covariation model* (1967) tries to explain how we make causal attributions where we have some knowledge of how the actor usually behaves in a variety of situations, and how others usually behave in those situations. The principle of covariation states that:

An effect is attributed to one of its possible causes with which, over time, it covaries.

In other words, if two events repeatedly occur together, we're more likely to infer that they're causally related than if they very rarely occur together. If the behaviour to be explained is thought of as an *effect,* the *cause* can be one of three kinds, and the extent to which the behaviour covaries with each of these three kinds of possible cause is what we base our attribution on. To illustrate the three kinds of causal information, let's take the hypothetical example of Sally, who's late for her psychology class.

- *Consensus* refers to the extent to which other people behave in the same way. In this example, are other students late for psychology? If all (or most) other students are late, then consensus is *high* (she's in good company), but if only Sally is late, consensus is *low.*
- *Distinctiveness* refers to the extent to which Sally behaves in a similar way towards other, similar, 'stimuli' or 'entities'. Is she late for other subjects? If she is, then distinctiveness is *low* (there's nothing special or distinctive about psychology), but if she's late only for psychology, then distinctiveness is *high.*
- *Consistency* refers to how stable Sally's behaviour is over time. Is she regularly late for psychology? If she is, consistency is *high*, but if she's not (this is a 'one-off'), then consistency is *low.*

Kelley believes that a combination of *low consensus* (Sally is the only one late), *low distinctiveness* (she's late for all her subjects), and *high consistency* (she's regularly late) will lead us to make a *person* (*internal* or *dispositional*) attribution. In other words, the cause of Sally's behaviour is something to do with Sally, such as being a poor timekeeper.

However, any other combination would normally result in an external or situational attribution. For example, if Sally is generally punctual (*low consistency*), or if most students are late for psychology (*high consensus*), then the cause of Sally's lateness might be 'extenuating circumstances' in the first case or the subject and/or the lecturer in the second.

Table 23.1 Causal attributions based on three different combinations of causal information (based on Kelley, 1967)

Consensus	Distinctiveness	Consistency	Causal attribution
Low	Low	High	Person (actor/internal)
Low	High	Low	Circumstances (external)
High	High	High	Stimulus/target (external)

Evaluation of Kelley's covariation model

ASK YOURSELF...

- Can you relate consensus, distinctiveness and consistency information to components of Jones and Davis's correspondent inference theory?

- According to Gilbert (1998), the similarities between Kelley's covariation model and CIT are often overlooked: (a) *consensus* is similar to Jones and Davis's *social desirability* (if consensus is high, then the behaviour is socially desirable); (b) *distinctiveness* is similar to Jones and Davis's concern with *uncommon/unique effects* (the more distinctive the choice, the more it has to do with the unique effects of the choice); (c) *consistency* reflects an enduring *disposition* (as opposed to temporary circumstances).

- A number of empirical studies have found support for Kelley.

KEY STUDY 23.3 A funny thing happened on the way to the laboratory (McArthur, 1972)

- McArthur presented participants with one-sentence descriptions of various behaviours relating to emotions, accomplishments, opinions and actions (for example, 'John laughs at the comedian', 'Sue is afraid of the dog', 'George translates the sentence incorrectly').
- Each description was accompanied by *high or low consensus information* ('Almost everyone ...' or 'Hardly anyone ...'), *high or low distinctiveness information* (this person does/does not respond the same way to 'almost every other ... comedian ... dog, etc.'), and *high or low consistency information* ('In the past ... has almost always ...' or 'almost never').
- The task was to attribute each behaviour to (a) characteristics of the actor, (b) the stimulus (target), (c) circumstances, or (d) some combination of these.
- Predictions based on Kelley's model were strongly supported.

- However, not all three types of causal information were used to the same extent. Distinctiveness influenced entity attributions the most, and consistency influenced circumstances attribution the most. Also, *contrary* to predictions, consensus *didn't* influence person attributions the most.
- Other laboratory studies have also found this uneven use of the three kinds of causal information. For example, Major (1980) found that participants show a marked preference for consistency over the other two, with consensus being the least preferred.
- Similarly, Nisbett & Borgida (1975) found surprisingly weak effects of consensus information when they asked university students to explain the behaviour of a participant in a psychology experiment. This participant, like most others involved, had agreed to tolerate a high level of electric shock. But the students who were told that 16 of the 34 participants had tolerated the highest possible shock level, were *no more likely* to make situational attributions than those who had been given no consensus information at all. According to Nisbett and Borgida, people's judgements are less responsive to the dull and abstract base rates that constitute consensus information than to the more vivid information regarding the behaviour of one, concrete target person.
- However, consensus information can have more of an impact if it's made more salient (for example, if it's contrary to what we might expect most people to do: Wells & Harvey, 1977).
- Consistent with Wells and Harvey's proposal is Hilton & Slugoski's (1986) *abnormal conditions focus model*. This can help explain why the three types of causal information aren't used to the same extent.

Box 23.1 The abnormal conditions focus model (Hilton & Slugoski, 1986)

- According to Hilton and Slugoski, Kelley's three types of information are useful to the extent that the behaviour requiring explanation contrasts with the information given. So, with *low consensus* information, the *person* is abnormal, whereas with *low consistency* information the *circumstances* are abnormal. With *high distinctiveness* information, the *stimulus/target* is abnormal.
- Another way of looking at 'abnormality' is, in Table 23.1, to read down the columns. Two 'values' are the same, and different from the third. For example, *high consensus* (the 'odd one out') corresponds to the *stimulus/target, low distinctiveness* corresponds to the *person/actor,* and *low consistency* corresponds to the *circumstances*.
- Here, then, 'abnormal' is taken to refer to the causal *information,* rather than the causal attribution. But the end result seems to be the same.
- The model proposes that we attribute as a cause the necessary condition that's abnormal when compared with the background of the target event (Slugoski & Hilton, 2000).

- Just because people make attributions as if they're using covariation 'rules', doesn't necessarily mean they are (Hewstone & Fincham, 1996). Kelley seems to have overestimated people's ability to assess covariation. He originally compared the social perceiver to a naïve scientist (as did Heider), trying to draw inferences in much the same way as the formal scientist draws conclusions from data. More significantly, it's a *normative* model which states how, ideally, people should come to draw inferences about others' behaviour. However, the actual procedures that people use aren't as logical, rational and systematic as the model suggests. (This criticism also applies to Jones and Davis's CIT: see the section on error and bias, below.)

The configuration model

Kelley recognised that in many situations (most notably when we don't know the actor), we might not have access to any or all of the covariation model's three types of information. Indeed, often the only information we have is a single occurrence of the behaviour of a particular individual. Yet we still feel able to explain the behaviour. The configuration model was Kelley's attempt to account for attributions about such single occurrence behaviours.

Causal schemata

When we make 'single event attributions' we do so using *causal schemata* (Kelley, 1972, 1983). These are general ideas (or ready-made beliefs, preconceptions, and even theories: Hewstone & Fincham, 1996) about 'how certain kinds of causes interact to produce a specific kind of effect' (Kelley, 1972). According to Fiske & Taylor (1991), causal schemata provide the social perceiver with a 'causal short-hand' for making complex inferences quickly and easily. They're based on our experience of cause–effect relationships, and what we've been taught by others about such relationships. They come into play when causal information is otherwise ambiguous and incomplete.

The two major kinds of causal schemata are *multiple necessary schemata* and *multiple sufficient schemata.*

Box 23.2 Multiple necessary and multiple sufficient schemata

- **Multiple necessary causes:** Experience tells us that to win a marathon, for example, you must not only be fit and highly motivated, but you must have trained hard for several months beforehand, you must wear the right kind of running shoes and so on.
- Even if all these conditions are met, there's no guarantee of success, but the absence of any one of them is likely to produce failure. So, in this sense, success is more informative than failure. Thus, there are many causes needed to produce certain behaviours – typically, those which are unusual or extreme.
- **Multiple sufficient causes:** With some behaviours, any number of causes are sufficient to explain their occurrence. For example, a footballer who advertises shampoo may do so because he genuinely believes it's a good product, or because he's being paid a large sum of money to advertise it – either of these is a sufficient cause.

David Beckham, almost as famous for his promotion of Adidas as for playing football

ASK YOURSELF...

- In this last example, do you think one of the proposed causes is more likely to be the real cause than the other (believing in the product or receiving a large fee)?
- If so, which one?
- What do you base this attribution on?

Since it's reasonable to assume that it's the fee which accounts for the footballer's appearance in the commercial, we're likely to reject the other cause ('belief' in the product) according to the *discounting principle* (Kelley, 1983). According to this:

> Given that different causes can produce the same effect, the role of a given cause is discounted if other plausible causes are present.

Multiple sufficient schemata are also associated with the *augmenting principle* (Kelley, 1983). This states that:

> The role of a given cause is augmented or increased if the effect occurs in the presence of an inhibitory factor.

So, we're more likely to make an internal attribution (to effort and ability) when a student passes an exam after (say) suffering the death of a relative, than would be the case for a student who'd passed without having suffered such a loss.

WEINER'S ATTRIBUTIONAL THEORY OF EMOTION AND MOTIVATION

As the name suggests, Weiner's (1986) theory is really an application of basic attributional principles to human emotion and motivation (see Chapters 9 and 10). According to Weiner, the attributions we make about our own and others' successes and failures produce specific kinds of emotional response, but these attributions are more complex than described by Heider, Jones and Davis or Kelley.

For Weiner, there are three dimensions of causality. These are:

1. the *locus dimension:* causes can be internal/external (person/situation)
2. the *stability dimension:* causes can be stable/transient (permanent/temporary)
3. the *controllability dimension:* causes can be controllable or uncontrollable.

For example, we may blame failure in an exam on a really difficult paper (external, stable, uncontrollable), which is likely to make us feel angry. Or we may blame the really bad headache we awoke with on the morning of the exam (internal, unstable, uncontrollable), which may make us feel both angry and disappointed. But a third possibility is that we blame our failure on our basic lack of ability (internal, stable, uncontrollable), which is likely to make us feel quite depressed (see Figure 10.7, page 166).

What's important here is that not all internal or external causes are of the same kind. For Weiner, causes are *multidimensional*.

ERROR AND BIAS IN THE ATTRIBUTION PROCESS

As we've already seen, people are far less logical and systematic (less 'scientific') than required by Kelley's covariation model. We also noted that both this and Jones and Davis's CIT are *normative* models: they describe people's *ideal* attribution processes. 'Normative' here means a model of people thinking according to the highest standards, an idealised view of how people would think if provided with all the available information, with unlimited time and displaying no bias (Fiske, 2004).

Research into sources of error and bias seems to provide a much more accurate account of how people *actually* make causal attributions. Zebrowitz (1990) defines sources of bias as:

> ... the tendency to favour one cause over another when explaining some effect. Such favouritism may result in causal attributions that deviate from predictions derived from rational attributional principles, like covariation ...

Even though almost all behaviour is the product of both the person and the situation, our causal explanations tend to emphasise one or the other. According to Jones & Nisbett (1971), we all want to see ourselves as competent interpreters of human behaviour, and so we naïvely assume that simple explanations are better than complex ones. To try to analyse the interactions between personal and situational factors would take time and energy, and we seldom have all the relevant information at our disposal.

One kind of bias is the uneven use of different kinds of causal information that relate to Kelley's covariation model. Although all three types have some influence on attributions (thus supporting the broad outline of Kelley's model), we've noted that they're not used to an equal extent. People use consistency the most, distinctiveness moderately and consensus the least (Kruglanski, 1977).

The fundamental attribution error (FAE)

The *fundamental attribution error* (FAE) refers to the general tendency to overestimate the importance of personal/dispositional factors relative to situational/environmental factors as causes of behaviour (Ross, 1977).

This will tend to make others' behaviour seem more predictable which, in turn, enhances our sense of control over the environment.

> *ASK YOURSELF...*
> - Can you relate the FAE to any of the Gestalt laws of perception (see Chapter 15)?

Heider (1958) believed that behaviour represents the 'figure' against the 'ground', comprising context, roles, situational pressures, and so on. In other words, behaviour is conspicuous, and situational factors are less easily perceived.

For Zebrowitz (1990):

> ... the fundamental attribution error is best viewed as a bias towards attributing an actor's behaviour to dispositional causes rather than as an attribution error. This bias may be limited to adults in Western societies and it may be most pronounced when they are constrained to attribute behaviour to a single cause ...

(See Critical Discussion 23.1, page 403.)

The FAE and the just world hypothesis (JWH)

Related to the FAE, but not usually cited as an example of an attribution error, is the *just world hypothesis* (JWH) (Lerner, 1965, 1980). According to this, 'I am a just person living in a just world, a world where people get what they deserve'. When 'bad' things happen to people, we believe it's because they're in some way 'bad' people, so that they have at least partly 'brought it on themselves'. This can help explain the phenomenon of 'blaming the victim'. In rape cases, for example, the woman is often accused of having 'led the man on' or giving him the sexual 'green light' before changing her mind.

Myers (1994) gives the example of a German civilian who, on being shown round the Bergen–Belsen concentration camp after the British liberation, commented 'What terrible criminals these prisoners must have been to receive such treatment'. What this person seems to have been saying is that s/he found it totally unbelievable that such horrors (as had obviously been perpetrated in that camp) could have happened to innocent people – if they happened to them, why couldn't they happen to me? Believing in a just world gives us a sense of being in control: so long as we're 'good', only 'good' things will happen to us.

Jodie Foster, in *The Accused*, victim of gang-rape. Defence lawyers accused her of being of 'questionable character'

Glenn Hoddle was sacked as England football manager in 1999 after allegedly claiming that disabled people were being punished for sins committed in a former life

The actor–observer effect (AOE)

Related to the FAE is the tendency for actors and observers to make different attributions about the same event. This is called the *actor–observer effect* (AOE) (Jones & Nisbett, 1971; Nisbett *et al.*, 1973).

- Actors usually see their own behaviour as primarily a response to the situation, and therefore as quite *variable* from situation to situation (the cause is *external*).
- The observer typically attributes the same behaviour to the actor's intentions and dispositions, and therefore as quite *consistent* across situations (the cause is *internal*). The observer's attribution to internal causes is, of course, the FAE.

Nisbett *et al.* (1973) found that students: (a) assumed that actors would behave in the future in ways similar to those they'd just witnessed; (b) described their best friend's choices of girlfriend and college major in terms referring to dispositional qualities of their best friend (while more often describing their own similar choices in terms of properties of the girlfriend or major); and (c) attributed more personality traits to other people than to themselves.

One explanation for the AOE is that what's *perceptually salient* or vivid for the actor is different from what's perceptually salient or vivid for the observer (this is the figure–ground explanation which we noted when discussing the FAE). An important study by Storms (1973) supports this perceptual salience explanation of the AOE.

KEY STUDY 23.4 Videotape and the attribution process (Storms, 1973)

- Two actor participants at a time engaged in a brief, unstructured conversation, while two observers looked on.
- Later, a questionnaire was used to measure the actors' attributions of their own behaviour in the conversation, and the observers' attributions of the behaviour of one of the two actors to whom they'd been assigned.
- Visual orientation was manipulated by the use of videotapes of the conversation so that:

  a the *no video* (control) group simply completed the questionnaire
  b the *same orientation* group simply saw a video of what they saw during the original conversation (before completing the questionnaire)
  c the *new orientation* group saw a video which reversed the original orientation: actors saw themselves and observers saw the other actor (again, before completing the questionnaire).

- As predicted, in the first two groups the usual AOE was found. But, also as predicted, the AOE was reversed in the third group: actors made more dispositional attributions than did observers.

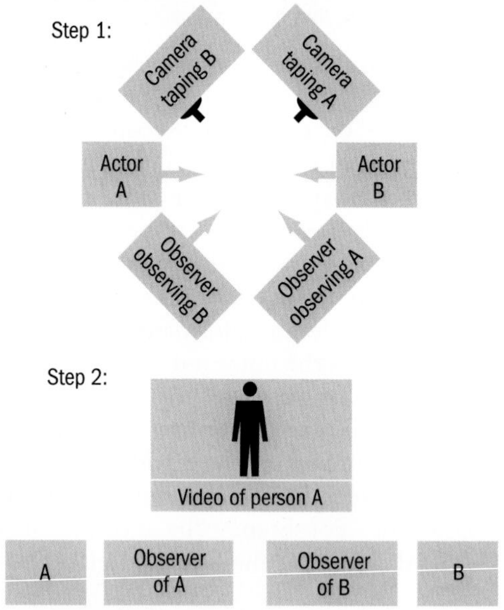

Figure 23.1 Diagram depicting the arrangement in the Storms (1973) experiment

The self-serving bias (SSB)

Several studies have found that the AOE is most pronounced when judging *negative* behaviours, and may be absent or even reversed for positive ones.

ASK YOURSELF...
- Try to account for this finding.

Naturally, no one wants to admit to being incompetent, so we're more likely to 'blame' our failures on something external to ourselves. This is the *self-protecting bias,* which protects our self-esteem. However, we're quite happy to take the credit for our successes. This is the *self-enhancing bias,* which enhances our self-esteem. Together, they constitute the *self-serving bias* (SSB) (Miller & Ross, 1975).

There's some evidence that positively valued outcomes (e.g. altruism) are more often attributed to people, and negatively valued outcomes (e.g. being late) to situational factors, regardless of who committed them. However, when either the self or someone closely associated with the self has committed the action, credit for positive events and denial of responsibility for negative ones are even stronger.

CRITICAL DISCUSSION 23.1 Cultural differences in attributional errors and biases

- Although the FAE has been assumed to be universal, more recent research suggests it may actually be specific to *individualist* (predominantly western) cultures (Fiske *et al.*, 1998: see Chapter 47).
- In *collectivist* (mainly non-western) cultures, people are more likely to attribute someone's behaviour to situational factors as opposed to personality characteristics. They don't expect people to be consistent on their behaviour: different behaviours may be required when the situation calls for it (Nagayama Hall & Barongan, 2002).
- English-language newspapers reporting murders emphasise dispositional causes (such as a deeply disturbed, driven personality, very bad temper/'short fuse'), while Chinese-language papers reporting the same crime emphasise situational causes (relationships, rivalry and isolation, the social availability of guns, achievement pressure, and the immediate context, such as having recently been sacked) (Morris & Peng, 1994).
- While all cultures encourage a search for invariant dispositions, some locate them more in individual actors, others in collective actors (Morris *et al.*, 2001).
- The SSB isn't found among Asians, who are more likely to attribute their successes to external factors (such as luck) and their failures to internal factors (such as lack of effort) (Kitayama & Markus, 1995). This, in turn, reflects a bias towards *self-effacement*, which is more likely to maintain one's self-esteem in a collectivist culture (where the achievements of the individual are minimised).
- This strategy for maintaining self-esteem is also often used by women in individualist cultures:

> *... whose belief system can also be characterized as collectivist in nature, in that they value relationships, put other people's needs before their own, and define themselves in terms of their connectedness to others ... (Nagayama Hall & Barongan, 2002)*

The importance of the consequences

The more serious the consequences of an actor's behaviour, the more likely the FAE is to be made: the more serious the outcome, the more likely we are to judge the actor as responsible, regardless of his/her perceived intentions.

KEY STUDY 23.5: Consequences of behaviour and the FAE (Walster, 1966)

- Walster gave participants an account of a car accident, in which a young man's car had been left at the top of a hill and then rolled down backwards.
- One group was told that very little damage was done to the car, and no other vehicle was involved.
- A second group was told that it collided with another car, causing some damage.
- A third group was told that the car crashed into a shop, injuring the shopkeeper and a small child.
- When participants had to assess how responsible the car owner was, the third group found him more 'guilty' or morally culpable than the second group, and the second group found him more guilty than the first.

If more serious consequences can result in greater blame and responsibility, can the reverse inference occur; that is, can belief that an act is intentional affect perception of the seriousness of the consequences? Darley & Huff (1990) found that judgements of the damage caused by an action depended on whether participants believed it was done intentionally, through negligence or accidentally. Although the damage done was described in an identical way, those who read that the act was done intentionally inflated their estimation of the amount of damage done, compared with those who believed the damage was caused unintentionally (either through negligence or accident).

Another facet of the consequences of behaviour is how they affect us personally (*personal* or *hedonic relevance*): the more they affect us (the greater the hedonic relevance), the more likely we are to hold the actor responsible. Going one step further, *personalism* is the perceiver's belief that the actor intended to harm the perceiver. In terms of Jones and Davis's theory, this increases the chances of making a *correspondent inference.*

Self-centred bias

This refers to the tendency for each person to think that s/he has contributed more to a joint project than the other thinks s/he has. This has been found in several settings, including married couples and household chores, students and ideas generated in a team's psychological assessment, and in basketball players and important turning points in a game (Ross & Sicoly, 1979).

In all these settings, the bias seems to depend on people's ability to *remember* their own contribution more than that of others, rather than a motivation to distort the extent of their contribution (Fiske, 2004).

CONCLUSIONS

All these errors and biases fall under the heading of *descriptive models.* They emphasise what people actually do when observed directly. What people 'ought' to do (according to normative models) if they're being completely rational, is often *not* what they actually do. According to Fiske (2004):

> ... The descriptive models, by documenting biases, capture that discrepancy. In the case of ordinary personology, people ignore the hidden power of situations and focus on other people's dispositions more than they should, and people attribute more personal responsibility to themselves for good events than they should.

CHAPTER SUMMARY

- **Attribution theory** refers to psychologists' attempts to explain the **attribution process**. **Theories of attribution** draw on the principles of attribution theory to predict how people will respond in particular life domains.
- Heider's 'common-sense' psychology sees people as **naïve scientists**, inferring unobservable causes (or meaning) from observable behaviour. In western culture, behaviour is explained in terms of both **personal** (**dispositional/internal**) and **situational** (**environmental/external**) factors.
- Jones and Davis were concerned with explaining why we make **correspondent inferences** about people's dispositions. One way of looking for dispositions that could have caused behaviour is through the **analysis of uncommon effects**.
- The likelihood of making dispositional attributions is influenced by **free choice**, **social desirability**, **roles** and **prior expectations**.
- Kelley's **covariation model** is concerned with the processes by which we make internal and external attributions for the causes of behaviour. The **principle of covariation** says that we're more likely to infer that two events are causally related if they repeatedly co-occur.
- Attributions about some effect/behaviour depend on the extent of its covariation with causal information regarding **consensus**, **consistency** and **distinctiveness.**
- Kelley's **configuration model** tries to account for 'single event attributions' in terms of **multiple necessary** and multiple **sufficient causal schemata.** The latter are associated with the **augmenting principle**, and we choose between two or more possible causes by using the **discounting principle**.
- Weiner's attribution theory identifies three dimensions of causality: **locus**, **stability** and **controllability**. It applies basic attributional principles to emotion and motivation.
- People are actually less rational and scientific than Jones and Davis's, and Kelley's **normative** models require. A more accurate account of the attribution process involves looking at **systematic biases** in the attribution of cause.
- The **fundamental attribution error** (FAE) is the tendency to exaggerate the importance of internal/dispositional factors relative to external/situational factors. The likelihood of making the error depends on the seriousness/importance of the **consequences** of behaviour, and **personal/hedonic relevance**.
- In the **actor–observer effect** (AOE), **actors** see their behaviours as responses to **situational factors**, whereas **observers** explain the same behaviours in **dispositional** terms.
- The AOE is most pronounced when one explains one's own negative behaviour (**self-protecting bias**). Personal successes tend to be explained in dispositional ways (**self-enhancing bias**). Together, they comprise **the self-serving bias** (SSB).
- There are important **cultural differences** with regard to the FAE and SSB in particular. These are related to **individualist** and **collectivist** cultures.
- Other biases include the **self-centred bias**.

Links with other topics/chapters

- Two of the traditions that form the backbone of attribution theory are Schachter's *cognitive labelling theory of emotion* (Chapter 10) and Bem's *self-perception theory of attitude change* (Chapter 24).
- The multidimensional nature of causes, combined with the emotional responses associated with different attributions (Weiner) have important implications for *impression management/self-presentation* (Chapter 22), *self-esteem* (especially in relation to *gender differences* in *achievement motivation*) (Chapters 9 and 36), and *helping behaviour* (Chapter 30).
- The claim that women's collectivist belief system is a means of maintaining their self-esteem is directly relevant to Gilligan's account of *female morality* (Chapter 35).
- In combination with the FAE, the JWH can help to explain certain aspects of *prejudice* (see Chapter 25) and *helping behaviour* (see Chapter 30).
- An interesting exception to the SSB is the case of *clinically depressed* people (Abramson *et al.*, 1978) (Chapter 44).
- There's also evidence that women are more likely than men to cope with stress by blaming themselves for their plight (Chapter 12).
- The SSB might be useful in the short run, but not adaptive in the long term. For example, blaming one's partners is correlated with *marital dissatisfaction,* and the data suggest that blame actually causes the unhappiness (not vice-versa) (Chapter 28).

24

ATTITUDES AND ATTITUDE CHANGE

INTRODUCTION AND OVERVIEW

According to Gordon Allport (1935):

> The concept of attitudes is probably the most distinctive and indispensable concept in contemporary American social psychology ...

More than 50 years later, Hogg & Vaughan (1995) claim that:

> Attitudes continue to fascinate research workers and remain a key, if controversial, part of social psychology.

However, the study of attitudes has undergone many important changes during that time, with different questions becoming the focus of theory and research.

According to Stainton Rogers *et al.* (1995), psychologists have tried to answer four fundamental questions over the last 70 years:

1. Where do attitudes come from? How are they moulded and formed in the first place?
2. How can attitudes be measured?
3. How and why do attitudes change? What forces are involved and what intrapsychic mechanisms operate when people shift in their opinions about particular 'attitude objects'?
4. How do attitudes relate to behaviour? What is it that links the way people think and feel about an attitude object, and what they do about it?

In this chapter, the emphasis is on some of the answers that have been offered to questions 3 and 4. This discussion is also relevant to prejudice, considered as an extreme attitude (see Chapter 25).

During the 1940s and 1950s, the focus of research was on attitude change, in particular *persuasive communication*. Much of the impetus for this came from the use of *propaganda* during the Second World War, as well as a more general concern over the growing influence of the mass media, especially in the USA. The power of advertising was also beginning to interest psychologists and other social scientists. This period also saw the birth of a number of theories of attitude change, the most influential of these being Festinger's *cognitive dissonance theory.*

The 1960s and 1970s was a period of decline and pessimism in attitude research, at least partly due to the apparent failure to find any reliable relationship between measured attitudes and behaviour (Hogg & Vaughan, 1995). However, the 1980s saw a revival of interest, stimulated largely by the cognitive approach, so attitudes represent another important aspect of *social cognition* (see Chapter 22).

WHAT ARE ATTITUDES?

Allport (1935) regarded the study of attitudes as the meeting ground for the study of social groups, culture and the individual. Similarly, Festinger (1950) emphasised the integral interdependence of individual and group: 'an attitude is correct, valid, and proper to the extent that it is anchored in a group of people with similar beliefs, opinions, and attitudes'. But, with a few notable exceptions, attitude research has focused on *internal* processes, ignoring the influence of groups on attitude formation and change (Cooper *et al.*, 2004). Even Allport's definition in Table 24.1 reflects this bias. Warren and Jahoda's definition is probably the most 'social'.

According to Rosenberg & Hovland (1960), attitudes are 'predispositions to respond to some class of stimuli with certain classes of response'. These classes of response are:

- *affective:* what a person feels about the attitude object, how favourably or unfavourably it's evaluated
- *cognitive:* what a person believes the attitude object is like, objectively
- *behavioural* (sometimes called the '*conative*'): how a person actually responds, or intends to respond, to the attitude object.

Table 24.1 Some definitions of attitudes

'An attitude is a mental and neural state of readiness, organised through experience, exerting a directive or dynamic influence upon the individual's response to all objects and situations with which it is related.' (Allport, 1935)
'A learned orientation, or disposition, toward an object or situation, which provides a tendency to respond favourably or unfavourably to the object or situation ...' (Rokeach, 1968)
'... attitudes have social reference in their origins and development and in their objects, while at the same time they have psychological reference in that they inhere in the individual and are intimately enmeshed in his behaviour and his psychological make-up.' (Warren & Jahoda, 1973)
'The term *attitude* should be used to refer to a general, enduring positive or negative feeling about some person, object, or issue.' (Petty & Cacioppo, 1981)
'An *attitude* is an *evaluative disposition toward some object*. It's an evaluation of something or someone along a continuum of like-to-dislike or favourable-to-unfavourable ....' (Zimbardo & Leippe, 1991)

This *three-component model,* which is much more a model of attitude structure than a simple definition (Stahlberg & Frey, 1988), is shown in Figure 24.1 (page 407). It sees an attitude as an intervening/mediating variable between observable stimuli and responses, illustrating the influence that behaviourism was still having, even in social psychology, at the start of the 1960s. A major problem with this multi-component model is the assumption that the three components are highly correlated (see below, pages 409–411).

Attitudes, beliefs and values

An attitude can be thought of as a blend or integration of beliefs and values. Beliefs represent the knowledge or information we have about the world (although these may be inaccurate or incomplete) and, in themselves, are *non-evaluative.* According to Fishbein & Ajzen (1975), 'a belief links an object to some attribute' (e.g. 'America' and 'capitalist state'). To convert a belief into an attitude, a 'value' ingredient is needed. Values refer to an individual's sense of what is desirable, good, valuable, worthwhile, and so on. While most adults will have many thousands of beliefs, they have only hundreds of attitudes and a few dozen values.

> *ASK YOURSELF...*
> - Try to identify some of your most cherished values (there should be a relatively small number of these). Then try to identify some related attitudes, which are less abstract than values.

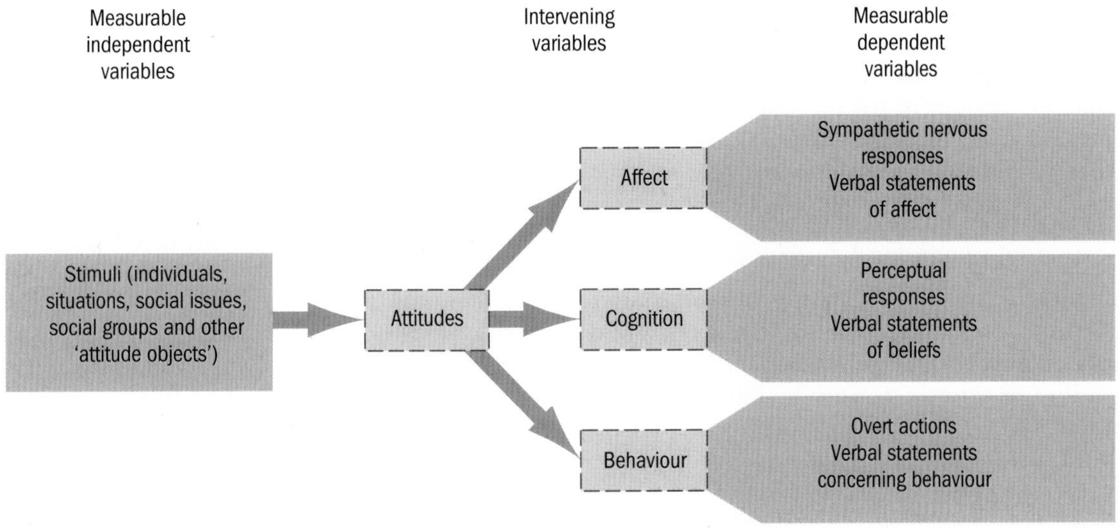

Figure 24.1 Three-component view of attitudes (Rosenberg & Hovland, 1960). From Stahlberg, D. & Frey, D. (1988) 'Attitudes 1: Structure, measurement and functions'. In Hewstone, M. *et al.* (Eds) *Introduction to Social Psychology*. Oxford, Blackwell.

WHAT ARE ATTITUDES FOR?

According to Hogg & Vaughan (1995):

> ... attitudes are basic and pervasive in human life ... Without the concept of attitude, we would have difficulty construing and reacting to events, trying to make decisions, and making sense of our relationships with people in everyday life ...

In other words, attitudes provide us with ready-made reactions to, and interpretations of events, just as other aspects of our cognitive 'equipment' do, such as schemas (see Chapter 21) and stereotypes (see Chapters 22 and 25). Attitudes save us energy, since we don't have to work out how we feel about objects or events each time we come into contact with them.

However, not all attitudes serve the same function. Katz (1960), influenced by Freud's psychoanalytic theory, believes that attitudes serve both conscious and unconscious motives. He identified four major functions of attitudes (see Table 24.2).

Katz's functional approach implies that some attitudes will be more resistant to efforts to change them than others, in particular those that serve an ego-defensive function. This is especially important when trying to account for prejudice and attempts to reduce it (see Chapter 25).

Table 24.2 Four major functions of attitudes (based on Katz, 1960)

Knowledge function	We seek a degree of predictability, consistency and stability in our perception of the world. Attitudes give meaning and direction to experience, providing frames of reference for judging events, objects and people.
Adjustive (instrumental or utilitarian) function	We obtain favourable responses from others by displaying socially acceptable attitudes, so they become associated with important rewards (such as others' acceptance and approval). These attitudes may be publicly expressed, but not necessarily believed, as is the case with compliance (see Chapter 26).
Value-expressive function	We achieve self-expression through cherished values. The reward may not be gaining social approval, but confirmation of the more positive aspects of our self-concept, especially our sense of personal integrity.
Ego-defensive function	Attitudes help protect us from admitting personal deficiencies. For example, prejudice helps us to sustain our self-concept by maintaining a sense of superiority over others. Ego defence often means avoiding and denying self-knowledge. This function comes closest to being unconscious in a Freudian sense (see Chapters 2 and 42).

THE MEASUREMENT OF ATTITUDES

An attitude cannot be measured directly, because it's a *hypothetical construct*. Consequently, it's necessary to find adequate attitude indicators, and most methods of attitude measurement are based on the assumption that they can be measured by people's beliefs or opinions about the attitude object (Stahlberg & Frey, 1988). Most attitude scales rely on verbal reports, and usually take the form of standardised statements which clearly refer to the attitude being measured. Such scales make two further assumptions: (i) the same statement has the *same meaning* for all respondents; and, more fundamentally, (ii) subjective attitudes, when expressed verbally, can be *quantified* (represented by a numerical score).

Thurstone's equal appearing intervals scale (1928)

Strictly, this is a technique for constructing an attitude scale. First, about 100 statements are collected, relevant to the attitude object. These statements must range from extreme positive to extreme negative, and should be short and unambiguous. Next, about 100 'judges' (representative of the population for whom the scale is intended) evaluate the statements on an eleven-point scale, assuming an equal interval scale. Any statements (items) which produce substantial disagreements are discarded, until 22 remain (two for each of the eleven points on the scale: eleven favourable, eleven unfavourable). The average numerical scale position of each statement is calculated.

Finally, the 22 statements are given, in random order, to participants who are asked to indicate every statement with which they agree. The final attitude score is the mean scale value for these statements. Though revolutionary in its time, the Thurstone scale is rarely used today, partly because it's so time-consuming, and partly because of the assumption that it's an interval (as opposed to an ordinal) scale.

> ***ASK YOURSELF...***
> - What's the difference between an ordinal and interval scale?
> - Why do you think this is a problem in relation to attitude measurement?

Likert scale (1932)

This comprises a number of statements, for each of which participants indicate whether they strongly agree/agree/undecided/disagree/strongly disagree. If possible, statements are selected so that for half 'agree' represents a positive attitude and for the other half a negative attitude. This controls for *acquiescence response set*, the tendency to agree or disagree with items consistently, or to tick the 'undecided' point on the scale.

LIKERT SCALE

'I believe that under no circumstances can animal experiments be justified'

5	4	3	2	1
Strongly agree	Agree	Undecided	Disagree	Strongly disagree

It's one of the most popular standard attitude scales, partly because it's more statistically reliable than the Thurstone scale, and partly because it's easier to construct. It makes no assumptions about equal intervals.

Sociometry (Moreno, 1953)

This represents a method for assessing interpersonal attitudes in 'natural' groups (at school, college, work); that is, it assesses who likes whom. Each group member is asked to name another who'd be his/her preferred partner for a specific activity or as a friend. The product of these choices is a *sociogram,* which charts the friendship patterns, revealing the popular and unpopular members, the 'isolates', and so on.

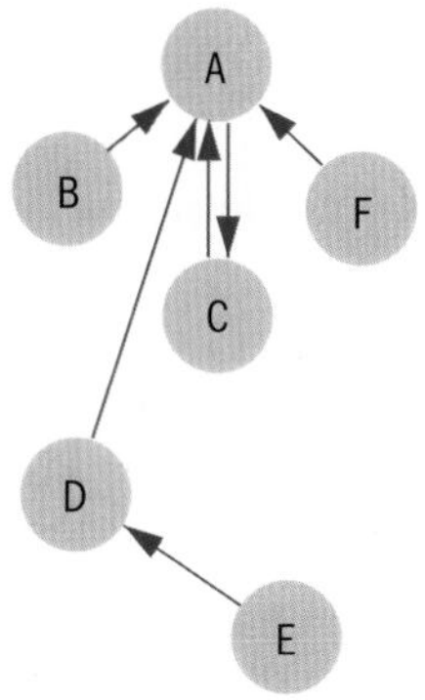

Each circle represents a group member, and the arrows indicate direction of preference.

> ***ASK YOURSELF...***
> - Who's the most popular member of the group?
> - Who's most isolated?

Guttman scalogram method

This is based on the assumption that a single, unidimensional trait can be measured by a set of statements that are ordered along a continuum of difficulty of acceptance. The statements range from those that are easy for most people to accept, to those that most people couldn't endorse. Such scale items are also *cumulative,* since accepting one item implies acceptance of all those 'below' it. It's constructed so that responses follow a step-like order (Hogg & Vaughan, 1995). See figure on page 409.

Semantic differential (Osgood *et al.*, 1957)

This assumes a hypothetical semantic space, in which the meaning or connotation of any word or concept can be represented somewhere on a seven-point scale. Unlike other scales, this allows different attitudes to be measured on the same scale. The attitude object is denoted by a single word (e.g. 'father'), and the scale comprises seven *bipolar* scales of adjectives (a value of seven usually being given to the positive end).

GUTTMAN SCALE
Attitude towards mixed-ethnic housing

How acceptable	Statement
Least	*Generally speaking, people should be able to live where they want.*
	Real estate agencies should not discriminate against minority groups.
	The local council should actively support the idea of open housing.
	There should be a local review board that would pass on cases of extreme discrimination of housing.
Most	*There should be laws to enforce mixed-ethnic housing.*

good_ _ _ _ _ _ _ _ _bad (illustrates the *evaluative factor*)
strong_ _ _ _ _ _ _ _ weak (illustrates the *potency factor*)
active _ _ _ _ _ _ _ _ passive (illustrates the *activity factor*)

Some alternative methods of measuring attitudes

- A problem with attitude scales (*self-report methods*) is that participants may be reluctant to reveal their true feelings. This can produce the effects of *social desirability*, in which participants give answers they think are expected or 'proper'. Incorporating a *lie scale* can help detect this tendency (see Chapter 42). Reassurance that their answers will remain anonymous, and stressing the importance of giving honest answers, can also help reduce the social desirability effect.
- A very different kind of solution is to use cleverly planned inconspicuous observation, such as Milgram's (1965) *lost letter technique*. This was designed to measure people's political attitudes, and involves the distribution, throughout a city, of large numbers of letters, stamped but unposted and addressed to different political organisations (such as 'Friends of the Nazi Party' and 'Friends of the Communist Party'). Depending on the rate at which the letters were returned, Milgram could assess the popularity of each organisation and the corresponding ideological bias of particular parts of the city. Milgram (1992) stresses that the technique guarantees the anonymity of those who took part.

> ***ASK YOURSELF...***
> - Despite Milgram's assurance regarding anonymity, can you think of any ethical objections to the lost letter technique?

- In the *bogus pipeline technique* (Jones & Sigall, 1971), participants are convinced they cannot hide their true attitudes. They're connected to a machine that resembles a lie detector and told that it can measure both the strength and direction of emotional responses, implying that there's no point in lying. Several studies have shown that participants are indeed convinced, and are less likely to conceal socially undesirable attitudes (such as racial prejudice: Hogg & Vaughan, 1995).

> ***ASK YOURSELF...***
> - Again, what's ethically dubious about the bogus pipeline technique?

THE RELATIONSHIP BETWEEN ATTITUDES AND BEHAVIOUR

Once we've established people's attitudes, can we then accurately predict how they'll behave? Rosenberg & Hovland's (1960) three-components model (see page 406) implies that the behavioural component will be highly correlated with the cognitive and affective components.

> ***ASK YOURSELF...***
> - Do people's expressed attitudes (cognitive and affective components) necessarily coincide with their overt actions (behavioural component)?
> - Do we always act in accordance with our attitudes?

An early study that shows the inconsistency of attitudes and behaviour is that of LaPiere (1934).

> **KEY STUDY 24.1 Some of my best friends are Chinese ... (LaPiere, 1934)**
> - Beginning in 1930 and for the next two years, LaPiere travelled around the USA with a Chinese couple (a young student and his wife), expecting to encounter anti-Oriental attitudes which would make it difficult for them to find accommodation.
> - But in the course of 10,000 miles of travel, they were discriminated against only once and there appeared to be no prejudice. They were given accommodation in 66 hotels, auto-camps and 'Tourist Homes' and refused at only one. They were also served in 184 restaurants and cafés and treated with '... more than ordinary consideration ...' in 72 of them.
> - However, when each of the 251 establishments visited was sent a letter six months later asking: 'Will you accept members of the Chinese race as guests in your establishment?', 91 per cent of the 128 which responded gave an emphatic 'No'. One establishment gave an unqualified 'Yes' and the rest said 'Undecided: depends upon circumstances'.

ASK YOURSELF...
- Try to account for LaPiere's findings.

Influences on behaviour

It's generally agreed that attitudes form only one determinant of behaviour. They represent *predispositions* to behave in particular ways, but how we actually act in a particular situation will depend on the immediate consequences of our behaviour, how we think others will evaluate our actions, and habitual ways of behaving in those kinds of situations. In addition, there may be specific *situational factors* influencing behaviour. For example, in the LaPiere study, the high quality of his Chinese friends' clothes and luggage and their politeness, together with the presence of LaPiere himself, may have made it more difficult to show overt prejudice. Thus, sometimes we experience a conflict of attitudes, and behaviour may represent a compromise between them.

Compatibility between attitudes and behaviour

The same attitude may be expressed in a variety of ways. For example, having a positive attitude towards the Labour Party doesn't necessarily mean that you actually become a member, or that you attend public meetings. But if you don't vote Labour in a general or local election, people may question your attitude. In other words, an attitude should predict behaviour to some extent, even if this is extremely limited and specific.

Indeed, Ajzen & Fishbein (1977) argue that attitudes can predict behaviour, provided that both are assessed at the same level of generality: there needs to be a high degree of *compatibility* (or *correspondence*) between them. They argue that much of the earlier research (LaPiere's study included) suffered from either trying to predict specific behaviours from general attitudes, or vice versa, and this accounts for the generally low correlations. A study by Davidson & Jaccard (1979) tried to overcome this limitation.

KEY STUDY 24.2 Attitudes can predict behaviour if you ask the right questions (Davidson & Jaccard, 1979)

- Davidson and Jaccard analysed correlations between married women's attitudes towards birth control and their actual use of oral contraceptives during the two years following the study.
- When 'attitude towards birth control' was used as the attitude measure, the correlation was 0.08. Clearly, the correspondence here was very low.
- But when 'attitudes towards oral contraceptives' were measured, the correlation rose to 0.32, and when 'attitudes towards using oral contraceptives' were measured, the correlation rose still further to 0.53.
- Finally, when 'attitudes towards using oral contraceptives during the next two years' was used, it rose still further, to 0.57. Clearly, in the last three cases, *correspondence* was much higher.

According to Ajzen and Fishbein, every single instance of behaviour involves four specific elements:

1. a specific action
2. performed with respect to a given target
3. in a given context
4. at a given point in time.

According to the *principle of compatibility,* measures of attitude and behaviour are compatible to the extent that the target, action, context and time element are assessed at identical levels of generality or specificity (Ajzen, 1988).

For example, a person's attitude towards a 'healthy lifestyle' specifies only the target, leaving the other three unspecified. A behavioural measure that would be compatible with this global attitude would have to aggregate a wide range of health behaviour across different contexts and times (Stroebe, 2000). Elaborating the psychological processes underlying the principle of compatibility, Ajzen (1996) suggested that to:

> ... the extent that the beliefs salient at the time of attitude assessment are also salient when plans are formulated or executed, strong attitude–behaviour correlations are expected.

The reliability and consistency of behaviour

Many of the classic studies which failed to find an attitude–behaviour relationship assessed just single instances of behaviour (Stroebe, 2000). As we noted earlier when discussing the LaPiere study, behaviour depends on many factors in addition to the attitude. This makes a single instance of behaviour an unreliable indicator of an attitude (Jonas *et al.*, 1995). Only by sampling many instances of the behaviour will the influence of specific factors 'cancel out'. This *aggregation principle* (Fishbein & Ajzen, 1974) has been demonstrated in a number of studies.

According to Hogg & Vaughan (1995), what emerged in the 1980s and 1990s is a view that attitudes and overt behaviour aren't related in a simple one-to-one fashion. In order to predict someone's behaviour, it must be possible to account for the interaction between attitudes, beliefs and behavioural intentions, as well as how all of these connect with the later action. One attempt to formalise these links is the *theory of reasoned action* (TRA) (Ajzen & Fishbein, 1970; Fishbein & Ajzen, 1975). This is discussed in relation to health behaviour in Chapter 12.

A demonstration of attitude–behaviour consistency that amazed the world; a pro-democracy Chinese student stands up for his convictions and defies tanks sent in against fellow rebels in Tiananmen Square, Beijing, China. Some 2000 demonstrators died in the subsequent massacre and the student was tried and shot a few days later

The strength of attitudes

Most modern theories agree that attitudes are represented in memory, and that an attitude's *accessibility* can exert a strong influence on behaviour (Fazio, 1986). By definition, strong attitudes exert more influence over behaviour, because they can be *automatically activated.* According to the MODE model ('motivation and opportunity as determinants': Fazio, 1986, 1990), spontaneous/automatic attitude–behaviour links occur when people hold highly accessible attitudes towards certain targets. These spontaneously guide behaviour, partly because they influence people's selective attention and perceptions of a particular target or situation.

One factor that seems to be important is *direct experience.* For example, Fazio & Zanna (1978) found that measures of students' attitudes towards psychology experiments were better predictors of their future participation if they'd already taken part in several experiments than if they'd only read about them.

MODE acknowledges that, in some situations, people engage in *deliberate, effortful* thinking about their attitudes when deciding how to act (forming behavioural intentions). For example, a student deciding which university to go to will probably scrutinise his/her attitudes before making a choice. But research conducted under MODE focuses on automatic processing (Cooper *et al.*, 2004). The *theory of planned behaviour* (TPB: Ajzen, 1991), which built on the TRA (see above), was designed to explain the relationship between attitudes and behaviour when deliberate, effortful processing is required. According to TPB, it's behavioural *intentions,* rather than attitudes, that directly influence behaviour (again, see Chapter 12).

CRITICAL DISCUSSION 24.1: So attitudes don't predict behaviour: what's the problem?

- The so-called *attitude–behaviour problem,* that is, the failure to find a reliable relationship between attitudes and behaviour, threatened to undermine the entire study of attitudes. As we saw in the *Introduction and overview,* attitude research was a cornerstone of social psychology in general, and social cognition in particular, for much of their history (Stainton Rogers *et al.*, 1995).
- But from the perspective of *discursive psychology* (DP) there's no reason to expect such a correlation: *inconsistency* between attitudes and behaviour is what we'd expect to find.
- Traditional, mainstream, attitude research is based on the fallacy of *individualism,* according to which attitudes 'belong' to individuals (see Chapter 3). This implies something fairly constant, and which is expressed and reflected in behaviour. From a discursive perspective, attitudes are versions of the world that are *constructed* by people in the course of their interactions with others.
- DP is concerned with *action,* as distinct from cognition. In saying or writing things, people are performing actions, whose nature can be revealed through a detailed study of the discourse (e.g. recordings of everyday conversations, newspaper articles, TV programmes). Social psychologists have underestimated the centrality of *conflict* in social life; an analysis of *rhetoric* highlights the point that people's versions of events, and their own mental life, are part of ongoing arguments, debates and dialogues (Billig, 1987, 1992, in Potter, 1996).
- Compared with traditional attitude research, DP tries to shift the focus away from single, isolated, individuals towards interactions between individuals and groups, a more *relational* or *distributed* focus (Potter, 1996).

SOCIAL INFLUENCE AND BEHAVIOUR CHANGE

Persuasive communication

According to Laswell (1948), in order to understand and predict the effectiveness of one person's attempt to change the attitude of another, we need to know 'Who says what in which channel to whom and with what effect'. Similarly, Hovland & Janis (1959) say that we need to study:

- *the source* of the persuasive communication, that is, the communicator (Laswell's 'who')
- *the message* itself (Laswell's 'what')
- *the recipient* of the message or the audience (Laswell's 'whom'), and
- the *situation* or *context.*

The basic paradigm in laboratory attitude-change research involves three steps or stages:

1. measure people's attitude towards the attitude object (*pre-test*)

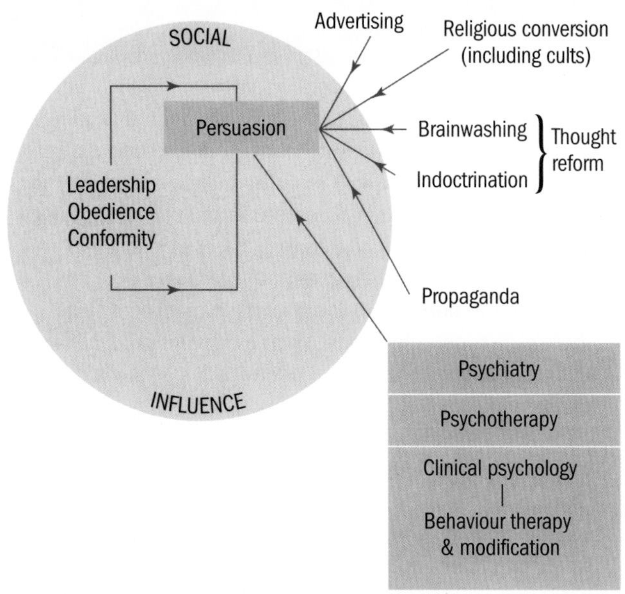

Figure 24.2 Different kinds of attempt to change people's attitudes and behaviour. These range from professional help for emotional and behavioural problems, through inevitable features of social interaction/social influence, to deliberate attempts to manipulate and control others for the benefit of the manipulator

2. expose them to a *persuasive communication* (manipulate a source, message or situational variable, or isolate a recipient-variable as the independent variable: see Figure 24.3)
3. measure their attitudes again (*post-test*).

If there's a difference between pre- and post-test measures, then the persuasive communication is judged to have 'worked'.

Theories of persuasion

The early research into persuasive communication was conducted for the US War Department's Information and Education Department. This largely pragmatic approach is known as the *Yale approach,* with Hovland being one of the leading figures involved. It told us a great deal regarding *when* attitude change is most likely to occur, and *how,* in practical terms, it can be produced. But it told us less about *why* people change their attitudes in response to persuasive messages.

Theories of systematic processing

According to *theories of systematic processing,* what's important is that the recipient processes the message content in a detailed way. This approach began with Hovland *et al.*'s (1953) proposal that the impact of persuasive messages can be understood in terms of a sequence of processes:

Attention to message ⟶ Comprehension of the content ⟶ Acceptance of its conclusions

If any of these fails to occur, persuasion is unlikely to be achieved.

McGuire (1969) proposed a longer chain of processes. We should ask if the recipient (i) attended to the message; (ii) comprehended it; (iii) yielded to it (accepted it); (iv) retained it; and (v) acted as a result. As with Hovland *et al.*'s theory, the failure of any one of these steps will cause the sequence to be broken.

Dual process/cognitive models

According to the *dual-process* or *cognitive perspective* (e.g. Chaiken, 1987), the key questions are as follows.

- What cognitive processes determine whether someone is actually persuaded?

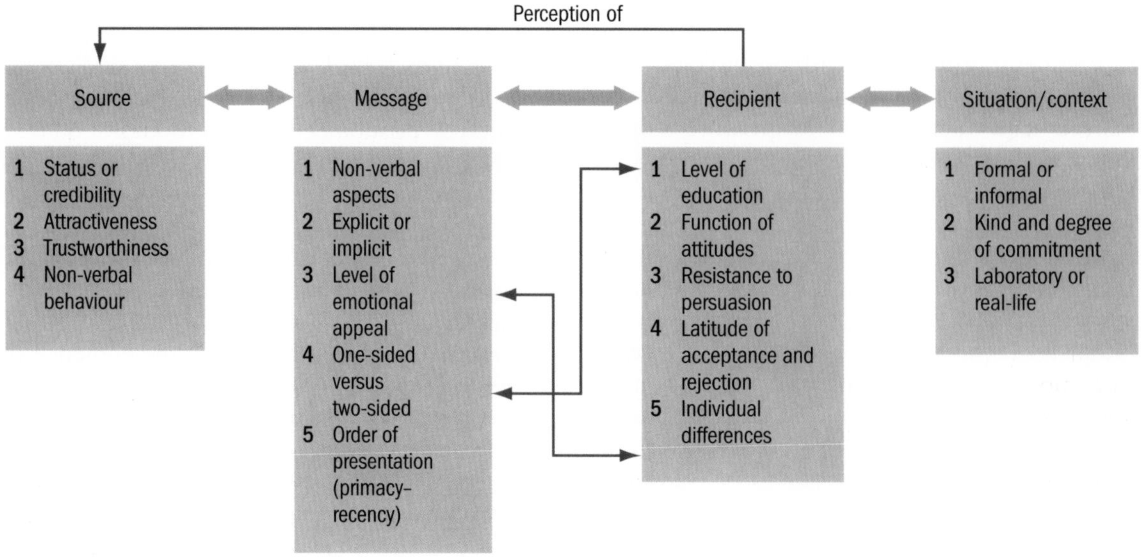

Figure 24.3 The four major factors involved in persuasive communication (arrows between boxes indicate examples of interaction between variables)

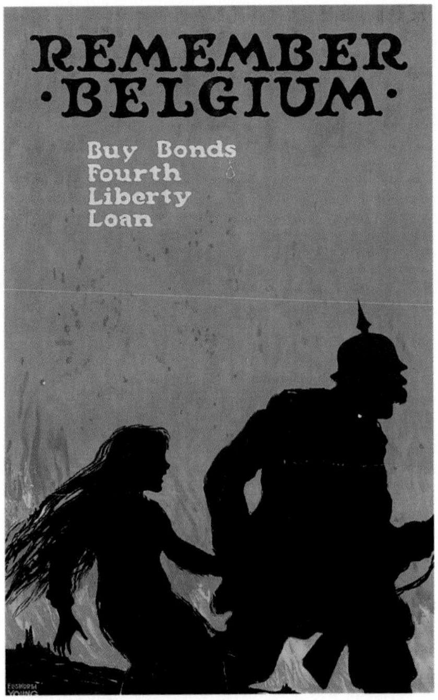

A First World War poster campaign, inducing people to invest in the war effort. Most people were sufficiently ego-involved that source credibility was irrelevant, nor was suspicion of the source's motives aroused since it was in everybody's best interest to invest in the war effort

- What do people think about when exposed to persuasive appeals?
- How do their various cognitive processes determine whether and to what extent they experience attitude changes (Baron & Byrne, 1991)?

Chaiken's (1987) answer to these questions is in the form of his *heuristic model of persuasion*. Heuristics are rules of thumb or mental shortcuts, which we use in processing social or any other kind of information (see Chapters 20 and 22). When a situation is personally involving (for example, it involves attitudes which are salient for the individual concerned), careful, cognitive analysis of the input occurs. The degree of attitude change depends largely on the quality of the arguments presented.

However, when personal involvement is low, individuals rely on various heuristics to determine whether to change their attitudes. Much of the Yale approach, in fact, deals with the content of these heuristics. For example, experts are more believable than non-experts, and so we're more easily persuaded by the former, as we are by likeable sources (compared with non-likeable). Other examples of heuristics include being more persuaded by a greater number of arguments backed up by statistics than a smaller number, and 'if other people think something is right (or wrong), then I should too'. These are essentially peripheral, non-content issues.

An evaluation of heuristic models

It's assumed that attitudes formed or changed on the basis of heuristic processing will be less stable, less resistant to counter-arguments, and less predictive of subsequent behaviour than those based on systematic processing. Several studies have shown that attitude change accompanied by high levels of issue-relevant cognitive activity is more persistent than that accompanied by little such activity (Stroebe, 2000).

Attitude function and persuasion

The functions of attitudes also represent an important feature of the cognitive analysis of persuasion (see Table 24.2). Shavitt (1990) argues that persuasive messages which emphasise the appropriate (primary) attitude function of a given product should be more successful in changing attitudes than those which focus on other attitude functions. For example, a commercial which emphasises the practical function of air conditioners should be more successful than one which emphasises their social identity function (they project a particular kind of social image). The reverse would be true for a commercial advertising perfume.

Fear and persuasion

A famous early attempt to induce attitude change through the manipulation of fear was made by Janis & Feshbach (1953).

KEY STUDY 24.3 Fear of the dentist as a means to healthier teeth (Janis & Feshbach, 1953)

- Janis and Feshbach randomly assigned American high-school students to one of four groups (one control and three experimental).
- The message was concerned with dental hygiene, and degree of fear arousal was manipulated by the number and nature of consequences of improper care of teeth (which were also shown in colour slides). Each message also contained factual information about the causes of tooth decay, and some advice about caring for teeth.
- The *high fear condition* involved 71 references to unpleasant effects (including toothache, painful treatment, and possible secondary diseases, such as blindness and cancer). The *moderate fear condition* involved 49 references, and the *low fear condition* just 18. The control group heard a talk about the eye.
- Before the experiment, participants' attitudes to dental health, and their dental habits, were assessed as part of a general health survey. The same questionnaire was given again immediately following the fear-inducing message, and one week later.
- The results show that the stronger the appeal to fear, the greater their anxiety (an index of attitude change). But as far as actual changes in dental *behaviour* were concerned, the high fear condition proved to be the least

effective. Eight per cent of the high fear group had adopted the recommendations (changes in teethbrushing and visiting the dentist in the weeks immediately following the experiment), compared with 22 per cent and 37 per cent in the moderate and low fear conditions respectively.

Similar results were reported by Janis & Terwillinger (1962), who presented a mild and strong fear message concerning the relationship between smoking and cancer.

These studies suggest that, in McGuire's terms, you can frighten people into attending to a message, comprehending it, yielding to it, and retaining it, but not necessarily into acting upon it. Indeed, fear may be so great that action is *inhibited* rather than facilitated. However, if the audience is told how to avoid undesirable consequences and believes that the preventative action is realistic and will be effective, then even high levels of fear in the message can produce changes in behaviour. The more specific and precise the instructions, the greater the behaviour change (the *high availability factor*).

ASK YOURSELF...

- Can you relate the high availability factor to one of the principles we identified when discussing the measurement of attitude–behaviour correlations?

Part of an anti-smoking commercial based on the appeal to fear

According to Stroebe (2000), mass media campaigns designed to change some specific health behaviour should use arguments aimed mainly at changing beliefs relating to that *specific* behaviour – rather than focusing on more general health concerns. This is another example of the compatibility principle. For example, to persuade people to lower their dietary cholesterol, it wouldn't be very effective merely to point out that coronary heart disease (CHD) is the major killer and/or that high levels of saturated fat are bad for one's heart. To influence diet, it would have to be argued that very specific dietary changes, such as less animal fats and red meat, would have a positive impact on blood cholesterol levels, which, in turn, should reduce the risk of developing CHD.

In situations of minimal or extreme fear, the message may fail to produce any attitude change, let alone any change in behaviour. According to McGuire (1968), there's an inverted U-shaped curve in the relationship between fear and attitude change.

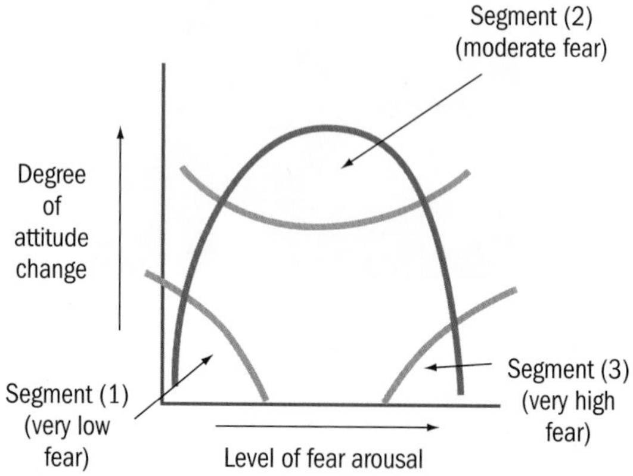

Figure 24.4 Inverted U curve showing relationship between attitude change and fear arousal (based on McGuire, 1968)

In segment 1 of the curve, the participant isn't particularly interested in (aroused by) the message: it's hardly attended to and may not even register. In segment 2, attention and arousal increase as fear increases, but the fear remains within manageable proportions. In segment 3, attention will decrease again, but this time because defences are being used to deal with extreme fear: the message may be denied ('it couldn't happen to me') or repressed (see Chapter 12). Despite evidence of defensive processing, Stroebe (2000) maintains that:

> ... the overwhelming majority of studies on fear appeals has found that higher levels of threat resulted in greater persuasion than did lower levels. However, the effectiveness of high-fear messages appeared to be somewhat reduced for respondents who feel highly vulnerable to the threat ...

The importance of feeling vulnerable

In order to arouse fear, it isn't enough that a health risk has serious consequences: the individual must also feel personally at risk (i.e. vulnerable). There's some evidence that unless individuals feel vulnerable to a threat, they're unlikely to form the intention to act on the recommendations in the message (Kuppens *et al.*, 1996). Fear appeals are also most likely to be effective for individuals who are unfamiliar with a given health risk. For example, when the dangers involved in unprotected anal intercourse among homosexuals became known in the early 1980s, the information appeared to produce an enormous reduction in such practices. But there was a core of men who were unaffected by the information, illustrating that simply repeating the dangers of HIV infection doesn't achieve risk reduction with such individuals (Stroebe, 2000: see Chapter 12).

Feeling vulnerable relates to what McGuire calls the *initial level of concern*. Clearly, someone who has a high level of initial concern will be more easily pushed into segment 3 of the curve than someone with a low level. The former may be overwhelmed by a high-fear message (in which case defences are used against it), while the latter may not become interested and aroused enough for the message to have an impact.

Propaganda and war

'Propaganda' comes from the Latin '*propagare*', which refers to the gardener's practice of pinning the fresh shoots of a plant into the earth in order to reproduce new plants which will later take on a life of their own. So, one implication of the term (as originally used in the seventeenth century) is the spread of ideas through their deliberate cultivation or artificial generation.

But in the twentieth century, propaganda implies something more sinister, a deliberate attempt to manipulate, often by concealed or underhand means, the minds of other people for ulterior ends (Brown, 1963). This change can be dated from the official use of propaganda as a weapon in the total warfare of modern times, beginning with World War I. But this was itself an effect of changes in the nature of communication within technically advanced societies. Pratkanis & Aronson (1991) define propaganda as:

> ... mass suggestion or influence, through the manipulation of symbols and the psychology of the individual. Propaganda is the communication of a point of view with the ulterior goal of having the recipient of the appeal come to 'voluntarily' accept this position as if it were his or her own.

The aims of propaganda

Regardless of the media used (such as pamphlets, leaflets, newspapers, posters, films and public speeches), and the particular war, the chief aims of wartime propaganda, according to Brown (1963) are to:

- mobilise and direct hatred against the enemy and undermine the enemy's morale
- convince the home public of the rightness of the [Allied] cause and to increase and maintain fighting spirit
- develop the friendship of neutrals and strengthen in their minds the belief that not only are the Allies in the right but they will be victorious in the end, and, if possible, to enlist their active support and cooperation
- promote a picture of the enemy (as brutal, committing atrocities, wholly responsible for the war in the first place, and so on) that justifies the entry of a (usually) peaceable nation into war to 'clear the conscience of the whole nation' (Brown, 1963)
- develop and strengthen the friendship of the Allies
- build up strong ingroup attitudes and feelings and opposed feelings of hatred towards the enemy as a dangerous outgroup.

George W. Bush rallying US troops in Iraq, 2004

As Brown (1963) claims:

> There is nothing like a war for breaking down class and other barriers and creating feelings of friendship and co-operation within a country because all its previously inwardly directed aggression and resentment comes to be directed against an external enemy, and it is only in the last stages of a losing effort or after a war has been won that disunity begins to show itself once more ...

ASK YOURSELF...

- How does Brown's quote relate to Tajfel's *social identity theory* (SIT) as one explanation of prejudice and discrimination, and to Allport's advocacy of *equal status contact* and the *pursuit of common goals* as one means of reducing them? (See Chapter 25.)

Propaganda tries to limit our choices deliberately, either by (a) avoiding arguments (the bald statement of one point of view to the exclusion of others), or (b) by emotional, non-objective criticism of the other side and its opinions by use of caricature, stereotypes and other methods.

Box 24.1 Some specific techniques used in propaganda

The use of stereotypes: The Nazi portrayal of Jews (as shown below) is a good illustration of how a generalised belief about an entire group of people is exaggerated in the form of a caricatured portrayal of that group – the negative characteristics are taken to an extreme form (see Chapter 22).

The substitution of names: Favourable or unfavourable names, with an emotional connotation, are substituted for neutral ones, for example, 'Red' (replaces Communist or Russian), 'Union bosses' (for the presidents of trade unions), 'Huns'/'Krauts' (Germans) and 'Yids' (Jews). Conversely, 'free enterprise' sounds better than 'capitalism'.

Selection: From a mass of complex facts, selection is made for propaganda purposes. Censorship is one way of achieving this and thus is a form of propaganda.

Repetition: If a statement or slogan is repeated often enough, it will eventually come to be accepted by the audience, such as Hitler's 'Ein Volk, ein Reich, ein Fuhrer' ('One people, one empire, one leader'). During the First World War, there were demands for 'A War to End War' and to 'Make the World Safe for Democracy'.

Assertion: Instead of argument, bald assertions are used to support the propagandist's case, as in the presentation of only one side of the picture, the deliberate limitation of free thought and questioning.

Pinpointing the enemy: It's useful to present a message not only *for* something but also *against* some real or imagined enemy who's supposedly frustrating the audience's will. This is demonstrated by the Nazi campaign against the Jews (the scapegoats for Germany's humiliation and economic hardships following World War I, which pervaded every aspect of life in Germany in the 1930s (see Chapter 25). An example of this is the beer-mat with the inscription 'Whoever buys from a Jew is a traitor to his people'. (The caricatured face also illustrates the use of stereotypes – see above.)

(Based on Brown, 1963)

Propaganda versus education

Although public health campaigns (such as those for safe sex and healthier eating: see above) fit Pratkanis and Aronson's definition of propaganda, these aren't usually what we have in mind when we use the term: such campaigns are aimed at *benefiting* the audience. Similarly, while education tries to encourage independence of judgement, individual responsibility and an open mind, as well as how to think, propaganda provides ready-made judgements for the un-thinking, promotes a closed mind, and tells people what to think.

However, what about the vast majority of high-school textbooks in US history that virtually ignore the contributions of blacks and other minorities 'to the US scene' (Aronson, 1992)? Are such books merely imparting knowledge? A recent demonstration of 'history as doctrine' is described in Box 24.2.

Box 24.2 Changing the history of war

- In 1997, a history professor in Japan won a 32-year fight to expose one of the darkest chapters in his country's wartime history. Saburo Ienaga won a Supreme Court ruling that censorship of references in his books to a germ warfare group (Unit 731) were 'unlawful'.
- Unit 731 conducted biological warfare experiments such as injecting prisoners with anthrax and cholera, exposing them to sub-zero temperatures, and manufacturing bubonic plague bombs (the latter killing thousands of Chinese civilians). None of the 3000 Chinese, Korean, Russian and Mongolian prisoners survived, many being dismembered alive to monitor the progress of the diseases through their bodies.
- The Japanese government has never acknowledged these activities, let alone apologised for them. In August 1997, the Supreme Court in Tokyo ruled that the Japanese education ministry acted illegally when it censored a proposed textbook by Mr Ienaga, but it upheld its right to continue screening all textbooks and removing anything it finds objectionable, including references to war crimes.

(Source: *Daily Mail,* 30 August 1997)

Advertising

An interesting link between psychology and advertising comes in the form of J.B. Watson, the founder of behaviourism (see Chapter 1). Following dismissal from his academic position at Johns Hopkins University, during which he devised health promotion films on venereal disease for the American military (propaganda?), Watson joined the J. Walter Thompson advertising agency, becoming one of the first and most successful applied psychologists (Banyard & Hayes, 1994).

Scott (1909, in Brown, 1963) wrote the first textbook published in Britain on advertising. In it, he identified a number of principles, the most fundamental being *association*. Not until the late 1930s did advertisers discover Freud – but little came of it until the late 1940s and early 1950s (Brown, 1963).

> *ASK YOURSELF...*
> - Taking some advertisements you're familiar with, try to identify the way that (a) association (as demonstrated by classical conditioning: see Chapter 11), and (b) aspects of Freud's psychoanalytic theory (see Chapter 42) are used. Are these 'techniques' more likely to influence:
>   - developing a need (i.e. convincing people they want or need the product)
>   - noticing the product
>   - purchasing the product
>   - behaviour after the purchase (encouraging repeat purchases)?
>
> Based on Banyard, 1996)

Subliminal advertising

This is by far the most controversial aspect of advertising. It originated with Jim Vicary, an American market researcher, who arranged with the owner of a New Jersey cinema to install a second special projector which, during a film, flashed on the screen phrases such as 'Hungry? Eat Popcorn' and 'Drink Coca-Cola'. These were either flashed so quickly, or printed so faintly, that they couldn't be consciously perceived ('*subliminal perception*' means recognition without awareness), even after a warning that they were about to appear.

Films treated in this way were alternated with untreated ones throughout the summer of 1956. In the former, sales of popcorn rose by almost 50 per cent and soft drinks by about 18 per cent. Vicary himself believed it unlikely that a subliminal stimulus could produce any

Linda Blair as Regan, the possessed child in *The Exorcist*

Judas Priest in concert (1990)

response at all, unless prospective customers already intended buying the product. Nevertheless, subliminal advertising caused a storm of protest in the American press, and, later on, in the UK too.

Seeking to scare, rather than sell, a movie producer used a similar technique to Vicary's to flash pictures of a skull and the word 'blood' at key points in pairs of horror movies (Packard, 1957). Despite subliminal messages being legally outlawed (even before it was established whether they really worked), they made a comeback in the mid-1970s. In *The Exorcist* (1974), for example, a death mask was flashed on to the screen subliminally and, more recently, in order to reduce theft, several department stores in America began mixing barely audible and rapidly repeated whispers (such as 'I am honest. I will not steal') with their piped music. Many stores reported dramatic decreases in shoplifting. Also, audio cassette tapes are readily available which supposedly cure stress with soothing sub-audible messages covered by mood music or the ambient sounds of nature (Zimbardo & Leippe, 1991).

In 1990, the heavy metal band Judas Priest went on trial for triggering a suicide attempt by two young fans through, allegedly, recording the repeated subliminal message 'Do it' in one of their album tracks ('Better By You Better Than Me'). They won their case on the grounds that there's no scientific evidence that subliminal messages, even if perceived, could produce such extreme behaviour. However, it was this aspect of the trial that the media emphasised, rather than details of the troubled lives of the two young people concerned (Wadeley, 1996).

Box 24.3 Are subliminal messages effective?

To be effective, subliminal stimuli:

- must be able to influence judgements when superimposed on consciously attended-to material; subliminals *can* have an impact even when presented simultaneously with something that dominates conscious attention

- must affect general reactions; so, in the popcorn/Coca-Cola example, Vicary didn't want the audience to like *the words* 'Hungry? Eat Popcorn' more than they did before, but to have an increased desire to eat popcorn that would lead to buying more
- need to be strong and persistent enough to affect the mental processes that lead to subsequent directed behaviour; there's little relevant evidence.

Subliminal *sounds* are less likely to be effective than visual messages, since they're apt to go *totally* unregistered if attention is given to other sounds. According to Pratkanis *et al.* (1990), subliminal 'self-help' tapes have little, if any, therapeutic effect (not even a potentially beneficial placebo effect: see Chapter 45).

According to Zimbardo & Leippe (1991):

... so far none of the more fabulous claims for subliminals have been borne out by well-controlled and replicable studies. And while some of the touted subliminal techniques merit scientific study, others are simply not possible given what is known about the functioning of the human mind ...

Based on Zimbardo & Leippe (1991)

Are subliminal messages ethically unacceptable?

ASK YOURSELF...
- Before reading on, try to identify some of the ethical objections to any form of subliminal advertising.
- How relevant is the evidence presented in Box 24.3 to the question of ethics?

As we noted earlier, subliminal advertising was banned in the 1950s both in the UK and the USA. The British Institute of Practitioners in Advertising published a booklet (*Subliminal Communication,* 1958, in Brown, 1963) and banned all its 243 affiliated agencies from using this type of advertising. It states:

The free choice by the public to accept or reject is an integral part of all forms of professionally accepted advertising and does not appear to be available to recipients of subliminal communication.

Whether subliminal messages are unethical depends on the ethics of social influence and persuasion in general (Zimbardo & Leippe, 1991). It's widely agreed that *any* technique used to influence others (excluding physical coercion) is unethical if it:

- *relies on deception* – subliminals are deceptive to the extent that their users keep their use a secret, but, conceivably, they might still be effective even when it's openly announced that they're present
- *prohibits exposure to opposing messages* ('denial of the other side') – this doesn't apply to subliminals (but is relevant for evaluating attempts to indoctrinate people, as used by the Moonies, for example: see above)
- *unfairly prevents efforts to resist it* – it's here that subliminals can be viewed as unethical in the extreme; we cannot defend against something we don't know about and, by definition, we don't know about subliminals. Unlike other forms of influence, such as the image-processing of political candidates, or classical conditioning, we cannot resist the influence of subliminals through being observant and mindful; it's only later on – at the time of behavioural decision – that we may ask ourselves why we feel a certain way.

For Zimbardo & Leippe (1991):

... if subliminal influence should prove to work outside the laboratory in advertising contexts, it would seem highly unethical to use it – mainly because it deprives people of much of their opportunity to resist it.

THEORIES OF ATTITUDE CHANGE

The most influential theories of attitude change have concentrated on the principle of *cognitive consistency.* Human beings are seen as internally active information-processors, who sort through and modify a large number of cognitive elements in order to achieve some kind of cognitive coherence. This need for cognitive consistency means that theories such as Heider's *balance theory* (1958), Osgood and Tannenbaum's *congruity theory* (1955), and Festinger's *cognitive dissonance theory* (1957) aren't just theories of attitude change, but are also theories of human motivation (see Chapter 9).

Cognitive dissonance theory (CDT)

According to *cognitive dissonance theory* (CDT), whenever we simultaneously hold two cognitions which are psychologically inconsistent, we experience *dissonance.* This is a negative drive state, a state of 'psychological discomfort or tension', which motivates us to reduce it by achieving consonance. Attitude change is a major way of reducing dissonance. Cognitions are 'the things a person knows about himself, about his behaviour and about his surroundings' (Festinger, 1957), and any two cognitions can be consonant (A implies B), dissonant (A implies not-B) or irrelevant to each other.

For example, the cognition 'I smoke' is psychologically inconsistent with the cognition 'smoking causes cancer' (assuming that we don't wish to get cancer).

ASK YOURSELF...
- How might someone who smokes try to reduce dissonance?

Perhaps the most efficient (and certainly the healthiest!) way to reduce dissonance is to stop smoking, but many people will work on the other cognition; for example, they might:

- belittle the evidence about smoking and cancer (e.g. 'The human data are only correlational')
- associate with other smokers (e.g. 'If so-and-so smokes, then it can't be very dangerous')
- smoke low-tar cigarettes
- convince themselves that smoking is an important and highly pleasurable activity.

These examples illustrate how CDT regards human beings not as rational but *rationalising* creatures: attempting to *appear* rational, both to others and to themselves.

Dissonance following a decision

If we have to choose between two equally attractive objects or activities, then one way of reducing the resulting dissonance is to emphasise the undesirable features of the one we've rejected. This adds to the number of consonant cognitions and reduces the number of dissonant ones.

This was demonstrated in a study by Brehm (1956). Female participants had to rate the desirability of several household appliances on an eight-point scale. They then had to choose between two of the items (their reward for participating). For one group the items were ½ to 1½ points apart on the scale (*high dissonance condition*), while for a second group they were a full three points apart (*low dissonance condition*). When they were asked to re-evaluate the items they'd chosen and rejected, the first group showed increased liking for the chosen item and decreased liking for the rejected one.

CDT also predicts that there'll be *selective exposure* to consonant information: seeking consistent information which isn't present at the time. However, selective perception also includes *selective attention* (looking at consistent information which is present) and *selective interpretation* (perceiving ambiguous information as being consistent with our other cognitions). According to Fiske & Taylor (1991), the evidence overall is stronger for selective attention and interpretation than for selective exposure.

Dissonance resulting from effort

When a voluntarily chosen experience turns out badly, the fact that we chose it motivates us to try to think that it actually turned out well. The greater the sacrifice or hardship associated with the choice, the greater the dissonance and, therefore, the greater the pressure towards attitude change (the *suffering-leads-to-liking effect*).

KEY STUDY 24.4 Preferring things that turn out for the worst (Aronson & Mills, 1959)

- Female college students volunteered for a discussion on the psychology of sex, with the understanding that the research was concerned with the dynamics of group discussion. Each student was interviewed individually, and asked if she could participate without embarrassment; all but one said yes.
- If a student had been assigned to the *control condition,* she was simply accepted. But for acceptance to the *severe embarrassment condition,* she had to take an 'embarrassment test' (reading out loud to a male experimenter a list of obscene words and some explicit sexual passages from modern novels – remember the year was 1959!). For acceptance to the *mild embarrassment condition,* she had to read aloud words like 'prostitute' and 'virgin'.
- They then all heard a tape-recording of an actual, extremely dull, discussion (by a group which they believed they'd later join) about sex in lower animals.
- They then had to rate the discussion, and the group members, in terms of how interesting and intelligent they found them.
- As predicted, the *severe embarrassment group* gave the *most positive* ratings – because they'd experienced the greatest dissonance!

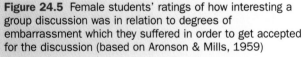

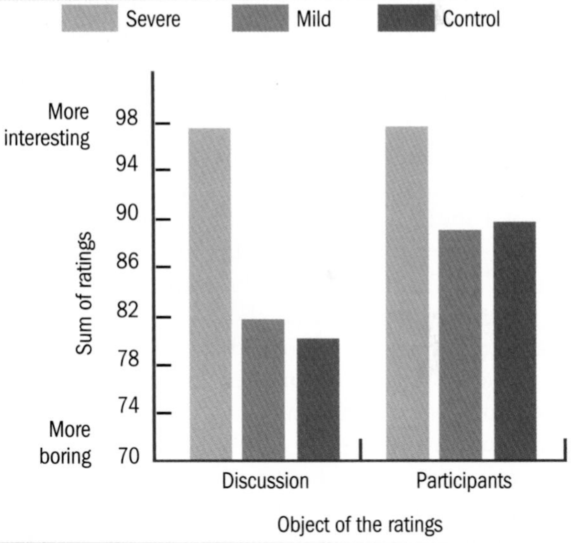

Figure 24.5 Female students' ratings of how interesting a group discussion was in relation to degrees of embarrassment which they suffered in order to get accepted for the discussion (based on Aronson & Mills, 1959)

Engaging in counter-attitudinal behaviour

This aspect of CDT is of most relevance to our earlier discussion of the relationship between attitudes and behaviour.

KEY STUDY 24.5 The '1 dollar/20 dollar' experiment (Festinger & Carlsmith, 1959)

- College students were brought, one at a time, into a small room to work for 30 minutes on two extremely dull and repetitive tasks (stacking spools and turning pegs).

- Later, they were offered either 1 dollar or 20 dollars to enter a waiting room and to try to convince the next 'participant' (in fact, a female stooge) that the tasks were interesting and enjoyable.
- Common sense would predict that the 20-dollar students would be more likely to change their attitudes in favour of the tasks (they had more reason to do so), and this is also what *reinforcement/incentive theory* (Janis *et al.*, 1965) would predict (the greater the reward/incentive, the greater the attitude change).
- However, as predicted by CDT, it was in fact the 1-dollar group that showed the greater attitude change (the *less-leads-to-more effect*).

ASK YOURSELF...

- How would CDT explain these findings? (You first need to ask yourself who experienced the greater dissonance.)

The large, 20-dollar incentive gave those participants ample justification for their counter-attitudinal behaviour, and so they experienced very *little* dissonance. But the 1-dollar group experienced considerable dissonance: they could hardly justify their counter-attitudinal behaviour in terms of the negligible reward (hence, the change of attitude to reduce the dissonance).

Festinger and Carlsmith's findings have been replicated by several studies, in which children are given either a mild or a severe threat not to play with an attractive toy (Aronson & Carlsmith, 1963; Freedman, 1965). If children obey a *mild* threat, they'll experience *greater* dissonance, because it's more difficult for them to justify their behaviour than for children given a severe threat. So, the mild threat condition produces greater reduction in liking of the toy.

However, dissonance occurs only when the behaviour is *volitional* (voluntary); that is, when we feel we've acted of our own free will. If we believe we had no choice, there's no dissonance, and hence no attitude change. A study by Freedman (1963) shows that dissonance theory and reinforcement theory aren't mutually exclusive; instead, they seem to apply to voluntary and involuntary behaviour respectively.

Self-perception theory (SPT)

According to Bem's *self-perception theory* (SPT) (1965, 1967), the concept of dissonance is both unnecessary and unhelpful. Any self-report of an attitude is an *inference* from observation of one's own behaviour, and the situation in which it occurs. This is because we don't have 'privileged access' to our own thoughts and feelings, but find out about them in the same way as we learn about other people's. (Bem was a behaviourist.)

If the situation contains cues (such as the offer of a large 20-dollar incentive) which imply that we might have behaved that way regardless of how we personally felt (we lie about the task being interesting even though it was boring), then we don't infer that the behaviour reflected our true attitudes. But in the absence of obvious situational pressures (1-dollar condition), we assume that our attitudes are what our behaviour suggests they are.

ASK YOURSELF...

- How could you account for Festinger and Carlsmith's results in terms of *attributional principles* (see Chapter 23)?

In attributional terms, the 20-dollar group can easily make a *situational attribution* ('I did it for the money'), whereas the one-dollar group had to make a *dispositional attribution* ('I did it because I really enjoyed it'). Bem combined attributional principles with his basic behaviourist beliefs.

An evaluation of CDT and SPT

- Eiser & van der Pligt (1988) believe that, conceptually, it's very difficult to distinguish between the two theories. Perhaps, as with CDT and incentive theories, both processes operate but to different extents under different circumstances. Fazio *et al.* (1977), for example, argue that dissonance may apply when people behave in a way which is contrary to their initial attitude (*counter-attitudinal behaviour*), while self-perception may apply better where their behaviour and initial attitude are broadly consistent (*attitude-congruent behaviour*). According to Fiske (2004), Bem's theory best accounts for those circumstances where we don't know our own mind or attitudes ahead of time.
- Zanna & Cooper's (1974) experiment provides support for *both* CDT and SPT.

KEY STUDY 24.6 Is there a dissonance-reduction pill? (Zanna & Cooper, 1974)

- Zanna and Cooper had participants write a counter-attitudinal essay under instructions that implied either high or low freedom of choice.
- Consistent with previous findings, the prediction that high-choice participants change their opinions more than low-choice participants was confirmed.
- The novel feature of the experiment was that participants were also given a placebo pill: they were either told it would make them feel tense or relaxed, or they were told nothing about it at all.

ASK YOURSELF...

- The dissonance theory prediction was upheld when participants were given no information about the pill, and upheld even more strongly when they were told it would relax them. But when they were told it would make them feel tense, no difference between the high- and low-choice conditions was found. How can you explain these findings?

- If participants believe the pill will either relax them or have no effect, and they also believe they're acting of their own free will, they change their opinions, presumably because they experience an internal state of dissonance. But if told the pill will make them tense, they will (mis)attribute their tension to the pill, and so little attitude change will occur (as is also true of low-freedom-of-choice participants). This attributional explanation is consistent with SPT, and so the Zanna and Cooper experiment offers support for both Festinger and Bem.
- Fiske (2004) believes that one of the most provocative lines of research to have emerged from SPT is the *over-justification effect*. If one has a situational justification for one's behaviour (such as an external reward), then one doesn't need to make a dispositional attribution for it. For example, if a child enjoys reading and receives a gold star for each book completed, s/he may infer that the reading is motivated by the reward. If the rewards are discontinued, the reading may too (the opposite effect to what was intended).
- Conflict or inconsistency often arise between two attitudes, rather than between an attitude and behaviour. Both situations can be explained by CDT, but because SPT is based on attribution principles, it requires some overt behaviour from which we then make an inference about our attitudes.
- According to some *impression management theorists* (e.g. Schlenker, 1982; Tedeschi & Rosenfield, 1981: see Chapter 22), many dissonance experiments might not reflect genuine cases of 'private' attitude change (a drive to be consistent). Rather, they reflect the need to *appear* consistent, and hence to avoid social anxiety and embarrassment, or to project positive views of one's own identity. So, the 1-dollar group's attitude change is genuine, but is motivated by *social* (rather than *cognitive*) factors.

CRITICAL DISCUSSION 24.2: Are theories of attitude change culturally biased?

- Although lying to another 'participant' (as in the 1-dollar/20-dollar experiment) may contravene the norms of many cultures, other commonly used dissonance paradigms may *not* induce the same level of dissonance in all cultures (Cooper *et al.*, 2004).
- For example, Heine & Lehman (1997) used the 'free choice' method used by Brehm (1956: see above, page 419). Japanese and Canadian participants were asked to rate a selection of western rock and pop CDs, then asked to choose between two that they'd rated similarly. The Canadians showed the usual dissonance effect, but the Japanese didn't. Heine and Lehman concluded that Japanese people may not be as concerned about the inconsistency that arises when they 'lose' the positive aspect of the unchosen option and 'accept' the negative aspects of the chosen option.
- The tendency to change one's attitude or behaviour in order to be more consistent (and so reduce dissonance) reflects a need to view behaviour as driven by *internal* factors. But members of *collectivist* cultures don't demonstrate these tendencies. They're willing to sacrifice consistency to maintain a sense of harmony with others (Nagayama Hall & Barongan, 2002). It may even be considered selfish to act according to one's own desires, or to express one's attitudes, if they make others feel uncomfortable (Fiske *et al.*, 1998).
- The evidence for the overjustification effect is strong in the USA, but it rests on that culture's bias towards individual autonomy and perceived choice (Fiske, 2004). In more *interdependent* (i.e. collectivist) cultures, children's intrinsic motivation increases when choices are made *for them* by trusted authorities and peers (Iyengar & Lepper, 1999).

- Despite these and other challenges and reconceptualisations, Hogg & Vaughan (1995) maintain that:

> ... cognitive dissonance theory remains one of the most widely accepted explanations of attitude change and many other social behaviours. It has generated over one thousand research studies and will probably continue to be an integral part of social psychological theory for many years ...

CHAPTER SUMMARY

- The **three-component model** of attitude structure sees attitudes as comprising **affective**, **cognitive** and **behavioural** components. Attitudes have much in common with beliefs and values, but they need to be distinguished.
- Katz identifies the **knowledge**, **adjustive**, **value-expressive** and **ego-defensive functions** of attitudes.
- Most methods of **attitude measurement** rely on verbal reports of people's opinions about the attitude object. They assume that attitudes can be quantified, and that the same statement has the same meaning for all respondents.
- Thurstone's **equal appearing interval scale**, the **Likert scale**, the **Guttman scalogram method**, the **semantic differential** and **sociometry** are some of the major **self-report methods** used in attitude measurement.

- Alternative methods attempt to get round problems such as **acquiescent response set** and the effects of **social desirability**. These include the **lost letter** and **bogus pipeline techniques**. Whatever their methodological advantages, they pose very serious ethical questions.
- Early research into the **relationship between attitudes and behaviour** showed that attitudes are very poor predictors of behaviour. But attitudes represent only one of several determinants of behaviour, including situational factors.
- Attitudes can predict behaviour, provided there's a close **correspondence** between the way the two variables are defined and measured (the **principle of compatibility**). Also, measures of a representative sample of behaviours relevant to the attitude must be made (the **aggregation principle**).
- According to **discursive psychologists**, attitudes are **constructed** in the course of social interaction, rather than possessed by isolated individuals.
- **Persuasive communication** has traditionally been studied in terms of the influence of four interacting factors: the **source** of the persuasive message, the **message** itself, the **recipient** of the message, and the **situation/context**.
- **Theories of systematic processing** see the impact of persuasive messages as dependent on a sequence of processes, including **attending** to the message, **comprehending** it, **accepting** its conclusions, **retaining** it and **acting** as a result.
- The more recent **cognitive perspective** focuses on **why** people change their attitudes, not merely **when** and **how** it's likely to happen. The **heuristic model of persuasion**, for example, explains why we're more likely to be persuaded when the situation isn't personally involving or if the arguments are convincing.
- People can be frightened into attending to, comprehending, accepting and retaining a message, but the **high availability factor** is necessary for any behaviour change to take place.
- People also need to feel personally **vulnerable** if fear appeals are to have any impact. There appears to be an **inverted U-shaped curve** in the relationship between fear and attitude change.
- **Propaganda** tries deliberately to limit people's choices, either through **censorship** or through use of **caricature**, **stereotypes**, **emotive names** and **repetitive slogans**. By contrast, **education** encourages independent thinking, individual responsibility and an open mind.
- **Subliminal messages** can influence judgements when superimposed on consciously attended-to material, producing general reactions (such as increasing the desire to eat popcorn). However, their influence on behaviour is much less certain.
- The major theories of attitude change share the basic principle of **cognitive consistency**. The most influential of these is Festinger's **cognitive dissonance theory** (CDT).
- **Dissonance** is most likely to occur after making a very **difficult choice/decision**, when putting ourselves through **hardship** or making a **sacrifice** only to find it was for nothing, or when engaging **voluntarily** in **counter-attitudinal behaviour**.
- Bem's **self-perception theory** (SPT) explains the results of dissonance experiments in terms of **attributional principles**. CDT may apply under conditions of 'true' counter-attitudinal behaviour, while SPT applies to attitude-congruent behaviour.
- **Impression management theory** stresses the **social** rather than the **cognitive** motivation underlying attitude change.
- Like most western psychology, theories of attitude change are **culturally biased**.

Links with other topics/chapters

- Strong attitudes influence behaviour partly through their automatic activation from within *memory* (Chapter 17).
- Personal (direct) experience also helps activate attitudes automatically. This can be explained by the *mere exposure effect* (Zajonc, 1968), according to which the more contact we have with something or somebody, the more we like them (Chapter 28).
- Heuristic models of attitude change have their counterparts in *problem-solving* (Chapter 20), *interpersonal perception* (Chapter 22) and *social cognition/attribution* (Chapter 23).
- The TRA and TPB are major theories used to explain and predict a wide range of *health-related behaviours* (Chapter 12).
- The *stereotyping* used in propaganda is the cognitive component of *prejudice* (Chapter 25).
- Aronson's point regarding US history books ignoring the contributions of blacks and other minorities is paralleled by the view that psychology discovers 'facts' about human behaviour, which exist *objectively* (Chapters 3) and *universally* (Chapter 47).
- The overjustification effect is sometimes referred to as the *paradox of reward,* which is relevant to the debate on *free will* (Chapter 49).

25

PREJUDICE AND DISCRIMINATION

... fifty years after the [Nazi] extermination and concentration camps were liberated, genocide continues unabated, neither punished nor prevented. In what used to be ... [Yugoslavia], torture, murder, rape, and starvation are everyday occurrences ... (Hirsch, 1995)

INTRODUCTION AND OVERVIEW

While genocide – the systematic destruction of an entire cultural, ethnic or racial group – is the most extreme form of discrimination, the prejudice that underlies it is essentially the same as that which underlies less extreme behaviours.

Prejudice is an *attitude* that can be expressed in many ways, or which may not be overtly or openly expressed at all. Like other attitudes, prejudice can be regarded as a *disposition* to behave in a prejudiced way (to practise *discrimination*), so the relationship between prejudice and discrimination is an example of the wider debate concerning the attitude–behaviour relationship. As we saw in Chapter 24, LaPiere's early study of this relationship was concerned with anti-Oriental prejudice and discrimination in the USA in the 1930s.

Theories of prejudice and discrimination try to explain their origins: how do people come to be prejudiced and to act in discriminatory ways? Answers to these questions potentially answer the further question: how can they be reduced or even prevented altogether? This, of course, has much greater practical significance for people's lives, as the quote from Hirsch conveys.

PREJUDICE AS AN ATTITUDE

As an *extreme* attitude, prejudice comprises the three components common to all attitudes:

- the *cognitive* component is the *stereotype* (see Chapter 22)
- the *affective* component is a *strong feeling of hostility*
- the *behavioural* component can take different forms.

Allport (1954) proposed five stages of this component:

1. *antilocution* – hostile talk, verbal denigration and insult, racial jokes
2. *avoidance* – keeping a distance but without actively inflicting harm
3. *discrimination* – exclusion from housing, civil rights, employment
4. *physical attack* – violence against the person and property
5. *extermination* – indiscriminate violence against an entire group (including genocide).

As we noted in the *Introduction and overview*, 'discrimination' is often used to denote the behavioural component, while 'prejudice' denotes the cognitive and affective components. But just as the cognitive and affective components may not necessarily be manifested behaviourally (as in LaPiere's study), so discrimination doesn't necessarily imply the presence of cognitive and affective components. People may discriminate if the prevailing social norms dictate that they do so, and if their wish to become or remain a member of the discriminating group is stronger than their wish to be fair and egalitarian (see below). According to Fiske (2004), the affective component is crucial. This is illustrated by the findings that (a) individual differences in emotional prejudice correlate with discrimination better than do stereotypes (Dovidio *et al.*, 1996), and (b) affective reactions to gay men predict discrimination far better than do stereotypes (Talaska *et al.*, 2003). Although the relationship between prejudice and discrimination is moderate, it's comparable to the general attitude–behaviour relationship (Fiske, 2004: see Chapter 24).

Definitions of prejudice

Although most definitions of prejudice stress the hostile, negative kind, prejudice can also be positive (just as stereotypes can be positive such as, 'women are caring', or neutral, such as 'men are tall'). However, the research which tries to identify how prejudice arises, and how it might be reduced, focuses on hostile prejudice.

Table 25.1 Some definitions of prejudice and discrimination

'... an antipathy based on faulty and inflexible generalisation directed towards a group as a whole or towards an individual because he is a member of that group. It may be felt or expressed.' (Allport, 1954)
'Prejudice is an attitude (usually negative) toward the members of some group, based solely on their membership in that group ...'. (Baron & Byrne, 1991)
'Prejudice is a learned attitude towards a target object that typically involves negative affect, dislike or fear, a set of negative beliefs that support the attitude and a behavioural intention to avoid, or to control or dominate, those in the target group ... Stereotypes are prejudiced beliefs ... when prejudice is acted out, when it becomes overt in various forms of behaviour, then discrimination is in practice ...'. (Zimbardo & Leippe, 1991)

The definitions in Table 25.1 locate prejudice squarely *within the individual* – it's an attitude which represents one aspect of social cognition. However, Vivian & Brown (1995) prefer to see prejudice as a special case of intergroup conflict. Although conceptually distinct, prejudice and intergroup conflict often coexist. For Vivian and Brown, intergroup conflict occurs when:

> ... people think or behave antagonistically towards another group or its members in terms of their group membership and seem motivated by concerns relating to those groups ...

They also distinguish intergroup conflict and *interpersonal* conflict, a distinction we shall return to when discussing attempts to reduce prejudice (see pages 435–438).

Defining prejudice in terms of intergroup conflict 'lifts' it to the social plane. Consistent with this is Fernando's (1991) distinction between 'racial prejudice' and 'racism': the former denotes an attitude possessed by an individual, while the latter refers to a political and economic ideology, which is a characteristic of society. Similarly, Littlewood & Lipsedge (1989) argue that:

Racist attitudes may be manifest as a highly articulated set of beliefs in the individual, but they are also found in less conscious presuppositions, located in society as a whole ...

Strictly, then, it is societies (or institutions, such as the police or the armed forces) that are racist, and individuals who are racially prejudiced.

ASK YOURSELF...
- Apart from racism, what other '-isms' are there that meet these criteria for being social, rather than individual, phenomena?

Until quite recently, most of the theory and research into prejudice and discrimination were concerned with racism, '... the quite specific belief that cultural differences between ethnic groups are of biological origin and that groups should be ranked in worth' (Littlewood & Lipsedge, 1989). However, gender (as in *sexism:* see Chapters 36 and 47), sexual orientation or preference (as in *heterosexism:* see Chapters 43 and 47) and age (as in *ageism:* see Chapter 39) can all be targets for hostility and discrimination.

CRITICAL DISCUSSION 25.1 Prejudice and discrimination in health care

- According to Rose & Platzer (1993), the attitudes of many nurses are grounded in their assumptions about people's heterosexual nature and their lack of knowledge about different lifestyles and how these affect people's health. Ignorance about how lesbians and gay men live can lead nurses to ask inappropriate questions during assessments, leading them to form mistaken judgements.
- For example, one lesbian patient who was receiving a cervical smear test was asked if she was sexually active. After saying she was, she was asked what contraceptive she used and replied 'none'. She was then asked if she was trying to become pregnant, which she wasn't. She had to disclose her lesbianism in order to ensure that health professionals didn't make incorrect assumptions about her, which could have led to an incorrect diagnosis.
- In another example, one patient's charts were labelled 'high risk'. These labels, which were clearly visible to other patients and members of staff, were there simply because he was gay and so was seen as being at risk of having HIV – the nurses simply assumed that gay men were likely to be HIV-positive and that heterosexual men weren't. Such assumptions are, of course, linked to stereotypes about what gay men do, rather than to a knowledge of sexual behaviours, which can differ widely regardless of sexual orientation.
- One nurse in an accident and emergency department refused to give a male patient an analgesic suppository (a pain-relieving capsule inserted into the anus) 'in case he liked it'. Such examples suggest that homosexuality is seen only in terms of sexual behaviour and not lifestyle, and this interferes with nurses' ability to see patients as individuals with particular nursing needs.
- Another false but commonplace belief is that lesbians and gay men are less discriminating in their sexual habits than heterosexuals, and that they'd want to engage in sexual activity in any setting and regardless of personal preferences (Rose & Platzer, 1993: see Chapter 28).

Sexual orientation is a target for hostility and discrimination in a heterosexist society

Institutionalised prejudice and discrimination

Critical Discussion 25.1 illustrates that a great deal of prejudice and discrimination is unconscious, reflected in basic, stereotyped assumptions that we make about others. These assumptions influence our behaviour towards them, which may not be necessarily overtly hostile or 'anti'. It's this pervasive form of prejudice and discrimination that's perhaps the most difficult to break down, because we're unaware of it, and because it reflects institutionalised heterosexism, racism and so on.

Both Cochrane (1983) and Littlewood & Lipsedge (1989) show how ethnic minorities in England are more often hospitalised for mental illness than non-black English. This is interpreted as reflecting an implicit, unwitting, prejudice against minority groups which pervades the National Health Service as an institution. This definition of 'institutionalised racism' as 'unwitting' was included in the Government Report (1999) on the behaviour of the police in their investigation of the murder of the black London teenager, Stephen Lawrence (in Horton, 1999).

Stephen Lawrence

CRITICAL DISCUSSION 25.2 The concept of race

- The classification of people into racial types based on physical appearance (mainly skin colour) has a long history in western culture. Darwin's (1859) theory of evolution introduced a new concept of 'race', based on his description of numerous 'races' within each species of animals. While human beings as a whole constitute 'a species' with fertile mating within it, individual (human) 'races' represent 'varieties' or 'subspecies', each being partially isolated reproductively from the others (Fernando, 1991). The essential point here is that *individuals* differ much more from each other than do groups.
- In his *Descent of Man* (1871), Darwin talked of the likely extinction of 'savage races', because of their inability to change habits when brought into contact with 'civilised races'. He then joined Galton in calling for the control of how different races breed (*eugenics*) in order to ensure the survival of the latter.
- Twentieth-century genetics at first described different races in terms of blood types, but this proved unreliable. More recently, scientific advances have enabled geneticists to identify human genes that code for specific enzymes and other proteins. But the genetic differences between the classically described races (European, Indian, African, East Asian, New World, and Oceanian) are, on average, only slightly higher (10 per cent) than those which exist between nations within a racial group (6 per cent), and the genetic differences between individual human beings within a population are far larger than either of these (84 per cent) (Fernando, 1991). According to Bamshad & Olson (2003), race defined as 'genetically discrete groups' *doesn't* exist.
- Nevertheless, the traditional view persists that people resembling each other in obvious physical ways (such as skin colour and hair texture) belong to a 'race' that represents a genetically distinct human type. Anthropologists, biologists and medical people are all guilty of perpetuating the myth, despite the widely held belief that 'race' has ceased to have a scientific meaning.
- These outward signs are determined by a handful of genes. But the other genes of two people of the same 'race' can be very different, and, conversely, two people of *different* 'races' can have more genes in common than two people of the *same* 'race' (Bamshad & Olson, 2003).
- 'Race' is a *social*, not a biological category. As Richards (1996a) points out:

  Any theory that puts Colin Powell, Shirley Bassey, Maya Angelou, Frank Bruno and Snoop Doggy Dogg in the same 'isolated inbreeding population' cannot have much going for it. Humanity is a single gene-pool, parts of which were relatively (rarely completely) isolated for longer or shorter periods of time.

- Similarly, Wetherell (1996) argues that 'race' is a social as opposed to a natural phenomenon:

  ... a process which gives significance to superficial physical differences, but where the construction of group divisions depends on ... economic, political and cultural processes ...

  She points out that many writers prefer to put quotation marks around 'race' to indicate that we're dealing with one possible social classification of people and groups, rather than an established biological or genetic reality.

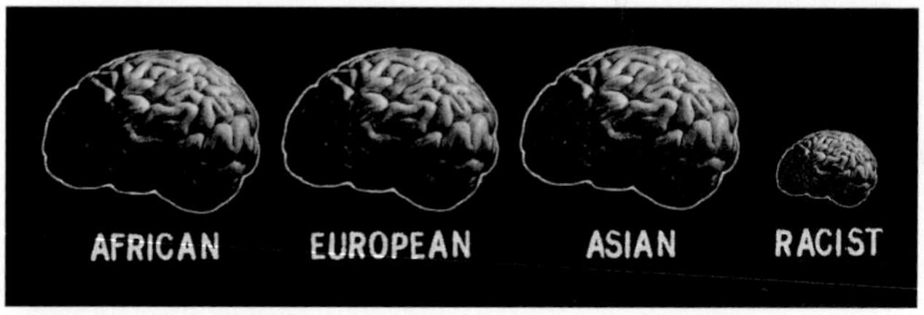

Poster used during the 1997 European Year against Racism
Reproduced by permission of The Commission for Racial Equality

Sexism and psychology

The sexist nature of psychology is demonstrated in a variety of ways, including the biased nature of the study of sex differences (e.g. Unger, 1979: see Chapters 36 and 47) and discrimination against women within psychology itself. According to Paludi (1992), for example, the history of psychology is the history of the contributions of men, with women psychologists being kept largely invisible, despite their enormous contribution, both historically and currently. One manifestation of this is the devaluation (by men) of the areas of psychology in which women are traditionally more numerous and which they seem to prefer, compared with the traditionally 'male' areas. The former include person-oriented/service-oriented fields, such as educational, developmental, clinical psychology and counselling, while the latter are the academic/experimental areas. These include learning and cognitive psychology, which are regarded (by men) as more scientifically rigorous and intellectually demanding (Paludi, 1992). Could it be that women are 'channelled' into certain fields of psychology, which then are defined as 'inferior' simply because they're populated mainly by women? Paludi sees certain individuals acting as *gatekeepers*, determining the career paths of others; in the case of psychology, the gatekeepers are usually men.

CRITICAL DISCUSSION 25.3 Scientific racism

- The attempt to present racist views as scientific 'fact' is revealed in the (not very subtle) form of 'scientific racism'. Chris Brand, a psychologist at the University of Edinburgh, had his book, *The g Factor: General intelligence and its implications*, withdrawn by the publisher (John Wiley) in April 1996 before its publication. He denies being a 'racist' while being 'perfectly proud to be a racist in the scientific sense', that is, a believer in the view that race and psychology have deep links (most likely genetic).
- According to Brand (quoted in Richards, 1996a), 'You won't find any psychologist of repute who has said anything different [than that black people have lower intelligence] since the turn of the century'.
- However, according to Richards, dozens of psychologists of unimpeachable repute (including Bartlett, Freud, Piaget and Skinner) have either disagreed or, more commonly, not even been interested in the question. Some who've agreed turn out not to have been so reputable after all. For example, Cattell (see Chapter 42) was pro-Hitler in the 1930s, a ruthless racist eugenicist all his life, who even contemplated genocide ('genthenasia'). Brand is simply wrong!

Racism in psychiatry

Cartwright (1851), an American psychiatrist, proposed two diagnostic categories meant to apply exclusively to black people (at the time of slavery).

- *Dysaesthesia Aethiopis* was a disease which afflicted all 'free negroes' without a white person to direct and take care of them, 'the natural offspring of negro liberty – the liberty to be idle … wallow in filth … indulge in improper food and drinks'. Symptoms included breaking, wasting and destroying everything they handled, tearing or burning their clothing, stealing from others to replace what they had destroyed, and apparent insensitivity to pain.
- *Drapetomania* was, quite simply, the disease which caused slaves to run away (Fernando, 1991: see Chapter 43).

THEORIES OF PREJUDICE AND DISCRIMINATION

Attempts to explain prejudice and discrimination fall into three broad categories:

1. those that see prejudice as stemming from *personality variables* and other aspects of the psychological make-up of individuals
2. those that emphasise the role of *environmental factors* (sometimes called the *conflict approach*)
3. those that focus on the effects of the mere fact of *group membership*.

Each approach may be important to a complete understanding of the causes of intergroup conflict and prejudice, and to their reduction (Vivian & Brown, 1995).

Prejudice and personality

The authoritarian personality

Adorno *et al.* (1950) proposed the concept of the *authoritarian personality* (in a book of the same name), someone who's prejudiced by virtue of specific personality traits which predispose them to be hostile towards ethnic, racial and other minority or outgroups.

Adorno *et al.* began by studying antisemitism in Nazi Germany in the 1940s, and drew on Freud's theories to help understand the relationship between 'collective ideologies' (such as fascism) and individual personality (Brown, 1985). After their emigration to the USA, studies began with over 2000 college students and other native-born, white, non-Jewish, middle-class Americans (including school teachers, nurses, prison inmates, and psychiatric patients). These involved interviews concerning their political views and childhood experiences, and the use of *projective tests* (in particular, the thematic apperception test/TAT: see Chapter 9) designed to reveal unconscious attitudes towards minority groups.

A banner reading 'Germans, don't buy from Jews' in front of a synagogue in Berlin, circa 1937

A number of scales were developed in the course of their research (see Table 25.2).

- *Antisemitism (AS) scale:* The 52 items were phrased so as to express a subtle hostility without seeming to offend the democratic values most respondents would feel bound to support, a kind of 'fair-minded and reasonable veneer' (Brown, 1965).
- *Ethnocentrism (E) scale:* The term 'ethnocentrism' was first defined by Sumner (1906) as: 'A view of things in which one's own group is the centre of everything, and all others are scaled and rated with reference to it … each group … boasts itself superior … and looks with contempt on outsiders. Each group thinks its own folkways the only right one'. The scale comprised 34 items.

Table 25.2 Sample items from the various scales used by Adorno *et al.* (1950)

Antisemitism (AS) scale	The trouble with letting Jews into a nice neighbourhood is that they gradually give it a typically Jewish atmosphere.
Ethnocentrism(E) scale	Negroes have their rights, but it's best to keep them in their own districts and schools and to prevent too much contact with whites.
Political and economic conservatism (PEC) scale	In general, full economic security is harmful; most men wouldn't work if they didn't need the money for eating and living.
Potentiality for fascism (F) scale	
1 Conventionalism	Obedience and respect for authority are the most important virtues children should learn.
2 Authoritarian submission	Young people sometimes get rebellious ideas, but as they grow up they ought to get over them and settle down.
3 Authoritarian aggression	Sex crimes, such as rape and attacks on children, deserve more than mere imprisonment; such criminals ought to be publicly whipped or worse.
4 Power and toughness	People can be divided into two distinct classes: the weak and the strong.
5 Projectivity	Nowadays when so many different kinds of people move around and mix together so much, a person has to protect himself especially carefully against catching an infection or disease from them.
6 Sex	Homosexuals are hardly better than criminals and ought to be severely punished.

- *Political and economic conservatism (PEC) scale:* The central component of conservatism is attachment to things as they are, and a resistance to social change. This is the only scale to include items supporting both sides of the issues.
- *Potentiality for fascism (F) scale:* According to Brown (1965), Adorno *et al.* never referred to the F scale as the authoritarianism scale. But since it's supposed to identify the kind of personality the book is talking about, it's reasonable to suppose that the scale could also be correctly called the authoritarianism scale (as it has been in many subsequent research reports). The scale was revised several times during the course of the research, but the items never referred directly to minority groups or politico-economic issues. It was intended to measure implicit authoritarian and antidemocratic trends in personality, making someone with such a personality susceptible to explicit fascist propaganda. The 38 items were subclassified under nine general headings (six of which are included in Table 25.2).

Table 25.3 shows the correlations between the different scales.

Table 25.3 Correlations between scores on the different scales used by Adorno *et al.* (1950)

	AS	E	PEC	F
AS		0.80	0.43	0.53
E			0.57	0.65
PEC				0.57
F (final version)		0.75		

ASK YOURSELF…
- What conclusions can you draw from the correlations in Table 25.3?

The pattern of intercorrelations suggests that:

- scores on the AS, E and F scales all correlate with each other much more strongly than any of them does with the PEC score, and, following from this
- people who are antisemitic are also likely to be hostile towards 'Negroes', 'Japs' and any other minority group or 'foreigner' (all *outgroups*) – the authoritarian personality is prejudiced in a very *generalised* way.

What's the authoritarian personality like?

Typically, the authoritarians are hostile to people of inferior status, servile to those of higher status, and contemptuous of weakness. They're also rigid and inflexible, intolerant of ambiguity and uncertainty, unwilling to introspect feelings, and upholders of conventional values and ways of life (such as religion). This belief in convention and intolerance of ambiguity combine to make minorities 'them' and the authoritarian's membership group 'us'; 'they' are by definition 'bad' and 'we' are by definition 'good'.

How does the authoritarian personality become prejudiced?

Based on the interview and TAT data, Adorno *et al.* claimed that authoritarians have often experienced a harsh, punitive, disciplinarian upbringing, with little affection. While they consciously have very high opinions of their parents, they often reveal considerable latent (unconscious) hostility towards them, stemming from the extreme frustration they experienced as children.

Drawing on Freudian theory, Adorno *et al.* proposed that such unconscious hostility may be *displaced* onto minority groups, which become the targets for the authoritarian's hostility. Authoritarians also *project* onto these groups their own unacceptable, antisocial impulses (especially sexual and aggressive), so that they feel threatened by members of these groups. They have very little self-understanding (insight), and their prejudice serves a vital *ego-defensive function:* it protects them from the unacceptable parts of themselves (see Table 24.2, page 407).

Evaluation of the authoritarian personality theory

While some evidence is broadly consistent with the theory, there are a number of serious methodological and other problems which make it untenable.

- The items on the AS, E and F scales (all Likert-type questions: see Chapter 24) were worded in such a way that agreement with them always implies antisemitism, ethnocentrism and potential fascism respectively. Adorno *et al.* recognised the possibility that *acquiescent response set* (see Chapter 24) might be a problem.
- The interview and TAT data were intended partly to validate the F scale. But the clinical interviews were flawed, since the interviewer knew the interviewee's F score. This represents a serious source of *experimenter bias* (see Chapter 3).
- According to Brown (1988), if prejudice is to be explained in terms of individual differences, how can it then be manifested in a whole population or at least a vast majority of that population? In pre-war Nazi Germany, for example (and in many other places since), consistent racist attitudes and behaviour were shown by hundreds of thousands of people, who must have differed on most other psychological characteristics.
- Similarly, how can the theory account for the sudden rise and fall of prejudice in particular societies at specific historical periods? Antisemitism in Nazi Germany grew during a decade or so, which is much too short a time for a whole generation of German families to have adopted new forms of childrearing practices giving rise to authoritarian and prejudiced children (Brown, 1988). Even more dramatic was the anti-Japanese prejudice among Americans following the attack on Pearl Harbor. Brown believes that such examples strongly suggest that:

> ... the attitudes held by members of different groups towards each other have more to do with the objective relations between the groups – relations of political conflict or alliance, economic interdependence and so on – than with the familial relation in which they grew up!

The attack by Japan on Pearl Harbor in 1941 brought the USA into the Second World War

The open and closed mind

Another criticism of the authoritarian personality theory is that it assumed that authoritarianism is a characteristic of the *political right,* implying that there's no equivalent authoritarianism on the left. According to Rokeach (1960) 'ideological dogmatism' refers to a relatively rigid outlook on life and intolerance of those with opposing beliefs. High scores on the *dogmatism scale* reveal: (i) closedness of mind; (ii) lack of flexibility; and (iii) authoritarianism, regardless of particular social and political ideology.

Dogmatism is a way of *thinking,* rather than a set of beliefs (Brown, 1965). The dogmatic individual tends to accentuate differences between 'us and them' and displays *self-aggrandisement* (e.g. 'If I had to choose between happiness and greatness, I'd choose greatness'). S/he also has a *paranoid* outlook on life ('I often feel people are looking at me critically'), and is *uncompromising* in his/her beliefs and intolerant of others. These characteristics serve as defences against a sense of personal inadequacy.

Rokeach (1960) gave the F scale and the dogmatism scale to five English groups of different political persuasions, including a group of 13 communist students. While the communists scored low on the F scale, they had the highest dogmatism scores. This supported Rokeach's claim that the F scale measures only right-wing authoritarianism.

Scapegoating: the frustration–aggression hypothesis

According to Dollard *et al.*'s (1939) *frustration–aggression hypothesis,* frustration always gives rise to aggression, and aggression is always caused by frustration (see Chapter 29). The source of frustration (whatever prevents us from achieving our goals) might often be seen as a fairly powerful threat (such as parents or employers) or may be difficult to identify. Drawing on Freudian theory, Dollard *et al.* claim that when we need to vent our frustration but are unable to do this directly, we do so *indirectly* by displacing it on to a substitute target (we find a *scapegoat*).

> ***ASK YOURSELF...***
> - Can you see any parallels between the frustration–aggression hypothesis and certain parts of Adorno *et al.*'s theory?

According to the frustration–aggression hypothesis, discrimination against outsiders (in this case eastern-European asylum seekers) is a form of displaced aggression

The choice of scapegoat isn't usually random. In England during the 1930s and 1940s, it was predominantly the Jews, who were replaced by West Indians during the 1950s and 1960s, and during the 1970s, 1980s and 1990s by Asians from Pakistan. In the southern USA, lynchings of blacks from 1880 to 1930 were related to the price of cotton: as the price dropped, so the number of lynchings increased (Hovland & Sears, 1940). While this is consistent with the concept of displaced aggression, the fact that whites chose blacks as scapegoats rather than some other minority group suggests that there are usually socially approved (legitimised) targets for frustration-induced aggression.

Limitations of the personality approach

- Several researchers (e.g. Billig, 1976; Brown, 1988; Hogg & Abrams, 1988) have argued that any account of prejudice and discrimination in terms of individuals (*intrapersonal behaviour*) is *reductionist* (see Chapter 49). In other words, the *social* nature of prejudice and discrimination requires a social explanation (in terms of *intergroup behaviour*).
- Adorno *et al.* imply that racism is the product of the abnormal personality of a small minority of human beings, rather than a social and political ideology. This distinction is of great practical as well as theoretical importance, because what's considered to be the cause of prejudice has very real implications for its reduction. Indeed, Adorno *et al.* recognised that *society* provides the content of attitudes and prejudice and defines the outgroups.
- According to Brown (1985), 'cultural or societal norms may be much more important than personality in accounting for ethnocentrism, outgroup rejection, prejudice and discrimination'.

The role of environmental factors

The impact of social norms: prejudice as conformity

Individual bigotry is only part of the explanation of racial discrimination. For example, even though overt discrimination has, traditionally, been greater in the southern USA, white southerners haven't scored higher than whites from the north on measures of authoritarianism (Pettigrew, 1959). So, clearly, *conformity to social norms* can prove more powerful as a determinant of behaviour than personality factors.

Racial discrimination in the southern USA during the 1950s was as much a way of life as apartheid in South Africa

Minard (1952) found that black and white coalminers in West Virginia followed a pattern of almost complete integration below ground, but almost complete segregation above! This makes sense only when viewed in terms of conformity to the norms which operated in those different situations.

> *ASK YOURSELF...*
> - What do you think the two sets of norms may have been?

Pettigrew (1971) also found that Americans in the south are no more antisemitic or hostile towards other minority groups than those from the north (as the authoritarian personality explanation would require). In other words, prejudice *isn't* the generalised attitude which Adorno *et al.* claimed. According to Reich & Adcock (1976), the need to conform and not be seen as different may cause milder prejudices. But active discrimination against, and ill treatment of, minorities reflects a prejudice which already exists, and which is maintained and legitimised by conformity.

Relative deprivation theory

According to the frustration–aggression hypothesis, people experience frustration when they feel deprived of something they believe they're entitled to. The discrepancy between our actual attainments (such as standard of living) and expectations (the standard of living we feel we deserve) is our *relative deprivation* (Davis, 1959). When attainments suddenly fall short of rising expectations, relative deprivation is particularly acute, resulting in collective unrest. This is expressed as a J-curve (Davies, 1969).

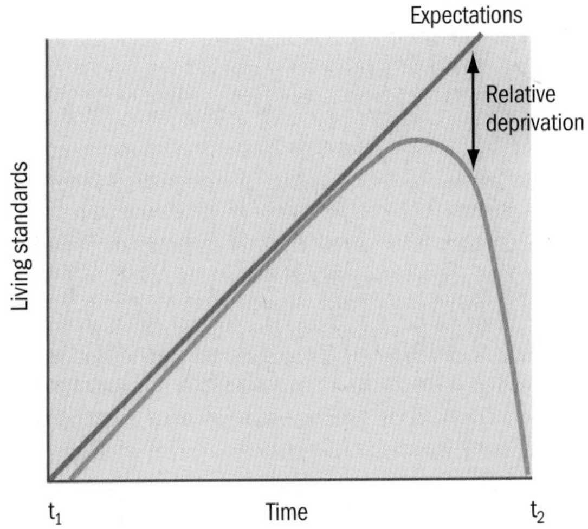

Figure 25.1 The J-curve hypothesis of relative deprivation (based on Davies, 1969)

The 1992 Los Angeles riots were triggered by an all-white jury's acquittal of four Los Angeles police officers accused of beating a black motorist, Rodney King

A good example of such acute relative deprivation is the 1992 Los Angeles riots. The immediate cause was the acquittal, by an all-white jury, of four LA police officers accused of beating a black motorist, Rodney King. Against a background of rising unemployment and continuing disadvantage, the acquittal was seen by blacks as symbolic of their low esteem in the eyes of the white majority (Hogg & Vaughan, 1995). The great sense of injustice at the acquittal seemed to demonstrate in acute form the injustice which is an inherent feature of discrimination – and of relative deprivation.

The LA riots illustrate *fraternalistic relative deprivation,* based on a comparison either with dissimilar others or with other groups (Runciman, 1966). This is contrasted with *egoistic relative deprivation,* which is based on comparison with other similar individuals. Vanneman & Pettigrew (1972) found that whites who expressed the most anti-black attitudes were those who felt most strongly that whites as a group were badly off relative to blacks. Objectively, they were actually better off, showing the subjective nature of relative deprivation. It has also been found that the most militant blacks seem to be those of higher socio-economic and educational status. They probably have higher expectations, both for themselves and for their group, and consequently experience relative deprivation more acutely (Vivian & Brown, 1995).

Realistic group conflict theory (RGCT)

According to Sherif's (1966) *realistic group conflict theory* (RGCT), intergroup conflict arises as a result of a conflict of interests. When two groups want to achieve the same goal but cannot both have it, hostility is produced between them. Indeed, Sherif claims that conflict of interest (or competition) is a *sufficient* condition for the occurrence of hostility or conflict. He bases this claim on the Robber's Cave experiment, which Brown (1986) describes as the most successful field experiment ever conducted on intergroup conflict.

KEY STUDY 25.1 The Robber's Cave experiment (Sherif *et al.*, 1961)

- The setting was Robber's Cave State Park in Oklahoma, where 22 white, middle-class, Protestant, well-adjusted boys spent two weeks at a summer camp. They were randomly assigned to two groups of eleven, each occupying a separate cabin, out of sight of each other. None of the boys knew any of the others prior to their arrival at the camp.

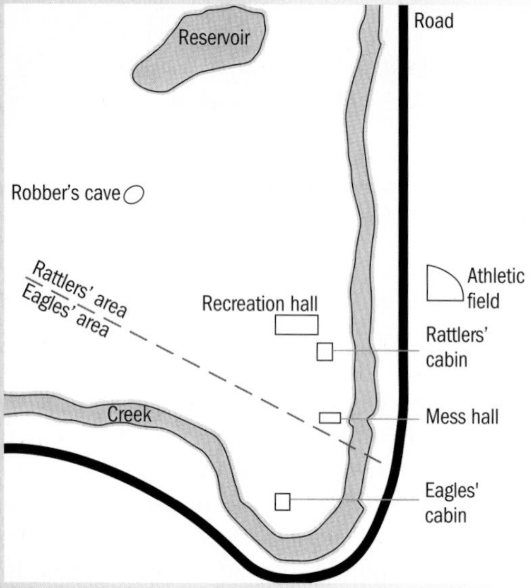

Figure 25.2 A map of Robber's Cave State Park

- During the *first stage* of the experiment, each group cooperated on a number of activities (pitching tents, making meals, a treasure hunt), and soon a distinct set of norms emerged which defined the group's identity. One group called itself 'the Rattlers', and the other 'the Eagles'. Towards the end of the first week, they were allowed to become aware of the other's existence, and an 'us and them' language quickly developed.
- The *second stage* began with the announcement that there was to be a grand tournament between the two groups, comprising ten sporting events, plus points awarded for the state of their cabins and so on. A splendid trophy, medals and four-bladed knives for each of the group members would be awarded to the winning group.
- Before the tournament began, the Rattlers' flag was burned, and the camp counsellors (the experimenters) had to break up a fight between the two groups. With some 'help' from the counsellors, the Eagles won and later the Rattlers stole their medals and knives.
- There was a strong ingroup preference. Rattlers stereotyped all Rattlers as brave, tough and friendly, and (almost) all Eagles as sneaky, stinkers and smart alecks. The reverse was true for the Eagles.

An evaluation of RGCT

- According to Fiske (2004), RGCT is the most obvious explanation for prejudice and discrimination. However, it has received only limited and inconsistent support, and the *perceived, symbolic threat* posed by outgroups matters more than any real or tangible threat. For this reason, the 'realistic' may as well be dropped from its name, and the theory renamed 'perceived group conflict theory'.
- Perceived conflict *does* predict negative attitudes towards outgroups (Brown *et al.*, 2001; Hennessy & West, 1999), and conflict only matters when people identify with their ingroups. More importantly, ingroup identification *by itself* can account for intergroup hostility, even in the absence of competition (Brewer & Brown, 1998). Intangible outcomes (such as group recognition, status, prestige) produce conflict far more often than do tangible resources. Even when the conflict appears to involve resources, often the real pay-off is pride in one's own identification with a group capable of winning them. As Fiske (2004) says:

> ... Group conflict is an inherently social competition that goes beyond concrete self-interest. One result of the struggle for positive identity is bias against the outgroup ...

This is related to *social identity theory* (see below, pages 433–435).

- Tyerman & Spencer (1983) challenged Sherif *et al.*'s conclusions that competition is a sufficient condition for intergroup conflict. They observed English boy scouts at their annual camp. The boys knew each other well before the start of camp, and much of what they did there was similar to what the Rattlers and Eagles did at Robber's Cave. They were divided into four 'patrols', competing in situations familiar to them from previous camps, but the friendship ties which existed prior to arrival at camp were maintained across the patrol groups. Competition remained friendly, and there was no increase of ingroup solidarity. The four groups continued to see themselves as part of the *whole* group, something that was deliberately encouraged by the leader.
- Tyerman and Spencer concluded that Sherif *et al.*'s results reflect the transitory nature of their experimental group. The fact that the English boys knew each other beforehand, had established friendships, were familiar with camp life, and had a leader who encouraged cooperation, were all important *contextual/situational* influences on the boys' behaviour.
- It seems, then, that 'competition' may not be a sufficient condition for intergroup conflict and hostility after all. If we accept this conclusion, the question arises whether it's even a necessary condition. In other words, can hostility arise in the absence of conflicting interests?

The influence of group membership

Minimal groups

According to Tajfel *et al.* (1971), the *mere perception* of another group's existence can produce discrimination. When people are arbitrarily and randomly divided into two groups, knowledge of the other group's existence is a sufficient condition for the development of pro-ingroup and anti-outgroup attitudes. These artificial groups are known as *minimal groups.*

Before any discrimination can occur, people must be categorised as members of an ingroup or an outgroup (making categorisation a *necessary* condition). More significantly, the very act of categorisation produces conflict and discrimination (making it also a *sufficient* condition). These conclusions are based on the creation of artificial groups among 14–15-year-old Bristol schoolboys. The criteria used to create the groups were arbitrary and superficial, and differed from experiment to experiment. They included:

- chronic 'overestimations' or 'underestimations' on a task involving estimating the number of dots appearing on slide projections
- preference for paintings by Klee or Kandinsky
- the toss of a coin.

Box 25.1 The minimal group paradigm (Tajfel *et al.*, 1971)

- Once these arbitrary groups had been formed, each boy worked alone in a cubicle on a task that required various matrices to be studied (see Figure 25.3).
- He had to decide how to allocate points to a member of his own group (but not himself) and a member of the other group. The boys were also told that the points could be converted to money after the study.
- The only information each boy had about another boy was whether he was a member of the same group or the other group; otherwise he was anonymous, unknown, unseen and identified only by a code number.
- The top line in the figure represents the points that can be allocated to the boy's own group, and the bottom line the points to the other group. For example, if 18 points are allocated to the boy's own group, then five are allocated to the other group. If 12 are allocated to the boy's own group, 11 are allocated to the other group, and so on.

MATRIX 4

18	17	16	15	14	13	12	11	10	9	8	7	6	5
5	6	7	8	9	10	11	12	13	14	15	16	17	18

Figure 25.3 One of the matrices used by Tajfel *et al.* (1971)

In the Tajfel *et al.* experiments, the actual group assignments were always made *randomly,* whatever the boys believed to be the basis for the categorisation.

An evaluation of minimal group experiments

- The minimal group experiment must stand as one of the most influential and provocative in the study of intergroup processes (Oakes, 2004).
- Billig & Tajfel (1973) and Locksley *et al.* (1980) went even further than Tajfel *et al.*, by actually telling the participants they were being randomly assigned, tossing the coin in front of them, and giving them obviously meaningless names (such as As and Bs, or Kappas and Phis). Even under these conditions, the groups still showed a strong ingroup preference.
- According to Brown (1988), intergroup discrimination in this minimal group situation has proved to be a remarkably robust phenomenon. In more than two dozen independent studies in several different countries, using a wide range of experimental participants of both sexes (from young children to adults), essentially the same result has been found: the mere act of allocating people into arbitrary social categories is sufficient to elicit biased judgements and discriminatory behaviours.
- Wetherell (1982) maintains that intergroup conflict *isn't* inevitable. She studied white and Polynesian children in New Zealand, and found the latter to be much more generous towards the outgroup, reflecting cultural norms which emphasised cooperation.
- The minimal group paradigm has been criticised on several methodological and theoretical grounds, especially its artificiality and *meaninglessness* (e.g. Schiffman & Wicklund, 1992; Gross, 2003a). Tajfel (1972), however, argues that it's precisely the need to find meaning in an 'otherwise empty situation' (especially for the *self*) that leads participants to act in terms of the minimal categories ('Klee' or 'Kandinsky', etc.). In fact, you can turn the meaninglessness argument on its head and argue that:

> ... the power of minimal categorizations to produce group-based behaviour reflects the customary significance and usefulness of categorical perception which participants import to the laboratory – when a context is defined in social categorical terms *participants expect the categories to mean something* ... (Oakes, 2004)

Social identity theory (SIT)

Tajfel (1978) and Tajfel & Turner (1986) explain the minimal group effect in terms of *social identity theory* (SIT). According to SIT, an individual strives to achieve or maintain a positive self-image. This has two components: *personal identity* (the personal characteristics and attributes which make each person unique), and *social identity* (a sense of who we are, derived from the groups we belong to).

In fact, each of us has several social identities, corresponding to the different groups with which we identify. In each case, the more positive the image of the group, the more positive will be our own social identity, and hence our self-image. By emphasising the desirability of the ingroup(s) and focusing on those distinctions which enable our own group to come out on top, we help to create for ourselves a satisfactory social identity. This can be seen as lying at the heart of prejudice.

Box 25.2 Group status and self-esteem

- Members of minimal groups in the laboratory (compared with controls who aren't assigned to a group) have been found to show higher self-esteem. For example, Lemyre & Smith (1985) claimed that it was the opportunity to display intergroup discrimination that increased self-esteem. Control participants who were categorised but could only distribute rewards between two ingroupers or two outgroupers, or couldn't distribute rewards at all, showed lower self-esteem than experimental participants able to make intergroup decisions.
- Outside the laboratory, groups with lower social status in a particular society strive to improve their social identities, and thus members' self-esteem. If group members feel its inferior status is unfair or illegitimate, then the group can become very well organised and assertive in trying to change its objective status. Good examples are those working for the Welsh language revival, and the Basque Separatists in Spain.
- Dominant or high status groups typically react very negatively to threats to their privileged position, and this can take the form of extreme prejudices being expressed (Hogg & Abrams, 2000).

Some individuals may be more prone to prejudice because they have an intense need for acceptance by others. Their personal and social identities may be much more interconnected than for those with a lesser need for social acceptance. Prejudice can be seen as an adjustive mechanism which bolsters the self-concept of individuals who have feelings of personal inadequacy – but with potentially undesirable social implications.

Evaluation of SIT

- While there's considerable empirical support for the theory, much of this comes from minimal group experiments. Not only have they been criticised (see above), but SIT was originally proposed to explain the findings from those experiments. So, there's a *circularity* involved, making it necessary to test SIT's predictions in other ways.
- SIT has been criticised on the grounds that it presents racism (and other forms of prejudice) as 'natural', helping to justify it. Stemming from Allport's (1954) claims that stereotypes are 'categories about people' and that 'the human mind must think with the aid of categories' (see Chapter 22), Tajfel (1969; Tajfel *et al.*, 1971) saw the process of *categorisation* as a basic characteristic of human thought. SIT implies that intergroup hostility is natural and built into our thought processes as a consequence of categorisation. If this is correct, then racism (conceived as a form of intergroup hostility or ingroup favouritism) may also be construed as natural. In terms of the distribution of resources, racism is thus justified as the norm ('charity begins at home') (Howitt & Owusu-Bempah, 1994).
- Of course, Tajfel never intended SIT to be seen as a justification of racism. Indeed, he was a life-long opponent of racism, having lost his family and community in the Holocaust. Taken out of context and elevated to the status of a universal human characteristic, SIT is easily *misrepresented* as an explanation and justification of racism (Milner, 1991, in Howitt & Owusu-Bempah, 1994).
- The evidence as it stands shows only a *positive ingroup bias,* and *not* derogatory attitudes or behaviour towards the outgroup, which is what we normally understand by 'prejudice'. In other words, although there's abundant evidence of intergroup discrimination, this appears to stem from raising the evaluation of the ingroup, rather than denigrating the outgroup (Vivian & Brown, 1995). Indeed, SIT suggests that prejudice consists largely of liking 'us' more than disliking 'them': favouring the ingroup is the core phenomenon, *not* outgroup hostility (Brewer, 1999; Hewstone *et al.*, 2002). However, one form that ingroup favouritism can take is 'modern racism'.

Box 25.3 Modern racism and subtle prejudice

- According to Fiske (2004), most estimates put 70–80 per cent of whites as relatively high on *modern/subtle* forms of racism. These are 'cool' and indirect, automatic, unconscious, unintentional, ambiguous and ambivalent. This is in sharp contrast with the crude and blatant racist abuse associated with Allport's 'antilocution' (see above).
- This is sometimes referred to as *symbolic* racism, and Henry & Sears' (2002) *Symbolic Racism Scale* attempts to assess this 'new' form of racism through items such as the following.

1. It's really a matter of some people not trying hard enough; if blacks would only try harder they could be just as well off as whites (1–4: *strongly agree to strongly disagree*).
2. Irish, Italian, Jewish and many other minorities overcame prejudice and worked their way up. Blacks should do the same (1–4: *strongly agree to strongly disagree*).
3. How much of the racial tension that exists in the United States today do you think blacks are responsible for creating? (1–4: *all of it – not much at all*).

- Subtle prejudice isn't a uniquely American, white-on-black phenomenon, however (Pettigrew, 1998; Pettigrew & Meertens, 1995). In Europe, there is French/North Africans, British/South Asians, Germans/Turks.
- Symptomatic of this form of racism (or perhaps a variety of it) is the belief that 'one is not a racist' while simultaneously engaging in racist talk. A classic recent example in the UK involved Ron Atkinson, an eminent ex-football manager and TV football pundit, who was heard to make 'old-fashioned' racist remarks about a black player when he thought his microphone was switched off. In his defence, he claimed, 'What I said was racist – but I'm not a racist. I am an idiot' (in Eboda, 2004). He was sacked from his job.

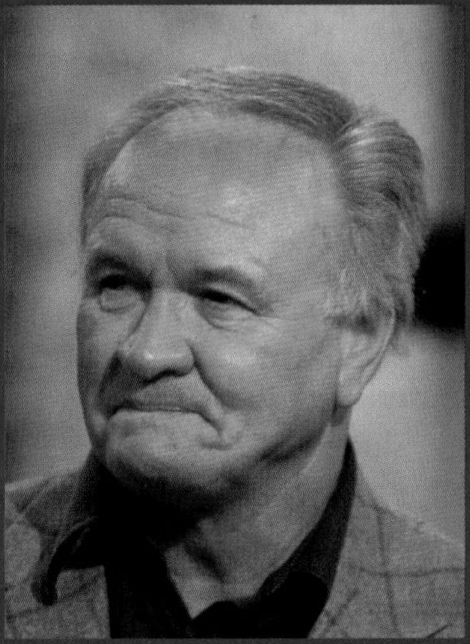

Ron Atkinson, self-declared non-racist

- Wetherell (1996) believes that SIT emphasises the 'ordinariness' of racism and its continuity with other forms of group behaviour. Intergroup conflict isn't seen as a psychopathology or the result of irrational prejudice, but as a form of behaviour involving complex psychological states which are also central to more positive group actions, such as developing a sense of solidarity with others, group loyalty, cohesiveness and national belonging. Racism is only inevitable given a particular social context, where 'racial' categories become significant and acquire meaning as group divisions. These categories aren't natural, but become powerful as a result of social history (see Critical Discussion 25.2, page 426).

REDUCING PREJUDICE AND DISCRIMINATION

ASK YOURSELF...

- What do the major theories we've discussed above imply about how prejudice and discrimination could be reduced – or prevented?

- The *authoritarian personality theory* implies that by changing the personality structure of the prejudiced individual, the need for an ego-defensive 'prop' such as prejudice is removed. By its nature, this is practically very difficult to achieve, even if it's theoretically possible. Equally difficult is the prevention of the kind of childrearing pattern which, according to Adorno *et al.*, determines the authoritarian personality in the first place.
- According to the *frustration–aggression hypothesis* and the *theory of relative deprivation,* preventing frustration, lowering people's expectations, and providing people with ways to vent their frustration in less antisocial ways than discrimination are all possible solutions. However, this would involve putting the historical clock back, or changing social conditions in quite fundamental ways.
- RGCT makes it very clear that removing competition and replacing it with superordinate goals and cooperation will remove or prevent hostility (this is discussed further below).
- SIT implies that if intergroup stereotypes can become less negative and automatic, and if boundaries between groups can be made more blurred or more flexible, then group memberships may become a less central part of the self-concept, making positive evaluation of the ingroup less inevitable. We shall return to this theme below.

The contact hypothesis

Probably the first formal proposal of a set of social–psychological principles for reducing prejudice was Allport's (1954) *contact hypothesis* (as it's come to be called), according to which:

> Prejudice (unless deeply rooted in the character structure of the individual) may be reduced by equal status contact between majority and minority groups in the pursuit of common goals. The effect is greatly enhanced if this contact is sanctioned by institutional supports (i.e. by law, custom or local atmosphere) and provided it is of a sort that leads to the perception of common interests and common humanity between members of the two groups.

Most programmes aimed at promoting harmonious relations between groups that were previously in conflict have operated according to Allport's 'principles', in particular *equal status contact* and the *pursuit of common (superordinate) goals.*

Equal status contact

When people are segregated, they're likely to experience *autistic hostility,* that is, ignorance of others, which results in a failure to understand the reasons for their actions. Lack of contact means there's no 'reality testing' against which to check our own interpretations of others' behaviour, and this in turn is likely to reinforce *negative stereotypes.* By the same token, ignorance of what 'makes

Francois Pienaar, the South African rugby union captain, receiving the Rugby World Cup from Nelson Mandela in 1995

them tick' will probably make 'them' seem more dissimilar from ourselves than they really are. Bringing people into contact with each other should make them seem more familiar, and at least offers the possibility that this negative cycle can be interrupted and even reversed.

Related to autistic hostility is the *mirror-image phenomenon* (Bronfenbrenner, 1960), whereby enemies come to see themselves as being in the right (with 'God on our side') and the other side as in the wrong. Both sides tend to attribute to each other the same negative characteristics (the 'assumed dissimilarity of beliefs'). Increased contact provides the opportunity to disconfirm our stereotypes. The outgroup loses its strangeness, and group members are more likely to be seen as unique individuals, rather than an 'undifferentiated mass' (see Figure 25.4). This represents a reduction in the *illusion of outgroup homogeneity* (see Chapter 22).

How effective is equal status contact?

It's generally agreed that increased contact alone won't reduce prejudice. Despite evidence that we prefer people who are familiar (see Chapter 28), if this contact is between people who are consistently of *unequal status,* then 'familiarity may breed contempt'. Aronson (1980) points out that many whites (in the USA) have always had a great deal of contact with blacks – as dishwashers, toilet attendants, domestic servants, and so on. Such contacts may simply reinforce the stereotypes held by whites of blacks as being inferior. Similarly, Amir (1994) argues that we need to ask 'Under what conditions does intergroup contact have an impact, for whom, and regarding what outcomes?'

One early study of equal status contact was that of Deutsch & Collins (1951). They compared two kinds of housing project, one of which was thoroughly integrated (blacks and whites were assigned houses regardless of race), and the other segregated. Both casual and neighbourly contact were greater in the integrated housing, with a corresponding decrease in prejudice among whites towards blacks.

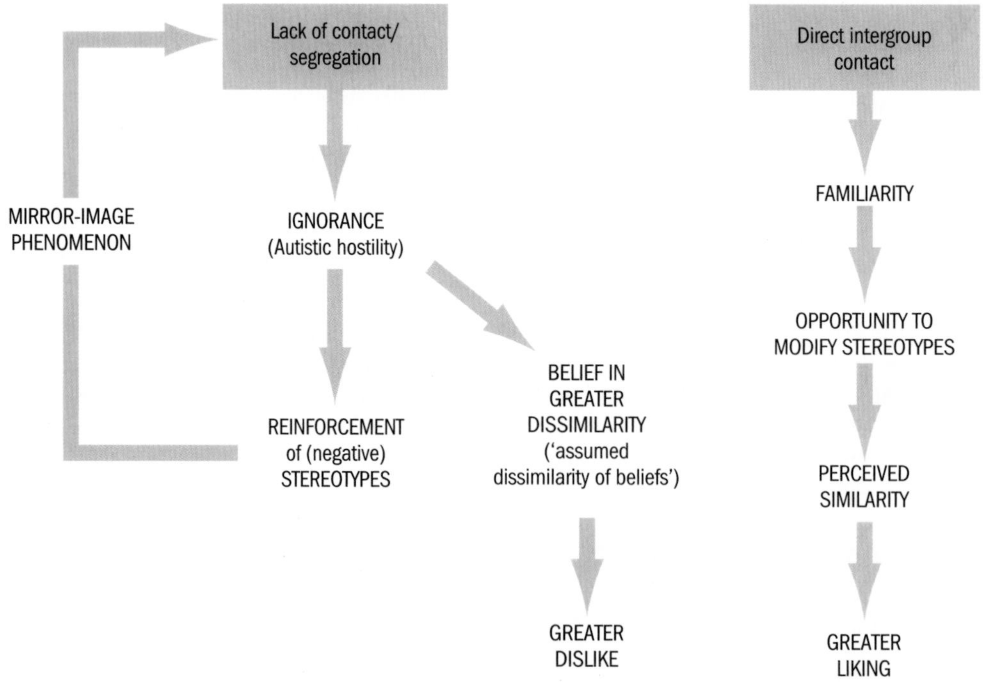

Figure 25.4 Summary of how the negative cycle of lack of contact/segregation between racial/ethnic groups and reinforcement of negative stereotypes can be broken by direct contact (as advocated by Allport's contact hypothesis)

As noted earlier, in Minard's study of miners in West Virginia, black and white miners were (equal status) colleagues in the mine, but the norms operating 'above ground' clearly didn't permit equality of status. Similarly, Stouffer *et al.* (1949) and Amir (1969) found that inter-racial attitudes improved markedly when blacks and whites served together as soldiers in battle and on ships, but relationships weren't so good at base camp.

Stephan (1978) reviewed a number of studies of *desegregation* of American schools, and concluded that white prejudice towards blacks wasn't reduced, while black prejudice towards whites seemed to have increased. Several studies have found that, at first, interaction and friendship are totally governed by group attitudes and then slowly start to take account of personal qualities. But racial attitudes change very little. Aronson (2000) believes that the main reason for this failure was that very few of the studies reviewed by Stephan involved a school situation where all three of Allport's requisites – equal status contact, pursuit of common goals, and sanction by authority – were in place at the same time.

Pursuit of common (superordinate) goals

In a *cooperative* situation, the attainment of one person's goal enhances the chances of attainment of the goals of other group members; this is the reverse of a competitive situation (Brown, 1986).

KEY STUDY 25.2 Robber's Cave revisited (Sherif *et al.*, 1961)

- Sherif *et al.* introduced a *third stage* (see Key Study 25.1), in which seven *equal status contact* situations were created (including filling out questionnaires, seeing movies, and having meals together). None of these, nor all of them in combination, did anything to reduce friction.
- But it was also arranged that the camp's drinking water supply was cut off, and the only way of restoring it was by a *cooperative* effort by the Rattlers and Eagles. In order to afford to hire a movie, both groups had to chip in, and on a trip to Cedar Lake, one of the trucks got stuck and they all had to pull on a rope together to get it started again.
- In the final few days, the group divisions disappeared and they actually suggested travelling home together in one bus. 65 per cent of their friendship choices were now made from the other group, and their stereotypes of the other group became much more favourable.

One influential attempt to realise both mutual cooperation and equal status contact is Aronson *et al.*'s (1978) *jigsaw method*.

Box 25.4 The jigsaw method (Aronson *et al.*, 1978)

- This is a highly structured method of interdependent learning, in which children are assigned to six-person, inter-racial learning groups.
- The day's lesson is divided into six parts, and each member is given material which represents one piece of the lesson to be learned.
- Each child must learn its part, and then communicate it to the rest of the group. At the end of the lesson, the children are tested on the whole lesson and each is given an individual score.
- So, each child is dependent on the others in the group for parts of the lesson that can only be learned from them. Hence, there's complete mutual interdependence.

Evaluation of the jigsaw method

ASK YOURSELF...

- What do you think are some of the benefits of the jigsaw method compared with the conventional classroom?
- How might these benefits contribute to a reduction in prejudice?

The aim of the research programme was to develop and evaluate a classroom atmosphere that could be sustained by the classroom teacher long after the researchers had left. Every student spends some time in the role of expert, and the most important, unique, aspect of this method is that each student has a special, vital gift for the other group members – a gift that's unattainable elsewhere (Aronson, 2000).

The experiment has been replicated in scores of classrooms with thousands of students. According to Aronson (1992, 2000), the jigsaw method consistently enhances students' self-esteem, improves academic performance, increases liking for classmates and improves some interracial perceptions, compared with children in traditional classrooms.

However, although the children of different racial/ethnic groups who'd actually worked together came to like each other better as individuals, their reduced prejudice didn't *generalise* to those ethnic groups as a whole. This may be partly accounted for by the fact that most experiments of this type are small-scale and relatively short-term interventions. The jigsaw method also works best with young children, before prejudiced attitudes have an opportunity to become deeply ingrained (Aronson, 1992).

Do common goals always work?

The imposition of superordinate goals may sometimes even increase antagonism towards the outgroup – if the cooperation fails to achieve its aims. Groups need distinctive and complementary roles to play, so that each group's contributions are clearly defined. When this doesn't happen, liking for the other group may actually *decrease,* perhaps because group members are concerned with the integrity of the ingroup (Brown, 1988).

Maintaining group boundaries (*mutual differentiation:* Fiske, 2004) is essential for promoting generalisation from the particular outgroup members to the whole outgroup (Hewstone, 2003). For example, Harwood *et al.* (2003) found that contact with grandparents was a much better predictor of more positive attitudes towards the elderly in general, when young people reported being aware of age groups during contact.

But isn't there the danger that emphasising group/category boundaries during contact will *reinforce* perceptions of group differences and increase intergroup anxiety (Islam & Hewstone, 1993: see below)? It certainly shouldn't be done in the initial stages of contact, especially when intergroup relationships are very negative. According to Hewstone (2003), the best approach is:

> ... to promote contact that is simultaneously both 'interpersonal' (e.g. involving personal exchange within a close relationship) and 'intergroup' (i.e. both members are still aware that they belong to different groups) ...

An evaluation of the contact hypothesis (CH)

- We noted above that the reduction in prejudice among children who participate in the jigsaw classroom doesn't generalise to those ethnic groups as a whole. This is a crucial criticism of the CH (Hewstone & Brown, 1986). But there's now much greater optimism that positive effects *can* generalise in several ways: across situations, from specific outgroup members to the whole outgroup, from the immediate outgroup to *other* outgroups, and across different types of responses (Gaertner & Dovidio, 2000; Hewstone, 1996; Pettigrew, 1997).
- But contact can also 'work' via more subtle processes than generalisation (Hewstone, 2003). For example, It can help reduce the 'almost automatic fear' caused by interacting with members of outgroups ('intergroup awe': Stephan & Stephan, 1985). Contact has been shown to play a crucial mediating role in reducing anxiety between Hindus and Muslims in Bangladesh, and between Catholics and Protestants in Northern Ireland (Hewstone, 2003). Pettigrew & Tropp (2003) have calculated that anxiety reduction accounts for over 20 per cent of the overall effectiveness of contact in reducing prejudice.
- According to Pettigrew (1998), generating affective (emotional) ties (including anxiety reduction) is the key mechanism involved in contact. Forming close friendships with outgroup members appears to be the most effective in reducing prejudice, and is certainly more effective than the rather superficial contact that occurs in the neighbourhood or at work.
- Pettigrew & Tropp (2003) carried out a meta-analysis ('study of studies') of 561 studies and found a highly significant inverse relationship between contact and prejudice. In other words, the more contact, the less prejudice. Although the results varied between studies, and well-controlled, experimental studies produced larger effects than cross-sectional surveys (the majority), they concluded, emphatically, that 'contact works'.
- The CH doesn't apply only to relationships between members of different ethnic/racial groups. The positive effects of contact have also been shown with attitudes towards psychiatric patients, gay men and disabled children (Hewstone, 2003).

CONCLUSIONS: WHAT TO DO WITH STEREOTYPES?

According to Brislin (1993):

> In many cultures, stereotypes of certain groups are so negative, so pervasive, and have existed for so many generations that they can be considered part of the culture into which children are socialised ...

As we saw in Chapter 22, stereotypes represent a way of simplifying the extraordinarily complex social world we inhabit by placing people into categories. This alone would explain why they're so resistant to change. But they also influence selective attention and selective remembering, processes that are to a large extent outside conscious control. For example, Devine (1989) found that both low- and high-prejudiced people are vulnerable to the automatic activation of the cultural stereotype of African-Americans (see Chapter 22).

However, these automatic stereotyped reactions (like one I'm still 'guilty' of, namely inferring that 'doctor' denotes 'he') can be seen simply as habits that can be broken. Prejudice reduction is a *process* (rather than an all-or-none event), which involves learning to inhibit these automatic reactions and deciding that prejudice is an inappropriate way of relating to others (Devine & Zuwerink, 1994). But trying to suppress your stereotypes may actually *strengthen* their automaticity. Hogg & Abrams (2000) argue that:

> The knack would seem to be to get people to have insight into their stereotypes – to understand them and see through them rather than merely to suppress them ...

Relying on stereotypes to form impressions of strangers (*category-driven processing*) represents the cognitively easiest, least strenuous, route, while relying on their unique characteristics (*attribute-driven processing*) represents the most strenuous route (Fiske & Neuberg, 1990). While people are very skilled at preserving their stereotypes ('You're OK, it's the others'), the more often they come into contact with members of a particular group who don't fit the stereotype, the more likely it is to lose its credibility. Motivating individuals in some way to pay careful attention to others, and to focus on their unique attributes rather than their 'group' attributes, can be effective.

Finally, propaganda, education and the raising of consciousness can all contribute to the reduction and prevention of prejudice.

KEY STUDY 25.3 The blue eyes–brown eyes experiment (Elliott, in Aronson & Osherow, 1980)

- Aronson and Osherow reported an experiment with *third-graders* (nine-year-olds) conducted by their teacher, Jane Elliott.
- She told her class one day that brown-eyed people are more intelligent and 'better' people than those with blue eyes. Brown-eyed students, though in the minority, would be the 'ruling class' over the inferior blue-eyed children and be given extra privileges. The blue-eyed students were to be 'kept in their place' by being last in line, seated at the back of the class, and given less break-time. They also had to wear special collars as a sign of their low status.
- Within a short time, the blue-eyed children began to do more poorly in their schoolwork, became depressed and angry, and described themselves more negatively. The brown-eyed group grew mean, oppressing the others and making derogatory comments about them.

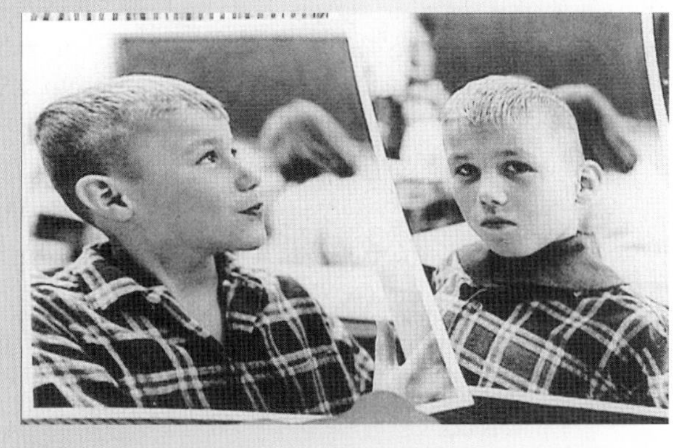

Stills from the film of Elliot's classroom experiment, in which wearing collars as an overt sign of low status was part of the discrimination sanctioned by the teacher

- The next day, Elliott announced that she'd made a mistake, and that it was really blue-eyed people who are superior. The pattern of prejudice and discrimination quickly switched from the blue-eyed as victims to the brown-eyed.
- At the end of the experiment, Elliott debriefed the children. She told them its purpose was to provide them with an opportunity to experience the evils of prejudice and discrimination in a protected environment.

In a follow-up study of the students when they were 18, Elliott (1990) found that they reported themselves as being more tolerant of differences between groups and actively opposed to prejudice.

Elliott's experiment (described in her book *The Eye of the Storm,* and featured in the TV programme *A Class Divided*) demonstrates the potential impact of experiencing prejudice and discrimination first-hand. Prejudice is mindless. If we teach people, especially children, to be mindful of others, to think of them as complex, whole individuals, stereotypic reactions could be reduced (Hogg & Vaughan, 1995).

CHAPTER SUMMARY

- As an extreme attitude, **prejudice** comprises **cognitive (stereotype)**, **affective (hostility)** and **behavioural components**. **Discrimination** usually refers to any kind of prejudiced behaviour.
- Most definitions of prejudice identify it as the characteristic of an individual, but it's often associated with **intergroup conflict**. Racism, sexism, heterosexism and ageism can all be regarded as **ideologies**, which are characteristics of society, not individuals.
- The most influential 'individual' theory of prejudice is the **authoritarian personality**. Adorno *et al.* concluded that the authoritarian personality is prejudiced in a **generalised** way.
- This reflects a personality structure that divides the world rigidly into 'us' and 'them', and a punitive, unloving upbringing, from which considerable **repressed hostility** towards the parents is **displaced** and **projected** onto minority groups.
- Methodological problems with these data include **acquiescent response set** and **experimenter bias**. A major theoretical problem is how a theory of individual differences can account for the uniformity of prejudice as found in Nazi Germany.
- Rokeach's theory of **ideological dogmatism** identifies authoritarianism as an extreme way of thinking (the 'closed mind'), rather than a particular political persuasion.
- According to Dollard *et al.*'s **frustration–aggression hypothesis**, frustration-induced aggression is often displaced onto minority groups, which act as **scapegoats**.
- **Relative deprivation theory** claims that we experience frustration when attainments fall short of expectations. **Fraternalistic relative deprivation** will produce intergroup hostility, particularly if there's a sudden shortfall of attainments.
- According to Sherif's realistic group conflict theory (RGCT), **competition** between groups for scarce resources is a sufficient condition for inter-group hostility. This was demonstrated in the Robber's Cave field experiment.
- **Minimal group experiments** demonstrate that intergroup conflict can occur without competition, and that the **mere categorisation** of oneself as

belonging to one group rather than another is sufficient for intergroup discrimination.

- The minimal group effect is explained in terms of Tajfel's **social identity theory** (SIT), according to which we try to increase self-esteem by accentuating the desirability of our ingroup(s). Prejudice can be seen as part of the attempt to boost self-image.
- An important framework for attempts to reduce prejudice is Allport's **contact hypothesis** (CH), which stresses the need for **equal status contact** and the **pursuit of common (superordinate) goals** between members of different ethnic groups.
- Group segregation can produce **autistic hostility** and the related **mirror-image phenomenon**, with the likely reinforcement of negative stereotypes. Unequal status contact can also reinforce stereotypes.
- In **equal status** situations, there needs to be a balance between **mutual group differentiation** (which maintains **intergroup contact**) and **interpersonal contact**.
- Cooperative learning in the classroom has been studied using the **jigsaw method**, which creates **mutual interdependence** between students. Despite its undoubted benefits for individuals and interpersonal relationships, it's unclear whether these generalise to intergroup attitudes.
- There's considerable support for the CH, which doesn't just apply to relationships between ethnic/racial groups but to a wide range of social groups. The key mechanism involved seems to be creating **affective ties**, including the reduction of **intergroup awe**.
- Stereotypes (**category-driven processing**) are very resistant to change, because they often form part of the culture. They can be activated automatically/unconsciously, but may be broken if people are encouraged to focus on the unique characteristics of individuals (**attribute-driven processing**).

Links with other topics/chapters

- Social institutions other than the police that may be guilty of institutional racism include *psychiatry* (Chapter 43) and *psychology* itself (the '-isms' including *sexism* and *heterosexism,* as well as *ethnocentrism* (Chapter 47).
- *Stereotypes* represent the cognitive component of prejudice (Chapter 22).
- The frustration–aggression hypothesis is, of course, relevant to understanding human *aggression* (Chapter 29).
- Explanations of prejudice and discrimination in terms of individual personality (intrapersonal behaviour), rather than interpersonal/intergroup, are *reductionist* (Chapter 49).
- The *ultimate attribution error* (UAE) (Pettigrew, 1979) refers to the belief that the negative behaviours of an outgroup member are caused by immutable, genetic characteristics of the group as a whole. Pettigrew describes this as the 'bedrock assumption of racist doctrine', and the FAE operating at the group level (Moghaddam, 1998) 'blended' with the SSB at the group level (Chapter 23).

26

CONFORMITY AND GROUP INFLUENCE

INTRODUCTION AND OVERVIEW

It's impossible to live amongst other people and not be influenced by them in some way. According to Allport (1968), social psychology as a discipline can be defined as:

> ... an attempt to understand and explain how the thoughts, feelings and behaviours of individuals are influenced by the actual, imagined, or implied presence of others.

Sometimes, other people's attempts to change our thoughts or behaviour are very obvious, as when, for example, a traffic warden tells us not to park our car in a particular place. If we do as we're told and move the car, we're demonstrating *obedience,* which implies that one person (in this example, the traffic warden, an authority figure) has more social power than others (motorists). Obedience is discussed in Chapter 27.

In common with obedience, other forms of *active social influence* involve deliberate attempts by one person to change another's thoughts or behaviour.

> ***ASK YOURSELF...***
> - Try to identify some other examples of active social influence (see previous chapters in the 'Social' part of this book and the 'Links with other topics/chapters' section at the end of this chapter).

However, on other occasions social influence is less direct and deliberate, and may not involve any explicit requests or demands at all. For example, sometimes the mere presence of other people can influence our behaviour. This can take the form of *inhibiting* our behaviour, as in bystander intervention (see Chapter 30) or social loafing, or *enhancing* it, as in social facilitation (see Chapter 31).

Another form of indirect or passive social influence occurs when your choice of clothes or taste in music is affected by what your friends wear or listen to. This is *conformity*. Your peers (equals) exert pressure on you to behave (and think) in particular ways, a case of the majority influencing the individual (*majority influence*). But majorities can also be influenced by minorities (*minority influence*). Related to conformity are other group processes, such as the *risky shift phenomenon* and *group polarisation*.

Is there anything that these different forms of social influence have in common? According to Turner (1991):

> The key idea in understanding what researchers mean by social influence is the concept of a *social norm*. Influence relates to the processes whereby people agree or disagree about appropriate behaviour, form, maintain or change social norms, and the social conditions that give rise to, and the effects of, such norms ...

Turner defines a social norm as:

> ... a rule, value or standard shared by the members of a social group that prescribes appropriate, expected or desirable attitudes and conduct in matters relevant to the group ...

CONFORMITY

What is conformity?

Conformity has been defined in a number of ways. For Crutchfield (1955), it is 'yielding to group pressure'. Mann (1969) agrees with Crutchfield, but argues that it may take different forms and be based on motives other than group pressure. Zimbardo & Leippe (1991) define conformity as:

> ... a change in belief or behaviour in response to real or imagined group pressure when there is no direct request to comply with the group nor any reason to justify the behaviour change.

> ***ASK YOURSELF...***
> - What do these definitions have in common?

Group pressure is the common denominator in definitions of conformity, although none of them specifies particular groups with particular beliefs or practices. Pressure is exerted by those groups that are important to the individual at a given time. Such groups may consist of 'significant others', such as family or peers (*membership groups*), or groups whose values a person admires or aspires to, but to which s/he doesn't actually belong (*reference groups*).

Conformity, then, doesn't imply adhering to any particular set of attitudes or values. Instead, it involves yielding to the real or imagined pressures of any group, whether it has majority or minority status (van Avermaet, 1996).

Experimental studies of conformity

A study by Jenness (1932) is sometimes cited as the very first experimental study of conformity, although it's usually discussed in the context of social facilitation (see Chapter 31). Jenness asked individual students to estimate the number of beans in a bottle, and then had them discuss it to arrive at a group estimate. When they were asked individually to make a second estimate, there was a distinct shift towards the group's estimate. Sherif (1935) used a similar procedure in one of the classic conformity experiments.

> **KEY STUDY 26.1 If the light appears to move, it must be the Sherif (Sherif, 1935)**
> - Sherif used a visual illusion called the *autokinetic effect*: a stationary spot of light seen in an otherwise dark room appears to move (see Chapter 15).
> - He told participants he was going to move the light, and their task was to say how far they thought the light moved.
> - They were tested individually at first, being asked to estimate the extent of movement several times. The estimates fluctuated to begin with, but then 'settled down' and became quite consistent. However, there were wide differences between participants.
> - They then heard the estimates of two other participants (the group condition). Under these conditions, the estimates of different participants *converged* (they became more *similar*). Thus, a *group norm* developed, which represented the average of the individual estimates.
> - Just as different individuals produced different estimates, so did different groups. This happened both under the conditions already described, and also when participants were tested in small groups right from the start.

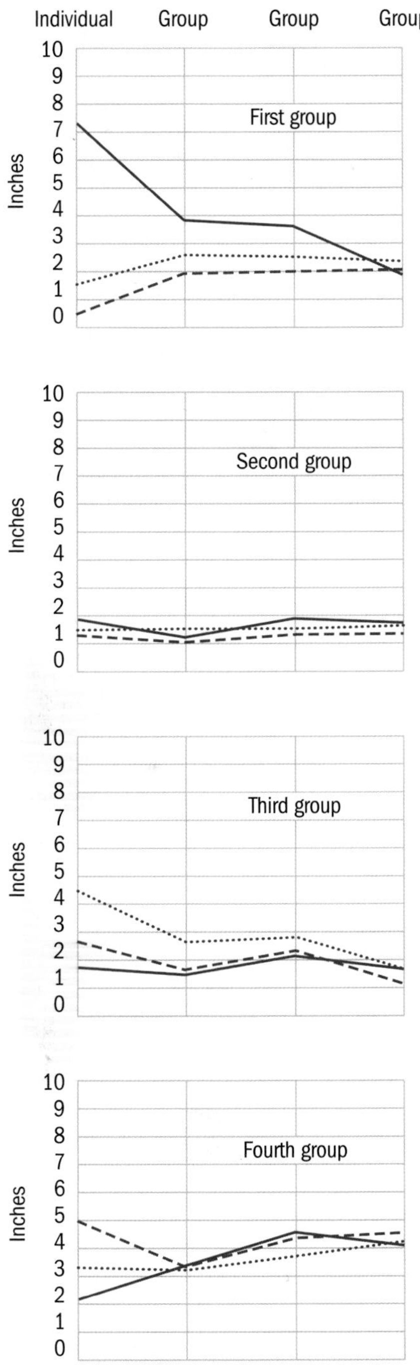

Figure 26.1 Median judgements of the apparent movement of a stationary point of light given by participants in Sherif's (1935) experiment. In the data shown, participants first made their estimates alone ('individual'), and then in groups of three on three occasions ('group'). The figure shows the estimates given by four groups. Sherif also found that when the procedure was reversed, that is, participants made three estimates in groups followed by an estimate alone, the 'individual' estimates did not deviate from one another (from Sherif, 1936)

According to Sherif, participants used others' estimates as a frame of reference in what was an ambiguous situation. Note that:

- participants weren't in any way instructed to agree with the others in the group (unlike the Jenness study), despite initially wide differences between individuals
- when participants were tested again individually, their estimates closely resembled the group norm (rather than their original, individual, estimates).

An evaluation of Sherif's experiment

According to Brown (1996), Sherif's study is one of the classics of social psychology. But it seems to raise questions rather than provide answers.

- In what sense can Sherif's participants be described as a group?
- Can we speak of group norms without any direct interaction taking place or participants seeing themselves as engaged in some kind of joint activity?

In post-experimental interviews, participants all denied being influenced by others' judgements. They also claimed that they struggled to arrive at the 'correct' answers on their own. In other words, they didn't consider themselves part of a group (although there's always doubt about taking participants' reports about the motivation for their behaviour at face value).

While Sherif believed he'd demonstrated conformity, others, notably Asch, disagreed. According to Asch, the fact that the task used by Sherif was *ambiguous* (there was no right or wrong answer) made it difficult to draw any definite conclusions about conformity. Conformity should be measured in terms of the individual's tendency to agree with other group members who unanimously give the *wrong answer* on a task where the solution is obvious or unambiguous. This is a much stricter test of conformity than where there's no correct or incorrect answer to begin with. Asch devised a simple perceptual task that involved participants deciding which of three comparison lines of different lengths matched a standard line.

In a pilot study, Asch tested 36 participants individually on 20 slightly different versions of the task shown in Figure 26.2. They made a total of only three mistakes in the 720 trials (an error rate of 0.42 per cent).

> ***ASK YOURSELF...***
> - What was the purpose of the pilot study?
> - What conclusions do you think Asch drew from its results?

The purpose of the pilot study (which involved participants who weren't to take part in the actual experiment)

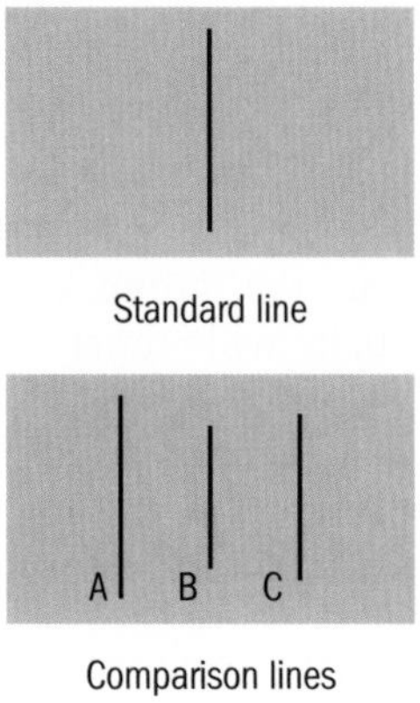

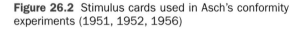

Figure 26.2 Stimulus cards used in Asch's conformity experiments (1951, 1952, 1956)

was to establish that the task really was simple, and the answers obvious and unambiguous. Asch concluded that they were. Because his procedure for studying conformity can be adapted to investigate the effects of different variables on conformity, it's known as the *Asch paradigm*.

Box 26.1 The Asch paradigm

- Some of the participants who'd taken part in the pilot study were asked to act as 'stooges' (or 'confederates: accomplices of the experimenter). The stooges were told they'd be doing the task again, but this time in a group. They were also told that the group would contain one person (a naïve participant) who was completely ignorant that they were stooges.
- On certain *critical* trials, which Asch would indicate by means of a secret signal, all the stooges were required to say out loud the same *wrong answer.* In Asch's original experiment, the stooges (usually seven to nine of them) and the naïve participant were seated either in a straight line or round a table. The situation was rigged so that the naïve participant was always the last or last but one to say the answer out loud.
- On the first two trials (*neutral* trials), all the stooges gave the correct answers. But the next trial was a critical trial (the stooges unanimously gave a wrong answer). This happened a further 11 times (making 12 critical trials in total), with four additional neutral trials (making six in total) between the critical trials.

The important measure in the Asch paradigm is whether the naïve participant conforms, and gives the same wrong answer as the unanimous stooges on the critical trials, or remains independent and gives the obviously correct answer. Asch found a mean conformity rate of 32 per cent; that is, participants agreed with the incorrect majority answer on about one-third of the critical trials.

As shown in Table 26.1, there were also wide individual differences:

A minority of one faces a unanimous majority (Courtesy William Vandivert and *Scientific American*, November 1955)

- no one conformed on all the critical trials, and 13 of the 50 participants (26 per cent) never conformed
- one person conformed on 11 of the 12 critical trials, and about 75 per cent conformed at least once.

Table 26.1 The findings from Asch's original experiment

No of conforming responses made	No of people making those responses
0	13
1	4
2	5
3	6
4	3
5	4
6	1
7	2
8	5
9	3
10	3
11	1
12	0

Given that the task was simple and unambiguous, such findings indicate a high level of conformity. As van Avermaet (1996) has remarked:

> The results reveal the tremendous impact of an 'obviously' incorrect but unanimous majority on the judgements of a lone individual.

How did the naïve participants explain their behaviour?

When interviewed at length following the experiment, participants gave a number of specific reasons for conforming.

- Some wanted to act in accordance with the experimenter's wishes and convey a favourable impression of themselves by not 'upsetting the experiment' (which they believed they would have done by disagreeing with the majority); they thought some obscure 'mistake' had been made.
- A few, who had no reason to believe that there was anything wrong with their eyesight, genuinely doubted the validity of their own judgements by wondering if they were suffering from eye-strain, or if their chairs had been moved so that they couldn't see the cards properly.
- Some denied being aware of having given incorrect answers – they'd unwittingly used the confederates as 'marker posts' (Smith, 1995).
- Others said they wanted to be like everyone else, didn't want to 'appear different', 'be made to look a fool', a 'social outcast' or 'inferior'. So, for these participants there was a discrepancy between the answer they gave in the group and what they *privately believed:* they *knew* the 'wrong' answer was wrong, but went along with it nonetheless. Contrast this with Sherif's participants, for whom there was no conflict between the group's estimate and their own, individual estimates.

Factors affecting conformity

So far, we've described the original, basic experiment. Asch (1952, 1955) subsequently manipulated different variables in order to identify the crucial influences on conformity.

Size of the majority and unanimity

With one naïve participant and just one stooge, conformity was very low (about 3 per cent), ('it's my word against yours'). Where there were two stooges and one participant, conformity increased to 14 per cent, and with three stooges it reached the 32 per cent that Asch originally reported. But beyond three, conformity didn't continue to rise. This suggests that it's the *unanimity* of the majority which is important (the stooges all agree with each other), rather than the actual size of the majority (the number of stooges).

This was demonstrated when one of the stooges (a *dissenter*) agreed with the naïve participant. With one 'supporter', conformity dropped from 32 to 5.5 per cent. Significantly, a dissenter who disagrees with *both* the naïve participant and the majority has almost as much effect on reducing conformity as one who gives the correct answer (that is, agrees with the naïve participant). In both cases, the majority is no longer unanimous. Thus, just breaking the unanimity of the majority is sufficient to reduce conformity (Allen & Levine, 1971). According to Asch (1951):

> ... a unanimous majority of three is, under the given conditions, far more effective than a majority of eight containing one dissenter ...

However, this reduction in conformity only seems to apply to unambiguous stimulus situations (like Asch's perceptual task), and not where opinions are being asked for (Allen & Levine, 1968).

Also, Gerard *et al.* (1968) and Latané & Wolf (1981) claim that adding more stooges *will* increase conformity, although the *rate of increase* falls with each extra majority member. Mann (1969) disagrees with Asch and these later studies, by arguing for a *linear relationship* between group size and conformity: as group size increases, so conformity goes on increasing.

However, adding more members will produce more conformity only if the majority members are perceived as independent judges, and not as sheep following each other or as members of a group who've jointly reached a judgement. According to Hogg & Vaughan (1995), the most robust finding is that conformity reaches its full extent with a three-to-five-person majority, with additional members having little effect.

Fear of ridicule

In the original experiment, it seems that participants were justified in fearing they'd be ridiculed by the rest of the group if they gave the answer they believed to be correct. When a group of 16 naïve participants and a single stooge were tested, the stooge's wrong answers on the critical trials were greeted with sarcasm, exclamations of disbelief, and mocking laughter!

Task difficulty

When Asch made the comparison lines more similar in length (making the task more difficult), participants were more likely to yield to the incorrect majority answer. This was especially true when they felt confident that there was a right answer. When tasks are more ambiguous, in the sense that they involve expressing opinions or stating preferences (there's no objectively correct answer), conformity actually *decreases.*

Giving answers in private

Critics of Asch's experiment have pointed out that participants may conform because they're reluctant or too embarrassed to expose their private views in face-to-face situations (as many of them indicated in post-experimental interviews). If so, the level of conformity should decrease if they're allowed to write their answers down, or where they remain anonymous in some other way. For example, Deutsch & Gerard (1955) used partitions which shielded participants from each other, with responses showing up on a light panel in front of them – the naïve participant had to press one of three buttons. Under these conditions, conformity was lower than in Asch's face-to-face situation. Indeed, when Asch himself allowed the naïve participant to answer in writing (while the stooges still gave their answers publicly), conformity dropped to 12.5 per cent.

Crutchfield (1954) also used a non-face-to-face procedure. He criticised Asch's experiments for being time-consuming and uneconomical, since only one participant could be tested at a time. So, he changed the experimental situation so that several (usually five) naïve participants could be tested at the same time. Altogether, he tested over 600.

Box 26.2 Testing conformity the Crutchfield way – private booths

- Each participant sits in an open cubicle which has a panel with an array of lights and switches; neighbouring panels cannot be seen. Questions, pictures and other kinds of stimuli are projected onto the wall, and participants are told that the lights on the display panel indicate the answers of other participants.
- In fact, everyone sees an identical display, and each believes that s/he is the last to respond. The answers are wrong on approximately half the trials.
- Crutchfield presented a variety of tasks and conformity to the wrong answers differed according to the type of task involved.

(i) On the Asch-type perceptual judgement, he found 30 per cent conformity.
(ii) When participants were asked to complete a series of numbers (as in IQ tests), he also found 30 per cent conformity.
(iii)When he presented a star which was obviously smaller in area than a circle (by about one-third), there was 46 per cent agreement that the circle was smaller than the star.
(iv)Some of his participants were army officers attending a three-day assessment programme. 37 per cent of them agreed with the statement 'I doubt whether I would make a good leader' when it was presented in the booth, but significantly, none of them agreed with it when tested without reference to anyone else.
(v) A substantial proportion of college students agreed with statements which, under more 'normal' circumstances, they probably wouldn't have agreed with. For example: 'American males are, on average, taller than American females, by eight or nine inches'; 'the life expectancy of American males is only about 25 years'; 'Americans sleep four to five hours per night, on average, and eat six meals a day'; 'free speech being a privilege rather than a right, it is proper for a society to suspend free speech when it feels itself threatened'.

Replications of Asch's research

Were Asch's findings a reflection of the times?

The Asch studies have stimulated a great deal of research. Larsen (1974) found significantly lower conformity rates than Asch had found among groups of American students, and suggested that this was because of a changed climate of opinion in America in the 1970s towards independence and criticism and away from conformity. However, in a later (1979) study, Larsen *et al.* found results very similar to those of Asch. Perhaps the pendulum had begun to swing back again. Why might this have happened?

Senator Joseph McCarthy (1908–1957)

The early 1950s was the McCarthyism era in America. This is named after the US Senator Joseph McCarthy, who claimed to have unearthed an anti-American Communist plot. This resulted in a witch-hunt of alleged Communist sympathisers, which included academics and Hollywood stars. Under these social and political conditions, high conformity is to be expected (Spencer & Perrin, 1998). By the early 1970s, there was a more liberal climate, but this may have changed again by the late 1970s.

In Britain, Perrin & Spencer (1981) found very low rates of conformity among university students during a period of self-expression and tolerance. As Spencer & Perrin (1998) say, 'The Asch findings are clearly an indicator of the prevailing culture'.

ASK YOURSELF...

- Perrin & Spencer (1981) tested young offenders on probation, with probation officers as stooges.
- How do you think conformity rates with these participants compared with those of Asch?
- Explain your answer.

We might expect the general social and political climate in Britain in the early 1980s to have had a different impact on university students than on young offenders. Additionally, the stooges were adult authority figures, which means that the group wasn't composed of peers (or equals). Not surprisingly, conformity rates were much higher than for the undergraduates and were similar to those reported by Asch.

It's also possible that experimenters exert an influence. As Brown (1985) has noted, experimenters may also have changed over time. Perhaps their expectations of the amount of conformity that will occur in an experiment are unwittingly conveyed to the participants, who respond accordingly (see Chapter 3).

Cross-cultural studies of conformity

As shown in Table 26.2 below, the vast majority of conformity studies using the Asch paradigm have been carried out in Britain and America. However, using a special statistical technique called meta-analysis (see Chapter 45), Bond & Smith (1996) were able to compare the British and American studies with the small number carried out in other parts of the world. After all relevant factors have been taken into account, the studies can be compared in terms of an *averaged effect size,* in this case, the conformity rate.

Table 26.2 Asch conformity studies by national culture (based on Bond & Smith, 1996; taken from Smith & Bond, 1998)

Nation	Number of studies	Averaged effect size
Asch's own US studies	18	1.16
Other US studies	79	0.90
Canada	1	1.37
UK	10	0.81
Belgium	4	0.91
France	2	0.56
Netherlands	1	0.74
Germany	1	0.92
Portugal	1	0.58
Japan	5	1.42
Brazil	3	1.60
Fiji	2	2.48
Hong Kong	1	1.93
Arab samples (Kuwait, Lebanon)	2	1.31
Africa (Zimbabwe, Republic of the Congo [Zaire], Ghana)	3	1.84

ASK YOURSELF...

- Are there any patterns in the conformity rates (averaged effect size) in Table 26.2?
- For example, are those countries with the highest and lowest conformity geographically and/or culturally related?

According to Smith & Bond (1998), the countries represented in Table 26.2 can be described as *individualist* (such as the USA, the UK, and other western European countries) or *collectivist* (such as Japan, Fiji, and the African countries). In individualist cultures, one's identity is defined by personal choices and achievements, while in collectivist cultures it's defined in terms of the collective group one belongs to (such as the family or religious group). As might be expected, the tendency is for more conformity in collectivist cultures (see Box 26.4, page 452).

An evaluation of the Asch paradigm

- According to Fiske (2004), Asch's research could be seen as focusing on a 'stripped-down' form of social influence, without any real interaction – 'Asch's groups weren't very groupy'. This mirrors Brown's criticism of Sherif's experiments (see above).
- He took an individualist view of groups, rather than a more social interactionist view – that is, he focused on participants as individuals within a group as distinct from a group process as such. None of his groups actually interacted, and he concentrated on individual naïve participants' *independence* rather than group members' *interdependence* (Leyens & Corneille, 1999).

Majority or minority influence in Asch-type experiments?

Typically, the findings from experiments using the Asch paradigm have been interpreted as showing the impact of a (powerful) majority on the (vulnerable) individual (who's usually in a minority of one). While the stooges are, numerically, the majority, Asch himself was interested in the social and personal conditions that induce individuals to resist group pressure. (In 1950s' America, this group pressure took the form of McCarthyism: see above.)

Spencer & Perrin (1998) ask if reports of Asch's experiments have overstated the power of the majority to force minority individuals to agree with obviously mistaken judgements. Indeed, Moscovici & Faucheux (1972) argued that it's more useful to think of the naïve participant as the majority (s/he embodies the 'conventional', self-evident 'truth') and the stooges as the minority (they reflect an unorthodox, unconventional, eccentric, and even outrageous viewpoint). This corresponds to the distinction between the ingroup and outgroup respectively: Moscovici wanted to demonstrate the conditions under which people actually conform to the outgroup. In Asch's experiments, this minority/outgroup influenced the majority 32 per cent of the time, and it's those participants remaining independent who are actually the conformists!

Is the majority always right?

Looked at from Moscovici and Faucheux's perspective, Asch-type experiments suggest how new ideas may come to be accepted (they explain *innovation*), rather than providing evidence about maintenance of the *status quo.* If groups always followed a majority decision rule ('the majority is always or probably right, so best go along with it'), or if social influence were about the inevitable conforming to the group, where would innovation come from? (Spencer & Perrin, 1998: see Box 26.3).

According to Moscovici (1976), there's a *conformity bias* in this area of research, such that all social influence is seen as serving the need to adapt to the *status quo* for the sake of uniformity and stability (the 'tyranny of the majority': Martin & Hewstone, 2001; Wood, 2000). However, change is sometimes needed to adapt to changing circumstances, and this is very difficult to explain given the conformity bias. Without *active minorities,* social and scientific innovations would simply never happen (van Avermaet, 1996).

How do minorities exert an influence?

Moscovici (1976b) reanalysed the data from one of Asch's (1955) experiments, in which he varied the proportion of neutral to critical trials. In the original experiment this proportion was 1:2 (see Box 26.1). When the proportion was 1:6, the conformity rate was 50 per cent, but when it was 4:1 it dropped to 26.2 per cent.

ASK YOURSELF...

- Try to account for these findings.
- Why should conformity rate *increase* as the ratio of neutral to critical trials *decreases,* but *decrease* when it *increases?*

Moscovici interpreted these findings in terms of *consistency.* When there were more critical than neutral trials (the ratio *decreases*), the stooges (who embody the *minority* viewpoint) appear *more consistent* as a group, and this produces a higher conformity rate. They're more often agreeing with each other about something unconventional or novel, which makes it more likely they'll change the views of the majority (as represented by the naïve participant).

KEY STUDY 26.2 Green colour slide experiment (Moscovici *et al.*, 1969)

- Moscovici *et al.* used groups of six participants, of whom four were naïve and two were stooges. The stooges played the role of the minority.
- Before the experiment began, participants' colour vision was tested. They all passed. This meant that the naïve participants couldn't explain the stooges' wrong answers by claiming they were colour blind.
- All the participants gave their answers out loud. The stooges sat either in the first and second position, or first and fourth.
- On 36 separate trials, a slide that was clearly blue was presented on a screen. In the *consistent condition*, the stooges called it green *every time*. In the *inconsistent condition*, they answered 'green' 24 times and 'blue' 12 times.
- In the *control condition*, the groups consisted of six naïve participants.
- In the *control condition*, there were fewer than 1 per cent green responses. This showed how obvious the correct response was.
- In the *inconsistent condition*, 1.25 per cent of responses were green. But in the *consistent condition*, green responses were made over 8 per cent of the time. This was significantly more than in the other two conditions; 32 per cent of naïve participants gave at least *one* green response.
- There were really two types of group: one where *nobody* was influenced by the majority, and one where *several* were influenced. Where the stooges sat made no difference.

Moscovici *et al.*'s experiment clearly showed that a consistent minority can affect the judgements made by the majority. Although the minority doesn't have a numerical advantage, their consistent behavioural style makes them influential. In conformity experiments, the influence of the (numerical) majority is evident from the start; but minority influence only begins to show after a while.

However, consistency doesn't necessarily have to involve repeating the same response. Nemeth *et al.* (1974) replicated the Moscovici *et al.* experiment, but added two conditions: the stooges said 'green' on half the trials and 'green-blue' on the other half. In the *random condition,* the green and green-blue responses were randomly distributed across the trials (there was *no consistency* in their responses). In the *correlated condition,* whether they said green or green-blue depended on the *brightness* of the slide (so, there was still a *pattern* to their responses).

Compared to a no-influence *control condition,* the random condition had no effect. But in the correlated condition, almost 21 per cent of the responses were wrong (minority) answers. Where stooges consistently repeated the green response, there was *no* minority influence. In other words, there's more to minority influence than just consistency. It also matters how the majority interprets the minority's answers. They must relate to the stimulus in some predictable way. In Nemeth *et al.*'s study, it was the brightness of the slide that counted.

Minority influence is achieved not so much by a particular style of behaviour in the group, but more by a combination of attributes and behaviour (Smith, 1995). Moscovici (1980) proposes that while majorities impose their views through directly requiring compliance (which often requires 'surveillance'), minorities use more *indirect* means to achieve a more lasting conversion.

Box 26.3 The importance of consistency and other factors in minority influence

According to Hogg & Vaughan (1998), consistency has five main effects.

1. It disrupts the majority norm, producing uncertainty and doubt.
2. It draws attention to itself as an entity.
3. It conveys the existence of an alternative, coherent point of view.
4. It demonstrates certainty and an unshakeable commitment to a particular point of view.
5. It shows that the only solution to the current conflict is the minority viewpoint.

Minorities are more efficient if they:

- are seen to have made significant personal/material sacrifices (*investment*)
- are perceived as acting out of principle rather than ulterior motives (*autonomy*)
- display a balance between being 'dogmatic' (*rigid*) and 'inconsistent' (*flexible*)
- are seen as being *similar* to the majority in terms of age, gender and social category, particularly if they're categorised as part of the ingroup.

ASK YOURSELF...

- Can you relate the importance of consistency to Kelley's covariation model of attribution? (See Chapter 23.)

When minority group members *consistently* adopt a unique (non-majority, unconventional) response (that is, there's *low consensus*), this is likely to lead majority members to make an *internal/dispositional* attribution (they sincerely believe in what they say).

According to Wood *et al.* (1994), minority influence most often occurs *privately* – that is, on measures that protect the converted majority individuals from appearing publicly to abandon their majority position. For the same reason, influence is often *indirect,* emerging on issues merely *related* to the controversial issues or *delayed* beyond the immediate context (Crano, 2000):

> ... Thus, majorities can be converted by minorities, but majority individuals do not admit it to others, and perhaps not to themselves, thereby avoiding public identification with the unpopular minority position ... (Fiske, 2004)

Why do people conform?

Different types of social influence

One very influential and widely accepted account of group influence is Deutsch & Gerard's (1955) distinction between *informational social influence* (ISI) and *normative social influence* (NSI).

Informational social influence (ISI)

Underlying ISI is the need to be right, to have an accurate perception of reality. So when we're uncertain or face an ambiguous situation, we look to others to help us perceive the stimulus situation accurately (or define the situation: see Chapter 30). This involves a *social comparison* with other group members in order to reduce the uncertainty.

As we saw earlier, Sherif's experiment involves an inherently ambiguous situation: there's no actual movement of the light, and so there cannot be any right or wrong answers. Under these conditions, participants were only too willing to validate their own estimates by comparing them with those of others. The results were consistent with Sherif's *social reality hypothesis,* which states that:

> The less one can rely on one's own direct perception and behavioural contact with the physical world, the more susceptible one should be to influence from others ... (Turner, 1991)

According to Festinger's (1954) *social comparison theory,* people have a basic need to evaluate their ideas and attitudes and, in turn, to confirm that they're correct. This can provide a reassuring sense of control over one's world, and a satisfying sense of competence. In novel or ambiguous situations, social reality is defined by what others think and do. Significantly, Sherif's participants were relatively unaware of being influenced by the other judges (see page 443). As Turner (1991) observes:

> They appear to be largely unconsciously adjusting their judgement in the light of others' reports to arrive at a stable, agreed picture of a shared but initially unstructured world.

Normative social influence (NSI)

Underlying NSI is the need to be accepted by other people, and to make a favourable impression on them. We conform in order to gain social approval and avoid rejection – we agree with others because of their power to reward, punish, accept, or reject us.

In Asch's experiment (and to a large extent in Crutchfield's too), most participants weren't unsure about the correct answer. Rather, they were faced with a *conflict* between two sources of information, which in unambiguous situations normally coincide, namely their own judgement and that of others. If they chose their own judgement, they risked rejection and ridicule by the majority. Recall, though, that some participants were unaware of any conflict or of having given an incorrect response.

Internalisation and compliance

Related to ISI and NSI are two kinds of conformity.

1. *Internalisation* occurs when a private belief or opinion becomes consistent with a public belief or opinion. In other words, we say what we believe and believe what

we say. Mann (1969) calls this *true conformity,* and it can be thought of as a *conversion* to other people's points of view, especially in ambiguous situations.

2. *Compliance* occurs when the answers given publicly aren't those that are privately believed (we say what we don't believe and what we believe we don't say). Compliance represents a compromise in situations where people face a conflict between what they privately believe and what others publicly say they believe.

> *ASK YOURSELF...*
> - Which kind of conformity was most common in Sherif's and Asch's experiments?
> - How are internalisation and compliance related to NSI and ISI?

In Sherif's experiment, participants were *internalising* others' judgements and making them their own. Faced with an ambiguous situation, participants were guided by what others believed to reduce their uncertainty. So, internalisation is related to ISI.

By contrast, most of Asch's participants knew that the majority answers on the critical trials were wrong, but often agreed with them publicly. They were *complying* with the majority to avoid ridicule or rejection. So, compliance is related to NSI.

Do we have to choose between ISI and NSI?

The ISI/NSI distinction has proved very influential. But like all distinctions, it faces the problem of being a *false dichotomy:* are they really separate, opposite forms of influence? A study by Insko *et al.* (1983) suggests that they can operate together.

KEY STUDY 26.3 The compatibility of ISI and NSI (Insko *et al.*, 1983)

- Insko *et al.* had participants, in groups of six, judge whether a colour shown on a slide was more similar to another colour shown to the left or to one shown to the right.
- On critical trials, four stooges who answered before the naïve participant, and another who answered last, gave answers which deviated from those given by most participants in a control condition who were tested alone.
- There were two independent variables:

  1. participants answered either *publicly* or *privately*
  2. the experimenter said that he either was or wasn't able to determine which response was more correct (in the '*determined*' condition, he referred to an apparatus through which he could accurately measure which response was more correct; in the '*undetermined*' condition, he said this was impossible).
- Two hypotheses were tested:

  1. there will be greater conformity in the public than the private condition due to NSI

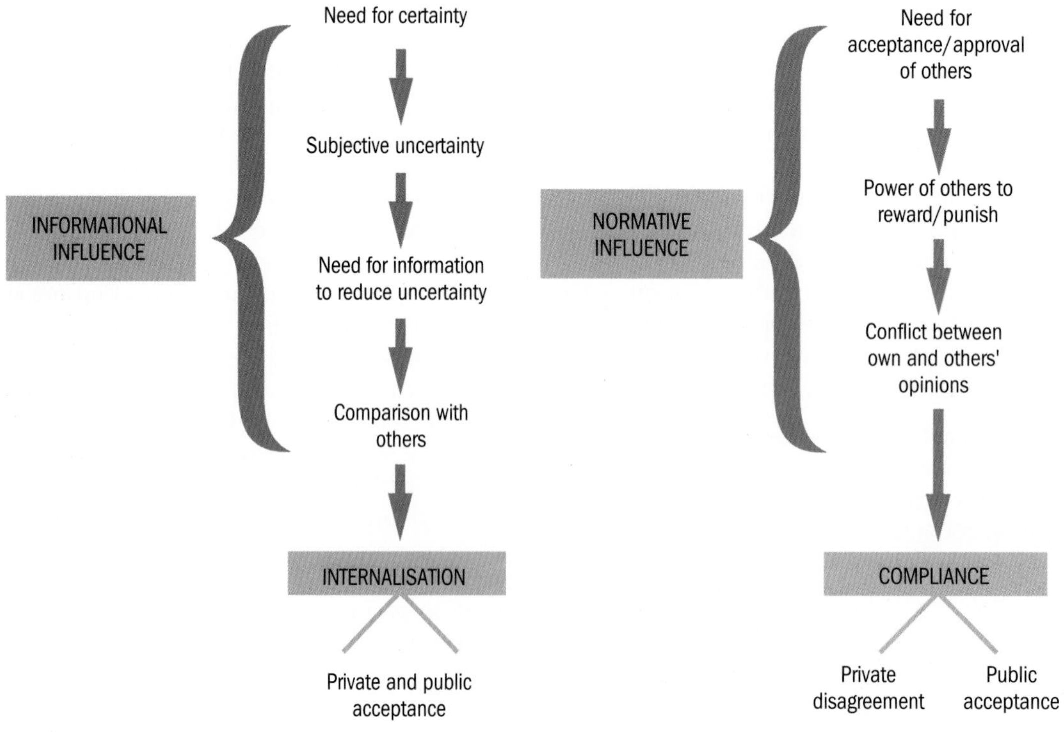

Figure 26.3 The relationship between different kinds of influence and different kinds of conformity

2. there will be greater conformity in the determined than the undetermined condition due to ISI.

- Both hypotheses were confirmed.
- Also, the determined condition produced greater conformity in both private and public conditions, and all four conditions produced greater conformity than the control condition. Hence, even with 'objective stimuli', ISI can add to the effect of NSI (van Avermaet, 1996).

Remember that when Asch made the three comparison lines much more similar – and hence the task more difficult – conformity increased. Clearly, ISI was involved here. If we believe there's a correct answer and are uncertain what it is, it seems quite logical to expect that we'd be more influenced by a unanimous majority. This is why having a supporter, or the presence of a dissenter, has the effect of reducing conformity. By breaking the group consensus, the participant is shown both that disagreement is possible and that the group is fallible. As Turner (1991) puts it:

> ... the more consensual the group and the more isolated the individual (i.e. the less others agree with the deviant), the greater the power of the group to define reality, induce self-doubt in the deviant as to both her competence and social position, and threaten her with ridicule and rejection for being different.

In other words, both ISI and NSI can operate in conjunction with each other, and shouldn't be seen as opposed processes of influence.

Conformity and group belongingness

The distinction between NSI and ISI has been called the *dual process dependency model* of social influence (e.g. Turner, 1991). But this model underestimates the role of group 'belongingness'. One important feature of conformity is that we're influenced by a group because, psychologically, we feel we belong to it. This is why a group's norms are relevant standards for our own attitudes and behaviour. The dual process dependency model emphasises the *interpersonal* aspects of conformity experiments, which could just as easily occur between individuals as group members.

Scene from *Twelve Angry Men,* starring Henry Fonda as the only dissenter in an (all-male) jury

The *self-categorisation approach* suggests that in Sherif's (1935) experiment, for example, participants assumed that the autokinetic effect was real, and expected to agree with each other. In support of this, it's been shown that when participants discover that the autokinetic effect is an illusion, mutual influence and convergence cease – the need to agree at all is removed (Sperling, 1946).

If, however, we believe that there *is* a correct answer, and we're uncertain what it is, then only those whom we categorise as belonging to 'our' group will influence our judgements. As Brown (1988) has remarked:

> There is more to conformity than simply 'defining social reality': it all depends on who is doing the defining.

KEY STUDY 26.4 Knowing what to think by knowing who you are (Abrams *et al.*, 1990)

- Abrams *et al.* replicated Sherif's experiment with psychology students, but manipulated categorisation: stooges were introduced as students at a nearby university, but were either fellow psychology students or students of ancient history.
- Convergence only occurred when others were categorised as being equivalent to self, that is, a member of the ingroup (fellow psychology students). So self-categorisation may set limits on ISI.
- It should also set limits on NSI, since individuals will presumably have a stronger desire to receive rewards, approval and acceptance from those categorised in the same way as themselves than from those categorised differently.
- Using the Asch paradigm but again manipulating categorisation, Abrams *et al.* found that conformity exceeded the usual level of 32 per cent in the ingroup condition, but was greatly below this level in the outgroup condition.

Abrams *et al.* (1990) argue that we experience uncertainty only when we disagree with those with whom we expect to agree. This is especially likely when we regard those others as members of the same category or group as ourselves with respect to judgements made in a shared stimulus situation. Social influence occurs, then, when we see ourselves as belonging to a group, and possessing the same characteristics and reactions as other group members.

Turner (1991) calls this kind of self-categorisation, in which group membership is relevant, *referent social influence*

(RSI). What's important isn't the validation of physical reality or the avoidance of social disapproval, but the upholding of a *group norm:* people are the source of information about the appropriate ingroup norm.

According to Fiske (2004), a social categorisation approach sees the NSI/SIS distinction as (another) false dichotomy (see Key Study 26.3), since 'Information is intrinsically social'.

> ***ASK YOURSELF...***
> - What do you understand Fiske to mean when she says that 'Information is intrinsically social'? (A look back at Chapter 3 should offer you some clues.)

Conformity: good or bad?

> ***ASK YOURSELF...***
> - Is conformity always and necessarily desirable, and is failure to conform always and necessarily undesirable?

Sometimes, dissent is just an expression of disagreement, a refusal to 'go along with the crowd' (Maslach *et al.*, 1985). On other occasions, it's more creative or constructive, as when someone suggests a better solution to a problem. A refusal to 'go along with the crowd' may be an attempt to remain independent *as a matter of principle* (what Willis, 1963, calls *anticonformity*), and may betray a basic fear of a loss of personal identity.

According to Zimbardo & Leippe (1991), in most circumstances conformity serves a valuable social purpose in that it:

> ... lubricates the machinery of social interaction [and] enables us to structure our social behaviour and predict the reactions of others.

For most people, though, the word 'conformity' has a negative connotation. As a result, it's implicitly assumed that independence is 'good' and conformity is 'bad', a value judgement made explicit by Asch (1952). However, conformity can be highly functional, helping us to satisfy social and non-social needs, as well as being necessary (at least to a degree) for social life to proceed at all.

Since each of us has a limited (and often biased) store of information on which to make decisions, other people can often provide valuable additional information and expertise. Conforming with others under these circumstances may be a rational judgement. However, while conformity can help preserve harmony:

> There are obvious dangers to conformity. Failure to speak our minds against dangerous trends or attitudes (for example, racism) can easily be interpreted as support ... (Krebs & Blackman, 1988)

Box 26.4 Japan: a straitjacket society?

- The Japanese government is encouraging people to stop being so 'typically' Japanese.
- An advisory panel set up by the conservative prime minister, Keizo Obuchi, advocated that Japan must abandon its obsession with conformity and equality if it is to tackle its growing social problems, such as juvenile crime, suicide, bankruptcy and unemployment.
- This promotion of 'individual empowerment' represents a rejection of many of Japan's core values, but the country is desperate for spontaneity, innovation and ambition.
- In education, for example, the panel calls for action to curb 'the excessive degree of homogeneity and uniformity'. What the panel is recommending is a shift from collectivist to individualist values (see text below).

Almost all Japanese school children aged up to 16 wear dark-blue sailor-style uniforms and follow the same rigid curriculum and textbooks (based on Watts, 2000)

The term conformity is often used to convey undesirable behaviour. In laboratory research, it has most often been studied in terms of the 'conspiratorial group ... [being] shown to limit, constrain, and distort the individual's response' (Milgram, 1965). However, in the context of his famous studies of obedience, Milgram showed that the presence of two defiant peers significantly reduced the obedience rate among naïve participants, and he wrote an article (1965) called 'Liberating effects of group pressure' (see Chapter 27).

Also, whether conformity is considered good or bad is a matter of *culture*. In *individualist* cultures, people are often distressed by the possibility that others can influence their behaviour against their will: they prefer to believe they're in control of their destiny. So 'conformity', 'compliance', 'obedience' and other similar terms have negative connotations. But in *collectivist* cultures, adjusting one's behaviour to fit the requests and expectations of others is highly valued, and sometimes even a moral imperative (Fiske *et al.*, 1998). In these cultures, conformity is seen as necessary for social functioning, rather than a sign of weakness (Nagayama Hall & Barongan, 2002).

Individual differences in conformity

Another way of trying to understand why people conform is to consider whether some people are more likely to conform than others and if so, why.

Crutchfield (1955) found that people who conform tend to be intellectually less effective, have less ego strength, less leadership ability, less mature social relationships, and feelings of inferiority. They also tend to be authoritarian, more submissive, narrow-minded and inhibited, and have relatively little insight into their own personalities compared with those who tend not to conform. However, *consistency across situations* isn't high (McGuire, 1968), and the authoritarian personality (Adorno *et al.*, 1950: see Chapter 25) is perhaps as close to a 'conforming personality type' as can be found.

In general, men conform less than women. This is at least partly because men are traditionally more likely to see dissent or independence as a way of expressing their competence, while women tend to see cooperation and agreement with others as expressing competence (Zimbardo & Leippe, 1991). However, men with personal qualities and interests that are stereotypically 'feminine' conform as much as women with these same qualities and interests. Conversely, women and men with stereotypically 'masculine' qualities and interests conform less (Maslach *et al.*, 1987).

OTHER GROUP PROCESSES

Risky shift

Based on the traditional interpretation of conformity studies as being concerned with majority influence and with how the *status quo* is maintained, the common-sense prediction is that groups, relative to individuals, will be more cautious and conservative. Convergence towards a group mean in Sherif's experiment is a clear demonstration of this prediction. However, Stoner (1961) found the *opposite* to be true. He presented participants with twelve decision dilemmas faced by hypothetical people, and their task was to advise the person about how much risk to take. Initially this was done individually, then in groups of about five.

To everyone's amazement, the group decisions were usually *riskier* than the individuals'. In other words, the group advised the hypothetical person to take a greater risk than the average of the individuals' advice (the *risky shift phenomenon*). Stoner sparked a wave of research into group decision-making, which initially found considerable support for risky shift, involving people of varying ages, occupations and from 12 different countries. However, it was eventually found that risky shift wasn't universal after all. It was possible to present decision dilemmas on which people became *more cautious* after discussion (Myers, 1994). So, is there a general principle that will predict how risky or cautious people's advice will be?

Group polarisation

One of the most robust findings in social psychology is that when group members with similar initial attitudes engage in group discussion to achieve agreement about difficult decisions, the discussion *strengthens* the average individual inclinations (Cooper *et al.*, 2004). For this reason, risky shift came to be seen as part of a much wider phenomenon called *group polarisation* (GP) (Moscovici & Zavalloni, 1969). This is the tendency for groups to make decisions that are more extreme than the mean of individuals' initial positions, in the direction already favoured by that mean (Myers & Lamm, 1975; Wetherell, 1987). So, groups are likely to adopt more extreme views than individual members, but this can be in either a riskier or a more cautious direction. Why does it occur?

- According to Brown (1986), the mere *exchange of information* about which members made which decisions can produce GP. In group discussion, group members may point out relevant information that others have missed, exposing individuals to *supportive arguments* they might not previously have thought of. This relates to ISI.
- Group members wish to define their identity more positively and distinctively, in contrast to members of other groups whom they might expect to adopt more average positions (Turner, 1991). This is supported by studies in which groups are told of the presumed decisions of other groups relevant to them (Smith, 1995). This is related to NSI.
- Several studies suggest that *social categorisation processes* also play a significant role in GP. It seems to occur through three steps: (i) categorisation of self as a member of a group (the ingroup); (ii) identification of the prototypical characteristics, behaviours and norms of the ingroup that differentiate it from other (out)groups; and (iii) stereotyping the self as a member of the ingroup (Cooper *et al.*, 2004).

Groupthink

Groupthink (Janis, 1971, 1982) is an example of how group decisions may become very extreme. Groupthink is defined as a mode of thinking in which the desire to reach unanimous agreement overrides the motivation to adopt proper, rational, decision-making procedures. Using archive material (people's retrospective accounts and content analysis), Janis analysed how the decisions were taken that led to certain major political/military fiascos, such as Pearl Harbor (1941), the Bay of Pigs invasion of Cuba (1961) which led to the Cuban Missile Crisis (1962), and the Vietnam War.

It's been suggested that groupthink is merely a specific instance of risky shift, in which a group that already tends towards making risky decisions polarises, through discussion, to an even riskier one (Myers & Lamm,

The American invasion of the Bay of Pigs, Cuba, in 1961

1975). Janis believes that groupthink stems from an excessively cohesive, closeknit group, the suppression of dissent in the interests of group harmony, and a directive leader who signals what decisions s/he favours.

CHAPTER SUMMARY

- **Social influence** can be **active** or **deliberate**, as in persuasive communication and obedience, or **passive** or **non-deliberate**, as in social facilitation and conformity. A common feature of all social influence is the concept of a **social norm**.
- Definitions of **conformity** commonly refer to group pressure, whether the group is a **membership** or a **reference** group.
- In Sherif's experiment using the **autokinetic effect**, individual estimates **converged** to form a group norm. Asch criticised Sherif's use of an ambiguous task, and in his own experiments used a comparison of lines task for which there was a correct answer.
- Asch found that the **unanimity/consensus of the majority** is crucial, not its size. The presence of a **supporter** or **dissenter** reduces conformity, because the majority is no longer unanimous.
- Conformity is increased when the task is made **more difficult** (more **ambiguous**), and reduced when participants give their answer **anonymously**. However, Crutchfield found that conformity rate still differs according to the type of task.
- Replications of Asch's experiment have produced higher or lower rates of conformity according to when and where they were conducted. Both **socio-historical** and **cultural factors** seem to play a part.
- Asch's findings are usually interpreted as showing the impact of **majority influence**. But Moscovici believes that the stooge majority should be thought of as embodying unconventional, minority beliefs, and that conformity experiments show how new ideas come to be accepted (**innovation**).
- One way in which **minority influence** works is by displaying **consistency**, together with **investment**, **autonomy**, and a balance between **rigidity** and **flexibility**.
- Two major **motives for conformity** are the need to be right (**informational social influence**/ISI) and the need to be accepted by others (**normative social influence**/NSI).
- ISI is related to Sherif's **social reality hypothesis** and Festinger's **social comparison theory**, and is demonstrated through **internalisation/true conformity**. NSI is linked to **compliance**.
- ISI and NSI aren't opposed forms of influence, but the **dual process dependency model** tends to emphasise the **interpersonal** aspects of conformity experiments. In contrast, **referent social influence**/RFI stresses the importance of **group membership** and **self-categorisation**.
- Despite evidence of **individual differences** in the tendency to conform, there's unlikely to be a 'conforming personality'.
- While **independence** is often seen as preferable to conformity, conformity also serves an important social function. Milgram has shown how it can have liberating effects in an obedience situation.
- Evidence for the **risky shift phenomenon** is mixed. It has come to be seen as part of **group polarisation**/GP, in which group decisions tend to become more extreme than the mean of individuals' initial positions.
- One demonstration of GP is **groupthink**, which stems from excessively cohesive groups with a directive leader.

Links with other topics/chapters

- Other examples of active social influence apart from *obedience* (Chapter 27) include *impression management* (Chapter 22), *persuasive communication,* and *propaganda and advertising* (Chapter 24).
- *Social loafing* and *social facilitation* are both forms of indirect/passive social influence that are relevant to the *social psychology of sport* (Chapter 31).
- The finding that conformity is generally higher in *collectivist cultures* demonstrates the importance of *cross-cultural research* in general, and the need to counteract *ethnocentrism* and *Eurocentrism* in particular (Chapter 47).
- Self-categorisation and intergroup relationships are crucial for understanding *prejudice and discrimination* (Chapter 25).

27

OBEDIENCE

INTRODUCTION AND OVERVIEW

As we saw at the beginning of Chapter 26, obedience is an active or deliberate form of social influence, which involves someone in authority requiring us to behave in a particular way in a particular situation. If we obey, we are said to be *complying* with the authority figure's request or instruction. We also discussed compliance as a major kind of conformity, namely one in which overt behaviour doesn't reflect private beliefs.

Compliance also occurs whenever we do what someone else 'asks' us to do, that is, whenever people make direct requests, such as when a friend asks us for a 'favour' or a salesperson 'invites' us to try a product or service. Many researchers believe that attempts to gain compliance through direct requests is the most common form of social influence (Hogg & Vaughan, 1995).

Cialdini (2004) identifies six basic tendencies of human behaviour that come into play in generating a positive response when one person tries to influence another's attitudes or actions. These are: *reciprocity* (*reciprocation*), *liking, consistency, social validation, authority* and *scarcity.* (We will look at each of these in more detail in the following section.) Most of these are best understood as 'tactics' used by a salesperson trying to sell a product (Cialdini, 1988). *Consistency* was discussed in Chapter 26 in relation to *minority influence,* and *authority* relates directly to *obedience* (see above).

Like the demands of an authority figure, these tactics (some more subtle than others) are active and deliberate attempts to make us behave in particular ways. Unlike both obedience and conformity, there's no obvious 'penalty' to pay for not complying. And as we find in some obedience and conformity situations, the salesperson may be perceived as an expert with access to information (and goods/services) that we need. So, it's clear that these various forms of social influence share many characteristics.

Migde Ure and Bob Geldof at the re-recording of 'Feed the World', 2004

COMPLIANCE: REQUESTING, SELLING, AND CONVINCING

- *The norm of reciprocity:* Giving away a free sample, or a free estimate for a job, or a 'free pen' in charity donation envelopes, may put the potential customer/donor under a sense of obligation. This is based on the social norm that 'we should treat others the way they treat us' (and on the further principle that 'there's no such thing as a free lunch'). Survey researchers have found that attaching a small incentive (financial or otherwise) increases return rate by almost 20 per cent, while a payment dependent on completing the questionnaire *doesn't have the same effect*. It's the unsolicited gift that does the trick (Tourangeau, 2004). This can apply to other relationships too, as in the belief that 'one good turn deserves another'.
- *Liking:* people prefer to say 'yes' to people they like. This can be manipulated through physical attractiveness, agreeing with others and in other ways showing them how we're similar to them, paying them compliments (even flattering them), and cooperating with them ('I'm on your side'). This is sometimes referred to as *ingratiation*. According to Fiske (2004), attractive people:

> ... sell products, win votes, raise funds, and shorten their jail sentences, all reflecting their success as compliance agents. This builds on the belonging principle of people going along with those they like.

- *Social validation:* requesters can stimulate compliance by demonstrating (or implying) that others 'just like you' have already complied (for example, telling us how many people have already subscribed to X or signed in support of Y). But this can backfire, as in:

> ... the understandable but potentially misguided tendency of health educators to call attention to a problem by depicting it as regrettably frequent. Information campaigns stress that alcohol and drug abuse are intolerably high, that adolescent suicide rates are alarming and that polluters are spoiling the environment ... (Cialdini, 2004)

Although the claims are both true and well intentioned:

> .. Within the statement 'Look at all the people who are doing this *undesirable* thing' lurks the powerful and undercutting message 'Look at all the people who *are* doing this undesirable thing ... (Cialdini, 2004)

This may produce a boomerang effect.

- *Scarcity:* This relates to people's tendency to value rare/scarce resources. They'll try to obtain items that are going out of stock ('while stocks last') or that are almost out of reach ('once-in-a-lifetime opportunity'). The resources can take the form of information (as in newspaper 'scoops' or exclusives). On the same principle, 'secret' affairs can be more exciting, and 'absence makes the heart grow fonder' (Cialdini, 2004: see Chapter 28).
- The *'foot in the door' tactic* (FITD) (Freedman & Fraser, 1966): Getting someone to agree to a small request makes them more likely to comply with a larger request at some later point, than if the larger request had been made initially. This can be explained partly in terms of people's need to appear *consistent* – to both themselves and others (see Chapter 24). To be effective, the FITD usually requires a delay between the initial small request and the later larger one. If they come too close together, people feel exploited and often refuse. Similarly, people refuse to comply when

the *same* person makes *both* requests (Fiske, 2004). For people to maintain their relationships, they must abide by the *norm of reciprocity* (Cialdini & Trost, 1998: see above).

- According to Hogg & Vaughan (1995), the FITD represents one of three multiple-request tactics, whereby an initial request functions as a set-up for a second (real) request. The other two are:

  (a) the '*door-in-the-face*' tactic (DIF), in which a large, unreasonable request is followed up with a second, much more reasonable request, which is more difficult to refuse. Compliance takes the form of a 'concession', and trades on the requester appearing to 'back off' and the target person feeling guilty and perhaps needing to reciprocate by agreeing to the more moderate request (Fiske, 2004); however it works, it works (O'Keefe & Hale, 2001)

  (b) the '*low-ball*' (LB) tactic – for example, having induced a customer to commit him/herself to a purchase, the salesperson then reveals certain hidden costs that weren't previously mentioned (the term comes from US baseball; in the UK, we might talk of 'moving the goal posts').

> *ASK YOURSELF...*
> - Can you identify any of these tactics in your own experience with salespeople?
> - Have you possibly employed one or more of them yourself?

DISTINGUISHING BETWEEN CONFORMITY AND OBEDIENCE

> *ASK YOURSELF...*
> - Based on what you know about conformity (see Chapter 26), try to identify some of the basic *similarities and differences* between conformity and obedience.

According to Milgram (1992), both conformity and obedience involve the 'abdication of individual judgement in the face of some external social pressure'. However, there are three major *differences* between them.

1. In conformity, there's no explicit requirement to act in a certain way, whereas in obedience we're being ordered or instructed to do something.
2. In conformity, those who influence us are our *peers (equals)* and people's behaviour becomes more *alike (homogenisation of behaviour)*. In obedience, there's a *difference in status* from the outset, with the authority figure influencing another person who has inferior power or status: there's no mutual influence.
3. Conformity has to do with the psychological 'need' for acceptance by others, and entails going along with one's peers in a group situation. Obedience has to do with the social power and status of an authority figure in a hierarchical situation. Although we typically deny that we conform (because it seems to detract from our sense of *individuality*), we usually *deny responsibility* for our behaviour in the case of obedience ('He made me do it', or 'I was only doing what I was told').

In addition, Brown (1986) says that conformity behaviour is affected by *example* (from peers or equals), while obedience is affected by *direction* (from somebody in higher authority).

EXPERIMENTAL STUDIES OF OBEDIENCE

In the experiments of Sherif, Asch and Crutchfield (see Chapter 25), participants showed conformity by giving a verbal response of some kind, or pressing buttons representing answers on various tasks. In the most famous and controversial of all obedience experiments, Milgram's participants were required to 'kill' another human being.

Milgram's research

Stanley Milgram (1933–1984)

Milgram was attempting to test 'the "Germans are different" hypothesis'. This has been used by historians to explain the systematic destruction of millions of Jews, Poles, and others by the Nazis during the 1930s and 1940s. It maintains that:

- Hitler couldn't have put his evil plans into operation without the cooperation of thousands of others, and

- the Germans have a basic character defect, namely a readiness to obey authority without question regardless of the acts demanded by the authority figure; it's this readiness to obey that provided Hitler with the cooperation he needed.

It's really the second part of the hypothesis that Milgram was trying to test. After piloting his research in America, he planned to continue it in Germany. But his results showed this was unnecessary.

The participants

The participants in the original (1963) experiment were 20–50-year-old men, from all walks of life. They answered advertisements that came by post or appeared in local newspapers, which asked for volunteers for a study of learning to be conducted at Yale University. It would take about one hour, and there'd be a payment of $4.50.

Public Announcement

WE WILL PAY YOU $4.00 FOR ONE HOUR OF YOUR TIME

Persons Needed for a Study of Memory

***We will pay five hundred New Haven men to help us complete a scientific study of memory and learning. The study is being done at Yale University.**

***Each person who participates will be paid $4.00 (plus 50c carfare) for approximately 1 hour's time. We need you for only one hour: there are no further obligations. You may choose the time you would like to come (evenings, weekdays, or weekends).**

***No special training, education, or experience is needed. We want:**

Factory workers	Businessmen	Construction workers
City employees	Clerks	Salespeople
Laborers	Professional people	White-collar workers
Barbers	Telephone workers	Others

All persons must be between the ages of 20 and 50. High school and college students cannot be used.

***If you meet these qualifications, fill out the coupon below and mail it now to Professor Stanley Milgram, Department of Psychology, Yale University, New Haven. You will be notified later of the specific time and place of the study. We reserve the right to decline any application.**

***You will be paid $4.00 (plus 50c carfare) as soon as you arrive at the laboratory.**

TO:
PROF. STANLEY MILGRAM, DEPARTMENT OF PSYCHOLOGY, YALE UNIVERSITY, NEW HAVEN, CONN. I want to take part in this study of memory and learning. I am between the ages of 20 and 50. I will be paid $4.00 (plus 50c carfare) if I participate.

NAME (Please Print)..

ADDRESS..

TELEPHONE NO................. Best time to call you ....

AGE........ OCCUPATION.................... SEX......
CAN YOU COME:

WEEKDAYS .... EVENINGS ......WEEKENDS.........

Announcement placed in a local newspaper to recruit participants (from Milgram, 1974)

The basic procedure

Box 27.1 The basic procedure used in Milgram's obedience experiment

- When participants arrived at Yale University psychology department, they were met by a young man in a grey laboratory coat, who introduced himself as Jack Williams, the experimenter. Also present was a Mr Wallace, introduced as another participant, in his late fifties, an accountant, a little overweight and generally a very mild and harmless-looking man.
- In fact, Mr Wallace was a stooge, and everything that happened after this was preplanned, staged, and scripted: everything, that is, except the degree to which the real participant obeyed the experimenter's instructions.
- The participant and Mr Wallace were told that the experiment was concerned with the effects of punishment on learning. One of them was to be the teacher and the other the learner. Their roles were determined by each drawing a piece of paper from a hat: both, in fact, had 'teacher' written on them. Mr Wallace drew first and called out 'learner', so, of course, the real participant was always the teacher.
- They all went into an adjoining room, where Mr Wallace was strapped into a chair with his arms attached to electrodes, which would deliver a shock from the shock generator situated in an adjacent room.
- The teacher and experimenter then moved next door, where the generator was situated. The teacher was given a 45-volt shock to convince him/her that it was real, for s/he was to operate the generator during the experiment. However, that was the only real shock that either the teacher or the learner was to receive throughout the entire experiment.
- The generator had a number of switches, each clearly marked with voltage levels and verbal descriptions, starting at 15 volts and going up to 450 in intervals of 15:

15–60	Slight shock
75–120	Moderate shock
135–180	Strong shock
195–240	Very strong shock
255–300	Intense shock
315–360	Intense to extreme shock
375–420	Danger: severe shock
435–450	XXX

- The teacher had to read out a series of word pairs (e.g. 'blue–girl', 'nice–day', 'fat–neck'), and then the first of one pair (the stimulus word) followed by five words, of which one was the original paired response. The learner had to choose the correct response to the stimulus word by pressing one of four switches, which turned on a light on a panel in the generator room. Each time he made a mistake, the teacher had to deliver a shock, and each successive mistake was punished by a shock 15 volts higher than the one before.

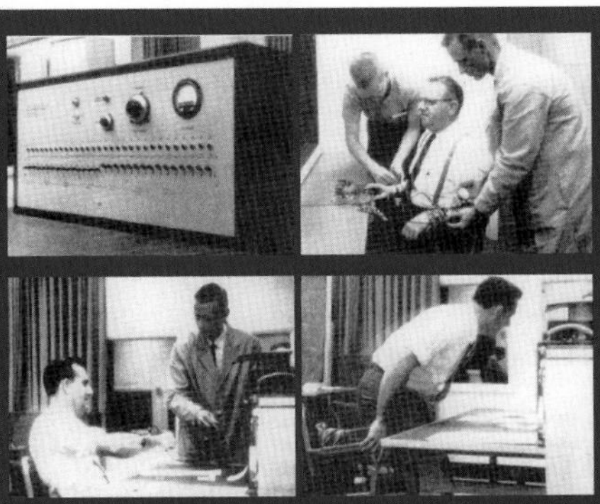

1 Shock generator used in the experiments. Fifteen of the 30 switches have already been depressed. 2 Learner is strapped into chair and electrodes are attached to his wrist. Electrode paste is applied by the experimenter. 3 Subject receives sample shock from the generator. 4 Subject breaks off experiment. (Copyright 1965 by Stanley Milgram from the film Obedience, distributed by the Pennsylvania State University, Audio Visual Services.) (From Milgram, 1974)

Milgram had asked 14 psychology students to predict what would happen for 100 participants in this situation. They thought that a few would break off early on, most would stop somewhere in the middle, and a few would continue right up to 450 volts. He also asked 40 psychiatrists, who predicted that, on average, less than one per cent would administer the highest voltage.

These estimates were based on what Milgram called the *remote-victim condition,* which was the first of a series of 18 different experiments, all variations on the same basic theme. In this particular experiment, Mr Wallace was scripted to pound loudly on the wall at 300 volts and, after 315 volts, to stop pounding and give no further answers. In the second experiment (*voice feedback*), teachers heard a tape-recorded series of verbal responses, which they believed were the spontaneous reactions of Mr Wallace to the increasing shock levels.

At 75, 90 and 105 volts, he made a little grunt.

At 120 volts, he shouted to the experimenter that the shocks were becoming painful.

At 135 volts, he made pained groans.

At 150 volts, he cried out, 'Experimenter, get me out of here! I won't be in the experiment any more! I refuse to go on!' This continued with rising intensity until at 180 volts, he shouted, 'I can't stand the pain!'

At 270 volts, he let out an agonised scream. (He continued to insist on being released.)

At 300 volts, he shouted desperately that he would no longer provide answers.

At 315 volts, he let out a violent scream, reaffirming vehemently that he was no longer participating.

After 330 volts, ominous silence!

The teacher was instructed to treat no response as if it were an incorrect response, so the shocks could continue beyond 300 volts. In addition, the experimenter had a script prepared for whenever the teacher refused to continue or showed any resistance or reluctance to do so:

- 'Please continue' or 'Please go on'
- 'The experiment requires that you continue'
- 'It's absolutely essential that you continue'
- 'You have no other choice, you must go on.'

There were also 'special prods' to reassure the participant that s/he wasn't doing the learner any permanent harm: 'Although the shocks may be painful there is no permanent tissue damage, so please go on.'

> ***ASK YOURSELF...***
> - If you'd been one of Milgram's teacher-participants, how far up the voltage scale would you have continued to punish 'wrong answers'?

The results

In the first (remote-victim) experiment, every teacher shocked up to at least 300 volts, and 65 per cent went all the way up to 450 volts. In the voice-feedback condition, 62.5 per cent of participants went on giving shocks up to 450 volts.

Many displayed great anguish, attacked the experimenter verbally, twitched nervously, or broke out into nervous laughter. Many were observed to:

> ... sweat, stutter, tremble, groan, bite their lips and dig their nails into their flesh. Full-blown, uncontrollable seizures were observed for three subjects. (Milgram, 1974)

Indeed, one experiment had to be stopped because the participant had a violently convulsive seizure.

To determine why the obedience levels were so high, Milgram conducted several variations using the voice-feedback condition as his baseline measure. In all, a further 16 variations were performed.

> **KEY STUDY 27.1 Some variations on Milgram's basic procedure**
>
> **Institutional context (variation 10):** In interviews following the first experiment, many participants said they continued delivering shocks because the research was being conducted at Yale University, a highly prestigious institution. So, Milgram transferred the experiment to a run-down office in downtown Bridgeport.
>
> **Proximity and touch proximity (variations 3 and 4):** In the original procedure, the teacher and learner were in adjacent rooms and couldn't see one another. But in variation 3, they were in the same room (about 1.5 ft/46 cm apart), and in variation 4 the teacher was required to force the learner's hand down on to the shock plate.

Remote authority (variation 7): The experimenter left the room (having first given the essential instructions), and gave subsequent instructions by telephone.
Two peers rebel (variation 17): The teacher was paired with two other (stooge) teachers. The stooge teachers read out the list of word-pairs, and informed the learner whether the response was correct. The naïve participant delivered the shocks. At 150 volts, the first stooge refused to continue and moved to another part of the room. At 210 volts, the second stooge did the same. The experimenter ordered the real teacher to continue.
A peer administers the shocks (variation 18): The teacher was paired with another (stooge) teacher and had only to read out the word-pairs (the shock being delivered by the stooge).

ASK YOURSELF...

- For each of the variations described in Key Study 27.1, estimate the rates of total obedience (those participants going all the way up to 450 volts).
- Try to explain why it might have been higher or lower than the 62.5 per cent in the voice-feedback condition.

- In variation 10, the obedience rate was 47.5 per cent. This still very high figure suggests that the institutional context played some part, but wasn't a crucial factor.
- In variation 3, the obedience rate dropped to 40 per cent, and in variation 4 it dropped further to 30 per cent. While it became much more uncomfortable for participants to see – as well as hear – the effects of their obedience, the figures are still very high.
- In variation 7, obedience dropped to 20.5 per cent. Indeed, participants often pretended to deliver a shock or delivered one lower than they were asked to. This suggests that they were trying to compromise between their conscience and the experimenter's instructions. In his absence, it was easier to follow their conscience.
- In variation 17, there was only 10 per cent obedience. Most stopped obeying when the first or second stooge refused to continue. According to Milgram (1965):

The effects of peer rebellion are most impressive in undercutting the experimenter's authority.

In other words, seeing other participants (our peers) disobey shows that it's *possible* to disobey, as well as *how* to disobey. Indeed, some participants said they didn't realise they *could*. This is a demonstration of the effects of *conformity*.

- In variation 18, obedience rose to 92.5 per cent. This shows that it's easier for participants to shift responsibility from themselves to the person who actually 'throws the switch'.

Why do people obey?

According to Milgram (1974):

The most fundamental lesson of our study is that ordinary people simply doing their jobs, and without any particular hostility on their part, can become agents in a terrible destructive process.

Unless there's reason to believe that people who go all the way up to 450 volts are especially sadistic and cruel, or are unusually obedient (which 'the 'Germans are different' hypothesis' claimed about a whole nation), explanations of obedience must look 'outside' the individual participant. In this way, the emphasis is shifted away from personal characteristics to the characteristics of the social situation: most people facing that situation would probably act in a similar (obedient) way. What might some of these situational factors be?

Personal responsibility

Many participants raised the issue of responsibility for any harm to the learner. Although the experimenter didn't always discuss this, when he did say 'I'm responsible for what goes on here', participants showed visible relief. Indeed, when participants are told they're responsible for what happens, obedience is sharply reduced (Hamilton, 1978).

Milgram saw this *diffusion of responsibility* as crucial to understanding the atrocities committed by the Nazis, and Eichmann's defence that he was 'just carrying out orders'. (Eichmann was in charge of the transportation of Jews and others to extermination camps, and was eventually tried in Jerusalem, in 1960). It can also explain the behaviour of William Calley, an American soldier who was court-martialled for the 1968 massacre by troops under his command of several hundred Vietnamese civilians at My Lai.

Eichmann at his trial in Jerusalem, 1960

The perception of legitimate authority

As we mentioned earlier, many participants showed signs of distress and conflict, and so diffusion of responsibility cannot tell the whole story. The conflict seems to be between two opposing sets of demands – the external authority of the experimenter who says 'Shock', and the internal authority of the conscience which says, 'Don't shock'. The point at which conscience triumphs is, of course, where the participant (finally) stops obeying the experimenter, who, in a sense, ceases to be a legitimate authority in the eyes of the participant. 35 per cent in the original experiment reached that point somewhere before 450 volts, and for many, the crucial 'prod' was when the experimenter said, 'You have no other choice, you *must* go on'. They were able to exercise the choice which, of course, they had from the start.

The most common mental adjustment in the obedient participant is to see him/herself as an agent of external authority (the *agentic state*). This represents the opposite of an *autonomous state,* and is what makes it possible for us to function in a *hierarchical* social system. For a group to function as a whole, individuals must give up responsibility and defer to others of higher status in the social hierarchy. Legitimate authority thus replaces a person's own self-regulation (Turner, 1991). In Milgram's (1974) words:

> The essence of obedience consists in the fact that a person comes to view himself as the instrument for carrying out another person's wishes, and he, therefore, no longer regards himself as responsible for his actions. Once this critical shift of viewpoint has occurred in the person, all the essential features of obedience follow.

ASK YOURSELF...

- What was it about Jack Williams, the experimenter, that conveyed to participants that he was 'in charge' in the experimental situation?

One of the many statues of Lenin brought crashing down in Eastern Europe after the collapse of Communism in 1989

Authority figures often possess highly visible symbols of their power or status that make it difficult to refuse their commands. In Milgram's experiments, the experimenter always wore a grey laboratory coat to indicate his position as an authority figure. The impact of such 'visible symbols' was demonstrated by Bickman (1974). When people were told by a stooge wearing a guard's uniform to pick up a paper bag or give a coin to a stranger, obedience was higher (80 per cent) than when the order was given by a stooge in civilian clothes (40 per cent). Similarly, a stooge wearing a firefighting uniform was obeyed more often than a stooge dressed as a civilian, even though the request (to give someone a dime) had nothing to do with the authority role in question (Bushman, 1984). For Milgram (1974):

> A substantial proportion of people do what they are told to do, irrespective of the content of the act and without limitations of conscience, so long as they perceive that the command comes from a legitimate authority.

Another major study that demonstrates the impact of uniforms and other symbols of authority is Zimbardo *et al.*'s (1973) 'prison simulation experiment', which is discussed on pages 464–465.

The 'foot in the door' and not knowing how to disobey

According to Gilbert (1981), Milgram's participants may have been 'sucked in' by the series of graduated demands. These began with the 'harmless' advertisement for volunteers for a study of learning and memory, and ended with the instruction to deliver what appeared to be potentially lethal electric shocks to another person. Having begun the experiment, participants may have found it difficult to remove themselves from it.

ASK YOURSELF...

- If the original advertisement had mentioned electric shocks, do you think there would have been many volunteers?
- In what ways might such volunteers have constituted a more biased sample than those who participated in the actual experiments?

Presumably, fewer volunteers would have come forward. Those who did may well have been more sadistic than Milgram's sample (assuming that they believed they'd be giving the electric shocks).

Socialisation

Despite our expressed ideal of independence, obedience is something we're socialised into from a very early age by significant others (including our parents and teachers). Obedience may be an ingrained habit that's difficult to resist (Brown, 1986).

An evaluation of Milgram's research

In evaluating Milgram's experiments, *ethical issues* are usually more prominent than scientific ones. These are discussed in detail in Chapter 48. However, Milgram asks whether the ethical criticisms are based as much on the nature of the (unexpected) results as on the procedure itself. Aronson (1988) asks if we'd question the ethics if none of the participants had gone beyond the 150-volt level, which is the point at which most people were expected to stop (according to Milgram's students and the 40 psychiatrists he consulted). Aronson manipulated the results experimentally, and found that the higher the percentage going right up to 450 volts, the more harmful the effects of the experiment are judged to be.

Methodological issues

- One criticism is that Milgram's sample was unrepresentative of the American population. However, a total of 636 participants were tested (in the 18 separate experiments as a whole), representing a cross-section of the population of New Haven, thought to be a fairly typical small American town. But Milgram admits that those who went on obeying up to 450 volts were more likely to see the learner as responsible for what happened to him, and not themselves! They seemed to have a stronger *authoritarian character* and a less advanced level of moral development. But as Rosenthal & Rosnow (1966a) and others have found, people who volunteer for experiments are, on the whole, considerably *less* authoritarian than those who don't.
- Only 40 women were included in Milgram's sample (Experiment 8). But they showed a 65 per cent obedience rate, just like their male counterparts.
- According to Orne & Holland (1968), Milgram's experiments lack *experimental realism,* that is, participants might not have believed the experimental set-up they found themselves in, and knew the learner wasn't really being given electric shocks. However, a study by Sheridan & King (1972) seems to exclude this.

KEY STUDY 27.2 Obedience training for puppies (Sheridan & King, 1972)

- Students trained a puppy to learn a discrimination task by punishing it with increasingly severe and real electric shocks whenever it made an error.
- Although the puppy actually received only a small shock, the participants could see it and hear its squeals.
- After a time, an odourless anaesthetic was released into the puppy's cage, causing it to fall asleep.
- Although participants complained about the procedure (and some even cried), they were reminded that the puppy's failure to respond was a punishable error, and that they should continue to give shocks.
- A total of 75 per cent of participants delivered the maximum shock possible.

- Orne and Holland also criticised Milgram's experiments for their lack of *mundane realism,* that is, the results don't extend beyond the particular laboratory setting in which they were collected. They base this claim on the further claim that cues in the experimental setting influenced the participants' perceptions of what was required of them. Obedience, then, might simply have been a response to the *demand characteristics* of the highly unusual experimental setting (see Chapter 3). However, naturalistic studies of obedience dispute this.

KEY STUDY 27.3 A naturalistic study of nurses (Hofling *et al.*, 1966)

- Twenty-two nurses working in various American hospitals received telephone calls from a stooge 'Dr Smith of the psychiatric department', instructing them to give Mr Jones (Dr Smith's patient) 20 mg of a drug called Astrofen.
- Dr Smith said that he was in a desperate hurry, and would sign the drug authorisation form when he came to see the patient in ten minutes' time.
- The label on the box containing the Astrofen (which was actually a harmless sugar pill) clearly stated that the maximum daily dose was 10 mg.
- So, if the nurse obeyed Dr Smith's instructions she'd be exceeding the maximum daily dose. Also, she'd be breaking the rules requiring written authorisation before any drug is given, and that a nurse be absolutely sure that 'Dr Smith' is a genuine doctor.

ASK YOURSELF...

- What do you think you'd have done if you'd been one of the nurses?

- In interviews, 22 graduate nurses who hadn't participated in the actual experiment were presented with the same situation as an issue to discuss; 21 said they wouldn't have given the drug without written authorisation, especially as it exceeded the maximum daily dose.
- A real doctor was posted nearby, unseen by the nurse, and observed what the nurse did following the telephone call. 21 out of the 22 nurses complied without hesitation, and 11 later said they hadn't noticed the dosage discrepancy!

But could the unfamiliarity of Astrofen (a dummy drug, invented for the purposes of the experiment) have influenced the nurses' responses? Also, Hofling *et al.* failed to report what proportion of nurses actually tried to check the instruction with fellow nurses or superiors – they reported only the number of those who (eventually) complied. Rank & Jacobson (1977) repeated the experiment, but with two important changes:

1. they recorded any checking that nurses did
2. they changed the prescription to 30 mg of Valium, with which they were familiar.

Under these conditions, only two out of 18 nurses were prepared to administer the drug without any checking; 10 prepared the drug but then tried to recontact the doctor, pharmacy, or a supervisor; and six tried to check the order before preparing the drug. The limitations of Hofling *et al.*'s experiment, therefore, offer only modest support to Milgram.

- A further methodological criticism concerns the *cross-cultural replicability* of Milgram's findings

Table 27.1 Cross-cultural replications of Milgram's obedience experiment (adapted from Smith & Bond, 1998)

Study	Country	Participants	Percentage obedient
Ancona & Pareyson (1968)	Italy	Students	85
Kilham & Mann (1974)	Australia	Male students Female students	40 16
Burley & McGuiness (1977)	UK	Male students	50
Shanab & Yahya (1978)	Jordan	Students	62
Miranda *et al.* (1981)	Spain	Students	over 90
Schurz (1985)	Austria	General population	80
Meeus & Raajimakers (1986)	The Netherlands	General population	92

Unfortunately, it's very difficult to compare these studies because of methodological discrepancies between them (Smith & Bond, 1998). For example, different types of stooges were used (e.g. a 'long-haired student' in Kilham and Mann's study), some of whom may have been perceived as more vulnerable – or more deserving of shocks – than others. In the Meeus and Raajimakers study, the task involved participants having to harass and criticise someone who was completing an important job application.

While Milgram found no gender differences (as noted above), the Australian female students were asked to shock another female (but the learner was always male in Milgram's experiments). Also, with the exception of Jordan (Shanab & Yahya, 1978), all the countries studied have been western industrialised nations, so we should be cautious when concluding that a universal aspect of social behaviour has been identified. But Smith & Bond (1998) observe that:

In none of the countries studied is obedience to authority the kind of blind process that some interpreters of Milgram's work have implied. Levels of obedience can and do vary greatly, depending on the social contexts that define the meaning of the orders given.

Issues of generalisation

As we noted earlier, Orne & Holland (1968), along with several other researchers, have argued that Milgram's experiments lack mundane realism (or *external* or *ecological validity*). But Milgram (1974) maintains that the process of complying with the demands of an authority figure is essentially the same whether the setting is the artificial one of the psychological laboratory or a naturally occurring one in the outside world. While there are, of course, differences between laboratory studies of obedience and the obedience observed in Nazi Germany:

Differences in scale, numbers and political context may turn out to be relatively unimportant as long as certain essential features are retained ...

The 'essential features' that Milgram refers to is the *agentic state* (see page 461).

What do Milgram's studies tell us about ourselves?

Perhaps one of the reasons Milgram's research has been so heavily criticised is that it paints an unacceptable picture of human beings. Thus, it's far easier for us to believe that a war criminal like Eichmann was an inhuman monster than that 'ordinary people' can be destructively obedient (what Arendt, 1965, called the *banality of evil*).

Yet atrocities, such as those committed in Rwanda, Kosovo and Sudan, continue to occur. According to Hirsch (1995), many of the greatest crimes against humanity are committed in the name of obedience.

Box 27.2 Genocide

Hirsch (1995) maintains that genocide, a term first used in 1944, tends to occur under conditions created by three social processes:

1. *authorisation* relates to the 'agentic state' – that is, obeying orders because of where they come from
2. *routinisation* refers to massacre becoming a matter of routine, or a mechanical and highly programmed operation
3. *dehumanisation* involves the victims being reduced to something less than human, allowing the perpetrators to suspend their usual moral prohibition on killing.

The ingredients of genocide were personified by Eichmann who, at his trial in 1960, denied ever killing anybody. However, he took great pride in the way he transported millions to their deaths 'with great zeal and meticulous care' (Arendt, 1965).

Social roles provide models of power and powerlessness, as in parent–child, teacher–student, and employer–employee relationships. Rather than asking what makes some people more obedient than others, or how we'd have reacted if we'd been one of Milgram's participants, we could instead ask how we would behave if put into a position of authority ourselves. How easily could we assume the role and use the power that goes with it?

Zimbardo's research

Almost as famous – and controversial – as Milgram's obedience studies is the *prison simulation experiment* (Zimbardo *et al.*, 1973). We mentioned earlier that this experiment illustrates the impact of uniforms and other visible symbols of authority, and for this reason it's usually discussed in relation to obedience. However, it's also relevant to certain aspects of *conformity,* as well as demonstrating the *power of social situations* on people's behaviour.

KEY STUDY 27.4 The prison simulation experiment (Zimbardo *et al.*, 1973)

- Zimbardo *et al.* recruited male participants through newspaper advertisements asking for student volunteers for a two-week study of prison life. From 75 volunteers, 24 were selected. They were judged to be emotionally stable, physically healthy, and 'normal to average' (based on personality tests). They also had no history of psychiatric problems and had never been in trouble with the police.
- Participants were told they'd be randomly assigned to the role of either 'prisoner' or 'prison guard'. At the beginning of the experiment, then, there were no differences between those selected to be prisoners and guards. They constituted a relatively homogeneous group of white, middle-class college students from all over America.
- The basement of the Stanford University psychology department was converted into a 'mock prison'. Zimbardo *et al.* wished to create a prison-like environment which was as *psychologically real* as possible. The aim was to study how prison life impacts upon both prisoners and guards.
- The experiment began one Sunday morning, when those allocated to the prisoner role were unexpectedly arrested by the local police. They were charged with a felony, read their rights, searched, handcuffed, and taken to the police station to be 'booked'. After being fingerprinted, each prisoner was taken blindfold to the basement prison.
- Upon arrival, the prisoners were stripped naked, skin-searched, deloused, and issued with uniforms and bedding. Each prisoner wore a loose-fitting smock with his identification number on the front and back, plus a chain bolted around one ankle. He also wore a nylon stocking to cover his hair (rather than having his head shaved). They were referred to by number only and accommodated in 6 × 9 ft 'cells', three to a cell.
- The guards wore military-style khaki uniforms, silver reflector sunglasses (making eye contact with them impossible), and carried clubs, whistles, handcuffs and keys to the cells and main gate.
- The guards were on duty 24 hours a day, each working eight-hour shifts. They had complete control over the prisoners, who were kept in their cells around the clock, except for meals, toilet privileges, head counts and work.

a

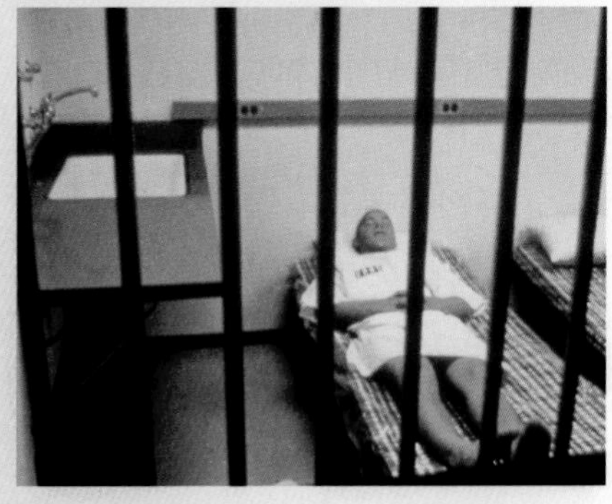

b

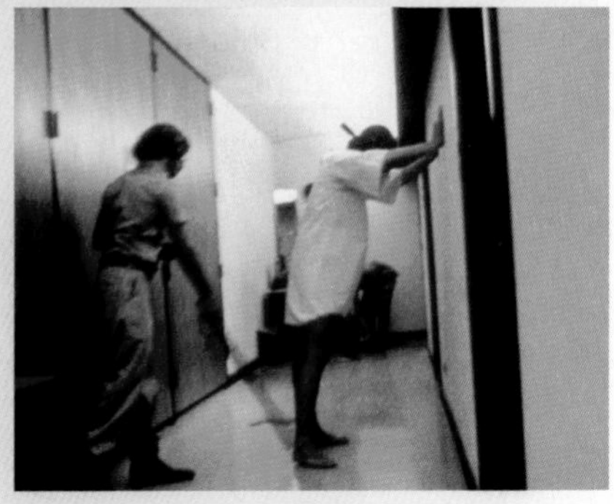

a A prisoner in one of the three-bedded cells
b A prison guard asserting his authority over a prisoner

After an initial 'rebellion' had been crushed, the prisoners began to react passively as the guards stepped up their aggression each day (by, for example, having a head count in the middle of the night simply to disrupt the prisoners' sleep). This made the prisoners feel helpless, and no longer in control of their lives.

Social power became the major dimension on which everyone and everything was defined. Every guard at some time or another behaved in an abusive, authoritarian way. Many seemed positively to enjoy the newfound power and the almost total control over the prisoners which went with the uniform.

- Guard A said: 'I was surprised at myself – I made them call each other names and clean the toilets out with their bare hands. I practically considered the prisoners cattle and I kept thinking I have to watch out for them in case they try something.'
- Guard B (preparing for the visitors' first night): 'I made sure I was one of the guards on the yard, because this was my first chance for the type of manipulative power that I really like – being a very noticed figure with complete control over what is said or not.'
- Guard C: 'Acting authoritatively can be fun. Power can be a great pleasure.'

After less than 36 hours, one prisoner had to be released because of uncontrolled crying, fits of rage, disorganised thinking and severe depression. Three others developed the same symptoms, and had to be released on successive days. Another prisoner developed a rash over his whole body, which was triggered when his 'parole' request was rejected. Prisoners became demoralised and apathetic, and even began to refer to themselves and others by their numbers. The whole experiment, planned to run for two weeks, was abandoned after six days because of the pathological reactions of the prisoners.

An evaluation of the prison simulation experiment

- An outside observer, who had a long history of imprisonment, believed that the mock prison, and both the guards' and prisoners' behaviours, were strikingly similar to real prison life. This supports Zimbardo *et al.*'s major conclusion that what make prisons such evil places are prisons themselves – not prisoners or guards. As Zimbardo (1973) says:

> Not that anyone ever doubted the horrors of prison, but rather it had been assumed that it was the predispositions of the guards ('sadistic') and prisoners ('sociopathic') that made prisons such evil places. Our study holds constant and positive the dispositional alternative and reveals the power of social, institutional forces to make good men engage in evil deeds.

> ***ASK YOURSELF...***
> - What does Zimbardo mean by 'Our study holds constant and positive the dispositional alternative'?

Volunteers were selected for their emotional stability and 'normality', and then randomly allocated to the prisoner/guard roles. Therefore, their different behaviours and reactions couldn't be attributed to their personal characteristics (or dispositions). Rather, the differences could only be explained in terms of the different roles they played in the context of the mock prison.

- But according to Banuazizi & Mohavedi (1975), the behaviour of both guards and prisoners may have arisen from the *stereotyped expectations* of their respective roles. The participants were 'merely' role-playing (based on their prior expectations about how guards and prisoners 'ought' to behave). However, one reply to this criticism is to ask at what point 'mere' role-playing becomes a 'real' experience. As Zimbardo (1971, quoted in Aronson, 1992) says:

> It was no longer apparent to us or most of the subjects where they ended and their roles began. The majority had indeed become 'prisoners' or 'guards', no longer able to clearly differentiate between role-playing and self.

This strongly suggests that their experiences were very real, and that even if they were 'merely' role-playing at the beginning, they were soon taking their roles very seriously indeed! This was 'aided and abetted' by the environmental conditions. A brutalising atmosphere, like the 'mock' prison, produces brutality. Had the roles been reversed, those who suffered as the prisoners may just as easily have inflicted suffering on those who were randomly chosen as guards.

- The study has provoked almost as much controversy regarding its ethics as did Milgram's experiments (see Chapter 48).

KEY STUDY 27.5 *The Experiment* (Reicher & Haslam, 2002)

- *The Experiment* was the BBC's version of Zimbardo *et al.*'s prison study, conducted by Reicher and Haslam in December 2001, and screened in April 2002.
- A newspaper advert appeared under the heading 'Do you really know yourself?', appealing for volunteers to take part in a 'university-backed social science experiment to be shown on TV'. It warned that successful candidates would be exposed to 'exercise, tasks, hardship, hunger, solitude, and anger'. No financial incentive was offered, nor was it implied that involvement would, as in most reality TV shows, be a short-cut to celebrity. Instead, the BBC promised that participation would 'change the way you think' (Brockes, 2001).
- According to Reicher (in Brockes, 2001), the motivation for the study was to ask:

> *... What are the conditions under which people accept oppression or act against it? We want to study how social systems work.*

- A studio at Elstree, in Hertfordshire, was converted into a 'social environment', within which the 15 volunteers were randomly allocated to the roles of oppressors and oppressed. They were encouraged, through a system of 'privileges' and 'punishments', to resent each other.
- Reicher plays down the prison analogy. He maintains that it works just as well as an office or a school, where one set of people has power over another. But the creative

director describes it as 'more of a detention centre or a prisoner-of-war camp'.

- The Exeter University Ethics Committee gave it the green light. There was 24-hour monitoring of the participants by a group of independent clinical psychologists, who were given the power to 'pull the plug' on the experiment if they felt the process was damaging the participants. Similarly, an independent ethics panel appointed to monitor the whole experiment was empowered to withdraw participants or stop the experiment if it was judged to be inappropriate.
- *The Experiment*, due to last ten days, was stopped after only nine. The independent psychologists became concerned that the participants' emotional and physical wellbeing was in danger of being compromised (Wells, 2002).
- Nevertheless, Reicher and Haslam were overjoyed with the results, which they feel will prove scientifically important. Far from producing an explosion of aggression, some of the participants felt that 'peacenik' tendencies dominated. According to Haslam, filming stopped a day early because the research had progressed so smoothly and had produced a wealth of data that would take months to process. This *wasn't* an attempt to replicate Zimbardo's study, but to extend his research and look at what drives positive group behaviour. But Haslam admits there were some 'darker sides' to the study (Farrar, 2002).
- According to Reicher and Haslam, the TV programmes were very faithful to the key events in the study, but they could only ever be a 'window' on the science.

CONCLUSIONS: HOW CAN WE RESIST OBEDIENCE?

In 1992, an East German judge sentenced a former East German border guard for having shot a man trying (three years earlier) to escape to the West. The judge's comments echo the spirit of the Nuremberg Accords which followed the Nazi war crimes trials:

> Not everything that is legal is right … At the end of the twentieth century, no one has the right to turn off his conscience when it comes to killing people on the orders of authorities … (cited in Berkowitz, 1993)

As we've seen, it's difficult to disobey authority. But we're most likely to rebel when we feel that social pressure is so strong that our freedom is under threat.

Milgram himself felt that obedience would be reduced by:

- educating people about the dangers of blind obedience
- encouraging them to question authority
- exposing them to the actions of disobedient models.

According to Brehm (1966), we need to believe that we have freedom of choice. When we believe that this isn't the case and when we believe we're entitled to freedom, we experience reactance, an unpleasant emotional state. To reduce it, and restore the sense of freedom, we disobey (see Chapter 49).

CHAPTER SUMMARY

- **Compliance** is a factor in different kinds of social influence, including conformity, obedience and our responses to other people's direct requests.
- Attempts to change people's opinions and behaviour used by salespeople and others include **reciprocity**, **liking (ingratiation)**, **scarcity**, **social validation**, **foot-in-the-door** (FITD), **door-in-the-face** (DIF) and **low-ball** (LB) **tactics**.
- While both conformity and obedience involve the **abdication of personal responsibility**, **obedience** involves orders from someone in **higher authority**, with influence being in one direction only.
- Milgram's series of 18 obedience experiments involve a basic procedure (**remote victim/voice feedback**) and variations on this, involving the manipulation of critical variables.
- Increasing the proximity to the victim, reducing the proximity of the experimenter and having the social support of 'rebel' fellow teachers all reduced obedience, while having someone else actually deliver the shock increased it.
- Two related variables that are crucial for understanding obedience are **acceptance/denial of responsibility** and the **agentic state**. The wearing of uniform and other such symbols of authority are also important.
- Milgram's experiments have caused great ethical controversy, but have also been criticised on scientific grounds. The results have been replicated **cross-culturally**, although identical procedures haven't always been used, making it difficult to draw comparisons. But blind obedience hasn't been found anywhere, and social context influences obedience levels.
- The **mundane realism** of the procedure is supported by Hofling *et al.*'s naturalistic experiment involving nurses, and Milgram believes that obedience is essentially the same process regardless of the particular context.
- Many of the greatest crimes against humanity are committed in the name of obedience. **Genocide** tends to occur under conditions of **authorisation**, **routinisation** and **dehumanisation**.
- Zimbardo's **prison simulation experiment**, like Milgram's obedience studies, demonstrates the **power of social situations** to make people act in uncharacteristic ways. A brutalising atmosphere, like a prison, can induce brutality in people who aren't usually brutal.

- Participants were selected for their emotional stability and general 'normality', and then randomly allocated to the roles of prisoner or prison guard. Therefore, their pathological reactions couldn't be attributed to their personal characteristics.
- While they may have been merely **role-playing** at the beginning of the experiment, they soon 'became' prisoners or guards.
- The BBC's ***The Experiment*** wasn't intended as a replication of Zimbardo's prison study, but was more concerned with the differences in **power** between people in any institutional setting (including schools and offices).

Links with other topics/chapters

- Liking as a tactic used to influence people's attitudes or behaviour is related to *interpersonal attraction,* part of the more general topic of *interpersonal relationships* (Chapter 28).
- Liking/ingratiation is a major component of *impression management,* and the norm of reciprocity is a factor influencing *self-disclosure* (Chapter 22).
- When people feel exploited by attempts to change their opinions/behaviour through the FITD, it may be because of *psychological reactance* (Chapter 49).
- Diffusion of responsibility is a factor involved in *helping behaviour/bystander intervention* (Chapter 30).
- Milgram's 'Two peers rebel' experiment demonstrates how obedience and *conformity* are two forms of social influence that can operate together (Chapter 26).
- Both Milgram's and Zimbardo's research highlights the debate regarding the obligation of psychologists to carry out socially meaningful/potentially beneficial research, and at the same time to protect participants from emotional harm – the *double obligation dilemma* (Chapter 48).
- Uniforms and other trappings of power and authority are important aspects of non-verbal 'behaviour', and so are important for understanding *interpersonal perception* (Chapter 22).
- The prison simulation experiment found support for the influence of social situations, rather than individual personality (the *dispositional hypothesis*), in explaining the behaviour of people in prisons (Chapters 23 and 47).

28

INTERPERSONAL RELATIONSHIPS

INTRODUCTION AND OVERVIEW

According to popular belief, it's love that makes the world go round. But according to Rubin & NcNeil (1983), liking perhaps more than loving is what keeps it spinning. How are liking and loving related? Are there different kinds of love, and can this help us understand how romantic relationships develop over time and why some break down? How do we get into relationships in the first place?

The importance of relationships, both sexual and non-sexual, is 'obvious'. According to Duck (1999):

... We need merely to reflect for a moment on the sources of our greatest pleasure and pain to appreciate that nothing else arouses the extremes of emotion that are experienced in the course of personal relationships with other human beings ...

Relationships make life meaningful, whether they're good or bad. When asked 'What's necessary for your happiness?', most people say, before anything else, satisfying close relationships with friends, family and romantic partners (Berscheid, 1985).

Most relationship research has focused on 'voluntary' relationships. When describing relationships breaking up (or down), we often use language that implies a degree of choice ('Why don't you get out of that relationship?', or 'I wish I'd never got involved in the first place.'). One way of trying to understand the *dissolution* of relationships is to see it as the process of relationship *formation* in reverse.

Traditionally, social psychologists have been interested in *interpersonal attraction* (really an aspect of interpersonal perception: see Chapter 22), which relates to the question 'How do relationships start?' But during the last 20 years or so, the emphasis has shifted to relationships *as a process* (Duck, 1999), reflected in two further questions: 'What makes people stay in relationships (maintenance and progression)?' and 'Why and how do relationships go wrong (breakdown or dissolution)?'

AFFILIATION: THE NEED FOR OTHER PEOPLE

Affiliation is the basic human need for the company of other human beings. The need to belong and to be accepted by others is one of Maslow's basic survival needs (see Chapter 9), and is also a major motive underlying conformity (see Chapter 26). We also saw in Chapter 26 that conformity can be explained in terms of the need to evaluate our beliefs and opinions by comparing them with other people's, especially in ambiguous or unstructured situations. This is the central idea in Festinger's (1954) *social comparison theory.*

According to Duck (1988), we're more 'affiliative' and inclined to seek others' company under certain conditions than others, for example when we're anxious, when we've just left a close relationship (the 'rebound' situation), and when we've moved to a new neighbourhood. One of the most powerful factors influencing affiliation is *anxiety.*

KEY STUDY 28.1 'Anxiety loves anxious company' (Schachter, 1959)

- Female psychology students were led to believe they'd be receiving electric shocks. One group was told the shocks would be painful (*high anxiety condition*), while another group was told they wouldn't be at all painful (*low anxiety condition*).
- They were then told that there'd be a delay while the equipment was set up, and they were given the option of waiting either alone or with another participant (this was the dependent variable and no actual shock was given).
- As predicted, the high anxiety group showed a greater preference for company (20 out of 32) than the low anxiety group (ten out of 30).
- In a separate, related experiment, all the participants were told that the shocks would be painful, but for half the choice was between waiting alone and waiting with another participant in the same experiment, and for the other half it was between waiting alone and waiting with another student who was waiting to see her teacher.
- For the first group, there was a strong preference for waiting with another high-anxiety participant, while the second group preferred to wait alone.

ASK YOURSELF...

- What do these results tell you about the students' motives for affiliation?

Schachter's results strongly suggest that *social comparison* was the motive for affiliation (rather than distraction) – if we have something to worry about, we prefer to be with other worriers.

Kulik & Mahler (1989) reached the same conclusions when studying patients about to undergo coronary bypass surgery. Most preferred to share a room with someone who'd already undergone coronary surgery, rather than another patient waiting for the same operation. The main motive for this preference seemed to be the need for information about the stress-inducing situation.

LIKING, LOVE AND INTIMACY

ASK YOURSELF...

- What is a relationship and what makes a relationship a close one?
- What different kinds of relationship are there?
- How does liking differ from loving?
- Is love just an intense form of liking?
- Are there different types of love?

Relationships and close relationships

According to Berscheid & Ammazzalorso (2004), the concept of a relationship:

... refers to two people whose behaviour is *interdependent* in that a change in behaviour in one is likely to produce a change in behaviour of the other ...

'Close' refers to an interaction pattern in which each partner's behaviour is highly dependent on the other's behaviour. So, a *close* relationship is usually seen as one in which partners are *highly interdependent*. The interaction takes place over a long period of time, the partners' influence on each other is strong and frequent, and many different types of behaviour are affected (Kelley *et al.*, 1983).

In common with other close relationships, *romantic relationships* involve interdependence, strong feelings, committed intent and overlapping self-concept. But unique to romantic relationships are passion and exclusive commitment (Fiske, 2004).

Different types of relationship

Voluntary/involuntary relationships

According to Moghaddam *et al.* (1993), interpersonal relationships in western cultures tend to be *individualistic, voluntary* and *temporary.* Those in non-western cultures are more *collectivist, involuntary* and *permanent.* As they say:

> The cultural values and environmental conditions in North America have led North American social psychologists to be primarily concerned with first-time acquaintances, friendships and intimate relationships, primarily because these appear to be the relationships most relevant to the North American urban cultural experience.

In other words, western psychologists tend to equate 'relationships' with 'western relationships' (a form of *ethnocentrism:* see Chapter 47).

The examples given in the quote from Moghaddam *et al.* are all *voluntary;* but western psychologists have studied a wide range of such relationships during the past 20 years or so, some of which may seem more voluntary than others. Duck (1999) gives the following examples: relationships of blended families, cross-sex non-romantic friendships, romantic or friendly relationships in the workplace, relationships between cooperative neighbours, relationships between prisoners and guards, sibling relationships, children relating to other children, and adults' relationships with their parents.

Marriage is found in all known cultures (Fletcher, 2002) and is usually taken to be a voluntary relationship. But there are several reasons for asking if it really is.

- There are wide and important cultural variations in marital arrangements. From a western perspective, the 'natural' form of marriage is *monogamy* (marriage to one spouse at any one time). This belief is enshrined in the law (bigamy is a criminal offence) and reflects basic Judeo-Christian doctrine. But monogamy is only one of the forms that marriage can take.

Box 28.1 Culture and marriage

- *Polygamy* refers to having two or more spouses at once.
- It can take the form of *polygyny* (one man having two or more wives) or (less commonly) *polyandry* (one women with two or more husbands).
- Another arrangement is *mandatory marriage to specific relatives,* as when a son marries the daughter of his father's brother (his first cousin: Triandis, 1994).
- A total of 84 per cent of known cultures allow polygyny, but only 5–10 per cent of men in such cultures actually have more than one wife (Fletcher, 2002).
- Probably fewer than 0.5 per cent of human societies have practised polyandry as a common or preferred form of marriage (Price & Crapo, 1999). However, throughout Tibet and the neighbouring Himalayan areas in India, Nepal and Bhutan, it's been common for generations. Usually, a woman marries two or more brothers (*fraternal polyandry*). This helps to keep family numbers down in order to cope with scarce resources. It also keeps brothers together. Land doesn't need to be divided between the brothers, and a single family is preserved as an economic unit.

Polygyny in Nevada, USA is alive and well!

- According to Duck (1999), the *choice to marry* is voluntary, presumably. But once the marriage is a few years old, it's much *less* voluntary than it was, since getting out of it is accompanied by a great deal of 'social and legal baggage':

> ... Thus when we talk about 'voluntary relationships', we need to recognize not only that the exercise of apparently free choice is always tempered by the social realities and constraints that surround us, but also that, once exercised, some choices are then disabled, and cannot be easily or straightforwardly remade. To that extent, therefore, their consequences become non-voluntary ... (Duck, 1999)

- According to Kerckhoff & Davis's (1962) *filter model* (see below, page 477), our choice of potential (realistic) marriage partners is limited by *demographic variables* (age, education, ethnic and religious background, and so on). To this extent, most relationships are 'arranged'. As Duck (1999) says:

  > Many of us would perhaps not recognize – or accept – that marriages are actually 'arranged' by religion, social position, wealth, class, opportunity and other things over which we have little control, even within our own culture ...

- Conversely, parentally arranged marriages in some cultures are gladly entered into, and are considered perfectly normal, natural relationships that are anticipated with pleasure (Duck, 1999).

A scene from *Monsoon Wedding* (2002)

Arranged marriages

> **ASK YOURSELF...**
> - Do you consider that arranged marriages are necessarily wrong or undesirable?
> - Do you come from a cultural background in which they are the norm?
> - Is there a sense in which all marriages are 'arranged'?

Gupta & Singh (1982) found that couples in Jaipur, India, who married for love reported *diminished* feelings of love if they'd been married for more than five years. By contrast, those who'd undertaken arranged marriages reported *more* love if they weren't newlyweds. These findings reveal that passionate love 'cools' over time, and that there's scope for love to flourish within an arranged marriage.

In cultures where arranged marriages occur, courtship is accepted to a certain degree, but love is left to be defined and discovered *after* marriage (Bellur, 1995). This, of course, is the reverse of the 'Hollywood' picture, where love is supposed to *precede* marriage and be what marriage is all about (see Box 28.5, page 475). But even in traditional cultures that practise arranged marriages, brides (and grooms) are typically given some choice in the matter (Fletcher, 2002). For example, in Sri Lanka men and women who like one another (or fall in love) usually let their parents know their choices in advance through indirect channels (de Munck, 1998). Families often use similar criteria that the individuals themselves might use if they had a free choice (including matching on attractiveness: see below). The classic example is the Jewish custom of having a *matchmaker* arrange a suitable match (Rockman, 1994).

Arranged marriages are far more common in *collectivist* (mainly non-western) *cultures,* where the whole extended family 'marries' the other extended family ('social networks motivate marriages': Fiske, 2004). For example, almost 25 per cent of marriages in Japan are arranged (Iwao, 1993). This contrasts with *individualist* (mainly western) *cultures,* in which the individuals marry one another (Triandis, 1994). Here, it's presumed that marriage is motivated by romantic love between two mutually attracted individuals, who freely choose to commit (Fiske, 2004).

In general, *divorce rates* among those who marry according to parents' wishes are much *lower* than among those who marry for love. This is an argument in favour of arranged marriages. Indeed, it's difficult to argue for the superiority of western (especially American) marital arrangements given the 50 per cent divorce rate and an average marriage that lasts for just seven years (Fiske, 2004). As Triandis (1994) argues:

> Marriage, when seen as a fifty-year relationship, is more likely to be a good one if people enter it after careful, rational analysis, which is more likely to be provided by older adults than by sexually aroused young people ...

Traditional forms of matchmaking are, however, on the wane in most cultures, reflecting the growing western influence, and divorce rates among 'arranged couples' are rising. Personal freedom is gaining in importance, and traditional structures that define set roles for family members are becoming less valid. Among the more liberal-minded Asians living in the West, arranged marriages operate more like a dating facility ('arranged meetings' rather than 'arranged marriages'). The transition from meeting to marrying occurs when both parties formally agree to the commitment.

Gay and lesbian relationships

> **ASK YOURSELF...**
> - Do you believe that the differences between gays and lesbians, and heterosexuals, are greater than the similarities?
> - What are the major differences and similarities?
> - What is your belief based on?

The focus on the long-term relationships of heterosexuals has now been supplemented with discussion of gay and lesbian relationships (Duck, 1999). This includes studies of their stability and dissolution (Kurdeck, 1991, 1992).

Compared with same-sex friendships and cross-sex non-romantic friendships, gay and lesbian partners experience extra social burdens in terms of the influence of other people's reactions (Huston & Schwartz, 1995). Weston (1991) argues that 'blood-family' is often replaced for homosexuals by 'families of choice'. Gays and lesbians often aren't 'out' to blood-family, or may be estranged from their blood-families specifically because of their homosexuality. As a result, the blood-family can function very differently for gays and lesbians compared with heterosexuals. Not only are they less likely to tell their parents and siblings of 'new' relationships; they're less likely to talk about intimate relationships that have already developed (Huston & Schwartz, 1995).

According to Kitzinger & Coyle (1995), psychological research into homosexuality since the mid-1970s has moved away from a 'pathology model' towards one comprising four overlapping themes:

1 rejection of the concept of homosexuality as a central organising principle of the personality in favour of recognising the diversity and variety of homosexuals as individuals
2 an assertion that homosexuality is as natural, normal and healthy as heterosexuality
3 denial of the idea that homosexuals pose any threat to children, the nuclear family or the future of society as we know it.

According to Bee (1994), homosexual partnerships are far more like heterosexual ones than they are different. In terms of sexual behaviour, apart from their sexual preferences, gays and lesbians don't look massively different from their heterosexual counterparts (Fletcher, 2002). Researchers have repeatedly found that many of the same gender differences between heterosexual men and women occur when comparing gays and lesbians. For example, straight men and gays have higher sex drives than straight women and lesbians, and females (straight or lesbian) are more relationship-focused than males (straight or gay). In other words:

> ... many central patterns of sexual attitudes and behaviour are more closely linked to gender than to sexual orientation. If one wants to understand gays and lesbians, a good place to start is by looking at heterosexual men and women respectively ... (Fletcher, 2002)

But Kitzinger and Coyle argue that certain factors are omitted or distorted when homosexual relationships are assessed in terms derived from heterosexual relationships.

Does this couple conform to the stereotype of how gays are supposed to look?

Box 28.2 Some key differences between homosexual and heterosexual relationships (Kitzinger & Coyle, 1995)

- *Cohabitation* (living together) is much less common for homosexuals than heterosexuals.
- *Sexual exclusivity* (having only one sexual partner at a time) is *less* common in lesbian relationships and *much less* common in gay relationships (Peplau, 1982). However, the ideal of sexual exclusivity is based on an assumed heterosexual norm or 'blueprint' (Yip, 1999), which many gays and lesbians reject. Sexual infidelity may cause heterosexual couples to break up, largely because it's 'secretive'. But homosexual couples are more likely to have open relationships, and so are 'less likely to experience their own, or their partners' sexual affairs as signalling the end of the couple relationship' (Kitzinger & Coyle, 1995).
- Most gays and lesbians actively reject traditional (i.e. heterosexual) husband/wife or masculine/feminine *sex roles* as a model for enduring relationships (Peplau, 1991). Gay and lesbian couples tend to adopt 'the ethic of equality and reciprocity. This is especially true for lesbians, who've previously been in 'unequal' heterosexual relationships (Yip, 1999).

'Electronic' friendships

ASK YOURSELF...
- Have you had an online relationship?
- What do you think the potential benefits and dangers of such a relationship might be?

Probably one of the most unexpected uses of the Internet is the development of *online relationships* (or *cyber affairs:* Griffiths, 2000). In the UK, one newspaper reported that there have been over 1000 weddings resulting from

Internet meetings. Cyberspace is becoming another 'singles bar'. There are now many sites aimed at those looking for romance or a sexual liaison. Some are directed at singles, while others seem to encourage or facilitate virtual adultery.

Online relationships can proceed through chat rooms, interactive games or newsgroups. What may begin as a simple e-mail exchange, or innocent chat-room encounter, can escalate into an intense and passionate cyber affair – and eventually into face-to-face sexual encounters. Griffiths (2000) claims that 'electronic communication is the easiest, most disinhibiting and most accessible way to meet potential new partners'.

Box 28.3 Three basic types of online relationship (Griffiths, 1999)

- *Purely virtual:* while these are usually sexually very explicit, the 'correspondents' never meet, just want sexual kicks and don't consider they're being unfaithful to their actual partners.
- Increasingly sexually intense *online contact* may eventually lead to the exchange of photographs, secret telephone calls, letters and meetings. Once the two people have met, and if practically possible, actual time spent together largely replaces online contact.
- An initial *offline* meeting will be maintained largely by an online relationship. This usually involves people living in different countries.

Some concerns about online relationships

The disinhibiting, anonymous nature of the Internet can make online relationships seductive and potentially addictive. As Griffiths (2000) points out:

> What might take months or years in an offline relationship may only take days or weeks online ... the perception of trust, intimacy, and acceptance has the potential to encourage online users to see these relationships as a primary source of companionship and comfort.

According to the sociologist Taylor (in Williams, 2000):

> Face-to-face relationships are steadily declining. Fewer and fewer people take part in civic activities such as ... political party involvement or trade unions as the mass movement towards faceless electronic liaisons continues to increase. In the long run we will become incapable of relating to each other in person at all.

Given the emphasis placed on physical attractiveness in our image-conscious society, the disembodied, anonymous nature of online relationships may help individuals' focus on the content of the message: 'there's no such thing as a bad hair day on the Internet' (Joinson, in Williams, 2000). For people who are normally inhibited, or those who are too cowardly to finish a romantic relationship in person, this is probably a godsend (Williams, 2000).

The other major concern relates to paedophiles. The text-based nature of the communication allows someone to pretend to be, say, a teenager, when in fact they are a 50-year-old man. In this way, vulnerable young people – especially girls – can be lured into an offline meeting, with potentially fatal consequences.

Liking and loving

Rubin (1973) defines liking as positively evaluating another. Loving is *qualitatively* different from liking and comprises three main components:

1. *attachment:* the need for the physical presence and emotional support of the loved one
2. *caring:* a feeling of concern and responsibility for the loved one
3. *intimacy:* the desire for close and confidential contact and communication, wanting to share certain thoughts and feelings with the loved one more fully than with anyone else.

The *Love Scale* can also be applied to same-sex friends, and Rubin found that females reported loving their friends more than men did. But there was no difference between males and females on the *Liking Scale.* Rubin & McNeil (1983) suggest that loving for men may be channelled into single, sexual relationships, while women may be better able to experience attachment, caring and intimacy in a wider range and variety of relationships.

Although love is a label that we learn to attach to our own state of physiological arousal (see Chapter 10), most of the time love doesn't involve intense physical symptoms. Love, therefore, is more usefully thought of as a particular sort of *attitude* that one person has towards another (Rubin & McNeil, 1983).

Different types of love

Berscheid & Walster (1978) distinguish between: (a) *companionate love* ('true love' or 'conjugal love'), 'the affection we feel for those with whom our lives are deeply entwined', including very close friends and marriage partners; and (b) *passionate love* (romantic love, obsessive love, infatuation, 'love sick' or 'being in love'). Romantic love is 'A state of intense absorption in another ... A state of intense physiological arousal.' These are qualitatively different, but companionate love is only a more extreme form of liking ('the affection we feel for casual acquaintances') and corresponds to Rubin's 'love'.

Similarly, Sternberg (1988b) has proposed a 'triangular' model of love, in which three basic components (intimacy, passion and decision/commitment) can be combined to produce *consummate love.* When only two are combined, the resulting love is *romantic, companionate* or *fatuous.*

Berscheid and Walster's, and Sternberg's models are *multidimensional,* in contrast with Rubin's, according to which love is a single, underlying dimension on which

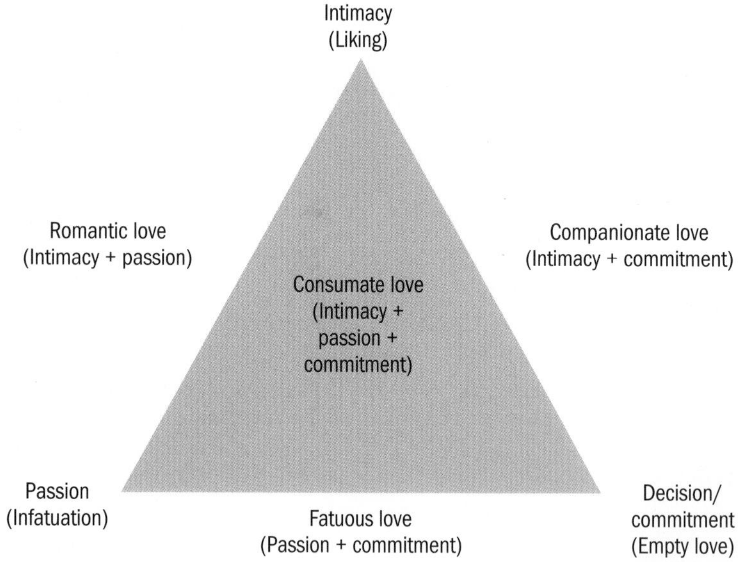

Figure 28.1 Robert Sternberg's (1988b) model of different kinds of love as combinations of three basic components of love (from Myers, D.G. (1994), *Exploring Social Psychology*. New York, McGraw-Hill)

individuals can be ranked in terms of the strength of feeling for a partner. These distinctions are important for understanding how intimate relationships change over time.

The power of love

Box 28.4 Fairy tales as 'carriers' of love

True love conquers all

- According to Moghaddam (2002), the process of teaching individuals about romantic love begins almost as soon as they are born. This takes place through countless *carriers*, which are 'the means by which styles of social thinking and doing are sustained and passed on from generation to generation'. *Symbolic* carriers include flags, conceptual constructions (such as 'nationalism') and fairy tales (such as 'Beauty and the Beast').
- By teenagehood, the ideal of romantic love is deeply ingrained in individuals' behaviour. After learning the story of 'Beauty and the Beast' as a three-year-old:

... the teenage girl now tries out different ways to realise her ideals in practice, exploring different ways to improve her skills in romantic relationships toward the ultimate goal that she and her prince will live happily ever after. (Moghaddam, 2002)

- When asked about their ideal lives in the future, 18-year-olds put romantic love at the centre of their stories. Reaching sexual maturity earlier and having more sexual experience hasn't lessened the belief of the younger generation in the fairy tale of romantic love (see Chapter 37).
- But age is no barrier to falling in love and the pursuit of happiness through romantic love. Increasingly, middle-aged and older people try to keep the romance in their lives. They're willing to go through the trauma of divorce and family break-up when they feel their marriage lacks magic:

... What begins as a fairy tale about the prince and princess living happily ever after in a far-away castle, takes such a strong grip and becomes so powerful in personal lives that its influence shapes lifelong development... (Moghaddam, 2002)

Is romantic love unique to western culture?

American researchers have focused mainly on romantic relationships as the basis for marriage (Fiske, 2004). The popular ('Hollywood') view is that people fall in love and then commit themselves to each other through marriage. Individuals learn that in order to be happy and fulfilled, they must be in love and live for love (Moghaddam, 2002). However, as we've seen, in cultures where arranged marriages occur, the relationship between love and marriage is the other way around, and marriage is seen as the basis on which to explore a loving relationship (Bellur, 1995). As Bellur notes, the cultural background in which people have learned about love is important in shaping their concept of it.

Box 28.5 Exporting love from Hollywood to the rest of the world

- According to Moghaddam (1998, 2002), romantic love isn't exclusive to western societies. The notion of people falling in love is found in one form or another in most human societies, even where marriages are traditionally arranged by families or friends. For example, an analysis of songs and folklore in 166 societies indicates that 'western' romantic love is recognised in more than 85 per cent of them (Jankowiak & Fischer, 1992). However, Moghaddam (1998) believes that:

  What is unique about romantic love in late twentieth-century Western societies is its pervasiveness: the idea that everyone should marry only when they are in love. Such an idea is fairly new historically and is still limited to Western societies.

- Moghaddam (2002) believes that modern romantic love is also distinct in that it involves two individuals who 'are free to fall in love and to make their own choices as to who will be their partner'.
- This 'democratisation' of romantic love was one consequence of women entering higher education and the labour market in large numbers during the twentieth century. Women's increasing financial independence gave them the power to make choices, including the choice of romantic partners.
- Perhaps no other feature of western culture is being exported or internationalised more than romantic love 'Hollywood style'. Over the last century, there's been an increasing acceptance in western societies of the idea that one should marry for love, and that it's right to end the relationship when love dies. As societies become industrialised and more individualistic, the percentage of people who believe that love must precede marriage increases.

ASK YOURSELF...

- If someone had all the other qualities you desired in a marriage partner, would you marry this person if you were not in love?

When Kephart (1967) asked Americans this question, well over twice as many men replied 'no' as did women. When Simpson *et al.* (1986) repeated the study, more than 80 per cent of both men and women said 'no'.

ASK YOURSELF...

- How might you account for the difference between Kephart's and Simpson *et al.*'s findings? (See Box 28.5.)

This can be explained at least partly by the fact that, 20 years later, financial independence has allowed women to choose marriage partners for reasons other than material necessity. But this doesn't explain why romantic love has become so central for both American men and women (Moghaddam, 1998).

As non-western societies become westernised, there's a greater tendency for young people to say 'no' to the question asked by Kephart and Simpson *et al.* Even in collectivist cultures (such as India and Pakistan), about 50 per cent of young people said 'no', and the indications are that this percentage is rising (Moghaddam, 2002).

Box 28.6 The politics of love

- According to Burr (2003), romantic love is a *discourse*, which, like other discourses, offers a framework against which people may understand their own experience and behaviour, and those of others. We're all subjected to this discourse, through film and television images of true love, young love, adulterous love, love-at-first-sight and unrequited love:

  ... As a way of formatting our thoughts, emotions and behaviour the discourse of romantic love must surely be one of the most prevalent in modern society ...

- This discourse presents romantic love as (a) a part of human nature, the 'emotional cement' that strengthens the sexual relationship between men and women, and (b) the foundation for marriage and family life. Marriage is the appropriate and natural culmination of a romantic alliance.
- While this might seem fairly 'obvious' (i.e. 'true'), feminists were among the first to criticise notions of romantic love.
- From a Marxist perspective, marriage and the family play a crucial role in maintaining the capitalist economy. Men-as-workers need to be 'healthy' and relieved of child-care responsibilities. This makes the role of women central.
- Not only do they look after their men so the latter can sell their labour, but they produce children and provide their caring and sexual services 'free of charge'. This is provided via marriage. This is legitimated by the idea of the 'family wage' – that is, a man should be paid enough money to support himself and his dependent wife and children.
- But if you ask people why men and women get married or what marriage is about, they're likely to say that it's because they love each other, and women care for their

husband and children because they love them. It's 'common sense'.

- But according to Foucault (1976), for example, the discourses of love, marriage and family life are a form of social control, obscuring the reality of the economic arrangements of capitalist society.

Nicole Kidman and Ewan McGregor in *Moulin Rouge* (2001)

However, cultural differences still exist. For example, Levine *et al.* (1995) studied young people in Australia, Brazil, England, Hong Kong, India, Japan, Mexico, Pakistan, the Philippines, Thailand and the USA. Participants from India, Thailand and Pakistan gave the highest proportion of 'yes' replies, while those from England and the USA gave the lowest. These are collectivist and individualist cultures, respectively.

Based on studies conducted in Canada, the Caribbean, Senegal, Uganda, the USA and South Africa, Smith & Bond (1998) conclude that:

> There are relatively universal ways in which people speak about their attachment to others. However, the more detail we add to the measures, explicating exactly what attitudes and behaviours are entailed within the generalised notion of love or romance, the more differences we start to find.

There are also important differences *within* culturally diverse societies, such as Britain, America and Canada. For example, first generation Indian immigrants to Canada (those born abroad who subsequently emigrated to Canada) tend to endorse the idea that marriage precedes love more than second generation Indian Canadians (whose parents came from abroad but who were themselves born in Canada: Vaidyanathan & Naidoo, 1991). Similarly, Dion & Dion (1993) found that Asian Canadians tend to interpret love as more friendship- and caring-based than something 'mysterious', compared with European Canadians. Both these findings are consistent with the distinction between collectivist and individualist cultural beliefs and practices, such as arranged marriages (see above).

An evolutionary theory of love: love as attachment

An *evolutionary* account of love focuses on the *functions* that love evolved to meet. Compared with other primates, humans are dependent on their parents for an exceptionally long period of time. As length of childhood (and related brain size) increased steadily over the last million years or so of *Homo* evolution, so there were strong selection pressures toward the development of (relatively) *monogamous* (one male, one female) *pair-bonding*. In other words:

> Love is ... an evolutionary device to persuade couples to stay together for long enough to give their children a good shot at making it to adulthood ... (Fletcher, 2002)

In our hunter-gatherer ancestral environment, two parents were better than one. Attachment bonds between procreative partners would have greatly enhanced the survival of their offspring (Zeifman & Hazan, 2000).

Bowlby (1969) identified three basic behavioural systems that bond male–female pairs together: attachment, caregiving and sex. Shaver *et al.* (1996) have proposed a theory of adult romantic love in terms of these three systems. So, when we say 'I love you', we can mean any or all of the following.

- *Love as attachment:* 'I am emotionally dependent on you for happiness, safety and security; I feel anxious and lonely when you're gone, relieved and stronger when you're near. I want to be comforted, supported emotionally, and taken care of by you ...'
- *Love as caregiving:* 'I get great pleasure from supporting, caring for and taking care of you; from facilitating your progress, health, growth and happiness ...'

Table 28.1 The four stages of adult attachment in relation to Bowlby's four phases of infant attachment development

Bowlby's phases of infant attachment	Pre-attachment (0–3/4 months)	Attachment-in-the-making (3/4–6/7 months)	Clear-cut attachment (6/7–12/18 months)	Goal-directed partnership (12–18 months onwards)
Four stages of adult attachment	Attraction and flirting	Falling in love	Loving	Life as usual

Based on Zeifman & Hazan (2000)

◎ *Love as sexual attraction:* 'I am sexually attracted to you and can't get you out of my mind. You excite me, "turn me on", make me feel alive ... I want to see you, devour you, touch you, merge with you, lose myself in you, "get off on you" ...'

Zeifman & Hazan (2000) believe that there are four stages of adult attachment that mirror Bowlby's (1969) four phases of infants' attachment to the mother(-figure). These are summarised in Table 28.1 (page 476).

STAGE THEORIES OF RELATIONSHIPS

> *ASK YOURSELF...*
> - Do you think there are any 'natural' stages that all intimate (romantic and non-romantic) relationships go through (assuming the 'romantic' ones last a reasonable amount of time – so one-night-stands don't count!).

Our own experience tells us that intimate relationships change and develop over time. Indeed, those which stagnate ('we're not going anywhere'), especially sexual/romantic relationships, may well be doomed to failure (Duck, 1988).

The filter model (Kerckhoff & Davis, 1962)

Kerckhoff and Davis compared 'short-term couples' (together for less than 18 months) with 'long-term couples' (18 months or more) over a seven-month period. According to their *filter model:*

◎ *similarity of sociological* (or *demographic*) *variables* determines the likelihood of individuals meeting in the first place. To some extent, our choice of friends and partners is made for us; social circumstances reduce the '*field of availables*' (Kerckhoff, 1974) – that is, the range of people that are *realistically* available for us to meet (as opposed to those who are theoretically available). There's considerable *preselection* of the types of people we come into contact with, namely those from our own ethnic, racial, religious, social class and educational groups; these are the types of people we tend to find most attractive initially, since similarity makes communication easier and we've something immediately in common with them, as a group. At this point, attraction has little to do with other people's individual characteristics (this is the first 'filter')

◎ the next filter involves the psychological characteristics of individuals, specifically *agreement on basic values.* This was found to be the best predictor of the relationship becoming more stable and permanent; those who'd been together for less than 18 months tended to have a stronger relationship when the partners' values coincided

◎ but with the long-term couples, similarity wasn't the most important factor. The best predictor of a longer-term commitment was *complementarity of emotional needs* (this constitutes the third filter).

Stimulus–value–role theory (Murstein, 1976, 1986, 1987)

According to Murstein's *stimulus-value-role* (SVR) *theory,* intimate relationships proceed from:

◎ a *stimulus stage,* in which attraction is based on external attributes (such as physical appearance), through

◎ a *value stage,* in which similarity of values and beliefs becomes much more important, and finally to

◎ a *role stage,* which involves a commitment based on successful performance of relationship roles, such as husband and wife.

Although all three factors have some influence throughout a relationship, each one assumes greatest significance during one particular stage.

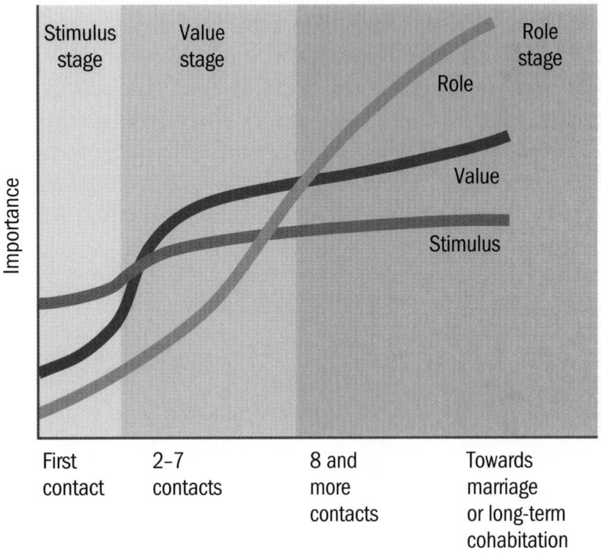

Figure 28.2 States of courtship in SVR theory (Murstein, 1987, based on Brehm, 1992)

An evaluation of stage theories

Brehm (1992) points out that many studies have provided only weak evidence for a fixed sequence of stages in intimate relationships. 'Stages' are probably best regarded as 'phases' that take place at different times for different couples. However, the claim that relationships change and develop isn't in dispute, and it's useful to think of this as involving a beginning, a middle and an end, corresponding to the three questions that were posed at the beginning of the chapter (see *Introduction and overview*). For example, how each partner understands the role of husband and wife, and how well each performs their role, are relatively late influences in a given courtship. The matching of partners' role concepts will be irrelevant to the success of the early stages of the courtship (Duck, 1999).

INTERPERSONAL ATTRACTION: HOW RELATIONSHIPS GET STARTED

A general theoretical framework for explaining initial attraction is that we're attracted to individuals whose presence is *rewarding* for us (e.g. Clore & Byrne, 1974; Lott & Lott, 1974). The more rewards someone provides for us, the more we should be attracted to that individual. A number of factors have been found to influence initial attraction through their reward value, including *proximity, exposure* and *familiarity, physical attractiveness,* and *similarity.*

Proximity, exposure and familiarity

Proximity

Proximity (physical or geographical closeness) represents a minimum requirement for attraction, because the further apart two people live, the lower the probability that they'll ever meet, let alone become friends or marry each other. Festinger *et al.* (1950) studied friendship patterns in a university campus housing complex for married students. People were more friendly with those who lived next door, next most friendly with those living two doors away, and least friendly with those who lived at the end of the corridor. Families separated by four flats hardly ever became friends, and in two-storey blocks of flats the residents tended to interact mainly with others living on the same floor. On any one floor, people who lived near stairways had more friends than those living at the end of a corridor.

Personal space

ASK YOURSELF...

- If you're sitting in an otherwise empty row of seats in a train and someone comes and sits right next to you, how do you think you'd react, and why?

In a series of studies by Sommer, the experimenter deliberately sat close to unsuspecting people when there was plenty of other available space, in order to see how likely they were to react to this invasion of their personal space.

KEY STUDY 28.2 Beware of space invaders in the library (Felipe & Sommer, 1966)

- The unsuspecting participants were female university students studying at a large table (1m x 5m) with six chairs evenly spaced on either side of the table. There were at least two empty chairs on either side of each student, and one opposite.
- There were five experimental conditions in which the female experimenter:

  a sat next to the student and moved her chair to within about 8 cm of the student's (about as close as possible without actually touching); if the student moved her chair away, the experimenter would move her chair nearer
  b sat in the chair next to the student at a normal, acceptable distance (about half a metre)
  c sat two seats away from her (leaving one chair between them)
  d sat three seats away
  e sat immediately opposite her (about a metre apart).

- About 55 per cent of the participants in condition (a) stayed in the library for longer than 10 minutes, compared with 90 per cent in conditions (b)–(e) combined; 100 per cent of participants in a control condition (who sat at the same-sized table, with the same number and arrangement of empty chairs, but weren't 'invaded' by the experimenter) stayed longer than 10 minutes.
- After 20 minutes, these percentages reduced to 45 per cent in the first condition, 80 per cent in (b)–(e). and just below 100 per cent in the control condition.
- By the end of the 30-minute experiment, the figures were 30 per cent, 73 per cent and 87 per cent respectively.
- Students were more likely to leave, move away, adjust their chair or erect barriers (such as putting a bag on the table between themselves and the 'intruder') in condition (a).

Similar results were found for male psychiatric patients (Felipe & Sommer, 1966), and for people sitting on park benches (Sommer, 1969). In Hall's (1959, 1966) terms, the stranger in Felipe and Sommer's studies was invading the student's *personal space.* This describes the human behaviour resembling the 'individual distance' of zoo animals (the distance that two individuals of the same species try to keep between each other: Hediger, 1951).

Box 28.7 Personal space

Personal space is a sort of invisible bubble that surrounds us. According to Hall, we learn *proxemic rules* that prescribe:

- the amount of physical distance that's appropriate in daily relationships, and
- the kinds of situations in which closeness or distance are proper.

Hall identifies four main regions or zones of personal space. (See Figure 28.3 on next page.)

There are important *cultural differences* regarding proxemic rules. Each zone of personal space allows the use of different cues of touch, smell, hearing and seeing, which are more important in some cultures than others. Watson & Graves (1966) observed discussion groups of Americans and those from Arab countries; in the latter, there was more direct face-to-face orientation, greater closeness and touching.

South Americans and Arabs have been called *'contact cultures'*, while the Scots and Swedes have been called *'non-contact cultures'*.

The *caste system* in India represents a highly formalised, institutionalised set of proxemic rules.

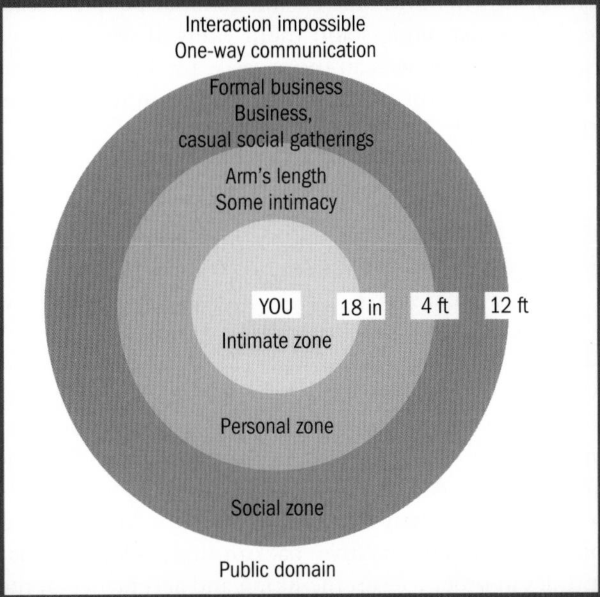

Figure 28.3 Hall's four zones of personal space (from Nicholson, 1977)

A similar concept to personal space is the *body-buffer zone,* the point at which a person begins to feel uncomfortable when approached by another. Criminals convicted of violent crimes compared with non-criminals, and schizophrenics compared with other kinds of psychiatric patients, tend to have *larger* body-buffer zones, that is, they more easily begin to feel uneasy when others walk towards them (Nicholson, 1977).

Our feelings for others may depend on whether proxemic rules are followed, and these rules are themselves influenced by the nature of the relationship. For instance, relatives and intimate friends are allowed much closer proximity – and bodily contact – than mere acquaintances or strangers. As far as bodily contact is concerned, there are different rules for different relatives depending on their gender, and this applies to friends too (see Figure 28.4).

Proximity is just one of several kinds of *social act* which make up the degree of intimacy that exists between two people. According to Argyle & Dean (1965), we all have a dual tendency to approach others and seek their company, and to avoid them and remain separate and independent. The balance between these two opposing tendencies is 'negotiated', non-verbally, in each social situation, so that we try to find a level of intimacy we feel comfortable with.

Successful friendships may require an initial establishment of *boundary understandings.* In Hall's terms, strangers must be 'invited' into our intimate zone and not 'trespass' from an initial casual personal distance. In terms of Argyle

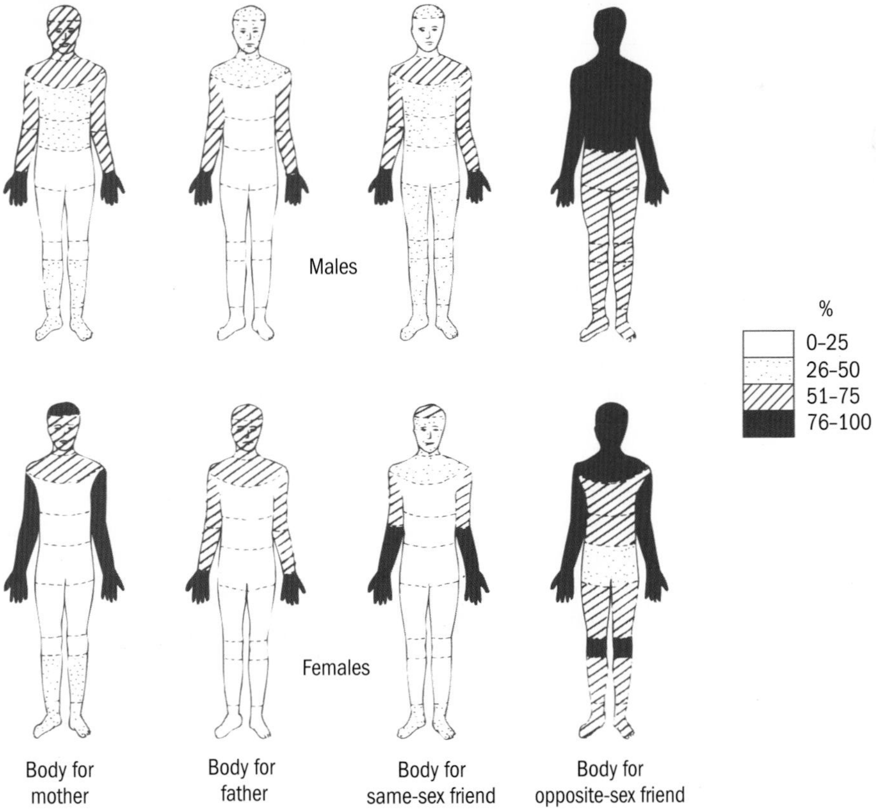

Figure 28.4 Male and female 'bodies for others', as experienced through the amount of touching received from others (Jourard, 1966)

and Dean's equilibrium model of intimacy, strangers (like the experimenter in Sommer's studies) who make a situation uncomfortably intimate too soon are unlikely to become friends.

> **ASK YOURSELF...**
> - Do you think it's ethically acceptable to conduct research like Sommer and Felipe's 'library study'?

Exposure and familiarity

Proximity increases the opportunity for interaction (*exposure*), which, in turn, increases *familiarity*. There's considerable evidence that, far from breeding contempt, familiarity breeds fondness (the *mere exposure effect*: Zajonc, 1968). For example, the more times university students saw photographs of men's faces, the more they liked them (Zajonc, 1968).

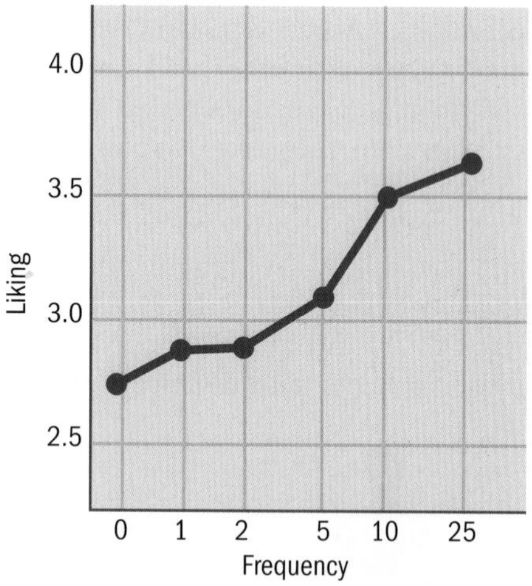

Figure 28.5 The relationship between frequency of exposure and liking. Participants were shown photographs of different faces and the number of times each face was shown was varied. The more they saw a particular face, the more they said they liked the person shown (based on Zajonc, 1968)

According to Argyle (1983), the more two people interact, the more *polarised* their attitudes towards each other become, usually in the direction of greater liking. This, in turn, increases the likelihood of further interaction, but only if the interaction is on an equal footing.

People form friendships with those they encounter frequently (as the mere exposure effect would predict). Asian-Americans date Euro-Americans when they're in close proximity (Fujino, 1997), high-school students form friendships within their own academic subjects (Kubitschek & Hallinan, 1998), and older, relocated adults make friends among their nearest neighbours (Dugan & Kivett, 1998).

This preference for what is familiar extends to our own facial appearance. Mita *et al.* (1977) photographed women students and later showed each student her actual picture together with a mirror-image of it. Most students preferred the latter – this is how we're used to seeing ourselves – while their friends preferred the former – this is how others are used to seeing us!

> **ASK YOURSELF...**
> - What is it about familiarity that makes it an influence on attraction?
> - Why should we prefer the familiar?

Fiske (2004) believes that we like familiar people because we feel we can understand them easily. If we (think we) understand them, we can more easily predict their behaviour, which, in turn, makes it easier to influence them. Familiar people are also safe.

Similarity

> **ASK YOURSELF...**
> - Do you consider your friends to be similar to you? If so, in what ways?
> - Does this also apply to sexual partners?

Evidence suggests that 'birds of a feather flock together', and that the critical similarities are those concerning *beliefs, attitudes* and *values*. For example, Newcomb (1943) studied students at an American college with a liberal tradition among teaching staff and senior students. Many students coming from conservative backgrounds adopted liberal attitudes in order to gain the liking and acceptance of their classmates. Griffitt & Veitch (1974) paid 13 males to spend ten days in a fall-out shelter. Those with similar attitudes and opinions liked each other most by the end of the study, particularly if they agreed on highly salient issues.

> **ASK YOURSELF...**
> - What is it about similarity that makes it an influence on attraction?
> - Why should we prefer people who (we believe) are like us?

Rubin (1973) suggests that similarity is rewarding because:

- agreement may provide a basis for engaging in joint activities
- a person who agrees with us helps to increase our confidence in our own opinions, which enhances our self-esteem; according to Duck (1992), the validation that friends give us is experienced as evidence of the accuracy of our *personal constructs* (see Chapter 42)
- most people are vain enough to believe that anyone who shares their views must be a sensitive and praiseworthy individual
- people who agree about things that matter to them generally find it easier to communicate
- we may assume that people with similar attitudes to ourselves will like us, and so we like them in turn (*reciprocal liking*).

According to Fiske (2004), if someone resembles prior experience or the self, then at least we have the illusion of knowing 'what makes them tick'. In this respect, familiarity and similarity influence attraction in comparable ways. We mostly seek out others who make us feel good about ourselves:

> ... People who resemble us or agree with us also reassure us. People who validate us and like us presumably won't do us any harm ... (Fiske, 2004)

According to the *similarity-attraction principle,* if familiarity underlies attraction, and if the most familiar people are those who are like us, then people like us are attractive. This stems in part from *consistency theories of attitude change* (see Chapter 24). The most relevant here is Heider's (1958) *balance theory.* People prefer and infer affective, cognitive and behavioural consistency – in themselves and others. Psychologically related individuals will see each other as similar if they like each other, and they'll see each other as likeable if they're similar. In other words, people like to agree with their friends and to befriend those who agree with them. This describes *interpersonal balance,* 'a harmonious state, one in which the entities comprising the situation and the feelings about them fit together without stress' (Heider, 1958).

Physical attractiveness

While it often takes time to find out about other people's attitudes and values, their physical attractiveness is immediately apparent. Physical attractiveness has been studied as an influence on attraction in its own right, as well as one aspect of similarity.

The attractiveness stereotype

As we saw in Chapter 22, we tend to perceive attractive-looking people as also having more attractive personalities (the *attractiveness stereotype*). Dion *et al.* (1972) found that photographs of attractive people, compared with unattractive people, were consistently credited with more desirable qualities – sexually warm and responsive, kind, strong, outgoing, nurturant, sensitive, interesting, poised, sociable, exciting dates, better character, happily married, socially and professionally successful and enjoying more fulfilling lives. So, 'what is beautiful is socially good' (Fiske, 2004).

The power of the physical attractiveness stereotype is demonstrated in a classic study by Snyder *et al.* (1977).

KEY STUDY 28.3 The self-fulfilling nature of the attractiveness stereotype (Snyder *et al.*, 1977)

- Male undergraduates received photographs of women before a getting-acquainted telephone conversation.
- The photographs, independently rated as either quite attractive or quite unattractive, didn't depict their actual partners, who were unaware of the experimental manipulation.
- Before the telephone conversation, the men rated the supposedly attractive partner as more sociable, poised, humorous and adept.
- During the conversation, independent judges rated these men as more sociable, sexually warm, outgoing, interesting, independent, bold, humorous and adept.
- In response, their (actual) partners, who'd been randomly allocated to the 'attractive' or 'unattractive' conditions, behaved in similar ways.
- The men's expectations about their partners, based on the photographs, created a *self-fulfilling prophecy.*

However, Dermer & Thiel (1975) found that extremely attractive women were judged (by female participants) to be egotistic, vain, materialistic, snobbish and less likely to be successfully married. This suggests that it's not always to our advantage to be seen as highly attractive, and one situation where this may apply is where a criminal's good looks played a part in the crime.

Dion & Dion (1995) observe that stereotyping based on facial attractiveness appears at least as early as six years old. They also suggest that this might be linked to the *just world hypothesis,* such that there's a positive bias towards 'winners', equivalent to 'blaming the victim' (see Chapter 23).

Is the attractiveness stereotype culturally relative?

Like most attractiveness research, studies of the attractiveness stereotype are American, the prime example of an individualist culture. Although a physical attractiveness stereotype can be found in some collectivist cultures (such as Korea and Taiwan), the content differs. For example, in Korea attractive people aren't seen as more powerful but as showing more concern for others and more integrity. In other words, 'the beautiful receive the benefits of social status, embodying that culture's ideal values' (Fiske, 2004).

What makes someone attractive?

Different cultures have different criteria concerning physical beauty. For example, chipped teeth, body scars, artificially elongated heads and bound feet have all been regarded as beautiful, and in western culture, definitions of beauty change over time, as in the 'ideal' figure for women (see Chapter 44.) Traditionally, men have emphasised physical attractiveness, including facial beauty, more than women have. But women haven't been disinterested in men's appearance: their stature, particularly height, plus a muscular body and (currently) firm, rounded buttocks influence how attractive they're judged to be (by women, anyway!). Nor are they indifferent about men's facial appearance.

According to Brehm (1992), in the context of personal ads and commercial dating services, the primary 'resource' (or reward) offered by females seeking a male partner is still physical attractiveness, which matches what men are actually seeking from a female partner. But this appears to be an almost universal male preference, not one confined to western culture (Buss, 1989: see below, page 487).

Jude Law in *The Talented Mr Ripley* (1999)

ASK YOURSELF...

- Think of someone you find extremely facially attractive, and try to specify what it is about their face that you like.

Defining facial attractiveness

The idea that beauty is in the eye of the beholder stems from the philosopher, Hume (1757). This implies, of course, that beauty cannot be defined objectively,. However, although any two individuals can vary widely in what they consider facially attractive, these differences actually vary around an underlying norm, which is surprisingly consistent across cultures (Berry, 2000; Langlois & Roggman, 1990). Langlois *et al.* (1987) found that when babies under one year are shown faces that adults consider attractive or unattractive, they spend longer looking at the former (implying that they prefer them: see Chapter 16). Clearly, they're too young to have learned cultural standards of beauty.

Langlois & Rogmann (1990) took photographs of faces with standard pose, expression and lighting, and then scanned them into a computer. Each image was then divided into a very large number of tiny squares (or *pixels*), and the brightnesses of corresponding pixels in different same-sex faces were *averaged* to produce *computer-composite images.* When people were asked to judge the attractiveness of these composite faces (made from four, eight, 16, or 32 faces), they rated them as increasingly attractive the more faces that went into each image. This applied to both male and female faces.

The greater the number of faces making up a composite image, the more the peculiarities of particular faces become ironed out. Hence, as Bruce & Young (1998) observe:

It seems that moving a facial image closer to the average ... increases its perceived attractiveness ...

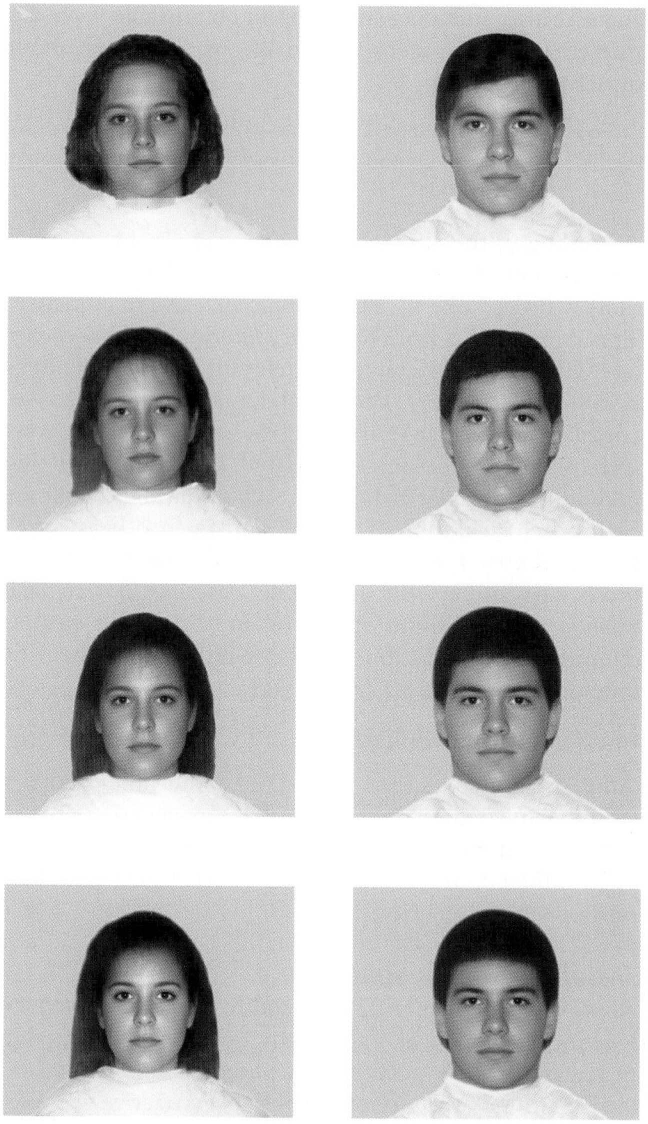

Computer-composite faces. The columns show composite sets created from female faces (left) or from male faces (right). From top to bottom, rows show composites created by averaging across 4, 8, 16 and 32 faces (from Bruce & Young, 1998)

If this is a genuine phenomenon, how can we explain it? Bruce and Young suggest two possible explanations:

- although we've not seen composite faces before, *averaged* faces (close to the average of faces we *have* see before) are preferred because they seem *familiar* (seen above, page 480). This is consistent with the idea that attractive people are seen as possessing high status – that is, they represent the 'culturally good and the socially desirable' (Fiske, 2004)
- individuals whose characteristics are close to the average of the population might be preferred, because they're less likely to carry harmful genetic mutations (Langlois & Roggman, 1990).

A third possible explanation (an almost 'obvious' one) is that average features (by definition) omit every 'too': too big, too small, too short, too long, and so on (Fiske, 2004).

Is attractiveness really no more than averageness? This seems unlikely. For example, if we describe someone as 'average looking', we usually mean that s/he is neither 'good-looking' nor 'ugly', and movie stars and sex symbols *aren't* obviously average (otherwise most of us would be sex symbols!).

According to Perret *et al.* (1994), the average derived from highly attractive faces is consistently preferred to the average of the entire set of photographs they were taken from. This wouldn't happen if 'attractive' equalled 'average. When the difference between the average shape of attractive faces and the average shape of the entire set was increased, perceived attractiveness of the former also increased. But the effect of this was to make the resulting faces *more different* from the average. Perret *et al.* found exactly the same pattern of results for European and Japanese faces, regardless of whether they were judged by European or Japanese people.

We also seem to prefer more *symmetrical* faces. While most faces (to varying degrees) are, in fact, asymmetrical around the vertical midline, even those with only slight asymmetry can be made more attractive (Bruce & Young, 1998).

In addition, having younger-looking features, for both sexes, seems to be an advantage. For women, 'favourites' include child-like features (large eyes, spaced far apart, small chin and nose), narrow face and prominent cheek-bones, expressive features (high eyebrows and large smile), and sexual cues (larger lower lip and well-groomed, full hair). The recent trend in cosmetic surgery for full lips has resulted, for some, in a bizarre change of appearance.

Actress Lesley Ash – the after photo

Facial attractiveness in men is less often studied, but high cheekbones and a rugged jaw seem to be favoured (Berry, 2000).

From a *sociobiological* perspective (see Chapter 2), attractive facial features may signal sexual maturity or fertility. This is also consistent with the tendency to equate beauty with youthfulness (but see Chapters 22 and 39, and Box 28.8).

Box 28.8 The sociobiology of beauty

- According to Singh (in Charter, 1995), anyone whose waist size exceeds their hip measurement (i.e. whose *waist-hip ratio* – WHR – is greater than one) is much more at risk from heart disease and diabetes.
- Furthermore, Singh claims to have shown that women with a waist-hip ratio of 0.7 have universal appeal as potential partners, because their body shape transmits signals about health, sexual maturity, and fertility. For males the ideal is more like 0.85–0.9.
- This fits in perfectly with Darwinian theories of human mate selection, which claim that both men and women select partners who enable them to enhance reproductive success, thus ensuring the survival of their genes into the next generation (see Chapter 2 and Gross & Rolls, 2004).
- Twiggy's WHR was a surprising 0.73 (her vital statistics were 31–24–33), and although *Playboy* centrefolds have shown a 20 per cent decline in plumpness over the years (see Chapter 44), they've shown a consistent WHR of 0.7.
- Singh has been criticised on several grounds. The diseases he claims are correlated with high WHRs affect mainly older (post-menopausal) women, and so aren't relevant to mating. They're also historically quite recent.

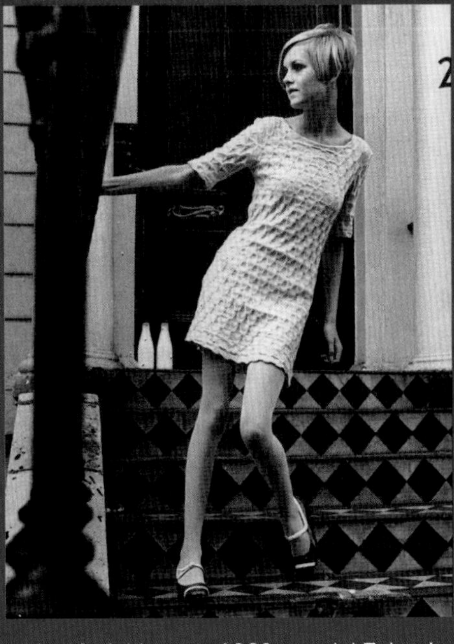

As well as her facial beauty, 1960s model Twiggy's waist-hip ratio was (surprisingly) an attractive 0.73

The matching hypothesis

According to *social exchange theory* (e.g. Thibaut & Kelley, 1959: see below), people are more likely to become romantically involved if they're fairly closely matched in their ability to reward one another. Ideally, we'd all have the 'perfect partner' because, the theory says, we're all selfish. But since this is impossible, we try to find a compromise solution. The best general bargain that can be struck is a *value-match,* a subjective belief that our partner is the most rewarding we could realistically hope to find.

Several studies have tested the *matching hypothesis* (Walster *et al.*, 1966; Dion & Berscheid, 1974; Berscheid *et al.*, 1971; Silverman, 1971; Murstein, 1972; Berscheid & Walster, 1974). These studies generally show that people rated as being of high, low or average attractiveness tend to choose partners of a corresponding level of attractiveness. Indeed, according to Price & Vandenberg (1979):

> The matching phenomenon [of physical attraction between marriage partners] is stable within and across generations.

The findings from the various matching hypothesis studies imply that the kind of partner we'd be satisfied with is one we feel won't reject us, rather than one we positively desire. Brown (1986), however, maintains that the matching phenomenon results from a well-learned sense of what's 'fitting', rather than a fear of being rebuffed. For Brown, we learn to adjust our expectations of rewards in line with what we believe we have to offer others.

An evaluation of attraction research

According to Duck (1999), the 'magnetic metaphor' of attraction implies that people are unwittingly, and almost against their will, pulled towards one another's inherent, pre-existing characteristics. It's a view of relationships as:

> ... implicitly independent of interaction, co-construction, mutually responsive behaviour, or shared understandings derived from active conversation ... In short, it leaves out most of the other things that humans do in everyday life, and so it serves to caricature social and personal relationships as the unthinking domain of reactive magnetism ...

More recent research has considered the *dynamics* of relationships (how they develop and unfold over time), and how relationships are actually conducted in real life. One feature of 'real' relationships is their inherent tensions, such as the need to balance our desire for disclosure and openness, connectedness and interdependence on the one hand, and the desire for autonomy and independence, privacy and the right to retain secrets on the other.

Not surprisingly, this shift has involved fewer controlled laboratory studies, and more exploration of life as it's lived 'out there' (Duck, 1999). This now includes such diverse research areas as *homosexual* and *electronic* (online or cyberspace) relationships (see above).

WHAT KEEPS PEOPLE TOGETHER?

> *ASK YOURSELF...*
> - What do all the important relationships in your life have in common?

You may say something to the effect that they provide you with security, happiness, contentment, fun and so on, and (if you're honest) that they can also be complex, demanding and, at times, even painful. If all relationships involve both positive and negative, desirable and undesirable aspects, what determines our continued involvement in them?

Social exchange theory

Social exchange theory (SET) provides a general framework for analysing all kinds of relationship, both intimate and non-intimate, and is really an extension of *reward theory* (see above, page 478).

According to Homans (1974), we view our feelings for others in terms of profits (the amount of reward obtained from a relationship minus the cost). The greater the reward and lower the cost, the greater the profit and hence the attraction. Blau (1964) argues that interactions are 'expensive': they take time, energy and commitment, and may involve unpleasant emotions and experiences. Because of this, what we get out of a relationship must be more than what we put in.

Similarly, Berscheid & Walster (1978) argue that in any social interaction there's an exchange of rewards (such as affection, information and status), and that the degree of attraction or liking will reflect how people evaluate the rewards they receive relative to those they give.

> *ASK YOURSELF...*
> - Is it appropriate to think of relationships in this economic, capitalistic, way?
> - Are relationships really like that?

An evaluation of SET

Social exchange theory sees people as fundamentally selfish and human relationships as based primarily on self-interest. But this is a *metaphor* for human relationships, and it shouldn't be taken too literally. However, although we like to believe that the joy of giving is as important as the desire to receive, we have to admit that our attitudes toward other people are determined to a large extent by our assessments of the rewards they hold for us (Rubin, 1973).

Equally, though, Rubin believes that SET doesn't provide an adequate, complete account:

> Human beings are sometimes altruistic in the fullest sense of the word. They make sacrifices for the sake of others without any consideration of the rewards they will obtain from them in return ...

Altruism is most often and most clearly seen in close interpersonal relationships (see Chapter 30).

Indeed, some psychologists make the distinction between 'true' love and friendship, which are altruistic, and less admirable forms which are based on considerations of exchange (Brown, 1986). Fromm (1962) defines true love as giving, as opposed to the false love of the 'marketing character' which depends upon expecting to have the favours returned. Support for this distinction comes from studies by Clark & Mills (1979, 1993),who identified two kinds of intimate relationship:

- the *communal couple,* in which each partner gives out of concern for the other
- the *exchange couple,* in which each keeps mental records of who's 'ahead' and who's 'behind'.

SET implies that *all* relationships are of the exchange variety. Exchange might describe some kinds of relationship, such as impersonal friendships and relationships between business associates, but in communal relationships, people don't track outcomes (who did what for whom: Clark, 1984). Instead, they track each other's needs, and one partner may need more than the other, at different times, or even throughout the relationship (Clark *et al.*, 1986). Fiske (2004) suggests that thinking of family relationships as communal explains why parents don't normally 'charge' their children for their upbringing. According to Clark & Grote (1998), communal relationships operate by different norms from exchange relationships.

One of those norms is *reciprocity,* which involves the repayment of specific benefits ('you scratch my back, and I'll scratch yours': see Chapter 27). Perhaps contrary to what most people would expect, reciprocity is particularly strong in most casual relationships, but weaker in more intimate communal relationships (Clark & Mills, 1993). Indeed, 'exchange' implies that people reciprocate benefit for benefit, resulting in an *equivalence* of outcomes (Fiske, 2004). The communal couple's responsiveness to each other's needs represents a broader type of reciprocity. In some form, reciprocity appears to be a fundamental aspect of human social exchanges (Dovidio & Penner, 2004), evident in all known cultures (Moghaddam *et al.*, 1993).

Clearly, SET is a greatly oversimplified account of human relationships. It simply cannot accommodate the rich diversity and complexity of relationships. At best, it may describe a certain type of superficial and probably short-term relationship.

Equity theory

SET is really a special case of a more general account of human relationships called *equity theory* (ET). The extra component in ET that's added to reward, cost and profit is *investment.* For Brown (1986):

> A person's investments are not just financial; they are anything at all that is believed to entitle him to his rewards, costs, and profits. An investment is any factor to be weighed in determining fair profits or losses.

Equity *doesn't* mean equality (as implied by 'exchange'), but a *constant ratio* of rewards to costs or profit to investment. So, equity theory involves a concern with *fairness,* and it's *changes* in the ratio of what you put in and what you get out of a relationship which are likely to cause changes in how you feel about it, rather than the initial ratio. You may believe it's fair and just that you give more than you get, but if you start giving very much more than you did and receiving proportionately less, then you're likely to become dissatisfied.

An evaluation of ET

ET is an improvement on SET, and it seemed to predict satisfaction and liking in relationships (Walster *et al.*, 1978). But relationships *don't* become more equitable over time, and equity *doesn't* predict the stability or quality of relationships over time (Van Yperen & Buunk, 1990).

However, some versions of SET do actually take account of factors other than the simple and crude profit motives of social interactors. One of these was introduced by Thibaut & Kelley (1959).

Box 28.9 The concepts of comparison level and comparison level for alternatives (Thibaut & Kelley, 1959)

- *Comparison level* (CL) is essentially the average level of rewards and costs you're used to in relationships, and is the basic level you expect in any future relationship. So, if your current reward:cost ratio falls below your CL, the relationship will be unsatisfying. If it's above your CL, you'll be satisfied with the relationship.
- *Comparison level for alternatives* (CL alt.) is essentially your expectation about the reward:cost ratio which *could* be obtained in other relationships. If your current ratio in a relationship exceeds the CL alt., then you're doing better in it than you could do elsewhere. As a result, the relationship should be satisfying and likely to continue. But if the CL alt. exceeds your current reward:cost ratio, then you're doing worse than you could do elsewhere. As a result, the relationship should be unsatisfying and unlikely to continue.

According to Duck (1988), the concept of CL alt. implies that the endurance of a relationship (as far as one partner is concerned) could be due to:

- the qualities of the other partner and the relationship
- the negative and unattractive features of the perceived alternatives, or
- the perceived costs of leaving.

But this still portrays people as being fundamentally selfish, and many researchers (e.g. Duck, 1988; Walster *et al.*, 1978) prefer to see relationships as being maintained by an equitable distribution of rewards and costs for both partners. In this approach, people are seen as being concerned with the equity of outcomes for both themselves and their partners.

Murstein *et al.* (1977) argue that concern with either exchange or equity is negatively correlated with marital adjustment. People in close relationships don't think in terms of rewards and costs at all – until they start to feel dissatisfied (Argyle, 1987). Murstein & MacDonald (1983) have argued that although the principles of exchange and equity play a significant role in intimate relationships, a conscious concern with 'getting a fair deal', especially in the short term, makes *compatibility* (see below) very hard to achieve. This is true in both friendship and, especially, marriage. This corresponds to Clark and Mills's *exchange couple* (see above).

Complementarity

> ***ASK YOURSELF...***
> - Think of your most successful relationship(s) – past and/or present.
> - What made it/them work?
> - Did the 'essential ingredients' change as the relationship(s) developed?

According to Kerckhoff & Davis's (1962) filter model (see above), *complementarity of needs* becomes increasingly important as relationships become long-term. According to Winch (1958), happy marriages are often based on each partner's ability to fulfil the needs of the other. For example, a domineering person could more easily satisfy a partner who needs to be dominated than one who's equally domineering, and Winch found some empirical support for this view.

Although some complementarity may evolve as a relationship develops, people seem, if anything, slightly more likely to marry those whose needs and personalities are *similar* (the *matching phenomenon*) (e.g. Berscheid & Walster, 1978). Indeed, Berscheid & Reis (1998) argue that the overwhelming evidence favours similarity:

> ... Altogether, support is weak for people's intuition that opposites, exotics, or mysteries form the primary basis for attraction, whereas support is strong for the similarity-attraction principle.

In direct contradiction of the opposites-attract hypothesis, Felmlee (1998) examined 'fatal attractions' to a partner with qualities that differed from the partner and from the average. Descriptions of these terminated relationships indicated that even when these dissimilar, unique or extreme qualities might have been intriguing or appealing to begin with, it was the self-same qualities that eventually produced disenchantment.

Complementarity of resources

Instead of complementary needs, what about complementarity in resources (Brehm, 1992)? As we noted earlier, men seem to give a universally higher priority to 'good looks' in their female partners than do women in their male partners, while the situation is reversed when it comes to 'good financial prospect' and 'good earning capacity'. Based on a study of 37 cultures (including Nigeria, South Africa, Japan, Estonia, Zambia, Columbia, Poland, Germany, Spain, France, China, Palestinian Arabs, Italy and The Netherlands) involving over 10,000 people, Buss (1989) concluded that these sex differences 'appear to be deeply rooted in the evolutionary history of our species'.

CRITICAL DISCUSSION 28.1 Do our genes dictate what we want in a mate?

- According to Buss (1988, 1989), the chances of reproductive success should be increased for men who mate with younger, healthy adult females, as opposed to older, unhealthy ones. Fertility is a function of the mother's age and health, which also affects pregnancy and her ability to care for her child.
- Men often have to rely on a woman's physical appearance in order to estimate her age and health, with younger, healthier women being perceived as more attractive (see Box 28.8).
- Women's mate selection depends on their need for a provider to take care of them during pregnancy and nursing: men seen as powerful and controlling resources that contribute to the mother and child's welfare will be seen as especially attractive.
- Buss's sociobiological explanation removes male–female relationships from their cultural or historical context. This

is captured in the use of the term 'mate selection', which is normally used to describe non-human animals.
- Perhaps women have been forced to obtain desirable resources through men, because they've been denied direct access to political and economic power. Traditionally, a woman has been regarded as the man's property, whereby her beauty increases his status and respect in others' eyes.
- Buss conveniently seems to overlook a major finding from his (1989) study: 'kind' and 'intelligent' were universally ranked as *more important* than 'physically attractive' or 'good earning power' by both men and women!
- Simpson *et al.*'s (1986) findings that women are increasingly marrying for reasons ***other than*** material necessity contradict Buss's sociobiological explanation (see above, page 475).
- How can Buss's argument account for homosexual relationships, which clearly don't contribute to the survival of the species, but which are subject to many of the same sociopsychological influences involved in heterosexual relationships (Brehm, 1992)?

Compatibility

The importance of similarity

Complementarity, as far as it exists, can be seen as a component of *compatibility,* but *similarity* plays a much larger part in keeping couples together. For example, individuals with similar needs (Meyer & Pepper, 1977), attitudes, likes and dislikes (Newcomb, 1978), and who are similar in attractiveness (White, 1980), are more likely to remain in a relationship than dissimilar individuals.

KEY STUDY 28.4 Do birds of a feather stay together?

- Hill *et al.* (1976) studied 231 steadily dating couples over a two-year period, at the end of which 103 couples (45 per cent) had broken up.
- The surviving couples tended to be more alike in terms of age, intelligence, educational and career plans, as well as physical attractiveness. Those who split up often mentioned differences in interests, background, sexual attitudes and ideas about marriage.
- About 80 per cent of the couples who described themselves as being 'in love' at the start stayed together, compared with 56 per cent who didn't. Of couples in which both members initially reported being equally involved in the relationship, only 23 per cent broke up, but where one member was much more involved than the other, 54 per cent did so.
- The latter is a highly unstable couple, in which the one who's more involved (putting more in but getting less in return) may feel dependent and exploited, while the one who's less involved (putting less in but getting more in return) may feel restless and guilty (which implies some sense of fairness).

Jack and Vera Duckworth from *Coronation Street* – complementarity personified!

Marital satisfaction

This is another way of looking at compatibility. In a review of studies looking at marital satisfaction and communication, Duck (1992) found that happy couples give more positive and consistent non-verbal cues than unhappy couples, express more agreement and approval for the other's ideas and suggestions, talk more about their relationship, and are more willing to compromise on difficult decisions.

Lauer & Lauer (1985) asked several hundred couples married for at least 15 years why they thought their marriage had lasted. They stressed *friendship* (e.g. 'My spouse is my best friend'), *commitment* ('Marriage is a long-term commitment'), *similarity* ('We agree on how and how often to show affection'), and *positive affect* ('We laugh together') as the basic elements in an enduring relationship. These findings could be seen as implying a successful transition from passionate to companionate love.

RELATIONSHIP BREAKDOWN AND DISSOLUTION

ASK YOURSELF...
- Think of your most unsuccessful relationship(s).
- Why did it/they go wrong?
- Was it to do with you as individuals, or 'circumstances', or a mixture of the two?

Why do relationships go wrong?

According to Duck (2001), there's an almost infinite number of reasons why relationships break up. But they can be put into three broad categories:

1. *pre-existing doom:* incompatibility and failure are almost predestined (for example, 'Schoolgirl, 17, marries her 50-year-old teacher, who's already a grandfather')

2. *mechanical failure:* two suitable people of goodwill and good nature nevertheless find they cannot live together (this is the most common cause)
3. *sudden death:* the discovery of a betrayal or infidelity can lead to the immediate termination of a romantic relationship (see below).

Duck believes that the 'official' reasons given to others (including the partner) to justify the break-up are far more interesting psychologically than the real reasons. The psychology of break-up involves a whole layer of individual psychological processes, group processes, cultural rules and self-presentation. But this applies mainly to romantic relationships, rather than friendships.

When you fall out with a friend, there's usually no formal or public 'announcement'. There's no need for this, because friendships aren't exclusive in the way that most sexual relationships are (it's 'normal' to have several friends at once, but not several partners!). As Duck says:

> ... Truly committed romantic relationships necessarily involve the foregoing of other romantic relationships and commitment to only one partner ('forsaking all others', as it says in the marriage ceremony) ...

Marital unhappiness and divorce

Duck (1988, 1992) has identified several factors that make it more likely that a marriage will be unhappy and/or end in divorce.

- Marriages in which the partners are *younger than average* tend to be more unstable. This can be understood by reference to Erikson's concept of *intimacy* (see Chapter 38). Such marriages often involve early parenthood; the young couple has little time to adjust to the new responsibilities of marriage before financial and housing problems are added with the arrival of a baby (Kellmer Pringle, 1986).
- Marriages between couples from *lower socio-economic groups* and *educational levels* tend to be more unstable. These are also the couples which tend to have their children very early in marriage.
- Marriages between partners from *different demographic backgrounds* (race, religion, and so on.) also tend to be more unstable. This can be related to Kerckhoff and Davis's filter model.
- Marriages between people who've experienced *parental divorce* as children, or who've had a greater *number of sexual partners* than average before marriage tend to be more unstable.

While these factors are important, only a proportion of marriages involving young, lower class individuals or those from different cultural backgrounds and so on actually end in divorce. Conversely, many divorces will involve couples who don't fit any of these descriptions. So what other factors may be involved?

According to Brehm (1992), there are two broad types of cause: *structural* (gender, duration of the relationship, the presence of children and role strain created by competing demands of work and family) and *conflict resolution*.

Gender differences

Men and women seem to differ in their perception of problems in a relationship. In general, women report more problems, and there's some evidence that the degree of female dissatisfaction is a better predictor than male unhappiness of whether the relationship will end. This could be because women are more sensitive to relationship problems than men. Alternatively, men and women may come into relationships with different expectations and hopes, with men's generally being fulfilled to a greater extent than women's.

Consistent with this possibility is evidence of gender differences in the specific type of problems that are reported. For example, divorcing men and women are equally likely to cite communication problems as a cause of their splitting up. But women stress basic unhappiness and incompatibility more than men do.

Men also seem particularly upset by 'sexual withholding' by a female partner, while women are distressed by a male partner's sexual aggression. This is consistent with the finding that men tend to fall in love more easily than women (Baumeister & Bratslavsky, 1999), which is contrary to the popular myth about women demanding commitment and men fighting shy of it. Men also seem to respond more quickly to any intimacy changes (positive and negative), at both earlier and later stages of a relationship (Fiske, 2004).

Duration of relationships and the passage of time

The longer partners have known each other before marriage, the more likely they are to be satisfied in the marriage, and the less likely they are to divorce. However,

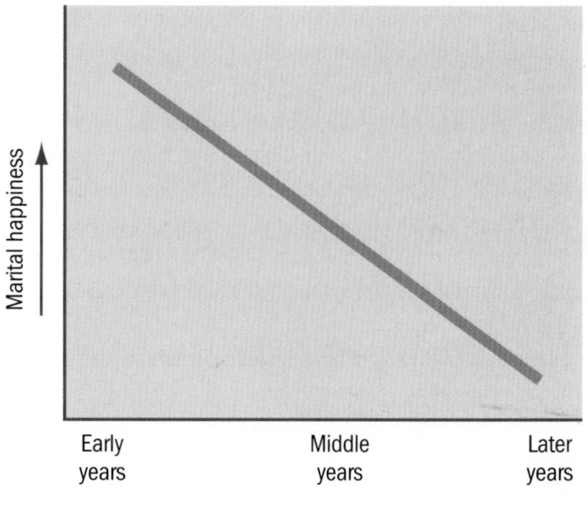

Figure 28.6 A linear life-cycle (based on Brehm, 1992)

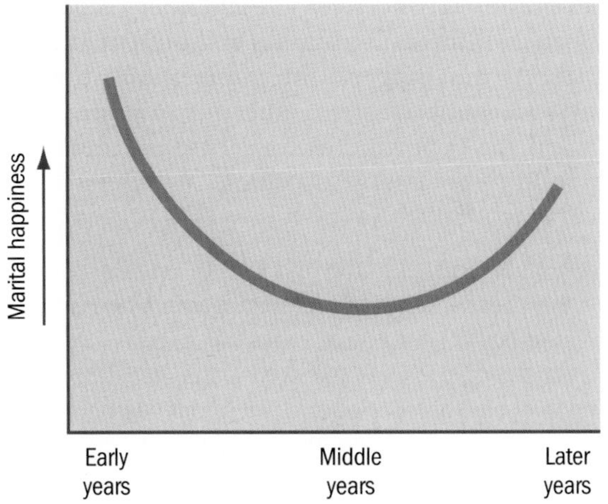

Figure 28.7 A curvilinear life cycle (based on Brehm, 1992)

couples who've have cohabited before marriage report fewer barriers to ending the marriage, and the longer a relationship lasts, the more people blame their partners for negative events.

Two major views of changes in marital satisfaction over time are Pineo's (1961) *linear model* and Burr's (1970) *curvilinear model.* According to the linear model, there's an inevitable fading of the romantic 'high' of courtship before marriage. Also, people marry because they've achieved a 'good fit' with their partner. So, any changes that occur in either partner will reduce their compatibility. For example, if one partner becomes more self-confident (ironically, through the support gained from the relationship), there may be increased conflict between two 'equals' competing for superiority.

The curvilinear model (see Figure 28.7) proposes that marital happiness is greatest in the earliest years. Marital satisfaction declines as children are born and grow up, then increases again as they mature and leave home.

While it's generally agreed that there's a decline in satisfaction during the early years, whether there's an actual increase or just a levelling off after that remains a matter of debate. Gilford & Bengtson (1979) argue that it's an oversimplification to talk about 'marital satisfaction'. Instead, we should look at two life cycles: the *pattern of positive rewards,* and the *pattern of negative costs.* The early years are associated with very high rewards and very high costs, while in the middle years there's a decline in both. In the later years, costs continue to decline, but there's an increase in rewards.

Conflict resolution

According to Duck (1988), some kind and degree of conflict is inevitable in all relationships. But the process of resolving conflicts can often be positive, promoting growth of the relationship (Wood & Duck, 1995).The important question, therefore, isn't whether there's conflict, but *how* it's handled. However, recurring conflicts may indicate an inability to resolve the underlying source; the partners may come to doubt each other as reasonable persons, leading to a 'digging in of the heels', a disaffection with each other and, ultimately, a 'strong falling out' (Berry & Willingham, 1997).

Some degree of overt conflict ('getting it out in the open') can improve a relationship – talking it through and working it out. But differences can result in destructive behaviour, in which partners fail to accommodate to each other's needs. This, in turn, can produce a *conflict spiral,* where one partner responds to the other's negative emotion with negative emotion, and so on. *Unregulated couples,* who don't balance their negative reactions with at least an equal number of positive ones, are headed for trouble (Fiske, 2004).

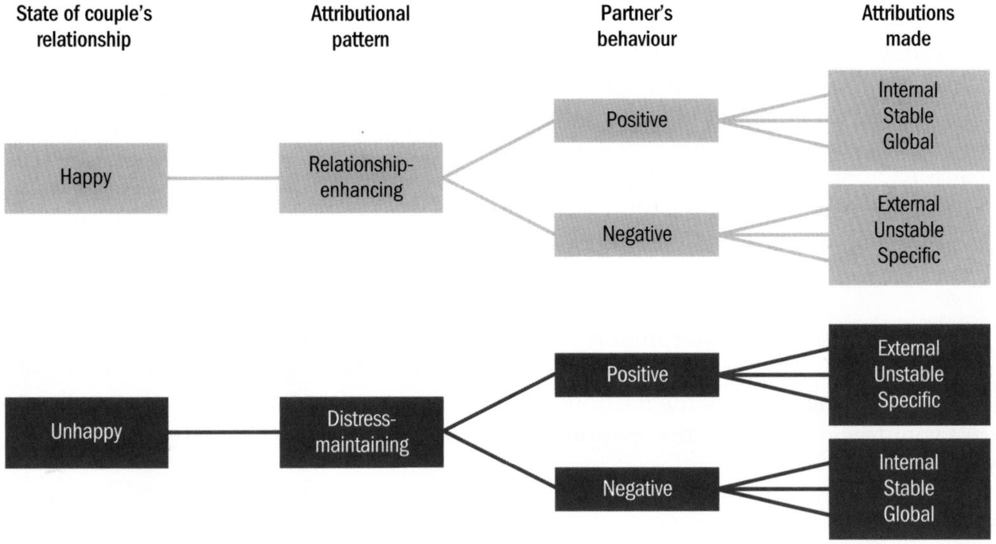

Figure 28.8 Attributions made by happy and unhappy couples according to Bradbury & Fincham (1990) (from Brehm, S.S. (1992) *Intimate Relationships* (2nd edition). New York, McGraw-Hill)

According to Bradbury & Fincham (1990), happy and unhappy couples resolve conflict in typically different ways, which can be understood as different *attributional patterns* (see Chapter 23). Happy couples use a *relationship-enhancing pattern,* while unhappy couples use a *distress-maintaining* (or *conflict-promoting*) *pattern*.

Causal attributions concern who or what produced an event, while *responsibility* attributions involves an assessment of who's accountable for the event once a cause is known. So, for example, the conflict-promoting attributional style shown in Figure 28.8 involves seeing the partner's negative behaviour as *intentional* ('you did it on purpose'), *selfish* ('you did it for what you could get out of it') and *blame* ('it's your fault') (Fincham, 2004).

According to Fincham, support for the attributional hypothesis accumulated during the 1990s. Indeed:

> ... the evidence for an association between attribution and marital satisfaction is overwhelming, making it possibly the most robust, replicable phenomenon in the study of marriage.

There's also increasing evidence that the causal link between attributions and marital satisfaction is *bidirectional*; in other words, they influence each other (Fincham, 2004). However, couples *don't* seem to have enduring attributional styles. Rather, their changing attributions over time predict their marital satisfaction, more than satisfaction predicts attributions (Karney & Bradbury, 2000).

Rule-breaking and deception

> ***ASK YOURSELF...***
> - What's the worst thing that a friend or partner could do as far as your relationship is concerned?
> - Is there anything that, *in principle,* you wouldn't tolerate?

Argyle & Henderson (1984) and Argyle *et al.* (1985) identified a number of rules thought to apply to all or most relationships, such as 'Should respect the other's privacy', 'Should not discuss what is said in confidence', 'Should be emotionally supportive'. There are additional rules for particular types of relationship. Relationships fall into clusters, with similar rules applying within a cluster. For example, one cluster includes spouse, siblings and close friends, and another includes doctor, teacher and boss.

Deception probably represents the most important rule that shouldn't be broken. Although what counts as deception will depend on the nature of the relationship, if you cannot trust your friend or partner, the relationship is almost certainly doomed.

Violation of expectations

As a relationship develops, partners learn more about each other and become increasingly close. This occurs through greater dependence on each other's activities for performance of the daily routines and fulfilment of plans and goals. As this happens, the number and strength of their *expectations* about each other increase. But, by the same token, the opportunities for *violation* of these expectations also increase. According to Berscheid & Ammazzalorso (2004):

> ... – when our partners turn out not to be the person we thought they were – we truly are endangered. The partner has become unfamiliar and thus, possibly unsafe. He or she becomes a stranger; hence, the word 'estranged' is often used to describe once close partners ... all of our customary behaviours and plans and goals that depend on the partner's behavioural contributions may be threatened.

Relationship dissolution as a process

Relationships are highly complex, and this applies to their break-up as much as it does to their formation and maintenance. It applies to the break-up of friendships and sexual relationships, and not just marriages, particularly if the relationship is a long-term one that has embraced many parts of the person's emotional, communicative, leisure and everyday life (Duck, 1988).

As we noted earlier, not all marriages involving young partners will break up while they're still young, so research needs to focus on the *processes* by which the lasting/non-lasting relationships may be distinguished (Gottman, 1994; Aldous, 1996). As Duck (1999) says:

> ... In accounting for break-up, therefore, we need to consider it as a long-term process in the lives of the partners and their associates ...

Also, people sometimes think about and plan their break-up, or maybe about how to prevent it: it doesn't always come at people 'out of the blue'. Recent research has begun to look more closely at the specific characteristics of those relationships that do break apart. What is it about the partners and their behaviour towards each other that accounts for their problems? For example, do troubled couples have particular ways of communicating and relating? (Duck, 1999). Researchers have also begun to look at the break-up of friendships, and the actions, strategies, and persuasive techniques people deliberately take to cause break-up. As Duck (1999) observes:

> ... Break-up is not just the waning of intimacy or reduction in feelings towards the partner ... the dissolution of relationships highlights the operation of relationship processes, such as interpersonal judgements, assessments of social exchange, and interactions that are present throughout a relationship but go unnoticed in routine interaction.

Duck's model

Duck's (1982) model comprises four phases, each of which is initiated when a threshold is broken.

The ending of a romantic relationship indicates that the two people are now legitimately available as partners for other relationships. This requires them to create a story for the end of the relationship that leaves them in a favourable light as potential partners. Romantic relationships are, therefore, typically ended publicly in a way that announces the ex-partners' freedom from the expectations of exclusive commitment.

Table 28.2 A sketch of the main phases of dissolving personal relationships (based on Duck, 1982, from Duck, 1988)

Breakdown–dissatisfaction with relationship
↓
Threshold: 'I can't stand this any more'
INTRAPSYCHIC PHASE
◎ Personal focus on partner's behaviour
◎ Assess adequacy of partner's role performance
◎ Depict and evaluate negative aspects of being in the relationship
◎ Consider costs of withdrawal
◎ Assess positive aspects of alternative relationships
◎ Face 'express/repress dilemma'
↓
Threshold: 'I'd be justified in withdrawing'
DYADIC PHASE
◎ Face 'confrontation/avoidance dilemma'
◎ Confront partner
◎ Negotiate in 'our relationship talks'
◎ Attempt repair and reconciliation?
◎ Assess joint costs of withdrawal or reduced intimacy
↓
Threshold: 'I mean it'
SOCIAL PHASE
◎ Negotiate post-dissolution state with partner
◎ Initiate gossip/discussion in social network
◎ Create publicly negotiable face-saving/blame-placing stories and accounts
◎ Consider and face up to implied social network effect, if any
◎ Call in intervention team
↓
Threshold: 'It's now inevitable'
GRAVE-DRESSING PHASE
◎ 'Getting over' activity
◎ Retrospective; reformative post-mortem attribution
◎ Public distribution of own version of break-up story

'Dressing the grave' involves 'erecting a tablet' that provides a credible, socially acceptable account of the life and death of the relationship. While helping to save face, it also serves to keep alive some memories and to 'justify' the original commitment to the ex-partner. As Duck (1988) puts it:

> ... Such stories are an integral and important part of the psychology of ending relationships ... By helping the person to get over the break-up they are immensely significant in preparing the person for future relationships as well as helping them out of old ones.

Duck (2001) identifies a number of classic formats for a break-up story (such as 'X suddenly changed and I had to get out'; 'X betrayed me'; 'We grew apart'). The crucial ingredients of such stories are those that show the speaker:

- is open to relationships but doesn't enter them thoughtlessly
- is aware of others' deficiencies but isn't overly critical
- is willing to work to improve a relationship or take decisive action when partners turn nasty or break the rules of relating
- is rational and sensible, and brings closure to relationships only after trauma, hard work or on reasonable grounds after real effort to make things work.

CONCLUSIONS: WHAT HAPPENS AFTER DIVORCE?

One growing area of research interest is 'postmarital' and 'remarital relationships', and family reorganisation after divorce. The increasing incidence of divorce is making blended families the norm. Indeed, there's shift in ideology, from viewing divorce as pathology to viewing it as an institution (Duck, 1999).

Once divorce is seen a common transition, rather than as pathological, researchers can reasonably begin to attend to a much wider range of issues, such as 'getting over ' and prevention, and as much to the processes of entering new relationships as to those to do with leaving the old ones (Masheter, 1997: see Chapter 38).

Even the most stable and loving relationships, inevitably, dissolve. As Berscheid & Ammazzalorso (2004) say:

> ... It is one of the saddest facts of the human condition that even the closest and happiest of relationships end – if not by some circumstance of fate that causes separation, then by the death of one of the partners ...

The loss, through death, of a loved one is often accompanied by the experience of the strongest negative emotions of which human beings are capable.

CHAPTER SUMMARY

- The **need for affiliation** represents a precondition for attraction, and can be related to the need for **social comparison**. Both are enhanced under conditions of increased anxiety.

- Interpersonal relationships in western cultures tend to be **individualistic**, **voluntary** and **temporary**, whereas those in non-western cultures tend to be more **collectivist**, **involuntary** and **permanent**.
- Western psychologists tend to equate 'relationships' with 'western relationships'. This is a form of **ethnocentrism**, specifically, **Anglo-** or **Eurocentrism**.
- **Marriage** is found in all cultures. But there are important cultural variations in marital arrangements, including **monogamy**, **polygamy** (**polygyny** or **polyandry**), **mandatory marriage to specific relatives** and **arranged marriages**.
- Arranged marriages are far more common in collectivist cultures. But, even here, brides and grooms are typically given some **choice** about who they marry. Traditionally, **divorce rates** have been much lower among 'arranged couples', but these are now increasing.
- The focus on long-term heterosexual relationships has now been supplemented with discussion of **gay** and **lesbian** relationships.
- Up to the mid-1970s, psychological research into homosexuality adopted a 'pathology model'. This has been replaced by a model that emphasises the underlying **similarity** between homosexuals and heterosexuals. This approach, however, omits or distorts certain key **differences**, such as those relating to **cohabitation**, **sexual exclusivity** and **sex roles.**
- One of the most unexpected uses of the Internet is in the development of **online relationships** (**cyber affairs** or **electronic friendships**). These can be **purely virtual**, progress to increasingly sexually intense **online contact** or eventually lead to an **offline** meeting that is then maintained online.
- Berscheid and Walster distinguish between **companionate** ('true' or 'conjugal') **love** and **passionate** (romantic or obsessive) **love**. These are **qualitatively** different, but companionate love is only a more extreme form of **liking**.
- Sternberg's **triangular theory of love** comprises three basic components (**intimacy**, **passion** and **decision/commitment**), which can be combined to form different kinds of love.
- These models of love fail to take **cultural background** into account. They reflect the popular western ('Hollywood') view of the relationship between love and marriage, which *isn't* universal.
- An **evolutionary** account of love focuses on love as **attachment**. This is one of three meanings of 'I love you', the others being **love as caregiving** and **love as sexual attraction**.
- The notion of people falling in love is found in one form or another in most human societies, even where marriages are traditionally arranged by families or friends.
- Kerckhoff and Davis's '**filter model**', and other 'stage' theories, aren't strongly supported by empirical evidence. But it's generally agreed that relationships change and develop.
- A general theoretical framework for explaining **initial attraction** is that the presence of others must be **rewarding**. This can help explain the impact of **proximity**, **exposure** and **familiarity**, **physical attractiveness** and **similarity**.
- **Proximity** provides increased opportunity for interaction, which increases **familiarity** through the **mere exposure effect**. But people can become too familiar by invading our **personal space**. **Proxemic rules** dictate the appropriate distance to keep between ourselves and another person in different situations.
- **Similarity** of attitudes and values is a powerful influence on attraction, but this usually only emerges as the relationship develops. However, **physical attractiveness** is immediately apparent.
- There are important **cultural differences** in what counts as physical beauty, but there's a universal tendency for men to regard physical attractiveness as more important than women.
- The **matching hypothesis** (MH) is derived from **social exchange theory** (SET), which is a major explanation of all kinds of relationships, both intimate and non-intimate. Its different versions see people as fundamentally **selfish**, concerned only with getting as much out of a relationship as possible. But humans are capable of **altruism** as well as selfishness.
- SET is a special case of **equity theory** (ET), which adds **investment** to SET's **reward**, **cost** and **profit**. Equity refers to a **constant ratio** of profit to investment and relates to the concept of **fairness**.
- While there's little evidence for the **complementarity of psychological needs**, there's more support for complementarity in **resources**. But sociobiologists' claim that the universal male preference for physical attractiveness and female preference for financial security are genetically determined ignores cultural and historical factors.
- Marriages are more **unstable** if the couple are teenagers, from lower socio-economic groups and different demographic backgrounds, whose parents were divorced, who've been sexually active prior to marriage, and who experience early parenthood.
- **Conflict** is an inherent part of all relationships, and what's crucial is how constructively it's resolved. Happy couples tend to deal with conflict in a **relationship-enhancing way**, while unhappy couples use a **distress-maintaining pattern** of conflict resolution.
- **Rule-breaking** is a major cause of relationship breakdown, especially **deception**.
- Relationship breakdown is a **process**, involving a number of stages or phases. Research is increasingly concerned with the **aftermath** of relationship breakdown, especially divorce, and not just the breakdown itself.

Links with other topics/chapters

- Interpersonal attraction is really one aspect of *interpersonal* (or social) *perception* (Chapter 22).
- Affiliation can be understood in relation to *conformity,* especially the need to belong. We also compare ourselves with others when we're unsure what to do or think (Chapter 26).
- Ethnocentricism is a form of *bias* involved when western psychologists assume that 'relationships' and 'western relationships' are the same. Other examples of ethnocentrism are discussed in Chapter 47. That chapter also discusses cross-cultural and cultural psychology, and the differences between *cultures* (such as collectivist and individualist).
- Homosexuality is discussed in relation to definitions and classification of *psychological abnormality* in Chapter 43.
- Seeing love as a label we attach to our state of physiological arousal is consistent with the *cognitive labelling theory* of emotion discussed in Chapter 10.
- The view of romantic love as a discourse that represents a form of social control is consistent with *social constructionism* (Chapter 2).
- An evolutionary theory of love (love as attachment) is one aspect of *evolutionary psychology* (Chapter 2). Attachment is discussed fully in Chapter 32.
- The similarity-attraction principle is related to *consistency theories of attitude change* (including Heider's balance theory) (Chapter 24).
- The attractiveness stereotype is discussed, along with other aspects of *social perception,* in Chapter 22.
- Ideas about what makes people (especially women) physically attractive are relevant to discussion of eating disorders (Chapter 44).
- Analysing the factors that account for facial attractiveness is related to *facial perception* (including face recognition). This is discussed in relation to *pattern recognition* in Chapter 14.
- Sociobiological accounts of beauty are related to the *evolutionary approach* within psychology (Chapter 2). The tendency to equate beauty with youthfulness (as claimed by sociobiologists) is the flip-side of prejudice against old age (*ageism:* Chapter 39).
- The SET view of people as fundamentally selfish is relevant to discussion of *altruism and pro-social behaviour* (Chapter 30).
- Erikson's concept of intimacy is discussed as part of his *psychosocial theory* of development in Chapter 38.
- Marriage, divorce and parenthood are discussed in Chapter 37.
- Attribution is discussed in Chapter 23.
- Grief is discussed in relation to *old age* in Chapter 39.

29

AGGRESSION AND ANTISOCIAL BEHAVIOUR

INTRODUCTION AND OVERVIEW

Philosophers and psychologists have been interested in human aggression for a long time. According to Hobbes (1651), people are naturally competitive and hostile, interested only in their own power and gaining advantage over others. Hobbes argued that to prevent conflict and mutual destruction, people need government.

This pessimistic view of human nature was shared by Freud and Lorenz, albeit for different theoretical reasons. Like McDougall, Freud and Lorenz saw aggression as an *instinct* (see Chapter 9). In Freud's psychoanalytic theory, aggression is inherently self-destructive, but in practice is directed outwards mainly at other people, demonstrated all too clearly in the carnage of war. According to Lorenz's *ethological theory,* human beings have lost the means of controlling their aggression that other species possess, and in addition have invented weapons that allow aggression to take place from a distance.

Other explanations of aggression have combined elements of instinct theories with those of *learning theory,* such as Dollard *et al.*'s *frustration–aggression hypothesis,* and Berkowitz's *aggressive-cue theory.* Bandura's study of *observational learning's* role in aggression stimulated research into the effects of violence in the media, in particular television, and, more recently, so-called 'video nasties'. Perhaps the 'purest' social psychological account of aggression is the theory of *deindividuation.*

Baron & Richardson (1994) define antisocial behaviours as those 'which show a lack of feeling and concern for the welfare of others'. While aggression represents just one such lack of feeling and concern, it's the one that psychologists have focused on. But aggression itself can take different forms, and can be linked to motives other than wishing to harm or injure another person.

DEFINING AGGRESSION

ASK YOURSELF...
- What do you understand by 'aggression'?
- Are there different kinds of aggression?
- Is aggression the same as violence?

We all seem to recognise aggression when we witness or encounter it, but defining it often proves much more difficult. When used as a noun, aggression usually conveys some behaviour which is intended to harm another (or at least which has that effect). Yet even this definition is too broad: self-defence and unprovoked attack may both involve similar 'acts' and degrees of aggression, but only the latter would normally be considered 'antisocial' (and the law also recognises this distinction). When used as an adjective, 'aggressive' can convey that an action is carried out with energy and persistence (Lloyd *et al.*, 1984), something which may be regarded as socially desirable.

The importance of intention

Moyer (1976) and Berkowitz (1993) see aggression as always involving behaviour, either physical or symbolic, performed with the intention of harming someone. Similarly, Fiske (2004) defines aggression as entailing 'any *behaviour* whose *proximate intention* is to harm another person'. Aggressive *thoughts,* without the behaviour, *aren't* aggressive. Bushman & Anderson (2001a) distinguish between two types of intention: *proximate* (the closest and most immediate) and *primary* (*ultimate*). Aggressors operate with *multiple motives.* For example, perpetrators of school shootings may have the primary intent of revenge, suicide or fame. Terrorist attacks may have various primary intentions, such as revenge, escalating tensions, genocide, political control, moral influence, personal salvation or publicity. Domestic abuse can be motivated by control, self-enhancement, and relief from tension. According to Fiske (2004):

> ... because people's motives are complex, focusing on the most immediate, closest, or proximate goal seems more fruitful than trying to decide the primary one.

Moyer and Berkowitz reserve the word violence to describe an extreme form of aggression involving a deliberate attempt to inflict serious physical injury on another person or damage property.

Other important distinctions include:

- *hostile aggression* is aimed solely at hurting another (gratuitous aggression or 'aggression for aggression's sake'); this would exclude self-defence; it's also angry, impulsive and automatic
- *instrumental aggression* is a means to an end (and so would include self-defence: Buss, 1961; Feshbach, 1964); it's controlled and premeditated.

ASK YOURSELF...
- Can you think of any exceptions to this distinction between hostile and instrumental aggression?

Hostile aggression can sometimes be controlled, as when an angry person plots revenge over time. Conversely, instrumental aggression can sometimes be impulsive, as when a child hits another child to get its toy back. Fiske (2004) believes that examples like these make the distinction less useful.

- *Natural* or *positive* aggression is aimed largely at self-defence, or combating prejudice and other social injustice.
- *Pathological aggression* or violence results when our inner nature has become twisted or frustrated (e.g. Maslow, 1968).

THEORIES OF AGGRESSION

Instinct theories

Lorenz's ethological approach

Ethologists consider aggression to be instinctive in all species and important in the evolutionary development of the species. It allows individuals to adapt to their environments, survive in them, and successfully reproduce (see Chapter 2 and Gross *et al.*, 2000). When space or food are scarce, many species limit their reproduction and survive by marking off living space which they defend against 'trespassers' (*territoriality*). Aggressiveness is clearly important in competing successfully for limited resources, in defending territory and for basic survival.

According to Lorenz (1966), it's legitimate to make direct comparisons between different species, although his theory of human aggression is based on the study of non-primates, and mainly non-mammals (mainly fish and insects). He defines aggression as:

> ... the fighting instinct in beast and man which is directed against members of the same species ...

Differences between non-human and human aggression

According to Lorenz, aggression in non-humans is basically *constructive,* but in humans it's become *distorted.*

- *Ritualisation* refers to a way of discharging aggression in a fixed, stereotyped pattern. Fights between members of the same species result in relatively little physical harm to either victor or vanquished, but at the same time allow a victor to emerge. For example, the fighting that takes place between stags is highly ritualised, and the triumphant one is the male who 'makes his point' rather than the one who kills or incapacitates his opponent. Similarly, wolves will end their fight with the loser exposing its jugular vein – but this is sufficient and no blood is spilled.

- Sometimes, antagonists may approach each other in a threatening manner - but not actually engage in combat. One will show *appeasement rituals* (or *gestures*), which prevent the other from engaging in actual conflict. For example, in one species of jackdaw, the nape section at the bottom of the head is clearly marked off from the rest of the body by its plumage and colouring. When one bird 'offers' its nape to an aggressor, the latter will never attack, even if on the verge of doing so.

> *ASK YOURSELF...*
> - Can you think of any examples of human appeasement rituals/gestures?
> - How effective do you consider these to be?

Although human appeasement responses (such as smiling, cowering, cringing, or begging for mercy) are normally very effective, we've developed a *technology* of aggression. However naturally aggressive we are as a species compared with other species, our superior brains have enabled us to construct weapons which remove combat from the eye-to-eye, face-to-face situation. This inevitably reduces the overall role – and effectiveness – of appeasement rituals. Indeed, the deadliest weapons (as measured by the number of victims who can be killed or injured at one time) are the very ones which can be used at the *greatest distance* from the intended victims (such as bombs and intercontinental nuclear missiles). According to Lea (1984):

> We have developed a technology which enables our intentions to override our instincts.

A passenger train destroyed in a NATO missile attack in Serbia in April, 1999, during the Kosovo conflict. At least ten people were killed and 16 others injured

An evaluation of Lorenz's theory

- In keeping with his belief that humans are naturally highly aggressive, Lorenz maintains that their 'natural condition' is that of 'warrior'. However, it's generally agreed that early human beings *weren't* warriors but 'hunter–gatherers' (such as the present-day Inuit Eskimos, Pygmies of the Ituri forest, Aborigines, Kalahari Bushmen, the Punan of Borneo, and so on), who live in small clans which hardly ever come into contact with other groups of people (Siann, 1985).
- Even without the most primitive weapons, other primates, including chimps, can and do kill each other.

Goodall (1978) describes warfare between two colonies of chimps, which ended in the killing of every male in one of the groups. Also, infanticide is one of the more common kinds of unrestrained aggression among non-human species. For example, male lions that succeed in taking over a 'pride' of females (so displacing other adult males) will often attack and kill any cubs that are present (which then makes the females available for mating). According to Lea (1984), Lorenz's claim that non-human aggression always stops before an animal is killed is basically a myth.

- Lorenz totally ignored the role of *learning* and *cultural influences,* which are far more important determinants of human aggression than biological factors. Whatever potential for aggression we may have inherited as a species, it's culturally overridden and repackaged into forms which fit current circumstances. Cultures differ in the degrees and kinds of aggression which are permissible, including gender-related aggression (see Chapter 36).
- Lorenz claims that aggression (like hunger, sexuality and flight, which collectively he calls the 'big four') isn't a response to environmental stimuli. Rather, it occurs spontaneously, when instinctive aggressive energy builds up and demands discharge (the *hydraulic model of instinct*). The evidence for this energy model is very sparse indeed (Siann, 1985), and many modern biologists and ethologists believe that aggression in animals is reactive and modifiable by a variety of internal and external conditions (Hinde, 1974).

Freud's psychoanalytic approach

As we saw in Chapter 9, Freud's theory is normally regarded as an *instinct theory.* It wasn't until late in his life that Freud recognised aggression as an instinct distinct from sexuality (libido). This change in his thinking occurred in response to the horrific carnage of the First World War. In *Beyond the Pleasure Principle* (1920) and *The Ego and the Id* (1923), he distinguished between the *life instinct* (or Eros), including sexuality, and the *death instinct* (*Thanatos*).

Thanatos represents an inborn destructiveness, directed primarily against *the self.* The aim (as with all instincts in Freud's view) is to reduce tension or excitation to a minimum and, ultimately, to eliminate it completely. This was the idyllic state we enjoyed in the womb, where our needs were met as soon as they arose, and, for a while, at our mother's breast. But after this, the only way of achieving such a *Nirvana* is through death.

Self-directed aggression, however, conflicts with the life instinct, especially the self-preservative component. But because the impulse to self-destruction is so strong, Freud believed that we must destroy some other thing or person if we're not to destroy ourselves. Conflict with the life instinct results in our aggression being *displaced* onto others. More positively, aggression can be *sublimated* into sport, physical occupations and domination and mastery of nature and the world in general. Like Freud, Lorenz also argued that we need to acknowledge our aggressiveness and to control it through sport (e.g. the Olympics), expeditions, explorations, and so on, especially if international cooperation is involved (Lorenz called these 'displacement' activities). Freud shared Lorenz's view that aggressive energy builds up until eventually it has to be discharged in some way.

Opening ceremony to the 2004 Athens Olympic Games

KEY STUDY 29.1 The overcontrolled violent criminal (Megargee, 1966)

- Megargee reported that brutally aggressive crimes are often committed by *overcontrolled* individuals. They repress their anger, and over a period of time the pressure to be aggressive builds up. Often it's an objectively trivial incident which provokes the destructive outburst. The aggressor then returns to his previously passive state, once again seeming incapable of violence.
- In Phoenix, an 11-year-old boy who stabbed his brother 34 times with a steak knife was described by all who knew him as being extremely polite and softly spoken, with no history of violent behaviour. In New York, an 18-year-old youth who confessed he'd assaulted and strangled a seven-year-old girl in a church, and later tried to burn her body in the furnace, was described in the press as an unemotional person who planned to be a minister. A 21-year-old man from Colorado accused of the rape and murder of two little girls had never been a discipline problem and, in fact, his stepfather reported, 'When he was in school the other kids would run all over him and he'd never fight back. There is just no violence in him.'
- In these cases, the homicide wasn't just one more aggressive offence in a person who'd always displayed

inadequate controls. Rather, it was a completely uncharacteristic act in a person who'd always displayed extraordinarily high levels of control. According to Megargee & Mendelsohn (1962):

> *... the extremely assaultive person is often a fairly mild-mannered, long-suffering individual who buries his resentment under rigid but brittle controls. Under certain circumstances he may lash out and release all his aggression in one, often disastrous, act. Afterwards he reverts to his usual overcontrolled defences. Thus he may be more of a menace than the verbally aggressive 'chip-on-the-shoulder' type who releases his aggression in small doses.*

An evaluation of Freud's theory

- Despite supportive evidence such as Megargee's, Freud's ideas on aggression made little impact either on the public imagination or on other psychologists (including other psychoanalysts) until Dollard *et al.* (1939) proposed their *frustration–aggression hypothesis* (see below).
- Fromm's *The Anatomy of Human Destructiveness* (1977) was influenced by Freud's ideas, as was Storr's *Human Aggression* (1968). Storr (like Fromm, a psychoanalyst) dedicated his book to Lorenz, and in the introduction he says:

> That man is an aggressive creature will hardly be disputed. With the exception of certain rodents, no other vertebrate habitually destroys members of his own species ... the extremes of 'brutal' behaviour are confined to man; and there is no parallel in nature to our savage treatment of each other ... we are the cruellest and most ruthless species that has ever walked the earth; and that, although we may recoil in horror when we read in newspaper or history book of the atrocities committed by man upon man, we know in our hearts that each one of us harbours within himself those same savage impulses which lead to murder, to torture and to war.

The frustration–aggression hypothesis (FAH)

Dollard *et al.*'s (1939) *frustration–aggression hypothesis* (FAH) was intended partly to 'translate' some of Freud's psychoanalytic concepts into learning theory terms. It claims that:

> ... aggression is always a consequence of frustration and, contrariwise ... the existence of frustration always leads to some form of aggression ...

While agreeing with Freud that aggression is an innate response, Dollard *et al.* argued that it would be triggered only by frustrating situations and events. Some support for this view comes from the *displacement* of aggression, as demonstrated in the *scapegoating* account of racial discrimination (see Chapter 25).

Indeed, evidence for this form of *indirect* aggression is stronger than for direct aggression (Fiske, 2004). A meta-analysis of laboratory studies found a sizeable effect of provocation on aggression towards innocent third parties when retaliation against the provoking person isn't possible (Marcus-Newhall *et al.*, 2000). Displaced aggression often focuses on a weaker, safer target than the frustrating agent. Related research into *bullying* and *partner abuse* shows that aggression towards others is an attempt to exert *control* over someone in a weaker position (Fiske, 2004).

ASK YOURSELF...

- Can you think of any exceptions to the claims made by the frustration–aggression hypothesis?
- Do we necessarily become aggressive when we're frustrated?

Some criticisms of the original FAH

Despite the evidence for displaced aggression, it soon became apparent that the FAH, in its original form, was an overstatement.

- Miller (1941) argued that frustration is an *instigator* of aggression, but situational factors (such as *learned inhibition* and *fear of retaliation*) may prevent actual aggressive behaviour from occurring. So, although frustration may make aggression more likely, it's far from being a sufficient cause of aggression.
- Bandura (1973) argued that frustration might be a source of *arousal*, but frustration-induced arousal (like other types of arousal) could have a variety of outcomes, of which aggression is only one. Whether it actually occurs is more the result of learned patterns of behaviour triggered by environmental cues.
- Frustration may also produce different responses in different people in different situations. For example, experiments seem to suggest that frustration is most likely to produce aggression if (a) the person is close to achieving his/her goal, or (b) the frustrating event seems arbitrary (Miell, 1990). Berkowitz (1993) says that if a frustration is either arbitrary or illegitimate, it's seen as unfair.

KEY STUDY 29.2 Don't frustrate me without a good reason (Kulik & Brown, 1979)

- Kulik and Brown found that frustration was more likely to produce aggression if it wasn't anticipated, and if participants believed that the person responsible for frustrating them did so deliberately and without good reason.
- This shows the importance of *cognitive factors* as cues for aggressive behaviour.
- Participants were told they could earn money by telephoning people and persuading them to make a pledge to charity. One group expected that about two-thirds of